443

COLLINS

Easy Learning

FRENCH

DICTIONARY

to notice → remarquer   to stress → accentuer
to mention → evoquer

M N O P Q R S T

HarperCollins*Publishers*

first published in this edition 1996

© **HarperCollins Publishers 1996**

ISBN 0 00 470714-1

project management
Ray Carrick, Michela Clari

general editor
Horst Kopleck

editorial coordination
Vivian Marr, Nicola Cooke

editors

Christine Penman	Daphne Day
Chantal Testa	Harry Campbell
Cécile Aubinière-Robb	Gavin Killip
Hélène Bernaërt	Elspeth Anderson
Sabine Citron	

computing staff
Ann Rautenbach

*our thanks to the following
for their help in researching the project*

Maree Airlie, Teresa Alvarez
Phyllis Gautier, Janet Gough, Sharon Hunter
Mary James, Carol MacLeod, Jill McNair

maps
HarperCollins Cartographic

series editor
Lorna Sinclair

Corpus Acknowledgements

We would like to acknowledge the assistance of the many hundreds of individuals and companies who have kindly given permission for copyright material to be used in The Bank of English. The written sources include many national and regional newspapers in Britain and overseas; magazine and periodical publishers; and book publishers in Britain, the United States and Australia. Extensive spoken data has been provided by radio and television broadcasting companies; research workers at many universities and other institutions; and individual numerous contributors. We are grateful to them all.

Typeset by Ray Carrick

A catalogue record for this book is available from the British Library

*Printed and bound in Great Britain by
Caledonian International Book Manufacturing Ltd, Glasgow, G64*

CONTENTS

INTRODUCTION

Collins Easy Learning French Dictionary is an innovative new dictionary designed specifically for anyone starting to learn French. We are grateful to all those teachers who have contributed to its development by advising us on how to tailor it to the needs of their students. We also gratefully acknowledge the help of the Northern Examining and Assessment Board, whom we have consulted throughout this project, and whose word lists and exam papers we carefully studied when compiling this dictionary.

HOW TO USE THE DICTIONARY

Using a dictionary is a skill you can improve with practice and by following some basic guidelines. This section gives you a detailed explanation of how to use the dictionary to ensure you get the most out of it.

The answers to all the questions in this section are on page 10.

MAKE SURE YOU LOOK IN THE RIGHT SIDE OF THE DICTIONARY

The French–English side comes first: you look there to find the meaning of a French word. The second part is English–French. That's what you need for translating into French. (To remind yourself which side is which, you could remember the phrase *French first*.) At the top of every page, you will see either **French → English** or **English → French**, so you can see immediately if you've got the side you want. The middle pages of the book have a grey border so that you can see where one side finishes and the other starts.

> **Check:** 1 Which side of the dictionary would you need to look up to translate *le fauteuil*?

FINDING THE WORD YOU WANT

When you are looking for a word, for example *nouveau*, look at the first letter – **n** – and find the **N** section in the French–English side. Look at page 170. At the top of the page, you'll find the words **nectar → n'importe**. These are the first and last words on that page. So **nouveau** is not going to be on page 170 because its second letter, **o**, comes after i, th second letter of **n'importe**. You have to go past all the words starting with **ne** and all words starting with **ni** until you get to words starting with **no**. Scan down these un you find the word you want. Remember that even if a letter has an accent on it akes no difference to the alphabetical order.

Check: 2 Which comes first – **nager** or **nécessaire**?
3 Does **nouveau** come before or after **Noël**?
4 Does **chou-fleur** come before or after **chocolat**?

MAKE SURE YOU LOOK AT THE RIGHT ENTRY

An entry is made up of a **word**, its translations and, often, example phrases to show you
how to use the translations. If there is more than one entry for the same word, then
there is a warning box to tell you so. Look at the following example entries:

flat ADJECTIVE
see also flat NOUN
1 **plat** ◇ *a flat roof* un toit plat
◇ *flat shoes* des chaussures plates
2 **crevé** *(tyre)* ◇ *I've got a flat tyre.*
J'ai un pneu crevé.

flat NOUN
see also flat ADJECTIVE
l' **appartement** MASC ◇ *She lives
in a flat.* Elle habite un
appartement.

Check: 5 Which of the two entries above will help you translate the
phrase *I live in a flat*?

Look for the two clues which are there to help you:
◇ an example similar to what you want to say
◇ the word NOUN

**Always pay attention to information boxes – they tell you if there is more than one entry for
the same word, give you guidance on grammatical points, and tell you about differences
between French and British life.**

NOUNS, PRONOUNS, ADJECTIVES, VERBS, ADVERBS, PREPOSITIONS

There are two entries for **flat** because this word can be a noun or an adjective. It helps to
choose correctly between entries if you know how to recognize these different types of
words.

Nouns and pronouns

Nouns often appear with words like *a, the, this, that, my, your* and *his*. They can be
singular (abbreviated to SING in the dictionary):

a friend   *the* street   *this* year   *my* dog   *your* car

or plural (abbreviated to PL in the dictionary):

the facts   *those* people   *his* shoes   *our* holidays

They can be the subject of a verb:

Vegetables are good for you

object of a verb:

tennis

ou, he, she, him, her and *they* are pronouns. They can be used instead
er to a person as *he* or *she* or to a thing as *it*.

> **Check:** *I bought my mother a box of chocolates.*
>
> **6** Which three words are nouns in this sentence?
> **7** Which of the nouns is plural?
> **8** Which word is a pronoun?

French nouns are either masculine or feminine (abbreviated to MASC and FEM). Masculine nouns are shown by **le**:

le bateau   *le* chien   *le* jardin

Feminine nouns are shown by **la**:

la porte   *la* robe   *la* souris

If a noun starts with a vowel or a vowel sound, then **le** or **la** becomes **l'**:

*l'*ami   *l'*eau   *l'*orage   *l'*histoire

The plural form of **le**, **la** and **l'** is **les**. As in English, the plural of most French nouns is made by adding **s**:

les chien*s*   *les* porte*s*   *les* table*s*

If the singular form already ends in **s** or if it ends in **x**, then you don't have to add anything:

l'ananas   *les ananas*
la voix   *les voix*

Sometimes, however, the plural form is irregular and this is shown in the entry:

le **cheval** NOUN   **horse** NOUN
   (PL les **chevaux**)   le **cheval**
   horse   (les **chevaux** PL)

> **Check:** *Je me brosse les dents tous les soirs.*
>
> **9** Two words in this sentence are nouns. Which ones?
> **10** Are they singular or plural?
> **11** What is the plural form of *le choix*?
> **12** Look in the dictionary to find the plural form of *le travail*.

Adjectives

Flat can be an adjective as well as a noun. Adjectives describe nouns: your tyre can be **flat**, you can have a pair of **flat** shoes.

> **Check:** **13** *dark* is an adjective in one of these sentences and a noun in the other. Which is which?
>
> *I'm not afraid of the dark.*
> *She's got dark hair.*

French adjectives can be masculine or feminine, singular or plural, depending on the noun they describe:

un **petit** garçon (MASC SING)
une **petite** fille (FEM SING = masculine singular + **e**)
trois **petits** garçons (MASC PL = masculine singular + **s**)
trois **petites** filles (FEM PL = masculine singular + **es**)

Only the masculine singular form of regular adjectives is shown in the dictionary. So if you want to find out what sort of shoes **des chaussures plates** are, look under **plat**.

If the feminine or the plural form of an adjective does *not* follow the above rules, then the irregular form is shown in the dictionary:

frais ADJECTIVE
(FEM SING **fraîche**)
fresh

fresh ADJECTIVE
frais MASC
fraîche FEM

bon ADJECTIVE
(FEM SING **bonne**)
good

good ADJECTIVE
bon MASC
bonne FEM

If the masculine form ends in **s** or **x**, then you don't need to add **s** to make the masculine plural. And if the masculine form ends in **e**, you don't add anything to form the feminine form. But remember – if the adjective ends in **é**, then it behaves like any regular adjective.

MASC SING	FEM SING	MASC PL	FEM PL
gris	grise	gris	grises
anxieux	anxieuse	anxieux	anxieuses
agréable	agréable	agréables	agréables
passé	passée	passés	passées

Some adjectives remain the same whether they're masculine, feminine or plural. This is also shown in the dictionary:

arrière ADJECTIVE (MASC, FEM, PL)
back

back ADJECTIVE
arrière MASC, FEM, PL

Check: **14** What is the feminine form of **vert**?
15 What is the masculine plural form of **aimable**?
16 What is the masculine singular form of **heureux**?
17 What is the masculine plural form of **gras**? And the feminine singular (look in the dictionary for this one)?

Verbs

His time in the race was a new world record.
She's going to record the programme for me.

Record in the first sentence is a noun. In the second, it is a verb.

One way to recognize a verb is that it frequently comes with a pronoun such as **I**, **you** or **she**, or with somebody's name. Verbs can relate to the present, the past or the future. They have a number of different forms to show this: **I'm going** (present), **he will go** (future), and **Nicola went by herself** (past). Often verbs appear with **to**: **they promised to go**. This basic form of the verb is called the infinitive.

In this dictionary, verbs are preceded by to, so you can identify them at a glance. No matter which of the four previous examples you want to translate, you should look up to **go**, not **going** or **went**. If you want to translate **I thought**, look up to **think**.

Check: **18** What would you look up to translate the verbs in these phrases?

I **went**	*she***'s crying**	*he* **was lying**
I **did** *it*	*he***'s out**	*they***'ve gone**

Verbs have different endings, depending on whether you are talking about **je, tu, nous, ils** etc: **j'aime, tu aimes, nous aimons, ils aiment** etc. They also have different forms for the present, future, past etc. **Nous mangeons** (*we eat* = present), **nous avons mangé** (*we ate* = past). **Manger** is the infinitive and is the form that appears in the dictionary.

Sometimes the verb changes completely between the infinitive form and the **je, tu, il** etc form. For example, *I go* is **je vais** but *to go* is **aller** and **nous faisons** (*we do*) comes from **faire** (*to do*). **J'ai fait** (*I have done* or *I did*) also comes from **faire**.

On pages 284–297 of the dictionary, you will find tables of the most important forms of 14 French verbs. And on pages 298–299, you will find a list of the main forms of other French irregular verbs.

Adverbs

An adverb is a word that describes a verb or an adjective:

> Write **soon**.   Check your work **carefully**.
> They arrived **late**.   The film was **very** good.

In the sentence *The swimming pool is open daily*, **daily** is an adverb describing the adjective **open**. In the phrase *my daily routine*, **daily** is an adjective describing the noun **routine**. We use the same word in English but to get the right French translation, it is important to know if it's being used as an adjective or an adverb. When you look up **daily** you find:

> **daily**   ADJECTIVE, ADVERB
>   1 **quotidien** MASC
>   **quotidienne** FEM
>   ◇ *It's part of my daily routine.* Ça fait
>   partie de mes occupations
>   quotidiennes.
>   2 **tous les jours**
> ► **The pool is open daily from 9 a.m. to**
>   **6 p.m.** La piscine est ouverte tous les
>   jours de neuf heures à dix-huit heures.

The examples show you **daily** being used as an adjective and as an adverb and will help you choose the right French translation.

> **Check:**   Take the sentence *The menu changes daily.*
>
>   **19** Does **daily** go with the noun **menu** or the verb **changes**?
>   **20** Is it an adverb or an adjective?
>   **21** How would you translate **daily** in this sentence?

Prepositions

Prepositions are words like **for, with** and **across**, which are followed by nouns or pronouns:

> I've got a present **for** David.   Come **with** me.   He ran **across** the road.

> **Check:** *The party's over.*
>   *The shop's just over the road.*
>
>   **22** In one of these sentences **over** is an adjective describing a noun, in the other it is a preposition followed by a noun. Which is which?

CHOOSING THE RIGHT TRANSLATION

The main translation of a word is shown on a new line with shading behind it to make it stand out from the rest of the entry. If there is more than one main translation for a word, each one is numbered. If an entry continues over the page, there is a signpost to indicate this.

Often you will see phrases in *italics*, preceded by a white diamond ◦. These show how the translation they follow can be used. They also help you choose the translation you want because they give examples of the context in which it can be used.

bouillant ADJECTIVE

1 **boiling** ◦ *Faites cuire les pâtes à l'eau bouillante.* Cook the pasta in boiling water.

2 **piping hot** ◦ *La soupe est servie bouillante.* The soup should be served piping hot.

to overlook VERB

1 **donner sur** (*have view of*) ◦ *The hotel overlooked the beach.* L'hôtel donnait sur la plage.

2 **négliger** (*forget about*) ◦ *He had overlooked one important problem.* Il avait négligé un problème important.

Check: **23** Use the dictionary to translate *That's a very hard question.*

Words often have more than one meaning and more than one translation: if you don't **get** to the station on time, you don't arrive on time, but if you say "I don't **get** it", you mean you don't understand. When you are translating from English, be careful to choose the French word that has the particular meaning you want. The dictionary offers you a lot of help with this. Look at the following entry:

pool NOUN

1 la **flaque** (*puddle*)

2 l' **étang** (*pond*)

3 la **piscine** (*for swimming*)

4 le **billard américain** (*game*)

A **pool** can be a puddle, a pond or a swimming pool; **pool** can also be a game. The shading highlights all the main translations, the numbers tell you that there is more than one possible translation and the words in brackets in *italics* after the translations help you choose which translation you want.

Check: **24** How would you translate *I like playing pool*?

Never take the first translation you see without looking at the others. Always look to see if there is more than one shaded translation.

Phrases in **bold type** preceded by a black diamond ◆ are phrases which are particularly common or important. Sometimes these phrases have a completely different translation from the main translation; sometimes the translation is the same. For example:

le **dommage** NOUN

damage ◦ *La tempête a causé d'importants dommages.* The storm caused a lot of damage.

◆ **C'est dommage.** It's a shame.
◦ *C'est dommage que tu ne puisses pas venir.* It's a shame you can't come.

to go out VERB

1 **sortir** (*person*) ◦ *Are you going out tonight?* Tu sors ce soir?

◆ **to go out with somebody** sortir avec quelqu'un ◦ *Are you going out with him?* Est-ce que tu sors avec lui?

2 **s'éteindre** (*light, fire, candle*)
◦ *Suddenly the lights went out.* Soudain, les lumières se sont éteintes.

When you look up a word, make sure you look beyond the main translations to see if the entry includes any **bold phrases**.

> **Check:** 25 In a job advert you read that applicants *doivent tous passer une visite médicale*. What must they all do?
>
> Look up **visite** and find the answer as quickly as possible by skimming down the **bold phrases**.

MAKING USE OF THE PHRASES IN THE DICTIONARY

Sometimes when you look up a word you will find not only the word, but the exact phrase you want. For example, you might want to say *What's the date today?* Look up **date** and you will find:

date NOUN
la **date** ◇ *my date of birth* ma date de
naissance
- **What's the date today?** Quel jour
sommes-nous?

Sometimes you have to adapt what you find in the dictionary. If you want to say *I play darts* and look up **darts** you will find:

dart NOUN
la **fléchette** ◇ *to play darts* jouer aux
fléchettes

You have to substitute *je joue* for the infinitive form *jouer*. You will often have to adapt the infinitive in this way, adding the correct ending for **je, tu, il** etc and choosing the present, future or past form. For help with this, look at the verb tables. **Jouer** is a verb ending in *–er* so it follows the same pattern as **aimer**, which is set out on page 284.

> **Check:** 26 How would you say *We played football*?

Phrases containing nouns and adjectives also need to be adapted. You may need to make the noun plural, or the adjective feminine or plural. Remember that some nouns and adjectives have irregular feminine or plural forms and that this is shown in the entry.

> **Check:** 27 How would you say *The jewels are beautiful*?

DON'T OVERUSE THE DICTIONARY

It takes time to look up words so try to avoid using the dictionary unnecessarily, **especially in exams**. Think carefully about what you want to say and see if you can put it another way, using words you already know. To rephrase things you can:

◇ Use a word with a similar meaning. This is particularly easy with adjectives, as there are a lot of words which mean good, bad, big etc and you're sure to know at least one.

◇ Use negatives: if the cake you made was a total disaster, you could just say it wasn't very good.

◇ Use particular examples instead of general terms. If you are asked to describe the sports facilities in your area, and time is short, don't look up *facilities* – say something like "In our town there is a swimming pool and a football ground."

> **Check:** **28** You want to ask *Have you got any pets?* How could you avoid
> the word *pet* if you don't know it?
> **29** How could you say *The palace of Versailles is huge* without
> looking up the word *huge*?

You can also often guess the meaning of a French word by using others to give you a
clue. If you see the sentence *j'écoute de la musique rap*, you may not know the meaning
of the word **écoute**, but you do know it's a verb because it's preceded by **j'**. Therefore it
must be something you can do to music: **listen**. So the translation is: *I listen to rap
music.*

> **Check:** **30** In a description of a holiday centre you see a picture of bikes
> and read *On peut louer des vélos: 20F la journée.* You may not know
> the meaning of *louer*, but you can see that you have to pay 20
> francs, which gives you a clue to what it could mean. What can
> you do – ride bikes, borrow bikes or hire bikes?

Answers

1 the French side
2 **nager**
3 **nouveau** comes after **Noël**
4 **chou–fleur** comes after **chocolat**
5 the second entry (the NOUN entry)
6 **mother**, **box** and **chocolates** are nouns
7 **chocolates** is plural
8 **I** is a pronoun
9 **dents** and **soirs** are nouns
10 they are both plural
11 **les choix**
12 **les travaux**
13 **dark** in the first sentence is a noun and in the second, it's an adjective
14 **verte**
15 **aimables**
16 **heureux**
17 the masculine plural form is **gras** and the feminine singular form is **grasse**
18 to **go**, to **cry**, to **lie**, to **do**, to **be**, to **go**
19 **daily** goes with the verb **changes**
20 it is an adverb
21 **tous les jours**
22 in the first sentence, **over** is an adjective and in the second, it's a preposition
23 **c'est une question très difficile**
24 **j'aime jouer au billard américain**
25 they must all have **a medical examination**
26 **nous avons joué au football**
27 **les bijoux sont beaux**
28 you could ask, "Have you got a cat or a dog?"
29 you could say, "Very big."
30 you can **hire** bikes

A

a VERB *see* **avoir**

> **a** *should not be confused with the preposition* **à.**

- **Il a beaucoup d'amis.** He has a lot of friends.
- **Il a mangé des frites.** He had some chips.
- **Il a neigé pendant la nuit.** It snowed during the night.
- **il y a (1)** there is ◇ *Il y a un bon film à la télé.* There's a good film on TV.
- **il y a (2)** there are ◇ *Il y a beaucoup de monde.* There are lots of people.

à PREPOSITION

> **à** *should not be confused with the verb form* **a.** *See also* **au (=à+le)** *and* **aux (=à+les).**

1. **at** ◇ *être à la maison* to be at home ◇ *à trois heures* at 3 o'clock
2. **in** ◇ *être à Paris* to be in Paris ◇ *habiter au Portugal* to live in Portugal ◇ *habiter à la campagne* to live in the country ◇ *au printemps* in the spring ◇ *au mois de juin* in June
3. **to** ◇ *aller à Paris* to go to Paris ◇ *aller au Portugal* to go to Portugal ◇ *aller à la campagne* to go to the country ◇ *donner quelque chose à quelqu'un* to give something to somebody ◇ *Cette veste appartient à Marie.* This jacket belongs to Marie. ◇ *Je n'ai rien à faire.* I've got nothing to do.

- **Ce livre est à Paul.** This book is Paul's.
- **Cette voiture est à nous.** This car is ours.

4. **by** ◇ *à bicyclette* by bicycle ◇ *être payé à l'heure* to be paid by the hour

- **à pied** on foot
- **C'est à côté de chez moi.** It's near my house.
- **C'est à dix kilomètres d'ici.** It's 10 kilometres from here.
- **cent kilomètres à l'heure** 100 kilometres an hour
- **À bientôt!** See you soon! ◇ *À demain!* See you tomorrow! ◇ *À samedi!* See you on Saturday! ◇ *À tout à l'heure!* See you later!

abandonner VERB

1. **to abandon** ◇ *Avant les vacances, beaucoup de chiens sont abandonnés par leurs maîtres.* Before the holidays, a lot of dogs are abandoned by their owners.
2. **to give up** ◇ *J'ai décidé d'abandonner la natation.* I've decided to give up swimming.

l'abeille FEM NOUN
  bee

abîmer VERB
  to damage
- **s'abîmer** to get damaged

l'abonnement MASC NOUN
  1. **season ticket**
  2. **subscription** (*to magazine*)

s'abonner VERB
- **s'abonner à une revue** to take out a subscription to a magazine

l'abord MASC NOUN
- **d'abord** first ◇ *Je vais rentrer chez moi d'abord.* I'll go home first.

aboyer VERB
  to bark

l'abri MASC NOUN
  shelter
- **être à l'abri** to be under cover
- **se mettre à l'abri** to shelter

l'abricot MASC NOUN
  apricot

s'abriter VERB
  to shelter

l'absence FEM NOUN
  absence
- **Il est passé pendant ton absence.** He came while you were away.

absent ADJECTIVE
  absent

absolument ADVERB
  absolutely

l'accélérateur MASC NOUN
  accelerator

accélérer VERB
  to accelerate

l'accent MASC NOUN
  accent ◇ *Il a l'accent de Marseille.* He has a Marseilles accent.
- **un accent aigu** an acute accent
- **un accent grave** a grave accent
- **un accent circonflexe** a circumflex

accentuer VERB
  to stress

accepter VERB
  to accept
- **accepter de faire quelque chose** to agree to do something

l'accessoire MASC NOUN
  1. **accessory** ◇ *les accessoires de mode* fashion accessories
  2. **prop**

l'accident MASC NOUN
  accident ◇ *un accident de la route* a road accident

accompagner VERB
  to accompany

l'**accord** MASC NOUN
  agreement
- **être d'accord** to agree ◇ *Tu es d'accord avec moi?* Do you agree with me?
- **se mettre d'accord** to come to an agreement
- **D'accord!** OK!

l'**accordéon** MASC NOUN
  accordion ◇ *Ray joue de l'accordéon.* Ray plays the accordion.

l'**accoudoir** MASC NOUN
  armrest

l'**accrochage** MASC NOUN
  collision

accrocher VERB
- **accrocher quelque chose à (1)** to hang something on ◇ *Il a accroché sa veste au portemanteau.* He hung his jacket on the coat rack.
- **accrocher quelque chose à (2)** to hitch something up to ◇ *Ils ont accroché la remorque à leur voiture.* They hitched the trailer up to their car.
- **s'accrocher à quelque chose** to catch on something ◇ *Sa jupe s'est accrochée aux ronces.* Her skirt got caught on the brambles.

s'**accroupir** VERB
  to squat down

l'**accueil** MASC NOUN
  welcome ◇ *Il nous a remerciés de notre accueil.* He thanked us for our welcome.
- **Elle s'occupe de l'accueil des visiteurs.** She's in charge of looking after visitors.

accueillir VERB
  to welcome

accumuler VERB
  to accumulate
- **s'accumuler** to pile up

l'**accusé** MASC NOUN
  accused ◇ *L'accusé a déclaré que...* The accused stated that...
- **un accusé de réception** an acknowledgement of receipt

l'**accusée** FEM NOUN
  accused

accuser VERB
  to accuse ◇ *accuser quelqu'un de quelque chose* to accuse somebody of something

l'**achat** MASC NOUN
  purchase
- **faire des achats** to do some shopping

acheter VERB
  to buy ◇ *J'ai acheté des gâteaux à la pâtisserie.* I bought some cakes at the cake shop.
- **acheter quelque chose à quelqu'un (1)** to buy something for somebody ◇ *Qu'est-ce que tu lui as acheté pour son anniversaire?* What did you buy him for his birthday?
- **acheter quelque chose à quelqu'un (2)** to buy something from somebody ◇ *J'ai acheté des œufs au fermier.* I bought some eggs from the farmer.

acide ADJECTIVE
  see also **acide** NOUN
  acid ◇ *Ce pamplemousse est trop acide.* This grapefruit is too acid.

l'**acide** MASC NOUN
  see also **acide** ADJECTIVE
  acid

l'**acier** MASC NOUN
  steel

l'**acné** FEM NOUN
  acne ◇ *Il a de l'acné.* He has acne.

acquérir VERB
  to acquire

acquis VERB *see* **acquérir**

acquitter VERB
  to acquit ◇ *L'accusé a été acquitté.* The accused was acquitted.

l'**acte** MASC NOUN
  act
- **un acte de naissance** a birth certificate

l'**acteur** MASC NOUN
  actor ◇ *Il est acteur.* He's an actor. ◇ *un acteur de cinéma* a film actor

actif ADJECTIVE
  (FEM SING **active**)
  active
- **la population active** the working population

l'**action** FEM NOUN
  action
- **une bonne action** a good deed

s'**activer** VERB
  1 **to bustle about** ◇ *Elle s'activait à préparer le repas.* She bustled about preparing the meal.
  2 **to move oneself** ◇ *Allez! Active-toi!* Come on! Get moving!

l'**activité** FEM NOUN
  activity

l'**actrice** FEM NOUN
  actress ◇ *Elle est actrice.* She's an actress. ◇ *une actrice de cinéma* a film actress

l'**actualité** FEM NOUN
  current events
- **un problème d'actualité** a topical issue

- **les actualités** the news
actuel ADJECTIVE
(FEM SING **actuelle**)
present ◇ *le système actuel* the present system
- **à l'heure actuelle** at the present time
actuellement ADVERB
at present
l'**adaptateur** MASC NOUN
adaptor
l'**addition** FEM NOUN
[1] **addition** ◇ *Il a fait une erreur dans son addition.* He made a mistake in his addition.
[2] **bill** ◇ *L'addition, s'il vous plaît!* Can we have the bill, please?
additionner VERB
to add up
adhésif ADJECTIVE
(FEM SING **adhésive**)
- **le ruban adhésif** sticky tape
l'**adjectif** MASC NOUN
adjective
admettre VERB
[1] **to admit** ◇ *Il refuse d'admettre qu'il s'est trompé.* He won't admit that he made a mistake.
[2] **to allow** ◇ *Les chiens ne sont pas admis dans le restaurant.* Dogs are not allowed in the restaurant.
l'**administration** FEM NOUN
administration
- **l'Administration** the Civil Service
admirable ADJECTIVE
wonderful
l'**admirateur** MASC NOUN
admirer
l'**admiratrice** FEM NOUN
admirer
admirer VERB
to admire
admis VERB *see* **admettre**
l'**adolescence** FEM NOUN
adolescence
l'**adolescent** MASC NOUN
teenager
l'**adolescente** FEM NOUN
teenager
adopter VERB
to adopt
adorable ADJECTIVE
lovely
adorer VERB
to love ◇ *Elle adore le chocolat.* She loves chocolate. ◇ *J'adore jouer au tennis.* I love playing tennis.
l'**adresse** FEM NOUN
address
adresser VERB

- **adresser la parole à quelqu'un** to speak to someone
- **s'adresser à quelqu'un (1)** to speak to somebody ◇ *C'est à toi que je m'adresse.* It's you I'm speaking to.
- **s'adresser à quelqu'un (2)** to go and see somebody ◇ *Adressez-vous au patron.* Go and see the boss. ◇ *Adressez-vous aux renseignements.* Ask at the enquiry desk.
- **s'adresser à quelqu'un (3)** to be aimed at somebody ◇ *Ce film s'adresse surtout aux enfants.* This film is aimed mainly at children.
l'**adulte** MASC/FEM NOUN
adult
l'**adverbe** MASC NOUN
adverb
l'**adversaire** MASC/FEM NOUN
opponent
aérien ADJECTIVE
(FEM SING **aérienne**)
- **une compagnie aérienne** an airline
l'**aérobic** MASC NOUN
aerobics ◇ *Teresa fait de l'aérobic.* Teresa does aerobics.
l'**aérogare** FEM NOUN
terminal
l'**aéroglisseur** MASC NOUN
hovercraft
l'**aéroport** MASC NOUN
airport
l'**affaire** FEM NOUN
see also les affaires
[1] **case** ◇ *une affaire de drogue* a drugs case
[2] **business** ◇ *Son affaire marche bien.* His business is doing well.
- **une bonne affaire** a real bargain
- **Ça fera l'affaire.** This will do nicely.
- **avoir affaire à quelqu'un** to deal with somebody
les **affaires** FEM NOUN
see also l'affaire
[1] **things** ◇ *Va chercher tes affaires!* Go and get your things!
[2] **business** ◇ *Les affaires marchent bien en ce moment.* Business is good at the moment. ◇ *Mêle-toi de tes affaires.* (*informal*) Mind your own business.
- **un homme d'affaires** a businessman
- **le ministre des Affaires étrangères** the Foreign Secretary
l'**affection** FEM NOUN
affection
affectueux ADJECTIVE
(FEM SING **affectueuse**)
affectionate

l'**affiche** FEM NOUN
  poster
afficher VERB
  to put up ◇ *Ils ont affiché les résultats dehors.* They've put the results up outside.
- **"Défense d'afficher"** "Stick no bills"
affilée
- **d'affilée** ADVERB
  at a stretch ◇ *Il a travaillé douze heures d'affilée.* He worked 12 hours at a stretch.
l'**affluence** FEM NOUN
- **les heures d'affluence** the rush hour
s'**affoler** VERB
  to panic ◇ *Ne t'affole pas!* Don't panic!
affranchir VERB
  to stamp
affreux ADJECTIVE
  (FEM SING **affreuse**)
  awful
affronter VERB
  to face ◇ *L'Allemagne affronte l'Italie en finale.* Germany will face Italy in the final.
afin de CONJUNCTION
- **afin de faire quelque chose** so as to do something ◇ *Je me suis levé très tôt afin d'être prêt à temps.* I got up very early so as to be ready on time.
afin que CONJUNCTION
  so that
  afin que *is followed by a verb in the subjunctive.*
  ◇ *Il m'a téléphoné afin que je sois prêt à temps.* He phoned me so that I'd be ready on time.
africain ADJECTIVE, NOUN
  (FEM SING **africaine**)
  African
- **un Africain** an African (*man*)
- **une Africaine** an African (*woman*)
l'**Afrique** FEM NOUN
  Africa
- **en Afrique (1)** in Africa
- **en Afrique (2)** to Africa
- **l'Afrique du Sud** South Africa
agacer VERB
  to get on somebody's nerves ◇ *Tu m'agaces avec tes questions!* You're getting on my nerves with all your questions!
l'**âge** MASC NOUN
  age
- **Quel âge as-tu?** How old are you?
âgé ADJECTIVE
  old ◇ *Son père est âgé.* His father's old. ◇ *Il est âgé de dix ans.* He's 10

years old.
- **les personnes âgées** the elderly
l'**agence** FEM NOUN
  1 **agency**
- **une agence de voyages** a travel agency
  2 **office** ◇ *Nous avons plusieurs agences à Londres.* We have several offices in London.
- **une agence immobilière** an estate agent's
l'**agenda** MASC NOUN
  diary (*for appointments*)
s'**agenouiller** VERB
  to kneel down
l'**agent** MASC NOUN
- **un agent de police** a policeman
l'**agglomération** FEM NOUN
  town
- **l'agglomération parisienne** Greater Paris
aggraver VERB
  to make worse
- **s'aggraver** to worsen
agir VERB
  to act ◇ *Il a agi par vengeance.* He acted out of vengeance.
- **Il s'agit de...** It's about... ◇ *Il s'agit du club de sport.* It's about the sports club. ◇ *De quoi s'agit-il?* What is it about?
- **Il s'agit de faire attention.** We must be careful.
agité ADJECTIVE
  1 **restless** ◇ *Les élèves sont agités.* The pupils are restless.
  2 **rough** ◇ *La mer est agitée.* The sea is rough.
- **un sommeil agité** broken sleep
agiter VERB
  to shake ◇ *Agitez la bouteille.* Shake the bottle.
l'**agneau** MASC NOUN
  (PL les **agneaux**)
  lamb
l'**agrafe** FEM NOUN
  staple (*for papers*)
l'**agrafeuse** FEM NOUN
  stapler
agrandir VERB
  1 **to enlarge** ◇ *J'ai fait agrandir mes photos.* I've had my photos enlarged.
  2 **to extend** ◇ *Ils ont agrandi leur jardin.* They've extended their garden.
- **s'agrandir** to expand ◇ *Leur magasin s'est agrandi.* Their shop has expanded.

agréable ADJECTIVE
nice

agréer VERB
- Veuillez agréer, Monsieur, l'expression de mes sentiments les meilleurs. Jean Ormal. Yours sincerely, Jean Ormal.

agressif ADJECTIVE
(FEM SING **agressive**)
aggressive

agricole ADJECTIVE
agricultural ◇ le matériel agricole agricultural machinery
- une exploitation agricole a farm

agriculteur MASC NOUN
farmer
- Il est agriculteur. He's a farmer.

agriculture FEM NOUN
farming

ai VERB see **avoir**
- J'ai deux chats. I have two cats.
- J'ai bien dormi. I slept well.

aide FEM NOUN
1 help ◇ J'ai besoin de ton aide. I need your help. ◇ appeler quelqu'un à l'aide to call to somebody for help
- À l'aide! Help!
2 aid ◇ une aide financière financial aid
- à l'aide de using ◇ J'ai réussi à ouvrir la boîte à l'aide d'un couteau. I managed to open the tin using a knife.

aider VERB
to help

aide-soignant MASC NOUN
(PL les **aides-soignants**)
auxiliary nurse ◇ Il est aide-soignant. He's an auxiliary nurse.

aide-soignante FEM NOUN
(PL les **aides-soignantes**)
auxiliary nurse ◇ Françoise est aide-soignante. Françoise is an auxiliary nurse.

aie VERB see **avoir**

aïe EXCLAMATION
Ouch!

aigre ADJECTIVE
sour

aiguille FEM NOUN
needle ◇ une aiguille à tricoter a knitting needle
- les aiguilles d'une montre the hands of a watch

ail MASC NOUN
garlic

aile FEM NOUN
wing

aille VERB see **aller**

ailleurs ADVERB
somewhere else
- partout ailleurs everywhere else
- nulle part ailleurs nowhere else
- d'ailleurs besides

aimable ADJECTIVE
kind

aimant MASC NOUN
magnet

aimer VERB
1 to love ◇ Elle aime ses enfants. She loves her children.
2 to like ◇ Tu aimes le chocolat? Do you like chocolate? ◇ J'aime bien ce garçon. I like this boy. ◇ J'aime bien jouer au tennis. I like playing tennis. ◇ J'aimerais aller en Grèce. I'd like to go to Greece.
- J'aimerais mieux ne pas y aller. I'd rather not go.

aîné ADJECTIVE
see also **aîné** NOUN
elder ◇ mon frère aîné my big brother

aîné MASC NOUN
see also **aîné** ADJECTIVE
oldest child ◇ Il est l'aîné. He's the oldest child.

aînée FEM NOUN
oldest child ◇ Elle est l'aînée. She's the oldest child.

ainsi ADVERB
in this way ◇ Il faut faire ainsi. This is the way to do it.
- C'est ainsi qu'il a réussi. That's how he succeeded.
- ainsi que as well as
- et ainsi de suite and so on

air MASC NOUN
1 air ◇ l'air chaud warm air
- prendre l'air to get some fresh air
2 tune ◇ Elle a joué un air au piano. She played a tune on the piano.
- Elle a l'air fatiguée. She looks tired.
- Il a l'air d'un clown. He looks like a clown.

aise FEM NOUN
- être à l'aise to be at ease ◇ Elle est à l'aise avec tout le monde. She's at ease with everybody.
- être mal à l'aise to be ill at ease
- se mettre à l'aise to make oneself comfortable

ait VERB see **avoir**

ajouter VERB
to add

alarme FEM NOUN
alarm ◇ donner l'alarme to raise the alarm

l' **Albanie** FEM NOUN
Albania

l' **album** MASC NOUN
album

l' **alcool** MASC NOUN
alcohol ◇ *Je ne bois pas d'alcool.* I
don't drink alcohol.
- **les alcools forts** spirits

alcoolisé ADJECTIVE
alcoholic
- **une boisson non alcoolisée** a soft
drink

les **alentours** MASC NOUN
- **dans les alentours** in the area
- **aux alentours de Paris** in the Paris
area
- **aux alentours de cinq heures** around
5 o'clock

l' **algèbre** FEM NOUN
algebra

Alger NOUN
Algiers

l' **Algérie** FEM NOUN
Algeria

algérien ADJECTIVE, NOUN
(FEM SING **algérienne**)
Algerian
- **un Algérien** an Algerian (*man*)
- **une Algérienne** an Algerian (*woman*)

l' **algue** FEM NOUN
seaweed

l' **aliment** MASC NOUN
food

l' **alimentation** FEM NOUN
1 **groceries** ◇ *le rayon
alimentation du supermarché* the
grocery department in the
supermarket
2 **diet** ◇ *Elle a une alimentation
saine.* She has a healthy diet.

l' **allée** FEM NOUN
1 **path** ◇ *les allées du parc* the
paths in the park
2 **drive** (*in street names*)
- **les allées et venues** comings and
goings

allégé ADJECTIVE
low-fat ◇ *un yaourt allégé* a low-fat
yoghurt

l' **Allemagne** FEM NOUN
Germany
- **en Allemagne (1)** in Germany
- **en Allemagne (2)** to Germany

allemand ADJECTIVE, NOUN
German ◇ *Elle parle allemand.* She
speaks German.
- **un Allemand** a German (*man*)
- **une Allemande** a German (*woman*)
- **les Allemands** the Germans

aller VERB
see also **aller** NOUN
Present tense:

je vais	nous allons
tu vas	vous allez
il/elle va	ils/elles vont

Past participle: *allé*
to go ◇ *Je suis allé à Londres.* I
went to London. ◇ *Je dois y aller.* I've
got to go. ◇ *Elle ira le voir.* She'll go
and see him. ◇ *Je vais me fâcher.* I'm
going to get angry.
- **s'en aller** to go away ◇ *Je m'en vais
demain.* I'm going tomorrow.
- **aller bien à quelqu'un** to suit
somebody ◇ *Cette robe te va bien.*
This dress suits you.
- **Allez! Dépêche-toi!** Come on! Hurry
up!
- **Comment allez-vous?–Je vais bien.**
How are you?–I'm fine.
- **Comment ça va?–Ça va bien.** How are
you?–I'm fine.
- **aller mieux** to be better

l' **aller** MASC NOUN
see also **aller** VERB
1 **outward journey** ◇ *L'aller nous a
pris trois heures.* The journey there
took us three hours.
2 **single** (*ticket*) ◇ *Je voudrais un
aller pour Angers.* I'd like a single to
Angers.
- **un aller retour (1)** a return ticket
◇ *Je voudrais un aller retour pour
Londres.* I'd like a return to London.
- **un aller retour (2)** a round trip ◇ *Il a
fait l'aller retour en dix heures.* He did
the round trip in ten hours.

allergique ADJECTIVE
- **allergique à** allergic to ◇ *Je suis
allergique aux poils de chat.* I'm allergic
to cat fur.

allô EXCLAMATION
Hello! ◇ *Allô! Je voudrais parler à
Monsieur Simon.* Hello! I'd like to speak
to Mr Simon.

l' **allocation** FEM NOUN
allowance
- **les allocations chômage**
unemployment benefit

s' **allonger** VERB
to lie down ◇ *Il s'est allongé sur son
lit.* He lay down on his bed.

allumer VERB
1 **to put on** (*light*) ◇ *Tu peux allumer
la lumière?* Can you put the light on?
2 **to light** ◇ *Elle a allumé une
cigarette.* She lit a cigarette.
- **s'allumer** (*light*) to come on ◇ *La*

lumière s'est allumée. The light came on.

allumette FEM NOUN
match ◇ *une boîte d'allumettes* a box of matches

allure FEM NOUN
1 **speed** ◇ *à toute allure* at top speed
2 **look** ◇ *avoir une drôle d'allure* to look odd

allusion FEM NOUN
reference

alors ADVERB
1 **then** ◇ *Tu as fini? Alors je m'en vais.* Have you finished? I'm going then.
2 **so** ◇ *Alors je lui ai dit de partir.* So I told him to leave.
- **Et alors?** So what?
3 **at that time** ◇ *Il habitait alors à Paris.* He was living in Paris at that time.
- **alors que (1)** as ◇ *Il est arrivé alors que je partais.* He arrived just as I was leaving.
- **alors que (2)** while ◇ *Alors que je travaillais dur, lui se reposait.* While I was working hard, he was resting.

Alpes FEM NOUN
Alps ◇ *dans les Alpes* in the Alps

alphabet MASC NOUN
alphabet

alphabétique ADJECTIVE
alphabetical ◇ *par ordre alphabétique* in alphabetical order

alpinisme MASC NOUN
mountaineering

alpiniste MASC/FEM NOUN
mountaineer

Alsace FEM NOUN
Alsace

amande FEM NOUN
almond
- **la pâte d'amandes** marzipan

amant MASC NOUN
lover

amateur ADJECTIVE
(FEM SING **amateur**)
see also amateur NOUN
amateur ◇ *Elle est pianiste amateur.* She's an amateur pianist.

amateur MASC NOUN
see also amateur ADJECTIVE
amateur
- **en amateur** as a hobby ◇ *Il fait de la photo en amateur.* He takes photos as a hobby.
- **C'est un amateur de musique.** He's a music lover.

l'ambassade FEM NOUN
embassy

l'ambassadeur MASC NOUN
ambassador

l'ambiance FEM NOUN
atmosphere ◇ *Je n'aime pas l'ambiance ici.* I don't like the atmosphere here. ◇ *Il y a de l'ambiance dans ce café.* This café has a lively atmosphere.
- **la musique d'ambiance** background music

l'ambulance FEM NOUN
ambulance

l'âme FEM NOUN
soul

améliorer VERB
to improve
- **s'améliorer** to improve ◇ *Le temps s'améliore.* The weather's improving.

l'amende FEM NOUN
fine ◇ *une amende de cinq cents francs* a 500 franc fine

amener VERB
to bring ◇ *Qu'est-ce qui t'amène?* What brings you here? ◇ *Est-ce que je peux amener un ami?* Can I bring a friend?

amer ADJECTIVE
(FEM SING **amère**)
bitter

américain ADJECTIVE, NOUN
(FEM SING **américaine**)
American
- **un Américain** an American (*man*)
- **une Américaine** an American (*woman*)

l'Amérique FEM NOUN
America
- **en Amérique (1)** in America
- **en Amérique (2)** to America
- **l'Amérique du Nord** North America
- **l'Amérique du Sud** South America

l'ami MASC NOUN
friend
- **C'est son petit ami.** He's her boyfriend.

amical ADJECTIVE
(MASC PL **amicaux**)
friendly

l'amie FEM NOUN
friend
- **C'est sa petite amie.** She's his girlfriend.

l'amitié FEM NOUN
friendship
- **Fais mes amitiés à Paul.** Give my regards to Paul.
- **Amitiés, Christèle.** (*in letter*) Best wishes, Christèle.

l'**amour** MASC NOUN
love
- **faire l'amour** to make love

amoureux ADJECTIVE
(FEM SING **amoureuse**)
in love ◇ *être amoureux de quelqu'un*
to be in love with somebody

l'**amour-propre** MASC NOUN
self-esteem

l'**amphithéâtre** MASC NOUN
lecture theatre

amplement ADVERB
- **Nous avons amplement le temps.** We
have plenty of time.

l'**ampoule** FEM NOUN
1 light bulb
2 blister ◇ *J'ai une ampoule au pied.*
I've got a blister on my foot.

amusant ADJECTIVE
amusing

les **amuse-gueule** MASC NOUN
party nibbles

amuser VERB
to amuse
- **s'amuser (1)** to play ◇ *Les enfants*
s'amusent dehors. The children are
playing outside.
- **s'amuser (2)** to enjoy oneself ◇ *On*
s'est bien amusés à cette soirée. We
really enjoyed ourselves at that party.

l'**an** MASC NOUN
year
- **le premier de l'an** New Year's Day
- **le nouvel an** New Year

l'**analyse** FEM NOUN
1 analysis
2 test (*medical*) ◇ *une analyse d'urine*
a urine test

l'**ananas** MASC NOUN
pineapple

l'**ancêtre** MASC/FEM NOUN
ancestor

l'**anchois** MASC NOUN
anchovy

ancien ADJECTIVE
(FEM SING **ancienne**)
1 former ◇ *C'est une ancienne*
élève. She's a former pupil.
2 old ◇ *notre ancienne voiture* our
old car
3 antique ◇ *un fauteuil ancien* an
antique chair

l'**ancre** FEM NOUN
anchor

Andorre FEM NOUN
Andorra

l'**âne** MASC NOUN
donkey

l'**ange** MASC NOUN
angel
- **être aux anges** to be over the moon

l'**angine** FEM NOUN
throat infection

anglais ADJECTIVE, NOUN
(FEM SING **anglaise**)
English ◇ *Est-ce que vous parlez*
anglais? Do you speak English?
- **un Anglais** an Englishman
- **une Anglaise** an Englishwoman
- **les Anglais** the English

l'**angle** MASC NOUN
1 angle ◇ *un angle droit* a right
angle
2 corner ◇ *à l'angle de la rue* at the
corner of the street

l'**Angleterre** FEM NOUN
England
- **en Angleterre (1)** in England
◇ *J'habite en Angleterre.* I live in
England.
- **en Angleterre (2)** to England ◇ *Je*
suis allée en Angleterre le mois dernier.
I went to England last month.

anglo- PREFIX
anglo-
- **les îles Anglo-Normandes** the
Channel Islands

anglophone ADJECTIVE
English-speaking

l'**animal** MASC NOUN
(PL les **animaux**)
animal

l'**animateur** MASC NOUN
1 host ◇ *Il est animateur à la télé.*
He's a TV host.
2 youth leader ◇ *Pierre est*
animateur au centre sportif. Pierre is a
youth leader at the sports centre.

l'**animatrice** FEM NOUN
1 host ◇ *Elle est animatrice à la télé.*
She's a TV host.
2 youth leader ◇ *Cécile est*
animatrice au centre sportif. Cécile is a
youth leader at the sports centre.

animé ADJECTIVE
lively ◇ *Cette rue est très animée.*
This is a very lively street.
- **un dessin animé** a cartoon

l'**anis** MASC NOUN
aniseed

l'**anneau** MASC NOUN
(PL les **anneaux**)
ring

l'**année** FEM NOUN
year ◇ *l'année dernière* last year
◇ *l'année prochaine* next year

l'**anniversaire** MASC NOUN
1 birthday ◇ *C'est l'anniversaire de*

Janet. It's Janet's birthday.

2 **anniversary** ◇ *un anniversaire de mariage* a wedding anniversary

l'**annonce** FEM NOUN

advert ◇ *J'ai lu votre annonce dans le journal.* I saw your advert in the newspaper. ◇ *passer une annonce* to place an ad

- **les petites annonces** the small ads

annoncer VERB

to announce ◇ *Ils ont annoncé leurs fiançailles.* They've announced their engagement.

l'**annuaire** MASC NOUN

phone book

annuel ADJECTIVE

(FEM SING **annuelle**)

annual

annuler VERB

to cancel

anonyme ADJECTIVE

anonymous

l'**anorak** MASC NOUN

anorak

ANPE ABBREVIATION (= *Agence nationale pour l'emploi*)

national employment agency ◇ *Je suis allé à l'ANPE.* I went to the job centre.

l'**Antarctique** MASC NOUN

Antarctic

l'**antenne** FEM NOUN

1 **aerial**

2 **antenna**

- **être à l'antenne** to be on the air

l'**antibiotique** MASC NOUN

antibiotic

l'**antigel** MASC NOUN

antifreeze

les **Antilles** FEM NOUN

West Indies

- **aux Antilles (1)** in the West Indies
- **aux Antilles (2)** to the West Indies

antipathique ADJECTIVE

unpleasant ◇ *Je le trouve plutôt antipathique.* I find him rather unpleasant.

antipelliculaire ADJECTIVE

anti-dandruff

l'**antiquaire** MASC/FEM NOUN

antique dealer ◇ *Elle est antiquaire.* She's an antique dealer.

l'**antiquité** FEM NOUN

antique ◇ *un magasin d'antiquités* an antique shop

- **pendant l'antiquité** in classical times

antiseptique ADJECTIVE

see also antiseptique NOUN

antiseptic

l'**antiseptique** MASC NOUN

see also antiseptique ADJECTIVE

antiseptic

anxieux ADJECTIVE

(FEM SING **anxieuse**)

anxious ◇ *Il est anxieux de nature.* He's a born worrier.

août MASC NOUN

August

- **en août** in August

apercevoir VERB

to see ◇ *J'aperçois la côte.* I can see the shore.

- **s'apercevoir de quelque chose** to notice something
- **s'apercevoir que...** to notice that...

l'**apéritif** MASC NOUN

aperitif ◇ *Venez donc prendre l'apéritif ce soir!* Come round for drinks this evening!

apparaître VERB

to appear

l'**appareil** MASC NOUN

device

- **un appareil dentaire** a brace (*for teeth*)
- **les appareils ménagers** domestic appliances
- **un appareil photo** a camera
- **Qui est à l'appareil?** Who's speaking? (*on phone*)

apparemment ADVERB

apparently

l'**apparence** FEM NOUN

appearance

l'**apparition** FEM NOUN

appearance ◇ *Il n'a fait qu'une brève apparition.* He only appeared briefly.

l'**appartement** MASC NOUN

flat

appartenir VERB

- **appartenir à quelqu'un** to belong to somebody

apparu VERB see **apparaître**

l'**appel** MASC NOUN

1 **cry** ◇ *un appel au secours* a cry for help

2 **phone call**

- **faire appel à quelqu'un** to appeal to somebody
- **faire l'appel** to call the register (*in school*)
- **faire un appel de phares** to flash one's headlights

appeler VERB

to call ◇ *Elle a appelé le médecin.* She called the doctor. ◇ *J'ai appelé Richard à Londres.* I called Richard in London.

- **s'appeler** to be called ◇ *Comment ça*

s'appelle? What is it called? ◇ *Elle s'appelle Muriel.* Her name's Muriel. ◇ *Comment tu t'appelles?* What's your name?

l'**appendicite** FEM NOUN
appendicitis

appétissant ADJECTIVE
appetizing

l'**appétit** MASC NOUN
appetite

◆ **Bon appétit!** Enjoy your meal!

applaudir VERB
to clap (*applaud*)

les **applaudissements** MASC NOUN
applause

appliquer VERB
1 to apply
2 to enforce ◇ *appliquer la loi* to enforce the law

◆ **s'appliquer** to apply oneself

apporter VERB
to bring

apprécier VERB
to appreciate

appréhender VERB
to dread ◇ *J'appréhende cette réunion.* I'm dreading this meeting.

apprendre VERB
1 to learn ◇ *apprendre quelque chose par cœur* to learn something by heart

◆ **apprendre à faire quelque chose** to learn to do something ◇ *J'apprends à faire la cuisine.* I'm learning to cook.
2 to hear ◇ *J'ai appris son départ.* I heard that she had left.

◆ **apprendre quelque chose à quelqu'un (1)** to teach somebody something ◇ *Ma mère m'a appris l'anglais.* My mother taught me English. ◇ *Elle lui a appris à conduire.* She taught him to drive.

◆ **apprendre quelque chose à quelqu'un (2)** to tell somebody something ◇ *Jean-Pierre m'a appris la nouvelle.* Jean-Pierre told me the news.

appris VERB *see* **apprendre**

approcher VERB
◆ **approcher de** to approach ◇ *Nous approchons de Paris.* We are approaching Paris.

◆ **s'approcher de** to come closer to ◇ *Ne t'approche pas, j'ai la grippe!* Don't get too close to me, I've got flu!

approuver VERB
to approve of ◇ *Je n'approuve pas ses méthodes.* I don't approve of his methods.

approximatif ADJECTIVE
(FEM SING **approximative**)
1 approximate ◇ *un prix approximatif* an approximate price
2 rough ◇ *un calcul approximatif* a rough calculation

l'**appui** MASC NOUN
support ◇ *J'ai besoin de votre appui.* I need your support.

appuyer VERB
1 to press ◇ *appuyer sur un bouton* to press a button
2 to lean ◇ *Elle a appuyé son vélo contre la porte.* She leaned her bike against the door.

◆ **s'appuyer** to lean ◇ *Elle s'est appuyée contre le mur.* She leaned against the wall. ◇ *Il s'est appuyé sur la table.* He leaned on the table.

après PREPOSITION, ADVERB
1 after ◇ *après le déjeuner* after lunch ◇ *après son départ* after he had left ◇ *après qu'il est parti* after he had left ◇ *Nous viendrons après avoir fait la vaisselle.* We'll come after we've done the dishes.
2 afterwards ◇ *aussitôt après* immediately afterwards

◆ **après coup** afterwards ◇ *J'y ai repensé après coup.* I thought about it again afterwards.

◆ **d'après** according to ◇ *D'après lui, c'est une erreur.* According to him, that's a mistake.

◆ **après tout** after all

après-demain ADVERB
the day after tomorrow

l'**après-midi** MASC OR FEM NOUN
afternoon

l'**aquarium** MASC NOUN
aquarium

arabe ADJECTIVE, NOUN
1 Arab ◇ *les pays arabes* the Arab countries
2 Arabic ◇ *la littérature arabe* Arabic literature ◇ *Il parle arabe.* He speaks Arabic.

◆ **un Arabe** an Arab (*man*)
◆ **une Arabe** an Arab (*woman*)

l'**Arabie Saoudite** FEM NOUN
Saudi Arabia

l'**araignée** FEM NOUN
spider

l'**arbitre** MASC NOUN
1 referee
2 umpire

l'**arbre** MASC NOUN
tree

◆ **un arbre généalogique** a family tree

l'**arbuste** MASC NOUN
shrub

l'**arc** MASC NOUN
bow ◇ *son arc et ses flèches* his bow and arrows

l'**arc-en-ciel** MASC NOUN
(PL les **arcs-en-ciel**)
rainbow

l'**archéologie** FEM NOUN
archaeology

l'**archéologue** MASC/FEM NOUN
archaeologist ◇ *Elle est archéologue.* She's an archaeologist.

l'**archipel** MASC NOUN
archipelago

l'**architecte** MASC NOUN
architect ◇ *Il est architecte.* He's an architect.

l'**architecture** FEM NOUN
architecture

l'**Arctique** MASC NOUN
Arctic

l'**ardoise** FEM NOUN
slate

l'**arène** FEM NOUN
bullring
- **des arènes romaines** a Roman amphitheatre
- **l'arène politique** the political arena

l'**arête** FEM NOUN
fish bone

l'**argent** MASC NOUN
1. **silver** ◇ *une bague en argent* a silver ring
2. **money** ◇ *Je n'ai plus d'argent.* I haven't got any more money.
- **l'argent de poche** pocket money
- **l'argent liquide** cash

argentin ADJECTIVE, NOUN
(FEM SING **argentine**)
Argentinian
- **un Argentin** an Argentinian (*man*)
- **une Argentine** an Argentinian (*woman*)

l'**Argentine** FEM NOUN
Argentina

l'**argile** FEM NOUN
clay

l'**argot** MASC NOUN
slang

l'**arme** FEM NOUN
weapon
- **une arme à feu** a firearm

l'**armée** FEM NOUN
army
- **l'armée de l'air** the Air Force

l'**armistice** MASC NOUN
armistice

l'**armoire** FEM NOUN
wardrobe

l'**armure** FEM NOUN
armour ◇ *un chevalier en armure* a knight in armour

arnaquer (*informal*) VERB
to con

aromatisé ADJECTIVE
flavoured

l'**arôme** MASC NOUN
1. **aroma**
2. **flavouring** (*added to food*)

arpenter VERB
to pace up and down ◇ *Il arpentait le couloir.* He was pacing up and down the corridor.

arrache-pied
- **d'arrache-pied** ADVERB
furiously ◇ *travailler d'arrache-pied* to work furiously

arracher VERB
1. **to take out** ◇ *Le dentiste m'a arraché une dent.* The dentist took one of my teeth out.
2. **to tear out** ◇ *Arrachez la page.* Tear the page out.
3. **to pull up** ◇ *Elle a arraché les mauvaises herbes.* She pulled up the weeds.
- **arracher quelque chose à quelqu'un** to snatch something from somebody

arranger VERB
1. **to arrange** ◇ *arranger des fleurs dans un vase* to arrange flowers in a vase
2. **to suit** ◇ *Ça m'arrange de partir plus tôt.* It suits me to leave earlier.
- **s'arranger** to come to an agreement ◇ *Arrangez-vous avec le patron.* You'll have to come to an agreement with the boss.
- **Je vais m'arranger pour venir.** I'll organize things so that I can come.
- **Ça va s'arranger.** Things will work themselves out.

l'**arrestation** FEM NOUN
arrest ◇ *en état d'arrestation* under arrest

l'**arrêt** MASC NOUN
stop ◇ *un arrêt de bus* a bus stop
- **sans arrêt (1)** non-stop ◇ *Elle travaille sans arrêt.* She works non-stop.
- **sans arrêt (2)** continually ◇ *Ils se disputent sans arrêt.* They quarrel continually.

arrêter VERB
1. **to stop**
- **Arrête!** Stop it!
- **arrêter de faire quelque chose** to stop doing something

2 **to switch off** ◇ *Il a arrêté le moteur.* He switched the engine off.

3 **to arrest** ◇ *Mon voisin a été arrêté.* My neighbour's been arrested.

- **s'arrêter** to stop ◇ *Elle s'est arrêtée devant une vitrine.* She stopped in front of a shop window.
- **s'arrêter de faire quelque chose** to stop doing something ◇ *s'arrêter de fumer* to stop smoking

les **arrhes** FEM NOUN
deposit ◇ *verser des arrhes* to pay a deposit

l' **arrière** MASC NOUN
see also arrière ADJECTIVE
back ◇ *l'arrière de la maison* the back of the house
- **à l'arrière** at the back
- **en arrière** behind ◇ *Ils sont restés en arrière.* They stayed behind.

arrière ADJECTIVE (MASC, FEM, PL)
see also arrière NOUN
back ◇ *le siège arrière* the back seat ◇ *les roues arrière* the rear wheels

l' **arrière-grand-mère** FEM NOUN
(PL les arrière-grands-mères)
great-grandmother

l' **arrière-grand-père** MASC NOUN
(PL les arrière-grands-pères)
great-grandfather

l' **arrivée** FEM NOUN
arrival

arriver VERB
1 **to arrive** ◇ *J'arrive à l'école à huit heures.* I arrive at school at 8 o'clock.
2 **to happen** ◇ *Qu'est-ce qui est arrivé à Christian?* What happened to Christian?
- **arriver à faire quelque chose** to manage to do something ◇ *J'espère que je vais y arriver.* I hope I'll manage it.
- **Il m'arrive de dormir jusqu'à midi.** I sometimes sleep till midday.

arrogant ADJECTIVE
arrogant

l' **arrondissement** MASC NOUN
district
Paris, Lyons and Marseilles are divided into numbered districts called arrondissements.

arroser VERB
to water ◇ *Daphne arrose ses tomates.* Daphne is watering her tomatoes.
- **Ils ont arrosé leur victoire.** They had a drink to celebrate their victory.

l' **arrosoir** MASC NOUN
watering can

l' **art** MASC NOUN

art

l' **artère** FEM NOUN
1 **artery**
2 **thoroughfare** ◇ *les grandes artères de Paris* the main roads of Paris

l' **artichaut** MASC NOUN
artichoke

l' **article** MASC NOUN
1 **article** ◇ *un article de journal* a newspaper article
2 **item** ◇ *les articles en promotion* items on special offer

l' **articulation** FEM NOUN
joint ◇ *l'articulation du genou* the knee joint

articuler VERB
to pronounce clearly

artificiel ADJECTIVE
(FEM SING artificielle)
artificial

l' **artisan** MASC NOUN
self-employed craftsman

l' **artiste** MASC/FEM NOUN
1 **artist**
2 **performer**

artistique ADJECTIVE
artistic

as VERB *see* avoir
see also **as** NOUN
- **Tu as de beaux cheveux.** You've got nice hair.

l' **as** MASC NOUN
see also **as** VERB
ace ◇ *l'as de trèfle* the ace of clubs

l' **ascenseur** MASC NOUN
lift

l' **Ascension** FEM NOUN
Ascension

asiatique ADJECTIVE
Asiatic ◇ *la cuisine asiatique* Oriental cooking ◇ *le Sud-Est asiatique* South East Asia

l' **Asie** FEM NOUN
Asia
- **en Asie (1)** in Asia
- **en Asie (2)** to Asia

l' **aspect** MASC NOUN
appearance

l' **asperge** FEM NOUN
asparagus

l' **aspirateur** MASC NOUN
vacuum cleaner
- **passer l'aspirateur** to vacuum

l' **aspirine** FEM NOUN
aspirin

assaisonner VERB
to season

l' **assassin** MASC NOUN
murderer

assassiner VERB
to murder
assembler VERB
to assemble
• **s'assembler** to gather ◦ *Une foule énorme s'était assemblée.* A huge crowd had gathered.
s'**asseoir** VERB
to sit down ◦ *Asseyez-vous!* Sit down! ◦ *Assieds-toi!* Sit down!
assez ADVERB
1 **enough** ◦ *Nous n'avons pas assez de temps.* We don't have enough time. ◦ *Est-ce qu'il y a assez de pain?* Is there enough bread?
• **J'en ai assez!** I've had enough!
2 **quite** ◦ *Il faisait assez beau.* The weather was quite nice.
l'**assiette** FEM NOUN
plate ◦ *une assiette creuse* a soup plate ◦ *une assiette à dessert* a dessert plate
• **une assiette anglaise** assorted cold meats
assis VERB *see* **asseoir**
assis ADJECTIVE
sitting ◦ *Il est assis par terre.* He's sitting on the floor.
l'**assistance** FEM NOUN
1 **audience** ◦ *Y a-t-il un médecin dans l'assistance?* Is there a doctor in the audience?
2 **aid** ◦ *l'assistance humanitaire* humanitarian aid
3 **assistance** ◦ *avec l'assistance de quelqu'un* with the assistance of somebody
l'**assistant** MASC NOUN
assistant ◦ *Il était assistant d'anglais à Tourcoing.* He was an English assistant in Tourcoing.
• **un assistant social** a social worker
l'**assistante** FEM NOUN
assistant ◦ *Elle est assistante de français à Oxford.* She's a French assistant in Oxford.
• **une assistante sociale** a social worker
assister VERB
• **assister à un accident** to witness an accident
• **assister à un cours** to attend a class
• **assister à un concert** to be at a concert
l'**association** FEM NOUN
association
l'**associé** MASC NOUN
partner (*in business*)
l'**associée** FEM NOUN
partner (*in business*)

s'**associer** VERB
to go into partnership
assommer VERB
to knock out ◦ *Il l'a assommé avec une bouteille.* He knocked him out with a bottle.
l'**Assomption** FEM NOUN
Assumption
assorti ADJECTIVE
1 **matching** ◦ *des couleurs assorties* matching colours
2 **assorted** ◦ *des chocolats assortis* assorted chocolates
• **être assorti à quelque chose** to match something ◦ *Son sac est assorti à ses chaussures.* Her bag matches her shoes.
l'**assortiment** MASC NOUN
assortment
l'**assurance** FEM NOUN
1 **insurance** ◦ *une assurance maladie* medical insurance
2 **confidence** ◦ *parler avec assurance* to speak with confidence
assurer VERB
1 **to insure** ◦ *La maison est assurée.* The house is insured. ◦ *être assuré contre quelque chose* to be insured against something
2 **to assure** ◦ *Je t'assure que c'est vrai!* I assure you it's true!
• **s'assurer de quelque chose** to make sure of something ◦ *Il s'est assuré que la porte était fermée.* He made sure the door was shut.
l'**asthme** MASC NOUN
asthma ◦ *une crise d'asthme* an asthma attack
l'**astronaute** MASC/FEM NOUN
astronaut
l'**astronomie** FEM NOUN
astronomy
astucieux ADJECTIVE
(FEM SING **astucieuse**)
clever
l'**atelier** MASC NOUN
1 **workshop**
2 **studio** (*artist's*)
Athènes NOUN
Athens
l'**athlète** MASC/FEM NOUN
athlete
l'**athlétisme** MASC NOUN
athletics ◦ *un championnat d'athlétisme* an athletics championship
l'**Atlantique** MASC NOUN
Atlantic
l'**atlas** MASC NOUN
atlas

l'**atmosphère** FEM NOUN
atmosphere

atomique ADJECTIVE
atomic ◇ *la bombe atomique* the atomic bomb

atroce ADJECTIVE
terrible

attachant ADJECTIVE
lovable ◇ *un enfant attachant* a lovable child

attacher VERB
to tie up ◇ *Elle a attaché ses cheveux avec un élastique.* She tied her hair up with an elastic band.
- **s'attacher à quelqu'un** to become attached to somebody
- **une poêle qui n'attache pas** a non-stick frying pan

attaquer VERB
to attack

atteindre VERB
to reach

attendant
- **en attendant** ADVERB
in the meantime

attendre VERB
to wait ◇ *attendre quelqu'un* to wait for someone ◇ *J'attends d'avoir un appartement à moi.* I'm waiting until I've got a flat of my own. ◇ *Attends qu'il ne pleuve plus.* Wait until it's stopped raining.
- **attendre un enfant** to be expecting a baby
- **s'attendre à** to expect ◇ *Je m'attends à ce qu'il soit en retard.* I expect he'll be late.

l'**attentat** MASC NOUN
- **un attentat à la bombe** a terrorist bombing

l'**attente** FEM NOUN
wait ◇ *deux heures d'attente* two hours' wait
- **la salle d'attente** the waiting room

attentif ADJECTIVE
(FEM SING **attentive**)
attentive

l'**attention** FEM NOUN
attention ◇ *à l'attention de* for the attention of
- **faire attention** to be careful
- **Attention!** Watch out! ◇ *Attention, tu vas te faire écraser!* Watch out, you'll get run over!

attentionné ADJECTIVE
thoughtful

atterrir VERB
to land

l'**atterrissage** MASC NOUN

landing (*of plane*)

attirant ADJECTIVE
attractive

attirer VERB
to attract ◇ *attirer l'attention de quelqu'un* to attract somebody's attention
- **s'attirer des ennuis** to get into trouble ◇ *Si tu continues, tu vas t'attirer des ennuis.* If you keep on like that, you'll get yourself into trouble.

l'**attitude** FEM NOUN
attitude

l'**attraction** FEM NOUN
- **un parc d'attractions** an amusement park

attraper VERB
to catch

attrayant ADJECTIVE
attractive

attrister VERB
to sadden

au PREPOSITION *see* **à**
au *is the contracted form of* **à + le.**
- **au printemps** in the spring

l'**aube** FEM NOUN
dawn ◇ *à l'aube* at dawn

l'**auberge de jeunesse** FEM NOUN
youth hostel

l'**aubergine** FEM NOUN
aubergine

aucun ADJECTIVE, PRONOUN
1 **no** ◇ *Il n'a aucun ami.* He's got no friends. ◇ *Aucun enfant ne pourrait le faire.* No child could do that.
2 **none** ◇ *Aucun d'entre eux n'est venu.* None of them came. ◇ *Aucune de mes amies n'aime le football.* None of my female friends like football. ◇ *Tu aimes ses films?—Je n'en ai vu aucun.* Do you like his films?—I haven't seen any of them.
- **sans aucun doute** without any doubt

au-delà ADVERB
- **au-delà de** beyond ◇ *Votre ticket n'est pas valable au-delà de cette limite.* Your ticket is not valid beyond this point.

au-dessous ADVERB
1 **downstairs** ◇ *Ils habitent au-dessous.* They live downstairs.
2 **underneath**
- **au-dessous de** under ◇ *au-dessous du pont* under the bridge ◇ *dix degrés au-dessous de zéro* ten degrees below zero

au-dessus ADVERB
1 **upstairs** ◇ *J'habite au-dessus.* I live upstairs.

A

2 **above**
- **au-dessus de** above ◇ *au-dessus de la table* above the table
audiovisuel ADJECTIVE
(FEM SING **audiovisuelle**)
audiovisual
l'**auditeur** MASC NOUN
listener (*to radio*)
l'**auditrice** FEM NOUN
listener (*to radio*)
l'**augmentation** FEM NOUN
rise
augmenter VERB
to increase
aujourd'hui ADVERB
today
auparavant ADVERB
first ◇ *Vous pouvez utiliser l'ordinateur mais auparavant vous devez taper le mot de passe.* You can use the computer but first you have to key in the password.
auquel PRONOUN
(MASC PL **auxquels**, FEM PL **auxquelles**)
auquel *is the contracted form of* **à + lequel**.
◇ *l'homme auquel j'ai parlé* the man I spoke to
aura, aurai, auras, aurez, aurons, auront VERB *see* **avoir**
l'**aurore** FEM NOUN
daybreak
ausculter VERB
- **Le médecin l'a ausculté.** The doctor listened to his chest.
aussi ADVERB
1 **too** ◇ *Dors bien.–Toi aussi.* Sleep well.–You too. ◇ *Lui aussi parle espagnol.* He too speaks Spanish.
2 **also** ◇ *J'aimerais aussi que tu achètes le journal.* I'd also like you to get the paper. ◇ *Je parle anglais et aussi allemand.* I speak English and also German.
- **aussi...que** as...as ◇ *aussi grand que moi* as big as me
aussitôt ADVERB
straight away ◇ *aussitôt après son retour* straight after his return
- **aussitôt que** as soon as ◇ *aussitôt que tu auras fini* as soon as you've finished
l'**Australie** FEM NOUN
Australia
- **en Australie (1)** in Australia
- **en Australie (2)** to Australia
australien ADJECTIVE, NOUN
(FEM SING **australienne**)
Australian
- **un Australien** an Australian (*man*)

- **une Australienne** an Australian (*woman*)
autant ADVERB
- **autant de (1)** so much ◇ *Je ne veux pas autant de gâteau.* I don't want so much cake.
- **autant de (2)** so many ◇ *Je n'ai jamais vu autant de monde.* I've never seen so many people.
- **autant...que (1)** as much...as ◇ *J'ai autant d'argent que toi.* I've got as much money as you have.
- **autant...que (2)** as many...as ◇ *J'ai autant d'amis que lui.* I've got as many friends as he has.
- **d'autant plus que** all the more since ◇ *Elle est d'autant plus déçue qu'il le lui avait promis.* She's all the more disappointed since he had promised her.
- **d'autant moins que** even less since ◇ *C'est d'autant moins pratique pour lui qu'il doit changer deux fois de train.* It's even less convenient for him since he has to change trains twice.
l'**auteur** MASC NOUN
author
l'**auto** FEM NOUN
car
l'**autobus** MASC NOUN
bus ◇ *en autobus* by bus
l'**autocar** MASC NOUN
coach ◇ *en autocar* by coach
autocollant ADJECTIVE
see also **autocollant** NOUN
self-adhesive ◇ *une étiquette autocollante* a self-adhesive label
- **une enveloppe autocollante** a self-seal envelope
l'**autocollant** MASC NOUN
see also **autocollant** ADJECTIVE
sticker
l'**auto-école** FEM NOUN
driving school
automatique ADJECTIVE
automatic
l'**automne** MASC NOUN
autumn
- **en automne** in autumn
automobile ADJECTIVE
see also **automobile** NOUN
- **une course automobile** a motor race
l'**automobile** FEM NOUN
see also **automobile** ADJECTIVE
car
l'**automobiliste** MASC/FEM NOUN
motorist
l'**autoradio** MASC NOUN
car radio

l'**autorisation** FEM NOUN

   1 **permission** ◇ *Il m'a donné l'autorisation de sortir ce soir.* He's given me permission to go out tonight.

   2 **permit** ◇ *Il faut une autorisation pour camper ici.* You need a permit to camp here.

autoriser VERB

   to give permission for ◇ *Il m'a autorisé à en parler.* He's given me permission to talk about it.

autoritaire ADJECTIVE

   authoritarian

l'**autorité** FEM NOUN

   authority

l'**autoroute** FEM NOUN

   motorway

l'**auto-stop** MASC NOUN

• **faire de l'auto-stop** to hitchhike

l'**auto-stoppeur** MASC NOUN

   hitchhiker

l'**auto-stoppeuse** FEM NOUN

   hitchhiker

autour ADVERB

   around ◇ *autour de la maison* around the house

autre ADJECTIVE, PRONOUN

   other ◇ *Je viendrai un autre jour.* I'll come some other day. ◇ *J'ai d'autres projets.* I've got other plans.

• **autre chose** something else

• **autre part** somewhere else

• **un autre** another ◇ *Tu veux un autre morceau de gâteau?* Would you like another piece of cake?

• **l'autre** the other ◇ *Non, pas celui-ci, l'autre.* No, not that one, the other one.

• **d'autres** others ◇ *Je t'en apporterai d'autres.* I'll bring you some others.

• **les autres** the others ◇ *Les autres sont arrivés plus tard.* The others arrived later.

• **ni l'un ni l'autre** neither of them

• **entre autres** among other things ◇ *Nous avons parlé, entre autres, de nos projets de vacances.* We talked about our holiday plans, among other things.

autrefois ADVERB

   in the old days ◇ *Autrefois Saint-Tropez n'était qu'un village de pêcheurs.* In the old days Saint-Tropez was just a fishing village.

autrement ADVERB

   1 **differently** ◇ *Il l'a fait autrement.* He did it differently.

   2 **otherwise** ◇ *Je n'ai pas pu faire autrement.* I couldn't do otherwise.

• **autrement dit** in other words

l'**Autriche** FEM NOUN

   Austria

• **en Autriche (1)** in Austria

• **en Autriche (2)** to Austria

autrichien ADJECTIVE, NOUN

   (FEM SING **autrichienne**)

   Austrian

• **un Autrichien** an Austrian (*man*)

• **une Autrichienne** an Austrian (*woman*)

l'**autruche** FEM NOUN

   ostrich

aux PREPOSITION *see* **à**

   aux *is the contracted form of* **à + les.**

   ◇ *J'ai dit aux enfants d'aller jouer.* I told the children to go and play.

auxquelles PRONOUN

   auxquelles *is the contracted form of* **à + lesquelles.**

   ◇ *les revues auxquelles il est abonné* the magazines to which he subscribes

auxquels PRONOUN

   auxquels *is the contracted form of* **à + lesquels.**

   ◇ *les enfants auxquels il a parlé* the children he spoke to

l'**avalanche** FEM NOUN

   avalanche

avaler VERB

   to swallow

l'**avance** FEM NOUN

• **être en avance** to be early

• **à l'avance** beforehand ◇ *réserver longtemps à l'avance* to book well beforehand

• **d'avance** in advance ◇ *payer d'avance* to pay in advance

avancé ADJECTIVE

   advanced ◇ *à un niveau avancé* at an advanced level

• **bien avancé** well under way ◇ *Les travaux sont déjà bien avancés.* The work is already well under way.

avancer VERB

   1 **to move forward** ◇ *Il avançait prudemment.* He was moving forward cautiously.

   2 **to bring forward** ◇ *La date de l'examen a été avancée.* The date of the exam has been brought forward.

   3 **to put forward** ◇ *Il a avancé sa montre d'une heure.* He put his watch forward an hour.

   4 **to be fast** (*watch*) ◇ *Ma montre avance d'une heure.* My watch is an hour fast.

   5 **to lend** ◇ *Peux-tu m'avancer cent francs?* Can you lend me 100 francs?

avant PREPOSITION, ADJECTIVE

   see also **avant** NOUN

1 before ◦ *avant qu'il ne pleuve* before it rains ◦ *avant de partir* before leaving

2 front ◦ *la roue avant* the front wheel ◦ *le siège avant* the front seat

l'**avant** MASC NOUN

see also avant PREPOSITION

front ◦ *l'avant de la voiture* the front of the car

- **à l'avant** in front
- **en avant** forward ◦ *Il a fait un pas en avant.* He took a step forward.

l'**avantage** MASC NOUN

advantage

l'**avant-bras** MASC NOUN

(PL les **avant-bras**)

forearm

avant-dernier ADJECTIVE

(FEM **avant-dernière**, MASC PL **avant-derniers**)

last but one ◦ *l'avant-dernière page* the last page but one ◦ *Ils sont arrivés avant-derniers.* They arrived last but one.

avant-hier ADVERB

the day before yesterday ◦ *Il est arrivé avant-hier.* He arrived the day before yesterday.

avare ADJECTIVE

see also avare NOUN

miserly

l'**avare** MASC/FEM NOUN

see also avare ADJECTIVE

miser

avec PREPOSITION

with ◦ *avec mon père* with my father

- **Et avec ça?** Anything else? (*in shop*)

l'**avenir** MASC NOUN

future

- **à l'avenir** in future ◦ *À l'avenir, essayez d'être à l'heure.* Try to be on time in future.
- **dans un proche avenir** in the near future

l'**aventure** FEM NOUN

adventure

l'**avenue** FEM NOUN

avenue

l'**averse** FEM NOUN

shower (*of rain*)

avertir VERB

to warn

- **avertir quelqu'un de quelque chose** to warn somebody about something

l'**avertissement** MASC NOUN

warning

aveugle ADJECTIVE

blind

l'**avion** MASC NOUN

plane

- **aller en avion** to go by plane ◦ *Il est allé en Italie en avion.* He flew to Italy.
- **par avion** by airmail

l'**aviron** MASC NOUN

rowing

l'**avis** MASC NOUN

1 opinion ◦ *J'aimerais avoir ton avis.* I'd like to have your opinion.

2 notice ◦ *jusqu'à nouvel avis* until further notice

- **changer d'avis** to change one's mind ◦ *J'ai changé d'avis.* I've changed my mind.

l'**avocat** MASC NOUN

1 lawyer ◦ *Il est avocat.* He's a lawyer.

2 avocado

l'**avocate** FEM NOUN

lawyer ◦ *Elle est avocate.* She's a lawyer.

l'**avoine** FEM NOUN

oats ◦ *les flocons d'avoine* porridge oats

avoir VERB

Present tense:	
j'ai	nous avons
tu as	vous avez
il/elle a	ils/elles ont
Past participle: *eu*	

1 to have ◦ *Ils ont deux enfants.* They have two children. ◦ *Il a les yeux bleus.* He's got blue eyes. ◦ *J'ai déjà mangé.* I've already eaten. ◦ *Est-ce que tu as vu ce film?* Have you seen this film? ◦ *Je lui ai parlé hier.* I spoke to him yesterday.

- **On t'a bien eu!** (*informal*) You've been had!

2 to be ◦ *Il a trois ans.* He's three. ◦ *J'avais dix ans quand je l'ai rencontré.* I was ten when I met him.

- **il y a (1)** there is ◦ *Il y a quelqu'un à la porte.* There's somebody at the door.
- **il y a (2)** there are ◦ *Il y a des chocolats sur la table.* There are some chocolates on the table.
- **il y a (3)** ago ◦ *Je l'ai rencontré il y a deux ans.* I met him two years ago.
- **Qu'est-ce qu'il y a?** What's the matter?
- **Il n'y a qu'à partir plus tôt.** We'll just have to leave earlier.

l'**avortement** MASC NOUN

abortion

avril MASC NOUN

April

- **en avril** in April

ayez, ayons VERB *see* **avoir**

B

le **baby-foot** NOUN
 table football ◇ *jouer au baby-foot*
 to play table football

le **baby-sitting** NOUN
 ◆ **faire du baby-sitting** to babysit

le **bac** = baccalauréat

le **baccalauréat** NOUN
 A levels ◇ *Elle a passé son baccalauréat l'année dernière.* She did her A levels last year.

> *The French* baccalauréat, *or* bac *for short, is taken at the age of 17 or 18. Students have to sit one of a variety of set subject combinations, rather than being able to choose any combination of subjects they want. If you pass you have the right to a place at university.*

bâcler VERB
 to botch up ◇ *Je déteste le travail bâclé!* I hate work that's not done properly!

le **bagage** NOUN
 luggage
 ◆ **faire ses bagages** to pack
 ◆ **les bagages à main** hand luggage
  ◇ *un bagage à main* a piece of hand luggage

la **bagarre** NOUN
 fight ◇ *Une bagarre a éclaté à la fermeture du pub.* A fight broke out when the pub closed.

se **bagarrer** VERB
 to fight ◇ *Il s'est encore bagarré avec son frère.* He's been fighting with his brother again.

la **bagnole** NOUN (*informal*)
 car

la **bague** NOUN
 ring

la **baguette** NOUN
 1 **stick of French bread**
 2 **chopstick** ◇ *manger avec des baguettes* to eat with chopsticks
 ◆ **une baguette magique** a magic wand

la **baie** NOUN
 bay

se **baigner** VERB
 to go swimming ◇ *Si on allait se baigner?* Shall we go swimming?

la **baignoire** NOUN
 bath (*bathtub*)

bâiller VERB
 to yawn

le **bain** NOUN
 bath ◇ *prendre un bain* to take a bath ◇ *prendre un bain de soleil* to sunbathe

le **baiser** NOUN
 kiss

baisser VERB
 1 **to turn down** ◇ *Il fait moins froid, tu peux baisser le chauffage.* It's not so cold, you can turn down the heating.
 2 **to fall** ◇ *Le prix des CD a baissé.* The price of CDs has fallen.
 ◆ **se baisser** to bend down ◇ *Il s'est baissé pour ramasser son mouchoir.* He bent down to pick up his handkerchief.

le **bal** NOUN
 dance ◇ *un bal populaire* a local dance
 ◆ **un bal costumé** a fancy dress ball

la **balade** NOUN (*informal*)
 walk ◇ *faire une balade* to go for a walk

se **balader** VERB (*informal*)
 to wander around ◇ *J'adore me balader dans les rues de Paris.* I love to wander around the streets of Paris.

le **baladeur** NOUN
 personal stereo

le **balai** NOUN
 broom ◇ *Je vais donner un coup de balai dans la cuisine.* I'm going to sweep the kitchen.

la **balance** NOUN
 scales PL (*for weighing*)
 ◆ **la Balance** Libra ◇ *Todd est Balance.* Todd is Libra.

se **balancer** VERB
 to swing

la **balançoire** NOUN
 swing

balayer VERB
 1 **to sweep** ◇ *Jean-Pierre a balayé la cuisine.* Jean-Pierre swept the kitchen.
 2 **to sweep up** ◇ *Va balayer les feuilles sur la terrasse.* Go and sweep up the leaves on the terrace.

le **balayeur** NOUN
 roadsweeper

balbutier VERB
 to stammer

le **balcon** NOUN
 balcony

la **baleine** NOUN
 whale

la **balle** NOUN
 1 **ball** ◇ *une balle de tennis* a tennis ball
 2 **bullet**

la **ballerine** NOUN

B

[1] **ballet dancer**
[2] **ballet shoe** ◇ *une paire de ballerines rouges* a pair of red ballet shoes

le **ballet** NOUN
ballet

le **ballon** NOUN
[1] **ball** ◇ *lancer le ballon* to throw the ball
- *un ballon de football* a football
[2] **balloon**

balnéaire ADJECTIVE
- *une station balnéaire* a seaside resort

banal ADJECTIVE
(MASC PL **banaux**)
[1] **commonplace** ◇ *La violence est devenue banale à la télévision.* Violence has become commonplace on television.
[2] **hackneyed** ◇ *L'intrigue du film est très banale.* The plot of the film is very hackneyed.

la **banane** NOUN
banana

le **banc** NOUN
bench

bancaire ADJECTIVE
- *une carte bancaire* a bank card

le **bandage** NOUN
bandage

la **bande** NOUN
[1] **gang** ◇ *une bande de voyous* a gang of louts
[2] **bunch** ◇ *C'est une bande d'idiots!* They are a bunch of idiots!
[3] **bandage** ◇ *une bande Velpeau* ® a crepe bandage
- *une bande dessinée* a comic strip
Comic strips are very popular in France with people of all ages.
- *une bande magnétique* a tape
- *la bande sonore* the sound track
- *Elle fait toujours bande à part.* She always keeps to herself.

le **bandeau** NOUN
(PL les **bandeaux**)
headband

bander VERB
to bandage ◇ *L'infirmière lui a bandé la jambe.* The nurse bandaged his leg.

le **bandit** NOUN
bandit

la **banlieue** NOUN
suburbs ◇ *Christèle habite en banlieue.* Christèle lives in the suburbs.
- *les lignes de banlieue* suburban lines
- *les trains de banlieue* commuter trains

la **banque** NOUN
bank

le **banquet** NOUN
dinner ◇ *le banquet annuel de l'association* the club's annual dinner

la **banquette** NOUN
seat ◇ *la banquette arrière de la voiture* the back seat of the car

le **banquier** NOUN
banker

le **baptême** NOUN
christening ◇ *le baptême de notre fille* our daughter's christening
- *C'était mon baptême de l'air.* It was the first time I had flown.

le **baquet** NOUN
tub

le **bar** NOUN
bar

la **baraque** NOUN (*informal*)
house ◇ *Elle habite dans une belle baraque.* She lives in a beautiful house.

barbare ADJECTIVE
barbaric

la **barbe** NOUN
beard ◇ *Il porte la barbe.* He's got a beard.
- *Quelle barbe!* (*informal*) What a drag!
- *la barbe à papa* candyfloss

barbouiller VERB
to daub ◇ *Les murs étaient barbouillés de graffitis.* The walls were daubed with graffiti.
- *J'ai l'estomac barbouillé.* (*informal*) I'm feeling queasy.

barbu ADJECTIVE
bearded ◇ *un grand barbu* a big, bearded man

barder VERB (*informal*)
- *Ça va barder!* There's going to be trouble!

le **baromètre** NOUN
barometer

la **barque** NOUN
rowing boat ◇ *Ils sont allés faire une promenade en barque.* They've gone for a row.

le **barrage** NOUN
dam
- *un barrage de police* a police roadblock

la **barre** NOUN
bar (*metal*) ◇ *une barre de fer* an iron bar

le **barreau** NOUN
(PL les **barreaux**)
bar (*on window*) ◇ *Il s'est retrouvé derrière les barreaux.* He ended up behind bars.

barrer VERB
to block ◇ *Il y a un tronc d'arbre qui*

barre la route. There's a tree trunk blocking the road.
- **se barrer** (*informal*) to clear off ◇ *Barre-toi!* Clear off!

la **barrette** NOUN
hair slide

la **barrière** NOUN
fence

le **bar-tabac** NOUN
(PL les **bars-tabacs**)
A bar-tabac is a bar which also sells cigarettes and stamps; you can tell a bar-tabac by the red diamond-shaped sign outside it.

le **bas** NOUN
see also **bas** ADJECTIVE
① **bottom** ◇ *en bas de la page* at the bottom of the page ◇ *en bas de l'escalier* at the bottom of the stairs
② **stocking** ◇ *une paire de bas* a pair of stockings

bas ADJECTIVE, ADVERB
(FEM SING **basse**)
see also **bas** NOUN
low ◇ *parler à voix basse* to speak in a low voice
- **en bas (1)** down ◇ *Ça me donne le vertige de regarder en bas.* I get dizzy if I look down.
- **en bas (2)** (down) at the bottom ◇ *Son nom est tout en bas.* His name is down at the bottom. ◇ *Il y a un marchand de journaux en bas de la rue.* There's a newsagent's at the bottom of the street.
- **en bas (3)** downstairs ◇ *Elle habite en bas.* She lives downstairs.

le **bas-côté** NOUN
verge ◇ *Il s'est garé sur le bas-côté de la route.* He stopped his car on the verge.

la **bascule** NOUN
- **un fauteuil à bascule** a rocking chair

la **base** NOUN
base ◇ *la base de la pyramide* the base of the pyramid
- **de base** basic ◇ *Le pain et le lait sont des aliments de base.* Bread and milk are basic foods.
- **à base de** made from ◇ *des produits de beauté à base de plantes* cosmetics made from plants
- **une base de données** a database

le **basket** NOUN
basketball ◇ *jouer au basket* to play basketball

les **baskets** FEM NOUN
trainers ◇ *une paire de baskets* a pair of trainers

le/la **Basque** NOUN

Basque (*person, language*)

basque ADJECTIVE
Basque

basse ADJECTIVE see **bas**

la **basse-cour** NOUN
(PL les **basses-cours**)
farmyard

le **bassin** NOUN
① **pond** ◇ *Il y a un bassin à poissons rouges dans le parc.* There's a goldfish pond in the park.
② **pelvis** ◇ *une fracture du bassin* a fractured pelvis

la **bassine** NOUN
bowl (*for washing*)

le **bas-ventre** NOUN
stomach ◇ *Elle se plaint de douleurs dans le bas-ventre.* She is complaining of pains in her stomach.

la **bataille** NOUN
battle

le **bateau** NOUN
(PL les **bateaux**)
boat

le **bateau-mouche** NOUN
(PL les **bateaux-mouches**)
pleasure boat

bâti ADJECTIVE
- **bien bâti** well-built

le **bâtiment** NOUN
building

bâtir VERB
to build

le **bâton** NOUN
stick ◇ *un coup de bâton* a blow with a stick

le **battement** NOUN
- **J'ai dix minutes de battement.** I've got ten minutes free.

la **batterie** NOUN
① **battery** ◇ *La batterie est à plat.* The battery is flat.
② **drums** ◇ *jouer de la batterie* to play drums
- **la batterie de cuisine** the pots and pans

le **batteur** NOUN
drummer

battre VERB
to beat ◇ *Quand je le vois, mon cœur bat plus vite.* When I see him, my heart beats faster.
- **se battre** to fight ◇ *Je me bats souvent avec mon frère.* I fight a lot with my brother.
- **battre son plein** to in be full swing ◇ *A minuit, la fête battait son plein.* At midnight, the party was in full swing.

B

bavard ADJECTIVE
  talkative
bavarder VERB
  to chat
baver VERB
  to dribble
baveux ADJECTIVE
  (FEM SING **baveuse**)
  runny ◇ *une omelette baveuse* a
  runny omelette
la **bavure** NOUN
  blunder ◇ *une bavure policière* a
  police blunder
le **bazar** NOUN
  general store
  ◆ **Quel bazar!** (*informal*) What a mess!
BCBG ADJECTIVE (= *bon chic bon genre*)
  posh
la **BD** NOUN (= *bande dessinée*)
  comic strip ◇ *Marguerite adore les*
  BD. Marguerite loves comic strips.
béant ADJECTIVE
  gaping ◇ *un trou béant* a gaping
  hole
beau ADJECTIVE, ADVERB
  (MASC SING ALSO **bel**, FEM SING **belle**, MASC PL
  beaux)

  beau *changes to* **bel** *before a vowel and most*
  words beginning with "h".

  1 **lovely** ◇ *un bel été* a lovely
  summer ◇ *une belle journée* a fine
  day
  2 **beautiful** ◇ *C'est une belle*
  femme. She is a beautiful woman.
  3 **good-looking** ◇ *C'est un beau*
  garçon. He is a good-looking boy.
  4 **handsome** ◇ *un bel homme* a
  handsome man
  ◆ **Il fait beau aujourd'hui.** It's a nice day
  today.
  ◆ **J'ai beau essayer, je n'y arrive pas.**
  However hard I try, I just can't do it.
beaucoup ADVERB
  1 **a lot** ◇ *Il boit beaucoup.* He drinks
  a lot.
  2 **much** ◇ *Elle n'a pas beaucoup*
  d'argent. She hasn't got much money.
  ◇ *Janet est beaucoup plus grande*
  que moi. Janet is much taller than me.
  ◆ **beaucoup de** a lot of ◇ *Il y avait*
  beaucoup de monde au concert. There
  were a lot of people at the concert.
  ◇ *Elle fait beaucoup de fautes.* She
  makes a lot of mistakes.
  ◆ **J'ai eu beaucoup de chance.** I was
  very lucky.
le **beau-fils** NOUN
  (PL les **beaux-fils**)
  1 **son-in-law**

  2 **stepson**
le **beau-frère** NOUN
  (PL les **beaux-frères**)
  brother-in-law
le **beau-père** NOUN
  (PL les **beaux-pères**)
  1 **father-in-law**
  2 **stepfather**
la **beauté** NOUN
  beauty
les **beaux-arts** MASC NOUN
  fine arts
les **beaux-parents** MASC NOUN
  in-laws
le **bébé** NOUN
  baby
le **bec** NOUN
  beak
la **bécane** NOUN (*informal*)
  bike
la **bêche** NOUN
  spade
bêcher VERB
  to dig ◇ *Il bêchait son jardin.* He was
  digging the garden.
bégayer VERB
  to stammer
beige ADJECTIVE
  beige
le **beignet** NOUN
  fritter ◇ *les beignets aux pommes*
  apple fritters
bel ADJECTIVE *see* **beau**
le/la **Belge** NOUN
  Belgian
belge ADJECTIVE
  Belgian
la **Belgique** NOUN
  Belgium
  ◆ **en Belgique (1)** in Belgium
  ◆ **en Belgique (2)** to Belgium
le **bélier** MASC NOUN
  ram
  ◆ **le Bélier** Aries ◇ *Christine est Bélier.*
  Christine's Aries.
belle ADJECTIVE *see* **beau**
la **belle-famille** NOUN
  in-laws
la **belle-fille** NOUN
  (PL les **belles-filles**)
  1 **daughter-in-law**
  2 **stepdaughter**
la **belle-mère** NOUN
  (PL les **belles-mères**)
  1 **mother-in-law**
  2 **stepmother**
la **belle-sœur** NOUN
  (PL les **belles-sœurs**)
  sister-in-law

la **bénédiction** NOUN
blessing

le **bénéfice** NOUN
profit ◇ *La société réalise de gros bénéfices.* The company is making big profits.

bénévole ADJECTIVE
voluntary ◇ *du travail bénévole* voluntary work

bénir VERB
to bless

bénit ADJECTIVE
consecrated ◇ *l'eau bénite* holy water

la **béquille** NOUN
crutch ◇ *Il marche avec des béquilles.* He walks on crutches.

le **berceau** NOUN
(PL les **berceaux**)
cradle

bercer VERB
to rock

la **berceuse** NOUN
lullaby

le **béret** NOUN
beret

la **berge** NOUN
bank (*of river*)

le **berger** NOUN
shepherd

la **bergère** NOUN
shepherdess

le **besoin** NOUN
need
- **avoir besoin de quelque chose** to need something ◇ *J'ai besoin d'argent.* I need some money. ◇ *J'ai besoin d'y réfléchir.* I need to think about it.
- **une famille dans le besoin** a needy family

le **bétail** NOUN
livestock

la **bête** NOUN
see also **bête** ADJECTIVE
animal

bête ADJECTIVE
see also **bête** NOUN
stupid

la **bêtise** NOUN
- **faire une bêtise** to do something stupid ◇ *Je crois que j'ai fait une bêtise.* I think I've done something stupid.
- **dire des bêtises** to talk nonsense ◇ *Tu dis des bêtises!* You're talking nonsense!

le **béton** NOUN
concrete

- **un alibi en béton** a cast-iron alibi

la **betterave** NOUN
beetroot ◇ *la salade de betterave* beetroot salad

le/la **beur** NOUN (*informal*)
A **beur** *is a young person of North African origin born in France.*

le **beurre** NOUN
butter ◇ *une sauce au beurre* a sauce made with butter

beurrer VERB
to butter

Beyrouth NOUN
Beirut

le **bibelot** NOUN
ornament

le **biberon** NOUN
baby's bottle

la **Bible** NOUN
Bible

le/la **bibliothécaire** NOUN
librarian

la **bibliothèque** NOUN
1 **library** ◇ *emprunter un livre à la bibliothèque* to borrow a book from the library
2 **bookcase** ◇ *une bibliothèque en chêne massif* a bookcase made of solid oak

le **bic** ® NOUN
Biro ®

la **biche** NOUN
doe

la **bicyclette** NOUN
bicycle

le **bidet** NOUN
bidet

le **bidon** NOUN
see also **bidon** ADJECTIVE
can ◇ *un bidon d'essence* a can of petrol

bidon ADJECTIVE (*informal*)
see also **bidon** NOUN
phoney ◇ *Son histoire est complètement bidon.* His story is a complete load of rubbish.

le **bidonville** NOUN
shanty town

la **Biélorussie** NOUN
Belarus

le **bien** NOUN
see also **bien** ADJECTIVE
1 **good** ◇ *le bien et le mal* good and evil ◇ *Jean m'a dit beaucoup de bien de toi.* Jean told me a lot of good things about you. ◇ *C'est pour son bien.* It's for his own good.
- **faire du bien à quelqu'un** to do somebody good ◇ *Ses vacances lui*

ont fait beaucoup de bien. His holiday has done him a lot of good.

② **possession** ◇ *son bien le plus précieux* his most treasured possession

bien ADJECTIVE, ADVERB

see also bien NOUN

① **well** ◇ *Daphne travaille bien.* Daphne works well. ◇ *Je me sens bien.* I feel fine. ◇ *Je ne me sens pas bien.* I don't feel well.

② **good** ◇ *Ce restaurant est vraiment bien.* This restaurant is really good.

③ **quite** ◇ *bien assez* quite enough

‣ **Je veux bien le faire.** I'm quite willing to do it.

‣ **bien mieux** much better

‣ **J'espère bien y aller.** I very much hope to go.

④ **right** ◇ *Ce n'est pas bien de dire du mal des gens.* It's not right to say nasty things about people. ◇ *Il croyait bien faire.* He thought he was doing the right thing.

‣ **C'est bien fait pour lui!** It serves him right!

le **bien-être** NOUN

well-being ◇ *une sensation de bien-être* a feeling of well-being

la **bienfaisance** NOUN

charity

‣ **une œuvre de bienfaisance** a charity

bien que CONJUNCTION

although ◇ *Il fait assez chaud bien qu'il n'y ait pas de soleil.* It's quite warm although there's no sun.

bien sûr ADVERB

of course

bientôt ADVERB

soon ◇ *À bientôt!* See you soon!

le **bienvenu** NOUN

‣ **Vous êtes le bienvenu!** You're welcome! ◇ *Vous êtes tous les bienvenus!* You're all welcome!

la **bienvenue** NOUN

welcome ◇ *Bienvenue à Paris!* Welcome to Paris! ◇ *Vous êtes la bienvenue!* You're welcome!

la **bière** NOUN

beer

‣ **la bière blonde** lager

‣ **la bière brune** brown ale

‣ **la bière pression** draught beer

le **bifteck** NOUN

steak

le **bigoudi** NOUN

roller (*in hair*)

le **bijou** NOUN

(PL les **bijoux**)

jewel

la **bijouterie** NOUN

jeweller's

le **bijoutier** NOUN

jeweller

la **bijoutière** NOUN

jeweller ◇ *Elle est bijoutière.* She's a jeweller.

le **bilan** NOUN

‣ **faire le bilan de quelque chose** to assess something ◇ *Il faut faire le bilan de la situation.* We need to assess the situation.

bilingue ADJECTIVE

bilingual

le **billard** NOUN

billiards

‣ **le billard américain** pool

la **bille** NOUN

marble (*toy*) ◇ *jouer aux billes* to play marbles

le **billet** NOUN

① **ticket** ◇ *un billet d'avion* a plane ticket

② **banknote** ◇ *un billet de cent francs* a 100 franc note

le **billion** NOUN

billion

la **biographie** NOUN

biography

la **biologie** NOUN

biology

biologique ADJECTIVE

① **organic** ◇ *des légumes biologiques* organic vegetables

② **biological** ◇ *des armes biologiques* biological weapons

la **Birmanie** NOUN

Burma

bis ADVERB

see also bis NOUN

◇ *Il habite au douze bis rue des Fleurs.* He lives at 12A rue des Fleurs.

le **bis** NOUN

see also bis ADVERB

encore

la **biscotte** NOUN

toasted bread (*sold in packets*)

le **biscuit** NOUN

biscuit

‣ **un biscuit de Savoie** a sponge cake

la **bise** NOUN

kiss ◇ *Grosses bises de Bretagne.* Love and kisses from Brittany.

bissextile ADJECTIVE

‣ **une année bissextile** a leap year

le **bistrot** NOUN (*informal*)

café

Cafés in France sell both alcoholic and non-alcoholic drinks.

bizarre ADJECTIVE
strange

la **blague** NOUN (informal)
[1] **joke** ◇ *raconter une blague* to tell a joke
- **Sans blague!** No kidding!
[2] **trick** ◇ *André nous a encore fait une blague!* André has played a trick on us again!

blaguer VERB (informal)
to joke

le **blaireau** NOUN
(PL les **blaireaux**)
shaving brush

blâmer VERB
to blame

blanc ADJECTIVE
(FEM SING **blanche**)
see also blanc NOUN
[1] **white** ◇ *un chemisier blanc* a white blouse
[2] **blank** ◇ *une page blanche* a blank page

le **blanc** NOUN
see also blanc ADJECTIVE
[1] **white** ◇ *Colette est habillée tout en blanc.* Colette is dressed all in white.
[2] **white wine** ◇ *un verre de blanc* a glass of white wine
- **un blanc d'œuf** an egg white
- **un blanc de poulet** a chicken breast

le **Blanc** NOUN
white man

la **Blanche** NOUN
white woman

blanche ADJECTIVE *see* **blanc**

la **blanchisserie** NOUN
laundry

le **blé** NOUN
wheat

blessé ADJECTIVE
see also blessé NOUN
injured

le **blessé** NOUN
see also blessé ADJECTIVE
injured person ◇ *L'accident a fait trois blessés.* Three people were injured in the accident.

la **blessée** NOUN
injured person

blesser VERB
[1] **to injure** ◇ *Il a été blessé dans un accident de voiture.* He was injured in a car accident.
[2] **to hurt** ◇ *Il a fait exprès de le blesser.* He hurt him on purpose.
- **se blesser** to hurt oneself ◇ *Je me suis blessé au pied.* I've hurt my foot.

la **blessure** NOUN
injury

bleu ADJECTIVE
see also bleu NOUN
[1] **blue** ◇ *une veste bleue* a blue jacket
- **bleu marine** navy blue
[2] **very rare** (steak)

le **bleu** NOUN
see also bleu ADJECTIVE
[1] **blue** ◇ *Le bleu est ma couleur préférée.* Blue is my favourite colour.
[2] **bruise** ◇ *Il a un bleu au front.* He's got a bruise on his forehead.

le **bleuet** NOUN
cornflower

le **bloc** NOUN
pad ◇ *un bloc de papier à lettres* a pad of writing paper
- **le bloc opératoire** the operating theatre

le **bloc-notes** NOUN
(PL les **blocs-notes**)
note pad

blond ADJECTIVE
blond
- **blond cendré** ash blond ◇ *Andrew a les cheveux blond cendré.* Andrew has ash blond hair.

bloquer VERB
to block ◇ *bloquer le passage* to block the way
- **être bloqué dans un embouteillage** to be stuck in a traffic jam

se **blottir** VERB
to huddle ◇ *Ils étaient blottis l'un contre l'autre.* They were huddled together.

la **blouse** NOUN
overall

le **blouson** NOUN
jacket ◇ *un blouson en cuir* a leather jacket

la **bobine** NOUN
reel ◇ *une bobine de fil* a reel of thread

le **bocal** NOUN
(PL les **bocaux**)
jar

le **bœuf** NOUN
[1] **ox**
[2] **beef** ◇ *un rôti de bœuf* a joint of beef

bof EXCLAMATION (informal)
- **Le film t'a plu?–Bof! C'était pas terrible!** Did you like the film?–Well...it wasn't that great!
- **Comment ça va?–Bof! Pas terrible.** How is it going?–Oh...not too well

B

actually.

le **bohémien** NOUN
  gipsy

la **bohémienne** NOUN
  gipsy

boire VERB
  to drink
- **boire un coup** (*informal*) to have a drink

le **bois** NOUN
  wood
- **en bois** wooden ◇ *une table en bois* a wooden table
- **avoir la gueule de bois** (*informal*) to have a hangover

la **boisson** NOUN
  drink

la **boîte** NOUN
  [1] **box** ◇ *une boîte d'allumettes* a box of matches
- **une boîte aux lettres** a letter box
- **une boîte postale** a PO Box
  [2] **tin** ◇ *une boîte de sardines* a tin of sardines
- **une boîte de conserve** a tin
- **en boîte** tinned ◇ *des petits pois en boîte* tinned peas
- **une boîte de nuit** a night club

boiter VERB
  to limp

le **bol** NOUN
  bowl
- **en avoir ras le bol** (*informal*) to be fed up ◇ *J'en ai ras le bol de ce boulot.* I'm fed up with this job.

bombarder VERB
  to bomb

la **bombe** NOUN
  [1] **bomb** ◇ *une bombe atomique* an atomic bomb
  [2] **aerosol** ◇ *du déodorant en bombe* aérosol aerosol deodorant

bon ADJECTIVE, ADVERB
  (FEM SING **bonne**)
  see also bon NOUN
  [1] **good** ◇ *un bon restaurant* a good restaurant ◇ *Le tabac n'est pas bon pour la santé.* Smoking isn't good for you.
- **être bon en maths** to be good at maths
- **sentir bon** to smell nice
- **Bon voyage!** Have a good trip!
- **Bonne chance!** Good luck!
- **Bonne nuit!** Good night!
- **Bon anniversaire!** Happy birthday!
- **Bonne année!** Happy New Year!
  [2] **right** ◇ *Il est arrivé au bon moment.* He arrived at the right

moment. ◇ *Ce n'est pas la bonne réponse.* That's not the right answer.
- **Il fait bon aujourd'hui.** It's nice today.
- **de bonne heure** early
- **bon marché** cheap ◇ *Les fraises ne sont pas bon marché en hiver.* Strawberries aren't cheap in winter.
- **Ah bon?** Really? ◇ *Je pars aux États-Unis la semaine prochaine.—Ah bon?* I'm going to the States next week.—Really?
- **J'aimerais vraiment que tu viennes! —Bon, d'accord.** I'd really like you to come!—OK then, I will.

le **bon** NOUN
  see also bon ADJECTIVE
  voucher ◇ *un bon d'achat* a voucher
- **pour de bon** for good ◇ *Cette fois, c'est pour de bon.* This time it's for good.

le **bonbon** NOUN
  sweet

bondé ADJECTIVE
  crowded

bondir VERB
  to leap

le **bonheur** NOUN
  happiness
- **porter bonheur** to bring luck

le **bonhomme** NOUN
  (PL les **bonshommes**)
- **un bonhomme de neige** a snowman

bonjour EXCLAMATION
  [1] **Hello!** ◇ *Donne le bonjour à tes parents de ma part.* Say hello to your parents for me.
  [2] **Good morning!**
  [3] **Good afternoon!**
  bonjour *is used in the morning and afternoon; in the evening* **bonsoir** *is used instead.*
- **C'est simple comme bonjour!** It's easy as pie!

bonne ADJECTIVE *see* **bon**

le **bonnet** NOUN
  hat ◇ *un bonnet de laine* a woolly hat
- **un bonnet de bain** a bathing cap

bonsoir EXCLAMATION
  Good evening!

la **bonté** NOUN
  kindness

le **bord** NOUN
  [1] **edge** ◇ *le bord de la table* the edge of the table
  [2] **side** ◇ *Jane a garé sa voiture au bord de la route.* Jane parked her car on the side of the road.
- **au bord de la mer** at the seaside
- **au bord de l'eau** by the water

- **monter à bord** to go on board
- **être au bord des larmes** to be on the verge of tears

le **bordeaux** NOUN
> see also bordeaux ADJECTIVE

Bordeaux wine
- **du bordeaux rouge** claret

bordeaux ADJECTIVE
> see also bordeaux NOUN

maroon ◇ *une jupe bordeaux* a maroon skirt

le **bordel** NOUN

brothel ◇ *Quel bordel!* (*informal*) What a bloody mess!

border VERB

1 to line ◇ *une route bordée d'arbres* a tree-lined street
2 to trim ◇ *un col bordé de dentelle* a collar trimmed with lace
3 to tuck up ◇ *Sa mère vient la border tous les soirs.* Her mother comes and tucks her up every night.

la **bordure** NOUN

border
- **une villa en bordure de mer** a villa right by the sea

la **Bosnie** NOUN

Bosnia
- **la Bosnie-Herzégovine** Bosnia-Herzegovina

la **bosse** NOUN

bump ◇ *Jacques a une grosse bosse au front.* Jacques has got a big bump on his forehead. ◇ *La route est pleine de bosses.* The road is very bumpy.

le **bossu** NOUN

hunchback

la **bossue** NOUN

hunchback

botanique ADJECTIVE
> see also botanique NOUN

botanic ◇ *les jardins botaniques* the botanic gardens

la **botanique** NOUN
> see also botanique ADJECTIVE

botany

la **botte** NOUN

1 boot ◇ *une paire de bottes* a pair of boots
- **les bottes de caoutchouc** wellington boots
2 bunch ◇ *une botte de radis* a bunch of radishes

le **bottin** ® NOUN

phone book

le **bouc** NOUN

1 goatee beard
2 billy goat
- **un bouc émissaire** a scapegoat

la **bouche** NOUN

mouth
- **le bouche à bouche** the kiss of life
- **une bouche d'égout** a manhole
- **une bouche de métro** an entrance to the underground

la **bouchée** NOUN

mouthful
- **une bouchée à la reine** a chicken vol-au-vent

boucher VERB
> see also boucher NOUN

1 to fill ◇ *boucher un trou* to fill a hole
2 to block ◇ *L'évier est bouché.* The sink is blocked. ◇ *J'ai le nez bouché.* My nose is blocked.

le **boucher** NOUN
> see also boucher VERB

butcher ◇ *Il est boucher.* He's a butcher.

la **bouchère** NOUN

butcher ◇ *Elle est bouchère.* She's a butcher.

la **boucherie** NOUN

butcher's

le **bouchon** NOUN

1 top (*of plastic bottle*)
2 cork (*of wine bottle*)
3 hold-up ◇ *Il y avait beaucoup de bouchons sur l'autoroute.* There were a lot of hold-ups on the motorway.

la **boucle** NOUN

curl (*of hair*)
- **une boucle d'oreille** an earring ◇ *une paire de boucles d'oreille* a pair of earrings

bouclé ADJECTIVE

curly

le **bouclier** NOUN

shield

le/la **bouddhiste** NOUN

Buddhist

bouder VERB

to sulk

le **boudin** NOUN

- **le boudin noir** black pudding
- **le boudin blanc** white pudding

la **boue** NOUN

mud

la **bouée** NOUN

buoy
- **une bouée de sauvetage** a life buoy

boueux ADJECTIVE
(FEM SING **boueuse**)

muddy

la **bouffe** NOUN (*informal*)

food ◇ *La bouffe est infecte à la cantine.* The food in the canteen is revolting.

la **bouffée** NOUN
- **une bouffée d'air frais** a breath of fresh air

bouffer VERB (*informal*)
to eat

le **bougeoir** NOUN
candlestick

bouger VERB
to move

la **bougie** NOUN
candle

la **bouillabaisse** NOUN
fish soup

bouillant ADJECTIVE
1 **boiling** ◦ *Faites cuire les pâtes à l'eau bouillante.* Cook the pasta in boiling water.
2 **piping hot** ◦ *La soupe est servie bouillante.* The soup should be served piping hot.

bouillir VERB
to boil ◦ *L'eau bout.* The water's boiling.
- **Je bous d'impatience.** I'm bursting with impatience.

la **bouilloire** NOUN
kettle

le **bouillon** NOUN
stock ◦ *du bouillon de légumes* vegetable stock

la **bouillotte** NOUN
hot-water bottle

le **boulanger** NOUN
baker ◦ *Il est boulanger.* He's a baker.

la **boulangère** NOUN
baker ◦ *Elle est boulangère.* She's a baker.

la **boulangerie** NOUN
baker's

la **boule** NOUN
ball ◦ *une boule de cristal* a crystal ball
- **une boule de neige** a snowball
- **jouer aux boules** to play bowls

le **boulevard** NOUN
boulevard

bouleverser VERB
1 **to move deeply** ◦ *Cette histoire déchirante m'a bouleversée.* This heartbreaking story moved me deeply.
2 **to shatter** ◦ *La mort de son ami l'a bouleversé.* He was shattered by the death of his friend.
3 **to turn upside down** ◦ *Cette rencontre a bouleversé sa vie.* This meeting turned his life upside down.

le **boulot** NOUN (*informal*)
1 **job** ◦ *Anita a trouvé du boulot.* Anita has found a job.
2 **work** ◦ *J'ai beaucoup de boulot en ce moment.* I've got a lot of work to do at the moment.

la **boum** NOUN (*informal*)
party

le **bouquet** NOUN
bunch of flowers ◦ *un bouquet de roses* a bunch of roses

le **bouquin** NOUN (*informal*)
book

bouquiner VERB (*informal*)
to read

bourdonner VERB
to buzz

le **bourg** NOUN
small market town

bourgeois ADJECTIVE
middle-class ◦ *un quartier bourgeois* a posh area

le **bourgeon** NOUN
bud

la **Bourgogne** NOUN
Burgundy

bourré ADJECTIVE
- **bourré de** stuffed with ◦ *un portefeuille bourré de billets* a wallet stuffed with banknotes
- **être bourré** (*informal*) to be plastered ◦ *Il était complètement bourré.* He was completely plastered.

le **bourreau** NOUN
(PL les **bourreaux**)
executioner
- **C'est un véritable bourreau de travail.** He's a real workaholic.

bourrer VERB
to stuff ◦ *bourrer une valise de vêtements* to stuff clothes into a case

la **bourse** NOUN
grant
- **la Bourse** the Stock Exchange

bous VERB *see* **bouillir**

la **bousculade** NOUN
crush ◦ *la bousculade dans les grands magasins au moment des soldes* the crush in the big stores at sale time

bousculer VERB
1 **to jostle** ◦ *être bousculé par la foule* to be jostled by the crowd
2 **to rush** ◦ *Je n'aime pas qu'on me bouscule.* I don't like to be rushed.

la **boussole** NOUN
compass

bout VERB *see* **bouillir**

le **bout** NOUN
1 **end** ◦ *Elle habite au bout de la rue.* She lives at the end of the street.

○ *Jane est assise en bout de table.*
Jane is sitting at the end of the table.
2 **tip** ○ *le bout du nez* the tip of the nose
3 **bit** ○ *un petit bout de fromage* a bit of cheese
- **un bout de papier** a scrap of paper
- **au bout de** after ○ *Au bout d'un moment, il s'est endormi.* After a while he fell asleep.
- **Elle est à bout.** She's at the end of her tether.

la **bouteille** NOUN
bottle ○ *une bouteille de vin rouge* a bottle of red wine
- **une bouteille de gaz** a gas cylinder

la **boutique** NOUN
shop

le **bouton** NOUN
1 **button**
2 **spot** (*on skin*) ○ *J'ai un bouton sur le nez.* I've got a spot on my nose.
3 **bud** ○ *un bouton de rose* a rosebud
- **un bouton d'or** a buttercup

le **bowling** NOUN
1 **tenpin bowling**
2 **bowling alley**

la **boxe** NOUN
boxing

le **boxeur** NOUN
boxer

le **bracelet** NOUN
bracelet

le **bracelet-montre** NOUN
wristwatch

le **brancard** NOUN
stretcher

le **brancardier** NOUN
stretcher-bearer

la **branche** NOUN
branch

branché ADJECTIVE (*informal*)
trendy ○ *avoir un look branché* to look trendy

brancher VERB
1 **to connect** ○ *Le téléphone est branché?* Is the phone connected?
2 **to plug in** ○ *L'aspirateur n'est pas branché.* The hoover isn't plugged in.

le **bras** NOUN
arm

la **brasse** NOUN
breaststroke ○ *nager la brasse* to do the breaststroke

la **brasserie** NOUN
café-restaurant

brave ADJECTIVE
nice ○ *C'est un brave type.* He's a

nice enough fellow.

bravo EXCLAMATION
Bravo!

le **break** NOUN
estate car

la **brebis** NOUN
ewe
- **le fromage de brebis** sheep's cheese

bref ADJECTIVE, ADVERB
(FEM SING **brève**)
short ○ *Sa lettre était brève.* His letter was short.
- **en bref** in brief ○ *l'actualité en bref* the news in brief
- **...bref, ça s'est bien terminé.** ...to cut a long story short, it turned out all right in the end.

le **Brésil** NOUN
Brazil

la **Bretagne** NOUN
Brittany

la **bretelle** NOUN
strap ○ *La bretelle de son soutien-gorge dépasse.* Her bra strap is showing.
- **les bretelles** braces ○ *Il porte des bretelles.* He's wearing braces.

breton ADJECTIVE, NOUN
(FEM SING **bretonne**)
Breton ○ *Ils parlent breton.* They speak Breton.
- **un Breton** a Breton (*man*)
- **une Bretonne** a Breton (*woman*)
- **les Bretons** the Bretons

brève ADJECTIVE *see* **bref**

le **brevet** NOUN
certificate

le **bricolage** NOUN
do-it-yourself ○ *Elle aime le bricolage.* She likes doing DIY. ○ *un magasin de bricolage* a DIY shop

la **bricole** NOUN (*informal*)
- **J'ai acheté une bricole pour le bébé de Sabine.** I've bought a little something for Sabine's baby.
- **J'ai encore quelques bricoles à faire avant de partir.** I've still got a few things to do before I go.

bricoler VERB
to do DIY ○ *Pascal aime bricoler.* Pascal loves doing DIY.

le **bricoleur** NOUN
DIY enthusiast

la **bricoleuse** NOUN
DIY enthusiast

le **bridge** NOUN
bridge (*game*) ○ *Horst adore jouer au bridge.* Horst loves playing bridge.

brièvement ADVERB

B

briefly ◦ *Expliquez-moi brièvement ce qui s'est passé.* Tell me briefly what happened.

la **brigade** NOUN
squad (*of police*) ◦ *la brigade des stups* (*informal*) the drugs squad

brillamment ADVERB
brilliantly ◦ *Il a réussi brillamment à son examen.* He did brilliantly in the exam.

brillant ADJECTIVE
1 **brilliant** ◦ *une brillante carrière* a brilliant career ◦ *Ses notes ne sont pas brillantes.* His marks aren't brilliant.
2 **shiny** ◦ *des cheveux brillants* shiny hair

briller VERB
to shine

le **brin** NOUN
- **un brin d'herbe** a blade of grass
- **un brin de muguet** a sprig of lily of the valley

la **brindille** NOUN
twig

la **brioche** NOUN
brioche bun

la **brique** NOUN
brick

le **briquet** NOUN
cigarette lighter

la **brise** NOUN
breeze

se **briser** VERB
to break ◦ *Le vase s'est brisé en mille morceaux.* The vase broke into a thousand pieces.

e/la **Britannique** NOUN
Briton
- **les Britanniques** the British

britannique ADJECTIVE
British

la **brocante** NOUN
junk ◦ *un magasin de brocante* a junk shop

le **brocanteur** NOUN
dealer in second-hand goods

la **brocanteuse** NOUN
dealer in second-hand goods

la **broche** NOUN
brooch ◦ *une broche en argent* a silver brooch
- **à la broche** spit-roasted ◦ *un poulet à la broche* a spit-roasted chicken

la **brochette** NOUN
skewer
- **les brochettes d'agneau** lamb kebabs

la **brochure** NOUN
brochure

broder VERB
to embroider

la **broderie** NOUN
embroidery

la **bronchite** NOUN
bronchitis ◦ *avoir une bronchite* to have bronchitis

le **bronze** NOUN
bronze ◦ *la médaille de bronze* the bronze medal

bronzer VERB
to get a tan ◦ *Il est bien bronzé.* He's got a good tan.
- **se bronzer** to sunbathe

la **brosse** NOUN
brush
- **une brosse à cheveux** a hairbrush
- **une brosse à dents** a toothbrush
- **Il est coiffé en brosse.** He's got a crew cut.

brosser VERB
to brush
- **se brosser les dents** to brush one's teeth ◦ *Je me brosse les dents tous les soirs.* I brush my teeth every night.

la **brouette** NOUN
wheelbarrow

le **brouillard** NOUN
fog ◦ *Il y a du brouillard.* It's foggy.

le **brouillon** NOUN
first draft ◦ *Ce n'est qu'un brouillon.* It's just a first draft.

les **broussailles** FEM NOUN
undergrowth

brouter VERB
to graze (*animals*)

broyer VERB
to crush
- **broyer du noir** to be down in the dumps

le **brugnon** NOUN
nectarine

le **bruit** NOUN
1 **noise** ◦ *J'ai entendu un bruit.* I heard a noise. ◦ *faire du bruit* to make a noise
- **sans bruit** without a sound
2 **rumour** ◦ *Des bruits circulent à son sujet.* There are rumours going round about him.

brûlant ADJECTIVE
1 **blazing** ◦ *un soleil brûlant* a blazing sun
2 **boiling hot** ◦ *Faith boit son café brûlant.* Faith drinks her coffee boiling hot.

le **brûlé** NOUN
smell of burning ◦ *Ça sent le brûlé.* There's a smell of burning.

brûler VERB
to burn
- **se brûler** to burn oneself
la **brûlure** NOUN
burn
- **des brûlures d'estomac** heartburn
la **brume** NOUN
mist
brun ADJECTIVE
brown
- **Catherine est brune.** Catherine's got dark hair.
le **brushing** NOUN
blow-dry ◇ *une coupe et un brushing* a cut and blow-dry
brusque ADJECTIVE
abrupt
- **d'un ton brusque** brusquely
brusquer VERB
to rush ◇ *Il ne faut pas la brusquer.* You mustn't rush her.
brut ADJECTIVE
- **le champagne brut** dry champagne
- **le pétrole brut** crude oil
- **son salaire brut** his gross salary
brutal ADJECTIVE
(MASC PL **brutaux**)
brutal
brutaliser VERB
to knock about ◇ *Il a été brutalisé par la police.* He was treated roughly by the police.
Bruxelles NOUN
Brussels
bruyamment ADVERB
noisily
bruyant ADJECTIVE
noisy
la **bruyère** NOUN
heather
bu VERB *see* **boire**
la **bûche** NOUN
log
- **la bûche de Noël** the Yule log
  This is what is usually eaten in France instead of Christmas pudding.
le **bûcheron** NOUN
woodcutter
le **budget** NOUN
budget
le **buffet** NOUN
1 **sideboard** ◇ *un buffet en chêne* an oak sideboard
2 **buffet** ◇ *un buffet froid* a cold buffet ◇ *un buffet de gare* a station buffet

le **buisson** NOUN
bush
la **Bulgarie** NOUN
Bulgaria
la **bulle** NOUN
bubble ◇ *une bulle de savon* a soap bubble
le **bulletin** NOUN
1 **bulletin**
- **le bulletin d'informations** the news bulletin
2 **report** ◇ *Ton bulletin n'est pas fameux ce mois-ci.* Your school report isn't very good this month.
- **le bulletin météorologique** the weather report
- **le bulletin de salaire** pay slip
- **le bulletin de vote** the ballot paper
le **bureau** NOUN
(PL les **bureaux**)
1 **desk** ◇ *Posez le dossier sur mon bureau.* Put the file on my desk.
2 **office** ◇ *Il vous attend dans son bureau.* He's waiting for you in his office.
- **un bureau de change** a bureau de change
- **le bureau de poste** the post office
- **le bureau de tabac** the tobacconist's
- **le bureau de vote** the polling station
bus VERB *see* **boire**
le **bus** NOUN
bus
le **buste** NOUN
bust
but VERB *see* **boire**
le **but** NOUN
1 **aim** ◇ *Ils n'ont pas de but dans la vie.* They have no aim in life.
- **Quel est le but de votre visite?** What's the reason for your visit?
- **dans le but de** with the intention of ◇ *Je suis venue dans le but de vous aider.* I came to help you.
2 **goal** ◇ *marquer un but* to score a goal
le **butane** NOUN
Calor gas ®
le **butin** NOUN
loot ◇ *Les cambrioleurs se sont partagé le butin.* The burglars shared the stolen goods.
buvais, buvait VERB *see* **boire**
le **buvard** NOUN
blotter

C

c' PRONOUN *see* **ce**

ça PRONOUN

  1 this ◇ *Est-ce que vous pouvez me donner un peu de ça?* Can you give me a bit of this?

  2 that ◇ *Est-ce que tu peux prendre ça, là-bas dans le coin?* Can you bring that from over there in the corner?

  3 it ◇ *Ça ne fait rien.* It doesn't matter.

  • **Comment ça va?** How are you?

  • **Ça alors!** Well, well!

  • **C'est ça.** That's right.

  • **Ça y est!** That's it!

çà ADVERB

  • **çà et là** here and there

la **cabane** NOUN

  hut

le **cabillaud** NOUN

  cod

la **cabine** NOUN

  cabin (*on a ship*)

  • **une cabine d'essayage** a fitting room

  • **une cabine téléphonique** a phone box

le **cabinet** NOUN

  surgery (*of doctor, of dentist*)

  • **une chambre avec cabinet de toilette** a room with washing facilities

les **cabinets** MASC NOUN

  toilet

le **câble** NOUN

  cable

  cabosser VERB

  to dent

la **cacahuète** NOUN

  peanut

  • **le beurre de cacahuète** peanut butter

le **cacao** NOUN

  cocoa

  • **le beurre de cacao** cocoa butter

  cache-cache MASC NOUN

  • **jouer à cache-cache** to play hide-and-seek

le **cachemire** NOUN

  cashmere ◇ *un pull en cachemire* a cashmere jumper

le **cache-nez** NOUN

  (PL les **cache-nez**)

  long woollen scarf

  cacher VERB

  to hide ◇ *J'ai caché les cadeaux sous le lit.* I hid the presents under the bed. ◇ *Tu me caches quelque chose!* You're hiding something!

  • **se cacher** to hide ◇ *Elle s'est cachée sous la table.* She's hiding under the table.

le **cachet** NOUN

  1 tablet

  • **un cachet d'aspirine** an aspirin

  2 fee (*for performer*) ◇ *Il a touché un gros cachet pour ce concert.* He got a big fee for the concert.

  • **le cachet de la poste** the postmark

la **cachette** NOUN

  hiding place

  • **en cachette** on the sly ◇ *Il est sorti en cachette sans réveiller ses parents.* He crept out on the sly without waking his parents.

le **cachot** NOUN

  dungeon

le **cactus** NOUN

  cactus

le **cadavre** NOUN

  corpse

le **caddie** ® NOUN

  supermarket trolley

le **cadeau** NOUN

  (PL les **cadeaux**)

  present

  • **faire un cadeau à quelqu'un** to give somebody a present

le **cadenas** NOUN

  padlock

  cadet ADJECTIVE

  (FEM SING **cadette**)

  see also **cadet** NOUN

  1 younger (*brother, sister*) ◇ *ma sœur cadette* my younger sister

  2 youngest (*son, daughter*) ◇ *son fils cadet* his youngest son

le **cadet** NOUN

  see also **cadet** ADJECTIVE

  youngest ◇ *C'est le cadet de la famille.* He's the youngest of the family.

la **cadette** NOUN

  youngest ◇ *C'est la cadette de la famille.* She's the youngest of the family.

le **cadre** NOUN

  1 frame ◇ *un cadre en bois* a wooden frame

  2 surroundings ◇ *L'hôtel est situé dans un très beau cadre.* The hotel is set in beautiful surroundings.

  3 executive ◇ *un cadre supérieur* a senior executive

le **cafard** NOUN

  cockroach

  • **avoir le cafard** (*informal*) to be feeling

down ◇ *J'ai le cafard.* I'm feeling down.

le **café** NOUN

1 **coffee** ◇ *un café au lait* a white coffee

2 **café**

Cafés in France sell both alcoholic and non-alcoholic drinks.

le **café-tabac** NOUN

A café-tabac is a bar which also sells cigarettes and stamps; you can tell a café-tabac by the red diamond-shaped sign outside it.

la **cafetière** NOUN

1 **coffee maker**

2 **coffee pot**

la **cage** NOUN

cage

- **la cage d'escalier** the stairwell

la **cagoule** NOUN

balaclava

le **cahier** NOUN

exercise book ◇ *mon cahier de brouillon* my rough book

la **caille** NOUN

quail

le **caillou** NOUN

(PL les **cailloux**)

pebble

la **caisse** NOUN

1 **box** ◇ *une caisse à outils* a tool box

2 **till** ◇ *le ticket de caisse* the till receipt

3 **checkout** ◇ *J'ai dû faire la queue à la caisse.* I had to queue at the checkout.

le **caissier** NOUN

cashier

la **caissière** NOUN

cashier

le **cake** NOUN

fruit cake

le **calcul** NOUN

1 **calculation** ◇ *Je me suis trompé dans mes calculs.* I made a mistake in my calculations.

2 **arithmetic** ◇ *Je ne suis pas très bon en calcul.* I'm not very good at arithmetic.

la **calculatrice** NOUN

calculator

calculer VERB

to work out ◇ *J'ai calculé combien ça allait coûter.* I worked out how much it was going to cost.

la **calculette** NOUN

pocket calculator

la **cale** NOUN

wedge

calé ADJECTIVE (*informal*)

- **Elle est calée en histoire.** She's really good at history.

le **caleçon** NOUN

1 **boxer shorts**

2 **leggings**

le **calendrier** NOUN

calendar

le **calepin** NOUN

notebook

caler VERB

to stall ◇ *La voiture a calé dans une côte.* The car stalled on a hill.

câlin ADJECTIVE

see also **câlin** NOUN

cuddly

le **câlin** NOUN

see also **câlin** ADJECTIVE

cuddle ◇ *faire un câlin à quelqu'un* to give somebody a cuddle

le **calmant** NOUN

tranquillizer

calme ADJECTIVE

see also **calme** NOUN

1 **quiet** ◇ *un endroit calme* a quiet place

2 **calm** ◇ *Elle est restée très calme.* She stayed very calm.

le **calme** NOUN

see also **calme** ADJECTIVE

peace and quiet ◇ *J'ai besoin de calme pour travailler.* I need peace and quiet to work.

calmer VERB

to soothe ◇ *Cette pommade calme les démangeaisons.* This ointment soothes itching.

- **se calmer** to calm down ◇ *Calme-toi!* Calm down!

la **calorie** NOUN

calorie

le/la **camarade** NOUN

friend

- **un camarade de classe** a school friend

le **cambriolage** NOUN

burglary

cambrioler VERB

to burgle

le **cambrioleur** NOUN

burglar

la **cambrioleuse** NOUN

burglar

la **camelote** NOUN (*informal*)

junk ◇ *C'est vraiment de la camelote.* It's absolute junk.

la **caméra** NOUN

camera (*cinema, TV*)

le **caméscope** NOUN
  camcorder
le **camion** NOUN
  lorry
la **camionnette** NOUN
  van
le **camionneur** NOUN
  lorry driver
la **camomille** NOUN
  camomile tea
le **camp** NOUN
  camp ◇ *un camp de prisonniers* a prison camp ◇ *un camp de vacances* a holiday camp
la **campagne** NOUN
  [1] country
  - **à la campagne** in the country ◇ *Nous passons nos vacances à la campagne.* We spend our holidays in the country.
  [2] campaign ◇ *une campagne de marketing* a marketing campaign
camper VERB
  to camp
le **campeur** NOUN
  camper
la **campeuse** NOUN
  camper
le **camping** NOUN
  camping ◇ *faire du camping* to go camping
  - **un terrain de camping** a campsite
le **Canada** NOUN
  Canada
  - **au Canada (1)** in Canada
  - **au Canada (2)** to Canada
canadien ADJECTIVE, NOUN
  (FEM SING **canadienne**)
  Canadian
  - **un Canadien** a Canadian (*man*)
  - **une Canadienne** a Canadian (*woman*)
le **canal** NOUN
  (PL les **canaux**)
  canal
le **canapé** NOUN
  [1] sofa
  [2] open sandwich
le **canard** NOUN
  duck
le **canari** NOUN
  canary
le **cancer** NOUN
  cancer ◇ *le cancer du poumon* lung cancer
  - **le Cancer** Cancer ◇ *Sabine est Cancer.* Sabine's Cancer.
le **candidat** NOUN
  [1] candidate (*in exam, election*)
  [2] applicant (*for job*)

la **candidate** NOUN
  [1] candidate (*in exam, election*)
  [2] applicant (*for job*)
la **candidature** NOUN
  - **poser sa candidature à un poste** to apply for a job ◇ *Il a posé sa candidature à des dizaines de postes.* He has applied for dozens of jobs.
le **caneton** NOUN
  duckling
la **canette** NOUN
  - **une canette de bière** a small bottle of beer
le **caniche** NOUN
  poodle
la **canicule** NOUN
  scorching heat
le **canif** NOUN
  penknife
le **caniveau** NOUN
  (PL les **caniveaux**)
  gutter
la **canne** NOUN
  walking stick
  - **une canne à pêche** a fishing rod
la **cannelle** NOUN
  cinnamon
le **canoë** NOUN
  [1] canoe
  [2] canoeing ◇ *faire du canoë* to go canoeing
le **canon** NOUN
  [1] gun ◇ *un canon antichar* an anti-tank gun
  [2] cannon ◇ *un boulet de canon* a cannon ball
le **canot** NOUN
  dinghy ◇ *un canot pneumatique* a rubber dinghy
  - **un canot de sauvetage** a lifeboat
la **cantatrice** NOUN
  opera singer
la **cantine** NOUN
  canteen
le **caoutchouc** NOUN
  rubber
  - **des bottes en caoutchouc** Wellington boots
le **cap** NOUN
  cape ◇ *le cap Horn* Cape Horn
capable ADJECTIVE
  - **Elle est capable de marcher pendant des heures.** She can walk for hours.
  - **Il est capable de changer d'avis au dernier moment.** He's capable of changing his mind at the last minute.
la **cape** NOUN
  cape

le **capitaine** NOUN
captain

la **capitale** NOUN
capital ◇ *la capitale de la France* the capital of France

le **capot** NOUN
bonnet (*of car*)

la **capote** NOUN (*informal*)
condom

la **câpre** NOUN
caper (*food*)

le **caprice** NOUN
- **faire des caprices** to make a fuss ◇ *Il n'aime pas les enfants qui font des caprices.* He doesn't like children who make a fuss.

capricieux ADJECTIVE
(FEM SING **capricieuse**)
- **un enfant capricieux** an awkward child

le **Capricorne** NOUN
Capricorn ◇ *Helen est Capricorne.* Helen's Capricorn.

captivant ADJECTIVE
fascinating

la **captivité** NOUN
captivity ◇ *en captivité* in captivity

capturer VERB
to capture

la **capuche** NOUN
hood ◇ *un manteau à capuche* a coat with a hood

le **capuchon** NOUN
cap (*of pen*)

la **capucine** NOUN
nasturtium

le **car** NOUN
see also **car** CONJUNCTION
coach ◇ *un car scolaire* a school bus

car CONJUNCTION
see also **car** NOUN
because ◇ *Nous sommes inquiets car il n'est pas encore rentré.* We're worried because he isn't back yet.

la **carabine** NOUN
rifle

le **caractère** NOUN
personality ◇ *Il a le même caractère que son père.* He's got the same personality as his father.
- **Il a bon caractère.** He's good-natured.
- **Elle a mauvais caractère.** She's bad-tempered.
- **Il n'a pas un caractère facile.** He isn't easy to get on with.

caractéristique ADJECTIVE
see also **caractéristique** NOUN
characteristic

la **caractéristique** NOUN

see also **caractéristique** ADJECTIVE
characteristic

la **carafe** NOUN
jug ◇ *une carafe d'eau* a jug of water

les **Caraïbes** FEM NOUN
Caribbean Islands

le **caramel** NOUN
1 **caramel** ◇ *la crème caramel* crème caramel
2 **toffee**

la **caravane** NOUN
caravan

carbonique ADJECTIVE
- **le gaz carbonique** carbon dioxide

le **carburant** NOUN
fuel

cardiaque ADJECTIVE
- **une crise cardiaque** a heart attack
- **Ma tante est cardiaque.** My aunt has heart trouble.

le **cardigan** NOUN
cardigan

le/la **cardiologue** NOUN
heart specialist

le **carême** NOUN
Lent

la **caresse** NOUN
stroke ◇ *faire des caresses à un chat* to stroke a cat

caresser VERB
to stroke

la **carie** NOUN
tooth decay ◇ *J'ai une carie.* I've got a hole in my tooth.

caritatif ADJECTIVE
(FEM SING **caritative**)
- **une organisation caritative** a charity

le **carnaval** NOUN
carnival

le **carnet** NOUN
1 **notebook**
2 **book** ◇ *un carnet d'adresses* an address book ◇ *un carnet de chèques* a cheque book ◇ *un carnet de timbres* a book of stamps ◇ *un carnet de tickets* a book of tickets
In the Paris metro it is cheaper to buy tickets in a book of ten, known as a **carnet**.
- **mon carnet de notes** my school report

la **carotte** NOUN
carrot ◇ *les carottes râpées* grated carrots

carré ADJECTIVE
see also **carré** NOUN
square
- **un mètre carré** a square metre

le **carré** NOUN
see also **carré** ADJECTIVE

square

le **carreau** NOUN

(PL les **carreaux**)

1 **check** ◇ *une chemise à carreaux* a checked shirt

2 **tile** (*on floor, wall*) ◇ *Je viens de laver les carreaux de la cuisine.* I've just washed the kitchen floor.

3 **pane** ◇ *Il a cassé un carreau.* He broke a windowpane.

4 **diamonds** (*cards*) ◇ *l'as de carreau* the ace of diamonds

le **carrefour** NOUN

junction

le **carrelage** NOUN

tiled floor

carrément ADVERB

1 **completely** ◇ *C'est carrément impossible.* It's completely impossible.

2 **straight out** ◇ *Dis-lui carrément ce que tu penses.* Tell him straight out what you think.

la **carrière** NOUN

career

- **un militaire de carrière** a professional soldier

la **carrure** NOUN

build ◇ *Il a une carrure d'athlète.* He has an athletic build.

le **cartable** NOUN

satchel

la **carte** NOUN

1 **card**

- **une carte d'anniversaire** a birthday card
- **une carte postale** a postcard
- **une carte de vœux** a Christmas card

*The French send greetings cards (**les cartes de vœux**) in January rather than at Christmas, with best wishes for the New Year.*

- **une carte bancaire** a cash card
- **une carte de crédit** a credit card
- **une carte d'embarquement** a boarding card
- **une carte d'identité** an identity card
- **une carte de séjour** a residence permit
- **une carte téléphonique** a phonecard
- **un jeu de cartes (1)** a pack of cards
- **un jeu de cartes (2)** a card game

2 **map** ◇ *une carte de France* a map of France ◇ *une carte routière* a road map

3 **menu** ◇ *la carte des vins* the wine list

- **manger à la carte** to eat à la carte ◇ *Nous avons décidé de manger à la carte.* We decided to choose from the à la carte menu.

le **carton** NOUN

1 **cardboard** ◇ *un morceau de carton* a piece of cardboard

2 **cardboard box** ◇ *un carton à chaussures* a shoe box

la **cartouche** NOUN

cartridge

- **une cartouche de cigarettes** a carton of cigarettes

le **cas** NOUN

(PL les **cas**)

case ◇ *plusieurs cas* several cases

- **ne faire aucun cas de** to take no notice of ◇ *Il ne fait aucun cas de ce qu'on lui dit.* He takes no notice of what people say to him.
- **en aucun cas** on no account
- **en tout cas** at any rate
- **au cas où** in case ◇ *Prends un sandwich au cas où la cantine serait fermée.* Take a sandwich in case the canteen's closed.
- **en cas de** in case of ◇ *En cas d'incendie, appelez ce numéro.* In case of fire, call this number.

la **cascade** NOUN

waterfall

le **cascadeur** NOUN

stuntman

la **caserne** NOUN

barracks

cash ADVERB

- **payer cash** to pay cash

le **casier** NOUN

locker

le **casque** NOUN

1 **helmet**

2 **headphones**

la **casquette** NOUN

cap

cassant ADJECTIVE

- **Il m'a parlé d'un ton cassant.** He spoke to me curtly.

le **casse-croûte** NOUN

(PL les **casse-croûte**)

snack

le **casse-noix** NOUN

(PL les **casse-noix**)

nutcrackers

casse-pieds ADJECTIVE (MASC, FEM, PL)

(*informal*)

- **Il est vraiment casse-pieds!** He's a real pain in the neck!

casser VERB

to break ◇ *J'ai cassé un verre.* I've broken a glass.

- **se casser** to break ◇ *Il s'est cassé la jambe au ski.* He broke his leg when he was skiing.

- **se casser la tête** (*informal*) to go to a lot of trouble ◇ *Je ne vais pas me casser la tête pour le dîner: je vais ouvrir une boîte de conserve.* I'm not going to go to a whole lot of trouble over dinner: I'll just open a tin.

la **casserole** NOUN
saucepan

le **casse-tête** NOUN
(PL les **casse-tête**)

- **C'est un vrai casse-tête!** It's a real headache!

la **cassette** NOUN
cassette

le **cassis** NOUN
blackcurrant

le **castor** NOUN
beaver

le **catalogue** NOUN
catalogue

la **catastrophe** NOUN
disaster

le **catch** NOUN
wrestling

le **catéchisme** NOUN
catechism

la **catégorie** NOUN
category

catégorique ADJECTIVE
firm ◇ *un refus catégorique* a flat refusal

la **cathédrale** NOUN
cathedral

catholique ADJECTIVE
see also **catholique** NOUN
Catholic

le/la **catholique** NOUN
see also **catholique** ADJECTIVE
Catholic

le **cauchemar** NOUN
nightmare ◇ *faire un cauchemar* to have a nightmare

la **cause** NOUN
cause

- **à cause de** because of ◇ *Nous n'avons pas pu sortir à cause du mauvais temps.* We couldn't go out because of the bad weather.

causer VERB
1 **to cause** ◇ *La tempête a causé beaucoup de dégâts.* The storm caused a lot of damage.
2 **to chat** ◇ *Nous n'avons pas beaucoup eu le temps de causer.* We didn't have much time to chat.

la **caution** NOUN
1 **bail**
2 **deposit**

le **cavalier** NOUN

1 **rider**
2 **partner** (*at dance*)

la **cavalière** NOUN
rider

la **cave** NOUN
cellar

la **caverne** NOUN
cave

le **CD** NOUN
(PL les **CD**)
CD

le **CD-ROM** NOUN
(PL les **CD-ROM**)
CD-ROM

la **CE** NOUN (= *Communauté européenne*)
EC

ce ADJECTIVE
(MASC SING **cet**, FEM SING **cette**, PL **ces**)
see also **ce** PRONOUN
ce *changes to* **cet** *before a vowel and most words beginning with "h".*
1 **this** ◇ *Tu peux prendre ce livre.* You can take this book. ◇ *cet après-midi* this afternoon ◇ *cet hiver* this winter

- **ce livre-ci** this book
- **cette voiture-ci** this car
2 **that** ◇ *Je n'aime pas du tout ce film.* I don't like that film at all.
- **ce livre-là** that book
- **cette voiture-là** that car

ce PRONOUN
see also **ce** ADJECTIVE
ce *changes to* **c'** *before the vowel in* **est**, **était** *and* **étaient**.
it ◇ *Ce n'est pas facile.* It's not easy.

- **c'est (1)** it is ◇ *C'est vraiment trop cher.* It's really too expensive. ◇ *Ouvre, c'est moi!* Open the door, it's me!
- **c'est (2)** he is ◇ *C'est un peintre du début du siècle.* He's a painter from the turn of the century.
- **c'est (3)** she is ◇ *C'est une romancière très célèbre.* She's a very famous novelist.
- **ce sont** they are ◇ *Ce sont des amis à mes parents.* They're friends of my parents'.
- **Qui est-ce?** Who is it?
- **Qu'est-ce que c'est?** What is it?
- **ce qui** what ◇ *C'est ce qui compte.* That's what matters.
- **tout ce qui** everything that ◇ *J'ai rangé tout ce qui traînait par terre.* I've tidied up everything that was on the floor.
- **ce que** what ◇ *Je vais lui dire ce que je pense.* I'm going to tell him what I

think.

- **tout ce que** everything ◇ *Tu peux avoir tout ce que tu veux.* You can have everything you want.

ceci PRONOUN

this ◇ *Prends ceci, tu en auras besoin.* Take this, you'll need it.

céder VERB

to give in ◇ *Elle a tellement insisté qu'il a fini par céder.* She went on so much that he eventually gave in.

- **céder à** to give in to ◇ *Je ne veux pas céder à ses caprices.* I'm not going to give in to her whims.

la **cédille** NOUN

cedilla

la **ceinture** NOUN

belt ◇ *une ceinture en cuir* a leather belt

- **votre ceinture de sécurité** your seatbelt

cela PRONOUN

1 **it** ◇ *Cela dépend.* It depends.

2 **that** ◇ *Je n'aime pas cela.* I don't like that.

- **C'est cela.** That's right.
- **à part cela** apart from that

célèbre ADJECTIVE

famous

célébrer VERB

to celebrate

le **céleri** NOUN

- **le céleri-rave** celeriac
- **le céleri en branche** celery

célibataire ADJECTIVE, NOUN

single

- **un célibataire** a bachelor
- **une célibataire** a single woman

celle PRONOUN *see* **celui**

celles PRONOUN *see* **ceux**

la **cellule** NOUN

cell

celui PRONOUN

(FEM **celle**, MASC PL **ceux**, FEM PL **celles**)

the one ◇ *Prends celui que tu préfères.* Take the one you like best. ◇ *Je n'ai pas d'appareil photo mais je peux emprunter celui de ma sœur.* I haven't got a camera but I can borrow my sister's. ◇ *Je n'ai pas de platine laser mais je peux emprunter celle de mon frère.* I haven't got a CD player but I can borrow my brother's.

- **celui-ci** this one
- **celle-ci** this one
- **celui-là** that one
- **celle-là** that one

la **cendre** NOUN

ash

le **cendrier** NOUN

ashtray

censé ADJECTIVE

- **être censé faire quelque chose** to be supposed to do something ◇ *Vous êtes censé arriver à l'heure.* You're supposed to get here on time.

cent NUMBER

a hundred ◇ *cent francs* a hundred francs

> **cent** *is spelt with an* **-s** *when there are two or more hundreds, but not when it is followed by another number, as in "a hundred and two".*

◇ *trois cents ans* three hundred years ◇ *cent deux kilomètres* a hundred and two kilometres ◇ *trois cent cinquante kilomètres* three hundred and fifty kilometres ◇ *trois cent mille kilomètres* three hundred thousand kilometres

la **centaine** NOUN

about a hundred ◇ *Il y avait une centaine de personnes dans la salle.* There were about a hundred people in the hall.

- **des centaines de** hundreds of ◇ *Des centaines de réfugiés se sont présentés à l'ambassade.* Hundreds of refugees came to the embassy.

le **centenaire** NOUN

centenary

centième ADJECTIVE

hundredth

le **centilitre** NOUN

centilitre

le **centime** NOUN

centime

> *The franc is divided into 100* centimes.

◇ *une pièce de cinquante centimes* a 50-centime coin

le **centimètre** NOUN

centimetre

central ADJECTIVE

(MASC PL **centraux**)

central

la **centrale** NOUN

power station ◇ *une centrale nucléaire* a nuclear power station

le **centre** NOUN

centre

- **un centre commercial** a shopping centre

le **centre-ville** NOUN

town centre

cependant ADVERB

however

le **cercle** NOUN

circle ◇ *Entourez d'un cercle la bonne réponse.* Put a circle round the right

answer.
- **un cercle vicieux** a vicious circle

le **cercueil** NOUN
coffin

la **céréale** NOUN
cereal ◇ *un bol de céréales* a bowl of cereal
- **un pain aux cinq céréales** a multigrain loaf

la **cérémonie** NOUN
ceremony

le **cerf** NOUN
stag

le **cerf-volant** NOUN
(PL les **cerfs-volants**)
kite

la **cerise** NOUN
cherry

le **cerisier** NOUN
cherry tree

cerné ADJECTIVE
- **avoir les yeux cernés** to have shadows under one's eyes ◇ *Elle avait les yeux cernés.* She had shadows under her eyes.

cerner VERB
- **J'ai du mal à le cerner.** I can't figure him out.

certain ADJECTIVE
1 certain ◇ *Je suis certain que je l'ai remis en place.* I'm certain that I put it back. ◇ *Ce n'est pas certain.* It's not certain.
2 some ◇ *Certaines personnes n'aiment pas la crème.* Some people don't like cream.
- **un certain temps** quite some time ◇ *J'ai mis un certain temps à comprendre ce qu'elle disait.* It took me quite some time to understand what she was saying.

certainement ADVERB
1 definitely ◇ *C'est certainement le meilleur film que j'ai vu cette année.* It's definitely the best film I've seen this year.
2 of course ◇ *Est-ce que je peux t'emprunter ton stylo?—Mais certainement!* Can I borrow your pen? –Of course!

certains PRONOUN
1 some ◇ *certains de ses amis* some of his friends ◇ *certains d'entre vous* some of you
2 some people ◇ *Certains pensent que le film est meilleur que le roman.* Some people think that the film is better than the novel.

certes ADVERB

certainly ◇ *Nous nous connaissons, certes, mais nous ne sommes pas amis.* We know each other, certainly, but we are not friends.

le **certificat** NOUN
certificate

le **cerveau** NOUN
(PL les **cerveaux**)
brain

la **cervelle** NOUN
brain
- **se creuser la cervelle** (*informal*) to rack one's brains

le **CES** NOUN (= *Collège d'enseignement secondaire*)
secondary school
In France pupils go to a CES between the ages of 11 and 15, and then to a lycée until the age of 18.

ces ADJECTIVE
1 these ◇ *Tu peux prendre ces photos si tu veux.* You can have these photos if you like.
- **ces photos-ci** these photos
2 those ◇ *Ces montagnes sont dangereuses en hiver.* Those mountains are dangerous in winter.
- **ces livres-là** those books

cesse
- **sans cesse** ADVERB
continually
- **Elle me dérange sans cesse.** She keeps interrupting me.

cesser VERB
to stop ◇ *cesser de faire quelque chose* to stop doing something

le **cessez-le-feu** NOUN
(PL les **cessez-le-feu**)
ceasefire

c'est-à-dire ADVERB
that is ◇ *Est-ce que tu peux venir lundi prochain, c'est-à-dire le quinze?* Can you come next Monday, that's the 15th?

cet ADJECTIVE
(FEM SING **cette**)
ce changes to cet before a vowel and most words beginning with "h".
1 this ◇ *cet après-midi* this afternoon ◇ *cet hiver* this winter ◇ *cette année* this year
- **cette semaine-ci** this week
2 that ◇ *Est-ce que tu peux me passer cette assiette?* Could you pass me that plate?
- **cet après-midi-là** that afternoon
- **cette nuit (1)** tonight ◇ *On prévoit de l'orage pour cette nuit.* A storm is forecast for tonight.

- **cette nuit (2)** last night ◇ *J'ai très mal dormi cette nuit.* I slept very badly last night.

cette PRONOUN *see* **ce**

ceux PRONOUN
(FEM PL **celles**)
the ones ◇ *Prends ceux que tu préfères.* Take the ones you like best. ◇ *Je n'ai pas de skis mais je peux emprunter ceux de ma sœur.* I haven't got any skis but I can borrow my sister's. ◇ *Je n'ai pas de jumelles mais je peux emprunter celles de mon frère.* I haven't got any binoculars but I can borrow my brother's.
- **ceux-ci** these ones
- **celles-ci** these ones
- **ceux-là** those ones
- **celles-là** those ones

chacun PRONOUN
[1] **each** ◇ *Il nous a donné un cadeau à chacun.* He gave us each a present. ◇ *Nous avons chacun donné dix francs.* We each gave 10 francs.
[2] **everyone** ◇ *Chacun fait ce qu'il veut.* Everyone does what they like.

le **chagrin** NOUN
- **avoir du chagrin** to be very upset ◇ *Elle a eu beaucoup de chagrin à la mort de sa tante.* She was terribly upset by the death of her aunt.

le **chahut** NOUN
bedlam ◇ *Il y avait du chahut dans la classe.* There was bedlam in the classroom.

la **chaîne** NOUN
[1] **chain** ◇ *une chaîne en or* a gold chain
[2] **channel** (*on TV*) ◇ *Le film passe sur quelque chaîne?* Which channel is the film on?
- **une chaîne hi-fi** a hi-fi system
- **une chaîne laser** a CD player
- **une chaîne stéréo** a music centre
- **travailler à la chaîne** to work on an assembly line

la **chair** NOUN
flesh
- **en chair et en os** in the flesh ◇ *J'ai vu Mel Gibson en chair et en os.* I saw Mel Gibson in the flesh.
- **avoir la chair de poule** to have goose pimples

la **chaise** NOUN
chair
- **une chaise longue** a deckchair

le **châle** NOUN
shawl

la **chaleur** NOUN

[1] **heat**
[2] **warmth**

chaleureux ADJECTIVE
(FEM SING **chaleureuse**)
warm ◇ *un accueil chaleureux* a warm welcome

se **chamailler** VERB (*informal*)
to squabble ◇ *Elle se chamaille sans cesse avec son frère.* She's always squabbling with her brother.

la **chambre** NOUN
room ◇ *C'est la chambre de Camille.* This is Camille's room.
- **une chambre à coucher** a bedroom
- **une chambre d'amis** a spare room
- **une chambre à un lit** a single room
- **une chambre pour deux personnes** a double room

le **chameau** NOUN
(PL les **chameaux**)
camel

le **champ** NOUN
field

le **champagne** NOUN
champagne

le **champignon** NOUN
mushroom ◇ *une omelette aux champignons* a mushroom omelette
- **un champignon de Paris** a button mushroom

le **champion** NOUN
champion

le **championnat** NOUN
championship ◇ *le championnat du monde* the world championship

la **championne** NOUN
champion

la **chance** NOUN
[1] **luck**
- **Bonne chance!** Good luck!
- **avoir de la chance** to be lucky ◇ *Tu as de la chance de partir au soleil!* You're lucky, going off to the sun!
[2] **chance** ◇ *Il n'a aucune chance.* He's got no chance. ◇ *Il a des chances de réussir.* He's got a good chance of passing.

le **change** NOUN
exchange ◇ *le taux de change* the exchange rate

le **changement** NOUN
change ◇ *Il n'aime pas le changement.* He doesn't like changes.

changer VERB
to change ◇ *Il n'a pas beaucoup changé.* He hasn't changed much. ◇ *J'ai changé les draps ce matin.* I changed the sheets this morning. ◇ *J'ai changé trois cents francs.* I

changed 300 francs.

- **se changer** to get changed ◇ *Je vais me changer avant de sortir.* I'm going to get changed before I go out.

- **changer de** to change ◇ *Je change de chaussures et j'arrive!* I'll change my shoes and then I'll be ready!

- **changer d'avis** to change one's mind ◇ *Appelle-moi si tu changes d'avis.* Give me a ring if you change your mind.

la **chanson** NOUN
song

le **chant** NOUN
singing ◇ *des cours de chant* singing lessons

- **un chant de Noël** a Christmas carol

le **chantage** NOUN
blackmail ◇ *faire du chantage à quelqu'un* to blackmail somebody

chanter VERB
to sing

le **chanteur** NOUN
singer

la **chanteuse** NOUN
singer

le **chantier** NOUN
building site

la **Chantilly** NOUN
whipped cream

chantonner VERB
to hum

le **chapeau** NOUN
(PL les **chapeaux**)
hat

la **chapelle** NOUN
chapel

le **chapitre** NOUN
chapter

chaque ADJECTIVE
1 **every** ◇ *chaque année* every year
2 **each** ◇ *Ces verres coûtent cinquante francs chaque.* These glasses cost 50 francs each.

le **char** NOUN
tank (military)

le **charabia** NOUN (informal)
gibberish ◇ *Je n'y comprends rien: c'est du charabia.* I don't understand any of it: it's gibberish.

la **charade** NOUN
1 **riddle**
2 **charade** ◇ *jouer aux charades* to play charades

le **charbon** NOUN
coal

- **le charbon de bois** charcoal

la **charcuterie** NOUN
1 **pork butcher's**
2 **cold meats**
A charcuterie *sells cuts of pork and pork products such as sausages, salami and pâté, as well as various cooked dishes and salads;* charcuterie *served at a meal is an assortment of ham, sausage and pâtés.*

le **charcutier** NOUN
pork butcher

la **charcutière** NOUN
pork butcher

le **chardon** NOUN
thistle

charger VERB
to load

- **charger quelqu'un de faire quelque chose** to tell somebody to do something ◇ *Paul m'a chargé de vous dire que la clé est sous le paillasson.* Paul told me to tell you that the key's under the mat.

le **chariot** NOUN
trolley (at supermarket)

charmant ADJECTIVE
charming

le **charme** NOUN
charm

charmer VERB
to charm

la **charrue** NOUN
plough

la **chasse** NOUN
1 **hunting** ◇ *un chien de chasse* a hunting dog
2 **shooting** ◇ *la chasse au canard* duck shooting

- **tirer la chasse d'eau** to flush the toilet

le **chasse-neige** NOUN
(PL les **chasse-neige**)
snowplough

chasser VERB
1 **to hunt** ◇ *Mon père chasse le lapin.* My father hunts rabbits.
2 **to chase away** ◇ *Ils ont chassé les cambrioleurs.* They chased away the robbers.
3 **to get rid of** ◇ *Ouvre donc la fenêtre pour chasser les odeurs de cuisine.* Open the window to get rid of the cooking smells.

le **chasseur** NOUN
hunter

le **chat** NOUN
cat

la **châtaigne** NOUN
chestnut

le **châtaignier** NOUN
chestnut tree

châtain ADJECTIVE (MASC, FEM, PL)
brown ◇ *J'ai les cheveux châtain.*

I've got brown hair.

le **château** NOUN
(PL les **châteaux**)
[1] **castle**
- **un château fort** a castle
[2] **palace** ◇ *le château de Versailles* the palace of Versailles

le **chaton** NOUN
kitten

chatouiller VERB
to tickle

chatouilleux ADJECTIVE
(FEM SING **chatouilleuse**)
ticklish

la **chatte** NOUN
cat (*female*)

chaud ADJECTIVE
[1] **warm** ◇ *des vêtements chauds* warm clothes
- **avoir chaud** to be warm ◇ *J'ai assez chaud.* I'm warm enough.
[2] **hot** ◇ *Il fait chaud aujourd'hui.* It's hot today. ◇ *un plat chaud* a hot dish ◇ *Attention, c'est chaud!* Mind, it's hot! ◇ *J'ai trop chaud!* I'm too hot!

le **chauffage** NOUN
heating ◇ *Le chauffage est en panne.* The heating isn't working.
- **le chauffage central** central heating

le **chauffe-eau** NOUN
(PL les **chauffe-eau**)
water heater

chauffer VERB
to warm ◇ *Je vais mettre de l'eau à chauffer pour faire du thé.* I'm going to put some water on to make tea.

le **chauffeur** NOUN
driver

le **chaume** NOUN
- **un toit de chaume** a thatched roof

chausser VERB
- **Vous chaussez du combien?** What size shoe do you take?

la **chaussette** NOUN
sock

le **chausson** NOUN
slipper
- **un chausson aux pommes** an apple turnover

la **chaussure** NOUN
shoe
- **les chaussures de ski** ski boots

chauve ADJECTIVE
bald

la **chauve-souris** NOUN
(PL les **chauves-souris**)
bat (*animal*)

le **chef** NOUN
[1] **head** ◇ *le chef de famille* the head of the family
- **le chef de l'État** the Head of State
[2] **boss** ◇ *Je dois demander la permission à mon chef.* I have to get permission from my boss.
- **un chef d'entreprise** a company director
[3] **chef** ◇ *la spécialité du chef* the chef's speciality
- **un chef d'orchestre** a conductor

le **chef-d'œuvre** NOUN
(PL les **chefs-d'œuvre**)
masterpiece

le **chemin** NOUN
[1] **path** ◇ *Je suis descendu à la plage par un petit chemin.* I went down a little path to the beach.
[2] **way** ◇ *Quel est le chemin le plus court pour aller à l'aéroport?* What's the quickest way to the airport?
- **en chemin** on the way ◇ *Je mangerai mon sandwich en chemin.* I'll eat my sandwich on the way.
- **les chemins de fer** the railways

la **cheminée** NOUN
[1] **chimney**
[2] **fireplace**

la **chemise** NOUN
[1] **shirt** ◇ *une chemise à carreaux* a checked shirt
- **une chemise de nuit** a nightdress
[2] **folder** ◇ *J'ai classé mes cours dans des chemises de couleurs différentes.* I've sorted my notes into different coloured folders.

le **chemisier** NOUN
blouse

le **chêne** NOUN
oak ◇ *une armoire en chêne* an oak wardrobe

le **chenil** NOUN
kennels

la **chenille** NOUN
caterpillar

le **chèque** NOUN
cheque
- **les chèques de voyage** traveller's cheques

le **chéquier** NOUN
cheque book

cher ADJECTIVE, ADVERB
(FEM SING **chère**)
[1] **dear** ◇ *Chère Mélusine...* Dear Mélusine...
[2] **expensive** ◇ *C'est trop cher.* It's too expensive. ◇ *coûter cher* to be expensive

chercher VERB
[1] **to look for** ◇ *Je cherche mes clés.*

I'm looking for my keys.

2 **to look up** ◇ *chercher un mot dans le dictionnaire* to look up a word in the dictionary

• **aller chercher (1)** to go to get ◇ *Elle est allée chercher du pain pour ce midi.* She's gone to get some bread for lunch.

• **aller chercher (2)** to pick up ◇ *J'irai te chercher à la gare.* I'll pick you up at the station.

le **chercheur** NOUN
scientist

la **chercheuse** NOUN
scientist

chère ADJECTIVE *see* **cher**

chéri ADJECTIVE
see also **chéri** NOUN
darling ◇ *ma petite fille chérie* my darling daughter

le **chéri** NOUN
see also **chéri** ADJECTIVE
darling

• **mon chéri** darling

la **chérie** NOUN
darling

• **ma chérie** darling

le **cheval** NOUN
(PL les **chevaux**)
horse ◇ *un cheval de course* a racehorse

• **à cheval** on horseback

• **faire du cheval** to go riding

le **chevalier** NOUN
knight

la **chevalière** NOUN
signet ring

chevalin ADJECTIVE

• **une boucherie chevaline** a horsemeat butcher's

les **chevaux** MASC NOUN *see* **cheval**

le **chevet** NOUN

• **une table de chevet** a bedside table

• **une lampe de chevet** a bedside lamp

les **cheveux** MASC NOUN
hair ◇ *Elle a les cheveux courts.* She's got short hair.

la **cheville** NOUN
ankle

la **chèvre** NOUN
goat

• **le fromage de chèvre** goat's cheese

le **chevreau** NOUN
(PL les **chevreaux**)
kid (*animal, leather*)

le **chèvrefeuille** NOUN
honeysuckle

le **chevreuil** NOUN
1 **roe deer**
2 **venison** ◇ *un rôti de chevreuil*

roast venison

le **chewing-gum** NOUN
chewing gum

chez PREPOSITION

• **chez Pierre (1)** at Pierre's house

• **chez Pierre (2)** to Pierre's house

• **chez moi (1)** at my house ◇ *Je suis resté chez moi ce week-end.* I stayed at home this weekend.

• **chez moi (2)** to my house ◇ *Je vais rentrer chez moi.* I'm going home.

• **chez le dentiste (1)** at the dentist's ◇ *J'ai rendez-vous chez le dentiste demain matin.* I've got an appointment at the dentist's tomorrow morning.

• **chez le dentiste (2)** to the dentist's ◇ *Je vais chez le dentiste.* I'm going to the dentist's.

chic ADJECTIVE
1 **smart** ◇ *une tenue chic* a smart outfit
2 **nice** ◇ *C'est chic de ta part de m'avoir invité.* (*informal*) It was nice of you to invite me.

la **chicorée** NOUN
endive

le **chien** NOUN
dog

• **"Attention, chien méchant"** "Beware of the dog"

la **chienne** NOUN
bitch (*dog*)

le **chiffon** NOUN
cloth

chiffonner VERB
to crease ◇ *Ma robe est toute chiffonnée.* My dress is all creased.

le **chiffre** NOUN
figure ◇ *en chiffres ronds* in round figures

• **les chiffres romains** Roman numerals

le **chignon** NOUN
bun (*in hair*) ◇ *Elle s'est fait un chignon.* She put her hair in a bun.

le **Chili** NOUN
Chile

la **chimie** NOUN
chemistry ◇ *un cours de chimie* a chemistry lesson

chimique ADJECTIVE
chemical ◇ *une réaction chimique* a chemical reaction

• **les produits chimiques** chemicals

la **Chine** NOUN
China

chinois ADJECTIVE, NOUN
Chinese ◇ *Il apprend le chinois.* He's learning Chinese.

• **un Chinois** a Chinese (*man*)

- **une Chinoise** a Chinese (*woman*)
- **les Chinois** the Chinese

le **chiot** NOUN
puppy

les **chips** FEM NOUN
crisps ◇ *un paquet de chips* a packet of crisps

chirurgical ADJECTIVE
(MASC PL **chirurgicaux**)
- **une intervention chirurgicale** an operation

la **chirurgie** NOUN
surgery
- **la chirurgie esthétique** plastic surgery

le **chirurgien** NOUN
surgeon

le **choc** NOUN
shock ◇ *Ça m'a fait un sacré choc de le voir comme ça.* It gave me a hell of a shock to see him in that state.
- **Elle est encore sous le choc.** She's still in shock.

le **chocolat** NOUN
chocolate
- **un chocolat chaud** a hot chocolate
- **le chocolat à croquer** dark chocolate

le **chœur** NOUN
choir

choisir VERB
to choose

le **choix** NOUN
1 **choice**
- **avoir le choix** to have the choice
2 **selection** ◇ *Il n'y a pas beaucoup de choix dans ce magasin.* There's not a very wide selection of things in this shop.

le **chômage** NOUN
unemployment
- **être au chômage** to be unemployed

le **chômeur** NOUN
unemployed person ◇ *Il est chômeur.* He's unemployed.

la **chômeuse** NOUN
unemployed woman ◇ *Elle est chômeuse.* She's unemployed.

choquer VERB
to shock ◇ *Cette remarque m'a choqué.* I was shocked by that remark.

la **chose** NOUN
thing ◇ *J'ai fait des choses intéressantes pendant les vacances.* I did some interesting things during the holidays.
- **C'est peu de chose.** It's nothing really.

le **chou** NOUN
(PL les **choux**)
cabbage

- **les choux de Bruxelles** Brussels sprouts
- **un chou à la crème** a choux bun

le **chouchou** NOUN (*informal*)
teacher's pet

la **chouchoute** NOUN (*informal*)
teacher's pet

la **choucroute** NOUN
sauerkraut (with sausages and ham)

la **chouette** NOUN
see also **chouette** ADJECTIVE
owl

chouette ADJECTIVE
see also **chouette** NOUN (*informal*)
brilliant ◇ *Chouette alors!* Brilliant!

le **chou-fleur** NOUN
(PL les **choux-fleurs**)
cauliflower

chrétien ADJECTIVE
(FEM SING **chrétienne**)
Christian ◇ *Il est chrétien.* He's a Christian.

le **Christ** NOUN
Christ

chronologique ADJECTIVE
chronological

le **chronomètre** NOUN
stopwatch

chronométrer VERB
to time

le **chrysanthème** NOUN
chrysanthemum
Chrysanthemums are strongly associated with funerals in France.

chuchoter VERB
to whisper

chut EXCLAMATION
Shh!

la **chute** NOUN
fall
- **faire une chute** to fall
- **une chute d'eau** a waterfall
- **la chute des cheveux** hair loss
- **les chutes de neige** snowfalls

Chypre NOUN
Cyprus

-ci ADVERB
- **ce livre-ci** this book
- **ces bottes-ci** these boots

la **cible** NOUN
target

la **ciboulette** NOUN
chives

la **cicatrice** NOUN
scar

se **cicatriser** VERB
to heal up ◇ *Cette plaie s'est vite cicatrisée.* This wound has healed up quickly.

ci-contre ADVERB
  opposite ◇ *la page ci-contre* the opposite page

ci-dessous ADVERB
  below ◇ *la photo ci-dessous* the picture below

ci-dessus ADVERB
  above

le **cidre** NOUN
  cider

le **ciel** NOUN
  ☐ **sky** ◇ *un ciel nuageux* a cloudy sky
  ☐ **heaven** ◇ *être au ciel* to be in heaven

le **cierge** NOUN
  candle (*in church*)

la **cigale** NOUN
  cicada

le **cigare** NOUN
  cigar ◇ *Il fume le cigare.* He smokes cigars.

la **cigarette** NOUN
  cigarette

la **cigogne** NOUN
  stork

ci-joint ADVERB
  enclosed ◇ *Veuillez trouver ci-joint mon curriculum vitae.* Please find enclosed my CV.

le **cil** NOUN
  eyelash

le **ciment** NOUN
  cement

le **cimetière** NOUN
  cemetery

le/la **cinéaste** NOUN
  film-maker

le **cinéma** NOUN
  cinema

cinq NUMBER
  five ◇ *Il est cinq heures du matin.* It's five in the morning. ◇ *Il a cinq ans.* He's five.
  → **le cinq février** the fifth of February

la **cinquantaine** NOUN
  about fifty ◇ *Il y avait une cinquantaine de personnes.* There were about fifty people there.
  → **Il a la cinquantaine.** He's in his fifties.

cinquante NUMBER
  fifty ◇ *Il a cinquante ans.* He's fifty.
  → **cinquante et un** fifty-one
  → **cinquante-deux** fifty-two

cinquième ADJECTIVE
  see also **cinquième** NOUN
  fifth ◇ *au cinquième étage* on the fifth floor

la **cinquième** NOUN
  see also **cinquième** ADJECTIVE
  second year
  In French secondary schools, years are counted from the **sixième** *(youngest) to* **première** *and* **terminale** *(oldest).*
  ◇ *Mon frère est en cinquième.* My brother's in second year.

le **cintre** NOUN
  coat hanger

le **cirage** NOUN
  shoe polish

circonflexe ADJECTIVE
  → **un accent circonflexe** a circumflex

la **circonstance** NOUN
  circumstance ◇ *dans les circonstances actuelles* in the present circumstances

la **circulation** NOUN
  ☐ **traffic** ◇ *Il y avait beaucoup de circulation.* There was a lot of traffic.
  ☐ **circulation** ◇ *Elle a des problèmes de circulation.* She has bad circulation.

circuler VERB
  to run ◇ *Il n'y a qu'un bus sur trois qui circule.* Only one bus in three is running.

la **cire** NOUN
  wax

le **ciré** NOUN
  oilskin jacket

cirer VERB
  to polish (*shoes, floor*)

le **cirque** NOUN
  circus

les **ciseaux** MASC NOUN
  → **une paire de ciseaux** a pair of scissors

le **citadin** NOUN
  city dweller

la **citation** NOUN
  quotation

la **cité** NOUN
  estate ◇ *J'habite dans une cité.* I live on an estate.
  → **une cité universitaire** halls of residence
  → **une cité-dortoir** a dormitory town

citer VERB
  to quote

le **citoyen** NOUN
  citizen

la **citoyenne** NOUN
  citizen

le **citron** NOUN
  lemon
  → **un citron vert** a lime

la **citronnade** NOUN
  still lemonade

la **citrouille** NOUN

pumpkin

le **civet** NOUN
   stew ◇ *du civet de lapin* rabbit stew

civil ADJECTIVE
   civilian
 • **en civil** in civilian clothes

la **civilisation** NOUN
   civilization

clair ADJECTIVE, ADVERB
   1 **light** ◇ *vert clair* light green
   ◇ *C'est une pièce très claire.* It's a
   very light room.
   2 **clear** (*water*)
 • **voir clair** to see clearly
 • **le clair de lune** moonlight

clairement ADVERB
   clearly

la **clairière** NOUN
   clearing

clandestin ADJECTIVE
 • **un passager clandestin** a stowaway

la **claque** NOUN
   slap ◇ *Elle m'a donné une claque.*
   She gave me a slap.

claquer VERB
   1 **to bang** ◇ *On entend des volets
   qui claquent.* You can hear shutters
   banging.
   2 **to slam** ◇ *Elle est partie en
   claquant la porte.* She left, slamming
   the door behind her.

les **claquettes** FEM NOUN
 • **faire des claquettes** to tap-dance

la **clarinette** NOUN
   clarinet ◇ *Gavin joue de la clarinette.*
   Gavin plays the clarinet.

la **classe** NOUN
   1 **class** ◇ *C'est la meilleure élève de
   la classe.* She's the best pupil in the
   class. ◇ *voyager en première classe* to
   travel first class
   2 **classroom**

classer VERB
   to arrange ◇ *Les livres sont classés
   par ordre alphabétique.* The books are
   arranged in alphabetical order.

le **classeur** NOUN
   ring binder

classique ADJECTIVE
   1 **classical** ◇ *de la musique classique*
   classical music
   2 **classic** ◇ *un style classique* a
   classic style

le **clavier** NOUN
   keyboard (*of computer, typewriter*)

la **clé** NOUN
   1 **key**
   2 **clef** ◇ *la clé de sol* the treble clef
   ◇ *la clé de fa* the bass clef

la **clef** = clé

le **client** NOUN
   customer

la **cliente** NOUN
   customer

la **clientèle** NOUN
   customers

cligner VERB
 • **cligner des yeux** to blink

le **clignotant** NOUN
   indicator ◇ *Il a mis son clignotant à
   gauche.* He's indicating left.

le **climat** NOUN
   climate

la **climatisation** NOUN
   air conditioning

climatisé ADJECTIVE
   air-conditioned ◇ *L'hôtel est
   climatisé.* The hotel is air-conditioned.

le **clin d'œil** NOUN
   (PL les **clins d'œil**)
   wink
 • **en un clin d'œil** in a flash

la **clinique** NOUN
   private hospital

le **clochard** NOUN
   tramp

la **cloche** NOUN
   bell

le **clocher** NOUN
   1 **church tower**
   2 **steeple**

le **clou** NOUN
   nail
 • **un clou de girofle** a clove

le **clown** NOUN
   clown

le **club** NOUN
   club

le **cobaye** NOUN
   guinea pig

le **coca** NOUN
   Coke ®

la **cocaïne** NOUN
   cocaine

la **coccinelle** NOUN
   ladybird

cocher VERB
   to tick ◇ *Cochez la bonne réponse.*
   Tick the right answer.

le **cochon** NOUN
   see also cochon ADJECTIVE
   pig
 • **un cochon d'Inde** a guinea pig

cochon ADJECTIVE (*informal*)
   see also cochon NOUN
   dirty ◇ *une histoire cochonne* a dirty
   story

le **cocktail** NOUN

1 **cocktail**
2 **cocktail party**
le **coco** NOUN
- **une noix de coco** a coconut
cocorico EXCLAMATION
1 **Cock-a-doodle-doo!**
2 **Three cheers for France!**
*The symbol of France is the cockerel and so
cocorico! is sometimes used as an
expression of French national pride.*
la **cocotte** NOUN
casserole (*pan*)
- **une cocotte-minute** ® a pressure
cooker
le **code** NOUN
code
- **le code de la route** the highway code
- **le code postal** the postcode
le **cœur** NOUN
heart
- **avoir bon cœur** to be kind-hearted
- **la dame de cœur** the queen of hearts
- **avoir mal au cœur** to feel sick
- **par cœur** by heart ◇ *apprendre
quelque chose par cœur* to learn
something by heart
le **coffre** NOUN
1 **boot** (*of car*)
2 **chest** (*furniture*)
le **coffre-fort** NOUN
(PL les **coffres-forts**)
safe
le **coffret** NOUN
- **un coffret à bijoux** a jewellery box
le **cognac** NOUN
brandy
se **cogner** VERB
- **se cogner à quelque chose** to bang
into something ◇ *Je me suis cogné à
la table.* I banged into the table. ◇ *Je
me suis cogné la tête contre la porte du
placard.* I banged my head on the
cupboard door.
coiffé ADJECTIVE
- **Tu es bien coiffée.** Your hair looks
nice.
coiffer VERB
- **se coiffer** to do one's hair
le **coiffeur** NOUN
hairdresser
la **coiffeuse** NOUN
hairdresser
la **coiffure** NOUN
hairstyle ◇ *Cette coiffure te va bien.*
That hairstyle suits you.
- **un salon de coiffure** a hairdresser's
le **coin** NOUN
corner
- **Tu habites dans le coin?** Do you live

near here?
- **Je ne suis pas du coin.** I'm not from
here.
- **le bistrot du coin** the local pub
coincé ADJECTIVE
1 **stuck** ◇ *La clé est coincée dans la
serrure.* The key is stuck in the
keyhole.
2 **stuffy** ◇ *Il est un peu coincé.*
(*informal*) He's a bit stuffy.
coincer VERB
to jam ◇ *La porte est coincée.* The
door's jammed.
la **coïncidence** NOUN
coincidence
le **col** NOUN
1 **collar**
2 **pass** (*of mountain*)
la **colère** NOUN
anger
- **Je suis en colère.** I'm angry.
- **se mettre en colère** to get angry
le **colin** NOUN
hake
la **colique** NOUN
diarrhoea
le **colis** NOUN
parcel
collaborer VERB
to collaborate
collant ADJECTIVE
see also **collant** NOUN
1 **sticky**
2 **clingy** ◇ *Je le trouve un peu
collant.* (*informal*) He's always hanging
around me.
le **collant** NOUN
see also **collant** ADJECTIVE
tights ◇ *un collant en laine* woollen
tights
la **colle** NOUN
1 **glue** ◇ *un tube de colle* a tube of
glue
2 **detention** ◇ *J'ai une heure de
colle samedi prochain.* (*informal*) I've got
an hour's detention next Saturday.
- **Je n'en sais rien: tu me poses une
colle.** (*informal*) I really don't know:
you've got me there.
la **collecte** NOUN
collection (*of money*) ◇ *On a fait une
collecte au profit des victimes.* There
was a collection for the victims.
la **collection** NOUN
collection ◇ *une collection de
timbres* a stamp collection
collectionner VERB
to collect
le **collège** NOUN

secondary school

In France pupils go to a collège *between the ages of 11 and 15, and then to a* lycée *until the age of 18.*

le **collégien** NOUN
schoolboy

la **collégienne** NOUN
schoolgirl

la **collègue** NOUN
colleague

coller VERB
1 **to stick** ◇ *Il y a un chewing-gum collé sous la chaise.* There's a bit of chewing gum stuck under the chair.
2 **to be sticky** ◇ *Ce timbre ne colle plus.* This stamp won't stick on.
3 **to press** ◇ *J'ai collé mon oreille au mur.* I pressed my ear against the wall.

le **collier** NOUN
1 **necklace** ◇ *un collier de perles* a pearl necklace
2 **collar** (*of dog, cat*)

la **colline** NOUN
hill

la **colombe** NOUN
dove

la **colonie** NOUN
- **aller en colonie de vacances** to go to summer camp

la **colonne** NOUN
column
- **la colonne vertébrale** the spine

le **colorant** NOUN
colouring

le **coloris** NOUN
colour

le **coma** NOUN
coma ◇ *être dans le coma* to be in a coma

le **combat** NOUN
fighting ◇ *Les combats ont repris ce matin.* Fighting started again this morning.
- **un combat de boxe** a boxing match

le **combattant** NOUN
- **un ancien combattant** a war veteran

combattre VERB
to fight

combien ADVERB
1 **how much** ◇ *Vous en voulez combien? Un kilo?* How much do you want? One kilo? ◇ *Combien est-ce que ça coûte?* How much does it cost? ◇ *Combien ça fait?* How much does it come to?
2 **how many** ◇ *Tu en veux combien? Deux?* How many do you want? Two?
- **combien de (1)** how much

◇ *Combien de purée est-ce que je vous sers?* How much mashed potato shall I give you?
- **combien de (2)** how many
◇ *Combien de personnes as-tu invitées?* How many people have you invited?
- **combien de temps** how long
◇ *Combien de temps est-ce que tu seras absente?* How long will you be away?
- **On est le combien aujourd'hui?—On est le vingt.** What's the date today?–It's the 20th.

la **combinaison** NOUN
1 **combination** ◇ *J'ai changé la combinaison de mon antivol.* I've changed the combination on my bike lock.
2 **slip** (*petticoat*)
- **une combinaison de plongée** a wetsuit
- **une combinaison de ski** a ski suit

le **comble** NOUN
- **Alors ça, c'est le comble!** That's the last straw!

la **comédie** NOUN
comedy
- **une comédie musicale** a musical

le **comédien** NOUN
actor

la **comédienne** NOUN
actress

comestible ADJECTIVE
edible

comique ADJECTIVE
see also comique NOUN
comical

le **comique** NOUN
see also comique ADJECTIVE
comedian

le **commandant** NOUN
captain (*of ship, plane*)

la **commande** NOUN
order ◇ *un bon de commande* an order form
- **être aux commandes** to be at the controls

commander VERB
1 **to order** ◇ *J'ai commandé une robe par catalogue.* I've ordered a dress from a catalogue.
2 **to give orders** ◇ *C'est moi qui commande ici, pas vous!* I give the orders here, not you!

comme CONJUNCTION, ADVERB
1 **like** ◇ *Il est comme son père.* He's like his father. ◇ *Je voudrais un manteau comme celui de la photo.* I'd

like a coat like the one in the picture.

② **for** ◇ *Qu'est-ce que tu veux comme dessert?* What would you like for pudding?

③ **as** ◇ *J'ai travaillé comme serveuse cet été.* I worked as a waitress this summer. ◇ *Faites comme vous voulez.* Do as you like.

- **comme ça** like this ◇ *Ça se plie comme ça.* You fold it like this. ◇ *C'était un poisson grand comme ça.* The fish was this big.

- **comme il faut** properly ◇ *Mets le couvert comme il faut!* Set the table properly!

- **Comme tu as grandi!** How you've grown!

- **Regarde comme c'est beau!** Look, isn't it lovely!

- **comme ci comme ça** so-so ◇ *Comment est-ce que tu as trouvé le film?—Comme ci comme ça.* What did you think of the film?–So-so.

le **commencement** NOUN
   beginning

commencer VERB
   to start ◇ *Les cours commencent à huit heures.* Lessons start at 8 o'clock. ◇ *Il a commencé à pleuvoir.* It started raining. ◇ *J'ai commencé de réviser pour les examens.* I've started revising for the exams.

comment ADVERB
   how ◇ *Comment arrives-tu à travailler dans ce bruit?* How can you possibly work with this noise?

- **Comment allez-vous?** How are you?

- **Comment s'appelle-t-il?** What's his name?

- **Comment?** What did you say?

le **commentaire** NOUN
   comment

les **commérages** MASC NOUN
   gossip

le **commerçant** NOUN
   shopkeeper

le **commerce** NOUN
   ① trade ◇ *le commerce extérieur* foreign trade
   ② business ◇ *Il fait des études de commerce.* He's studying business.
   ③ shop ◇ *On trouve ça facilement dans ce commerce.* You can easily find it in the shops.

commercial ADJECTIVE
   (MASC PL **commerciaux**)

- **un centre commercial** a shopping centre

le **commissaire** NOUN

   police superintendent

le **commissariat** NOUN
   police station

les **commissions** FEM NOUN
   shopping ◇ *J'ai quelques commissions à faire.* I've got some shopping to do.

commode ADJECTIVE
   see also **commode** NOUN
   handy ◇ *Ce sac est très commode pour les voyages.* This bag is very handy for travelling.

- **Son père n'est pas commode.** His father is a difficult character.

la **commode** NOUN
   see also **commode** ADJECTIVE
   chest of drawers

commun ADJECTIVE
   shared ◇ *une salle de bain commune* a shared bathroom ◇ *Nous avons des intérêts communs.* We have interests in common.

- **en commun** in common ◇ *Ils n'ont rien en commun.* They've got nothing in common.

- **les transports en commun** public transport

- **mettre quelque chose en commun** to share something ◇ *Nous mettons tous nos livres en commun.* We share all our books.

la **communauté** NOUN
   community

la **communication** NOUN
   communication

- **une communication téléphonique** a telephone call

la **communion** NOUN
   communion ◇ *faire sa première communion* to make one's first communion

communiquer VERB
   to communicate

communiste ADJECTIVE
   communist ◇ *le Parti communiste* the Communist Party

compact ADJECTIVE
   compact

- **un disque compact** a compact disc

la **compagne** NOUN
   ① companion
   ② partner (*living together*)

la **compagnie** NOUN
   company ◇ *J'aime avoir de la compagnie.* I like to have company. ◇ *Je viendrai te tenir compagnie.* I'll come to keep you company.

- **une compagnie d'assurances** an insurance company

- **une compagnie aérienne** an airline
le **compagnon** NOUN
   1 **companion**
   2 **partner** (*living together*)
la **comparaison** NOUN
   comparison ◇ *en comparaison de* in comparison with
comparer VERB
   to compare
le **compartiment** NOUN
   compartment (*on train*)
le **compas** NOUN
   compass (*for drawing circles*)
compatible ADJECTIVE
   compatible
la **compétence** NOUN
   competence
compétent ADJECTIVE
   competent
la **compétition** NOUN
   competition
complet ADJECTIVE, ADVERB
   (FEM SING **complète**)
   see also complet NOUN
   1 **complete** ◇ *les œuvres complètes de Shakespeare* the complete works of Shakespeare
   2 **full** ◇ *L'hôtel est complet.* The hotel is full.
- **"complet"** "no vacancies"
- **le pain complet** wholemeal bread
le **complet** NOUN
   see also complet ADJECTIVE
   suit (*for man*)
complètement ADVERB
   completely ◇ *J'avais complètement oublié que tu viendrais.* I'd completely forgotten that you were coming.
compléter VERB
   to complete ◇ *Complétez les phrases suivantes.* Complete the following phrases.
complexe ADJECTIVE
   complex
complexé ADJECTIVE
   screwed-up
la **complication** NOUN
   complication
la **complice** NOUN
   accomplice
les **compliments** MASC NOUN
   compliment SING
- **faire des compliments** to compliment ◇ *Il m'a fait des compliments sur ma robe.* He complimented me on my dress.
compliqué ADJECTIVE
   complicated ◇ *C'est une histoire compliquée.* It's a complicated story.

le **complot** NOUN
   plot
le **comportement** NOUN
   behaviour
comporter VERB
   1 **to consist of** ◇ *Le château comporte trois parties.* The castle consists of three parts.
   2 **to have** ◇ *Ce modèle comporte un écran couleur.* This model has a colour screen.
- **se comporter** to behave ◇ *Il s'est comporté de façon odieuse.* He behaved atrociously.
composer VERB
   to compose (*music, text*)
- **composer un numéro** to dial a number
- **se composer de** to consist of ◇ *L'uniforme se compose d'une veste, d'un pantalon et d'une cravate.* The uniform consists of a jacket, trousers and a tie.
le **compositeur** NOUN
   composer
la **composition** NOUN
   test ◇ *Nous avons une composition de français cet après-midi.* We've got a French test this afternoon.
la **compositrice** NOUN
   composer
composter VERB
   to punch ◇ *N'oublie pas de composter ton billet avant de monter dans le train.* Remember to punch your ticket before you get on the train.
   In France you have to punch your ticket on the platform to validate it before getting onto the train.
la **compote** NOUN
   stewed fruit
- **la compote de prunes** stewed plums
compréhensible ADJECTIVE
   understandable
compréhensif ADJECTIVE
   (FEM SING **compréhensive**)
   understanding
comprendre VERB
   1 **to understand** ◇ *Je ne comprends pas ce que vous dites.* I don't understand what you're saying.
   2 **to include** ◇ *Le forfait ne comprend pas la location des skis.* The price doesn't include ski hire.
le **comprimé** NOUN
   tablet ◇ *un comprimé d'aspirine* an aspirin
compris ADJECTIVE
   included ◇ *Le service n'est pas*

compris. Service is not included.

- **y compris** including ◇ *Ils ont tout vendu, y compris leur voiture.* They sold everything, including their car.
- **non compris** excluding ◇ *un menu à cent francs, vin non compris* a set menu for 100 francs, excluding wine
- **cent francs tout compris** 100 francs all-inclusive

la **comptabilité** NOUN
accounting ◇ *un cours de comptabilité* a course in accounting

le/la **comptable** NOUN
accountant ◇ *Il est comptable.* He's an accountant.

comptant ADVERB
- **payer comptant** to pay cash

le **compte** NOUN
account ◇ *J'ai déposé le chèque sur mon compte.* I've paid the cheque into my account.
- **Le compte est bon.** That's the right amount.
- **tenir compte de (1)** to take into account ◇ *Ils ont tenu compte de mon expérience.* They took my experience into account.
- **tenir compte de (2)** to take notice of ◇ *Il n'a pas tenu compte de mes conseils.* He took no notice of my advice.
- **travailler à son compte** to be self-employed
- **en fin de compte** all things considered ◇ *Le voyage ne s'est pas mal passé, en fin de compte.* The journey wasn't bad, all things considered.

compter VERB
to count

le **compte rendu** NOUN
(PL les **comptes rendus**)
report

le **compteur** NOUN
meter

le **comptoir** NOUN
bar ◇ *au comptoir* at the bar

con ADJECTIVE *(rude)*
(FEM SING **conne**)
bloody stupid

se **concentrer** VERB
to concentrate ◇ *J'ai du mal à me concentrer.* I find it hard to concentrate.

la **conception** NOUN
design

concerner VERB
to concern ◇ *en ce qui me concerne* as far as I'm concerned
- **Je ne me sens pas concerné.** I don't feel it's anything to do with me.

le **concert** NOUN
concert

le/la **concierge** NOUN
caretaker

conclure VERB
to conclude

la **conclusion** NOUN
conclusion

le **concombre** NOUN
cucumber

concorder VERB
to tally ◇ *Les dates concordent.* The dates tally.

le **concours** NOUN
1 **competition** ◇ *un concours de chant* a singing competition
2 **competitive exam**

concret ADJECTIVE
(FEM SING **concrète**)
concrete

conçu VERB
designed ◇ *Ces appartements sont très mal conçus.* These flats are very badly designed.

la **concurrence** NOUN
competition ◇ *La concurrence est vive sur ce marché.* There's a lot of competition in this market.

le **concurrent** NOUN
competitor

la **concurrente** NOUN
competitor

condamner VERB
to sentence ◇ *Il a été condamné à deux ans de prison.* He was sentenced to two years in prison. ◇ *condamner à mort* to sentence to death

la **condition** NOUN
condition ◇ *Je le ferai à une condition...* I'll do it, on one condition...
- **à condition que** provided that ◇ *Je viendrai à condition qu'il me le demande.* I'll come provided he asks me to.
- **les conditions de travail** working conditions

le **conditionnel** NOUN
conditional tense

le **conducteur** NOUN
driver

la **conductrice** NOUN
driver

conduire VERB
to drive ◇ *Est-ce que tu sais conduire?* Can you drive? ◇ *Je te conduirai chez le docteur.* I'll drive you to the doctor's.
- **se conduire** to behave ◇ *Il s'est mal*

conduit. He behaved badly.

conduite NOUN
behaviour

conférence NOUN
1 **lecture** ◇ *donner une conférence* to give a lecture
2 **conference** ◇ *une conférence internationale* an international conference

confesser VERB
to go to confession

confiance NOUN
1 **trust**
- **avoir confiance en quelqu'un** to trust somebody ◇ *Je n'ai pas confiance en lui.* I don't trust him.
2 **confidence**
- **Tu peux avoir confiance. Il sera à l'heure.** You don't need to worry. He'll be on time.
- **confiance en soi** self-confidence ◇ *Elle manque de confiance en elle.* She lacks self-confidence.

confiant ADJECTIVE
confident

confidences FEM NOUN
- **faire des confidences à quelqu'un** to confide in someone ◇ *Elle me fait quelquefois des confidences.* She sometimes confides in me.

confidentiel ADJECTIVE
(FEM SING **confidentielle**)
confidential

confier VERB
- **se confier à quelqu'un** to confide in somebody ◇ *Elle s'est confiée à sa meilleure amie.* She confided in her best friend.

confirmer VERB
to confirm

confiserie NOUN
sweet shop

confisquer VERB
to confiscate

confit ADJECTIVE
- **des fruits confits** crystallized fruits

confiture NOUN
jam ◇ *la confiture de fraises* strawberry jam
- **la confiture d'oranges** marmalade

conflit NOUN
conflict

confondre VERB
to mix up ◇ *On le confond souvent avec son frère.* People often mix him up with his brother.

confort NOUN
comfort
- **tout confort** with all mod cons ◇ *un appartement tout confort* a flat with all mod cons

confortable ADJECTIVE
comfortable ◇ *des chaussures confortables* comfortable shoes

confus ADJECTIVE
1 **unclear** ◇ *J'ai trouvé ses explications confuses.* I thought his explanation was unclear.
2 **embarrassed** ◇ *Il avait l'air confus.* He looked embarrassed.

la **confusion** NOUN
1 **confusion**
2 **embarrassment** ◇ *rougir de confusion* to go red with embarrassment

le **congé** NOUN
holiday ◇ *une semaine de congé* a week's holiday
- **en congé** on holiday ◇ *Je serai en congé la semaine prochaine.* I'll be on holiday next week.
- **un congé de maladie** sick leave ◇ *Il est en congé de maladie.* He's on sick leave.

le **congélateur** NOUN
freezer

congeler VERB
to freeze

la **conjonctivite** NOUN
conjunctivitis

la **conjugaison** NOUN
conjugation

la **connaissance** NOUN
1 **knowledge** ◇ *...pour approfondir vos connaissances* ...to increase your knowledge
2 **acquaintance** ◇ *Ce n'est pas vraiment une amie, juste une connaissance.* She's not really a friend, just an acquaintance.
- **perdre connaissance** to lose consciousness

connaître VERB
to know ◇ *Je ne connais pas du tout cette région.* I don't know this area at all. ◇ *Je le connais de vue.* I know him by sight.
- **Ils se sont connus à Nantes.** They first met in Nantes.
- **s'y connaître en quelque chose** to know about something ◇ *Je ne m'y connais pas beaucoup en musique classique.* I don't know much about classical music.

la **connerie** NOUN *(rude)*
bloody stupid thing ◇ *faire une connerie* to do something bloody stupid

connu ADJECTIVE
well-known ◇ *C'est un acteur connu.* He's a well-known actor.

conquérir VERB
to conquer

consacrer VERB
to devote ◇ *Il consacre beaucoup de temps à ses enfants.* He devotes a lot of time to his children. ◇ *Je suis désolé, je n'ai pas beaucoup de temps à vous consacrer.* I'm afraid I can't spare much time for you.

la **conscience** NOUN
conscience ◇ *avoir mauvaise conscience* to have a guilty conscience
• **prendre conscience de** to become aware of ◇ *Ils ont fini par prendre conscience de la gravité de la situation.* They eventually became aware of the seriousness of the situation.

consciencieux ADJECTIVE
(FEM SING **consciencieuse**)
conscientious

conscient ADJECTIVE
conscious

consécutif ADJECTIVE
(FEM SING **consécutive**)
consecutive

le **conseil** NOUN
advice ◇ *Est-ce que je peux te demander conseil?* Can I ask you for some advice?
• **un conseil** a piece of advice

conseiller VERB
1 **to advise** ◇ *Il a été mal conseillé.* He has been badly advised.
2 **to recommend** ◇ *Il m'a conseillé ce livre.* He recommended this book to me.

le **consentement** NOUN
consent ◇ *le consentement des parents* the parents' consent

consentir VERB
to agree ◇ *consentir à quelque chose* to agree to something

la **conséquence** NOUN
consequence
• **en conséquence** consequently

conséquent ADJECTIVE
• **par conséquent** consequently

le **conservatoire** NOUN
school of music ◇ *Elle fait du piano au conservatoire.* She's learning the piano at the school of music.

la **conserve** NOUN
tin ◇ *Je vais ouvrir une conserve.* I'll open a tin.
• **une boîte de conserve** a tin
• **les conserves** tinned food ◇ *Il n'est pas bon de manger tous les jours des conserves.* It's not healthy to eat tinned food every day.
• **en conserve** tinned ◇ *des petits pois en conserve* tinned peas

conserver VERB
to keep ◇ *J'ai conservé toutes ses lettres.* I've kept all her letters.
• **se conserver** to keep ◇ *Ce pain se conserve plus d'une semaine.* This bread will keep for more than a week.

considérable ADJECTIVE
considerable ◇ *Il a fait des progrès considérables.* He's made considerable progress.

la **considération** NOUN
• **prendre quelque chose en considération** to take something into consideration

considérer VERB
• **considérer que** to believe that ◇ *Je considère que le gouvernement devrait investir davantage dans l'éducation.* I believe that the government should invest more money in education.

la **consigne** NOUN
left-luggage office
• **une consigne automatique** a left-luggage locker

consistant ADJECTIVE
substantial ◇ *un petit déjeuner consistant* a substantial breakfast

consister VERB
• **consister à** to consist of ◇ *Mon travail consiste à répondre au téléphone et à recevoir les clients.* My job consists of answering the phone and welcoming the customers. ◇ *En quoi consiste votre travail?* What does your job involve?

consoler VERB
to console

le **consommateur** NOUN
1 **consumer**
2 **customer** (*in café*)

la **consommation** NOUN
1 **consumption** ◇ *la consommation d'électricité* electricity consumption
2 **drink** ◇ *Le billet d'entrée donne droit à une consommation gratuite.* The ticket entitles you to one free drink.

la **consommatrice** NOUN
1 **consumer**
2 **customer** (*in café*)

consommer VERB
1 **to use** ◇ *Ces grosses voitures consomment beaucoup d'essence.* These big cars use a lot of petrol.
2 **to have a drink** ◇ *Est-ce qu'on*

peut consommer à la terrasse? Can we have drinks outside?

consonne NOUN
consonant

constamment ADVERB
constantly ◇ *Elle se plaint constamment.* She's constantly complaining.

constant ADJECTIVE
constant

constater VERB
to notice

constipé ADJECTIVE
constipated

constitué ADJECTIVE
- **être constitué de** to consist of

constituer VERB
to make up ◇ *les États qui constituent la Fédération russe* the states which make up the Russian Federation

construction NOUN
building ◇ *des matériaux de construction* building materials
- **une maison en construction** a house being built

construire VERB
to build ◇ *Ils font construire une maison neuve.* They're having a new house built.

consultation NOUN
- **les heures de consultation** surgery hours

consulter VERB
1 to consult ◇ *Tu devrais consulter un médecin.* You should see a doctor.
2 to see patients ◇ *Le docteur ne consulte pas le samedi.* The doctor doesn't see patients on Saturdays.

contact NOUN
contact ◇ *les contacts humains* human contact
- **Il a le contact facile.** He's very approachable.
- **garder le contact avec quelqu'un** to keep in touch with somebody

contacter VERB
to get in touch with ◇ *Je te contacterai dès que j'aurai des nouvelles.* I'll get in touch with you as soon as I have some news.

contagieux ADJECTIVE
(FEM SING **contagieuse**)
infectious ◇ *une maladie contagieuse* an infectious disease ◇ *Restez chez vous si vous êtes contagieux.* Stay at home if you've got something infectious.

contaminer VERB

to contaminate

le **conte de fées** NOUN
(PL les **contes de fées**)
fairy tale

contempler VERB
to gaze at

contemporain ADJECTIVE
contemporary
- **un auteur contemporain** a modern writer

contenir VERB
to contain ◇ *un portefeuille contenant de l'argent* a wallet containing money

content ADJECTIVE
glad ◇ *Je suis content que tu sois venu.* I'm glad you've come.
- **content de** pleased with ◇ *Elle m'a dit qu'elle était contente de mon travail.* She told me she was pleased with my work.

contenter VERB
to please ◇ *Il est difficile à contenter.* He's hard to please.
- **Je me contente de peu.** I can make do with very little.

contesté ADJECTIVE
controversial ◇ *Cette décision est très contestée.* This is a very controversial decision.

le **continent** NOUN
continent

continu ADJECTIVE
continuous
- **faire la journée continue** to work without taking a full lunch break

continuellement ADVERB
constantly

continuer VERB
to carry on ◇ *Continuez sans moi!* Carry on without me! ◇ *Il ne veut pas continuer ses études.* He doesn't want to go on studying.
- **continuer à faire quelque chose** to go on doing something ◇ *Ils ont continué à regarder la télé sans me dire bonjour.* They went on watching TV without saying hello to me.
- **continuer de faire quelque chose** to go on doing something ◇ *Il continue de fumer malgré son asthme.* He keeps on smoking, despite his asthma.

contourner VERB
to go round ◇ *La route contourne la ville.* The road goes round the town.

le **contraceptif** NOUN
contraceptive

la **contraception** NOUN
contraception

le **contractuel** NOUN
traffic warden

la **contractuelle** NOUN
traffic warden

la **contradiction** NOUN
contradiction

- **par esprit de contradiction** just to be
awkward ◇ *Il a refusé de venir par
esprit de contradiction.* He refused to
come, just to be awkward.

le **contraire** NOUN
opposite ◇ *Il a fait le contraire de ce
que je lui avais demandé.* He did the
opposite of what I asked him.
- **au contraire** on the contrary

contrarier VERB
1 **to annoy** ◇ *Il avait l'air contrarié.*
He looked annoyed.
2 **to upset** ◇ *Est-ce que tu serais
contrariée si je ne venais pas?* Would
you be upset if I didn't come?

le **contraste** NOUN
contrast

le **contrat** NOUN
contract ◇ *un contrat de travail* an
employment contract

la **contravention** NOUN
parking ticket

contre PREPOSITION
1 **against** ◇ *Ne mets pas ton vélo
contre le mur.* Don't put your bike
against the wall. ◇ *Tu es pour ou
contre ce projet?* Are you for or against
this plan?
2 **for** ◇ *échanger quelque chose
contre quelque chose* to swap
something for something
- **par contre** on the other hand

la **contrebande** NOUN
smuggling
- **des produits de contrebande**
smuggled goods

la **contrebasse** NOUN
double bass

contrecœur
- **à contrecœur** ADVERB
reluctantly ◇ *Il est venu à
contrecœur.* He came reluctantly.

contredire VERB
to contradict ◇ *Il ne supporte pas
d'être contredit.* He can't stand being
contradicted.

la **contre-indication** NOUN
- **"Contre-indication en cas d'eczéma"**
"Should not be used by people with
eczema"

le **contresens** NOUN
mistranslation

le **contretemps** NOUN

- **Désolé d'être en retard: j'ai eu un
contretemps.** Sorry I'm late: I was
held up.

contribuer VERB
- **contribuer à** to contribute to
◇ *Est-ce que tu veux contribuer au
cadeau pour Marie?* Do you want to
contribute to Marie's present?

le **contrôle** NOUN
1 **control** ◇ *le contrôle des
passeports* passport control
2 **check**
- **un contrôle d'identité** an identity
check
- **le contrôle des billets** ticket
inspection
3 **test** ◇ *un contrôle antidopage* a
drugs test
- **le contrôle continu** continuous
assessment

contrôler VERB
to check ◇ *Personne n'a contrôlé
mon billet.* Nobody checked my ticket.

le **contrôleur** NOUN
ticket inspector

la **contrôleuse** NOUN
ticket inspector

controversé ADJECTIVE
controversial

convaincre VERB
1 **to persuade** ◇ *Il a essayé de me
convaincre de rester.* He tried to
persuade me to stay.
2 **to convince** ◇ *Tu n'as pas l'air
convaincu.* You don't look convinced.

la **convalescence** NOUN
convalescence

convenable ADJECTIVE
decent ◇ *un hôtel convenable* a
decent hotel
- **Ce n'est pas convenable.** It's bad
manners.

convenir VERB
- **convenir à** to suit ◇ *Est-ce que cette
date te convient?* Does this date suit
you? ◇ *J'espère que cela vous
conviendra.* I hope this will suit you.
- **convenir de** to agree on ◇ *Nous
avons convenu d'une date.* We've
agreed on a date.

conventionné ADJECTIVE
- **un médecin conventionné** a Health
Service doctor

*All doctors in France charge for treatment, but
patients of Health Service doctors get their
money refunded by the government.*

convenu ADJECTIVE
agreed ◇ *au moment convenu* at the
agreed time

conversation NOUN
   conversation
convocation NOUN
   notification
convoquer VERB
+ **convoquer quelqu'un à une réunion**
   to invite somebody to a meeting
   ◇ *Le directeur a convoqué tous les
   parents à la réunion.* The headmaster
   has invited all the parents to the
   meeting.
coopération NOUN
   co-operation
coopérer VERB
   to co-operate
copain NOUN (*informal*)
   1 **friend** ◇ *C'est un bon copain.* He's
   a good friend.
   2 **boyfriend** ◇ *Je l'ai vue avec son
   copain.* I saw her with her boyfriend.
copie NOUN
   1 **copy** ◇ *Ce tableau n'est qu'une
   copie.* This picture is only a copy.
   2 **paper** ◇ *Il a des copies à corriger
   ce week-end.* He's got some papers to
   mark this weekend.
copier VERB
   to copy
copieux ADJECTIVE
   (FEM SING **copieuse**)
   hearty ◇ *un repas copieux* a hearty
   meal
copine NOUN (*informal*)
   1 **friend** ◇ *Je sors avec une copine
   ce soir.* I'm going out with a friend
   tonight.
   2 **girlfriend** ◇ *Je ne savais pas qu'il
   avait une copine.* I didn't know he had
   a girlfriend.
coq NOUN
   cockerel
coque NOUN
   hull (*of boat*)
+ **un œuf à la coque** a soft-boiled egg
coquelicot NOUN
   poppy
coqueluche NOUN
   whooping cough
coquillage NOUN
   1 **shellfish**
   2 **shell** ◇ *Nous avons ramassé des
   coquillages sur la plage.* We picked up
   some shells on the beach.
coquille NOUN
   shell
+ **une coquille d'œuf** an eggshell
+ **une coquille Saint-Jacques** a scallop
coquin ADJECTIVE
   cheeky ◇ *Il m'a regardé d'un air*

coquin. He gave me a cheeky look.
le cor NOUN
   horn ◇ *Je joue du cor.* I play the
   horn.
le corbeau NOUN
   (PL les **corbeaux**)
   crow
la corbeille NOUN
   basket ◇ *une corbeille de fruits* a
   basket of fruit
+ **une corbeille à papier** a wastepaper
   basket
la corde NOUN
   1 **rope**
   2 **string** (*of violin, tennis racket*)
+ **une corde à linge** a clothes line
la cordonnerie NOUN
   shoe repair shop
le cordonnier NOUN
   cobbler
coriace ADJECTIVE
   tough
la corne NOUN
   horn
la cornemuse NOUN
   bagpipes ◇ *jouer de la cornemuse* to
   play the bagpipes
le cornet NOUN
+ **un cornet de frites** a bag of chips
+ **un cornet de glace** an ice cream cone
le cornichon NOUN
   gherkin
la Cornouailles NOUN
   Cornwall
le corps NOUN
   body
correct ADJECTIVE
   1 **correct** ◇ *Ce n'est pas tout à fait
   correct.* That's not quite correct.
   2 **reasonable** ◇ *un salaire correct* a
   reasonable salary ◇ *Le repas était tout
   à fait correct.* The meal was quite
   reasonable.
la correction NOUN
   correction
la correspondance NOUN
   1 **correspondence**
+ **un cours par correspondance** a
   correspondence course
   2 **connection** (*train, plane*) ◇ *Il y a
   une correspondance pour Toulouse à dix
   heures.* There's a connection for
   Toulouse at ten o'clock.
le correspondant NOUN
   penfriend
la correspondante NOUN
   penfriend
correspondre VERB
   to correspond

le **corridor** NOUN
corridor

corriger VERB
to mark ◇ *Le prof n'a pas encore corrigé nos copies.* The teacher hasn't marked our papers yet.

corse ADJECTIVE, NOUN
Corsican
- **un Corse** a Corsican (*man*)
- **une Corse** a Corsican (*woman*)

la **Corse** NOUN
Corsica

la **corvée** NOUN
chore ◇ *Quelle corvée!* What a chore!

costaud ADJECTIVE
brawny

le **costume** NOUN
[1] **suit** (*man's*) ◇ *Tu devrais mettre un costume et une cravate pour l'entretien.* You should wear a suit and tie for the interview.
[2] **costume** (*theatre*) ◇ *Nous avons fait nous-mêmes tous les costumes pour la pièce.* We made all the costumes for the play ourselves.

la **côte** NOUN
[1] **coastline** ◇ *La route longe la côte.* The road follows the coastline.
- **la Côte d'Azur** the French Riviera
[2] **hill** ◇ *J'ai grimpé la côte.* I went up the hill.
[3] **rib** ◇ *Il s'est cassé une côte en tombant.* He broke a rib when he fell.
[4] **chop** ◇ *une côte de porc* a pork chop
- **une côte de bœuf** a rib of beef
- **côte à côte** side by side

le **côté** NOUN
side
- **à côté de (1)** next to ◇ *Le café est à côté du sucre.* The coffee's next to the sugar.
- **à côté de (2)** next door to ◇ *Il habite à côté de chez moi.* He lives next door to me.
- **de l'autre côté** on the other side ◇ *La pharmacie est de l'autre côté de la rue.* The chemist's is on the other side of the street.
- **De quel côté est-il parti?** Which way did he go?
- **mettre quelque chose de côté** to save something ◇ *J'ai mis de l'argent de côté.* I've saved some money.

la **côtelette** NOUN
chop ◇ *une côtelette d'agneau* a lamb chop

le **coton** NOUN
cotton ◇ *une chemise en coton* a cotton shirt
- **le coton hydrophile** cotton wool

le **cou** NOUN
neck

couchant ADJECTIVE
- **le soleil couchant** the setting sun

la **couche** NOUN
[1] **layer** ◇ *la couche d'ozone* the ozone layer
[2] **coat** (*of paint, varnish*)
[3] **nappy**

couché ADJECTIVE
[1] **lying down** ◇ *Il était couché sur le tapis.* He was lying on the carpet.
[2] **in bed** ◇ *À huit heures, il était déjà couché.* He was already in bed at 8 o'clock.

le **coucher** NOUN
see also coucher VERB
- **un coucher de soleil** a sunset

se **coucher** VERB
see also coucher NOUN
[1] **to go to bed** ◇ *Je me suis couché tard hier soir.* I went to bed late last night.
[2] **to set** (*sun*)

la **couchette** NOUN
[1] **couchette** (*on train*)
[2] **bunk** (*on boat*)

le **coude** NOUN
elbow

coudre VERB
[1] **to sew** ◇ *J'aime coudre.* I like sewing.
[2] **to sew on** ◇ *Il ne sait même pas coudre un bouton.* He can't even sew a button on.

la **couette** NOUN
duvet

les **couettes** FEM NOUN
bunches ◇ *Quand j'étais petite, ma mère me faisait des couettes.* When I was little, my mother put my hair in bunches.

couler VERB
[1] **to run** ◇ *Ne laissez pas couler les robinets.* Don't leave the taps running. ◇ *J'ai le nez qui coule.* My nose is running.
[2] **to flow** ◇ *La rivière coulait lentement.* The river was flowing slowly.
[3] **to leak** ◇ *Mon stylo coule.* My pen's leaking.
[4] **to sink** ◇ *Un bateau a coulé pendant la tempête.* A boat sank during the storm.

la **couleur** NOUN

colour ◇ *une pellicule couleur* a colour film
- **Tu as pris des couleurs.** You've got a tan.

a **couleuvre** NOUN
grass snake

s **coulisses** FEM NOUN
wings (*in theatre*)
- **dans les coulisses** behind the scenes

e **couloir** NOUN
corridor

e **coup** NOUN
1 **knock** ◇ *donner un coup à quelque chose* to give something a knock
2 **blow** ◇ *Il m'a donné un coup!* He hit me!
- **un coup de pied** a kick
- **un coup de poing** a punch
3 **shock** ◇ *Ça m'a fait un coup de le voir comme ça!* (*informal*) It gave me a shock to see him like that!
- **un coup de feu** a shot
- **un coup de fil** (*informal*) a ring ◇ *Je te donnerai un coup de fil dans la soirée.* I'll give you a ring this evening.
- **donner un coup de main à quelqu'un** to give somebody a hand ◇ *Je viendrai te donner un coup de main.* I'll come and give you a hand.
- **un coup d'œil** a quick look ◇ *jeter un coup d'œil* to have a quick look
- **attraper un coup de soleil** to get sunburnt
- **un coup de téléphone** a phone call
- **un coup de tonnerre** a clap of thunder
- **boire un coup** (*informal*) to have a drink
- **après coup** afterwards ◇ *Après coup j'ai regretté de m'être mis en colère.* Afterwards I was sorry I'd got angry.
- **à tous les coups** (*informal*) every time ◇ *Je me trompe de rue à tous les coups.* I get the street wrong every time.
- **du premier coup** first time ◇ *Il a été reçu au permis du premier coup.* He passed his driving test first time.
- **sur le coup** at first ◇ *Sur le coup je ne l'ai pas reconnu.* I didn't recognize him at first.

coupable ADJECTIVE
see also coupable NOUN
guilty

a **coupable** NOUN
see also coupable ADJECTIVE
culprit

a **coupe** NOUN
cup (*sport*) ◇ *Ils ont remporté la coupe du monde.* They won the World Cup.

- **une coupe de cheveux** a haircut
- **une coupe de champagne** a glass of champagne

couper VERB
1 **to cut**
2 **to turn off** ◇ *couper le courant* to turn off the electricity
3 **to take a short-cut** ◇ *On peut couper par la forêt.* There's a short-cut through the woods.
- **couper l'appétit** to spoil one's appetite
- **se couper** to cut oneself ◇ *Je me suis coupé le doigt avec une boîte de conserve.* I cut my finger on a tin.
- **couper la parole à quelqu'un** to interrupt somebody

le **couple** NOUN
couple

le **couplet** NOUN
verse ◇ *le premier couplet* the first verse

la **coupure** NOUN
cut
- **une coupure de courant** a power cut

la **cour** NOUN
1 **yard** ◇ *la cour de l'école* the school yard
2 **court** ◇ *la cour de Louis XIV* the court of Louis XIV ◇ *la cour d'assises* the criminal court

le **courage** NOUN
courage

courageux ADJECTIVE
(FEM SING **courageuse**)
brave

couramment ADVERB
1 **fluently** ◇ *Elle parle couramment japonais.* She speaks Japanese fluently.
2 **commonly** ◇ *C'est une expression que l'on emploie couramment.* It's a commonly used phrase.

courant ADJECTIVE
see also courant NOUN
1 **common** ◇ *C'est une erreur courante.* It's a common mistake.
2 **standard** ◇ *C'est un modèle courant.* It's a standard model.

le **courant** NOUN
see also courant ADJECTIVE
1 **current** (*of river*)
- **un courant d'air** a draught
2 **power** ◇ *une panne de courant* a power cut
- **Je le ferai dans le courant de la semaine.** I'll do it some time during the week.
- **être au courant de quelque chose** to know about something ◇ *Je ne suis*

pas au courant de ses projets pour l'été. I don't know about her plans for the summer.
- **mettre quelqu'un au courant de quelque chose** to tell somebody about something
- **Tu es au courant?** Have you heard about it?
- **se tenir au courant de quelque chose** to keep up with something ◇ *J'essaie de me tenir au courant de l'actualité.* I try to keep up with the news.

le**coureur** NOUN
runner
- **un coureur à pied** a runner
- **un coureur cycliste** a racing cyclist
- **un coureur automobile** a racing driver

la**coureuse** NOUN
runner

la**courgette** NOUN
courgette

courir VERB
to run ◇ *Elle a traversé la rue en courant.* She ran across the street.
- **courir un risque** to run a risk

la**couronne** NOUN
crown

courons, courez VERB *see* **courir**

le**courrier** NOUN
post ◇ *Est-ce qu'il y avait du courrier ce matin?* Was there any post this morning? ◇ *N'oublie pas de poster le courrier.* Don't forget to post the letters.
- **le courrier électronique** E-mail

la**courroie** NOUN
- **la courroie du ventilateur** fan belt

le**cours** NOUN
1 **lesson** ◇ *un cours d'espagnol* a Spanish lesson ◇ *des cours particuliers* private lessons
2 **course** ◇ *un cours intensif* a crash course
3 **rate** ◇ *le cours du change* the exchange rate
- **au cours de** during ◇ *Il a été réveillé trois fois au cours de la nuit.* He was woken up three times during the night.

la**course** NOUN
1 **running** ◇ *la course de fond* long-distance running
2 **race** ◇ *une course hippique* a horse race
3 **shopping** ◇ *J'ai juste une course à faire.* I've just got a bit of shopping to do.
- **faire les courses** to go shopping ◇ *Elle est partie faire les courses de*

la semaine. She's gone to do her weekly shopping.

court ADJECTIVE
see also **court** NOUN
short

le**court** NOUN
see also **court** ADJECTIVE
- **un court de tennis** a tennis court

couru VERB *see* **courir**

le**couscous** NOUN
couscous
couscous *is a spicy North African dish made with meat, vegetables and steamed semolina.*

le**cousin** NOUN
cousin

la**cousine** NOUN
cousin

le**coussin** NOUN
cushion

le**coût** NOUN
cost ◇ *le coût de la vie* the cost of living

le**couteau** NOUN
(PL les **couteaux**)
knife

coûter VERB
to cost ◇ *Est-ce que ça coûte cher?* Does it cost a lot?
- **Combien ça coûte?** How much is it?

coûteux ADJECTIVE
(FEM SING **coûteuse**)
expensive

la**coutume** NOUN
custom

la**couture** NOUN
1 **sewing** ◇ *Je n'aime pas la couture.* I don't like sewing.
- **faire de la couture** to sew
2 **seam** ◇ *La couture de mon pantalon s'est défaite.* The seam of my trousers has come undone.

le**couturier** NOUN
fashion designer ◇ *un grand couturier* a top designer

la**couturière** NOUN
dressmaker

le**couvercle** NOUN
1 **lid** (*of pan*)
2 **top** (*of tube, jar, spray can*)

couvert VERB *see* **couvrir**

couvert ADJECTIVE
see also **couvert** NOUN
- **couvert de** covered with ◇ *Cet arbre est couvert de fleurs au printemps.* This tree is covered with blossom in spring.
overcast (*sky*)

le**couvert** NOUN
see also **couvert** ADJECTIVE
- **mettre le couvert** to lay the table

es couverts MASC NOUN
  cutlery ◇ *Les couverts sont dans le tiroir de gauche.* The cutlery is in the left-hand drawer.

a couverture NOUN
  blanket

e couvre-lit NOUN
  bedspread

couvrir VERB
  to cover ◇ *Le chien est revenu couvert de boue.* The dog came back covered with mud.
  ➡ **se couvrir (1)** to wrap up ◇ *Couvre-toi bien: il fait très froid dehors.* Wrap up well: it's very cold outside.
  ➡ **se couvrir (2)** to cloud over ◇ *Le ciel se couvre.* The sky's clouding over.

e crabe NOUN
  crab

cracher VERB
  to spit

e crachin NOUN
  drizzle

a craie NOUN
  chalk

craindre VERB
  to fear ◇ *Tu n'as rien à craindre.* You've got nothing to fear.

a crainte NOUN
  fear
  ➡ **de crainte de** for fear of ◇ *Il n'ose rien dire de crainte de la vexer.* He daren't say anything for fear of upsetting her.

craintif ADJECTIVE
  (FEM SING **craintive**)
  timid

a crampe NOUN
  cramp ◇ *J'ai une crampe au mollet.* I've got a cramp in my calf.

e cran NOUN
  hole (*in belt*)
  ➡ **avoir du cran** (*informal*) to have guts

e crâne NOUN
  skull

crâner VERB (*informal*)
  to show off

e crapaud NOUN
  toad

cracquer VERB
  ① to creak ◇ *Le plancher craque.* The floor creaks.
  ② to burst ◇ *Ma fermeture éclair a craqué.* My zip's burst.
  ③ to crack up ◇ *Je vais finir par craquer!* (*informal*) I'm going to crack up at this rate!
  ➡ **Quand j'ai vu cette robe, j'ai craqué!**

(*informal*) When I saw that dress, I couldn't resist it!

la crasse NOUN
  filth

la cravate NOUN
  tie

le crawl NOUN
  crawl ◇ *nager le crawl* to do the crawl

le crayon NOUN
  pencil ◇ *un crayon de couleur* a coloured pencil
  ➡ **un crayon feutre** a felt-tip pen

la création NOUN
  creation

la crèche NOUN
  ① nursery ◇ *Elle dépose ses enfants à la crèche à huit heures.* She leaves her children at the nursery at 8 o'clock.
  ② nativity scene

le crédit NOUN
  credit

créer VERB
  to create

la crémaillère NOUN
  ➡ **pendre la crémaillère** to have a house-warming party

la crème NOUN
  see also le crème
  cream
  ➡ **la crème Chantilly** whipped cream
  ➡ **la crème fouettée** whipped cream
  ➡ **une crème caramel** a crème caramel
  ➡ **une crème au chocolat** a chocolate dessert

le crème NOUN
  see also la crème
  white coffee ◇ *un grand crème* a large white coffee

crémeux ADJECTIVE
  (FEM SING **crémeuse**)
  creamy

la crêpe NOUN
  pancake

la crêperie NOUN
  pancake restaurant

le crépuscule NOUN
  dusk

le cresson NOUN
  watercress

la Crète NOUN
  Crete

creuser VERB
  to dig (*a hole*)
  ➡ **Ça creuse!** That gives you a real appetite!
  ➡ **se creuser la cervelle** (*informal*) to rack one's brains

creux ADJECTIVE
(FEM SING **creuse**)
    hollow
la **crevaison** NOUN
    puncture
    crevé ADJECTIVE
    1 **punctured** ◇ *un pneu crevé* a
    puncture
    2 **knackered** ◇ *Je suis
    complètement crevé!* (*informal*) I'm
    knackered!
    crever VERB
    1 **to burst** (*balloon*)
    2 **to have a puncture** (*motorist*)
    ◇ *J'ai crevé sur l'autoroute.* I had a
    puncture on the motorway.
- **Je crève de faim!** (*informal*) I'm
    starving!
- **Je crève de froid!** (*informal*) I'm
    freezing!
la **crevette** NOUN
    prawn
- **une crevette rose** a prawn
- **une crevette grise** a shrimp
le **cri** NOUN
    1 **scream** ◇ *J'ai entendu un cri.* I
    heard a scream. ◇ *pousser des cris de
    douleur* to scream with pain
    2 **call** ◇ *Il sait reconnaître les cris
    des oiseaux.* He can identify the calls
    of birds.
- **C'est le dernier cri.** It's the latest
    fashion. ◇ *Ces chaussures sont du
    dernier cri.* These shoes are the latest
    fashion.
    criard ADJECTIVE
    garish (*colours*)
le **cric** NOUN
    jack (*for car*)
    crier VERB
    to shout
- **crier de douleur** to scream with pain
le **crime** NOUN
    1 **crime** ◇ *un crime de guerre* a war
    crime
    2 **murder** ◇ *Un crime a été commis
    ici.* There was a murder here.
le **criminel** NOUN
    1 **criminal** ◇ *un criminel de guerre* a
    war criminal
    2 **murderer**
la **criminelle** NOUN
    1 **criminal**
    2 **murderer**
le **crin** NOUN
    horsehair
la **crinière** NOUN
    mane
le **criquet** NOUN

    grasshopper
la **crise** NOUN
    1 **crisis**
- **la crise économique** the recession
    2 **attack** ◇ *une crise d'asthme* an
    asthma attack ◇ *une crise cardiaque* a
    heart attack
- **une crise de foie** an upset stomach
- **piquer une crise de nerfs** to go
    hysterical
- **avoir une crise de fou rire** to have a
    fit of the giggles
le **cristal** NOUN
    (PL LES **cristaux**)
    crystal ◇ *un verre en cristal* a crystal
    glass
le **critère** NOUN
    criterion
    critique ADJECTIVE
    see also critique NOUN
    critical
le **critique** NOUN
    see also la critique *and* critique ADJECTIVE
    critic ◇ *un critique de cinéma* a film
    critic
la **critique** NOUN
    see also le critique *and* critique ADJECTIVE
    1 **criticism** ◇ *Elle ne supporte pas
    les critiques.* She can't stand being
    criticized.
    2 **review** ◇ *Le film a reçu de bonnes
    critiques.* The film's had good reviews.
    critiquer VERB
    to criticize
la **Croatie** NOUN
    Croatia
le **crochet** NOUN
    1 **hook**
    2 **detour** ◇ *faire un crochet* to make
    a detour
    3 **crochet** ◇ *un pull au crochet* a
    crocheted sweater
le **crocodile** NOUN
    crocodile
    croire VERB
    to believe ◇ *Il croit tout ce qu'on lui
    raconte.* He believes everything he's
    told.
- **croire que** to think that ◇ *Tu crois
    qu'il fera meilleur demain?* Do you
    think the weather will be better
    tomorrow?
- **croire à quelque chose** to believe in
    something
- **croire en Dieu** to believe in God
    crois VERB *see* **croire**
    croîs VERB *see* **croître**
le **croisement** NOUN
    crossroads ◇ *Tournez à gauche au*

croisement. Turn left at the crossroads.

croiser VERB
- **J'ai croisé Anne-Laure dans la rue.** I bumped into Anne-Laure in the street.
- **croiser les bras** to fold one's arms
- **croiser les jambes** to cross one's legs
- **se croiser** to pass each other ◇ *Nous nous croisons dans l'escalier tous les matins.* We pass each other on the stairs every morning.

la **croisière** NOUN
cruise

la **croissance** NOUN
growth

le **croissant** NOUN
croissant ◇ *un croissant au beurre* a butter croissant

croit VERB *see* **croire**

croître VERB
to grow

la **croix** NOUN
cross
- **la Croix-Rouge** the Red Cross

le **croque-monsieur** NOUN
(PL les **croque-monsieur**)
toasted ham and cheese sandwich

croquer VERB
to munch ◇ *croquer une pomme* to munch an apple
- **le chocolat à croquer** plain chocolate

le **croquis** NOUN
sketch

la **crotte** NOUN
- **une crotte de chien** dog dirt

le **crottin** NOUN
1 manure ◇ *du crottin de cheval* horse manure
2 small goat's cheese

croustillant ADJECTIVE
crusty

la **croûte** NOUN
1 crust (*of bread*)
- **en croûte** in pastry
2 rind (*of cheese*)
3 scab (*on skin*)

le **croûton** NOUN
1 crust (*end of loaf*)
2 crouton ◇ *des croûtons frottés d'ail* garlic croutons

croyons, croyez VERB *see* **croire**

les **CRS** MASC NOUN
French riot police

cru VERB *see* **croire**

cru ADJECTIVE
raw ◇ *la viande crue* raw meat
- **le jambon cru** Parma ham

crû VERB *see* **croître**

la **cruauté** NOUN
cruelty

la **cruche** NOUN
jug

les **crudités** FEM NOUN
assorted raw vegetables

cruel ADJECTIVE
(FEM SING **cruelle**)
cruel

les **crustacés** MASC NOUN
shellfish

le **cube** NOUN
cube
- **un mètre cube** a cubic metre

la **cueillette** NOUN
picking ◇ *la cueillette des champignons* mushroom picking

cueillir VERB
to pick (*flowers, fruit*)

la **cuiller** NOUN
spoon
- **une cuiller à café** a teaspoon
- **une cuiller à soupe** a soup spoon

la **cuillère** NOUN
spoon
- **une cuillère à café** a teaspoon
- **une cuillère à soupe** a soup spoon

la **cuillerée** NOUN
spoonful

le **cuir** NOUN
leather ◇ *un sac en cuir* a leather bag
- **le cuir chevelu** the scalp

cuire VERB
to cook ◇ *cuire quelque chose à feu vif* to cook something on a high heat
- **cuire quelque chose au four** to bake something
- **cuire quelque chose à la vapeur** to steam something
- **bien cuit** well done
- **trop cuit** overdone

la **cuisine** NOUN
1 kitchen
2 cooking ◇ *la cuisine française* French cooking
- **faire la cuisine** to cook

cuisiné ADJECTIVE
- **un plat cuisiné** a ready-made meal

cuisiner VERB
to cook ◇ *J'aime beaucoup cuisiner.* I love cooking.

le **cuisinier** NOUN
cook

la **cuisinière** NOUN
1 cook
2 cooker ◇ *une cuisinière à gaz* a gas cooker

la **cuisse** NOUN
thigh
- **une cuisse de poulet** a chicken leg

la **cuisson** NOUN
cooking ◦ *"une heure de cuisson"* "cooking time: one hour"

cuit VERB *see* **cuire**

le **cuivre** NOUN
copper

le **cul** NOUN (*rude*)
bum

le **culot** NOUN (*informal*)
cheek ◦ *Quel culot!* What a cheek! ◦ *Il a un sacré culot!* He's got a damn cheek!

la **culotte** NOUN
knickers

la **culpabilité** NOUN
guilt

le **cultivateur** NOUN
farmer

la **cultivatrice** NOUN
farmer

cultivé ADJECTIVE
cultured ◦ *Il est très cultivé.* He's very cultured.

cultiver VERB
to grow ◦ *Il cultive la vigne.* He grows grapes.
◆ **cultiver la terre** to farm the land

la **culture** NOUN
1 **farming** ◦ *les cultures intensives* intensive farming
2 **education** ◦ *Pour cet emploi, on demande une bonne culture générale.* For this job, a good general education is needed.
◆ **la culture physique** physical education

le **culturisme** NOUN
body-building

le **curé** NOUN
parish priest

le **cure-dent** NOUN
toothpick

curieux ADJECTIVE
(FEM SING **curieuse**)
curious

la **curiosité** NOUN
curiosity

la **cuvette** NOUN
bowl ◦ *une cuvette en plastique* a plastic bowl

cyclable ADJECTIVE
◆ **une piste cyclable** a cycle track

le **cycle** NOUN
cycle

le/la **cycliste** NOUN
cyclist

le **cyclomoteur** NOUN
moped

le **cyclone** NOUN
hurricane

le **cygne** NOUN
swan

D

d' PREPOSITION, ARTICLE *see* **de**

la **dactylo** NOUN

[1] **typist** ⋄ *Elle est dactylo.* She's a typist.

[2] **typing** ⋄ *Je prends des cours de dactylo.* I'm doing typing lessons.

le **daim** NOUN

suede ⋄ *une veste en daim* a suede jacket

la **dame** NOUN

[1] **lady**

[2] **queen** (*in cards, chess*)

les **dames** FEM NOUN

draughts

le **Danemark** NOUN

Denmark

dangereux ADJECTIVE

(FEM SING **dangereuse**)

dangerous

danois ADJECTIVE, NOUN

(FEM SING **danoise**)

Danish ⋄ *Il parle danois.* He speaks Danish.

- **un Danois** a Dane (*man*)
- **une Danoise** a Dane (*woman*)
- **les Danois** the Danish

dans PREPOSITION

[1] **in** ⋄ *Il est dans sa chambre.* He's in his bedroom. ⋄ *dans deux mois* in two months' time

[2] **into** ⋄ *Il est entré dans mon bureau.* He came into my office.

[3] **out of** ⋄ *On a bu dans des verres en plastique.* We drank out of plastic glasses.

la **danse** NOUN

[1] **dance** ⋄ *la danse moderne* modern dance ⋄ *des danses folkloriques* folk dances

- **la danse classique** ballet

[2] **dancing** ⋄ *des cours de danse* dancing lessons

danser VERB

to dance

le **danseur** NOUN

dancer

la **danseuse** NOUN

dancer

la **date** NOUN

date ⋄ *votre date de naissance* your date of birth ⋄ *la date limite de vente* the sell-by date

- **un ami de longue date** an old friend

dater VERB

- **dater de** to date from ⋄ *Cette coutume date du moyen âge.* This

custom dates from the Middle Ages.

la **datte** NOUN

date (*fruit*)

le **dauphin** NOUN

dolphin

davantage ADVERB

- **davantage de** more ⋄ *Il faudrait davantage de stages de formation.* There should be more training courses.

de PREPOSITION, ARTICLE

see also **du** (=de+le) *and* **des** (=de+les). **de** *changes to* **d'** *before a vowel and most words beginning with "h"*

[1] **of** ⋄ *le toit de la maison* the roof of the house ⋄ *la voiture de Paul* Paul's car ⋄ *la voiture de mes parents* my parents' car ⋄ *la voiture d'Hélène* Hélène's car ⋄ *deux bouteilles de vin* two bottles of wine ⋄ *un litre d'essence* a litre of petrol

- **un bébé d'un an** a one-year-old baby
- **un billet de cinquante francs** a 50-franc note

[2] **from** ⋄ *Il vient de Londres.* He comes from London. ⋄ *une lettre de Victor* a letter from Victor

[3] **by** ⋄ *augmenter de dix francs* to increase by ten francs

You use **de** *to form expressions with the meaning of* **some** *and* **any**.

- **Je voudrais de l'eau.** I'd like some water. ⋄ *du pain et de la confiture* bread and jam
- **Il n'a pas de famille.** He hasn't got any family.
- **Il n'y a plus de biscuits.** There aren't any more biscuits.

le **dé** NOUN

[1] **dice**

[2] **thimble**

le **dealer** NOUN (*informal*)

drug-pusher

déballer VERB

to unpack

le **débardeur** NOUN

tank top

débarquer VERB

to disembark ⋄ *Nous avons dû débarquer à Marseille.* We had to disembark at Marseilles.

- **débarquer chez quelqu'un** (*informal*) to descend on somebody ⋄ *Ils ont débarqué chez nous à dix heures du soir.* They descended on us at ten o'clock at night.

le **débarras** NOUN
junk room
- **Bon débarras!** Good riddance!
débarrasser VERB
to clear ◇ *Tu peux débarrasser la table, s'il te plaît?* Can you clear the table please?
- **se débarrasser de quelque chose** to get rid of something ◇ *Je me suis débarrassé de mon vieux frigo.* I got rid of my old fridge.
le **débat** NOUN
debate
se **débattre** VERB
to struggle
débile ADJECTIVE
crazy ◇ *C'est complètement débile!* (*informal*) That's totally crazy!
débordé ADJECTIVE
- **être débordé** to be snowed under
déborder VERB
to overflow (*river*)
- **déborder d'énergie** to be full of energy
le **débouché** NOUN
job prospect ◇ *Quels débouchés y a-t-il après ces études?* What sort of job does this course qualify you for?
déboucher VERB
[1] **to unblock** (*sink, pipe*)
[2] **to open** (*bottle*)
- **déboucher sur** to lead into ◇ *La rue débouche sur une place.* The street leads into a square.
debout ADVERB
[1] **standing up** ◇ *Il a mangé ses céréales debout.* He ate his cereal standing up.
[2] **upright** ◇ *Mets les livres debout sur l'étagère.* Put the books upright on the shelf.
[3] **up** ◇ *Tu es déjà debout?* Are you up already?
- **Debout!** Get up!
déboutonner VERB
to unbutton
débraillé ADJECTIVE
sloppily dressed
débrancher VERB
to unplug
le **débris** NOUN
- **des débris de verre** bits of glass
débrouillard ADJECTIVE
streetwise
se **débrouiller** VERB
to manage ◇ *C'était difficile, mais je ne me suis pas trop mal débrouillé.* It was difficult, but I managed OK.
- **Débrouille-toi tout seul.** Sort things

out for yourself.
le **début** NOUN
beginning ◇ *au début* at the beginning
- **début mai** in early May
le **débutant** NOUN
beginner
la **débutante** NOUN
beginner
débuter VERB
to start
décaféiné ADJECTIVE
decaffeinated
le **décalage horaire** NOUN
time difference (*between time zones*) ◇ *Il y a une heure de décalage horaire entre la France et la Grande-Bretagne.* There's an hour's time difference between France and Britain.
décalquer VERB
to trace
décapiter VERB
to behead
décapotable ADJECTIVE
convertible
décapsuler VERB
- **décapsuler une bouteille** to take the top off a bottle
le **décapsuleur** NOUN
bottle-opener
décéder VERB
to die ◇ *Son père est décédé il y a trois ans.* His father died three years ago.
décembre MASC NOUN
December
- **en décembre** in December
décemment ADVERB
decently
décent ADJECTIVE
decent
la **déception** NOUN
disappointment
décerner VERB
to award
le **décès** NOUN
death
décevoir VERB
to disappoint
décharger VERB
to unload
se **déchausser** VERB
to take off one's shoes
les **déchets** MASC NOUN
waste ◇ *les déchets nucléaires* nuclear waste ◇ *les déchets toxiques* toxic waste
déchiffrer VERB

to decipher

déchirant ADJECTIVE

heart-rending

déchirer VERB

1 **to tear** (*clothes*)

2 **to tear up** ◇ *déchirer une lettre* to tear up a letter

3 **to tear out** ◇ *déchirer une page d'un livre* to tear a page out of a book

• **se déchirer** to tear ◇ *se déchirer un muscle* to tear a muscle

la **déchirure** NOUN

tear (*rip*)

• **une déchirure musculaire** a torn muscle

décidé ADJECTIVE

determined

• **C'est décidé.** It's decided.

décidément ADVERB

certainly ◇ *Décidément, je n'ai pas de chance aujourd'hui.* I'm certainly not having much luck today.

décider VERB

to decide

• **décider de faire quelque chose** to decide to do something ◇ *Ils ont décidé de passer leurs vacances en Normandie.* They decided to go to Normandy for their holiday.

• **se décider** to make up one's mind ◇ *Elle n'arrive pas à se décider.* She can't make up her mind.

décisif ADJECTIVE

(FEM SING **décisive**)

decisive

la **décision** NOUN

decision

la **déclaration** NOUN

statement ◇ *Je n'ai aucune déclaration à faire.* I have no statement to make.

• **faire une déclaration de vol** to report something as stolen

déclarer VERB

to declare ◇ *déclarer la guerre à un pays* to declare war on a country

• **se déclarer** to break out ◇ *Le feu s'est déclaré dans la cantine.* The fire broke out in the canteen.

déclencher VERB

to set off (*alarm, explosion*)

• **se déclencher** to go off

le **déclic** NOUN

click

décoiffé ADJECTIVE

• **Elle était toute décoiffée.** Her hair was in a real mess.

le **décollage** NOUN

takeoff (*of plane*)

décollé ADJECTIVE

• **avoir les oreilles décollées** to have sticking-out ears

décoller VERB

1 **to unstick** ◇ *décoller une étiquette* to unstick a label

• **se décoller** to come unstuck

2 **to take off** ◇ *L'avion a décollé avec dix minutes de retard.* The plane took off ten minutes late.

décolleté ADJECTIVE

see also **décolleté** NOUN

low-cut

le **décolleté** NOUN

see also **décolleté** ADJECTIVE

• **un décolleté plongeant** a plunging neckline

se **décolorer** VERB

to fade ◇ *Ce tee-shirt s'est décoloré au lavage.* This T-shirt has faded in the wash.

• **se faire décolorer les cheveux** to have one's hair bleached

les **décombres** MASC NOUN

rubble

se **décommander** VERB

to cry off ◇ *Elle devait venir mais elle s'est décommandée à la dernière minute.* She was supposed to be coming, but she cried off at the last minute.

décongeler VERB

to thaw

déconner VERB (*rude*)

to talk rubbish ◇ *Non mais, sans déconner, c'est vrai?* No kidding, is that true?

déconseiller VERB

• **déconseiller à quelqu'un de faire quelque chose** to advise somebody not to do something ◇ *Je lui ai déconseillé d'y aller.* I advised him not to go.

• **C'est déconseillé.** It's not recommended.

décontracté ADJECTIVE

relaxed

• **s'habiller décontracté** to dress casually

se **décontracter** VERB

to relax ◇ *Il est allé faire du footing pour se décontracter.* He went jogging to relax.

le **décor** NOUN

décor

le **décorateur** NOUN

interior decorator

la **décoration** NOUN

decoration

la **décoratrice** NOUN
interior decorator
décorer VERB
to decorate
les **décors** MASC NOUN
1 **scenery** (*in play*)
2 **set** (*in film*)
décortiquer VERB
to shell
- **des crevettes décortiquées** peeled shrimps
découdre VERB
to unpick
- **se découdre** to come unstitched
découper VERB
1 **to cut out** ◇ *J'ai découpé cet article dans le journal.* I cut this article out of the paper.
2 **to carve** (*meat*)
décourageant ADJECTIVE
discouraging
décourager VERB
to discourage
- **se décourager** to get discouraged ◇ *Ne te décourage pas!* Don't give up!
décousu ADJECTIVE
unstitched ◇ *L'ourlet est décousu.* The hem's come unstitched.
le **découvert** NOUN
overdraft
la **découverte** NOUN
discovery
découvrir VERB
to discover
décrire VERB
to describe
décrocher VERB
1 **to take down** ◇ *Tu peux m'aider à décrocher les rideaux?* Can you help me take down the curtains?
2 **to pick up the phone** ◇ *Il a décroché et a composé le numéro.* He picked up the phone and dialled the number.
- **décrocher le téléphone** to take the phone off the hook
déçu VERB
disappointed
dédaigneux ADJECTIVE
(FEM SING **dédaigneuse**)
disdainful ◇ *d'un air dédaigneux* disdainfully
le **dédain** NOUN
disdain ◇ *avec dédain* with disdain
dedans ADVERB
inside ◇ *C'est une jolie boîte: qu'est-ce qu'il y a dedans?* That's a nice box: what's in it?

- **là-dedans (1)** in there ◇ *J'ai trouvé les clés là-dedans.* I found the keys in there.
- **là-dedans (2)** in that ◇ *Il y a du vrai là-dedans.* There's some truth in that.
dédicacé ADJECTIVE
- **un exemplaire dédicacé** a signed copy
dédier VERB
to dedicate
déduire VERB
to take off ◇ *Tu as déduit les vingt francs que je te devais?* Did you take off the twenty francs I owed you?
- **déduire que** to deduce that ◇ *J'en déduis qu'il m'a menti.* That means he must have been lying.
défaire VERB
to undo
- **se défaire** to come undone
la **défaite** NOUN
defeat
le **défaut** NOUN
fault
défavorable ADJECTIVE
unfavourable
défavorisé ADJECTIVE
underprivileged
défectueux ADJECTIVE
(FEM SING **défectueuse**)
faulty
défendu ADJECTIVE
forbidden ◇ *C'est défendu.* It's not allowed.
la **défense** NOUN
1 **defence** ◇ *prendre la défense de quelqu'un* to back somebody up
- **"défense de fumer"** "no smoking"
2 **tusk** (*of elephant*)
le **défi** NOUN
challenge
- **d'un air de défi** defiantly
- **sur un ton de défi** defiantly
défier VERB
1 **to challenge** ◇ *Je te défie de trouver un meilleur exemple.* I challenge you to find a better example.
2 **to dare** ◇ *Il m'a défié d'aller à l'école en pyjama.* He dared me to go to school in my pyjamas.
défigurer VERB
to disfigure
le **défilé** NOUN
1 **parade**
- **un défilé de mode** a fashion show
2 **march**
défiler VERB
to march
définir VERB
to define

définitif ADJECTIVE
(FEM SING **définitive**)
final
- **en définitive** in the end ◦ *En définitive, ils ont décidé de rester.* In the end, they decided to stay.

définitivement ADVERB
for good ◦ *Elle s'est définitivement installée en Écosse en 1980.* She settled in Scotland for good in 1980.

déformer VERB
to stretch ◦ *Ne tire pas sur ton pull, tu vas le déformer.* Don't pull at your sweater, you'll stretch it.
- **se déformer** to stretch ◦ *Ce tee-shirt s'est déformé au lavage.* This T-shirt has stretched in the wash.

se **défouler** VERB
to unwind ◦ *Je fais du step pour me défouler.* I do step aerobics to unwind.

dégagé ADJECTIVE
- **d'un air dégagé** casually
- **sur un ton dégagé** casually

dégager VERB
1 **to free** ◦ *Ils ont mis une heure à dégager les victimes.* They took an hour to free the victims.
2 **to clear** ◦ *des gouttes qui dégagent le nez* drops to clear your nose
- **Ça se dégage.** It's clearing up. (*weather*)

se **dégarnir** VERB
to go bald

les **dégâts** MASC NOUN
damage

le **dégel** NOUN
thaw

dégeler VERB
to thaw ◦ *faire dégeler un poulet congelé* to thaw out a frozen chicken

dégivrer VERB
1 **to defrost**
2 **to de-ice**

dégonfler VERB
to let down ◦ *Quelqu'un a dégonflé mes pneus.* Somebody let down my tyres.
- **se dégonfler** (*informal*) to chicken out

dégouliner VERB
to trickle

dégourdi ADJECTIVE
smart ◦ *Il n'est pas très dégourdi.* He's pretty clueless.

dégourdir VERB
- **se dégourdir les jambes** to stretch one's legs

le **dégoût** NOUN
disgust ◦ *une expression de dégoût* a disgusted expression

- **avec dégoût** disgustedly

dégoûtant ADJECTIVE
disgusting

dégoûté ADJECTIVE
disgusted
- **être dégoûté de tout** to be sick of everything

dégoûter VERB
to disgust ◦ *Ce genre de comportement me dégoûte.* That kind of behaviour makes me sick.
- **dégoûter quelqu'un de quelque chose** to put somebody off something ◦ *Ça m'a dégoûté de la viande.* That put me off meat.

se **dégrader** VERB
to deteriorate

le **degré** NOUN
degree
- **de l'alcool à 90 degrés** surgical spirit

dégringoler VERB
1 **to rush down** ◦ *Il a dégringolé l'escalier.* He rushed down the stairs.
2 **to collapse** ◦ *Elle a fait dégringoler la pile de livres.* She knocked over the stack of books.

dégueulasse ADJECTIVE (*rude*)
disgusting

le **déguisement** NOUN
disguise

déguiser VERB
- **se déguiser en quelque chose** to dress up as something ◦ *Elle s'était déguisée en vampire.* She was dressed up as a vampire.

déguster VERB
1 **to taste** (*food, wine*)
2 **to enjoy**

dehors ADVERB
outside ◦ *Je t'attends dehors.* I'll wait for you outside.
- **jeter quelqu'un dehors** to throw somebody out
- **en dehors de** apart from ◦ *En dehors de lui, tout le monde était content.* Apart from him, everybody was happy.

déjà ADVERB
1 **already** ◦ *J'ai déjà fini.* I've already finished.
2 **before** ◦ *Tu es déjà venu en France?* Have you been to France before?

déjeuner VERB
see also **déjeuner** NOUN
to have lunch

le **déjeuner** NOUN
see also **déjeuner** VERB
lunch

D

le **délai** NOUN

[1] **extension** ◇ *J'ai demandé un délai d'une semaine.* I've asked for a week's extension.

[2] **time limit** ◇ *être dans les délais* to be within the time limit

délasser VERB

to relax ◇ *La lecture délasse.* Reading's relaxing.

- **se délasser** to relax ◇ *J'ai pris un bain pour me délasser.* I had a bath to relax.

délavé ADJECTIVE

faded ◇ *un jean délavé* a pair of faded jeans

le **délégué** NOUN

representative ◇ *les délégués de classe* the class representatives

In French schools, each class elects two representatives or délégués de classe, *one boy and one girl.*

la **déléguée** NOUN

representative

déléguer VERB

to delegate

délibéré ADJECTIVE

deliberate

délicat ADJECTIVE

[1] **delicate** ◇ *avoir la peau délicate* to have delicate skin

[2] **tricky** ◇ *une situation délicate* a tricky situation

[3] **tactful** ◇ *Il est toujours très délicat.* He's always very tactful.

[4] **thoughtful** ◇ *C'est une attention délicate de sa part.* That was a kind thought on his part.

délicatement ADVERB

[1] **gently**

[2] **tactfully**

le **délice** NOUN

delight ◇ *Vivre ici est un vrai délice.* Living here is a real delight. ◇ *Ce gâteau est un vrai délice.* This cake's a real treat.

délicieux ADJECTIVE

(FEM SING **délicieuse**)

delicious

la **délinquance** NOUN

crime ◇ *de nouvelles mesures pour combattre la délinquance juvénile* new measures to fight juvenile delinquency

le **délinquant** NOUN

criminal

la **délinquante** NOUN

criminal

délirer VERB

- **Mais tu délires!** (*informal*) You're crazy!

le **délit** NOUN

criminal offence

délivrer VERB

to set free (*prisoner*)

le **deltaplane** NOUN

hang-glider

- **faire du deltaplane** to go hang-gliding

demain ADVERB

tomorrow

- **À demain!** See you tomorrow!

la **demande** NOUN

request

- **une demande en mariage** an offer of marriage

- **"demandes d'emploi"** "situations wanted"

demandé ADJECTIVE

- **très demandé** very much in demand

demander VERB

[1] **to ask for** ◇ *J'ai demandé la permission.* I've asked for permission. ◇ *Nous avons demandé notre chemin à un chauffeur de taxi.* We asked a taxi driver the way. ◇ *Je lui ai demandé de m'aider.* I asked him to help me.

[2] **to require** ◇ *un travail qui demande beaucoup de concentration* a job that requires a lot of concentration

- **se demander** to wonder ◇ *Je me demande à quelle heure il va venir.* I wonder what time he'll come.

le **demandeur d'emploi** NOUN

job-seeker

la **démangeaison** NOUN

itching

démanger VERB

to itch ◇ *Ça me démange.* It itches.

le **démaquillant** NOUN

make-up remover

démaquiller VERB

- **se démaquiller** to remove one's make-up

la **démarche** NOUN

[1] **walk** ◇ *Il a une drôle de démarche.* He's got a funny walk.

[2] **step** ◇ *faire les démarches nécessaires pour obtenir quelque chose* to take the necessary steps to obtain something

démarrer VERB

to start (*car*)

démêler VERB

to untangle

le **déménagement** NOUN

move ◇ *C'était le jour de notre déménagement.* It was the day we moved house.

- **un camion de déménagement** a removal van

déménager VERB

to move house
le **déménageur** NOUN
removal man
dément ADJECTIVE
crazy
démentiel ADJECTIVE
(FEM SING démentielle)
insane ◇ *un projet démentiel* an
insane scheme
se **démerder** VERB (*rude*)
to get by ◇ *Ne t'inquiète pas, il saura
se démerder.* Don't worry, he'll get by.
• **Démerde-toi tout seul.** Sort things out
for yourself.
demi ADJECTIVE, ADVERB
see also demi NOUN
half ◇ *Il a trois ans et demi.* He's
three and a half.
• **Il est trois heures et demie.** It's half
past three.
• **Il est midi et demi.** It's half past
twelve.
• **à demi endormi** half-asleep
le **demi** NOUN
see also demi ADJECTIVE
half pint of beer
• **Un demi, s'il vous plaît!** A beer please!
la **demi-baguette** NOUN
half a baguette
le **demi-cercle** NOUN
semicircle
la **demi-douzaine** NOUN
half-dozen ◇ *une demi-douzaine
d'œufs* half a dozen eggs
la **demie** NOUN
half-hour ◇ *Le bus passe à la demie.*
The bus comes by on the half-hour.
demi-écrémé ADJECTIVE
semi-skimmed
la **demi-finale** NOUN
semifinal
le **demi-frère** NOUN
half-brother
la **demi-heure** NOUN
half an hour ◇ *dans une demi-heure*
in half an hour ◇ *toutes les
demi-heures* every half an hour
la **demi-journée** NOUN
half-day ◇ *On peut louer un parasol
à la demi-journée.* You can hire a sun
umbrella for a half-day.
le **demi-litre** NOUN
half litre ◇ *un demi-litre de lait* half a
litre of milk
la **demi-livre** NOUN
half-pound ◇ *une demi-livre de
tomates* half a pound of tomatoes
demi-sel ADJECTIVE
• **du beurre demi-sel** slightly salted

butter
la **demi-sœur** NOUN
half-sister
la **démission** NOUN
resignation
• **donner sa démission** to resign
démissionner VERB
to resign
le **demi-tarif** NOUN
1 half-price ◇ *un billet à demi-tarif* a
half-price season ticket
2 half-fare ◇ *voyager à demi-tarif* to
travel half-fare
le **demi-tour** NOUN
• **faire demi-tour** to turn back ◇ *La
nuit commence à tomber; il est temps de
faire demi-tour.* It's getting dark; it's
time we turned back.
la **démocratie** NOUN
democracy
démocratique ADJECTIVE
democratic
démodé ADJECTIVE
old-fashioned
la **demoiselle** NOUN
young lady
• **une demoiselle d'honneur** a
bridesmaid
démolir VERB
to demolish
le **démon** NOUN
devil
démonter VERB
1 to take down (*tent*)
2 to take apart (*machine*)
démontrer VERB
to show
dénoncer VERB
to denounce
• **se dénoncer** to give oneself up ◇ *Il
s'est dénoncé à la police.* He gave
himself up to the police.
le **dénouement** NOUN
outcome
la **densité** NOUN
density
la **dent** NOUN
tooth ◇ *une dent de lait* a milk
tooth ◇ *une dent de sagesse* a
wisdom tooth
dentaire ADJECTIVE
dental
la **dentelle** NOUN
lace ◇ *un chemisier en dentelle* a lacy
blouse
le **dentier** NOUN
denture
le **dentifrice** NOUN
toothpaste

D

le/la **dentiste** NOUN
dentist ◇ *Elle est dentiste.* She's a dentist.

le **déodorant** NOUN
deodorant

le **dépannage** NOUN
- **un service de dépannage** a breakdown service

dépanner VERB
[1] **to fix** ◇ *Il a dépanné la voiture en cinq minutes.* He fixed the car in five minutes.
[2] **to help out** ◇ *Il m'a prêté cent francs pour me dépanner.* (*informal*) He lent me 100 francs to help me out.

la **dépanneuse** NOUN
breakdown lorry

le **départ** NOUN
departure ◇ *Le départ est à onze heures quinze.* The departure is at 11.15.
- **Je lui téléphonerai la veille de son départ.** I'll phone him the day before he leaves.

le **département** NOUN
[1] **department** ◇ *le département d'anglais à l'université* the English department at the university
[2] **administrative area**
France is divided into 96 départements, administrative areas rather like counties.
◇ *le département du Vaucluse* the Vaucluse region

dépasser VERB
[1] **to overtake** ◇ *Il y a une voiture qui essaie de nous dépasser.* There's a car trying to overtake us.
[2] **to pass** ◇ *Nous avons dépassé Dijon.* We've passed Dijon.
[3] **to exceed** (*sum, limit*)

dépaysé ADJECTIVE
- **se sentir un peu dépaysé** to feel a bit lost

se **dépêcher** VERB
to hurry ◇ *Dépêche-toi!* Hurry up!

dépendre VERB
- **dépendre de** to depend on ◇ *Ça dépend du temps.* It depends on the weather.
- **dépendre de quelqu'un** to be dependent on somebody
- **Ça dépend.** It depends.

dépenser VERB
to spend (*money*)

dépensier ADJECTIVE
(FEM SING **dépensière**)
- **Il est dépensier.** He's a big spender.
- **Elle n'est pas dépensière.** She's not exactly extravagant.

dépilatoire ADJECTIVE
- **une crème dépilatoire** a hair-removing cream

le **dépit** NOUN
- **en dépit de** in spite of ◇ *Il y est allé en dépit de mes conseils.* He went in spite of my advice.

déplacé ADJECTIVE
uncalled-for ◇ *C'était une remarque déplacée.* That remark was uncalled-for.

le **déplacement** NOUN
trip ◇ *Ça vaut le déplacement.* It's worth the trip.

déplacer VERB
[1] **to move** ◇ *Tu peux m'aider à déplacer la table?* Can you help me move the table?
[2] **to put off** ◇ *déplacer un rendez-vous* to put off an appointment
- **se déplacer (1)** to travel around ◇ *Il se déplace beaucoup pour son travail.* He travels around a lot for his work.
- **se déplacer (2)** to get around ◇ *Il a du mal à se déplacer.* He has difficulty getting around.
- **se déplacer une vertèbre** to slip a disc

déplaire VERB
- **Cela me déplaît.** I dislike this.

déplaisant ADJECTIVE
unpleasant

le **dépliant** NOUN
leaflet

déplier VERB
to unfold

déposer VERB
[1] **to leave** ◇ *J'ai déposé mon sac à la consigne.* I left my bag at the left luggage office.
[2] **to put down** ◇ *Déposez le paquet sur la table.* Put the parcel down on the table.
- **déposer quelqu'un** to drop somebody off

dépourvu ADJECTIVE
- **prendre quelqu'un au dépourvu** to take somebody by surprise ◇ *Sa question m'a pris au dépourvu.* His question took me by surprise.

la **dépression** NOUN
depression
- **faire de la dépression** to be suffering from depression
- **faire une dépression** to have a breakdown

déprimant ADJECTIVE
depressing

déprimer VERB
to get depressed ◇ *Il déprime tout le*

temps. He gets depressed all the time.
- **Ce genre de temps me déprime.** This kind of weather makes me depressed.

depuis PREPOSITION, ADVERB
  [1] **since** ◇ *Il habite Paris depuis 1983.* He's been living in Paris since 1983. ◇ *Je ne lui ai pas parlé depuis.* I haven't spoken to him since.
- **depuis que** since ◇ *Il a plu tous les jours depuis qu'elle est arrivée.* It's rained every day since she arrived.
  [2] **for** ◇ *Il habite Paris depuis cinq ans.* He's been living in Paris for five years.
- **Depuis combien de temps?** How long? ◇ *Depuis combien de temps est-ce que vous le connaissez?* How long have you known him?
- **Depuis quand?** How long? ◇ *Depuis quand est-ce que vous le connaissez?* How long have you known him?

le **député** NOUN
  Member of Parliament
la **députée** NOUN
  Member of Parliament
déraciner VERB
  to uproot
le **dérangement** NOUN
- **en dérangement** out of order ◇ *Le téléphone est en dérangement.* The phone's out of order.
déranger VERB
  [1] **to bother** ◇ *Excusez-moi de vous déranger.* I'm sorry to bother you.
- **Ne vous dérangez pas, je vais répondre au téléphone.** You stay there, I'll answer the phone.
  [2] **to disorganize** ◇ *Ne dérange pas mes livres, s'il te plaît.* Don't disorganize my books, please.
déraper VERB
  to skid
e/la **dermatologue** NOUN
  dermatologist ◇ *Elle est dermatologue.* She's a dermatologist.
dernier ADJECTIVE
  (FEM SING **dernière**)
  [1] **last** ◇ *Il est arrivé dernier.* He arrived last. ◇ *la dernière fois* the last time
  [2] **latest** ◇ *le dernier film de Spielberg* Spielberg's latest film
- **en dernier** last ◇ *Ajoutez le lait en dernier.* Put the milk in last.
dernièrement ADVERB
  recently
dérouler VERB
  [1] **to unroll**
  [2] **to unwind**

- **se dérouler** to take place ◇ *L'action se déroule dans les années vingt.* The action takes place in the 1920s.
- **Tout s'est déroulé comme prévu.** Everything went as planned.

derrière ADVERB, PREPOSITION
  see also **derrière** NOUN
  behind
le **derrière** NOUN
  see also **derrière** ADVERB
  [1] **back** ◇ *la porte de derrière* the back door
  [2] **backside** ◇ *un coup de pied dans le derrière* a kick up the backside

des ARTICLE
  des *is the contracted form of* **de + les.**
  [1] **some** ◇ *Tu veux des chips?* Would you like some crisps?
  des *is sometimes not translated.*
  ◇ *J'ai des cousins en France.* I have cousins in France. ◇ *pendant des mois* for months
  [2] **any** ◇ *Tu as des frères?* Have you got any brothers? ◇ *la fin des vacances* the end of the holidays ◇ *la voiture des Durand* the Durands' car ◇ *Il arrive des États-Unis.* He's arriving from the United States.

dès PREPOSITION
  as early as ◇ *dès le mois de novembre* from November
- **dès le début** right from the start
- **Il vous appellera dès son retour.** He'll call you as soon as he gets back.
- **dès que** as soon as ◇ *Il m'a reconnu dès qu'il m'a vu.* He recognized me as soon as he saw me.

désabusé ADJECTIVE
  disillusioned
le **désaccord** NOUN
  disagreement
désagréable ADJECTIVE
  unpleasant
désaltérer VERB
- **L'eau gazeuse désaltère bien.** Sparkling water is very thirst-quenching.
- **se désaltérer** to quench one's thirst ◇ *Nous sommes allés dans un café pour nous désaltérer.* We went into a café to have a drink.
désapprobateur ADJECTIVE
  (FEM SING **désapprobatrice**)
  disapproving ◇ *un regard désapprobateur* a disapproving look
le **désastre** NOUN
  disaster
le **désavantage** NOUN
  disadvantage

désavantager VERB
- **désavantager quelqu'un** to put somebody at a disadvantage ◦ *Cette nouvelle loi va désavantager les femmes.* The new law will put women at a disadvantage.

descendre VERB
1. **to go down** ◦ *Je suis tombé en descendant l'escalier.* I fell as I was going down the stairs.
2. **to come down** ◦ *Attends en bas; je descends!* Wait downstairs; I'm coming down!
3. **to get down** ◦ *Vous pouvez descendre ma valise, s'il vous plaît?* Can you get my suitcase down, please?
4. **to get off** ◦ *Nous descendons à la prochaine station.* We're getting off at the next station.

la **descente** NOUN
way down ◦ *Je t'attendrai au bas de la descente.* I'll wait for you at the bottom of the hill.
- **une descente de police** a police raid

déséquilibré ADJECTIVE
unbalanced

déséquilibrer VERB
- **déséquilibrer quelqu'un** to throw somebody off balance ◦ *Le coup de poing l'a déséquilibré.* The punch threw him off balance.

désert ADJECTIVE
see also **désert** NOUN
deserted ◦ *Le dimanche, le centre commercial est désert.* On Sundays, the shopping centre is deserted.
- **une île déserte** a desert island

le **désert** NOUN
see also **désert** ADJECTIVE
desert

déserter VERB
to desert

désertique ADJECTIVE
desert ◦ *une région désertique* a desert region

désespéré ADJECTIVE
desperate

désespérer VERB
to despair ◦ *Il ne faut pas désespérer.* Don't despair.

le **désespoir** NOUN
despair

déshabiller VERB
to undress
- **se déshabiller** to get undressed

déshériter VERB
to disinherit
- **les déshérités** the underprivileged

déshydraté ADJECTIVE
dehydrated

désigner VERB
to choose ◦ *On l'a désignée pour remettre le prix.* She was chosen to present the prize.
- **désigner quelque chose du doigt** to point at something

le **désinfectant** NOUN
disinfectant

désinfecter VERB
to disinfect

désintéressé ADJECTIVE
1. **unselfish** ◦ *un acte désintéressé* an unselfish action
2. **impartial** ◦ *un conseil désintéressé* impartial advice

désintéresser VERB
- **se désintéresser de quelque chose** to lose interest in something

le **désir** NOUN
1. **wish** ◦ *Vos désirs sont des ordres.* Your wish is my command.
2. **will** ◦ *le désir de réussir* the will to succeed
3. **desire** ◦ *Ses yeux brillaient de désir.* Her eyes were shining with desire.

désirer VERB
to want ◦ *Vous désirez?* (in shop) What would you like?

désobéir VERB
- **désobéir à quelqu'un** to disobey somebody

désobéissant ADJECTIVE
disobedient

désobligeant ADJECTIVE
unpleasant ◦ *faire une remarque désobligeante* to make an unpleasant remark

le **désodorisant** NOUN
air freshener

désolé ADJECTIVE
sorry ◦ *Je suis vraiment désolé.* I'm very sorry.
- **Désolé!** Sorry!

désopilant ADJECTIVE
hilarious

désordonné ADJECTIVE
untidy

le **désordre** NOUN
untidiness
- **Quel désordre!** What a mess!
- **en désordre** untidy ◦ *Sa chambre est toujours en désordre.* His bedroom is always untidy.

désormais ADVERB
from now on ◦ *Désormais, je boirai de l'eau.* From now on I'll drink water.

desquelles PRONOUN

> desquelles is the contracted form of de + lesquelles.

◇ des négociations au cours desquelles les patrons ont fait des concessions negotiations during which the employers made concessions

desquels PRONOUN

> desquels is the contracted form of de + lesquels.

◇ les lacs au bord desquels nous avons campé the lakes on the banks of which we camped

dessécher VERB

to dry out ◇ Le soleil dessèche la peau. The sun dries your skin out.

desserrer VERB

to loosen

le **dessert** NOUN

pudding ◇ Qu'est-ce que vous désirez comme dessert? What would you like for pudding?

le **dessin** NOUN

drawing ◇ C'est un dessin de ma petite sœur. It's a drawing my little sister did.

- **un dessin animé** a cartoon (film)
- **un dessin humoristique** a cartoon (drawing)

le **dessinateur** NOUN

- **un dessinateur industriel** a draughtsman

dessiner VERB

to draw

dessous ADVERB

> see also dessous NOUN

underneath

- **en dessous** underneath ◇ Soulève le pot de fleurs, la clé est en dessous. Lift the flowerpot, the key's underneath.
- **par-dessous** underneath ◇ Le grillage ne sert à rien, les lapins passent par-dessous. The fence is useless, the rabbits get in underneath.
- **là-dessous** under there ◇ Il s'est caché là-dessous. He hid under there.
- **ci-dessous** below ◇ Complétez les phrases ci-dessous. Complete the sentences below.
- **au-dessous de** below ◇ vingt degrés au-dessous de zéro 20 degrees below zero

le **dessous** NOUN

> see also dessous ADVERB

underneath

- **les voisins du dessous** the downstairs neighbours
- **les dessous** underwear ◇ des

dessous en soie silk underwear

le **dessous-de-plat** NOUN

(PL les dessous-de-plat)

tablemat

dessus ADVERB

> see also dessus NOUN

on top ◇ un gâteau avec des bougies dessus a cake with candles on top

- **par-dessus** over ◇ Nous avons sauté par-dessus la barrière. We jumped over the gate.
- **au-dessus** above ◇ la taille au-dessus the size above ◇ au-dessus du lit above the bed
- **là-dessus (1)** on there ◇ Tu peux écrire là-dessus. You can write on there.
- **là-dessus (2)** with that ◇ "Je démissionne!" Là-dessus, il est parti. "I resign!" With that, he left.
- **ci-dessus** above ◇ l'exemple ci-dessus the example above

le **dessus** NOUN

> see also dessus ADVERB

top

- **les voisins du dessus** the upstairs neighbours

le/la **destinataire** NOUN

addressee

la **destination** NOUN

destination

- **les passagers à destination de Paris** passengers travelling to Paris

le **détachant** NOUN

stain remover

détacher VERB

to undo

le **détail** NOUN

detail

- **en détail** in detail

le **détective** NOUN

detective ◇ un détective privé a private detective

déteindre VERB

to fade (in wash)

détendre VERB

to relax ◇ La lecture, ça me détend. I find reading relaxing.

- **se détendre** to relax ◇ Il est allé prendre un bain pour se détendre. He's gone to have a bath to relax.

la **détente** NOUN

relaxation

le **détenu** NOUN

prisoner

la **détenue** NOUN

prisoner

se **détériorer** VERB

to deteriorate

déterminé ADJECTIVE

  1 **determined** ◇ *C'est un homme déterminé.* He's a determined man.

  2 **specific** ◇ *un but déterminé* a specific aim

détestable ADJECTIVE

  horrible

détester VERB

  to hate

la **détonation** NOUN

  bang ◇ *J'ai entendu une détonation.* I heard a bang.

le **détour** NOUN

  detour

  • **Ça vaut le détour.** It's worth the trip.

le **détournement** NOUN

  • **un détournement d'avion** a hijacking

détrempé ADJECTIVE

  waterlogged

les **détritus** MASC NOUN

  litter

détruire VERB

  to destroy

la **dette** NOUN

  debt

le **deuil** NOUN

  • **être en deuil** to be in mourning

deux NUMBER

  two ◇ *Il était deux heures.* It was two o'clock. ◇ *Elle a deux ans.* She's two.

  • **deux fois** twice

  • **tous les deux** both ◇ *Nous y sommes allées toutes les deux.* We both went.

  • **le deux février** the second of February

deuxième ADJECTIVE

  second ◇ *au deuxième étage* on the second floor

deuxièmement ADVERB

  secondly

devais, devait, devaient VERB *see* **devoir**

dévaliser VERB

  to rob

devant ADVERB, PREPOSITION

  see also **devant** NOUN

  1 **in front** ◇ *Il marchait devant.* He was walking in front.

  2 **in front of** ◇ *Il était assis devant moi.* He was sitting in front of me.

  • **passer devant** to go past ◇ *Nous sommes passés devant chez toi.* We went past your house.

le **devant** NOUN

  see also **devant** ADVERB

  front ◇ *le devant de la maison* the front of the house

  • **les pattes de devant** the front legs

le **développement** NOUN

development

  • **les pays en voie de développement** developing countries

développer VERB

  to develop ◇ *donner une pellicule à développer* to take a film to be developed

  • **se développer** to develop

devenir VERB

  to become

devez VERB *see* **devoir**

la **déviation** NOUN

  diversion

deviez VERB *see* **devoir**

deviner VERB

  to guess

la **devinette** NOUN

  riddle ◇ *poser une devinette à quelqu'un* to ask somebody a riddle

devions VERB *see* **devoir**

dévisager VERB

  • **dévisager quelqu'un** to stare at somebody

la **devise** NOUN

  currency ◇ *les devises étrangères* foreign currency

dévisser VERB

  to unscrew

dévoiler VERB

  to unveil

devoir VERB

  see also **devoir** NOUN

  Present tense:

je dois	nous devons
tu dois	vous devez
il/elle doit	ils/elles doivent

  Past participle: dû

  1 **to have to** ◇ *Je dois partir.* I've got to go.

  2 **must** ◇ *Tu dois être fatigué.* You must be tired.

  3 **to be due to** ◇ *Le nouveau centre commercial doit ouvrir en mai.* The new shopping centre is due to open in May.

  • **devoir quelque chose à quelqu'un** to owe somebody something ◇ *Combien est-ce que je vous dois?* How much do I owe you?

le **devoir** NOUN

  see also **devoir** VERB

  1 **exercise**

  • **les devoirs** homework

  • **un devoir sur table** a written test

  2 **duty** ◇ *Aller voter fait partie des devoirs du citoyen.* Voting is part of one's duty as a citizen.

devons VERB *see* **devoir**

dévorer VERB

  to devour

dévoué ADJECTIVE
  devoted
devra, devrai, devras, devrez, devrons, devront VERB *see* **devoir**
le **diabète** NOUN
  diabetes
diabétique ADJECTIVE
  diabetic ◇ *Je suis diabétique.* I'm diabetic.
le **diable** NOUN
  devil
le **diabolo** NOUN
  fruit cordial and lemonade
  - **un diabolo menthe** a mint cordial and lemonade
diagonal ADJECTIVE
  (MASC PL **diagonaux**)
  diagonal
la **diagonale** NOUN
  diagonal
  - **en diagonale** diagonally
le **diagramme** NOUN
  diagram
le **dialecte** NOUN
  dialect
le **diamant** NOUN
  diamond
le **diamètre** NOUN
  diameter
la **diapo** NOUN (*informal*)
  slide
  - **une pellicule diapo** a slide film
la **diapositive** NOUN
  slide ◇ *projeter des diapositives* to show some slides
la **diarrhée** NOUN
  diarrhoea ◇ *avoir la diarrhée* to have diarrhoea
le **dictateur** NOUN
  dictator
la **dictature** NOUN
  dictatorship
la **dictée** NOUN
  dictation
  dicter VERB
  to dictate
le **dictionnaire** NOUN
  dictionary
diététique ADJECTIVE
  - **un magasin diététique** a health food shop
le **dieu** NOUN
  (PL les **dieux**)
  god ◇ *Dieu* God ◇ *Mon Dieu!* Oh my God!
différent ADJECTIVE
  1 **different** ◇ *pour des raisons différentes* for different reasons
  2 **various** ◇ *pour différentes raisons*

for various reasons
  - **différent de** different to ◇ *Son point de vue est différent du mien.* His point of view is different to mine.
difficile ADJECTIVE
  difficult ◇ *Son accent est difficile à comprendre.* His accent is difficult to understand.
difficilement ADVERB
  - **faire quelque chose difficilement** to have trouble doing something ◇ *Ma grand-mère se déplace difficilement.* My grandmother has trouble getting around.
  - **Je pouvais difficilement refuser.** It was difficult for me to refuse.
la **difficulté** NOUN
  difficulty ◇ *avec difficulté* with difficulty
  - **être en difficulté** to be in difficulties
digérer VERB
  to digest
le **digestif** NOUN
  after-dinner liqueur
digne ADJECTIVE
  - **digne de** worthy of ◇ *digne de confiance* trustworthy
la **dignité** NOUN
  dignity
le **dilemme** NOUN
  dilemma ◇ *être devant un dilemme* to be faced with a dilemma
diluer VERB
  to dilute
le **dimanche** NOUN
  1 **Sunday** ◇ *Aujourd'hui, nous sommes dimanche.* It's Sunday today.
  2 **on Sunday** ◇ *Dimanche, nous allons déjeuner chez mes grands-parents.* On Sunday we're having lunch at my grandparents'.
  - **le dimanche** on Sundays ◇ *Le dimanche, je fais la grasse matinée.* I have a lie-in on Sundays.
  - **tous les dimanches** every Sunday
  - **dimanche dernier** last Sunday
  - **dimanche prochain** next Sunday
diminuer VERB
  to decrease ◇ *Est-ce que tu peux diminuer le son?* Could you turn down the sound?
le **diminutif** NOUN
  pet name
la **diminution** NOUN
  1 **reduction**
  2 **decrease**
la **dinde** NOUN
  turkey ◇ *la dinde de Noël* the Christmas turkey

le **dindon** NOUN
turkey
le dindon *refers to a live turkey, whereas* **la dinde** *refers to the meat.*

le **dîner** NOUN
see also dîner VERB
dinner *(evening meal)*

dîner VERB
see also dîner NOUN
to have dinner *(evening meal)*

dingue ADJECTIVE *(informal)*
crazy

diplomate ADJECTIVE
see also diplomate NOUN
diplomatic

le **diplomate** NOUN
see also diplomate ADJECTIVE
diplomat

la **diplomatie** NOUN
diplomacy

le **diplôme** NOUN
qualification

diplômé ADJECTIVE
qualified

dire VERB
1 to say ◇ *Il a dit qu'il ne viendrait pas.* He said he wouldn't come.
- **on dit que...** they say that... ◇ *On dit que la nourriture est excellente là-bas.* They say that the food is excellent there.
2 to tell
- **dire quelque chose à quelqu'un** to tell somebody something ◇ *Elle m'a dit la vérité.* She told me the truth. ◇ *Il nous a dit de regarder cette émission.* He told us to watch this programme.
- **On dirait qu'il va pleuvoir.** It looks as if it's going to rain.

direct ADJECTIVE
direct
- **en direct** live ◇ *une émission en direct* a live broadcast

directement ADVERB
straight ◇ *Il est rentré directement chez lui.* He went straight home.

le **directeur** NOUN
1 headteacher ◇ *Il est directeur.* He's a headteacher.
2 manager ◇ *Il est directeur du personnel.* He's a personnel manager.

la **direction** NOUN
1 management ◇ *la direction et les ouvriers* the management and the workers
2 direction ◇ *"toutes directions"* "all directions"

la **directrice** NOUN
1 headteacher ◇ *Elle est directrice.*

She's a headteacher.
2 manager ◇ *Elle est directrice commerciale.* She's a sales manager.

dirent VERB *see* **dire**

le **dirigeant** NOUN
leader

la **dirigeante** NOUN
leader

diriger VERB
to manage ◇ *Il dirige une petite entreprise.* He manages a small company.
- **se diriger vers** to head for ◇ *Il se dirigeait vers la gare.* He was heading for the station.

dis VERB *see* **dire**
- **Dis-moi la vérité!** Tell me the truth!
- **dis donc** hey ◇ *Il a drôlement changé, dis donc!* Hey, he's really changed! ◇ *Dis donc, tu te souviens de Sam?* Hey, do you remember Sam?

disaient, disais, disait VERB *see* **dire**

la **discothèque** NOUN
disco *(club)*

le **discours** NOUN
speech

discret ADJECTIVE
(FEM SING **discrète**)
discreet

la **discrimination** NOUN
discrimination ◇ *la discrimination raciale* racial discrimination ◇ *la discrimination sexuelle* sex discrimination

la **discussion** NOUN
discussion

discutable ADJECTIVE
debatable

discuter VERB
1 to talk ◇ *Nous avons discuté pendant des heures.* We talked for hours.
2 to argue ◇ *C'est ce que j'ai décidé, alors ne discutez pas!* That's what I've decided, so don't argue!

disent, disiez, disions VERB *see* **dire**

disons VERB *see* **dire**
let's say ◇ *C'est à, disons, une demi-heure à pied.* It's half an hour's walk, say.

disparaître VERB
to disappear
- **faire disparaître quelque chose (1)** to make something disappear ◇ *Il a fait disparaître le lapin dans son chapeau.* He made the rabbit disappear in his hat.

- **faire disparaître quelque chose (2)** to get rid of something ◇ *Ils ont fait disparaître tous les documents compromettants.* They got rid of all the incriminating documents.

la **disparition** NOUN
disappearance

- **une espèce en voie de disparition** an endangered species

disparu ADJECTIVE

- **être porté disparu** to be reported missing

le **dispensaire** NOUN
community clinic

dispensé ADJECTIVE

- **être dispensé de quelque chose** to be excused something ◇ *Elle est dispensée de gymnastique.* She's excused gym.

disperser VERB
to break up ◇ *La police a dispersé les manifestants.* The police broke up the demonstrators.

- **se disperser** to break up ◇ *Une fois l'ambulance partie, la foule s'est dispersée.* Once the ambulance had left, the crowd broke up.

disponible ADJECTIVE
available

disposé ADJECTIVE

- **être disposé à faire quelque chose** to be willing to do something ◇ *Il était disposé à m'aider.* He was willing to help me.

disposer VERB

- **disposer de quelque chose** to have access to something ◇ *Je dispose d'un ordinateur.* I have access to a computer.

la **disposition** NOUN

- **prendre ses dispositions** to make arrangements ◇ *Est-ce que vous avez pris vos dispositions pour partir en France?* Have you made arrangements to go to France?

- **avoir quelque chose à sa disposition** to have something at one's disposal
  ◇ *J'ai une voiture à ma disposition pour la semaine.* I have a car at my disposal for the week.

- **Je suis à votre disposition.** I am at your service.

- **Je tiens ces livres à votre disposition.** The books are at your disposal.

la **dispute** NOUN
argument

se **disputer** VERB
to argue

le **disquaire** NOUN
record dealer

le **disque** NOUN
record

- **un disque compact** a compact disc
- **le disque dur** hard disk

la **disquette** NOUN
diskette

disséminé ADJECTIVE
scattered

disséquer VERB
to dissect

la **dissertation** NOUN
essay

dissimuler VERB
to conceal

se **dissiper** VERB
to clear ◇ *Le brouillard va se dissiper dans l'après-midi.* The fog will clear during the afternoon.

le **dissolvant** NOUN
nail polish remover

dissoudre VERB
to dissolve

- **se dissoudre** to dissolve

dissuader VERB

- **dissuader quelqu'un de faire quelque chose** to dissuade somebody from doing something ◇ *Elle m'a dissuadé d'aller voir ce film.* She dissuaded me from going to see the film.

la **distance** NOUN
distance

la **distillerie** NOUN
distillery

distingué ADJECTIVE
distinguished

distinguer VERB
to distinguish

la **distraction** NOUN
entertainment ◇ *Il lit beaucoup: c'est sa seule distraction.* He reads a lot: it's his only form of entertainment.

distraire VERB

- **Va voir un film, ça te distraira.** Go and see a film, it'll take your mind off things.

distrait ADJECTIVE
absent-minded

distribuer VERB
1 to give out ◇ *Distribue les livres, s'il te plaît.* Give out the books, please.
2 to deal *(cards)*

le **distributeur** NOUN

- **un distributeur automatique** a vending machine
- **un distributeur de billets** a cash dispenser

dit VERB *see* dire

dit ADJECTIVE
> known as ◇ *Pierre, dit Pierrot* Pierre, known as Pierrot

dites VERB *see* **dire**
- **Dites-moi ce que vous pensez.** Tell me what you think.
- **dites donc** hey ◇ *Dites-donc, vous, là-bas!* Hey, you there!

divers ADJECTIVE
> diverse
- **pour diverses raisons** for various different reasons

se **divertir** VERB
> to enjoy oneself

divin ADJECTIVE
> divine

diviser VERB
> to divide ◇ *Quatre divisé par deux égalent deux.* 4 divided by 2 equals 2.

le **divorcé** NOUN
> divorcee

la **divorcée** NOUN
> divorcee

divorcer VERB
> to get divorced

dix NUMBER
> ten ◇ *Elle a dix ans.* She's ten. ◇ *à dix heures* at ten o'clock
- **le dix février** the tenth of February

dix-huit NUMBER ◇ *Elle a dix-huit ans.* She's eighteen. ◇ *à dix-huit heures* at 6 p.m.

dixième ADJECTIVE
> tenth ◇ *au dixième étage* on the tenth floor

dix-neuf NUMBER ◇ *Elle a dix-neuf ans.* She's nineteen. ◇ *à dix-neuf heures* at 7 p.m.

dix-sept NUMBER ◇ *Elle a dix-sept ans.* She's seventeen. ◇ *à dix-sept heures* at 5 p.m.

la **dizaine** NOUN
> about ten ◇ *une dizaine de jours* about ten days

le **do** NOUN
> 1 C ◇ *en do majeur* in C major
> 2 do ◇ *do, ré, mi...* do, re, mi...

le **docteur** NOUN
> doctor ◇ *Elle est docteur.* She's a doctor.

le **documentaire** NOUN
> documentary

le/la **documentaliste** NOUN
> librarian

documenter VERB
- **se documenter sur quelque chose** to gather information on something

dodu ADJECTIVE
> plump

le **doigt** NOUN
> finger
- **les doigts de pied** the toes

dois, doit, doivent VERB *see* **devoir**

le **domaine** NOUN
> 1 estate ◇ *Il possède un immense domaine en Normandie.* He owns a huge estate in Normandy.
> 2 field ◇ *La chimie n'est pas mon domaine.* Chemistry's not my field.

domestique ADJECTIVE
> see also **domestique** NOUN
> domestic
- **les animaux domestiques** pets

le/la **domestique** NOUN
> see also **domestique** ADJECTIVE
> servant

le **domicile** NOUN
> place of residence
- **à domicile** at home ◇ *Il travaille à domicile.* He works at home.

domicilié ADJECTIVE
- **"domicilié à:..."** "address:..."

dominer VERB
> to dominate
- **se dominer** to control oneself

les **dominos** MASC NOUN
> dominoes ◇ *jouer aux dominos* to play dominoes

le **dommage** NOUN
> damage ◇ *La tempête a causé d'importants dommages.* The storm caused a lot of damage.
- **C'est dommage.** It's a shame. ◇ *C'est dommage que tu ne puisses pas venir.* It's a shame you can't come.

dompter VERB
> to tame

le **dompteur** NOUN
> animal tamer

la **dompteuse** NOUN
> animal tamer

le **don** NOUN
> 1 donation
> 2 gift ◇ *avoir un don pour quelque chose* to have a gift for something
- **Elle a le don de m'énerver.** She's got a knack of getting on my nerves.

donc CONJUNCTION
> so

le **donjon** NOUN
> keep (*of castle*)

les **données** FEM NOUN
> data

donner VERB
> 1 to give
- **donner quelque chose à quelqu'un** to give somebody something ◇ *Elle m'a donné son adresse.* She gave me her

address.
- **Ça m'a donné faim.** That made me feel hungry.
  2 **to give away** ◇ *Tu as toujours ta veste en daim?–Non, je l'ai donnée.* Have you still got your suede jacket? –No, I gave it away.
- **donner sur quelque chose** to overlook something ◇ *une fenêtre qui donne sur la mer* a window overlooking the sea

dont PRONOUN
  1 **of which** ◇ *deux livres, dont l'un est en anglais* two books, one of which is in English ◇ *le prix dont il est si fier* the prize he's so proud of
  2 **of whom** ◇ *dix blessés, dont deux grièvement* ten people injured, two of them seriously ◇ *la fille dont je t'ai parlé* the girl I told you about

doré ADJECTIVE
  golden ◇ *une étoile dorée* a golden star

dorénavant ADVERB
  from now on ◇ *Dorénavant, tu feras attention.* From now on, you'll be careful.

dorloter VERB
  to pamper

dormir VERB
  1 **to sleep** ◇ *Tu as bien dormi?* Did you sleep well?
  2 **to be asleep** ◇ *Ne faites pas de bruit, il dort.* Don't make any noise, he's asleep.

le **dortoir** NOUN
  dormitory

le **dos** NOUN
  back ◇ *dos à dos* back to back
- **faire quelque chose dans le dos de quelqu'un** to do something behind somebody's back ◇ *Elle me critique dans mon dos.* She criticizes me behind my back.
- **de dos** from behind
- **nager le dos crawlé** to swim backstroke
- **"voir au dos"** "see over"

la **dose** NOUN
  dose ◇ *Ne pas dépasser la dose prescrite.* Do not exceed the stated dose.

le **dossier** NOUN
  1 **file** ◇ *une pile de dossiers* a stack of files
  2 **report** ◇ *un bon dossier scolaire* a good school report
  3 **feature** (*in magazine*)
  4 **back** (*of chair*)

la **douane** NOUN
  customs

le **douanier** NOUN
  customs officer

le **double** NOUN
- **le double** twice as much ◇ *Il gagne le double.* He earns twice as much. ◇ *le double du prix normal* twice the normal price
- **en double** in duplicate ◇ *Garde cette photo, je l'ai en double.* Keep this photo, I've got a copy of it.
- **le double messieurs** the men's doubles (*tennis*)

doubler VERB
  1 **to double** ◇ *Le prix a doublé en dix ans.* The price has doubled in 10 years.
  2 **to overtake** ◇ *Il est dangereux de doubler sur cette route.* It's dangerous to overtake on this road.
- **un film doublé** a dubbed film

douce ADJECTIVE *see* **doux**

doucement ADVERB
  1 **gently** ◇ *Il a frappé doucement à la porte.* He knocked gently at the door.
  2 **slowly** ◇ *Roulez doucement!* Drive slowly! ◇ *Je ne comprends pas, parle plus doucement.* I don't understand, speak more slowly.

la **douceur** NOUN
  1 **softness** ◇ *Cette crème maintient la douceur de votre peau.* This cream keeps your skin soft.
  2 **gentleness** ◇ *parler avec douceur* to speak gently
- **L'avion a atterri en douceur.** The plane made a smooth landing.

la **douche** NOUN
  shower
- **les douches** the shower room

se **doucher** VERB
  to have a shower

doué ADJECTIVE
  talented
- **être doué en quelque chose** to be good at something ◇ *Il est doué en maths.* He's good at maths.

douillet ADJECTIVE
  (FEM SING **douillette**)
  1 **cosy** ◇ *un anorak douillet* a cosy anorak
  2 **soft** ◇ *Je ne supporte pas la douleur: je suis très douillette.* I can't stand pain: I'm a real softie.

la **douleur** NOUN
  pain

douloureux ADJECTIVE
  (FEM SING **douloureuse**)
  painful

le **doute** NOUN
 doubt
- **sans doute** probably

douter VERB
 to doubt
- **douter de quelque chose** to doubt
  something ◇ *Je doute de sa sincérité.*
  I have my doubts about his sincerity.
- **se douter de quelque chose** to
  suspect something ◇ *Je ne me
  doutais de rien.* I didn't suspect
  anything.
- **Je m'en doutais.** I suspected as much.

douteux ADJECTIVE
 (FEM SING **douteuse**)
 1 **dubious** ◇ *une plaisanterie d'un
 goût douteux* a joke in dubious taste
 2 **suspicious-looking** ◇ *un individu
 douteux* a suspicious-looking person

Douvres NOUN
 Dover

doux ADJECTIVE
 (FEM SING **douce**, MASC PL **doux**)
 1 **soft** ◇ *un tissu doux* soft material
 ◇ *les drogues douces* soft drugs
 2 **sweet** ◇ *du cidre doux* sweet cider
 3 **mild** ◇ *Il fait doux aujourd'hui.* It's
 mild today.
 4 **gentle** ◇ *C'est quelqu'un de très
 doux.* He's a very gentle person.
- **en douce** on the quiet ◇ *Il m'a
  donné cinquante francs en douce.* He
  slipped me 50 francs on the quiet.

la **douzaine** NOUN
 dozen ◇ *une douzaine d'œufs* a
 dozen eggs
- **une douzaine de personnes** about
  twelve people

douze NUMBER
 twelve ◇ *Il a douze ans.* He's twelve.
- **le douze février** the twelfth of
  February

douzième ADJECTIVE
 twelfth ◇ *au douzième étage* on the
 twelfth floor

la **dragée** NOUN
 sugared almond

draguer VERB (*informal*)
- **draguer quelqu'un** to chat somebody
  up ◇ *Il est en train de la draguer.* He's
  chatting her up.
- **se faire draguer** to get chatted up
  ◇ *Elle aime se faire draguer.* She
  likes being chatted up.

le **dragueur** NOUN (*informal*)
 flirt (*person*)

la **dragueuse** NOUN (*informal*)
 flirt (*person*)

dramatique ADJECTIVE
 tragic ◇ *une situation dramatique* a
 tragic situation
- **l'art dramatique** drama

le **drame** NOUN
 drama (*incident*)
- **Ça n'est pas un drame si tu ne viens
  pas.** It's not the end of the world if
  you don't come.

le **drap** NOUN
 sheet (*for bed*)

le **drapeau** NOUN
 (PL les **drapeaux**)
 flag ◇ *le drapeau français* the
 French flag

dressé ADJECTIVE
 trained ◇ *un chien bien dressé* a
 well-trained dog

dresser VERB
 1 **to draw up** ◇ *dresser une liste* to
 draw up a list
 2 **to train** ◇ *dresser un chien* to
 train a dog
- **dresser l'oreille** to prick up one's ears
  ◇ *Quand elle a dit ça, il a dressé
  l'oreille.* When she said that, he
  pricked up his ears.

la **drogue** NOUN
 drug ◇ *le problème de la drogue* the
 drugs problem ◇ *la lutte contre la
 drogue* the war against drugs
- **les drogues douces** soft drugs
- **les drogues dures** hard drugs

le **drogué** NOUN
 drug addict

la **droguée** NOUN
 drug addict

droguer VERB
- **droguer quelqu'un** to drug somebody
- **se droguer** to take drugs

la **droguerie** NOUN
 hardware shop

droit ADJECTIVE, ADVERB
 see also **droit** NOUN
 1 **right** ◇ *le bras droit* the right arm
 ◇ *le côté droit* the right-hand side
 2 **straight** ◇ *une ligne droite* a
 straight line ◇ *Tiens-toi droite!* Stand
 up straight!
- **tout droit** straight on

le **droit** NOUN
 see also **droit** ADJECTIVE
 1 **right** ◇ *les droits de l'homme*
 human rights
- **avoir le droit de faire quelque chose**
  to be allowed to do something ◇ *On
  n'a pas le droit de fumer à l'école.* We're
  not allowed to smoke at school.
 2 **law** ◇ *faire son droit* to study law
 ◇ *un étudiant en droit* a law student

la droite NOUN

see also droit ADJECTIVE

right ◇ *sur votre droite* on your right
- **à droite (1)** on the right ◇ *la troisième rue à droite* the third street on the right
- **à droite (2)** to the right ◇ *à droite de la fenêtre* to the right of the window ◇ *Tournez à droite.* Turn right.
- **la voie de droite** the right-hand lane
- **la droite** the right (*in politics*) ◇ *Elle est très à droite.* She's very right-wing.

droitier ADJECTIVE

(FEM SING **droitière**)

right-handed ◇ *Elle est droitière.* She's right-handed.

drôle ADJECTIVE

funny ◇ *Ça n'est pas drôle.* It's not funny.
- **un drôle de temps** funny weather

drôlement ADVERB (*informal*)

really ◇ *C'est drôlement bon.* It's really good.

du ARTICLE

du *is the contracted form of* **de + le.**

1 **some** ◇ *Tu veux du fromage?* Would you like some cheese?
2 **any** ◇ *Tu as du chocolat?* Have you got any chocolate? ◇ *la porte du garage* the door of the garage ◇ *la femme du directeur* the headmaster's wife

dû VERB *see* **devoir**

see also dû ADJECTIVE
- **Nous avons dû nous arrêter.** We had to stop.

dû ADJECTIVE

(FEM **due**, MASC PL **dus**)

see also dû VERB
- **dû à** due to ◇ *un retard dû au mauvais temps* a delay due to bad weather

le duc NOUN

duke

la duchesse NOUN

duchess

dupe ADJECTIVE
- **Elle me ment mais je ne suis pas dupe.** She lies to me but I'm not taken in by that.

duquel PRONOUN

(MASC PL **desquels**, FEM PL **desquelles**)

duquel *is the contracted form of* **de + lequel.**
◇ *l'homme duquel il parle* the man he is talking about

dur ADJECTIVE, ADVERB

hard ◇ *travailler dur* to work hard ◇ *être dur avec quelqu'un* to be hard on somebody

durant PREPOSITION

1 **during** ◇ *durant la nuit* during the night
2 **for** ◇ *durant des années* for years ◇ *des mois durant* for months

la durée NOUN

length ◇ *Quelle est la durée des études d'ingénieur?* How long does it take to train as an engineer?
- **pour une durée de quinze jours** for a period of two weeks
- **de courte durée** short ◇ *un séjour de courte durée* a short stay
- **de longue durée** long ◇ *une absence de longue durée* a long absence

durement ADVERB

harshly

durer VERB

to last

la dureté NOUN

harshness ◇ *traiter quelqu'un avec dureté* to treat somebody harshly

dynamique ADJECTIVE

dynamic

dyslexique ADJECTIVE

dyslexic

E

l' eau FEM NOUN
(PL les **eaux**)
water
- **l'eau minérale** mineral water
- **l'eau plate** still water
- **tomber à l'eau** to fall through ◇ *Nos projets sont tombés à l'eau.* Our plans have fallen through.

éblouir VERB
to dazzle

l' éboueur MASC NOUN
dustman

ébouillanter VERB
to scald

l' écaille FEM NOUN
scale (*of fish*)

s' écailler VERB
to flake

l' écart MASC NOUN
gap
- **à l'écart de** away from ◇ *Ils se sont assis à l'écart des autres.* They sat down away from the others.

écarté ADJECTIVE
remote
- **les bras écartés** arms outstretched
- **les jambes écartées** legs apart

écarter VERB
to open wide (*arms, legs*)
- **s'écarter** to move ◇ *Ils se sont écartés pour le laisser passer.* They moved to let him pass.

l' échafaudage MASC NOUN
scaffolding

l' échalote FEM NOUN
shallot

l' échange MASC NOUN
exchange ◇ *en échange de* in exchange for

échanger VERB
to swap ◇ *Je t'échange ce timbre contre celui-là.* I'll swap you this stamp for that one.

l' échantillon MASC NOUN
sample

échapper VERB
- **échapper à** to escape from ◇ *Le prisonnier a réussi à échapper à la police.* The prisoner managed to escape from the police.
- **s'échapper** to escape ◇ *Il s'est échappé de prison.* He escaped from prison.
- **l'échapper belle** to have a narrow escape ◇ *Nous l'avons échappé belle.* We had a narrow escape.

l' écharde FEM NOUN
splinter of wood

l' écharpe FEM NOUN
scarf

s' échauffer VERB
to warm up (*before exercise*)

l' échec MASC NOUN
failure

les **échecs** MASC NOUN
chess ◇ *jouer aux échecs* to play chess

l' échelle FEM NOUN
1. **ladder**
2. **scale** (*of map*)

échevelé ADJECTIVE
dishevelled

l' écho MASC NOUN
echo

échouer VERB
- **échouer à un examen** to fail an exam

éclabousser VERB
to splash

l' éclair MASC NOUN
flash of lightning
- **un éclair au chocolat** a chocolate éclair

l' éclairage MASC NOUN
lighting

l' éclaircie FEM NOUN
bright interval

éclairer VERB
- **Cette lampe éclaire bien.** This lamp gives a good light.

l' éclat MASC NOUN
1. **fragment** (*of glass*) ◇ *La vase a volé en éclats.* The vase smashed into pieces.
2. **brightness** (*of sun, colour*)
- **des éclats de rire** roars of laughter

éclatant ADJECTIVE
brilliant ◇ *des dents d'une blancheur éclatante* brilliant white teeth

éclater VERB
1. **to burst** (*tyre, balloon*)
- **éclater de rire** to burst out laughing
- **éclater en sanglots** to burst into tears
2. **to break out** ◇ *La Seconde Guerre mondiale a éclaté en 1939.* The Second World War broke out in 1939.

écœurant ADJECTIVE
sickly

écœurer VERB
- **Tous ces mensonges m'écœurent.** All these lies make me sick.

l' école FEM NOUN
school ◇ *aller à l'école* to go to

school ◇ *une école publique* a state school ◇ *une école maternelle* a nursery school

The école maternelle is a state school for 2-6 year-olds.

l'**écolier** MASC NOUN
schoolboy

l'**écolière** FEM NOUN
schoolgirl

l'**écologie** FEM NOUN
ecology

écologique ADJECTIVE
ecological ◇ *une lessive écologique* an ecological washing powder

l'**économie** FEM NOUN
1 **economy** ◇ *l'économie de la France* the French economy
2 **economics** ◇ *un cours d'économie* an economics class

les **économies** FEM NOUN
savings
- **faire des économies** to save up ◇ *Je fais des économies pour partir en vacances.* I'm saving up for my holidays.

économique ADJECTIVE
1 **economic** ◇ *une crise économique* an economic crisis
2 **economical** ◇ *Il est plus économique d'acheter une grande boîte de lessive.* It's more economical to buy a big box of washing powder. ◇ *Cette petite voiture est économique.* This little car is cheap to run.

économiser VERB
to save

l'**écorce** FEM NOUN
1 **bark** (*of tree*)
2 **peel** (*of orange, lemon*)

s'**écorcher** VERB
- **Je me suis écorché le genou.** I've grazed my knee.

écossais ADJECTIVE, NOUN
(FEM SING **écossaise**)
1 **Scottish** ◇ *Elle est écossaise.* She's Scottish.
- **un Écossais** a Scot (*man*)
- **une Écossaise** a Scot (*woman*)
- **les Écossais** the Scots
2 **tartan** ◇ *une jupe écossaise* a tartan skirt

l'**Écosse** FEM NOUN
Scotland
- **en Écosse (1)** in Scotland ◇ *Il a passé une semaine en Écosse.* He spent a week in Scotland.
- **en Écosse (2)** to Scotland ◇ *Nous allons en Écosse l'été prochain.* We're going to Scotland next summer.

s'**écouler** VERB
1 **to flow out** (*water*)
2 **to pass** ◇ *Le temps s'écoule trop vite.* Time passes too quickly.

écouter VERB
to listen to ◇ *J'aime écouter de la musique.* I like listening to music.
- **Écoute-moi!** Listen!

l'**écouteur** MASC NOUN
earpiece (*of phone*)

l'**écran** MASC NOUN
screen
- **le petit écran** television
- **l'écran total** sunblock

écraser VERB
1 **to crush** ◇ *Écrasez une gousse d'ail.* Crush a clove of garlic.
2 **to run over** ◇ *Regarde bien avant de traverser, sinon tu vas te faire écraser.* Look carefully before you cross or you'll get run over.
- **s'écraser** to crash ◇ *L'avion s'est écrasé dans le désert.* The plane crashed in the desert.

l'**écrevisse** FEM NOUN
crayfish

écrire VERB
to write ◇ *Nous nous écrivons régulièrement.* We write to each other regularly.
- **Ça s'écrit comment?** How do you spell that?

l'**écrit** MASC NOUN
written paper ◇ *L'écrit d'anglais a lieu la semaine prochaine.* The written paper in English is next week.
- **par écrit** in writing

l'**écriteau** MASC NOUN
(PL les **écriteaux**)
notice

l'**écriture** FEM NOUN
writing ◇ *J'ai du mal à lire son écriture.* I can't read his writing.

l'**écrivain** MASC NOUN
writer ◇ *Elle est écrivain.* She's a writer.

l'**écrou** MASC NOUN
nut (*metal*)

s'**écrouler** VERB
to collapse

écru ADJECTIVE
off-white

l'**écureuil** MASC NOUN
squirrel

l'**écurie** FEM NOUN
stable

EDF ABBREVIATION (= *Électricité de France*)
French electricity company

Édimbourg NOUN
Edinburgh

éditer VERB
to publish ◇ *On vient d'éditer un nouveau dictionnaire.* A new dictionary has just been published.

l'**éditeur** MASC NOUN
publisher

l'**édition** FEM NOUN
[1] edition ◇ *une édition de poche* a paperback edition
[2] publishing ◇ *Il travaille dans l'édition.* He works in publishing.

l'**édredon** MASC NOUN
eiderdown

l'**éducateur** MASC NOUN
teacher (*of people with special needs*)

éducatif ADJECTIVE
(FEM SING **éducative**)
educational ◇ *un jeu éducatif* an educational game

l'**éducation** FEM NOUN
[1] education ◇ *l'éducation physique* physical education ◇ *Il n'a pas beaucoup d'éducation.* He's not very well educated.
[2] upbringing ◇ *Il a reçu une éducation très stricte.* He had a very strict upbringing.

l'**éducatrice** FEM NOUN
teacher (*of people with special needs*)

éduquer VERB
to educate

effacer VERB
to rub out

effarant ADJECTIVE
amazing ◇ *Il a mangé une quantité effarante de pain.* He ate an amazing amount of bread.

effectivement ADVERB
indeed ◇ *Il est effectivement plus rapide de passer par là.* It is indeed quicker to go this way. ◇ *Oui, effectivement.* Yes, indeed.

effectuer VERB
[1] to make ◇ *Ils ont effectué de nombreux changements.* They have made a lot of changes.
[2] to do ◇ *On vient d'effectuer des travaux dans le bâtiment.* They have just done some work in the building.

effervescent ADJECTIVE
effervescent ◇ *un comprimé effervescent* an effervescent tablet

l'**effet** MASC NOUN
effect
• faire de l'effet to take effect ◇ *Ce médicament fait rapidement de l'effet.* This medicine takes effect quickly.

• Ça m'a fait un drôle d'effet de le revoir. It gave me a strange feeling to see him again.

• en effet yes indeed ◇ *Je ne me sens pas très bien.–En effet, tu as l'air pâle.* I don't feel very well.–Yes, you do look pale.

efficace ADJECTIVE
[1] efficient ◇ *C'est une femme efficace.* She's an efficient woman.
[2] effective ◇ *un remède efficace* an effective remedy

s'**effondrer** VERB
to collapse

s'**efforcer** VERB
• s'efforcer de faire quelque chose to try hard to do something ◇ *Il s'efforce d'être aimable avec la clientèle.* He tries hard to be polite to the customers.

l'**effort** MASC NOUN
effort ◇ *faire un effort* to make an effort

effrayant ADJECTIVE
frightening

effrayer VERB
to frighten

effronté ADJECTIVE
cheeky ◇ *Ce gamin est vraiment effronté.* This kid's really cheeky.

effroyable ADJECTIVE
horrifying

égal ADJECTIVE
(MASC PL **égaux**)
equal ◇ *une quantité égale de farine et de sucre* an equal quantity of flour and sugar
• Ça m'est égal. (1) I don't mind. ◇ *Tu préfères du riz ou des pâtes? –Ça m'est égal.* Would you rather have rice or pasta?–I don't mind.
• Ça m'est égal. (2) I don't care. ◇ *Fais ce que tu veux, ça m'est égal.* Do what you like, I don't care.

également ADVERB
also ◇ *On appelle également la France l'Hexagone à cause de sa forme.* France is also called the Hexagon because of its shape.

égaler VERB
to equal

l'**égalité** FEM NOUN
equality
• être à égalité to be level ◇ *Maintenant les deux joueurs sont à égalité.* The two players are now level.

l'**égard** MASC NOUN
• à cet égard in this respect

égarer VERB

to mislay ◇ *J'ai égaré mes clés.* I've mislaid my keys.
- **s'égarer** to get lost ◇ *Ils se sont égarés dans la forêt.* They got lost in the forest.

l'**église** FEM NOUN
church ◇ *aller à l'église* to go to church

l'**égoïsme** MASC NOUN
selfishness

égoïste ADJECTIVE
selfish

l'**égratignure** FEM NOUN
scratch

l'**Égypte** FEM NOUN
Egypt

égyptien ADJECTIVE
(FEM SING **égyptienne**)
Egyptian

l'**élan** MASC NOUN
- **prendre de l'élan** to gather speed

s'**élancer** VERB
to hurl oneself

élargir VERB
to widen

l'**élastique** MASC NOUN
rubber band

l'**électeur** MASC NOUN
voter (*man*)

l'**élection** FEM NOUN
election ◇ *les élections présidentielles* the presidential election

l'**électrice** FEM NOUN
voter (*woman*)

l'**électricien** MASC NOUN
electrician

l'**électricité** FEM NOUN
electricity ◇ *une facture d'électricité* an electricity bill
- **allumer l'électricité** to turn on the light
- **éteindre l'électricité** to turn off the light

électrique ADJECTIVE
electric ◇ *le courant électrique* the electric current

l'**électronique** FEM NOUN
electronics

élégant ADJECTIVE
smart

élémentaire ADJECTIVE
elementary

l'**éléphant** MASC NOUN
elephant

l'**élevage** MASC NOUN
cattle rearing ◇ *faire de l'élevage* to rear cattle
- **un élevage de porcs** a pig farm
- **un élevage de poulets** a chicken farm

- **les truites d'élevage** farmed trout

élevé ADJECTIVE
high ◇ *Le prix est trop élevé.* The price is too high.
- **être bien élevé** to have good manners
- **être mal élevé** to have bad manners

l'**élève** MASC/FEM NOUN
pupil

élever VERB
1 **to bring up** ◇ *Il a été élevé par sa grand-mère.* He was brought up by his grandmother.
2 **to breed** ◇ *Son oncle élève des chevaux.* His uncle breeds horses.
- **élever la voix** to raise one's voice
- **s'élever à** to come to ◇ *À combien s'élèvent les dégâts?* How much does the damage come to?

l'**éleveur** MASC NOUN
breeder

éliminatoire ADJECTIVE
- **une note éliminatoire** a fail mark
- **une épreuve éliminatoire** a qualifying round (*sport*)

éliminer VERB
to eliminate

élire VERB
to elect

elle PRONOUN
1 **she** ◇ *Elle est institutrice.* She is a primary school teacher.
2 **her** ◇ *Vous pouvez avoir confiance en elle.* You can trust her.
3 **it** ◇ *Prends cette chaise: elle est plus confortable.* Take this chair: it's more comfortable.
| elle *is also used for emphasis.* |
◇ *Elle, elle est toujours en retard!* Oh, SHE's always late!
- **elle-même** herself ◇ *Elle l'a choisi elle-même.* She chose it herself.

elles PRONOUN
they ◇ *Où sont Anne et Rachel?—Elles sont allées au cinéma.* Where are Anne and Rachel?–They've gone to the cinema.
- **elles-mêmes** themselves

éloigné ADJECTIVE
distant

s'**éloigner** VERB
to go far away ◇ *Ne vous éloignez pas: le dîner est bientôt prêt!* Don't go far away: dinner will soon be ready!
- **Vous vous éloignez du sujet.** You are getting off the point.

l'**Élysée** MASC NOUN
Élysée Palace
| The Élysée *is the residence of the French president.* |

l'**emballage** MASC NOUN
- le papier d'emballage wrapping paper

emballer VERB
  to wrap
- s'emballer (*informal*) to get excited ◇ *Il s'est emballé pour ce projet.* He got really excited about this plan.

l'**embarquement** MASC NOUN
  boarding ◇ *L'embarquement des passagers n'a pas encore été annoncé.* Passenger boarding has not been announced yet.

l'**embarras** MASC NOUN
  embarrassment ◇ *Votre question me met dans l'embarras.* It's difficult for me to answer your question.
- Vous n'avez que l'embarras du choix. The only problem is choosing.

embarrassant ADJECTIVE
  embarrassing

embarrasser VERB
  to embarrass ◇ *Cela m'embarrasse de vous demander encore un service.* I feel embarrassed to ask you to do something more for me.

embaucher VERB
  to take on ◇ *L'entreprise vient d'embaucher cinquante ouvriers.* The firm has just taken on fifty workers.

les **embêtements** MASC NOUN
  trouble

embêter VERB
  to bother
- s'embêter to be bored ◇ *Qu'est-ce qu'on s'embête ici!* Isn't it boring here!

l'**embouteillage** MASC NOUN
  traffic jam

embrasser VERB
  to kiss ◇ *Ils se sont embrassés.* They kissed each other.

s'**embrouiller** VERB
  to get confused ◇ *Il s'embrouille dans ses explications.* He gets confused when he explains things.

émerveiller VERB
  to dazzle

l'**émeute** FEM NOUN
  riot

émigrer VERB
  to emigrate

l'**émission** FEM NOUN
  programme ◇ *une émission de télévision* a TV programme

s'**emmêler** VERB
  to get tangled ◇ *Ma laine s'est emmêlée.* My wool has got tangled.

emménager VERB
  to move in ◇ *Nous venons d'emménager dans une nouvelle maison.* We've just moved into a new house.

emmener VERB
  to take ◇ *Ils m'ont emmené au cinéma pour mon anniversaire.* They took me to the cinema for my birthday.

emmerder VERB (*rude*)
- Ça m'emmerde! It pisses me off!
- Je t'emmerde! Piss off!
- s'emmerder to be bored stiff

émotif ADJECTIVE
(FEM SING émotive)
  emotional ◇ *Il est très émotif.* He's very emotional.

l'**émotion** FEM NOUN
  emotion

émouvoir VERB
  to move ◇ *Sa lettre l'a beaucoup émue.* She was deeply moved by his letter.

emparer VERB
- s'emparer de to grab ◇ *Il s'est emparé de ma valise.* He grabbed my case.

l'**empêchement** MASC NOUN
- Nous avons eu un empêchement de dernière minute. We were held up at the last minute.

empêcher VERB
  to prevent ◇ *Le café le soir m'empêche de dormir.* Coffee at night keeps me awake.
- Il n'a pas pu s'empêcher de rire. He couldn't help laughing.

l'**empereur** MASC NOUN
  emperor

s'**empiffrer** VERB (*informal*)
  to stuff one's face ◇ *Arrête de t'empiffrer!* Stop stuffing your face!

empiler VERB
  to pile up

empirer VERB
  to worsen ◇ *La situation a encore empiré.* The situation got even worse.

l'**emplacement** MASC NOUN
  site ◇ *Un panneau indique l'emplacement de la vieille abbaye.* A sign shows the site of the old abbey.

l'**emploi** MASC NOUN
  1 use ◇ *prêt à l'emploi* ready for use
- le mode d'emploi directions for use
  2 job ◇ *la création d'emplois* job creation
- un emploi du temps a timetable

l'**employé** MASC NOUN
  employee
- un employé de bureau an office worker

l'**employée** FEM NOUN
employee
→ **une employée de banque** a bank clerk
employer VERB
☐1 **to use** ◇ *Quelle méthode employez-vous?* What method do you use?
☐2 **to employ** ◇ *L'entreprise emploie dix ingénieurs.* The firm employs ten engineers.
l'**employeur** MASC NOUN
employer
empoisonner VERB
to poison
emporter VERB
to take ◇ *N'emportez que le strict nécessaire.* Only take the bare minimum.
→ **plats à emporter** take-away meals
→ **s'emporter** to lose one's temper ◇ *Je m'emporte facilement et finis souvent par le regretter.* I'm quick to lose my temper and I'm often sorry afterwards.
l'**empreinte** FEM NOUN
→ **une empreinte digitale** a fingerprint
s'**empresser** VERB
→ **s'empresser de faire quelque chose** to be quick to do something ◇ *Ils se sont empressés de nous annoncer la nouvelle.* They were quick to tell us the news.
emprisonner VERB
to imprison
l'**emprunt** MASC NOUN
loan
emprunter VERB
to borrow
→ **emprunter quelque chose à quelqu'un** to borrow something from somebody ◇ *Est-ce que je peux t'emprunter dix francs?* Can I borrow ten francs from you?
ému ADJECTIVE
touched ◇ *J'ai été très ému par sa gentillesse.* I was very touched by her kindness.
en PREPOSITION, PRONOUN
☐1 **in** ◇ *Il habite en France.* He lives in France. ◇ *La mariée est en blanc.* The bride is in white. ◇ *Je le verrai en mai.* I'll see him in May.
☐2 **to** ◇ *Je vais en France cet été.* I'm going to France this summer.
☐3 **by** ◇ *C'est plus rapide en voiture.* It's quicker by car.
☐4 **made of** ◇ *C'est en verre.* It's made of glass. ◇ *un collier en argent* a silver necklace

☐5 **while** ◇ *Il s'est coupé le doigt en ouvrant une boîte de conserve.* He cut his finger while opening a tin.
→ **Elle est sortie en courant.** She ran out.

When en is used with avoir and il y a, it is not translated in English.

◇ *Est-ce que tu as un dictionnaire?–Oui, j'en ai un.* Have you got a dictionary? –Yes, I've got one. ◇ *Combien d'élèves y a-t-il dans ta classe?–Il y en a trente.* How many pupils are there in your class?–There are 30.

en is also used with verbs and expressions normally followed by de to avoid repeating the same word.

◇ *Si tu as un problème, tu peux m'en parler.* If you've got a problem, you can talk about it with me. ◇ *Est-ce que tu peux me rendre ce livre? J'en ai besoin.* Can you give me back that book? I need it. ◇ *Il adore son petit-fils et il en est très fier.* He loves his grandson and is very proud of him.
→ **J'en ai assez.** I've had enough.
enceinte ADJECTIVE
pregnant ◇ *Elle est enceinte de six mois.* She's 6 months pregnant.
enchanté ADJECTIVE
delighted ◇ *Ma mère est enchantée de sa nouvelle voiture.* My mother's delighted with her new car.
→ **Enchanté!** Pleased to meet you!
encombrant ADJECTIVE
bulky
encombrer VERB
to clutter
encore ADVERB
☐1 **still** ◇ *Il est encore au travail.* He's still at work. ◇ *Il reste encore deux morceaux de gâteau.* There are two bits of cake left.
☐2 **even** ◇ *C'est encore mieux.* That's even better.
☐3 **again** ◇ *Il m'a encore demandé de l'argent.* He asked me for money again.
→ **encore une fois** once again
→ **pas encore** not yet ◇ *Je n'ai pas encore fini.* I haven't finished yet.
encourager VERB
to encourage
l'**encre** FEM NOUN
ink
l'**encyclopédie** FEM NOUN
encyclopaedia
l'**endive** FEM NOUN
chicory
endommager VERB
to damage

endormi ADJECTIVE
asleep
endormir VERB
to deaden ◇ *Cette piqûre sert à endormir le nerf.* This injection is to deaden the nerve.
- **s'endormir** to go to sleep
l'**endroit** MASC NOUN
place ◇ *C'est un endroit très tranquille.* It's a very quiet place.
- **à l'endroit (1)** the right way out
- **à l'endroit (2)** the right way up
endurant ADJECTIVE
tough (*person*)
endurcir VERB
to toughen up ◇ *Ces exercices servent à endurcir les soldats.* These exercises are to toughen up the soldiers.
- **s'endurcir** to become hardened
endurer VERB
to endure
l'**énergie** FEM NOUN
1 **energy** ◇ *Je n'ai pas beaucoup d'énergie ce matin.* I haven't got much energy this morning.
2 **power** ◇ *l'énergie nucléaire* nuclear power
- **avec énergie** vigorously ◇ *Il a protesté avec énergie.* He protested vigorously.
énergique ADJECTIVE
energetic ◇ *C'est une femme très énergique.* She's a very energetic woman.
- **des mesures énergiques** strong measures
énerver VERB
- **Il m'énerve!** He gets on my nerves!
- **Ce bruit m'énerve.** This noise gets on my nerves.
- **s'énerver** to get worked up
- **Ne t'énerve pas!** Take it easy!
l'**enfance** FEM NOUN
childhood
- **Je le connais depuis l'enfance.** I've known him since I was a child.
l'**enfant** MASC/FEM NOUN
child
l'**enfer** MASC NOUN
hell
s'enfermer VERB
- **Il s'est enfermé dans sa chambre.** He shut himself up in his bedroom.
enfiler VERB
1 **to put on** ◇ *J'ai rapidement enfilé un pull avant de sortir.* I quickly put on a sweater before going out.
2 **to thread** ◇ *J'ai du mal à enfiler cette aiguille.* I am having difficulty

threading this needle.
enfin ADVERB
at last ◇ *J'ai enfin réussi à le joindre.* I have at last managed to contact him.
enflé ADJECTIVE
swollen
enfler VERB
to swell
enfoncer VERB
- **Il marchait, les mains enfoncées dans les poches.** He was walking with his hands thrust into his pockets.
- **s'enfoncer** to sink ◇ *Les roues de la voiture s'enfonçaient dans la boue.* The wheels of the car were sinking into the mud.
s'enfuir VERB
to run off
l'**engagement** MASC NOUN
commitment
s'engager VERB
to commit oneself ◇ *Le Premier ministre s'est engagé à combattre le chômage.* The Prime Minister has committed himself to fighting unemployment.
- **Il s'est engagé dans l'armée à dix-huit ans.** He joined the army when he was 18.
les **engelures** FEM NOUN
chilblains
l'**engin** MASC NOUN
machine
s'engourdir VERB
to go numb ◇ *Mes doigts se sont engourdis avec le froid.* My fingers have gone numb with the cold.
engueuler VERB (*informal*)
- **engueuler quelqu'un** to tell somebody off ◇ *Tu vas te faire engueuler!* You're going to get a telling-off!
l'**énigme** FEM NOUN
riddle
s'enivrer VERB
to get drunk
enjamber VERB
to stride over ◇ *enjamber une barrière* to stride over a fence
l'**enlèvement** MASC NOUN
kidnapping
enlever VERB
1 **to take off** ◇ *Enlève donc ton manteau!* Take off your coat!
2 **to kidnap** ◇ *Un groupe terroriste a enlevé la femme de l'ambassadeur.* A terrorist group has kidnapped the ambassador's wife.
enneigé ADJECTIVE
snowed up ◇ *Les routes sont encore*

enneigées. The roads are still snowed up.

l'**ennemi** MASC NOUN
enemy

l'**ennemie** FEM NOUN
enemy

l'**ennui** MASC NOUN
1 **boredom** ◇ C'est à mourir d'ennui. It's enough to bore you to death.
2 **problem** ◇ avoir des ennuis to have problems

ennuyer VERB
to bother ◇ J'espère que cela ne vous ennuie pas trop. I hope it doesn't bother you too much.
- **s'ennuyer** to be bored

ennuyeux ADJECTIVE
(FEM SING **ennuyeuse**)
1 **boring**
2 **awkward** ◇ Tu ne peux pas venir plus tôt? C'est bien ennuyeux. You can't come any earlier? That's rather awkward.

énorme ADJECTIVE
huge

énormément ADVERB
- **Il a énormément grossi.** He's got terribly fat.
- **Il y a énormément de neige.** There's an enormous amount of snow.

l'**enquête** FEM NOUN
1 **investigation** ◇ La police a ouvert une enquête. The police have begun an investigation.
2 **survey** ◇ une enquête parmi les étudiants a montré que... a survey of students has shown that...

enquêter VERB
to investigate ◇ La police enquête actuellement sur le crime. The police are currently investigating the crime.

enrageant ADJECTIVE
infuriating

enrager VERB
to be furious ◇ J'enrage de n'avoir pas pu profiter de cette occasion. I'm furious I wasn't able to take advantage of this opportunity.

l'**enregistrement** MASC NOUN
recording
- **l'enregistrement des bagages** baggage check-in

enregistrer VERB
1 **to record** ◇ Ils viennent d'enregistrer un nouvel album. They've just recorded a new album.
2 **to check in** ◇ Vous pouvez enregistrer plusieurs valises. You can check in several cases.

s'**enrhumer** VERB
to catch a cold ◇ Je suis enrhumé. I've got a cold.

s'**enrichir** VERB
to get rich

enrouler VERB
to wind ◇ Enroulez le fil autour de la bobine. Wind the thread round the bobbin.

l'**enseignant** MASC NOUN
teacher

l'**enseignante** FEM NOUN
teacher

l'**enseignement** MASC NOUN
1 **education** ◇ les réformes de l'enseignement education reforms
2 **teaching** ◇ l'enseignement des langues étrangères the teaching of foreign languages

enseigner VERB
to teach ◇ Mon père enseigne les maths dans un lycée. My father teaches maths in a secondary school.

ensemble ADVERB
see also **ensemble** NOUN
together ◇ tous ensemble all together

l'**ensemble** NOUN
see also **ensemble** ADVERB
outfit ◇ Elle portait un ensemble vert. She was wearing a green outfit.
- **l'ensemble de** the whole of ◇ La grève a été suivie par l'ensemble du personnel. The whole workforce went on strike.
- **dans l'ensemble** on the whole

ensoleillé ADJECTIVE
sunny

ensuite ADVERB
then ◇ Nous sommes allés au cinéma et ensuite au restaurant. We went to the cinema and then to a restaurant.

entamer VERB
to start ◇ Qui a entamé le gâteau? Who's started the cake?

s'**entasser** VERB
to cram ◇ Ils se sont tous entassés dans ma voiture. They all crammed into my car.

entendre VERB
1 **to hear** ◇ Je ne t'entends pas. I can't hear you.
- **J'ai entendu dire qu'il est dangereux de nager ici.** I've heard that it's dangerous to swim here.
2 **to mean** ◇ Qu'est-ce que tu entends par là? What do you mean by that?
- **s'entendre** to get on ◇ Il s'entend

bien avec sa sœur. He gets on well with his sister.

entendu ADJECTIVE
- **C'est entendu!** Agreed! ◇ *Je passerai te prendre à sept heures, c'est entendu.* That's agreed then, I'll pick you up at 7 o'clock.
- **bien entendu** of course ◇ *Il est bien entendu que je n'en parlerai à personne.* I won't tell anybody about it of course.

l'**enterrement** MASC NOUN
funeral (*burial*)

enterrer VERB
to bury

entêté ADJECTIVE
stubborn

s'**entêter** VERB
to persist ◇ *Il s'entête à refuser de voir le médecin.* He persists in refusing to go to the doctor.

l'**enthousiasme** MASC NOUN
enthusiasm

s'**enthousiasmer** VERB
to get enthusiastic ◇ *Il s'enthousiasme facilement.* He gets very enthusiastic about things.

entier ADJECTIVE
(FEM SING **entière**)
whole ◇ *Il a mangé une quiche entière.* He ate the whole quiche. ◇ *Je n'ai pas lu le livre en entier.* I haven't read the whole book.
- **le lait entier** full fat milk

entièrement ADVERB
completely

l'**entorse** FEM NOUN
sprain ◇ *Il s'est fait une entorse à la cheville.* He's sprained his ankle.

entourer VERB
to surround ◇ *Le jardin est entouré d'un mur de pierres.* The garden is surrounded by a stone wall.

l'**entracte** MASC NOUN
interval

l'**entraînement** MASC NOUN
training

entraîner VERB
1. **to lead** ◇ *Il se laisse facilement entraîner par les autres.* He's easily led.
2. **to train** ◇ *Il entraîne l'équipe de France depuis cinq ans.* He's been training the French team for five years.
3. **to involve** ◇ *Un mariage entraîne beaucoup de dépenses.* A wedding involves a lot of expense.
- **s'entraîner** to train ◇ *Il s'entraîne au foot tous les samedis matins.* He does football training every Saturday morning.

l'**entraîneur** MASC NOUN
trainer

entre PREPOSITION
between ◇ *Il est assis entre son père et son oncle.* He's sitting between his father and his uncle.
- **entre eux** among themselves
- **l'un d'entre eux** one of them

l'**entrecôte** FEM NOUN
rib steak

l'**entrée** FEM NOUN
1. **entrance**
2. **starter** (*of meal*) ◇ *Qu'est ce que vous prenez comme entrée?* What would like for the starter?

entreprendre VERB
to start on ◇ *Elle a entrepris des démarches pour essayer d'adopter un enfant.* She's started on the procedures for adopting a child.

l'**entrepreneur** MASC NOUN
contractor

l'**entreprise** FEM NOUN
firm

entrer VERB
1. **to come in** ◇ *Entrez donc!* Come on in!
2. **to go in** ◇ *Ils sont tous entrés dans la maison.* They all went into the house.
- **entrer à l'hôpital** to go into hospital

entre-temps ADVERB
meanwhile

l'**entretien** MASC NOUN
1. **maintenance** ◇ *un contrat d'entretien* a maintenance contract
2. **interview** ◇ *On m'a convoqué à un entretien pour un travail.* I've been called for a job interview.

l'**entrevue** FEM NOUN
interview ◇ *une entrevue avec le ministre* an interview with the minister

entrouvert ADJECTIVE
half-open ◇ *La porte était entrouverte.* The door was half open.

envahir VERB
to invade

l'**enveloppe** FEM NOUN
envelope

envelopper VERB
to wrap

envers PREPOSITION
see also **envers** NOUN
towards ◇ *Il est bien disposé envers elle.* He's well disposed towards her. ◇ *son attitude envers moi* his attitude to me

l'**envers** MASC NOUN
see also **envers** PREPOSITION

- **à l'envers** inside out ◇ *Je dois repasser ce chemisier à l'envers.* I have to iron this blouse inside out.

l'**envie** FEM NOUN
- **avoir envie de faire quelque chose** to feel like doing something ◇ *J'avais envie de pleurer.* I felt like crying. ◇ *J'ai envie d'aller aux toilettes.* I want to go to the toilet.
- **Cette glace me fait envie.** I fancy some of that ice cream.

envier VERB
 to envy

environ ADVERB
 about ◇ *C'est à soixante kilomètres environ.* It's about 60 kilometres.

l'**environnement** MASC NOUN
 environment

les**environs** MASC NOUN
 area ◇ *les environs de Nantes* the Nantes area ◇ *Il y a beaucoup de choses intéressantes à voir dans les environs.* There are a lot of interesting things to see in the area.
- **aux environs de dix-neuf heures** around 7 p.m.

envisager VERB
 to consider ◇ *Est-ce que vous envisagez de travailler à l'étranger?* Are you considering working abroad?

s'**envoler** VERB
 1 **to fly away** ◇ *Le papillon s'est envolé.* The butterfly flew away.
 2 **to blow away** ◇ *Toutes mes feuilles de cours se sont envolées.* All my lecture notes blew away.

envoyer VERB
 to send ◇ *Ma tante m'a envoyé une carte pour mon anniversaire.* My aunt sent me a card for my birthday.
- **envoyer quelqu'un chercher quelque chose** to send somebody to get something ◇ *Sa mère l'a envoyé chercher du pain.* His mother sent him to get some bread.

épais ADJECTIVE
 (FEM SING **épaisse**)
 thick

l'**épaisseur** FEM NOUN
 thickness

épatant ADJECTIVE (*informal*)
 great ◇ *C'est un type épatant.* He's a great guy.

l'**épaule** FEM NOUN
 shoulder

l'**épée** FEM NOUN
 sword

épeler VERB
 to spell ◇ *Est-ce que vous pouvez*

épeler votre nom s'il vous plaît? Can you spell your name please?

l'**épice** FEM NOUN
 spice

épicé ADJECTIVE
 spicy ◇ *Ce n'est pas assez épicé pour moi: je trouve ça trop fade.* It's not spicy enough for me: I think it's too bland.

l'**épicerie** FEM NOUN
 grocer's shop

l'**épicier** MASC NOUN
 grocer

l'**épicière** FEM NOUN
 grocer

l'**épidémie** FEM NOUN
 epidemic

épiler VERB
- **s'épiler les jambes** to shave one's legs
- **s'épiler les sourcils** to pluck one's eyebrows

les**épinards** MASC NOUN
 spinach

l'**épine** FEM NOUN
 thorn

l'**épingle** FEM NOUN
 pin
- **une épingle de sûreté** a safety pin

l'**épisode** MASC NOUN
 episode

éplucher VERB
 to peel

l'**éponge** FEM NOUN
 sponge

l'**époque** FEM NOUN
 time ◇ *à cette époque de l'année* at this time of year
- **à l'époque** at that time ◇ *À l'époque, beaucoup de gens n'avaient pas l'eau courante.* At that time a lot of people didn't have running water.

l'**épouse** FEM NOUN
 wife

épouser VERB
 to marry

épouvantable ADJECTIVE
 awful

l'**épouvante** FEM NOUN
 terror
- **un film d'épouvante** a horror film

épouvanter VERB
 to terrify

l'**époux** MASC NOUN
 husband
- **les nouveaux époux** the newly-weds

l'**épreuve** FEM NOUN
 1 **test** ◇ *une épreuve orale* an oral test ◇ *une épreuve écrite* a written test

2 **event** (*sport*)

éprouver VERB

to feel ◇ *Qu'est-ce que vous avez éprouvé à ce moment-là?* What did you feel at that moment?

épuisé ADJECTIVE

exhausted

épuiser VERB

to wear out ◇ *Ce travail m'a complètement épuisé.* This job has completely worn me out.

◆ **s'épuiser** to wear oneself out ◇ *Il s'épuise à garder un jardin impeccable.* He wears himself out keeping his garden immaculate.

l'**Équateur** MASC NOUN

Ecuador

l'**équateur** MASC NOUN

equator

l'**équation** FEM NOUN

equation

l'**équerre** FEM NOUN

set square

l'**équilibre** MASC NOUN

balance ◇ *J'ai failli perdre l'équilibre.* I nearly lost my balance.

équilibré ADJECTIVE

well-balanced

l'**équipage** MASC NOUN

crew

l'**équipe** FEM NOUN

team

équipé ADJECTIVE

◆ **bien équipé** well-equipped

l'**équipement** MASC NOUN

equipment

les **équipements** MASC NOUN

facilities ◇ *les équipements sportifs* sports facilities

l'**équitation** FEM NOUN

riding ◇ *faire de l'équitation* to go riding

l'**équivalent** MASC NOUN

equivalent

l'**erreur** FEM NOUN

mistake

◆ **faire erreur** to be mistaken

es VERB *see* **être**

◆ **Tu es très gentille.** You're very kind.

l'**escabeau** MASC NOUN

(PL les **escabeaux**)

stepladder

l'**escalade** FEM NOUN

climbing ◇ *faire de l'escalade* to go climbing

escalader VERB

to climb

l'**escale** FEM NOUN

◆ **faire escale** to stop off

l'**escalier** MASC NOUN

stairs

l'**escargot** MASC NOUN

snail

l'**esclavage** MASC NOUN

slavery

l'**esclave** MASC/FEM NOUN

slave

l'**escrime** FEM NOUN

fencing

l'**escroc** MASC NOUN

crook

l'**espace** MASC NOUN

space

s'**espacer** VERB

to become less frequent ◇ *Ses visites se sont peu à peu espacées.* His visits became less and less frequent.

l'**espadrille** FEM NOUN

rope-soled sandal

l'**Espagne** FEM NOUN

Spain

◆ **en Espagne (1)** in Spain

◆ **en Espagne (2)** to Spain

espagnol ADJECTIVE, NOUN

Spanish ◇ *J'apprends l'espagnol.* I'm learning Spanish.

◆ **un Espagnol** a Spaniard (*man*)

◆ **une Espagnole** a Spaniard (*woman*)

l'**espèce** FEM NOUN

1 **sort** ◇ *Elle portait une espèce de cape en velours.* She was wearing a sort of velvet cloak.

2 **species** ◇ *une espèce en voie de disparition* an endangered species

◆ **Espèce d'idiot!** You idiot!

les **espèces** FEM NOUN

cash ◇ *payer en espèces* to pay cash

espérer VERB

to hope

◆ **J'espère bien.** I hope so. ◇ *Tu penses avoir réussi?—Oui, j'espère bien.* Do you think you've passed?–Yes, I hope so.

espiègle ADJECTIVE

mischievous

l'**espion** MASC NOUN

spy

l'**espionnage** MASC NOUN

spying

◆ **un roman d'espionnage** a spy novel

l'**espionne** FEM NOUN

spy

l'**espoir** MASC NOUN

hope

l'**esprit** MASC NOUN

mind ◇ *Ça ne m'est pas venu à l'esprit.* It didn't cross my mind.

◆ **avoir de l'esprit** to be witty ◇ *Il a*

beaucoup d'esprit. He's very witty.

l'**esquimau** ®
(PL les esquimaux) MASC NOUN
ice lolly

l'**Esquimau** MASC NOUN
(PL les Esquimaux)
Eskimo

l'**Esquimaude** FEM NOUN
Eskimo

l'**essai** MASC NOUN
attempt ◇ *Ce n'est pas mal pour un coup d'essai.* It's not bad for a first attempt.
- **prendre quelqu'un à l'essai** to take somebody on for a trial period

essayer VERB
[1] **to try** ◇ *Essaie de rentrer de bonne heure.* Try to come home early.
[2] **to try on** ◇ *Essaie donc ce pull: il devrait bien t'aller.* Try this sweater on: it ought to look good on you.

l'**essence** FEM NOUN
petrol

essentiel ADJECTIVE
(FEM SING essentielle)
essential
- **Tu es là: c'est l'essentiel.** You're here: that's the main thing.

s'**essouffler** VERB
to get out of breath

l'**essuie-glace** MASC NOUN
windscreen wiper

essuyer VERB
to wipe
- **essuyer la vaisselle** to dry the dishes
- **s'essuyer** to dry oneself ◇ *Vous pouvez vous essuyer les mains avec cette serviette.* You can dry your hands on this towel.

est VERB *see* **être**
[see also est ADJECTIVE, NOUN]
- **Elle est merveilleuse.** She's marvellous.

est ADJECTIVE
[see also est VERB, NOUN]
[1] **east** ◇ *la côte est des États-Unis* the east coast of the United States
[2] **eastern** ◇ *dans la partie est du pays* in the eastern part of the country

l'**est** MASC NOUN
[see also est VERB, ADJECTIVE]
east ◇ *Je vis dans l'est de la France.* I live in the East of France.
- **vers l'est** eastwards
- **à l'est de Paris** east of Paris
- **l'Europe de l'Est** Eastern Europe
- **le vent d'est** the east wind

est-ce que ADVERB
- **Est-ce que c'est cher?** Is it expensive?

- **Quand est-ce qu'il part?** When is he leaving?

l'**esthéticienne** FEM NOUN
beautician

l'**estime** FEM NOUN
- **J'ai beaucoup d'estime pour elle.** I think a lot of her.

estimer VERB
- **estimer quelqu'un** to have great respect for somebody ◇ *Mon père l'estime beaucoup.* My father has a lot of respect for him.
- **estimer que** to consider that ◇ *J'estime que c'est de sa faute.* I consider that it's his fault.

l'**estivant** MASC NOUN
holiday-maker

l'**estivante** FEM NOUN
holiday-maker

l'**estomac** MASC NOUN
stomach

l'**Estonie** FEM NOUN
Estonia

l'**estrade** FEM NOUN
platform

et CONJUNCTION
and

établir VERB
to establish
- **s'établir à son compte** to set up in business

l'**établissement** MASC NOUN
establishment
- **un établissement scolaire** a school

l'**étage** MASC NOUN
floor ◇ *au premier étage* on the first floor
- **à l'étage** upstairs

l'**étagère** FEM NOUN
shelf

étaient VERB *see* **être**

l'**étain** MASC NOUN
tin

étais, était VERB *see* **être**
- **Il était très jeune.** He was very young.

l'**étalage** MASC NOUN
display

étaler VERB
to spread ◇ *Il a étalé la carte sur la table.* He spread the map on the table.

étanche ADJECTIVE
[1] **watertight** ◇ *La toiture n'est pas étanche.* The roof isn't watertight.
[2] **waterproof** (*watch*)

l'**étang** MASC NOUN
pond

étant VERB *see* **être**
- **Mes revenus étant limités...** My income being limited...

l' **étape** FEM NOUN
stage ◇ *une étape importante de la vie* an important stage in life
+ **faire étape** to stop off

l' **État** MASC NOUN
state (*nation*) ◇ *un chef d'État* a head of state

l' **état** MASC NOUN
1 **state** (*country*)
2 **condition** ◇ *en mauvais état* in poor condition
+ **remettre quelque chose en état** to repair something
+ **le bureau d'état civil** the registry office

les **États-Unis** MASC NOUN
United States
+ **aux États-Unis (1)** in the United States
+ **aux États-Unis (2)** to the United States

été VERB *see* **être**
see also été NOUN
+ **Il a été promu.** He's been promoted.

l' **été** MASC NOUN
see also été VERB
summer
+ **en été** in the summer

éteindre VERB
1 **to switch off** ◇ *N'oubliez pas d'éteindre la lumière en sortant.* Don't forget to switch off the light when you leave.
2 **to put out** (*cigarette*)

étendre VERB
to spread ◇ *Elle a étendu une nappe propre sur la table.* She spread a clean cloth on the table.
+ **étendre le linge** to hang out the washing
+ **s'étendre** to lie down ◇ *Je vais m'étendre cinq minutes.* I'm going to lie down for five minutes.

l' **éternité** FEM NOUN
+ **J'ai attendu une éternité chez le médecin.** I waited for ages at the doctor's.

éternuer VERB
to sneeze

êtes VERB *see* **être**
+ **Vous êtes en retard.** You're late.

étiez VERB *see* **être**

étinceler VERB
to sparkle

étions VERB *see* **être**

l' **étiquette** FEM NOUN
label ◇ *L'étiquette du pot de confiture s'est décollée.* The label has come off the jam pot.

s' **étirer** VERB
to stretch ◇ *Elle s'est étirée paresseusement.* She stretched lazily.

l' **étoile** FEM NOUN
star
+ **une étoile de mer** a starfish
+ **une étoile filante** a shooting star
+ **dormir à la belle étoile** to sleep under the stars

étonnant ADJECTIVE
amazing

étonner VERB
to surprise ◇ *Cela m'étonnerait que le colis soit déjà arrivé.* I'd be surprised if the parcel had arrived yet.

étouffer VERB
+ **On étouffe ici: ouvre donc les fenêtres.** It's stifling in here: open the windows.
+ **s'étouffer** to choke ◇ *Ne mange pas si vite: tu vas t'étouffer!* Don't eat so fast: you'll choke!

l' **étourderie** FEM NOUN
absent-mindedness
+ **une erreur d'étourderie** a slip

étourdi ADJECTIVE
scatterbrained

l' **étourdissement** MASC NOUN
+ **avoir des étourdissements** to feel dizzy

étrange ADJECTIVE
strange

étranger ADJECTIVE
(FEM SING **étrangère**)
see also étranger NOUN
foreign ◇ *un pays étranger* a foreign country
+ **une personne étrangère** a stranger

l' **étranger** MASC NOUN
see also étranger ADJECTIVE
1 **foreigner**
2 **stranger**
+ **à l'étranger** abroad

l' **étrangère** FEM NOUN
1 **foreigner**
2 **stranger**

étrangler VERB
to strangle

l' **être** MASC NOUN
see also être VERB
+ **un être humain** a human being

être VERB
see also être NOUN

Present tense:	
je suis	nous sommes
tu es	vous êtes
il/elle est	ils/elles sont
Past participle: été	

1 **to be** ◇ *Je suis heureux.* I'm happy. ◇ *Mon père est instituteur.* My father's a primary school teacher. ◇ *Il est dix heures.* It's 10 o'clock.

2 to have ⋄ *Il n'est pas encore arrivé.* He hasn't arrived yet.

les **étrennes** FEM NOUN
- **Nous avons donné des étrennes à la gardienne.** We gave the caretaker a New Year gift.

étroit ADJECTIVE
   narrow
- **être à l'étroit** to be cramped ⋄ *Nous sommes un peu à l'étroit dans cet appartement.* We're a bit cramped in this flat.

l' **étude** FEM NOUN
   study ⋄ *une étude de cas* a case study
- **faire des études** to be studying ⋄ *Il fait des études de droit.* He's studying law.

l' **étudiant** MASC NOUN
   student

l' **étudiante** FEM NOUN
   student

étudier VERB
   to study

l' **étui** MASC NOUN
   case ⋄ *un étui à lunettes* a glasses case

eu VERB *see* **avoir**
- **J'ai eu une bonne note.** I got a good mark.

euh EXCLAMATION
   er ⋄ *Euh...je ne m'en souviens pas.* Er...I can't remember.

l' **Europe** FEM NOUN
   Europe
- **en Europe (1)** in Europe
- **en Europe (2)** to Europe

européen ADJECTIVE
   (FEM SING **européenne**)
   European

eux PRONOUN
   them ⋄ *Je pense souvent à eux.* I often think of them.
   eux *is also used for emphasis.*
   ⋄ *Elle a accepté l'invitation, mais eux ont refusé.* She accepted the invitation, but THEY refused.

évacuer VERB
   to evacuate

s' **évader** VERB
   to escape

l' **évangile** MASC NOUN
   gospel

s' **évanouir** VERB
   to faint

s' **évaporer** VERB
   to evaporate

évasif ADJECTIVE
   (FEM SING **évasive**)

evasive

l' **évasion** FEM NOUN
   escape ⋄ *Ils ont préparé leur évasion pendant des mois.* They spent months planning their escape.

éveillé ADJECTIVE
   1 awake ⋄ *Il est resté éveillé toute la nuit.* He stayed awake all night.
   2 bright ⋄ *C'est un enfant très éveillé pour son âge.* He's very bright for his age.

s' **éveiller** VERB
   to awaken

l' **événement** MASC NOUN
   event

l' **éventail** MASC NOUN
   fan (*hand-held*)
- **un large éventail de prix** a wide range of prices

l' **éventualité** FEM NOUN
- **dans l'éventualité d'un retard** in the event of a delay

éventuel ADJECTIVE
   (FEM SING **éventuelle**)
   possible ⋄ *une solution éventuelle* a possible solution ⋄ *les conséquences éventuelles* the possible consequences

éventuellement ADVERB
   possibly ⋄ *Nous pourrions éventuellement avoir besoin de vous.* We may need you. ⋄ *les difficultés que vous pourriez éventuellement rencontrer* the difficulties that you may have

l' **évêque** MASC NOUN
   bishop

évidemment ADVERB
   1 obviously ⋄ *Les tomates sont évidemment chères en cette saison.* Tomatoes are obviously dear at this time of year.
   2 of course ⋄ *Est-ce que je peux utiliser ton téléphone?–Évidemment, tu n'as pas besoin de demander.* Can I use your phone?–Of course, you don't need to ask.

l' **évidence** FEM NOUN
- **C'est une évidence.** It's quite obvious.
- **de toute évidence** obviously ⋄ *De toute évidence, il ne veut pas nous voir.* Obviously he doesn't want to see us.
- **être en évidence** to be clearly visible ⋄ *La lettre était en évidence sur la table.* The letter was clearly visible on the table.
- **mettre en évidence** to reveal

évident ADJECTIVE
   obvious

l' **évier** MASC NOUN
   sink

éviter VERB
to avoid

évolué ADJECTIVE
advanced

évoluer VERB
to progress ◇ *La chirurgie esthétique a beaucoup évolué.* Plastic surgery has progressed a great deal.
- **Il a beaucoup évolué.** He has come on a great deal.

l'**évolution** FEM NOUN
1 **development** ◇ *une évolution rapide* rapid development
2 **evolution** ◇ *la théorie de l'évolution* the theory of evolution

évoquer VERB
to mention ◇ *Il a évoqué divers problèmes dans son discours.* He mentioned various problems in his speech.

exact ADJECTIVE
1 **right** ◇ *Avez-vous l'heure exacte?* Have you got the right time? ◇ *Votre voiture est garée dehors, n'est-ce pas? –C'est exact.* Your car's parked outside, isn't it?–That's right.
2 **exact** ◇ *Est-ce que vous pouvez m'indiquer le prix exact du billet?* Can you tell me the exact price of the ticket?

exactement ADVERB
exactly ◇ *C'est exactement ce que je cherchais.* That's exactly what I was looking for.

ex aequo ADJECTIVE
- **Ils sont arrivés ex aequo.** They finished neck and neck.

exagérer VERB
1 **to exaggerate** ◇ *Vous exagérez!* You're exaggerating!
2 **to go too far** ◇ *Ça fait trois fois que tu arrives en retard: tu exagères!* That's three times you've been late: you really go too far sometimes!

l'**examen** MASC NOUN
exam ◇ *Nous allons passer l'examen d'anglais vendredi matin.* We're doing our English exam on Friday morning. ◇ *un examen de français* a French exam
- **un examen médical** a medical

examiner VERB
to examine

exaspérant ADJECTIVE
infuriating

exaspérer VERB
to infuriate

l'**excédent** MASC NOUN
- **l' excédent de bagages** excess baggage

excéder VERB
to exceed ◇ *un contrat dont la durée n'excède pas deux ans* a contract for a period not exceeding two years
- **excéder quelqu'un** to drive somebody mad ◇ *Les cris des enfants l'excédaient.* The noise of the children was driving her mad.

excellent ADJECTIVE
excellent

excentrique ADJECTIVE
eccentric

excepté PREPOSITION
except ◇ *Toutes les chaussures excepté les sandales sont en solde.* All the shoes except sandals are reduced.

l'**exception** FEM NOUN
exception

exceptionnel ADJECTIVE
(FEM SING **exceptionnelle**)
exceptional

l'**excès** MASC NOUN
- **faire des excès** to overindulge ◇ *On fait souvent des excès aux environs de Noël.* People often overindulge around Christmas.
- **les excès de vitesse** speeding

excessif ADJECTIVE
(FEM SING **excessive**)
excessive

excitant ADJECTIVE
see also excitant NOUN
exciting

l'**excitant** MASC NOUN
see also excitant ADJECTIVE
stimulant ◇ *Le thé et le café sont des excitants.* Tea and coffee are stimulants.

l'**excitation** FEM NOUN
excitement

exciter VERB
to excite ◇ *Il était tout excité à l'idée de revoir ses cousins.* He was all excited about seeing his cousins again.
- **s'exciter** (*informal*) to get excited ◇ *Ne t'excite pas trop vite: ça ne va peut-être pas marcher!* Don't get excited too soon: it may not work!

l'**exclamation** FEM NOUN
exclamation

exclu ADJECTIVE
- **Il n'est pas exclu que...** It's not impossible that...

exclusif ADJECTIVE
(FEM SING **exclusive**)
exclusive

l'**excursion** FEM NOUN
1 **trip** ◇ *faire une excursion* to go on a trip

2 **walk** ◇ *une excursion dans la montagne* a walk in the hills

l'**excuse** FEM NOUN
1 **excuse** ◇ *Il trouve toujours une bonne excuse pour ne pas faire la vaisselle.* He always finds a good excuse for not doing the washing-up.
2 **apology** ◇ *présenter ses excuses* to offer one's apologies
- **un mot d'excuse** a note ◇ *Vous devez apporter un mot d'excuse signé par vos parents.* You have to bring a note signed by your parents.

excuser VERB
to excuse
- **Excusez-moi. (1)** Sorry!
  ◇ *Excusez-moi, je ne vous avais pas vu.* Sorry, I didn't see you.
- **Excusez-moi. (2)** Excuse me.
  ◇ *Excusez-moi, est-ce que vous avez l'heure?* Excuse me, have you got the time?
- **s'excuser** to apologize ◇ *Il s'est excusé de son retard.* He apologized for being late.

exécuter VERB
1 **to execute** ◇ *Le prisonnier a été exécuté à l'aube.* The prisoner was executed at dawn.
2 **to perform** ◇ *Le pianiste va maintenant exécuter une valse de Chopin.* The pianist is now going to perform a waltz by Chopin.

l'**exemplaire** MASC NOUN
copy

l'**exemple** MASC NOUN
example ◇ *donner l'exemple* to set an example
- **par exemple** for example

s'**exercer** VERB
to practise

l'**exercice** MASC NOUN
exercise

exhiber VERB
to show off ◇ *Il aime bien exhiber ses décorations.* He likes showing off his medals.
- **s'exhiber** to expose oneself

l'**exhibitionniste** MASC NOUN
flasher

exigeant ADJECTIVE
hard to please ◇ *Elle est vraiment exigeante.* She's really hard to please.

exiger VERB
1 **to demand** ◇ *Le propriétaire exige d'être payé immédiatement.* The landlord is demanding to be paid immediately.
2 **to require** ◇ *Ce travail exige*

beaucoup de patience. This job requires a lot of patience.

l'**exil** MASC NOUN
exile

exister VERB
to exist ◇ *Ça n'existe pas.* It doesn't exist. ◇ *Ce manteau existe également en rose.* This coat's also available in pink.

exotique ADJECTIVE
exotic ◇ *une plante exotique* an exotic plant ◇ *un yaourt aux fruits exotiques* a tropical fruit yoghurt

expédier VERB
to send ◇ *expédier un colis* to send a parcel

l'**expéditeur** MASC NOUN
sender

l'**expédition** FEM NOUN
expedition
- **l'expédition du courrier** the dispatch of the mail

l'**expéditrice** FEM NOUN
sender

l'**expérience** FEM NOUN
1 **experience** ◇ *Elle a plusieurs années d'expérience.* She's got several years' experience.
2 **experiment** ◇ *une expérience de chimie* a chemistry experiment

expérimenter VERB
to test ◇ *Ces produits de beauté n'ont pas été expérimentés sur des animaux.* These cosmetics have not been tested on animals.

l'**expert** MASC NOUN
expert

l'**explication** FEM NOUN
explanation
- **une explication de texte** a critical analysis (of a text)

expliquer VERB
to explain ◇ *Il m'a expliqué comment faire.* He explained to me how to do it.
- **ça s'explique** it's understandable

l'**exploit** MASC NOUN
achievement

l'**exploitation** FEM NOUN
exploitation ◇ *Cet organisme lutte contre l'exploitation des femmes.* This organization fights against the exploitation of women.
- **une exploitation agricole** a farm

exploiter VERB
to exploit ◇ *Il s'est fait exploiter par le patron du restaurant.* He was exploited by the owner of the restaurant.

explorer VERB
  to explore
exploser VERB
  to explode ◇ *La bombe a explosé en pleine rue.* The bomb exploded in the middle of the street.
l'**explosif** MASC NOUN
  explosive
l'**explosion** FEM NOUN
  explosion
l'**exportateur** MASC NOUN
  exporter
l'**exportation** FEM NOUN
  export
l'**exportatrice** FEM NOUN
  exporter
exporter VERB
  to export
l'**exposé** MASC NOUN
  talk ◇ *On nous a demandé de faire un exposé sur l'environnement.* We were asked to give a talk on the environment.
exposer VERB
  1 to show ◇ *Il expose ses peintures dans une galerie d'art.* He shows his paintings in a private art gallery.
  2 to expose ◇ *N'exposez pas la pellicule à la lumière.* Do not expose the film to light.
  3 to set out ◇ *Il nous a exposé les raisons de son départ.* He set out the reasons for his departure.
  • **s'exposer au soleil** to stay out in the sun ◇ *Ne vous exposez pas trop longtemps au soleil.* Don't stay out too long in the sun.
l'**exposition** FEM NOUN
  exhibition ◇ *une exposition de peinture* an exhibition of paintings
exprès ADVERB
  1 on purpose ◇ *Je suis sûr qu'il l'a fait exprès.* I'm sure he did it on purpose.
  2 specially ◇ *Goûtes-y: j'ai fait ce gâteau exprès pour toi.* Have a taste: I made this cake specially for you.
l'**express** MASC NOUN
  1 espresso *(coffee)*
  2 fast train ◇ *Il a décidé de prendre l'express de dix heures.* He decided to catch the fast train at 10 o'clock.
l'**expression** FEM NOUN

  1 expression
  2 phrase
exprimer VERB
  to express
  • **s'exprimer** to express oneself ◇ *Il s'exprime très bien pour un enfant de huit ans.* For a child of 8, he expresses himself very well.
exquis ADJECTIVE
  exquisite
extérieur ADJECTIVE
  see also **extérieur** NOUN
  outside
l'**extérieur** MASC NOUN
  see also **extérieur** ADJECTIVE
  outside
  • **à l'extérieur** outside ◇ *Les toilettes sont à l'extérieur.* The toilet is outside.
l'**externat** MASC NOUN
  day school
l'**externe** MASC/FEM NOUN
  day pupil
l'**extincteur** MASC NOUN
  fire extinguisher
extra ADJECTIVE (MASC, FEM, PL)
  excellent ◇ *Ce fromage est extra!* This cheese is excellent!
  • **des haricots extra fins** top quality French beans
extraire VERB
  to extract
l'**extrait** MASC NOUN
  extract
extraordinaire ADJECTIVE
  extraordinary
extravagant ADJECTIVE
  extravagant
extrême ADJECTIVE
  see also **extrême** NOUN
  extreme ◇ *l'extrême droite et l'extrême gauche* the far right and the far left
l'**extrême** MASC NOUN
  see also **extrême** ADJECTIVE
  extreme
extrêmement ADVERB
  extremely
l'**Extrême-Orient** MASC NOUN
  the Far East
l'**extrémité** FEM NOUN
  end ◇ *La gare est à l'autre extrémité de la ville.* The station is at the other end of the town.

F

F. ABBREVIATION
   franc
fa NOUN
   F
fabrication NOUN
   manufacture
fabriquer VERB
   to make ◇ *fabriqué en France* made in France
 - **Qu'est-ce qu'il fabrique?** (*informal*) What's he up to?
fac NOUN (*informal*)
   university
face NOUN
 - **face à face** face to face
 - **en face de** opposite ◇ *Le bus s'arrête en face de chez moi.* The bus stops opposite my house.
 - **faire face à quelque chose** to face something
 - **Pile ou face?—Face.** Heads or tails? —Heads.
fâché ADJECTIVE
   angry
 - **être fâché contre quelqu'un** to be angry with somebody ◇ *Elle est fâchée contre moi.* She's angry with me.
 - **être fâché avec quelqu'un** to be on bad terms with somebody ◇ *Elle est fâchée avec sa sœur.* She's on bad terms with her sister.
fâcher VERB
 - **se fâcher contre quelqu'un** to lose one's temper with somebody
 - **se fâcher avec quelqu'un** to fall out with somebody ◇ *Il s'est fâché avec son frère.* He's fallen out with his brother.
facile ADJECTIVE
   easy
 - **facile à faire** easy to do
facilement ADVERB
   easily
façon NOUN
   way ◇ *De quelle façon?* In what way?
 - **de toute façon** anyway
facteur NOUN
   postman ◇ *Il est facteur.* He's a postman.
facture NOUN
   bill ◇ *une facture de gaz* a gas bill
facultatif ADJECTIVE
   (FEM SING **facultative**)
   optional

fade ADJECTIVE
   tasteless ◇ *La soupe est un peu fade.* The soup is a bit tasteless.
faible ADJECTIVE
   weak ◇ *Je me sens encore faible.* I still feel a bit weak.
 - **Il est faible en maths.** He's not very good at maths.
la faiblesse NOUN
   weakness
la faïence NOUN
   pottery
faillir VERB
 - **J'ai failli tomber.** I nearly fell.
la faim NOUN
   hunger
 - **avoir faim** to be hungry
fainéant ADJECTIVE
   lazy
faire VERB

Present tense:	
je fais	nous faisons
tu fais	vous faites
il/elle fait	ils/elles font
Past participle: *fait*	

   1 to make ◇ *Je vais faire un gâteau pour ce soir.* I'm going to make a cake for tonight. ◇ *Ils font trop de bruit.* They're making too much noise. ◇ *Je voudrais me faire de nouveaux amis.* I'd like to make new friends.
   2 to do ◇ *Qu'est-ce que tu fais?* What are you doing? ◇ *Il fait de l'italien.* He's doing Italian. ◇ *Qui veut bien faire la vaisselle?* Who'll do the dishes?
   3 to play ◇ *Il fait du piano.* He plays the piano.
   4 to be ◇ *Qu'est-ce qu'il fait chaud!* Isn't it hot! ◇ *Espérons qu'il fera beau demain.* Let's hope it'll be nice weather tomorrow.
 - **faire tomber** to knock over ◇ *Le chat a fait tomber le vase.* The cat knocked over the vase.
 - **faire faire quelque chose** to get something done ◇ *Je dois faire réparer ma voiture.* I've got to get my car repaired.
 - **Je vais me faire couper les cheveux.** I'm going to get my hair cut.
 - **Ne t'en fais pas!** Don't worry!
fais, faisaient, faisais, faisait VERB
   see **faire**
le faisan NOUN
   pheasant

faisiez, faisions, faisons, fait
VERB *see* **faire**

le **fait** NOUN
fact ◇ *Le fait que...* The fact that...
- **au fait** by the way ◇ *Au fait, est-ce que tu as aimé le film d'hier?* By the way, did you enjoy the film yesterday?
- **en fait** actually ◇ *En fait je n'ai pas beaucoup de temps.* I haven't got much time actually.

faites VERB *see* **faire**

la **falaise** NOUN
cliff

falloir VERB *see* **faut, faudra, faudrait**

famé ADJECTIVE
- **un quartier mal famé** a rough area

fameux ADJECTIVE
(FEM SING **fameuse**)
- **Ce n'est pas fameux.** It's not great.

familial ADJECTIVE
(MASC PL **familiaux**)
family ◇ *une atmosphère familiale* a family atmosphere
- **les allocations familiales** child benefit

familier ADJECTIVE
(FEM SING **familière**)
familiar ◇ *C'est un nom qui m'est familier.* The name's familiar.

la **famille** NOUN
1 family ◇ *une famille nombreuse* a big family ◇ *Nous passons Noël en famille.* We have a family Christmas.
2 relatives ◇ *Il a de la famille à Paris.* He's got relatives in Paris.

la **famine** NOUN
famine

la **fanfare** NOUN
band

fantaisie ADJECTIVE
- **des bijoux fantaisie** costume jewellery

fantastique ADJECTIVE
fantastic

le **fantôme** NOUN
ghost

la **farce** NOUN
1 stuffing (*for chicken, turkey*)
2 practical joke ◇ *André aime faire des farces.* André likes to play practical jokes.

farci ADJECTIVE
stuffed ◇ *des tomates farcies* stuffed tomatoes

la **farine** NOUN
flour

fasciner VERB
to fascinate

fasse, fassent, fasses, fassiez, fassions VERB *see* **faire**
- **Pourvu qu'il fasse beau demain!** Let's

hope it'll be fine tomorrow!

fatal ADJECTIVE
fatal
- **C'était fatal.** It was bound to happen.

la **fatalité** NOUN
fate

fatigant ADJECTIVE
tiring

la **fatigue** NOUN
tiredness

fatigué ADJECTIVE
tired

se **fatiguer** VERB
to get tired

fauché ADJECTIVE (*informal*)
hard up

faudra VERB
faudra *is the future tense of* **falloir.**
- **Il faudra qu'on soit plus rapide demain.** We'll have to be quicker tomorrow.

faudrait VERB
faudrait *is the conditional tense of* **falloir.**
- **Il faudrait qu'on fasse attention.** We ought to be careful.

se **faufiler** VERB
- **Il s'est faufilé à travers la foule.** He made his way through the crowd.

la **faune** NOUN
wildlife

fausse ADJECTIVE *see* **faux**

faut VERB
faut *is the present tense of* **falloir.**
- **Il faut faire attention.** You've got to be careful.
- **Nous n'avons pas le choix, il faut y aller.** We've no choice, we've got to go.
- **Il faut que je parte.** I've got to go.
- **Il faut du courage pour faire ce métier.** It takes courage to do that job.

la **faute** NOUN
1 mistake ◇ *faire une faute* to make a mistake
2 fault ◇ *Ce n'est pas de ma faute.* It's not my fault.
- **sans faute** without fail ◇ *Je t'appellerai sans faute.* I'll phone you without fail.

le **fauteuil** NOUN
armchair
- **un fauteuil roulant** a wheelchair

faux ADJECTIVE, ADVERB
(FEM SING **fausse**)
see also faux NOUN
untrue ◇ *C'est entièrement faux.* It's totally untrue.
- **faire un faux pas** to trip
- **Il chante faux.** He sings out of tune.

faux NOUN

see also **faux** ADJECTIVE

fake ◇ *Ce tableau est un faux.* This painting is a fake.

faveur NOUN

favour

favori ADJECTIVE

(FEM SING **favorite**)

favourite

favoriser VERB

to favour ◇ *Ce système d'examen favorise ceux qui ont de la mémoire.* This exam system favours people with good memories.

fax NOUN

fax

fée NOUN

fairy

feignant ADJECTIVE (*informal*)

lazy

félicitations FEM NOUN

congratulations

féliciter VERB

to congratulate

femelle NOUN

female (*animal*)

féminin ADJECTIVE

[1] **female** ◇ *les personnages féminins du roman* the female characters in the novel

[2] **feminine** ◇ *Elle est très féminine.* She's very feminine.

[3] **women's** ◇ *Elle joue dans l'équipe féminine de France.* She plays in the French women's team.

féministe ADJECTIVE

feminist

femme NOUN

[1] **woman**

[2] **wife** ◇ *C'est la femme du directeur.* She's the headmaster's wife.

- **une femme au foyer** a housewife
- **une femme de ménage** a cleaning woman

fendre VERB

to crack

fenêtre NOUN

window

fenouil NOUN

fennel

fente NOUN

slot

fer NOUN

iron

- **un fer à cheval** a horseshoe
- **un fer à repasser** an iron

fera, ferai, feras, ferez VERB *see* **faire**

férié ADJECTIVE

- **un jour férié** a public holiday

feriez, ferions VERB *see* **faire**

ferme ADJECTIVE

see also **ferme** NOUN

firm ◇ *Elle s'est montrée très ferme à mon égard.* She was very firm with me.

la **ferme** NOUN

see also **ferme** ADJECTIVE

farm

fermé ADJECTIVE

[1] **closed** ◇ *La pharmacie est fermée.* The chemist's is closed.

[2] **off** ◇ *Est-ce que le gaz est fermé?* Is the gas off?

fermer VERB

[1] **to close** ◇ *N'oublie pas de fermer la fenêtre.* Don't forget to close the window.

[2] **to turn off** ◇ *As-tu bien fermé le robinet?* Have you turned the tap off?

la **fermeture** NOUN

- **les heures de fermeture** closing times
- **une fermeture éclair** ® a zip

le **fermier** NOUN

farmer

la **fermière** NOUN

[1] **woman farmer**

[2] **farmer's wife**

féroce ADJECTIVE

fierce ◇ *un animal féroce* a fierce animal

ferons, feront VERB *see* **faire**

les **fesses** FEM NOUN

buttocks

le **festival** NOUN

festival

la **fête** NOUN

[1] **party** ◇ *Nous organisons une petite fête pour son anniversaire.* We're having a little party for his birthday.

- **faire la fête** to party

[2] **name day** ◇ *C'est sa fête aujourd'hui.* It's his name day today.

- **une fête foraine** a funfair
- **la Fête Nationale** Bastille Day
- **les fêtes de fin d'année** the festive season

fêter VERB

to celebrate

le **feu** NOUN

(PL les **feux**)

[1] **fire** ◇ *prendre feu* to catch fire ◇ *faire du feu* to make a fire

- **Au feu!** Fire!

[2] **traffic light** ◇ *un feu rouge* a red light ◇ *Tournez à gauche aux feux.* Turn left at the lights.

- **Avez-vous du feu?** Have you got a

F

light?

3 heat ◦ ...*mijoter à feu doux*
...simmer over a gentle heat
- **un feu d'artifice** a firework display

le **feuillage** NOUN
leaves

la **feuille** NOUN
1 leaf ◦ *des feuilles mortes* fallen
leaves
2 sheet ◦ *une feuille de papier* a
sheet of paper
- **une feuille de maladie** a claim form
for medical expenses

feuilleté ADJECTIVE
- **de la pâte feuilletée** flaky pastry

feuilleter VERB
to leaf through

le **feuilleton** NOUN
serial

le **feutre** NOUN
felt
- **un stylo-feutre** a felt-tip pen

la **fève** NOUN
broad bean

février MASC NOUN
February
- **en février** in February

fiable ADJECTIVE
reliable

les **fiançailles** FEM NOUN
engagement SING

fiancé ADJECTIVE
- **être fiancé à quelqu'un** to be engaged
to somebody

se **fiancer** VERB
to get engaged

la **ficelle** NOUN
1 string ◦ *Passe-moi un bout de
ficelle.* Give me a piece of string.
2 thin baguette (*bread*)

la **fiche** NOUN
form ◦ *Remplissez cette fiche s'il
vous plaît.* Fill in this form please.

se **ficher** VERB (*informal*)
- **Je m'en fiche!** I don't care!
- **Fiche-moi la paix!** Leave me alone!
- **Quoi, tu n'as fait que ça? Tu te fiches
de moi!** You've only done that much?
You can't be serious!

fichu ADJECTIVE (*informal*)
- **Ce parapluie est fichu.** This
umbrella's knackered.

fidèle ADJECTIVE
faithful

fier ADJECTIVE
(FEM SING **fière**)
proud

la **fierté** NOUN
pride

la **fièvre** NOUN
fever ◦ *J'ai de la fièvre.* I've got a
temperature. ◦ *Il a trente-neuf de
fièvre.* He's got a temperature of 39°C.

fiévreux ADJECTIVE
(FEM SING **fiévreuse**)
feverish

la **figue** NOUN
fig

la **figure** NOUN
1 face ◦ *Il a reçu le ballon en pleine
figure.* The ball hit him smack in the
face.
2 figure (*illustration*) ◦ *Voir figure 2.1,
page 32.* See figure 2.1, page 32.

le **fil** NOUN
thread ◦ *le fil à coudre* sewing
thread
- **le fil de fer** wire
- **un coup de fil** a phone call

la **file** NOUN
line (*of people, objects*)
- **une file d'attente** a queue ◦ *se
mettre à la file* to join the queue
- **à la file** one after the other
- **en file indienne** in single file

filer VERB
to speed along ◦ *Les voitures
filent sur l'autoroute.* The cars are
speeding along the motorway.
- **File dans ta chambre!** Off to your
room with you!

le **filet** NOUN
net

la **fille** NOUN
1 girl ◦ *C'est une école de filles.* It's
a girls' school.
2 daughter ◦ *C'est leur fille aînée.*
She's their oldest daughter.

la **fillette** NOUN
little girl

le **filleul** NOUN
godson

la **filleule** NOUN
goddaughter

le **film** NOUN
film
- **un film policier** a thriller
- **un film d'aventures** an adventure film
- **un film d'épouvante** a horror film

le **fils** NOUN
son

la **fin** NOUN
see also **fin** ADJECTIVE
end
- **sans fin** endless

fin ADJECTIVE
see also **fin** NOUN
fine

des fines herbes mixed herbs

la **finale** NOUN
final ◇ *les quarts de finale* the quarter finals

finalement ADVERB
[1] **at last** ◇ *Nous sommes finalement arrivés.* At last we arrived.
[2] **after all** ◇ *Finalement, tu avais raison.* You were right after all.

fini ADJECTIVE
finished

finir VERB
to finish ◇ *Le cours finit à onze heures.* The lesson finishes at 11 o'clock. ◇ *Je viens de finir ce livre.* I've just finished this book.
Il a fini par se décider. He made up his mind in the end.

finlandais ADJECTIVE, NOUN
Finnish ◇ *Ils parlent finlandais.* They speak Finnish.
un Finlandais a Finn *(man)*
une Finlandaise a Finn *(woman)*
les Finlandais the Finnish

Finlande NOUN
Finland

firme NOUN
firm

fis VERB *see* **faire**

fissure NOUN
crack

fit VERB *see* **faire**

fixe ADJECTIVE
[1] **steady** ◇ *Il n'a pas d'emploi fixe.* He hasn't got a steady job.
[2] **set** ◇ *Il mange toujours à heures fixes.* He always eats at set times.
un menu à prix fixe a set menu

fixer VERB
[1] **to fix** ◇ *Les volets sont fixés avec des crochets.* The shutters are fixed with hooks. ◇ *Nous avons fixé une heure pour nous retrouver.* We fixed a time to meet.
[2] **to stare at** ◇ *Ne fixe pas les gens comme ça!* Don't stare at people like that!

flacon NOUN
bottle ◇ *un flacon de parfum* a bottle of perfume

flageolet NOUN
small haricot bean

flamand ADJECTIVE, NOUN
(FEM SING **flamande**)
[1] **Flemish** ◇ *Il parle flamand chez lui.* He speaks Flemish at home.
[2] **Fleming** *(Dutch-speaking Belgian)*
les Flamands the Dutch-speaking Belgians

flambé ADJECTIVE
des bananes flambées flambéed bananas

la **flamme** NOUN
flame
en flammes on fire

le **flan** NOUN
baked custard

flâner VERB
to stroll

la **flaque** NOUN
puddle *(of water)*

le **flash** NOUN
(PL les **flashes**)
flash *(of camera)*
un flash d'information a newsflash

flatter VERB
to flatter

la **flèche** NOUN
arrow

les **fléchettes** FEM NOUN
darts ◇ *jouer aux fléchettes* to play darts

la **fleur** NOUN
flower

fleuri ADJECTIVE
[1] **full of flowers** ◇ *Son jardin était très fleuri.* Her garden was full of flowers.
[2] **flowery** ◇ *un papier peint fleuri* flowery wallpaper

fleurir VERB
to flower ◇ *Cette plante fleurit en automne.* This plant flowers in autumn.

le/la **fleuriste** NOUN
florist

le **fleuve** NOUN
river

le **flic** *(informal)* NOUN
cop

le **flipper** NOUN
pinball machine

flirter VERB
to flirt

le **flocon** NOUN
flake

flotter VERB
to float

flou ADJECTIVE
blurred

le **fluor** NOUN
le dentifrice au fluor fluoride toothpaste

la **flûte** NOUN
flute ◇ *Je joue de la flûte.* I play the flute.
Flûte! *(informal)* Heck!

la **foi** NOUN
  faith
le **foie** NOUN
  liver
  • **une crise de foie** a stomach upset
le **foin** NOUN
  hay
  • **un rhume des foins** hay fever
la **foire** NOUN
  fair
la **fois** NOUN
  time ◇ *la première fois* the first time
  ◇ *deux fois deux font quatre* 2 times 2
  is 4
  • **une fois** once
  • **deux fois** twice ◇ *deux fois plus de
  gens* twice as many people
  • **une fois que** once ◇ *Tu te sentiras
  mieux une fois que tu auras mangé.*
  You'll feel better once you've had
  something to eat.
  • **à la fois** at once ◇ *Je ne peux pas
  faire deux choses à la fois.* I can't do
  two things at once.
la **folie** NOUN
  madness ◇ *C'est de la folie pure!* It's
  absolute madness!
  • **faire une folie** to be extravagant
folklorique ADJECTIVE
  folk ◇ *de la musique folklorique* folk
  music
folle ADJECTIVE
  (MASC SING **fou**)
  mad
foncé ADJECTIVE
  dark ◇ *bleu foncé* dark blue
foncer VERB (*informal*)
  • **Je vais foncer à la boulangerie.** I'm
  just going to dash to the baker's.
la **fonction** NOUN
  function
  • **une voiture de fonction** a company
  car
le/la **fonctionnaire** NOUN
  civil servant
fonctionner VERB
  to work
le **fond** NOUN
  1 **bottom** ◇ *Mon porte-monnaie est
  au fond de mon sac.* My purse is at the
  bottom of my bag.
  2 **end** ◇ *Les toilettes sont au fond du
  couloir.* The toilets are at the end of the
  corridor.
  • **dans le fond** all things considered
  ◇ *Dans le fond, ce n'est pas si grave.*
  All things considered, it's not that bad.
fonder VERB
  to found

fondre VERB
  to melt ◇ *La tablette de chocolat a
  fondu dans ma poche.* The bar of
  chocolate melted in my pocket.
  • **fondre en larmes** to burst into tears
fondu ADJECTIVE
  • **du beurre fondu** melted butter
font VERB *see* **faire**
la **fontaine** NOUN
  fountain
le **foot** NOUN (*informal*)
  football
le **football** NOUN
  football ◇ *jouer au football* to play
  football
le **footballeur** NOUN
  footballer
le **footing** NOUN
  jogging ◇ *faire du footing* to go
  jogging
forain ADJECTIVE
  see also **forain** NOUN
  • **une fête foraine** a funfair
le **forain** NOUN
  see also **forain** ADJECTIVE
  fairground worker
la **force** NOUN
  strength ◇ *Je n'ai pas beaucoup de
  force dans les bras.* I haven't got much
  strength in my arms.
  • **à force de** by ◇ *Il a grossi à force de
  manger autant.* He got fat by eating so
  much.
  • **de force** by force ◇ *Ils lui ont enlevé
  son pistolet de force.* They took the gun
  from him by force.
forcé ADJECTIVE
  forced ◇ *un sourire forcé* a forced
  smile
  • **C'est forcé.** (*informal*) It's inevitable.
forcément ADVERB
  • **Ça devait forcément arriver.** That was
  bound to happen.
  • **pas forcément** not necessarily
la **forêt** NOUN
  forest
le **forfait** NOUN
  all-in price
  • **C'est compris dans le forfait.** It's
  included in the price.
la **formalité** NOUN
  formality ◇ *Ce n'est qu'une simple
  formalité.* It's just a formality.
le **format** NOUN
  size
la **formation** NOUN
  training ◇ *la formation
  professionnelle* vocational training
  • **Il a une formation d'ingénieur.** He is a

trained engineer.

forme NOUN
shape
- **être en forme** to be in good shape
- **Je ne suis pas en forme aujourd'hui.** I'm not feeling too good today.
- **Tu as l'air en forme.** You're looking well.

formellement ADVERB
strictly ◇ *Il est formellement interdit de fumer dans les couloirs.* It is strictly forbidden to smoke in the corridors.

former VERB
to form

formidable ADJECTIVE
great

formulaire NOUN
form

fort ADJECTIVE, ADVERB
[1] **strong** ◇ *Le café est trop fort.* The coffee's too strong.
[2] **good** ◇ *Il est très fort en espagnol.* He's very good at Spanish.
[3] **loud** ◇ *Est-ce vous pouvez parler plus fort?* Can you speak louder?
- **frapper fort** to hit hard

fortifiant NOUN
tonic (*medicine*)

fortune NOUN
fortune
- **de fortune** makeshift ◇ *Ils ont traversé la rivière sur un radeau de fortune.* They crossed the river on a makeshift raft.

fossé NOUN
ditch

fou ADJECTIVE
(FEM SING **folle**)
mad
- **Il y a un monde fou sur la plage!** (*informal*) There are loads of people on the beach!
- **attraper le fou rire** to get the giggles

foudre NOUN
lightning ◇ *L'arbre a été frappé par la foudre.* The tree was struck by lightning.

foudroyant ADJECTIVE
instant ◇ *un succès foudroyant* an instant hit

fouet NOUN
whisk

fougère NOUN
fern

fouiller VERB
to rummage

fouillis NOUN
mess ◇ *Il y a du fouillis dans sa chambre.* His bedroom is a mess.

foulard NOUN
scarf ◇ *un foulard en soie* a silk scarf

foule NOUN
crowd
- **une foule de** masses of ◇ *J'ai une foule de choses à faire ce week-end.* I've got masses of things to do this weekend.

four NOUN
oven ◇ *un four à micro-ondes* a microwave oven

fourchette NOUN
fork

fourmi NOUN
ant
- **avoir des fourmis dans les jambes** to have pins and needles

fourneau NOUN
(PL les **fourneaux**)
stove

fourni ADJECTIVE
thick (*beard, hair*)

fournir VERB
to supply

fournitures FEM NOUN
- **les fournitures scolaires** school stationery

fourré ADJECTIVE
filled ◇ *un gâteau fourré à la confiture d'abricot* a cake filled with apricot jam

fourrer (*informal*) VERB
to put ◇ *Où est-ce que tu as fourré mon passeport?* Where have you put my passport?

fourre-tout NOUN
(PL les **fourre-tout**)
holdall

fourrure NOUN
fur ◇ *un manteau de fourrure* a fur coat

foutre VERB (*rude*)
to do ◇ *Qu'est-ce qu'il fout?* What the hell is he doing?
- **Je n'en ai rien à foutre!** I don't give a damn!

foutu ADJECTIVE (*rude*)
[1] **knackered** ◇ *Mon stylo est foutu.* My pen's knackered.
[2] **bloody** ◇ *Qu'est-ce que j'ai fait de ce foutu stylo?* Where did I put that bloody pen?

foyer NOUN
home ◇ *dans la plupart des foyers français* in most French homes
- **un foyer de jeunes** a youth club

fracture NOUN
fracture

fragile ADJECTIVE
fragile ◇ *Attention, c'est fragile!* Be

careful, it's fragile!

la**fragilité** NOUN
fragility

fraîche ADJECTIVE *see* **frais**

la**fraîcheur** NOUN
1 cool ◇ *la fraîcheur du soir* the cool of the evening
2 freshness ◇ *Je ne suis pas sûre de la fraîcheur du poisson.* I'm not sure about the freshness of the fish.

frais ADJECTIVE
(FEM SING **fraîche**)
see also **frais** NOUN
1 fresh ◇ *des œufs frais* fresh eggs ◇ *Cette salade n'est pas très fraîche.* This lettuce isn't very fresh.
2 chilly ◇ *Il fait un peu frais ce soir.* It's a bit chilly this evening.
3 cool ◇ *des boissons fraîches* cool drinks
• "servir frais" "serve chilled"
• mettre au frais to put in a cool place

les**frais** MASC NOUN
see also **frais** ADJECTIVE
expenses

la**fraise** NOUN
strawberry ◇ *une fraise des bois* a wild strawberry

la**framboise** NOUN
raspberry

franc ADJECTIVE
(FEM SING **franche**)
see also **franc** NOUN
frank

le**franc** NOUN
see also **franc** ADJECTIVE
franc
The franc *is the unit of currency in France, Belgium, Switzerland and many former French colonies; it is divided into 100* centimes.

français ADJECTIVE, NOUN
(FEM SING **française**)
French ◇ *Il parle français couramment.* He speaks French fluently.
• un Français a Frenchman
• une Française a Frenchwoman
• les Français the French

la**France** NOUN
France
• en France (1) in France ◇ *Je suis né en France.* I was born in France.
• en France (2) to France ◇ *Je pars en France pour Noël.* I'm going to France for Christmas.

franche ADJECTIVE *see* **franc**

franchement ADVERB
1 frankly ◇ *Il m'a parlé franchement.* He spoke to me frankly.

2 really ◇ *C'est franchement mauvais.* It's really bad.

franchir VERB
to get over

la**franchise** NOUN
frankness

francophone ADJECTIVE
French-speaking

la**frange** NOUN
fringe

la**frangipane** NOUN
almond cream

frapper VERB
to strike ◇ *Il l'a frappée au visage.* He struck her in the face. ◇ *Son air fatigué m'a frappé.* I was struck by how tired she looked.

fredonner VERB
to hum

le**freezer** NOUN
freezing compartment

le**frein** NOUN
brake
• le frein à main handbrake

freiner VERB
to brake

frêle ADJECTIVE
frail

le**frelon** NOUN
hornet

frémir VERB
shudder ◇ *Cette idée me fait frémir.* The idea makes me shudder.

fréquemment ADVERB
frequently

fréquent ADJECTIVE
frequent

fréquenté ADJECTIVE
busy ◇ *une rue très fréquentée* a very busy street
• un bar mal fréquenté a rough pub

fréquenter VERB
to see (*person*) ◇ *Je ne le fréquente pas beaucoup.* I don't see him often.

le**frère** NOUN
brother

le**friand** NOUN
• un friand au fromage a cheese puff

la**friandise** NOUN
sweet

le**fric** NOUN (*informal*)
cash

le**frigidaire** ® NOUN
refrigerator

le**frigo** NOUN (*informal*)
fridge

frileux ADJECTIVE
(FEM SING **frileuse**)
• être frileux to feel the cold ◇ *Je suis*

très frileuse. I really feel the cold.
frimer VERB (*informal*)
  to show off
les **fringues** FEM NOUN (*informal*)
  clothes
fripé ADJECTIVE
  crumpled
frire VERB
- **faire frire** to fry ◦ *Faites frire les boulettes dans de l'huile très chaude.* Fry the meatballs in very hot oil.
frisé ADJECTIVE
  curly ◦ *Elle est très frisée.* She's got very curly hair.
le **frisson** NOUN
  shiver
frissonner VERB
  to shiver
frit ADJECTIVE
  fried ◦ *du poisson frit* fried fish
les **frites** FEM NOUN
  chips
la **friture** NOUN
  ① **fried food** ◦ *On lui a conseillé d'éviter les fritures.* He's been advised to avoid fried food.
  ② **fried fish** ◦ *Nous allons faire une friture ce soir.* We are going to have fried fish tonight.
froid ADJECTIVE
  see also **froid** NOUN
  cold ◦ *Ça me laisse froid.* It leaves me cold. ◦ *de la viande froide* cold meat
le **froid** NOUN
  see also **froid** ADJECTIVE
  cold
- **Il fait froid.** It's cold.
- **avoir froid** to be cold ◦ *Est-ce que tu as froid?* Are you cold?
se **froisser** VERB
  ① **to crease** ◦ *Ce tissu se froisse très facilement.* This material creases very easily.
  ② **to take offence** ◦ *Paul se froisse très facilement.* Paul's very quick to take offence.
- **se froisser un muscle** to strain a muscle
frôler VERB
  ① **to brush against** ◦ *Le chat m'a frôlé au passage.* The cat brushed against me as it went past.
  ② **to narrowly avoid** ◦ *Nous avons frôlé la catastrophe.* We narrowly avoided disaster.
le **fromage** NOUN
  cheese
- **du fromage blanc** soft white cheese

le **froment** NOUN
  wheat
- **une crêpe de froment** a pancake (*made with wheat flour*)
froncer VERB
- **froncer les sourcils** to frown
le **front** NOUN
  forehead
la **frontière** NOUN
  border
frotter VERB
  to rub ◦ *se frotter les yeux* to rub one's eyes
- **frotter une allumette** to strike a match
le **fruit** NOUN
  fruit
- **un fruit** a piece of fruit ◦ *Est-ce que vous voulez manger un fruit?* Would you like some fruit?
- **les fruits de mer** seafood
fruité ADJECTIVE
  fruity
frustrer VERB
  to frustrate
la **fugue** NOUN
- **faire une fugue** to run away
fuir VERB
  ① **to flee** ◦ *fuir devant un danger* to flee from danger
  ② **to drip** ◦ *Le robinet fuit.* The tap's dripping.
la **fuite** NOUN
  ① **leak** ◦ *Il y a une fuite de gaz.* There is a gas leak.
  ② **flight** (*escape*)
- **être en fuite** to be on the run
fumé ADJECTIVE
  smoked ◦ *du saumon fumé* smoked salmon
la **fumée** NOUN
  smoke
fumer VERB
  to smoke
le **fumeur** NOUN
  smoker
la **fumeuse** NOUN
  smoker
fur
- **au fur et à mesure** ADVERB
  as you go along ◦ *Je vérifie mon travail au fur et à mesure.* I check my work as I go along.
- **au fur et à mesure que** as ◦ *Je réponds à mon courrier au fur et à mesure que je le reçois.* I answer my mail as I receive it.
la **fureur** NOUN
  fury
- **faire fureur** to be all the rage ◦ *Ce*

genre de sac fait fureur actuellement.
This sort of bag is all the rage at the moment.

furieux ADJECTIVE
(FEM SING **furieuse**)
furious

le **furoncle** NOUN
boil (on skin)

fus VERB see **être**

le **fuseau** NOUN
(PL les **fuseaux**)
ski pants

la **fusée** NOUN
rocket

le **fusil** NOUN
gun

fut VERB see **être**

futé ADJECTIVE
crafty

le **futur** NOUN
future

G

gâcher VERB
to waste ◦ *Je n'aime pas gâcher la nourriture.* I don't like to waste food.

le **gâchis** NOUN
waste

la **gaffe** NOUN
- **faire une gaffe** to do something stupid
- **Fais gaffe!** (*informal*) Watch out!
  ◦ *Fais gaffe: la peinture est encore humide!* Watch out: the paint's still wet!

le **gage** NOUN
forfeit (*in a game*) ◦ *recevoir un gage* to pay a forfeit

le **gagnant** NOUN
winner

la **gagnante** NOUN
winner

gagner VERB
to win ◦ *Qui a gagné?* Who won?
- **gagner du temps** to gain time
- **Il gagne bien sa vie.** He makes a good living.

gai ADJECTIVE
cheerful ◦ *Elle est très gaie.* She's very cheerful.

la **gaieté** NOUN
cheerfulness

la **galerie** NOUN
gallery ◦ *une galerie de peinture* an art gallery
- **une galerie marchande** a shopping arcade

le **galet** NOUN
pebble

la **galette** NOUN
[1] **round flat cake** ◦ *une galette de blé noir* a buckwheat pancake
[2] **biscuit** ◦ *des galettes pur beurre* shortbread biscuits
- **la galette des Rois**

  A galette des Rois *is a cake eaten on Twelfth Night containing a figurine. The person who finds it is the king (or queen) and gets a paper crown. They then choose someone else to be their queen (or king).*

Galles FEM NOUN
- **le pays de Galles** Wales
- **le prince de Galles** the Prince of Wales

gallois ADJECTIVE, NOUN
Welsh ◦ *un peintre gallois* a Welsh painter
- **un Gallois** a Welshman
- **une Galloise** a Welshwoman
- **les Gallois** the Welsh

le **galop** NOUN
gallop

galoper VERB
to gallop

le **gamin** NOUN (*informal*)
kid

la **gamine** NOUN (*informal*)
kid

la **gamme** NOUN
scale (*in music*) ◦ *Je dois faire des gammes tous les soirs.* I have to do my scales every night.
- **une gamme de produits** a range of products

gammée ADJECTIVE
- **la croix gammée** the swastika

le **gant** NOUN
glove ◦ *des gants en laine* woollen gloves
- **un gant de toilette** a face cloth

le **garage** NOUN
garage

le/la **garagiste** NOUN
[1] **garage owner**
[2] **mechanic**

la **garantie** NOUN
guarantee

garantir VERB
to guarantee

le **garçon** NOUN
[1] **boy**
[2] **waiter** (*in a café*)
- **un vieux garçon** a bachelor

le **garde** NOUN
see also la **garde**
[1] **warder** (*in prison*)
[2] **security man**
- **un garde du corps** a bodyguard

la **garde** NOUN
see also le **garde**
[1] **guarding** ◦ *Il est chargé de la garde des prisonniers.* He's responsible for guarding the prisoners.
[2] **guard** ◦ *la relève de la garde* the changing of the guard
- **être de garde** to be on duty ◦ *Mon père est de garde ce soir.* My father is on duty tonight. ◦ *La pharmacie de garde ce week-end est...* The duty chemist this weekend is...
- **mettre en garde** to warn ◦ *Elle m'a mis en garde contre les pickpockets.* She warned me about pickpockets.

garder VERB
[1] **to keep** ◦ *Est-ce que tu as gardé toutes ses lettres?* Have you kept all

PTO

his letters?

2 to look after ◇ *Je garde ma nièce samedi après-midi.* I'm looking after my niece on Saturday afternoon.

3 to guard ◇ *Ils ont pris un gros chien pour garder la maison.* They got a big dog to guard the house.

- **se garder** to keep ◇ *Ces crêpes se gardent bien.* These pancakes keep well.

la **garderie** NOUN

nursery

la **garde-robe** NOUN

wardrobe (*clothes*) ◇ *Elle a une garde-robe bien fournie.* She's got an extensive wardrobe.

le **gardien** NOUN

1 caretaker

2 attendant (*in a museum*)

- **un gardien de but** a goalkeeper
- **un gardien de la paix** a police officer

la **gardienne** NOUN

1 caretaker

2 attendant (*in a museum*)

la **gare** NOUN

see also **gare** EXCLAMATION

station ◇ *la gare routière* the bus station

gare EXCLAMATION

see also **gare** NOUN

- **Gare aux serpents!** Watch out for snakes!

garer VERB

to park

- **se garer** to park ◇ *Où t'es-tu garé?* Where are you parked?

garni ADJECTIVE

- **un plat garni** a dish served with accompaniments (*vegetables, chips, rice etc*)

le **gars** NOUN (*informal*)

guy

gaspiller VERB

to waste

le **gâteau** NOUN

(PL les **gâteaux**)

cake

- **les gâteaux secs** biscuits

gâter VERB

to spoil ◇ *Il aime gâter ses petits enfants.* He likes to spoil his grandchildren.

- **se gâter** to go bad ◇ *Le temps va se gâter.* The weather's going to break.

gauche ADJECTIVE

see also **gauche**

left ◇ *le bras gauche* the left arm ◇ *le côté gauche* the left-hand side

la **gauche** NOUN

see also **gauche** ADJECTIVE

left ◇ *sur votre gauche* on your left

- **à gauche (1)** on the left ◇ *la deuxième rue à gauche* the second street on the left
- **à gauche (2)** to the left ◇ *à gauche de l'armoire* to the left of the cupboard ◇ *Tournez à gauche.* Turn left.
- **la voie de gauche** the left-hand lane
- **la gauche** the left (*in politics*) ◇ *Il est de gauche.* He's left-wing.

gaucher ADJECTIVE

(FEM SING **gauchère**)

left-handed

la **gaufre** NOUN

waffle

la **gaufrette** NOUN

wafer

le **Gaulois** NOUN

Gaul ◇ *Astérix le Gaulois* Asterix the Gaul

gaulois ADJECTIVE

Gallic

le **gaz** NOUN

gas

gazeux ADJECTIVE

(FEM SING **gazeuse**)

- **une boisson gazeuse** a fizzy drink
- **de l'eau gazeuse** sparkling water

le **gazole** NOUN

diesel (*fuel*)

le **gazon** NOUN

lawn

le **géant** NOUN

giant

le **gel** NOUN

frost

la **gelée** NOUN

jelly

geler VERB

to freeze ◇ *Il a gelé cette nuit.* There was a frost last night.

la **gélule** NOUN

capsule (*containing medicine*)

les **Gémeaux** MASC NOUN

Gemini ◇ *Henry est Gémeaux.* Henry's Gemini.

gémir VERB

to moan

gênant ADJECTIVE

awkward ◇ *un silence gênant* an awkward silence

la **gencive** NOUN

gum (*in mouth*)

le **gendarme** NOUN

policeman

la **gendarmerie** NOUN

1 police force

2 police station ⋄ *Vous devriez porter plainte à la gendarmerie.* You should go to the police station and report it.

le **gendre** NOUN
son-in-law

gêné ADJECTIVE
embarrassed

gêner VERB
1 to bother ⋄ *Je ne voudrais pas vous gêner.* I don't want to bother you.
2 to feel awkward ⋄ *Son regard la gênait.* The way he was looking at her made her feel awkward.

général ADJECTIVE
(MASC PL **généraux**)
see also général NOUN
general

• **en général** usually

le **général** NOUN
(PL les **généraux**)
see also général ADJECTIVE
general

généralement ADVERB
generally

e/la **généraliste** NOUN
family doctor

la **génération** NOUN
generation

généreux ADJECTIVE
(FEM SING **généreuse**)
generous

la **générosité** NOUN
generosity

le **genêt** NOUN
broom (*bush*)

la **génétique** NOUN
genetics

Genève NOUN
Geneva

génial ADJECTIVE (*informal*)
(MASC PL **géniaux**)
great ⋄ *Le film d'hier soir était génial.* The film last night was great.

le **genou** NOUN
(PL les **genoux**)
knee ⋄ *Elle est à genoux.* She's on her knees. ⋄ *se mettre à genoux* to kneel down

le **genre** NOUN
kind ⋄ *C'est un genre de gâteau à la crème.* It's a kind of cream cake.

les **gens** MASC NOUN
people

gentil ADJECTIVE
(FEM SING **gentille**)
1 nice ⋄ *Nos voisins sont très gentils.* Our neighbours are very nice.
2 kind ⋄ *C'était très gentil de votre part.* It was very kind of you.

la **gentillesse** NOUN
kindness ⋄ *Je l'ai remerciée de sa gentillesse.* I thanked her for her kindness. ⋄ *C'est un homme d'une grande gentillesse.* He is a very nice man.

gentiment ADVERB
1 nicely ⋄ *Demande-le lui gentiment.* Ask him nicely.
2 kindly ⋄ *Ils nous ont gentiment proposé de rester dîner.* They kindly invited us to stay for dinner.

la **géographie** NOUN
geography

la **géométrie** NOUN
geometry

gérer VERB
to manage

germain ADJECTIVE
• **un cousin germain** a first cousin

le **geste** NOUN
gesture ⋄ *Il a voulu faire un geste.* He wanted to make a gesture.
• **Ne faites pas un geste!** Don't move!

la **gestion** NOUN
management

la **gifle** NOUN
slap across the face

gifler VERB
to slap across the face

gigantesque ADJECTIVE
gigantic

le **gigot** NOUN
leg of lamb

le **gilet** NOUN
1 waistcoat ⋄ *un gilet en cuir* a leather waistcoat
2 cardigan ⋄ *un gilet tricoté main* a hand-knitted cardigan
• **un gilet de sauvetage** a life jacket

le **gingembre** NOUN
ginger

la **girafe** NOUN
giraffe

le **gitan** NOUN
gipsy

la **gitane** NOUN
gipsy

le **gîte** NOUN
• **un gîte rural** a holiday house

la **glace** NOUN
1 ice ⋄ *L'étang est recouvert de glace.* The pond is covered with ice.
2 ice cream ⋄ *une glace à la fraise* a strawberry ice cream
3 mirror ⋄ *Il se regarde souvent dans la glace.* He often looks at himself in the mirror.

glacé ADJECTIVE
1 **icy** ◇ *Il soufflait un vent glacé.* An icy wind was blowing.
2 **iced** ◇ *un thé glacé* an iced tea

glacial ADJECTIVE
(MASC PL **glaciaux**)
icy

le **glaçon** NOUN
ice cube

glissant ADJECTIVE
slippery

glisser VERB
1 **to slip** ◇ *Il a glissé sur une peau de banane.* He slipped on a banana skin.
2 **to be slippery** ◇ *Attention, ça glisse!* Watch out, it's slippery!

global ADJECTIVE
(MASC PL **globaux**)
total ◇ *la somme globale* the total amount

la **gloire** NOUN
glory

la **godasse** NOUN (*informal*)
shoe

le **goéland** NOUN
seagull

le **golf** NOUN
1 **golf** ◇ *Il joue au golf.* He plays golf.
2 **golf course** ◇ *un golf dix-huit trous* an 18-hole golf course

le **golfe** NOUN
gulf
- **le golfe de Gascogne** the Bay of Biscay

la **gomme** NOUN
rubber

gommer VERB
to rub out

gonfler VERB
1 **to blow up** ◇ *gonfler un ballon* to blow up a balloon
2 **to pump up** ◇ *Tu devrais gonfler ton pneu arrière.* You should pump up your back tyre.

la **gorge** NOUN
1 **throat** ◇ *J'ai mal à la gorge.* I've got a sore throat.
2 **gorge** ◇ *les gorges du Tarn* the Tarn gorges

la **gorgée** NOUN
sip ◇ *une gorgée d'eau* a sip of water

le **gorille** NOUN
gorilla

le/la **gosse** NOUN (*informal*)
kid

le **goudron** NOUN
tar

le **gouffre** NOUN
chasm
- **Cette voiture est un vrai gouffre!** This car eats up money!

la **gourde** NOUN
water bottle

gourmand ADJECTIVE
greedy

la **gourmandise** NOUN
greed

la **gousse** NOUN
- **une gousse d'ail** a clove of garlic

le **goût** NOUN
taste ◇ *Ça n'a pas de goût.* It's got no taste. ◇ *Elle a très bon goût.* She's got very good taste.

goûter VERB
see also **goûter** NOUN
1 **to taste** ◇ *Goûte donc ce fromage: tu verras comme il est bon!* Have a taste of this cheese: you'll see how nice it is!
2 **to have a snack** (*in the afternoon*) ◇ *Les enfants goûtent généralement vers quatre heures.* The children usually have a snack around 4 o'clock.

le **goûter** NOUN
see also **goûter** VERB
afternoon snack

la **goutte** NOUN
drop

le **gouvernement** NOUN
government

gouverner VERB
to govern

la **grâce** NOUN
- **grâce à** thanks to ◇ *Je suis arrivé à l'heure grâce à toi.* I arrived on time thanks to you.

gracieux ADJECTIVE
(FEM SING **gracieuse**)
graceful

les **gradins** MASC NOUN
terraces (*in stadium*)

graduel ADJECTIVE
(FEM SING **graduelle**)
gradual

le **grain** NOUN
grain ◇ *un grain de sable* a grain of sand
- **un grain de beauté** a beauty spot
- **un grain de café** a coffee bean
- **un grain de raisin** a grape

la **graine** NOUN
seed

la **graisse** NOUN
fat

la **grammaire** NOUN
grammar

le **gramme** NOUN
gramme

grand ADJECTIVE, ADVERB
[1] **tall** ◇ *Il est grand pour son âge.* He's tall for his age.
[2] **big** ◇ *une grande valise* a big suitcase ◇ *C'est sa grande sœur.* She's his big sister.
- **une grande personne** a grown-up
[3] **long** ◇ *un grand voyage* a long journey
- **les grandes vacances** the summer holidays
[4] **great** ◇ *C'est un grand ami à moi.* He's a great friend of mine.
- **un grand magasin** a department store
- **une grande surface** a hypermarket
- **les grandes écoles** top ranking colleges (*at university level*)
- **au grand air** out in the open air ◇ *Ça te fera beaucoup de bien d'être au grand air.* It'll be very good for you to be out in the open air.
- **grand ouvert** wide open

grand-chose NOUN
- **pas grand-chose** not much ◇ *Je n'ai pas acheté grand-chose au marché.* I didn't buy much at the market. ◇ *Voici un petit cadeau: ce n'est pas grand-chose.* Here's a little present: it's nothing much.

la **Grande-Bretagne** NOUN
Britain

la **grandeur** NOUN
size

grandir VERB
to grow ◇ *Il a beaucoup grandi.* He's grown a lot.

la **grand-mère** NOUN
(PL les **grands-mères**)
grandmother

grand-peine NOUN
- **à grand-peine** ADVERB
with great difficulty

le **grand-père** NOUN
(PL les **grands-pères**)
grandfather

les **grands-parents** MASC NOUN
grandparents

la **grange** NOUN
barn

la **grappe** NOUN
- **une grappe de raisin** a bunch of grapes

gras ADJECTIVE
(FEM SING **grasse**)
[1] **fatty** (*food*) ◇ *Évitez les aliments gras.* Avoid fatty foods.
[2] **greasy** ◇ *des cheveux gras* greasy

hair
[3] **oily** ◇ *une peau grasse* oily skin
- **faire la grasse matinée** to have a lie-in

gratis ADJECTIVE, ADVERB
free ◇ *J'ai eu ce stylo gratis.* I got this pen free.

le **gratte-ciel** NOUN
(PL les **gratte-ciel**)
skyscraper

gratter VERB
[1] **to scratch** ◇ *Ne gratte pas tes piqûres de moustiques!* Don't scratch your mosquito bites!
[2] **to be itchy** ◇ *C'est épouvantable comme ça gratte!* It's terribly itchy!

gratuit ADJECTIVE
free ◇ *entrée gratuite* entrance free

grave ADJECTIVE
[1] **serious** ◇ *une maladie grave* a serious illness ◇ *Il avait l'air grave.* He was looking serious.
[2] **deep** ◇ *Il a une voix grave.* He's got a deep voice.
- **Ce n'est pas grave.** It doesn't matter. ◇ *J'ai oublié ma clé.—Ce n'est pas grave, j'ai la mienne.* I've forgotten my key.–It doesn't matter, I've got mine.

gravement ADVERB
seriously ◇ *Il a été gravement blessé.* He was seriously injured.

grec ADJECTIVE, NOUN
(FEM SING **grecque**)
Greek
- **J'apprends le grec.** I'm learning Greek.
- **un Grec** a Greek (*man*)
- **une Grecque** a Greek (*woman*)
- **les Grecs** the Greeks

la **Grèce** NOUN
Greece
- **en Grèce (1)** in Greece
- **en Grèce (2)** to Greece

la **grêle** NOUN
hail

grêler VERB
- **Il grêle.** It's hailing.

grelotter VERB
to shiver

la **grenade** NOUN
[1] **pomegranate**
[2] **grenade**

le **grenier** NOUN
attic

la **grenouille** NOUN
frog

la **grève** NOUN
[1] **strike**
- **en grève** on strike ◇ *Les ouvriers sont en grève depuis dix jours.* The

workers have been on strike for ten days.

- **faire grève** to be on strike

2 **shore** ◇ *Nous nous sommes promenés le long de la grève.* We went for a walk along the shore.

le/la **gréviste** NOUN
striker

grièvement ADVERB

- **grièvement blessé** seriously injured

la **griffe** NOUN

1 **claw** ◇ *Le chat m'a donné un coup de griffe.* The cat scratched me.

2 **label** ◇ *la griffe d'un grand couturier* the label of a top designer

griffer VERB
to scratch ◇ *Le chat m'a griffé.* The cat scratched me.

grignoter VERB
to nibble

la **grillade** NOUN
grilled food ◇ *une grillade d'agneau* grilled lamb

la **grille** NOUN

1 **wire fence** ◇ *L'usine est entourée d'une haute grille.* The factory is surrounded by a high wire fence.

2 **metal gate** ◇ *Le facteur a sonné à la grille du jardin.* The postman rang at the garden gate.

le **grille-pain** NOUN
(PL les **grille-pain**)
toaster

griller VERB

1 **to toast**

- **du pain grillé** toast

2 **to grill** ◇ *des saucisses grillées* grilled sausages

la **grimace** NOUN

- **faire des grimaces** to make faces

grimper VERB
to climb

grincer VERB
to creak

grincheux ADJECTIVE
(FEM SING **grincheuse**)
grumpy

la **grippe** NOUN
flu

- **avoir la grippe** to have flu ◇ *J'ai eu une mauvaise grippe l'hiver dernier.* I had a bad attack of flu last winter.

grippé ADJECTIVE

- **être grippé** to have flu

gris ADJECTIVE
grey

le **Groenland** NOUN
Greenland

grogner VERB

1 **to growl** ◇ *Le chien a grogné quand je me suis approché de lui.* The dog growled when I went near it.

2 **to complain** ◇ *Arrête donc de grogner!* Stop complaining!

gronder VERB

- **se faire gronder** to get a telling off ◇ *Tu vas te faire gronder par ton père!* You're going to get a telling off from your father!

gros ADJECTIVE
(FEM SING **grosse**)

1 **big** ◇ *une grosse pomme* a big apple

2 **fat** ◇ *Je suis trop grosse pour porter ça!* I'm too fat to wear that!

la **groseille** NOUN

- **la groseille rouge** redcurrant
- **la groseille à maquereau** gooseberry

la **grossesse** NOUN
pregnancy

grossier ADJECTIVE
(FFM SING **grossière**)
rude ◇ *Ne sois pas si grossier!* Don't be so rude!

- **une erreur grossière** a bad mistake

grossir VERB
to put on weight ◇ *Il a beaucoup grossi.* He's put on a lot of weight.

grosso modo ADVERB
roughly ◇ *Dis-moi grosso modo ce que tu en penses.* Give me a rough idea what you think of it.

la **grotte** NOUN
cave

le **groupe** NOUN
group ◇ *votre groupe sanguin* your blood group

grouper VERB
to group ◇ *On nous a groupés dans différentes classes selon notre niveau.* We were grouped in different classes according to our level.

- **se grouper** to gather ◇ *Nous nous sommes groupés autour du feu.* We gathered round the fire.

le **guépard** NOUN
cheetah

la **guêpe** NOUN
wasp

guérir VERB
to recover ◇ *Il est maintenant complètement guéri.* He's now completely recovered.

la **guérison** NOUN
recovery

la **guerre** NOUN
war ◇ *en guerre* at war

guetter VERB
to look out for ◇ *Elle guette l'arrivée du facteur tous les matins.* She looks out for the postman every morning.

la **gueule** NOUN
mouth (*rude when used for people*) ◇ *Le chat a ramené une souris dans sa gueule.* The cat brought in a mouse in its mouth.
- **Ta gueule!** (*rude*) Shut your face!
- **avoir la gueule de bois** (*informal*) to have a hangover

gueuler (*informal*) VERB
to bawl

le **guichet** NOUN
counter (*in bank, booking office*)

le **guide** NOUN
guide

guider VERB
to guide

le **guidon** NOUN
handlebars

les **guillemets** MASC NOUN
inverted commas ◇ *entre guillemets* in inverted commas

la **guirlande** NOUN
tinsel ◇ *Nous avons décoré le sapin de Noël avec des guirlandes.* We decorated the Christmas tree with tinsel.
- **des guirlandes en papier** paper chains

la **guitare** NOUN
guitar ◇ *Sais-tu jouer de la guitare?* Can you play the guitar?

le **gymnase** NOUN
gym ◇ *Le lycée a un nouveau gymnase.* The school's got a new gym.

la **gymnastique** NOUN
gymnastics ◇ *faire de la gymnastique* to do one's exercises

H

habile ADJECTIVE
  skilful ◦ *Il est très habile de ses mains.* He is very clever with his hands.

habillé ADJECTIVE
  1 **dressed** ◦ *Il n'est pas encore habillé.* He's not dressed yet.
  2 **smart** ◦ *Cette robe fait très habillé.* This dress looks very smart.

s'**habiller** VERB
  1 **to get dressed** ◦ *Je me suis rapidement habillé.* I got dressed quickly.
  2 **to dress up** ◦ *Est-ce qu'il faut s'habiller pour la réception?* Do you have to dress up to go to the party?

l'**habitant** MASC NOUN
  inhabitant ◦ *Les habitants du quartier sont contre ce projet.* The local people are against this plan.

l'**habitante** FEM NOUN
  inhabitant

habiter VERB
  to live ◦ *Il habite à Montpellier.* He lives in Montpellier.

les **habits** MASC NOUN
  clothes

l'**habitude** FEM NOUN
  habit ◦ *une mauvaise habitude* a bad habit
  - **avoir l'habitude de quelque chose** to be used to something ◦ *Elle a l'habitude des enfants.* She's used to children. ◦ *Je n'ai pas l'habitude de parler en public.* I'm not used to speaking in public.
  - **d'habitude** usually
  - **comme d'habitude** as usual

habituel ADJECTIVE
  (FEM SING **habituelle**)
  usual

s'**habituer** VERB
  - **s'habituer à quelque chose** to get used to something ◦ *Il faudra que tu t'habitues à te lever tôt.* You'll have to get used to getting up early.

le **hachis** NOUN
  mince
  - **le hachis Parmentier** shepherd's pie

la **haie** NOUN
  hedge

la **haine** NOUN
  hatred

haïr VERB
  to hate

l'**haleine** FEM NOUN

breath ◦ *avoir mauvaise haleine* to have bad breath ◦ *être hors d'haleine* to be out of breath

les **halles** FEM NOUN
  covered market

la **halte** NOUN
  stop ◦ *faire halte* to make a stop
  - **Halte!** Stop!

l'**haltérophilie** FEM NOUN
  weightlifting

l'**hameçon** MASC NOUN
  fish hook

le **hamster** NOUN
  hamster

la **hanche** NOUN
  hip

le **handball** NOUN
  handball ◦ *jouer au handball* to play handball

le **handicapé** NOUN
  handicapped man

la **handicapée** NOUN
  handicapped woman

le **hareng** NOUN
  herring
  - **un hareng saur** a kipper

le **haricot** NOUN
  bean
  - **les haricots verts** runner beans
  - **les haricots blancs** haricot beans

l'**harmonica** MASC NOUN
  mouth organ

la **harpe** NOUN
  harp

le **hasard** NOUN
  coincidence ◦ *C'était un pur hasard.* It was pure coincidence.
  - **au hasard** at random ◦ *Choisis un numéro au hasard.* Choose a number at random.
  - **par hasard** by chance ◦ *Je l'ai rencontrée tout à fait par hasard au supermarché.* I met her at the supermarket quite by chance.
  - **à tout hasard (1)** just in case ◦ *Prends un parapluie à tout hasard.* Take an umbrella just in case.
  - **à tout hasard (2)** on the off chance ◦ *Je ne sais pas s'il est chez lui, mais je vais l'appeler à tout hasard.* I don't know if he's at home, but I'll phone on the off chance.

la **hâte** NOUN
  - **à la hâte** hurriedly ◦ *Elle s'est habillée à la hâte.* She got dressed hurriedly.

J'ai hâte de te voir. I can't wait to see you.

la **hausse** NOUN
1 **increase** ◇ *la hausse des prix* price increase
2 **rise** ◇ *On annonce une légère hausse de température.* The forecast is for a slight rise in temperature.

hausser VERB
- **hausser les épaules** to shrug one's shoulders

haut ADJECTIVE, ADVERB
see also **haut** NOUN
1 **high** ◇ *une haute montagne* a high mountain
2 **aloud** ◇ *penser tout haut* to think aloud

le **haut** NOUN
see also **haut** ADJECTIVE
top
- **un mur de trois mètres de haut** a wall 3 metres high
- **en haut (1)** upstairs ◇ *La salle de bain est en haut.* The bathroom is upstairs.
- **en haut (2)** at the top ◇ *Le nid est tout en haut de l'arbre.* The nest is right at the top of the tree.

la **hauteur** NOUN
height

le **haut-parleur** NOUN
loudspeaker

l' **hebdomadaire** MASC NOUN
weekly *(magazine)*

héberger VERB
to put up ◇ *Mon cousin a dit qu'il nous hébergerait.* My cousin said he would put us up.

hélas ADVERB
unfortunately ◇ *Hélas, il ne restait plus de billets.* Unfortunately there were no tickets left.

l' **hélicoptère** MASC NOUN
helicopter

l' **hémorragie** FEM NOUN
haemorrhage

l' **herbe** FEM NOUN
grass
- **les herbes de Provence** mixed herbs

le **hérisson** NOUN
hedgehog

hériter VERB
to inherit

l' **héritier** MASC NOUN
heir

l' **héritière** FEM NOUN
heiress

hermétique ADJECTIVE
airtight

l' **héroïne** FEM NOUN
1 **heroine** ◇ *l'héroïne du roman* the heroine of the novel
2 **heroin** *(drug)*

le **héros** NOUN
hero

l' **hésitation** FEM NOUN
hesitation

hésiter VERB
to hesitate ◇ *Il n'a pas hésité à nous aider.* He didn't hesitate to help us. ◇ *J'ai hésité entre le pull vert et le cardigan jaune.* I couldn't decide between the green pullover and the yellow cardigan. ◇ *Est-ce que tu viens ce soir?–J'hésite...* Are you coming this evening?–I'm not sure...
- **sans hésiter** without hesitating

l' **heure** FEM NOUN
1 **hour** ◇ *Le trajet dure six heures.* The journey lasts six hours.
2 **time** ◇ *Vous avez l'heure?* Have you got the time?
- **Quelle heure est-il?** What time is it?
- **À quelle heure?** What time? ◇ *À quelle heure arrivons-nous?* What time do we arrive?
- **deux heures du matin** 2 o'clock in the morning
- **être à l'heure** to be on time
- **une heure de français** a period of French

heureusement ADVERB
luckily ◇ *Heureusement qu'il n'a pas été blessé.* Luckily he wasn't hurt.

heureux ADJECTIVE
(FEM SING **heureuse**)
happy

heurter VERB
to hit

l' **hexagone** MASC NOUN
hexagon
- **l'Hexagone** France
France is often referred to as l'Hexagone because of its six-sided shape.

le **hibou** NOUN
(PL les **hiboux**)
owl

hier ADVERB
yesterday
- **avant-hier** the day before yesterday

la **hi-fi** NOUN
stereo
- **une chaîne hi-fi** a stereo system

hippique ADJECTIVE
- **un club hippique** a riding centre
- **un concours hippique** a horse show

l' **hippopotame** MASC NOUN
hippopotamus

l'**hirondelle** FEM NOUN
swallow (*bird*)

l'**histoire** FEM NOUN
[1] **history** ◇ *un cours d'histoire* a history lesson
[2] **story** ◇ *Ce roman raconte l'histoire de deux enfants.* This novel tells the story of two children.
- **Ne fais pas d'histoires!** Don't make a fuss!

historique ADJECTIVE
historic ◇ *un monument historique* a historic monument

l'**hiver** MASC NOUN
winter
- **en hiver** in winter

la **HLM** NOUN (= *habitation à loyer modéré*)
council flat
- **des HLM** council housing

le **hockey** NOUN
hockey
- **le hockey sur glace** ice hockey

hollandais ADJECTIVE, NOUN
Dutch
- **J'apprends le hollandais.** I'm learning Dutch.
- **un Hollandais** a Dutch man
- **une Hollandaise** a Dutch woman
- **les Hollandais** the Dutch

la **Hollande** NOUN
Holland
- **en Hollande (1)** in Holland
- **en Hollande (2)** to Holland

le **homard** NOUN
lobster

homéopathique ADJECTIVE
homeopathic

l'**hommage** MASC NOUN
tribute

l'**homme** MASC NOUN
man
- **un homme d'affaires** a businessman

homosexuel ADJECTIVE
(FEM SING **homosexuelle**)
homosexual

la **Hongrie** NOUN
Hungary

hongrois ADJECTIVE
Hungarian

honnête ADJECTIVE
honest

l'**honnêteté** FEM NOUN
honesty

l'**honneur** MASC NOUN
honour

la **honte** NOUN
shame ◇ *avoir honte de quelque chose* to be ashamed of something

l'**hôpital** MASC NOUN
(PL les **hôpitaux**)
hospital

le **hoquet** NOUN
- **avoir le hoquet** to have hiccups

l'**horaire** MASC NOUN
timetable
- **les horaires de train** the train timetable

l'**horizon** MASC NOUN
horizon

horizontal ADJECTIVE
(MASC PL **horizontaux**)
horizontal

l'**horloge** FEM NOUN
clock

l'**horreur** FEM NOUN
horror ◇ *un film d'horreur* a horror film
- **avoir horreur de** to hate ◇ *J'ai horreur du chou.* I hate cabbage.

horrible ADJECTIVE
horrible

hors PREPOSITION
- **hors de** out of ◇ *Elle est hors de danger maintenant.* She's out of danger now.
- **hors taxes** duty-free

le **hors-d'œuvre** NOUN
(PL les **hors-d'œuvre**)
starter (*food*)

hospitalier ADJECTIVE
(FEM SING **hospitalière**)
hospitable ◇ *Ils sont très hospitaliers.* They're very hospitable.
- **les services hospitaliers** hospital services

l'**hospitalité** FEM NOUN
hospitality

hostile ADJECTIVE
hostile

l'**hôte** MASC/FEM NOUN
[1] **host** ◇ *N'oubliez pas de remercier vos hôtes.* Don't forget to thank your hosts.
[2] **guest** ◇ *Cette ferme accueille des hôtes payants.* This farm takes paying guests.

l'**hôtel** MASC NOUN
hotel
- **l'hôtel de ville** the town hall

l'**hôtesse** FEM NOUN
hostess
- **une hôtesse de l'air** a stewardess

le **houx** NOUN
holly

l'**huile** FEM NOUN
oil
- **l'huile solaire** suntan oil

huit NUMBER

eight ◇ *Il est huit heures du matin.* It's eight in the morning. ◇ *Il a huit ans.* He's eight.

– **le huit février** the eighth of February

la **huitaine** NOUN

– **une huitaine de jours** about a week ◇ *Nous serons de retour dans une huitaine de jours.* We'll be back in about a week.

huitième ADJECTIVE

eighth ◇ *au huitième étage* on the eighth floor

l' **huître** FEM NOUN

oyster

humain ADJECTIVE

see also humain NOUN

human

l' **humain** MASC NOUN

see also humain ADJECTIVE

human being

l' **humeur** FEM NOUN

mood ◇ *Il est de bonne humeur.* He's in a good mood. ◇ *Elle était de mauvaise humeur.* She was in a bad mood.

humide ADJECTIVE

damp ◇ *L'herbe est humide.* The grass is damp. ◇ *un climat humide* a damp climate

humilier VERB

to humiliate

humoristique ADJECTIVE

humorous

– **des dessins humoristiques** cartoons

l' **humour** MASC NOUN

humour ◇ *Il n'a pas beaucoup d'humour.* He hasn't got much sense of humour.

hurler VERB

to howl

la **hutte** NOUN

hut

hydratant ADJECTIVE

– **une crème hydratante** a moisturizing cream

hygiénique ADJECTIVE

hygienic

– **une serviette hygiénique** a sanitary towel

– **le papier hygiénique** toilet paper

l' **hymne** MASC NOUN

– **l'hymne national** the national anthem

l' **hypermarché** MASC NOUN

hypermarket

hypermétrope ADJECTIVE

long-sighted

hypocrite ADJECTIVE

hypocritical ◇ *Il est hypocrite.* He's a hypocrite.

l' **hypothèse** FEM NOUN

hypothesis

H

I

l' **iceberg** MASC NOUN
iceberg

ici ADVERB
here ◦ *Les assiettes sont ici.* The plates are here.
- **La mer monte parfois jusqu'ici.** The sea sometimes comes in as far as this.
- **Jusqu'ici nous n'avons eu aucun problème avec la voiture.** So far we haven't had any problems with the car.

idéal ADJECTIVE
(MASC PL **idéaux**)
ideal ◦ *C'est l'endroit idéal pour faire un pique-nique.* It's an ideal place to have a picnic.

l' **idée** FEM NOUN
idea ◦ *C'est une bonne idée.* It's a good idea.

identifier VERB
to identify ◦ *La police a identifié le meurtrier.* The police have identified the murderer.

identique ADJECTIVE
identical ◦ *Ils ont obtenu des résultats identiques.* They obtained identical results.

l' **identité** FEM NOUN
identity
- **une pièce d'identité** a form of identification ◦ *Avez-vous une pièce d'identité?* Have you got any form of identification?

idiot ADJECTIVE
see also **idiot** NOUN
1 **stupid** ◦ *une plaisanterie idiote* a stupid joke
2 **silly** ◦ *Ne sois pas idiot!* Don't be silly!

l' **idiot** MASC NOUN
see also **idiot** ADJECTIVE
idiot

l' **idiote** FEM NOUN
idiot

ignorant ADJECTIVE
ignorant

ignorer VERB
1 **not to know** ◦ *J'ignore son nom.* I don't know his name.
2 **to ignore** ◦ *Il m'a complètement ignoré.* He completely ignored me.

il PRONOUN
1 **he** ◦ *Il est parti ce matin de bonne heure.* He left early this morning.
2 **it** ◦ *Méfie-toi de ce chien: il mord.* Be careful of that dog: it bites. ◦ *Il pleut.* It's raining.

l' **île** FEM NOUN
island
- **les îles Anglo-Normandes** the Channel Islands
- **les îles Britanniques** the British Isles
- **les îles Féroé** the Faroe Islands

illégal ADJECTIVE
(MASC PL **illégaux**)
illegal

illimité ADJECTIVE
unlimited

illisible ADJECTIVE
illegible ◦ *une écriture illisible* illegible handwriting

illuminer VERB
to floodlight ◦ *Le château est illuminé tous les soirs pendant l'été.* The castle is floodlit every night in the summer.

l' **illusion** FEM NOUN
illusion ◦ *Tu te fais des illusions!* You're deluding yourself!

l' **illustration** FEM NOUN
illustration

illustré ADJECTIVE
see also **illustré** NOUN
illustrated

l' **illustré** MASC NOUN
see also **illustré** ADJECTIVE
comic

illustrer VERB
to illustrate ◦ *Vous pouvez illustrer votre rédaction avec des exemples.* You may illustrate your essay with examples.

ils PRONOUN
they ◦ *Ils nous ont appelés hier soir.* They phoned us last night.

l' **image** FEM NOUN
picture ◦ *Les films donnent une fausse image de l'Amérique.* Films give a false picture of America.

l' **imagination** FEM NOUN
imagination ◦ *Elle a beaucoup d'imagination.* She's got a vivid imagination.

imaginer VERB
to imagine

l' **imbécile** MASC/FEM NOUN
idiot

l' **imitation** FEM NOUN
imitation

imiter VERB
to imitate

l' **immatriculation** FEM NOUN
- **une plaque d'immatriculation** a

numberplate

l' **immédiat** MASC NOUN
- **dans l'immédiat** for the moment
  ◇ *Je n'ai pas besoin de ce livre dans l'immédiat.* I don't need this book for the moment.

immédiatement ADVERB
immediately

immense ADJECTIVE
1 huge ◇ *une immense fortune* a huge fortune
2 tremendous ◇ *un immense soulagement* a tremendous relief

l' **immeuble** MASC NOUN
block of flats

l' **immigration** FEM NOUN
immigration

l' **immigré** MASC NOUN
immigrant

l' **immigrée** FEM NOUN
immigrant

immobile ADJECTIVE
motionless

immobilier ADJECTIVE
(FEM SING **immobilière**)
- **une agence immobilière** an estate agent's

immobiliser VERB
to immobilize

immunisé ADJECTIVE
immunized

l' **impact** MASC NOUN
impact

impair ADJECTIVE
odd ◇ *un nombre impair* an odd number

impardonnable ADJECTIVE
unforgivable

l' **impasse** FEM NOUN
cul-de-sac

l' **impatience** FEM NOUN
impatience

impatient ADJECTIVE
impatient

impeccable ADJECTIVE
1 immaculate ◇ *Elle est toujours impeccable.* She's always immaculate.
2 perfect ◇ *Il a fait un travail impeccable.* He's done a perfect job.
◇ *C'est impeccable!* That's perfect!

l' **impératif** MASC NOUN
imperative

l' **impératrice** FEM NOUN
empress

l' **imperméable** MASC NOUN
raincoat

impertinent ADJECTIVE
cheeky ◇ *Ne sois pas impertinent!* Don't be cheeky!

impitoyable ADJECTIVE
merciless

impliquer VERB
to mean ◇ *Si tu vas à l'université, ça implique que tu vas devoir nous quitter.* If you go to university, it'll mean that you have to leave us.
- **être impliqué dans** to be involved in
  ◇ *Il est impliqué dans un scandale financier.* He's involved in a financial scandal.

impoli ADJECTIVE
rude

l' **importance** FEM NOUN
importance ◇ *C'est sans importance.* It doesn't matter.

important ADJECTIVE
1 important ◇ *un rôle important* an important role
2 considerable ◇ *une somme importante* a considerable sum

l' **importation** FEM NOUN
import ◇ *Les importations de pétrole ont baissé.* Oil imports have fallen.

importer VERB
see also n'importe
1 to import (*goods*)
2 to matter ◇ *Peu importe.* It doesn't matter.

imposant ADJECTIVE
imposing

imposer VERB
to impose
- **imposer quelque chose à quelqu'un** to make somebody do something

impossible ADJECTIVE
see also impossible NOUN
impossible

l' **impossible** MASC NOUN
see also impossible ADJECTIVE
- **Nous ferons l'impossible pour finir à temps.** We'll do our utmost to finish on time.

l' **impôt** MASC NOUN
tax

imprécis ADJECTIVE
imprecise

l' **impression** FEM NOUN
impression ◇ *Il a fait bonne impression à ma mère.* He made a good impression on my mother.

impressionnant ADJECTIVE
impressive

impressionner VERB
to impress

imprévisible ADJECTIVE
unpredictable

imprévu ADJECTIVE
unexpected

l' **imprimante** FEM NOUN
printer (for computer)

imprimé ADJECTIVE
printed ◇ un tissu imprimé a printed
fabric ◇ C'est imprimé en grandes
lettres. It's printed in large letters.

imprimer VERB
to print

impropre ADJECTIVE
◆ **impropre à la consommation** unfit for
human consumption

improviser VERB
to improvise

improviste ADVERB
◆ **arriver à l'improviste** to arrive
unexpectedly

l' **imprudence** FEM NOUN
carelessness
◆ **Ne fais pas d'imprudences!** Don't do
anything silly!

imprudent ADJECTIVE
[1] **unwise** ◇ Il serait imprudent de
prendre la voiture aujourd'hui. It would
be unwise to take the car today.
[2] **careless** ◇ un conducteur
imprudent a careless driver

impuissant ADJECTIVE
helpless ◇ Elle se sentait
complètement impuissante. She felt
completely helpless.

impulsif ADJECTIVE
(FEM SING **impulsive**)
impulsive

inabordable ADJECTIVE
prohibitive ◇ des prix inabordables
prohibitive prices

inaccessible ADJECTIVE
inaccessible ◇ Cette plage est
inaccessible par la route. This beach is
inaccessible by road.

inachevé ADJECTIVE
unfinished

inadmissible ADJECTIVE
intolerable ◇ Ce type de
comportement est inadmissible! This
sort of behaviour is intolerable!

inanimé ADJECTIVE
unconscious ◇ On l'a retrouvé
inanimé sur la route. He was found
unconscious on the road.

inaperçu ADJECTIVE
◆ **passer inaperçu** to go unnoticed

inattendu ADJECTIVE
unexpected

l' **inattention** FEM NOUN
◆ **une faute d'inattention** a careless
mistake

inaugurer VERB
to open (an exhibition)

incapable ADJECTIVE
incapable ◇ être incapable de faire
quelque chose to be incapable of
doing something

incassable ADJECTIVE
unbreakable

l' **incendie** MASC NOUN
fire ◇ un incendie de forêt a forest
fire

incertain ADJECTIVE
[1] **uncertain** ◇ Son avenir est encore
incertain. His future is still uncertain.
[2] **unsettled** ◇ Le temps est incertain.
The weather is unsettled.

l' **incident** MASC NOUN
incident

inciter VERB
◆ **inciter quelqu'un à faire quelque
chose** to encourage somebody to do
something ◇ J'ai incité mes parents à
partir en voyage. I encouraged my
parents to go on a trip.

inclure VERB
to enclose ◇ Veuillez inclure une
enveloppe timbrée libellée à votre
adresse. Please enclose a stamped
addressed envelope.
◆ **jusqu'au dix mars inclus** until 10th
March inclusive

incohérent ADJECTIVE
incoherent

incollable ADJECTIVE
◆ **être incollable sur quelque chose**
(informal) to know everything there is to
know about something
◆ **le riz incollable** non-stick rice

incolore ADJECTIVE
colourless

incompétent ADJECTIVE
incompetent

incompris ADJECTIVE
misunderstood

l' **inconnu** MASC NOUN
stranger ◇ Ne parle pas à des
inconnus. Don't speak to strangers.
◆ **l'inconnu** the unknown ◇ la peur de
l'inconnu the fear of the unknown

l' **inconnue** FEM NOUN
stranger

inconsciemment ADVERB
unconsciously

inconscient ADJECTIVE
unconscious ◇ Il est resté
inconscient quelques minutes. He was
unconscious for several minutes.

incontestable ADJECTIVE
indisputable

incontournable ADJECTIVE
inevitable ◇ l'incontournable petite

robe noire the inevitable little black dress

l' **inconvénient** MASC NOUN
disadvantage
- **si vous n'y voyez pas d'inconvénient** if you have no objection

incorrect ADJECTIVE
[1] **incorrect** ◇ *une réponse incorrecte* an incorrect answer
[2] **rude** ◇ *Il a été incorrect avec la voisine.* He was rude to the woman next door.

incroyable ADJECTIVE
incredible

inculper VERB
- **inculper de** to charge with ◇ *Il a été inculpé de meurtre.* He was charged with murder.

l' **Inde** FEM NOUN
India

indécis ADJECTIVE
[1] **indecisive** ◇ *Il est constamment indécis.* He's always indecisive.
[2] **undecided** ◇ *Je suis encore indécis.* I'm still undecided.

indéfiniment ADVERB
indefinitely

indélicat ADJECTIVE
tactless

indemne ADJECTIVE
unharmed ◇ *Il s'en est sorti indemne.* He escaped unharmed.

indemniser VERB
to compensate ◇ *Les victimes demandent maintenant à être indemnisées.* The victims are now demanding compensation.

indépendamment ADVERB
independently
- **indépendamment de** irrespective of ◇ *Les allocations familiales sont versées indépendamment des revenus.* Child benefit is given irrespective of income.

l' **indépendance** FEM NOUN
independence

indépendant ADJECTIVE
independent

l' **index** MASC NOUN
[1] **index finger**
[2] **index** (*in book*)

indicatif ADJECTIVE
(FEM SING **indicative**)
see also **indicatif** NOUN
- **à titre indicatif** for your information

l' **indicatif** MASC NOUN
see also **indicatif** ADJECTIVE
[1] **dialling code**
[2] **indicative** (*of verb*)

[3] **theme tune** (*of TV programme*)

les **indications** FEM NOUN
instructions ◇ *Il suffit de suivre les indications.* You just have to follow the instructions.

l' **indice** MASC NOUN
clue ◇ *La police cherche des indices.* The police are looking for clues.

indien ADJECTIVE, NOUN
(FEM SING **indienne**)
Indian
- **un Indien** an Indian (*man*)
- **une Indienne** an Indian (*woman*)

l' **indifférence** FEM NOUN
indifference

indifférent ADJECTIVE
indifferent

l' **indigène** MASC/FEM NOUN
native

indigeste ADJECTIVE
indigestible

l' **indigestion** FEM NOUN
indigestion

indigne ADJECTIVE
unworthy

indigner VERB
- **s'indigner de quelque chose** to get indignant about something

indiqué ADJECTIVE
advisable ◇ *Ce n'est pas très indiqué.* It's not really advisable.

indiquer VERB
to point out ◇ *Il m'a indiqué la mairie.* He pointed out the town hall.

indirect ADJECTIVE
indirect

indiscipliné ADJECTIVE
unruly

indiscret ADJECTIVE
(FEM SING **indiscrète**)
indiscreet

indispensable ADJECTIVE
indispensable

indisposé ADJECTIVE
indisposed
- **être indisposée** to be having one's period

l' **individu** MASC NOUN
individual

individuel ADJECTIVE
(FEM SING **individuelle**)
individual ◇ *servi en portions individuelles* served in individual portions
- **Vous aurez une chambre individuelle.** You'll have a room of your own.

indolore ADJECTIVE
painless

l' **Indonésie** FEM NOUN
Indonesia

indulgent ADJECTIVE
indulgent

◆ Elle est trop indulgente avec son fils.
She's not firm enough with her son.

l' **industrie** FEM NOUN
industry

industriel ADJECTIVE
(FEM SING **industrielle**)
see also industriel NOUN
industrial

l' **industriel** MASC NOUN
see also industriel ADJECTIVE
industrialist

inédit ADJECTIVE
unpublished

inefficace ADJECTIVE
1 ineffective (*treatment*)
2 inefficient ◇ *un service de transports publics inefficace* an inefficient public transport system

inégal ADJECTIVE
(MASC PL **inégaux**)
1 unequal ◇ *un combat inégal* an unequal struggle
2 uneven ◇ *la qualité est inégale* the quality varies

inévitable ADJECTIVE
unavoidable

◆ C'était inévitable! That was bound to happen!

inexact ADJECTIVE
inaccurate

in extremis ADVERB
◆ Il a réussi à attraper son train in extremis. He just managed to catch his train.
◆ Ils ont évité un accident in extremis. They avoided an accident by the skin of their teeth.

l' **infarctus** MASC NOUN
coronary

infatigable ADJECTIVE
indefatigable ◇ *Il est infatigable.* He's indefatigable.

infect ADJECTIVE
revolting (*meal*)

s' **infecter** VERB
to go septic ◇ *La plaie s'est infectée.* The wound has gone septic.

l' **infection** FEM NOUN
infection

inférieur ADJECTIVE
lower ◇ *les membres inférieurs* the lower limbs ◇ *C'est moins cher, mais de qualité inférieure.* It's cheaper but of lower quality.

infernal ADJECTIVE
(MASC PL **infernaux**)
terrible ◇ *Ils faisaient un bruit infernal.* They were making a terrible noise.

l' **infini** MASC NOUN
◆ à l'infini indefinitely ◇ *On pourrait en parler à l'infini.* We could discuss this indefinitely.

l' **infinitif** MASC NOUN
infinitive

l' **infirme** MASC/FEM NOUN
disabled person

l' **infirmerie** FEM NOUN
medical room ◇ *Elle est à l'infirmerie.* She's in the medical room.

l' **infirmier** MASC NOUN
nurse

l' **infirmière** FEM NOUN
nurse

inflammable ADJECTIVE
inflammable

l' **influence** FEM NOUN
influence

influencer VERB
to influence

l' **informaticien** MASC NOUN
computer scientist

l' **informaticienne** FEM NOUN
computer scientist

les **informations** FEM NOUN
1 news (*on TV*) ◇ *les informations de vingt heures* the 8 o'clock news
2 information ◇ *Je voudrais quelques informations, s'il vous plaît.* I'd like some information, please.
◆ une information a piece of information

l' **informatique** FEM NOUN
computing

informer VERB
to inform
◆ s'informer to find out ◇ *Je ne connais pas les heures de fermeture, mais je vais m'informer.* I don't know when they close, but I'm going to find out.

infuser VERB
1 to brew (*tea*)
2 to infuse (*herbal tea*)

l' **infusion** FEM NOUN
herbal tea

l' **ingénieur** MASC NOUN
engineer

ingrat ADJECTIVE
ungrateful

l' **ingrédient** MASC NOUN
ingredient

inhabituel ADJECTIVE
(FEM SING **inhabituelle**)
unusual

inhumain ADJECTIVE
inhuman

initial ADJECTIVE
(MASC PL **initiaux**)
initial

l' **initiale** FEM NOUN
initial

l' **initiation** FEM NOUN
introduction ◇ *un stage d'initiation à la planche à voile* an introductory course in windsurfing

l' **initiative** FEM NOUN
initiative ◇ *avoir de l'initiative* to have initiative

injecter VERB
to inject

l' **injection** FEM NOUN
injection

l' **injure** FEM NOUN
1 **insult** ◇ *Il a pris ça comme une injure.* He took this as an insult.
2 **abuse** ◇ *lancer des injures à quelqu'un* to hurl abuse at somebody

injurieux ADJECTIVE
(FEM SING **injurieuse**)
abusive (*language*)

injuste ADJECTIVE
unfair

innocent ADJECTIVE
innocent

innombrable ADJECTIVE
innumerable

innover VERB
to break new ground

inoccupé ADJECTIVE
empty ◇ *un appartement inoccupé* an empty flat

inoffensif ADJECTIVE
(FEM SING **inoffensive**)
harmless

l' **inondation** FEM NOUN
flood

inoubliable ADJECTIVE
unforgettable

inoxydable ADJECTIVE
• **l'acier inoxydable** stainless steel

inquiet ADJECTIVE
(FEM SING **inquiète**)
worried

inquiétant ADJECTIVE
worrying

s' **inquiéter** VERB
to worry ◇ *Ne t'inquiète pas!* Don't worry!

l' **inquiétude** FEM NOUN
anxiety

insatisfait ADJECTIVE
dissatisfied

l' **inscription** FEM NOUN
registration (*for school, course*)

s' **inscrire** VERB
• **s'inscrire à (1)** to join ◇ *Je me suis inscrit au club de tennis.* I've joined the tennis club.
• **s'inscrire à (2)** to register ◇ *N'attends pas trop pour t'inscrire à la fac.* Don't leave it too long to register at the university.

l' **insecte** MASC NOUN
insect

insensible ADJECTIVE
insensitive ◇ *Il la trouve insensible.* He thinks she's insensitive.

l' **insigne** MASC NOUN
badge

insignifiant ADJECTIVE
insignificant

insister VERB
to insist
• **N'insiste pas!** Don't keep on!

l' **insolation** FEM NOUN
sunstroke

insolent ADJECTIVE
cheeky

insouciant ADJECTIVE
carefree

insoutenable ADJECTIVE
unbearable ◇ *une douleur insoutenable* an unbearable pain

inspecter VERB
to inspect

l' **inspecteur** MASC NOUN
inspector

l' **inspection** FEM NOUN
inspection

l' **inspectrice** FEM NOUN
inspector

inspirer VERB
to inspire
• **s'inspirer de** to take one's inspiration from ◇ *Le peintre s'est inspiré d'un poème.* The painter took his inspiration from a poem.

instable ADJECTIVE
1 **unsteady** (*piece of furniture*)
2 **unstable** (*person*)

les **installations** FEM NOUN
facilities ◇ *Cet appartement est pourvu de toutes les installations modernes.* This flat has all modern facilities.

installer VERB
1 **to put up** (*shelves*)
2 **to install** (*gas, telephone*)
• **s'installer** to settle in ◇ *Nous nous*

sommes installés dans notre nouvel appartement. We've settled into our new flat.

→ **Installez-vous, je vous en prie.** Have a seat please.

l' **instant** MASC NOUN
moment ◇ *dans un instant* in a moment ◇ *Le dîner sera prêt dans un instant.* Dinner will be ready in a moment. ◇ *pour l'instant* for the moment

instantané ADJECTIVE
instant ◇ *du café instantané* instant coffee

l' **instinct** MASC NOUN
instinct

l' **institut** MASC NOUN
institute

l' **instituteur** MASC NOUN
primary school teacher

l' **institution** FEM NOUN
institution

l' **institutrice** FEM NOUN
primary school teacher

l' **instruction** FEM NOUN
1 instruction ◇ *J'ai suivi soigneusement ses instructions.* I followed his instructions carefully.
2 education ◇ *Il n'a pas beaucoup d'instruction.* He's not very well-educated.

s' **instruire** VERB
to educate oneself

instruit ADJECTIVE
educated

l' **instrument** MASC NOUN
instrument ◇ *un instrument de musique* a musical instrument

insuffisant ADJECTIVE
insufficient

→ **"travail insuffisant"** (*on school report*) "must make more effort"

l' **insuline** FEM NOUN
insulin

l' **insulte** FEM NOUN
insult

insulter VERB
to insult

insupportable ADJECTIVE
unbearable

intact ADJECTIVE
intact

intégral ADJECTIVE
(MASC PL **intégraux**)
→ **le texte intégral** unabridged version
→ **un remboursement intégral** a full refund

l' **intégrisme** MASC NOUN
fundamentalism

l' **intelligence** FEM NOUN
intelligence

intelligent ADJECTIVE
intelligent

intense ADJECTIVE
intense

intensif ADJECTIVE
(FEM SING **intensive**)
intensive
→ **un cours intensif** a crash course

l' **intention** FEM NOUN
intention
→ **avoir l'intention de faire quelque chose** to intend to do something ◇ *J'ai l'intention de lui en parler.* I intend to speak to him about it.

l' **interdiction** FEM NOUN
→ **"interdiction de stationner"** "no parking"
→ **"interdiction de fumer"** "no smoking"

interdire VERB
to forbid ◇ *Ses parents lui ont interdit de sortir.* His parents have forbidden him to go out.

interdit ADJECTIVE
forbidden ◇ *Il est interdit de fumer dans les couloirs.* Smoking in the corridors is forbidden.

intéressant ADJECTIVE
interesting ◇ *un livre intéressant* an interesting book
→ **On lui a fait une offre intéressante.** They made him an attractive offer.
→ **On trouve des CD à des prix très intéressants dans ce magasin.** You can get very cheap CDs in this shop.

intéresser VERB
to interest
→ **s'intéresser à** to be interested in ◇ *Est-ce que vous vous intéressez à la politique?* Are you interested in politics?

l' **intérêt** MASC NOUN
interest
→ **avoir intérêt à faire quelque chose** to do well to do something ◇ *Tu as intérêt à te dépêcher si tu veux prendre le train de dix heures.* You'd better hurry up if you want to catch the 10 o'clock train.

l' **intérieur** MASC NOUN
inside ◇ *Il fait plus frais à l'intérieur de la maison.* It's cooler inside the house.

l' **interlocuteur** MASC NOUN
→ **son interlocuteur** the man he's speaking to

l' **interlocutrice** FEM NOUN
→ **son interlocutrice** the woman he's speaking to

l'**intermédiaire** MASC NOUN
intermediary
- **par l'intermédiaire de** through ◇ *Je l'ai rencontré par l'intermédiaire de sa sœur.* I met him through his sister.

l'**internat** MASC NOUN
boarding school

international ADJECTIVE
(MASC PL **internationaux**)
international

l'**interne** MASC/FEM NOUN
boarder

l'**Internet** MASC NOUN
Internet ◇ *sur Internet* on the Internet

l'**interphone** MASC NOUN
intercom

l'**interprète** MASC/FEM NOUN
interpreter

interpréter VERB
to interpret

interrogatif ADJECTIVE
(FEM SING **interrogative**)
interrogative

l'**interrogation** FEM NOUN
1 **question**
2 **test** ◇ *une interrogation écrite* a written test ◇ *une interrogation orale* an oral test

l'**interrogatoire** MASC NOUN
questioning
- **C'est un interrogatoire ou quoi?** Am I being cross-examined?

interroger VERB
to question

interrompre VERB
to interrupt

l'**interrupteur** MASC NOUN
switch

l'**interruption** FEM NOUN
interruption
- **sans interruption** without stopping ◇ *Il a parlé pendant deux heures sans interruption.* He spoke for two hours without stopping.

l'**intervalle** MASC NOUN
interval
- **dans l'intervalle** in the meantime

intervenir VERB
1 **to intervene**
2 **to take action** ◇ *La police est intervenue.* The police took action.

l'**intervention** FEM NOUN
intervention ◇ *une intervention militaire* a military intervention
- **une intervention chirurgicale** a surgical operation

l'**interview** FEM NOUN
interview (*on radio, TV*)

l'**intestin** MASC NOUN
intestine

intime ADJECTIVE
intimate
- **un journal intime** a diary

intimider VERB
to intimidate

l'**intimité** FEM NOUN
- **dans l'intimité** in private ◇ *Ce que vous faites dans l'intimité ne m'intéresse pas.* What you do in private doesn't interest me.
- **Le mariage a eu lieu dans l'intimité.** The wedding ceremony was private.

intitulé ADJECTIVE
entitled

intolérable ADJECTIVE
intolerable

l'**intoxication** FEM NOUN
- **une intoxication alimentaire** food poisoning

intransigeant ADJECTIVE
uncompromising

l'**intrigue** FEM NOUN
plot (*of book, film*)

l'**introduction** FEM NOUN
introduction

introduire VERB
to introduce

l'**intuition** FEM NOUN
intuition

inusable ADJECTIVE
hard-wearing

inutile ADJECTIVE
useless

l'**invalide** MASC/FEM NOUN
disabled person

l'**invasion** FEM NOUN
invasion

inventer VERB
1 **to invent**
2 **to make up** ◇ *inventer une excuse* to make up an excuse

l'**inventeur** MASC NOUN
inventor

l'**invention** FEM NOUN
invention

inverse ADJECTIVE
see also **inverse** NOUN
- **dans l'ordre inverse** in reverse order
- **en sens inverse** in the opposite direction

l'**inverse** MASC NOUN
see also **inverse** ADJECTIVE
reverse
- **Tu t'es trompé, c'est l'inverse.** You've got it wrong, it's the other way round.

l'**investissement** MASC NOUN
investment

invisible ADJECTIVE
　invisible

l'**invitation** FEM NOUN
　invitation

l'**invité** MASC NOUN
　guest

l'**invitée** FEM NOUN
　guest

inviter VERB
　to invite

involontaire ADJECTIVE
　unintentional　◇ *C'était tout à fait involontaire.* It was quite unintentional.

invraisemblable ADJECTIVE
　unlikely　◇ *une histoire invraisemblable* an implausible story

ira, irai, iraient, irais VERB *see* **aller**
→ *J'irai demain au supermarché.* I'll go to the supermarket tomorrow.

l'**Irak** MASC NOUN
　Iraq

l'**Iran** MASC NOUN
　Iran

iras, irez VERB *see* **aller**

irlandais ADJECTIVE, NOUN
　(FEM SING **irlandaise**)
　Irish
→ **un Irlandais** an Irishman
→ **une Irlandaise** an Irishwoman
→ **les Irlandais** the Irish

l'**Irlande** FEM NOUN
　Ireland
→ **en Irlande (1)** in Ireland
→ **en Irlande (2)** to Ireland
→ **la République d'Irlande** the Irish Republic
→ **l'Irlande du Nord** Northern Ireland

l'**ironie** FEM NOUN
　irony

ironique ADJECTIVE
　ironical

irons, iront VERB *see* **aller**
→ **Nous irons à la plage cet après-midi.** We'll go to the beach this afternoon.

irrationnel ADJECTIVE
　(FEM SING **irrationnelle**)
　irrational

irréel ADJECTIVE
　(FEM SING **irréelle**)
　unreal

irrégulier ADJECTIVE
　(FEM SING **irrégulière**)
　irregular

irrésistible ADJECTIVE
　irresistible

irritable ADJECTIVE
　irritable

irriter VERB
　to irritate

islamique ADJECTIVE
　Islamic

l'**Islande** FEM NOUN
　Iceland

isolé ADJECTIVE
　isolated　◇ *une ferme isolée* an isolated farm

Israël MASC NOUN
　Israel

israélien ADJECTIVE, NOUN
　(FEM SING **israélienne**)
　Israeli
→ **un Israélien** an Israeli (*man*)
→ **une Israélienne** an Israeli (*woman*)
→ **les Israéliens** the Israelis

israélite ADJECTIVE
　Jewish

l'**issue** FEM NOUN
→ **une voie sans issue** a dead end
→ **l'issue de secours** emergency exit

l'**Italie** FEM NOUN
　Italy
→ **en Italie (1)** in Italy
→ **en Italie (2)** to Italy

italien ADJECTIVE, NOUN
　(FEM SING **italienne**)
　Italian　◇ *J'apprends l'italien.* I'm learning Italian.
→ **un Italien** an Italian (*man*)
→ **une Italienne** (*woman*)
→ **les Italiens** the Italians

l'**itinéraire** MASC NOUN
　route

l'**IUT** MASC NOUN (= *Institut universitaire de technologie*)
　institute of technology (*at university level*)

ivre ADJECTIVE
　drunk

l'**ivrogne** MASC/FEM NOUN
　drunkard

J

j' PRONOUN *see* **je**

la **jalousie** NOUN
  jealousy

jaloux ADJECTIVE
  (FEM SING **jalouse**)
  jealous

jamais ADVERB
  ① **never** ◇ *Est-ce que tu vas souvent au cinéma?–Non, jamais.* Do you go to the cinema often?–No, never. ◇ *Il ne boit jamais d'alcool.* He never drinks alcohol.
  ② **ever**
  Phrases with **jamais** *meaning* **ever** *are followed by a verb in the subjunctive.*
  ◇ *C'est la plus belle chose que j'aie jamais vue.* It's the most beautiful thing I've ever seen.

la **jambe** NOUN
  leg

le **jambon** NOUN
  ham
  ‣ **le jambon cru** Parma ham

le **jambonneau** NOUN
  (PL les **jambonneaux**)
  knuckle of ham

janvier MASC NOUN
  January
  ‣ **en janvier** in January

le **Japon** NOUN
  Japan
  ‣ **au Japon (1)** in Japan
  ‣ **au Japon (2)** to Japan

japonais ADJECTIVE, NOUN
  Japanese ◇ *Elle parle japonais.* She speaks Japanese.
  ‣ **un Japonais** a Japanese (*man*)
  ‣ **une Japonaise** a Japanese (*woman*)
  ‣ **les Japonais** the Japanese

le **jardin** NOUN
  garden

le **jardinage** NOUN
  gardening

le **jardinier** NOUN
  gardener

la **jardinière** NOUN
  gardener

jaune ADJECTIVE
  see also **jaune** NOUN
  yellow

le **jaune** NOUN
  see also **jaune** ADJECTIVE
  yellow
  ‣ **un jaune d'œuf** an egg yolk

jaunir VERB
  to turn yellow

la **jaunisse** NOUN
  jaundice

Javel NOUN
  ‣ **l'eau de Javel** bleach

J.-C. ABBREVIATION (= *Jésus-Christ*)
  ‣ **44 avant J.-C.** 44 BC
  ‣ **115 après J.-C.** 115 AD

je PRONOUN
  je *changes to* **j'** *before a vowel and most words beginning with "h".*
  I ◇ *Je t'appellerai ce soir.* I'll phone you this evening. ◇ *J'arrive!* I'm coming! ◇ *J'hésite.* I'm not sure.

le **jean** NOUN
  jeans

Jésus-Christ MASC NOUN
  Jesus Christ

le **jet** NOUN
  ① **jet** (*of water*)
  ② **jet plane**

jetable ADJECTIVE
  disposable

la **jetée** NOUN
  jetty

jeter VERB
  ① **to throw** ◇ *Il a jeté son manteau sur le lit.* He threw his coat onto the bed.
  ② **to throw away** ◇ *Mes parents ne jettent jamais rien.* My parents never throw anything away.
  ‣ **jeter un coup d'œil** to have a look ◇ *Jette un coup d'œil pour voir s'il y a des erreurs.* Have a look to see if there are any mistakes.

le **jeton** NOUN
  counter (*in board game*)

le **jeu** NOUN
  (PL les **jeux**)
  game ◇ *Je n'aime pas les jeux de société.* I don't like board games.
  ‣ **un jeu de cartes (1)** a pack of cards
  ‣ **un jeu de cartes (2)** a card game
  ‣ **un jeu de mots** a pun
  ‣ **en jeu** at stake ◇ *Des vies humaines sont en jeu.* Human lives are at stake.

le **jeudi** NOUN
  ① **Thursday** ◇ *Aujourd'hui, nous sommes jeudi.* It's Thursday today.
  ② **on Thursday** ◇ *Il arrivera jeudi matin.* He's arriving on Thursday morning.
  ‣ **le jeudi** on Thursdays ◇ *Le musée est fermé le jeudi.* The museum is closed on Thursdays.
  ‣ **tous les jeudis** every Thursday

PTO

- **jeudi dernier** last Thursday
- **jeudi prochain** next Thursday

jeun
- **à jeun** ADVERB
  on an empty stomach ◇ *à prendre à jeun* to be taken on an empty stomach ◇ *Il faut être à jeun pour la prise de sang.* You mustn't have eaten anything before giving a blood sample.

jeune ADJECTIVE
young ◇ *un jeune homme* a young man ◇ *une jeune femme* a young woman
- **une jeune fille** a girl

la **jeunesse** NOUN
youth

la **joie** NOUN
joy

joindre VERB
1 to put together ◇ *On va joindre les deux tables.* We're going to put the two tables together.
2 to contact ◇ *Vous arriverez peut-être à le joindre chez lui.* Maybe you'll be able to contact him at home.

joint ADJECTIVE
- **une pièce jointe** an enclosure (*in letter*)

joli ADJECTIVE
pretty

le **jonc** NOUN
rush

la **jonquille** NOUN
daffodil

la **joue** NOUN
cheek

jouer VERB
1 to play ◇ *Elle est allée jouer avec les petits voisins.* She's gone to play with the children next door.
- **jouer de** to play (*instrument*) ◇ *Il joue de la guitare et du piano.* He plays the guitar and the piano.
- **jouer à** to play (*sport, game*) ◇ *Elle joue au tennis.* She plays tennis. ◇ *jouer aux dames* to play draughts
2 to act ◇ *Je trouve qu'il joue très bien dans ce film.* I think he acts very well in this film.
- **On joue Hamlet au Théâtre de la Ville.** Hamlet is on at the Théâtre de la Ville.

le **jouet** NOUN
toy

le **joueur** NOUN
player
- **être mauvais joueur** to be a bad loser

la **joueuse** NOUN
player

le **jour** NOUN
day ◇ *J'ai passé trois jours chez mes cousins.* I stayed with my cousins for three days.
- **Il fait jour.** It's daylight.
- **mettre quelque chose à jour** to update something
- **un jour férié** a public holiday

le **journal** NOUN
(PL les **journaux**)
1 newspaper
- **le journal télévisé** the television news
2 diary ◇ *Elle tient un journal depuis l'âge de douze ans.* She has been keeping a diary since she was 12.

journalier ADJECTIVE
(FEM SING **journalière**)
daily

le **journalisme** NOUN
journalism

le/la **journaliste** NOUN
journalist ◇ *Elle est journaliste.* She's a journalist.

la **journée** NOUN
day

joyeux ADJECTIVE
(FEM SING **joyeuse**)
happy
- **Joyeux anniversaire!** Happy birthday!
- **Joyeux Noël!** Merry Christmas!

le **judo** NOUN
judo

le **juge** NOUN
judge

juger VERB
to judge

juif ADJECTIVE
(FEM SING **juive**)
Jewish ◇ *la cuisine juive* Jewish cooking
- **un juif** a Jew (*man*)
- **une juive** a Jew (*woman*)

juillet MASC NOUN
July
- **en juillet** in July

juin MASC NOUN
June
- **en juin** in June

le **jumeau** NOUN
(PL les **jumeaux**)
twin

jumeler VERB
to twin ◇ *Saint-Brieuc est jumelée avec Aberystwyth.* Saint-Brieuc is twinned with Aberystwyth.

la **jumelle** NOUN
twin

les **jumelles** FEM NOUN
binoculars

la **jument** NOUN
mare

la **jungle** NOUN
  jungle
la **jupe** NOUN
  skirt
jurer VERB
  to swear   ◇ *Je jure que c'est vrai!* I swear it's true!
juridique ADJECTIVE
  legal
le **jury** NOUN
  jury
le **jus** NOUN
  juice
- **un jus de fruit** a fruit juice
jusqu'à PREPOSITION
  [1] as far as   ◇ *Nous avons marché jusqu'au village.* We walked as far as the village.
  [2] until   ◇ *Il fait généralement chaud jusqu'à la mi-août.* It's usually hot until mid-August.
- **jusqu'à ce que** until   ◇ *Tu peux rester ici jusqu'à ce qu'il cesse de pleuvoir.* You can stay here until it stops raining.

- **jusqu'à présent** so far
juste ADJECTIVE, ADVERB
  [1] fair   ◇ *Il est sévère, mais juste.* He's strict but fair.
  [2] tight   ◇ *Cette veste est un peu juste.* This jacket is a bit tight.
- **juste assez** just enough
- **chanter juste** to sing in tune
justement ADVERB
  just   ◇ *C'est justement pour cela qu'il est parti!* That's just the reason why he left!
la **justesse** NOUN
- **de justesse** only just   ◇ *Il a eu son permis de justesse.* He only just passed his driving test.
la **justice** NOUN
  justice
justifier VERB
  to justify
juteux ADJECTIVE
  (FEM SING **juteuse**)
  juicy
juvénile ADJECTIVE
  youthful

J

K

kaki ADJECTIVE
khaki

le **kangourou** NOUN
kangaroo

le **karaté** NOUN
karate

la **kermesse** NOUN
fair

kidnapper VERB
to kidnap

le **kilo** NOUN
kilo

le **kilogramme** NOUN
kilogramme

le **kilomètre** NOUN
kilometre

le/la **kinésithérapeute** NOUN
physiotherapist

le **kiosque** NOUN
- un kiosque à journaux a news stand

le **klaxon** NOUN
horn (of car)

klaxonner VERB
to sound the horn

km ABBREVIATION (= kilomètre)
- km/h kph (= kilometres per hour)

K.-O. ADJECTIVE
knocked out
- mettre quelqu'un K.-O. to knock
somebody out ◇ Il l'a mis K.-O. au
troisième round. He knocked him out
in the third round.
- Je suis complètement K.-O. (informal)
I'm knackered.

le **K-way** NOUN
cagoule

L

l' ARTICLE, PRONOUN *see* **la, le**

la ARTICLE, PRONOUN

> *see also* **la** NOUN

> **la** *changes to* **l'** *before a vowel and most words beginning with "h".*

1. **the** ◇ *la maison* the house ◇ *l'actrice* the actress ◇ *l'herbe* the grass

2. **her** ◇ *Je la connais depuis longtemps.* I've known her for a long time. ◇ *C'est une femme intelligente: je l'admire beaucoup.* She's an intelligent woman: I admire her very much.

3. **it** ◇ *C'est une bonne émission: je la regarde toutes les semaines.* It's a good programme: I watch it every week.

4. **one's**

- **se mordre la langue** to bite one's tongue ◇ *Je me suis mordu la langue.* I've bitten my tongue.

- **dix francs la douzaine** 10 francs a dozen

le la NOUN

> *see also* **la** ARTICLE

1. **A** ◇ *en la bémol* in A flat

2. **la** ◇ *sol, la, si, do* so, la, ti, do

là ADVERB

1. **there** ◇ *Ton livre est là, sur la table.* Your book's there, on the table.

2. **here** ◇ *Elle n'est pas là.* She isn't here.

- **C'est là que... (1)** That's where... ◇ *C'est là que je suis né.* That's where I was born.

- **C'est là que... (2)** That's when... ◇ *C'est là que j'ai réalisé que je m'étais trompé.* That's when I realized that I had made a mistake.

là-bas ADVERB
over there

le labo NOUN *(informal)*
lab

le laboratoire NOUN
laboratory

labourer VERB
to plough

le labyrinthe NOUN
maze

le lac NOUN
lake

lacer VERB
to do up *(shoes)*

le lacet NOUN
lace

- **des chaussures à lacets** lace-up shoes

lâche ADJECTIVE

> *see also* **lâche** NOUN

1. **loose** ◇ *Le nœud est trop lâche.* The knot's too loose.

2. **cowardly**

- **Il est lâche.** He's a coward.

le lâche NOUN

> *see also* **lâche** ADJECTIVE

coward

lâcher VERB

1. **to let go of** ◇ *Il n'a pas lâché ma main de tout le film.* He didn't let go of my hand until the end of the film.

2. **to drop** ◇ *Il a été tellement surpris qu'il a lâché son verre.* He was so surprised that he dropped his glass.

3. **to fail** ◇ *Les freins ont lâché.* The brakes failed.

la lâcheté NOUN
cowardice

lacrymogène ADJECTIVE

- **le gaz lacrymogène** tear gas

la lacune NOUN
gap

là-dedans ADVERB
in there ◇ *Qu'est-ce qu'il y a là-dedans?* What's in there?

là-dessous ADVERB

1. **under there** ◇ *Mon carnet d'adresses est quelque part là-dessous.* My address book is under there somewhere.

2. **behind it** ◇ *Il y a quelque chose de louche là-dessous.* There's something fishy behind it.

là-dessus ADVERB
on there

là-haut ADVERB
up there

laid ADJECTIVE
ugly

la laideur NOUN
ugliness

le lainage NOUN
woollen garment

la laine NOUN
wool ◇ *un pull en laine* a wool jumper

laïque ADJECTIVE

- **une école laïque** a state school

la laisse NOUN
lead ◇ *Tenez votre chien en laisse.* Keep your dog on a lead.

laisser VERB

1. **to leave** ◇ *J'ai laissé mon parapluie à la maison.* I've left my

umbrella at home.

2 to let ◦ *Laisse-le parler.* Let him speak.

→ **Elle se laisse aller.** She's letting herself go.

le **laisser-aller** NOUN
    carelessness

le **lait** NOUN
    milk

→ **un café au lait** a white coffee

la **laitue** NOUN
    lettuce

les **lambeaux** MASC NOUN

→ **en lambeaux** tattered

la **lame** NOUN
    blade ◦ *une lame de rasoir* a razor blade

la **lamelle** NOUN
    thin strip

lamentable ADJECTIVE
    appalling

se **lamenter** VERB
    to moan

le **lampadaire** NOUN
    standard lamp

la **lampe** NOUN
    lamp

→ **une lampe de poche** a torch

la **lance** NOUN
    spear

le **lancement** NOUN
    launch

lancer VERB
    see also lancer NOUN

    1 to throw ◦ *Lance-moi le ballon!* Throw me the ball!

    2 to launch ◦ *Ils viennent de lancer un nouveau modèle.* They've just launched a new model.

→ **se lancer** to embark on ◦ *Il s'est lancé là-dedans sans bien réfléchir.* He embarked on it without thinking properly.

le **lancer** NOUN
    see also lancer VERB

→ **le lancer de poids** putting the shot

lancinant ADJECTIVE

→ **une douleur lancinante** a shooting pain

le **landau** NOUN
    pram

la **lande** NOUN
    moor

le **langage** NOUN
    language

la **langouste** NOUN
    crayfish

la **langue** NOUN
    1 tongue ◦ *Un petit garçon m'a tiré la langue.* A little boy stuck out his tongue at me.

→ **sa langue maternelle** his mother tongue

    2 language ◦ *une langue vivante* a modern language

la **lanière** NOUN
    strap

le **lapin** NOUN
    rabbit

le **laps** NOUN

→ **un laps de temps** a space of time

la **laque** NOUN
    hair spray

laquelle PRONOUN
    (PL **lesquelles**)

    1 which ◦ *Laquelle de ces photos préfères-tu?* Which of these photos do you prefer? ◦ *À laquelle de tes sœurs ressembles-tu?* Which of your sisters do you look like?

    2 whom ◦ *la personne à laquelle vous faites référence* the person to whom you are referring

    laquelle *is often not translated in English.*
    ◦ *la personne à laquelle je pense* the person I'm thinking of

le **lard** NOUN
    streaky bacon

les **lardons** MASC NOUN
    chunks of bacon

large ADJECTIVE, ADVERB
    see also large NOUN
    wide

→ **voir large** to allow a bit extra ◦ *Achète un autre pain: il vaut mieux voir large.* Buy another loaf of bread: it's better to have a bit extra.

le **large** NOUN
    see also large ADJECTIVE

→ **cinq mètres de large** 5 m wide

→ **le large** the open sea

→ **au large de** off the coast of ◦ *Le bateau est actuellement au large du Portugal.* The boat is off the coast of Portugal at the moment.

largement ADVERB

→ **Vous avez largement le temps.** You have plenty of time.

→ **C'est largement suffisant.** That's ample.

la **largeur** NOUN
    width

la **larme** NOUN
    tear ◦ *être en larmes* to be in tears

la **laryngite** NOUN
    laryngitis

le **laser** NOUN
    laser

- **une chaîne laser** a compact disc player
- **un disque laser** a compact disc

lasser VERB
- **se lasser de** to get tired of ◇ *Il s'est lassé de la tapisserie à fleurs du salon.* He's got tired of the flowery wallpaper in the sitting room.

le **latin** NOUN
Latin

le **laurier** NOUN
laurel tree ◇ *une feuille de laurier* a bay leaf

lavable ADJECTIVE
washable

le **lavabo** NOUN
washbasin

le **lavage** NOUN
wash ◇ *Ce pull a rétréci au lavage.* This jumper has shrunk in the wash.

la **lavande** NOUN
lavender

le **lave-linge** NOUN
(PL les **lave-linge**)
washing machine

laver VERB
to wash
- **se laver** to wash ◇ *se laver les mains* to wash one's hands

la **laverie** NOUN
- **une laverie automatique** a launderette

le **lave-vaisselle** NOUN
(PL les **lave-vaisselle**)
dishwasher

le ARTICLE, PRONOUN
le *changes to* l' *before a vowel and most words beginning with "h".*
1 the ◇ *le livre* the book ◇ *l'arbre* the tree ◇ *l'hélicoptère* the helicopter
2 him ◇ *Daniel est un vieil ami: je le connais depuis plus de vingt ans.* Daniel is an old friend: I've known him for over 20 years.
3 it ◇ *Où est mon stylo? Je ne le trouve plus.* Where's my pen? I can't find it. ◇ *Où est le fromage?-Je l'ai mis au frigo.* Where's the cheese?-I've put it in the fridge.
4 one's
- **se laver le visage** to wash one's face ◇ *Évitez de vous laver le visage avec du savon.* Avoid washing your face with soap.
- **dix francs le kilo** 10 francs a kilo

lécher VERB
to lick

le **lèche-vitrine** NOUN
- **faire du lèche-vitrine** to go window-shopping

la **leçon** NOUN
lesson

le **lecteur** NOUN
1 reader
2 foreign language assistant (*at a university*)
- **un lecteur de cassettes** a cassette player
- **un lecteur de CD** a CD player

la **lectrice** NOUN
1 reader
2 foreign language assistant (*at a university*)

la **lecture** NOUN
reading

légal ADJECTIVE
(MASC PL **légaux**)
legal

la **légende** NOUN
1 legend
2 key (*of map*)

léger ADJECTIVE
(FEM SING **légère**)
1 light
2 slight ◇ *un léger retard* a slight delay
- **à la légère** thoughtlessly ◇ *Il a agi à la légère.* He acted thoughtlessly.

légèrement ADVERB
1 lightly ◇ *Habille-toi légèrement: il va faire chaud.* Wear light clothes: it's going to be hot.
2 slightly ◇ *Il est légèrement plus grand que son frère.* He's slightly taller than his brother.

les **législatives** FEM NOUN
general election

le **légume** NOUN
vegetable

le **lendemain** NOUN
next day ◇ *le lendemain de son arrivée* the day after he arrived
- **le lendemain matin** the next morning

lent ADJECTIVE
slow

lentement ADVERB
slowly

la **lenteur** NOUN
slowness

la **lentille** NOUN
1 contact lens ◇ *Est-ce que tu portes des lentilles?* Do you wear contact lenses?
2 lentil ◇ *un rôti de porc aux lentilles* roast pork with lentils

le **léopard** NOUN
leopard

lequel PRONOUN
(FEM SING **laquelle**, MASC PL **lesquels**, FEM PL **lesquelles**)

1 **which** ◇ *Lequel de ces films as-tu préféré?* Which of the films did you prefer?

2 **whom** ◇ *l'homme avec lequel elle a été vue pour la dernière fois* the man with whom she was last seen

lequel *is often not translated in English.*
◇ *le garçon avec lequel elle est sortie* the boy she went out with

les ARTICLE, PRONOUN

1 **the** ◇ *les arbres* the trees

2 **them** ◇ *Elle les a invités à dîner.* She invited them to dinner.

3 **one's**

- **se brosser les dents** to brush one's teeth ◇ *Elle s'est brossé les dents.* She brushed her teeth.

- **dix francs les cinq** 10 francs for 5

la **lesbienne** NOUN
lesbian

lesquels PRONOUN
(FEM **lesquelles**)

1 **which** ◇ *Lesquelles de ces photos as-tu choisies?* Which of the photos did you choose?

2 **whom** ◇ *les personnes avec lesquelles il est associé* the people with whom he is in partnership

lesquels *is often not translated in English.*
◇ *les gens chez lesquels nous avons dîné* the people we had dinner with

la **lessive** NOUN

1 **washing powder** ◇ *une marque de lessive* a brand of washing powder

2 **wash** ◇ *Est-ce que vous avez quelque chose à mettre à la lessive?* Have you got anything to go in the wash?

leste ADJECTIVE
nimble

la **Lettonie** NOUN
Latvia

la **lettre** NOUN
letter ◇ *écrire une lettre* to write a lettre

les **lettres** FEM NOUN
arts ◇ *la faculté de lettres* the Faculty of Arts

leur ADJECTIVE, PRONOUN

1 **their** ◇ *leur ami* their friend

2 **them** ◇ *Je leur ai dit la vérité.* I told them the truth.

- **le leur** theirs ◇ *mon camion et le leur* my truck and theirs ◇ *Ma voiture est rouge, la leur est bleue.* My car's red, theirs is blue.

leurs ADJECTIVE, PRONOUN
their ◇ *leurs amis* their friends

- **les leurs** theirs ◇ *tes livres et les leurs* your books and theirs

levé ADJECTIVE

- **être levé** to be up ◇ *Est-ce qu'il est levé?* Is he up?

lever VERB
see also **lever** NOUN
to raise ◇ *Levez vos verres!* Raise your glasses! ◇ *Levez la main si vous connaissez la réponse.* Put your hand up if you know the answer.

- **lever les yeux** to look up

- **se lever (1)** to get up ◇ *Il se lève tous les jours à six heures.* He gets up at 6 o'clock every day.

- **se lever (2)** to rise ◇ *Le soleil se lève actuellement à cinq heures.* At the moment the sun rises at 5 o'clock.

le **lever** NOUN
see also **lever** VERB

- **le lever du soleil** sunrise

le **levier** NOUN
lever

la **lèvre** NOUN
lip

le **lévrier** NOUN
greyhound

la **levure** NOUN
yeast

- **la levure chimique** baking powder

le **lexique** NOUN
word list

le **lézard** NOUN
lizard

la **liaison** NOUN
affair ◇ *Ils ont eu une liaison dans leur jeunesse.* They had an affair when they were younger.

la **libellule** NOUN
dragonfly

libérer VERB
to free ◇ *Les otages ont été libérés hier soir.* The hostages were freed last night.

- **se libérer** to find time ◇ *J'essaierai de me libérer cet après-midi.* I'll try to find time this afternoon.

la **liberté** NOUN
freedom

- **mettre en liberté** to release ◇ *Il a été mis en liberté au bout d'un an de prison.* He was released after a year in prison.

le/la **libraire** NOUN
bookseller

la **librairie** NOUN
bookshop

libre ADJECTIVE

① **free** ◇ *Tu es libre de faire ce que tu veux.* You are free to do as you wish. ◇ *Est-ce que cette place est libre?* Is this seat free?

② **clear** ◇ *La route est libre: vous pouvez traverser.* The road is clear: you can cross.

- **une école libre** a private school

le **libre-service** NOUN
(PL les **libres-services**)
self-service store

la **Libye** NOUN
Libya

la **licence** NOUN
① **degree** ◇ *une licence de droit* a law degree
② **licence** ◇ *une licence d'exportation* an export licence

le **licencié** NOUN
graduate

la **licenciée** NOUN
graduate

licencier VERB
to make redundant ◇ *Ils viennent de licencier sept employés.* They've just made 7 employees redundant.

le **liège** NOUN
cork ◇ *des sets en liège* cork mats
- **un bouchon en liège** a cork *(for bottle)*

le **lien** NOUN
connection ◇ *Il n'y aucun lien entre ces deux événements.* There's no connection between these two events.
- **un lien de parenté** a family tie

lier VERB
- **lier conversation avec quelqu'un** to get into conversation with somebody
- **se lier avec quelqu'un** to make friends with somebody ◇ *Je ne me lie pas facilement.* I don't make friends easily.

le **lierre** NOUN
ivy

le **lieu** NOUN
(PL les **lieux**)
place ◇ *votre lieu de travail* your place of work
- **avoir lieu** to take place ◇ *La cérémonie a eu lieu dans la salle des fêtes.* The ceremony took place in the village hall.
- **au lieu de** instead of ◇ *J'aimerais une pomme au lieu de la glace.* I'd like an apple instead of ice cream.

le **lièvre** NOUN
hare

la **ligne** NOUN
① **line** *(phone, train)* ◇ *La ligne est mauvaise.* It's a bad line. ◇ *la ligne d'autobus numéro douze* the number

12 bus
② **figure** ◇ *C'est mauvais pour la ligne.* It's bad for your figure.

ligoter VERB
to tie up

la **ligue** NOUN
league

le **lilas** NOUN
lilac

la **limace** NOUN
slug

la **lime** NOUN
- **une lime à ongles** a nail file

la **limitation** NOUN
- **la limitation de vitesse** the speed limit

la **limite** NOUN
① **boundary** *(of property, football pitch)*
② **limit** ◇ *Est-ce qu'il y a une limite d'âge?* Is there an age limit?
- **la date limite** the deadline
- **la date limite de vente** the sell-by-date

limiter VERB
to limit ◇ *Le nombre de billets est limité à deux par personne.* The number of tickets is limited to two per person.

la **limonade** NOUN
lemonade

le **lin** NOUN
linen ◇ *une veste en lin* a linen jacket

le **linge** NOUN
① **linen** ◇ *le linge sale* dirty linen
② **washing** ◇ *laver le linge* to do the washing
- **du linge de corps** underwear

la **lingerie** NOUN
underwear *(women's)*

le **lion** NOUN
lion
- **le Lion** Leo ◇ *Louise est Lion.* Louise is Leo.

la **lionne** NOUN
lioness

la **liqueur** NOUN
liqueur

liquide ADJECTIVE
see also **liquide** NOUN
liquid

le **liquide** NOUN
see also **liquide** ADJECTIVE
liquid
- **payer quelque chose en liquide** to pay cash for something

lire VERB
to read ◇ *Tu as lu "Madame Bovary"?* Have you read "Madame Bovary"?

lis, lisent, lisez VERB *see* **lire**
- **Je lis beaucoup.** I read a lot.

lisible ADJECTIVE
legible
lisse ADJECTIVE
smooth
la **liste** NOUN
list
- **faire la liste de** to make a list of
  ◇ *J'ai fait la liste de tout ce dont j'ai besoin.* I've made a list of all the things I need.
lit VERB *see* **lire**
le **lit** NOUN
bed ◇ *aller au lit* to go to bed
- **faire son lit** to make one's bed ◇ *Je n'ai pas eu le temps de faire mon lit ce matin.* I haven't had time to make my bed this morning.
- **un lit de camp** a campbed
la **literie** NOUN
bedding
la **litière** NOUN
1 **litter** (*for cat*)
2 **bedding** (*of caged pet*)
le **litre** NOUN
litre
littéraire ADJECTIVE
- **une œuvre littéraire** a work of literature
la **littérature** NOUN
literature
le **littoral** NOUN
(PL les **littoraux**)
coast
la **Lituanie** NOUN
Lithuania
la **livraison** NOUN
delivery
- **la livraison des bagages** baggage reclaim
le **livre** NOUN
see also la **livre**
book
- **un livre de poche** a paperback
la **livre** NOUN
see also le **livre**
pound
The French livre *is 500 grams.*
◇ *une livre de beurre* a pound of butter
- **la livre sterling** the pound sterling
  ◇ *Le guide coûte trois livres.* The guide book costs £3.
livrer VERB
to deliver
le **livret** NOUN
booklet
- **le livret scolaire** the school report book
le **livreur** NOUN
delivery man

local ADJECTIVE
(MASC PL **locaux**)
see also **local** NOUN
local
le **local** NOUN
(PL les **locaux**)
see also **local** ADJECTIVE
premises ◇ *Nous cherchons un local pour les répétitions.* We are looking for premises to rehearse in.
le/la **locataire** NOUN
1 **tenant**
2 **lodger** ◇ *Ils ont décidé de prendre un locataire.* They have decided to take a lodger.
la **location** NOUN
- **location de voitures** car rental
- **location de skis** ski hire
locaux ADJECTIVE, NOUN *see* **local**
la **locomotive** NOUN
locomotive
la **loge** NOUN
dressing room
le **logement** NOUN
1 **housing**
2 **accommodation**
loger VERB
to stay ◇ *Elle loge chez sa cousine quand elle revient dans la région.* She stays with her cousin when she comes back to the area.
- **trouver à se loger** to find somewhere to live ◇ *J'ai eu du mal à trouver à me loger.* I had difficulty finding somewhere to live.
le **logiciel** NOUN
software
logique ADJECTIVE
see also **logique** NOUN
logical
la **logique** NOUN
see also **logique** ADJECTIVE
logic
la **loi** NOUN
law
loin ADVERB
1 **far** ◇ *La gare n'est pas très loin d'ici.* The station is not very far from here.
2 **far off** ◇ *Noël n'est plus tellement loin.* Christmas isn't far off now.
3 **a long time ago** ◇ *Les vacances paraissent déjà tellement loin!* The holidays already seem such a long time ago!
- **au loin** in the distance ◇ *On aperçoit la mer au loin.* You can see the sea in the distance.
- **de loin (1)** from a long way away

◇ *On voit l'église de loin.* You can see the church from a long way away.
- **de loin (2)** by far   ◇ *C'est de loin l'élève la plus brillante.* She is by far the brightest pupil.

lointain   ADJECTIVE
see also lointain NOUN
distant   ◇ *un pays lointain* a distant country   ◇ *C'est un parent lointain de ma mère.* He's a distant relation of my mother.

le **lointain**   NOUN
see also lointain ADJECTIVE
- **dans le lointain** in the distance

le **loir**   NOUN
dormouse
- **dormir comme un loir** to sleep like a log

les **loisirs**   MASC NOUN
1 **free time**   ◇ *Qu'est-ce que vous faites pendant vos loisirs?* What do you do in your free time?
2 **hobby**   ◇ *Le ski et l'équitation sont des loisirs coûteux.* Skiing and riding are expensive hobbies.

le **Londonien**   NOUN
Londoner

la **Londonienne**   NOUN
Londoner

Londres   NOUN
London   ◇ *le métro de Londres* the London underground
- **à Londres (1)** in London
- **à Londres (2)** to London

long   ADJECTIVE
(FEM SING **longue**)
see also long NOUN
long

le **long**   NOUN
see also long ADJECTIVE
- **un bateau de trois mètres de long** a boat 3 m long
- **tout le long de** all along   ◇ *Il y a des chemins de randonnée tout le long de la côte.* There are footpaths all along the coast.
- **marcher de long en large** to walk up and down

longtemps   ADVERB
a long time   ◇ *J'ai attendu longtemps chez le dentiste.* I waited a long time at the dentist's.
- **pendant longtemps** for a long time   ◇ *On a cru pendant longtemps que la Terre était plate.* For a long time people thought the Earth was flat.
- **mettre longtemps à faire quelque chose** to take a long time to do something   ◇ *Il a mis longtemps à répondre à ma lettre.* He took a long

time to answer my letter.
longue   ADJECTIVE *see* **long**

la **longue**   NOUN
- **à la longue** in the end   ◇ *Elle a fini par agacer tout le monde à la longue.* In the end she got on everybody's nerves.

longuement   ADVERB
at length   ◇ *Elle m'a longuement parlé de ses projets d'avenir.* She talked to me at length about her plans for the future.

la **longueur**   NOUN
length
- **à longueur de journée** all day long   ◇ *Elle mâche du chewing-gum à longueur de journée.* She chews gum all day long.

les **loques**   FEM NOUN
- **être en loques** to be torn to bits   ◇ *Sa chemise était en loques.* His shirt was torn to bits.

lors de   PREPOSITION
during   ◇ *Je l'ai rencontré lors de mon stage en entreprise.* I met him during my work placement.

lorsque   CONJUNCTION
when   ◇ *J'allais composer ton numéro lorsque tu as appelé.* I was about to dial your number when you called.

le **lot**   NOUN
prize
- **le gros lot** the jackpot

la **loterie**   NOUN
1 **lottery**   ◇ *la loterie nationale* the National Lottery
2 **raffle**   ◇ *J'ai gagné cet ours en peluche dans une loterie.* I won this teddy in a raffle.

la **lotion**   NOUN
lotion   ◇ *une bouteille de lotion solaire* a bottle of suntan lotion
- **une lotion après-rasage** an aftershave

le **lotissement**   NOUN
housing estate

le **loto**   NOUN
lottery
- **le loto sportif** the pools

le **loubard**   NOUN (*informal*)
lout

louche   ADJECTIVE
see also louche NOUN
fishy   ◇ *une histoire louche* a fishy story

la **louche**   NOUN
see also louche ADJECTIVE
ladle

loucher   VERB
to squint

louer   VERB

1 **to let** ◇ *Ils louent des chambres à des étudiants.* They let rooms to students.
- **"à louer"** "to let"
2 **to rent** ◇ *Je loue un petit appartement au centre-ville.* I rent a little flat in the centre of town.
3 **to hire** ◇ *Est-ce que vous louez des vélos?* Do you hire bikes? ◇ *Nous allons louer une voiture pour le week-end.* We're going to hire a car for the weekend.
4 **to praise** ◇ *Les journaux ont loué le courage des pompiers.* The newspapers praised the courage of the firefighters.

le **loup** NOUN
wolf

la **loupe** NOUN
magnifying glass

louper VERB (*informal*)
to miss ◇ *Dépêche-toi, tu vas louper ton train!* Hurry up, you'll miss your train!

lourd ADJECTIVE
heavy ◇ *Mon sac est très lourd.* My bag's very heavy.

la **loutre** NOUN
otter

la **loyauté** NOUN
loyalty

le **loyer** NOUN
rent

lu VERB *see* **lire**

la **lucarne** NOUN
skylight

la **luge** NOUN
sledge

lugubre ADJECTIVE
gloomy

lui PRONOUN
1 **him** ◇ *Il a été très content du cadeau que je lui ai offert.* He was very pleased with the present I gave him. ◇ *C'est bien lui!* It's definitely him! ◇ *J'ai pensé à lui toute la journée.* I thought about him all day long.
2 **to him** ◇ *Mon père est d'accord: je lui ai parlé ce matin.* My father said yes: I spoke to him this morning.
3 **her** ◇ *Elle a été très contente du cadeau que je lui ai offert.* She was very pleased with the present I gave her.
4 **to her** ◇ *Ma mère est d'accord: je lui ai parlé ce matin.* My mother said yes: I spoke to her this morning.
5 **it** ◇ *Qu'est-ce que tu donnes à ton chat?–Je lui donne de la viande crue.* What do you give your cat?–I give it

raw meat.
lui is also used for emphasis.
◇ *Lui, il est toujours en retard!* Oh him, he's always late!
- **lui-même** himself ◇ *Il a construit son bateau lui-même.* He built his boat himself.

la **lumière** NOUN
light
- **la lumière du jour** daylight

lumineux ADJECTIVE
(FEM SING **lumineuse**)
- **une enseigne lumineuse** a neon sign

lunatique ADJECTIVE
temperamental ◇ *Il est plutôt lunatique.* He's rather temperamental.

le **lundi** NOUN
1 **Monday** ◇ *Aujourd'hui, nous sommes lundi.* It's Monday today.
2 **on Monday** ◇ *Ils sont arrivés lundi.* They arrived on Monday.
- **le lundi** on Mondays ◇ *Le lundi, je vais à la piscine.* I go swimming on Mondays.
- **tous les lundis** every Monday
- **lundi dernier** last Monday
- **lundi prochain** next Monday
- **le lundi de Pâques** Easter Monday

la **lune** NOUN
moon
- **la lune de miel** honeymoon

les **lunettes** FEM NOUN
glasses
- **des lunettes de soleil** sunglasses
- **des lunettes de plongée** swimming goggles

la **lutte** NOUN
1 **fight** ◇ *la lutte contre le racisme* the fight against racism
2 **wrestling** ◇ *une épreuve de lutte* a wrestling bout

lutter VERB
to fight

le **luxe** NOUN
luxury
- **de luxe** luxury ◇ *un hôtel de luxe* a luxury hotel

luxueux ADJECTIVE
(FEM SING **luxueuse**)
luxurious

le **lycée** NOUN
secondary school
In France pupils go to a **collège** *between the ages of 11 and 15, and then to a* **lycée** *until the age of 18.*

le **lycéen** NOUN
secondary school pupil

la **lycéenne** NOUN
secondary school pupil

M

M. ABBREVIATION (= *Monsieur*)
  Mr ○ *M. Bernard* Mr Bernard
m' PRONOUN *see* me
ma ADJECTIVE
  my ○ *ma mère* my mother ○ *ma montre* my watch
les **macaronis** MASC NOUN
  macaroni
la **Macédoine** NOUN
  Macedonia
la **macédoine** NOUN
  • **la macédoine de fruits** fruit salad
  • **la macédoine de légumes** mixed vegetables
mâcher VERB
  to chew
le **machin** NOUN (*informal*)
  thingy ○ *Passe-moi le machin pour râper les carottes.* Pass me the thingy for grating carrots. ○ *Qu'est-ce que c'est que ce vieux machin?* What's this old thing?
la **machine** NOUN
  machine
  • **une machine à laver** a washing machine
  • **une machine à écrire** a typewriter
  • **une machine à coudre** a sewing machine
  • **une machine à sous** a fruit machine
la **mâchoire** NOUN
  jaw
mâchonner VERB
  to chew
le **maçon** NOUN
  bricklayer
Madame FEM NOUN
  (PL **Mesdames**)
  ① **Mrs** ○ *Madame Legall* Mrs Legall
  ② **lady** ○ *Occupez-vous de Madame.* Could you look after this lady?
  ③ **Madam** ○ *Madame,...* Dear Madam,... (*in letter*) ○ *Madame! Vous avez oublié votre parapluie!* Excuse me! You've forgotten your umbrella!
Mademoiselle FEM NOUN
  (PL **Mesdemoiselles**)
  ① **Miss** ○ *Mademoiselle Martin* Miss Martin
  ② **Madam** ○ *Mademoiselle,...* Dear Madam,... (*in letter*)
le **magasin** NOUN
  shop ○ *Les magasins ouvrent à huit heures.* The shops open at 8 o'clock.
le **magazine** NOUN
  magazine

le **magicien** NOUN
  magician
la **magicienne** NOUN
  magician
la **magie** NOUN
  magic ○ *un tour de magie* a magic trick
magique ADJECTIVE
  magic ○ *une baguette magique* a magic wand
magistral ADJECTIVE
  (MASC PL **magistraux**)
  • **un cours magistral** a lecture (*at university*)
magnétique ADJECTIVE
  magnetic
le **magnétophone** NOUN
  tape recorder
  • **un magnétophone à cassettes** a cassette recorder
le **magnétoscope** NOUN
  video recorder
magnifique ADJECTIVE
  superb
mai MASC NOUN
  May
  • **en mai** in May
maigre ADJECTIVE
  ① **skinny** ○ *Ma mère me trouve trop maigre.* My mother says I'm too skinny.
  ② **lean** (*meat*)
  ③ **low-fat** (*cheese, yoghurt*)
maigrir VERB
  to lose weight ○ *Il fait un régime pour essayer de maigrir.* He's on a diet, to try to lose weight. ○ *Elle a maigri de deux kilos en un mois.* She's lost two kilos in a month.
le **maillot de bain** NOUN
  ① **swimsuit**
  ② **swimming trunks**
la **main** NOUN
  hand ○ *Donne-moi la main!* Give me your hand!
  • **serrer la main à quelqu'un** to shake hands with somebody
  • **se serrer la main** to shake hands ○ *Les deux présidents se sont serré la main.* The two presidents shook hands.
  • **sous la main** to hand ○ *Est-ce que tu as son adresse sous la main?* Have you got his address to hand?
maintenant ADVERB
  ① **now** ○ *Qu'est-ce que tu veux faire*

maintenant? What do you want to do now? ◇ *C'est maintenant ou jamais.* It's now or never.

2 **nowadays** ◇ *Maintenant la plupart des gens font leurs courses au supermarché.* Nowadays most people do their shopping at the supermarket.

maintenir VERB
to maintain ◇ *Il maintient qu'il n'était pas là le jour du crime.* He maintains he wasn't there on the day of the crime.

- **se maintenir** to hold ◇ *Espérons que le beau temps va se maintenir pour le week-end!* Let's hope the good weather will hold over the weekend!

le **maire** NOUN
mayor

la **mairie** NOUN
town hall

mais CONJUNCTION
but ◇ *C'est cher mais de très bonne qualité.* It's expensive, but very good quality.

le **maïs** NOUN
1 **maize**
2 **sweetcorn**

la **maison** NOUN
see also **maison** ADJECTIVE
house ◇ *Ils habitent dans la maison qui est au bout de la rue.* They live in the house at the end of the street.

- **à la maison (1)** at home ◇ *Je serai à la maison cet après-midi.* I'll be at home this afternoon.
- **à la maison (2)** home ◇ *Elle est rentrée à la maison.* She's gone home.

maison ADJECTIVE (MASC, FEM, PL)
see also **maison** NOUN
home-made ◇ *Je préfère les tartes maison à celles qui sont achetées.* I prefer home-made pies to bought ones.

le **maître** NOUN
1 **teacher** (*in primary school*)
2 **master** (*of dog*)

- **un maître d'hôtel** a head waiter (*in restaurant*)
- **un maître nageur** a lifeguard

la **maîtresse** NOUN
1 **teacher** (*in primary school*)
2 **mistress** ◇ *Il paraît qu'il a une maîtresse.* They say he's got a mistress.

la **maîtrise** NOUN
master's degree ◇ *Elle a une maîtrise d'anglais.* She's got a master's degree in English.

- **la maîtrise de soi** self-control

maîtriser VERB
- **se maîtriser** to control oneself ◇ *Il se met facilement en colère et a du mal à se maîtriser.* He loses his temper easily and finds it hard to control himself.

majestueux ADJECTIVE
(FEM SING **majestueuse**)
majestic

majeur ADJECTIVE
- **être majeur** to be 18 ◇ *Tu feras ce que tu voudras quand tu seras majeure.* You can do what you like once you're 18. ◇ *Elle sera majeure en août.* She comes of age in August.
- **la majeure partie** most ◇ *la majeure partie de mon salaire* most of my salary

la **majorité** NOUN
majority ◇ *dans la majorité des cas* in the majority of cases
- **la majorité et l'opposition** the government and the opposition

Majorque FEM NOUN
Majorca

la **majuscule** NOUN
capital letter ◇ *un M majuscule* a capital M

mal ADVERB, ADJECTIVE (MASC, FEM, PL)
see also **mal** NOUN
1 **badly** ◇ *Ce travail a été mal fait.* The work was badly done. ◇ *Il a mal compris.* He misunderstood.
2 **wrong** ◇ *C'est mal de mentir.* It's wrong to tell lies.

- **aller mal** to be ill ◇ *Son grand-père va très mal.* His grandfather is very ill.
- **pas mal** quite good ◇ *Je te trouve pas mal sur cette photo.* I think you look quite good in this photo.

le **mal** NOUN
(PL les **maux**)
see also **mal** ADVERB
1 **ache** ◇ *J'ai mal à la tête.* I've got a headache. ◇ *J'ai mal aux dents.* I've got toothache. ◇ *J'ai mal au dos.* My back hurts. ◇ *Est-ce que vous avez mal à la gorge?* Have you got a sore throat?

- **Ça fait mal.** It hurts.
- **Où est-ce que tu as mal?** Where does it hurt?
- **faire mal à quelqu'un** to hurt somebody ◇ *Attention, tu me fais mal!* Be careful, you're hurting me!
- **se faire mal** to hurt oneself ◇ *Je me suis fait mal au bras.* I hurt my arm.
- **se donner du mal pour faire quelque chose** to go to a lot of trouble to do something ◇ *Il s'est donné beaucoup de mal pour que cette soirée soit réussie.* He went to a lot of trouble to make the party a success.
- **avoir le mal de mer** to be seasick

- **avoir le mal du pays** to be homesick
  [2] **evil** ◇ *le bien et le mal* good and evil
- **dire du mal de quelqu'un** to speak ill of somebody

malade ADJECTIVE
> see also **malade** NOUN

ill
- **tomber malade** to fall ill

e/la **malade** NOUN
> see also **malade** ADJECTIVE

patient

la **maladie** NOUN
illness

maladif ADJECTIVE
(FEM SING **maladive**)
sickly ◇ *C'est un enfant maladif.* He's a sickly child.

la **maladresse** NOUN
clumsiness

maladroit ADJECTIVE
clumsy

le **malaise** NOUN
- **avoir un malaise** to feel faint ◇ *Elle a eu un malaise après le déjeuner.* She felt faint after lunch.
- **Son arrivée a créé un malaise parmi les invités.** Her arrival made the guests feel uncomfortable.

la **malchance** NOUN
bad luck

mâle ADJECTIVE
male

la **malédiction** NOUN
curse

mal en point ADJECTIVE (MASC, FEM, PL)
- **Il avait l'air mal en point quand je l'ai vu hier soir.** He didn't look too good when I saw him last night.

le **malentendu** NOUN
misunderstanding

le **malfaiteur** NOUN
criminal

mal famé ADJECTIVE
(FEM **mal famée**, MASC PL **mal famés**)
- **un quartier mal famé** a seedy area

malgache ADJECTIVE
from Madagascar ◇ *Sa mère est malgache.* His mother's from Madagascar.

malgré PREPOSITION
in spite of ◇ *Il est toujours généreux malgré ses problèmes d'argent.* He's always generous in spite of his financial problems.
- **malgré tout** all the same ◇ *Il faisait mauvais mais nous sommes sortis malgré tout.* The weather was bad but we went out all the same.

le **malheur** NOUN
tragedy ◇ *Elle a eu beaucoup de malheurs dans sa vie.* She's had a lot of tragedy in her life.
- **faire un malheur** (*informal*) to be a smash hit ◇ *Leur dernier album a fait un malheur.* Their latest album was a smash hit.

malheureusement ADVERB
unfortunately

malheureux ADJECTIVE
(FEM SING **malheureuse**)
miserable ◇ *Qu'est-ce que tu as? Tu as l'air malheureux.* What's wrong with you? You look miserable.

malhonnête ADJECTIVE
dishonest

la **malice** NOUN
mischief ◇ *Son regard était plein de malice.* His eyes were full of mischief.

malicieux ADJECTIVE
(FEM SING **malicieuse**)
mischievous

malin ADJECTIVE
(FEM SING **maligne**)
crafty
- **C'est malin!** (*informal*) That's clever! ◇ *Ah c'est malin! Nous voilà enfermés à cause de toi!* That's clever! You've got us locked in!

la **malle** NOUN
trunk

malodorant ADJECTIVE
foul-smelling

malpropre ADJECTIVE
dirty

malsain ADJECTIVE
unhealthy

Malte MASC NOUN
Malta

maltraiter VERB
to ill-treat ◇ *Il maltraite son chien.* He ill-treats his dog.
- **des enfants maltraités** battered children

malveillant ADJECTIVE
malicious ◇ *des rumeurs malveillantes* malicious rumours

la **maman** NOUN
mum

la **mamie** NOUN
granny

le **mammifère** NOUN
mammal

la **manche** NOUN
> see also **le manche**

[1] **sleeve** (*of clothes*)
[2] **leg** (*of game*) ◇ *Ils ont remporté la première manche du match.* They won

M

the first leg of the match.
- **la Manche** the Channel

le **manche** NOUN
see also la manche
handle (of pan)

la **mandarine** NOUN
mandarin orange

le **manège** NOUN
merry-go-round

la **manette** NOUN
lever

mangeable ADJECTIVE
edible ◇ C'est à peine mangeable! It's practically inedible!

manger VERB
to eat

la **mangue** NOUN
mango

maniaque ADJECTIVE
fussy

la **manie** NOUN
1 **obsession**
- **avoir la manie de** to be obsessive about ◇ Il a la manie du rangement. He's obsessive about tidying up.
2 **habit** ◇ J'essaie de respecter ses petites manies. I try to go along with her little ways.

manier VERB
to handle

la **manière**
see also les manières NOUN
way
- **de manière à** so as to ◇ Nous sommes partis tôt de manière à éviter la circulation. We left early so as to avoid the traffic.
- **de toute manière** in any case ◇ Je n'aurais pas pu venir de toute manière. I couldn't have come in any case.

maniéré ADJECTIVE
affected

les **manières**
see also la manière FEM NOUN
1 **manners** ◇ apprendre les bonnes manières to learn good manners
2 **fuss** ◇ Ne fais pas de manières: mange ta soupe! Don't make a fuss: eat your soup!

le **manifestant** NOUN
demonstrator

la **manifestante** NOUN
demonstrator

la **manifestation** NOUN
demonstration ◇ une manifestation pour la paix a peace demonstration

manifester VERB
to demonstrate

manipuler VERB

1 **to handle** ◇ Ce vase doit être manipulé avec soin. This vase must be handled with care.
2 **to manipulate** ◇ Tous les partis essaient de manipuler l'opinion publique. All the parties are trying to manipulate public opinion.

le **mannequin** NOUN
model ◇ Elle est mannequin. She's a model.

manœuvrer VERB
to manœuvre

le **manque** NOUN
- **le manque de** lack of ◇ Le manque de sommeil peut provoquer toutes sortes de troubles. Lack of sleep can cause all sorts of problems.
withdrawal ◇ un drogué en état de manque a drug addict suffering withdrawal symptoms

manqué ADJECTIVE
- **un garçon manqué** a tomboy

manquer VERB
to miss ◇ Tu n'as rien manqué: le film n'était pas très bon. You didn't miss anything: the film wasn't very good. ◇ Il manque des pages à ce livre. There are some pages missing from this book.
- **Mes parents me manquent.** I miss my parents.
- **Ma sœur me manque.** I miss my sister.
- **Il manque encore cent francs.** We are still 100 francs short.
- **manquer de** to lack ◇ La quiche manque de sel. The quiche hasn't got enough salt in it. ◇ Je trouve qu'il a manqué de tact. I don't think he was very tactful.
- **Il a manqué se tuer.** He nearly got killed.

le **manteau** NOUN
(PL les **manteaux**)
coat

manuel ADJECTIVE
(FEM SING **manuelle**)
see also manuel NOUN
manual

le **manuel** NOUN
see also manuel ADJECTIVE
1 **textbook**
2 **handbook**

le **maquereau** NOUN
(PL les **maquereaux**)
mackerel

la **maquette** NOUN
model ◇ une maquette de bateau a model boat

le **maquillage** NOUN
  make-up
se **maquiller** VERB
  to put on one's make-up ◇ *Je vais me maquiller en vitesse.* I'll just quickly put on my make-up.
le **marais** NOUN
  marsh
le **marbre** NOUN
  marble ◇ *une statue en marbre* a marble statue
le **marchand** NOUN
  ① **shopkeeper**
  • **un marchand de journaux** a newsagent
  ② **stallholder** (*in market*)
la **marchande** NOUN
  ① **shopkeeper**
  • **une marchande de fruits et de légumes** a greengrocer
  ② **stallholder** (*in market*)
marchander VERB
  to haggle
la **marchandise** NOUN
  goods
la **marche** NOUN
  ① **step** ◇ *Fais attention à la marche!* Mind the step!
  ② **walking** ◇ *La marche me fait du bien.* Walking does me good.
  • **être en état de marche** to be in working order ◇ *Cette voiture est en parfait état de marche.* This car is in perfect running order.
  • **Ne montez jamais dans un train en marche.** Never try to get into a moving train.
  • **mettre en marche** to start ◇ *Comment est-ce qu'on met la machine à laver en marche?* How do you start the washing machine?
  • **la marche arrière** reverse gear
  • **faire marche arrière** to reverse
  ③ **march** ◇ *une marche militaire* a military march
le **marché** NOUN
  market
  • **un marché aux puces** a flea market
marcher VERB
  ① **to walk** ◇ *Elle marche cinq kilomètres par jour.* She walks 5 kilometres every day.
  ② **to run** ◇ *Le métro marche normalement aujourd'hui.* The underground is running normally today.
  ③ **to work** ◇ *Est-ce que l'ascenseur marche?* Is the lift working?
  ④ **to go well** ◇ *Est-ce que les* *affaires marchent actuellement?* Is business going well at the moment?
  • **Alors les études, ça marche?** (*informal*) How are you getting on at school?
  • **faire marcher quelqu'un** to pull somebody's leg ◇ *Il essaie de te faire marcher.* He's pulling your leg.
le **marcheur** NOUN
  walker
la **marcheuse** NOUN
  walker
le **mardi** NOUN
  ① **Tuesday** ◇ *Aujourd'hui, nous sommes mardi.* It's Tuesday today.
  ② **on Tuesday** ◇ *Ils reviennent mardi.* They're coming back on Tuesday.
  • **le mardi** on Tuesdays ◇ *Le mardi, je vais à la gym.* I go to the gym on Tuesdays.
  • **tous les mardis** every Tuesday
  • **mardi dernier** last Tuesday
  • **mardi prochain** next Tuesday
  • **Mardi gras** Shrove Tuesday
la **mare** NOUN
  pond
le **marécage** NOUN
  marsh
la **marée** NOUN
  tide ◇ *la marée haute* high tide ◇ *la marée basse* low tide ◇ *la marée montante* the rising tide ◇ *la marée descendante* the ebb tide
la **margarine** NOUN
  margarine
la **marge** NOUN
  margin
le **mari** NOUN
  husband ◇ *son mari* her husband
le **mariage** NOUN
  ① **marriage**
  ② **wedding** ◇ *un mariage civil* a registry office wedding ◇ *un mariage religieux* a church wedding
marié ADJECTIVE
  see also **marié** NOUN
  married
le **marié** NOUN
  see also **marié** ADJECTIVE
  bridegroom
  • **les mariés** the bride and groom
la **mariée** NOUN
  bride
se **marier** VERB
  to marry ◇ *Elle s'est mariée avec un ami d'enfance.* She married a childhood friend.
marin ADJECTIVE
  see also **marin** NOUN
  sea ◇ *l'air marin* the sea air

M

- **un pull marin** a sailor's jersey

le **marin** NOUN

see also marin ADJECTIVE

sailor

marine ADJECTIVE (MASC, FEM, PL)

see also marine NOUN

- **bleu marine** navy-blue ◇ *un pull bleu marine* a navy-blue sweater

la **marine** NOUN

see also marine ADJECTIVE

navy

- **la marine nationale** the French navy

la **marionnette** NOUN

puppet

la **marmelade** NOUN

stewed fruit

- **la marmelade de pommes** stewed apple
- **la marmelade d'oranges** marmalade

la **marmite** NOUN

cooking pot

marmonner VERB

to mumble

le **Maroc** NOUN

Morocco

marocain ADJECTIVE

Moroccan

la **maroquinerie** NOUN

leather goods shop

marquant ADJECTIVE

significant ◇ *un événement marquant* a significant event

la **marque** NOUN

1 mark ◇ *des marques de doigts* fingermarks

2 make ◇ *De quelle marque est ton jean?* What make are your jeans?

3 brand ◇ *une grande marque de cognac* a well-known brand of cognac

- **l'image de marque** the public image ◇ *Le ministre tient à son image de marque.* The minister cares about his public image.
- **une marque déposée** a registered trademark
- **A vos marques! prêts! partez!** Ready, steady, go!

marquer VERB

1 to mark ◇ *Peux-tu marquer sur la carte où se trouve le village?* Can you mark where the village is on the map?

2 to score ◇ *L'équipe adverse a marqué dix points.* The opposing team scored ten points.

3 to celebrate ◇ *On va sortir au restaurant pour marquer ton anniversaire.* We'll eat out to celebrate your birthday.

la **marraine** NOUN

godmother

marrant ADJECTIVE (*informal*)

funny

marre ADVERB (*informal*)

- **en avoir marre de quelque chose** to be fed up with something ◇ *J'en ai marre de faire la vaisselle.* I'm fed up with doing the dishes.

se **marrer** VERB (*informal*)

to have a good laugh ◇ *On s'est bien marrés.* We had a good laugh.

le **marron** NOUN

see also marron ADJECTIVE

chestnut ◇ *la crème de marrons* chestnut purée

marron ADJECTIVE (MASC, FEM, PL)

see also marron NOUN

brown ◇ *des chaussures marron* brown shoes

le **marronnier** NOUN

chestnut tree

mars MASC NOUN

March

- **en mars** in March

le **marteau** NOUN

(PL les **marteaux**)

hammer

martyriser VERB

to batter ◇ *des enfants martyrisés* battered children

masculin ADJECTIVE

1 men's ◇ *la mode masculine* men's fashion

2 masculine ◇ *"chat" est un nom masculin.* "chat" is a masculine noun. ◇ *Elle a une allure assez masculine.* She looks rather masculine.

le **masque** NOUN

mask

le **massacre** NOUN

massacre

massacrer VERB

to massacre

le **massage** NOUN

massage

la **masse** NOUN

- **une masse de** (*informal*) masses of ◇ *J'ai une masse de choses à faire.* I've got masses of things to do.
- **produire en masse** to mass-produce ◇ *Ces jouets sont produits en masse en Chine.* These toys are mass-produced in China.
- **venir en masse** to come en masse ◇ *Les gens sont venus en masse pour accueillir Nelson Mandela.* People came en masse to welcome Nelson Mandela.

masser VERB

to massage
- **se masser** to gather ◇ *Les manifestants se sont massés devant l'ambassade.* The demonstrators gathered in front of the embassy.

massif ADJECTIVE
(FEM SING **massive**)
1 **solid** (*gold, silver, wood*) ◇ *un bracelet en or massif* a solid gold bracelet
2 **massive** ◇ *une dose massive d'antibiotiques* a massive dose of antibiotics
3 **mass** ◇ *des départs massifs* a mass exodus

mat ADJECTIVE
matt ◇ *blanc mat* matt white ◇ *Je voudrais mes photos en mat.* I would like my photos matt.
- **être mat** to be checkmate (*chess*)

match NOUN
match ◇ *un match de football* a football match
- **le match aller** the first leg
- **le match retour** the second leg
- **faire match nul** to draw

matelas NOUN
mattress
- **un matelas pneumatique** an air bed

matelassé ADJECTIVE
quilted ◇ *une veste matelassée* a quilted jacket

matelot NOUN
sailor

matériaux MASC NOUN
materials

matériel NOUN
1 **equipment** ◇ *du matériel de laboratoire* laboratory equipment
2 **gear** ◇ *Il a pris tout son matériel de pêche avec lui.* He took all his fishing gear with him.

maternel ADJECTIVE
(FEM SING **maternelle**)
motherly ◇ *Elle est très maternelle.* She's very motherly.
- **ma grand-mère maternelle** my mother's mother
- **mon oncle maternel** my mother's brother

maternelle NOUN
nursery school
The maternelle *is a state school for 2-6 year-olds.*

maternité NOUN
- **le congé de maternité** maternity leave ◇ *Notre professeur de musique est en congé de maternité.* Our music teacher is on maternity leave.

les mathématiques FEM NOUN
mathematics

les maths FEM NOUN (*informal*)
maths

la matière NOUN
subject ◇ *Le latin est une matière facultative.* Latin is an optional subject.
- **sans matières grasses** fat-free
- **les matières premières** raw materials

le matin NOUN
morning ◇ *à trois heures du matin* at 3 o'clock in the morning ◇ *du matin au soir* from morning till night
- **Je suis du matin.** I'm at my best in the morning.
- **de bon matin** early in the morning

matinal ADJECTIVE
(MASC PL **matinaux**)
morning ◇ *Je fais ma gymnastique matinale avant de déjeuner.* I do my morning exercises before breakfast.
- **être matinal** to be up early ◇ *Tu es bien matinal aujourd'hui!* You're up early today!

la matinée NOUN
morning ◇ *Je t'appellerai demain dans la matinée.* I'll call you sometime tomorrow morning. ◇ *en début de matinée* early in the morning

le matou NOUN
tomcat

matrimonial ADJECTIVE
(MASC PL **matrimoniaux**)
- **une agence matrimoniale** a marriage bureau

maudire VERB
to curse

maudit ADJECTIVE (*informal*)
blasted ◇ *Où est passé ce maudit parapluie?* Where's that blasted umbrella got to?

maussade ADJECTIVE
sullen

mauvais ADJECTIVE, ADVERB
1 **bad** ◇ *une mauvaise note* a bad mark ◇ *Tu arrives au mauvais moment.* You've come at a bad time.
- **Il fait mauvais.** The weather's bad.
- **être mauvais en** to be bad at ◇ *Je suis mauvais en allemand.* I'm bad at German.
2 **poor** ◇ *J'ai trouvé que le film était mauvais.* I thought the film was poor. ◇ *Il est en mauvaise santé.* His health is poor.
- **Tu as mauvaise mine.** You don't look well.
3 **wrong** ◇ *Vous avez fait le mauvais numéro.* You've dialled the wrong

M

number.

- **des mauvaises herbes** weeds
- **sentir mauvais** to smell

les **maux** MASC NOUN

- **des maux de ventre** stomachache
- **des maux de tête** headache

le **maximum** NOUN

maximum

- **au maximum (1)** as much as one can ◇ *Remplis le seau au maximum.* Fill the bucket as full as you can.
- **au maximum (2)** at the very most ◇ *Ça va vous coûter deux cents francs au maximum.* It'll cost you 200 francs at the very most.

la **mayonnaise** NOUN

mayonnaise

le **mazout** NOUN

fuel oil

me PRONOUN

me *changes to* **m'** *before a vowel and most words beginning with "h".*

1 me ◇ *Elle me téléphone tous les jours.* She phones me every day. ◇ *Il m'attend depuis une heure.* He's been waiting for me for an hour.

2 to me ◇ *Il me parle en allemand.* He talks to me in German. ◇ *Elle m'a expliqué la situation.* She explained the situation to me.

3 myself ◇ *Je vais me préparer quelque chose à manger.* I'm going to make myself something to eat.

With reflexive verbs, **me** *is often not translated.* ◇ *Je me lève à sept heures tous les matins.* I get up at 7 every morning.

le **mec** NOUN *(informal)*

guy

le **mécanicien** NOUN

mechanic

la **mécanicienne** NOUN

mechanic

la **mécanique** NOUN

1 mechanics

2 mechanism *(of watch, clock)*

le **mécanisme** NOUN

mechanism

méchamment ADVERB

nastily ◇ *Il lui a répondu méchamment.* He answered him nastily.

la **méchanceté** NOUN

nastiness

méchant ADJECTIVE

nasty ◇ *C'est un homme méchant.* He's a nasty man. ◇ *Ne sois pas méchant avec ton petit frère.* Don't be nasty to your little brother.

- **"Attention, chien méchant"** "Beware of the dog"

la **mèche** NOUN

lock *(of hair)*

mécontent ADJECTIVE

- **mécontent de** unhappy with ◇ *Elle est mécontente de sa coupe de cheveux.* She's unhappy with her haircut.

le **mécontentement** NOUN

displeasure ◇ *Il a exprimé son mécontentement.* He expressed his displeasure.

la **médaille** NOUN

medal

le **médecin** NOUN

doctor ◇ *aller chez le médecin* to go to the doctor

la **médecine** NOUN

medicine *(subject)* ◇ *Il fait médecine.* He's studying medicine.

les **médias** MASC NOUN

media

médical ADJECTIVE

(MASC PL **médicaux**)

medical ◇ *la recherche médicale* medical research

- **passer une visite médicale** to have a medical

le **médicament** NOUN

medicine *(drug)*

médiéval ADJECTIVE

(MASC PL **médiévaux**)

medieval

médiocre ADJECTIVE

poor ◇ *des notes médiocres* poor marks

méditer VERB

to meditate

la **Méditerranée** NOUN

Mediterranean

méditerranéen ADJECTIVE

(FEM SING **méditerranéenne**)

Mediterranean

la **méduse** NOUN

jellyfish

la **méfiance** NOUN

mistrust

méfiant ADJECTIVE

mistrustful

se **méfier** VERB

- **se méfier de quelqu'un** to distrust somebody ◇ *Si j'étais toi, je me méfierais de lui.* If I were you, I wouldn't trust him.

la **mégarde** NOUN

- **par mégarde** by mistake ◇ *J'ai emporté son livre par mégarde.* I took his book by mistake.

le **mégot** NOUN

cigarette end

meilleur ADJECTIVE, ADVERB, NOUN
- **better** ◦ *Ce serait meilleur avec du fromage râpé.* It would be better with grated cheese. ◦ *Il paraît que le film est meilleur que le livre.* They say that the film is better than the book.
- **le meilleur** the best ◦ *C'est elle qui est la meilleure en sport.* She's the best at sport. ◦ *Je préfère garder le meilleur pour la fin.* I like to keep the best for last.
- **le meilleur des deux** the better of the two
- **meilleur marché** cheaper ◦ *La bière est meilleur marché en France.* Beer's cheaper in France.

mélancolique ADJECTIVE
melancholy

mélange NOUN
mixture

mélanger VERB
1. **to mix** ◦ *Mélangez le tout.* Mix everything together.
2. **to muddle up** ◦ *Tu mélanges tout!* You're muddling everything up!

mêlée NOUN
scrum

mêler VERB
- **se mêler** to mix ◦ *Il ne cherche pas à se mêler aux autres.* He doesn't try to mix with the others.
- **Mêle-toi de ce qui te regarde!** (*informal*) Mind your own business!

mélodie NOUN
melody

melon NOUN
melon

membre NOUN
1. **limb**
2. **member** ◦ *les pays membres de l'Union européenne* the member countries of the European Union

mémé NOUN (*informal*)
granny

même ADJECTIVE, ADVERB, PRONOUN
1. **same** ◦ *J'ai le même manteau.* I've got the same coat. ◦ *Tiens, c'est curieux j'ai le même!* That's strange, I've got the same one!
- **en même temps** at the same time
- **moi-même** myself ◦ *Je l'ai fait moi-même.* I did it myself.
2. **even** ◦ *Il n'a même pas pleuré.* He didn't even cry.

mémoire NOUN
memory

menace NOUN
threat

menacer VERB
to threaten

le ménage NOUN
housework ◦ *faire le ménage* to do the housework
- **une femme de ménage** a cleaning woman

ménager ADJECTIVE
(FEM SING **ménagère**)
- **les travaux ménagers** housework

la ménagère NOUN
housewife

le mendiant NOUN
beggar

la mendiante NOUN
beggar

mendier VERB
to beg

mener VERB
to lead ◦ *Cette rue mène directement à la gare.* This street leads straight to the station.
- **Cela ne vous mènera à rien!** That will get you nowhere!

la méningite NOUN
meningitis

les menottes FEM NOUN
handcuffs

le mensonge NOUN
lie

la mensualité NOUN
monthly payment ◦ *en dix mensualités* in ten monthly payments

mensuel ADJECTIVE
(FEM SING **mensuelle**)
monthly

les mensurations FEM NOUN
measurements

la mentalité NOUN
mentality

le menteur NOUN
liar

la menteuse NOUN
liar

la menthe NOUN
mint

la mention NOUN
grade ◦ *Il a été reçu avec mention bien.* He got a grade B pass.

mentionner VERB
to mention

mentir VERB
to lie ◦ *Tu mens!* You're lying!

le menton NOUN
chin

menu ADJECTIVE, ADVERB
see also **menu** NOUN
1. **slim** ◦ *Elle est menue.* She's slim. ◦ *Elle est petite et menue.* She's petite.

M

2 **very fine** ◇ *Les oignons doivent être coupés menu.* The onions have to be cut up very fine.

le **menu** NOUN

see also menu ADJECTIVE

menu ◇ *le menu du jour* today's menu

la **menuiserie** NOUN

woodwork

le **menuisier** NOUN

joiner

le **mépris** NOUN

contempt ◇ *Il nous a traités avec mépris.* He treated us with contempt.

méprisant ADJECTIVE

contemptuous

mépriser VERB

to despise

la **mer** NOUN

1 **sea** ◇ *en mer* at sea

◆ **au bord de la mer** at the seaside

◆ **la mer du Nord** the North Sea

2 **tide** ◇ *La mer est basse.* The tide is out. ◇ *La mer sera haute à sept heures.* It'll be high tide at 7 o'clock.

la **mercerie** NOUN

1 **haberdashery**

2 **haberdasher's shop**

merci EXCLAMATION

thank you ◇ *Merci de m'avoir raccompagné.* Thank you for taking me home.

◆ **merci beaucoup** thank you very much

le **mercredi** NOUN

1 **Wednesday** ◇ *Aujourd'hui, nous sommes mercredi.* It's Wednesday today.

2 **on Wednesday** ◇ *Nous comptons partir mercredi.* We plan to leave on Wednesday.

◆ **le mercredi** on Wednesdays ◇ *Le musée est fermé le mercredi.* The museum is shut on Wednesdays.

◆ **tous les mercredis** every Wednesday

◆ **mercredi dernier** last Wednesday

◆ **mercredi prochain** next Wednesday

la **merde** NOUN (*rude*)

shit ◇ *Merde!* Shit!

la **mère** NOUN

mother

méridional ADJECTIVE

(MASC PL **méridionaux**)

southern ◇ *Il a un accent méridional.* He's got a southern accent.

la **meringue** NOUN

meringue

mériter VERB

to deserve

le **merlan** NOUN

whiting

le **merle** NOUN

blackbird

la **merveille** NOUN

◆ *Cet ordinateur est une vraie merveille!* This computer's really wonderful!

◆ **à merveille** wonderfully ◇ *Elle se porte à merveille depuis son opération.* She's been wonderfully well since the operation.

merveilleux ADJECTIVE

(FEM SING **merveilleuse**)

marvellous

mes ADJECTIVE

my ◇ *mes parents* my parents

Mesdames FEM NOUN

ladies ◇ *Bonjour, Mesdames.* Good morning, ladies.

Mesdemoiselles FEM NOUN

ladies ◇ *Bonjour, Mesdemoiselles.* Good morning, ladies.

mesquin ADJECTIVE

mean

le **message** NOUN

message

la **messe** NOUN

mass ◇ *aller à la messe* to go to mass ◇ *la messe de minuit* midnight mass

messieurs MASC NOUN

gentlemen ◇ *Que puis-je faire pour vous, Messieurs?* What can I do for you, gentlemen?

◆ **Messieurs,...** Dear Sirs,... (*in letter*)

la **mesure** NOUN

1 **measurement** ◇ *J'ai pris les mesures de la fenêtre.* I took the measurements of the window.

◆ **sur mesure** tailor-made ◇ *un costume sur mesure* a tailor-made suit

2 **measure** ◇ *L'établissement a pris des mesures pour lutter contre le vandalisme.* The school has taken measures to combat vandalism.

◆ **au fur et à mesure** as one goes along ◇ *Quand je cuisine, je préfère faire la vaisselle au fur et à mesure.* When I'm cooking, I prefer to wash up as I go along.

◆ **être en mesure de faire quelque chose** to be in a position to do something ◇ *Nous ne sommes pas en mesure de vous renseigner.* We are not in a position to give you any information.

mesurer VERB

to measure ◇ *Mesurez la longueur et la largeur.* Measure the length and the width.

- **Il mesure un mètre quatre-vingts.** He's 1 m 80 tall.

met VERB *see* **mettre**

le **métal** NOUN

(PL les **métaux**)

metal

métallique ADJECTIVE

metallic

la **météo** NOUN

weather forecast ◇ *Qu'est-ce que dit la météo pour cet après-midi?* What's the weather forecast for this afternoon?

la **méthode** NOUN

[1] method ◇ *des méthodes d'enseignement modernes* modern teaching methods

[2] tutor ◇ *une méthode de guitare* a guitar tutor

le **métier** NOUN

job ◇ *Quel métier est-ce que tu aimerais faire plus tard?* What job would you like to do when you're older?

le **mètre** NOUN

metre

- **un mètre ruban** a tape measure

le **métro** NOUN

underground ◇ *prendre le métro* to go by underground

mets VERB *see* **mettre**

le **metteur en scène** NOUN

(PL les **metteurs en scène**)

[1] producer (*of play*)

[2] director (*of film*)

mettre VERB

Present tense:	
je mets	nous mettons
tu mets	vous mettez
il/elle met	ils/elles mettent
Past participle: *mis*	

[1] to put ◇ *Où est-ce que tu as mis les clés?* Where have you put the keys?

[2] to put on ◇ *Je mets mon manteau et j'arrive.* I'll put on my coat and then I'll be ready. ◇ *Il fait froid, je vais mettre le chauffage.* It's cold, I'm going to put the heating on.

[3] to wear ◇ *Elle ne met pas souvent de jupe.* She doesn't often wear a skirt. ◇ *Je n'ai rien à me mettre!* I've got nothing to wear!

[4] to take ◇ *Combien de temps as-tu mis pour aller à Lille?* How long did it take you to get to Lille? ◇ *Elle met des heures à se préparer.* She takes hours getting ready.

- **mettre en marche** to start

◇ *Comment met-on la machine à laver en marche?* How do you start the washing machine?

- **Vous pouvez vous mettre là.** You can sit there.

- **se mettre au lit** to get into bed

- **se mettre en maillot de bain** to put on one's swimsuit

- **se mettre à** to start ◇ *Il s'est mis à la peinture à cinquante ans.* He started painting when he was 50. ◇ *Il est temps de se mettre au travail.* It's time to start work. ◇ *Elle s'est mise à pleurer.* She started crying.

le **meuble** NOUN

piece of furniture ◇ *Je me suis cogné contre un meuble.* I bumped into a piece of furniture. ◇ *Ce magasin vend de beaux meubles.* This shop sells nice furniture.

le **meublé** NOUN

[1] furnished flat

[2] furnished room

meubler VERB

to furnish

le **meurtre** NOUN

murder

le **meurtrier** NOUN

murderer

la **meurtrière** NOUN

murderess

Mexico NOUN

Mexico City

le **Mexique** NOUN

Mexico

le **mi** NOUN

[1] E ◇ *mi bémol* E flat

[2] mi ◇ *do, ré, mi...* do, re, mi...

mi- PREFIX

[1] half- ◇ *mi-clos* half-shut

[2] mid- ◇ *à la mi-janvier* in mid-January

miauler VERB

to mew

la **miche** NOUN

loaf

mi-chemin

- **à mi-chemin** ADVERB

halfway

le **micro** NOUN

microphone

le **microbe** NOUN

germ

le **micro-ondes** NOUN

microwave oven

le **micro-ordinateur** NOUN

microcomputer

le **microscope** NOUN

microscope

M

le **midi** NOUN
- **1** **midday** ◇ *à midi* at midday
- **midi et demi** half past twelve
- **2** **lunchtime** ◇ *On a bien mangé à midi.* We had a good meal at lunchtime.
- **le Midi** the South of France

la **mie** NOUN
breadcrumbs

le **miel** NOUN
honey

mien PRONOUN
- **le mien** mine ◇ *Ce vélo-là, c'est le mien.* That bike's mine.

mienne PRONOUN
- **la mienne** mine ◇ *Cette valise-là, c'est la mienne.* That case is mine.

miennes PRONOUN
- **les miennes** mine ◇ *Heureusement que tu as tes clés: j'ai oublié les miennes.* It's lucky you've got your keys: I forgot mine.

miens PRONOUN
- **les miens** mine ◇ *Ces CD-là, ce sont les miens.* Those CDs are mine.

la **miette** NOUN
crumb *(of bread, cake)*

mieux ADVERB, ADJECTIVE, NOUN
better ◇ *Je la connais mieux que son frère.* I know her better than her brother. ◇ *Elle va mieux.* She's better. ◇ *Les cheveux courts lui vont mieux.* She looks better with short hair.
- **Il vaut mieux que tu appelles ta mère.** You'd better phone your mother.
- **le mieux** the best ◇ *C'est la région que je connais le mieux.* It's the region I know best.
- **faire de son mieux** to do one's best ◇ *Essaie de faire de ton mieux.* Try to do your best.

mignon ADJECTIVE
(FEM SING **mignonne**)
sweet ◇ *Qu'est-ce qu'il est mignon!* Isn't he sweet!

la **migraine** NOUN
migraine ◇ *J'ai la migraine.* I've got a migraine.

mijoter VERB
to simmer

le **milieu** NOUN
(PL les **milieux**)
1 **middle**
- **au milieu de** in the middle of ◇ *Place le vase au milieu de la table.* Put the vase in the middle of the table.
- **au beau milieu de** in the middle of ◇ *Quelqu'un a sonné à la porte au beau milieu de la nuit.* Somebody rang

the bell in the middle of the night.
- **2** **background** ◇ *le milieu familial* the family background ◇ *Il vient d'un milieu modeste.* He comes from a modest background.
- **3** **environment** ◇ *le milieu marin* the marine environment

militaire ADJECTIVE
see also militaire NOUN
military ◇ *faire son service militaire* to do one's military service

le **militaire** NOUN
see also militaire ADJECTIVE
serviceman ◇ *Son père est militaire.* His father is in the services.
- **un militaire de carrière** a professional soldier

mille NUMBER
a thousand ◇ *mille francs* a thousand francs ◇ *deux mille personnes* two thousand people

le **millefeuille** NOUN
vanilla slice

le **milliard** NOUN
thousand million ◇ *cinq milliards de francs* five thousand million francs

le/la **milliardaire** NOUN
multimillionaire

le **millier** NOUN
thousand ◇ *des milliers de personnes* thousands of people
- **par milliers** by the thousand

le **milligramme** NOUN
milligramme

le **millimètre** NOUN
millimetre

le **million** NOUN
million ◇ *deux millions de personnes* two million people

le/la **millionnaire** NOUN
millionaire

le/la **mime** NOUN
mime artist

mimer VERB
to mimic

minable ADJECTIVE
1 **shabby** ◇ *un imperméable minable* a shabby raincoat
2 **pathetic** ◇ *Mon moniteur de ski était minable.* My skiing instructor was pathetic.

mince ADJECTIVE
1 **thin** ◇ *une mince tranche de jambon* a thin slice of ham
2 **slim** ◇ *Il est grand et mince.* He's tall and slim.
- **Mince alors!** *(informal)* Oh bother!

la **minceur** NOUN
1 **thinness** ◇ *la minceur des murs*

the thinness of the walls
2 **slimness** ◇ *Elle enviait la minceur de sa sœur.* She envied her sister's slimness.

la **mine** NOUN
1 **expression**
2 **look** ◇ *Tu as bonne mine.* You look well. ◇ *Il a mauvaise mine.* He doesn't look well. ◇ *Elle avait une mine fatiguée.* She was looking tired.
3 **appearance** ◇ *Il ne faut pas juger les gens d'après leur mine.* You shouldn't judge people by their appearance.
4 **lead** (*of pencil*)
5 **mine** ◇ *une mine de charbon* a coal mine
• **faire mine de faire quelque chose** to pretend to do something ◇ *Elle a fait mine de le croire.* She pretended to believe him.
• **mine de rien** somehow or other ◇ *Elle a réussi mine de rien à le faire parler de lui.* Somehow or other she got him to talk about himself.

minéral ADJECTIVE
(MASC PL **minéraux**)
mineral ◇ *l'eau minérale* mineral water

minéralogique ADJECTIVE
• **une plaque minéralogique** a number plate

e **minet** NOUN
pussycat

a **minette** NOUN
pussycat (*female*)

mineur ADJECTIVE
see also mineur NOUN
minor

e **mineur** NOUN
see also mineur ADJECTIVE
1 **boy under 18**
• **les mineurs** the under-18s
2 **miner** ◇ *Mon grand-père était mineur.* My grandfather was a miner.

a **mineure** NOUN
girl under 18

a **minijupe** NOUN
miniskirt

e **minimum** NOUN
minimum ◇ *Il en fait le minimum.* He does the absolute minimum.
• **au minimum** at the very least

e **ministère** NOUN
ministry ◇ *le ministère des Affaires étrangères* the Foreign Office

e **ministre** NOUN
minister ◇ *le ministre des Affaires étrangères* the Foreign Secretary

le **Minitel** ® NOUN
Minitel *is France Telecom's online data service. You can use it instead of a phone directory, and to make bookings for transport, exhibitions etc.*

la **minorité** NOUN
minority

Minorque FEM NOUN
Minorca

le **minuit** NOUN
midnight ◇ *à minuit et quart* at a quarter past midnight

minuscule ADJECTIVE
see also minuscule NOUN
tiny

la **minuscule** NOUN
see also minuscule ADJECTIVE
small letter

la **minute** NOUN
minute
• **à la minute** just this minute ◇ *Je viens de l'appeler à la minute.* I've just this minute called him.

minutieux ADJECTIVE
(FEM SING **minutieuse**)
meticulous
• **C'est un travail minutieux.** It's a fiddly job.

la **mirabelle** NOUN
small yellow plum

le **miracle** NOUN
miracle

le **miroir** NOUN
mirror

mis VERB *see* **mettre**

mis ADJECTIVE
• **bien mis** well turned out ◇ *Elle est toujours bien mise.* She's always well turned out.

miser VERB (*informal*)
to bank on ◇ *On ne peut pas miser là-dessus.* We can't bank on it.

misérable ADJECTIVE
shabby-looking ◇ *une femme d'aspect misérable* a shabby-looking woman

la **misère** NOUN
extreme poverty
• **un salaire de misère** starvation wages

le/la **missionnaire** NOUN
missionary

mit VERB *see* **mettre**

la **mi-temps** NOUN
1 **half** (*of match*) ◇ *la première mi-temps* the first half ◇ *la deuxième mi-temps* the second half
2 **half-time** ◇ *Je lui parlerai à la mi-temps.* I'll speak to him at half-time.
• **travailler à mi-temps** to work part-time

la **mitraillette** NOUN
submachine gun

mixte ADJECTIVE
- **une école mixte** a mixed school

Mlle ABBREVIATION (= *Mademoiselle*)
(PL **Mlles**)
Miss ◇ *Mlle Renoir* Miss Renoir

Mme ABBREVIATION (= *Madame*)
(PL **Mmes**)
Mrs ◇ *Mme Leroy* Mrs Leroy

le **mobile** NOUN
motive ◇ *Quel était le mobile du crime?* What was the motive for the crime?

le **mobilier** NOUN
furniture

moche ADJECTIVE (*informal*)
[1] **awful** ◇ *Cette couleur est vraiment moche.* That colour's really awful. ◇ *Je me trouve moche!* I think I look awful!
[2] **rotten** ◇ *Il a la grippe, c'est moche pour lui.* He's got flu, that's rotten for him.

la **mode** NOUN
see also le mode
fashion ◇ *être à la mode* to be fashionable

le **mode** NOUN
see also la mode
- **le mode d'emploi** directions for use
- **le mode de vie** the way of life

le **modèle** NOUN
[1] **model** ◇ *Le nouveau modèle sort en septembre.* The new model is coming out in September.
[2] **style** (*of clothes*) ◇ *Est-ce que vous avez le même modèle en plus grand?* Have you got the same style in a bigger size?

modéré ADJECTIVE
moderate

moderne ADJECTIVE
modern

moderniser VERB
to modernize

modeste ADJECTIVE
modest ◇ *Ne sois pas si modeste!* Don't be so modest!

la **modestie** NOUN
modesty

moelleux ADJECTIVE
(FEM SING **moelleuse**)
soft ◇ *un coussin moelleux* a soft cushion

moi PRONOUN
me ◇ *Coucou, c'est moi!* Hello, it's me!
- **Moi, je pense que tu as tort.** I

personally think you're wrong.
- **à moi** mine ◇ *Ce livre n'est pas à moi.* This book isn't mine. ◇ *un ami à moi* a friend of mine

moi-même PRONOUN
myself ◇ *J'ai tricoté ce pull moi-même.* I knitted this jumper myself.

moindre ADJECTIVE
- **le moindre** the slightest ◇ *Il ne fait pas le moindre effort.* He doesn't make the slightest effort. ◇ *Je n'en ai pas la moindre idée.* I haven't the slightest idea.

le **moine** NOUN
monk

le **moineau** NOUN
(PL les **moineaux**)
sparrow

moins ADVERB, PREPOSITION
[1] **less** ◇ *Ça coûte moins de deux cents francs.* It costs less than 200 francs.
[2] **fewer** ◇ *Il y a moins de gens aujourd'hui.* There are fewer people today.
- **Il est cinq heures moins dix.** It's 10 to 5.
[3] **minus** ◇ *quatre moins trois* 4 minus 3 ◇ *Il a fait moins cinq la nuit dernière.* It was minus five last night.
- **le moins** the least ◇ *C'est le modèle le moins cher.* It's the least expensive model. ◇ *Ce sont les plages qui sont les moins polluées.* These are the least polluted beaches. ◇ *C'est l'album que j'aime le moins.* This is the album I like the least.
- **de moins en moins** less and less ◇ *Il vient nous voir de moins en moins.* He comes to see us less and less often.
- **Il a trois ans de moins que moi.** He's three years younger than me.
- **au moins** at least ◇ *Ne te plains pas: au moins il ne pleut pas!* Don't complain: at least it's not raining!
- **à moins que** unless
à moins que *is followed by a verb in the subjunctive.*
◇ *Je te retrouverai à dix heures à moins que le train n'ait du retard.* I'll meet you at 10 o'clock unless the train's late.

le **mois** NOUN
month

le **moisi** NOUN
- **Ça sent le moisi.** It smells musty.

moisir VERB
to go mouldy ◇ *Le pain a moisi.* The bread's gone mouldy.

la **moisson** NOUN
harvest

moite ADJECTIVE
sweaty ◇ *J'ai toujours les mains moites.* My hands are always sweaty.

la **moitié** NOUN
half ◇ *Il a mangé la moitié du gâteau à lui seul.* He ate half the cake all by himself.
- **la moitié du temps** half the time
- **à la moitié de** halfway through ◇ *Elle est partie à la moitié du film.* She left halfway through the film.
- **à moitié** half ◇ *Ton verre est encore à moitié plein.* Your glass is still half-full. ◇ *Ce sac était à moitié prix.* This bag was half-price.
- **partager moitié moitié** to go halves ◇ *On partage moitié moitié, d'accord?* We'll go halves, OK?

a **molaire** NOUN
back tooth

a **Moldavie** NOUN
Moldova

molle ADJECTIVE
lethargic ◇ *Je la trouve un peu molle.* I find her a bit lethargic.

e **mollet** NOUN
see also **mollet** ADJECTIVE
calf (*of leg*)

mollet ADJECTIVE
see also **mollet** NOUN
- **un œuf mollet** a soft-boiled egg

a **môme** (*informal*) NOUN
kid

e **moment** NOUN
moment
- **en ce moment** at the moment ◇ *Nous avons beaucoup de travail en ce moment.* We have a lot of work at the moment.
- **pour le moment** for the moment ◇ *Nous ne pensons pas déménager pour le moment.* We're not thinking of moving for the moment.
- **au moment où** just as ◇ *Il est arrivé au moment où j'allais partir.* He turned up just as I was leaving.
- **à tout moment (1)** at any moment ◇ *Elle peut arriver à tout moment.* She could arrive at any moment.
- **à tout moment (2)** constantly ◇ *Il nous dérange à tout moment pour des riens.* He's constantly bothering us about silly little things.
- **sur le moment** at the time ◇ *Sur le moment je n'ai rien dit.* At the time I didn't say anything.
- **par moments** at times ◇ *Elle se sent*

seule par moments. She feels lonely at times.

momentané ADJECTIVE
momentary

la **momie** NOUN
mummy (*Egyptian*)

mon ADJECTIVE
(FEM SING **ma**, PL **mes**)
my ◇ *mon frère* my brother ◇ *mon ami* my friend

la **monarchie** NOUN
monarchy

le **monastère** NOUN
monastery

le **monde** NOUN
world ◇ *faire le tour du monde* to go round the world
- **Il y a du monde.** There are a lot of people.
- **beaucoup de monde** a lot of people ◇ *Il y avait beaucoup de monde au concert.* There were a lot of people at the concert.
- **peu de monde** not many people

mondial ADJECTIVE
(MASC PL **mondiaux**)
[1] **world** ◇ *la population mondiale* the world population
[2] **world-wide** ◇ *une crise mondiale* a world-wide crisis

le **moniteur** NOUN
[1] **instructor** ◇ *un moniteur de voile* a sailing instructor
[2] **supervisor**

la **monitrice** NOUN
[1] **instructor** ◇ *une monitrice de ski* a ski instructor
[2] **supervisor**

la **monnaie** NOUN
- **une pièce de monnaie** a coin
- **avoir de la monnaie** to have change ◇ *Est-ce que tu as de la monnaie?* Have you got any change? ◇ *Est-ce que vous avez la monnaie de cent francs?* Do you have change for 100 francs?
- **rendre la monnaie à quelqu'un** to give somebody their change

monotone ADJECTIVE
monotonous

Monsieur MASC NOUN
(PL **Messieurs**)
[1] **Mr** ◇ *Monsieur Dupont* Mr Dupont
[2] **man** ◇ *Il y a un monsieur qui veut te voir.* There's a man to see you.
[3] **Sir** ◇ *Monsieur,...* Dear Sir,... (*in letter*) ◇ *Monsieur! Vous avez oublié votre parapluie!* Excuse me! You've

M

PTO

forgotten your umbrella!

le **monstre** NOUN

see also monstre ADJECTIVE

monster

monstre ADJECTIVE

see also monstre NOUN

- **Nous avons un travail monstre.**
We've got a terrific amount of work.

le **mont** NOUN

mount

- **le mont Everest** Mount Everest

- **le mont Blanc** Mont Blanc

la **montagne** NOUN

mountain ◇ *de hautes montagnes* high mountains ◇ *Nous passons tous les ans un mois à la montagne.* We spend a month in the mountains every year.

- **les montagnes russes** roller coaster

montagneux ADJECTIVE

(FEM SING **montagneuse**)

mountainous ◇ *une région montagneuse* a mountainous area

montant ADJECTIVE

[1] rising ◇ *la marée montante* the rising tide

[2] high ◇ *un pull à col montant* a high-necked jumper

monter VERB

[1] to go up ◇ *Elle a du mal à monter les escaliers.* She has difficulty going upstairs. ◇ *Les prix ont encore monté.* Prices have gone up again.

[2] to assemble ◇ *Est-ce que ces étagères sont difficiles à monter?* Are these shelves difficult to assemble?

- **monter dans** to get on ◇ *Il est temps de monter dans l'avion.* It's time to get on the plane.

- **monter sur** to stand on ◇ *Tu vas devoir monter sur une chaise pour changer l'ampoule.* You'll have to stand on a chair to change the light bulb.

- **monter à cheval** to ride

la **montre** NOUN

watch

montrer VERB

to show ◇ *Est-ce que vous pouvez me montrer la gare sur le plan?* Can you show me the station on the map?

la **monture** NOUN

frames *(of glasses)*

le **monument** NOUN

monument

se **moquer** VERB

- **se moquer de (1)** to make fun of
◇ *Ils se sont moqués de mes*

chaussures jaunes. They made fun of my yellow shoes.

- **se moquer de (2)** *(informal)* not to care about ◇ *Il se moque complètement de la mode.* He couldn't care less about fashion.

la **moquette** NOUN

fitted carpet

moqueur ADJECTIVE

(FEM SING **moqueuse**)

mocking

le **moral** NOUN

- **Elle a le moral.** She's in good spirits.

- **J'ai le moral à zéro.** I'm feeling really down.

la **morale** NOUN

moral ◇ *La morale de cette histoire est...* The moral of the story is...

- **faire la morale à quelqu'un** to lecture somebody

le **morceau** NOUN

(PL les **morceaux**)

piece ◇ *un morceau de pain* a piece of bread

mordre VERB

to bite

mordu ADJECTIVE

- **Il est mordu de jazz.** *(informal)* He's crazy about jazz.

la **morgue** NOUN

mortuary

le **morse** NOUN

walrus

la **morsure** NOUN

bite

la **mort** NOUN

see also mort ADJECTIVE

death

mort ADJECTIVE

see also mort NOUN

dead ◇ *Nous avons trouvé un oiseau mort.* We found a dead bird. ◇ *Napoléon est mort en 1821.* Napoleon died in 1821.

- **Il était mort de peur.** He was scared to death.

- **Je suis morte de fatigue.** I'm dead tired.

mortel ADJECTIVE

(FEM SING **mortelle**)

[1] deadly ◇ *un poison mortel* a deadly poison ◇ *Ces réunions de famille sont mortelles!* *(informal)* These family gatherings are deadly!

[2] fatal ◇ *une chute mortelle* a fatal fall

la **morue** NOUN

cod

Moscou NOUN

Moscow
la mosquée NOUN
  mosque
le mot NOUN
  [1] **word** ◇ *mot à mot* word for word
  [2] **line** ◇ *Je vais lui écrire un mot pour lui dire qu'on arrive.* I'll drop her a line to say we're coming.
  ◆ **des mots croisés** a crossword
le motard NOUN
  [1] **biker**
  [2] **motorcycle cop** (*informal*) ◇ *Il s'est fait arrêter par un motard pour excès de vitesse.* He was stopped for speeding by a motorcycle cop.
le moteur NOUN
  engine
  ◆ **un bateau à moteur** a motor boat
le motif NOUN
  pattern ◇ *des rideaux avec un motif d'oiseaux* curtains with a bird pattern
  ◆ **sans motif** for no reason ◇ *Il s'est fâché sans motif.* He got angry for no reason.
la moto NOUN
  motorbike
la motocycliste NOUN
  motorcyclist
mou ADJECTIVE
  (FEM SING **molle**)
  [1] **soft** ◇ *Mon matelas est trop mou.* My mattress is too soft.
  [2] **lethargic** ◇ *Je le trouve un peu mou.* I find him a bit lethargic.
la mouche NOUN
  fly
se moucher VERB
  to blow one's nose
le moucheron NOUN
  midge
le mouchoir NOUN
  handkerchief
  ◆ **un mouchoir en papier** a tissue
moudre VERB
  to grind
la moue NOUN
  pout
  ◆ **faire la moue** to pout
la mouette NOUN
  seagull
la moufle NOUN
  mitt
mouillé ADJECTIVE
  wet
mouiller VERB
  to get wet ◇ *J'ai mouillé les manches de mon pull.* I got the sleeves of my jumper wet.
  ◆ **se mouiller** to get wet ◇ *Attention, tu*

vas te mouiller! Careful, you'll get wet!
moulant ADJECTIVE
  figure-hugging ◇ *une robe moulante* a figure-hugging dress
la moule NOUN
  see also **le moule**
  mussel
le moule NOUN
  see also **la moule**
  ◆ **un moule à gâteaux** a cake tin
le moulin NOUN
  mill
moulu VERB *see* **moudre**
mourir VERB
  to die
  ◆ **mourir de faim** to starve ◇ *Des centaines de personnes sont mortes de faim.* Hundreds of people starved to death.
  ◆ **Je meurs de faim!** I'm starving!
  ◆ **mourir de froid** to die of exposure
  ◆ **Je meurs de froid!** I'm freezing!
  ◆ **mourir d'envie de faire quelque chose** to be dying to do something ◇ *Je meurs d'envie d'aller me baigner.* I'm dying to go for a swim.
la mousse NOUN
  [1] **moss** ◇ *un rocher recouvert de mousse* a rock covered with moss
  [2] **froth** (*on beer*)
  [3] **lather** (*of soap, shampoo*)
  [4] **mousse** ◇ *une mousse au chocolat* a chocolate mousse ◇ *une mousse de poisson* a fish mousse
  ◆ **la mousse à raser** shaving foam
mousseux ADJECTIVE
  (FEM SING **mousseuse**)
  ◆ **un vin mousseux** a sparkling wine
la moustache NOUN
  moustache
  ◆ **les moustaches** whiskers
le moustique NOUN
  mosquito
la moutarde NOUN
  mustard
le mouton NOUN
  [1] **sheep** ◇ *une peau de mouton* a sheepskin
  [2] **mutton** ◇ *un gigot de mouton* a leg of mutton
le mouvement NOUN
  movement
mouvementé ADJECTIVE
  eventful ◇ *des vacances mouvementées* eventful holidays
moyen ADJECTIVE
  (FEM SING **moyenne**)
  see also **moyen** NOUN
  [1] **average** ◇ *Je suis plutôt moyenne*

M

en langues. I'm just average at languages.

2 **medium** ◇ *Elle est de taille moyenne.* She's of medium height.
- **le moyen âge** the Middle Ages

le **moyen** NOUN

see also moyen ADJECTIVE

way ◇ *Quel est le meilleur moyen de le convaincre?* What's the best way of convincing him?
- **Je n'en ai pas les moyens.** I can't afford it.
- **Ils n'ont pas les moyens de s'acheter une voiture.** They can't afford to buy a car.
- **un moyen de transport** a means of transport
- **par tous les moyens** by every possible means

la **moyenne** NOUN
- **avoir la moyenne** to get a pass mark ◇ *J'espère avoir la moyenne en maths.* I hope to get a pass mark in maths.
- **en moyenne** on average
- **la moyenne d'âge** the average age

le **Moyen-Orient** NOUN
Middle East

muet ADJECTIVE
(FEM SING **muette**)
dumb
- **un film muet** a silent film

le **muguet** NOUN
lily of the valley

multiple ADJECTIVE
numerous ◇ *en de multiples occasions* on numerous occasions

multiplier VERB
to multiply

municipal ADJECTIVE
(MASC PL **municipaux**)
- **la bibliothèque municipale** the public library

la **municipalité** NOUN
town council

les **munitions** FEM NOUN
ammunition

le **mur** NOUN
wall

mûr ADJECTIVE
1 **ripe** (*fruit*)
2 **mature** (*person*)

la **mûre** NOUN
bramble

mûrir VERB
1 **to ripen** ◇ *Les fraises ont mis du*

temps à mûrir. The strawberries took a while to ripen.

2 **to make mature** ◇ *Cette expérience l'a beaucoup mûrie.* That experience has made her much more mature.

murmurer VERB
to whisper ◇ *Il m'a murmuré à l'oreille qu'il allait partir.* He whispered in my ear that he was going to go.

la **muscade** NOUN
nutmeg

le **muscat** NOUN
1 **muscat grape**
2 **muscatel** (*wine*) ◇ *un verre de muscat* a glass of muscatel

le **muscle** NOUN
muscle

musclé ADJECTIVE
muscular

le **museau** NOUN
(PL les **museaux**)
muzzle

le **musée** NOUN
museum

musical ADJECTIVE
(MASC PL **musicaux**)
musical
- **avoir l'oreille musicale** to be musical

le **music-hall** NOUN
variety ◇ *une chanteuse de music-hall* a variety singer

le **musicien** NOUN
musician

la **musicienne** NOUN
musician

la **musique** NOUN
music

musulman ADJECTIVE, NOUN
Muslim
- **un musulman** a Muslim (*man*)
- **une musulmane** a Muslim (*woman*)

la **mutation** NOUN
transfer ◇ *Il a demandé sa mutation à Paris.* He asked for a transfer to Paris.

myope ADJECTIVE
short-sighted

le **mystère** NOUN
mystery

mystérieux ADJECTIVE
(FEM SING **mystérieuse**)
mysterious

le **mythe** NOUN
myth

N

n' PRONOUN *see* **ne**

la **nage** NOUN
- **traverser une rivière à la nage** to swim across a river

la **nageoire** NOUN
  fin

nager VERB
  to swim

le **nageur** NOUN
  swimmer

la **nageuse** NOUN
  swimmer

naïf ADJECTIVE
  (FEM SING **naïve**)
  naïve

le **nain** NOUN
  dwarf

la **naissance** NOUN
  birth
- **votre date de naissance** your date of birth

naître VERB
  to be born
- **Il est né en 1982.** He was born in 1982.

naïve ADJECTIVE *see* **naïf**

la **nana** NOUN (*informal*)
  girl

la **nappe** NOUN
  tablecloth

la **narine** NOUN
  nostril

natal ADJECTIVE
  native ◇ *mon pays natal* my native country

la **natation** NOUN
  swimming ◇ *La natation est mon sport favori.* Swimming's my favourite sport.

national ADJECTIVE
  (MASC PL **nationaux**)
  national
- **la fête nationale espagnole** the national day of Spain

la **nationalité** NOUN
  nationality

la **natte** NOUN
  plait ◇ *Cécile avait des nattes.* Cécile had plaits.

la **nature** NOUN
  [see also nature ADJECTIVE]
  nature

nature ADJECTIVE
  [see also nature NOUN]
  plain ◇ *un yaourt nature* a plain yoghurt

naturel ADJECTIVE
  (FEM SING **naturelle**)
  natural

naturellement ADVERB
  of course ◇ *Vous viendrez à notre fête?–Naturellement!* Are you coming to our party?–Of course!
  ◇ *Naturellement, il est encore en retard.* Of course, he's late again.

le **naufrage** NOUN
  shipwreck

nautique ADJECTIVE
  water
- **les sports nautiques** water sports
- **le ski nautique** water-skiing

le **navet** NOUN
  turnip

la **navette** NOUN
  shuttle ◇ *la navette entre la gare et l'aéroport* the shuttle between the station and the airport
- **faire la navette** to commute ◇ *Je fais la navette entre Paris et Ivry.* I commute between Paris and Ivry.

la **navigation** NOUN
- **La navigation est interdite ici.** Boats are not allowed here.

naviguer VERB
  to sail

le **navire** NOUN
  ship

ne ADVERB

  > **ne** *is combined with words such as* **pas,**
  > **personne, plus** *and* **jamais** *to form negative phrases.*

  ◇ *Je ne peux pas venir.* I can't come.
  ◇ *Ils ne vont jamais en boîte.* They never go to discos. ◇ *Je ne connais personne ici.* I don't know anyone here.

  > **ne** *changes to* **n'** *before a vowel and most words beginning with "h".*

  ◇ *Je n'ai pas d'argent.* I haven't got any money. ◇ *Il n'habite plus à Paris.* He doesn't live in Paris any more.

  > **ne** *is sometimes not translated.*

  ◇ *C'est plus loin que je ne le croyais.* It's further than I thought.

né VERB *see* **naître**
  born ◇ *Elle est née en 1980.* She was born in 1980.

néanmoins ADVERB
  nevertheless

nécessaire ADJECTIVE
  necessary ◇ *Il est nécessaire de réserver.* It's necessary to book.

le **nectar** NOUN
- **le nectar d'abricot** apricot drink

néerlandais ADJECTIVE, NOUN
(FEM SING **néerlandaise**)
Dutch ◇ *Manon parle néerlandais.* Manon speaks Dutch.
- **un Néerlandais** a Dutchman
- **une Néerlandaise** a Dutchwoman
- **les Néerlandais** the Dutch

négatif ADJECTIVE
(FEM SING **négative**)
see also négatif NOUN
negative

le **négatif** NOUN
see also négatif ADJECTIVE
negative (*of photo*)

négligé ADJECTIVE
scruffy ◇ *une tenue négligée* scruffy clothes

la **neige** NOUN
snow
- **un bonhomme de neige** a snowman

neiger VERB
to snow

le **nénuphar** NOUN
water lily

le **néon** NOUN
neon ◇ *une lampe au néon* a neon light ◇ *La cuisine est éclairée au néon.* The kitchen has a neon light.

néo-zélandais ADJECTIVE, NOUN
(FEM SING **néo-zélandaise**)
New Zealand ◇ *Le champion néo-zélandais a gagné la course.* The New Zealand champion won the race.
- **un Néo-Zélandais** a New Zealander (*man*)
- **une Néo-Zélandaise** a New Zealander (*woman*)

le **nerf** NOUN
nerve
- **taper sur les nerfs de quelqu'un** to get on somebody's nerves ◇ *Il me tape sur les nerfs.* He's getting on my nerves.

nerveux ADJECTIVE
(FEM SING **nerveuse**)
nervous

la **nervosité** NOUN
nervousness

n'est-ce pas ADVERB
n'est-ce pas *is used to check that something is true.*
◇ *Nous sommes le douze aujourd'hui, n'est-ce pas?* It's the 12th today, isn't it? ◇ *Ils sont venus l'an dernier, n'est-ce pas?* They came last year, didn't they? ◇ *Elle aura dix-huit ans en octobre, n'est-ce pas?* She'll be 18 in October, won't she?

net ADJECTIVE, ADVERB
(FEM SING **nette**)
1 **clear** ◇ *L'image n'est pas nette.* The picture isn't very clear.
2 **net** ◇ *Poids net: 500 g.* Net weight: 500 g.
3 **flatly** ◇ *Il a refusé net de nous aider.* He flatly refused to help us.
- **s'arrêter net** to stop dead

nettement ADVERB
much ◇ *Ce magasin est nettement plus cher.* This shop is much more expensive.

le **nettoyage** NOUN
cleaning
- **le nettoyage à sec** dry cleaning

nettoyer VERB
to clean

neuf NUMBER
see also neuf ADJECTIVE
nine ◇ *Claire a neuf ans.* Claire's nine. ◇ *Il est neuf heures du matin.* It's nine in the morning.
- **le neuf février** the ninth of February

neuf ADJECTIVE
(FEM SING **neuve**)
see also neuf NUMBER
new ◇ *des chaussures neuves* new shoes

neutre ADJECTIVE
neutral

neuve ADJECTIVE *see* **neuf**

neuvième ADJECTIVE
ninth ◇ *au neuvième étage* on the ninth floor

le **neveu** NOUN
(PL les **neveux**)
nephew

le **nez** NOUN
nose
- **se trouver nez à nez avec quelqu'un** to come face to face with somebody

ni CONJUNCTION
- **ni...ni...** neither...nor... ◇ *Je n'aime ni les lentilles ni les épinards.* I like neither lentils nor spinach. ◇ *Elles ne sont venues ni l'une ni l'autre.* Neither of them came.

la **niche** NOUN
kennel

le **nid** NOUN
nest

la **nièce** NOUN
niece

nier VERB
to deny

n'importe ADVERB
- **n'importe qui** anybody ◇ *N'ouvre*

pas la porte à n'importe qui. Don't open the door to just anybody.
- **n'importe quoi** anything ◦ *Je ferais n'importe quoi pour elle.* I'd do anything for her.
- **Tu dis n'importe quoi.** You're talking rubbish.
- **n'importe où** anywhere ◦ *On trouve ces fleurs n'importe où.* You can find these flowers anywhere.
- **Ne laisse pas tes affaires n'importe où.** Don't leave your things lying everywhere.
- **n'importe quand** any time ◦ *Tu peux venir n'importe quand.* You can come any time.
- **n'importe comment** any old how ◦ *Ces livres sont rangés n'importe comment.* These books have been put away any old how.

le **niveau** NOUN
(PL les **niveaux**)
1 **level** ◦ *le niveau de l'eau* the water level
2 **standard** ◦ *Ces deux enfants n'ont pas le même niveau.* These two children aren't at the same level.
- **le niveau de vie** the standard of living

noble ADJECTIVE
noble

la **noblesse** NOUN
nobility

la **noce** NOUN
wedding
- **un repas de noce** a wedding reception

nocif ADJECTIVE
(FEM SING **nocive**)
harmful ◦ *une substance nocive* a harmful substance

nocturne ADJECTIVE
see also nocturne NOUN
1 **nocturnal** ◦ *un oiseau nocturne* a nocturnal bird
2 **by night** ◦ *Découvrez le Paris nocturne!* Discover Paris by night!

la **nocturne** NOUN
see also nocturne ADJECTIVE
late-night opening ◦ *Nocturne le vendredi jusqu'à vingt-trois heures.* Late-night opening until 11 p.m. on Fridays.

le **Noël** NOUN
Christmas ◦ *Qu'est-ce que tu as eu pour Noël?* What did you get for Christmas?
- **Joyeux Noël!** Merry Christmas!

le **nœud** NOUN
1 **knot** ◦ *Il a fait un nœud à la corde.* He tied a knot in the rope.

2 **bow** ◦ *Janet avait un nœud dans les cheveux.* Janet had a bow in her hair.
- **un nœud papillon** a bow tie

noir ADJECTIVE
see also noir NOUN
1 **black** ◦ *Elle porte une robe noire.* She's wearing a black dress. ◦ *Elle est noire.* She's black.
2 **dark** ◦ *Il fait noir dehors.* It's dark outside.

le **noir** NOUN
see also noir ADJECTIVE
dark ◦ *J'ai peur du noir.* I'm afraid of the dark.
- **le travail au noir** moonlighting

le **Noir** NOUN
black man
- **les Noirs** black people

la **Noire** NOUN
black woman

la **noisette** NOUN
hazelnut

la **noix** NOUN
(PL les **noix**)
walnut
- **une noix de coco** a coconut
- **les noix de cajou** cashew nuts
- **une noix de beurre** a knob of butter

le **nom** NOUN
1 **name** ◦ *votre nom* your name
- **mon nom de famille** my surname
- **son nom de jeune fille** her maiden name
2 **noun** (in grammar)

le **nombre** NOUN
number ◦ *Treize est un nombre impair.* Thirteen is an odd number. ◦ *un grand nombre d'amis* a large number of friends

nombreux ADJECTIVE
(FEM SING **nombreuse**)
1 **many** ◦ *Il a gagné de nombreux matchs.* He's won many matches.
2 **large** ◦ *une famille nombreuse* a large family
- **peu nombreux** few ◦ *Nous étions peu nombreux à la réunion.* There were few of us at the meeting.

le **nombril** NOUN
navel

nommer VERB
1 **to name** ◦ *Il n'a voulu nommer personne.* He didn't want to name anybody.
2 **to appoint** ◦ *Il a été nommé directeur.* He was appointed director.

non ADVERB
no ◦ *Tu as vu Jean-Pierre?—Non.*

Have you seen Jean-Pierre?–No.

- **non seulement** not only ◇ *Il est non seulement intelligent, mais aussi très gentil.* Not only is he intelligent, he's also very nice.
- **moi non plus** Neither do I. ◇ *Je n'aime pas les hamburgers.–Moi non plus.* I don't like hamburgers.–Neither do I. ◇ *Il n'y est pas allé et moi non plus.* He didn't go and neither did I.

non alcoolisé ADJECTIVE
non-alcoholic ◇ *les boissons non alcoolisées* non-alcoholic drinks

le **non-fumeur** NOUN
non-smoker ◇ *Gavin est un non-fumeur.* Gavin's a non-smoker.
- **une voiture non-fumeurs** a no-smoking carriage

le **nord** NOUN
see also nord ADJECTIVE
north ◇ *Ils vivent dans le nord de l'île.* They live in the north of the island.
- **vers le nord** northwards
- **au nord de Paris** north of Paris
- **l'Afrique du Nord** North Africa
- **le vent du nord** the north wind

nord ADJECTIVE
see also nord NOUN
[1] **north** ◇ *la face nord du Mont-Blanc* the north face of Mont-Blanc
- **le pôle Nord** the North Pole
[2] **northern** ◇ *Nous avons visité la partie nord de l'île.* We visited the northern part of the island.

le **nord-est** NOUN
north-east ◇ *les régions du nord-est* north-eastern regions

le **nord-ouest** NOUN
north-west
- **l'Europe du nord-ouest** north-west Europe

normal ADJECTIVE
(MASC PL **normaux**)
[1] **normal** ◇ *un bébé normal* a normal baby
[2] **natural** ◇ *C'est tout à fait normal.* It's perfectly natural.
- **Vous trouvez que c'est normal?** Does that seem right to you?

normalement ADVERB
normally ◇ *Les aéroports fonctionnent tous normalement.* The airports are all working normally.
- **Normalement, elle doit arriver à huit heures.** She's supposed to arrive at 8 o'clock.
- **Tu es libre ce week-end?–Oui, normalement.** Are you free this

weekend?–Yes, I should be.

normand ADJECTIVE
- **un village normand** a village in Normandy
- **la côte normande** the coast of Normandy

la **Normandie** NOUN
Normandy

la **Norvège** NOUN
Norway

norvégien ADJECTIVE, NOUN
(FEM SING **norvégienne**)
Norwegian
- **Elle parle norvégien.** She speaks Norwegian.
- **un Norvégien** a Norwegian (*man*)
- **une Norvégienne** a Norwegian (*woman*)

nos ADJECTIVE
our ◇ *Où sont nos affaires?* Where are our things?

le **notaire** NOUN
solicitor ◇ *Son père est notaire.* His father's a solicitor.

la **note** NOUN
[1] **note** ◇ *J'ai pris des notes pendant la conférence.* I took notes at the lecture. ◇ *Il a joué quelques notes au piano.* He played a few notes on the piano.
[2] **mark** ◇ *Vincent a de bonnes notes en maths.* Vincent's got good marks in maths.
[3] **bill** ◇ *Il n'a pas payé sa note.* He didn't pay his bill.

noter VERB
to make a note of ◇ *Tu as noté leur adresse?* Did you make a note of their address?

les **notions** FEM NOUN
basics ◇ *Il faut avoir des notions d'anglais.* You have to have some basic English. ◇ *Elle a des notions de comptabilité.* She knows the basics of accounting.

notre ADJECTIVE
(PL **nos**)
our ◇ *Voici notre maison.* Here's our house.

nôtre PRONOUN
- **le nôtre** ours ◇ *À qui est ce chien? –C'est le nôtre.* Whose dog is it? –It's ours. ◇ *Leur voiture est rouge, la nôtre est bleue.* Their car is red, ours is blue.

nôtres PRONOUN
- **les nôtres** ours ◇ *Ces places-là sont les nôtres.* Those seats are ours.

nouer VERB

to tie

les **nouilles** FEM NOUN
  noodles

nourrir VERB
  to feed

la **nourriture** NOUN
  food

nous PRONOUN
  1 **we** ◇ *Nous avons deux enfants.*
  We have two children.
  2 **us** ◇ *Viens avec nous.* Come with
  us.
  ‣ **nous-mêmes** ourselves

nouveau ADJECTIVE
  (MASC SING ALSO **nouvel**, FEM SING **nouvelle**,
  MASC PL **nouveaux**)
  see also nouveau NOUN
  new ◇ *Il me faut un nouveau*
  pantalon. I need some new trousers.
  ◇ *Elle a une nouvelle voiture.* She's
  got a new car.

  nouveau *changes to* **nouvel** *before a vowel*
  and most words beginning with "h".

  ◇ *Il y a un nouvel élève dans ma classe.*
  There's a new boy in my class.
  ‣ **le nouvel an** New Year

le **nouveau** NOUN
  (PL les **nouveaux**)
  see also nouveau ADJECTIVE
  new pupil ◇ *Il y a plusieurs*
  nouveaux dans la classe. There are
  several new pupils in the class.
  ‣ **de nouveau** again ◇ *Il pleut de*
  nouveau. It's raining again.

la **nouveauté** NOUN
  novelty

nouvel, nouvelle ADJECTIVE *see*
  nouveau

la **nouvelle** NOUN
  1 **news** ◇ *Tu connais la nouvelle?*
  Teresa a gagné au loto. Have you heard
  the news? Teresa won the lottery.
  ◇ *C'est une bonne nouvelle.* That's
  good news.
  2 **short story** ◇ *une nouvelle de*
  Maupassant a short story by
  Maupassant
  ‣ **les nouvelles** the news ◇ *J'ai écouté*
  les nouvelles à la radio. I listened to
  the news on the radio.
  ‣ **avoir des nouvelles de quelqu'un** to
  hear from somebody ◇ *Je n'ai pas eu*
  de nouvelles de lui. I haven't heard
  from him.

la **Nouvelle-Zélande** NOUN
  New Zealand

novembre MASC NOUN
  November

‣ **en novembre** in November

le **noyau** NOUN
  (PL les **noyaux**)
  stone *(of fruit)* ◇ *un noyau d'abricot*
  an apricot stone

le **noyer** NOUN
  see also noyer VERB
  walnut tree

se **noyer** VERB
  see also noyer NOUN
  to drown ◇ *Il s'est noyé dans la*
  rivière. He drowned in the river.

nu ADJECTIVE
  1 **naked** ◇ *Ils se sont baignés nus.*
  They went for a swim naked. ◇ *tout*
  nus stark naked
  2 **bare** ◇ *Elle avait les bras nus.* Her
  arms were bare. ◇ *Les murs étaient*
  nus. The walls were bare.

le **nuage** NOUN
  cloud
  ‣ **un nuage de lait** a drop of milk

nuageux ADJECTIVE
  (FEM SING **nuageuse**)
  cloudy

nucléaire ADJECTIVE
  nuclear ◇ *l'énergie nucléaire* nuclear
  power

le/la **nudiste** NOUN
  nudist

la **nuit** NOUN
  night ◇ *Ils ont fait du bruit toute la*
  nuit. They were noisy all night.
  ‣ **Il fait nuit.** It's dark.
  ‣ **cette nuit** tonight ◇ *Il va rentrer*
  cette nuit. He'll be back tonight.
  ‣ **Bonne nuit!** Good night!

nul ADJECTIVE
  (FEM SING **nulle**)
  rubbish
  ‣ **Ce film est nul.** *(informal)* This film's
  rubbish.
  ‣ **un match nul** a draw *(in sport)* ◇ *Ils*
  ont fait match nul. It was a draw.
  ‣ **nulle part** nowhere ◇ *Je ne le vois*
  nulle part. I can't see it anywhere.

le **numéro** NOUN
  number ◇ *J'habite au numéro trois.* I
  live at number 3.
  ‣ **mon numéro de téléphone** my phone
  number

nu-pieds ADJECTIVE, ADVERB
  barefoot ◇ *Il se promenait nu-pieds.*
  He was walking barefoot.

la **nuque** NOUN
  nape of the neck

le **nylon** NOUN
  nylon

N

O

obéir VERB
to obey
- **obéir à quelqu'un** to obey somebody ◇ *Elle refuse d'obéir à ses parents.* She refuses to obey her parents.

obéissant ADJECTIVE
obedient

l'**objet** MASC NOUN
object
- **les objets de valeur** valuables
- **les objets trouvés** the lost property office

obligatoire ADJECTIVE
compulsory

obliger VERB
- **obliger quelqu'un à faire quelque chose** to force somebody to do something
- **Je suis bien obligé d'accepter.** I can't really refuse.

obscur ADJECTIVE
dark

l'**obscurité** FEM NOUN
darkness ◇ *dans l'obscurité* in the dark

l'**obsédé** MASC NOUN
sex maniac
- **un obsédé sexuel** a sex maniac

obséder VERB
to obsess ◇ *Il est obsédé par le travail.* He's obsessed by work.

l'**observation** FEM NOUN
comment ◇ *J'ai une ou deux observations à faire.* I've got one or two comments to make.

observer VERB
1 **to watch** ◇ *Il observait les canards sur le lac.* He watched the ducks on the lake.
2 **to observe** ◇ *Ils observent le règlement.* They observe the rules.

l'**obstacle** MASC NOUN
1 **obstacle** ◇ *surmonter un obstacle* to overcome an obstacle
2 **fence** (*in show jumping*)
- **une course d'obstacles** an obstacle race

obtenir VERB
1 **to get** ◇ *Ils ont obtenu cinquante pour cent des voix.* They got 50% of the votes.
2 **to achieve** ◇ *Nous avons obtenu de bons résultats.* We achieved good results.

l'**occasion** FEM NOUN
1 **opportunity** ◇ *C'est une occasion à ne pas manquer.* It's an opportunity not to be missed.
2 **occasion** ◇ *à l'occasion de son anniversaire* on the occasion of his birthday ◇ *à plusieurs occasions* on several occasions
3 **bargain** ◇ *Cet ordinateur est une bonne occasion.* This computer's a real bargain.
- **d'occasion** second-hand ◇ *une voiture d'occasion* a second-hand car

l'**Occident** MASC NOUN
West
- **en Occident** in the West

occidental ADJECTIVE
(MASC PL **occidentaux**)
western
- **les pays occidentaux** the West

l'**occupation** FEM NOUN
occupation ◇ *la France sous l'Occupation* France during the Occupation

occupé ADJECTIVE
1 **busy** ◇ *Le directeur est très occupé.* The director's very busy.
2 **taken** ◇ *Est-ce que cette place est occupée?* Is this seat taken?
3 **engaged** ◇ *Les toilettes sont occupées.* The toilet's engaged. ◇ *La ligne est occupée.* The line's engaged.

occuper VERB
to occupy ◇ *Les enfants ne sont pas faciles à occuper quand il pleut.* Children aren't easy to keep occupied when it rains.
- **s'occuper de quelque chose (1)** to be in charge of something ◇ *Elle s'occupe d'un club de sport.* She's in charge of a sports club.
- **s'occuper de quelque chose (2)** to deal with something ◇ *Je vais m'occuper de ce dossier.* I'm going to deal with this file.
- **On s'occupe de vous?** (*in a shop*) Are you being attended to?

l'**océan** MASC NOUN
ocean ◇ *l'océan Indien* the Indian Ocean

octobre MASC NOUN
October
- **en octobre** in October

l'**odeur** FEM NOUN
smell ◇ *Il y a une drôle d'odeur ici.* There's a funny smell round here.

l'**œil** MASC NOUN
(PL **les yeux**)

eye ◇ *J'ai quelque chose dans l'œil.*
I've got something in my eye.
- **à l'œil** (*informal*) for free ◇ *Il est
entré à l'œil.* He got in for free.

l'**œillet** MASC NOUN
carnation

l'**œuf** MASC NOUN
egg
- **un œuf à la coque** a soft-boiled egg
- **un œuf dur** a hard-boiled egg
- **un œuf au plat** a fried egg
- **les œufs brouillés** scrambled eggs
- **un œuf de Pâques** an Easter egg

l'**œuvre** FEM NOUN
work ◇ *J'étudie une œuvre de
Molière.* I'm studying one of Molière's
works.
- **une œuvre d'art** a work of art

offert VERB *see* **offrir**

l'**office** MASC NOUN
- **un office de tourisme** a tourist office

officiel ADJECTIVE
(FEM SING **officielle**)
official

l'**officier** MASC NOUN
officer ◇ *Il est officier de marine.*
He's a naval officer.

l'**offre** FEM NOUN
offer ◇ *une offre spéciale* a special
offer
- **"offres d'emploi"** "situations vacant"

offrir VERB
- **offrir quelque chose (1)** to offer
something ◇ *On lui a offert un poste
de secrétaire.* They offered her a
secretarial post. ◇ *Elle lui a offert à
boire.* She offered him a drink.
- **offrir quelque chose (2)** to give
something ◇ *Il lui a offert des roses.*
He gave her roses.
- **s'offrir quelque chose** to treat oneself
to something ◇ *Je me suis offert une
nouvelle paire de chaussures.* I treated
myself to a new pair of shoes.

l'**oie** FEM NOUN
goose

l'**oignon** MASC NOUN
onion

l'**oiseau** MASC NOUN
(PL les **oiseaux**)
bird

l'**olive** FEM NOUN
olive ◇ *l'huile d'olive* olive oil

olympique ADJECTIVE
- **les Jeux Olympiques** the Olympic
Games

l'**ombre** FEM NOUN
1 **shade** ◇ *Je vais me mettre à
l'ombre.* I'm going to sit in the shade.

2 **shadow**
- **l'ombre à paupières** eye shadow

l'**omelette** FEM NOUN
omelette

on PRONOUN
1 **we** ◇ *On va à la plage demain.*
We're going to the beach tomorrow.
◇ *On a pensé que ça te ferait plaisir.*
We thought you'd be pleased.
2 **someone** ◇ *On m'a volé mon
porte-monnaie.* Someone has stolen my
purse.
- **On m'a dit d'attendre.** I was told to
wait.
- **On vous demande au téléphone.**
There's a phone call for you.
3 **you** ◇ *On peut visiter le château
en été.* You can visit the castle in the
summer. ◇ *D'ici on peut voir la côte
française.* From here you can see the
French coast.

l'**oncle** MASC NOUN
uncle

l'**onde** FEM NOUN
wave (*on radio*) ◇ *sur les grandes
ondes* on long wave

l'**ongle** MASC NOUN
nail
- **se couper les ongles** to cut one's nails
◇ *Elle s'est coupé les ongles.* She cut
her nails.

ont VERB *see* **avoir**
- **Ils ont beaucoup d'argent.** They've
got lots of money.
- **Elles ont passé de bonnes vacances.**
They had a good holiday.

l'**ONU** FEM NOUN (= *Organisation des Nations
unies*)
UN (= United Nations)

onze NUMBER
eleven ◇ *Elle a onze ans.* She's
eleven. ◇ *à onze heures* at eleven
o'clock
- **le onze février** the eleventh of
February

onzième ADJECTIVE
eleventh ◇ *au onzième étage* on the
eleventh floor

l'**opéra** MASC NOUN
opera

l'**opération** FEM NOUN
operation

opérer VERB
to operate on ◇ *Elle a été opérée de
l'appendicite.* She was operated on for
appendicitis.
- **se faire opérer** to have an operation
◇ *Elle s'est fait opérer.* She's had an
operation.

O

l' **opinion** FEM NOUN
opinion

opposé ADJECTIVE
see also opposé NOUN
opposite ◇ *Elle est partie dans la direction opposée.* She went off in the opposite direction.
- **être opposé à quelque chose** to be opposed to something

l' **opposé** MASC NOUN
see also opposé ADJECTIVE
the opposite

opposer VERB
- **opposer quelqu'un à quelqu'un** to pit somebody against somebody ◇ *Ce match oppose les Français aux Allemands.* This match pits the French against the Germans.
- **s'opposer** to conflict ◇ *Ces deux points de vue s'opposent.* These two points of view conflict.
- **s'opposer à quelque chose** to oppose something ◇ *Son père s'oppose à son mariage.* Her father's against her marriage.

l' **opposition** FEM NOUN
opposition
- **par opposition à** as opposed to ◇ *la littérature contemporaine par opposition à la littérature classique* modern literature, as opposed to classics
- **faire opposition à un chèque** to stop a cheque

l' **opticien** MASC NOUN
optician ◇ *Il est opticien.* He's an optician.

l' **opticienne** FEM NOUN
optician ◇ *Elle est opticienne.* She's an optician.

optimiste ADJECTIVE
optimistic

l' **option** FEM NOUN
option
- **une matière à option** an optional subject

l' **or** MASC NOUN
see also or CONJUNCTION
gold ◇ *un bracelet en or* a gold bracelet

or CONJUNCTION
see also or NOUN
and yet ◇ *Il était sûr de gagner, or il a perdu.* He was sure he would win, and yet he lost.

l' **orage** MASC NOUN
thunderstorm

orageux ADJECTIVE
(FEM SING **orageuse**)
stormy

oral ADJECTIVE
(MASC PL **oraux**)
see also oral NOUN
- **une épreuve orale** an oral exam
- **à prendre par voie orale** to be taken orally

l' **oral** MASC NOUN
(PL les **oraux**)
see also oral ADJECTIVE
oral (*exam*) ◇ *un oral de français* a French oral

l' **orange** FEM NOUN
see also orange ADJECTIVE
orange (*fruit*)

orange ADJECTIVE (MASC, FEM, PL)
see also orange NOUN
orange (*in colour*) ◇ *des fleurs orange* orange flowers

l' **orchestre** MASC NOUN
1 orchestra ◇ *un orchestre symphonique* a symphony orchestra
2 band ◇ *un orchestre de jazz* a jazz band

ordinaire ADJECTIVE
see also ordinaire NOUN
1 ordinary ◇ *des gens ordinaires* ordinary people
2 standard ◇ *un format ordinaire* a standard size

l' **ordinaire** MASC NOUN
see also ordinaire ADJECTIVE
two-star (petrol)
- **sortir de l'ordinaire** to be out of the ordinary

l' **ordinateur** MASC NOUN
computer

l' **ordonnance** FEM NOUN
prescription

ordonné ADJECTIVE
tidy

ordonner VERB
- **ordonner à quelqu'un de faire quelque chose** to order somebody to do something ◇ *Il m'a ordonné de sortir.* He ordered me to leave.

l' **ordre** MASC NOUN
order ◇ *par ordre alphabétique* in alphabetical order
- **mettre en ordre** to tidy up
- **jusqu'à nouvel ordre** until further notice

les **ordures** FEM NOUN
rubbish
- **jeter quelque chose aux ordures** to throw something in the bin

l' **oreille** FEM NOUN
ear

l' **oreiller** MASC NOUN
pillow

les **oreillons** MASC NOUN
mumps

l' **organe** MASC NOUN
organ (*in body*)

l' **organisateur** MASC NOUN
organizer

l' **organisation** FEM NOUN
organization

l' **organisatrice** FEM NOUN
organizer

organiser VERB
to organize

- **s'organiser** to get organized ◇ *Il ne sait pas s'organiser.* He can't get himself organized.

l' **organisme** MASC NOUN
body (*organization*)

l' **orgue** MASC NOUN
organ ◇ *Carl joue de l'orgue.* Carl plays the organ.

orgueilleux ADJECTIVE
(FEM SING **orgueilleuse**)
proud

l' **Orient** MASC NOUN
East

- **en Orient** in the East

oriental ADJECTIVE
(MASC PL **orientaux**)
[1] oriental ◇ *un palais oriental* an oriental palace
[2] eastern ◇ *la frontière orientale de la Pologne* Poland's eastern border

l' **orientation** FEM NOUN
orientation

- **avoir le sens de l'orientation** to have a good sense of direction
- **l'orientation professionnelle** careers advice

originaire ADJECTIVE

- **Elle est originaire de Paris.** She's from Paris.

original ADJECTIVE
(MASC PL **originaux**)
see also original NOUN
original ◇ *un film en version originale* a film in the original language

l' **original** MASC NOUN
(PL les **originaux**)
see also original ADJECTIVE
original ◇ *L'original est au Louvre.* The original is in the Louvre.

- **un vieil original** an old eccentric

l' **origine** FEM NOUN
origin

- **à l'origine** originally

l' **orphelin** MASC NOUN
orphan

l' **orpheline** FEM NOUN
orphan

l' **orteil** MASC NOUN
toe

l' **orthographe** FEM NOUN
spelling

l' **os** MASC NOUN
bone

oser VERB
to dare

- **oser faire quelque chose** to dare to do something

l' **otage** MASC NOUN
hostage

ôter VERB
[1] to take off ◇ *Elle a ôté son manteau.* She took off her coat.
[2] to take away

ou CONJUNCTION
or

- **ou...ou...** either...or...
- **ou bien** or else ◇ *On pourrait aller au cinéma ou bien rentrer directement.* We could go to the cinema or else go straight home.

où PRONOUN, ADVERB
[1] where ◇ *Où est Nick?* Where's Nick? ◇ *Où allez-vous?* Where are you going? ◇ *Je sais où il est.* I know where he is. ◇ *C'est la maison où je suis né.* That's the house where I was born. ◇ *la ville d'où je viens* the town I come from
[2] that ◇ *Le jour où il est parti, tout le monde a pleuré.* The day that he left, everyone cried.

- **Par où allons-nous passer?** Which way are we going to go?

l' **ouate** FEM NOUN
cotton wool

oublier VERB
[1] to forget ◇ *N'oublie pas de fermer la porte.* Don't forget to shut the door.
[2] to leave ◇ *J'ai oublié mon sac chez Sabine.* I left my bag at Sabine's.

l' **ouest** MASC NOUN
see also ouest ADJECTIVE
west ◇ *Elle vit dans l'ouest de l'Angleterre.* She lives in the West of England.

- **à l'ouest de Paris** west of Paris
- **vers l'ouest** westwards
- **l'Europe de l'Ouest** Western Europe
- **le vent d'ouest** the west wind

ouest ADJECTIVE (MASC, FEM, PL)
see also ouest NOUN
[1] west ◇ *la côte ouest de l'Écosse* the west coast of Scotland
[2] western ◇ *la partie ouest du pays* the western part of the country

ouf EXCLAMATION
phew!

oui ADVERB
yes

l'**ouragan** MASC NOUN
hurricane

l'**ourlet** MASC NOUN
seam

l'**ours** MASC NOUN
bear

- **un ours en peluche** a teddy bear

l'**outil** MASC NOUN
tool

ouvert VERB see **ouvrir**

ouvert ADJECTIVE

① **open** ◇ *Le magasin est ouvert.*
The shop's open.

② **on** ◇ *Il a laissé le robinet ouvert.*
He left the tap on.

- **avoir l'esprit ouvert** to be
open-minded

l'**ouverture** FEM NOUN

opening ◇ *les heures d'ouverture*
opening hours

l'**ouvre-boîte** MASC NOUN
tin opener

l'**ouvre-bouteille** MASC NOUN
bottle-opener

l'**ouvrier** NOUN
worker ◇ *Son père est ouvrier dans
une usine.* His father's a factory
worker.

l'**ouvrière** NOUN
worker

ouvrir VERB
to open ◇ *Ouvrez!* Open up! ◇ *Elle
a ouvert la porte.* She opened the door.

- **s'ouvrir** to open ◇ *La porte s'est
ouverte.* The door opened.

l'**ovni** MASC NOUN (= objet volant non identifié)
UFO

l'**oxygène** MASC NOUN
oxygen

P

le **Pacifique** NOUN
Pacific ◇ *l'océan Pacifique* the
Pacific Ocean

la **pagaille** NOUN
mess SING ◇ *Quelle pagaille!* What a
mess!

la **page** NOUN
page ◇ *Tournez la page.* Turn the
page.

la **paie** NOUN
wages

le **paiement** NOUN
payment

le **paillasson** NOUN
doormat

la **paille** NOUN
straw

le **pain** NOUN
1 **bread** ◇ *un morceau de pain* a
piece of bread ◇ *une tranche de pain* a
slice of bread
2 **loaf** ◇ *J'ai acheté un pain.* I
bought a loaf of bread.
- **le pain complet** wholemeal bread
- **le pain d'épice** gingerbread
- **le pain de mie** sandwich loaf
- **le pain grillé** toast

pair ADJECTIVE
even ◇ *un nombre pair* an even
number
- **une jeune fille au pair** an au pair

la **paire** NOUN
pair ◇ *une paire de chaussures* a
pair of shoes

paisible ADJECTIVE
peaceful ◇ *un village paisible* a
peaceful village

la **paix** NOUN
peace
- **faire la paix (1)** to make peace ◇ *Les
deux pays ont fait la paix.* The two
countries have made peace with each
other.
- **faire la paix (2)** to make it up
◇ *Laure a fait la paix avec son frère.*
Laure made it up with her brother.
- **avoir la paix** to have peace and quiet
◇ *J'aimerais bien avoir la paix.* I'd
like to have a bit of peace and quiet.
- **Fiche-lui la paix!** (*informal*) Leave him
alone!

le **palais** NOUN
1 **palace** ◇ *le palais de Buckingham*
Buckingham Palace
2 **palate** (*in mouth*)

pâle ADJECTIVE

pale ◇ *bleu pâle* pale blue

la **Palestine** NOUN
Palestine

la **pâleur** NOUN
paleness

le **palier** NOUN
landing ◇ *Il m'attendait sur le palier.*
He was waiting for me on the landing.

pâlir VERB
to go pale

la **palme** NOUN
flipper (*for swimming*)

palmé ADJECTIVE
webbed ◇ *Les canards ont les pieds
palmés.* Ducks have webbed feet.

le **palmier** NOUN
palm tree

palpitant ADJECTIVE
thrilling ◇ *un roman palpitant* a
thrilling novel

le **pamplemousse** NOUN
grapefruit

le **panaché** NOUN
shandy

la **pancarte** NOUN
sign ◇ *Il y a une pancarte dans la
vitrine.* There's a sign in the window.

pané ADJECTIVE
fried in breadcrumbs ◇ *du poisson
pané* fish in breadcrumbs

le **panier** NOUN
basket

la **panique** NOUN
panic

paniquer VERB
to panic

la **panne** NOUN
breakdown
- **être en panne** to have broken down
◇ *L'ascenseur est en panne.* The
lift's not working.
- **tomber en panne** to break down
◇ *Nous sommes tombés en panne
sur l'autoroute.* We broke down on the
motorway. ◇ *Nous sommes tombés
en panne d'essence.* We've run out of
petrol.
- **une panne de courant** a power cut

le **panneau** NOUN
(PL les **panneaux**)
sign ◇ *Ce panneau dit que la maison
est à vendre.* This sign says that the
house is for sale.
- **panneau d'affichage (1)** advertising
hoarding
- **panneau d'affichage (2)** arrivals and

P

PTO

departures board (*in station*)

le **panorama** NOUN
panorama

le **pansement** NOUN
1 dressing (*bandage*)
2 sticking plaster

le **pantalon** NOUN
trousers PL ◇ *Son pantalon est trop court.* His trousers are too short.
- un pantalon de ski a pair of ski pants

la **panthère** NOUN
panther

la **pantoufle** NOUN
slipper

le **paon** NOUN
peacock

le **papa** NOUN
dad

le **pape** NOUN
pope

la **papeterie** NOUN
stationer's

le **papi** NOUN (*informal*)
granddad

le **papier** NOUN
paper ◇ *une feuille de papier* a sheet of paper
- Vos papiers, s'il vous plaît. Your identity papers, please.
- les papiers d'identité identity papers
- le papier à lettres writing paper
- le papier hygiénique toilet paper
- le papier peint wallpaper

le **papillon** NOUN
butterfly

le **paquebot** NOUN
liner

la **pâquerette** NOUN
daisy

Pâques MASC NOUN
Easter ◇ *Je viendrai te voir à Pâques.* I'll come and see you at Easter.
- les œufs de Pâques Easter eggs

> *In France, Easter eggs are said to be brought by the Easter bells or* cloches de Pâques *which fly from Rome and drop them in people's gardens.*

le **paquet** NOUN
1 packet ◇ *Je voudrais un paquet de cigarettes.* I'd like a packet of cigarettes.
2 parcel ◇ *Sa mère lui a envoyé un paquet.* His mother sent him a parcel.

le **paquet-cadeau** NOUN
(PL les **paquets-cadeaux**)
gift-wrapped parcel ◇ *La vendeuse m'a fait un paquet-cadeau.* The shop assistant gift-wrapped it for me.

par PREPOSITION
1 by ◇ *Le Tour de France a été remporté par un Écossais.* The Tour de France was won by a Scotsman.
- deux par deux two by two ◇ *Les élèves sont entrés deux par deux.* The pupils went in two by two.
2 with ◇ *Son nom commence par un H.* His name begins with H.
3 out of ◇ *Elle regardait par la fenêtre.* She was looking out of the window. ◇ *par habitude* out of habit
4 via ◇ *Nous sommes passés par Lyon pour aller à Grenoble.* We went via Lyons to Grenoble.
5 through ◇ *Il faut passer par la douane avant de prendre l'avion.* You have to go through customs before boarding the plane.
6 per ◇ *Prenez trois cachets par jour.* Take three tablets per day. ◇ *Le voyage coûte deux mille francs par personne.* The trip costs two thousand francs per person.
- par ici (1) this way ◇ *Il faut passer par ici pour y arriver.* You have to go this way to get there.
- par ici (2) round here ◇ *Il y a beaucoup de touristes par ici.* There are lots of tourists round here.
- par-ci, par-là here and there

le **parachute** NOUN
parachute

le/la **parachutiste** NOUN
parachutist

le **paradis** NOUN
heaven

les **parages** MASC NOUN
- dans les parages in the area ◇ *Il n'y a pas d'hôtel dans les parages.* There are no hotels in the area.

le **paragraphe** NOUN
paragraph

paraître VERB
1 to seem ◇ *Ça paraît incroyable.* It seems unbelievable.
2 to look ◇ *Elle paraît plus jeune que son frère.* She looks younger than her brother.
- il paraît que it seems that ◇ *Il paraît que c'est la faute de la direction.* It seems that it's the management's fault.

le **parallèle** NOUN
see also la parallèle
parallel ◇ *Il a fait un parallèle entre ces deux événements.* He drew a parallel between the two events.

la **parallèle** NOUN
see also le parallèle

parallel line
paralysé ADJECTIVE
  paralysed
le **parapluie** NOUN
  umbrella
le **parasol** NOUN
  parasol
le **parc** NOUN
  [1] **park** ◇ *Le dimanche, Chantal va se promener au parc.* On Sundays Chantal goes for a walk in the park.
  • **un parc d'attractions** an amusement park
  [2] **grounds** ◇ *Le château est situé au milieu d'un grand parc.* The castle is surrounded by extensive grounds.
parce que CONJUNCTION
  because ◇ *Il n'est pas venu parce qu'il n'avait pas de voiture.* He didn't come because he didn't have a car.
le **parcmètre** NOUN
  parking meter
parcourir VERB
  [1] **to cover** ◇ *Gavin a parcouru cinquante kilomètres à vélo.* Gavin covered 50 kilometres on his bike.
  [2] **to glance through** ◇ *J'ai parcouru le journal d'aujourd'hui.* I glanced through today's newspaper.
le **parcours** NOUN
  journey
par-dessous ADVERB
  underneath ◇ *Il portait un pull et une chemise par-dessous.* He was wearing a jumper with a shirt underneath.
le **pardessus** NOUN
  overcoat
par-dessus ADVERB, PREPOSITION
  [1] **on top** ◇ *Elle porte un chemisier et un pull rouge par-dessus.* She's wearing a blouse with a red jumper on top.
  [2] **over** ◇ *Elle a sauté par-dessus le mur.* She jumped over the wall.
  • **en avoir par-dessus la tête** to have had enough ◇ *J'en ai par-dessus la tête de tous ces problèmes.* I've had enough of all these problems.
le **pardon** NOUN
  see also pardon EXCLAMATION
  forgiveness
pardon EXCLAMATION
  see also pardon NOUN
  [1] **sorry!** ◇ *Oh, pardon! J'espère que je ne vous ai pas fait mal.* Oh, sorry! I hope I didn't hurt you.
  • **demander pardon à quelqu'un** to apologize to somebody ◇ *Il leur a demandé pardon.* He apologized to them.

• **Je vous demande pardon.** I'm sorry.
  [2] **excuse me!** ◇ *Pardon, madame! Pouvez-vous me dire où se trouve la poste?* Excuse me! Could you tell me where the post office is?
  [3] **pardon?** ◇ *Pardon? Je n'ai pas compris ce que vous avez dit.* Pardon? I didn't understand what you said.
pardonner VERB
  to forgive ◇ *Nous lui avons pardonné de nous avoir menti.* We forgave him for lying to us.
le **pare-brise** NOUN
  (PL les **pare-brise**)
  windscreen
le **pare-chocs** NOUN
  bumper
pareil ADJECTIVE
  (FEM SING **pareille**)
  [1] **the same** ◇ *Ces deux maisons ne sont pas pareilles.* These two houses aren't the same.
  [2] **like that** ◇ *J'aime bien sa voiture. J'en voudrais une pareille.* I like his car. I'd like one like that.
  [3] **such** ◇ *Je refuse d'écouter des bêtises pareilles.* I won't listen to such nonsense.
  • **sans pareil** unequalled ◇ *Il a joué cette symphonie avec un talent sans pareil.* He played this symphony with unequalled talent.
la **parenthèse** NOUN
  bracket ◇ *entre parenthèses* in brackets
les **parents** MASC NOUN
  parents
la **paresse** NOUN
  laziness
paresseux ADJECTIVE
  (FEM SING **paresseuse**)
  lazy
parfait ADJECTIVE
  perfect
parfaitement ADVERB
  perfectly ◇ *Il parle parfaitement l'arabe.* He speaks perfect Arabic.
parfois ADVERB
  sometimes
le **parfum** NOUN
  [1] **perfume**
  [2] **flavour** ◇ *Je voudrais une glace. —Quel parfum veux-tu?* I'd like an ice cream. —What flavour would you like?
parfumé ADJECTIVE
  [1] **fragrant** ◇ *une rose très parfumée* a very fragrant rose
  [2] **flavoured** ◇ *des biscuits parfumés*

P

PTO

au café coffee-flavoured biscuits

la **parfumerie** NOUN
perfume shop

le **pari** NOUN
bet

parier VERB
to bet

Paris NOUN
Paris

- **à Paris (1)** in Paris
- **à Paris (2)** to Paris

parisien ADJECTIVE, NOUN
(FEM SING **parisienne**)
[1] Parisian ◇ *un célèbre couturier parisien* a famous Parisian designer
[2] Paris ◇ *le métro parisien* the Paris metro

- **un Parisien** a Parisian (*man*)
- **une Parisienne** a Parisian (*woman*)

le **parking** NOUN
car park

le **parlement** NOUN
parliament

parler VERB
[1] to speak ◇ *Vous parlez français?* Do you speak French?
[2] to talk ◇ *Nous étions en train de parler quand le directeur est entré.* We were talking when the headmaster came in.

- **parler de quelque chose à quelqu'un** to tell somebody about something ◇ *Il m'a parlé de sa nouvelle voiture.* He told me about his new car.

parmi PREPOSITION
among ◇ *Ils étaient parmi les meilleurs de la classe.* They were among the best pupils in the class.

la **paroi** NOUN
wall

la **paroisse** NOUN
parish

la **parole** NOUN
[1] speech ◇ *l'usage de la parole* the power of speech
[2] word ◇ *Il m'a donné sa parole.* He gave me his word. ◇ *Elle a tenu parole.* She kept her word.

- **les paroles** lyrics ◇ *J'aime les paroles de cette chanson.* I like the lyrics of this song.

le **parquet** NOUN
floor (*wooden*)

le **parrain** NOUN
godfather

parrainer VERB
to sponsor ◇ *Cette entreprise parraine notre équipe de rugby.* This firm is sponsoring our rugby team.

pars VERB *see* **partir**

la **part** NOUN
[1] share ◇ *Vous n'avez pas eu votre part.* You haven't had your share.
[2] piece ◇ *une part de gâteau* a piece of cake

- **prendre part à quelque chose** to take part in something ◇ *Il va prendre part à la réunion.* He's going to take part in the meeting.
- **de la part de (1)** on behalf of ◇ *Je dois vous remercier de la part de mon frère.* I must thank you on behalf of my brother.
- **de la part de (2)** from ◇ *C'est un cadeau pour toi, de la part de Françoise.* It's a present for you, from Françoise.
- **à part** except ◇ *Ils sont tous venus, à part Christian.* They all came, except Christian.

partager VERB
[1] to share ◇ *Ils partagent un appartement.* They share a flat.
[2] to divide ◇ *Janet a partagé le gâteau en quatre.* Janet divided the cake into four.

le/la **partenaire** NOUN
partner

le **parti** NOUN
party ◇ *le Parti socialiste* the Socialist Party

le **participant** NOUN
participant

la **participante** NOUN
participant

la **participation** NOUN
participation

le **participe** NOUN
participle

- **le participe passé** the past participle
- **le participe présent** the present participle

participer VERB

- **participer à quelque chose (1)** to take part in something ◇ *André va participer à la course.* André is going to take part in the race.
- **participer à quelque chose (2)** to contribute to something ◇ *Je voudrais participer aux frais.* I would like to contribute to the cost.

la **particularité** NOUN
characteristic

particulier ADJECTIVE
(FEM SING **particulière**)
[1] private ◇ *une maison particulière* a private house
[2] distinctive ◇ *Ce vin a un arôme particulier.* This wine has a distinctive

flavour.

3 **particular** ◇ *Dans ce cas particulier, je ne peux rien faire.* In this particular case, I can't do anything.

- **en particulier (1)** particularly ◇ *J'aime les fruits, en particulier les fraises.* I like fruit, particularly strawberries.
- **en particulier (2)** in private ◇ *Est-ce que je peux vous parler en particulier?* Can I speak to you in private?

particulièrement ADVERB
particularly

la **partie** NOUN

1 **part** ◇ *Une partie du groupe partira en Italie.* Part of the group will go to Italy.

2 **game** ◇ *Nous avons fait une partie de tennis.* We played a game of tennis. ◇ *une partie de cartes* a game of cards

- **en partie** partly ◇ *Cela explique en partie le problème.* That partly explains the problem.
- **en grande partie** largely ◇ *Son histoire est en grande partie vraie.* His story is largely true.
- **faire partie de** to be part of ◇ *Ce tableau fait partie d'une très belle collection.* This picture is part of a very beautiful collection.

partiel ADJECTIVE
(FEM SING **partielle**)
partial

partir VERB

to go ◇ *Je lui ai téléphoné mais il était déjà parti.* I phoned him but he'd already gone.

- **partir en vacances** to go on holiday
- **partir de** to leave ◇ *Il est parti de Nice à sept heures.* He left Nice at 7.
- **à partir de** from ◇ *Je serai chez moi à partir de huit heures.* I'll be at home from eight o'clock onwards.

la **partition** NOUN

score (*in music*) ◇ *une partition de piano* a piano score

partout ADVERB
everywhere

paru VERB *see* **paraître**

la **parution** NOUN

publication ◇ *Ce roman a eu beaucoup de succès dès sa parution.* This novel was very successful from the moment it came out.

parvenir VERB

- **parvenir à faire quelque chose** to manage to do something ◇ *Elle est finalement parvenue à ouvrir la porte.* She finally managed to open the door.

- **faire parvenir quelque chose à quelqu'un** to send something to somebody ◇ *Je vous ferai parvenir le colis avant lundi.* I'll send you the parcel before Monday.

pas ADVERB
see also **pas** NOUN

- **ne...pas** not ◇ *Il ne pleut pas.* It's not raining. ◇ *Elle n'est pas venue.* She didn't come. ◇ *Ils n'ont pas de voiture.* They haven't got a car.
- **Vous viendrez à notre soirée, n'est-ce pas?** You're coming to our party, aren't you?
- **C'est Harry qui a gagné, n'est-ce pas?** Harry won, didn't he?
- **pas moi** not me ◇ *Elle veut aller au cinéma, pas moi.* She wants to go to the cinema, but I don't.
- **pas du tout** not at all ◇ *Je n'aime pas du tout ça.* I don't like that at all.
- **pas mal** not bad ◇ *Ce n'est pas mal pour un début.* That's not bad for a first attempt. ◇ *Comment allez-vous?–Pas mal.* How are you?–Not bad.
- **pas mal de** quite a lot of ◇ *Il y avait pas mal de monde au concert.* There were quite a lot of people at the concert.

le **pas** NOUN
see also **pas** ADVERB

1 **pace** ◇ *Il marchait d'un pas rapide.* He walked at a fast pace.

2 **step** ◇ *Faites trois pas en avant.* Take three steps forward.

3 **footstep** ◇ *J'entends des pas dans l'escalier.* I can hear footsteps on the stairs.

- **au pas** at walking pace ◇ *Le cheval est parti au pas.* The horse set off at walking pace.
- **faire les cent pas** to pace up and down ◇ *Il faisait les cent pas dans le corridor.* He was pacing up and down the corridor.

le **passage** NOUN

passage ◇ *J'ai traduit un passage de ce livre.* I translated a passage from this book.

- **Il a été éclaboussé au passage de la voiture.** He was soaked by a passing car.
- **de passage** passing through ◇ *Nous sommes de passage à Toulouse.* We're just passing through Toulouse.
- **un passage clouté** a pedestrian crossing
- **un passage souterrain** a subway

P

passager ADJECTIVE
(FEM SING **passagère**)
see also passager NOUN
temporary

le **passager** NOUN
see also passager ADJECTIVE
passenger
- **un passager clandestin** a stowaway

la **passagère** NOUN
passenger

le **passant** NOUN
passer-by

la **passante** NOUN
passer-by

passé ADJECTIVE
see also passé NOUN
1 **last** ◇ Je l'ai vu la semaine passée. I saw him last week.
2 **past** ◇ Il est minuit passé. It's past midnight.

le **passé** NOUN
see also passé ADJECTIVE
1 **past** ◇ dans le passé in the past
2 **past tense** ◇ Mettez ce verbe au passé. Put this verb into the past tense.
- **le passé composé** the perfect tense
- **le passé simple** the past historic

le **passeport** NOUN
passport

passer VERB
1 **to cross** ◇ Nous avons passé la frontière belge. We crossed the Belgian border.
2 **to go through** ◇ Il faut passer la douane en sortant. You have to go through customs on the way out.
3 **to take** ◇ Gordon a passé ses examens la semaine dernière. Gordon took his exams last week.
4 **to spend** ◇ Elle a passé la journée à ne rien faire. She spent the day doing nothing. ◇ Ils passent toujours leurs vacances au Danemark. They always spend their holidays in Denmark.
5 **to pass** ◇ Passe-moi le sel, s'il te plaît. Pass me the salt, please.
6 **to show** ◇ On passe "Le Kid" au cinéma cette semaine. They're showing "The Kid" at the cinema this week.
7 **to call in** ◇ Je passerai chez vous cet soir. I'll call in this evening.
- **Ne quittez pas, je vous passe Madame Chevalier.** Hold on please, I'm putting you through to Mrs Chevalier.
- **passer par** to go through ◇ Ils sont passés par Paris pour aller à Tours. They went through Paris to get to Tours.

- **en passant** in passing ◇ Je lui ai dit en passant que j'allais me marier. I told him in passing that I was getting married.
- **laisser passer** to let through ◇ Il m'a laissé passer. He let me through.
- **se passer (1)** to take place ◇ Cette histoire se passe au moyen âge. This story takes place in the Middle Ages.
- **se passer (2)** to go ◇ Comment se sont passés tes examens? How did your exams go?
- **se passer (3)** to happen ◇ Que s'est-il passé? Un accident? What happened? Was there an accident?
- **Qu'est-ce qui se passe? Pourquoi est-ce qu'elle pleure?** What's the matter? Why is she crying?
- **se passer de** to do without ◇ Je me passerai de café ce matin. I'll do without coffee this morning.

la **passerelle** NOUN
1 **footbridge** (over river)
2 **gangway** (onto plane, boat)

le **passe-temps** NOUN
pastime

passif ADJECTIVE
(FEM SING **passive**)
see also passif NOUN
passive

le **passif** NOUN
see also passif ADJECTIVE
passive ◇ Mettez ce verbe au passif. Put this verb into the passive.

la **passion** NOUN
passion

passionnant ADJECTIVE
fascinating

passionné ADJECTIVE
keen ◇ Donald est un lecteur passionné. Donald is a keen reader.
- **Il est passionné de voile.** He's a sailing fanatic.

passionner VERB
- **Son travail le passionne.** He's passionate about his work.
- **se passionner pour quelque chose** to have a passion for something ◇ Harry se passionne pour les perroquets. Harry has a passion for parrots.

la **passoire** NOUN
sieve

la **pastèque** NOUN
watermelon

le **pasteur** NOUN
minister (priest)

la **patate** NOUN (informal)
potato

- **une patate douce** a sweet potato
la **pâte**   NOUN
  1. **pastry**
  2. **dough**
  3. **cake mixture**
- **la pâte à crêpes** pancake batter
- **la pâte à modeler** Plasticine ®
- **la pâte d'amandes** marzipan
le **pâté**   NOUN
  pâté ◦ *Nous avons mangé du pâté en entrée.* We had pâté as a starter.
- **un pâté de maisons** a block (*of houses*)
paternel   ADJECTIVE
  (FEM SING **paternelle**)
- **ma grand-mère paternelle** my father's mother
- **mon oncle paternel** my father's brother
les **pâtes**   FEM NOUN
  pasta
la **patience**   NOUN
  patience
patient   ADJECTIVE
  see also patient NOUN
  patient
le **patient**   NOUN
  see also patient ADJECTIVE
  patient
la **patiente**   NOUN
  patient
patienter   VERB
  to wait ◦ *Veuillez patienter un instant, s'il vous plaît.* Please wait a moment.
le **patin**   NOUN
  1. **skate** ◦ *Nic a enfilé ses patins.* Nic put her skates on.
  2. **skating** ◦ *Ils font du patin tous les mercredis.* They go skating every Wednesday.
- **les patins à glace** ice skates
- **les patins à roulettes** roller skates
le **patinage**   NOUN
  skating
- **le patinage artistique** figure skating
patiner   VERB
  to skate
le **patineur**   NOUN
  skater
la **patineuse**   NOUN
  skater
la **patinoire**   NOUN
  ice rink
la **pâtisserie**   NOUN
  cake shop
- **faire de la pâtisserie** to bake
  ◦ *J'adore faire de la pâtisserie.* I love baking.
- **les pâtisseries** cakes

le **pâtissier**   NOUN
  confectioner
la **pâtissière**   NOUN
  confectioner
la **patrie**   NOUN
  homeland
le **patron**   NOUN
  1. **boss**
  2. **pattern** (*for dressmaking*)
la **patronne**   NOUN
  boss
- **Elle est patronne de café.** She runs a café.
patronner   VERB
  to sponsor ◦ *Le festival est patronné par des entreprises locales.* The festival is sponsored by local businesses.
la **patrouille**   NOUN
  patrol
la **patte**   NOUN
  1. **paw** (*of dog, cat*)
  2. **leg** (*of bird, animal*)
paumer   VERB (*informal*)
  to lose ◦ *J'ai paumé mes clefs.* I've lost my keys.
la **paupière**   NOUN
  eyelid
la **pause**   NOUN
  1. **break** ◦ *Ils font une pause.* They're having a break.
  2. **pause** ◦ *Il y a eu une pause dans la conversation.* There was a pause in the conversation.
pauvre   ADJECTIVE
  poor ◦ *Sa famille est pauvre.* His family is poor. ◦ *Pauvre Jean-Pierre! Il n'a pas eu de chance!* Poor Jean-Pierre! He was unlucky!
la **pauvreté**   NOUN
  poverty
pavé   ADJECTIVE
  cobbled ◦ *Les rues étaient pavées.* The streets were cobbled.
le **pavillon**   NOUN
  house ◦ *Ils habitent un pavillon de banlieue.* They've got a house in the suburbs.
payant   ADJECTIVE
  paying ◦ *Ce sont des hôtes payants.* They're paying guests.
- **C'est payant.** You have to pay.
  ◦ *L'entrée de la boîte est payante.* You have to pay to get into the nightclub.
la **paye**   NOUN
  wages
payer   VERB
  1. **to pay for** ◦ *Combien as-tu payé ta voiture?* How much did you pay for

P

your car?
- **J'ai payé ce T-shirt vingt francs.** I paid 20 francs for this T-shirt.
  2 **to pay** ◇ *Elle a été payée aujourd'hui.* She got paid today. ◇ *Son métier paye bien.* His job pays good money.
- **faire payer quelque chose à quelqu'un** to charge somebody for something ◇ *Il me l'a fait payer dix francs.* He charged me 10 francs for it.
- **payer quelque chose à quelqu'un** to buy somebody something ◇ *Allez, je vous paye un verre.* Come on, I'll buy you a drink.

le **pays** NOUN
  country
- **du pays** local ◇ *le vin du pays* the local wine

le **paysage** NOUN
  landscape

le **paysan** NOUN
  farmer

la **paysanne** NOUN
  farmer

les **Pays-Bas** MASC NOUN
  Netherlands
- **aux Pays-Bas (1)** in the Netherlands
- **aux Pays-Bas (2)** to the Netherlands

le **Pays de Galles** NOUN
  Wales
- **au Pays de Galles (1)** in Wales ◇ *Daphne habite au Pays de Galles.* Daphne lives in Wales.
- **au Pays de Galles (2)** to Wales ◇ *Elle part au Pays de Galles la semaine prochaine.* She is going to Wales next week.

le **PC** NOUN
  see also **PC** ABBREVIATION
  PC (= personal computer) ◇ *Il a tapé le rapport sur son PC.* He typed the report on his PC.
  PC ABBREVIATION (= *Parti communiste*)
  see also **PC** NOUN
  Communist Party

le **PDG** ABBREVIATION (= *président-directeur général*)
  MD (= managing director)

le **péage** NOUN
  1 **toll** ◇ *Nous avons payé cinquante francs de péage.* We paid a toll of 50 francs.
  2 **tollbooth** ◇ *Sabine s'est arrêtée au péage de l'autoroute.* Sabine stopped at the motorway tollbooth.
  French motorways charge a toll.

la **peau** NOUN
  (PL les **peaux**)
  skin ◇ *Elle a la peau douce.* She's got soft skin.

le/la **Peau-Rouge** NOUN
  (PL les **Peaux-Rouges**)
  Red Indian

la **pêche** NOUN
  1 **peach**
  2 **fishing**
- **aller à la pêche** to go fishing
- **la pêche à la ligne** angling

le **péché** NOUN
  sin

pêcher VERB
  1 **to fish for** ◇ *Ils sont partis pêcher la truite.* They've gone fishing for trout.
  2 **to catch** ◇ *Jacques a pêché deux saumons.* Jacques caught two salmon.

le **pêcheur** NOUN
  fisherman ◇ *Son père est pêcheur.* His father's a fisherman.
- **un pêcheur à la ligne** an angler

pédagogique ADJECTIVE
  educational

la **pédale** NOUN
  pedal

pédestre ADJECTIVE
- **une randonnée pédestre** a ramble

le **peigne** NOUN
  comb

peigner VERB
  to comb ◇ *Elle peigne sa poupée.* She's combing her doll's hair.
- **se peigner** to comb one's hair ◇ *Il faut que je me peigne.* I must comb my hair.

le **peignoir** NOUN
  dressing gown
- **un peignoir de bain** a bathrobe

peindre VERB
  to paint

la **peine** NOUN
  trouble
- **avoir de la peine à faire quelque chose** to have trouble doing something ◇ *J'ai eu beaucoup de peine à la convaincre.* I had a lot of trouble convincing her.
- **se donner de la peine** to make a real effort ◇ *Il s'est donné beaucoup de peine pour obtenir ces renseignements.* He made a real effort to get this information.
- **prendre la peine de faire quelque chose** to go to the trouble of doing something ◇ *Il a pris la peine de me rapporter ma valise.* He went to the trouble of returning my case to me.
- **faire de la peine à quelqu'un** to upset somebody ◇ *Ça me fait de la peine de*

la voir pleurer. It upsets me to see her crying.

- **ce n'est pas la peine** there's no point ◇ *Ce n'est pas la peine de téléphoner.* There's no point in phoning.
- **à peine (1)** hardly ◇ *J'ai à peine eu le temps de me changer.* I hardly had time to get changed.
- **à peine (2)** only just ◇ *Elle vient à peine de se lever.* She's only just got up.

le **peintre** NOUN
painter

la **peinture** NOUN
1 **painting** ◇ *On expose des peintures de Gautier au musée.* There's an exhibition of Gautier's paintings at the museum.
2 **paint** ◇ *J'ai acheté de la peinture verte.* I bought some green paint.
- **"peinture fraîche"** "wet paint"

pêle-mêle ADVERB
higgledy-piggledy

la **pelle** NOUN
1 **shovel**
2 **spade**

la **pellicule** NOUN
film ◇ *une pellicule couleur* a colour film

les **pellicules** FEM NOUN
dandruff SING

la **pelote** NOUN
ball ◇ *une pelote de laine* a ball of wool

la **pelouse** NOUN
lawn

la **peluche** NOUN
- **un animal en peluche** a soft toy

pencher VERB
to tilt ◇ *Ce tableau penche vers la droite.* The picture's tilting to the right.
- **se pencher (1)** to lean over ◇ *Françoise s'est penchée sur son cahier.* Françoise leant over her exercise book.
- **se pencher (2)** to bend down ◇ *Il s'est penché pour ramasser sa casquette.* He bent down to pick his cap up.
- **se pencher (3)** to lean out ◇ *Annick s'est penchée par la fenêtre.* Annick leant out of the window.

pendant PREPOSITION
during ◇ *Ça s'est passé pendant l'été.* It happened during the summer.
- **pendant que** while ◇ *Christian a téléphoné pendant que Chantal prenait son bain.* Christian phoned while Chantal was having a bath.

le **pendentif** NOUN
pendant

la **penderie** NOUN
wardrobe (*for hanging clothes*)

pendre VERB
to hang ◇ *Il a pendu sa veste dans l'armoire.* He hung his jacket in the wardrobe.
- **pendre quelqu'un** to hang somebody ◇ *L'assassin a été pendu.* The murderer was hanged.

la **pendule** NOUN
clock

pénétrer VERB
1 **to enter** ◇ *Ils ont pénétré dans la maison en passant par le jardin.* They entered the house through the garden.
2 **to penetrate** ◇ *L'armée a pénétré sur le territoire ennemi.* The army penetrated enemy territory.

pénible ADJECTIVE
hard ◇ *Travailler sur un chantier est pénible.* Working on a building site is hard.
- **Il est vraiment pénible.** He's a real nuisance.

péniblement ADVERB
with difficulty

la **péniche** NOUN
barge

le **pénis** NOUN
penis

la **pénombre** NOUN
half-light

la **pensée** NOUN
thought ◇ *Il était perdu dans ses pensées.* He was lost in thought.

penser VERB
to think ◇ *Je pense que Yann a eu raison de partir.* I think Yann was right to leave.
- **penser à quelque chose** to think about something ◇ *Je pense à mes vacances.* I'm thinking about my holidays. ◇ *C'est une bonne occasion, pensez-y.* It's a good opportunity, think about it.
- **faire penser quelqu'un à quelque chose** to remind someone of something ◇ *Cette photo me fait penser à la Grèce.* This photo reminds me of Greece.
- **faire penser quelqu'un à faire quelque chose** to remind somecone to do something ◇ *Fais-moi penser à téléphoner à Claire.* Remind me to phone Claire.
- **penser faire quelque chose** to be planning to do something ◇ *Ils*

P

pensent partir en Espagne en juillet.
They're planning to go to Spain in July.

la **pension** NOUN
　1 **boarding school** ◇ *Leur fille est en pension.* Their daughter is at boarding school.
　2 **pension** ◇ *Ma grand-mère reçoit sa pension tous les mois.* My grandma gets her pension every month.
　3 **boarding house**
- **la pension complète** full board

le/la **pensionnaire** NOUN
　boarder

le **pensionnat** NOUN
　boarding school

la **pente** NOUN
　slope ◇ *une pente raide* a steep slop
- **en pente** sloping ◇ *Le toit de cette maison est en pente.* This house has a sloping roof.

la **Pentecôte** NOUN
　Whitsun

le **pépin** NOUN
　1 **pip** ◇ *Cette orange est pleine de pépins.* This orange is full of pips.
　2 **problem** ◇ *avoir un pépin* (*informal*) to have a slight problem

perçant ADJECTIVE
　1 **sharp** ◇ *Il a une vue perçante.* He has very sharp eyes.
　2 **piercing** ◇ *un cri perçant* a piercing cry

percer VERB
　to pierce ◇ *Christèle s'est fait percer les oreilles.* Christèle has had her ears pierced.

le **perdant** NOUN
　loser

la **perdante** NOUN
　loser

perdre VERB
　to lose ◇ *Cécile a perdu ses clés.* Cécile's lost her keys.
- **J'ai perdu mon chemin.** I've lost my way.
- **perdre du temps** to waste time ◇ *J'ai perdu beaucoup de temps ce matin.* I've wasted a lot of time this morning. ◇ *Nous avons perdu notre temps à cette réunion.* That meeting was a waste of time.
- **se perdre** to get lost ◇ *Je me suis perdu en route.* I got lost on the way here.

perdu VERB *see* **perdre**

le **père** NOUN
　father
- **le père Noël** Father Christmas

perfectionné ADJECTIVE

sophisticated

perfectionner VERB
　to improve ◇ *Elle a besoin de perfectionner son anglais.* She needs to improve her English.

périmé ADJECTIVE
　out-of-date ◇ *Mon passeport est périmé.* My passport's out of date.
- **Ces yaourts sont périmés.** These yoghurts are past their use-by date.

la **période** NOUN
　period

périodique ADJECTIVE
　periodic

périphérique ADJECTIVE
　see also **périphérique** NOUN
　outlying ◇ *un quartier périphérique* an outlying district

le **périphérique** NOUN
　see also **périphérique** ADJECTIVE
　ring road

la **perle** NOUN
　pearl

la **permanence** NOUN
- **assurer une permanence** to operate a basic service ◇ *Ma banque assure une permanence le samedi matin.* My bank operates a basic service on Saturday mornings.
- **être de permanence** to be on duty ◇ *Sophie ne peut pas venir, elle est de permanence ce soir.* Sophie can't come, she's on duty tonight.
- **en permanence** permanently ◇ *Elle se plaint en permanence.* She's always complaining.

permanent ADJECTIVE
　1 **permanent** ◇ *Il a un poste permanent.* He has a permanent job.
　2 **continuous** ◇ *J'en ai assez de tes critiques permanentes.* I've had enough of your constant criticism.

la **permanente** NOUN
　perm

permettre VERB
　to allow
- **permettre à quelqu'un de faire quelque chose** to allow somebody to do something ◇ *Sa mère lui permet de sortir le soir.* His mother allows him to go out at night.

le **permis** NOUN
　permit ◇ *Il vous faut un permis pour camper ici.* You need a permit to camp here.
- **le permis de conduire** driving licence
- **un permis de séjour** a residence permit
- **un permis de travail** a work permit

la **permission** NOUN
  permission ◇ *Qui t'a donné la permission d'entrer?* Who gave you permission to come in?
  - **avoir la permission de faire quelque chose** to have permission to do something ◇ *J'ai la permission d'utiliser sa chaîne hi-fi.* I've got his permission to use his hi-fi.
  - **être en permission** to be on leave (*from the army*)
le **Pérou** NOUN
  Peru
  perpétuel ADJECTIVE
  (FEM SING **perpétuelle**)
  perpetual
le **perroquet** NOUN
  parrot
la **perruche** NOUN
  budgie
la **perruque** NOUN
  wig
le **persil** NOUN
  parsley
le **personnage** NOUN
  1 **figure** ◇ *les grands personnages de l'histoire de France* the important figures in French history
  2 **character** ◇ *le personnage principal du film* the main character in the film
la **personnalité** NOUN
  1 **personality** ◇ *Ray a une personnalité forte.* Ray has a strong personality.
  2 **prominent figure** ◇ *Il y avait beaucoup de personnalités politiques à ce dîner.* There were lots of prominent political figures at the dinner.
la **personne** NOUN
  see also personne PRONOUN
  person ◇ *Il y avait une trentaine de personnes dans la pièce.* There were about 30 people in the room. ◇ *une personne âgée* an elderly person
  - **en personne** in person
  personne PRONOUN
  see also personne NOUN
  1 **nobody** ◇ *Il n'y a personne à la maison.* There's nobody at home. ◇ *Personne n'est venu le chercher.* Nobody came to fetch him.
  2 **anybody** ◇ *Elle ne veut voir personne.* She doesn't want to see anybody.
  personnel ADJECTIVE
  (FEM SING **personnelle**)
  see also personnel NOUN
  personal

le **personnel** NOUN
  see also personnel ADJECTIVE
  staff ◇ *Il nous faut plus de personnel.* We need more staff.
  - **le service du personnel** the personnel department
  personnellement ADVERB
  personally ◇ *Personnellement, je ne suis pas d'accord.* Personally, I don't agree.
la **perspective** NOUN
  prospect ◇ *Les perspectives sont encourageantes.* The prospects are encouraging.
  - **perspectives d'avenir** prospects ◇ *Il y a des perspectives d'avenir dans ce métier.* This job has good prospects.
  - **en perspective (1)** in prospect ◇ *Il y a des changements en perspective.* Changes are in prospect.
  - **en perspective (2)** in perspective ◇ *Il a dessiné la maison en perspective.* He drew the house in perspective.
  persuader VERB
  to persuade
  - **persuader quelqu'un de faire quelque chose** to persuade somebody to do something ◇ *Elle m'a persuadé de l'accompagner au cinéma.* She persuaded me to go to the cinema with her.
la **perte** NOUN
  1 **loss** ◇ *des pertes d'emploi* job losses
  2 **waste** ◇ *Cette réunion a été une perte de temps.* The meeting was a waste of time.
  perturber VERB
  to disrupt ◇ *Un camion en panne perturbait la circulation.* A lorry had broken down and was disrupting the traffic.
le **pèse-personne** NOUN
  bathroom scales PL
  peser VERB
  to weigh ◇ *Elle pèse cent kilos.* She weighs 100 kilos.
  pessimiste ADJECTIVE
  pessimistic
le **pétale** NOUN
  petal
la **pétanque** NOUN
  pétanque *is a type of bowls played in France, especially in the south.*
le **pétard** NOUN
  firecracker
  péter VERB (*rude*)
  to fart

P

petit ADJECTIVE

[1] **small** ◇ *Sonia habite une petite ville.* Sonia lives in a small town.

[2] **little** ◇ *Phyllis a une jolie petite maison.* Phyllis has a nice little house.

- **petit à petit** bit by bit
- **un petit ami** a boyfriend
- **une petite amie** a girlfriend
- **le petit déjeuner** breakfast
- **un petit pain** a bread roll
- **les petites annonces** the small ads
- **des petits pois** garden peas
- **les petits** young (*of animal*) ◇ *la lionne et ses petits* the lioness and her young

la **petite-fille** NOUN

(PL les petites-filles)

granddaughter

le **petit-fils** NOUN

(PL les petits-fils)

grandson

les **petits-enfants** MASC NOUN

grandchildren

le **pétrole** NOUN

oil ◇ *une lampe à pétrole* an oil lamp

peu ADVERB, NOUN

not much ◇ *J'ai peu mangé à midi.* I didn't eat much for lunch. ◇ *Il voyage peu.* He doesn't travel much.

- **un peu** a bit ◇ *Elle est un peu timide.* She's a bit shy. ◇ *un peu de gâteau* a bit of cake
- **un petit peu** a little bit ◇ *un petit peu de crème* a little bit of cream
- **peu de (1)** not many ◇ *Il y a peu de bons films au cinéma.* There aren't very many good films on at the cinema. ◇ *Elle a peu d'amis.* She hasn't got many friends.
- **peu de (2)** not much ◇ *Il a peu d'espoir de réussir.* He doesn't have much hope of succeeding. ◇ *Il lui reste peu d'argent.* He hasn't got much money left.
- **à peu près (1)** more or less ◇ *J'ai à peu près fini.* I've more or less finished.
- **à peu près (2)** about ◇ *Le voyage prend à peu près deux heures.* The journey takes about two hours.
- **peu à peu** little by little
- **peu avant** shortly before
- **peu après** shortly afterwards
- **de peu** only just ◇ *Chantal a manqué son train de peu.* Chantal only just missed her train.

le **peuple** NOUN

people ◇ *le peuple français* the French people

la **peur** NOUN

fear

- **avoir peur de** to be afraid of ◇ *Il a peur du noir.* He's afraid of the dark.
- **avoir peur de faire quelque chose** to be frightened of doing something ◇ *Elle a peur d'y aller toute seule.* She's frightened of going on her own.
- **faire peur à quelqu'un** to frighten somebody ◇ *Cet homme-là me fait peur.* That man frightens me.

peureux ADJECTIVE

(FEM SING **peureuse**)

fearful

peut VERB *see* **pouvoir**

- **Il ne peut pas venir.** He can't come.

peut-être ADVERB

perhaps ◇ *Je l'ai peut-être oublié à la maison.* Perhaps I've left it at home.

- **peut-être que** perhaps ◇ *Peut-être qu'elles n'ont pas pu téléphoner.* Perhaps they weren't able to phone.

peuvent, peux VERB *see* **pouvoir**

- **Je ne peux pas le faire.** I can't do it.

p. ex. ABBREVIATION (= *par exemple*)

e.g.

le **phare** NOUN

[1] **lighthouse** ◇ *On voit le phare depuis le pont du bateau.* You can see the lighthouse from the ship's deck.

[2] **headlight** ◇ *Il a laissé les phares de sa voiture allumés.* He left his headlights on.

la **pharmacie** NOUN

chemist's

Chemist's shops in France are identified by a special green cross outside the shop.

le **pharmacien** NOUN

pharmacist

la **pharmacienne** NOUN

pharmacist

le **phénomène** NOUN

phenomenon

la **philosophie** NOUN

philosophy

le **phoque** NOUN

seal (*animal*)

la **photo** NOUN

photograph ◇ *Elle a fait développer ses photos.* She's had her photographs developed.

- **en photo** in photographs ◇ *Je n'ai vu Venise qu'en photo.* I've only seen Venice in photographs.
- **prendre quelqu'un en photo** to take a photo of somebody ◇ *Claire nous a pris en photo.* Claire took a photo of us.

- **une photo d'identité** a passport photograph

la **photocopie** NOUN
  photocopy

photocopier VERB
  to photocopy

la **photocopieuse** NOUN
  photocopier

e/la **photographe** NOUN
  photographer

la **photographie** NOUN
  1 photography
  2 photograph

photographier VERB
  to photograph

la **phrase** NOUN
  sentence

physique ADJECTIVE
  see also physique NOUN
  physical

le **physique** NOUN
  see also la physique *and* physique ADJECTIVE
- **Il a un physique agréable.** He's quite good-looking.

la **physique** NOUN
  see also le physique *and* physique ADJECTIVE
  physics ◇ *Il est professeur de physique.* He's a physics teacher.

e/la **pianiste** NOUN
  pianist ◇ *Elle est pianiste.* She's a pianist.

le **piano** NOUN
  piano

le **pic** NOUN
  peak ◇ *les pics enneigés des Pyrénées* the snowy peaks of the Pyrenees
- **à pic (1)** vertically ◇ *La falaise tombe à pic dans la mer.* The cliff drops vertically into the sea.
- **à pic (1)** just at the right time ◇ *Tu es arrivé à pic.* You arrived just at the right time.

la **pièce** NOUN
  1 room ◇ *Mon lit est au centre de la pièce.* My bed is in the middle of the room.
- **un cinq-pièces** a five-roomed flat
  2 play ◇ *On joue une pièce d'Anouilh au théâtre.* There's a play by Anouilh on at the theatre.
  3 part ◇ *Il faut changer une pièce du moteur.* There's an engine part which needs changing.
  4 coin ◇ *des pièces d'un franc* some one-franc coins
- **cinquante francs pièce** 50 francs each ◇ *J'ai acheté ces T-shirts dix francs pièce.* I bought these T-shirts for ten

francs each.
- **un maillot une pièce** a one-piece swimsuit
- **un maillot deux-pièces** a bikini
- **Avez-vous une pièce d'identité?** Have you got any identification?

le **pied** NOUN
  foot ◇ *J'ai mal aux pieds.* My feet are hurting.
- **à pied** on foot
- **avoir pied** to be able to touch the bottom ◇ *Justine n'aime pas nager là où elle n'a pas pied.* Justine doesn't like swimming where she can't touch the bottom.

le **pied-noir** NOUN
  (PL les **pieds-noirs**)
  A pied-noir *is a French person born in Algeria; most of them moved to France during the Algerian war in the 1950s.*
  ◇ *Sa grand-mère est pied-noir.* His grandmother was born in Algeria.

le **piège** NOUN
  trap
- **prendre quelqu'un au piège** to trap somebody

piéger VERB
  to trap
- **un colis piégé** a parcel bomb
- **une voiture piégée** a car bomb

la **pierre** NOUN
  stone
- **une pierre précieuse** a precious stone

le **piéton** NOUN
  pedestrian

la **piétonne** NOUN
  pedestrian

piétonnier ADJECTIVE
  (FEM SING **piétonnière**)
- **une rue piétonnière** a pedestrianized street
- **un quartier piétonnier** a pedestrianized area

la **pieuvre** NOUN
  octopus

le **pigeon** NOUN
  pigeon

piger VERB (*informal*)
  to understand

la **pile** NOUN
  see also pile ADVERB
  1 pile ◇ *Il y a une pile de disques sur la table.* There's a pile of records on the table.
  2 battery ◇ *Les piles de mon magnétophone sont usées.* The batteries in my tape recorder have run out.

P

pile ADVERB

see also **pile** NOUN

- **à deux heures pile** at two on the dot
- **jouer à pile ou face** to toss up
- **Pile ou face?** Heads or tails?

le **pilote** NOUN

pilot

- **un pilote de course** a racing driver
- **un pilote de ligne** an airline pilot

piloter VERB

to fly (*a plane*)

la **pilule** NOUN

pill

- **prendre la pilule** to be on the pill

le **piment** NOUN

chilli

le **pin** NOUN

pine

le **pinard** NOUN (*informal*)

wine

la **pince** NOUN

1. **pliers** PL (*tool*)
2. **pincer** (*of crab*)

- **une pince à épiler** tweezers
- **une pince à linge** a clothes peg

le **pinceau** NOUN

(PL les **pinceaux**)

paintbrush

la **pincée** NOUN

- **une pincée de sel** a pinch of salt

pincer VERB

to pinch ◇ *Elle m'a pincé le bras.* She pinched my arm.

le **pingouin** NOUN

penguin

le **ping-pong** NOUN

table tennis ◇ *jouer au ping-pong* to play table tennis

la **pintade** NOUN

guinea fowl

le **pion** NOUN

1. **pawn** (*in chess*)
2. **piece** (*in draughts*)
3. **supervisor** (*man*)

In French secondary schools, the teachers are not responsible for supervising the pupils outside class. This job is done by people called pions *or* surveillants.

la **pionne** NOUN

supervisor (*woman*)

la **pipe** NOUN

pipe ◇ *Mon grand-père fume la pipe.* My granddad smokes a pipe.

piquant ADJECTIVE

1. **prickly**
2. **spicy**

le **pique** NOUN

see also **la pique**

spades PL ◇ *l'as de pique* the ace of spades

la **pique** NOUN

see also **le pique**

cutting remark ◇ *envoyer des piques à quelqu'un* to make cutting remarks to somebody

le **pique-nique** NOUN

picnic

piquer VERB

1. **to bite** ◇ *Nous avons été piqués par les moustiques.* We were bitten by mosquitoes.
2. **to burn** ◇ *Cette sauce me pique la langue.* This sauce is burning my tongue.
3. **to steal** ◇ *On m'a piqué mon porte-monnaie.* (*informal*) I've had my purse stolen.

- **se piquer** to prick oneself ◇ *Il s'est piqué avec une aiguille.* He pricked himself with a needle.

le **piquet** NOUN

1. **post** ◇ *Le chien est attaché à un piquet.* The dog is tied to a post.
2. **peg** ◇ *Il nous manque un des piquets de la tente.* One of our tent pegs is missing.

la **piqûre** NOUN

1. **injection** ◇ *Le médecin lui a fait une piqûre.* The doctor gave him an injection.
2. **bite** ◇ *une piqûre de moustique* a mosquito bite
3. **sting** ◇ *une piqûre d'abeille* a bee sting

le **pirate** NOUN

pirate

pire ADJECTIVE, NOUN

worse ◇ *C'est encore pire qu'avant.* It's even worse than before.

- **le pire** the worst ◇ *C'est la pire journée que j'aie jamais passée.* That's the worst day I've ever had. ◇ *Ce gamin est le pire de la bande.* That boy is the worst in the group.

- **le pire de** the worst of ◇ *Le pire de tout, c'est qu'on s'ennuie tout le temps.* The worst of it is that we're always bored.

la **piscine** NOUN

swimming pool

la **pistache** NOUN

pistachio ◇ *une glace à la pistache* a pistachio ice cream

la **piste** NOUN

1. **lead** ◇ *La police est sur une piste.* The police are following a lead.
2. **runway** ◇ *L'avion s'est posé sur la piste.* The plane landed on the runway.

3 **ski run** ◇ *Le skieur a descendu la piste.* The skier came down the ski run.
- **une piste artificielle** a dry ski slope
- **la piste de danse** the dance floor
- **une piste cyclable** a cycle track

le **pistolet** NOUN
pistol

pistonner VERB
- **Il a été pistonné pour avoir ce travail.** They pulled some strings to get him this job.

la **pitié** NOUN
pity
- **Il me fait pitié.** I feel sorry for him.
- **avoir pitié de quelqu'un** to feel sorry for somebody

pittoresque ADJECTIVE
picturesque

le **placard** NOUN
cupboard

la **place** NOUN
1 **place** ◇ *Vincent a eu la troisième place au concours.* Vincent got third place in the competition.
2 **square** ◇ *la place du village* the village square
3 **space** ◇ *Il ne reste plus de place pour se garer.* There's no more space to park. ◇ *Ça prend de la place.* It takes up a lot of room.
4 **seat** ◇ *Toutes les places ont été vendues.* All the seats have been sold. ◇ *Il y a vingt places assises.* There are 20 seats. ◇ *remettre quelque chose en place* to put something back in its place
- **sur place** on the spot
- **à la place** instead ◇ *Il ne reste plus de tarte; désirez-vous quelque chose d'autre à la place?* There's no pie left; would you like something else instead?
- **à la place de** instead of

placer VERB
1 **to seat** ◇ *Nous étions placés à côté du directeur.* We were seated next to the manager.
2 **to invest** ◇ *Il a placé ses économies en Bourse.* He invested his money on the Stock Exchange.

le **plafond** NOUN
ceiling

la **plage** NOUN
beach

la **plaie** NOUN
wound

plaindre VERB
- **plaindre quelqu'un** to feel sorry for somebody ◇ *Je te plains.* I feel sorry for you.
- **se plaindre** to complain ◇ *Il n'arrête pas de se plaindre.* He never stops complaining.
- **se plaindre à quelqu'un** to complain to somebody ◇ *Ils se sont plaints au directeur.* They complained to the manager.
- **se plaindre de quelque chose** to complain about something ◇ *Elle s'est plainte du bruit.* She complained about the noise.

la **plaine** NOUN
plain (*level area*)

la **plainte** NOUN
complaint
- **porter plainte** to lodge a complaint

plaire VERB
- **Ce cadeau me plaît beaucoup.** I like this present a lot.
- **Ce film plaît beaucoup aux jeunes.** The film is very popular with young people.
- **Elle lui plaît.** He fancies her.
- **s'il te plaît** please
- **s'il vous plaît** please

plaisanter VERB
to joke

la **plaisanterie** NOUN
joke

le **plaisir** NOUN
pleasure
- **faire plaisir à quelqu'un** to please somebody ◇ *J'y suis allé pour lui faire plaisir.* I went there to please him. ◇ *Ce cadeau me fait très plaisir.* I'm very pleased with this present.

plaît VERB *see* **plaire**

le **plan** NOUN
plan
- **au premier plan** in the foreground

la **planche** NOUN
plank
- **une planche à repasser** an ironing board
- **une planche à roulettes** a skateboard

le **plancher** NOUN
floor

planer VERB
1 **to glide** ◇ *L'avion planait dans le ciel.* The plane was gliding in the sky.
2 **to have one's head in the clouds** ◇ *Ce garçon plane complètement.* (*informal*) He's not with us at all.

la **planète** NOUN
planet

la **plante** NOUN
plant

planter VERB

P

1 **to plant** ◇ *Daphné a planté des tomates.* Daphne planted some tomatoes.

2 **to hammer in** ◇ *Jean-Pierre a planté un clou dans le mur.* Jean-Pierre hammered a nail into the wall.

3 **to pitch** ◇ *André a planté sa tente au bord du lac.* André pitched his tent next to the lake.

→ **Ne reste pas planté là!** Don't just stand there!

→ **se planter** (*informal*) to fail ◇ *Je me suis planté en maths.* I failed maths.

la **plaque** NOUN
(metal) plate
→ **une plaque de verglas** a patch of ice
→ **une plaque de chocolat** a bar of chocolate
→ **une plaque d'immatriculation** a number plate (*of car*)

plaqué ADJECTIVE
→ **plaqué or** gold-plated
→ **plaqué argent** silver-plated

plaquer VERB (*informal*)
1 **to ditch** ◇ *Elle a plaqué son copain.* She ditched her boyfriend.
2 **to pack in** ◇ *Il a plaqué son boulot.* He packed in his job.

la **plaquette** NOUN
→ **une plaquette de chocolat** a bar of chocolate
→ **une plaquette de beurre** a pack of butter

le **plastique** NOUN
plastic

plat ADJECTIVE
see also plat NOUN
flat
→ **être à plat ventre** to be lying face down
→ **l'eau plate** still water

le **plat** NOUN
see also plat ADJECTIVE
1 **dish** ◇ *un plat en inox* a stainless steel dish
2 **course** ◇ *le plat principal* the main course
→ **un plat cuisiné** a pre-cooked meal
→ **le plat de résistance** the main course
→ **le plat du jour** the dish of the day

le **platane** NOUN
plane tree

le **plateau** NOUN
(PL les **plateaux**)
1 **tray**
→ **un plateau de fromages** a selection of cheeses
2 **plateau**

le **platine** NOUN
see also la platine
platinum

la **platine** NOUN
see also le platine
turntable (*of record player*)
→ **une platine laser** a CD player

le **plâtre** NOUN
plaster ◇ *une statue en plâtre* a statue made of plaster ◇ *avoir un bras dans le plâtre* to have an arm in plaster

plein ADJECTIVE
see also plein NOUN
full
→ **à plein temps** full-time ◇ *Elle travaille à plein temps.* She works full-time.
→ **en plein air** in the open air
→ **en pleine nuit** in the middle of the night
→ **en plein jour** in broad daylight

le **plein** NOUN
see also plein ADJECTIVE
→ **faire le plein** to fill up (*petrol tank*) ◇ *Faites le plein, s'il vous plaît.* Fill it up, please.

pleurer VERB
to cry

pleut VERB *see* pleuvoir

pleuvoir VERB
to rain ◇ *Il pleut.* It's raining.

le **pli** NOUN
1 **fold**
2 **pleat** ◇ *Elle a repassé les plis de sa jupe.* She ironed the pleats of her skirt.
3 **crease** ◇ *Il y a un pli sur la manche de ta chemise.* There's a crease in the sleeve of your shirt.

pliant ADJECTIVE
folding ◇ *un lit pliant* a folding bed

plier VERB
1 **to fold** ◇ *Elle a plié sa serviette.* She folded her towel.
2 **to bend** ◇ *Elle a plié le bras.* She bent her arm.

le **plomb** NOUN
1 **lead** ◇ *Ces jouets sont en plomb.* These toys are made of lead.
2 **fuse** ◇ *Les plombs ont sauté.* The fuses have blown.
→ **l'essence sans plomb** unleaded petrol

le **plombier** NOUN
plumber
→ **Il est plombier.** He's a plumber.

la **plongée** NOUN
diving ◇ *faire de la plongée* to go diving

le **plongeoir** NOUN
   diving board
le **plongeon** NOUN
   dive
plonger VERB
   to dive ◊ *Jean a plongé dans la piscine.* Jean dived into the swimming pool.
 ◆ **J'ai plongé ma main dans l'eau.** I plunged my hand into the water.
plu VERB *see* **plaire, pleuvoir**
la **pluie** NOUN
   rain ◊ *sous la pluie* in the rain
la **plume** NOUN
   feather ◊ *une plume d'oiseau* a bird's feather
 ◆ **un stylo à plume** a fountain pen
plupart
 ◆ **la plupart** PRONOUN
   most (of them) ◊ *La plupart ont moins de quinze ans.* Most of them are under 15.
 ◆ **la plupart des** most ◊ *La plupart des gens ont vu ce film.* Most people have seen this film.
 ◆ **la plupart du temps** most of the time
le **pluriel** NOUN
   plural
plus ADVERB, PREPOSITION
 ◆ **ne...plus (1)** not...any more ◊ *Je ne veux plus le voir.* I don't want to see him any more.
 ◆ **ne...plus (2)** no longer ◊ *Il ne travaille plus ici.* He's no longer working here.
 ◆ **Je n'ai plus de pain.** I've got no bread left.
 ◆ **plus...que** more...than ◊ *Il est plus intelligent que son frère.* He's more intelligent than his brother. ◊ *Il travaille plus que moi.* He works more than me. ◊ *Elle est plus grande que moi.* She's bigger than me.
 ◆ **C'est le plus grand de la famille.** He's the tallest in his family.
 ◆ **plus...plus...** the more...the more... ◊ *Plus il gagne d'argent, plus il en veut.* The more money he earns, the more he wants.
 ◆ **plus de (1)** more ◊ *Il nous faut plus de pain.* We need more bread.
 ◆ **plus de (2)** more than ◊ *Il y avait plus de dix personnes.* There were more than 10 people.
 ◆ **de plus** more ◊ *Il nous faut un joueur de plus.* We need one more player. ◊ *Le voyage a pris trois heures de plus que prévu.* The journey took 3 hours more than planned.

 ◆ **en plus** more ◊ *J'ai apporté quelques gâteaux en plus.* I brought a few more cakes.
 ◆ **de plus en plus** more and more ◊ *Il y a de plus en plus de touristes par ici.* There are more and more tourists round here. ◊ *Il fait de plus en plus chaud.* It's getting hotter and hotter.
 ◆ **plus ou moins** more or less
 ◆ **Quatre plus deux égalent six.** 4 plus 2 is 6.
plusieurs PRONOUN
   several ◊ *Elle a acheté plusieurs chemises.* She bought several shirts. ◊ *Il y en a plusieurs.* There are several of them.
le **plus-que-parfait** NOUN
   pluperfect
plutôt ADVERB
   [1] **quite** ◊ *Elle est plutôt jolie.* She's quite pretty.
   [2] **rather** ◊ *L'eau est plutôt froide.* The water's rather cold.
   [3] **instead** ◊ *Demande-leur plutôt de venir avec toi.* Ask them to come with you instead.
 ◆ **plutôt que** rather than ◊ *Invite Marie plutôt que Nathalie.* Invite Marie rather than Nathalie.
pluvieux ADJECTIVE
   (FEM SING **pluvieuse**)
   rainy
le **pneu** NOUN
   tyre
la **pneumonie** NOUN
   pneumonia
la **poche** NOUN
   pocket
 ◆ **l'argent de poche** pocket money
 ◆ **un livre de poche** a paperback
la **poêle** NOUN
   frying pan
 ◆ **une poêle à frire** a frying pan
le **poème** NOUN
   poem
la **poésie** NOUN
   [1] **poetry**
   [2] **poem**
le **poète** NOUN
   poet
le **poids** NOUN
   weight ◊ *vendre quelque chose au poids* to sell something by weight
 ◆ **prendre du poids** to put on weight ◊ *Il a pris du poids.* He's put on weight.
 ◆ **perdre du poids** to lose weight ◊ *Elle a perdu du poids.* She's lost weight.

P

- **un poids lourd** a lorry

la **poignée** NOUN
1 **handful** ◇ *une poignée de sel* a handful of salt
2 **handle** ◇ *la poignée de la porte* the door handle
- **une poignée de main** a handshake

le **poignet** NOUN
1 **wrist** ◇ *Je me suis fait mal au poignet.* I've hurt my wrist.
2 **cuff** (*of shirt*)

le **poil** NOUN
1 **hair** ◇ *Il y a des poils de chat partout sur la moquette.* There are cat hairs all over the carpet.
2 **fur** ◇ *Ton chien a un beau poil.* Your dog's got lovely fur.

poilu ADJECTIVE
hairy

poinçonner VERB
to punch ◇ *Le contrôleur a poinçonné les billets.* The conductor punched the tickets.

le **poing** NOUN
fist
- **un coup de poing** a punch

le **point** NOUN
1 **point** ◇ *Je ne suis pas d'accord sur ce point.* I don't agree with this point. ◇ *Son point faible, c'est qu'elle est trop gentille.* Her weak point is she's too nice.
- **point de vue** point of view
2 **full stop**
- **être sur le point de faire quelque chose** to be just about to do something ◇ *J'étais sur le point de te téléphoner.* I was just about to phone you.
- **mettre au point** to finalize
- **Ce n'est pas encore au point.** It's not finalized yet.
- **à point** medium ◇ *Comment voulez-vous votre steak?–À point.* How would you like your steak?–Medium.
- **un point d'exclamation** an exclamation mark
- **un point d'interrogation** a question mark

la **pointe** NOUN
point ◇ *la pointe d'un couteau* the point of a knife
- **être à la pointe du progrès** to be in the forefront of progress
- **sur la pointe des pieds** on tiptoe
- **les heures de pointe** peak hours

le **pointillé** NOUN
dotted line

pointu ADJECTIVE

pointed ◇ *un chapeau pointu* a pointed hat

la **pointure** NOUN
size (*of shoes*) ◇ *Quelle est votre pointure?* What size shoes do you take?

le **point-virgule** NOUN
semicolon

la **poire** NOUN
pear

le **poireau** NOUN
(PL les **poireaux**)
leek ◇ *la soupe aux poireaux* leek soup

le **pois** NOUN
pea
- **les petits pois** peas
- **les pois chiches** chickpeas
- **à pois** spotted ◇ *une robe à pois* a spotted dress

le **poison** NOUN
poison

le **poisson** NOUN
fish ◇ *Je n'aime pas le poisson.* I don't like fish. ◇ *André a pêché deux poissons.* André caught two fish.
- **les Poissons** Pisces ◇ *Monique est Poissons.* Monique is Pisces.
- **Poisson d'avril!** April fool!
Pinning a paper fish to somebody's back is a traditional April fool joke in France.
- **un poisson rouge** a goldfish

la **poissonnerie** NOUN
fish shop

le **poissonnier** NOUN
fishmonger

la **poitrine** NOUN
1 **chest** ◇ *J'ai mal à la poitrine.* My chest hurts.
2 **bust** ◇ *Quel est votre tour de poitrine?* What's your bust size?

le **poivre** NOUN
pepper (*spice*)

le **poivron** NOUN
pepper (*vegetable*)

le **pôle** NOUN
pole
- **le pôle Nord** the North Pole
- **le pôle Sud** the South Pole

poli ADJECTIVE
polite

la **police** NOUN
police ◇ *La police recherche le voleur.* The police are looking for the thief.
- **police secours** emergency services ◇ *Ils ont appelé police secours.* They phoned the emergency services.
- **une police d'assurance** an insurance policy

policier ADJECTIVE
(FEM SING **policière**)
see also policier NOUN
- **un roman policier** a detective novel

le policier NOUN
see also policier ADJECTIVE
policeman ◇ *Il est policier.* He's a policeman.

la politesse NOUN
politeness

la politique NOUN
politics ◇ *La politique ne l'intéresse pas du tout.* He's not at all interested in politics.
- **un homme politique** a politician

la pollution NOUN
pollution

le polo NOUN
polo shirt

la Pologne NOUN
Poland

polonais ADJECTIVE, NOUN
(FEM SING **polonaise**)
Polish ◇ *Elle parle polonais.* She speaks Polish.
- **un Polonais** a Pole (*man*)
- **une Polonaise** a Pole (*woman*)
- **les Polonais** the Polish

la Polynésie NOUN
Polynesia

la pommade NOUN
ointment

la pomme NOUN
apple
- **les pomme de terre** potatoes
- **les pommes frites** chips

la pompe NOUN
pump
- **une pompe à essence** a petrol pump
- **les pompes funèbres** undertakers

le pompier NOUN
fireman

pondre VERB
to lay (*eggs*)

le poney NOUN
pony

le pont NOUN
1 **bridge**
2 **deck** (*of ship*)
- **faire le pont** to take a long weekend
  ◇ *Nous faisons le pont pour la Pentecôte.* We're taking a long weekend for Whitsun.

populaire ADJECTIVE
1 **popular** ◇ *Ce chanteur est très populaire en France.* This singer's very popular in France.
2 **working-class** ◇ *un quartier populaire de la ville* a working-class

area of town

la population NOUN
population

le porc NOUN
1 **pig** ◇ *Ils élèvent des porcs.* They breed pigs.
2 **pork** ◇ *du rôti de porc* roast pork

la porcelaine NOUN
china ◇ *une tasse en porcelaine* a china cup

le port NOUN
1 **harbour**
2 **port**

le portail NOUN
gate

portatif ADJECTIVE
(FEM SING **portative**)
portable

la porte NOUN
1 **door** ◇ *Ferme la porte, s'il te plaît.* Close the door, please.
- **la porte d'entrée** the front door
2 **gate** ◇ *Vol 432 à destination de Paris: porte numéro trois.* Flight 432 to Paris: gate 3.
- **mettre quelqu'un à la porte** to sack somebody

le porte-bagages NOUN
luggage rack

le porte-clés NOUN
key ring

la portée NOUN
- **à portée de la main** within arm's reach
- **hors de portée** out of reach

le portefeuille NOUN
wallet

le portemanteau NOUN
(PL les **portemanteaux**)
1 **coat hanger**
2 **coat rack**

le porte-monnaie NOUN
(PL les **porte-monnaie**)
purse

porter VERB
1 **to carry** ◇ *Il portait une valise.* He was carrying a suitcase.
2 **to wear** ◇ *Elle porte une jolie robe bleue.* She's wearing a lovely blue dress.
- **se porter bien** to be well
- **se porter mal** to be unwell

la portière NOUN
door (*of car*)

la portion NOUN
portion

le porto NOUN
port (*wine*)

le portrait NOUN
portrait

P

portugais ADJECTIVE, NOUN
(FEM SING **portugaise**)
Portuguese ◇ *Il parle portugais.* He speaks Portuguese.
- **un Portugais** a Portuguese (*man*)
- **une Portugaise** a Portuguese (*woman*)
- **les Portugais** the Portuguese

le **Portugal** NOUN
Portugal
- **au Portugal (1)** in Portugal
- **au Portugal (2)** to Portugal

poser VERB
[1] to put down ◇ *J'ai posé la cafetière sur la table.* I put the coffee pot down on the table.
[2] to pose ◇ *Cela pose un problème.* That poses a problem.
- **poser une question à quelqu'un** to ask somebody a question
- **se poser** to land ◇ *L'avion s'est posé à huit heures.* The plane landed at 8 o'clock.

positif ADJECTIVE
(FEM SING **positive**)
positive

la **position** NOUN
position

posséder VERB
to own ◇ *Ils possèdent une jolie maison.* They own a lovely house.

la **possibilité** NOUN
possibility

possible ADJECTIVE
possible ◇ *Alain leur a dit que ce n'était pas possible.* Alain told them it wasn't possible.
- **le plus de gens possible** as many people as possible
- **le plus tôt possible** as early as possible
- **le moins d'argent possible** as little money as possible
- **Il travaille le moins possible.** He works as little as possible.
- **dès que possible** as soon as possible
- **faire son possible** to do all one can
◇ *Je ferai tout mon possible.* I'll do all I can.

la **poste** NOUN
see also le poste
[1] post ◇ *Je vais l'envoyer par la poste.* I'm going to send it by post.
[2] post office ◇ *Je vais à la poste pour acheter des timbres.* I'm going to the post office to buy some stamps.
- **mettre une lettre à la poste** to post a letter

le **poste** NOUN
see also la poste
[1] post ◇ *Jean-Pierre a trouvé un poste de professeur.* Jean-Pierre has found a teaching post.
[2] extension (*phone*) ◇ *Pouvez-vous me passer le poste de M. Salzedo?* Can you put me through to Mr Salzedo's extension?
[3] set ◇ *un poste de radio* a radio set
- **un poste de police** a police station

poster VERB
see also poster NOUN
to post ◇ *Je vais poster ce colis.* I'm going to post this parcel.

le **poster** NOUN
see also poster VERB
poster ◇ *un poster de la Grèce* a poster of Greece

postérieur ADJECTIVE
[1] later ◇ *Ce document est postérieur à mille trois cent quatorze.* This document is from later than 1314.
[2] back ◇ *la partie postérieure de ma jambe* the back of my leg

le **pot** NOUN
jar ◇ *J'ai fait trois pots de confiture.* I've made three jars of jam.
- **prendre un pot** (*informal*) to have a drink ◇ *On va prendre un pot ce soir.* We're going for a drink tonight.
- **un pot de fleurs** a plant pot

potable ADJECTIVE
- **eau potable** drinking water
- **"eau non potable"** "not drinking water"

le **potage** NOUN
soup

le **potager** NOUN
vegetable garden

le **pot-au-feu** NOUN
(PL les **pot-au-feu**)
beef stew

le **pote** NOUN (*informal*)
mate ◇ *Je sors avec mes potes ce soir.* I'm going out with my mates tonight.

le **poteau** NOUN
(PL les **poteaux**)
post ◇ *Il s'est appuyé contre un poteau.* He leant against a post.
- **un poteau indicateur** a signpost

potentiel ADJECTIVE
(FEM SING **potentielle**)
potential

la **poterie** NOUN
[1] pottery ◇ *Elle fait de la poterie à l'école.* She does pottery at school.
[2] piece of pottery ◇ *J'ai acheté deux poteries.* I bought two pieces of pottery.

le **potier** NOUN
potter

le **pou** NOUN
(PL les **poux**)
louse

la **poubelle** NOUN
dustbin

le **pouce** NOUN
1 **thumb** ◇ *Je me suis coincé le pouce dans la porte.* I trapped my thumb in the door.
2 **inch** ◇ *Un pouce fait à peu près deux virgule cinq centimètres.* 1 inch equals roughly 2.5 centimetres.
- **manger sur le pouce** to have a quick snack

la **poudre** NOUN
1 **powder**
2 **face powder**
- **la poudre à laver** washing powder
- **le lait en poudre** powdered milk
- **le café en poudre** instant coffee

le **poulain** NOUN
foal

la **poule** NOUN
hen

le **poulet** NOUN
1 **chicken** ◇ *J'adore le poulet.* I love chicken.
2 **cop** ◇ *Il s'est fait attraper par les poulets.* (*informal*) He got caught by the cops.

le **pouls** NOUN
pulse ◇ *Il m'a pris le pouls.* He took my pulse.

le **poumon** NOUN
lung

la **poupée** NOUN
doll

pour PREPOSITION
for ◇ *C'est un cadeau pour toi.* It's a present for you. ◇ *Qu'est-ce que tu veux pour ton petit déjeuner?* What would you like for breakfast?
- **pour faire quelque chose** to do something ◇ *Je lui ai téléphoné pour l'inviter.* I phoned him to invite him.
- **pour que** so that
  pour que *is followed by a verb in the subjunctive.*
  ◇ *Je lui ai prêté mon pull pour qu'elle n'ait pas froid.* I lent her my jumper so that she wouldn't be cold.
- **pour cent** per cent

le **pourboire** NOUN
tip ◇ *Il a donné un pourboire au garçon.* He gave the waiter a tip.

le **pourcentage** NOUN
percentage

pourquoi ADVERB, CONJUNCTION
why ◇ *Pourquoi est-ce qu'il ne vient pas avec nous?* Why isn't he coming with us? ◇ *Elle ne m'a pas dit pourquoi.* She didn't tell me why.

pourra, pourrai, pourras, pourrez VERB *see* **pouvoir**

pourri ADJECTIVE
rotten

pourrir VERB
to go bad ◇ *Ces poires ont pourri.* These pears have gone bad.

pourrons, pourront VERB *see* **pouvoir**

la **poursuite** NOUN
chase
- **se lancer à la poursuite de quelqu'un** to chase after somebody

poursuivre VERB
to carry on with ◇ *Ils ont poursuivi leur travail.* They carried on with their work.
- **se poursuivre** to go on ◇ *Le concert s'est poursuivi très tard.* The concert went on very late.

pourtant ADVERB
yet ◇ *Il a raté son examen. Pourtant, il n'est pas bête.* He failed his exam, yet he's not stupid.
- **C'est pourtant facile!** But it's easy!

pourvu ADJECTIVE
- **pourvu que...** let's hope that...
  pourvu que *is followed by a verb in the subjunctive.*
  ◇ *Pourvu qu'il ne pleuve pas!* Let's hope it doesn't rain!

pousser VERB
1 **to push** ◇ *Ils ont dû pousser la voiture.* They had to push the car.
2 **to grow** ◇ *Mes cheveux poussent vite.* My hair grows quickly.
- **pousser un cri** to give a cry
- **se pousser** to move over
  ◇ *Pousse-toi, je ne vois rien.* Move over, I can't see a thing.

la **poussette** NOUN
pushchair

la **poussière** NOUN
1 **dust** ◇ *La table est couverte de poussière.* The table's covered in dust.
2 **speck of dust** ◇ *J'ai une poussière dans l'œil.* I've got a speck of dust in my eye.

poussiéreux ADJECTIVE
(FEM SING **poussiéreuse**)
dusty

le **poussin** NOUN
chick

P

le **pouvoir** NOUN
see also pouvoir VERB
power ◇ *Le Premier ministre a beaucoup de pouvoir.* The prime minister has a lot of power.

pouvoir VERB
see also pouvoir NOUN
Present tense:
je peux	nous pouvons
tu peux	vous pouvez
il/elle peut	ils/elles peuvent
Past participle: *pu*
can ◇ *Je peux lui téléphoner si tu veux.* I can phone her if you want.
◇ *Puis-je venir vous voir samedi?* May I come and see you on Saturday?
◇ *Je ne pourrai pas venir samedi.* I can't come on Saturday. ◇ *J'ai fait tout ce que j'ai pu.* I did all I could.
• **Je n'en peux plus.** I'm exhausted.
• **Il se peut que...** It's possible that...
il se peut que is followed by a verb in the subjunctive.
◇ *Il se peut qu'elle ait déménagé.* It's possible that she's moved house. ◇ *Il se peut que j'y aille.* I might go.

la **prairie** NOUN
meadow

la **pratique** NOUN
see also pratique ADJECTIVE
practice ◇ *Je manque de pratique.* I'm out of practice.

pratique ADJECTIVE
see also pratique NOUN
practical ◇ *Ce sac est très pratique.* This bag's very practical.

pratiquement ADVERB
virtually ◇ *J'ai pratiquement fini.* I've virtually finished.

pratiquer VERB
to practise ◇ *Je dois pratiquer mon espagnol.* I need to practise my Spanish.
• **Pratiquez-vous un sport?** Do you do any sport?

le **pré** NOUN
meadow

la **précaution** NOUN
precaution ◇ *prendre ses précautions* to take precautions
• **par précaution** as a precaution ◇ *Il a pris une assurance par précaution.* He took out insurance as a precaution.
• **"à manipuler avec précaution"** "handle with care"

précédemment ADVERB
previously

précédent ADJECTIVE
previous

précieux ADJECTIVE
(FEM SING **précieuse**)
precious
• **une pierre précieuse** a precious stone
• **de précieux conseils** invaluable advice

le **précipice** NOUN
ravine ◇ *Leur voiture est tombée dans un précipice.* Their car fell into a ravine.

précipitamment ADVERB
hurriedly ◇ *Chantal est partie précipitamment.* Chantal left hurriedly.

la **précipitation** NOUN
haste ◇ *Il a agi avec précipitation.* He acted hastily.

se **précipiter** VERB
to rush

précis ADJECTIVE
precise

précisément ADVERB
precisely

préciser VERB
1 **to be more specific about** ◇ *Pouvez-vous préciser ce que vous voulez dire?* Can you be more specific about what you want to say?
2 **to specify** ◇ *Pouvez-vous préciser les raisons de ce changement?* Can you specify the reasons for this change?

la **précision** NOUN
1 **precision**
2 **detail** ◇ *Je vais vous donner quelques précisions.* I'm going to give you some details.

la **préfecture** NOUN
A préfecture is the headquarters of a département, *one of the 96 administrative areas of France.*
• **la préfecture de police** the police headquarters

préférable ADJECTIVE
preferable

préféré ADJECTIVE
favourite

la **préférence** NOUN
preference ◇ *Je n'ai pas de préférence.* I've no preference.
• **de préférence** preferably

préférer VERB
to prefer ◇ *Je préfère la cuisine de Teresa.* I prefer Teresa's cooking. ◇ *Je préfère manger à la cantine.* I prefer to eat in the canteen.
• **Je préférerais du thé.** I'd rather have tea.
• **préférer quelqu'un à quelqu'un** to prefer somebody to somebody ◇ *Je le préfère à son frère.* I prefer him to

his brother.

préhistorique ADJECTIVE

prehistoric

le**préjugé** NOUN

prejudice ◇ *avoir des préjugés contre quelqu'un* to be prejudiced against somebody

premier ADJECTIVE

(FEM SING **première**)

see also **première** NOUN

first ◇ *au premier étage* on the first floor ◇ *C'est notre premier jour de vacances.* It's the first day of our holiday. ◇ *C'est la première fois que je viens ici.* It's the first time I've been here. ◇ *le premier mai* the first of May ◇ *Il est arrivé premier.* He came first.

- **le Premier ministre** the Prime Minister

la**première** NOUN

see also **premier** ADJECTIVE

[1] **first class** ◇ *Nous avons voyagé en première.* We travelled first class.

[2] **first gear** ◇ *Passe en première pour prendre ce virage.* Change into first to go round this bend.

[3] **lower sixth form**

In French secondary schools, years are counted from the **sixième** *(youngest) to* **première** *and* **terminale** *(oldest).*

◇ *Ma sœur est en première.* My sister's in the lower sixth.

premièrement ADVERB

firstly

prendre VERB

to take ◇ *Prends tes affaires et viens avec moi.* Take your things and come with me.

- **prendre quelque chose à quelqu'un** to take something from somebody ◇ *Il m'a pris mon stylo!* He's taken my pen!

- **passer prendre** to pick up ◇ *Je dois passer prendre Richard.* I have to pick up Richard.

- **prendre à gauche** to turn left ◇ *Prenez à gauche en arrivant au rond-point.* Turn left at the roundabout.

- **Il se prend pour Napoléon.** He thinks he's Napoleon.

- **s'en prendre à quelqu'un** to lay into somebody *(verbally)* ◇ *Il s'en est pris à moi.* He laid into me.

- **s'y prendre** to set about it ◇ *Tu t'y prends mal!* You're setting about it the wrong way!

le**prénom** NOUN

first name ◇ *Quel est votre prénom?* What's your first name?

la**préparation** NOUN

preparation

préparer VERB

[1] **to prepare** ◇ *Elle prépare le dîner.* She's preparing dinner.

[2] **to make** ◇ *Je vais préparer le café.* I'm going to make the coffee.

[3] **to prepare for** ◇ *Laure prépare son examen d'économie.* Laure's preparing for her economics exam.

- **se préparer** to get ready ◇ *Ils se préparent à partir.* They're getting ready to go.

la**préposition** NOUN

preposition

près ADVERB

- **tout près** nearby ◇ *J'habite tout près.* I live nearby.

- **près de (1)** near (to) ◇ *Est-ce que c'est près d'ici?* Is it near here?

- **près de (2)** next to ◇ *Assied-toi près de moi.* Sit down next to me.

- **près de (3)** nearly ◇ *Il y avait près de cinq cents spectateurs.* There were nearly 500 spectators.

- **de près** closely ◇ *Il a regardé la photo de près.* He looked closely at the photo.

- **à peu de chose près** more or less

la**présence** NOUN

[1] **presence** ◇ *Sa présence est rassurante.* His presence is reassuring.

[2] **attendance** ◇ *La présence aux cours est obligatoire.* Attendance at lessons is compulsory.

présent ADJECTIVE

see also **présent** NOUN

present

le**présent** NOUN

see also **présent** ADJECTIVE

present tense

- **à présent** now

la**présentation** NOUN

presentation

- **faire les présentations** to do the introductions

présenter VERB

to present ◇ *Il présentait le spectacle.* He presented the show.

- **présenter quelqu'un à quelqu'un** to introduce somebody to somebody ◇ *Il m'a présenté à sa sœur.* He introduced me to his sister.

- **Marc, je te présente Anaïs.** Marc, this is Anaïs.

- **se présenter (1)** to introduce oneself ◇ *Elle s'est présentée à ses collègues.* She introduced herself to her colleagues.

P

◆ **se présenter (2)** to arise ◇ *Si l'occasion se présente, nous irons en Écosse.* If the chance arises, we'll go to Scotland.

◆ **se présenter (3)** to stand ◇ *Monsieur Legros se présente encore aux élections.* Mr Legros is standing for election again.

le **préservatif** NOUN
condom

préserver VERB
to protect

◆ **préserver de** to protect from ◇ *Nous avons ramassé les chaises du jardin pour les préserver de l'humidité.* We brought the garden chairs in to protect them from the damp.

le **président** NOUN
1 president ◇ *le président des États-Unis* the president of the United States
2 chairman ◇ *le président du conseil d'administration* the chairman of the board of directors

◆ **le président directeur général** the chairman and managing director

présider VERB
1 to chair ◇ *Duncan a présidé la réunion.* Duncan chaired the meeting.
2 to be the guest of honour ◇ *Il présidait à table.* He was the guest of honour at the table.

presque ADVERB
nearly ◇ *Il est presque six heures.* It's nearly 6 o'clock. ◇ *Nous sommes presque arrivés.* We're nearly there.

◆ **presque rien** hardly anything ◇ *Elle n'a presque rien mangé.* She's hardly eaten anything.

◆ **presque pas** hardly at all ◇ *Il ne dort presque pas.* He hardly sleeps at all.

◆ **presque pas de** hardly any ◇ *Il n'y a presque pas de place.* There's hardly any space.

la **presqu'île** NOUN
peninsula

la **presse** NOUN
press ◇ *les représentants de la presse* representatives of the press

pressé ADJECTIVE
1 in a hurry ◇ *Je ne peux pas rester, je suis pressé.* I can't stay, I'm in a hurry.
2 urgent ◇ *Ce n'est pas très pressé.* It's not very urgent.

◆ **une orange pressée** a fresh orange juice

presser VERB
1 to squeeze ◇ *Tu peux me presser un citron?* Can you squeeze me a lemon?
2 to be urgent ◇ *Est-ce que ça presse?* Is it urgent?

◆ **se presser** to hurry up ◇ *Allez, presse-toi, on va être en retard!* Come on, hurry up, we're going to be late!

◆ **Rien ne presse.** There's no hurry.

le **pressing** NOUN
dry-cleaner's

la **pression** NOUN
1 pressure

◆ **faire pression sur quelqu'un** to put pressure on somebody
2 draught beer *(informal)*

prêt ADJECTIVE
see also **prêt** NOUN
ready ◇ *Le déjeuner est prêt.* Lunch is ready. ◇ *Tu es prête?* Are you ready?

le **prêt** NOUN
see also **prêt** ADJECTIVE
loan

le **prêt-à-porter** NOUN
ready-to-wear clothes

prétendre VERB
◆ **prétendre que** to claim that ◇ *Il prétend qu'il ne la connaît pas.* He claims he doesn't know her.

prétendu ADJECTIVE
so-called ◇ *un prétendu expert* a so-called expert

prétentieux ADJECTIVE
(FEM SING **prétentieuse**)
pretentious

prêter VERB
◆ **prêter quelque chose à quelqu'un** to lend something to someone ◇ *Il m'a prêté sa voiture.* He lent me his car.

◆ **prêter attention à quelque chose** to pay attention to something

le **prétexte** NOUN
excuse ◇ *Il avait un prétexte pour ne pas venir.* He had an excuse for not coming.

◆ **sous aucun prétexte** on no account ◇ *Ne le dérangez sous aucun prétexte.* On no account must you disturb him.

prétexter VERB
to give as an excuse ◇ *Elle a prétexté une réunion.* She gave a meeting as her excuse. ◇ *Il a prétexté qu'il avait un rendez-vous.* He gave the excuse that he had an appointment.

le **prêtre** NOUN
priest

la **preuve** NOUN
1 evidence ◇ *Il y a des preuves*

contre lui. There's evidence against him.

2 **proof** ◇ *Vous n'avez aucune preuve.* You haven't got any proof.

- **faire preuve de courage** to show courage
- **faire ses preuves** to prove oneself ◇ *Pour être embauché ici, il faut faire ses preuves.* To be employed here, you need to prove yourself.

prévenir VERB

- **prévenir quelqu'un** to warn somebody ◇ *Je te préviens, il est de mauvaise humeur.* I'm warning you, he's in a bad mood.

la **prévention** NOUN
prevention

- **des mesures de prévention** preventative measures
- **la prévention routière** road safety

la **prévision** NOUN

- **les prévisions météorologiques** the weather forecast
- **en prévision de quelque chose** in anticipation of something

prévoir VERB

1 **to plan** ◇ *Nous prévoyons un pique-nique pour dimanche.* We're planning to have a picnic on Sunday.

- **Le départ est prévu pour dix heures.** The departure's scheduled for 10 o'clock.

2 **to allow** ◇ *J'ai prévu assez à manger pour quatre.* I allowed enough food for four.

3 **to foresee** ◇ *J'avais prévu qu'il serait en retard.* I'd foreseen that he'd be late.

- **Je prévois qu'il me faudra une heure de plus.** I reckon on it taking me another hour.

prier VERB
to pray to ◇ *Les Grecs priaient Dionysos.* The Greeks prayed to Dionysos.

- **prier quelqu'un de faire quelque chose** to ask somebody to do something ◇ *Elle l'a prié de sortir.* She asked him to leave.
- **je vous en prie (1)** please do ◇ *Je peux m'asseoir?–Je vous en prie.* May I sit down?–Please do.
- **je vous en prie (2)** please ◇ *Je vous en prie, ne me laissez pas seule.* Please, don't leave me alone.
- **je vous en prie (3)** don't mention it ◇ *Merci pour votre aide.–Je vous en prie.* Thanks for your help.–Don't mention it.

la **prière** NOUN
prayer ◇ *faire ses prières* to say one's prayers

- **"prière de ne pas fumer"** "no smoking please"

le **primaire** NOUN
primary education ◇ *Ses enfants sont encore en primaire.* His children are still in primary education.

- **l'école primaire** primary school

la **prime** NOUN

1 **bonus** ◇ *Il a eu une prime en récompense de son travail.* He received a bonus for his work.

2 **free gift** ◇ *J'ai eu ce stylo en prime avec l'agenda.* I got this pen as a free gift with the diary.

3 **premium** ◇ *une prime d'assurance* an insurance premium

la **primevère** NOUN
primrose

le **prince** NOUN
prince ◇ *le prince Charles* Prince Charles

la **princesse** NOUN
princess ◇ *la princesse Diana* Princess Diana

principal ADJECTIVE
(MASC PL **principaux**)
see also principal NOUN
main ◇ *le rôle principal* the main role

le **principal** NOUN
(PL les **principaux**)
see also principal ADJECTIVE

1 **headmaster** ◇ *le principal du collège* the headmaster of the school

2 **main thing** ◇ *Personne n'a été blessé; c'est le principal.* Nobody was injured; that's the main thing.

le **principe** NOUN
principle

- **pour le principe** on principle
- **en principe (1)** as a rule ◇ *Il déjeune en principe à midi et demi.* As a rule he has lunch at 12.30.
- **en principe (2)** in theory ◇ *En principe Anne doit arriver lundi.* In theory, Anne should arrive on Monday.

le **printemps** NOUN
spring

- **au printemps** in spring

la **priorité** NOUN

1 **priority** ◇ *C'est à faire en priorité.* It needs to be done as a priority.

2 **right of way** ◇ *Tu n'as pas la priorité.* You haven't got right of way.

P

pris VERB see **prendre**

pris ADJECTIVE

  1 taken ◇ *Est-ce que cette place est prise?* Is this seat taken?

  2 busy ◇ *Je serai très pris la semaine prochaine.* I'll be very busy next week.

- **avoir le nez pris** to have a stuffy nose
- **être pris de panique** to be panic-stricken

la **prise** NOUN

  1 plug

  2 socket

- **une prise de courant** a power point
- **une prise multiple** an adaptor
- **une prise de sang** a blood test

la **prison** NOUN

  prison ◇ *aller en prison* to go to prison ◇ *être en prison* to be in prison

prisonnier ADJECTIVE

  see also prisonnier NOUN

  captive

le **prisonnier** NOUN

  see also prisonnier ADJECTIVE

  prisoner

la **prisonnière** NOUN

  prisoner

prit VERB see **prendre**

privé ADJECTIVE

  private ◇ *la propriété privée* private property ◇ *ma vie privée* my private life

- **en privé** in private

priver VERB

- **priver quelqu'un de quelque chose** to deprive somebody of something ◇ *Le prisonnier a été privé de nourriture.* The prisoner was deprived of food.
- **Tu seras privé de dessert!** You won't get any pudding!

le **prix** NOUN

  1 price ◇ *Je n'arrive pas à lire le prix de ce livre.* I can't see the price of this book.

  2 prize ◇ *Cécile a eu le prix de la meilleure actrice.* Cécile got the prize for best actress.

- **hors de prix** exorbitantly priced ◇ *Les repas sont hors de prix ici!* The price of meals here is exorbitant!
- **à aucun prix** not at any price ◇ *Je n'irai là-bas à aucun prix.* I'm not going there, not at any price.
- **à tout prix** at all costs ◇ *Je veux à tout prix voir ce film.* I want to see this film at all costs.

probable ADJECTIVE

  likely ◇ *Il est probable qu'elle*

viendra. It's likely she'll come.

- **C'est peu probable.** That's unlikely.

probablement ADVERB

  probably

le **problème** NOUN

  problem

le **procédé** NOUN

  process

le **procès** NOUN

  trial ◇ *Le procès du meurtrier commence mardi.* The murder trial starts on Tuesday.

- **Il est en procès avec son employeur.** He's involved in a lawsuit with his employer.

prochain ADJECTIVE

  next ◇ *Nous descendons au prochain arrêt.* We're getting off at the next stop.

- **la prochaine fois** next time
- **la semaine prochaine** next week
- **À la prochaine!** See you!

prochainement ADVERB

  soon

proche ADJECTIVE

  1 near ◇ *Les magasins les plus proches étaient à trois kilomètres.* The nearest shops were 3 kilometres away. ◇ *dans un proche avenir* in the near future

  2 close ◇ *un ami proche* a close friend

- **proche de** near to ◇ *La cathédrale est proche du château.* The cathedral is near the castle.
- **le Proche-Orient** the Middle East

les **proches** MASC NOUN

  close relatives

proclamer VERB

  to proclaim

procurer VERB

- **procurer quelque chose à quelqu'un** to get something for somebody ◇ *C'est lui qui m'a procuré ce travail.* He got me this job.
- **se procurer quelque chose** to get something ◇ *Je me suis procuré leur dernier catalogue.* I got their latest catalogue.

le **producteur** NOUN

  producer

la **production** NOUN

  production

la **productrice** NOUN

  producer

produire VERB

  to produce

- **se produire** to take place ◇ *Ces changements se sont produits l'an* dernier. The changes took place last year.

le **produit** NOUN

product ◇ les produits de beauté beauty products

le **prof** NOUN (informal)

teacher ◇ Elle est prof de maths. She's a maths teacher.

le **professeur** NOUN

[1] **teacher** ◇ Philippe est professeur d'histoire. Philippe's a history teacher.

[2] **professor** ◇ le professeur Dupont Professor Dupont

• **un professeur de faculté** a university lecturer

la **profession** NOUN

profession ◇ Quelle est votre profession? What's your profession?

• "sans profession" "unemployed"

professionnel ADJECTIVE

(FEM SING **professionnelle**)

professional

le **profil** NOUN

[1] **profile** (of person) ◇ de profil in profile

[2] **contours** (of object)

le **profit** NOUN

profit ◇ La société a fait des profits importants. The company made significant profits.

• **tirer profit de quelque chose** to profit from something

• **au profit de** in aid of ◇ un spectacle au profit de l'UNICEF a show in aid of UNICEF

profiter VERB

• **profiter de quelque chose** to take advantage of something ◇ Profitez du beau temps pour aller faire du vélo. Take advantage of the good weather and go cycling.

• **Profitez-en bien!** Make the most of it!

profond ADJECTIVE

deep

la **profondeur** NOUN

depth

le **programme** NOUN

[1] **programme** ◇ le programme du festival the festival programme

[2] **syllabus** ◇ le programme de littérature the literature syllabus

[3] **program** ◇ un programme informatique a computer program

programmer VERB

[1] **to show** ◇ Ce film est programmé dimanche soir. The film is scheduled for Sunday evening.

[2] **to program** ◇ Mon ordinateur n'est pas programmé pour ça. My

computer isn't programmed to do that.

le **progrès** NOUN

progress ◇ faire des progrès to make progress

progresser VERB

to progress

progressif ADJECTIVE

(FEM SING **progressive**)

progressive

le **projecteur** NOUN

[1] **projector** ◇ Le projecteur de diapositives est en panne. The slide projector is broken.

[2] **spotlight** ◇ Elle était sous les projecteurs. She was under the spotlight.

le **projet** NOUN

[1] **plan** ◇ des projets de vacances holiday plans

[2] **draft** ◇ le projet de construction d'un musée the draft for the construction of a museum

• **un projet de loi** a bill (in parliament)

projeter VERB

[1] **to plan** ◇ Ils projettent d'acheter une maison. They're planning to buy a house.

[2] **to cast** ◇ une ombre projetée sur le mur a shadow cast onto the wall

• **Elle a été projetée hors de la voiture.** She was thrown out of the car.

prolonger VERB

[1] **to prolong** ◇ Je vais prolonger mes vacances en Espagne. I'm going to prolong my holidays in Spain.

[2] **to extend** ◇ Je vais prolonger mon abonnement. I'm going to extend my subscription.

• **se prolonger** to go on ◇ La réunion s'est prolongée tard. The meeting went on late.

la **promenade** NOUN

walk ◇ Il y a de belles promenades par ici. There are some nice walks round here.

• **faire une promenade** to go for a walk

• **faire une promenade en voiture** to go for a drive

• **faire une promenade à vélo** to go for a bike ride

promener VERB

to take for a walk ◇ Cordelia promène son chien tous les jours. Cordelia takes her dog for a walk every day.

• **se promener** to go for a walk ◇ Chantal est partie se promener. Chantal has gone for a walk.

P

la **promesse** NOUN
promise ◇ *faire une promesse* to make a promise ◇ *tenir sa promesse* to keep one's promise

promettre VERB
to promise ◇ *On m'a promis une augmentation.* They promised me a pay rise. ◇ *Elle m'a promis de me téléphoner.* She promised to phone me.

la **promotion** NOUN
promotion ◇ *Il espère avoir bientôt une promotion.* He's hoping to get promotion soon.
➤ **être en promotion** to be on special offer ◇ *Les côtes de porc sont en promotion.* Pork chops are on special offer.

le **pronom** NOUN
pronoun

prononcer VERB
1 to pronounce ◇ *Le russe est difficile à prononcer.* Russian is difficult to pronounce.
2 to deliver ◇ *prononcer un discours* to deliver a speech
➤ **se prononcer** to be pronounced ◇ *Le "e" final ne se prononce pas.* The final "e" isn't pronounced.

la **prononciation** NOUN
pronunciation

la **propagande** NOUN
propaganda

se **propager** VERB
to spread ◇ *Le feu s'est propagé rapidement.* The fire spread quickly.

la **proportion** NOUN
proportion

le **propos** NOUN
➤ **à propos** by the way ◇ *À propos, quand est-ce que tu viens?* By the way, when are you coming?
➤ **à propos de quelque chose** about something ◇ *C'est à propos de la soirée de vendredi.* It's about the party on Friday.

proposer VERB
➤ **proposer quelque chose à quelqu'un (1)** to suggest something to somebody ◇ *Nous lui avons proposé une promenade en bateau.* We suggested going on a boat ride to him.
➤ **proposer quelque chose à quelqu'un (2)** to offer somebody something ◇ *Ils m'ont proposé des chocolats.* They offered me some chocolates.

la **proposition** NOUN
offer ◇ *J'accepte ta proposition avec plaisir.* I'll be pleased to accept your offer.

propre ADJECTIVE
see also **propre** NOUN
1 clean ◇ *Ce mouchoir n'est pas propre.* This handkerchief isn't clean.
2 own ◇ *Gordon l'a fabriqué de ses propres mains.* Gordon made it with his own hands.
➤ **propre à** characteristic of ◇ *C'est une coutume propre au Berry.* It's a custom you find in the Berry region.

le **propre** NOUN
see also **propre** ADJECTIVE
➤ **recopier quelque chose au propre** to make a fair copy of something

proprement ADVERB
properly ◇ *Mange proprement!* Eat properly!
➤ **le village proprement dit** the village itself
➤ **à proprement parler** strictly speaking

la **propreté** NOUN
cleanliness

le **propriétaire** NOUN
see also **la propriétaire**
1 owner
2 landlord

la **propriétaire** NOUN
see also **le propriétaire**
1 owner
2 landlady

la **propriété** NOUN
property ◇ *la propriété privée* private property

le **prospectus** NOUN
leaflet

prospère ADJECTIVE
prosperous

la **prostituée** NOUN
prostitute

protecteur ADJECTIVE
(FEM SING **protectrice**)
1 protective ◇ *un vernis protecteur* a protective varnish
2 patronizing ◇ *un ton protecteur* a patronizing tone

la **protection** NOUN
protection

protéger VERB
to protect

la **protéine** NOUN
protein

protestant ADJECTIVE
(FEM SING **protestante**)
Protestant ◇ *une église protestante* a Protestant church
➤ **Il est protestant.** He's a Protestant.

la **protestation** NOUN
protest

protester VERB
  to protest ◦ *Ils protestent contre leurs conditions de travail.* They're protesting about their working conditions.

prouver VERB
  to prove

la **provenance** NOUN
  origin
- **un avion en provenance de Berlin** a plane arriving from Berlin

provenir VERB
- **provenir de (1)** to come from ◦ *Ces tomates proviennent d'Espagne.* These tomatoes come from Spain.
- **provenir de (2)** to be the result of ◦ *Cela provient d'un manque d'organisation.* This is the result of a lack of organization.

le **proverbe** NOUN
  proverb

la **province** NOUN
  province
- **en province** in the provinces ◦ *Ils habitent en province.* They live in the provinces.

le **proviseur** NOUN
  headteacher *(of state secondary school)* ◦ *Elle est proviseur.* She's a headteacher.

la **provision** NOUN
  supply ◦ *une provision de pommes de terre* a supply of potatoes

les **provisions** FEM NOUN
  food ◦ *Nous n'avons plus beaucoup de provisions.* We haven't got much food left.

provisoire ADJECTIVE
  temporary ◦ *un emploi provisoire* a temporary job

provoquer VERB
  1 to provoke ◦ *Il l'a provoquée en la traitant d'imbécile.* He provoked her by calling her stupid.
  2 to cause ◦ *Cet accident a provoqué la mort de quarante personnes.* The accident caused the death of 40 people.

la **proximité** NOUN
  proximity
- **à proximité** nearby ◦ *Sabine habite à proximité.* Sabine lives nearby.

prudemment ADVERB
  1 carefully ◦ *Conduisez prudemment.* Drive carefully.
  2 wisely ◦ *Prudemment, il a fait des économies.* Wisely, he saved some money.

la **prudence** NOUN
  caution
- **avec prudence** carefully ◦ *Ils ont conduit avec prudence.* They drove carefully.

prudent ADJECTIVE
  1 careful ◦ *Soyez prudents!* Be careful!
  2 wise ◦ *Laisse ton passeport à la maison, c'est plus prudent.* It would be wiser to leave your passport at home.

la **prune** NOUN
  plum

le **pruneau** NOUN
  (PL les **pruneaux**)
  prune

le/la **psychiatre** NOUN
  psychiatrist

la **psychologie** NOUN
  psychology

psychologique ADJECTIVE
  psychological

le/la **psychologue** NOUN
  psychologist

les **PTT** FEM NOUN (= *Postes et Télécommunications*)
  Post Office

pu VERB *see* **pouvoir**
- **Je n'ai pas pu venir.** I couldn't come.

la **pub** NOUN *(informal)*
  1 advertising ◦ *Il y a trop de pub à la télé.* There's too much advertising on TV.
  2 adverts ◦ *Le film a été coupé par la pub.* The film was interrupted by adverts.

public ADJECTIVE
  (FEM SING **publique**)
  see also public NOUN
  public ◦ *un jardin public* a public park
- **une école publique** a state school

le **public** NOUN
  see also public ADJECTIVE
  1 public ◦ *Ce parc est ouvert au public.* The park's open to the public.
  2 audience ◦ *Le public a applaudi le chanteur.* The audience applauded the singer.
- **en public** in public ◦ *Je déteste parler en public.* I hate speaking in public.

publicitaire ADJECTIVE
- **une agence publicitaire** an advertising agency
- **un film publicitaire** a publicity film

la **publicité** NOUN
  1 advertising ◦ *Muriel travaille dans la publicité.* Muriel works in advertising.

P

2 **advert** ◇ *Il y a trop de publicités dans ce journal.* There are too many adverts in this newspaper.

publier VERB
to publish ◇ *Bob vient de publier son nouveau roman.* Bob has just published his new novel.

publique ADJECTIVE *see* **public**

la **puce** NOUN
1 **flea** ◇ *Ce chien a des puces.* This dog has fleas.
2 **chip** ◇ *une puce électronique* a microchip
- **une carte à puce** a smart card

les **puces** FEM NOUN
flea market

puer VERB
to stink ◇ *Ça pue le tabac ici!* It stinks of tobacco round here!

puéril ADJECTIVE
childish

puis VERB
see also puis ADVERB *see* **pouvoir**
- **Puis-je venir vous voir samedi?** May I come and see you on Saturday?

puis ADVERB
see also puis VERB
then ◇ *Faites dorer le poulet, puis ajoutez le vin blanc.* Fry the chicken till golden, then add white wine.

puisque CONJUNCTION
since ◇ *Puisque c'est si cher, nous irons manger ailleurs.* Since it's so expensive, we'll eat elsewhere.

la **puissance** NOUN
power

puissant ADJECTIVE
powerful

le **puits** NOUN
well ◇ *Il a un puits dans son jardin.* He's got a well in his garden.

le **pull** NOUN
jumper

le **pull-over** NOUN
jumper

le **pulvérisateur** NOUN
spray ◇ *un pulvérisateur de parfum* a perfume spray

pulvériser VERB
1 **to pulverize** ◇ *L'explosion a pulvérisé le bâtiment.* The explosion pulverized the building.
2 **to spray** ◇ *Il a pulvérisé de l'insecticide sur ses plantes.* He sprayed insecticide on his plants.

la **punaise** NOUN
drawing pin

punir VERB
to punish ◇ *Il a été puni pour avoir menti.* He was punished for lying.

la **punition** NOUN
punishment

le **pupitre** NOUN
desk *(for pupil)*

pur ADJECTIVE
1 **pure** ◇ *L'eau de cette source est très pure.* The water from this spring is very pure.
2 **neat** *(undiluted)* ◇ *du whisky pur* neat whisky ◇ *de l'eau de Javel pure* concentrated bleach
- **c'est de la folie pure** it's sheer madness

la **purée** NOUN
mashed potatoes
- **la purée de marrons** chestnut purée

la **putain** NOUN *(rude)*
whore

le **puzzle** NOUN
jigsaw puzzle

le **p.-v.** NOUN *(= procès-verbal)*
parking ticket

le **pyjama** NOUN
pyjamas PL

la **pyramide** NOUN
pyramid

les **Pyrénées** FEM NOUN
Pyrenees
- **dans les Pyrénées** in the Pyrenees

Q

le **QI** NOUN (= *quotient intellectuel*)

IQ

le **quai** NOUN

    1 **quay** ◇ *être à quai* to be alongside the quay

    2 **platform** ◇ *Le train partira du quai numéro quatre.* The train will leave from platform 4.

qualifier VERB

◆ **se qualifier** to qualify ◇ *Bob s'est qualifié pour la demi-finale.* Bob has qualified for the semifinal.

la **qualité** NOUN

    quality ◇ *Ces outils sont de très bonne qualité.* These are very good quality tools.

quand CONJUNCTION, ADVERB

    when ◇ *Quand est-ce que tu pars en vacances?* When are you going on holiday? ◇ *Quand je serai riche, j'achèterai une belle maison.* When I'm rich, I'll buy a nice house.

◆ **quand même** all the same ◇ *Je ne voulais pas de dessert, mais j'en ai mangé quand même.* I didn't want any dessert, but I had some all the same.

quant à PREPOSITION

    regarding ◇ *Quant au problème de chauffage...* Regarding the problem with the heating... ◇ *Quant à moi, je n'arriverai qu'à dix heures.* As for me, I won't be arriving till 10 o'clock.

la **quantité** NOUN

    amount

◆ **des quantités de** a great deal of ◇ *Ils ont invité des quantités de gens.* They invited a lot of people.

la **quarantaine** NOUN

    about forty ◇ *une quarantaine de personnes* about forty people

◆ **Elle a la quarantaine.** She's in her forties.

quarante NUMBER

    forty ◇ *Elle a quarante ans.* She's forty.

◆ **quarante et un** forty-one

◆ **quarante-deux** forty-two

e **quart** NOUN

    quarter

◆ **le quart de** a quarter of ◇ *Elle a mangé le quart du gâteau.* She ate a quarter of the cake.

◆ **trois quarts** three quarters

◆ **un quart d'heure** a quarter of an hour

◆ **deux heures et quart** a quarter past two

◆ **dix heures moins le quart** a quarter to ten

◆ **Un quart d'eau minérale, s'il vous plaît.** A small bottle of mineral water, please.

le **quartier** NOUN

    1 **area** (*of town*) ◇ *un quartier tranquille* a quiet area

◆ **un cinéma de quartier** a local cinema

    2 **piece** ◇ *un quartier d'orange* a piece of orange

le **quartz** NOUN

◆ **une montre à quartz** a quartz watch

quasi ADVERB

    nearly ◇ *La quasi-totalité des récoltes a été détruite.* Nearly all of the crop was destroyed.

quasiment ADVERB

    nearly ◇ *Le film est quasiment fini.* The film's nearly finished.

◆ **quasiment jamais** hardly ever ◇ *Ils ne vont quasiment jamais en boîte.* They hardly ever go clubbing.

quatorze NUMBER

    fourteen ◇ *Mon frère a quatorze ans.* My brother's fourteen. ◇ *à quatorze heures* at 2 p.m.

◆ **le quatorze février** the fourteenth of February

quatre NUMBER

    four ◇ *Il est quatre heures du matin.* It's four in the morning. ◇ *Il a quatre ans.* He's four.

◆ **le quatre février** the fourth of February

◆ **faire les quatre cents coups** to be a bit wild ◇ *Todd a fait les quatre cents coups dans sa jeunesse.* Todd was a bit wild in his youth.

quatre-vingts NUMBER

    eighty

    quatre-vingts is spelt with an **-s** *when it is followed by a noun, but not when it is followed by another number.*

    ◇ *quatre-vingts francs* eighty francs

    ◇ *Elle a quatre-vingt-deux ans.* She's eighty-two.

◆ **quatre-vingt-dix** ninety

◆ **quatre-vingt-onze** ninety-one

◆ **quatre-vingt-quinze** ninety-five

◆ **quatre-vingt-dix-huit** ninety-eight

quatrième ADJECTIVE

    see also quatrième NOUN

    fourth ◇ *au quatrième étage* on the fourth floor

la **quatrième** NOUN

    see also quatrième ADJECTIVE

third year

In French secondary schools, years are counted from the sixième *(youngest) to* première *and* terminale *(oldest).*

◇ *Mon frère est en quatrième.* My brother's in third year.

que CONJUNCTION, PRONOUN, ADVERB

[1] **that** ◇ *Il sait que tu es là.* He knows that you're here. ◇ *la dame que j'ai rencontrée hier* the lady that I met yesterday ◇ *Le gâteau qu'elle a fait est délicieux.* The cake she's made is delicious.

- **Je veux que tu viennes.** I want you to come.

[2] **what** ◇ *Que fais-tu?* What are you doing? ◇ *Que vas-tu lui dire?* What are you going to tell him?

- **Qu'est-ce que...?** What...?
◇ *Qu'est-ce que tu fais?* What are you doing? ◇ *Qu'est-ce que c'est?* What's that?

- **plus...que** more...than ◇ *C'est plus difficile que je ne le pensais.* It's more difficult than I thought. ◇ *Il est plus grand que moi.* He's bigger than me.

- **aussi...que** as...as ◇ *Elle est aussi jolie que sa sœur.* She's as pretty as her sister. ◇ *Le train est aussi cher que l'avion.* The train is as expensive as the plane.

- **ne...que** only ◇ *Il ne boit que de l'eau.* He only drinks water. ◇ *Je ne l'ai vu qu'une fois.* I've only seen him once.

- **Qu'il est bête!** He's so silly!

quel ADJECTIVE

(FEM SING **quelle**)

[1] **who** ◇ *Quel est ton chanteur préféré?* Who's your favourite singer?

[2] **what** ◇ *Quelle est ta couleur préférée?* What's your favourite colour? ◇ *Quelle heure est-il?* What time is it? ◇ *Quelle bonne surprise!* What a surprise!

[3] **which** ◇ *Quel groupe préfères-tu?* Which band do you like best?

- **quel que soit (1)** whoever ◇ *quel que soit le coupable* whoever is guilty

- **quel que soit (2)** whatever ◇ *quel que soit votre avis* whatever your opinion

quelle ADJECTIVE *see* **quel**

quelque ADJECTIVE, ADVERB

[1] **some** ◇ *Il a quelques amis à Paris.* He has some friends in Paris. ◇ *J'ai acheté quelques disques.* I bought some records.

[2] **a few** ◇ *Il reste quelques bouteilles.* There are a few bottles left.

[3] **few** ◇ *Ils ont fini les quelques bouteilles qui restaient.* They finished the few bottles that were left.

- **quelque chose (1)** something ◇ *J'ai quelque chose pour toi.* I've got something for you. ◇ *Je voudrais quelque chose de moins cher.* I'd like something cheaper.

- **quelque chose (2)** anything ◇ *Avez-vous quelque chose à déclarer?* Have you got anything to declare? ◇ *Tu as pensé à quelque chose d'autre?* Did you think of anything else?

- **quelque part (1)** somewhere ◇ *J'ai oublié mon sac quelque part.* I've left my bag somewhere.

- **quelque part (2)** anywhere ◇ *Vous allez quelque part ce week-end?* Are you going anywhere this weekend?

quelquefois ADVERB

sometimes

quelques-uns PRONOUN

(FEM **quelques-unes**)

some ◇ *As-tu vu ses films? J'en ai vu quelques-uns.* Have you seen his films? I've seen some of them.

quelqu'un PRONOUN

[1] **somebody** ◇ *Quelqu'un t'a appelé.* Somebody phoned you. ◇ *Il y a quelqu'un à la porte.* There's somebody at the door.

[2] **anybody** ◇ *Est-ce que quelqu'un a vu mon parapluie?* Has anybody seen my umbrella? ◇ *Il y a quelqu'un?* Is there anybody there?

la **querelle** NOUN

quarrel

qu'est-ce que *see* **que**

qu'est-ce qui *see* **qui**

la **question** NOUN

[1] **question** ◇ *Je t'ai posé une question.* I asked you a question.

[2] **matter** ◇ *Ils se sont disputés pour des questions d'argent.* They argued over money matters.

- **Il n'en est pas question.** There's no question of it. ◇ *Il n'est pas question que je paye.* There's no question of me paying.

- **De quoi est-il question?** What's it about?

- **Il est question de l'organisation du concert.** It's about the organization of the concert.

- **hors de question** out of the question ◇ *Il est hors de question que nous restions ici.* It's out of the question that we stay here.

le **questionnaire** NOUN
questionnaire

questionner VERB
to question

la **queue** NOUN
1. **tail** ◦ *Le chien a agité la queue.* The dog wagged its tail.
- **faire la queue** to queue
- **une queue de cheval** a ponytail
2. **rear** ◦ *en queue du train* at the rear of the train
3. **bottom** ◦ *en queue de liste* at the bottom of the list
4. **stalk** (*of fruit, leaf*) ◦ *la queue d'une cerise* a cherry stalk

qui PRONOUN
1. **who** ◦ *Qui a téléphoné?* Who phoned? ◦ *Le peintre qui a peint ce tableau est un génie.* The artist who painted this picture is a genius.
2. **whom** ◦ *C'est la personne à qui j'ai parlé hier.* It's the person whom I spoke to yesterday.
3. **that** ◦ *Donne-moi la veste qui est sur la chaise.* Give me the jacket that's on the chair.
- **Qui est-ce qui...?** Who...? ◦ *Qui est-ce qui t'emmène au spectacle?* Who's taking you to the show?
- **Qui est-ce que...?** Who...? ◦ *Qui est-ce que tu as vu à cette soirée?* Who did you see at the party?
- **Qu'est-ce qui...?** What...? ◦ *Qu'est-ce qui est sur la table?* What's on the table? ◦ *Qu'est-ce qui te prend?* What's the matter with you?
- **À qui est ce sac?** Whose bag is this?
- **À qui parlais-tu?** Who were you talking to?

la **quille** NOUN
- **un jeu de quilles** skittles

la **quincaillerie** NOUN
ironmonger's (shop)

la **quinzaine** NOUN
about fifteen ◦ *Il y avait une quinzaine de personnes.* There were about fifteen people there.
- **une quinzaine de jours** a fortnight

quinze NUMBER
fifteen ◦ *Anaïs a quinze ans.* Anaïs is fifteen. ◦ *à quinze heures* at 3 p.m.
- **le quinze février** the fifteenth of February
- **dans quinze jours** in a fortnight's time

quitter VERB
to leave ◦ *J'ai quitté la maison à huit heures.* I left the house at 8 o'clock.
- **se quitter** to part ◦ *Les deux amis se sont quittés devant le café.* The two friends parted in front of the café.
- **Ne quittez pas.** (*on telephone*) Hold the line. ◦ *Ne quittez pas, je vous passe Monsieur Divan.* Hold the line, I'll put you through to Monsieur Divan.

quoi PRONOUN
what? ◦ *À quoi penses-tu?* What are you thinking about?
- **Quoi de neuf?** What's new?
- **As-tu de quoi écrire?** Have you got anything to write with?
- **Je n'ai pas de quoi acheter une voiture.** I can't afford to buy a car.
- **Quoi qu'il arrive.** Whatever happens.
- **Il n'y a pas de quoi.** Don't mention it.
- **Il n'y a pas de quoi s'énerver.** There's no reason for getting worked up.
- **En quoi puis-je vous aider?** How may I help you?

quoique CONJUNCTION
even though ◦ *Il va l'acheter quoique ce soit cher.* He's going to buy it even though it's expensive.

quotidien ADJECTIVE
(FEM SING **quotidienne**)
see also quotidien NOUN
daily ◦ *Il est parti faire sa promenade quotidienne.* He's gone for his daily walk.

le **quotidien** NOUN
see also quotidien ADJECTIVE
daily paper ◦ *Le Monde est un quotidien.* Le Monde is a daily paper.

R

le **rab** NOUN (*informal*)
seconds (*of meal*) ◇ *Il y a du rab?* Are there any seconds?

le **rabais** NOUN
reduction (*in price*)
- **au rabais** at a discount

raccompagner VERB
to take home ◇ *Tu peux me raccompagner?* Can you take me home?

le **raccourci** NOUN
shortcut

raccrocher VERB
to hang up (*telephone*)

la **race** NOUN
1 **race** ◇ *la race humaine* the human race
2 **breed** ◇ *De quelle race est ton chat?* What breed is your cat?
- **de race** pedigree ◇ *un chien de race* a pedigree dog

racheter VERB
1 **to buy another** ◇ *J'ai racheté un portefeuille.* I've bought another wallet. ◇ *racheter du lait* to buy more milk
2 **to buy** ◇ *Il m'a racheté ma moto.* He bought my bike from me.

la **racine** NOUN
root

raciste ADJECTIVE
racist

raconter VERB
- **raconter quelque chose à quelqu'un** to tell somebody about something ◇ *Raconte-moi ce qui s'est passé.* Tell me what happened. ◇ *Raconte-moi une histoire.* Tell me a story.
- **Qu'est-ce que tu racontes?** What are you talking about?

le **radar** NOUN
radar

le **radiateur** NOUN
radiator
- **un radiateur électrique** an electric heater

radin ADJECTIVE (*informal*)
stingy

la **radio** NOUN
1 **radio** ◇ *à la radio* on the radio
2 **X-ray**
- **passer une radio** to have an X-ray ◇ *Elle a passé une radio des poumons.* She had a chest X-ray.

le **radio-réveil** NOUN

(PL les **radios-réveils**)
clock radio

le **radis** NOUN
radish

raffoler VERB
- **raffoler de** to be crazy about ◇ *Elle raffole de la tarte aux pommes.* She really loves apple tart.

rafraîchir VERB
to cool down
- **se rafraîchir (1)** to get cooler ◇ *Le temps se rafraîchit.* The weather's getting cooler.
- **se rafraîchir (2)** to freshen up ◇ *Il a pris une douche pour se rafraîchir.* He had a shower to freshen up.

rafraîchissant ADJECTIVE
refreshing

la **rage** NOUN
rabies
- **une rage de dents** raging toothache

le **ragoût** NOUN
stew

raide ADJECTIVE
1 **steep** ◇ *Cette pente est raide.* This is a steep slope.
2 **straight** ◇ *Laure a les cheveux raides.* Laure has straight hair.
3 **stiff** ◇ *Son bras est encore raide.* His arm's still stiff.
4 **flat broke** ◇ *Je suis raide ce mois-ci.* (*informal*) I'm flat broke this month.

la **raie** NOUN
1 **skate** (*fish*)
2 **parting** (*in hair*)

le **rail** NOUN
rail ◇ *par rail* by rail

le **raisin** NOUN
grapes ◇ *le raisin blanc* green grapes
- **des raisins secs** raisins

la **raison** NOUN
reason ◇ *sans raison* for no reason ◇ *Raison de plus pour y aller.* All the more reason for going.
- **Ce n'est pas une raison.** That's no excuse.
- **avoir raison** to be right ◇ *Tu as raison.* You're right.
- **en raison de** because of ◇ *en raison d'une grève* because of a strike

raisonnable ADJECTIVE
sensible ◇ *Elle est très raisonnable pour son âge.* She's very sensible for her age.

le **raisonnement** NOUN

reasoning ◇ *J'ai du mal à suivre son raisonnement.* I have difficulty following his reasoning.

rajouter VERB
to add

ralentir VERB
to slow down

râler VERB (*informal*)
to moan

le **ramassage** NOUN
- **le ramassage scolaire** the school bus service

ramasser VERB
1 **to pick up** ◇ *Il a ramassé son crayon.* He picked up his pencil.
2 **to take in** ◇ *Il a ramassé les copies.* He took in the exam papers.

la **rame** NOUN
1 **oar** (*of boat*)
2 **train** (*on the underground*)

le **rameau** NOUN
(PL les **rameaux**)
branch
- **le dimanche des Rameaux** Palm Sunday

ramener VERB
1 **to bring back** ◇ *Je t'ai ramené un souvenir de Grèce.* I've brought you back a present from Greece.
2 **to take home** ◇ *Tu me ramènes?* Will you take me home?

ramer VERB
to row ◇ *C'est Jean-Pierre qui ramait.* Jean-Pierre was rowing.

la **rampe** NOUN
banister

la **rancune** NOUN
- **garder rancune à quelqu'un** to bear somebody a grudge
- **Sans rancune!** No hard feelings!

rancunier ADJECTIVE
(FEM SING **rancunière**)
vindictive

la **randonnée** NOUN
- **une randonnée à vélo** a bike ride
- **une randonnée pédestre** a ramble

le **rang** NOUN
row (*line*) ◇ *au premier rang* in the front row ◇ *se mettre en rangs* to get into rows

la **rangée** NOUN
row (*line*) ◇ *une rangée de chaises* a row of chairs

ranger VERB
1 **to put away** ◇ *J'ai rangé tes affaires.* I've put your things away.
2 **to tidy up** ◇ *Va ranger ta chambre.* Go and tidy up your room.

le **rap** NOUN

rap ◇ *Robert est chanteur de rap.* Robert's a rap singer.

râper VERB
to grate ◇ *le fromage râpé* grated cheese

rapide ADJECTIVE
1 **fast** ◇ *Cette voiture est très rapide.* This is a very fast car.
2 **quick** ◇ *J'ai jeté un coup d'œil rapide sur ton travail.* I had a quick glance at your work.

rapidement ADVERB
quickly

le **rappel** NOUN
1 **booster** (*vaccination*)
2 **curtain call**

rappeler VERB
to call back ◇ *Je te rappelle dans cinq minutes.* I'll call you back in 5 minutes.
- **rappeler quelque chose à quelqu'un** to remind somebody of something ◇ *Cette odeur me rappelle mon enfance.* This smell reminds me of my childhood.
- **rappeler à quelqu'un de faire quelque chose** to remind somebody to do something ◇ *Rappelle-moi d'acheter des billets.* Remind me to get tickets.
- **se rappeler** to remember ◇ *Il s'est rappelé qu'il avait une course à faire.* He remembered he had some shopping to do.

le **rapport** NOUN
see also les **rapports**
1 **report** ◇ *Il a écrit un rapport.* He wrote a report.
2 **connection** ◇ *Je ne vois pas le rapport.* I can't see the connection.
- **par rapport à** in comparison with

rapporter VERB
to bring back ◇ *Je leur ai rapporté un cadeau.* I brought them back a present.

le **rapporteur** NOUN
telltale

la **rapporteuse** NOUN
telltale

les **rapports** MASC NOUN
see also le **rapport**
relations ◇ *Leurs rapports avec leurs voisins se sont améliorés.* Their relations with their neighbours have improved.
- **les rapports sexuels** sexual intercourse

rapprocher VERB
1 **to bring together** ◇ *Cet accident a rapproché les deux frères.* The

R

accident brought the two brothers together.

[2] **to bring closer** ◇ *Il a rapproché le fauteuil de la télé.* He brought the armchair closer to the TV.

• **se rapprocher** to come closer ◇ *Rapproche-toi, tu verras mieux.* Come closer, you'll see better.

la **raquette** NOUN
[1] **racket** (*tennis*)
[2] **bat** (*table tennis*)

rare ADJECTIVE
rare ◇ *une plante rare* a rare plant

rarement ADVERB
rarely

ras ADJECTIVE, ADVERB
short ◇ *un chien à poil ras* a short-haired dog
• **à ras bords** to the brim ◇ *Il a rempli son verre à ras bords.* He filled his glass to the brim.
• **en avoir ras le bol de quelque chose** (*informal*) to be fed up with something
• **un pull ras du cou** a crew-neck jumper

raser VERB
to shave off ◇ *Ray a rasé sa barbe.* Ray has shaved off his beard.
• **se raser** to shave

le **rasoir** NOUN
see also rasoir ADJECTIVE
razor

rasoir ADJECTIVE (MASC, FEM, PL) (*informal*)
see also rasoir NOUN
dead boring

rassembler VERB
to assemble ◇ *Il a rassemblé les enfants dans la cour.* He assembled the children in the playground.
• **se rassembler** to gather together ◇ *Les passagers se sont rassemblés près du car.* The passengers gathered near the coach.

rassurer VERB
to reassure
• **Je suis rassuré.** I don't need to worry any more.
• **se rassurer** to be reassured ◇ *Rassure-toi!* Don't worry!

le **rat** NOUN
rat

raté ADJECTIVE
unsuccessful ◇ *Le gâteau est raté.* The cake's a failure.

le **râteau** NOUN
(PL les **râteaux**)
rake

rater VERB
[1] **to miss** ◇ *Chantal a raté son train.* Chantal missed her train.

[2] **to fail** ◇ *J'ai raté mon examen de maths.* I failed my maths exam.
◇ *Elle a raté sa quiche.* Her quiche didn't turn out right.

RATP ABBREVIATION
Paris transport authority

rattacher VERB
to tie up again ◇ *rattacher ses lacets* to tie up one's laces

rattraper VERB
[1] **to recapture** ◇ *La police a rattrapé le voleur.* The police recaptured the thief.
[2] **to catch up with** ◇ *Je vais rattraper Cécile.* I'll catch up with Cécile.
[3] **to make up for** ◇ *Il faut rattraper le temps perdu.* We must make up for lost time.
• **se rattraper** to make up for it ◇ *Je n'ai pas le temps de sortir mais je me rattraperai après les examens.* I haven't got time to go out, but I'll make up for it after the exams.

la **rature** NOUN
correction ◇ *un texte sans ratures* a text with no corrections

ravi ADJECTIVE
• **être ravi** to be delighted ◇ *Ils étaient ravis de nous voir.* They were delighted to see us. ◇ *Je suis ravi que vous puissiez venir.* I'm delighted that you can come.

rayé ADJECTIVE
striped ◇ *une chemise rayée* a striped shirt

rayer VERB
[1] **to scratch** ◇ *Il a rayé la peinture de sa voiture.* He scratched the paintwork of his car.
[2] **to cross off** ◇ *Son nom a été rayé de la liste.* His name has been crossed off the list.

le **rayon** NOUN
[1] **ray** ◇ *un rayon de soleil* a ray of sunshine
[2] **radius** ◇ *le rayon d'un cercle* the radius of a circle
[3] **shelf** ◇ *les rayons d'une bibliothèque* the shelves of a bookcase
[4] **department** ◇ *le rayon hi-fi vidéo* the hi-fi and video department
• **les rayons X** X-rays

la **rayure** NOUN
stripe

le **ré** NOUN
[1] **D** ◇ *en ré majeur* in D major
[2] **re** ◇ *do, ré, mi...* do, re, mi...

la **réaction** NOUN
reaction

réagir VERB
to react

le **réalisateur** NOUN
director (of film) ◦ Il est réalisateur. He's a film director.

la **réalisatrice** NOUN
director (of film) ◦ Elle est réalisatrice. She's a film director.

réaliser VERB
[1] **to carry out** ◦ Ils ont réalisé leur projet. They carried out their plan.
[2] **to fulfil** ◦ Il a réalisé son rêve. He has fulfilled his dream.
[3] **to realize** ◦ Tu réalises ce que tu dis? Do you realize what you're saying?
[4] **to make** ◦ réaliser un film to make a film
‣ **se réaliser** to come true ◦ Mon rêve s'est réalisé. My dream has come true.

réaliste ADJECTIVE
realistic

la **réalité** NOUN
reality
‣ **en réalité** in fact

rebondir VERB
to bounce

le **rebord** NOUN
edge ◦ le rebord du lavabo the edge of the washbasin
‣ **le rebord de la fenêtre** the window ledge

recaler VERB (informal)
‣ **J'ai été recalé en maths.** I failed maths.

récemment ADVERB
recently

récent ADJECTIVE
recent

la **réception** NOUN
reception desk

/la **réceptionniste** NOUN
receptionist ◦ Elle est réceptionniste. She's a receptionist.

la **recette** NOUN
recipe

recevoir VERB
[1] **to receive** ◦ J'ai reçu une lettre. I received a letter.
[2] **to see** ◦ Il a reçu trois clients ce matin. He has seen three clients this morning.
[3] **to have round** ◦ Je reçois des amis à dîner. I'm having friends for dinner.
‣ **être reçu à un examen** to pass an exam

le **rechange** NOUN
‣ **de rechange** spare (battery, bulb)
◦ des vêtements de rechange a change of clothes

la **recharge** NOUN
refill

le **réchaud** NOUN
stove

réchauffer VERB
[1] **to reheat** ◦ Je vais réchauffer les légumes. I'll reheat the vegetables.
[2] **to warm up** ◦ Un bon café va te réchauffer. A nice cup of coffee will warm you up.
‣ **se réchauffer** to warm oneself ◦ Je vais me réchauffer près du feu. I'll go and warm myself by the fire.

la **recherche** NOUN
research ◦ Je voudrais faire de la recherche. I'd like to do research.
‣ **être à la recherche de quelque chose** to be looking for something ◦ Je suis à la recherche d'un emploi. I'm looking for a job.
‣ **les recherches** search ◦ La police a interrompu les recherches. The police called off the search.

rechercher VERB
to look for ◦ La police recherche l'assassin. The police are looking for the killer.

la **rechute** NOUN
relapse

le **récipient** NOUN
container

le **récit** NOUN
story

réciter VERB
to recite

la **réclamation** NOUN
complaint ◦ J'ai une réclamation à faire. I want to make a complaint.
‣ **les réclamations** the complaints department

la **réclame** NOUN
advert ◦ une réclame de lessive an advert for washing powder
‣ **en réclame** on special offer ◦ Le saumon était en réclame au supermarché. Salmon was on special offer at the supermarket.

réclamer VERB
[1] **to demand** ◦ Nous réclamons la semaine de trente heures. We demand a 30-hour week.
[2] **to complain** ◦ Elles sont toujours en train de réclamer. They're always complaining about something.

reçois VERB see **recevoir**

R

la **récolte** NOUN
  harvest
récolter VERB
  ⒈ to harvest ◇ *Ils ont récolté le blé.*
  They harvested the wheat.
  ⒉ to collect ◇ *Ils ont récolté deux*
  mille francs. They collected 2000
  francs.
  ⒊ to get ◇ *Il a récolté une amende.*
  (*informal*) He got a fine.
le **recommandé** NOUN
  • en recommandé by registered mail
  ◇ *Je voudrais envoyer ce paquet en*
  recommandé. I'd like to send this
  parcel registered.
recommander VERB
  to recommend ◇ *Je vous*
  recommande ce restaurant. I
  recommend this restaurant.
recommencer VERB
  ⒈ to start again ◇ *Il a recommencé à*
  pleuvoir. It's started raining again.
  ⒉ to do again ◇ *S'il n'est pas puni, il*
  va recommencer. If he's not punished
  he'll do it again.
la **récompense** NOUN
  reward
récompenser VERB
  to reward ◇ *Il m'a récompensée de*
  mes efforts. He rewarded me for my
  efforts.
réconcilier VERB
  • se réconcilier avec quelqu'un to be
  make it up with somebody ◇ *Il s'est*
  réconcilié avec sa sœur. He has made
  it up with his sister.
reconnaissant ADJECTIVE
  grateful
reconnaître VERB
  ⒈ to recognize ◇ *Je ne l'ai pas*
  reconnu. I didn't recognize him.
  ⒉ to admit ◇ *Je reconnais que j'ai*
  eu tort. I admit I was wrong.
reconstruire VERB
  to rebuild
le **record** NOUN
  record ◇ *battre un record* to break a
  record
recouvrir VERB
  to cover ◇ *La neige recouvre le sol.*
  The ground is covered in snow.
la **récréation** NOUN
  break ◇ *Les élèves sont en*
  récréation. The pupils are having their
  break.
  • la cour de récréation the playground
  (*of school*)
le **rectangle** NOUN
  rectangle

rectangulaire ADJECTIVE
  rectangular
rectifier VERB
  to correct
le **reçu** NOUN
  see also reçu VERB
  receipt
reçu VERB *see* **recevoir**
  see also reçu NOUN
  • J'ai reçu un colis ce matin. I received
  a parcel this morning.
  • être reçu à un examen to pass an
  exam
reculer VERB
  ⒈ to step back ◇ *Il a reculé pour la*
  laisser entrer. He stepped back to let
  her in.
  ⒉ to reverse ◇ *J'ai reculé pour laisser*
  passer le camion. I reversed to let the
  lorry past.
  ⒊ to postpone ◇ *Ils ont reculé la*
  date du spectacle. They postponed the
  show.
reculons
  • à reculons ADVERB
  backwards ◇ *Elle est entrée à*
  reculons. She came in backwards.
récupérer VERB
  ⒈ to get back ◇ *Je vais récupérer ma*
  voiture au garage. I'm going to get my
  car back from the garage.
  ⒉ to make up ◇ *J'ai des heures à*
  récupérer. I've got time to make up.
  ⒊ to recover ◇ *J'ai besoin de*
  récupérer. I need to recover.
recycler VERB
  to recycle
  • se recycler to retrain ◇ *Il a décidé*
  de se recycler en informatique. He
  decided to retrain as a computer
  programmer.
la **rédaction** NOUN
  essay
redemander VERB
  ⒈ to ask again for ◇ *Je vais lui*
  redemander son adresse. I'll ask him
  for his address again.
  ⒉ to ask for more ◇ *Je vais*
  redemander des carottes. I'm going to
  ask for more carrots.
redescendre VERB
  to go back down ◇ *Il est redescendu*
  au premier étage. He went back down
  to the first floor. ◇ *Elle a redescendu*
  l'escalier. She went back down the
  stairs.
rédiger VERB
  to write (*an essay*)
redoubler VERB

to repeat a year ◇ *Il a raté son examen et doit redoubler.* He's failed his exam and will have to repeat the year.

la **réduction** NOUN
- 1 **reduction** ◇ *une réduction du nombre des touristes* a reduction in the number of tourists
- 2 **discount** ◇ *une réduction de cent francs* a 100 franc discount

réduire VERB
- **to cut** ◇ *Ils ont réduit leurs prix.* They've cut their prices. ◇ *Il a réduit de moitié ses dépenses.* He has cut his spending by half.

réel ADJECTIVE
(FEM SING **réelle**)
- **real**

réellement ADVERB
- **really**

refaire VERB
- 1 **to do again** ◇ *Je dois refaire ce rapport.* I've got to do this report again.
- 2 **to take up again** ◇ *Je voudrais refaire de la gym.* I'd like to take up gymnastics again.

le **réfectoire** NOUN
- **refectory**

la **référence** NOUN
- **reference**
- **faire référence à quelque chose** to refer to something
- **Ce n'est pas une référence!** That's no recommendation!

réfléchi ADJECTIVE
- **reflexive** (*verb*)
- **C'est tout réfléchi.** My mind's made up.

réfléchir VERB
- **to think** ◇ *Il est en train de réfléchir.* He's thinking.
- **réfléchir à quelque chose** to think about something ◇ *Je vais réfléchir à ta proposition.* I'll think about your suggestion.

le **reflet** NOUN
- **reflection** ◇ *les reflets du soleil sur la mer* the reflection of the sun on the sea

refléter VERB
- **to reflect**

le **réflexe** NOUN
- **reflex** ◇ *avoir de bons réflexes* to have good reflexes

la **réflexion** NOUN
- 1 **thought** ◇ *Elle est en pleine réflexion.* She's deep in thought.
- 2 **remark** ◇ *faire des réflexions désagréables* to make nasty remarks

- **réflexion faite** on reflection

le **refrain** NOUN
- **chorus** (*of song*)

le **réfrigérateur** NOUN
- **refrigerator**

refroidir VERB
- **to cool** ◇ *Laissez le gâteau refroidir.* Leave the cake to cool.
- **se refroidir** to get colder ◇ *Le temps se refroidit.* It's getting colder.

se **réfugier** VERB
- **to take shelter** ◇ *Je me suis réfugié sous un arbre.* I took shelter under a tree.

le **refus** NOUN
- **refusal**
- **Ce n'est pas de refus.** I wouldn't say no. ◇ *Voulez-vous une bière?–Ce n'est pas de refus.* Would you like a beer?–I wouldn't say no.

refuser VERB
- **to refuse** ◇ *Il a refusé de payer sa part.* He refused to pay his share. ◇ *On lui a refusé une augmentation.* He was refused a pay rise.
- **Je refuse qu'on me parle ainsi!** I won't let anybody talk to me like that!

se **régaler** VERB
- **Merci beaucoup: je me suis régalé!** Thank you very much: it was absolutely delicious!

le **regard** NOUN
- **look** ◇ *Il lui a jeté un regard interrogateur.* He gave him an enquiring look. ◇ *On voyait à son regard qu'elle était contrariée.* You could tell from the look in her eyes that she was upset.
- **Tous les regards se sont tournés vers lui.** All eyes turned towards him.

regarder VERB
- 1 **to look at** ◇ *Il regardait ses photos de vacances.* He was looking at his holiday photos. ◇ *Regarde! J'ai presque fini.* Look! I've nearly finished.
- 2 **to watch** ◇ *Je regarde la télévision.* I'm watching television. ◇ *Regarde où tu mets les pieds!* Watch where you put your feet!
- 3 **to concern** ◇ *Ça ne nous regarde pas.* It doesn't concern us.
- **ne pas regarder à la dépense** to spare no expense

le **régime** NOUN
- 1 **régime** (*of a country*)
- 2 **diet** ◇ *un régime sans sel* a salt-free diet ◇ *se mettre au régime* to go on a diet ◇ *suivre un régime* to be on a diet

R

+ **un régime de bananes** a bunch of bananas

la **région** NOUN
  region

régional ADJECTIVE
  (MASC PL **régionaux**)
  regional

le **registre** NOUN
  register

la **règle** NOUN
  ① **ruler** ◇ *Il a souligné son nom avec une règle.* He underlined his name with a ruler.
  ② **rule** ◇ *C'est la règle.* That's the rule. ◇ *en règle générale* as a general rule
  + **être en règle** to be in order ◇ *Mes papiers sont en règle.* My papers are in order.
  + **les règles** period (*menstruation*)

le **règlement** NOUN
  rules ◇ *Le règlement est affiché à l'entrée.* The rules are up on the wall by the entrance.

régler VERB
  ① **to adjust** ◇ *Il faut que je règle mon rétroviseur.* I'll have to adjust my rear-view mirror.
  ② **to tune** ◇ *J'ai réglé ma radio sur 476 FM.* I tuned my radio to 476 FM.
  ③ **to set** ◇ *J'ai réglé le thermostat à vingt degrés.* I've set the thermostat to 20 degrees.
  ④ **to solve** ◇ *Le problème est réglé.* The problem's solved.
  ⑤ **to settle** ◇ *Elle a réglé sa facture.* She's settled her bill. ◇ *J'ai réglé Jean-Pierre pour l'essence.* I've settled up with Jean-Pierre for the petrol.

la **réglisse** NOUN
  liquorice

le **règne** NOUN
  reign ◇ *sous le règne de Henri IV* in the reign of Henry IV

régner VERB
  to reign

le **regret** NOUN
  regret
  + **à regret** reluctantly

regretter VERB
  ① **to regret** ◇ *Elle regrette ce qu'elle a dit.* She regrets saying what she did.
  + **Je regrette.** I'm sorry. ◇ *Je regrette, je ne peux pas vous aider.* I'm sorry, I can't help you.
  ② **to miss** ◇ *Je regrette mon ancien travail.* I miss my old job.

regrouper VERB
  to group together ◇ *Nous avons*

regroupé les enfants suivant leur âge. We grouped the children together according to age.
  + **se regrouper** to gather together ◇ *Les agriculteurs se sont regroupés pour constituer un syndicat.* The farmers joined together to form a union.

régulier ADJECTIVE
  (FEM SING **régulière**)
  ① **regular** ◇ *des livraisons régulières* regular deliveries ◇ *des bus réguliers* a regular bus service
  ② **steady** ◇ *à un rythme régulier* at a steady rate
  ③ **scheduled** ◇ *des vols réguliers pour Marseille* scheduled flights to Marseilles

régulièrement ADVERB
  regularly

le **rein** NOUN
  kidney
  + **les reins** back (*of body*) ◇ *J'ai mal aux reins.* My back hurts.

la **reine** NOUN
  queen

rejoindre VERB
  to go back to ◇ *J'ai rejoint mes amis.* I went back to my friends.
  + **Je te rejoins au café.** I'll see you at the café.
  + **se rejoindre** to meet up ◇ *Elles se sont rejointes une heure après.* They met up an hour later.

relâcher VERB
  to release (*prisoner, animal*)
  + **se relâcher** to get slack ◇ *Il se relâche dans son travail.* His work is getting careless.

le **relais** NOUN
  relay race ◇ *le relais quatre fois cent mètres* the 4 x 100 metre relay
  + **prendre le relais** to take over

la **relation** NOUN
  relationship
  + **les relations franco-britanniques** Anglo-French relations

se **relaxer** VERB
  to relax

se **relayer** VERB
  + **se relayer pour faire quelque chose** to take it in turns to do something

le **relevé** NOUN
  + **un relevé de compte** a bank statement

relever VERB
  ① **to collect** ◇ *Je relève les copies dans cinq minutes.* I'll collect the papers in five minutes.
  ② **to react to** ◇ *Je n'ai pas relevé sa*

réflexion. I didn't react to his remark.

- **relever la tête** to look up
- **se relever** to get up ◇ *Il est tombé mais s'est relevé aussitôt.* He fell, but got up immediately.

la **religieuse** NOUN
[1] nun ◇ *Marie est religieuse.* Marie is a nun.
[2] choux cream bun ◇ *des religieuses au chocolat* choux buns with chocolate cream and icing

religieux ADJECTIVE
(FEM **religieuse**)
religious

la **religion** NOUN
religion

relire VERB
[1] to read over ◇ *Il a relu sa copie avant de la rendre.* He read his exam paper over before handing it in.
[2] to read again ◇ *Je voudrais relire ce roman.* I'd like to read this novel again.

remarquable ADJECTIVE
remarkable

la **remarque** NOUN
[1] remark ◇ *Il a fait une remarque désagréable.* He made a nasty remark.
[2] comment ◇ *Avez-vous des remarques à faire?* Have you any comments to make?

remarquer VERB
to notice ◇ *J'ai remarqué qu'elle avait l'air triste.* I noticed she was looking sad.

- **faire remarquer quelque chose à quelqu'un** to point something out to somebody ◇ *Je lui ai fait remarquer que c'était un peu cher.* I pointed out to him that it was rather expensive.
- **Remarque, il n'est pas si bête que ça.** Mind you, he's not as stupid as all that.
- **se remarquer** to be noticeable ◇ *David ne s'est pas rasé ce matin. Ça se remarque.* It's obvious David didn't shave this morning.
- **se faire remarquer** to call attention to oneself

le **remboursement** NOUN
refund

rembourser VERB
to pay back ◇ *Il m'a remboursé l'argent qu'il me devait.* He paid me back the money he owed me.

- **"satisfait ou remboursé"** "satisfaction or your money back"

remercier VERB
to thank ◇ *Je te remercie pour ton*

cadeau. Thank you for your present.

- **remercier quelqu'un d'avoir fait quelque chose** to thank somebody for doing something ◇ *Je vous remercie de m'avoir invité.* Thank you for inviting me.

remettre VERB
[1] to put back on ◇ *Elle a remis son pull.* She put her sweater back on.
[2] to put back ◇ *Il a remis sa veste dans l'armoire.* He put his jacket back in the wardrobe.
[3] to put off ◇ *J'ai dû remettre mon rendez-vous.* I've had to put my appointment off.

- **se remettre** to recover *(from illness)* ◇ *Mélusine s'est bien remise de son opération.* Mélusine has fully recovered from her operation.

le **remonte-pente** NOUN
ski-lift

remonter VERB
[1] to go back up ◇ *Il est remonté au premier étage.* He has gone back up to the first floor.
[2] to go up ◇ *Ils ont remonté la pente.* They went up the hill.
[3] to buck up ◇ *Cette nouvelle m'a un peu remontée.* The news bucked me up a bit.

- **remonter le moral à quelqu'un** to cheer somebody up

le **remords** NOUN
- **avoir des remords** to feel remorse

la **remorque** NOUN
trailer *(of car)*

le **remplaçant** NOUN
supply teacher

la **remplaçante** NOUN
supply teacher

remplacer VERB
to replace ◇ *Il faut remplacer cette ampoule.* We need to replace this bulb. ◇ *Il remplace le prof de maths.* He's replacing the maths teacher.

- **remplacer par** to replace with

rempli ADJECTIVE
busy ◇ *une journée bien remplie* a very busy day

- **rempli de** full of ◇ *La salle était remplie de monde.* The room was full of people.

remplir VERB
[1] to fill up ◇ *Elle a rempli son verre de vin.* She filled her glass with wine.
[2] to fill in ◇ *Tu as rempli ton formulaire?* Have you filled in your form?

- **se remplir** to fill up ◇ *La salle s'est*

R

remplie de monde. The room filled up with people.

remuer VERB

1 **to move** ◇ *Elle a remué le bras.* She moved her arm.

2 **to stir** ◇ *Remuez la sauce pendant deux minutes.* Stir the sauce for two minutes.

• **se remuer** (*informal*) to go to a lot of trouble ◇ *Ils se sont beaucoup remués pour organiser cette soirée.* They went to a lot of trouble organizing this party.

le **renard** NOUN
fox

la **rencontre** NOUN

• **faire la rencontre de quelqu'un** to meet somebody ◇ *J'ai fait la rencontre de personnes intéressantes ce soir.* I met some interesting people this evening.

• **aller à la rencontre de quelqu'un** to go and meet somebody ◇ *Je viendrai à ta rencontre.* I'll come and meet you.

rencontrer VERB
to meet

• **se rencontrer** to meet ◇ *Ils se sont rencontrés il y a deux ans.* They met two years ago.

le **rendez-vous** NOUN

1 **appointment** ◇ *J'ai rendez-vous chez le coiffeur.* I've got an appointment at the hairdresser's. ◇ *prendre rendez-vous avec quelqu'un* to make an appointment with somebody

2 **date** ◇ *Tu sors ce soir?–Oui, j'ai un rendez-vous.* Are you going out tonight?–Yes, I've got a date.

• **donner rendez-vous à quelqu'un** to arrange to meet somebody

rendre VERB

1 **to give back** ◇ *J'ai rendu ses disques à Christine.* I've given Christine her records back.

2 **to take back** ◇ *J'ai rendu mes livres à la bibliothèque.* I've taken my books back to the library.

• **rendre quelqu'un célèbre** to make somebody famous

• **se rendre** to give oneself up ◇ *Le meurtrier s'est rendu à la police.* The murderer gave himself up to the police.

• **se rendre compte de quelque chose** to realize something

le **renfermé** NOUN

• **sentir le renfermé** to smell stuffy

renifler VERB
to sniff

le **renne** NOUN
reindeer

renommé ADJECTIVE
renowned ◇ *La Bretagne est renommée pour ses plages.* Brittany is renowned for its beaches.

renoncer VERB

• **renoncer à** to give up ◇ *Ils ont renoncé à leur projet.* They've given up their plan.

• **renoncer à faire quelque chose** to give up the idea of doing something

renouveler VERB
to renew (*passport, contract*)

• **se renouveler** to happen again ◇ *J'espère que ça ne se renouvellera pas.* I hope that won't happen again.

le **renseignement** NOUN
piece of information ◇ *Il me manque un renseignement.* There's one piece of information I still need.

• **les renseignements (1)** information ◇ *Il m'a donné des renseignements.* He gave me some information.

• **les renseignements (2)** information desk

• **les renseignements (3)** directory inquiries

renseigner VERB

• **renseigner quelqu'un sur quelque chose** to give somebody information about something

• **Est-ce que je peux vous renseigner?** Can I help you?

• **se renseigner** to find out ◇ *Je vais me renseigner pour voir s'il n'y a pas un vol direct.* I'm going to find out if there's a direct flight.

rentable ADJECTIVE
profitable

la **rentrée** NOUN

• **la rentrée (des classes)** the start of the new school year

rentrer VERB

1 **to come in** ◇ *Rentre, tu vas prendre froid.* Come in, you'll catch cold.

2 **to go in** ◇ *Elle est rentrée dans le magasin.* She went into the shop.

3 **to get home** ◇ *Je suis rentré à sept heures hier soir.* I got home at 7 o'clock last night.

4 **to put away** ◇ *Tu as rentré la voiture?* Have you put the car away?

• **rentrer dans** to crash into ◇ *Sa voiture est rentrée dans un arbre.* He crashed into a tree.

• **rentrer dans l'ordre** to get back to normal

la **renverse** NOUN
- **tomber à la renverse** to fall backwards

renverser VERB

  1 **to knock over** ◇ *J'ai renversé mon verre.* I knocked my glass over.

  2 **to knock down** ◇ *Elle a été renversée par une voiture.* She was knocked down by a car.

  3 **to spill** ◇ *Il a renversé de l'eau partout.* He has spilt water everywhere.

- **se renverser** to fall over (*glass, vase*)

renvoyer VERB

  1 **to send back** ◇ *Je t'ai renvoyé ton courrier.* I've sent your mail back to you.

  2 **to dismiss** ◇ *On a renvoyé deux employés.* Two employees have been dismissed.

la **réparation** NOUN

  repair

réparer VERB

  to repair

repartir VERB

  to set off again ◇ *Il s'est arrêté pour déjeuner avant de repartir.* He stopped for lunch before setting off again. ◇ *Maree était là tout à l'heure, mais elle est repartie.* Maree was here a moment ago, but she's gone again.

- **repartir à zéro** to start again from scratch

le **repas** NOUN

  meal

- **le repas de midi** lunch
- **le repas du soir** dinner

repasser VERB

  1 **to come back** ◇ *Je repasserai demain.* I'll come back tomorrow.

  2 **to go back** ◇ *Je dois repasser au magasin.* I've got to go back to the shop.

  3 **to iron** ◇ *J'ai repassé ma chemise.* I've ironed my shirt.

  4 **to resit** ◇ *Elle doit repasser son examen de maths.* She's got to resit her maths exam.

repérer VERB

  to spot ◇ *J'ai repéré deux fautes.* I spotted two mistakes.

- **se repérer** to find one's way around ◇ *J'ai du mal à me repérer de nuit.* I have difficulty finding my way around when it's dark.

répéter VERB

  1 **to repeat** ◇ *Elle répète toujours la même chose.* She keeps repeating the same thing.

  2 **to rehearse** ◇ *Les acteurs répètent une scène.* The actors are rehearsing a scene.

- **se répéter** to happen again ◇ *J'espère que cela ne se répétera pas!* I hope this won't happen again!

la **répétition** NOUN

  1 **repetition** ◇ *Il y a beaucoup de répétitions dans ce texte.* There's a lot of repetition in this text.

- **des grèves à répétition** repeated strikes

  2 **rehearsal** ◇ *Ils ont une répétition cet après-midi.* They've got a rehearsal this afternoon.

- **la répétition générale** the dress rehearsal

le **répondeur** NOUN

  answering machine

répondre VERB

  to answer ◇ *répondre à quelqu'un* to answer somebody

la **réponse** NOUN

  answer ◇ *C'est la bonne réponse.* That's the right answer.

le **reportage** NOUN

  1 **report** ◇ *J'ai vu ce reportage aux informations.* I saw that report on the news.

  2 **story** ◇ *J'ai lu ce reportage dans "La Gazette".* I read that story in "La Gazette".

le **reporter** NOUN

  reporter ◇ *Christian est reporter.* Christian is a reporter.

le **repos** NOUN

  rest

reposer VERB

  to put back down ◇ *Elle a reposé son verre sur la table.* She put her glass back down on the table.

- **se reposer** to have a rest ◇ *Tu pourras te reposer demain.* You'll be able to have a rest tomorrow.
- **se reposer sur quelqu'un** to rely on somebody

repousser VERB

  1 **to grow again** ◇ *Ses cheveux ont repoussé.* Her hair has grown again.

  2 **to postpone** ◇ *Le voyage est repoussé.* The trip's been postponed.

reprendre VERB

  1 **to take back** ◇ *Il a repris son livre.* He's taken his book back.

  2 **to go back to** ◇ *Elle a repris le travail.* She went back to work.

  3 **to start again** ◇ *La réunion reprendra à deux heures.* The meeting will start again at 2 o'clock.

- **reprendre du pain** to take more bread
- **reprendre la route** to set off again

R

- **reprendre son souffle** to get one's breath back

le **représentant** NOUN

rep ◇ *Il est représentant chez Harper Collins.* He's a rep for Harper Collins.

la **représentante** NOUN

rep ◇ *Elle est représentante.* She'a a sales rep.

la **représentation** NOUN

performance ◇ *la dernière représentation d'une pièce* the final performance of a play

représenter VERB

to show ◇ *Le tableau représente un enfant et un chat.* The picture shows a child with a cat.

- **se représenter** to arise again ◇ *Cette occasion ne se représentera pas.* This opportunity won't arise again.

le **reproche** NOUN

- **faire des reproches à quelqu'un** to reproach somebody

reprocher VERB

- **reprocher quelque chose à quelqu'un** to reproach somebody for something ◇ *Il m'a reproché mon retard.* He reproached me for being late.
- **Qu'est-ce que tu lui reproches?** What have you got against him?

la **reproduction** NOUN

reproduction

reproduire VERB

to reproduce

- **se reproduire** to happen again ◇ *Je te promets que ça ne se reproduira pas!* I promise it won't happen again!

républicain ADJECTIVE

republican

la **république** NOUN

republic ◇ *la République française* the French Republic

répugnant ADJECTIVE

repulsive

la **réputation** NOUN

reputation

le **requin** NOUN

shark

le **RER** NOUN

Greater Paris high-speed train service

le **réseau** NOUN

(PL les **réseaux**)

network

la **réservation** NOUN

reservation

la **réserve** NOUN

stock ◇ *avoir quelque chose en réserve* to have a stock of something

- **mettre quelque chose en réserve** to put something aside

réserver VERB

[1] **to reserve** ◇ *Cette table est réservée.* This table is reserved.

[2] **to book** ◇ *Nous avons réservé une chambre.* We've booked a room.

[3] **to save** ◇ *Je t'ai réservé une part de gâteau.* I've saved you a piece of cake.

le **réservoir** NOUN

petrol tank

la **résidence** NOUN

block of flats

- **une résidence secondaire** a second home

résistant ADJECTIVE

[1] **hard-wearing** ◇ *Ce tissu est résistant.* This fabric is hard-wearing.

[2] **robust** ◇ *Il est très résistant.* He's very robust.

résister VERB

to resist

résolu ADJECTIVE

- **Le problème est résolu.** The problem's solved.

résoudre VERB

to solve

le **respect** NOUN

respect

respecter VERB

to respect

la **respiration** NOUN

breathing

respirer VERB

to breathe

la **responsabilité** NOUN

responsibility

responsable ADJECTIVE

see also responsable NOUN

responsible ◇ *être responsable de quelque chose* to be responsible for something

le/la **responsable** NOUN

see also responsable ADJECTIVE

[1] **person in charge** ◇ *Je voudrais parler au responsable.* I'd like to speak to the person in charge.

[2] **person responsible** ◇ *Il faut punir les responsables.* Those responsible must be punished.

ressembler VERB

- **ressembler à (1)** to look like ◇ *Elle ne ressemble pas à sa sœur.* She doesn't look like her sister.
- **ressembler à (2)** to be like ◇ *Ça ressemble à un conte de fées.* It's like a fairy tale.
- **se ressembler (1)** to look alike ◇ *Les deux frères ne se ressemblent pas.* The two brothers don't look alike.

* **se rassembler (2)** to be alike ◇ *Ces deux pays ne se ressemblent pas.* These two countries aren't alike.

le **ressort** NOUN
  spring (*metal*) ◇ *Le ressort est cassé.* The spring is broken.

ressortir VERB
  to go out again

le **restaurant** NOUN
  restaurant

le **reste** NOUN
  rest
* **un reste de poulet** some left-over chicken
* **les restes** the left-overs

rester VERB
  1 **to stay** ◇ *Je reste à la maison ce week-end.* I'm staying at home this weekend.
  2 **to be left** ◇ *Il reste du pain.* There's some bread left. ◇ *Il me reste assez de temps.* I still have enough time.
* **Il ne me reste plus qu'à...** I've just got to... ◇ *Il ne me reste plus qu'à ranger mes affaires.* I've just got to put my things away.
* **Restons-en là.** Let's leave it at that.

le **résultat** NOUN
  result ◇ *le résultat des examens* the exam results

le **résumé** NOUN
  summary

résumer VERB
  to summarize

le **retard** NOUN
  delay ◇ *un retard de livraison* a delay in delivery
* **avoir du retard** to be late
* **être en retard de deux heures** to be two hours late
* **prendre du retard** to be delayed

retarder VERB
  1 **to be slow** ◇ *Ma montre retarde.* My watch is slow.
  2 **to put back** ◇ *Je dois retarder la pendule d'une heure.* I've got to put the clock back an hour.
* **être retardé** to be delayed ◇ *J'ai été retardé par un coup de téléphone.* I was held up by a phone call.

retenir VERB
  1 **to remember** ◇ *Tu as retenu leur adresse?* Do you remember their address?
  2 **to book** ◇ *J'ai retenu une chambre à l'hôtel.* I've booked a room at the hotel.
* **retenir son souffle** to hold one's breath

retenu ADJECTIVE
  1 **reserved** ◇ *Cette place est retenue.* This seat is reserved.
  2 **held up** ◇ *J'ai été retenu par un coup de téléphone.* I was held up by a phone call.

la **retenue** NOUN
  detention ◇ *Gerry est en retenue.* Gerry's in detention.

retirer VERB
  1 **to withdraw** ◇ *Elle a retiré de l'argent.* She withdrew some money.
  2 **to take off** ◇ *Il a retiré son pull.* He took off his sweater.

le **retour** NOUN
  return
* **être de retour** to be back ◇ *Je serai de retour la semaine prochaine.* I'll be back next week.

retourner VERB
  1 **to go back** ◇ *Est-ce que tu es retourné à Londres?* Have you been back to London?
  2 **to turn over** ◇ *Elle a retourné la crêpe.* She turned the pancake over. ◇ *Il a retourné la poubelle.* He turned the bin upside down.
* **se retourner (1)** to turn round ◇ *Janet s'est retournée.* Janet turned round.
* **se retourner (2)** to turn over ◇ *La voiture s'est retournée.* The car turned over.

la **retraite** NOUN
* **être à la retraite** to be retired
* **prendre sa retraite** to retire

retraité ADJECTIVE
  see also retraité NOUN
  retired ◇ *Mon oncle est maintenant retraité.* My uncle's now retired.

le **retraité** NOUN
  see also retraité ADJECTIVE
  pensioner

la **retraitée** NOUN
  pensioner

rétrécir VERB
  to shrink ◇ *Son pull a rétréci au lavage.* Her sweater shrank in the wash.
* **se rétrécir** to get narrower ◇ *La rue se rétrécit.* The street gets narrower.

retrouver VERB
  1 **to find** ◇ *J'ai retrouvé mon portefeuille.* I've found my wallet.
  2 **to meet up with** ◇ *Je te retrouve au café à trois heures.* I'll meet you at the café at 3 o'clock.
* **se retrouver (1)** to meet up ◇ *Ils se*

R

sont retrouvés devant le cinéma. They met up in front of the cinema.
- **se retrouver (2)** to find one's way around ○ *Je n'arrive pas à me retrouver.* I can't find my way around.

le **rétroviseur** NOUN
  rear-view mirror

la **réunion** NOUN
  meeting

se **réunir** VERB
  to meet ○ *Ils se sont réunis à cinq heures.* They met at 5 o'clock.

réussi ADJECTIVE
  successful ○ *une soirée très réussie* a very successful party
- **être réussi** to be a success ○ *Le repas était très réussi.* The meal was delicious.

réussir VERB
  to be successful ○ *Tous ses enfants ont très bien réussi.* All her children are very successful.
- **réussir à faire quelque chose** to succeed in doing something
- **réussir à un examen** to pass an exam

la **réussite** NOUN
  success

la **revanche** NOUN
  return match
- **prendre sa revanche** to get one's own back ○ *Il a pris sa revanche en refusant de lui prêter son vélo.* He got his own back by refusing to lend him his bike.
- **en revanche** on the other hand ○ *C'est cher mais en revanche c'est de la bonne qualité.* It is dear but on the other hand it's good quality.

le **rêve** NOUN
  dream
- **de rêve** fantastic ○ *des vacances de rêve* fantastic holidays

le **réveil** NOUN
  alarm clock

le **réveille-matin** NOUN
  (PL les **réveille-matin**)
  alarm clock

réveiller VERB
  to wake up ○ *réveiller quelqu'un* to wake somebody up
- **se réveiller** to wake up

le **réveillon** NOUN
- **le réveillon du premier de l'an** New Year's Eve celebrations
- **le réveillon de Noël** Christmas Eve celebrations

réveillonner VERB
  ① **to celebrate New Year's Eve**
  ② **to celebrate Christmas Eve**

revenir VERB
  to come back ○ *Reviens vite!* Come back soon! ○ *Son nom m'est revenu cinq minutes après.* His name came back to me five minutes later.
- **Ça revient au même.** It comes to the same thing.
- **Ça revient cher.** It costs a lot.
- **Je n'en reviens pas!** I can't get over it!
- **revenir sur ses pas** to retrace one's steps

le **revenu** NOUN
  income

rêver VERB
  to dream
- **rêver de quelque chose** to dream of something ○ *J'ai rêvé de mes vacances cette nuit.* I dreamt about my holidays last night.

le **réverbère** NOUN
  street lamp

le **revers** NOUN
  ① **backhand** ○ *Becker a un excellent revers.* Becker has an excellent backhand.
  ② **lapel** (*of jacket*)
- **le revers de la médaille** the other side of the coin

revient VERB *see* **revenir**

réviser VERB
  ① **to revise** ○ *Je dois réviser mon anglais.* I've got to revise my English.
  ② **to service** ○ *Je dois faire réviser ma voiture.* I must get my car serviced.

la **révision** NOUN
  revision

revoir VERB
  ① **to see again** ○ *J'ai revu Sophie hier soir.* I saw Sophie again last night.
  ② **to revise** ○ *Il est en train de revoir sa géographie.* He's revising his geography.
- **au revoir** goodbye

la **révolution** NOUN
  revolution ○ *la Révolution française* the French Revolution

le **revolver** NOUN
  revolver

la **revue** NOUN
  magazine

le **rez-de-chaussée** NOUN
  ground floor ○ *au rez-de-chaussée* on the ground floor

le **Rhin** NOUN
  Rhine

le **rhinocéros** NOUN
  rhinoceros

le **Rhône** NOUN
  Rhone

la **rhubarbe** NOUN
  rhubarb

le **rhum** NOUN
  rum

le **rhume** NOUN
  cold ◇ *J'ai attrapé un rhume.* I've caught a cold.
- **un rhume de cerveau** a head cold
- **le rhume des foins** hay fever

ri VERB *see* **rire**
- **Nous avons bien ri.** We had a good laugh.

riche ADJECTIVE
  1 **well-off** ◇ *Sa famille est très riche.* His family's very well-off.
  2 **rich** ◇ *riche en vitamines* rich in vitamins

le **rideau** NOUN
  (PL les **rideaux**)
  curtain ◇ *tirer les rideaux* to draw the curtains

ridicule ADJECTIVE
  ridiculous ◇ *Je trouve ça complètement ridicule.* I think that's absolutely ridiculous.

rien PRONOUN
  see also **rien** NOUN
  1 **nothing** ◇ *Qu'est-ce que tu as acheté?–Rien.* What have you bought? –Nothing. ◇ *Ça n'a rien à voir.* It has nothing to do with it.
- **rien d'intéressant** nothing interesting
- **rien d'autre** nothing else
- **rien du tout** nothing at all
  2 **anything** ◇ *Il n'a rien dit.* He didn't say anything.
- **rien que (1)** just ◇ *rien que pour lui faire plaisir* just to please him ◇ *Rien que la voiture coûte un million.* The car alone costs a million.
- **rien que (2)** nothing but ◇ *rien que la vérité* nothing but the truth
- **De rien!** Not at all! ◇ *Merci beaucoup!–De rien!* Thank you very much!–Not at all!

le **rien** NOUN
  see also **rien** PRONOUN
- **pour un rien** at the slightest thing ◇ *Il se met en colère pour un rien.* He loses his temper over the slightest thing.
- **en un rien de temps** in no time at all

rigoler VERB (*informal*)
  1 **to laugh** ◇ *Elle a rigolé en le voyant tomber.* She laughed when she saw him fall.
  2 **to have fun** ◇ *On a bien rigolé hier soir.* We had good fun last night.
  3 **to be joking** ◇ *Ne te fâche pas, je*

rigolais. Don't get upset, I was only joking.
- **pour rigoler** for a laugh

rigolo ADJECTIVE (*informal*)
  (FEM SING **rigolote**)
  funny

rincer VERB
  to rinse

rire VERB
  see also **rire** NOUN
  to laugh ◇ *Ce film m'a vraiment fait rire.* That film really made me laugh. ◇ *Nous avons bien ri.* We had a good laugh.
- **pour rire** for a laugh

le **rire** NOUN
  see also **rire** VERB
  laughter ◇ *Il a un rire communicatif.* He has an infectious laugh.

le **risque** NOUN
  1 **risk** ◇ *prendre des risques* to take risks ◇ *à tes risques et périls* at your own risk
  2 **danger** ◇ *Il n'y a pas de risque qu'il le sache.* There's no danger of him finding out.

risqué ADJECTIVE
  risky

risquer VERB
  to risk
- **Ça ne risque rien.** It's quite safe.
- **Il risque de se tuer.** He could get himself killed.
- **C'est ce qui risque de se passer.** That's what might well happen.

le **rivage** NOUN
  shore

la **rivière** NOUN
  river

le **riz** NOUN
  rice

le **RMI** NOUN
  Income Support ◇ *Il touche le RMI.* He's on Income Support.

RN ABBREVIATION (= *route nationale*)
  A road

la **robe** NOUN
  dress
- **une robe de soirée** an evening dress
- **une robe de mariée** a wedding dress
- **une robe de chambre** a dressing gown

le **robinet** NOUN
  tap

le **robot** NOUN
  robot

la **roche** NOUN
  rock (*stone*)

le **rocher** NOUN
  rock

R

le **rock** NOUN
  rock (*music*) ◇ *un chanteur de rock* a rock singer

les **rognons** MASC NOUN
  kidneys (*in cooking*)

le **roi** NOUN
  king
  - **le jour des Rois** Twelfth Night

le **rôle** NOUN
  role

romain ADJECTIVE
  Roman ◇ *des ruines romaines* Roman remains

le **roman** NOUN
  novel
  - **un roman policier** a detective story
  - **un roman d'espionnage** a spy story

le **romancier** NOUN
  novelist

rompre VERB
  [1] to split up ◇ *Paul et Justine ont rompu.* Paul and Justine have split up.
  [2] to break off ◇ *Ils ont rompu leurs fiançailles.* They've broken off their engagement.

les **ronces** FEM NOUN
  brambles

ronchonner VERB (*informal*)
  to grouse

rond ADJECTIVE
  see also rond NOUN
  [1] round ◇ *La Terre est ronde.* The earth is round.
  - **ouvrir des yeux ronds** to stare in amazement
  [2] chubby ◇ *Il a les joues rondes.* He has chubby cheeks.
  [3] drunk ◇ *Il est complètement rond.* (*informal*) He's completely drunk.

le **rond** NOUN
  see also rond ADJECTIVE
  circle ◇ *Elle a dessiné un rond sur le sable.* She drew a circle in the sand.
  - **en rond** in a circle ◇ *Ils se sont assis en rond.* They sat down in a circle.
  - **tourner en rond** to go round in circles
  - **Je n'ai plus un rond.** (*informal*) I haven't a penny left.

la **rondelle** NOUN
  slice ◇ *une rondelle de citron* a slice of lemon

le **rond-point** NOUN
  (PL les **ronds-points**)
  roundabout ◇ *La voiture s'est arrêtée au rond-point.* The car stopped at the roundabout.

ronfler VERB
  to snore

le **rosbif** NOUN
  roast beef

la **rose** NOUN
  see also rose ADJECTIVE
  rose

rose ADJECTIVE
  see also rose NOUN
  pink

le **rosé** NOUN
  rosé (*wine*) ◇ *Je prendrai un verre de rosé.* I'll have a glass of rosé.

le **rosier** NOUN
  rosebush

le **rôti** NOUN
  roast meat
  - **un rôti de bœuf** a joint of beef

rôtir VERB
  to roast ◇ *faire rôtir quelque chose* to roast something

la **roue** NOUN
  wheel ◇ *une roue de secours* a spare wheel

rouge ADJECTIVE
  see also rouge NOUN
  red

le **rouge** NOUN
  see also rouge ADJECTIVE
  [1] red ◇ *Le rouge est ma couleur préférée.* Red is my favourite colour.
  [2] red wine ◇ *un verre de rouge* a glass of red wine
  - **passer au rouge (1)** to change to red ◇ *Le feu est passé au rouge.* The light changed to red.
  - **passer au rouge (2)** to go through a red light ◇ *Jean-Pierre est passé au rouge.* Jean-Pierre went through a red light.
  - **un rouge à lèvres** a lipstick

la **rougeole** NOUN
  measles

rougir VERB
  [1] to blush ◇ *Il a rougi en me voyant.* He blushed when he saw me.
  [2] to flush ◇ *Il a rougi de colère.* He flushed with anger.

la **rouille** NOUN
  rust

rouillé ADJECTIVE
  rusty

rouiller VERB
  to go rusty

roulant ADJECTIVE
  - **un fauteuil roulant** a wheelchair
  - **une table roulante** a trolley

le **rouleau** NOUN
  (PL les **rouleaux**)
  roll ◇ *un rouleau de papier peint* a roll of wallpaper

- **un rouleau à pâtisserie** a rolling pin

rouler VERB

1. **to go** ◇ *Le train roulait à 250 km/h.* The train was going at 250 km an hour.
2. **to drive** ◇ *Il a roulé sans s'arrêter.* He drove without stopping.
3. **to roll** ◇ *Gilles a roulé une cigarette.* Gilles rolled a cigarette.
4. **to roll up** ◇ *Il a roulé le tapis.* He rolled the carpet up.
5. **to con** ◇ *Ils se sont fait rouler.* (informal) They were conned.

- **Alors, ça roule?** (informal) How's it going?

la **Roumanie** NOUN

Romania

le **rouquin** NOUN (informal)

redhead

la **rouquine** NOUN (informal)

redhead

rousse ADJECTIVE see **roux**

la **rousse** NOUN

redhead

la **route** NOUN

1. **road** ◇ *au bord de la route* at the roadside

- **une route nationale** an A road

2. **way** ◇ *Je ne connais pas la route.* I don't know the way.

- **Il y a trois heures de route.** It's a 3-hour journey.

- **en route** on the way ◇ *Ils se sont arrêtés en route pour pique-niquer.* They stopped on the way for a picnic.

- **mettre en route** to start up ◇ *Il a mis le moteur en route.* He started the engine up.

- **se mettre en route** to set off ◇ *Il s'est mis en route à cinq heures.* He set off at 5 o'clock.

le **routier** NOUN

1. **lorry driver** ◇ *Son père est routier.* His father's a lorry driver.

2. **transport café** ◇ *Nous avons mangé dans un routier.* We ate in a transport café.

la **routine** NOUN

routine

roux ADJECTIVE

(FEM SING **rousse**)

see also **roux** NOUN

1. **red** ◇ *Harry a les cheveux roux.* Harry has red hair.

2. **red-haired** ◇ *Isobel est rousse.* Isobel's red-haired.

le **roux** NOUN

see also **roux** ADJECTIVE

redhead

royal ADJECTIVE

(MASC PL **royaux**)

royal

le **royaume** NOUN

kingdom

- **le Royaume-Uni** the United Kingdom

le **ruban** NOUN

ribbon

- **le ruban adhésif** adhesive tape

la **rubéole** NOUN

German measles

la **ruche** NOUN

hive

rudement ADVERB (informal)

terribly ◇ *C'était rudement bon.* It was terribly good.

la **rue** NOUN

street

la **ruelle** NOUN

alley

le **rugby** NOUN

rugby ◇ *Yann joue au rugby.* Yann plays rugby.

la **ruine** NOUN

ruin ◇ *les ruines de la cathédrale* the ruins of the cathedral

ruiner VERB

to ruin

le **ruisseau** NOUN

(PL les **ruisseaux**)

stream

la **rumeur** NOUN

rumour

la **rupture** NOUN

break-up

la **ruse** NOUN

trickery ◇ *une ruse* a trick

rusé ADJECTIVE

cunning

russe ADJECTIVE, NOUN

Russian ◇ *Il parle russe.* He speaks Russian.

- **un Russe** a Russian (man)

- **une Russe** a Russian (woman)

- **les Russes** the Russians

la **Russie** NOUN

Russia

le **rythme** NOUN

1. **rhythm** ◇ *J'aime le rythme de cette musique.* I like the beat of this music.

2. **pace** ◇ *Il marche à un bon rythme.* He walks at a good pace.

S

s' PRONOUN *see* **se**

sa ADJECTIVE

[1] **his** ◇ *Paul est allé voir sa grand-mère.* Paul's gone to see his grandmother.

[2] **her** ◇ *Elle a embrassé sa mère.* She kissed her mother.

le **sable** NOUN

sand

- **des sables mouvants** quicksand

le **sablé** NOUN

shortbread biscuit

le **sabot** NOUN

[1] **clog**

[2] **hoof** (*of horse*)

le **sac** NOUN

bag

- **un sac de voyage** a travel bag
- **un sac de couchage** a sleeping bag
- **un sac à main** a handbag
- **un sac à dos** a rucksack

le **sachet** NOUN

sachet (*of sugar, coffee*)

- **du potage en sachet** packet soup
- **un sachet de thé** a tea bag

la **sacoche** NOUN

bag

- **une sacoche de bicyclette** a saddlebag

sacré ADJECTIVE

sacred

sage ADJECTIVE

[1] **good** (*well-behaved*) ◇ *Sois sage.* Be good.

[2] **wise** (*sensible*) ◇ *Il serait plus sage d'attendre.* It would be wiser to wait.

la **sagesse** NOUN

wisdom ◇ *Il a eu la sagesse de ne pas y aller.* He wisely didn't go.

- **une dent de sagesse** a wisdom tooth

le **Sagittaire** NOUN

Sagittarius ◇ *Michèle est Sagittaire.* Michèle is Sagittarius.

saignant ADJECTIVE

rare (*meat*)

saigner VERB

to bleed

- **saigner du nez** to have a nosebleed

sain ADJECTIVE

healthy

- **sain et sauf** safe and sound

saint ADJECTIVE

see also **saint** NOUN

holy ◇ *la semaine sainte* Holy Week ◇ *le Saint-Esprit* the Holy Spirit

- **la Sainte Vierge** the Blessed Virgin

- **le vendredi saint** Good Friday

le **saint** NOUN

see also **saint** ADJECTIVE

saint

la **sainte** NOUN

saint

sais VERB *see* **savoir**

- **Je ne sais pas.** I don't know.

saisir VERB

to take hold of

- **saisir l'occasion de faire quelque chose** to seize the opportunity to do something

la **saison** NOUN

season ◇ *Ce n'est pas la saison des fraises.* Strawberries are out of season. ◇ *un temps de saison* seasonable weather

- **la saison des vendanges** harvest time

sait VERB *see* **savoir**

- **Il sait que...** He knows that...

la **salade** NOUN

[1] **lettuce**

[2] **salad** ◇ *une salade composée* a mixed salad ◇ *une salade de fruits* a fruit salad

le **saladier** NOUN

salad bowl

le **salaire** NOUN

salary

le **salarié** NOUN

salaried employee

la **salariée** NOUN

salaried employee

le **salaud** NOUN (*rude*)

bastard

sale ADJECTIVE

dirty

salé ADJECTIVE

[1] **salty** ◇ *La soupe est trop salée.* The soup's too salty.

[2] **salted** ◇ *du beurre salé* salted butter

[3] **savoury** ◇ *des biscuits salés* savoury biscuits

saler VERB

to put salt in ◇ *J'ai oublié de saler la soupe.* I forgot to put salt in the soup.

la **saleté** NOUN

dirt ◇ *J'ai horreur de la saleté.* I hate dirt. ◇ *Il y a une saleté sur ta chemise.* There's some dirt on your shirt.

- **faire des saletés** to make a mess

salir VERB

- **salir quelque chose** to get something dirty

- **se salir** to get oneself dirty ◦ *Mets un tablier, sinon tu vas te salir.* Put on an apron or you'll get yourself dirty.

la **salle** NOUN
- 1 **room**
- 2 **audience** ◦ *Toute la salle l'a applaudi.* The whole audience applauded him.
- 3 **ward** (*in hospital*) ◦ *Il est à la salle douze.* He's in Ward 12.
- **la salle à manger** the dining room
- **la salle de séjour** the living room
- **la salle de bains** the bathroom
- **la salle d'attente** the waiting room
- **une salle de classe** a classroom
- **une salle de concert** a concert hall
- **la salle d'embarquement** the departure lounge

le **salon** NOUN
- **lounge**
- **un salon de thé** a tearoom
- **un salon de coiffure** a hair salon
- **un salon de beauté** a beauty salon

la **salope** NOUN (*rude*)
- **bitch**

la **salopette** NOUN
- 1 **dungarees**
- 2 **overalls**

saluer VERB
- **saluer quelqu'un (1)** to say hello to somebody ◦ *Je l'ai croisé dans la rue et il m'a salué.* I met him in the street and he said hello.
- **saluer quelqu'un (2)** to say goodbye to somebody ◦ *Il nous a salués et il est parti.* He said goodbye and left.

salut EXCLAMATION (*informal*)
- **Hi!**

le **samedi** NOUN
- 1 **Saturday** ◦ *Aujourd'hui, nous sommes samedi.* It's Saturday today.
- 2 **on Saturday** ◦ *Nous sommes allés au cinéma samedi.* We went to the cinema on Saturday.
- **le samedi** on Saturdays ◦ *Le magasin ferme à dix-huit heures le samedi.* The shop closes at 6 p.m. on Saturdays.
- **tous les samedis** every Saturday
- **samedi dernier** last Saturday
- **samedi prochain** next Saturday

le **SAMU** NOUN
- **ambulance service**

la **sandale** NOUN
- **sandal**

le **sang** NOUN
- **blood**
- **en sang** covered in blood

le **sang-froid** NOUN

- **garder son sang-froid** to keep calm
- **perdre son sang-froid** to lose one's cool
- **faire quelque chose de sang-froid** to do something in cold blood

le **sanglier** NOUN
- **wild boar**

le **sanglot** NOUN
- **éclater en sanglots** to burst into tears

la **sanisette** ® NOUN
- **Superloo** ®

sans PREPOSITION
- **without** ◦ *Elle est venue sans son frère.* She came without her brother.
- **un pull sans manches** a sleeveless sweater

le/la **sans-abri** NOUN
- (PL les **sans-abri**)
- **homeless person** ◦ *les sans-abri* the homeless

sans-gêne ADJECTIVE
- **inconsiderate**

la **santé** NOUN
- **health** ◦ *en bonne santé* in good health
- **Santé!** Cheers!

saoudien ADJECTIVE, NOUN
- (FEM SING **saoudienne**)
- **Saudi Arabian**
- **un Saoudien** a Saudi Arabian (*man*)
- **une Saoudienne** a Saudi Arabian (*woman*)

le **sapeur-pompier** NOUN
- (PL les **sapeurs-pompiers**)
- **fireman**
- **les sapeurs-pompiers** the fire brigade

le **sapin** NOUN
- **fir tree**
- **un sapin de Noël** a Christmas tree

la **Sardaigne** NOUN
- **Sardinia**

satisfaire VERB
- **to satisfy**

satisfaisant ADJECTIVE
- **satisfactory**

satisfait ADJECTIVE
- **satisfied** ◦ *être satisfait de quelque chose* to be satisfied with something

la **sauce** NOUN
- 1 **sauce**
- 2 **gravy**

la **saucisse** NOUN
- **sausage**

le **saucisson** NOUN
- **salami**

sauf PREPOSITION
- **except** ◦ *Tout le monde est venu sauf lui.* Everyone came except him.
- **sauf si** unless ◦ *Nous irons*

S

pique-niquer, *sauf s'il fait mauvais.*
We'll go for a picnic, unless the
weather's bad.
- **sauf que** except that ⋄ *Tout s'est
bien passé, sauf que nous sommes
arrivés en retard.* Everything went OK,
except that we arrived late.

le **saumon** NOUN
salmon

saur ADJECTIVE
- **un hareng saur** a kipper

le **saut** NOUN
jump
- **le saut en longueur** the long jump
- **le saut en hauteur** the high jump
- **le saut à la perche** the pole vault
- **le saut à l'élastique** bungee jumping
- **un saut périlleux** a somersault

sauter VERB
to jump ⋄ *Nous avons sauté
par-dessus la barrière.* We jumped
over the gate.
- **sauter à la corde** to skip (*with a rope*)
- **faire sauter quelque chose** to blow
something up ⋄ *On a fait sauter le
commissariat de police la nuit dernière.*
The police station was blown up last
night.

la **sauterelle** NOUN
grasshopper

sauvage ADJECTIVE
1 **wild** ⋄ *les animaux sauvages*
wild animals ⋄ *faire du camping
sauvage* to camp in the wild
- **une région sauvage** an unspoiled area
2 **shy** ⋄ *Il est un peu sauvage.* He's
a bit shy.

sauver VERB
to save
- **se sauver (1)** to run away ⋄ *Il s'est
sauvé à toutes jambes.* He ran away as
fast as he could.
- **se sauver (2)** (*informal*) to be off
⋄ *Allez, je me sauve!* Right, I'm off.

le **sauvetage** NOUN
rescue

le **sauveur** NOUN
saviour

savais, savait VERB *see* **savoir**
- **Je ne savais pas qu'il devait venir.** I
didn't know he was going to come.

le **savant** NOUN
scientist

savent VERB *see* **savoir**
- **Ils ne savent pas ce qu'ils veulent.**
They don't know what they want.

la **saveur** NOUN
flavour

savez VERB *see* **savoir**

- **Est-ce que vous savez où elle habite?**
Do you know where she lives?

savoir VERB
to know ⋄ *Je ne sais pas où il est
allé.* I don't know where he's gone.
⋄ *Nous ne savons pas s'il est bien
arrivé.* We don't know if he's arrived
safely. ⋄ *Tu savais que Canberra était
la capitale de l'Australie?* Did you know
that Canberra was the capital of
Australia? ⋄ *Il ne sait pas ce qu'il va
faire ce week-end.* He doesn't know
what he's going to do this weekend.
- **Tu sais nager?** Can you swim?

le **savon** NOUN
soap

la **savonnette** NOUN
bar of soap

savons VERB *see* **savoir**

savoureux ADJECTIVE
(FEM SING **savoureuse**)
tasty

le **saxo** NOUN (*informal*)
see also **la saxo**
1 sax
2 sax player

la **saxo** NOUN (*informal*)
see also **le saxo**
sax player

le **scandale** NOUN
scandal
- **faire scandale** to cause a scandal
⋄ *Ce film a fait scandale.* The film
caused a scandal.

scandaleux ADJECTIVE
(FEM SING **scandaleuse**)
outrageous

le/la **Scandinave** NOUN
Scandinavian

scandinave ADJECTIVE
Scandinavian

la **Scandinavie** NOUN
Scandinavia

le **scarabée** NOUN
beetle

la **scène** NOUN
scene ⋄ *une scène d'amour* a love
scene ⋄ *la scène du crime* the scene of
the crime ⋄ *Il m'a fait une scène.* He
made a scene.
- **une scène de ménage** a domestic row

sceptique ADJECTIVE
sceptical

le **schéma** NOUN
diagram

schématique ADJECTIVE
- **l'explication schématique d'une
théorie** the broad outline of a
theory

‣ **Cette interprétation est un peu trop schématique.** This interpretation is a bit oversimplified.

la **scie** NOUN

saw

‣ **une scie à métaux** a hacksaw

la **science** NOUN

science

‣ **les sciences physiques** physics
‣ **les sciences naturelles** biology
‣ **sciences po** (*informal*) politics ◇ *Mon frère fait sciences po à Paris.* My brother is studying politics in Paris.

scientifique ADJECTIVE

see also scientifique NOUN

scientific

le/la **scientifique** NOUN

see also scientifique ADJECTIVE

1 **scientist**
2 **science student**

scier VERB

to saw

scolaire ADJECTIVE

school ◇ *l'année scolaire* the school year ◇ *les vacances scolaires* the school holidays ◇ *mon livret scolaire* my school report

le **Scorpion** NOUN

Scorpio ◇ *Catherine est Scorpion.* Catherine is Scorpio.

le **Scotch** ® NOUN

adhesive tape

le **scrupule** NOUN

scruple

sculpter VERB

to sculpt

le **sculpteur** NOUN

sculptor

la **sculpture** NOUN

sculpture

le/la **SDF** NOUN (= *sans domicile fixe*)

homeless person

‣ **les SDF** the homeless

se PRONOUN

se forms part of reflexive constructions.

1 **himself** ◇ *Il se regarde dans la glace.* He's looking at himself in the mirror.
2 **herself** ◇ *Elle se regarde dans la glace.* She's looking at herself in the mirror.
3 **itself** ◇ *Le chien s'est fait mal.* The dog hurt itself.
4 **oneself** ◇ *se regarder dans une glace* to look at oneself in a mirror
5 **themselves** ◇ *Ils se sont regardés dans la glace.* They looked at themselves in the mirror.

se changes to **s'** *before a vowel and most words beginning with "h".*

◇ *Elle s'admire dans sa nouvelle robe.* She's admiring herself in her new dress.

6 **each other** ◇ *Ils s'aiment.* They love each other.

la **séance** NOUN

1 **session** ◇ *une séance de rééducation* a physiotherapy session
2 **showing** (*at the cinema*) ◇ *La prochaine séance est à dix-neuf heures.* The next showing is at 7 p.m.

le **seau** NOUN

(PL les **seaux**)

bucket

sec ADJECTIVE

(FEM SING **sèche**)

1 **dry** ◇ *Mon jean n'est pas encore sec.* My jeans aren't dry yet.
2 **dried** ◇ *des figues sèches* dried figs

le **sèche-cheveux** NOUN

(PL les **sèche-cheveux**)

hair dryer

le **sèche-linge** NOUN

(PL les **sèche-linge**)

tumble dryer

sécher VERB

1 **to dry**
2 **to be stumped** ◇ *J'ai complètement séché à l'interro de maths.* (*informal*) I was completely stumped in the maths test.

‣ **se sécher** to dry oneself ◇ *Sèche-toi avec cette serviette.* Dry yourself with this towel.

la **sécheresse** NOUN

drought ◇ *une terrible sécheresse* a terrible drought

second ADJECTIVE

see also second NOUN

second ◇ *Il est arrivé second.* He came second.

le **second** NOUN

see also second ADJECTIVE

second floor ◇ *Elle habite au second.* She lives on the second floor.

secondaire ADJECTIVE

secondary ◇ *l'enseignement secondaire* secondary education

‣ **des effets secondaires** side effects

la **seconde** NOUN

1 **second** ◇ *Attends une seconde!* Wait a second!
2 **fifth year**

In French secondary schools, years are counted from the **sixième** (*youngest*) *to* **première** *and* **terminale** (*oldest*).

S

◇ *Ma sœur est en seconde.* My sister's in fifth year.

[3] **second class** ◇ *voyager en seconde* to travel second-class

secouer VERB

to shake ◇ *secouer la tête* to shake one's head

secourir VERB

to rescue

le **secourisme** NOUN

first aid ◇ *J'ai un brevet de secourisme.* I've got a first aid qualification.

le **secours** NOUN

help ◇ *Il est allé chercher du secours.* He went to get help. ◇ *Au secours!* Help!

• **les premiers secours** first aid

• **une sortie de secours** an emergency exit

• **la roue de secours** the spare wheel

le **secret** NOUN

see also **secret** ADJECTIVE

secret

secret ADJECTIVE

(FEM SING **secrète**)

see also **secret** NOUN

secret

le **secrétaire** NOUN

see also **la secrétaire**

[1] **secretary**

[2] **writing desk**

la **secrétaire** NOUN

see also **le secrétaire**

secretary

le **secrétariat** NOUN

secretary's office

le **secteur** NOUN

sector ◇ *le secteur public* the public sector ◇ *le secteur privé* the private sector

la **sécu** NOUN (informal)

Social Security

la **sécurité** NOUN

[1] **safety**

• **être en sécurité** to be safe ◇ *On ne se sent pas en sécurité dans ce quartier.* You don't feel safe in this neighbourhood.

• **la sécurité routière** road safety

• **une ceinture de sécurité** a seatbelt

[2] **security** ◇ *par mesure de sécurité* as a security measure

• **la sécurité sociale** Social Security

• **la sécurité de l'emploi** job security

séduisant ADJECTIVE

attractive

le **seigle** NOUN

rye ◇ *un pain de seigle* a loaf of rye

bread

le **seigneur** NOUN

lord

• **le Seigneur** the Lord

le **sein** NOUN

breast

• **au sein de** within ◇ *Chaque pays est autonome au sein de l'Europe.* Each country is independent within Europe.

seize NUMBER

sixteen ◇ *Elle a seize ans.* She's sixteen. ◇ *à seize heures* at 4 p.m.

• **le seize février** the sixteenth of February

seizième ADJECTIVE

sixteenth

le **séjour** NOUN

stay ◇ *J'ai fait un séjour d'une semaine en Italie.* I stayed in Italy for a week.

le **sel** NOUN

salt

sélectionner VERB

to select

le **self** NOUN (informal)

self-service restaurant

le **self-service** NOUN

self-service restaurant

la **selle** NOUN

saddle

selon PREPOSITION

according to ◇ *selon lui* according to him ◇ *selon mon humeur* according to what mood I'm in ◇ *Ils sont répartis selon leur âge.* They're divided up according to age.

la **semaine** NOUN

week

• **en semaine** on weekdays

semblable ADJECTIVE

similar

le **semblant** NOUN

• **faire semblant de faire quelque chose** to pretend to do something ◇ *Il fait semblant de dormir.* He's pretending to be asleep.

sembler VERB

to seem ◇ *Le temps semble s'améliorer.* The weather seems to be improving. ◇ *Il me semble inutile de s'en inquiéter.* It seems pointless to me to worry about it.

la **semelle** NOUN

[1] **sole**

[2] **insole**

la **semoule** NOUN

semolina

le **sens** NOUN

[1] **sense** ◇ *avoir le sens de l'humour*

to have a sense of humour ⋄ *Je n'ai pas le sens de l'orientation.* I've got no sense of direction. ⋄ *Ça n'a pas de sens.* It doesn't make sense.
- **le bon sens** common sense
  [2] **direction** ⋄ *Tu tournes la poignée dans le mauvais sens.* You're turning the handle in the wrong direction.
- **sens dessus dessous** upside down
- **un sens interdit** a one-way street ⋄ *J'ai failli prendre un sens interdit.* I nearly went the wrong way down a one-way street.
- **un sens unique** a one-way street

sensé ADJECTIVE
  sensible

sensible ADJECTIVE
  [1] **sensitive** ⋄ *Elle est très sensible.* She's very sensitive. ⋄ *Ce film est déconseillé aux personnes sensibles.* This film contains scenes which some viewers may find disturbing.
  [2] **visible** ⋄ *une amélioration sensible* a visible improvement

sensiblement ADVERB
  [1] **visibly** ⋄ *Elle a sensiblement progressé.* She's made visible progress.
  [2] **approximately** ⋄ *Nous sommes sensiblement de la même taille.* We're approximately the same height.

la **sentence** NOUN
  sentence (*judgement*)

le **sentier** NOUN
  path

le **sentiment** NOUN
  feeling

sentimental ADJECTIVE
  (MASC PL **sentimentaux**)
  sentimental

sentir VERB
  [1] **to smell** ⋄ *Ça sent bon.* That smells good. ⋄ *Ça sent mauvais.* It smells bad.
  [2] **to smell of** ⋄ *Ça sent les frites ici.* It smells of chips in here.
  [3] **to taste** ⋄ *Est-ce que tu sens l'ail dans le rôti?* Can you taste the garlic in the roast?
  [4] **to feel** ⋄ *Ça t'a fait mal?–Non, je n'ai rien senti.* Did it hurt?–No, I didn't feel a thing. ⋄ *Je ne me sens pas bien.* I don't feel well.
- **Il ne peut pas la sentir.** (*informal*) He can't stand her.

séparé ADJECTIVE
  separated ⋄ *Mes parents sont séparés.* My parents are separated.

séparément ADVERB

separately

séparer VERB
  to separate ⋄ *Séparez le blanc du jaune.* Separate the yolk from the white.
- **se séparer** to separate ⋄ *Mes parents se sont séparés l'année dernière.* My parents separated last year.

sept NUMBER
  seven ⋄ *Il est arrivé à sept heures.* He arrived at seven o'clock. ⋄ *Elle a sept ans.* She's seven.
- **le sept février** the seventh of February

septembre MASC NOUN
  September
- **en septembre** in September

le **septennat** NOUN
  le septennat *is the seven-year term of office of the French President.*

septième ADJECTIVE
  seventh ⋄ *au septième étage* on the seventh floor

sera, serai, seras, serez VERB *see* être
- **Je serai de retour à dix heures.** I'll be back at 10 o'clock.

la **série** NOUN
  series

sérieusement ADVERB
  seriously

sérieux ADJECTIVE
  (FEM SING **sérieuse**)
  see also **sérieux** NOUN
  [1] **serious** ⋄ *Il plaisantait?–Non, il était sérieux.* Was he joking?–No, he was serious.
  [2] **responsible** ⋄ *C'est un employé très sérieux.* He's a very responsible employee.

le **sérieux** NOUN
  see also **sérieux** ADJECTIVE
- **garder son sérieux** to keep a straight face ⋄ *J'ai eu du mal à garder mon sérieux.* I had trouble keeping a straight face.
- **prendre quelque chose au sérieux** to take something seriously
- **prendre quelqu'un au sérieux** to take somebody seriously
- **Il manque un peu de sérieux.** He's not very responsible.

la **seringue** NOUN
  syringe

séronégatif ADJECTIVE
  (FEM SING **séronégative**)
  HIV-negative

serons, seront VERB *see* être

séropositif ADJECTIVE
(FEM SING **séropositive**)
    HIV-positive
le **serpent** NOUN
    snake
la **serre** NOUN
    greenhouse
- **l'effet de serre** the greenhouse effect
serré ADJECTIVE
    [1] tight   ◦ *Mon pantalon est trop
    serré.* My trousers are too tight.
    [2] close-fought   ◦ *Ça a été un match
    serré.* It was a close-fought game.
serrer VERB
- **Ce pantalon me serre trop.** These
  trousers are too tight for me.
- **serrer la main à quelqu'un** to shake
  hands with somebody
- **se serrer** to squeeze up
    ◦ *Serrez-vous un peu pour que je
    puisse m'asseoir.* Squeeze up a bit so I
    can sit down.
- **serrer quelqu'un dans ses bras** to
  hug somebody
la **serrure** NOUN
    lock
sers, sert VERB *see* **servir**
le **serveur** NOUN
    waiter
la **serveuse** NOUN
    waitress
serviable ADJECTIVE
    helpful
le **service** NOUN
    [1] service (*in restaurant*)   ◦ *Le service
    est compris.* Service is included.
- **être de service** to be on duty
- **hors service** out of order
- **faire le service** to serve (*at table*)
    ◦ *Tu peux faire le service s'il te plaît?*
    Could you serve please?
    [2] favour   ◦ *rendre service à
    quelqu'un* to do somebody a favour
    ◦ *Est-ce que je peux te demander un
    service?* Can I ask you a favour?
    [3] serve (*sport*)   ◦ *Il a un bon service.*
    He's got a good serve.
- **le service militaire** military service
- **les services sociaux** the social
  services
- **les services secrets** the secret service
la **serviette** NOUN
    [1] towel   ◦ *une serviette de bain* a
    bath towel
- **une serviette hygiénique** a sanitary
  towel
    [2] serviette (*napkin*)
    [3] briefcase
servir VERB

to serve   ◦ *On vous sert?* Are you
being served?
- **À toi de servir.** (*tennis*) It's your serve.
- **se servir** to help oneself
    ◦ *Servez-vous.* Help yourself.
- **se servir de** to use   ◦ *Tu te sers
  souvent de ton vélo?* Do you use your
  bike a lot?
- **servir à quelqu'un** to be of use to
  somebody   ◦ *Ça m'a beaucoup servi.*
  It was very useful.
- **À quoi ça sert?** What's it for?
- **Ça ne sert à rien.** It's no use.   ◦ *Ça
  ne sert à rien d'insister.* It's no use
  insisting.
ses ADJECTIVE
    [1] his   ◦ *Il est parti voir ses
    grands-parents.* He's gone to see his
    grandparents.
    [2] her   ◦ *Delphine a oublié ses
    baskets.* Delphine's forgotten her
    trainers.
    [3] its   ◦ *la ville et ses alentours* the
    town and its surroundings
seul ADJECTIVE, ADVERB
    [1] alone   ◦ *vivre seul* to live alone
    [2] by oneself   ◦ *Elle est venue seule.*
    She came by herself.
- **faire quelque chose tout seul** to do
  something by oneself   ◦ *Elle a fait ça
  toute seule?* Did she do it by herself?
- **se sentir seul** to feel lonely
- **un seul livre** one book only   ◦ *Vous
  avez droit à un seul livre.* You're
  entitled to one book only.
- **Il reste une seule nectarine.** There's
  only one nectarine left.
- **le seul livre que...** the only book that...
    ◦ *C'est le seul Agatha Christie que je
    n'aie pas lu.* That's the only Agatha
    Christie I haven't read.
- **le seul** the only one   ◦ *C'est la seule
  que je ne connaisse pas.* She's the only
  one I don't know.
seulement ADVERB
    only
- **non seulement...mais** not only...but
    ◦ *Non seulement il a plu, mais en
    plus il a fait froid.* Not only did it rain,
    but it was cold as well.
sévère ADJECTIVE
    strict   ◦ *Mon prof de maths est très
    sévère.* My maths teacher is very strict.
sexuel ADJECTIVE
(FEM SING **sexuelle**)
    sexual   ◦ *la discrimination sexuelle*
    sexual discrimination   ◦ *l'éducation
    sexuelle* sex education
le **shampooing** NOUN

shampoo
- **se faire un shampooing** to wash one's hair

le **short** NOUN
  shorts ◇ *Il était en short.* He was wearing shorts.

le **si** NOUN
  see also **si** CONJUNCTION
  [1] **B** ◇ *en si bémol* in B flat
  [2] **ti** ◇ *la, si, do* la, ti, do

si CONJUNCTION, ADVERB
  see also **si** NOUN
  [1] **if** ◇ *si tu veux* if you like ◇ *Je me demande si elle va venir.* I wonder if she'll come. ◇ *si seulement* if only
  [2] **so** ◇ *Elle est si gentille.* She's so kind. ◇ *Tout s'est passé si vite.* Everything happened so fast.
  [3] **yes** ◇ *Tu n'es pas allé à l'école habillé comme ça?–Si.* You didn't go to school dressed like that?–Yes I did.

la **Sicile** NOUN
  Sicily

le **sida** NOUN
  AIDS ◇ *Il a le sida.* He's got AIDS.

le **siècle** NOUN
  century ◇ *le vingtième siècle* the twentieth century

le **siège** NOUN
  [1] **seat** (*in vehicle*)
  [2] **head office**

sien PRONOUN
- **le sien (1)** his ◇ *C'est le vélo de Paul?–Oui, c'est le sien.* Is this Paul's bike?–Yes, it's his.
- **le sien (2)** hers ◇ *C'est le vélo d'Isabelle?–Oui, c'est le sien.* Is this Isabelle's bike?–Yes, it's hers.

sienne PRONOUN
- **la sienne (1)** his ◇ *C'est la montre de Paul?–Oui, c'est la sienne.* Is this Paul's watch?–Yes, it's his.
- **la sienne (2)** hers ◇ *C'est la montre d'Isabelle?–Oui, c'est la sienne.* Is this Isabelle's watch?–Yes, it's hers.

siennes PRONOUN
- **les siennes (1)** his ◇ *Ce sont les cassettes de Christian?–Oui, ce sont les siennes.* Are these Christian's cassettes?–Yes, they're his.
- **les siennes (2)** hers ◇ *Ce sont les lunettes de Daphne?–Oui, ce sont les siennes.* Are these Daphne's glasses? –Yes, they're hers.

siens PRONOUN
- **les siens (1)** his ◇ *Ce sont les sandwichs de Pierre?–Oui, ce sont les siens.* Are these Pierre's sandwiches? –Yes, they're his.

- **les siens (2)** hers ◇ *Ce sont les sandwichs de Justine?–Oui, ce sont les siens.* Are these Justine's sandwiches? –Yes, they're hers.

la **sieste** NOUN
  nap ◇ *faire la sieste* to have a nap

siffler VERB
  to whistle

le **sifflet** NOUN
  whistle

le **sigle** NOUN
  acronym

le **signal** NOUN
  (PL les **signaux**)
  signal

le **signe** NOUN
  sign
- **faire un signe de la main** to wave
- **faire signe à quelqu'un d'entrer** to beckon to somebody to come in

signer VERB
  to sign

la **signification** NOUN
  meaning

signifier VERB
  to mean ◇ *Que signifie ce mot?* What does this word mean?

silencieux ADJECTIVE
  (FEM SING **silencieuse**)
  [1] **silent** ◇ *Elle est restée silencieuse.* She remained silent.
  [2] **quiet** ◇ *C'est très silencieux ici.* It's very quiet here.

la **silhouette** NOUN
  figure ◇ *J'ai vu une silhouette dans le brouillard.* I saw a figure in the mist.

similaire ADJECTIVE
  similar

le **simple** NOUN
  singles (*tennis*) ◇ *le simple messieurs* the men's singles ◇ *le simple dames* the ladies' singles

simuler VERB
  to simulate

simultané ADJECTIVE
  simultaneous

sincère ADJECTIVE
  sincere

la **sincérité** NOUN
  sincerity

le **singe** NOUN
  monkey

le **singulier** NOUN
  singular ◇ *au féminin singulier* in the feminine singular

sinistre ADJECTIVE
  sinister

sinon CONJUNCTION
  otherwise ◇ *Dépêche-toi, sinon je*

S

pars sans toi. Hurry up, otherwise I'll leave without you.

la **sinusite** NOUN

  sinusitis ◇ *avoir de la sinusite* to have sinusitis

la **sirène** NOUN

  mermaid

- **la sirène d'alarme** the fire alarm

le **sirop** NOUN

  syrup

- **le sirop contre la toux** cough mixture

le **site** NOUN

  setting ◇ *un site très sauvage* a totally unspoiled setting

- **un site pittoresque** a beauty spot
- **un site touristique** a tourist attraction
- **un site archéologique** an archaeological site

sitôt ADVERB

- **sitôt dit, sitôt fait** no sooner said than done
- **pas de sitôt** not for a long time ◇ *On ne le reverra pas de sitôt.* We won't see him again for a long time.

la **situation** NOUN

  ①**situation**

- **la situation de famille** marital status

  ②**job** ◇ *Il a une belle situation.* He's got a good job.

se **situer** VERB

  to be situated ◇ *Versailles se situe à l'ouest de Paris.* Versailles is situated to the west of Paris.

- **bien situé** well situated

six NUMBER

  six ◇ *Il est rentré à six heures.* He got back at six o'clock. ◇ *Il a six ans.* He's six.

- **le six février** the sixth of February

sixième ADJECTIVE

  see also sixième NOUN

  sixth ◇ *au sixième étage* on the sixth floor

la **sixième** NOUN

  see also sixième ADJECTIVE

  first year

  In French secondary schools, years are counted from the sixième *(youngest) to* première *and* terminale *(oldest).*

  ◇ *Mon frère est en sixième.* My brother's in first year.

le **ski** NOUN

  ①**ski** ◇ *J'ai loué des skis.* I hired skis.

  ②**skiing** ◇ *J'adore le ski.* I love skiing. ◇ *faire du ski* to go skiing

- **le ski de fond** cross-country skiing
- **le ski nautique** water-skiing
- **le ski de piste** downhill skiing

- **le ski de randonnée** cross-country skiing

skier VERB

  to ski

le **skieur** NOUN

  skier

la **skieuse** NOUN

  skier

le **slip** NOUN

  pants

- **un slip de bain** swimming trunks

la **Slovaquie** NOUN

  Slovakia

la **Slovénie** NOUN

  Slovenia

le **SMIC** NOUN

  guaranteed minimum wage ◇ *Il touche le SMIC.* He's on the legal minimum wage.

le **smoking** NOUN

  dinner suit

la **SNCF** NOUN (= *Société nationale des chemins de fer français*)

  French railways

snob ADJECTIVE

  (FEM SING **snob**)

  snobbish

sobre ADJECTIVE

  ①**sober**

  ②**plain** ◇ *C'est une veste très sobre.* It's a very plain jacket.

social ADJECTIVE

  (MASC PL **sociaux**)

  social

le/la **socialiste** NOUN

  socialist

la **société** NOUN

  ①**society**

  ②**company** ◇ *une société d'ingénierie* an engineering company

la **sociologie** NOUN

  sociology

la **socquette** NOUN

  ankle sock

la **sœur** NOUN

  sister

- **une bonne sœur** (*informal*) a nun

soi PRONOUN

  oneself ◇ *avoir confiance en soi* to have confidence in oneself

- **rester chez soi** to stay at home
- **Ça va de soi.** It goes without saying.

soi-disant ADVERB, ADJECTIVE

  supposedly ◇ *Il était soi-disant parti à Paris.* He had supposedly left for Paris.

- **un soi-disant poète** a so-called poet

la **soie** NOUN

  silk

la **soif** NOUN

thirst
- **avoir soif** to be thirsty

soigner VERB

to look after (*ill person, animal*)
◇ *Soigne-toi bien ce week-end!* Take good care of yourself this weekend!

soigneux ADJECTIVE

(FEM SING **soigneuse**)

careful ◇ *Tu devrais être plus soigneux avec tes livres.* You should be more careful with your books.

soi-même PRONOUN

oneself ◇ *Il vaut mieux le faire soi-même.* It's better to do it oneself.

le **soin** NOUN

care
- **prendre soin de quelque chose** to take care of something ◇ *Prends bien soin de ce livre.* Take good care of this book.

les **soins** MASC NOUN

treatment
- **les premiers soins** first aid
- **"aux bons soins de Madame Martin"** (*on letter*) "c/o Mrs Martin"

le **soir** NOUN

evening ◇ *ce soir* this evening
- **demain soir** tomorrow night
- **hier soir** last night

la **soirée** NOUN

evening ◇ *en tenue de soirée* in evening dress

sois VERB *see* **être**
- **Sois tranquille!** Be quiet!

soit CONJUNCTION
- **soit..., soit...** either...or... ◇ *soit lundi, soit mardi* either Monday or Tuesday

la **soixantaine** NOUN

about sixty ◇ *une soixantaine de personnes* about sixty people
- **Elle a la soixantaine.** She's in her sixties.

soixante NUMBER

sixty ◇ *Il a soixante ans.* He's sixty.
◇ *soixante et un* sixty-one
◇ *soixante-deux* sixty-two
- **soixante et onze** seventy-one
- **soixante-quinze** seventy-five

soixante-dix NUMBER

seventy ◇ *Il a soixante-dix ans.* He's seventy.

le **soja** NOUN

soya
- **des germes de soja** beansprouts

le **sol** NOUN

[1] **floor** ◇ *un sol carrelé* a tiled floor
- **à même le sol** on the floor
[2] **soil** ◇ *sur le sol français* on

French soil
[3] **G** ◇ *sol dièse* G sharp
[4] **so** ◇ *do, ré, mi, fa, sol...* do, re, mi, fa, so...

solaire ADJECTIVE

solar ◇ *le système solaire* the solar system
- **la crème solaire** sun cream

le **soldat** NOUN

soldier

le **solde** NOUN
- **être en solde** to be reduced ◇ *Les chemisiers sont en solde.* The blouses are reduced.
- **les soldes** the sales ◇ *faire les soldes* to go round the sales ◇ *les soldes de janvier* the January sales

soldé ADJECTIVE
- **être soldé** to be reduced ◇ *un article soldé à dix francs* an item reduced to 10 francs

la **sole** NOUN

sole (*fish*)

le **soleil** NOUN

sun ◇ *au soleil* in the sun
- **Il y a du soleil.** It's sunny.

le **solfège** NOUN

musical theory ◇ *Il joue du violon sans connaître le solfège.* He plays the violin but he can't read music.

solidaire ADJECTIVE
- **être solidaire de quelqu'un** to back somebody up

solide ADJECTIVE

[1] **strong** (*person*)
[2] **solid** (*object*)

solitaire ADJECTIVE

see also **solitaire** NOUN

solitary

le/la **solitaire** NOUN

see also **solitaire** ADJECTIVE

loner

la **solitude** NOUN

loneliness

la **solution** NOUN

solution
- **une solution de facilité** an easy way out

sombre ADJECTIVE

dark

la **somme** NOUN

see also **le somme**

sum

le **somme** NOUN

see also **la somme**

nap ◇ *faire un somme* to take a nap

le **sommeil** NOUN

sleep
- **avoir sommeil** to be sleepy

S

sommes VERB *see* **être**
- **Nous sommes en vacances.** We're on holiday.

le **sommet** NOUN
  summit

le **somnifère** NOUN
  sleeping pill

somptueux ADJECTIVE
  (FEM SING **somptueuse**)
  sumptuous

son ADJECTIVE
  (FEM SING **sa**, PL **ses**)
  see also **son** NOUN
  [1] **his** ◇ *son père* his father ◇ *Il a perdu son portefeuille.* He's lost his wallet.
  [2] **her** ◇ *son père* her father ◇ *Elle a perdu son sac.* She's lost her bag.

le **son** NOUN
  see also **son** ADJECTIVE
  [1] **sound** ◇ *Le son n'est pas très bon.* The sound's not very good. ◇ *baisser le son* to turn the sound down
  [2] **bran**
- **le pain de son** brown bread

le **sondage** NOUN
  survey
- **un sondage d'opinion** an opinion poll

sonner VERB
  to ring ◇ *On a sonné.* Somebody rang the doorbell. ◇ *Le téléphone a sonné.* The phone rang.

la **sonnerie** NOUN
  bell (*electric*) ◇ *La sonnerie du téléphone l'a réveillé.* He was woken by the phone ringing.

la **sonnette** NOUN
  bell ◇ *la sonnette d'alarme* the alarm bell

la **sono** NOUN (*informal*)
  sound system

sont VERB *see* **être**
- **Ils sont en vacances.** They're on holiday.

sophistiqué ADJECTIVE
  sophisticated

le **sort** NOUN
  [1] **spell** ◇ *jeter un sort à quelqu'un* to cast a spell on somebody
- **un mauvais sort** a curse
  [2] **fate** ◇ *abandonner quelqu'un à son triste sort* to leave somebody to their fate
- **tirer au sort** to draw lots

la **sorte** NOUN
  sort ◇ *C'est une sorte de gâteau.* It's a sort of cake. ◇ *toutes sortes de choses* all sorts of things

la **sortie** NOUN
  way out ◇ *Où est la sortie?* Where's the way out?
- **la sortie de secours** the emergency exit
- **Attends-moi à la sortie de l'école.** Meet me after school.

sortir VERB
  [1] **to go out** ◇ *Il est sorti sans rien dire.* He went out without saying a word. ◇ *Il est sorti acheter un journal.* He's gone out to buy a newspaper. ◇ *J'aime sortir.* I like going out.
  [2] **to come out** ◇ *Elle sort de l'hôpital demain.* She's coming out of hospital tomorrow. ◇ *Je l'ai rencontré en sortant de la pharmacie.* I met him coming out of the chemist's. ◇ *Ce modèle vient juste de sortir.* This model has just come out.
  [3] **to take out** ◇ *Elle a sorti son porte-monnaie de son sac.* She took her purse out of her handbag. ◇ *Je vais sortir la voiture du garage.* I'll get the car out of the garage.
- **sortir avec quelqu'un** to be going out with somebody ◇ *Tu sors avec lui?* Are you going out with him?
- **s'en sortir** to manage ◇ *Ne t'en fais pas, tu t'en sortiras.* Don't worry, you'll manage OK.

la **sottise** NOUN
- **Ne fais pas de sottises.** Don't do anything silly.
- **Ne dis pas de sottises.** Don't talk nonsense.

le **sou** NOUN
- **une machine à sous** a fruit machine
- **Je n'ai pas un sou sur moi.** I haven't got a penny on me.
- **être près de ses sous** (*informal*) to be tight-fisted

le **souci** NOUN
  worry
- **se faire du souci** to worry

soucieux ADJECTIVE
  (FEM SING **soucieuse**)
  worried ◇ *Tu as l'air soucieux.* You look worried.

la **soucoupe** NOUN
  saucer
- **une soucoupe volante** a flying saucer

soudain ADJECTIVE, ADVERB
  [1] **sudden** ◇ *une douleur soudaine* a sudden pain
  [2] **suddenly** ◇ *Soudain, il s'est fâché.* Suddenly, he got angry.

le **souffle** NOUN
  breath

- **à bout de souffle** out of breath

le **soufflé** NOUN
soufflé ◇ *un soufflé au fromage* a cheese soufflé

souffler VERB
1 **to blow** ◇ *Le vent soufflait fort.* The wind was blowing hard.
2 **to blow out** ◇ *Souffle les bougies!* Blow out the candles!

la **souffrance** NOUN
suffering

souffrir VERB
to be in pain ◇ *Il souffre beaucoup.* He's in a lot of pain.
- **Il ne peux pas la souffrir.** (*informal*) He can't stand her.

le **souhait** NOUN
wish ◇ *faire un souhait* to make a wish ◇ *Tous nos souhaits de réussite.* All our best wishes for your success. ◇ *les souhaits de bonne année* New Year's wishes
- **Atchoum!–À tes souhaits!** Atchoo! –Bless you!

souhaiter VERB
to wish ◇ *Il souhaite aller à l'université.* He wishes to go to university. ◇ *Nous vous souhaitons une bonne année.* We wish you a happy New Year.

soûl ADJECTIVE (*informal*)
drunk

soulager VERB
to relieve

soulever VERB
1 **to lift** ◇ *Je n'arrive pas à soulever cette valise.* I can't lift this suitcase.
2 **to raise** ◇ *Il faudra soulever la question lors de la réunion.* We'll have to raise the matter at the meeting.

le **soulier** NOUN
shoe

souligner VERB
to underline

le **soupçon** NOUN
suspicion
- **un soupçon de** a dash of ◇ *Ajoutez un soupçon de rhum.* Add a dash of rum.

soupçonner VERB
to suspect

la **soupe** NOUN
soup

le **soupir** NOUN
sigh

soupirer VERB
to sigh

souple ADJECTIVE
1 **supple** (*person*)
2 **flexible** (*system*)

la **source** NOUN
spring ◇ *l'eau de source* spring water

le **sourcil** NOUN
eyebrow

sourd ADJECTIVE
deaf

souriant ADJECTIVE
cheerful

le **sourire** NOUN
see also **sourire** VERB
smile

sourire VERB
see also **sourire** NOUN
to smile ◇ *sourire à quelqu'un* to smile at somebody

la **souris** NOUN
mouse

sournois ADJECTIVE
sly

sous PREPOSITION
under
- **sous terre** underground
- **sous la pluie** in the rain

sous-entendu ADJECTIVE
see also **sous-entendu** NOUN
implied

le **sous-entendu** NOUN
see also **sous-entendu** ADJECTIVE
insinuation

sous-marin ADJECTIVE
see also **sous-marin** NOUN
underwater

le **sous-marin** NOUN
see also **sous-marin** ADJECTIVE
submarine

le **sous-sol** NOUN
basement

le **sous-titre** NOUN
subtitle

la **soustraction** NOUN
subtraction

les **sous-vêtements** MASC NOUN
underwear SING

soutenir VERB
to support ◇ *Il m'a toujours soutenu contre elle.* He's always supported me against her.
- **soutenir que** to maintain that ◇ *Elle soutenait que c'était impossible.* She maintained that it was impossible.
- **soutenir l'allure** to keep up ◇ *Il marchait trop vite et je n'arrivais pas à soutenir l'allure.* He was walking too fast and I couldn't keep up.

souterrain ADJECTIVE
see also **souterrain** NOUN
underground

S

le **souterrain** NOUN

see also **souterrain** ADJECTIVE

underground passage

le **soutien** NOUN

support

le **soutien-gorge** NOUN

(PL les **soutiens-gorge**)

bra

le **souvenir** NOUN

see also **se souvenir** VERB

1 **memory** ◇ garder un bon souvenir de quelque chose to have happy memories of something

2 **souvenir** ◇ un souvenir de Lourdes a souvenir of Lourdes

- **Garde ce livre en souvenir de moi.** Keep the book: it'll remind you of me.

se **souvenir** VERB

see also **souvenir** NOUN

- **se souvenir de quelque chose** to remember something ◇ Je ne me souviens pas de son adresse. I can't remember his address.

- **se souvenir que** to remember that ◇ Je me souviens qu'il neigeait ce jour-là. I remember it was snowing that day.

souvent ADVERB

often

soyez, soyons VERB see **être**

- **Soyons clairs!** Let's be clear about this!

spacieux ADJECTIVE

(FEM SING **spacieuse**)

spacious

les **spaghettis** MASC NOUN

spaghetti

le **sparadrap** NOUN

sticking plaster

le **speaker** NOUN

announcer

la **speakerine** NOUN

announcer

spécial ADJECTIVE

(MASC PL **spéciaux**)

1 **special** ◇ Qu'est-ce que tu fais ce week-end?–Rien de spécial. What are you doing this weekend?–Nothing special.

- **les effets spéciaux** special effects

2 **peculiar** ◇ Elle a des goûts un peu spéciaux. She has rather peculiar tastes.

spécialement ADVERB

1 **specially** ◇ Il est venu spécialement pour te parler. He came specially to speak to you.

2 **particularly** ◇ Ce n'est pas spécialement difficile. It's not particularly difficult.

se **spécialiser** VERB

- **se spécialiser dans quelque chose** to specialize in something ◇ Je me suis spécialisé en histoire contemporaine. I specialized in modern history.

le/la **spécialiste** NOUN

specialist

la **spécialité** NOUN

speciality

spécifier VERB

to specify

le **spectacle** NOUN

show

spectaculaire ADJECTIVE

spectacular

le **spectateur** NOUN

1 **member of the audience**

2 **spectator**

la **spectatrice** NOUN

1 **member of the audience**

2 **spectator**

la **spéléologie** NOUN

potholing

spirituel ADJECTIVE

1 **spiritual**

2 **witty**

splendide ADJECTIVE

magnificent

spontané ADJECTIVE

spontaneous

le **sport** NOUN

see also **sport** ADJECTIVE

sport ◇ faire du sport to do sport

- **les sports d'hiver** winter sports

sport ADJECTIVE (MASC, FEM, PL)

see also **sport** NOUN

casual ◇ une veste sport a casual jacket

sportif ADJECTIVE

(FEM SING **sportive**)

see also **sportif** NOUN

1 **sporty** ◇ Elle est très sportive. She's very sporty.

2 **sports** ◇ un club sportif a sports club

le **sportif** NOUN

see also **sportif** ADJECTIVE

sportsman

la **sportive** NOUN

sportswoman

le **spot** NOUN

spotlight

- **un spot publicitaire** a commercial break

le **square** NOUN

public gardens

le **squelette** NOUN

skeleton

stable ADJECTIVE
stable
- **un emploi stable** a steady job
le **stade** NOUN
stadium
le **stage** NOUN
training course
e/la **stagiaire** NOUN
see also stagiaire ADJECTIVE
trainee
stagiaire ADJECTIVE
see also stagiaire NOUN
trainee ◇ *un professeur stagiaire* a
trainee teacher
le **stand** NOUN
[1] **stand** (*at exhibition*)
[2] **stall** (*at fair*)
e/la **standardiste** NOUN
operator
la **station** NOUN
- **une station de métro** an underground
station
- **une station de taxis** a taxi rank
- **une station de ski** a ski resort
le **stationnement** NOUN
parking
- "**stationnement interdit**" "no parking"
stationner VERB
to park
la **station-service** NOUN
(PL les **stations-service**)
service station
la **statistique** NOUN
statistic
le **steak** NOUN
steak
- **un steak frites** steak and chips
- **un steak haché** a hamburger
la **sténo** NOUN
shorthand ◇ *un cours de sténo* a
shorthand course
la **sténodactylo** NOUN
shorthand typist
stérile ADJECTIVE
sterile
stimulant ADJECTIVE
stimulating
stimuler VERB
to stimulate
le **stop** NOUN
stop sign
- **faire du stop** to hitchhike
stopper VERB
to stop
le **store** NOUN
[1] **blind** (*on window*)
[2] **awning**
le **strapontin** NOUN
foldaway seat

la **stratégie** NOUN
strategy
stratégique ADJECTIVE
strategic
stressant ADJECTIVE
stressful
strict ADJECTIVE
[1] **strict** (*person*) ◇ *Ma prof de français
est très stricte.* My French teacher's
very strict.
[2] **severe** (*clothes*) ◇ *une tenue très
stricte* a very severe outfit
- **le strict minimum** the bare
minimum
la **strophe** NOUN
stanza
studieux ADJECTIVE
(FEM SING **studieuse**)
studious
le **studio** NOUN
[1] **studio flat**
[2] **studio** ◇ *un studio de télévision* a
television studio
stupéfait ADJECTIVE
astonished
les **stupéfiants** MASC NOUN
narcotics
stupéfier VERB
to astonish ◇ *Sa réponse m'a
stupéfié.* I was astonished by his
answer.
la **stupidité** NOUN
stupidity
le/la **styliste** NOUN
designer
le **stylo** NOUN
pen
- **un stylo plume** a fountain pen
- **un stylo bille** a ballpoint pen
- **un stylo-feutre** a felt-tip pen
su VERB *see* **savoir**
- **Si j'avais su...** If I'd known...
subir VERB
to suffer (*defeat*)
- **subir une opération** to have an
operation
subit ADJECTIVE
sudden
subitement ADVERB
suddenly
subjectif ADJECTIVE
(FEM SING **subjective**)
subjective
le **subjonctif** NOUN
subjunctive
substituer VERB
to substitute ◇ *substituer un mot à
un autre* to substitute one word for
another

S

subtil ADJECTIVE
   subtle
la **subvention** NOUN
   subsidy
subventionner VERB
   to subsidize
le **succès** NOUN
   success ◇ *avoir du succès* to be
   successful
le **successeur** NOUN
   successor
la **succursale** NOUN
   branch (*of company*)
sucer VERB
   to suck
la **sucette** NOUN
   lollipop
le **sucre** NOUN
   sugar
   • **un sucre** a sugar-lump ◇ *Je prends
   deux sucres dans mon café.* I take two
   lumps of sugar in my coffee.
   • **du sucre en morceaux** lump sugar
   • **un sucre d'orge** a barley sugar
   • **du sucre en poudre** caster sugar
   • **du sucre glace** icing sugar
sucré ADJECTIVE
   [1] **sweet** ◇ *Ce gâteau est un peu
   trop sucré.* This cake is a bit too
   sweet.
   [2] **sweetened** ◇ *du lait concentré
   sucré* sweetened condensed milk
les **sucreries** FEM NOUN
   sweet things
le **sucrier** NOUN
   sugar bowl
le **sud** NOUN
   see also sud ADJECTIVE
   south ◇ *Ils vivent dans le sud de la
   France.* They live in the South of
   France.
   • **vers le sud** southwards
   • **au sud de Paris** south of Paris
   • **l'Amérique du Sud** South America
   • **le vent du sud** the south wind
sud ADJECTIVE
   see also sud NOUN
   [1] **south** ◇ *la côte sud de l'Espagne*
   the south coast of Spain
   • **le pôle sud** the South Pole
   [2] **southern** ◇ *Nous avons visité la
   partie sud du pays.* We visited the
   southern part of the country.
sud-africain ADJECTIVE
   South African
sud-américain ADJECTIVE
   South American
le **sud-est** NOUN
   south-east ◇ *au sud-est* in the

le **sud-ouest** NOUN
   south-west ◇ *au sud-ouest* in the
   south-west
la **Suède** NOUN
   Sweden
suédois ADJECTIVE, NOUN
   (FEM SING **suédoise**)
   Swedish ◇ *Ils parlent suédois.* They
   speak Swedish.
   • **un Suédois** a Swede (*man*)
   • **une Suédoise** a Swede (*woman*)
   • **les Suédois** the Swedes
suer VERB
   to sweat
la **sueur** NOUN
   sweat
   • **en sueur** sweating
suffire VERB
   to be enough ◇ *Tiens, voilà dix
   francs. Ça te suffit?* Here's 10 francs. Is
   that enough for you?
   • **Ça suffit!** That's enough!
suffisamment ADVERB
   enough ◇ *Ça n'est pas suffisamment
   grand.* It's not big enough. ◇ *Il n'y a
   pas suffisamment de chaises.* There
   aren't enough chairs.
suffisant ADJECTIVE
   [1] **sufficient** ◇ *Ça n'est pas une
   raison suffisante.* That's not sufficient
   reason.
   [2] **smug** ◇ *Il est un peu trop suffisant.*
   He's rather smug.
suffoquer VERB
   to suffocate
suggérer VERB
   to suggest
se **suicider** VERB
   to commit suicide
suis VERB *see* être, *see* suivre
   • **Je suis écossais.** I'm Scottish.
   • **Suis-moi.** Follow me.
suisse ADJECTIVE, NOUN
   see also la Suisse
   Swiss ◇ *le franc suisse* the Swiss
   franc
   • **un Suisse** a Swiss man
   • **une Suisse** a Swiss woman
   • **les Suisses** the Swiss
la **Suisse** NOUN
   see also suisse ADJECTIVE
   Switzerland ◇ *la Suisse allemande*
   German-speaking Switzerland ◇ *la
   Suisse romande* French-speaking
   Switzerland
la **suite** NOUN
   [1] **rest** ◇ *Je vous raconterai la suite
   de l'histoire demain.* I'll tell you the rest

of the story tomorrow.

2 **sequel** (to book, film)

- **tout de suite** straightaway ◇ *J'y vais tout de suite.* I'll go straightaway.
- **de suite** in succession ◇ *Il a commis la même erreur trois fois de suite.* He made the same mistake three times in succession.
- **par la suite** subsequently ◇ *Il s'est avéré par la suite qu'il était coupable.* He subsequently turned out to be guilty.

suivant ADJECTIVE

following ◇ *le jour suivant* the following day ◇ *l'exercice suivant* the following exercise

- **Au suivant!** Next!

suivre VERB

1 **to follow** ◇ *Il m'a suivie jusque chez moi.* He followed me home. ◇ *Vous me suivez ou est-ce que je parle trop vite?* Are you following me or am I speaking too fast?

2 **to do** ◇ *Je suis un cours d'anglais à la fac.* I'm doing an English course at college.

3 **to keep up** ◇ *Il n'arrive pas à suivre en maths.* He can't keep up in maths. ◇ *J'aime suivre l'actualité.* I like to keep up with the news.

- **"à suivre"** "to be continued"
- **suivre un régime** to be on a diet

sujet ADJECTIVE

(FEM SING **sujette**)

see also **sujet** NOUN

- **être sujet à** to be prone to ◇ *Il est sujet au vertige.* He suffers from vertigo.

le **sujet** NOUN

see also **sujet** ADJECTIVE

subject

- **au sujet de** about ◇ *C'est à quel sujet?–C'est au sujet de l'annonce parue dans "Le Monde" d'aujourd'hui.* What's it about?–It's about the advertisement in today's "Le Monde".
- **un sujet de conversation** a topic of conversation
- **un sujet d'examen** an examination question
- **un sujet de plaisanterie** something to joke about

le **super** NOUN

4-star petrol

superficiel ADJECTIVE

(FEM SING **superficielle**)

superficial

superflu ADJECTIVE

superfluous

supérieur ADJECTIVE

see also **supérieur** NOUN

1 **upper** ◇ *la lèvre supérieure* the upper lip

2 **superior** ◇ *qualité supérieure* superior quality ◇ *Il a toujours l'air tellement supérieur!* He always looks so superior!

- **supérieur à** greater than ◇ *Choisissez un nombre supérieur à cent.* Choose a number greater than 100.

le **supérieur** NOUN

see also **supérieur** ADJECTIVE

superior ◇ *mon supérieur hiérarchique* my immediate superior

le **superlatif** NOUN

superlative

le **supermarché** NOUN

supermarket

superposé ADJECTIVE

- **des lits superposés** bunk beds

superstitieux ADJECTIVE

(FEM SING **superstitieuse**)

superstitious

le **suppléant** NOUN

supply teacher

la **suppléante** NOUN

supply teacher

le **supplément** NOUN

- **payer un supplément** to pay an additional charge
- **Le vin est en supplément.** Wine is extra.
- **un supplément de travail** extra work

supplémentaire ADJECTIVE

additional ◇ *Voici quelques exercices supplémentaires.* Here are some additional exercises.

- **faire des heures supplémentaires** to do overtime

le **supplice** NOUN

torture ◇ *C'était un supplice.* It was torture.

supplier VERB

- **supplier quelqu'un de faire quelque chose** to beg somebody to do something ◇ *Je t'en supplie!* I'm begging you!

supportable ADJECTIVE

bearable

supporter VERB

to stand (tolerate) ◇ *Je ne supporte pas l'hypocrisie.* I can't stand hypocrisy. ◇ *Elle ne supporte pas qu'on la critique.* She can't stand being criticized. ◇ *Je ne peux pas la supporter.* I can't stand her. ◇ *Je*

S

supporte mal la chaleur. I can't stand hot weather.

supposer VERB
to suppose

supprimer VERB
1 **to cut** ◇ *Deux mille emplois ont été supprimés dans le secteur public.* Two thousand jobs have been cut in the public sector.
2 **to cancel** ◇ *Le train de Londres a été supprimé.* The train to London has been cancelled.
3 **to get rid of** ◇ *Ils ont supprimé les témoins gênants.* They got rid of the awkward witnesses.

sur PREPOSITION
1 **on** ◇ *Pose-le sur la table.* Put it down on the table. ◇ *Vous verrez l'hôpital sur votre droite.* You'll see the hospital on your right. ◇ *une conférence sur Balzac* a lecture on Balzac
2 **in** ◇ *une personne sur dix* 1 person in 10
3 **out of** ◇ *J'ai eu quatorze sur vingt en maths.* I got 14 out of 20 in maths.
4 **by** ◇ *quatre mètres sur deux* 4 metres by 2

sûr ADJECTIVE
1 **sure** ◇ *Tu es sûr?* Are you sure?
• **sûr et certain** absolutely certain
2 **reliable** ◇ *C'est quelqu'un de très sûr.* He's a very reliable person.
3 **safe** ◇ *Ce quartier n'est pas très sûr la nuit.* This neighbourhood isn't very safe at night.
• **sûr de soi** self-confident ◇ *Elle est très sûre d'elle.* She's very self-confident.

sûrement ADVERB
certainly ◇ *Sûrement pas!* Certainly not! ◇ *Il est sûrement déjà parti.* He's sure to have already left.

la **sûreté** NOUN
• **mettre quelque chose en sûreté** to put something in a safe place

le **surf** NOUN
surfing

la **surface** NOUN
surface
• **les grandes surfaces** the supermarkets

surgelé ADJECTIVE
frozen ◇ *des frites surgelées* frozen chips

les **surgelés** MASC NOUN
frozen food

surhumain ADJECTIVE
superhuman

sur-le-champ ADVERB
immediately

le **surlendemain** NOUN
• **le surlendemain de son arrivée** two days after he arrived
• **le surlendemain dans la matinée** two days later, in the morning

se **surmener** VERB
to work too hard ◇ *Ne te surmène pas trop pendant le week-end.* Don't work too hard over the weekend.

surmonter VERB
to overcome ◇ *Il nous reste de nombreux obstacles à surmonter.* We still have many obstacles to overcome.

surnaturel ADJECTIVE
(FEM SING **surnaturelle**)
supernatural

le **surnom** NOUN
nickname

surnommer NOUN
to nickname ◇ *On l'a surnommé "Kiki".* We nicknamed him "Kiki".

surpeuplé ADJECTIVE
overpopulated

surprenant ADJECTIVE
surprising

surprendre VERB
to surprise ◇ *Ça me surprendrait beaucoup qu'il arrive à l'heure.* I'd be very surprised if he arrived on time.
• **surprendre quelqu'un en train de faire quelque chose** to catch somebody doing something ◇ *Je l'ai surpris en train de fouiller dans mon placard.* I caught him rummaging in my cupboard.

surpris ADJECTIVE
surprised ◇ *Il était surpris de me voir.* He was surprised to see me.

la **surprise** NOUN
surprise ◇ *faire une surprise à quelqu'un* to give somebody a surprise

sursauter VERB
to jump ◇ *J'ai sursauté en entendant mon nom.* I jumped when I heard my name.

surtout ADVERB
1 **especially** ◇ *Il est assez timide, surtout avec les filles.* He's rather shy, especially with girls.
2 **above all** ◇ *Ce canapé est joli et surtout, il n'est pas salissant.* This sofa is pretty, and even more important, it doesn't show the dirt. ◇ *Surtout, ne répète pas ce que je t'ai dit!* Whatever you do, don't repeat what I told you!

le **surveillant** NOUN
supervisor (*man*)
> *In French secondary schools, the teachers are
> not responsible for supervising the pupils outside
> class. This job is done by people called
> surveillants or pions.*

la **surveillante** NOUN
supervisor (*woman*)

surveiller VERB
1. **to keep an eye on** ⋄ *Tu peux
surveiller mes bagages?* Can you keep
an eye on my luggage?
2. **to keep a watch on** ⋄ *La police a
surveillé la maison pendant une
semaine.* The police kept the house
under surveillance for a week.
3. **to supervise** ⋄ *Nous sommes
toujours surveillés pendant la récréation.*
We're always supervised during break.
- **surveiller un examen** to invigilate an
exam
- **surveiller sa ligne** to watch one's
figure

le **survêtement** NOUN
tracksuit ⋄ *un haut de survêtement* a
tracksuit top ⋄ *un pantalon de
survêtement* tracksuit bottoms

la **survie** NOUN
survival

le **survivant** NOUN
survivor

la **survivante** NOUN
survivor

survivre VERB
to survive ⋄ *survivre à un accident*
to survive an accident

survoler VERB
to fly over

susceptible ADJECTIVE
touchy

suspect ADJECTIVE
suspicious ⋄ *dans des circonstances
suspectes* under suspicious
circumstances

suspecter VERB
to suspect

le **suspense** NOUN
suspense
- **un film à suspense** a thriller

la **suture** NOUN
- **un point de suture** a stitch

svelte ADJECTIVE
slender

SVP ABBREVIATION (= *s'il vous plaît*)
please

la **syllabe** NOUN
syllable

symbolique ADJECTIVE
symbolic

symboliser VERB
to symbolize

symétrique ADJECTIVE
symmetrical

sympa ADJECTIVE (*informal*)
nice ⋄ *Elle est très sympa.* She's a
really nice person.

la **sympathie** NOUN
- **J'ai beaucoup de sympathie pour lui.**
I like him a lot.

sympathique ADJECTIVE
nice ⋄ *Ce sont des gens très
sympathiques.* They're very nice
people.

sympathiser VERB
to get on well ⋄ *Nous avons
immédiatement sympathisé avec nos
voisins.* We got on well with our
neighbours straight away.

le **symptôme** NOUN
symptom

le **syndicat** NOUN
trade union
- **le syndicat d'initiative** the tourist
information office

synonyme ADJECTIVE
see also synonyme NOUN
synonymous ⋄ *être synonyme de* to
be synonymous with

le **synonyme** NOUN
see also synonyme ADJECTIVE
synonym

synthétique ADJECTIVE
synthetic

la **Syrie** NOUN
Syria

syrien ADJECTIVE
(FEM SING **syrienne**)
Syrian

systématique ADJECTIVE
systematic

le **système** NOUN
system

T

t' PRONOUN *see* **te**

ta ADJECTIVE

your ◇ *J'ai vu ta sœur hier.* I saw your sister yesterday.

le **tabac** NOUN

[1] **tobacco** ◇ *le tabac blond* light tobacco ◇ *le tabac brun* dark tobacco

[2] **smoking** ◇ *Le tabac est mauvais pour la santé.* Smoking is bad for you.

la **table** NOUN

table

- **mettre la table** to lay the table
- **se mettre à table** to sit down to eat
- **À table!** Dinner's ready!
- **une table de nuit** a bedside table
- **"table des matières"** "contents"

le **tableau** NOUN

(PL les **tableaux**)

painting ◇ *un tableau de Monet* a painting by Monet

- **le tableau d'affichage** the notice board
- **le tableau noir** the blackboard

la **tablette** NOUN

- **une tablette de chocolat** a bar of chocolate

le **tablier** NOUN

apron

le **tabouret** NOUN

stool

la **tache** NOUN

mark (*stain*)

- **des taches de rousseur** freckles

la **tâche** NOUN

task

tacher VERB

to leave a stain

le **tact** NOUN

tact ◇ *avoir du tact* to be tactful

la **tactique** NOUN

tactics

- **changer de tactique** to try something different

la **taie** NOUN

- **une taie d'oreiller** a pillowcase

la **taille** NOUN

[1] **waist** ◇ *Elle a la taille fine.* She has a slim waist.

[2] **height** ◇ *un homme de taille moyenne* a man of average height

[3] **size** ◇ *Avez-vous ma taille?* Have you got my size?

le **taille-crayon** NOUN

pencil sharpener

le **tailleur** NOUN

[1] **tailor**

[2] **suit** (*lady's*)

- **Il est assis en tailleur.** He's sitting cross-legged.

se **taire** VERB

to stop talking

- **Taisez-vous!** Be quiet!

le **talon** NOUN

heel

le **tambour** NOUN

drum

la **Tamise** NOUN

Thames

le **tampon** NOUN

pad ◇ *un tampon à récurer* a scouring pad

- **un tampon hygiénique** a tampon

tamponneuse ADJECTIVE

- **les autos tamponneuses** dodgems

tandis que CONJUNCTION

while ◇ *Il a toujours de bonnes notes, tandis que les miennes sont mauvaises.* He always gets good marks, while mine are poor.

tant ADVERB

so much ◇ *Je l'aime tant!* I love him so much!

- **tant de (1)** so much ◇ *tant de nourriture* so much food
- **tant de (2)** so many ◇ *tant de livres* so many books
- **tant que (1)** until ◇ *Tu ne sortiras pas tant que tu n'auras pas fini tes devoirs.* You're not going out until you've finished your homework.
- **tant que (2)** while ◇ *Profites-en tant que tu peux.* Make the most of it while you can.
- **tant mieux** so much the better
- **tant pis** never mind

la **tante** NOUN

aunt

tantôt ADVERB

sometimes ◇ *Nous venons tantôt à pied, tantôt en bus.* Sometimes we walk, sometimes we come by bus.

le **tapage** NOUN

[1] **racket** ◇ *Ils ont fait du tapage toute la nuit.* They made a racket all night long.

[2] **fuss** ◇ *On a fait beaucoup de tapage autour de cette affaire.* There was a lot of fuss about that business.

taper VERB

to beat down ◇ *Le soleil tape.* The sun's really beating down.

- **taper quelqu'un** to hit somebody

◇ *Maman, il m'a tapé!* Mum, he hit me!

- **taper sur quelque chose** to bang on something
- **taper des pieds** to stamp one's feet
- **taper des mains** to clap one's hands
- **taper à la machine** to type ◇ *Tu sais taper à la machine?* Can you type? ◇ *Je vais taper cette lettre.* I'm going to type this letter.

le **tapis** NOUN
    carpet

tapisser VERB
    to paper

la **tapisserie** NOUN
    ① wallpaper ◇ *Tu aimes la tapisserie de ma chambre?* Do you like the wallpaper in my bedroom?
    ② tapestry

taquiner VERB
    to tease

tard ADVERB
    late
- **plus tard** later on
- **au plus tard** at the latest

tardif ADJECTIVE
    (FEM SING **tardive**)
    late ◇ *un petit déjeuner tardif* a late breakfast

le **tarif** NOUN
- **le tarif des consommations** the price list (*in café*)
- **une communication à tarif réduit** an off-peak phone call
- **un billet de train à tarif réduit** a concessionary train ticket
- **un billet de train à plein tarif** a full-price train ticket
- **Est-ce que vous faites un tarif de groupe?** Is there a reduction for groups?

la **tarte** NOUN
    tart

la **tartine** NOUN
    slice of bread ◇ *une tartine de confiture* a slice of bread and jam

tartiner VERB
    to spread
- **le fromage à tartiner** cheese spread

le **tas** NOUN
    heap ◇ *un tas de charbon* a heap of coal
- **un tas de** (*informal*) loads of ◇ *J'ai lu un tas de livres pendant les vacances.* I read loads of books in the holidays.

la **tasse** NOUN
    cup

le **taureau** NOUN
    (PL les **taureaux**)
    bull
- **le Taureau** Taurus ◇ *Ils sont tous les deux Taureau.* They're both Taurus.

le **taux** NOUN
    rate ◇ *le taux de change* the exchange rate

la **taxe** NOUN
    tax
- **la boutique hors taxes** the duty-free shop

le **taxi** NOUN
    taxi

tchèque ADJECTIVE
    Czech
- **la République tchèque** the Czech Republic

te PRONOUN
    te *changes to* **t'** *before a vowel and most words beginning with "h".*
    ① you ◇ *Je te vois.* I can see you. ◇ *Il t'a vu?* Did he see you?
    ② to you ◇ *Est-ce qu'il te parle en français?* Does he talk to you in French? ◇ *Elle t'a parlé?* Did she speak to you?
    ③ yourself ◇ *Tu vas te rendre malade.* You'll make yourself sick.
    With reflexive verbs, **te** *is often not translated.*
    ◇ *Comment tu t'appelles?* What's your name?

le **technicien** NOUN
    technician

la **technicienne** NOUN
    technician

technique ADJECTIVE
    see also **technique** NOUN
    technical

la **technique** NOUN
    see also **technique** ADJECTIVE
    technique

la **technologie** NOUN
    technology

le **teint** NOUN
    complexion ◇ *Elle a le teint clair.* She's got a fair complexion.

la **teinte** NOUN
    shade (*colour*)

le **teinturier** NOUN
    dry cleaner's ◇ *Je vais porter ce manteau chez le teinturier.* I'm going to take this coat to the dry cleaner's.

tel ADJECTIVE
    (FEM SING **telle**)
- **Il a un tel enthousiasme!** He's got such enthusiasm!
- **rien de tel** nothing like ◇ *Il n'y a rien de tel qu'une bonne nuit de sommeil.* There's nothing like a good night's sleep.

- **J'ai tout laissé tel quel.** I left everything as it was.
- **tel que** such as

la **télé** NOUN
   telly ◇ *à la télé* on telly

la **télécarte** NOUN
   phonecard

la **télécommande** NOUN
   remote control

la **télécopie** NOUN
   fax

le **télégramme** NOUN
   telegram

le **téléphérique** NOUN
   cable car

le **téléphone** NOUN
   telephone ◇ *Elle est au téléphone.*
   She's on the phone.

téléphoner VERB
   to phone ◇ *Je vais téléphoner à Claire.* I'll phone Claire. ◇ *Je peux téléphoner?* Can I make a phone call?

le **télésiège** NOUN
   chairlift

le **téléski** NOUN
   ski-tow

le **téléspectateur** NOUN
   viewer *(TV)*

la **téléspectatrice** NOUN
   viewer *(TV)*

le **téléviseur** NOUN
   television set

la **télévision** NOUN
   television ◇ *à la télévision* on television

telle ADJECTIVE
- **Je n'ai jamais eu une telle peur.** I've never had such a fright.
- **telle que** such as

tellement ADVERB
   [1] **so** ◇ *Andrew est tellement gentil.* Andrew's so nice. ◇ *Il travaille tellement.* He works so hard.
   [2] **so much** ◇ *Il a tellement mangé que...* He ate so much that...
   [3] **so many** ◇ *Il y avait tellement de monde.* There were so many people.

telles ADJECTIVE
   such ◇ *Je n'ai jamais entendu de telles âneries!* I've never heard such nonsense!

tels ADJECTIVE
   such ◇ *Nous n'avons pas de tels orages chez nous.* We don't have such storms back home.

le **témoignage** NOUN
   testimony

témoigner VERB
   to testify

le **témoin** NOUN
   witness

la **température** NOUN
   temperature ◇ *avoir de la température* to have a temperature

la **tempête** NOUN
   storm

temporaire ADJECTIVE
   temporary

le **temps** NOUN
   [1] **weather** ◇ *Quel temps fait-il?* What's the weather like?
   [2] **time** ◇ *Je n'ai pas le temps.* I haven't got time. ◇ *Prends ton temps.* Take your time. ◇ *Il est temps de partir.* It's time to go.
- **juste à temps** just in time
- **de temps en temps** from time to time
- **en même temps** at the same time
- **à temps** in time ◇ *Il est arrivé à temps pour le match.* He arrived in time for the match.
- **à plein temps** full time ◇ *Elle travaille à plein temps.* She works full time.
- **à temps partiel** part time ◇ *le travail à temps partiel* part-time work
- **dans le temps** at one time ◇ *Dans le temps, on pouvait circuler en vélo sans danger.* At one time, it was safe to go around by bike.
   [3] **tense** *(of verb)*

tenais, tenait VERB *see* **tenir**

la **tendance** NOUN
- **avoir tendance à faire quelque chose** to tend to do something ◇ *Il a tendance à exagérer.* He tends to exaggerate.

tendre ADJECTIVE
   see also **tendre** VERB
   tender

tendre VERB
   see also **tendre** ADJECTIVE
   to stretch out ◇ *Ils ont tendu une corde entre deux arbres.* They stretched out a rope between two trees.
- **tendre quelque chose à quelqu'un** to hold something out to somebody ◇ *Il lui a tendu les clés.* He held out the keys to her.
- **tendre la main** to hold out one's hand
- **tendre le bras** to reach out
- **tendre un piège à quelqu'un** to set a trap for someone

tendrement ADVERB
   tenderly

la **tendresse** NOUN
   tenderness

tendu ADJECTIVE

tense ◦ *Il était très tendu aujourd'hui.* He was very tense today.

tenir VERB

to hold ◦ *Tu peux tenir la lampe, s'il te plaît?* Can you hold the torch, please? ◦ *Il tenait un enfant par la main.* He was holding a child by the hand.

→ **Tenez votre chien en laisse.** Keep your dog on the lead.

→ **tenir à quelqu'un** to be attached to somebody ◦ *Il tient beaucoup à elle.* He's very attached to her.

→ **tenir à faire quelque chose** to be determined to do something ◦ *Elle tient à y aller.* She's determined to go.

→ **tenir de quelqu'un** to take after somebody ◦ *Il tient de son père.* He takes after his father.

→ **Tiens, voilà un stylo.** Here's a pen.

→ **Tiens, c'est Alain là-bas!** Look, that's Alain over there!

→ **Tiens?** Really?

→ **se tenir (1)** to stand ◦ *Il se tenait près de la porte.* He was standing by the door.

→ **se tenir (2)** to be held ◦ *La foire va se tenir place du marché.* The fair will be held in the market place.

→ **se tenir droit (1)** to stand up straight ◦ *Tiens-toi droit pour que je puisse te mesurer.* Stand up straight so I can measure you.

→ **se tenir droit (2)** to sit up straight ◦ *Arrête de manger le nez dans ton assiette, tiens-toi droit.* Don't slouch while you're eating, sit up straight.

→ **Tiens-toi bien!** Behave yourself!

le **tennis** NOUN

1. **tennis** ◦ *Elle joue au tennis.* She plays tennis.

2. **tennis court** ◦ *Il est au tennis.* He's at the tennis court.

→ **les tennis** trainers

tentant ADJECTIVE

tempting

la **tentation** NOUN

temptation

la **tentative** NOUN

attempt

la **tente** NOUN

tent

tenter VERB

to tempt ◦ *J'ai été tenté de tout abandonner.* I was tempted to give up. ◦ *Ça ne me tente vraiment pas d'aller à la piscine.* I don't really fancy going to the swimming pool.

→ **tenter de faire quelque chose** to try

to do something ◦ *Il a tenté plusieurs fois de s'évader.* He tried several times to escape.

tenu VERB *see* **tenir**

la **tenue** NOUN

clothes

→ **en tenue de soirée** in evening dress

le **terme** NOUN

→ **à court terme** short-term

→ **à long terme** long-term

la **terminale** NOUN

final year

In French secondary schools, years are counted from the sixième *(youngest) to* première *and* terminale *(oldest).*

terminer VERB

to finish

→ **se terminer** to end ◦ *Les vacances se terminent demain.* The holidays end tomorrow.

le **terminus** NOUN

terminus

le **terrain** NOUN

land ◦ *Il veut acheter un terrain en Normandie.* He wants to buy some land in Normandy.

→ **un terrain de camping** a campsite

→ **un terrain de football** a football pitch

→ **un terrain de golf** a golf course

→ **un terrain de jeu** a playground

→ **un terrain de sport** a sports ground

→ **un terrain vague** a piece of waste ground

la **terrasse** NOUN

terrace

→ **Si on s'asseyait en terrasse?** Shall we sit outside? (*at café*)

la **terre** NOUN

earth

→ **la Terre** the Earth

→ **Elle s'est assise par terre.** She sat on the floor.

→ **Il est tombé par terre.** He fell down.

→ **la terre cuite** terracotta ◦ *un pot en terre cuite* a terracotta pot

→ **la terre glaise** clay

terrible ADJECTIVE

terrible ◦ *Quelque chose de terrible est arrivé.* Something terrible has happened.

→ **pas terrible** (*informal*) nothing special ◦ *Ce film n'est pas terrible.* The film's nothing special.

la **terrine** NOUN

pâté

le **territoire** NOUN

territory

le/la **terroriste** NOUN

terrorist

tes ADJECTIVE
  your ◇ *J'aime bien tes baskets.* I like your trainers.

le **test** NOUN
  test

le **testament** NOUN
  will ◇ *Il est mort sans testament.* He died without leaving a will.

  tester VERB
  to test

le **tétanos** NOUN
  tetanus

le **têtard** NOUN
  tadpole

la **tête** NOUN
  head ◇ *de la tête aux pieds* from head to foot
  ➤ **se laver la tête** to wash one's hair
  ➤ **la tête la première** headfirst
  ➤ **tenir tête à quelqu'un** to stand up to somebody
  ➤ **faire la tête** to sulk
  ➤ **en avoir par-dessus la tête** to be fed up

têtu ADJECTIVE
  stubborn

le **texte** NOUN
  text

le **TGV** NOUN (= *train à grande vitesse*)
  high-speed train

le **thé** NOUN
  tea ◇ *Je vous offre un thé?* Would you like a cup of tea?

le **théâtre** NOUN
  theatre
  ➤ **faire du théâtre** to act ◇ *Est-ce que tu as déjà fait du théâtre?* Have you ever acted?

la **théière** NOUN
  teapot

le **thème** NOUN
  1 **subject** ◇ *Quel est le thème de l'émission?* What's the programme about?
  2 **prose** (*translation into the foreign language*)

la **théorie** NOUN
  theory

le **thermomètre** NOUN
  thermometer

le **thon** NOUN
  tuna

le **tibia** NOUN
  1 **shinbone** ◇ *une fracture du tibia* a broken shinbone
  2 **shin** ◇ *Il m'a donné un coup de pied dans le tibia.* He kicked me in the shin.

le **tic** NOUN
  nervous twitch

le **ticket** NOUN
  ticket ◇ *un ticket de métro* an underground ticket
  ➤ **le ticket de caisse** the till receipt

tiède ADJECTIVE
  1 **warm** (*water, air*)
  2 **lukewarm** (*food, drink*)

tien PRONOUN
  ➤ **le tien** yours ◇ *J'ai oublié mon stylo. Tu peux me prêter le tien?* I've forgotten my pen. Can you lend me yours?

tienne PRONOUN
  ➤ **la tienne** yours ◇ *Ce n'est pas ma raquette, c'est la tienne.* It's not my racket, it's yours.
  ➤ **À la tienne!** Cheers!

tiennes PRONOUN
  ➤ **les tiennes** yours ◇ *J'ai pris mes baskets, mais j'ai oublié les tiennes.* I've brought my trainers, but I've forgotten yours.

tiens PRONOUN
  ➤ **les tiens** yours ◇ *Je ne trouve pas mes feutres. Je peux utiliser les tiens?* I can't find my felt pens. Can I use yours?

tiens, tient VERB *see* **tenir**

le **tiers** NOUN
  third ◇ *Un tiers de la classe était pour.* A third of the class were in favour.
  ➤ **le tiers monde** the Third World

la **tige** NOUN
  stem

le **tigre** NOUN
  tiger

le **tilleul** NOUN
  lime tea

le **timbre** NOUN
  stamp

timide ADJECTIVE
  shy

timidement ADVERB
  shyly

la **timidité** NOUN
  shyness

le **tir** NOUN
  shooting
  ➤ **le tir à l'arc** archery

le **tirage** NOUN
  ➤ **par tirage au sort** by drawing lots ◇ *Les prix seront attribués par tirage au sort.* The prizes will be awarded by drawing lots.

le **tire-bouchon** NOUN
  corkscrew

la **tirelire** NOUN
  money box

tirer VERB

　[1] **to pull** ◇ *Elle a tiré un mouchoir de son sac.* She pulled a handkerchief out of her bag. ◇ *Il m'a tiré les cheveux.* He pulled my hair. ◇ *"Tirer"* "Pull"

　[2] **to draw** ◇ *tirer les rideaux* to draw the curtains ◇ *tirer un trait* to draw a line ◇ *tirer des conclusions* to draw conclusions

　► **tirer au sort** to draw lots

　[3] **to fire** ◇ *Il a tiré plusieurs coups de feu.* He fired several shots. ◇ *Il a tiré sur les policiers.* He fired at the police.

le **tiret** NOUN

　dash (*hyphen*)

le **tiroir** NOUN

　drawer

la **tisane** NOUN

　herbal tea

tisser VERB

　to weave

le **tissu** NOUN

　material

　► **un sac en tissu** a cloth bag

le **titre** NOUN

　title

　► **les gros titres** the headlines

　► **un titre de transport** a travel ticket

tituber VERB

　to stagger

le **toast** NOUN

　[1] **piece of toast**

　[2] **toast** ◇ *porter un toast à quelqu'un* to drink a toast to somebody

le **toboggan** NOUN

　slide

toi PRONOUN

　you ◇ *Ça va?–Oui, et toi?* How are you?–Fine, and you? ◇ *J'ai faim, pas toi?* I'm hungry, aren't you?

　► **Assieds-toi.** Sit down.

　► **C'est à toi de jouer.** It's your turn to play.

　► **Est-ce que ce stylo est à toi?** Is this pen yours?

la **toile** NOUN

　► **un pantalon de toile** cotton trousers

　► **un sac de toile** a canvas bag

　► **une toile cirée** an oilcloth

　► **une toile d'araignée** a cobweb

la **toilette** NOUN

　[1] **wash** ◇ *faire sa toilette* to have a wash

　[2] **outfit** ◇ *une toilette élégante* an elegant outfit

les **toilettes** FEM NOUN

　toilet

toi-même PRONOUN

yourself ◇ *Tu as fait ça toi-même?* Did you do it yourself?

le **toit** NOUN

　roof

　► **un toit ouvrant** a sunroof

tolérant ADJECTIVE

　tolerant

tolérer VERB

　to tolerate

la **tomate** NOUN

　tomato

la **tombe** NOUN

　grave

le **tombeau** NOUN

　(PL les **tombeaux**)

　tomb

la **tombée** NOUN

　► **à la tombée de la nuit** at nightfall

tomber VERB

　to fall ◇ *Attention, tu vas tomber!* Be careful, you'll fall!

　► **laisser tomber (1)** to drop ◇ *Elle a laissé tomber son stylo.* She dropped her pen.

　► **laisser tomber (2)** to give up ◇ *Il a laissé tomber le piano.* He gave up the piano.

　► **laisser tomber (3)** to let down ◇ *Il ne laisse jamais tomber ses amis.* He never lets his friends down.

　► **tomber sur quelqu'un** to bump into someone ◇ *Je suis tombé sur lui en sortant de chez Pierre.* I bumped into him coming out of Pierre's place.

　► **Ça tombe bien.** That's lucky.

　► **Il tombe de sommeil.** He's asleep on his feet.

ton ADJECTIVE

　(FEM SING **ta**, PL **tes**)

　see also **ton** NOUN

　your ◇ *C'est ton stylo?* Is this your pen?

le **ton** NOUN

　see also **ton** ADJECTIVE

　[1] **tone of voice** ◇ *Ne me parle pas sur ce ton.* Don't speak to me in that tone of voice.

　[2] **colour** ◇ *J'adore les tons pastel.* I love pastel colours.

la **tonalité** NOUN

　dialling tone

la **tondeuse** NOUN

　lawnmower

tondre VERB

　to mow

tonique ADJECTIVE

　fortifying

la **tonne** NOUN

　tonne

T

le **tonneau** NOUN
(PL les **tonneaux**)
  barrel

le **tonnerre** NOUN
  thunder

le **tonus** NOUN
- **avoir du tonus** to be energetic

le **torchon** NOUN
  tea towel

tordre VERB
- **se tordre la cheville** to twist one's ankle

tordu ADJECTIVE
1 bent ◇ *Ce clou est un peu tordu.* This nail's a bit bent.
2 crazy ◇ *une histoire complètement tordue* a crazy story

le **torrent** NOUN
  mountain stream

le **torse** NOUN
  chest ◇ *Il était torse nu.* He was bare-chested.

le **tort** NOUN
- **avoir tort** to be wrong
- **donner tort à quelqu'un** to lay the blame on somebody

le **torticolis** NOUN
  stiff neck ◇ *J'ai le torticolis.* I've got a stiff neck.

la **tortue** NOUN
  tortoise

la **torture** NOUN
  torture

torturer VERB
  to torture

tôt ADVERB
  early
- **au plus tôt** at the earliest
- **tôt ou tard** sooner or later

total ADJECTIVE
(MASC PL **totaux**)
see also **total** NOUN
  total

le **total** NOUN
(PL les **totaux**)
see also **total** ADJECTIVE
  total ◇ *faire le total* to work out the total
- **au total** in total

totalement ADVERB
  totally

la **totalité** NOUN
- **la totalité des profs** all the teachers
- **la totalité du personnel** the entire staff

touchant ADJECTIVE
  touching

toucher VERB
1 to touch ◇ *Ne touche pas à mes livres!* Don't touch my books!

- **Nos deux jardins se touchent.** Our gardens are next to each other.
2 to feel ◇ *Ce pull a l'air doux. Je peux toucher?* That sweater looks soft. Can I feel it?
3 to hit ◇ *La balle l'a touché en pleine poitrine.* The bullet hit him right in the chest.
4 to affect ◇ *Ces nouvelles réformes ne nous touchent pas.* The new reforms don't affect us.
5 to receive ◇ *Il a touché une grosse somme d'argent.* He received a large sum of money.

toujours ADVERB
1 always ◇ *Il est toujours très gentil.* He's always very nice.
- **pour toujours** forever
2 still ◇ *Quand nous sommes revenus, il était toujours là.* When we got back he was still there.

le **toupet** NOUN (*informal*)
- **avoir du toupet** to have a nerve

la **tour** NOUN
see also **le tour**
1 tower ◇ *la Tour Eiffel* the Eiffel Tower
2 tower block ◇ *Il y a beaucoup de tours dans ce quartier.* There are a lot of tower blocks in this area.

le **tour** NOUN
see also **la tour**
  turn ◇ *C'est ton tour de jouer.* It's your turn to play.
- **faire un tour** to go for a walk ◇ *Allons faire un tour dans le parc.* Let's go for a walk in the park.
- **faire un tour en voiture** to go for a drive
- **faire un tour à vélo** to go for a ride ◇ *Tu veux aller faire un tour à vélo?* Do you want to go for a bike ride?
- **faire le tour du monde** to travel round the world

le **tourbillon** NOUN
  whirlpool

le/la **touriste** NOUN
  tourist

se **tourmenter** VERB
  to fret ◇ *Ne te tourmente pas, ça s'arrangera.* Don't fret about it, it'll be all right.

le **tournant** NOUN
1 bend ◇ *Il y a beaucoup de tournants dangereux sur cette route.* There are a lot of dangerous bends on this road.
2 turning point ◇ *Ça a été un tournant dans sa vie.* It was a turning

point in his life.

tournée NOUN

[1] **round** ◇ *Le facteur commence sa tournée à sept heures du matin.* The postman starts his round at 7 o'clock in the morning. ◇ *Allez, qu'est-ce que vous voulez boire? C'est ma tournée.* Right, what are you drinking? It's my round.

[2] **tour** ◇ *Il est en tournée aux États-Unis.* He's on tour in the United States.

tourner VERB

[1] **to turn** ◇ *Tournez à droite au prochain feu.* Turn right at the lights. ◇ *Tourne-toi un peu plus vers moi, et souris!* Turn towards me a bit more, and smile!

[2] **to go sour** ◇ *Le lait a tourné.* The milk's gone sour.

‣ **mal tourner** to go wrong ◇ *Ça a mal tourné.* It all went wrong.

‣ **tourner le dos à quelqu'un** to have one's back to somebody

le **tournesol** NOUN
   sunflower

le **tournevis** NOUN
   screwdriver

le **tournoi** NOUN
   tournament

la **tourte** NOUN
   pie ◇ *une tourte aux poireaux* a leek pie

tous ADJECTIVE, PRONOUN *see* **tout**

la **Toussaint** NOUN
   All Saints' Day

tousser VERB
   to cough

tout ADJECTIVE, ADVERB, PRONOUN
(MASC PL **tous**, FEM PL **toutes**)

[1] **all** ◇ *tout le lait* all the milk ◇ *toute la nuit* all night ◇ *tous les livres* all the books ◇ *toutes les filles* all the girls ◇ *tout le temps* all the time ◇ *Je les connais tous.* I know them all. ◇ *Nous y sommes toutes allées.* We all went. ◇ *Ça fait combien en tout?* How much is that all together?

‣ **Il est tout seul.** He's all alone.

‣ **pas du tout** not at all

[2] **every** ◇ *tous les jours* every day ◇ *tous les deux jours* every two days

‣ **tout le monde** everybody

‣ **tous les deux** both ◇ *Nous y sommes allés tous les deux.* We both went.

‣ **tous les trois** all three ◇ *Je les ai invités tous les trois.* I invited all three

of them.

[3] **everything** ◇ *Il a tout organisé.* He organized everything.

[4] **very** ◇ *Elle habite tout près.* She lives very close.

‣ **tout en haut** right at the top

‣ **tout droit** straight ahead

‣ **tout d'abord** first of all

‣ **tout à coup** suddenly

‣ **tout à fait** absolutely

‣ **tout à l'heure (1)** just now ◇ *Je l'ai vu tout à l'heure.* I saw him just now.

‣ **tout à l'heure (2)** in a moment ◇ *Je finirai ça tout à l'heure.* I'll finish it in a moment.

‣ **À tout à l'heure!** See you later!

‣ **tout de suite** straight away

toutefois ADVERB
   however

toutes ADJECTIVE, PRONOUN *see* **tout**

la **toux** NOUN
   cough

le/la **toxicomane** NOUN
   drug addict

le **trac** NOUN

‣ **avoir le trac** to be feeling nervous

la **trace** NOUN

[1] **trace** ◇ *Le voleur n'a pas laissé de traces.* The thief left no traces.

[2] **mark** ◇ *des traces de doigts* finger marks

‣ **des traces de pas** footprints

tracer VERB
   to draw ◇ *tracer un trait* to draw a line

le **tracteur** NOUN
   tractor

la **tradition** NOUN
   tradition

traditionnel ADJECTIVE
(FEM SING **traditionnelle**)
   traditional

le **traducteur** NOUN
   translator

la **traduction** NOUN
   translation

la **traductrice** NOUN
   translator

traduire VERB
   to translate

le **trafic** NOUN
   traffic

‣ **le trafic de drogue** drug trafficking

le **trafiquant** NOUN

‣ **un trafiquant de drogue** a drug trafficker

tragique ADJECTIVE
   tragic

T

trahir VERB
to betray

la **trahison** NOUN
betrayal

le **train** NOUN
train
- **un train électrique** a train set

le **traîneau** NOUN
(PL les **traîneaux**)
sledge

traîner VERB
[1] **to wander around** ◇ *J'ai vu des jeunes qui traînaient en ville.* I saw some young people wandering around town.
[2] **to hang about** ◇ *Dépêche-toi, ne traîne pas!* Hurry up, don't hang about!
[3] **to drag on** ◇ *La réunion a traîné jusqu'à midi.* The meeting dragged on till 12 o'clock.
- **traîner des pieds** to drag one's feet

le **train-train** NOUN
humdrum routine

traire VERB
to milk

le **trait** NOUN
[1] **line** ◇ *Tracez un trait.* Draw a line.
[2] **feature** ◇ *Elle a les traits fins.* She has delicate features.
- **boire quelque chose d'un trait** to drink something down in one gulp
- **un trait d'union** a hyphen

le **traitement** NOUN
treatment
- **le traitement de texte** word processing

traiter VERB
to treat ◇ *Elle le traite comme un chien.* She treats him like a dog.
- **Il m'a traité d'imbécile.** He called me an idiot.
- **traiter de** to be about ◇ *Cet article traite des sans-abri.* This article is about the homeless.

le **traiteur** NOUN
caterer

le **trajet** NOUN
[1] **journey** ◇ *Il n'a pas arrêté de parler pendant tout le trajet.* He talked for the whole journey. ◇ *J'ai une heure de trajet pour aller au travail.* My journey to work takes an hour.
[2] **route** ◇ *C'est le trajet le plus court.* It's the shortest route.

le **tramway** NOUN
tram

tranchant ADJECTIVE
sharp (*knife*)

la **tranche** NOUN
slice

tranquille ADJECTIVE
quiet ◇ *Cette rue est très tranquille.* This is a very quiet street.
- **Sois tranquille, il ne va rien lui arriver.** Don't worry, nothing will happen to him.
- **Tiens-toi tranquille!** Be quiet!
- **Laisse-moi tranquille.** Leave me alone.
- **Laisse ça tranquille.** Leave it alone.

la **tranquillité** NOUN
peace and quiet

transférer VERB
to transfer

transformer VERB
[1] **to transform** ◇ *Son séjour en France l'a transformé.* His stay in France has transformed him.
[2] **to convert** ◇ *Ils ont transformé la grange en garage.* They've converted the barn into a garage.
- **se transformer en** to turn into ◇ *La chenille se transforme en papillon.* The caterpillar turns into a butterfly.

la **transfusion** NOUN
- **une transfusion sanguine** a blood transfusion

transiger VERB
to compromise

transmettre VERB
- **transmettre quelque chose à quelqu'un** to pass something on to somebody

transpercer VERB
to go through ◇ *La pluie a transpercé mes vêtements.* The rain went through my clothes.

la **transpiration** NOUN
perspiration

transpirer VERB
to perspire

le **transport** NOUN
transport
- **les transports en commun** public transport

transporter VERB
[1] **to carry** ◇ *Le train transportait des marchandises.* The train was carrying freight.
[2] **to move** ◇ *Je ne sais pas comment je vais transporter mes affaires.* I don't know how I'm going to move my stuff.

traumatiser VERB
to traumatize

le **travail** NOUN
(PL les **travaux**)

1 **work** ◇ *J'ai beaucoup de travail.*
I've got a lot of work.
2 **job** ◇ *Il a un travail intéressant.*
He's got an interesting job.
- **le travail au noir** moonlighting
travailler VERB
to work
travailleur ADJECTIVE
(FEM SING **travailleuse**)
see also travailleur NOUN
hard-working
travailleur NOUN
see also travailleur ADJECTIVE
worker
travailleuse NOUN
worker
travaillistes MASC NOUN
the Labour Party
travaux MASC NOUN
1 **work** ◇ *des travaux de
construction* building work
2 **roadworks** ◇ *Il y a beaucoup de
bruit à cause des travaux dans la rue.*
There's a lot of noise from the
roadworks.
- **être en travaux** to be undergoing
alterations
- **les travaux dirigés** supervised
practical work
- **les travaux manuels** handicrafts
- **les travaux ménagers** housework
travers NOUN
- **en travers de** across ◇ *Il y avait un
arbre en travers de la route.* There was a
tree lying across the road.
- **de travers** crooked ◇ *Son chapeau
était de travers.* His hat was crooked.
- **comprendre de travers** to
misunderstand ◇ *Elle comprend
toujours tout de travers.* She always gets
the wrong idea.
- **J'ai avalé de travers.** Something went
down the wrong way.
- **à travers** through ◇ *Cette vitre est
tellement sale qu'on ne voit rien à
travers.* This window is so dirty you
can't see anything through it.
traversée NOUN
crossing
traverser VERB
1 **to cross** ◇ *Traversez la rue.* Cross
the street.
2 **to go through** ◇ *Nous avons
traversé la France pour aller en Espagne.*
We went through France on the way
to Spain. ◇ *La pluie a traversé mon
manteau.* The rain went through my
coat.
traversin NOUN

bolster
trébucher VERB
to trip up
le **trèfle** NOUN
1 **clover**
2 **clubs** (at cards) ◇ *le roi de trèfle*
the king of clubs
treize NUMBER
thirteen ◇ *Il a treize ans.* He's
thirteen. ◇ *à treize heures* at 1 p.m.
- **le treize février** the thirteenth of
February
treizième ADJECTIVE
thirteenth
le **tréma** NOUN
diaeresis
le **tremblement de terre** NOUN
earthquake
trembler VERB
to shake ◇ *trembler de peur* to shake
with fear
- **trembler de froid** to shiver
trempé ADJECTIVE
soaking wet
tremper VERB
to soak
- **tremper sa main dans l'eau** to dip
one's hand in the water
le **tremplin** NOUN
springboard
la **trentaine** NOUN
about thirty ◇ *une trentaine de
personnes* about thirty people
- **Il a la trentaine.** He's in his
thirties.
trente NUMBER
thirty ◇ *Elle a trente ans.* She's
thirty.
- **le trente janvier** the thirtieth of
January
- **trente et un** thirty-one
- **trente-deux** thirty-two
trentième ADJECTIVE
thirtieth
très ADVERB
very
le **trésor** NOUN
treasure
la **tresse** NOUN
plait
la **tribu** NOUN
tribe
le **tribunal** NOUN
(PL les **tribunaux**)
court
tricher VERB
to cheat
tricolore ADJECTIVE
three-coloured

T

PTO

le drapeau tricolore the French tricolour

le drapeau tricolore *is the French flag which is blue, white and red.*

le **tricot** NOUN

[1] knitting ◇ *On fait du tricot à l'école.* We do knitting at school.

[2] sweater ◇ *Mets un tricot, il fait froid.* Put a sweater on, it's cold.

tricoter VERB
to knit

trier VERB
to sort out ◇ *Je vais trier mes papiers avant de partir en vacances.* I'm going to sort out my papers before I go on holiday.

le **trimestre** NOUN
term

trinquer VERB
to clink glasses

le **triomphe** NOUN
triumph

triompher VERB
to triumph

les **tripes** FEM NOUN
tripe

le **triple** NOUN

• **Ça m'a coûté le triple.** It cost me three times as much.

• **Il gagne le triple de mon salaire.** He earns three times my salary.

tripler VERB
to treble

les **triplés** MASC NOUN
triplets

triste ADJECTIVE
sad

la **tristesse** NOUN
sadness

le **trognon** NOUN
core ◇ *un trognon de pomme* an apple core

trois NUMBER
three ◇ *à trois heures du matin* at three in the morning ◇ *Elle a trois ans.* She's three. ◇ *trois fois* three times

• **le trois février** the third of February

troisième ADJECTIVE
see also troisième NOUN
third ◇ *au troisième étage* on the third floor

la **troisième** NOUN
see also troisième ADJECTIVE
fourth year
In French secondary schools, years are counted from the sixième *(youngest) to* première *and* terminale *(oldest).*
◇ *Mon frère est en troisième.* My

brother's in fourth year.

les **trois-quarts** MASC NOUN
three-quarters ◇ *les trois-quarts de la classe* three-quarters of the class

le **trombone** NOUN

[1] trombone ◇ *Il joue du trombone.* He plays the trombone.

[2] paper clip

la **trompe** NOUN
trunk ◇ *la trompe d'un éléphant* an elephant's trunk

tromper VERB
to deceive

• **se tromper** to make a mistake ◇ *Tout le monde peut se tromper.* Anyone can make a mistake.

• **se tromper de jour** to get the wrong day

• **Vous vous êtes trompé de numéro.** You've got the wrong number.

la **trompette** NOUN
trumpet ◇ *Il joue de la trompette.* He plays the trumpet.

• **Il a le nez en trompette.** He's got a turned-up nose.

le **tronc** NOUN
trunk ◇ *un tronc d'arbre* a tree trunk

trop ADVERB

[1] too ◇ *Il conduit trop vite.* He drives too fast.

[2] too much ◇ *J'ai trop mangé.* I've eaten too much.

• **trop de (1)** too much ◇ *J'ai acheté trop de pain.* I bought too much bread. ◇ *trois francs de trop* 3 francs too much

• **trop de (2)** too many ◇ *J'ai apporté trop de vêtements.* I've brought too many clothes.

• **trois personnes de trop** 3 people too many

le **tropique** NOUN
tropic

le **trottoir** NOUN
pavement

le **trou** NOUN
hole

• **J'ai eu un trou de mémoire.** My mind went blank.

trouble ADJECTIVE, ADVERB
cloudy ◇ *L'eau est trouble.* The water's cloudy.

• **Sans mes lunettes je vois trouble.** Without my glasses I can't see properly.

les **troubles** MASC NOUN

• **une période de troubles politiques** a period of political instability

trouer VERB
to make a hole in ◇ *Il a troué la*

moquette avec sa cigarette. He made a
hole in the carpet with his cigarette.

trouille NOUN
- **avoir la trouille** (*informal*) to be scared
to death

troupe NOUN
troop
- **une troupe de théâtre** a theatre
company

troupeau NOUN
(PL les **troupeaux**)
- **un troupeau de moutons** a flock of
sheep
- **un troupeau de vaches** a herd of cows

trousse NOUN
pencil case
- **une trousse de toilette** a toilet bag

trouver VERB
1 **to find** ◇ Je ne trouve pas mes
lunettes. I can't find my glasses.
2 **to think** ◇ Je trouve que c'est
bête. I think it's stupid.
- **se trouver** to be ◇ Où se trouve la
poste? Where is the post office?
◇ Marseille se trouve dans le sud de
la France. Marseilles is in the South of
France.
- **se trouver mal** to pass out

truc NOUN (*informal*)
1 **thing** ◇ un truc en plastique a
thing made of plastic ◇ J'ai plein de
trucs à faire ce week-end. I've got loads
of things to do this weekend.
2 **trick** ◇ Je vais te montrer un truc
qui réussit à tous les coups. I'll show
you a trick that never fails.

truite NOUN
trout

TSVP ABBREVIATION (= tournez s'il vous plaît)
PTO (= please turn over)

tu PRONOUN
you ◇ Est-ce que tu as un animal
familier? Have you got a pet?

tuba NOUN
1 **tuba** ◇ Je joue du tuba. I play the
tuba.
2 **snorkel**

tube NOUN
1 **tube** ◇ un tube de dentifrice a tube
of toothpaste
- **un tube de rouge à lèvres** a lipstick
2 **hit** ◇ Ça va être le tube de l'été.
It's going to be this summer's hit.

tuer VERB
to kill
- **se tuer** to get killed ◇ Il s'est tué
dans un accident de voiture. He got
killed in a car accident.

tue-tête

- **à tue-tête** ADVERB
at the top of one's voice ◇ crier à
tue-tête to shout at the top of one's
voice ◇ Il chantait à tue-tête. He was
singing at the top of his voice.

tuile NOUN
tile ◇ un toit en tuiles a tiled roof

tunique NOUN
tunic

Tunisie NOUN
Tunisia

tunisien ADJECTIVE
(FEM SING **tunisienne**)
Tunisian

tunnel NOUN
tunnel
- **le tunnel sous la Manche** the Channel
Tunnel

turbulent ADJECTIVE
boisterous

turc ADJECTIVE, NOUN
(FEM SING **turque**)
Turkish ◇ Il parle turc. He speaks
Turkish.
- **un Turc** a Turk (*man*)
- **une Turque** a Turk (*woman*)

Turquie NOUN
Turkey

tutoyer VERB
- **tutoyer quelqu'un** to address
somebody as "tu"

tutoyer quelqu'un means to use **tu** when
speaking to someone, rather than **vous**. Use **tu**
only when talking to one person and when that
person is someone of your own age or whom you
know well; use **vous** to everyone else. If in
doubt use **vous**.

- **On se tutoie?** Shall we use "tu" to each
other?

tuyau NOUN
(PL les **tuyaux**)
1 **pipe**
- **un tuyau d'arrosage** a hosepipe
2 **tip** ◇ Il m'a donné un bon tuyau.
(*informal*) He gave me a handy tip.

TVA NOUN (= taxe sur la valeur ajoutée)
VAT

tympan NOUN
eardrum

type NOUN (*informal*)
guy ◇ C'est un type formidable. He's
a great guy.

typique ADJECTIVE
typical

tyran NOUN
tyrant ◇ C'est un vrai tyran. He's a
real tyrant.

tzigane NOUN
gipsy

U

un ARTICLE, PRONOUN, ADJECTIVE

1 **a** ◦ *un garçon* a boy
an ◦ *un œuf* an egg
2 **one** ◦ *l'un des meilleurs* one of
the best ◦ *un citron et deux oranges*
one lemon and two oranges
◦ *Combien de timbres?—Un.* How
many stamps? One. ◦ *Elle a un an.*
She's one year old.

- **l'un..., l'autre...** one..., the other...
◦ *L'un est grand, l'autre est petit.*
One is tall, the other is short.
- **les uns..., les autres...** some...,
others... ◦ *Les uns marchaient, les
autres couraient.* Some were walking,
others were running.
- **l'un ou l'autre** either of them
◦ *Prends l'un ou l'autre, ça m'est
égal.* Take either of them, I don't
mind.
- **un par un** one by one ◦ *Ils entraient
un par un.* They went in one by one.

unanime ADJECTIVE
unanimous

l'**unanimité** FEM NOUN

- **à l'unanimité** unanimously

une ARTICLE, PRONOUN, ADJECTIVE

1 **a** ◦ *une fille* a girl
an ◦ *une pomme* an apple
2 **one** ◦ *une pomme et deux
bananes* one apple and two bananas
◦ *Combien de cartes postales?—Une.*
How many postcards?—One. ◦ *à une
heure du matin* at one in the morning
◦ *l'une des meilleures* one of the
best

- **l'une..., l'autre...** one..., the other...
◦ *L'une est grande, l'autre est petite.*
One is tall, the other is short.
- **les unes..., les autres...** some...,
others... ◦ *Les unes marchaient, les
autres couraient.* Some were walking,
others were running.
- **l'une ou l'autre** either of them
◦ *Prends l'une ou l'autre, ça m'est
égal.* Take either of them, I don't
mind.
- **une par une** one by one ◦ *Elles
entraient une par une.* They went in
one by one.

uni ADJECTIVE

1 **plain** ◦ *un tissu uni* a plain fabric
2 **close-knit** ◦ *une famille unie* a
close-knit family

l'**uniforme** MASC NOUN
uniform

l'**union** FEM NOUN
union

- **l'ex-Union soviétique** the former
Soviet Union

unique ADJECTIVE
unique ◦ *Tout individu a des
empreintes uniques.* Everyone's
fingerprints are unique. ◦ *C'est une
occasion unique.* It's a unique
opportunity.

- **Il est fils unique.** He's an only child.
- **Elle est fille unique.** She's an only
child.

uniquement ADVERB
only

l'**unité** FEM NOUN

1 **unity** ◦ *l'unité européenne*
European unity
2 **unit** ◦ *une unité de mesure* a unit
of measurement

l'**univers** MASC NOUN
universe

universitaire ADJECTIVE
university ◦ *un diplôme universitaire*
a university degree

- **faire des études universitaires** to
study at university

l'**université** FEM NOUN
university ◦ *aller à l'université* to go
to university

l'**urgence** FEM NOUN

- **C'est une urgence.** It's urgent.
- **Il n'y a pas urgence.** It's not urgent.
- **le service des urgences** the accident
and emergency department
- **Il a été transporté d'urgence à
l'hôpital.** He was rushed to hospital.
- **Téléphonez d'urgence.** Phone as soon
as possible.

urgent ADJECTIVE
urgent

l'**urine** FEM NOUN
urine

les **USA** MASC NOUN
USA

- **aux USA (1)** in the USA
- **aux USA (2)** to the USA

l'**usage** MASC NOUN
use ◦ *à usage interne* for internal
use ◦ *à usage externe* for external use
only

- **hors d'usage** out of action ◦ *Cet
appareil est hors d'usage.* That
machine's out of action.

usagé ADJECTIVE

1 **old** ◦ *un manteau usagé* an old

coat

2 used ⋄ *une seringue usagée* a used syringe

l'**usager** MASC NOUN

user ⋄ *les usagers de la route* road users

usé ADJECTIVE

worn ⋄ *Mon jean est un peu usé.* My jeans are a bit worn.

s'**user** VERB

to wear out ⋄ *Mes baskets se sont usées en quinze jours.* My trainers wore out in two weeks.

l'**usine** FEM NOUN

factory ⋄ *une usine de sardines* a sardine factory

l'**ustensile** MASC NOUN

- **un ustensile de cuisine** a kitchen utensil

usuel ADJECTIVE

(FEM SING **usuelle**)

everyday ⋄ *la langue usuelle* everyday language

utile ADJECTIVE

useful

l'**utilisation** FEM NOUN

use ⋄ *L'utilisation des calculatrices est interdite.* It is forbidden to use calculators.

utiliser VERB

to use

l'**utilité** FEM NOUN

use ⋄ *Ce gadget n'est pas d'une grande utilité.* This gadget isn't much use.

U

V

va VERB *see* **aller**

les **vacances** FEM NOUN
>   **holidays** ◇ *aller en vacances* to go
>   on holiday ◇ *être en vacances* to be
>   on holiday
>   - **les grandes vacances** the summer
>   holidays

le **vacancier** NOUN
>   **holiday-maker**

la **vacancière** NOUN
>   **holiday-maker**

le **vacarme** NOUN
>   **racket** ◇ *Qu'est-ce que c'est que ce
>   vacarme?* What's all this racket?

le **vaccin** NOUN
>   **vaccination**

la **vaccination** NOUN
>   **vaccination** ◇ *La vaccination est
>   obligatoire.* Vaccination is compulsory.

vacciner VERB
>   **to vaccinate** ◇ *se faire vacciner
>   contre la rubéole* to be vaccinated
>   against German measles

la **vache** NOUN
>   *see also* **vache** ADJECTIVE
>   **cow**

vache ADJECTIVE (*informal*)
>   *see also* **vache** NOUN
>   **mean** ◇ *C'est vraiment vache, ce qu'il
>   a dit.* What he said was really mean.
>   ◇ *Il est vache.* He's a mean sod.

vachement ADVERB (*informal*)
>   **really** ◇ *Viens te baigner, l'eau est
>   vachement chaude.* Come in the water,
>   it's really warm.

le **vagabond** NOUN
>   **tramp**

le **vagin** NOUN
>   **vagina**

la **vague** NOUN
>   *see also* **vague** ADJECTIVE
>   **wave** (*in sea*)

vague ADJECTIVE
>   *see also* **vague** NOUN
>   **vague** ◇ *J'ai un vague souvenir de lui.*
>   I vaguely remember him.

vain ADJECTIVE
>   - **en vain** in vain

vaincre VERB
>   1 **to defeat** ◇ *L'armée a été vaincue.*
>   The army was defeated.
>   2 **to overcome** ◇ *Il a réussi à
>   vaincre sa timidité.* He managed to
>   overcome his shyness.

le **vainqueur** NOUN
>   **winner**

vais VERB *see* **aller**
>   - **Je vais écrire à mes cousins.** I'm
>   going to write to my cousins.

le **vaisseau** NOUN
>   (PL les **vaisseaux**)
>   - **un vaisseau spatial** a spaceship
>   - **un vaisseau sanguin** a blood
>   vessel

la **vaisselle** NOUN
>   1 **washing-up** ◇ *Je vais faire la
>   vaisselle.* I'll do the washing-up.
>   2 **dishes** ◇ *Tu peux ranger la
>   vaisselle s'il te plaît?* Can you put the
>   dishes away please?

valable ADJECTIVE
>   **valid** ◇ *Ce billet d'avion est valable
>   un an.* This plane ticket is valid for one
>   year.

le **valet** NOUN
>   **jack** (*in card games*) ◇ *le valet de
>   carreau* the jack of diamonds

la **valeur** NOUN
>   **value** ◇ *sans valeur* of no value
>   - **des objets de valeur** valuables ◇ *Ne
>   laissez pas d'objets de valeur dans votre
>   chambre.* Don't leave any valuables in
>   your room.

valider VERB
>   **to stamp** ◇ *Vous devez faire valider
>   votre billet avant votre départ.* You must
>   get your ticket stamped before you
>   leave.

la **valise** NOUN
>   **suitcase**

la **vallée** NOUN
>   **valley**

valoir VERB
>   **to be worth** ◇ *Ça vaut combien?*
>   How much is it worth? ◇ *Cette voiture
>   vaut très cher.* This car's worth a lot of
>   money.
>   - **Ça vaut mieux.** That would be better.
>   ◇ *Il vaut mieux ne rien dire.* It would
>   be better to say nothing.
>   - **valoir la peine** to be worth it ◇ *Ça
>   vaudrait la peine d'essayer.* It would be
>   worth a try.

le **vampire** NOUN
>   **vampire**

le **vandalisme** NOUN
>   **vandalism**

la **vanille** NOUN
>   **vanilla** ◇ *une glace à la vanille* a
>   vanilla ice cream

la **vanité** NOUN
>   **vanity**

vaniteux ADJECTIVE
(FEM SING **vaniteuse**)
   conceited
se **vanter** VERB
   to boast
la **vapeur** NOUN
   steam ◦ *des légumes cuits à la vapeur* steamed vegetables
la **varappe** NOUN
   rock climbing ◦ *faire de la varappe* to go rock climbing
variable ADJECTIVE
   changeable *(weather)*
la **varicelle** NOUN
   chickenpox ◦ *Elle a la varicelle.* She's got chickenpox.
varié ADJECTIVE
   varied ◦ *Son travail est très varié.* His job is very varied.
varier VERB
   to vary
- **Le menu varie tous les jours.** The menu changes every day.
la **variété** NOUN
   variety ◦ *Il n'y a pas beaucoup de variété.* There isn't much variety.
- **une émission de variétés** a television variety show
vas VERB *see* **aller**
le **vase** NOUN
   see also la vase
   vase
la **vase** NOUN
   see also le vase
   mud
vaste ADJECTIVE
   vast
vaudrait, vaut VERB *see* **valoir**
le **vautour** NOUN
   vulture
le **veau** NOUN X
(PL les **veaux**)
   1 calf *(animal)*
   2 veal *(meat)*
vécu VERB *see* **vivre**
- **Il a vécu à Paris pendant dix ans.** He lived in Paris for ten years.
la **vedette** NOUN
   1 star ◦ *une vedette de cinéma* a film star
   2 motor boat
- **une vedette de police** a police launch
végétal ADJECTIVE
(MASC PL **végétaux**)
   vegetable ◦ *l'huile végétale* vegetable oil
végétarien ADJECTIVE
(FEM SING **végétarienne**)
   vegetarian ◦ *Je suis végétarien.* I'm

a vegetarian.
la **végétation** NOUN
   vegetation
le **véhicule** NOUN
   vehicle
la **veille** NOUN
   the day before ◦ *la veille de son départ* the day before he left ◦ *la veille au soir* the previous evening
- **la veille de Noël** Christmas Eve
- **la veille du jour de l'An** New Year's Eve
veinard ADJECTIVE *(informal)*
- **Qu'est-ce qu'il est veinard!** He's such a lucky devil!
la **veine** NOUN
   vein
- **avoir de la veine** *(informal)* to be lucky
le/la **véliplanchiste** NOUN
   windsurfer
le **vélo** NOUN
   bike ◦ *faire du vélo* to go cycling
- **un vélo tout-terrain** a mountain bike
le **vélomoteur** NOUN
   moped
le **velours** NOUN
   velvet ◦ *une robe en velours* a velvet dress
- **le velours côtelé** corduroy ◦ *un pantalon en velours côtelé* corduroy trousers
les **vendanges** FEM NOUN
   grape harvest ◦ *On fait les vendanges en septembre.* The grape harvest is in September.
le **vendeur** NOUN
   shop assistant
la **vendeuse** NOUN
   shop assistant
vendre VERB
   to sell
- **vendre quelque chose à quelqu'un** to sell somebody something ◦ *Il m'a vendu son vélo.* He sold me his bike.
- **"à vendre"** "for sale"
le **vendredi** NOUN
   1 Friday ◦ *Aujourd'hui, nous sommes vendredi.* It's Friday today.
   2 on Friday ◦ *Il est venu vendredi.* He came on Friday.
- **le vendredi** on Fridays ◦ *Je joue au foot le vendredi.* I play football on Fridays.
- **tous les vendredis** every Friday
- **vendredi dernier** last Friday
- **vendredi prochain** next Friday
- **le Vendredi saint** Good Friday
vénéneux ADJECTIVE
(FEM SING **vénéneuse**)

V

poisonous (*plant*) ◇ *un champignon vénéneux* a poisonous mushroom

la **vengeance** NOUN
revenge

se **venger** VERB
to get revenge

venimeux ADJECTIVE
(FEM SING **venimeuse**)
poisonous (*animal*) ◇ *un serpent venimeux* a poisonous snake

le **venin** NOUN
poison

venir VERB
to come ◇ *Il viendra demain.* He'll come tomorrow. ◇ *Il est venu nous voir.* He came to see us.
◆ **venir de** to have just ◇ *Je viens de le voir.* I've just seen him. ◇ *Je viens de lui téléphoner.* I've just phoned him.
◆ **faire venir quelqu'un** to call somebody out ◇ *faire venir le médecin* to call the doctor out

le **vent** NOUN
wind ◇ *Il y a du vent.* It's windy.

la **vente** NOUN
sale ◇ *une vente de charité* a jumble sale
◆ **une vente aux enchères** an auction

le **ventilateur** NOUN
fan (*for cooling*)

le **ventre** NOUN
stomach ◇ *avoir mal au ventre* to have stomachache

venu VERB see **venir**

le **ver** NOUN
worm
◆ **un ver de terre** an earthworm

le **verbe** NOUN
verb

le **verdict** NOUN
verdict

le **verger** NOUN
orchard

verglacé ADJECTIVE
icy ◇ *La route était verglacée.* The road was icy.

le **verglas** NOUN
black ice

véridique ADJECTIVE
truthful

la **vérification** NOUN
check ◇ *une vérification d'identité* an identity check

vérifier VERB
to check

véritable ADJECTIVE
real ◇ *C'était un véritable cauchemar.* It was a real nightmare.

◆ **en cuir véritable** made of real leather

la **vérité** NOUN
truth ◇ *dire la vérité* to tell the truth

verni ADJECTIVE
varnished
◆ **des chaussures vernies** patent leather shoes

vernir VERB
to varnish

le **vernis** NOUN
varnish ◇ *le vernis à ongles* nail varnish

verra, verrai, verras VERB see **voir**
◆ **on verra...** we'll see...

le **verre** NOUN
⑴ **glass** ◇ *une table en verre* a glass table ◇ *un verre d'eau* a glass of water
◆ **boire un verre** to have a drink
⑵ **lens** (*of spectacles*) ◇ *des verres de contact* contact lenses

verrez, verrons, verront VERB see **voir**

le **verrou** NOUN
bolt (*on door*)

verrouiller VERB
to bolt ◇ *N'oublie pas de verrouiller la porte du garage.* Don't forget to bolt the garage door.

la **verrue** NOUN
wart

le **vers** NOUN
see also **vers** PREPOSITION
line (*of poetry*) ◇ *au troisième vers* in the third line

vers PREPOSITION
see also **vers** NOUN
⑴ **towards** ◇ *Il allait vers la gare.* He was going towards the station.
⑵ **at about** ◇ *Il est rentré chez lui vers cinq heures.* He came home at about 5 o'clock.

verse
◆ **à verse** ADVERB ◇ *Il pleut à verse.* It's pouring with rain.

le **Verseau** NOUN
Aquarius ◇ *Georges est Verseau.* Georges is Aquarius.

le **versement** NOUN
instalment ◇ *en cinq versements* in 5 instalments

verser VERB
to pour ◇ *Est-ce que tu peux me verser un verre d'eau?* Could you pour me a glass of water?

la **version** NOUN
⑴ **version**
⑵ **translation** (*from the foreign language*)
◆ **un film en version originale** a film in the original language

le **verso** NOUN
  back (*of sheet of paper*)
- **voir au verso** see overleaf

vert ADJECTIVE
  green

la **vertèbre** NOUN
  vertebra

vertical ADJECTIVE
  (MASC PL **verticaux**)
  vertical

le **vertige** NOUN
  vertigo ◇ *avoir le vertige* to have
  vertigo

la **verveine** NOUN
  verbena tea

la **vessie** NOUN
  bladder

la **veste** NOUN
  jacket

le **vestiaire** NOUN
  1 **cloakroom** (*in theatre, museum*)
  2 **changing room** (*at sports ground*)

le **vestibule** NOUN
  hall

le **vêtement** NOUN
  garment
- **les vêtements** clothes

la **vétérinaire** NOUN
  vet ◇ *Elle est vétérinaire.* She's a vet.

le **veuf** NOUN
  widower ◇ *Il est veuf.* He's a
  widower.

**veuille, veuillez, veuillons,
veulent, veut** VERB *see* **vouloir**
- **Veuillez fermer la porte en sortant.**
  Please shut the door when you go out.

la **veuve** NOUN
  widow ◇ *Elle est veuve.* She's a
  widow.

veux VERB *see* **vouloir**

vexer VERB
- **vexer quelqu'un** to hurt somebody's
  feelings
- **se vexer** to be offended

la **viande** NOUN
  meat
- **la viande hachée** mince

vibrer VERB
  to vibrate

le **vice** NOUN
  vice

vicieux ADJECTIVE
  (FEM SING **vicieuse**)
  lecherous ◇ *Il est un peu vicieux.*
  He's a bit of a lecher.

la **victime** NOUN
  victim

la **victoire** NOUN
  victory

vide ADJECTIVE
  see also **vide** NOUN
  empty

le **vide** NOUN
  see also **vide** ADJECTIVE
  vacuum ◇ *emballé sous vide*
  vacuum-packed
- **avoir peur du vide** to be afraid of
  heights

la **vidéo** NOUN
  see also **vidéo** ADJECTIVE
  video

vidéo ADJECTIVE (MASC, FEM, PL)
  see also **vidéo** NOUN
  video ◇ *une cassette vidéo* a video
  cassette ◇ *un jeu vidéo* a video game
  ◇ *une caméra vidéo* a video camera

le **vidéoclip** NOUN
  music video

le **vidéoclub** NOUN
  video shop

vider VERB
  to empty

la **vie** NOUN
  life
- **être en vie** to be alive

vieil ADJECTIVE
  vieil *is used with a masculine singular noun in*
  place of **vieux** *when the noun begins with a*
  vowel sound.
  old ◇ *un vieil arbre* an old tree ◇ *un*
  vieil homme an old man

le **vieillard** NOUN
  old man

vieille ADJECTIVE
  (MASC SING **vieux**)
  see also **vieille** NOUN
  old ◇ *une vieille dame* an old lady
- **une vieille fille** an old maid

la **vieille** NOUN
  see also **vieille** ADJECTIVE
  old woman
- **Eh bien, ma vieille...** (*informal*) Well,
  my dear...

la **vieillesse** NOUN
  old age

vieillir VERB
  to age ◇ *Il a beaucoup vieilli depuis la*
  dernière fois que je l'ai vu. He's aged a
  lot since I last saw him.

viendrai, vienne, viens VERB *see*
venir
- **Je viendrai dès que possible.** I'll
  come as soon as possible.
- **Je voudrais que tu viennes.** I'd like
  you to come.
- **Viens ici!** Come here!

la **Vierge** NOUN
  see also **vierge** ADJECTIVE

V

Virgo ◇ *Pascal est Vierge.* Pascal is Virgo.
- **la Vierge** the Virgin Mary

vierge ADJECTIVE
see also **Vierge** NOUN
1 **virgin** ◇ *Il est vierge.* He's a virgin.
2 **blank** ◇ *une cassette vierge* a blank cassette

le **Viêt-Nam** NOUN
Vietnam

vietnamien ADJECTIVE, NOUN
(FEM SING **vietnamienne**)
Vietnamese
- **un Vietnamien** a Vietnamese (*man*)
- **une Vietnamienne** a Vietnamese (*woman*)
- **les Vietnamiens** the Vietnamese

vieux ADJECTIVE
(FEM SING **vieille**)
see also **vieux** NOUN
old ◇ *Il fait plus vieux que son âge.* He looks older than he is.
- **un vieux garçon** a bachelor

le **vieux** NOUN
see also **vieux** ADJECTIVE
old man ◇ *Eh bien, mon vieux...* (*informal*) Well, my old mate...
- **les vieux** old people

vieux jeu ADJECTIVE (MASC, FEM, PL)
old-fashioned ◇ *Il est un peu vieux jeu.* He's a bit old-fashioned.

vif ADJECTIVE
(FEM SING **vive**)
1 **sharp** (*mentally*) ◇ *Il est très vif.* He's very sharp.
- **avoir l'esprit vif** to be quick-witted
2 **crisp** ◇ *L'air est plus vif à la campagne qu'en ville.* The air is crisper in the country than in the town.
3 **bright** (*colour*) ◇ *un bleu vif* a bright blue

la **vigne** NOUN
vine
- **des champs de vigne** vineyards

le **vigneron** NOUN
wine grower

la **vignette** NOUN
tax disc

le **vignoble** NOUN
vineyard

vilain ADJECTIVE
1 **naughty** ◇ *C'est très vilain de dire des mensonges.* It's very naughty to tell lies.
2 **ugly** ◇ *Il n'est pas vilain.* He's not bad-looking.

la **villa** NOUN
villa ◇ *une villa en multipropriété* a time-share villa

le **village** NOUN
village

le **villageois** NOUN
villager

la **villageoise** NOUN
villager

la **ville** NOUN
town
- **une grande ville** a city

le **vin** NOUN
wine ◇ *le vin de pays* local wine ◇ *le vin ordinaire* table wine

le **vinaigre** NOUN
vinegar

la **vinaigrette** NOUN
French dressing

vingt NUMBER
twenty ◇ *Elle a vingt ans.* She's twenty. ◇ *à vingt heures* at 8 p.m.
- **le vingt février** the twentieth of February
- **vingt et un** twenty-one
- **vingt-deux** twenty-two

la **vingtaine** NOUN
about twenty ◇ *une vingtaine de personnes* about twenty people
- **Il a une vingtaine d'années.** He's about twenty.

vingtième ADJECTIVE
twentieth

le **viol** NOUN
rape

violemment ADVERB
violently

la **violence** NOUN
violence

violent ADJECTIVE
violent

violer VERB
to rape

violet ADJECTIVE
(FEM SING **violette**)
purple

la **violette** NOUN
violet (*flower*)

le **violon** NOUN
violin ◇ *Je joue du violon.* I play the violin.

le **violoncelle** NOUN
cello ◇ *Elle joue du violoncelle.* She plays the cello.

le/la **violoniste** NOUN
violinist

la **vipère** NOUN
viper

le **virage** NOUN
bend ◇ *une route pleine de virages dangereux* a road full of dangerous

bends

la **virgule** NOUN

⊡ **comma**

⊡ **decimal point** ◇ *trois virgule cinq* three point five

le **virus** NOUN

virus

vis VERB *see* **vivre**

see also **vis** NOUN

- **Je vis en Écosse.** I live in Scotland.

la **vis** NOUN

see also **vis** VERB

screw

le **visa** NOUN

visa

le **visage** NOUN

face ◇ *Elle a le visage rond.* She's got a round face.

vis-à-vis PREPOSITION

with regard to ◇ *Ce n'est pas très juste vis-à-vis de lui.* It's not very fair to him.

viser VERB

to aim at ◇ *Il faut viser la cible.* You have to aim at the target.

la **visibilité** NOUN

visibility

visible ADJECTIVE

visible

la **visière** NOUN

peak (*of cap*)

la **visite** NOUN

visit

- **rendre visite à quelqu'un** to visit somebody ◇ *Je vais rendre visite à mon grand-père.* I'm going to visit my grandfather.
- **avoir de la visite** to have visitors ◇ *Nous avons de la visite aujourd'hui.* We've got visitors today.
- **une visite médicale** a medical examination

visiter VERB

to visit

le **visiteur** NOUN

visitor

la **visiteuse** NOUN

visitor

le **vison** NOUN

mink (*fur*) ◇ *un manteau en vison* a mink coat

vit VERB *see* **vivre**

- **Il vit chez ses parents.** He lives with his parents.

vital ADJECTIVE

(MASC PL **vitaux**)

vital ◇ *C'est une question vitale.* It's of vital importance.

la **vitamine** NOUN

vitamin

vite ADVERB

⊡ **quick** ◇ *Vite, ils arrivent!* Quick, they're coming! ◇ *Je peux aller dire au revoir à Claire?—Oui, mais fais vite!* Can I go and say goodbye to Claire?—Yes, but be quick! ◇ *Prenons la voiture, ça ira plus vite.* Let's take the car, it'll be quicker.

- **Le temps passe vite.** Time flies.

⊡ **fast** ◇ *Il roule trop vite.* He drives too fast.

⊡ **soon** ◇ *Il va vite oublier.* He'll soon forget.

- **Il a vite compris.** He understood immediately.

la **vitesse** NOUN

⊡ **speed** ◇ *à toute vitesse* at top speed ◇ *Nous sommes rentrés à toute vitesse.* We rushed back home.

⊡ **gear** ◇ *en première vitesse* in first gear

le **vitrail** NOUN

(PL les **vitraux**)

stained-glass window

la **vitre** NOUN

window ◇ *Il a cassé une vitre.* He broke a window.

la **vitrine** NOUN

shop window

vivant ADJECTIVE

⊡ **living** ◇ *les êtres vivants* living creatures ◇ *les expériences sur les animaux vivants* experiments on live animals

⊡ **lively** ◇ *Elle est très vivante.* She's very lively.

vive ADJECTIVE

(MASC SING **vif**)

see also **vive** EXCLAMATION

⊡ **sharp** (*mentally*) ◇ *Elle est très vive.* She's very sharp.

⊡ **bright** (*colour*)

- **à vive allure** at a brisk pace
- **de vive voix** in person ◇ *Je te le dirai de vive voix.* I'll tell you about it when I see you.

vive EXCLAMATION

see also **vive** ADJECTIVE

- **Vive le roi!** Long live the king!

vivement EXCLAMATION

- **Vivement les vacances!** Roll on the holidays!

vivre VERB

to live ◇ *J'aimerais vivre à l'étranger.* I'd like to live abroad. ◇ *Et ton grand-père? Il vit encore?* What about your grandfather? Is he still alive?

vlan EXCLAMATION
wham!

le **vocabulaire** NOUN
vocabulary

la **vocation** NOUN
vocation

le **vœu** NOUN
(PL les **vœux**)
wish ◇ *faire un vœu* to make a wish
◇ *Meilleurs vœux de bonne année!*
Best wishes for the New Year!

la **vogue** NOUN
fashion ◇ *C'est très en vogue en ce moment.* It's very fashionable at the moment.

voici PREPOSITION
1 **this is** ◇ *Voici mon frère et voilà ma sœur.* This is my brother and that's my sister.
2 **here is** ◇ *Tu as perdu ton stylo? Tiens, en voici un autre.* Have you lost your pen? Here's another one.
- **Le voici!** Here you are! ◇ *Tu veux tes clés? Tiens, les voici!* You want your keys? Here you are!

la **voie** NOUN
lane ◇ *une route à trois voies* a 3-lane road
- **par voie buccale** orally ◇ *à prendre par voie buccale* to be taken orally
- **la voie ferrée** the railway track

voilà PREPOSITION
1 **there is** ◇ *Tiens! Voilà Paul.* Look! There's Paul. ◇ *Tu as perdu ton stylo? Tiens, en voilà un autre.* Have you lost your pen? There's another one.
- **Les voilà!** There they are!
2 **that is** ◇ *Voilà ma sœur.* That's my sister.

le **voile** NOUN
see also la voile
veil ◇ *un voile de mariée* a wedding veil

la **voile** NOUN
see also le voile
1 **sail**
2 **sailing** ◇ *faire de la voile* to go sailing
- **un bateau à voiles** a sailing boat

le **voilier** NOUN
sailing boat

voir VERB

Present tense:	
je vois	nous voyons
tu vois	vous voyez
il/elle voit	ils/elles voient
Past participle: *vu*	

to see ◇ *Venez me voir quand vous serez à Paris.* Come and see me when

you're in Paris. ◇ *Je ne vois pas pourquoi il a fait ça.* I can't see why he did that.
- **faire voir quelque chose à quelqu'un** to show somebody something ◇ *Il m'a fait voir sa collection de timbres.* He showed me his stamp collection.
- **se voir** to be obvious ◇ *Est-ce que cette tache se voit?* Does that stain show? ◇ *Ça fait des années qu'elle n'a pas joué au tennis—Oui, ça se voit!* She hasn't played tennis for years—Yes, you can tell!
- **avoir quelque chose à voir avec** to have something to do with ◇ *Ça n'a rien à voir avec lui, c'est entre toi et moi.* It's nothing to do with him, it's between you and me.
- **Je ne peux vraiment pas la voir.** (*informal*) I really can't stand her.

le **voisin** NOUN
neighbour

le **voisinage** NOUN
- **dans le voisinage** in the vicinity

la **voisine** NOUN
neighbour

la **voiture** NOUN
car ◇ *une voiture de sport* a sports car

la **voix** NOUN
(PL les **voix**)
1 **voice** ◇ *à voix basse* in a low voice
- **à haute voix** aloud
2 **vote** ◇ *Il a obtenu cinquante pour cent des voix.* He got 50% of the votes.

le **vol** NOUN
1 **flight**
- **à vol d'oiseau** as the crow flies
- **le vol à voile** gliding
2 **theft** ◇ *un vol à main armée* an armed robbery

la **volaille** NOUN
poultry

le **volant** NOUN
1 **steering wheel** ◇ *Est-ce que tu veux que je prenne le volant?* Do you want me to take the wheel?
2 **shuttlecock**

le **volcan** NOUN
volcano

la **volée** NOUN
volley (*in tennis*)
- **rattraper une balle à la volée** to catch a ball in mid-air

voler VERB
1 **to fly** ◇ *J'aimerais savoir voler.* I'd like to be able to fly.
2 **to steal** ◇ *On a volé mon appareil*

photo. My camera's been stolen.
- **voler quelque chose à quelqu'un** to steal something from somebody ◇ *Ça n'est pas son stylo, il me l'a volé.* That's not his pen, he stole it from me.
- **voler quelqu'un** to rob somebody

le **volet** NOUN
shutter

le **voleur** NOUN
thief

la **voleuse** NOUN
thief

le **volley** NOUN
volleyball ◇ *jouer au volley* to play volleyball

le/la **volontaire** NOUN
volunteer

la **volonté** NOUN
willpower ◇ *Il a beaucoup de volonté.* He's got a lot of willpower.
- **la bonne volonté** goodwill
- **la mauvaise volonté** lack of goodwill

volontiers ADVERB
[1] **gladly** ◇ *Je l'aiderais volontiers s'il me le demandais.* I'd gladly help him if he asked me.
[2] **please** ◇ *Voulez-vous boire quelque chose?–Volontiers!* Would you like something to drink?–Yes, please!

le **volume** NOUN
volume ◇ *un dictionnaire en deux volumes* a two-volume dictionary

volumineux ADJECTIVE
(FEM SING **volumineuse**)
bulky

vomir VERB
to vomit ◇ *Il a vomi toute la nuit.* He was vomiting all night.

vont VERB *see* **aller**

vos ADJECTIVE
your ◇ *Rangez vos jouets, les enfants!* Children, put your toys away! ◇ *Merci pour vos fleurs, M. Durand.* Thanks for your flowers, Mr Durand.

le **vote** NOUN
vote

voter VERB
to vote

votre ADJECTIVE
(PL **vos**)
your ◇ *C'est votre manteau?* Is this your coat?

vôtre PRONOUN
- **le vôtre** yours ◇ *J'aime bien notre prof de maths, mais le vôtre est plus patient.* I like our maths teacher, but yours is more patient. ◇ *À qui est cette*

écharpe? C'est la vôtre? Whose is this scarf? Is it yours?
- **À la vôtre!** Cheers!

vôtres PRONOUN
- **les vôtres** yours ◇ *J'ai oublié mes lunettes de soleil. Vous avez apporté les vôtres?* I've forgotten my sunglasses. Have you brought yours?

voudra, voudrai, voudrais, voudras, voudrez, voudrons, voudront VERB *see* **vouloir**
- **Je voudrais...** I'd like... ◇ *Je voudrais deux litres de lait, s'il vous plaît.* I'd like two litres of milk, please.

vouloir VERB

Present tense:	
je veux	nous voulons
tu veux	vous voulez
il/elle veut	ils/elles veulent
Past participle: *voulu*	

to want ◇ *Elle veut un vélo pour Noël.* She wants a bike for Christmas.
◇ *Je ne veux pas de dessert.* I don't want any pudding. ◇ *Il ne veut pas venir.* He doesn't want to come. ◇ *On va au cinéma?–Si tu veux.* Shall we go to the cinema?–If you like.
- **Je veux bien.** I'll be happy to. ◇ *Je veux bien le faire à ta place si ça t'arrange.* I don't mind doing it for you if you prefer.
- **Voulez-vous une tasse de thé?–Je veux bien.** Would you like a cup of tea?–Yes please.
- **sans le vouloir** without meaning to ◇ *Je l'ai vexé sans le vouloir.* I upset him without meaning to.
- **en vouloir à quelqu'un** to be angry at somebody ◇ *Il m'en veut de ne pas l'avoir invité à mon anniversaire.* He's angry at me for not inviting me to my birthday party.
- **vouloir dire** to mean ◇ *Qu'est-ce que ça veut dire?* What does that mean?

voulu VERB *see* **vouloir**

vous PRONOUN
[1] **you** ◇ *Vous aimez la pizza?* Do you like pizza?
[2] **to you** ◇ *Je vous écrirai bientôt.* I'll write to you soon.
[3] **yourself** ◇ *Vous vous êtes fait mal?* Have you hurt yourself?
- **vous-même** yourself ◇ *Vous l'avez fait vous-même?* Did you do it yourself?

vouvoyer VERB
- **vouvoyer quelqu'un** to address

somebody as "vous"

> **vouvoyer quelqu'un** *means to use* **vous**
> *when speaking to someone, rather than* **tu**. *Use*
> **tu** *only when talking to one person and when*
> *that person is someone of your own age or*
> *whom you know well; use* **vous** *to everyone else.*
> *If in doubt use* **vous**.

- **Est-ce que je dois vouvoyer ta sœur?**
  Should I use "vous" to your sister?

le **voyage** NOUN
  journey ◇ *Avez-vous fait bon*
  voyage? Did you have a good journey?
- **Bon voyage!** Have a good trip!

voyager VERB
  to travel

le **voyageur** NOUN
  passenger

la **voyageuse** NOUN
  passenger

voyaient, voyais, voyait VERB *see*
  voir

la **voyelle** NOUN
  vowel

voyez, voyiez, voyions VERB *see*
  voir

voyons VERB *see* **voir**
  1 **let's see** ◇ *Voyons ce qu'on peut*
  faire. Let's see what we can do.
  2 **come on** ◇ *Voyons, sois*
  raisonnable! Come on, be reasonable!

le **voyou** NOUN
  hooligan

vrac
- **en vrac** ADVERB

  loose ◇ *du thé en vrac* loose tea
vrai ADJECTIVE
  true ◇ *une histoire vraie* a true story
  ◇ *C'est vrai?* Is that true?
- **à vrai dire** to tell the truth
vraiment ADVERB
  really
vraisemblable ADJECTIVE
  likely ◇ *C'est peu vraisemblable.*
  That's not very likely. ◇ *Il va falloir*
  trouver une excuse vraisemblable. We'll
  have to find a convincing excuse.
le **VTT** NOUN (= *vélo tout-terrain*)
  mountain bike
vu VERB *see* **voir**
- **être bien vu** to be popular (*person*)
  ◇ *Est-ce qu'il est bien vu à l'école?* Is
  he popular at school?
- **être mal vu** to be disapproved of
  ◇ *C'est mal vu de fumer ici.* They
  don't like people smoking here.
la **vue** NOUN
  1 **eyesight** ◇ *J'ai une mauvaise vue.*
  I've got bad eyesight.
  2 **view** ◇ *Il y a une belle vue d'ici.*
  There's a lovely view from here.
- **à vue d'œil** visibly ◇ *Elle grandit à*
  vue d'œil. Every time you see her, she's
  got taller.
vulgaire ADJECTIVE
  vulgar ◇ *Ne dit pas ça, c'est très*
  vulgaire. Don't say that, it's very
  vulgar.

W

le **wagon** NOUN
> railway carriage

le **wagon-lit** NOUN
> (PL les **wagons-lits**)
> sleeper (*on train*)

le **wagon-restaurant** NOUN
> (PL les **wagons-restaurants**)
> restaurant car

le **walkman** ® NOUN
> Walkman ®

wallon ADJECTIVE, NOUN
> (FEM SING **wallonne**)
> Walloon (*French-speaking Belgian*)

- **les Wallons** the French-speaking Belgians

la **Wallonie** NOUN
> French-speaking Belgium

les **W.-C.** MASC NOUN
> toilet

le **week-end** NOUN
> weekend

le **western** NOUN
> western (*film*)

le **whisky** NOUN
> (PL les **whiskies**)
> whisky

X

le **xylophone** NOUN
> xylophone ⋄ *Elle joue du xylophone.* She plays the xylophone.

Y

y PRONOUN
> there ⋄ *Nous y sommes allés l'été dernier.* We went there last summer. ⋄ *Regarde dans le tiroir: je pense que les clés y sont.* Look in the drawer: I think the keys are in there.
>
> y *replaces phrases with* **à** *in constructions like the ones below.*

- **Je pensais à l'examen.–Mais arrête d'y penser!** I was thinking about the exam.–Well, stop thinking about it!
- **Je ne m'attendais pas à ça.–Eh bien moi, je m'y attendais.** I wasn't expecting that.–Well, I was expecting it.

le **yaourt** NOUN
> yoghurt ⋄ *un yaourt nature* a plain yoghurt ⋄ *un yaourt aux fruits* a fruit yoghurt

les **yeux** MASC NOUN
> (SING **œil**)
> eyes ⋄ *Elle a les yeux bleus.* She's got blue eyes.

le **yoga** NOUN
> yoga

le **yoghourt** NOUN
> yoghurt

la **Yougoslavie** NOUN
> Yugoslavia

- **l'ex-Yougoslavie** the former Yugoslavia

youpi EXCLAMATION
> Yippee!

le **yoyo** NOUN
> yo-yo

Z

zapper VERB
  to channel hop

le **zèbre** NOUN
  zebra

le **zéro** NOUN
  zero
  - **Ils ont gagné trois à zéro.** They won three-nil.

zézayer VERB
  to lisp ◇ *Il zézaie.* He's got a lisp.

le **zigzag** NOUN
  - **faire des zigzags** to zigzag

la **zone** NOUN
  zone
  - **une zone industrielle** an industrial estate

le **zoo** NOUN
  zoo

zut EXCLAMATION
  Oh heck!

PUZZLES AND WORDGAMES

Introduction

The puzzles and wordgames on the following pages have been designed to give you practice in using your dictionary. Make sure you read the "How to use the dictionary" section at the front of this book before you start. Don't worry, there are answers at the end of the wordgames in case you get really stuck!

CHOOSING THE RIGHT TRANSLATION

Complete the crossword below by looking up the English words in the list and finding the correct French translations. There is a slight catch, however! All the English words have more than one French translation, but only one will fit correctly into each part of the crossword.

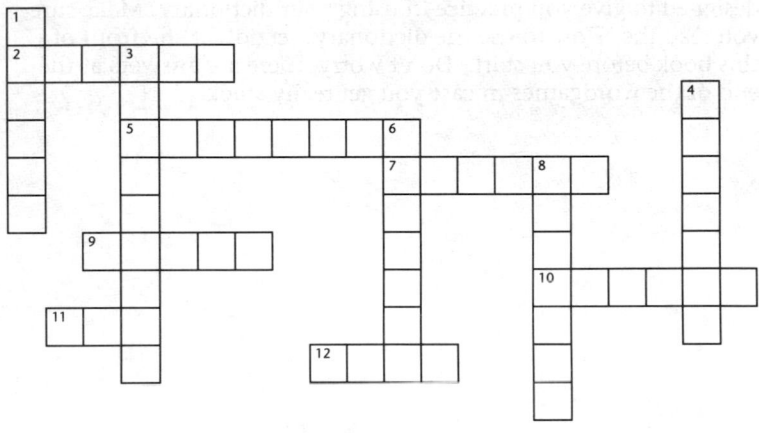

1. CLASS	5. NUT	9. DINNER
2. THROW	6. TAKE	10. STAY
3. KNOW	7. CALF	11. HARD
4. FIND	8. PLACE	12. LATE

NOUNS, ADJECTIVES, ADVERBS & VERBS

In each sentence below a word has been shaded. Put a tick in the appropriate box to show whether it's a **noun**, **adjective**, adverb or **verb** each time. Look in the section "How to use the dictionary" at the front of the book to remind you what nouns, adjectives, adverbs and verbs are. Remember, there may be more than one entry for each word.

SENTENCE	Noun	Adj	Adv	Verb
1. La ferme de mes parents est en Alsace.				
2. Il n'est pas franc.				
3. Le magasin ferme dans deux minutes.				
4. Le dîner est à 20 heures.				
5. Tu veux goûter ma mousse au chocolat?				
6. Je n'aime pas la bière.				
7. C'est un faux passeport.				
8. J'entends des pas dans l'escalier.				
9. Ce film nous a fait rire.				
10. Cette voiture est mal garée.				

NOUNS

This list contains the feminine form of some French nouns. Use your dictionary to find the **masculine** form. Remember, the masculine form usually appears in a separate entry.

Use your dictionary to find the **plural** of the following nouns. Remember, the plural form appears in brackets and in bold on the line below the singular form.

MASCULINE	FEMININE	SINGULAR	PLURAL
	danseuse	chou	
	boulangère	canal	
	Américaine	bateau	
	animatrice	sapeur–pompier	
	avocate	neveu	
	Parisienne	travail	
	libraire	vœu	
	téléspectatrice	voix	
	pionne	œil	
	veuve	croque-monsieur	

WORDGAME 4

ADJECTIVES

Use the French–English side of your dictionary to find the
feminine singular form of these adjectives. Remember, the
feminine singular form appears in brackets and in bold on the line
below the masculine form.

MASCULINE	FEMININE
1. naturel	
2. beau	
3. heureux	
4. américain	
5. gros	
6. blanc	
7. faux	
8. sec	
9. favori	
10. frais	
11. bon	
12. fou	
13. public	
14. naïf	

WORDGAME 5

VERB TENSES

Use the verb tables on pages 284 to 297 to help you fill in the blanks in the table below.

INFINITIVE	PRESENT	IMPERFECT	FUTURE
faire		je	
se laver	il		
voir			nous
finir			elle
avoir		il	
aller	vous		
être	elles		
vouloir		ils	
devoir	tu		
mettre			je
dire		il	
pouvoir			nous

WORDGAME 6

«MOTS CODÉS»

In the boxes below, the letters of eight French words have been replaced by numbers. A number represents the same letter each time.

Try to crack the code and find the eight words. If you need help, use your dictionary.

Here is a clue: all the words you are looking for have something to do with CLOTHES.

1. | P¹ | 2 | 3 | 4 | 2 | 5 | 6 | 3 |

2. | 7 | 8 | P¹ | E⁹ |

3. | 10 | 11 | 3 | 11 | 7 | 8 | P¹ | 9 |

4. | 10 | 2 | 3 | 4 | 9 | 2 | 8 |

5. | P¹ | 8 | 5 | 5 |

6. | 12 | 13 | 2 | P¹ | 9 | 2 | 8 |

7. | 12 | 13 | 2 | 8 | 14 | 14 | 9 | 4 | 4 | 9 |

8. | 12 | 13 | 2 | 8 | 14 | 14 | 8 | 15 | 9 |

«MOTS CUISINÉS»

Here is a list of French words for things you will find in the kitchen.
Unfortunately, they have all been jumbled up. Try to work out what
each word is and put the word in the boxes on the right. You will
see there are five shaded boxes below. The five letters in the shaded
boxes make up *another* French word for an object you can find in
the kitchen.

1 féac   Tu prends du sucre
               dans ton _____ ?

2 rever   Encore un _____
               de vin ?

3 lesvisale   Je déteste faire
               la _____.

4 rascosele   Elle a fait cuire les pâtes
               dans une grande _____.

5 grifo   Le fromage est
               dans le _____ .

The word you are looking for is:

ANSWERS

WORDGAME 1
1. classe
2. lancer
3. connaître
4. trouver
5. noisette
6. emmener
7. mollet
8. endroit
9. dîner
10. rester
11. dur
12. tard

WORDGAME 2
1. noun
2. adjective
3. verb
4. noun
5. verb
6. adverb
7. adjective
8. noun
9. verb
10. adverb

WORDGAME 3
Masculine forms
1. danseur
2. boulanger
3. Américain
4. animateur
5. avocat
6. Parisien
7. libraire
8. téléspectateur
9. pion
10. veuf

WORDGAME 3
Plural forms
1. choux
2. canaux
3. bateaux
4. sapeurs–pompiers
5. neveux
6. travaux
7. vœux
8. voix
9. yeux
10. croque–monsieur

WORDGAME 4
1. naturelle
2. belle
3. heureuse
4. américaine
5. grosse
6. blanche
7. fausse
8. sèche
9. favorite
10. fraîche
11. bonne
12. folle
13. publique
14. naïve

WORDGAME 5
1. je faisais
2. il se lave
3. nous verrons
4. elle finira
5. il avait
6. vous allez
7. elles sont
8. ils voulaient
9. tu dois
10. je mettrai
11. il disait
12. nous pourrons

WORDGAME 6
1. pantalon
2. jupe
3. minijupe
4. manteau
5. pull
6. chapeau
7. chaussette
8. chaussure

WORDGAME 7
1. café
2. verre
3. vaisselle
4. casserole
5. frigo
missing word – évier

FRENCH VERB TABLES

CONTENTS

FRENCH VERB TABLES

This section contains fourteen important French verbs that you need to learn. All French verbs fall into two main categories – **regular** and **irregular** – and it is important to learn which verbs fall into which category.

The tables are arranged in the following order:

1. Regular verbs – **aimer, finir, attendre** and **se laver**
2. Very important irregular verbs – **avoir** and **être**
3. Other common irregular verbs – **aller, devoir, dire, faire, mettre, pouvoir, voir** and **vouloir**

At the top of each table you will find the infinitive, the imperative and the past participle. The lower section of the table shows you how to form six tenses of the verb:

PRESENT	e.g. je fais = I do *or* I **am doing**
*PRESENT SUBJUNCTIVE**	e.g. je fasse = I **do**
IMPERFECT	e.g. je faisais = I **was doing** *or* I **did**
PERFECT	e.g. j'ai fait = I **did** *or* I **have done**
FUTURE	e.g. je ferai = I **will do**
CONDITIONAL	e.g. je ferais = I **would do**

> * The French side of your dictionary will tell you which words must be followed by the subjunctive.

1. REGULAR VERBS

There are three groups of regular verbs:

1. "–ER" verbs = verbs that end in –er like **aimer** on p284 and **se laver** on p287
2. "–IR" verbs = verbs that end in –ir like **finir** on p285
3. "–RE" verbs = verbs that end in –re like **attendre** on p286

They are called regular verbs because they follow one of three set patterns. When you have learnt these patterns, you will be able to form *any* regular verb.

HOW TO FORM A REGULAR VERB

i. a) To form the present, imperfect or present subjunctive tense, take the infinitive minus the last two letters. This is called the **stem** e.g. *aimer* → **aim–** , *finir* → **fin–** , and *attendre* → **attend–**

b) To form the future or conditional tense, the stem is the whole infinitive for "–ER" and "–IR" verbs and the infinitive minus its final "e" for "–RE" verbs e.g. *aimer* → **aimer**, *finir* → **finir** and *attendre* → **attendr–**

ii) Next add the appropriate **ending**. You need to ask yourself three questions:

a) **What sort of verb** am I using (–ER, –IR or –RE)?
b) **Who** is doing the verb (je, tu, il *etc*)?
c) **When** are they doing it (in the present, the past or the future)?

Look at the verb tables for **aimer, finir** and **attendre**. The verb endings are in bold and underlined. These endings can be tagged onto the stem of *any* regular verb.

2. AVOIR AND ÊTRE

Avoir (to have) and **être** (to be) are very important verbs which **must** be learnt. You use them when you want to say "I have" *etc* or "I am" *etc*. The present tense of **avoir** or **être** is also used to form the **perfect tense**. In most cases, **avoir** is used to form the perfect, but verbs of movement like **aller** (to go) and **venir** (to come) use **être** – e.g. the French for both "he's gone" and "he went" is **il *est* allé**, not **il *a* allé**. You will have to learn which verbs use **être**.

HOW TO FORM THE PERFECT TENSE

a) Take the infinitive of a French verb e.g. **donner**

b) Does it use **avoir** or **être** to form the perfect tense? e.g. **donner** uses **avoir**

c) Take the present tense form of **avoir** or **être** that goes with the person who **did** the action e.g. **he** gave – the French for "he" is **il**, so to form the perfect tense of **donner** we use **il a**

d) Add the **past participle** – this is shown near the top of each verb table. If you want to form the past participle of *any* regular verb, simply take the infinitive of the verb, knock off the last two letters and add the following endings:

"–ER" verbs add **é** – e.g. aimer → aim**é**
"–IR" verbs add **i** – e.g. finir → fin**i**
"–RE" verbs add **u** – e.g. attendre → attend**u**

In our example, **donner** is a regular "–ER" verb, so the past participle is donn + é → **donné**

e) The French for "he gave" is "**il a donné**"

3. IRREGULAR VERBS

Many French verbs are irregular and this means you have to learn them individually. There are tables of the most important irregular verbs such as **avoir** (to have), **être** (to be) and **faire** (to do) in this section. When you are translating from French and meet an unfamiliar verb form, you may be able to guess from the context that it comes from one of these verbs, and you can use the verb table to check. The most common irregular verb parts are listed on the French side of the dictionary, so you could also look there.

HOW TO USE THE VERB TABLES

You will find some useful example phrases at the top of each verb table, but if you can't find what you need to say or write in French there, use the verb table itself to help you. Imagine that you want to find the French for "he wants". Here's how to do it:

a) Look up **want** on the English–French side of the dictionary to find the French translation

b) French translation = **vouloir**

c) Turn to the verb tables section of your dictionary and find **vouloir**

d) When does he want it? He wants it **now**, so look for the heading *PRESENT*

e) Who wants it? **He** does. The French for "he" is **il** so look for **il** under the *PRESENT* heading

f) The French for "he wants" is "**il veut**"

aimer

to like *or* to love

IMPERATIVE
aim**e**
aim**ons**
aim**ez**

PAST PARTICIPLE
aim**é**

EXAMPLE PHRASES

*Tu **aimes** le chocolat?* Do you like chocolate?

*Je t'**aime**.* I love you.

*J'**aimerais** aller en Grèce.* I'd like to go to Greece.

PRESENT

j' aim**e**
tu aim**es**
il aim**e**
nous aim**ons**
vous aim**ez**
ils aim**ent**

PRESENT SUBJUNCTIVE

j' aim**e**
tu aim**es**
il aim**e**
nous aim**ions**
vous aim**iez**
ils aim**ent**

PERFECT

j' ai aim**é**
tu as aim**é**
il a aim**é**
nous avons aim**é**
vous avez aim**é**
ils ont aim**é**

IMPERFECT

j' aim**ais**
tu aim**ais**
il aim**ait**
nous aim**ions**
vous aim**iez**
ils aim**aient**

FUTURE

j' aimer**ai**
tu aimer**as**
il aimer**a**
nous aimer**ons**
vous aimer**ez**
ils aimer**ont**

CONDITIONAL

j' aimer**ais**
tu aimer**ais**
il aimer**ait**
nous aimer**ions**
vous aimer**iez**
ils aimer**aient**

finir

to finish

EXAMPLE PHRASES

Finis *ta soupe!* Finish your soup!

J'ai fini! I've finished!

Je **finirai** *mes devoirs demain.* I'll finish
my homework tomorrow.

IMPERATIVE
fin**is**
fin**issons**
fin**issez**

PAST PARTICIPLE
fin**i**

PRESENT
    je fin**is**
    tu fin**is**
    il fin**it**
  nous fin**issons**
  vous fin**issez**
    ils fin**issent**

PERFECT
    j' ai fin**i**
    tu as fin**i**
    il a fin**i**
  nous avons fin**i**
  vous avez fin**i**
    ils ont fin**i**

FUTURE
    je finir**ai**
    tu finir**as**
    il finir**a**
  nous finir**ons**
  vous finir**ez**
    ils finir**ont**

PRESENT SUBJUNCTIVE
    je fin**isse**
    tu fin**isses**
    il fin**isse**
  nous fin**issions**
  vous fin**issiez**
    ils fin**issent**

IMPERFECT
    je fin**issais**
    tu fin**issais**
    il fin**issait**
  nous fin**issions**
  vous fin**issiez**
    ils fin**issaient**

CONDITIONAL
    je finir**ais**
    tu finir**ais**
    il finir**ait**
  nous finir**ions**
  vous finir**iez**
    ils finir**aient**

attendre

to wait

IMPERATIVE
attend**s**
attend**ons**
attend**ez**

PAST PARTICIPLE
attend**u**

EXAMPLE PHRASES

Attends–moi! Wait for me!

Tu attends *depuis longtemps?* Have you been waiting long?

Je l'ai attendu à la poste. I waited for him at the post office.

PRESENT
j' attend**s**
tu attend**s**
il attend
nous attend**ons**
vous attend**ez**
ils attend**ent**

PERFECT
j' ai attend**u**
tu as attend**u**
il a attend**u**
nous avons attend**u**
vous avez attend**u**
ils ont attend**u**

FUTURE
j' attendr**ai**
tu attendr**as**
il attendr**a**
nous attendr**ons**
vous attendr**ez**
ils attendr**ont**

PRESENT SUBJUNCTIVE
j' attend**e**
tu attend**es**
il attend**e**
nous attend**ions**
vous attend**iez**
ils attend**ent**

IMPERFECT
j' attend**ais**
tu attend**ais**
il attend**ait**
nous attend**ions**
vous attend**iez**
ils attend**aient**

CONDITIONAL
j' attendr**ais**
tu attendr**ais**
il attendr**ait**
nous attendr**ions**
vous attendr**iez**
ils attendr**aient**

se laver

to wash (oneself)

EXAMPLE PHRASES

Je me lave chaque matin. I have a wash every morning.

Il s'est lavé les mains. He washed his hands.

Elle va se laver les cheveux. She's going to wash her hair.

IMPERATIVE

lave–toi
lavons–nous
lavez–vous

PAST PARTICIPLE

lavé

PRESENT

je	me lave
tu	te laves
il	se lave
nous	nous lavons
vous	vous lavez
ils	se lavent

PERFECT

je	me suis lavé
tu	t'es lavé
il	s'est lavé
nous	nous sommes lavés
vous	vous êtes lavé(s)
ils	se sont lavés

FUTURE

je	me laverai
tu	te laveras
il	se lavera
nous	nous laverons
vous	vous laverez
ils	se laveront

PRESENT SUBJUNCTIVE

je	me lave
tu	te laves
il	se lave
nous	nous lavions
vous	vous laviez
ils	se lavent

IMPERFECT

je	me lavais
tu	te lavais
il	se lavait
nous	nous lavions
vous	vous laviez
ils	se lavaient

CONDITIONAL

je	me laverais
tu	te laverais
il	se laverait
nous	nous laverions
vous	vous laveriez
ils	se laveraient

avoir

to have

aie
ayons
ayez

EXAMPLE PHRASES

*Il **a** les yeux bleus.* He's got blue eyes.

*Quel âge **as**–tu?* How old are you?

*Il **a eu** un accident.* He's had an accident.

*J'**avais** faim.* I was hungry.

PAST PARTICIPLE
eu

PRESENT

j'	**ai**
tu	**as**
il	**a**
nous	av**ons**
vous	av**ez**
ils	**ont**

PRESENT SUBJUNCTIVE

j'	**aie**
tu	**aies**
il	**ait**
nous	**ayons**
vous	**ayez**
ils	**aient**

PERFECT

j'	ai **eu**
tu	as **eu**
il	a **eu**
nous	avons **eu**
vous	avez **eu**
ils	ont **eu**

IMPERFECT

j'	av**ais**
tu	av**ais**
il	av**ait**
nous	av**ions**
vous	av**iez**
ils	av**aient**

FUTURE

j'	**aurai**
tu	**auras**
il	**aura**
nous	**aurons**
vous	**aurez**
ils	**auront**

CONDITIONAL

j'	**aurais**
tu	**aurais**
il	**aurait**
nous	**aurions**
vous	**auriez**
ils	**auraient**

être

to be

Mon père est professeur. My father's a
teacher.

Quelle heure est–il? – Il est 10 heures.
What time is it? – It's 10 o'clock.

Ils ne sont pas encore arrivés. They haven't
arrived yet.

IMPERATIVE
sois
soyons
soyez

PAST PARTICIPLE
été

PRESENT

je **suis**
tu **es**
il **est**
nous **sommes**
vous **êtes**
ils **sont**

PERFECT

j' ai **été**
tu as **été**
il a **été**
nous avons **été**
vous avez **été**
ils ont **été**

FUTURE

je **serai**
tu **seras**
il **sera**
nous **serons**
vous **serez**
ils **seront**

PRESENT SUBJUNCTIVE

je **sois**
tu **sois**
il **soit**
nous **soyons**
vous **soyez**
ils **soient**

IMPERFECT

j' **étais**
tu **étais**
il **était**
nous **étions**
vous **étiez**
ils **étaient**

CONDITIONAL

je **serais**
tu **serais**
il **serait**
nous **serions**
vous **seriez**
ils **seraient**

aller

to go

IMPERATIVE
va
all**ons**
all**ez**

PAST PARTICIPLE
all**é**

EXAMPLE PHRASES

*Vous **allez** au cinéma?* Are you going to the cinema?

*Je **suis allé** à Londres.* I went to London.

*Est–ce que tu **es** déjà **allé** en Allemagne?* Have you ever been to Germany?

PRESENT
je **vais**
tu **vas**
il **va**
nous all**ons**
vous all**ez**
ils **vont**

PERFECT
je suis all**é**
tu es all**é**
il est all**é**
nous sommes all**és**
vous êtes all**é(s)**
ils sont all**és**

FUTURE
j' **irai**
tu **iras**
il **ira**
nous **irons**
vous **irez**
ils **iront**

PRESENT SUBJUNCTIVE
j' **aille**
tu **ailles**
il **aille**
nous all**ions**
vous all**iez**
ils **aillent**

IMPERFECT
j' all**ais**
tu all**ais**
il all**ait**
nous all**ions**
vous all**iez**
ils all**aient**

CONDITIONAL
j' **irais**
tu **irais**
il **irait**
nous **irions**
vous **iriez**
ils **iraient**

devoir

to have to

EXAMPLE PHRASES

*Je **dois** aller faire les courses ce matin.*
I have to do the shopping this morning.

*Il **a dû** faire ses devoirs hier soir.* He had to
do his homework last night.

*Il **devait** prendre le train pour aller travailler.*
He had to go to work by train.

IMPERATIVE
dois
dev**ons**
dev**ez**

PAST PARTICIPLE
dû

PRESENT

je	**dois**
tu	**dois**
il	**doit**
nous	dev**ons**
vous	dev**ez**
ils	**doivent**

PRESENT SUBJUNCTIVE

je	**doive**
tu	**doives**
il	**doive**
nous	dev**ions**
vous	dev**iez**
ils	**doivent**

PERFECT

j'	ai	**dû**
tu	as	**dû**
il	a	**dû**
nous	avons	**dû**
vous	avez	**dû**
ils	ont	**dû**

IMPERFECT

je	dev**ais**
tu	dev**ais**
il	dev**ait**
nous	dev**ions**
vous	dev**iez**
ils	dev**aient**

FUTURE

je	dev**rai**
tu	dev**ras**
il	dev**ra**
nous	dev**rons**
vous	dev**rez**
ils	dev**ront**

CONDITIONAL

je	dev**rais**
tu	dev**rais**
il	dev**rait**
nous	dev**rions**
vous	dev**riez**
ils	dev**raient**

dire

to say

dis
disons
dites

EXAMPLE PHRASES

*Qu'est-ce qu'elle **dit**?* What is she saying?

*"Bonjour!" **a-t-il dit**.* "Hello!" he said.

*Il m'**a dit** que le film était nul.* He told me that the film was rubbish.

PAST PARTICIPLE
dit

PRESENT

je **dis**
tu **dis**
il **dit**
nous **disons**
vous **dites**
ils **disent**

PRESENT SUBJUNCTIVE

je **dise**
tu **dises**
il **dise**
nous **disions**
vous **disiez**
ils **disent**

PERFECT

j' ai **dit**
tu as **dit**
il a **dit**
nous avons **dit**
vous avez **dit**
ils ont **dit**

IMPERFECT

je **disais**
tu **disais**
il **disait**
nous **disions**
vous **disiez**
ils **disaient**

FUTURE

je dir**ai**
tu dir**as**
il dir**a**
nous dir**ons**
vous dir**ez**
ils dir**ont**

CONDITIONAL

je dir**ais**
tu dir**ais**
il dir**ait**
nous dir**ions**
vous dir**iez**
ils dir**aient**

faire

to do *or* to make

EXAMPLE PHRASES

Qu'est–ce que tu fais? What are you doing?

Qu'est–ce qu'il a fait? What has he done *or* What did he do?

J'ai fait un gâteau. I've made a cake *or* I made a cake.

IMPERATIVE
fais
faisons
faites

PAST PARTICIPLE
fait

PRESENT

je **fais**
tu **fais**
il **fait**
nous **faisons**
vous **faites**
ils **font**

PERFECT

j' ai **fait**
tu as **fait**
il a **fait**
nous avons **fait**
vous avez **fait**
ils ont **fait**

FUTURE

je **ferai**
tu **feras**
il **fera**
nous **ferons**
vous **ferez**
ils **feront**

PRESENT SUBJUNCTIVE

je **fasse**
tu **fasses**
il **fasse**
nous **fassions**
vous **fassiez**
ils **fassent**

IMPERFECT

je **faisais**
tu **faisais**
il **faisait**
nous **faisions**
vous **faisiez**
ils **faisaient**

CONDITIONAL

je **ferais**
tu **ferais**
il **ferait**
nous **ferions**
vous **feriez**
ils **feraient**

mettre

to put

mets
mett**ons**
mett**ez**

PAST PARTICIPLE
mis

EXAMPLE PHRASES

***Mets** ton manteau!* Put your coat on!

*Où est–ce que tu **as mis** les clés?* Where have you put the keys?

*J'**ai mis** le livre sur la table.* I put the book on the table.

PRESENT

je **mets**
tu **mets**
il **met**
nous mett**ons**
vous mett**ez**
ils mett**ent**

PERFECT

j' ai **mis**
tu as **mis**
il a **mis**
nous avons **mis**
vous avez **mis**
ils ont **mis**

FUTURE

je mettr**ai**
tu mettr**as**
il mettr**a**
nous mettr**ons**
vous mettr**ez**
ils mettr**ont**

PRESENT SUBJUNCTIVE

je mett**e**
tu mett**es**
il mett**e**
nous mett**ions**
vous mett**iez**
ils mett**ent**

IMPERFECT

je mett**ais**
tu mett**ais**
il mett**ait**
nous mett**ions**
vous mett**iez**
ils mett**aient**

CONDITIONAL

je mettr**ais**
tu mettr**ais**
il mettr**ait**
nous mettr**ions**
vous mettr**iez**
ils mettr**aient**

pouvoir

to be able

EXAMPLE PHRASES

*Je **peux** t'aider, si tu veux.* I can help you if you like.

*J'ai fait tout ce que j'**ai pu**.* I did all I could.

*Je ne **pourrai** pas venir samedi.* I won't be able to come on Saturday.

IMPERATIVE

the imperative of **pouvoir** is not used

PAST PARTICIPLE

pu

PRESENT

je	**peux**
tu	**peux**
il	**peut**
nous	**pouvons**
vous	**pouvez**
ils	**peuvent**

PERFECT

j'	ai **pu**
tu	as **pu**
il	a **pu**
nous	avons **pu**
vous	avez **pu**
ils	ont **pu**

FUTURE

je	**pourrai**
tu	**pourras**
il	**pourra**
nous	**pourrons**
vous	**pourrez**
ils	**pourront**

PRESENT SUBJUNCTIVE

je	**puisse**
tu	**puisses**
il	**puisse**
nous	**puissions**
vous	**puissiez**
ils	**puissent**

IMPERFECT

je	**pouvais**
tu	**pouvais**
il	**pouvait**
nous	**pouvions**
vous	**pouviez**
ils	**pouvaient**

CONDITIONAL

je	**pourrais**
tu	**pourrais**
il	**pourrait**
nous	**pourrions**
vous	**pourriez**
ils	**pourraient**

voir

to see

IMPERATIVE

voi<u>s</u>
voyons
voyez

PAST PARTICIPLE

vu

EXAMPLE PHRASES

*Venez me **voir** quand vous serez à Paris.*
Come and see me when you're in Paris.

*Je ne **vois** rien sans mes lunettes.* I can't
see anything without my glasses.

*Est–ce que tu l'**as vu**?* Did you see him? *or*
Have you seen him?

PRESENT

je voi<u>s</u>
tu voi<u>s</u>
il voi<u>t</u>
nous **voyons**
vous **voyez**
ils voi**ent**

PRESENT SUBJUNCTIVE

je voi**e**
tu voi**es**
il voi**e**
nous **voyions**
vous **voyiez**
ils voi**ent**

PERFECT

j' ai **vu**
tu as **vu**
il a **vu**
nous avons **vu**
vous avez **vu**
ils ont **vu**

IMPERFECT

je **voyais**
tu **voyais**
il **voyait**
nous **voyions**
vous **voyiez**
ils **voyaient**

FUTURE

je **verrai**
tu **verras**
il **verra**
nous **verrons**
vous **verrez**
ils **verront**

CONDITIONAL

je **verrais**
tu **verrais**
il **verrait**
nous **verrions**
vous **verriez**
ils **verraient**

vouloir

to want

EXAMPLE PHRASES

*Elle **veut** un vélo pour Noël.* She wants a bike for Christmas.

*Ils **voulaient** aller au cinéma.* They wanted to go to the cinema.

*Tu **voudrais** une tasse de thé?* Would you like a cup of tea?

IMPERATIVE
veuille
veuillons
veuillez

PAST PARTICIPLE
voul<u>u</u>

PRESENT

je	**veux**
tu	**veux**
il	**veut**
nous	voul<u>ons</u>
vous	voul<u>ez</u>
ils	**veulent**

PRESENT SUBJUNCTIVE

je	**veuille**
tu	**veuilles**
il	**veuille**
nous	voul<u>ions</u>
vous	voul<u>iez</u>
ils	**veuillent**

PERFECT

j'	ai voul<u>u</u>
tu	as voul<u>u</u>
il	a voul<u>u</u>
nous	avons voul<u>u</u>
vous	avez voul<u>u</u>
ils	ont voul<u>u</u>

IMPERFECT

je	voul<u>ais</u>
tu	voul<u>ais</u>
il	voul<u>ait</u>
nous	voul<u>ions</u>
vous	voul<u>iez</u>
ils	voul<u>aient</u>

FUTURE

je	**voudrai**
tu	**voudras**
il	**voudra**
nous	**voudrons**
vous	**voudrez**
ils	**voudront**

CONDITIONAL

je	**voudrais**
tu	**voudrais**
il	**voudrait**
nous	**voudrions**
vous	**voudriez**
ils	**voudraient**

FRENCH IRREGULAR VERB FORMS

The following list is a summary of the main forms of other irregular verbs that are you are likely to come across. The **infinitive** appears in bold and is followed by a series of numbers from 1 to 5. These tell you which **tenses** are listed:

1 = Present
2 = Past participle
3 = Imperfect

4 = Future
5 = Present subjunctive

For the present tense, all **je** and **nous** forms are shown. The **il, vous** and **ils** forms are also included wherever the part of the verb that goes with them follows an unusual pattern. For the imperfect, future and present subjunctive tenses, only the **je** form is given.

acheter 1 j'achète, nous achetons, ils achètent **2** acheté **3** j'achetais **4** j'achèterai **5** j'achète

appeler 1 j'appelle, il appelle, nous appelons **2** appelé **3** j'appelais **4** j'appellerai **5** j'appelle

apprendre 1 j'apprends, nous apprenons, vous apprenez, ils apprennent **2** appris **3** j'apprenais **4** j'apprendrai **5** j'apprenne

s'asseoir 1 je m'assieds, nous nous asseyons, vous vous asseyez, ils s'asseyent **2** assis **3** je m'asseyais **4** je m'assiérai **5** je m'asseye

battre 1 je bats, il bat, nous battons **2** battu **3** je battais **5** je batte

boire 1 je bois, nous buvons, ils boivent **2** bu **3** je buvais **4** je boirai **5** je boive

bouillir 1 je bous, nous bouillons **2** bouilli **3** je bouillais **5** je bouille

conclure 1 je conclus, nous concluons **2** conclu **3** je concluais **5** je conclue

conduire 1 je conduis, nous conduisons **2** conduit **3** je conduisais **5** je conduise

connaître 1 je connais, il connaît, nous connaissons **2** connu **3** je connaissais **4** je connaîtrai **5** je connaisse

coudre 1 je couds, nous cousons, vous cousez, ils cousent **2** cousu **3** je cousais **4** je coudrai **5** je couse

courir 1 je cours, nous courons **2** couru **3** je courais **4** je courrai **5** je coure

couvrir 1 je couvre, nous couvrons **2** couvert **3** je couvrais **4** je couvrirai **5** je couvre

craindre 1 je crains, nous craignons **2** craint **3** je craignais **5** je craigne

créer 1 je crée, nous créons **2** créé **3** je créais **4** je créerai **5** je crée

croire 1 je crois, nous croyons, ils croient **2** cru **3** je croyais **4** je croirai **5** je croie

croître 1 je croîs, nous croissons **2** crû, crue, crus, crues **3** je croissais **5** je croisse

cueillir 1 je cueille, nous cueillons **2** cueilli **3** je cueillais **4** je cueillerai **5** je cueille

cuire 1 je cuis, nous cuisons, ils cuisent **2** cuit **3** je cuisais **4** je cuirai **5** je cuise

dormir 1 je dors, nous dormons **2** dormi **3** je dormais **4** je dormirai **5** je dorme

écrire 1 j'écris, nous écrivons **2** écrit **3** j'écrivais **4** j'écrirai **5** j'écrive

falloir 1 il faut 2 fallu 3 il fallait 4 il faudra 5 il faille

fuir 1 je fuis, nous fuyons, ils fuient 2 fui 3 je fuyais 5 je fuie

haïr 1 je hais, nous haïssons, ils haïssent 2 haï 3 je haïssais 4 je haïrai 5 je haïsse

jeter 1 je jette, nous jetons, ils jettent 2 jeté 3 je jetais 4 je jetterai 5 je jette

joindre 1 je joins, nous joignons 2 joint 3 je joignais 5 je joigne

lever 1 je lève, nous levons, ils lèvent 2 levé 3 je levais 4 je lèverai 5 je lève

lire 1 je lis, nous lisons 2 lu 3 je lisais 4 je lirai 5 je lise

manger 1 je mange, nous mangeons 2 mangé 3 je mangeais 4 je mangerai 5 je mange

mentir 1 je mens, nous mentons 2 menti 3 je mentais 5 je mente

mourir 1 je meurs, nous mourons, ils meurent 2 mort 3 je mourais 4 je mourrai 5 je meure

naître 1 je nais, il naît, nous naissons 2 né 3 je naissais 4 je naîtrai 5 je naisse

offrir 1 j'offre, nous offrons 2 offert 3 j'offrais 5 j'offre

paraître 1 je parais, il paraît, nous paraissons 2 paru 3 je paraissais 4 je paraîtrai 5 je paraisse

partir 1 je pars, nous partons 2 parti 3 je partais 4 je partirai 5 je parte

plaire 1 je plais, il plaît, nous plaisons 2 plu 3 je plaisais 4 je plairai 5 je plaise

pleuvoir 1 il pleut 2 plu 3 il pleuvait 4 il pleuvra 5 il pleuve

prendre 1 je prends, nous prenons, ils prennent 2 pris 3 je prenais 4 je prendrai 5 je prenne

recevoir 1 je reçois, il reçoit, ils reçoivent 2 reçu 3 je recevais 4 je recevrai 5 je reçoive

rire 1 je ris, nous rions 2 ri 3 je riais 4 je rirai 5 je rie

savoir 1 je sais, nous savons, ils savent 2 su 3 je savais 4 je saurai 5 je sache

servir 1 je sers, nous servons 2 servi 3 je servais 5 je serve

sortir 1 je sors, nous sortons 2 sorti 3 je sortais 5 je sorte

souffrir 1 je souffre, nous souffrons 2 souffert 3 je souffrais 5 je souffre

suffire 1 je suffis, nous suffisons 2 suffi 3 je suffisais 5 je suffise

suivre 1 je suis, nous suivons 2 suivi 3 je suivais 4 je suivrai 5 je suive

se taire 1 je me tais, nous nous taisons 2 tu 3 je me taisais 4 je me tairai 5 je me taise

tenir 1 je tiens, nous tenons, ils tiennent 2 tenu 3 je tenais 4 je tiendrai 5 je tienne

vaincre 1 je vaincs, il vainc, nous vainquons 2 vaincu 3 je vainquais 5 je vainque

valoir 1 je vaux, il vaut, nous valons 2 valu 3 je valais 4 je vaudrai 5 je vaille

venir 1 je viens, nous venons, ils viennent 2 venu 3 je venais 4 je viendrai 5 je vienne

vivre 1 je vis, nous vivons 2 vécu 3 je vivais 4 je vivrai 5 je vive

If you would like to see fuller tables for these verbs, look in **Collins Pocket French Verb Tables.**

LES NOMBRES

1	un (une)	1st	premier (1ᵉʳ), première (1ʳᵉ)
2	deux	2nd	deuxième (2ᵉ or 2ᵉᵐᵉ)
3	trois	3rd	troisième (3ᵉ or 3ᵉᵐᵉ)
4	quatre	4th	quatrième (4ᵉ or 4ᵉᵐᵉ)
5	cinq	5th	cinquième (5ᵉ or 5ᵉᵐᵉ)
6	six	6th	sixième (6ᵉ or 6ᵉᵐᵉ)
7	sept	7th	septième (7ᵉ or 7ᵉᵐᵉ)
8	huit	8th	huitième (8ᵉ or 8ᵉᵐᵉ)
9	neuf	9th	neuvième (9ᵉ or 9ᵉᵐᵉ)
10	dix	10th	dixième (10ᵉ or 10ᵉᵐᵉ)
11	onze	11th	onzième (11ᵉ or 11ᵉᵐᵉ)
12	douze	12th	douzième (12ᵉ or 12ᵉᵐᵉ)
13	treize	13th	treizième (13ᵉ or 13ᵉᵐᵉ)
14	quatorze	14th	quatorzième (14ᵉ or 14ᵉᵐᵉ)
15	quinze	15th	quinzième (15ᵉ or 15ᵉᵐᵉ)
16	seize	16th	seizième (16ᵉ or 16ᵉᵐᵉ)
17	dix–sept	17th	dix–septième (17ᵉ or 17ᵉᵐᵉ)
18	dix–huit	18th	dix–huitième (18ᵉ or 18ᵉᵐᵉ)
19	dix–neuf	19th	dix–neuvième (19ᵉ or 19ᵉᵐᵉ)
20	vingt	20th	vingtième (20ᵉ or 20ᵉᵐᵉ)
21	vingt et un (une)	21st	vingt et unième (21ᵉ or 21ᵉᵐᵉ)
22	vingt–deux	22nd	vingt–deuxième (22ᵉ or 22ᵉᵐᵉ)
30	trente	30th	trentième (30ᵉ or 30ᵉᵐᵉ)
40	quarante	100th	centième (100ᵉ or 100ᵉᵐᵉ)
50	cinquante	101st	cent unième (101ᵉ or 101ᵉᵐᵉ)
60	soixante	1000th	millième (1000ᵉ or 1000ᵉᵐᵉ)
70	soixante–dix		
71	soixante et onze		
72	soixante–douze		
80	quatre–vingts		
81	quatre–vingt–un (–une)		
90	quatre–vingt–dix		
91	quatre–vingt–onze		
100	cent		
101	cent un (une)		
300	trois cents		
301	trois cent un (une)		
1000	mille		
2000	deux mille		
1,000,000	un million		

Fractions etc

$\frac{1}{2}$	un demi
$\frac{1}{3}$	un tiers
$\frac{2}{3}$	deux tiers
$\frac{1}{4}$	un quart
$\frac{1}{5}$	un cinquième
0.5	zéro virgule cinq (0,5)
3.4	trois virgule quatre (3,4)
10%	dix pour cent
100%	cent pour cent

EXEMPLES

il habite au dix
à la page dix–neuf
au chapitre sept
il habite au cinquième (étage)
il est arrivé troisième
échelle au vingt–cinq millième

EXAMPLES

he lives at number ten
on page nineteen
in chapter seven
he lives on the fifth floor
he came in third
scale one to twenty–five thousand

L'HEURE

Quelle heure est–il? What time is it?
Il est... It's...

À quelle heure? At what time?

 une heure

 une heure dix

 une heure et quart

 une heure et demie

 deux heures moins vingt

 deux heures moins le quart

 à minuit

 à midi

 à une heure (de l'après–midi)

 à huit heures (du soir)

> *In France times are often given in the twenty-four hour clock.*

 à 11.15 *or* onze heures quinze

 à 20.45 *or* vingt heures quarante–cinq

LA DATE

LES JOURS DE LA SEMAINE

lundi
mardi
mercredi
jeudi
vendredi
samedi
dimanche

Quand?

lundi
le lundi
tous les lundis
mardi dernier
vendredi prochain
samedi en huit
samedi en quinze

DAYS OF THE WEEK

Monday
Tuesday
Wednesday
Thursday
Friday
Saturday
Sunday

When?

on Monday
on Mondays
every Monday
last Tuesday
next Friday
a week on Saturday
two weeks on Saturday

LES MOIS

janvier
février
mars
avril
mai
juin
juillet
août
septembre
octobre
novembre
décembre

MONTHS OF THE YEAR

January
February
March
April
May
June
July
August
September
October
November
December

Quand?

en février
le 1ᵉʳ décembre
le premier décembre
en 1997
en mille neuf cent quatre–vingt–dix–sept

When?

in February
on December 1st
on December first
in 1997
in nineteen ninety–seven

Quel jour sommes–nous? What day is it?

Nous sommes le... It's...

 lundi 26 février *or*
lundi vingt–six février

 dimanche 1ᵉʳ octobre *or*
dimanche premier octobre

VOCABULAIRE

Quand?

aujourd'hui
ce matin
cet après–midi
ce soir

Souvent?

tous les jours
tous les deux jours
une fois par semaine
deux fois par semaine
une fois par mois

Ça s'est passé quand?

le matin
le soir
hier
hier soir
avant–hier
il y a une semaine
il y a quinze jours
l'an dernier *or* l'année dernière

Ça va se passer quand?

demain
demain matin
après–demain
dans deux jours
dans une semaine
dans quinze jours
le mois prochain
l'an prochain *or* l'année prochaine

USEFUL VOCABULARY

When?

today
this morning
this afternoon
this evening

How often?

every day
every other day
once a week
twice a week
once a month

When *did* it happen?

in the morning
in the evening
yesterday
yesterday evening
the day before yesterday
a week ago
two weeks ago
last year

When *is it going* to happen?

tomorrow
tomorrow morning
the day after tomorrow
in two days
in a week
in two weeks
next month
next year

A

a ARTICLE

Use **un** *for masculine nouns,* **une** *for feminine nouns.*

un MASC ◇ *a book* un livre ◇ *a year ago* il y a un an

une FEM ◇ *an apple* une pomme

You do not translate **a** *when you want to describe somebody's job in French.*

◇ *He's a butcher.* Il est boucher.
◇ *She's a doctor.* Elle est médecin.

- **once a week** une fois par semaine
- **10 km an hour** dix kilomètres à l'heure
- **30 pence a kilo** trente pence le kilo
- **a hundred pounds** cent livres

to **abandon** VERB
abandonner

abbey NOUN
l' **abbaye** FEM

abbreviation NOUN
l' **abréviation** FEM

ability NOUN
- **to have the ability to do something** être capable de faire quelque chose

able ADJECTIVE
- **to be able to do something** être capable de faire quelque chose

to **abolish** VERB
abolir

abortion NOUN
l' **avortement** MASC
- **She had an abortion.** Elle s'est fait avorter.

about PREPOSITION, ADVERB
[1] **à propos de** (*concerning*) ◇ *I'm phoning you about tomorrow's meeting.* Je vous appelle à propos de la réunion de demain.
[2] **environ** (*approximately*) ◇ *It takes about 10 hours.* Ça prend dix heures environ.
- **about a hundred pounds** une centaine de livres
- **at about 11 o'clock** vers onze heures
[3] **dans** (*around*) ◇ *to walk about the town* se promener dans la ville
[4] **sur** ◇ *a book about London* un livre sur Londres
- **to be about to do something** être sur le point de faire quelque chose ◇ *I was about to go out.* J'étais sur le point de sortir.
- **to talk about something** parler de quelque chose
- **What's it about?** De quoi s'agit-il?
- **How about going to the cinema?** Et si nous allions au cinéma?

above PREPOSITION, ADVERB
[1] **au-dessus de** (*higher than*) ◇ *He put his hands above his head.* Il a mis ses mains au-dessus de sa tête.
- **the flat above** l'appartement du dessus
- **mentioned above** mentionné ci-dessus
- **above all** par-dessus tout
[2] **plus de** (*more than*) ◇ *above 40 degrees* plus de quarante degrés

abroad ADVERB
à l'étranger ◇ *to go abroad* partir à l'étranger

abrupt ADJECTIVE
brusque ◇ *He was a bit abrupt with me.* Il s'est montré un peu brusque avec moi.

abruptly ADVERB
brusquement ◇ *He got up abruptly.* Il s'est levé brusquement.

absence NOUN
l' **absence** FEM

absent ADJECTIVE
absent

absent-minded ADJECTIVE
distrait ◇ *She's a bit absent-minded.* Elle est un peu distraite.

absolutely ADVERB
[1] **tout à fait** (*completely*) ◇ *Chantal's absolutely right.* Chantal a tout à fait raison.
[2] **absolument** ◇ *Do you think it's a good idea?—Absolutely!* Tu trouves que c'est une bonne idée?–Absolument!

absurd ADJECTIVE
absurde ◇ *That's absurd!* C'est absurde!

academic ADJECTIVE
universitaire ◇ *the academic year* l'année universitaire FEM

academy NOUN
le **collège** ◇ *a military academy* un collège militaire

to **accelerate** VERB
accélérer

accelerator NOUN
l' **accélérateur** MASC

accent NOUN
l' **accent** MASC ◇ *He's got a French accent.* Il a l'accent français.

to **accept** VERB
accepter

acceptable ADJECTIVE
acceptable

access NOUN
[1] l' **accès** MASC ◇ *He has access to confidential information.* Il a accès à des

renseignements confidentiels.

[2] le **droit de visite** ◇ *Her ex-husband has access to the children.* Son ex-mari a le droit de visite.

accessible ADJECTIVE
accessible

accessory NOUN
l' **accessoire** MASC ◇ *fashion accessories* les accessoires de mode

accident NOUN
l' **accident** MASC ◇ *to have an accident* avoir un accident
- **by accident (1)** (*by mistake*) accidentellement ◇ *The burglar killed him by accident.* Le cambrioleur l'a tué accidentellement.
- **by accident (2)** (*by chance*) par hasard ◇ *She met him by accident.* Elle l'a rencontré par hasard.

accidental ADJECTIVE
accidentel MASC
accidentelle FEM

to **accommodate** VERB
recevoir ◇ *The hotel can accommodate 50 people.* L'hôtel peut recevoir cinquante personnes.

accommodation NOUN
le **logement**

to **accompany** VERB
accompagner

accord NOUN
- **of his own accord** de son plein gré ◇ *He left of his own accord.* Il est parti de son plein gré.

according to PREPOSITION
selon ◇ *According to him, everyone had gone.* Selon lui, tout le monde était parti.

account NOUN
[1] le **compte** ◇ *a bank account* un compte en banque
- **to do the accounts** tenir la comptabilité
[2] le **compte rendu** (*report*) ◇ *He gave a detailed account of what happened.* Il a donné un compte rendu détaillé des événements.
- **to take something into account** tenir compte de quelque chose
- **on account of** à cause de ◇ *We couldn't go out on account of the bad weather.* Nous n'avons pas pu sortir à cause du mauvais temps.

accountancy NOUN
la **comptabilité**

accountant NOUN
le/la **comptable** ◇ *She's an accountant.* Elle est comptable.

accuracy NOUN

l' **exactitude** FEM

accurate ADJECTIVE
précis ◇ *accurate information* les renseignements précis MASC

accurately ADVERB
avec précision

to **accuse** VERB
- **to accuse somebody of something** accuser quelqu'un de quelque chose ◇ *The police are accusing her of murder.* La police l'accuse de meurtre.

ace NOUN
l' **as** MASC ◇ *the ace of hearts* l'as de cœur

ache NOUN
see also **ache** VERB
la **douleur**

to **ache** VERB
see also **ache** NOUN
- **My leg's aching.** J'ai mal à la jambe.

to **achieve** VERB
[1] **atteindre** (*an aim*)
[2] **remporter** (*victory*)

achievement NOUN
l' **exploit** MASC ◇ *That was quite an achievement.* C'était un véritable exploit.

acid NOUN
l' **acide** MASC

acid rain NOUN
les **pluies acides** FEM PL

acne NOUN
l' **acné** FEM

acrobat NOUN
l' **acrobate** MASC/FEM ◇ *He's an acrobat.* Il est acrobate.

across PREPOSITION, ADVERB
de l'autre côté de ◇ *the shop across the road* la boutique de l'autre côté de la rue
- **to walk across the road** traverser la rue
- **to run across the road** traverser la rue en courant
- **across from** (*opposite*) en face de ◇ *He sat down across from her.* Il s'est assis en face d'elle.

to **act** VERB
see also **act** NOUN
[1] **jouer** (*in play, film*) ◇ *He acts really well.* Il joue vraiment bien. ◇ *She's acting the part of Juliet.* Elle joue le rôle de Juliette.
[2] **agir** (*take action*) ◇ *The police acted quickly.* La police a agi rapidement.
- **She acts as his interpreter.** Elle lui sert d'interprète.

act NOUN
see also **act** VERB
l' **acte** MASC (*in play*) ◇ *in the first act*

au premier acte

action NOUN
l' **action** FEM ◇ *The film was full of
action.* Il y avait beaucoup d'action
dans le film.
• **to take firm action against** prendre des
mesures énergiques contre

active ADJECTIVE
actif MASC
active FEM
◇ *He's a very active person.* Il est très
actif.
• **an active volcano** un volcan en
activité

activity NOUN
l' **activité** FEM ◇ *outdoor activities* les
activités de plein air

actor NOUN
l' **acteur** MASC ◇ *Brad Pitt is a
well-known actor.* Brad Pitt est un
acteur connu.

actress NOUN
l' **actrice** FEM ◇ *Julia Roberts is a
well-known actress.* Julia Roberts est
une actrice connue.

actually ADVERB
[1] **vraiment** (*really*) ◇ *Did it actually
happen?* Est-ce que c'est vraiment
arrivé?
[2] **en fait** (*in fact*) ◇ *Actually, I don't
know him at all.* En fait, je ne le connais
pas du tout.

ad NOUN
[1] l' **annonce** FEM (*in paper*)
[2] la **pub** (*on TV, radio*)

AD ABBREVIATION
ap. J.-C. (= après Jésus-Christ) ◇ *in
800 AD* en huit cent après Jésus-Christ

to **adapt** VERB
adapter ◇ *His novel was adapted for
television.* Son roman a été adapté pour
la télévision.
• **to adapt to something** (*get used to*)
s'adapter à quelque chose ◇ *He
adapted to his new school very quickly.* Il
s'est adapté très vite à sa nouvelle
école.

adaptor NOUN
l' **adaptateur** MASC

to **add** VERB
ajouter ◇ *Add two eggs to the mixture.*
Ajoutez deux œufs au mélange.
• **to add up** additionner ◇ *Add the
figures up.* Additionnez les chiffres.

addict NOUN
(*drug addict*)
le **drogué**
la **droguée**
• **Jean-Pierre's a football addict.**

Jean-Pierre est un mordu de football.

addicted ADJECTIVE
• **to be addicted to** (*drug*) s'adonner à
◇ *She's addicted to heroin.* Elle
s'adonne à l'héroïne.
• **She's addicted to soap operas.** C'est
une mordue des soaps.

addition NOUN
• **in addition** en plus ◇ *He's broken his
leg and, in addition, he's caught a cold.*
Il s'est cassé la jambe et en plus, il a
attrapé un rhume.
• **in addition to** en plus de ◇ *In
addition to the price of the cassette,
there's a charge for postage.* En plus du
prix de la cassette, il y a des frais de
port.

address NOUN
l' **adresse** FEM ◇ *What's your address?*
Quelle est votre adresse?

adjective NOUN
l' **adjectif** MASC

to **adjust** VERB
régler ◇ *You can adjust the height of
the chair.* Tu peux régler la hauteur de
la chaise.
• **to adjust to something** (*get used to*)
s'adapter à quelque chose ◇ *He
adjusted to his new school very quickly.*
Il s'est adapté très vite à sa nouvelle
école.

adjustable ADJECTIVE
réglable

administration NOUN
l' **administration** FEM

admiral NOUN
l' **amiral** MASC

to **admire** VERB
admirer

admission NOUN
l' **entrée** FEM ◇ *"admission free"*
"entrée gratuite"

to **admit** VERB
[1] **admettre** (*agree*) ◇ *I must admit
that...* Je dois admettre que...
[2] **reconnaître** (*confess*) ◇ *He admitted
that he'd done it.* Il a reconnu qu'il
l'avait fait.

adolescence NOUN
l' **adolescence** FEM

adolescent NOUN
l' **adolescent** MASC
l' **adolescente** FEM

to **adopt** VERB
adopter ◇ *Phil was adopted.* Phil a
été adopté.

adopted ADJECTIVE
adoptif MASC
adoptive FEM

◇ *an adopted son* un fils adoptif
adoption NOUN
   l' **adoption** FEM
to **adore** VERB
   adorer
Adriatic Sea NOUN
   la **mer Adriatique**
adult NOUN
   l' **adulte** MASC/FEM
◆ **adult education** l'enseignement pour adultes MASC
to **advance** VERB
   see also advance NOUN
   1 **avancer** (*move forward*) ◇ *The troops are advancing.* Les troupes avancent.
   2 **progresser** (*progress*) ◇ *Technology has advanced a lot.* La technologie a beaucoup progressé.
advance NOUN
   see also advance VERB
◆ **in advance** à l'avance ◇ *They bought the tickets in advance.* Ils ont acheté les billets à l'avance.
advance booking NOUN
◆ **Advance booking is essential.** Il est indispensable de réserver.
advanced ADJECTIVE
   avancé
advantage NOUN
   l' **avantage** MASC ◇ *Going to university has many advantages.* Aller à l'université présente de nombreux avantages.
◆ **to take advantage of something** profiter de quelque chose ◇ *He took advantage of the good weather to go for a walk.* Il a profité du beau temps pour faire une promenade.
◆ **to take advantage of somebody** exploiter quelqu'un ◇ *The company was taking advantage of its employees.* La société exploitait ses employés.
adventure NOUN
   l' **aventure** FEM
adverb NOUN
   l' **adverbe** MASC
advert, advertisement NOUN
   1 la **publicité** (*on TV*)
   2 l' **annonce** FEM (*in newspaper*)
advertising NOUN
   la **publicité**
advice NOUN
   les **conseils** MASC PL ◇ *to give somebody advice* donner des conseils à quelqu'un
◆ **a piece of advice** un conseil ◇ *He gave me a good piece of advice.* Il m'a donné un bon conseil.
to **advise** VERB

conseiller ◇ *He advised me to wait.* Il m'a conseillé d'attendre. ◇ *He advised me not to go there.* Il m'a conseillé de ne pas y aller.
aerial NOUN
   l' **antenne** FEM
aerobics PL NOUN
   l' **aérobic** FEM ◇ *I'm going to aerobics tonight.* Je vais au cours d'aérobic ce soir.
aeroplane NOUN
   l' **avion** MASC
aerosol NOUN
   la **bombe**
affair NOUN
   1 l' **aventure** FEM (*romantic*) ◇ *to have an affair with somebody* avoir une aventure avec quelqu'un
   2 l' **affaire** FEM (*event*)
to **affect** VERB
   affecter
affectionate ADJECTIVE
   affectueux MASC ˙
   affectueuse FEM
to **afford** VERB
   avoir les moyens d'acheter ◇ *I can't afford a new pair of jeans.* Je n'ai pas les moyens d'acheter un nouveau jean.
◆ **We can't afford to go on holiday.** Nous n'avons pas les moyens de partir en vacances.
afraid ADJECTIVE
◆ **to be afraid of something** avoir peur de quelque chose ◇ *I'm afraid of spiders.* J'ai peur des araignées.
◆ **I'm afraid I can't come.** Je crains de ne pouvoir venir.
◆ **I'm afraid so.** Hélas oui.
◆ **I'm afraid not.** Hélas non.
Africa NOUN
   l' **Afrique** FEM
◆ **in Africa** en Afrique
African ADJECTIVE
   see also African NOUN
   africain MASC
   africaine FEM
African NOUN
   see also African ADJECTIVE
   l' **Africain** MASC
   l' **Africaine** FEM
after PREPOSITION, ADVERB, CONJUNCTION
   après ◇ *after dinner* après le dîner
◇ *He ran after me.* Il a couru après moi. ◇ *soon after* peu après
◆ **after I'd had a rest** après m'être reposé
◆ **after having asked** après avoir demandé
◆ **after all** après tout
afternoon NOUN

l' **après-midi** MASC/FEM ◇ *3 o'clock in the afternoon* trois heures de l'après-midi ◇ *this afternoon* cet après-midi ◇ *on Saturday afternoon* le samedi après-midi

afters NOUN
le **dessert**

after-shave NOUN
l' **after-shave** MASC

afterwards ADVERB
après ◇ *She left not long afterwards.* Elle est partie peu de temps après.

again ADVERB
1 **de nouveau** (*once more*) ◇ *They're friends again.* Ils sont de nouveau amis.
2 **encore une fois** (*one more time*) ◇ *Can you tell me again?* Tu peux me le dire encore une fois?
◆ not...again ne...plus ◇ *I won't go there again.* Je n'y retournerai plus.
◆ Do it again! Refais-le!
◆ again and again à plusieurs reprises

against PREPOSITION
contre ◇ *He leant against the wall.* Il s'est appuyé contre le mur. ◇ *I'm against nuclear testing.* Je suis contre les essais nucléaires.

age NOUN
l' **âge** MASC ◇ *at the age of 16* à l'âge de seize ans ◇ *an age limit* une limite d'âge
◆ I haven't been to the cinema for ages. Ça fait une éternité que je ne suis pas allé au cinéma.

aged ADJECTIVE
◆ aged 10 âgé de dix ans

agenda NOUN
l' **ordre du jour** MASC

agent NOUN
l' **agent** MASC ◇ *an estate agent* un agent immobilier ◇ *a travel agent* un agent de voyage

aggressive ADJECTIVE
agressif MASC
agressive FEM

ago ADVERB
◆ two days ago il y a deux jours
◆ two years ago il y a deux ans
◆ not long ago il n'y a pas longtemps
◆ How long ago did it happen? Il y a combien de temps que c'est arrivé?

agony NOUN
◆ to be in agony souffrir le martyre
◇ *He was in agony.* Il souffrait le martyre.

to **agree** VERB
◆ to agree with être d'accord avec ◇ *I agree with Carol.* Je suis d'accord avec Carol.

◆ to agree to do something accepter de faire quelque chose ◇ *He agreed to go and pick her up.* Il a accepté d'aller la chercher.
◆ to agree that... admettre que... ◇ *I agree that it's difficult.* J'admets que c'est difficile.
◆ Garlic doesn't agree with me. Je ne supporte pas l'ail.

agreed ADJECTIVE
convenu ◇ *at the agreed time* au moment convenu

agreement NOUN
l' **accord** MASC
◆ to be in agreement être d'accord ◇ *Everybody was in agreement with Ray.* Tout le monde était d'accord avec Ray.

agricultural ADJECTIVE
agricole

agriculture NOUN
l' **agriculture** FEM

ahead ADVERB
devant ◇ *She looked straight ahead.* Elle regardait droit devant elle.
◆ ahead of time en avance
◆ to plan ahead organiser à l'avance
◆ The French are 5 points ahead. Les Français ont cinq points d'avance.
◆ Go ahead! Allez-y!

aid NOUN
◆ in aid of charity au profit d'associations caritatives

AIDS NOUN
le **sida**

to **aim** VERB
see also aim NOUN
◆ to aim at braquer sur ◇ *He aimed a gun at me.* Il a braqué un revolver sur moi.
◆ The film is aimed at children. Le film est destiné aux enfants.
◆ to aim to do something avoir l'intention de faire quelque chose ◇ *Janice aimed to leave at 5 o'clock.* Janice avait l'intention de partir à cinq heures.

aim NOUN
see also aim VERB
l' **objectif** ◇ *The aim of the festival is to raise money.* L'objectif du festival est de collecter des fonds.

air NOUN
l' **air** MASC ◇ *to get some fresh air* prendre l'air
◆ by air en avion ◇ *I prefer to travel by air.* Je préfère voyager en avion.

air-conditioned ADJECTIVE
climatisé

air conditioning NOUN
la **climatisation**
Air Force NOUN
l' **armée de l'air** FEM
air hostess NOUN
l' **hôtesse de l'air** ◇ *She's an air hostess.* Elle est hôtesse de l'air.
airline NOUN
la **compagnie aérienne**
airmail NOUN
- **by airmail** par avion
airport NOUN
l' **aéroport** MASC
aisle NOUN
l' **allée centrale** FEM
alarm NOUN
l' **alarme** FEM (*warning*)
- **a fire alarm** un avertisseur d'incendie
alarm clock NOUN
le **réveil**
album NOUN
l' **album** MASC
alcohol NOUN
l' **alcool** MASC
alcoholic NOUN
see also alcoholic ADJECTIVE
l' **alcoolique** MASC/FEM ◇ *He's an alcoholic.* C'est un alcoolique.
alcoholic ADJECTIVE
see also alcoholic NOUN
alcoolisé ◇ *alcoholic drinks* des boissons alcoolisées
alert ADJECTIVE
1 (*bright*)
vif MASC
vive FEM
◇ *He's a very alert baby.* C'est un bébé très vif.
2 (*paying attention*)
vigilant ◇ *We must stay alert.* Nous devons rester vigilants.
A levels PL NOUN
le **baccalauréat** SING
The baccalauréat (*or* bac *for short*) *is taken at the age of 17 or 18. Students have to sit one of a variety of set subject combinations, rather than being able to choose any combination of subjects they want. If you pass you have the right to a place at university.*
Algeria NOUN
l' **Algérie** FEM
- **in Algeria** en Algérie
alike ADVERB
- **to look alike** se ressembler ◇ *The two sisters look alike.* Les deux sœurs se ressemblent.
alive ADJECTIVE
vivant
all ADJECTIVE, PRONOUN, ADVERB

tout
(**tous** MASC PL)
◇ *all the time* tout le temps ◇ *I ate all of it.* J'ai tout mangé. ◇ *all day* toute la journée ◇ *all the books* tous les livres ◇ *all the apples* toutes les pommes
- **All of us went.** Nous y sommes tous allés.
- **after all** après tout ◇ *After all, nobody can make us go.* Après tout, personne ne peut nous obliger à y aller.
- **all alone** tout seul ◇ *She's all alone.* Elle est toute seule.
- **not at all** pas du tout ◇ *I'm not tired at all.* Je ne suis pas du tout fatigué.
- **The score is 5 all.** Le score est de cinq partout.
allergic ADJECTIVE
allergique
- **to be allergic to something** être allergique à quelque chose ◇ *I'm allergic to cats' hair.* Je suis allergique aux poils de chat.
alley NOUN
la **ruelle**
to **allow** VERB
- **to be allowed to do something** être autorisé à faire quelque chose ◇ *He's not allowed to go out at night.* Il n'est pas autorisé à sortir le soir.
- **to allow somebody to do something** permettre à quelqu'un de faire quelque chose ◇ *His mum allowed him to go out.* Sa mère lui a permis de sortir.
all right ADVERB
1 **bien** (*okay*) ◇ *Everything turned out all right.* Tout s'est bien terminé.
- **Are you all right?** Ça va?
2 **pas mal** (*not bad*) ◇ *The film was all right.* Le film n'était pas mal.
3 **d'accord** (*when agreeing*) ◇ *We'll talk about it later.—All right.* On en reparlera plus tard.—D'accord.
- **Is that all right with you?** Tu es d'accord?
almond NOUN
l' **amande** FEM
almost ADVERB
presque ◇ *I've almost finished.* J'ai presque fini.
alone ADJECTIVE, ADVERB
seul ◇ *She lives alone.* Elle habite seule.
- **to leave somebody alone** laisser quelqu'un tranquille ◇ *Leave her alone!* Laisse-la tranquille!
- **to leave something alone** ne pas toucher à quelque chose ◇ *Leave my*

things alone! Ne touche pas à mes affaires!

along PREPOSITION, ADVERB

le long de ◇ *Chris was walking along the beach.* Chris se promenait le long de la plage.

- **all along** depuis le début ◇ *He was lying to me all along.* Il m'a menti depuis le début.

aloud ADVERB

à haute voix ◇ *He read the poem aloud.* Il a lu le poème à haute voix.

alphabet NOUN

l' **alphabet** MASC

Alps PL NOUN

les **Alpes** FEM PL

already ADVERB

déjà ◇ *Liz had already gone.* Liz était déjà partie.

also ADVERB

aussi

altar NOUN

l' **autel** MASC

to **alter** VERB

changer

alternate ADJECTIVE

- **on alternate days** tous les deux jours

alternative NOUN

see also alternative ADJECTIVE

le **choix** ◇ *You have no alternative.* Tu n'as pas le choix.

- **Fruit is a healthy alternative to chocolate.** Les fruits sont plus sains que le chocolat.
- **There are several alternatives.** Il y a plusieurs possibilités.

alternative ADJECTIVE

see also alternative NOUN

autre ◇ *They made alternative plans.* Ils ont pris d'autres dispositions.

- **an alternative solution** une solution de rechange
- **alternative medicine** la médecine douce

alternatively ADVERB

- **Alternatively, we could just stay at home.** On pourrait aussi rester à la maison.

although CONJUNCTION

bien que

bien que *has to be followed by a verb in the subjunctive.*

◇ *Although she was tired, she stayed up late.* Bien qu'elle soit fatiguée, elle s'est couchée tard.

altogether ADVERB

[1] **en tout** (*in total*) ◇ *You owe me £20 altogether.* Tu me dois vingt livres en tout.

[2] **tout à fait** (*completely*) ◇ *I'm not altogether happy with your work.* Je ne suis pas tout à fait satisfait de votre travail.

aluminium NOUN

l' **aluminium** MASC

always ADVERB

toujours ◇ *He's always moaning.* Il est toujours en train de ronchonner.

am VERB *see* **be**

a.m. ABBREVIATION

du matin ◇ *At 4 a.m.* à quatre heures du matin

amateur NOUN

l' **amateur** MASC

to **amaze** VERB

- **to be amazed** être stupéfait ◇ *I was amazed that I managed to do it.* J'étais stupéfait d'avoir réussi.

amazing ADJECTIVE

[1] (*surprising*)

stupéfiant ◇ *That's amazing news!* C'est une nouvelle stupéfiante!

[2] (*excellent*)

exceptionnel MASC

exceptionnelle FEM

◇ *Vivian's an amazing cook.* Vivian est une cuisinière exceptionnelle.

ambassador NOUN

l' **ambassadeur** MASC

l' **ambassadrice** FEM

amber ADJECTIVE

- **an amber light** un feu orange

ambition NOUN

l' **ambition** FEM

ambitious ADJECTIVE

ambitieux MASC

ambitieuse FEM

◇ *She's very ambitious.* Elle est très ambitieuse.

ambulance NOUN

l' **ambulance** FEM

amenities PL NOUN

les **aménagements** MASC

- **The hotel has very good amenities.** L'hôtel est très bien aménagé.

America NOUN

l' **Amérique** FEM

- **in America** en Amérique
- **to America** en Amérique

American ADJECTIVE

see also American NOUN

américain ◇ *He's American.* Il est américain. ◇ *She's American.* Elle est américaine.

American NOUN

see also American ADJECTIVE

l' **Américain** MASC

l' **Américaine** FEM

- **the Americans** les Américains

amount NOUN

[1] la **somme** ◇ *a large amount of money* une grosse somme d'argent

[2] la **quantité**

- **a huge amount of rice** une énorme quantité de riz

amp NOUN

[1] l' **ampère** MASC (*of electricity*)

[2] l' **ampli** MASC (*for hi-fi*)

amplifier NOUN

l' **amplificateur** MASC (*for hi-fi*)

to **amuse** VERB

amuser ◇ *He was most amused by the story.* L'histoire l'a beaucoup amusé.

amusement arcade NOUN

la **salle de jeux électroniques**

an ARTICLE *see* **a**

to **analyse** VERB

analyser

analysis NOUN

l' **analyse** FEM

ancestor NOUN

l' **ancêtre** MASC/FEM

anchor NOUN

l' **ancre** FEM

ancient ADJECTIVE

[1] (*civilization*)

antique ◇ *ancient Greece* la Grèce antique

[2] (*custom, building*)

ancien MASC

ancienne FEM

◇ *an ancient monument* un monument ancien

and CONJUNCTION

et ◇ *you and me* toi et moi ◇ *2 and 2 are 4* deux et deux font quatre

- **Please try and come!** Essaie de venir!
- **He talked and talked.** Il n'a pas arrêté de parler.
- **better and better** de mieux en mieux

angel NOUN

l' **ange** MASC

anger NOUN

la **colère**

angle NOUN

l' **angle** MASC

angler NOUN

le **pêcheur à la ligne**

la **pêcheuse à la ligne**

angling NOUN

la **pêche à la ligne**

angry ADJECTIVE

en colère ◇ *Dad looks very angry.* Papa a l'air très en colère.

- **to be angry with somebody** être furieux contre quelqu'un ◇ *Mum's*

really angry with you. Maman est vraiment furieuse contre toi.

- **to get angry** se fâcher

animal NOUN

l' **animal** MASC

(les **animaux** PL)

ankle NOUN

la **cheville**

anniversary NOUN

l' **anniversaire** MASC ◇ *a wedding anniversary* un anniversaire de mariage

to **announce** VERB

annoncer

announcement NOUN

l' **annonce** FEM

to **annoy** VERB

agacer ◇ *He's really annoying me.* Il m'agace vraiment.

- **to get annoyed** se fâcher ◇ *Don't get so annoyed!* Ne vous fâchez pas!

annoying ADJECTIVE

agaçant ◇ *It's really annoying.* C'est vraiment agaçant.

annual ADJECTIVE

annuel MASC

annuelle FEM

◇ *an annual meeting* une réunion annuelle

anorak NOUN

l' **anorak** MASC

another ADJECTIVE

un autre

une autre

◇ *Would you like another piece of cake?* Tu veux un autre morceau de gâteau?

◇ *Have you got another skirt?* Tu as une autre jupe?

to **answer** VERB

see also **answer** NOUN

répondre à ◇ *Can you answer my question?* Peux-tu répondre à ma question? ◇ *to answer the phone* répondre au téléphone

- **to answer the door** aller ouvrir

◇ *Can you answer the door please?* Tu peux aller ouvrir s'il te plaît?

answer NOUN

see also **answer** VERB

[1] la **réponse** (*to question*)

[2] la **solution** (*to problem*)

answering machine NOUN

le **répondeur**

ant NOUN

la **fourmi**

Antarctic NOUN

l' **Antarctique** FEM

anthem NOUN

- **the national anthem** l'hymne national MASC

antibiotic NOUN
l' **antibiotique** MASC
antique NOUN
le **meuble ancien** (furniture)
antique shop NOUN
le **magasin d'antiquités**
antiseptic NOUN
l' **antiseptique** MASC
any ADJECTIVE, PRONOUN, ADVERB

> Use **du**, **de la** or **des** to translate any
> according to the gender of the French noun that
> follows it. **du** and **de la** become **de l'** when
> they're followed by a noun starting with a
> vowel.

[1] **du**   ◇ Would you like any bread?
Voulez-vous du pain?
de la   ◇ Would you like any beer?
Voulez-vous de la bière?
de l'   ◇ Have you got any mineral
water? Avez-vous de l'eau minérale?
des   ◇ Have you got any Blur CDs?
Avez-vous des CD de Blur?

> If you want to say you haven't got any of
> something, use **de** whatever the gender of the
> following noun is. **de** becomes **d'** when it comes
> before a noun starting with a vowel.

[2] **de**   ◇ I haven't got any books. Je
n'ai pas de livres.
d'   ◇ I haven't got any money. Je n'ai
pas d'argent.

> Use **en** where there is no noun after any.

[3] **en**   ◇ Sorry, I haven't got any.
Désolé, je n'en ai pas.
• **any more (1)** (additional) encore de
   ◇ Would you like any more coffee?
Est-ce que tu veux encore du café?
• **any more (2)** (no longer) ne...plus ◇ I
don't love him any more. Je ne l'aime
plus.
anybody PRONOUN
[1] **quelqu'un** (in question) ◇ Has
anybody got a pen? Est-ce que
quelqu'un a un stylo?
[2] **n'importe qui** (no matter who)
   ◇ Anybody can learn to swim.
N'importe qui peut apprendre à nager.

> Use **ne...personne** in a negative sentence. **ne**
> comes before the verb, **personne** after it.

[3] **ne...personne**   ◇ I can't see
anybody. Je ne vois personne.
anyhow ADVERB
de toute façon   ◇ He doesn't want to
go out and anyhow he's not allowed. Il
ne veut pas sortir et de toute façon il n'y
est pas autorisé.
anyone PRONOUN
[1] **quelqu'un** (in question) ◇ Has
anyone got a pen? Est-ce que quelqu'un
a un stylo?

[2] **n'importe qui** (no matter who)
   ◇ Anyone can learn to swim.
N'importe qui peut apprendre à nager.

> Use **ne...personne** in a negative sentence. **ne**
> comes before the verb, **personne** after it.

[3] **ne...personne**   ◇ I can't see
anyone. Je ne vois personne.
anything PRONOUN
[1] **quelque chose** (in question)
   ◇ Would you like anything to eat? Tu
veux manger quelque chose?
[2] **n'importe quoi** (no matter what)
   ◇ Anything could happen. Il pourrait
arriver n'importe quoi.

> Use **ne...rien** in a negative sentence. **ne** comes
> before the verb, **rien** after it.

[3] **ne...rien**   ◇ I can't hear anything. Je
n'entends rien.
anyway ADVERB
de toute façon   ◇ He doesn't want to
go out and anyway he's not allowed. Il
ne veut pas sortir et de toute façon il n'y
est pas autorisé.
anywhere ADVERB
[1] **quelque part** (in question) ◇ Have
you seen my coat anywhere? Est-ce que
tu as vu mon manteau quelque part?
[2] **n'importe où**   ◇ You can buy
stamps almost anywhere. On peut
acheter des timbres presque n'importe
où.

> Use **ne...nulle part** in a negative sentence. **ne**
> comes before the verb, **nulle part** after it.

[3] **ne...nulle part**   ◇ I can't find it
anywhere. Je ne le trouve nulle part.
apart ADVERB
• **The two towns are 10 kilometres apart.**
Les deux villes sont à dix kilomètres
l'une de l'autre.
• **apart from** à part   ◇ Apart from that,
everything's fine. À part ça, tout va
bien.
apartment NOUN
l' **appartement** MASC
to **apologize** VERB
s'excuser   ◇ He apologized for being
late. Il s'est excusé de son retard.
• **I apologize!** Je vous prie de m'excuser.
apology NOUN
les **excuses** FEM PL
apostrophe NOUN
l' **apostrophe** FEM
apparatus NOUN
[1] le **matériel** (in lab)
[2] les **agrès** MASC PL (in gym)
apparent ADJECTIVE
apparent
apparently ADVERB
apparemment

to **appeal** VERB
> *see also* appeal NOUN

  lancer un appel ◇ *They appealed for help.* Ils ont lancé un appel au secours.
- **Greece doesn't appeal to me.** Ça ne me tente pas d'aller en Grèce.
- **Does that appeal to you?** Ça te tente?

appeal NOUN
> *see also* appeal VERB

  l' **appel** MASC ◇ *They have launched an appeal.* Ils ont lancé un appel.

to **appear** VERB
  1 **apparaître** (*come into view*) ◇ *The bus appeared around the corner.* Le bus est apparu au coin de la rue.
- **to appear on TV** passer à la télé
  2 **paraître** (*seem*) ◇ *She appeared to be asleep.* Elle paraissait dormir.

appearance NOUN
  l' **apparence** FEM (*looks*) ◇ *She takes great care over her appearance.* Elle prend grand soin de son apparence.

appendicitis NOUN
  l' **appendicite** FEM

appetite NOUN
  l' **appétit** MASC

to **applaud** VERB
  applaudir

applause NOUN
  les **applaudissements** MASC PL

apple NOUN
  la **pomme**
- **an apple tree** un pommier

application NOUN
- **a job application** une candidature

application form NOUN
  1 le **dossier de candidature** (*for job*)
  2 le **dossier d'inscription** (*for university*)

to **apply** VERB
- **to apply for a job** poser sa candidature à un poste
- **to apply to** (*be relevant*) s'appliquer à ◇ *This rule doesn't apply to us.* Ce règlement ne s'applique pas à nous.

appointment NOUN
  le **rendez-vous** ◇ *I've got a dental appointment.* J'ai rendez-vous chez le dentiste.

to **appreciate** VERB
  être reconnaissant de ◇ *I really appreciate your help.* Je vous suis extrêmement reconnaissant de votre aide.

apprentice NOUN
  l' **apprenti** MASC
  l' **apprentie** FEM

to **approach** VERB
  1 **s'approcher de** (*get nearer to*) ◇ *He approached the house.* Il s'est approché de la maison.
  2 **aborder** (*tackle*) ◇ *to approach a problem* aborder un problème

appropriate ADJECTIVE
  approprié ◇ *That dress isn't very appropriate for an interview.* Cette robe n'est pas très appropriée pour un entretien.

to **approve** VERB
- **to approve of** approuver ◇ *I don't approve of his choice.* Je n'approuve pas son choix.
- **They didn't approve of his girlfriend.** Sa copine ne leur a pas plu.

approximate ADJECTIVE
  approximatif MASC
  approximative FEM

apricot NOUN
  l' **abricot** MASC

April NOUN
  avril MASC
- **in April** en avril
- **April Fool's Day** le premier avril

apron NOUN
  le **tablier**

Aquarius NOUN
  le **Verseau** ◇ *I'm Aquarius.* Je suis Verseau.

Arab ADJECTIVE
> *see also* Arab NOUN

  arabe ◇ *the Arab countries* les pays arabes

Arab NOUN
> *see also* Arab ADJECTIVE

  l' **Arabe** MASC/FEM

arch NOUN
  l' **arc** MASC

archaeologist NOUN
  l' **archéologue** MASC/FEM ◇ *He's an archaeologist.* Il est archéologue.

archaeology NOUN
  l' **archéologie** FEM

archbishop NOUN
  l' **archevêque** MASC

architect NOUN
  l' **architecte** MASC/FEM ◇ *She's an architect.* Elle est architecte.

architecture NOUN
  l' **architecture** FEM

Arctic NOUN
  l' **Arctique** MASC

are VERB *see* be

area NOUN
  1 la **région** ◇ *She lives in the Paris area.* Elle habite dans la région parisienne.
  2 le **quartier** ◇ *My favourite area of Paris is Montmartre.* Montmartre est le quartier de Paris que je préfère.

3 la **superficie** ◇ *The field has an area of 1500m².* Le champ a une superficie de mille cinq cent mètres carrés.

Argentina NOUN

l' **Argentine** FEM

- **in Argentina** en Argentine

Argentinian ADJECTIVE

argentin

to **argue** VERB

se disputer ◇ *They never stop arguing.* Ils n'arrêtent pas de se disputer.

argument NOUN

- **to have an argument** se disputer ◇ *They had an argument.* Ils se sont disputés.

Aries NOUN

le **Bélier** ◇ *I'm Aries.* Je suis Bélier.

arm NOUN

le **bras**

armchair NOUN

le **fauteuil**

armour NOUN

l' **armure** FEM

army NOUN

l' **armée** FEM

around PREPOSITION, ADVERB

1 **autour de** ◇ *She wore a scarf around her neck.* Elle portait une écharpe autour du cou.

2 **environ** (*approximately*) ◇ *It costs around £100.* Cela coûte environ cent livres.

3 **vers** (*date, time*) ◇ *Let's meet at around 8 p.m.* Retrouvons-nous vers vingt heures.

- **around here (1)** (*nearby*) près d'ici ◇ *Is there a chemist's around here?* Est-ce qu'il y a une pharmacie près d'ici?

- **around here (2)** (*in this area*) dans les parages ◇ *He lives around here.* Il habite dans les parages.

to **arrange** VERB

- **to arrange to do something** prévoir de faire quelque chose ◇ *They arranged to go out together on Friday.* Ils ont prévu de sortir ensemble vendredi.

- **to arrange a meeting** convenir d'un rendez-vous ◇ *Can we arrange a meeting?* Pouvons-nous convenir d'un rendez-vous?

- **to arrange a party** organiser une fête

arrangement NOUN

l' **arrangement** MASC (*plan*)

- **They made arrangements to go out on Friday night.** Ils ont organisé une sortie vendredi soir.

to **arrest** VERB

see also **arrest** NOUN

arrêter ◇ *The police have arrested 5 people.* La police a arrêté cinq personnes.

arrest NOUN

see also **arrest** VERB

l' **arrestation** FEM ◇ *You're under arrest!* Vous êtes en état d'arrestation!

arrival NOUN

l' **arrivée** FEM

to **arrive** VERB

arriver ◇ *I arrived at 5 o'clock.* Je suis arrivé à cinq heures.

arrow NOUN

la **flèche**

art NOUN

l' **art** MASC

artery NOUN

l' **artère** FEM

art gallery NOUN

le **musée**

article NOUN

l' **article** MASC ◇ *a newspaper article* un article de journal

artificial ADJECTIVE

artificiel MASC

artificielle FEM

artist NOUN

l' **artiste** MASC/FEM ◇ *She's an artist.* C'est une artiste.

artistic ADJECTIVE

artistique

as CONJUNCTION, ADVERB

1 **au moment où** (*while*) ◇ *He came in as I was leaving.* Il est arrivé au moment où je partais.

2 **puisque** (*since*) ◇ *As it's Sunday, you can have a lie-in.* Tu peux faire la grasse matinée, puisque c'est dimanche.

- **as...as** aussi...que ◇ *Pierre's as tall as Michel.* Pierre est aussi grand que Michel.

- **twice as...as** deux fois plus...que ◇ *Her coat cost twice as much as mine.* Son manteau a coûté deux fois plus cher que le mien.

- **as much...as** autant...que ◇ *I haven't got as much money as you.* Je n'ai pas autant d'argent que toi.

- **as soon as possible** dès que possible ◇ *I'll do it as soon as possible.* Je le ferai dès que possible.

- **as from tomorrow** à partir de demain ◇ *As from tomorrow, the shop will stay open until 10 p.m.* À partir de demain, le magasin restera ouvert jusqu'à vingt-deux heures.

- **as though** comme si ◇ *She acted as though she hadn't seen me.* Elle a fait comme si elle ne m'avait pas vu.
- **as if** comme si
- **He works as a waiter in the holidays.** Il travaille comme serveur pendant les vacances.

asap ABBREVIATION (= *as soon as possible*) **dès que possible**

ashamed ADJECTIVE
- **to be ashamed** avoir honte ◇ *You should be ashamed of yourself!* Tu devrais avoir honte!

ashtray NOUN
le **cendrier**

Asia NOUN
l' **Asie** FEM
- **in Asia** en Asie

Asian ADJECTIVE
see also Asian NOUN
asiatique ◇ *He's Asian.* C'est un Asiatique. ◇ *She's Asian.* C'est une Asiatique.

Asian NOUN
see also Asian ADJECTIVE
l' **Asiatique** MASC/FEM

to **ask** VERB
1 **demander** (*inquire, request*) ◇ *"Have you finished?" she asked.* "Tu as fini?" a-t-elle demandé.
- **to ask somebody something** demander quelque chose à quelqu'un ◇ *He asked her how old she was.* Il lui a demandé quel âge elle avait.
- **to ask for something** demander quelque chose ◇ *He asked for a cup of tea.* Il a demandé une tasse de thé.
- **to ask somebody to do something** demander à quelqu'un de faire quelque chose ◇ *She asked him to do the shopping.* Elle lui a demandé de faire les courses.
- **to ask about something** se renseigner sur quelque chose ◇ *I asked about train times to Leeds.* Je me suis renseigné sur les horaires des trains pour Leeds.
- **to ask somebody a question** poser une question à quelqu'un
2 **inviter** ◇ *Have you asked Matthew to the party?* Est-ce que tu as invité Matthew à la fête?
- **He asked her out.** (*on a date*) Il lui a demandé de sortir avec lui.

asleep ADJECTIVE
- **to be asleep** dormir ◇ *He's asleep.* Il dort.
- **to fall asleep** s'endormir ◇ *I fell asleep in front of the TV.* Je me suis endormi devant la télé.

asparagus NOUN
les **asperges** FEM PL

aspect NOUN
l' **aspect** MASC

aspirin NOUN
l' **aspirine** FEM

assignment NOUN
le **devoir** (*in school*)

assistance NOUN
l' **aide** FEM

assistant NOUN
1 (*in shop*)
le **vendeur**
la **vendeuse**
2 (*helper*)
l' **assistant** MASC
l' **assistante** FEM

association NOUN
l' **association** FEM

assortment NOUN
l' **assortiment** MASC

to **assume** VERB
supposer ◇ *I assume she won't be coming.* Je suppose qu'elle ne viendra pas.

to **assure** VERB
assurer ◇ *He assured me he was coming.* Il m'a assuré qu'il viendrait.

asthma NOUN
l' **asthme** MASC ◇ *I've got asthma.* J'ai de l'asthme.

astrology NOUN
l' **astrologie** FEM

astronaut NOUN
l' **astronaute** MASC/FEM

astronomy NOUN
l' **astronomie** FEM

at PREPOSITION
à+le *becomes* **au**, **à+les** *becomes* **aux**.
à ◇ *at 4 o'clock* à quatre heures ◇ *at Christmas* à Noël ◇ *at 50 km/h* à cinquante km/h ◇ *at home* à la maison ◇ *two at a time* deux à la fois ◇ *at school* à l'école
au ◇ *at the office* au bureau
aux ◇ *at the races* aux courses
- **at night** la nuit
- **What are you doing at the weekend?** Qu'est-ce que tu fais ce week-end?

ate VERB *see* **eat**

Athens NOUN
Athènes
- **in Athens** à Athènes

athlete NOUN
l' **athlète** MASC/FEM

athletic ADJECTIVE
athlétique

athletics NOUN

l' **athlétisme**   ◦ *I like watching the athletics on TV.* J'aime bien regarder les épreuves d'athlétisme à la télé.

Atlantic   NOUN
l' **océan Atlantique** MASC

atlas   NOUN
l' **atlas** MASC

atmosphere   NOUN
l' **atmosphère** FEM

atom   NOUN
l' **atome** MASC

atomic   ADJECTIVE
atomique   ◦ *an atomic bomb* une bombe atomique

to **attach**   VERB
fixer   ◦ *They attached a rope to the car.* Ils ont fixé une corde à la voiture.
- **Please find attached...** Veuillez trouver ci-joint...

attached   ADJECTIVE
- **to be attached to** être attaché à ◦ *He's very attached to his family.* Il est très attaché à sa famille.

to **attack**   VERB
see also attack NOUN
attaquer   ◦ *The dog attacked her.* Le chien l'a attaquée.

attack   NOUN
see also attack VERB
l' **attaque** FEM

attempt   NOUN
see also attempt VERB
la **tentative**   ◦ *She gave up after several attempts.* Elle y a renoncé après plusieurs tentatives.

to **attempt**   VERB
see also attempt NOUN
- **to attempt to do something** essayer de faire quelque chose ◦ *I attempted to write a song.* J'ai essayé d'écrire une chanson.

to **attend**   VERB
assister à   ◦ *to attend a meeting* assister à une réunion

attention   NOUN
l' **attention** FEM
- **to pay attention to** faire attention à ◦ *He didn't pay attention to what I was saying.* Il ne faisait pas attention à ce que je disais.

attic   NOUN
le **grenier**

attitude   NOUN
l' **attitude** FEM (*way of thinking*) ◦ *I really don't like your attitude!* Je n'aime pas du tout ton attitude!

to **attract**   VERB
attirer   ◦ *The Lake District attracts lots of tourists.* La région des lacs attire de

nombreux touristes.

attraction   NOUN
l' **attraction** FEM   ◦ *a tourist attraction* une attraction touristique

attractive   ADJECTIVE
séduisant   ◦ *She's very attractive.* Elle est très séduisante.

aubergine   NOUN
l' **aubergine** FEM

auction   NOUN
la **vente aux enchères**

audience   NOUN
les **spectateurs** MASC PL (*in theatre*)

audition   NOUN
l' **audition** FEM

August   NOUN
août MASC
- **in August** en août

aunt, aunty   NOUN
la **tante**   ◦ *my aunt* ma tante

au pair   NOUN
la **jeune fille au pair**   ◦ *She's an au pair.* Elle est jeune fille au pair.

Australia   NOUN
l' **Australie** FEM
- **in Australia** en Australie
- **to Australia** en Australie

Australian   ADJECTIVE
see also Australian NOUN
australien MASC
australienne FEM
◦ *He's Australian.* Il est australien.

Australian   NOUN
see also Australian ADJECTIVE
l' **Australien** MASC
l' **Australienne** FEM
- **the Australians** les Australiens

Austria   NOUN
l' **Autriche** FEM
- **in Austria** en Autriche

Austrian   ADJECTIVE
see also Austrian NOUN
autrichien MASC
autrichienne FEM
◦ *She's Austrian.* Elle est autrichienne.

Austrian   NOUN
see also Austrian ADJECTIVE
l' **Autrichien** MASC
l' **Autrichienne** FEM
- **the Austrians** les Autrichiens

author   NOUN
l' **auteur** MASC   ◦ *She's a famous author.* C'est un auteur connu.

autobiography   NOUN
l' **autobiographie** FEM

autograph   NOUN
l' **autographe** MASC

automatic   ADJECTIVE
automatique   ◦ *an automatic door*

une porte automatique

automatically ADVERB
automatiquement

autumn NOUN
l' automne MASC
- **in autumn** en automne

availability NOUN
la disponibilité

available ADJECTIVE
disponible ◇ *Free brochures are available on request.* Des brochures gratuites sont disponibles sur demande. ◇ *Is Mr Cooke available today?* Est-ce que Monsieur Cooke est disponible aujourd'hui?

avalanche NOUN
l' avalanche FEM

avenue NOUN
l' avenue FEM

average NOUN
see also average ADJECTIVE
la moyenne ◇ *on average* en moyenne

average ADJECTIVE
see also average NOUN
moyen MASC
moyenne FEM
◇ *the average price* le prix moyen

avocado NOUN
l' avocat MASC

to **avoid** VERB
éviter ◇ *He avoids her when she's in a bad mood.* Il l'évite lorsqu'elle est de mauvaise humeur.
- **to avoid doing something** éviter de faire quelque chose ◇ *Avoid going out on your own at night.* Évite de sortir seul le soir.

awake ADJECTIVE
- **to be awake** être réveillé ◇ *Is she*

awake? Elle est réveillée?
- **He was still awake.** Il ne dormait pas encore.

award NOUN
le prix ◇ *He's won an award.* Il a remporté un prix. ◇ *the award for the best actor* le prix du meilleur acteur

away ADJECTIVE, ADVERB
absent (*not here*) ◇ *André's away today.* André est absent aujourd'hui.
- **He's away for a week.** Il est parti pour une semaine.
- **The town's 2 kilometres away.** La ville est à deux kilomètres d'ici.
- **The coast is 2 hours away by car.** La côte est à deux heures de route.
- **Go away!** Va-t'en!
- **to put something away** ranger quelque chose ◇ *He put his toys away in the cupboard.* Il a rangé ses jouets dans le placard.

away match NOUN
le match à l'extérieur
(les matchs à l'extérieur PL)

awful ADJECTIVE
affreux MASC
affreuse FEM
◇ *That's awful!* C'est affreux!
- **an awful lot of...** énormément de...

awkward ADJECTIVE
1 délicat (*difficult to deal with*) ◇ *an awkward situation* une situation délicate
2 gênant (*embarrassing*) ◇ *an awkward question* une question gênante
- **It's a bit awkward for me to come and see you.** Ce n'est pas très pratique pour moi de venir vous voir.

axe NOUN
la hache

B

baby NOUN
le **bébé**

to **babysit** VERB
faire du baby-sitting

babysitter NOUN
le/la **baby-sitter**

babysitting NOUN
le **baby-sitting**

bachelor NOUN
le **célibataire** ◇ He's a bachelor. Il est célibataire.

back NOUN
see also back ADJECTIVE, VERB
[1] le **dos** (of person, horse, book)
[2] l' **arrière** MASC (of car, house) ◇ in the back à l'arrière
[3] le **verso** (of page) ◇ on the back au verso
[4] le **fond** (of room, garden) ◇ at the back au fond

back ADJECTIVE, ADVERB
see also back NOUN, VERB
arrière MASC, FEM, PL ◇ the back seat le siège arrière ◇ the back wheel of my bike la roue arrière de mon vélo
- **the back door** la porte de derrière
- **to get back** rentrer ◇ What time did you get back? À quelle heure est-ce que tu es rentré?
- **We went there by bus and walked back.** Nous y sommes allés en bus et nous sommes rentrés à pied.
- **He's not back yet.** Il n'est pas encore rentré.
- **to call somebody back** rappeler quelqu'un ◇ I'll call back later. Je rappellerai plus tard.

to **back** VERB
see also back NOUN, ADJECTIVE
soutenir (support) ◇ I'm backing Tony Blair. Je soutiens Tony Blair.
- **to back a horse** parier sur un cheval
- **to back out** se désister ◇ They promised to help and then backed out. Ils avaient promis de nous aider et ils se sont désistés.
- **to back somebody up** soutenir quelqu'un

backache NOUN
le **mal au dos** ◇ to have backache avoir mal au dos

backbone NOUN
la **colonne vertébrale**

to **backfire** VERB
échouer (go wrong)

background NOUN

[1] l' **arrière-plan** MASC (of picture) ◇ a house in the background une maison à l'arrière-plan
- **background noise** les bruits de fond MASC PL
[2] le **milieu**
(les **milieux** PL)
◇ his family background son milieu familial

backhand NOUN
le **revers**

backing NOUN
le **soutien** (support)

backpack NOUN
le **sac à dos**

back pain NOUN
le **mal au dos** ◇ to have back pain avoir mal au dos

backside NOUN
le **derrière**

backup NOUN
le **soutien** (support)
- **a backup file** une sauvegarde

backwards ADVERB
en arrière ◇ to take a step backwards faire un pas en arrière
- **to fall backwards** tomber à la renverse

back yard NOUN
la **cour**

bacon NOUN
[1] le **lard** (French type)
[2] le **bacon** (British type) ◇ bacon and eggs des œufs au bacon

bad ADJECTIVE
[1] **mauvais** ◇ a bad film un mauvais film ◇ the bad weather le mauvais temps ◇ to be in a bad mood être de mauvaise humeur
- **to be bad at something** être mauvais en quelque chose ◇ I'm really bad at maths. Je suis vraiment mauvais en maths.
[2] **grave** (serious) ◇ a bad accident un accident grave
[3] **vilain** (naughty) ◇ You bad boy! Vilain!
- **to go bad** (food) se gâter
- **I feel bad about it.** Ça m'ennuie.
- **not bad** pas mal ◇ That's not bad at all. Ce n'est pas mal du tout.

badge NOUN
le **badge**

badly ADVERB
mal ◇ badly paid mal payé
- **badly wounded** grièvement blessé
- **He badly needs a rest.** Il a

PTO

sérieusement besoin de se reposer.

badminton NOUN
le **badminton** ◇ to play badminton
jouer au badminton

bad-tempered ADJECTIVE
- **to be bad-tempered (1)** (by nature) avoir
  mauvais caractère ◇ He's a really
  bad-tempered person. Il a vraiment
  mauvais caractère.
- **to be bad-tempered (2)** (temporarily) être
  de mauvaise humeur ◇ He was really
  bad-tempered yesterday. Il était
  vraiment de mauvaise humeur hier.

bag NOUN
le **sac**
- **an old bag** (person) une vieille peau

baggage NOUN
les **bagages** MASC PL

baggage reclaim NOUN
la **livraison des bagages**

bagpipes PL NOUN
la **cornemuse** SING ◇ Ed plays the
bagpipes. Ed joue de la cornemuse.

to **bake** VERB
- **to bake a cake** faire un gâteau

baker NOUN
le **boulanger**
la **boulangère**
◇ He's a baker. Il est boulanger.

bakery NOUN
la **boulangerie**

baking ADJECTIVE
- **It's baking in here!** Il fait une chaleur
  torride ici!

balance NOUN
l' **équilibre** MASC ◇ to lose one's
balance perdre l'équilibre

balanced ADJECTIVE
équilibré

balcony NOUN
le **balcon**

bald ADJECTIVE
chauve

ball NOUN
1 la **balle** (tennis, golf, cricket)
2 le **ballon** (football, rugby)

ballet NOUN
le **ballet** ◇ We went to a ballet. Nous
sommes allés voir un ballet.
- **ballet lessons** les cours de danse

ballet dancer NOUN
le **danseur classique**
la **danseuse classique**

ballet shoes PL NOUN
les **chaussons de danse** MASC PL

balloon NOUN
le **ballon** (for parties)
- **a hot-air balloon** une montgolfière

ballpoint pen NOUN
le **stylo à bille**

ban NOUN
see also ban VERB
l' **interdiction** FEM

to **ban** VERB
see also ban NOUN
interdire

banana NOUN
la **banane** ◇ a banana skin une peau
de banane

band NOUN
1 le **groupe** (rock band)
2 la **fanfare** (brass band)

bandage NOUN
see also bandage VERB
le **bandage**

to **bandage** VERB
see also bandage NOUN
mettre un bandage à ◇ The nurse
bandaged his arm. L'infirmière lui a mis
un bandage au bras.

bandit NOUN
le **bandit**

bang NOUN
see also bang VERB
1 la **détonation** ◇ I heard a loud
bang. J'ai entendu une forte
détonation.
2 le **coup** ◇ a bang on the head un
coup sur la tête
- **Bang!** Pan!

to **bang** VERB
see also bang NOUN
se cogner (part of body) ◇ I banged my
head. Je me suis cogné la tête.
- **to bang the door** claquer la porte
- **to bang on the door** cogner à la porte

bank NOUN
1 la **banque** (financial)
2 le **bord** (of river, lake)

bank account NOUN
le **compte en banque**

banker NOUN
le **banquier**

bank holiday NOUN
le **jour férié**

banknote NOUN
le **billet de banque**

banned ADJECTIVE
interdit

bar NOUN
1 le **bar** (pub)
2 le **comptoir** (counter)
- **a bar of chocolate** une tablette de
  chocolat
- **a bar of soap** une savonnette

barbaric ADJECTIVE
barbare

barbecue NOUN

le **barbecue**
barber NOUN
le **coiffeur pour hommes**
bare ADJECTIVE
nu
barefoot ADJECTIVE, ADVERB
nu-pieds MASC, FEM, PL ◇ *The children go around barefoot.* Les enfants se promènent nu-pieds.
- **to be barefoot** avoir les pieds nus ◇ *She was barefoot.* Elle avait les pieds nus.
bargain NOUN
l' **affaire** FEM ◇ *It was a bargain!* C'était une affaire!
barge NOUN
la **péniche**
bark VERB
aboyer
barmaid NOUN
la **barmaid** ◇ *She's a barmaid.* Elle est barmaid.
barman NOUN
le **barman** ◇ *He's a barman.* Il est barman.
barn NOUN
la **grange**
barrel NOUN
le **tonneau**
(les **tonneaux** PL)
barrier NOUN
la **barrière**
base NOUN
la **base**
baseball NOUN
le **base-ball**
- **a baseball cap** une casquette de base-ball
based ADJECTIVE
- **based on** fondé sur
basement NOUN
le **sous-sol**
bash VERB
see also bash NOUN
- **to bash something** taper sur quelque chose
bash NOUN
see also bash VERB
- **I'll have a bash.** Je vais essayer.
basic ADJECTIVE
1 **de base** ◇ *It's a basic model.* C'est un modèle de base.
2 **rudimentaire** ◇ *The accommodation is pretty basic.* Le logement est plutôt rudimentaire.
basically ADVERB
tout simplement ◇ *Basically, I just don't like him.* Tout simplement, je ne

l'aime pas.
basics PL NOUN
les **rudiments** MASC PL
basin NOUN
le **lavabo** (*washbasin*)
basis NOUN
- **on a daily basis** quotidiennement
- **on a regular basis** régulièrement
basketball NOUN
le **basket**
bass NOUN
1 la **basse** (*guitar, singer*) ◇ *He plays the bass.* Il joue de la basse. ◇ *He's a bass.* Il est basse.
- **a bass guitar** une guitare basse
- **a double bass** une contrebasse
2 les **graves** MASC PL (*on hi-fi*)
bass drum NOUN
la **grosse caisse**
bassoon NOUN
le **basson** ◇ *I play the bassoon.* Je joue du basson.
bastard NOUN
le **salaud** (*rude*) ◇ *You bastard!* Salaud!
bat NOUN
1 (*for cricket, rounders*)
la **batte**
2 (*for table tennis*)
la **raquette**
3 (*animal*)
la **chauve-souris**
(les **chauves-souris** PL)
bath NOUN
1 le **bain** ◇ *to have a bath* prendre un bain
- **a hot bath** un bain chaud
2 la **baignoire** (*bathtub*) ◇ *There's a spider in the bath.* Il y a une araignée dans la baignoire.
bathe VERB
se baigner
bathroom NOUN
la **salle de bains**
baths PL NOUN
la **piscine** SING
bath towel NOUN
la **serviette de bain**
batter NOUN
la **pâte à frire**
battery NOUN
1 la **pile** (*for torch, toy*)
2 la **batterie** (*of car*)
battle NOUN
la **bataille** ◇ *the Battle of Hastings* la bataille de Hastings
- **It was a battle, but we managed in the end.** Il a fallu se battre, mais on a fini par y arriver.

battleship NOUN
le **cuirassé**

bay NOUN
la **baie**

BC ABBREVIATION (= before Christ)
av. J.-C. (= avant Jésus-Christ) ◇ in
200 BC en deux cent avant Jésus-Christ

to **be** VERB
être ◇ I'm tired. Je suis fatigué.
◇ You're late. Tu es en retard.
◇ She's English. Elle est anglaise.
◇ Edinburgh is in Scotland.
Édimbourg est en Écosse. ◇ It's 4
o'clock. Il est quatre heures. ◇ We are
all happy. Nous sommes tous heureux.
◇ They are in Paris at the moment. Ils
sont à Paris en ce moment. ◇ I've
been ill. J'ai été malade.
- **It's the 28th of October today.** Nous
sommes le vingt-huit octobre.
- **Have you been to Greece before?**
Est-ce que tu es déjà allé en Grèce?
- **I've never been to Paris.** Je ne suis
jamais allé à Paris.
- **to be killed** être tué

*When you are saying what somebody's
occupation is, you leave out the "a" in French.*
◇ She's a doctor. Elle est médecin.
◇ He's a student. Il est étudiant.

*With certain adjectives, such as "cold", "hot",
"hungry" and "thirsty", use **avoir** instead of
être.*
- **I'm cold.** J'ai froid.
- **I'm hungry.** J'ai faim.

*When saying how old somebody is, use **avoir**
not être.*
- **I'm fourteen.** J'ai quatorze ans.
- **How old are you?** Quel âge as-tu?

*When referring to the weather, use **faire**.*
- **It's cold.** Il fait froid.
- **It's too hot.** Il fait trop chaud.
- **It's a nice day.** Il fait beau.

beach NOUN
la **plage**

bead NOUN
la **perle**

beam NOUN
le **rayon**

beans NOUN
① les **haricots** MASC PL
② les **haricots blancs à la sauce
tomate** MASC PL (baked beans) ◇ I had
beans on toast. J'ai mangé des haricots
blancs à la sauce tomate sur du pain
grillé.
- **broad beans** les fèves FEM
- **green beans** les haricots verts MASC
- **kidney beans** les haricots rouges MASC

bear NOUN

see also bear VERB
l' **ours** MASC

to **bear** VERB

see also bear NOUN
- **I can't bear it!** C'est insupportable!
- **to bear up** tenir le coup
- **Bear up!** Tiens bon!

beard NOUN
la **barbe**
- **He's got a beard.** Il est barbu.
- **a man with a beard** un barbu

bearded ADJECTIVE
barbu

beat NOUN

see also beat VERB
le **rythme**

to **beat** VERB

see also beat NOUN
battre ◇ We beat them 3-0. On les a
battus trois à zéro.
- **Beat it!** Fiche le camp! (informal)
- **to beat somebody up** tabasser
quelqu'un (informal)

beautiful ADJECTIVE
beau MASC
belle FEM
(**beaux** MASC PL)

beautifully ADVERB
admirablement

beauty NOUN
la **beauté**

beauty spot NOUN
le **site pittoresque**

became VERB see **become**

because CONJUNCTION
parce que ◇ I did it because... Je l'ai
fait parce que...
- **because of** à cause de ◇ because of
the weather à cause du temps

to **become** VERB
devenir ◇ He became a famous
writer. Il est devenu un grand écrivain.

bed NOUN
le **lit** ◇ in bed au lit
- **to go to bed** aller se coucher
- **to go to bed with somebody** coucher
avec quelqu'un

bed and breakfast NOUN
la **chambre d'hôte** ◇ We stayed in a
bed and breakfast. Nous avons logé
dans une chambre d'hôte.
- **How much is it for bed and breakfast?**
C'est combien pour la chambre et le
petit déjeuner?

bedclothes PL NOUN
les **draps et les couvertures** MASC PL

bedding NOUN
la **literie**

bedroom NOUN

la **chambre**

bedspread NOUN

le **dessus-de-lit**

(les **dessus-de-lit** PL)

bedtime NOUN

- **Ten o'clock is my usual bedtime.** Je me couche généralement à dix heures.
- **Bedtime!** Au lit!

bee NOUN

l' **abeille** FEM

beef NOUN

le **bœuf**

- **roast beef** le rosbif

beefburger NOUN

le **hamburger**

been VERB *see* **be**

beer NOUN

la **bière**

beetle NOUN

le **scarabée**

beetroot NOUN

la **betterave rouge**

before PREPOSITION, CONJUNCTION, ADVERB

1 **avant** ◦ *before Tuesday* avant mardi

2 **avant de** ◦ *before going* avant de partir ◦ *Before opening the packet, read the instructions.* Avant d'ouvrir le paquet, lisez le mode d'emploi. ◦ *I'll phone before I leave.* J'appellerai avant de partir.

3 **déjà** (*already*) ◦ *I've seen this film before.* J'ai déjà vu ce film. ◦ *Have you been to Scotland before?* Vous êtes déjà venu en Écosse?

- **the day before** la veille
- **the week before** la semaine précédente

beforehand ADVERB

à l'avance

● **beg** VERB

1 **mendier** (*for money*)

2 **supplier** ◦ *He begged me to stop.* Il m'a supplié d'arrêter.

began VERB *see* **begin**

beggar NOUN

le **mendiant**

la **mendiante**

● **begin** VERB

commencer

- **to begin doing something** commencer à faire quelque chose

beginner NOUN

le **débutant**

la **débutante**

◦ *I'm just a beginner.* Je ne suis qu'un débutant.

beginning NOUN

le **début** ◦ *in the beginning* au début

behalf NOUN

- **on behalf of somebody** pour quelqu'un

to **behave** VERB

se comporter ◦ *He behaved like an idiot.* Il s'est comporté comme un idiot. ◦ *She behaved very badly.* Elle s'est très mal comportée.

- **to behave oneself** être sage ◦ *Did the children behave themselves?* Est-ce que les enfants ont été sages?
- **Behave!** Sois sage!

behaviour NOUN

le **comportement**

behind PREPOSITION, ADVERB

see also behind NOUN

derrière ◦ *behind the television* derrière la télévision

- **to be behind** (*late*) avoir du retard ◦ *I'm behind with my revision.* J'ai du retard dans mes révisions.

behind NOUN

see also behind PREPOSITION, ADVERB

le **derrière**

beige ADJECTIVE

beige

Belgian ADJECTIVE

see also Belgian NOUN

belge ◦ *Belgian chocolate* le chocolat belge ◦ *She's Belgian.* Elle est belge.

Belgian NOUN

see also Belgian ADJECTIVE

le/la **Belge**

- **the Belgians** les Belges

Belgium NOUN

la **Belgique**

- **in Belgium** en Belgique

to **believe** VERB

croire ◦ *I don't believe you.* Je ne te crois pas.

- **to believe in something** croire à quelque chose ◦ *Do you believe in ghosts?* Tu crois aux fantômes?
- **to believe in God** croire en Dieu

bell NOUN

1 la **sonnette** (*doorbell*)

- **to ring the bell** sonner à la porte

2 la **cloche** (*in church*)

3 la **sonnerie** (*in school*)

4 la **clochette** ◦ *Our cat has a bell on its neck.* Notre chat a une clochette sur son collier.

belly NOUN

le **ventre**

to **belong** VERB

- **to belong to somebody** être à quelqu'un ◦ *Who does it belong to?* C'est à qui? ◦ *That belongs to me.* C'est à moi.
- **Do you belong to any clubs?** Est-ce

que tu es membre d'un club?
- **Where does this belong?** Où est-ce que ça va?

belongings PL NOUN
les **affaires** FEM PL

below PREPOSITION, ADVERB
1 **au-dessous de** ◇ *below the castle* au-dessous du château
2 **en dessous** ◇ *on the floor below* à l'étage en dessous
- **10 degrees below freezing** moins dix

belt NOUN
la **ceinture**

bench NOUN
1 le **banc** (*seat*)
2 l' **établi** MASC (*for woodwork*)

bend NOUN
see also bend VERB
1 le **virage** (*in road*)
2 le **coude** (*in river*)

to **bend** VERB
see also bend NOUN
1 **courber** (*back*)
2 **plier** (*leg, arm*) ◇ *I can't bend my arm* Je n'arrive pas à plier le bras.
- **"do not bend"** "ne pas plier"
3 **tordre** (*object*) ◇ *You've bent it.* Tu l'as tordu.
4 **se tordre** ◇ *It bends easily.* Ça se tord facilement.
- **to bend down** se baisser
- **to bend over** se pencher

beneath PREPOSITION
sous

benefit NOUN
see also benefit VERB
l' **avantage** MASC (*advantage*)
- **unemployment benefit** les allocations de chômage

to **benefit** VERB
see also benefit NOUN
- **He'll benefit from the change.** Le changement lui fera du bien.

bent VERB *see* **bend**

bent ADJECTIVE
tordu ◇ *a bent fork* une fourchette tordue

beret NOUN
le **béret**

berserk ADJECTIVE
- **to go berserk** devenir fou furieux
  ◇ *She went berserk.* Elle est devenue folle furieuse.

berth NOUN
la **couchette**

beside PREPOSITION
à côté de ◇ *beside the television* à côté de la télévision
- **He was beside himself.** Il était hors de

lui.
- **That's beside the point.** Cela n'a rien à voir.

besides ADVERB
en plus ◇ *Besides, it's too expensive.* En plus, c'est trop cher.

best ADJECTIVE, ADVERB
1 **meilleur** ◇ *He's the best player in the team.* Il est le meilleur joueur de l'équipe. ◇ *Janet's the best at maths.* Janet est la meilleure en maths.
2 **le mieux** ◇ *Emma sings best.* C'est Emma qui chante le mieux.
◇ *That's the best I can do.* Je ne peux pas faire mieux.
- **to do one's best** faire de son mieux
◇ *It's not perfect, but I did my best.* Ça n'est pas parfait, mais j'ai fait de mon mieux.
- **to make the best of it** s'en contenter
◇ *We'll have to make the best of it.* Il va falloir nous en contenter.

best man NOUN
le **garçon d'honneur**

bet NOUN
see also bet VERB
le **pari** ◇ *to make a bet* faire un pari

to **bet** VERB
see also bet NOUN
parier ◇ *I bet you he won't come.* Je te parie qu'il ne viendra pas. ◇ *I bet he forgot.* Je parie qu'il a oublié.

to **betray** VERB
trahir

better ADJECTIVE, ADVERB
1 **meilleur** ◇ *This one's better than that one.* Celui-ci est meilleur que celui-là. ◇ *a better way to do it* une meilleure façon de le faire
2 **mieux** ◇ *That's better!* C'est mieux comme ça.
- **better still** encore mieux ◇ *Go and see her tomorrow, or better still, go today.* Va la voir demain, ou encore mieux, vas-y aujourd'hui.
- **to get better (1)** (*improve*) s'améliorer
◇ *I hope the weather gets better soon.* J'espère que le temps va s'améliorer bientôt. ◇ *My French is getting better.* Mon français s'améliore.
- **to get better (2)** (*from illness*) se remettre
◇ *I hope you get better soon.* J'espère que tu vas vite te remettre.
- **to feel better** se sentir mieux ◇ *Are you feeling better now?* Tu te sens mieux maintenant?
- **You'd better do it straight away.** Vous feriez mieux de le faire immédiatement.
- **I'd better go home.** Je ferais mieux de

rentrer.

betting shop NOUN
le **bureau de paris**

between PREPOSITION
entre ◇ *Stroud is between Oxford and Bristol.* Stroud est entre Oxford et Bristol. ◇ *between 15 and 20 minutes* entre quinze et vingt minutes

beyond PREPOSITION
au-delà de ◇ *There was a lake beyond the mountain.* Il y avait un lac au-delà de la montagne.
- **beyond belief** incroyable
- **beyond repair** irréparable

biased ADJECTIVE
partial

Bible NOUN
la **Bible**

bicycle NOUN
le **vélo**

bifocals PL NOUN
les **verres à double foyer** MASC PL

big ADJECTIVE
[1] **grand** ◇ *a big house* une grande maison ◇ *my big brother* mon grand frère ◇ *her big sister* sa grande sœur
- **He's a big guy.** C'est un grand gaillard.
[2] (*car, animal, book, parcel*)
gros MASC
grosse FEM
◇ *a big car* un grosse voiture

bigheaded ADJECTIVE
- **to be bigheaded** avoir la grosse tête

bike NOUN
le **vélo** ◇ *by bike* en vélo

bikini NOUN
le **bikini**

bilingual ADJECTIVE
bilingue

bill NOUN
[1] l' **addition** FEM (*in restaurant*) ◇ *Can we have the bill, please?* L'addition, s'il vous plaît.
[2] la **facture** (*for gas, electricity, telephone*)

billiards NOUN
le **billard** ◇ *to play billiards* jouer au billard

billion NOUN
le **milliard**

bin NOUN
la **poubelle**

binoculars PL NOUN
les **jumelles** FEM PL
- **a pair of binoculars** des jumelles

biochemistry NOUN
la **biochimie**

biography NOUN
la **biographie**

biology NOUN

la **biologie**

bird NOUN
l' **oiseau** MASC
(les **oiseaux** PL)

birdwatching NOUN
- **My hobby's birdwatching.** Mon passe-temps favori est d'observer les oiseaux.

Biro ® NOUN
le **bic** ®

birth NOUN
la **naissance** ◇ *date of birth* la date de naissance

birth certificate NOUN
l' **acte de naissance** MASC

birth control NOUN
la **contraception**

birthday NOUN
l' **anniversaire** MASC ◇ *When's your birthday?* Quelle est la date de ton anniversaire?
- **a birthday cake** un gâteau d'anniversaire
- **I'm going to have a birthday party.** Je vais faire une fête pour mon anniversaire.

biscuit NOUN
le **gâteau sec**

bishop NOUN
l' **évêque** MASC

bit VERB *see* **bite**

bit NOUN
le **morceau**
(les **morceaux** PL)
◇ *Would you like another bit?* Est-ce que tu en veux un autre morceau?
- **a bit of (1)** (*piece of*) un morceau de ◇ *a bit of cake* un morceau de gâteau
- **a bit of (2)** (*a little*) un peu de ◇ *a bit of music* un peu de musique
- **It's a bit of a nuisance.** C'est ennuyeux.
- **a bit** un peu ◇ *He's a bit mad.* Il est un peu fou. ◇ *a bit too hot* un peu trop chaud ◇ *Wait a bit!* Attends un peu! ◇ *Do you play football?—A bit.* Tu joues au football?—Un peu.
- **to fall to bits** se désintégrer
- **to take something to bits** démonter quelque chose
- **bit by bit** petit à petit

bitch NOUN
[1] la **garce** (*person*)
[2] la **chienne** (*female dog*)

to **bite** VERB
see also **bite** NOUN
[1] **mordre** (*person, dog*)
[2] **piquer** (*insect*) ◇ *I got bitten by mosquitoes.* Je me suis fait piquer par

des moustiques.
- **to bite one's nails** se ronger les ongles

bite NOUN

see also bite VERB

1 la **piqûre** (*insect bite*)

2 la **morsure** (*animal bite*)

- **to have a bite to eat** manger un morceau

bitter ADJECTIVE

see also bitter NOUN

1 **amer** MASC
amère FEM

2 (*weather, wind*)
glacial
(**glaciaux** MASC PL)
○ *It's bitter today.* Il fait glacial aujourd'hui.

bitter NOUN

see also bitter ADJECTIVE

la **bière brune**

black ADJECTIVE

noir ○ *a black jacket* une veste noire
○ *She's Black.* Elle est noire.

blackberry NOUN

la **mûre**

blackbird NOUN

le **merle**

blackboard NOUN

le **tableau noir**

black coffee NOUN

le **café**

blackcurrant NOUN

le **cassis**

blackmail NOUN

see also blackmail VERB

le **chantage** ○ *That's blackmail!* C'est du chantage!

to **blackmail** VERB

see also blackmail NOUN

- **to blackmail somebody** faire chanter quelqu'un ○ *He blackmailed her.* Il l'a fait chanter.

blackout NOUN

la **panne d'électricité** (*power cut*)

- **to have a blackout** (*faint*) s'évanouir

black pudding NOUN

le **boudin**

blade NOUN

la **lame**

to **blame** VERB

- **Don't blame me!** Ça n'est pas ma faute!
- **I blame the police.** À mon avis, c'est la faute de la police.
- **He blamed it on my sister.** Il a dit que c'était la faute de ma sœur.

blank ADJECTIVE

see also blank NOUN

1 (*paper*)
blanc MASC

blanche FEM

2 (*cassette, video, page*)
vierge

- **My mind went blank.** J'ai eu un trou.

blank NOUN

see also blank ADJECTIVE

le **blanc** ○ *Fill in the blanks.*
Remplissez les blancs.

blank cheque NOUN

le **chèque en blanc**

blanket NOUN

la **couverture**

blast NOUN

- **a bomb blast** une explosion

blatant ADJECTIVE

flagrant

blaze NOUN

l' **incendie** MASC

blazer NOUN

le **blazer**

bleach NOUN

l' **eau de Javel** FEM

bleached ADJECTIVE

décoloré ○ *bleached hair* les cheveux décolorés

to **bleed** VERB

saigner ○ *My nose is bleeding.* Je saigne du nez.

bleeper NOUN

le **bip**

blender NOUN

le **mixer**

to **bless** VERB

bénir (*religiously*)

- **Bless you!** (*after sneezing*) À tes souhaits!

blew VERB *see* **blow**

blind ADJECTIVE

see also blind NOUN

aveugle

blind NOUN

see also blind ADJECTIVE

le **store** (*for window*)

blindfold NOUN

see also blindfold VERB

le **bandeau**
(les **bandeaux** PL)

to **blindfold** VERB

see also blindfold NOUN

- **to blindfold somebody** bander les yeux à quelqu'un

to **blink** VERB

cligner des yeux

bliss NOUN

- **It was bliss!** C'était merveilleux!

blister NOUN

l' **ampoule** FEM

blizzard NOUN

la **tempête de neige**

blob NOUN
la **goutte** ◇ *a blob of glue* une goutte de colle

block NOUN
see also block VERB
l' **immeuble** MASC ◇ *He lives in our block.* Il habite dans notre immeuble.
- **a block of flats** un immeuble

to **block** VERB
see also block NOUN
bloquer

blockage NOUN
l' **obstruction** FEM

bloke NOUN
le **mec** (*informal*)

blonde ADJECTIVE
blond ◇ *She's got blonde hair.* Elle a les cheveux blonds.

blood NOUN
le **sang**

blood pressure NOUN
- **to have high blood pressure** faire de la tension

blood sports NOUN
les **sports sanguinaires** MASC PL

blood test NOUN
la **prise de sang**

bloody ADJECTIVE
- **bloody difficult** sacrément difficile
- **that bloody television** cette putain de télévision
- **Bloody hell!** Merde!

blouse NOUN
le **chemisier**

blow NOUN
see also blow VERB
le **coup**

to **blow** VERB
see also blow NOUN
souffler (*wind, person*)
- **to blow one's nose** se moucher
- **to blow a whistle** siffler
- **to blow out a candle** éteindre une bougie
- **to blow up (1)** faire sauter ◇ *The terrorists blew up a police station.* Les terroristes ont fait sauter un commissariat de police.
- **to blow up (2)** gonfler ◇ *to blow up a balloon* gonfler un ballon
- **The house blew up.** La maison a sauté.

blow-dry NOUN
le **brushing**
- **A cut and blow-dry, please.** Une coupe brushing, s'il vous plaît.

blue ADJECTIVE
bleu ◇ *a blue dress* une robe bleue
- **a blue film** un film pornographique

- **It came out of the blue.** C'était complètement inattendu.

blues PL NOUN
le **blues** SING

to **bluff** VERB
see also bluff NOUN
bluffer

bluff NOUN
see also bluff VERB
le **bluff** ◇ *It's just a bluff.* C'est du bluff.

blunder NOUN
la **gaffe**

blunt ADJECTIVE
1 **brusque** (*person*)
2 **émoussé** (*knife*)

to **blush** VERB
rougir

board NOUN
1 (*wooden*)
la **planche**
2 (*blackboard*)
le **tableau**
(les **tableaux** PL)
◇ *on the board* au tableau
3 (*noticeboard*)
le **panneau**
(les **panneaux** PL)
4 (*for board games*)
le **jeu**
(les **jeux** PL)
5 (*for chess*)
l' **échiquier** MASC
- **on board** à bord
- **"full board"** "pension complète"

boarder NOUN
l' **interne** MASC/FEM

board game NOUN
le **jeu de société**
(les **jeux de société** PL)

boarding card NOUN
la **carte d'embarquement**

boarding school NOUN
le **pensionnat**
- **I go to boarding school.** Je suis interne.

to **boast** VERB
se vanter ◇ *Stop boasting!* Arrête de te vanter!
- **to boast about something** se vanter de quelque chose

boat NOUN
le **bateau**
(les **bateaux** PL)

body NOUN
le **corps**

bodybuilding NOUN
le **culturisme**

bodyguard NOUN
le **garde du corps**

bog NOUN
la **tourbière** (*marsh*)

boil NOUN
see also boil VERB
le **furoncle**

to **boil** VERB
see also boil NOUN
[1] **faire bouillir** ◇ *to boil some water*
faire bouillir de l'eau
- **to boil an egg** faire cuire un œuf
[2] **bouillir** ◇ *The water's boiling.*
L'eau bout. ◇ *The water's boiled.* L'eau
a bouilli.
- **to boil over** déborder

boiled ADJECTIVE
à l'eau ◇ *boiled potatoes* des
pommes de terre à l'eau
- **a boiled egg** un œuf à la coque

boiling ADJECTIVE
- **It's boiling in here!** Il fait une chaleur
torride ici!
- **boiling hot** torride ◇ *a boiling hot
day* une journée torride

bolt NOUN
[1] le **verrou** (*on door*)
[2] le **boulon** (*with nut*)

bomb NOUN
see also bomb VERB
la **bombe**

to **bomb** VERB
see also bomb NOUN
bombarder

bomber NOUN
le **bombardier**

bombing NOUN
l' **attentat à la bombe** MASC

bond NOUN
le **lien**

bone NOUN
[1] l' **os** MASC (*of human, animal*)
[2] l' **arête** FEM (*of fish*)

bone dry ADJECTIVE
complètement sec MASC
complètement sèche FEM

bonfire NOUN
le **feu**
(les **feux** PL)

bonnet NOUN
le **capot** (*of car*)

book NOUN
see also book VERB
le **livre**

to **book** VERB
see also book NOUN
réserver ◇ *We haven't booked.* Nous
n'avons pas réservé.

bookcase NOUN
la **bibliothèque**

booklet NOUN

la **brochure**

bookshelf NOUN
l' **étagère à livres** FEM

bookshop NOUN
la **librairie**

boot NOUN
[1] le **coffre** (*of car*)
[2] la **botte** (*fashion boot*)
[3] la **chaussure de marche** (*for hiking*)
- **football boots** des chaussures foot

booze NOUN
l' **alcool** MASC

border NOUN
la **frontière**

bored ADJECTIVE
- **to be bored** s'ennuyer ◇ *I was bored.*
Je m'ennuyais.
- **to get bored** s'ennuyer

boredom NOUN
l' **ennui** MASC

boring ADJECTIVE
ennuyeux MASC
ennuyeuse FEM

born ADJECTIVE
- **to be born** naître ◇ *I was born in
1982.* Je suis né en mille neuf cent
quatre-vingt-deux.

to **borrow** VERB
emprunter ◇ *Can I borrow your pen?*
Je peux emprunter ton stylo?
- **to borrow something from somebody**
emprunter quelque chose à quelqu'un
◇ *I borrowed some money from a friend.*
J'ai emprunté de l'argent à un ami.

Bosnia NOUN
la **Bosnie**

Bosnian ADJECTIVE
bosniaque

boss NOUN
le **patron**
la **patronne**

to **boss around** VERB
- **to boss somebody around** donner des
ordres à quelqu'un

bossy ADJECTIVE
autoritaire

both ADJECTIVE, PRONOUN
tous les deux MASC PL
(**toutes les deux** FEM PL)
◇ *We both went.* Nous y sommes allés
tous les deux. ◇ *Emma and Jane both
went.* Emma et Jane y sont allées toutes
les deux. ◇ *Both of your answers are
wrong.* Vos réponses sont toutes les
deux mauvaises. ◇ *Both of them have
left.* Ils sont partis tous les deux.
◇ *Both of us went.* Nous y sommes
allés tous les deux. ◇ *Both Maggie and
John are against it.* Maggie et John sont

tous les deux contre.
- **He speaks both German and Italian.** Il parle allemand et italien.

to **bother** VERB
  1 **tracasser** (*worry*) ◇ *What's bothering you?* Qu'est-ce qui te tracasse?
  2 **déranger** (*disturb*) ◇ *I'm sorry to bother you.* Je suis désolé de vous déranger.
- **no bother** aucun problème
- **Don't bother!** Ça n'est pas la peine!
- **to bother to do something** prendre la peine de faire quelque chose ◇ *He didn't bother to tell me about it.* Il n'a pas pris la peine de m'en parler.

bottle NOUN
  la **bouteille**

bottle bank NOUN
  le **conteneur à verre**

bottle-opener NOUN
  l' **ouvre-bouteille** MASC

bottom NOUN
  see also bottom ADJECTIVE
  1 le **fond** (*of container, bag, sea*)
  2 le **derrière** (*buttocks*)
  3 le **bas** (*of page, list*)

bottom ADJECTIVE
  see also bottom NOUN
  inférieur ◇ *the bottom shelf* l'étagère inférieure
- **the bottom sheet** le drap de dessous

bought VERB *see* **buy**

to **bounce** VERB
  rebondir

bouncer NOUN
  le **videur**

bound ADJECTIVE
- **He's bound to fail.** Il va sûrement échouer.

boundary NOUN
  la **frontière**

bow NOUN
  see also bow VERB
  1 le **nœud** (*knot*) ◇ *to tie a bow* faire un nœud
  2 l' **arc** MASC ◇ *a bow and arrows* un arc et des flèches

to **bow** VERB
  see also bow NOUN
  faire une révérence

bowels PL NOUN
  les **intestins** MASC PL

bowl NOUN
  see also bowl VERB
  le **bol** (*for soup, cereal*)

to **bowl** VERB
  see also bowl NOUN
  lancer la balle (*in cricket*)

bowler NOUN
  le **lanceur** (*in cricket*)

bowling NOUN
  le **bowling**
- **to go bowling** jouer au bowling
- **a bowling alley** un bowling

bowls NOUN
  les **boules** FEM PL ◇ *to play bowls* jouer aux boules

bow tie NOUN
  le **nœud papillon**

box NOUN
  la **boîte** ◇ *a box of matches* une boîte d'allumettes
- **a cardboard box** un carton

boxer NOUN
  le **boxeur**

boxer shorts PL NOUN
  le **caleçon** SING

boxing NOUN
  la **boxe**

Boxing Day NOUN
  le **lendemain de Noël** ◇ *on Boxing Day* le lendemain de Noël

boy NOUN
  le **garçon**

boyfriend NOUN
  le **copain** ◇ *Have you got a boyfriend?* Est-ce que tu as un copain?

bra NOUN
  le **soutien-gorge**

brace NOUN
  l' **appareil** MASC (*on teeth*) ◇ *She wears a brace.* Elle a un appareil.

bracelet NOUN
  le **bracelet**

brackets PL NOUN
- **in brackets** entre parenthèses

brain NOUN
  le **cerveau**
  (les **cerveaux** PL)

brainy ADJECTIVE
  intelligent

brake NOUN
  see also brake VERB
  le **frein**

to **brake** VERB
  see also brake NOUN
  freiner

branch NOUN
  1 la **branche** (*of tree*)
  2 l' **agence** FEM (*of bank*)

brand-new ADJECTIVE
  tout neuf MASC
  toute neuve FEM

brandy NOUN
  le **cognac**

brass NOUN
  le **cuivre**
- **the brass section** les cuivres

brass band NOUN
la **fanfare**

brat NOUN
- He's a spoiled brat. C'est un enfant gâté.

brave ADJECTIVE
courageux MASC
courageuse FEM

Brazil NOUN
le **Brésil**
- in Brazil au Brésil

bread NOUN
le **pain** ◇ brown bread le pain complet ◇ white bread le pain blanc
- bread and butter les tartines de pain beurrées FEM

break NOUN
see also break VERB
1 la **pause** (rest) ◇ to take a break faire une pause
2 la **récréation** (at school) ◇ during morning break pendant la récréation du matin
- the Christmas break les vacances de Noël
- Give me a break! Laisse-moi tranquille!

to **break** VERB
see also break NOUN
1 **casser** ◇ Careful, you'll break something! Attention, tu vas casser quelque chose!
2 **se casser** (get broken) ◇ Careful, it'll break! Attention, ça va se casser!
- to break one's leg se casser la jambe ◇ I broke my leg. Je me suis cassé la jambe.
- He broke his arm. Il s'est cassé le bras.
- to break a promise rompre une promesse
- to break a record battre un record
- to break the law violer la loi

to **break down** VERB
tomber en panne ◇ The car broke down. La voiture est tombée en panne.

breakdown NOUN
1 la **panne** (in vehicle) ◇ to have a breakdown tomber en panne
2 la **dépression** (mental) ◇ to have a breakdown faire une dépression

breakdown van NOUN
la **dépanneuse**

breakfast NOUN
le **petit déjeuner** ◇ What would you like for breakfast? Qu'est-ce vous voulez pour le petit déjeuner?

to **break in** VERB
entrer par effraction

break-in NOUN
le **cambriolage**

to **break open** VERB
forcer (door, cupboard)

to **break out** VERB
1 **se déclarer** (fire)
2 **éclater** (war)
3 **s'évader** (prisoner)
- to break out in a rash être couvert de boutons

to **break up** VERB
1 **se disperser** (crowd)
2 **se terminer** (meeting, party)
3 **se séparer** (couple)
- to break up a fight mettre fin à une bagarre
- We break up next Wednesday. Nos vacances commencent mercredi.

breast NOUN
le **sein** (of woman)
- chicken breast le blanc de poulet

to **breast-feed** VERB
allaiter

breaststroke NOUN
la **brasse**

breath NOUN
l' **haleine** FEM ◇ to have bad breath avoir mauvaise haleine
- to be out of breath être essoufflé
- to get one's breath back reprendre son souffle

to **breathe** VERB
respirer

to **breed** VERB
see also breed NOUN
se reproduire (reproduce)
- to breed dogs faire de l'élevage de chiens

breed NOUN
see also breed VERB
la **race**

breeze NOUN
la **brise**

brewery NOUN
la **brasserie**

brick NOUN
la **brique**
- a brick wall un mur en brique

bricklayer NOUN
le **maçon**

bride NOUN
la **mariée**

bridegroom NOUN
le **marié**

bridesmaid NOUN
la **demoiselle d'honneur**

bridge NOUN
1 le **pont** ◇ a suspension bridge un pont suspendu
2 le **bridge** ◇ to play bridge jouer au bridge

brief ADJECTIVE
  bref MASC
  brève FEM
briefcase NOUN
  la **serviette**
briefly ADVERB
  brièvement
briefs PL NOUN
  le **slip** SING
- **a pair of briefs** un slip
bright ADJECTIVE
  1 (colour, light)
  vif MASC
  vive FEM
  ◇ a bright colour une couleur vive
- **bright blue** bleu vif ◇ a bright blue
  car une voiture bleu vif
  2 **intelligent** ◇ He's not very bright.
  Il n'est pas très intelligent.
brilliant ADJECTIVE
  1 (wonderful)
  génial
  (**géniaux** MASC PL)
  ◇ Brilliant! Génial!
  2 (clever)
  brillant ◇ a brilliant scientist un
  savant brillant
to **bring** VERB
  1 **apporter** ◇ Bring warm clothes.
  Apportez des vêtements chauds.
  ◇ Could you bring me my trainers?
  Tu peux m'apporter mes baskets?
  2 **amener** (person) ◇ Can I bring a
  friend? Est-ce que je peux amener un
  ami?
- **to bring back** rapporter
- **to bring up** élever ◇ She brought up 5
  children on her own. Elle a élevé cinq
  enfants toute seule.
Britain NOUN
  la **Grande-Bretagne**
- **in Britain** en Grande-Bretagne
- **to Britain** en Grande-Bretagne
- **I'm from Britain.** Je suis britannique.
- **Great Britain** la Grande-Bretagne
British ADJECTIVE
  britannique
- **the British** les Britanniques MASC PL
- **the British Isles** les îles Britanniques
  FEM PL
Brittany NOUN
  la **Bretagne**
- **in Brittany** en Bretagne
- **to Brittany** en Bretagne
- **She's from Brittany.** Elle est bretonne.
broad ADJECTIVE
  large (wide)
- **in broad daylight** en plein jour
broadcast NOUN

see also **broadcast** VERB
  l' **émission** FEM
to **broadcast** VERB
  see also **broadcast** NOUN
  diffuser ◇ The interview was
  broadcast all over the world. L'interview
  a été diffusé dans le monde entier.
- **to broadcast live** retransmettre en
  direct
broad-minded ADJECTIVE
  large d'esprit
broccoli NOUN
  les **brocolis** MASC PL
brochure NOUN
  la **brochure**
broke VERB see **break**
broke ADJECTIVE
- **to be broke** (without money) être fauché
broken ADJECTIVE
  cassé ◇ It's broken. C'est cassé. ◇ a
  broken leg une jambe cassée ◇ He's
  got a broken arm. Il a le bras cassé.
bronchitis NOUN
  la **bronchite**
bronze NOUN
  le **bronze** ◇ the bronze medal la
  médaille de bronze
brooch NOUN
  la **broche**
broom NOUN
  le **balai**
brother NOUN
  le **frère** ◇ my brother mon frère
  ◇ my big brother mon grand frère
brother-in-law NOUN
  le **beau-frère**
  (les **beaux-frères** PL)
brought VERB see **bring**
brown ADJECTIVE
  1 (clothes)
  marron MASC, FEM, PL
  2 (hair)
  brun
  3 (tanned)
  bronzé
- **brown bread** le pain complet
bruise NOUN
  le **bleu**
brush NOUN
  see also **brush** VERB
  1 la **brosse**
  2 (paintbrush)
  le **pinceau**
  (les **pinceaux** PL)
to **brush** VERB
  see also **brush** NOUN
  brosser
- **to brush one's hair** se brosser les
  cheveux ◇ I brushed my hair. Je me

suis brossé les cheveux.
- **to brush one's teeth** se brosser les dents ◇ *I brush my teeth every night.* Je me brosse les dents tous les soirs.

Brussels NOUN
Bruxelles
- **in Brussels** à Bruxelles
- **to Brussels** à Bruxelles

Brussels sprouts PL NOUN
les **choux de Bruxelles** MASC PL

brutal ADJECTIVE
brutal
(**brutaux** MASC PL)

bubble NOUN
la **bulle**

bubble bath NOUN
le **bain moussant**

bubble gum NOUN
le **chewing-gum**

bucket NOUN
le **seau**
(les **seaux** PL)

buckle NOUN
la **boucle** (*on belt, watch, shoe*)

Buddhism NOUN
le **bouddhisme**

Buddhist ADJECTIVE
bouddhiste

budget NOUN
le **budget**

budgie NOUN
la **perruche**

buffet NOUN
le **buffet**

buffet car NOUN
la **voiture-bar**

bug NOUN
1 l' **insecte** MASC (*insect*)
2 le **microbe** (*infection*) ◇ *There's a bug going round.* Il y a un microbe qui traîne.
- **a stomach bug** une gastroentérite
3 le **bug** (*in computer*)

bugged ADJECTIVE
sur écoute ◇ *The room was bugged.* La pièce était sur écoute.

to **build** VERB
construire ◇ *They're going to build houses here.* On va construire des maisons ici.
- **to build up** (*increase*) s'accumuler

builder NOUN
1 l' **entrepreneur** MASC (*owner of firm*)
2 le **maçon** (*worker*)

building NOUN
le **bâtiment**

built VERB *see* **build**

bulb NOUN
l' **ampoule** FEM (*electric*)

bull NOUN
le **taureau**
(les **taureaux** PL)

bullet NOUN
la **balle**

bullfighting NOUN
la **tauromachie**

bully NOUN
see also **bully** VERB
la **brute** ◇ *He's a big bully.* C'est une brute.

to **bully** VERB
see also **bully** NOUN
tyranniser

bum NOUN
le **derrière** (*bottom*)

bump NOUN
see also **bump** VERB
1 la **bosse** (*lump*)
2 l' **accrochage** MASC (*minor accident*) ◇ *We had a bump.* Nous avons eu un accrochage.

to **bump** VERB
see also **bump** NOUN
- **to bump into something** rentrer dans quelque chose ◇ *We bumped into his car.* Nous sommes rentrés dans sa voiture.
- **I bumped into the headteacher.** Je suis tombé sur le directeur par hasard.

bumper NOUN
le **pare-chocs**
(les **pare-chocs** PL)

bumpy ADJECTIVE
cahoteux MASC
cahoteuse FEM

bun NOUN
le **petit pain au lait**

bunch NOUN
- **a bunch of flowers** un bouquet de fleurs
- **a bunch of grapes** une grappe de raisin
- **a bunch of keys** un trousseau de clés

bunches PL NOUN
les **couettes** FEM ◇ *She has her hair in bunches.* Elle a des couettes.

bungalow NOUN
le **bungalow**

bunk NOUN
la **couchette**

burglar NOUN
le **cambrioleur**
la **cambrioleuse**

burglary NOUN
le **cambriolage**

burn NOUN
see also **burn** VERB
la **brûlure**

to **burn** VERB
see also burn NOUN
1 **brûler** (*rubbish, documents*)
2 **faire brûler** (*food*) ◇ *I burned the cake.* J'ai fait brûler le gâteau.
- **to burn oneself** se brûler ◇ *I burned myself on the oven door.* Je me suis brûlé sur la porte du four.
- **I've burned my hand.** Je me suis brûlé la main.
- **to burn down** brûler ◇ *The factory burned down.* L'usine a brûlé.

to **burst** VERB
éclater ◇ *The balloon burst.* Le ballon a éclaté.
- **to burst a balloon** faire éclater un ballon
- **to burst out laughing** éclater de rire
- **to burst into flames** prendre feu
- **to burst into tears** fondre en larmes

to **bury** VERB
enterrer

bus NOUN
l' **autobus** MASC ◇ *the bus driver* le conducteur d'autobus ◇ *a bus stop* un arrêt d'autobus
- **the school bus** le car scolaire
- **a bus pass** une carte d'abonnement pour le bus
- **a bus station** une gare routière
- **a bus ticket** un ticket de bus

bush NOUN
le **buisson**

business NOUN
1 l' **entreprise** FEM (*firm*) ◇ *He's got his own business.* Il a sa propre entreprise.
2 les **affaires** FEM PL (*commerce*) ◇ *He's away on business.* Il est en voyage d'affaires.
- **a business trip** un voyage d'affaires
- **It's none of my business.** Ça ne me regarde pas.

businessman NOUN
l' **homme d'affaires** MASC

businesswoman NOUN
la **femme d'affaires**

busker NOUN
le **musicien de rue**
la **musicienne de rue**

bust NOUN
la **poitrine** (*chest*)

busy ADJECTIVE
1 **occupé** (*person, phone line*)
2 **chargé** (*day, schedule*)
3 **très fréquenté** (*shop, street*)

but CONJUNCTION
mais ◇ *I'd like to come, but I'm busy.* J'aimerais venir mais je suis occupé.

butcher NOUN
le **boucher** ◇ *He's a butcher.* Il est boucher.

butcher's NOUN
la **boucherie**

butter NOUN
le **beurre**

butterfly NOUN
le **papillon**

buttocks PL NOUN
les **fesses** FEM PL

button NOUN
le **bouton**

to **buy** VERB
see also buy NOUN
acheter ◇ *He bought me an ice cream.* Il m'a acheté une glace. ◇ *I bought him an ice cream.* Je lui ai acheté une glace.
- **to buy something from somebody** acheter quelque chose à quelqu'un ◇ *I bought a watch from him.* Je lui ai acheté une montre.

buy NOUN
see also buy VERB
- **It was a good buy.** C'était une bonne affaire.

by PREPOSITION
1 **par** ◇ *The thieves were caught by the police.* Les voleurs ont été arrêtés par la police.
2 **de** ◇ *a painting by Picasso* un tableau de Picasso ◇ *a book by Balzac* un livre de Balzac
3 **en** ◇ *by car* en voiture ◇ *by train* en train ◇ *by bus* en autobus
4 **à côté de** (*close to*) ◇ *Where's the bank?—It's by the post office.* Où est la banque?—Elle est à côté de la poste.
5 **avant** (*not later than*) ◇ *We have to be there by 4 o'clock.* Nous devons y être avant quatre heures.
- **by the time...** quand... ◇ *By the time I got there it was too late.* Quand je suis arrivé il était déjà trop tard. ◇ *It'll be ready by the time you get back.* Ça sera prêt quand vous reviendrez.
- **That's fine by me.** Ça me va.
- **all by himself** tout seul
- **all by herself** toute seule
- **I did it all by myself.** Je l'ai fait tout seul.
- **by the way** au fait

bypass NOUN
la **route de contournement**

C

cab NOUN
le **taxi**

cabbage NOUN
le **chou**
(les **choux** PL)

cabin NOUN
la **cabine** (*on ship*)

cabinet NOUN
- **a bathroom cabinet** une armoire de salle de bain
- **a drinks cabinet** un bar

cable NOUN
le **câble**

cable car NOUN
le **téléphérique**

cable television NOUN
la **télévision par câble**

cactus NOUN
le **cactus**

cadet NOUN
- **a police cadet** un élève policier
- **a cadet officer** un élève officier

café NOUN
le **café**

Cafés in France sell both alcoholic and non-alcoholic drinks.

cage NOUN
la **cage**

cagoule NOUN
le **K-way** ®

cake NOUN
le **gâteau**
(les **gâteaux** PL)

to **calculate** VERB
calculer

calculation NOUN
le **calcul**

calculator NOUN
la **machine à calculer**

calendar NOUN
le **calendrier**

calf NOUN
1 (*of cow*)
le **veau**
(les **veaux** PL)
2 (*of leg*)
le **mollet**

call NOUN
see also **call** VERB
l' **appel** MASC (*by phone*) ◇ *Thanks for your call.* Merci de votre appel.
- **a phone call** un coup de téléphone
- **to be on call** (*doctor*) être de permanence ◇ *He's on call this evening.* Il est de permanence ce soir.

to **call** VERB

see also **call** NOUN
appeler ◇ *I'll tell him you called.* Je lui dirai que vous avez appelé. ◇ *This is the number to call.* C'est le numéro à appeler. ◇ *We called the police.* Nous avons appelé la police. ◇ *Everyone calls him Jimmy.* Tout le monde l'appelle Jimmy.
- **to be called** s'appeler ◇ *He's called Fluffy.* Il s'appelle Fluffy. ◇ *What's she called?* Elle s'appelle comment?
- **to call somebody names** insulter quelqu'un
- **He called me an idiot.** Il m'a traité d'idiot.
- **to call back** (*phone again*) rappeler ◇ *I'll call back at 6 o'clock.* Je rappellerai à six heures.
- **to call for** passer prendre ◇ *I'll call for you at 2.30.* Je passerai te prendre à deux heures et demie.
- **to call off** annuler ◇ *The match was called off.* Le match a été annulé.

call box NOUN
la **cabine téléphonique**

calm ADJECTIVE
calme

to **calm down** VERB
se **calmer** ◇ *Calm down!* Calme-toi!

Calor gas ® NOUN
le **butane**

calorie NOUN
la **calorie**

calves PL NOUN *see* **calf**

Cambodia NOUN
le **Cambodge**
- **in Cambodia** au Cambodge

camcorder NOUN
le **caméscope**

came VERB *see* **come**

camel NOUN
le **chameau**
(les **chameaux** PL)

camera NOUN
1 (*for photos*)
l' **appareil photo** MASC
(les **appareils photo** PL)
2 (*for filming, TV*)
la **caméra**

cameraman NOUN
le **caméraman**

to **camp** VERB
see also **camp** NOUN
camper

camp NOUN
see also **camp** VERB

le **camp**
- **a camp bed** un lit de camp

campaign NOUN
la **campagne**

camper NOUN
1 (*person*)
le **campeur**
la **campeuse**
2 (*van*)
le **camping-car**

camping NOUN
le **camping**
- **to go camping** faire du camping
  ◇ *We went camping in Cornwall.*
  Nous avons fait du camping en
  Cornouailles.

camping gas ® NOUN
le **butane**

campsite NOUN
le **terrain de camping**

campus NOUN
le **campus**

can NOUN
see also **can** VERB
1 la **boîte** (*tin*) ◇ *a can of sweetcorn*
une boîte de maïs ◇ *a can of beer* une
boîte de bière
2 le **bidon** (*jerry can*) ◇ *a can of petrol*
un bidon d'essence

can VERB
see also **can** NOUN
1 **pouvoir** (*be able to, be allowed to*) ◇ *I
can't come.* Je ne peux pas venir.
◇ *Can I help you?* Est-ce que je peux
vous aider? ◇ *Can I use your phone?*
Est-ce que je peux me servir de votre
téléphone? ◇ *You could hire a bike.* Tu
pourrais louer un vélo. ◇ *I couldn't
sleep because of the noise.* Je ne
pouvais pas dormir à cause du bruit.
can *is sometimes not translated.*
◇ *I can't hear you.* Je ne t'entends pas.
◇ *I can't remember.* Je ne m'en
souviens pas. ◇ *Can you speak
French?* Parlez-vous français?
2 **savoir** (*have learnt how to*) ◇ *I can
swim.* Je sais nager. ◇ *He can't drive.* Il
ne sait pas conduire.
- **That can't be true!** Ce n'est pas
possible!
- **You could be right.** Vous avez peut-être
raison.

Canada NOUN
le **Canada**
- **in Canada** au Canada
- **to Canada** au Canada

Canadian ADJECTIVE
see also **Canadian** NOUN
canadien MASC

canadienne FEM

Canadian NOUN
see also **Canadian** ADJECTIVE
le **Canadien**
la **Canadienne**

canal NOUN
le **canal**
(les **canaux** PL)

canary NOUN
le **canari**

to **cancel** VERB
annuler ◇ *The match was cancelled.*
Le match a été annulé.

cancellation NOUN
l' **annulation** FEM

cancer NOUN
1 le **cancer** ◇ *He's got cancer.* Il a le
cancer.
2 le **Cancer** ◇ *I'm Cancer.* Je suis
Cancer.

candidate NOUN
le **candidat**
la **candidate**

candle NOUN
la **bougie**

candyfloss NOUN
la **barbe à papa**

cannabis NOUN
le **cannabis**

canned ADJECTIVE
en conserve (*food*)

cannot VERB see **can**

canoe NOUN
le **canoë**

canoeing NOUN
- **to go canoeing** faire du canoë ◇ *We
went canoeing.* Nous avons fait du
canoë.

can-opener NOUN
l' **ouvre-boîte** MASC

can't VERB see **can**

canteen NOUN
la **cantine**

to **canter** VERB
aller au petit galop

canvas NOUN
la **toile**

cap NOUN
1 la **casquette** (*hat*)
2 le **bouchon** (*of bottle, tube*)

capable ADJECTIVE
capable

capacity NOUN
la **capacité**

capital NOUN
1 la **capitale** ◇ *Cardiff is the capital of
Wales.* Cardiff est la capitale du pays
de Galles.
2 la **majuscule** (*letter*) ◇ *Write your*

PTO

address in capitals. Écris ton adresse en majuscules.

capitalism NOUN
le capitalisme

capital punishment NOUN
la peine capitale

Capricorn NOUN
le Capricorne ◇ I'm Capricorn. Je suis Capricorne.

to **capsize** VERB
chavirer

captain NOUN
le capitaine ◇ She's captain of the hockey team. Elle est capitaine de l'équipe de hockey.

to **capture** VERB
capturer

car NOUN
la voiture
◆ to go by car aller en voiture ◇ We went by car. Nous y sommes allés en voiture.
◆ a car crash un accident de voiture

caramel NOUN
le caramel

caravan NOUN
la caravane ◇ a caravan site un camping pour caravanes

card NOUN
la carte
◆ a card game un jeu de cartes

cardboard NOUN
le carton

cardigan NOUN
le cardigan

cardphone NOUN
le téléphone à carte

care NOUN
see also care VERB
le soin ◇ with care avec soin
◆ to take care of s'occuper de ◇ I take care of the children on Saturdays. Le samedi, je m'occupe des enfants.
◆ Take care! (1) (Be careful!) Fais attention!
◆ Take care! (2) (Look after yourself!) Prends bien soin de toi!

to **care** VERB
see also care NOUN
◆ to care about se soucier de ◇ They don't care about their image. Ils se soucient peu de leur image.
◆ I don't care! Ça m'est égal! ◇ She doesn't care. Ça lui est égal.
◆ to care for somebody (patients, old people) s'occuper de quelqu'un

career NOUN
la carrière

careful ADJECTIVE

◆ Be careful! Fais attention!

carefully ADVERB
[1] soigneusement ◇ She carefully avoided talking about it. Elle évitait soigneusement d'en parler.
[2] prudemment (safely) ◇ Drive carefully! Conduisez prudemment!
◆ Think carefully! Réfléchis bien!

careless ADJECTIVE
[1] (work)
peu soigné
◆ a careless mistake une faute d'inattention
[2] (person)
peu soigneux MASC
peu soigneuse FEM
◇ She's very careless. Elle est bien peu soigneuse.
[3] imprudent ◇ a careless driver un conducteur imprudent

caretaker NOUN
le gardien
la gardienne

car-ferry NOUN
le ferry

cargo NOUN
la cargaison

car hire NOUN
la location de voitures

Caribbean ADJECTIVE
see also Caribbean NOUN
antillais ◇ Caribbean food la cuisine antillaise

Caribbean NOUN
see also Caribbean ADJECTIVE
[1] les Caraïbes FEM PL (islands) ◇ We're going to the Caribbean. Nous allons aux Caraïbes.
◆ He's from the Caribbean. Il est antillais.
[2] la mer des Caraïbes (sea)

carnation NOUN
l' œillet MASC

carnival NOUN
le carnaval

carol NOUN
◆ a Christmas carol un chant de Noël

car park NOUN
le parking

carpenter NOUN
le charpentier ◇ He's a carpenter. Il est charpentier.

carpentry NOUN
la menuiserie

carpet NOUN
[1] le tapis ◇ a Persian carpet un tapis persan
[2] la moquette (fitted)

car phone NOUN

le **téléphone de voiture**
carriage NOUN
la **voiture**
carrier bag NOUN
le **sac en plastique**
carrot NOUN
la **carotte**
to **carry** VERB
1. **porter** ◇ *I'll carry your bag.* Je vais porter ton sac.
2. **transporter** ◇ *a plane carrying 100 passengers* un avion transportant cent passagers
- **to carry on** continuer ◇ *Carry on!* Continue! ◇ *She carried on talking.* Elle a continué à parler.
- **to carry out** (*orders*) exécuter
carrycot NOUN
le **porte-bébé**
cart NOUN
la **charrette**
carton NOUN
la **brique** (*of milk, juice*)
cartoon NOUN
1. le **dessin animé** (*film*)
2. le **dessin humoristique** (*in newspaper*)
- **a strip cartoon** une bande dessinée
cartridge NOUN
la **cartouche**
to **carve** VERB
découper (*meat*)
case NOUN
1. la **valise** ◇ *I've packed my case.* J'ai fait ma valise.
2. le **cas**
(les **cas** PL)
◇ *in some cases* dans certains cas
- **in that case** dans ce cas ◇ *I don't want it.–In that case, I'll take it.* Je n'en veux pas.–Dans ce cas, je le prends.
- **in case** au cas où ◇ *in case it rains* au cas où il pleuvrait
- **just in case** à tout hasard ◇ *Take some money, just in case.* Prends de l'argent à tout hasard.
cash NOUN
l' **argent** MASC ◇ *I'm a bit short of cash.* Je suis un peu à court d'argent.
- **in cash** en liquide ◇ *£2000 in cash* deux mille livres en liquide
- **to pay cash** payer comptant
- **a cash card** une carte de retrait
- **a cash desk** la caisse
- **a cash dispenser** un distributeur automatique de billets
- **a cash register** une caisse
cashew NOUN
la **noix de cajou**
cashier NOUN

le **caissier**
la **caissière**
cashmere NOUN
le **cachemire** ◇ *a cashmere sweater* un pull en cachemire
casino NOUN
le **casino**
casserole NOUN
le **ragoût** ◇ *I'm going to make a casserole.* Je vais faire un ragoût.
- **a casserole dish** une cocotte
cassette NOUN
la **cassette**
- **a cassette player** une lecteur de cassettes
- **a cassette recorder** un magnétophone
cast NOUN
les **acteurs** MASC PL ◇ *After the play, we met the cast.* Après la représentation, nous avons rencontré les acteurs.
castle NOUN
le **château**
(les **châteaux** PL)
casual ADJECTIVE
1. **décontracté** ◇ *I prefer casual clothes.* Je préfère les vêtements décontractés.
2. **désinvolte** ◇ *a casual attitude* une attitude désinvolte
3. **en passant** ◇ *It was just a casual remark.* C'était juste une remarque en passant.
casually ADVERB
- **to dress casually** s'habiller de façon décontractée
casualty NOUN
les **urgences** FEM PL (*in hospital*)
cat NOUN
le **chat**
la **chatte** (*female*)
◇ *Have you got a cat?* Est-ce que tu as un chat?
catalogue NOUN
le **catalogue**
catalytic converter NOUN
le **catalyseur**
catarrh NOUN
le **rhume chronique**
catastrophe NOUN
la **catastrophe**
to **catch** VERB
1. **attraper** ◇ *to catch a thief* attraper un voleur ◇ *My cat catches birds.* Mon chat attrape des oiseaux.
- **to catch somebody doing something** attraper quelqu'un en train de faire quelque chose ◇ *If they catch you smoking...* S'ils t'attrapent en train de fumer...

- **to catch a cold** attraper un rhume
  2 prendre (bus, train) ◇ *We caught
  the last bus.* Nous avons pris le dernier
  bus.
  3 saisir (hear) ◇ *I didn't catch his
  name.* Je n'ai pas saisi son nom.
- **to catch up** rattraper son retard
  ◇ *I've got to catch up: I was away last
  week.* Je dois rattraper mon retard:
  j'étais absent la semaine dernière.

catching ADJECTIVE
  contagieux MASC
  contagieuse FEM
  ◇ *It's not catching.* Ce n'est pas
  contagieux.

catering NOUN
  la **restauration**

cathedral NOUN
  la **cathédrale**

Catholic ADJECTIVE
  see also Catholic NOUN
  catholique

Catholic NOUN
  see also Catholic ADJECTIVE
  le/la **catholique** ◇ *I'm a Catholic.* Je
  suis catholique.

cattle PL NOUN
  le **bétail** SING

caught VERB *see* **catch**

cauliflower NOUN
  le **chou-fleur**
  (les **choux-fleurs** PL)

cause NOUN
  see also cause VERB
  la **cause**

to **cause** VERB
  see also cause NOUN
  provoquer ◇ *to cause an accident*
  provoquer un accident

cautious ADJECTIVE
  prudent

cave NOUN
  la **grotte**

CD NOUN
  le **CD**
  (les **CD** PL)

CD player NOUN
  la **platine laser**

CD-ROM NOUN
  le **CD-ROM**
  (les **CD-ROM** PL)

ceiling NOUN
  le **plafond**

to **celebrate** VERB
  fêter (birthday)

celebrity NOUN
  la **célébrité**

celery NOUN
  le **céleri**

cell NOUN
  la **cellule**

cellar NOUN
  la **cave** ◇ *a wine cellar* une cave à vins

cello NOUN
  le **violoncelle** ◇ *I play the cello.* Je
  joue du violoncelle.

cement NOUN
  le **ciment**

cemetery NOUN
  le **cimetière**

cent NOUN
  le **cent** ◇ *twenty cents* vingt cents

centenary NOUN
  le **centenaire**

centigrade ADJECTIVE
  centigrade ◇ *20 degrees centigrade*
  vingt degrés centigrade

centimetre NOUN
  le **centimètre**

central ADJECTIVE
  central
  (**centraux** MASC PL)

central heating NOUN
  le **chauffage central**

centre NOUN
  le **centre** ◇ *a sports centre* un centre
  sportif

century NOUN
  le **siècle** ◇ *the 20th century* le
  vingtième siècle ◇ *the 21st century* le
  vingt-et-unième siècle

cereal NOUN
  les **céréales** FEM PL ◇ *I have cereal for
  breakfast.* Je prends des céréales au
  petit déjeuner.

ceremony NOUN
  la **cérémonie**

certain ADJECTIVE
  certain ◇ *a certain person* une
  certaine personne ◇ *I'm absolutely
  certain it was him.* Je suis absolument
  certain que c'était lui.
- **I don't know for certain.** Je n'en suis
  pas certain.
- **to make certain** s'assurer ◇ *I made
  certain the door was locked.* Je me suis
  assuré que la porte était fermée à clé.

certainly ADVERB
  vraiment ◇ *I certainly expected
  something better.* Je m'attendais
  vraiment à quelque chose de mieux.
- **Certainly not!** Certainement pas!
- **So it was a surprise?—It certainly was!**
  C'était donc une surprise?–Ça oui alors!

certificate NOUN
  le **certificat**

chain NOUN
  la **chaîne**

chair NOUN

[1] la **chaise** ◇ *a table and 4 chairs*
une table et quatre chaises

[2] le **fauteuil** *(armchair)*

chairlift NOUN

le **télésiège**

chairman NOUN

le **président**

chalet NOUN

le **chalet**

chalk NOUN

la **craie**

challenge NOUN

see also challenge VERB

le **défi**

to **challenge** VERB

see also challenge NOUN

◆ **She challenged me to a race.** Elle m'a
proposé de faire la course avec elle.

challenging ADJECTIVE

stimulant ◇ *a challenging job* un
travail stimulant

champagne NOUN

le **champagne**

champion NOUN

le **champion**
la **championne**

championship NOUN

le **championnat**

chance NOUN

[1] la **chance** ◇ *Do you think I've got
any chance?* Tu crois que j'ai une
chance? ◇ *Their chances of winning are
very good.* Ils ont de fortes chances de
gagner.

◆ **No chance!** Pas question!

[2] l' **occasion** FEM ◇ *I'd like to have a
chance to travel.* J'aimerais avoir
l'occasion de voyager.

◆ **I'll write when I get the chance.**
J'écrirai quand j'aurai un moment.

◆ **by chance** par hasard ◇ *We met by
chance.* Nous nous sommes rencontrés
par hasard.

◆ **to take a chance** prendre un risque
◇ *I'm taking no chances!* Je ne veux
prendre aucun risque!

Chancellor of the Exchequer
NOUN

le **chancelier de l'Échiquier**

to **change** VERB

see also change NOUN

[1] **changer** ◇ *The town has changed
a lot.* La ville a beaucoup changé. ◇ *I'd
like to change £50.* Je voudrais changer
cinquante livres.

Use **changer de** *when you change one thing for
another.*

[2] **changer de** ◇ *You have to change*

trains in Paris. Il faut changer de train à
Paris. ◇ *I'm going to change my shoes.*
Je vais changer de chaussures. ◇ *He
wants to change his job.* Il veut changer
d'emploi.

◆ **to change one's mind** changer d'avis
◇ *I've changed my mind.* J'ai changé
d'avis.

◆ **to change gear** changer de vitesse

[3] **se changer** ◇ *She's changing to go
out.* Elle est en train de se changer
pour sortir.

◆ **to get changed** se changer ◇ *I'm
going to get changed.* Je vais me
changer.

[4] **échanger** *(swap)* ◇ *Can I change
this sweater? It's too small.* Est-ce que je
peux échanger ce pull? Il est trop petit.

change NOUN

see also change VERB

[1] le **changement** ◇ *There's been a
change of plan.* Il y a eu un
changement de programme.

[2] la **monnaie** *(money)* ◇ *I haven't got
any change.* Je n'ai pas de monnaie.

◆ **a change of clothes** des vêtements de
rechange

◆ **for a change** pour changer ◇ *Let's
play tennis for a change.* Si on jouait au
tennis pour changer?

changeable ADJECTIVE

variable

changing room NOUN

[1] le **salon d'essayage** *(in shop)*

[2] le **vestiaire** *(for sport)*

channel NOUN

la **chaîne** *(TV)* ◇ *There's football on
the other channel.* Il y a du football sur
l'autre chaîne.

◆ **the Channel** la Manche

◆ **the Channel Islands** les îles
Anglo-Normandes MASC PL

◆ **the Channel Tunnel** le tunnel sous la
Manche

chaos NOUN

le **chaos**

chap NOUN

le **type** ◇ *He's a nice chap.* C'est un
type sympa.

chapel NOUN

la **chapelle** *(part of church)*

chapter NOUN

le **chapitre**

character NOUN

[1] le **caractère** ◇ *Give me some idea of
his character.* Décris-moi un peu son
caractère.

◆ **She's quite a character.** C'est un drôle
de numéro.

2 le **personnage** (*in play, film*) ◇ *The character played by Depardieu...* Le personnage joué par Depardieu...

characteristic NOUN
le **caractéristique**

charcoal NOUN
le **charbon de bois**

charge NOUN
see also charge VERB
les **frais** MASC PL ◇ *Is there a charge for delivery?* Est-ce qu'il y a des frais de livraison?
- **an extra charge** un supplément
- **free of charge** gratuit
- **to reverse the charges** Appeler en P.C.V. ◇ *I'd like to reverse the charges.* Je voudrais appeler en P.C.V.
- **to be on a charge** être inculpé ◇ *He's on a charge of murder.* Il est inculpé de meurtre.
- **to be in charge** être responsable ◇ *Mrs Munday was in charge of the group.* Madame Munday était responsable du groupe.

to **charge** VERB
see also charge NOUN
1 **prendre** (*money*) ◇ *How much did he charge you?* Combien est-ce qu'il vous a pris? ◇ *They charge £10 an hour.* Ils prennent dix livres de l'heure.
2 **inculper** (*with crime*) ◇ *The police have charged him with murder.* La police l'a inculpé de meurtre.

charity NOUN
l' **association caritative** FEM ◇ *He gave the money to charity.* Il a donné l'argent à une association caritative.

charm NOUN
le **charme** ◇ *He's got a lot of charm.* Il a beaucoup de charme.

charming ADJECTIVE
charmant

chart NOUN
le **tableau**
(les **tableaux** PL)
◇ *The chart shows the rise of unemployment.* Le tableau indique la progression du chômage.
- **the charts** le hit-parade ◇ *This album is number one in the charts.* Cet album est numéro un au hit-parade.

charter flight NOUN
le **charter**

to **chase** VERB
see also chase NOUN
pourchasser

chase NOUN
see also chase VERB
la **poursuite** ◇ *a car chase* une poursuite en voiture

chat NOUN
- **to have a chat** bavarder

chat show NOUN
le **talk-show**

cheap ADJECTIVE
bon marché MASC, FEM, PL ◇ *a cheap T-shirt* un T-shirt bon marché

cheaper ADJECTIVE
moins cher MASC
moins chère FEM
◇ *It's cheaper by bus.* C'est moins cher en bus.

to **cheat** VERB
see also cheat NOUN
tricher ◇ *You're cheating!* Tu triches!

cheat NOUN
see also cheat VERB
le **tricheur**
la **tricheuse**

check NOUN
see also check VERB
le **contrôle** ◇ *a security check* un contrôle de sécurité

to **check** VERB
see also check NOUN
vérifier ◇ *I'll check the time of the train.* Je vais vérifier l'heure du train. ◇ *Could you check the oil, please?* Pourriez-vous vérifier le niveau d'huile, s'il vous plaît?
- **to check in** (1) (*at airport*) se présenter à l'enregistrement ◇ *What time do I have to check in?* À quelle heure est-ce que je dois me présenter à l'enregistrement?
- **to check in** (2) (*in hotel*) se présenter à la réception
- **to check out** (*from hotel*) régler sa note

check-in NOUN
l' **enregistrement** MASC

checkout NOUN
la **caisse**

check-up NOUN
l' **examen de routine** MASC

cheek NOUN
1 la **joue** ◇ *He kissed her on the cheek.* Il l'a embrassée sur la joue.
2 le **culot** ◇ *What a cheek!* Quel culot!

cheeky ADJECTIVE
effronté ◇ *Don't be cheeky!* Ne sois pas effronté!
- **a cheeky smile** un sourire malicieux

cheer NOUN
see also cheer VERB
les **hourras** MASC PL
- **to give a cheer** pousser des hourras
- **Cheers!** (1) (*good health*) À la vôtre!

- **Cheers! (2)** (*thanks*) Merci!
to **cheer** VERB
  see also **cheer** NOUN
  applaudir
- **to cheer somebody up** remonter le moral à quelqu'un ◇ *I was trying to cheer him up.* J'essayais de lui remonter le moral.
- **Cheer up!** Ne te laisse pas abattre!
cheerful ADJECTIVE
  gai
cheerio EXCLAMATION
  salut!
cheese NOUN
  le **fromage**
chef NOUN
  le **chef**
chemical NOUN
  le **produit chimique**
chemist NOUN
  1 (*dispenser*)
  le **pharmacien**
  la **pharmacienne**
  2 (*shop*)
  la **pharmacie** ◇ *You get it from the chemist.* C'est vendu en pharmacie.
  Chemist's shops in France are identified by a special green cross outside the shop.
  3 (*scientist*)
  le/la **chimiste**
chemistry NOUN
  la **chimie** ◇ *the chemistry lab* la laboratoire de chimie
cheque NOUN
  le **chèque** ◇ *to write a cheque* faire un chèque ◇ *to pay by cheque* payer par chèque
chequebook NOUN
  le **carnet de chèques**
cherry NOUN
  la **cerise**
chess NOUN
  les **échecs** MASC PL ◇ *to play chess* jouer aux échecs
chessboard NOUN
  l' **échiquier** MASC
chest NOUN
  la **poitrine** (*of person*) ◇ *his chest measurement* son tour de poitrine
- **a chest of drawers** une commode
chestnut NOUN
  le **marron** ◇ *We have turkey with chestnuts.* Nous mangeons de la dinde aux marrons.
chewing gum NOUN
  le **chewing-gum**
chicken NOUN
  le **poulet**
chickenpox NOUN

la **varicelle**
child NOUN
  l' **enfant** MASC/FEM ◇ *all the children* tous les enfants
childish ADJECTIVE
  puéril
child minder NOUN
  la **nourrice**
children PL NOUN *see* **child**
Chile NOUN
  le **Chili**
- **in Chile** au Chili
to **chill** VERB
  mettre au frais ◇ *Put the wine in the fridge to chill.* Mets le vin au frais dans le réfrigérateur.
chilli NOUN
  le **piment**
chimney NOUN
  la **cheminée**
chin NOUN
  le **menton**
china NOUN
  la **porcelaine** ◇ *a china plate* une assiette en porcelaine
China NOUN
  la **Chine**
- **in China** en Chine
Chinese ADJECTIVE
  see also **Chinese** NOUN
  chinois ◇ *a Chinese restaurant* un restaurant chinois
- **a Chinese man** un Chinois
- **a Chinese woman** une Chinoise
Chinese NOUN
  see also **Chinese** ADJECTIVE
  le **chinois** (*language*)
- **the Chinese** (*people*) les Chinois
chip NOUN
  1 la **frite** (*food*) ◇ *We bought some chips.* Nous avons acheté des frites.
  2 la **puce** (*in computer*)
chiropodist NOUN
  le/la **pédicure** ◇ *He's a chiropodist.* Il est pédicure.
chives PL NOUN
  la **ciboulette** SING
chocolate NOUN
  le **chocolat** ◇ *a chocolate cake* un gâteau au chocolat
- **hot chocolate** le chocolat chaud
choice NOUN
  le **choix** ◇ *I had no choice.* Je n'avais pas le choix.
choir NOUN
  la **chorale** ◇ *I sing in the school choir.* Je chante dans la chorale de l'école.
to **choose** VERB
  choisir ◇ *It's difficult to choose.* C'est

difficile de choisir.

to **chop** VERB

see also **chop** NOUN

émincer ◇ *Chop the onions.* Émincez les oignons.

chop NOUN

see also **chop** VERB

la **côte** ◇ *a pork chop* une côte de porc

chopsticks PL NOUN

les **baguettes** FEM PL

chose, chosen VERB see **choose**

Christ NOUN

le **Christ** ◇ *the birth of Christ* la naissance du Christ

christening NOUN

le **baptême**

Christian NOUN

see also **Christian** ADJECTIVE

le **chrétien**

la **chrétienne**

Christian ADJECTIVE

see also **Christian** NOUN

chrétien MASC

chrétienne FEM

Christian name NOUN

le **prénom**

Christmas NOUN

Noël MASC ◇ *Happy Christmas!* Joyeux Noël!

- **Christmas Day** le jour de Noël
- **Christmas Eve** la veille de Noël
- **a Christmas tree** un arbre de Noël
- **a Christmas card** une carte de Noël

The French more often send greetings cards (une carte de vœux) in January rather than at Christmas, with best wishes for the New Year.

- **Christmas dinner** le repas de Noël

Most French people have their Christmas meal (réveillon de Noël) on the evening of Christmas Eve, though some have a repas de Noël *on Christmas Day.*

- **Christmas pudding**

The French usually have a Yule log (une bûche de Noël) for pudding at the Christmas meal. You could explain what Christmas pudding is using the example given.

◇ *Christmas pudding is made with dried fruit and spices, and steamed.* Le "Christmas pudding" est un gâteau avec des raisins secs, parfumé avec des épices et cuit à la vapeur.

chunk NOUN

le **gros morceau**

(les **gros morceaux** PL)

◇ *Cut the meat into chunks.* Coupez la viande en gros morceaux.

church NOUN

l' **église** FEM ◇ *I don't go to church every Sunday.* Je ne vais pas à l'église tous les dimanches.

- **the Church of England** l'Église anglicane

cider NOUN

le **cidre**

cigar NOUN

le **cigare**

cigarette NOUN

la **cigarette**

cinema NOUN

le **cinéma** ◇ *I'm going to the cinema this evening.* Je vais au cinéma ce soir.

circle NOUN

le **cercle**

circular ADJECTIVE

circulaire

circulation NOUN

1 la **circulation** (*of blood*)

2 le **tirage** (*of newspaper*)

circumflex NOUN

l' **accent circonflexe** MASC

circumstances PL NOUN

les **circonstances** FEM PL

circus NOUN

le **cirque**

citizen NOUN

le **citoyen**

la **citoyenne**

◇ *a French citizen* un citoyen français

city NOUN

la **ville**

- **the city centre** le centre-ville ◇ *It's in the city centre.* C'est au centre-ville.

city technology college NOUN

le **collège technique**

civilization NOUN

la **civilisation**

civil servant NOUN

le/la **fonctionnaire** ◇ *She's a civil servant.* Elle est fonctionnaire.

civil war NOUN

la **guerre civile**

to **claim** VERB

see also **claim** NOUN

1 **prétendre** ◇ *He claims to have found the money.* Il prétend avoir trouvé l'argent.

2 **percevoir** (*receive*) ◇ *She's claiming unemployment benefit.* Elle perçoit des allocations chômage.

- **She can't claim unemployment benefit.** Elle n'a pas droit aux allocations chômage.

- **to claim on one's insurance** se faire rembourser par son assurance ◇ *We claimed on our insurance.* Nous nous sommes fait rembourser par notre assurance.

claim NOUN
> see also **claim** VERB

la **demande d'indemnité** (*on insurance policy*) ◇ *to make a claim* faire une demande d'indemnité

to **clap** VERB
applaudir (*applaud*)
- *to clap one's hands* frapper dans ses mains ◇ *I've trained my dog to sit when I clap my hands.* J'ai dressé mon chien à s'asseoir quand je frappe dans mes mains.

clarinet NOUN
la **clarinette** ◇ *I play the clarinet.* Je joue de la clarinette.

to **clash** VERB
1 **jurer** (*colours*) ◇ *These two colours clash.* Ces deux couleurs jurent.
2 **tomber en même temps** (*events*) ◇ *The concert clashes with Ann's party.* Le concert tombe en même temps que la soirée d'Ann.

clasp NOUN
le **fermoir** (*of necklace*)

class NOUN
1 la **classe** (*group*) ◇ *We're in the same class.* Nous sommes dans la même classe.
2 le **cours** (*lesson*) ◇ *I go to dancing classes.* Je vais à des cours de danse.

classic ADJECTIVE
> see also **classic** NOUN

classique ◇ *a classic example* un cas classique

classic NOUN
> see also **classic** ADJECTIVE

le **classique** (*book, film*)

classical ADJECTIVE
classique ◇ *I like classical music.* J'aime la musique classique.

classroom NOUN
la **classe**

claw NOUN
1 la **griffe** (*of cat, dog*)
2 la **serre** (*of bird*)
3 la **pince** (*of crab, lobster*)

clean ADJECTIVE
> see also **clean** VERB

propre ◇ *a clean shirt* une chemise propre

to **clean** VERB
> see also **clean** ADJECTIVE

nettoyer

cleaner NOUN
la **femme de ménage** ◇ *She's a cleaner.* Elle est femme de ménage.

cleaner's NOUN
la **teinturerie**

clear ADJECTIVE
> see also **clear** VERB

1 **clair** ◇ *a clear explanation* une explication claire ◇ *It's clear you don't believe me.* Il est clair que tu ne me crois pas.
2 **libre** (*road, way*) ◇ *The road's clear now.* La route est libre maintenant.

to **clear** VERB
> see also **clear** ADJECTIVE

1 **dégager** ◇ *The police are clearing the road after the accident.* La police dégage la route après l'accident.
2 **se dissiper** (*fog, mist*) ◇ *The mist soon cleared.* La brume s'est vite dissipée.
- *to be cleared of a crime* être reconnu non coupable d'un crime ◇ *She was cleared of murder.* Elle a été reconnue non coupable du meurtre.
- *to clear the table* débarrasser la table ◇ *I'll clear the table.* Je vais débarrasser la table.
- *to clear up* ranger ◇ *Who's going to clear all this up?* Qui va ranger tout ça?
- **I think it's going to clear up.** (*weather*) Je pense que le temps va se lever.

clearly ADVERB
1 **clairement** ◇ *She explained it very clearly.* Elle l'a expliqué très clairement.
2 **nettement** ◇ *The French coast was clearly visible.* On distinguait nettement la côte française.
3 **distinctement** ◇ *to speak clearly* parler distinctement

clementine NOUN
la **clémentine**

clever ADJECTIVE
1 **intelligent** ◇ *She's very clever.* Elle est très intelligente.
2 (*ingenious*)
astucieux MASC
astucieuse FEM
◇ *a clever system* un système astucieux
- **What a clever idea!** Quelle bonne idée!

client NOUN
le **client**
la **cliente**

cliff NOUN
la **falaise**

climate NOUN
le **climat**

to **climb** VERB
1 **escalader** ◇ *We're going to climb Snowdon.* Nous allons escalader le Snowdon.
2 **monter** (*stairs*)

climber NOUN
le **grimpeur**
la **grimpeuse**

climbing NOUN
l' **escalade** FEM
- **to go climbing** faire de l'escalade
  ◇ *We're going climbing in Scotland.*
  Nous allons faire de l'escalade en
  Écosse.

clinic NOUN
le **centre médical**
(les **centres médicaux** PL)

cloakroom NOUN
[1] le **vestiaire** (*for coats*)
[2] les **toilettes** FEM PL (*toilet*)

clock NOUN
[1] l' **horloge** FEM ◇ *a grandfather clock*
une horloge de grand-père
[2] la **pendule** (*smaller*)
- **an alarm clock** un réveil
- **a clock-radio** un radio-réveil

clog NOUN
le **sabot**

close ADJECTIVE, ADVERB
> *see also* close VERB

[1] **près** (*near*) ◇ *The shops are very
close.* Les magasins sont tout près.
- **close to** près de ◇ *The youth hostel is
close to the station.* L'auberge de
jeunesse est près de la gare.
- **Come closer.** Rapproche-toi.
[2] **proche** (*in relationship*) ◇ *We're just
inviting close relations.* Nous n'invitons
que les parents proches. ◇ *She's a
close friend of mine.* C'est une proche
amie. ◇ *I'm very close to my sister.* Je
suis très proche de ma sœur.
[3] **très serré** (*contest*) ◇ *It's going to be
very close.* Ça va être très serré.
[4] **lourd** (*weather*) ◇ *It's close this
afternoon.* Il fait lourd cet après-midi.

to **close** VERB
> *see also* close ADJECTIVE

[1] **fermer** ◇ *What time does the pool
close?* La piscine ferme à quelle heure?
◇ *The shops close at 5.30.* Les
magasins ferment à cinq heures et
demie. ◇ *Please close the door.*
Fermez la porte, s'il vous plaît.
[2] **se fermer** ◇ *The doors close
automatically.* Les portes se ferment
automatiquement.

closed ADJECTIVE
fermé ◇ *The bank's closed.* La
banque est fermée.

closely ADVERB
de près (*look, examine*)

cloth NOUN
le **tissu** (*material*)
- **a cloth** un chiffon ◇ *Wipe it with a
damp cloth.* Nettoyez-le avec un chiffon
humide.

clothes PL NOUN
les **vêtements** MASC PL ◇ *new clothes*
des vêtements neufs
- **a clothes line** un fil à linge
- **a clothes peg** une pince à linge

cloud NOUN
le **nuage**

cloudy ADJECTIVE
nuageux MASC
nuageuse FEM

clove NOUN
- **a clove of garlic** une gousse d'ail

clown NOUN
le **clown**

club NOUN
le **club** ◇ *a golf club* (*society and for
playing golf*) un club de golf
- **the youth club** la maison des jeunes
- **clubs** (*in cards*) le trèfle ◇ *the ace of
clubs* l'as de trèfle

to **club together** VERB
se cotiser ◇ *We clubbed together to
buy her a present.* Nous nous sommes
cotisés pour lui acheter un cadeau.

clue NOUN
l' **indice** MASC ◇ *an important clue* un
indice important
- **I haven't a clue.** Je n'en ai pas la
moindre idée.

clumsy ADJECTIVE
maladroit

coach NOUN
[1] le **car** MASC ◇ *We went there by
coach.* Nous y sommes allés en car.
- **the coach station** la gare routière
- **a coach trip** une excursion en car
[2] l' **entraîneur** MASC (*trainer*) ◇ *the
French coach* l'entraîneur de l'équipe
de France

coal NOUN
le **charbon**
- **a coal mine** une mine de charbon
- **a coal miner** un mineur

coast NOUN
la **côte** ◇ *It's on the west coast of
Scotland.* C'est sur la côte ouest de
l'Écosse.

coat NOUN
le **manteau**
(les **manteaux** PL)
◇ *a warm coat* un manteau chaud
- **a coat of paint** une couche de peinture

coat hanger NOUN
le **cintre**

cocaine NOUN
la **cocaïne**

cockerel NOUN
le **coq**

cockney NOUN

le **cockney** ◇ *I'm a cockney.* Je suis cockney.

cocoa NOUN

le **cacao** ◇ *a cup of cocoa* une tasse de cacao

coconut NOUN

la **noix de coco**

cod NOUN

le **cabillaud**

code NOUN

le **code**

coffee NOUN

le **café**

- **A cup of coffee, please.** Un café, s'il vous plaît.

coffeepot NOUN

la **cafetière**

coffee table NOUN

la **table basse**

coffin NOUN

le **cercueil**

coin NOUN

la **pièce de monnaie**

- **a 5 franc coin** une pièce de cinq francs

coincidence NOUN

la **coïncidence**

coinphone NOUN

le **téléphone à pièces**

Coke ® NOUN

le **coca** ◇ *a can of Coke* ® une boîte de coca

colander NOUN

la **passoire**

cold ADJECTIVE

see also cold NOUN

froid ◇ *The water's cold.* L'eau est froide.

- **It's cold today.** Il fait froid aujourd'hui.

- **to be cold** (*person*) avoir froid ◇ *I'm cold.* J'ai froid. ◇ *Are you cold?* Est-ce que tu as froid?

cold NOUN

see also cold ADJECTIVE

1 le **froid** ◇ *I can't stand the cold.* Je ne supporte pas le froid.

2 le **rhume** ◇ *to catch a cold* attraper un rhume

- **to have a cold** avoir un rhume ◇ *I've got a bad cold.* J'ai un gros rhume.

- **a cold sore** un bouton de fièvre

coleslaw NOUN

la **salade de chou cru à la mayonnaise**

to **collapse** VERB

s'effondrer ◇ *He collapsed.* Il s'est effondré.

collar NOUN

1 le **col** (*of coat, shirt*)

2 le **collier** (*for animal*)

collarbone NOUN

la **clavicule** ◇ *I broke my collarbone.* Je me suis cassé la clavicule.

colleague NOUN

le/la **collègue**

to **collect** VERB

1 **ramasser** ◇ *The teacher collected the exercise books.* Le professeur a ramassé les cahiers. ◇ *They collect the rubbish twice a week.* Ils ramassent les ordures deux fois par semaine.

2 **faire collection de** ◇ *I collect stamps.* Je fais collection de timbres.

3 **aller chercher** ◇ *Their mother collects them from school.* Leur mère va les chercher à l'école.

4 **faire une collecte** ◇ *They're collecting for charity.* Ils font une collecte pour une association caritative.

collection NOUN

1 la **collection** ◇ *my CD collection* ma collection de CD

2 la **collecte** ◇ *a collection for charity* une collecte pour une association caritative

collector NOUN

le **collectionneur**

la **collectionneuse**

college NOUN

le **collège** ◇ *a technical college* un collège technique

to **collide** VERB

entrer en collision

collie NOUN

le **colley**

colliery NOUN

la **houillère**

collision NOUN

la **collision**

colonel NOUN

le **colonel**

colour NOUN

la **couleur** ◇ *What colour is it?* C'est de quelle couleur?

- **a colour film** (*for camera*) une pellicule en couleur

colourful ADJECTIVE

coloré

colouring NOUN

le **colorant** (*for food*)

comb NOUN

see also comb VERB

le **peigne**

to **comb** VERB

see also comb NOUN

- **to comb one's hair** se peigner ◇ *You haven't combed your hair.* Tu ne t'es pas peigné.

combination NOUN
la **combinaison**

to **combine** VERB
  1 **allier** ◇ *The film combines humour with suspense.* Le film allie l'humour au suspense.
  2 **concilier** ◇ *It's difficult to combine a career with a family.* Il est difficile de concilier carrière et vie de famille.

to **come** VERB
  1 **venir** ◇ *Can I come too?* Est-ce que je peux venir aussi? ◇ *Some friends came to see us.* Quelques amis sont venus nous voir. ◇ *I'll come with you.* Je viens avec toi.
  2 **arriver** (*arrive*) ◇ *I'm coming!* J'arrive! ◇ *They came late.* Ils sont arrivés en retard. ◇ *The letter came this morning.* La lettre est arrivée ce matin.
- **to come back** revenir ◇ *Come back!* Reviens!
- **to come down (1)** (*person, lift*) descendre
- **to come down (2)** (*prices*) baisser
- **to come from** venir de ◇ *Where do you come from?* Tu viens d'où?
- **to come in** entrer ◇ *Come in!* Entrez!
- **Come on!** Allez!
- **to come out** sortir ◇ *when we came out of the cinema* quand nous sommes sortis du cinéma ◇ *It's just come out on video.* Ça vient de sortir en vidéo.
- **None of my photos came out.** Mes photos n'ont rien donné.
- **to come round** reprendre connaissance (*after faint, operation*)
- **to come up** monter ◇ *Come up here!* Monte!
- **to come up to somebody (1)** s'approcher de quelqu'un ◇ *She came up to me and kissed me.* Elle s'est approchée de moi et m'a embrassé.
- **to come up to somebody (2)** (*to speak to them*) aborder quelqu'un ◇ *A man came up to me and said...* Un homme m'a abordé et m'a dit...

comedian NOUN
le **comique**

comedy NOUN
la **comédie**

comfortable ADJECTIVE
  1 **confortable** (*bed, chair*)
  2 **à l'aise** (*person*) ◇ *I'm very comfortable, thanks.* Je suis parfaitement à l'aise, merci.

comic NOUN
l' **illustré** MASC (*magazine*)

comic strip NOUN
la **bande dessinée**

coming ADJECTIVE
prochain ◇ *in the coming months* au cours des prochains mois

comma NOUN
la **virgule**

command NOUN
l' **ordre** MASC

comment NOUN
  see also comment VERB
le **commentaire** ◇ *He made no comment.* Il n'a fait aucun commentaire.
- **No comment!** Je n'ai rien à dire!

to **comment** VERB
  see also comment NOUN
- **to comment on something** faire des commentaires sur quelque chose

commentary NOUN
le **reportage en direct** (*on TV, radio*)

commentator NOUN
le **commentateur sportif**
la **commentatrice sportive**

commercial NOUN
le **spot publicitaire**

commission NOUN
la **commission** ◇ *Salesmen work on commission.* Les représentants travaillent à la commission.

to **commit** VERB
- **to commit a crime** commettre un crime
- **to commit oneself** s'engager ◇ *I don't want to commit myself.* Je ne veux pas m'engager.
- **to commit suicide** se suicider ◇ *He committed suicide.* Il s'est suicidé.

committee NOUN
le **comité**

common ADJECTIVE
  see also common NOUN
courant ◇ *"Smith" is a very common surname.* "Smith" est un nom de famille très courant.
- **in common** en commun ◇ *We've got a lot in common.* Nous avons beaucoup de choses en commun.

common NOUN
  see also common ADJECTIVE
le **terrain communal** ◇ *We went for a walk on the common.* Nous sommes allés nous promener sur le terrain communal.

common sense NOUN
le **bon sens** ◇ *Use your common sense!* Sers-toi de ton bon sens!

to **communicate** VERB
communiquer

communication NOUN
la **communication**

communion NOUN
  la **communion** ◇ *my First Communion* ma première communion

communism NOUN
  le **communisme**

communist NOUN
  see also communist ADJECTIVE
  le/la **communiste**

communist ADJECTIVE
  see also communist NOUN
  communiste
- **the Communist Party** le Parti communiste

community NOUN
  la **communauté**

to **commute** VERB
  faire la navette ◇ *She commutes between Liss and London.* Elle fait la navette entre Liss et Londres.

compact disc NOUN
  le **disque compact**
- **a compact disc player** une platine laser

companion NOUN
  le **compagnon**
  la **compagne**

company NOUN
  [1] la **société** ◇ *He works for a big company.* Il travaille pour une grosse société.
  [2] la **compagnie** ◇ *an insurance company* une compagnie d'assurance ◇ *a theatre company* une compagnie théâtrale
- **to keep somebody company** tenir compagnie à quelqu'un ◇ *I'll keep you company.* Je vais te tenir compagnie.

comparatively ADVERB
  relativement

to **compare** VERB
  comparer ◇ *People always compare him with his brother.* On le compare toujours à son frère.
- **compared with** en comparaison de ◇ *Oxford is small compared with London.* Oxford est une petite ville en comparaison de Londres.

comparison NOUN
  la **comparaison**

compartment NOUN
  le **compartiment**

compass NOUN
  la **boussole**

compensation NOUN
  l' **indemnité** FEM ◇ *They got £2000 compensation.* Ils ont reçu une indemnité de deux mille livres.

compere NOUN

  l' **animateur** MASC
  l' **animatrice** FEM

to **compete** VERB
  participer ◇ *I'm competing in the marathon.* Je participe au marathon.
- **to compete for something** se disputer quelque chose ◇ *There are 50 students competing for 6 places.* Ils sont cinquante étudiants à se disputer six places.

competent ADJECTIVE
  compétent

competition NOUN
  le **concours** ◇ *a singing competition* un concours de chant

competitor NOUN
  le **concurrent**
  la **concurrente**

to **complain** VERB
  se plaindre ◇ *I'm going to complain to the manager.* Je vais me plaindre au directeur. ◇ *We complained about the noise.* Nous nous sommes plaints du bruit.

complaint NOUN
  la **plainte** ◇ *There were lots of complaints about the food.* Il y eu beaucoup de plaintes à propos de la nourriture.

complete ADJECTIVE
  complet MASC
  complète FEM

completely ADVERB
  complètement

complexion NOUN
  le **teint**

complicated ADJECTIVE
  compliqué

compliment NOUN
  see also compliment VERB
  le **compliment**

to **compliment** VERB
  see also compliment NOUN
  complimenter ◇ *They complimented me on my French.* Ils m'ont complimenté sur mon français.

composer NOUN
  le **compositeur**
  la **compositrice**

comprehensive school NOUN
  [1] le **collège**
  [2] le **lycée**
  In France pupils go to a collège *between the ages of 11 and 15, and then to a* lycée *until the age of 18.*

compromise NOUN
  le **compromis** ◇ *We reached a compromise.* Nous sommes parvenus à un compromis.

compulsory ADJECTIVE
  obligatoire
computer NOUN
  l' **ordinateur** MASC
computer game NOUN
  le **jeu électronique**
  (les **jeux électroniques** PL)
computer programmer NOUN
  le **programmeur**
  la **programmeuse**
  ◇ *She's a computer programmer.* Elle
  est programmeuse.
computing NOUN
  l' **informatique** FEM
to **concentrate** VERB
  se concentrer ◇ *I couldn't*
  concentrate. Je n'arrivais pas à me
  concentrer.
concentration NOUN
  la **concentration**
concerned ADJECTIVE
  • **to be concerned** s'inquiéter ◇ *His*
  mother is concerned about him. Sa mère
  s'inquiète à son sujet.
  • **as far as I'm concerned** en ce qui me
  concerne
concert NOUN
  le **concert**
concrete NOUN
  le **béton**
condition NOUN
  [1] la **condition** ◇ *I'll do it, on one*
  condition... Je veux bien le faire, à une
  condition...
  [2] l' **état** MASC ◇ *in good condition* en
  bon état
conditional NOUN
  le **conditionnel**
conditioner NOUN
  le **baume démêlant** (*for hair*)
condom NOUN
  le **préservatif**
to **conduct** VERB
  diriger (*orchestra*)
conductor NOUN
  le **chef d'orchestre**
cone NOUN
  le **cornet** ◇ *an ice-cream cone* un
  cornet de glace
conference NOUN
  la **conférence**
to **confess** VERB
  avouer ◇ *He finally confessed.* Il a
  fini par avouer. ◇ *He confessed to the*
  murder. Il a avoué avoir commis le
  meurtre.
confession NOUN
  la **confession**
confidence NOUN

[1] la **confiance** ◇ *I've got confidence*
in you. J'ai confiance en toi.
[2] l' **assurance** FEM ◇ *She lacks*
confidence. Elle manque d'assurance.
confident ADJECTIVE
  sûr ◇ *I'm confident everything will be*
  okay. Je suis sûr que tout ira bien.
  • **She's seems quite confident.** Elle a
  l'air sûre d'elle.
confidential ADJECTIVE
  confidentiel MASC
  confidentielle FEM
to **confirm** VERB
  confirmer (*booking*)
confirmation NOUN
  la **confirmation**
conflict NOUN
  le **conflit**
to **confuse** VERB
  • **to confuse somebody** embrouiller les
  idées de quelqu'un ◇ *Don't confuse*
  me! Ne m'embrouille pas les idées!
confused ADJECTIVE
  désorienté
confusing ADJECTIVE
  • **The traffic signs are confusing.** Les
  panneaux de signalisation ne sont pas
  clairs.
confusion NOUN
  la **confusion**
to **congratulate** VERB
  féliciter ◇ *My friends congratulated*
  me on passing the test. Mes amis m'ont
  félicité d'avoir réussi à l'examen.
congratulations PL NOUN
  les **félicitations** FEM PL
  ◇ *Congratulations on your new job!*
  Félicitations pour votre nouveau poste!
conjurer NOUN
  le **prestidigitateur**
connection NOUN
  [1] le **rapport** ◇ *There's no connection*
  between the two events. Il n'y a aucun
  rapport entre les deux événements.
  [2] le **contact** (*electrical*) ◇ *There's a*
  loose connection. Il y a un mauvais
  contact.
  [3] la **correspondance** (*of trains, planes*)
  ◇ *We missed our connection.* Nous
  avons raté la correspondance.
to **conquer** VERB
  conquérir
conscience NOUN
  la **conscience**
conscious ADJECTIVE
  conscient
consciousness NOUN
  la **connaissance**
  • **to lose consciousness** perdre

connaissance ◇ *I lost consciousness.*
J'ai perdu connaissance.
consequently ADVERB
 par conséquent
conservation NOUN
 la **protection**
conservative ADJECTIVE
 see also conservative NOUN
 conservateur MASC
 conservatrice FEM
- **the Conservative Party** le Parti
conservateur
Conservative NOUN
 see also conservative ADJECTIVE
 le **conservateur**
 la **conservatrice**
- **to vote Conservative** voter
conservateur
- **the Conservatives** les conservateurs
conservatory NOUN
 le **jardin d'hiver**
to **consider** VERB
 1 **considérer** ◇ *He considers it a*
waste of time. Il considère que c'est une
perte de temps.
 2 **envisager** ◇ *We considered*
cancelling our holiday. Nous avons
envisagé d'annuler nos vacances.
- **I'm considering the idea.** J'y songe.
considerate ADJECTIVE
 délicat
considering PREPOSITION
 1 **étant donné** ◇ *Considering we*
were there for a month... Étant donné
que nous étions là pour un mois...
 2 **tout compte fait** ◇ *I got a good*
mark, considering. J'ai eu une bonne
note, tout compte fait.
to **consist** VERB
- **to consist of** être composé de ◇ *The*
band consists of three guitarists and a
drummer. Le groupe est composé de
trois guitaristes et un batteur.
consonant NOUN
 la **consonne**
constant ADJECTIVE
 constant
constantly ADVERB
 constamment
constipated ADJECTIVE
 constipé
to **construct** VERB
 construire
construction NOUN
 la **construction**
to **consult** VERB
 consulter
contact NOUN
 see also contact VERB

le **contact** ◇ *I'm in contact with her.* Je
suis en contact avec elle.
to **contact** VERB
 see also contact NOUN
 joindre ◇ *Where can we contact you?*
Où pouvons-nous vous joindre?
contact lenses PL NOUN
 les **verres de contact** MASC PL
to **contain** VERB
 contenir
container NOUN
 le **récipient**
contest NOUN
 le **concours**
contestant NOUN
 le **concurrent**
 la **concurrente**
context NOUN
 le **contexte**
continent NOUN
 le **continent** ◇ *How many continents*
are there? Combien y a-t-il de
continents?
- **the Continent** l'Europe FEM ◇ *I've*
never been to the Continent. Je ne suis
jamais allé en Europe.
continental breakfast NOUN
 le **petit déjeuner à la française**
to **continue** VERB
 1 **continuer** ◇ *She continued talking*
to her friend. Elle a continué à parler à
son amie.
 2 **reprendre** (*after interruption*) ◇ *We*
continued working after lunch. Nous
avons repris le travail après le déjeuner.
continuous ADJECTIVE
 continu
- **continuous assessment** le contrôle
continu
contraceptive NOUN
 le **contraceptif**
contract NOUN
 le **contrat**
to **contradict** VERB
 contredire
contrary NOUN
 le **contraire**
- **on the contrary** au contraire
contrast NOUN
 le **contraste**
to **contribute** VERB
 1 **contribuer** (*to success, achievement*)
◇ *The treaty will contribute to world*
peace. Le traité va contribuer à la paix
dans le monde.
 2 **participer** (*share in*) ◇ *He didn't*
contribute to the discussion. Il n'a pas
participé à la discussion.
 3 **donner** (*give*) ◇ *She contributed*

£10. Elle a donné dix livres.

contribution NOUN
la **contribution**

control NOUN
see also control VERB
le **contrôle**
- **to lose control** (*of vehicle*) perdre le contrôle ◇ *He lost control of the car.* Il a perdu le contrôle de son véhicule.
- **the controls** les commandes FEM (*of machine*)
- **to be in control** être maître de la situation
- **to keep control** (*of people*) se faire obéir ◇ *He can't keep control of the class.* Il n'arrive pas à se faire obéir de sa classe.
- **out of control** (*child, class*) déchaîné

to control VERB
see also control NOUN
1 **diriger** (*country, organization*)
2 **se faire obéir de** ◇ *He can't control the class.* Il n'arrive pas à se faire obéir de sa classe.
3 **maîtriser** ◇ *I couldn't control the horse.* Je ne suis pas arrivé à maîtriser le cheval.
- **to control oneself** se contrôler

controversial ADJECTIVE
controversé ◇ *a controversial book* un livre controversé

convenient ADJECTIVE
bien situé (*place*) ◇ *The hotel's convenient for the airport.* L'hôtel est bien situé par rapport à l'aéroport.
- **It's not a convenient time for me.** C'est une heure qui ne m'arrange pas.
- **Would Monday be convenient for you?** Est-ce que lundi vous conviendrait?

conventional ADJECTIVE
conventionnel MASC
conventionnelle FEM

convent school NOUN
l' **institution religieuse** FEM

conversation NOUN
la **conversation** ◇ *a French conversation class* un cours de conversation française

to convert VERB
transformer ◇ *We've converted the loft into a spare room.* Nous avons transformé le grenier en chambre d'amis.

to convict VERB
reconnaître coupable ◇ *He was convicted of the murder.* Il a été reconnu coupable du meurtre.

to convince VERB
persuader ◇ *I'm not convinced.* Je n'en suis pas persuadé.

to cook VERB
see also cook NOUN
1 **faire la cuisine** ◇ *I can't cook.* Je ne sais pas faire la cuisine.
2 **préparer** ◇ *She's cooking lunch.* Elle est en train de préparer le déjeuner.
3 **faire cuire** ◇ *Cook the pasta for 10 minutes.* Faites cuire les pâtes pendant dix minutes.
- **to be cooked** être cuit ◇ *When the potatoes are cooked...* Lorsque les pommes de terre sont cuites...

cook NOUN
see also cook VERB
le **cuisinier**
la **cuisinière**
◇ *Matthew's an excellent cook.* Matthew est un excellent cuisinier.

cookbook NOUN
le **livre de cuisine**

cooker NOUN
la **cuisinière** ◇ *a gas cooker* une cuisinière à gaz

cookery NOUN
la **cuisine**

cooking NOUN
la **cuisine** ◇ *I like cooking.* J'aime bien faire la cuisine.

cool ADJECTIVE
frais MASC
fraîche FEM
◇ *a cool place* un endroit frais
- **to stay cool** (*keep calm*) garder son calme ◇ *He stayed cool.* Il a gardé son calme.

cooperation NOUN
la **coopération**

cop NOUN
le **flic** (*informal*)

to cope VERB
se débrouiller ◇ *It was hard, but we coped.* C'était dur, mais nous nous sommes débrouillés.
- **to cope with** faire face à ◇ *She's got a lot of problems to cope with.* Elle doit faire face à de nombreux problèmes.

copper NOUN
1 le **cuivre** ◇ *a copper bracelet* un bracelet en cuivre
2 le **flic** (*policeman*)

copy NOUN
see also copy VERB
1 la **copie** (*of letter, document*)
2 l' **exemplaire** MASC (*of book*)

to copy VERB
see also copy NOUN
copier ◇ *The teacher accused him of copying.* Le professeur l'a accusé d'avoir copié.

cork NOUN
  [1] le **bouchon** (*of bottle*)
  [2] le **liège** (*material*) ⋄ *a cork table mat* un set de table en liège

corkscrew NOUN
  le **tire-bouchon**

corn NOUN
  [1] le **blé** (*wheat*)
  [2] le **maïs** (*sweetcorn*)
- **corn on the cob** l'épi de maïs MASC

corner NOUN
  [1] le **coin** ⋄ *in a corner of the room* dans un coin de la pièce
- **the shop on the corner** la boutique au coin de la rue
- **He lives just round the corner.** Il habite tout près d'ici.
  [2] le **corner** (*in football*)

cornet NOUN
  [1] le **cornet à pistons** ⋄ *He plays the cornet.* Il joue du cornet à pistons.
  [2] le **cornet** (*ice cream*)

cornflakes PL NOUN
  les **corn-flakes** MASC PL

Cornwall NOUN
  la **Cornouailles**
- **in Cornwall** en Cornouailles

corporal NOUN
  le **caporal**

corporal punishment NOUN
  le **châtiment corporel**

corpse NOUN
  le **cadavre**

correct ADJECTIVE
  see also correct VERB
  exact ⋄ *That's correct.* C'est exact.
- **the correct choice** le bon choix
- **the correct answer** la bonne réponse

to **correct** VERB
  see also correct ADJECTIVE
  corriger

correction NOUN
  la **correction**

corridor NOUN
  le **couloir**

corruption NOUN
  la **corruption**

Corsica NOUN
  la **Corse**
- **in Corsica** en Corse

cosmetics PL NOUN
  les **produits de beauté** MASC PL

to **cost** VERB
  see also cost NOUN
  coûter ⋄ *The meal costs a hundred francs.* Le repas coûte cent francs. ⋄ *How much does it cost?* Combien est-ce que ça coûte? ⋄ *It costs too much.* Ça coûte trop cher.

cost NOUN
  see also cost VERB
  le **coût**
- **the cost of living** le coût de la vie
- **at all costs** à tout prix

costume NOUN
  le **costume**

cosy ADJECTIVE
  douillet MASC
  douillette FEM

cot NOUN
  le **lit d'enfant**

cottage NOUN
  le **cottage**
- **a thatched cottage** une chaumière

cotton NOUN
  le **coton** ⋄ *a cotton shirt* une chemise en coton
- **cotton wool** le coton hydrophile

couch NOUN
  le **canapé**

couchette NOUN
  la **couchette**

to **cough** VERB
  see also cough NOUN
  tousser

cough NOUN
  see also cough VERB
  la **toux** ⋄ *a bad cough* une mauvaise toux
- **I've got a cough.** Je tousse.

could VERB see **can**

council NOUN
  le **conseil**
  The nearest French equivalent of a local council would be a conseil municipal, *which administers a* commune.
- **He's on the council.** Il fait partie du conseil municipal.
- **a council estate** une cité HLM
- **a council house** une HLM
  HLM *stands for* habitation à loyer modéré *which means "low-rent home".*

councillor NOUN
- **She's a local councillor.** Elle fait partie du conseil municipal.

to **count** VERB
  compter
- **to count on** compter sur ⋄ *You can count on me.* Tu peux compter sur moi.

counter NOUN
  [1] le **comptoir** (*in shop*)
  [2] le **guichet** (*in post office, bank*)
  [3] le **jeton** (*in game*)

country NOUN
  [1] le **pays** ⋄ *the border between the two countries* la frontière entre les deux pays
  [2] la **campagne** ⋄ *I live in the country.* ⟨PTO⟩

J'habite à la campagne.
- **country dancing** la danse folklorique

countryside NOUN
la **campagne**

county NOUN
le **comté**
> The nearest French equivalent of a county would be a département.

- **the county council**
> The nearest French equivalent of a county council would be a conseil général, which administers a département.

couple NOUN
le **couple** ◇ the couple who live next door le couple qui habite à côté
- **a couple** deux ◇ a couple of hours deux heures
- **Could you wait a couple of minutes?** Pourriez-vous attendre quelques minutes?

courage NOUN
le **courage**

courier NOUN
1 (for tourists)
l' **accompagnateur** MASC
l' **accompagnatrice** FEM
2 (delivery service)
le **coursier** ◇ They sent it by courier. Ils l'ont envoyé par coursier.

course NOUN
1 le **cours** ◇ a French course un cours de français ◇ to go on a course suivre un cours
2 le **plat** ◇ the main course le plat principal
- **the first course** l'entrée FEM
3 le **terrain** ◇ a golf course un terrain de golf
- **of course** bien sûr ◇ Do you love me?–Of course I do! Tu m'aimes?–Bien sûr que oui!

court NOUN
1 (of law)
le **tribunal**
(les **tribunaux** PL)
◇ He was in court last week. Il est passé devant le tribunal la semaine dernière.
2 (tennis)
le **court** ◇ There are tennis and squash courts. Il y a des courts de tennis et de squash.

courtyard NOUN
la **cour**

cousin NOUN
le **cousin**
la **cousine**

cover NOUN
see also cover VERB
1 la **couverture** (of book)

2 la **housse** (of duvet)

to **cover** VERB
see also cover NOUN
1 **couvrir** ◇ My face was covered with mosquito bites. J'avais le visage couvert de piqûres de moustique.
2 **prendre en charge** ◇ Our insurance didn't cover it. Notre assurance ne l'a pas pris en charge.
- **to cover up a scandal** étouffer un scandale

cow NOUN
la **vache**

coward NOUN
le **lâche** ◇ She's a coward. Elle est lâche.

cowardly ADJECTIVE
lâche

cowboy NOUN
le **cow-boy**

crab NOUN
le **crabe**

crack NOUN
see also crack VERB
1 la **fissure** (in wall)
2 la **fêlure** (in cup, window)
3 le **crack** (drug)
- **I'll have a crack at it.** Je vais tenter le coup.

to **crack** VERB
see also crack NOUN
casser (nut, egg)
- **to crack a joke** sortir une blague

cracked ADJECTIVE
fêlé (cup, window)

cracker NOUN
1 le **cracker** (biscuit)
2 le **diablotin** (Christmas cracker)

cradle NOUN
le **berceau**
(les **berceaux** PL)

craft NOUN
les **travaux manuels** MASC PL ◇ We do craft at school. Nous avons des cours de travaux manuels à l'école.
- **a craft centre** un centre artisanal

craftsman NOUN
l' **artisan** MASC

to **cram** VERB
1 **entasser** ◇ We crammed our stuff into the boot. Nous avons entassé nos affaires dans le coffre.
2 **bachoter** (for exams)

to **crash** VERB
see also crash NOUN
avoir un accident ◇ He's crashed his car. Il a eu un accident de voiture.
- **The plane crashed.** L'avion s'est écrasé.

crash NOUN
> *see also* crash VERB
1. la **collision** (*of car*)
2. l' **accident** MASC (*of plane*)
- a **crash helmet** un casque
- a **crash course** un cours intensif

to **crawl** VERB
> *see also* crawl NOUN
marcher à quatre pattes (*baby*)

crawl NOUN
> *see also* crawl VERB
le **crawl** ◦ *to do the crawl* nager le crawl

crazy ADJECTIVE
fou MASC
folle FEM

cream ADJECTIVE
> *see also* cream NOUN
crème MASC, FEM, PL (*colour*)

cream NOUN
> *see also* cream ADJECTIVE
la **crème** ◦ *strawberries and cream* les fraises à la crème
- a **cream cake** un gâteau à la crème
- **cream cheese** le fromage à la crème
- **sun cream** la crème solaire

crease NOUN
le **pli**

creased ADJECTIVE
froissé

to **create** VERB
créer

creation NOUN
la **création**

creative ADJECTIVE
créatif MASC
créative FEM

creature NOUN
la **créature**

crèche NOUN
la **crèche**

credit NOUN
le **crédit** ◦ *on credit* à crédit

credit card NOUN
la **carte de crédit**

cress NOUN
le **cresson**

crew NOUN
1. l' **équipage** MASC (*of ship, plane*)
2. l' **équipe** FEM ◦ *a film crew* une équipe de tournage

crew cut NOUN
les **cheveux en brosse** MASC PL

cricket NOUN
1. le **cricket** ◦ *I play cricket.* Je joue au cricket.
- a **cricket bat** une batte de cricket
2. le **grillon** (*insect*)

crime NOUN
1. le **délit** ◦ *Murder is a crime.* Le meurtre est un délit.
2. la **criminalité** (*lawlessness*)
- **Crime is rising.** La criminalité augmente.

criminal NOUN
> *see also* criminal ADJECTIVE
le **criminel**
la **criminelle**

criminal ADJECTIVE
> *see also* criminal NOUN
criminel MASC
criminelle FEM
◦ *It's criminal!* C'est criminel!
- **It's a criminal offence.** C'est un crime puni par la loi.
- to **have a criminal record** avoir un casier judiciaire

crisis NOUN
la **crise**

crisp ADJECTIVE
croquant (*food*)

crisps PL NOUN
les **chips** FEM PL ◦ *a bag of crisps* un paquet de chips

criterion NOUN
le **critère**

critic NOUN
le **critique**

critical ADJECTIVE
critique
- a **critical remark** une critique

criticism NOUN
la **critique**

to **criticize** VERB
critiquer

Croatia NOUN
la **Croatie**
- **in Croatia** en Croatie

to **crochet** VERB
crocheter

crocodile NOUN
le **crocodile**

crook NOUN
l' **escroc** MASC (*criminal*)

crop NOUN
la **récolte** ◦ *a good crop of apples* une bonne récolte de pommes

cross NOUN
> *see also* cross ADJECTIVE, VERB
la **croix**

cross ADJECTIVE
> *see also* cross NOUN, VERB
fâché ◦ *to be cross about something* être fâché à propos de quelque chose

to **cross** VERB
> *see also* cross ADJECTIVE, NOUN
traverser (*street, bridge*)
- to **cross out** barrer

◆ **to cross over** traverser

cross-country NOUN
le **cross** (race)
◆ **cross-country skiing** le ski de fond

crossing NOUN
1 la **traversée** (by boat) ◇ the crossing from Dover to Calais la traversée de Douvres à Calais
2 le **passage clouté** (for pedestrians)

crossroads NOUN
le **carrefour**

crossword NOUN
les **mots croisés** MASC PL ◇ I like doing crosswords. J'aime faire les mots croisés.

crow NOUN
le **corbeau**
(les **corbeaux** PL)

crowd NOUN
la **foule**
◆ **the crowd** (at sports match) les spectateurs

crowded ADJECTIVE
bondé

crown NOUN
la **couronne**

crucifix NOUN
le **crucifix**

crude ADJECTIVE
(vulgar)
grossier MASC
grossière FEM

cruel ADJECTIVE
cruel MASC
cruelle FEM

cruise NOUN
la **croisière** ◇ to go on a cruise faire une croisière

crumb NOUN
la **miette**

to **crush** VERB
écraser

crutch NOUN
la **béquille**

to **cry** VERB
pleurer ◇ The baby's crying. Le bébé pleure.

crystal NOUN
le **cristal**

CTC NOUN (= city technology college)
le **collège technique**

cub NOUN
1 (animal)
le **petit**
2 (scout)
le **louveteau**
(les **louveteaux** PL)

cube NOUN

le **cube**

cubic ADJECTIVE
◆ **a cubic metre** un mètre cube

cucumber NOUN
le **concombre**

cue NOUN
la **queue de billard** (for snooker, pool)

culottes PL NOUN
la **jupe-culotte** SING

culture NOUN
la **culture**

cunning ADJECTIVE
1 (person)
rusé
2 (plan, idea)
astucieux MASC
astucieuse FEM

cup NOUN
1 la **tasse** ◇ a china cup une tasse en porcelaine
◆ **a cup of coffee** un café
2 la **coupe** (trophy)

cupboard NOUN
le **placard**

to **cure** VERB
see also **cure** NOUN
guérir

cure NOUN
see also **cure** VERB
le **remède**

curious ADJECTIVE
curieux MASC
curieuse FEM

curly ADJECTIVE
1 **bouclé** (loosely curled)
2 **frisé** (tightly curled)

currant NOUN
le **raisin de Corinthe** (dried fruit)

currency NOUN
la **devise** ◇ foreign currency les devises étrangères

current NOUN
see also **current** ADJECTIVE
le **courant** ◇ The current is very strong. Le courant est très fort.

current ADJECTIVE
see also **current** NOUN
actuel MASC
actuelle FEM
◇ the current situation la situation actuelle

current affairs PL NOUN
l' **actualité** FEM

curriculum NOUN
le **programme**

curriculum vitae NOUN
le **curriculum vitae**

curry NOUN
le **curry**

curse NOUN
  la **malédiction** (*spell*)
curtain NOUN
  le **rideau**
  (les **rideaux** PL)
- **to draw the curtains** tirer les rideaux
cushion NOUN
  le **coussin**
custard NOUN
  la **crème anglaise** (*for pouring*)
custody NOUN
  la **garde** (*of child*)
custom NOUN
  la **coutume** MASC ◇ *It's an old custom.*
  C'est une ancienne coutume.
customer NOUN
  le **client**
  la **cliente**
customs PL NOUN
  la **douane** SING
customs officer NOUN
  le **douanier**
  la **douanière**
cut NOUN
  see also cut VERB
  1 la **coupure** ◇ *He's got a cut on his*
  forehead. Il a une coupure au front.
  2 la **coupe** ◇ *a cut and blow-dry* une
  coupe brushing
  3 la **réduction** (*in price, spending*)
to **cut** VERB
  see also cut NOUN
  1 **couper** ◇ *I'll cut some bread.* Je
  vais couper du pain.
- **to cut oneself** se couper ◇ *I cut my*
  foot on a piece of glass. Je me suis
  coupé au pied avec un morceau de
  verre.
  2 **réduire** (*price, spending*)

- **to cut down** abattre (*tree*)
- **to cut off** couper ◇ *The electricity*
  was cut off. L'électricité a été coupé.
- **to cut up** hacher (*vegetables, meat*)
cutlery NOUN
  les **couverts** MASC PL
CV NOUN
  le **C.V.**
to **cycle** VERB
  see also cycle NOUN
  faire de la bicyclette ◇ *I like cycling.*
  J'aime faire de la bicyclette.
- **I cycle to school.** Je vais à l'école à
  bicyclette.
cycle NOUN
  see also cycle VERB
  la **bicyclette**
- **a cycle ride** une promenade à
  bicyclette
cycling NOUN
  le **cyclisme**
cyclist NOUN
  le/la **cycliste**
cylinder NOUN
  le **cylindre**
Cyprus NOUN
  la **Chypre**
- **in Cyprus** à Chypre
- **We went to Cyprus.** Nous sommes allés
  à Chypre.
Czech ADJECTIVE
  see also Czech NOUN
  tchèque
- **the Czech Republic** la République
  tchèque
Czech NOUN
  see also Czech ADJECTIVE
  1 le/la **Tchèque** (*person*)
  2 le **tchèque** (*language*)

D

dad NOUN
1 le **père** ◇ *my dad* mon père ◇ *his dad* son père
2 le **papa**
Use **papa** *only when you are talking to your father or using it as his name; otherwise use* **père**.
- **Dad!** Papa! ◇ *I'll ask Dad.* Je vais demander à papa.

daffodil NOUN
la **jonquille**

daft ADJECTIVE
idiot

daily ADJECTIVE, ADVERB
1 **quotidien** MASC
quotidienne FEM
◇ *It's part of my daily routine.* Ça fait partie de mes occupations quotidiennes.
2 **tous les jours** ◇ *The pool is open daily from 9 a.m. to 6 p.m.* La piscine est ouverte tous les jours de neuf heures à dix-huit heures.

dairy NOUN
la **crémerie** (*shop*)

dairy products PL NOUN
les **produits laitiers** MASC PL

daisy NOUN
la **pâquerette**

dam NOUN
le **barrage**

damage NOUN
see also damage VERB
les **dégâts** MASC PL ◇ *The storm did a lot of damage.* La tempête a fait beaucoup de dégâts.

to damage VERB
see also damage NOUN
endommager

damn NOUN
see also damn ADJECTIVE
- **I don't give a damn!** Je m'en fiche! (*informal*)
- **Damn!** Zut! (*informal*)

damn ADJECTIVE, ADVERB
see also damn NOUN
- **It's a damn nuisance!** Quelle barbe!

damp ADJECTIVE
humide

dance NOUN
see also dance VERB
1 la **danse** ◇ *The last dance was a waltz.* La dernière danse était une valse.
2 le **bal** ◇ *Are you going to the dance tonight?* Tu vas au bal ce soir?

to dance VERB

see also dance NOUN
danser
- **to go dancing** aller danser ◇ *Let's go dancing!* Si on allait danser?

dancer NOUN
le **danseur**
la **danseuse**

dandruff NOUN
les **pellicules** FEM PL

Dane NOUN
1 le **Danois**
2 la **Danoise**

danger NOUN
le **danger**
- **in danger** en danger ◇ *His life is in danger.* Sa vie est en danger.
- **to be in danger of** risquer de ◇ *We were in danger of missing the plane.* Nous risquions de rater l'avion.

dangerous ADJECTIVE
dangereux MASC
dangereuse FEM

Danish ADJECTIVE
see also Danish NOUN
danois

Danish NOUN
see also Danish ADJECTIVE
le **danois** (*language*)

to dare VERB
oser
- **to dare to do something** oser faire quelque chose ◇ *I didn't dare to tell my parents.* Je n'ai pas osé le dire à mes parents.
- **I dare say it'll be okay.** Je suppose que ça va aller.

daring ADJECTIVE
audacieux MASC
audacieuse FEM

dark ADJECTIVE
see also dark NOUN
1 **sombre** (*room*) ◇ *It's dark.* (*inside*) Il fait sombre.
- **It's dark outside.** Il fait nuit dehors.
- **It's getting dark.** La nuit tombe.
2 **foncé** (*colour*) ◇ *She's got dark hair.* Elle a les cheveux foncés. ◇ *a dark green sweater* un pull vert foncé

dark NOUN
see also dark ADJECTIVE
le **noir** ◇ *I'm afraid of the dark.* J'ai peur du noir.
- **after dark** après la tombée de la nuit

darkness NOUN
l' **obscurité** FEM ◇ *The room was in darkness.* La chambre était dans

l'obscurité.

darling NOUN
le **chéri**
la **chérie**
◇ *Thank you, darling!* Merci, chéri!

dart NOUN
la **fléchette** ◇ *to play darts* jouer aux fléchettes

data PL NOUN
les **données** FEM PL

database NOUN
la **base de données** (*on computer*)

date NOUN
1 la **date** ◇ *my date of birth* ma date de naissance
- **What's the date today?** Quel jour sommes-nous?
- **to have a date with somebody** sortir avec quelqu'un ◇ *She's got a date with Ian tonight.* Elle sort avec Ian ce soir.
- **out of date (1)** (*passport*) périmé
- **out of date (2)** (*technology*) dépassé
- **out of date (3)** (*clothes*) démodé
2 la **datte** (*fruit*)

daughter NOUN
la **fille**

daughter-in-law NOUN
la **belle-fille**
(les **belles-filles** PL)

dawn NOUN
l' **aube** FEM ◇ *at dawn* à l'aube

day NOUN
> Use **jour** *to refer to the whole 24-hour period.* **journée** *only refers to the time when you are awake.*
1 le **jour** ◇ *We stayed in Nice for three days.* Nous sommes restés trois jours à Nice.
- **every day** tous les jours
2 la **journée** ◇ *during the day* dans la journée ◇ *I stayed at home all day.* Je suis resté à la maison toute la journée.
- **the day before** la veille ◇ *the day before my birthday* la veille de mon anniversaire
- **the day after** le lendemain
- **the day after tomorrow** après-demain ◇ *We're leaving the day after tomorrow.* Nous partons après-demain.
- **the day before yesterday** avant-hier ◇ *He arrived the day before yesterday.* Il est arrivé avant-hier.

dead ADJECTIVE, ADVERB
1 **mort** ◇ *He was already dead when the doctor came.* Il était déjà mort quand le docteur est arrivé.
- **He was shot dead.** Il a été abattu.
2 **absolument** (*totally*) ◇ *You're dead*

right! Tu as absolument raison!
- **dead on time** à l'heure pile ◇ *The train arrived dead on time.* Le train est arrivé à l'heure pile.

dead end NOUN
l' **impasse** FEM

deadline NOUN
la **date limite** ◇ *The deadline for entries is May 2nd.* La date limite d'inscription est le deux mai.

deaf ADJECTIVE
sourd

deafening ADJECTIVE
assourdissant

deal NOUN
> *see also* **deal** VERB
le **marché**
- **It's a deal!** Marché conclu!
- **a great deal** beaucoup ◇ *a great deal of money* beaucoup d'argent

to **deal** VERB
> *see also* **deal** NOUN
donner (*cards*) ◇ *It's your turn to deal.* C'est à toi de donner.
- **to deal with something** s'occuper de quelque chose ◇ *He promised to deal with it immediately.* Il a promis de s'en occuper immédiatement.

dear ADJECTIVE
1 **cher** MASC
chère FEM
◇ *Dear Mrs Duval* Chère Madame Duval
- **Dear Sir/Madam** (*in a circular*) Madame, Monsieur
2 (*expensive*)
coûteux MASC
coûteuse FEM

death NOUN
la **mort** ◇ *after his death* après sa mort
- **I was bored to death.** Je me suis ennuyé à mourir.

debate NOUN
> *see also* **debate** VERB
le **débat**

to **debate** VERB
> *see also* **debate** NOUN
débattre

debt NOUN
la **dette** ◇ *He's got a lot of debts.* Il a beaucoup de dettes.
- **to be in debt** avoir des dettes

decade NOUN
la **décennie**

decaffeinated ADJECTIVE
décaféiné

to **deceive** VERB
tromper

December NOUN

décembre MASC
- **in December** en décembre

decent ADJECTIVE
convenable ◇ *a decent education* une éducation convenable

to **decide** VERB
[1] **décider** ◇ *I decided to write to her.* J'ai décidé de lui écrire. ◇ *I decided not to go.* J'ai décidé de ne pas y aller.
[2] **se décider** ◇ *I can't decide.* Je n'arrive pas à me décider. ◇ *Haven't you decided yet?* Tu ne t'es pas encore décidé?

decimal ADJECTIVE
décimal ◇ *the decimal system* le système décimal

decision NOUN
la **décision**
- **to make a decision** prendre une décision

decisive ADJECTIVE
décidé (*person*)

deck NOUN
[1] (*of ship*)
le **pont**
- **on deck** sur le pont
[2] (*of cards*)
le **jeu**
(les **jeux** PL)

deckchair NOUN
la **chaise longue**

to **declare** VERB
déclarer

to **decorate** VERB
[1] **décorer** ◇ *I decorated the cake with glacé cherries.* J'ai décoré le gâteau avec des cerises confites.
[2] **peindre** (*paint*)
[3] **tapisser** (*wallpaper*)

decrease NOUN
see also decrease VERB
la **diminution** ◇ *a decrease in the number of unemployed people* une diminution du nombre de chômeurs

to **decrease** VERB
see also decrease NOUN
diminuer

dedicated ADJECTIVE
dévoué ◇ *a very dedicated teacher* un professeur très dévoué

to **deduct** VERB
déduire

deep ADJECTIVE
[1] (*water, hole, cut*)
profond ◇ *Is it deep?* Est-ce que c'est profond?
- **How deep is the lake?** Quelle est la profondeur du lac?
- **a hole 4 metres deep** un trou de

quatre mètres de profondeur
[2] (*layer*)
épais MASC
épaisse FEM
◇ *a deep layer of snow* une épaisse couche de neige ◇ *The snow was really deep.* Il y avait une épaisse couche de neige.
- **He's got a deep voice.** Il a la voix grave.
- **to take a deep breath** respirer à fond

deeply ADVERB
profondément (*depressed*)

deer NOUN
[1] le **cerf** (*red deer*)
[2] le **daim** (*fallow deer*)
[3] le **chevreuil** (*roe deer*)

defeat NOUN
see also defeat VERB
la **défaite**

to **defeat** VERB
see also defeat NOUN
battre

defect NOUN
le **défaut**

defence NOUN
la **défense**

to **defend** VERB
défendre

defender NOUN
le **défenseur**

to **define** VERB
définir

definite ADJECTIVE
[1] **précis** ◇ *I haven't got any definite plans.* Je n'ai pas de projets précis.
[2] **net** MASC
nette FEM
◇ *It's a definite improvement.* Cela constitue une nette amélioration.
[3] **sûr** ◇ *Perhaps we'll go to Spain, but it's not definite.* Nous irons peut-être en Espagne, mais ce n'est pas sûr.
- **He was definite about it.** Il a été catégorique.

definitely ADVERB
vraiment ◇ *He's definitely the best player.* C'est vraiment lui le meilleur joueur.
- **He's the best player.–Definitely!** C'est le meilleur joueur.–C'est sûr!
- **I definitely think he'll come.** Je suis sûr qu'il va venir.

definition NOUN
la **définition**

degree NOUN
[1] le **degré** ◇ *a temperature of 30 degrees* une température de trente degrés

[2] la **licence**　◇ *a degree in English*
une licence d'anglais

to **delay** VERB
see also delay NOUN
[1] **retarder**　◇ *We decided to delay our departure.* Nous avons décidé de retarder notre départ.
[2] **tarder**　◇ *Don't delay!* Ne tarde pas!
- **to be delayed** être retardé　◇ *Our flight was delayed.* Notre vol a été retardé.

delay NOUN
see also delay VERB
le **délai**　◇ *without delay* sans délai

to **delete** VERB
effacer (*on computer, tape*)

deliberate ADJECTIVE
délibéré

deliberately ADVERB
exprès　◇ *She did it deliberately.* Elle l'a fait exprès.

delicate ADJECTIVE
délicat

delicatessen NOUN
l' **épicerie fine** FEM

delicious ADJECTIVE
délicieux MASC
délicieuse FEM

delighted ADJECTIVE
ravi　◇ *He'll be delighted to see you.* Il sera ravi de vous voir.

delightful ADJECTIVE
(*meal, evening*)
délicieux MASC
délicieuse FEM

to **deliver** VERB
[1] **livrer**　◇ *I deliver newspapers.* Je livre les journaux.
[2] **distribuer** (*mail*)

delivery NOUN
la **livraison**

to **demand** VERB
see also demand NOUN
exiger

demand NOUN
see also demand VERB
la **demande** (*for product*)

demanding ADJECTIVE
astreignant　◇ *It's a very demanding job.* C'est un travail très astreignant.

demo NOUN
la **manif** (*protest*)

democracy NOUN
la **démocratie**

democratic ADJECTIVE
démocratique

to **demolish** VERB
démolir

to **demonstrate** VERB

[1] **faire une démonstration de** (*show*)
◇ *She demonstrated the technique.* Elle a fait une démonstration de la technique.
[2] **manifester** (*protest*)
- **to demonstrate against something** manifester contre quelque chose

demonstration NOUN
[1] la **démonstration** (*of method, technique*)
[2] la **manifestation** (*protest*)

demonstrator NOUN (*protester*)
le **manifestant**
la **manifestante**

denim NOUN
le **jean**　◇ *a denim jacket* une veste en jean

denims PL NOUN
le **jean** SING (*jeans*)

Denmark NOUN
le **Danemark**
- **in Denmark** au Danemark
- **to Denmark** au Danemark

dense ADJECTIVE
[1] (*crowd, fog*)
dense
[2] (*smoke*)
épais MASC
épaisse FEM
- **He's so dense!** Il est vraiment bouché!

dent NOUN
see also dent VERB
la **bosse**

to **dent** VERB
see also dent NOUN
cabosser

dental ADJECTIVE
dentaire
- **dental floss** le fil dentaire

dentist NOUN
le/la **dentiste**　◇ *Catherine is a dentist.* Catherine est dentiste.

to **deny** VERB
nier　◇ *She denied everything.* Elle a tout nié.

deodorant NOUN
le **déodorant**

to **depart** VERB
partir

department NOUN
[1] le **rayon** (*in shop*)　◇ *the shoe department* le rayon chaussures
[2] le **département** (*university, school*)
◇ *the English department* le département d'anglais

department store NOUN
le **grand magasin**

departure NOUN
le **départ**

to **depend** VERB

- **to depend on** dépendre de ◇ *The price depends on the quality.* Le prix dépend de la qualité.
- **depending on the weather** selon le temps
- **It depends.** Ça dépend.

to **deport** VERB
  expulser

deposit NOUN
  [1] les **arrhes** FEM PL (*part payment*) ◇ *You have to pay a deposit when you book.* Il faut verser des arrhes lors de la réservation.
  [2] la **caution** (*when hiring something*) ◇ *You get the deposit back when you return the bike.* On vous remboursera la caution quand vous ramènerez le vélo.
  [3] la **consigne** (*on bottle*)

depressed ADJECTIVE
  déprimé ◇ *I'm feeling depressed.* Je suis déprimé.

depressing ADJECTIVE
  déprimant

depth NOUN
  la **profondeur**

deputy head NOUN
  le **directeur adjoint**
  la **directrice adjointe**

to **descend** VERB
  descendre

to **describe** VERB
  décrire

description NOUN
  la **description**

desert NOUN
  le **désert**

desert island NOUN
  l' **île déserte** FEM

to **deserve** VERB
  mériter

design NOUN
  see also design VERB
  [1] la **conception** ◇ *It's a completely new design.* C'est une conception entièrement nouvelle.
  [2] le **motif** ◇ *a geometric design* un motif géométrique
- **fashion design** le stylisme

to **design** VERB
  see also design NOUN
  dessiner (*clothes, furniture*)

designer NOUN
  le/la **styliste** (*of clothes*)
- **designer clothes** les vêtements griffés

desire NOUN
  see also desire VERB
  le **désir**

to **desire** VERB
  see also desire NOUN

désirer

desk NOUN
  [1] (*in office*)
  le **bureau**
  (les **bureaux** PL)
  [2] (*for pupil*)
  le **pupitre**
  [3] (*in hotel*)
  la **réception**
  [4] (*at airport*)
  le **comptoir**

despair NOUN
  le **désespoir**
- **I was in despair.** J'étais désespéré.

desperate ADJECTIVE
  désespéré ◇ *a desperate situation* une situation désespérée
- **to get desperate** désespérer ◇ *I was getting desperate.* Je commençais à désespérer.

to **despise** VERB
  mépriser

despite PREPOSITION
  malgré

dessert NOUN
  le **dessert** ◇ *for dessert* comme dessert

destination NOUN
  la **destination**

to **destroy** VERB
  détruire

destruction NOUN
  la **destruction**

detached house NOUN
  le **pavillon**

detail NOUN
  le **détail** ◇ *in detail* en détail

detailed ADJECTIVE
  détaillé

detective NOUN
  l' **inspecteur de police**
- **a private detective** un détective privé
- **a detective story** un roman policier

detention NOUN
- **to get a detention** être consigné

detergent NOUN
  le **détergent**

determined ADJECTIVE
  déterminé
- **to be determined to do something** être déterminé à faire quelque chose ◇ *She's determined to succeed.* Elle est déterminée à réussir

detour NOUN
  le **détour**

devaluation NOUN
  la **dévaluation**

devastated ADJECTIVE
  anéanti ◇ *I was devastated.* J'étais

anéanti.

devastating ADJECTIVE

1 (*upsetting*)

accablant

2 (*flood, storm*)

dévastateur MASC

dévastatrice FEM

to **develop** VERB

1 **développer** ◇ *to get a film developed* faire développer un film

2 **se développer** ◇ *Girls develop faster than boys.* Les filles se développent plus vite que les garçons.

- **to develop into** se transformer en ◇ *The argument developed into a fight.* La dispute s'est transformée en bagarre.

- **a developing country** un pays en voie de développement

development NOUN

le **développement** ◇ *the latest developments* les derniers développements

devil NOUN

le **diable** ◇ *Poor devil!* Pauvre diable!

to **devise** VERB

concevoir

devoted ADJECTIVE

dévoué ◇ *He's completely devoted to her.* Il lui est très dévoué.

diabetes NOUN

le **diabète**

diabetic NOUN

le/la **diabétique** ◇ *I'm a diabetic.* Je suis diabétique.

diagonal ADJECTIVE

diagonal

(**diagonaux** MASC PL)

diagram NOUN

le **diagramme**

to **dial** VERB

composer (*number*)

dialling tone NOUN

la **tonalité**

dialogue NOUN

le **dialogue**

diamond NOUN

le **diamant** ◇ *a diamond ring* une bague en diamant

- **diamonds** (*at cards*) le carreau SING

diarrhoea NOUN

la **diarrhée** ◇ *I've got diarrhoea.* J'ai la diarrhée.

diary NOUN

1 l' **agenda** MASC ◇ *I've got her phone number in my diary.* J'ai son numéro de téléphone dans mon agenda.

2 le **journal**

(les **journaux** PL)

◇ *I keep a diary.* Je tiens un journal.

dice NOUN

le **dé**

dictation NOUN

la **dictée**

dictionary NOUN

le **dictionnaire**

did VERB *see* **do**

to **die** VERB

mourir ◇ *He died last year.* Il est mort l'année dernière.

- **to be dying to do something** mourir d'envie de faire quelque chose ◇ *I'm dying to see you.* Je meurs d'envie de te voir.

diesel NOUN

1 le **gazole** (*fuel*) ◇ *30 litres of diesel, please.* Trente litres de gazole, s'il vous plaît.

2 la **voiture diesel** (*car*) ◇ *Our car's a diesel.* Nous avons une voiture diesel.

diet NOUN

1 l' **alimentation** FEM ◇ *a healthy diet* une alimentation saine

2 le **régime** (*for slimming*) ◇ *I'm on a diet.* Je suis au régime.

difference NOUN

la **différence** ◇ *There's not much difference in age between us.* Il n'y a pas une grande différence d'âge entre nous.

- **It makes no difference.** Ça revient au même.

different ADJECTIVE

différent ◇ *We are very different.* Nous sommes très différents. ◇ *Paris is different from London.* Paris est différent de Londres.

difficult ADJECTIVE

difficile ◇ *It's difficult to choose.* C'est difficile de choisir.

difficulty NOUN

la **difficulté** ◇ *without difficulty* sans difficulté

- **to have difficulty doing something** avoir du mal à faire quelque chose

to **dig** VERB

1 **creuser** (*hole*)

2 **bêcher** (*garden*)

- **to dig something up** déterrer quelque chose

digestion NOUN

la **digestion**

digital watch NOUN

la **montre à affichage numérique**

dim ADJECTIVE

1 **faible** (*light*)

2 **limité** (*stupid*)

dimension NOUN
la **dimension**

to **diminish** VERB
diminuer

din NOUN
le **vacarme**

dinghy NOUN
- **a rubber dinghy** un canot pneumatique
- **a sailing dinghy** un dériveur

dining car NOUN
le **wagon-restaurant**

dining room NOUN
la **salle à manger**

dinner NOUN
1 le **déjeuner** (at midday)
2 le **dîner** (in the evening)

dinner party NOUN
le **dîner**

dinner time NOUN
1 l' **heure du déjeuner** FEM (midday)
2 l' **heure du dîner** FEM (in the evening)

dinosaur NOUN
le **dinosaure**

diploma NOUN
le **diplôme** ⋄ a diploma in social work un diplôme d'assistante sociale

diplomat NOUN
le/la **diplomate**

diplomatic ADJECTIVE
diplomatique

direct ADJECTIVE, ADVERB
see also direct VERB
direct ⋄ the most direct route le chemin le plus direct ⋄ You can't fly to Marseilles direct from Manchester. Il n'y a pas de vols directs de Manchester à Marseille.

to **direct** VERB
see also direct ADJECTIVE
1 **réaliser** (film, programme)
2 **mettre en scène** (play, show)

direction NOUN
la **direction** ⋄ We're going in the wrong direction. Nous allons dans la mauvaise direction.
- **to ask somebody for directions** demander son chemin à quelqu'un

director NOUN
1 (of company)
le **directeur**
la **directrice**
2 (of play)
le **metteur en scène**
(les **metteurs en scène** PL)
3 (of film, programme)
le **réalisateur**
la **réalisatrice**

directory NOUN

l' **annuaire** MASC

dirt NOUN
la **saleté**

dirty ADJECTIVE
sale
- **to get dirty** se salir
- **to get something dirty** salir quelque chose

disabled ADJECTIVE
handicapé
- **the disabled** les handicapés

disadvantage NOUN
le **désavantage**

to **disagree** VERB
- **We always disagree.** Nous ne sommes jamais d'accord.
- **I disagree!** Je ne suis pas d'accord!
- **He disagrees with me.** Il n'est pas d'accord avec moi.

disagreement NOUN
le **désaccord**

to **disappear** VERB
disparaître

disappearance NOUN
la **disparition**

disappointed ADJECTIVE
déçu

disappointing ADJECTIVE
décevant

disappointment NOUN
la **déception**

disaster NOUN
le **désastre**

disastrous ADJECTIVE
désastreux MASC
désastreuse FEM

discipline NOUN
la **discipline**

disc jockey NOUN
le **disc-jockey**

disco NOUN
la **soirée disco** ⋄ There's a disco at the school tonight. Il y a une soirée disco à l'école ce soir.

to **disconnect** VERB
1 **débrancher** (electrical equipment)
2 **couper** (telephone, water supply)

discount NOUN
la **réduction** ⋄ a discount for students une réduction pour les étudiants

to **discourage** VERB
décourager
- **to get discouraged** se décourager
⋄ Don't get discouraged! Ne te décourage pas!

to **discover** VERB
découvrir

discrimination NOUN
la **discrimination** ⋄ racial

discrimination la discrimination raciale

to **discuss** VERB

1 **discuter de** ◇ *I'll discuss it with my parents.* Je vais en discuter avec mes parents.

2 **discuter sur** (*topic*) ◇ *We discussed the problem of pollution.* Nous avons discuté du problème de la pollution.

discussion NOUN
la **discussion**

disease NOUN
la **maladie**

disgraceful ADJECTIVE
scandaleux MASC
scandaleuse FEM

to **disguise** VERB
déguiser ◇ *He was disguised as a policeman.* Il était déguisé en policier.

disgusted ADJECTIVE
dégoûté ◇ *I was absolutely disgusted.* J'étais complètement dégoûté.

disgusting ADJECTIVE

1 **dégoûtant** (*food, smell*) ◇ *It looks disgusting.* Ça a l'air dégoûtant.

2 **honteux** (*disgraceful*) ◇ *That's disgusting!* C'est honteux!

dish NOUN
le **plat** ◇ *a china dish* un plat en porcelaine ◇ *a vegetarian dish* un plat végétarien

- **to do the dishes** faire la vaisselle ◇ *He never does the dishes.* Il ne fait jamais la vaisselle.

dishonest ADJECTIVE
malhonnête

dishwasher NOUN
le **lave-vaisselle**
(les **lave-vaisselle** PL)

disinfectant NOUN
le **désinfectant**

disk NOUN
le **disque**

- **a floppy disk** une disquette
- **the hard disk** le disque dur

to **dislike** VERB
see also dislike NOUN
ne pas aimer ◇ *I really dislike cabbage.* Je n'aime vraiment pas le chou.

dislike NOUN
see also dislike VERB

- **my likes and dislikes** ce que j'aime et ce que je n'aime pas

to **dismiss** VERB
renvoyer (*employee*)

disobedient ADJECTIVE
désobéissant

display NOUN
see also display VERB

l' **étalage** MASC ◇ *There was a lovely display of fruit in the window.* Il y avait un superbe étalage de fruits en vitrine.

- **to be on display** être exposé ◇ *Her best paintings were on display.* Ses meilleurs tableaux étaient exposés.
- **a firework display** un feu d'artifice

to **display** VERB
see also display NOUN

1 **montrer** ◇ *She proudly displayed her medal.* Elle a montré sa médaille avec fierté.

2 **exposer** (*in shop window*)

disposable ADJECTIVE
jetable

to **disqualify** VERB
disqualifier

- **to be disqualified** être disqualifié ◇ *He was disqualified.* Il a été disqualifié.

to **disrupt** VERB
perturber ◇ *Protesters disrupted the meeting.* Des manifestants ont perturbé la réunion. ◇ *Train services are being disrupted by the strike.* Les horaires de train sont perturbés par la grève.

dissatisfied ADJECTIVE

- **We were dissatisfied with the service.** Nous n'étions pas satisfaits du service.

to **dissolve** VERB
dissoudre

distance NOUN
la **distance** ◇ *a distance of 40 kilometres* une distance de quarante kilomètres

- **It's within walking distance.** On peut y aller à pied.
- **in the distance** au loin

distant ADJECTIVE
lointain ◇ *in the distant future* dans un avenir lointain

distillery NOUN
la **distillerie** ◇ *a whisky distillery* une distillerie de whisky

distinction NOUN

1 la **distinction** ◇ *to make a distinction between...* faire la distinction entre...

2 la **mention très bien** ◇ *I got a distinction in my piano exam.* J'ai eu la mention très bien à mon examen de piano.

distinctive ADJECTIVE
distinctif MASC
distinctive FEM

to **distract** VERB
distraire

to **distribute** VERB
distribuer

district NOUN
[1] le **quartier** (of town)
[2] la **région** (of country)

to **disturb** VERB
déranger ◇ I'm sorry to disturb you. Je suis désolé de vous déranger.

ditch NOUN
| see also ditch VERB |
le **fossé**

to **ditch** VERB
| see also ditch NOUN |
plaquer (informal) ◇ She's just ditched her boyfriend. Elle vient de plaquer son copain.

dive NOUN
| see also dive VERB |
le **plongeon**

to **dive** VERB
| see also dive NOUN |
plonger

diver NOUN
le **plongeur**
la **plongeuse**

diversion NOUN
la **déviation** (for traffic)

to **divide** VERB
[1] **diviser** ◇ Divide the pastry in half. Divisez la pâte en deux. ◇ 12 divided by 3 is 4. Douze divisé par trois égalent quatre.
[2] **se diviser** ◇ We divided into two groups. Nous nous sommes divisés en deux groupes.

diving NOUN
la **plongée**
- **a diving board** un plongeoir

division NOUN
la **division**

divorce NOUN
le **divorce**

divorced ADJECTIVE
divorcé ◇ My parents are divorced. Mes parents sont divorcés.

DIY NOUN
le **bricolage** ◇ to do DIY faire du bricolage ◇ a DIY shop un magasin de bricolage

dizzy ADJECTIVE
- **to feel dizzy** avoir la tête qui tourne ◇ I feel dizzy. J'ai la tête qui tourne.

DJ NOUN
le **disc-jockey**

to **do** VERB
[1] **faire** ◇ What are you doing this evening? Qu'est-ce que tu fais ce soir? ◇ I do a lot of cycling. Je fais beaucoup de vélo. ◇ I haven't done my homework. Je n'ai pas fait mes devoirs. ◇ She did it by herself. Elle l'a fait

toute seule. ◇ I'll do my best. Je ferai de mon mieux.
- **to do well** marcher bien ◇ The firm is doing well. L'entreprise marche bien. ◇ She's doing well at school. Ses études marchent bien.
[2] **aller** (be enough) ◇ It's not very good, but it'll do. Ce n'est pas très bon, mais ça ira.
- **That'll do, thanks.** Ça ira, merci.

*In English do is used to make questions. In French questions are made either with **est-ce que** or by reversing the order of verb and subject.*

◇ Do you like French food? Est-ce que vous aimez la cuisine française? ◇ Where does he live? Où est-ce qu'il habite? ◇ Do you speak English? Parlez-vous anglais? ◇ What do you do in your free time? Qu'est-ce que vous faites pendant vos loisirs? ◇ Where did you go for your holidays? Où es-tu allé pendant tes vacances?

*Use **ne...pas** in negative sentences for don't.*

◇ I don't understand. Je ne comprends pas. ◇ Why didn't you come? Pourquoi n'êtes-vous pas venus?

do is not translated when it is used in place of another verb.

◇ I hate maths.–So do I. Je déteste les maths.–Moi aussi. ◇ I didn't like the film. –Neither did I. Je n'ai pas aimé le film.–Moi non plus. ◇ Do you like horses?–No I don't. Est-ce que tu aimes les chevaux?–Non.

*Use **n'est-ce pas** to check information.*

◇ You go swimming on Fridays, don't you? Tu fais de la natation le vendredi, n'est-ce pas? ◇ The bus stops at the youth hostel, doesn't it? Le bus s'arrête à l'auberge de jeunesse, n'est-ce pas?

- **How do you do?** Enchanté!
- **to do up (1)** (shoes) lacer ◇ Do up your shoes! Lace tes chaussures!
- **to do up (2)** (renovate) retaper ◇ They're doing up an old cottage. Ils retapent une vieille maison.
- **to do up (3)** (shirt, cardigan) boutonner
- **Do up your zip!** (on trousers) Ferme ta braguette!
- **to do without** se passer de ◇ I couldn't do without my computer. Je ne pourrais pas me passer de mon ordinateur.

dock NOUN
le **dock** (for ships)

doctor NOUN
le **médecin** ◇ She's a doctor. Elle est médecin. ◇ I'd like to be a doctor. Je voudrais être médecin.

document NOUN
le **document**
documentary NOUN
le **documentaire**
to **dodge** VERB
échapper à (*attacker*)
dodgems PL NOUN
les **autos tamponneuses** FEM PL ◇ *to go on the dodgems* aller faire un tour d'autos tamponneuses
does VERB *see* **do**
doesn't = does not
dog NOUN
le **chien**
la **chienne** (*female*)
◇ *Have you got a dog?* Est-ce que tu as un chien?
do-it-yourself NOUN
le **bricolage**
dole NOUN
les **allocations chômage** FEM PL
- **to be on the dole** toucher le chômage
◇ *A lot of people are on the dole.* Beaucoup de gens touchent le chômage.
- **to go on the dole** s'inscrire au chômage
doll NOUN
la **poupée**
dollar NOUN
le **dollar**
dolphin NOUN
le **dauphin**
domestic ADJECTIVE
- **a domestic flight** un vol intérieur
dominoes PL NOUN
- **to have a game of dominoes** faire une partie de dominos
to **donate** VERB
donner
done VERB *see* **do**
donkey NOUN
l' **âne** MASC
don't = do not
door NOUN
1 la **porte** ◇ *the first door on the right* la première porte à droite
2 la **portière** (*of car, train*)
doorbell NOUN
la **sonnette**
- **to ring the doorbell** sonner
- **Suddenly the doorbell rang.** Soudain, on a sonné.
doorman NOUN
le **portier**
doorstep NOUN
le **pas de la porte**
dormitory NOUN
le **dortoir**
dose NOUN

la **dose**
dosh NOUN
le **fric** (*informal: money*)
dot NOUN
le **point** (*on letter "i", in e-mail address*)
- **on the dot** à l'heure pile ◇ *He arrived at 9 o'clock on the dot.* Il est arrivé à neuf heures pile.
to **double** VERB
see also **double** ADJECTIVE
doubler ◇ *The number of attacks has doubled.* Le nombre d'agressions a doublé.
double ADJECTIVE, ADVERB
see also **double** VERB
double ◇ *a double helping* une double portion
- **to cost double** coûter le double
◇ *First-class tickets cost double.* Les billets de première classe coûtent le double.
- **a double bed** un grand lit
- **a double room** une chambre pour deux personnes
- **a double-decker bus** un autobus à impériale
double bass NOUN
la **contrebasse** ◇ *I play the double bass.* Je joue de la contrebasse.
double glazing NOUN
le **double vitrage**
doubles PL NOUN
le **double** SING (*in tennis*) ◇ *to play mixed doubles* jouer en double mixte
doubt NOUN
see also **doubt** VERB
le **doute** ◇ *I have my doubts.* J'ai des doutes.
to **doubt** VERB
see also **doubt** NOUN
douter de
- **I doubt it.** J'en doute.
- **to doubt that** douter que
douter que *has to be followed by a verb in the subjunctive.*
◇ *I doubt he'll agree.* Je doute qu'il soit d'accord.
doubtful ADJECTIVE
- **to be doubtful about doing something** hésiter à faire quelque chose ◇ *I'm doubtful about going by myself.* J'hésite à y aller tout seul.
- **It's doubtful.** Ce n'est pas sûr.
- **You sound doubtful.** Tu n'as pas l'air sûr.
dough NOUN
la **pâte**
doughnut NOUN
le **beignet** ◇ *a jam doughnut* un

beignet à la confiture

Dover NOUN

Douvres ◇ *We went from Dover to Boulogne.* Nous sommes allés de Douvres à Boulogne.
- **in Dover** à Douvres

down ADVERB, ADJECTIVE, PREPOSITION

[1] **en bas** (*below*) ◇ *His office is down on the first floor.* Son bureau est en bas, au premier étage. ◇ *It's down there.* C'est là bas.

[2] **à terre** (*to the ground*) ◇ *He threw down his racket.* Il a jeté sa raquette à terre.
- **They live just down the road.** Ils habitent tout à côté.
- **to come down** descendre ◇ *Come down here!* Descends!
- **to go down** descendre ◇ *The rabbit went down the hole.* Le lapin est descendu dans le terrier.
- **to sit down** s'asseoir ◇ *Sit down!* Asseyez-vous!
- **to feel down** avoir le cafard ◇ *I'm feeling a bit down.* J'ai un peu le cafard.
- **The computer's down.** L'ordinateur est en panne.

downpour NOUN

la **pluie torrentielle** ◇ *a sudden downpour* une pluie soudaine et torrentielle

downstairs ADVERB, ADJECTIVE

[1] **au rez-de-chaussée** ◇ *The bathroom's downstairs.* La salle de bain est au rez-de-chaussée.

[2] **du rez-de-chaussée** ◇ *the downstairs bathroom* la salle de bain du rez-de-chaussée
- **the people downstairs** les voisins du dessous

to **doze** VERB

sommeiller
- **to doze off** s'assoupir

dozen NOUN

la **douzaine** ◇ *two dozen* deux douzaines ◇ *a dozen eggs* une douzaine d'œufs
- **I've told you that dozens of times.** Je t'ai dit ça des centaines de fois.

drab ADJECTIVE

terne (*clothes*)

to **drag** VERB

see also drag NOUN

traîner (*thing, person*)

drag NOUN

see also drag VERB
- **It's a real drag!** C'est la barbe! (*informal*)
- **in drag** travesti ◇ *He was in drag.* Il était travesti.

dragon NOUN

le **dragon**

drain NOUN

see also drain VERB

l' **égout** MASC ◇ *The drains are blocked.* Les égouts sont bouchés.

to **drain** VERB

see also drain NOUN

égoutter (*vegetables, pasta*)

draining board NOUN

l' **égouttoir** MASC

drainpipe NOUN

le **tuyau d'écoulement**

drama NOUN

l' **art dramatique** MASC ◇ *Drama is my favourite subject.* L'art dramatique est ma matière préférée.
- **drama school** l'école d'art dramatique ◇ *I'd like to go to drama school.* J'aimerais entrer dans une école d'art dramatique.
- **Greek drama** le théâtre grec

dramatic ADJECTIVE

spectaculaire ◇ *It was really dramatic!* C'était vraiment spectaculaire! ◇ *a dramatic improvement* une amélioration spectaculaire
- **dramatic news** une nouvelle extraordinaire

drank VERB *see* **drink**

drastic ADJECTIVE

radical (*change*)
- **to take drastic action** prendre des mesures énergiques

draught NOUN

le **courant d'air**

draughts NOUN

les **dames** FEM PL ◇ *to play draughts* jouer aux dames

to **draw** VERB

see also draw NOUN

[1] **dessiner** ◇ *He's good at drawing.* Il dessine bien.
- **to draw a picture** faire un dessin
- **to draw a picture of somebody** faire le portrait de quelqu'un
- **to draw a line** tirer un trait

[2] **faire match nul** (*sport*) ◇ *We drew 2-2.* Nous avons fait match nul deux à deux.
- **to draw the curtains** tirer les rideaux
- **to draw lots** tirer au sort

draw NOUN

see also draw VERB

[1] le **match nul** (*sport*) ◇ *The game ended in a draw.* La partie s'est soldée par un match nul.

[2] le **tirage au sort** (*in lottery*) ◇ *The draw takes place on Saturday.* Le tirage

au sort a lieu samedi.

drawback NOUN
l' **inconvénient** MASC

drawer NOUN
le **tiroir**

drawing NOUN
le **dessin**

drawing pin NOUN
la **punaise**

drawn VERB see **draw**

dreadful ADJECTIVE
☐1 **terrible** ◇ a dreadful mistake une terrible erreur
☐2 **affreux** MASC
affreuse FEM
◇ The weather was dreadful. Il a fait un temps affreux.
• **I feel dreadful.** Je ne me sens vraiment pas bien.
• **You look dreadful.** (ill) Tu as une mine affreuse.

to **dream** VERB
see also **dream** NOUN
rêver ◇ I dreamed I was in Belgium. J'ai rêvé que j'étais en Belgique.

dream NOUN
see also **dream** VERB
le **rêve** ◇ It was just a dream. Ce n'était qu'un rêve.
• **a bad dream** un cauchemar

to **drench** VERB
• **to get drenched** se faire tremper
◇ We got drenched. Nous nous sommes fait tremper.

dress NOUN
see also **dress** VERB
la **robe**

to **dress** VERB
see also **dress** NOUN
s'habiller ◇ I got up, dressed, and went downstairs. Je me suis levé, je me suis habillé et je suis descendu.
• **to dress somebody** habiller quelqu'un
◇ She dressed the children. Elle a habillé les enfants.
• **to get dressed** s'habiller ◇ I got dressed quickly. Je me suis habillé rapidement.
• **to dress up** se déguiser ◇ I dressed up as a ghost. Je me suis déguisé en fantôme.

dressed ADJECTIVE
habillé ◇ I'm not dressed yet. Je ne suis pas encore habillé. ◇ How was she dressed? Comment est-ce qu'elle était habillée?
• **She was dressed in a green sweater and jeans.** Elle portait un pull vert et un jean.

dresser NOUN
le **vaisselier** (furniture)

dressing gown NOUN
la **robe de chambre**

dressing table NOUN
la **coiffeuse**

drew VERB see **draw**

drier NOUN
le **séchoir**

drift NOUN
see also **drift** VERB
• **a snow drift** une congère

to **drift** VERB
see also **drift** NOUN
☐1 **aller à la dérive** (boat)
☐2 **s'amonceler** (snow)

drill NOUN
see also **drill** VERB
la **perceuse**

to **drill** VERB
see also **drill** NOUN
percer

to **drink** VERB
see also **drink** NOUN
boire ◇ What would you like to drink? Qu'est-ce que voulez boire? ◇ She drank three cups of tea. Elle a bu trois tasses de thé. ◇ He'd been drinking. Il avait bu.
• **I don't drink.** Je ne bois pas d'alcool.

drink NOUN
see also **drink** VERB
☐1 la **boisson** ◇ a cold drink une boisson fraîche ◇ a hot drink une boisson chaude
☐2 le **verre** (alcoholic) ◇ They've gone out for a drink. Ils sont allés prendre un verre.
• **to have a drink** prendre un verre

drive NOUN
see also **drive** VERB
☐1 le **tour en voiture**
• **to go for a drive** aller faire un tour en voiture ◇ We went for a drive in the country. Nous sommes allés faire un tour à la campagne.
• **We've got a long drive tomorrow.** Nous avons une longue route à faire demain.
☐2 l' **allée** FEM (of house) ◇ He parked his car in the drive. Il a garé sa voiture dans l'allée.

to **drive** VERB
see also **drive** NOUN
☐1 **conduire** (a car) ◇ She's learning to drive. Elle apprend à conduire. ◇ Can you drive? Tu sais conduire?
☐2 **aller en voiture** (go by car) ◇ Did you go by train?—No, we drove. Vous

D

êtes partis en train?–Non, nous y sommes allés en avion.

3 **emmener en voiture** ◇ *My mother drives me to school.* Ma mère m'emmène à l'école en voiture.

- **to drive somebody home** raccompagner quelqu'un ◇ *He offered to drive me home.* Il m'a proposé de me raccompagner.

- **to drive somebody mad** rendre quelqu'un fou ◇ *He drives her mad.* Il la rend folle.

driver NOUN

1 le **conducteur**
la **conductrice**
◇ *She's an excellent driver.* C'est une excellente conductrice.

2 le **chauffeur** (*of taxi, bus*) ◇ *He's a bus driver.* Il est chauffeur d'autobus.

driving instructor NOUN
le **moniteur d'auto-école** ◇ *He's a driving instructor.* Il est moniteur d'auto-école.

driving lesson NOUN
la **leçon de conduite**

driving licence NOUN
le **permis de conduire**

driving test NOUN

- **to take one's driving test** passer son permis de conduire ◇ *He's taking his driving test tomorrow.* Il passe son permis de conduire demain.

- **She's just passed her driving test.** Elle vient d'avoir son permis.

drop NOUN
see also drop VERB
la **goutte** ◇ *a drop of water* une goutte d'eau

to **drop** VERB
see also drop NOUN
1 **laisser tomber** ◇ *I dropped the glass and it broke.* J'ai laissé tomber le verre et il s'est cassé. ◇ *I'm going to drop chemistry.* Je vais laisser tomber la chimie.
2 **déposer** ◇ *Could you drop me at the station?* Pouvez-vous me déposer à la gare?

drought NOUN
la **sécheresse**

drove VERB see **drive**

to **drown** VERB
se noyer ◇ *A boy drowned here yesterday.* Un jeune garçon s'est noyé ici hier.

drug NOUN
1 le **médicament** (*medicine*) ◇ *They need food and drugs.* Ils ont besoin de nourriture et de médicaments.

2 la **drogue** (*illegal*) ◇ *hard drugs* les drogues dures ◇ *soft drugs* les drogues douces

- **to take drugs** se droguer

- **a drug addict** un drogué ◇ *She's a drug addict.* C'est une droguée.

- **a drug pusher** un dealer

- **a drug smuggler** un trafiquant de drogue

- **the drugs squad** la brigade antidrogue

drum NOUN
le **tambour** ◇ *an African drum* un tambour africain

- **a drum kit** une batterie

- **drums** la batterie SING ◇ *I play drums.* Je joue de la batterie.

drummer NOUN
(*in rock group*)
le **batteur**
la **batteuse**

drunk ADJECTIVE
see also drunk NOUN
ivre ◇ *He was drunk.* Il était ivre.

drunk NOUN
see also drunk ADJECTIVE
l' **ivrogne** MASC/FEM ◇ *The streets were full of drunks.* Les rues étaient pleines d'ivrognes.

dry ADJECTIVE
see also dry VERB
1 **sec** MASC
sèche FEM
◇ *The paint isn't dry yet.* La peinture n'est pas encore sèche.
2 **sans pluie** (*weather*) ◇ *a long dry period* une longue période sans pluie

to **dry** VERB
see also dry ADJECTIVE
1 **sécher** ◇ *The washing will dry quickly in the sun.* Le linge va sécher vite au soleil. ◇ *some dried flowers* des fleurs séchées

- **to dry one's hair** se sécher les cheveux ◇ *I haven't dried my hair yet.* Je ne me suis pas encore séché les cheveux.

2 **faire sécher** (*clothes*) ◇ *There's nowhere to dry clothes here.* Il n'y a pas d'endroit où faire sécher les vêtements ici.

- **to dry the dishes** essuyer la vaisselle

dry-cleaner's NOUN
la **teinturerie**

dryer NOUN
le **séchoir** (*for clothes*)

- **a tumble dryer** séchoir à linge

- **a hair dryer** un sèche-cheveux

dubbed ADJECTIVE
doublé ◇ *The film was dubbed into French.* Le film était doublé en français.

dubious ADJECTIVE
réticent ◇ *My parents were a bit dubious about it.* Mes parents étaient un peu réticents à ce sujet.

duck NOUN
le canard

due ADJECTIVE, ADVERB
- **to be due to do something** devoir faire quelque chose ◇ *He's due to arrive tomorrow.* Il doit arriver demain.
- **The plane's due in half an hour.** L'avion doit arriver dans une demi-heure.
- **When's the baby due?** Le bébé est prévu pour quand?
- **due to** à cause de ◇ *The trip was cancelled due to bad weather.* Le voyage a été annulé à cause du mauvais temps.

dug VERB *see* **dig**

dull ADJECTIVE
1 ennuyeux MASC
ennuyeuse FEM
◇ *He's nice, but a bit dull.* Il est sympathique, mais un peu ennuyeux.
2 maussade (*weather, day*)

dumb ADJECTIVE
1 muet MASC
muette FEM
- **She's deaf and dumb.** Elle est sourde-muette.
2 bête (*stupid*) ◇ *That was a really dumb thing I did!* C'était vraiment bête de ma part!

dummy NOUN
la tétine (*for baby*)

dump NOUN
see also dump VERB
- **It's a real dump!** C'est un endroit minable!
- **a rubbish dump** un décharge

to dump VERB
see also dump NOUN
1 déposer (*waste*) ◇ *"no dumping"* "défense de déposer des ordures"
2 plaquer (*informer*) ◇ *He's just dumped his girlfriend.* Il vient de plaquer sa copine.

dungarees PL NOUN
la salopette SING

dungeon NOUN
le cachot

duration NOUN
la durée

during PREPOSITION

pendant ◇ *during the day* pendant la journée

dusk NOUN
le crépuscule ◇ *at dusk* au crépuscule

dust NOUN
see also dust VERB
la poussière

to dust VERB
see also dust NOUN
épousseter ◇ *I dusted the shelves.* J'ai épousseté les étagères.
- **I hate dusting!** Je déteste faire les poussières!

dustbin NOUN
la poubelle

dustman NOUN
l' éboueur MASC ◇ *He's a dustman.* Il est éboueur.

dusty ADJECTIVE
poussiéreux MASC
poussiéreuse FEM

Dutch ADJECTIVE
see also Dutch NOUN
hollandais ◇ *She's Dutch.* Elle est hollandaise.

Dutch NOUN
see also Dutch ADJECTIVE
le hollandais (*language*)
- **the Dutch** les Hollandais

Dutchman NOUN
le Hollandais

Dutchwoman NOUN
la Hollandaise

duty NOUN
le devoir ◇ *It was his duty to tell the police.* C'est son devoir de prévenir la police.
- **to be on duty (1)** (*policeman*) être de service
- **to be on duty (2)** (*doctor, nurse*) être de garde

duty-free ADJECTIVE
hors taxes FEM+PL
- **the duty-free shop** la boutique hors taxes

duvet NOUN
la couette

dwarf NOUN
le nain
la naine

dynamic ADJECTIVE
dynamique

dyslexia NOUN
la dyslexie

D

E

each ADJECTIVE, PRONOUN

[1] **chaque** ◇ *each day* chaque jour ◇ *Each house in our street has its own garden.* Chaque maison dans notre rue a son propre jardin.

[2] **chacun** MASC
chacune FEM
◇ *The girls each have their own bedroom.* Les filles ont chacune leur chambre. ◇ *They have 10 points each.* Ils ont dix points chacun. ◇ *The plates cost £5 each.* Les assiettes coûtent cinq livres chacune. ◇ *He gave each of us £10.* Il nous a donné dix livres à chacun.

Use a reflexive verb to translate each other.

- **They hate each other.** Ils se détestent.
- **We wrote to each other.** Nous nous sommes écrit.
- **They don't know each other.** Ils ne se connaissent pas.

ear NOUN
l' **oreille** FEM

earache NOUN
- **to have earache** avoir mal aux oreilles

earlier ADVERB
[1] **tout à l'heure** ◇ *I saw him earlier.* Je l'ai vu tout à l'heure.
[2] **plus tôt** (*in the morning*) ◇ *I ought to get up earlier.* Je devrais me lever plus tôt.

early ADVERB, ADJECTIVE
[1] **tôt** (*early in the day*) ◇ *I have to get up early.* Je dois me lever tôt.
- **to have an early night** se coucher tôt
[2] **en avance** (*ahead of time*) ◇ *I came early to get a good seat.* Je suis venu en avance pour avoir une bonne place.

to **earn** VERB
gagner ◇ *She earns £5 an hour.* Elle gagne cinq livres de l'heure.

earnings PL NOUN
le **salaire** SING

earring NOUN
la **boucle d'oreille**

earth NOUN
la **terre**

earthquake NOUN
le **tremblement de terre**

easily ADVERB
facilement

east ADJECTIVE, ADVERB
see also **east** NOUN
[1] **est** MASC, FEM, PL ◇ *the east coast* la côte est
- **an east wind** un vent d'est

- **east of** à l'est de ◇ *It's east of London.* C'est à l'est de Londres.
[2] **vers l'est** ◇ *We were travelling east.* Nous allions vers l'est.

east NOUN
see also **east** ADJECTIVE
l' **est** MASC ◇ *in the east* dans l'est

Easter NOUN
Pâques FEM ◇ *at Easter* à Pâques ◇ *We went to my grandparents' for Easter.* Nous sommes allés chez mes grands-parents à Pâques.

Easter egg NOUN
l' **œuf de Pâques** MASC

eastern ADJECTIVE
- **the eastern part of the island** la partie est de l'île
- **Eastern Europe** l'Europe de l'Est

easy ADJECTIVE
facile

easy chair NOUN
le **fauteuil**

easy-going ADJECTIVE
facile à vivre
(**faciles à vivre** PL)
◇ *She's very easy-going.* Elle est très facile à vivre.

to **eat** VERB
manger
- **Would you like something to eat?** Est-ce que tu veux manger quelque chose?

EC NOUN (= *European Community*)
la **CE** (= Communauté européenne)

eccentric ADJECTIVE
excentrique

echo NOUN
l' **écho** MASC

ecology NOUN
l' **écologie** FEM

economic ADJECTIVE
rentable (*profitable*)

economics NOUN
l' **économie** FEM ◇ *He's studying economics.* Il fait des études d'économie.

to **economize** VERB
faire des économies ◇ *to economize on something* faire des économies sur quelque chose

economy NOUN
l' **économie** FEM

ecstasy NOUN
l' **ecstasy** (*drug*)
- **to be in ecstasy** s'extasier

ecu NOUN (= *European Currency Unit*)

l' **écu** MASC
eczema NOUN
  l' **eczéma** MASC
edge NOUN
  le **bord**
edgy ADJECTIVE
  tendu
Edinburgh NOUN
  Édimbourg
editor NOUN
  (*of newspaper*)
  le **rédacteur en chef**
  la **rédactrice en chef**
educated ADJECTIVE
  cultivé
education NOUN
  1 l' **éducation** FEM ◇ *There should be more investment in education.* On devrait investir plus dans l'éducation.
  2 l' **enseignement** MASC (*teaching*) ◇ *She works in education.* Elle travaille dans l'enseignement.
educational ADJECTIVE
  (*experience, toy*)
  éducatif MASC
  éducative FEM
  ◇ *It was very educational.* C'était très éducatif.
effect NOUN
  l' **effet** MASC ◇ *special effects* les effets spéciaux
effective ADJECTIVE
  efficace
efficient ADJECTIVE
  efficace
effort NOUN
  l' **effort** MASC
e.g. ABBREVIATION
  p. ex. (= par exemple)
egg NOUN
  l' **œuf** MASC ◇ *a hard-boiled egg* un œuf dur ◇ *a soft-boiled egg* un œuf à la coque ◇ *a fried egg* un œuf sur le plat
- **scrambled eggs** les œufs brouillés
egg cup NOUN
  le **coquetier**
Egypt NOUN
  l' **Égypte** FEM
- **in Egypt** en Égypte
Eiffel Tower NOUN
  la **tour Eiffel**
eight NUMBER
  huit ◇ *She's eight.* Elle a huit ans.
eighteen NUMBER
  dix-huit ◇ *She's eighteen.* Elle a dix-huit ans.
eighth ADJECTIVE
  huitième ◇ *the eighth floor* le

huitième étage
- **the eighth of August** le huit août
eighty NUMBER
  quatre-vingts
Eire NOUN
  la **République d'Irlande**
- **in Eire** en République d'Irlande
either ADVERB, CONJUNCTION, PRONOUN
  non plus ◇ *I don't like milk, and I don't like eggs either.* Je n'aime pas le lait, et je n'aime pas les œufs non plus. ◇ *I've never been to Spain.–I haven't either.* Je ne suis jamais allé en Espagne.–Moi non plus.
- **either...or...** soit...soit... ◇ *You can have either ice cream or yoghurt.* Tu peux prendre soit une glace soit un yaourt.
- **either of them** l'un ou l'autre ◇ *Take either of them.* Prends l'un ou l'autre.
- **I don't like either of them.** Je n'aime ni l'un ni l'autre.
elastic NOUN
  l' **élastique** MASC
elastic band NOUN
  l' **élastique** MASC
elbow NOUN
  le **coude**
elder ADJECTIVE
  aîné ◇ *my elder sister* ma sœur aînée
elderly ADJECTIVE
  âgé
- **the elderly** les personnes âgées
eldest ADJECTIVE
  aîné ◇ *my eldest sister* ma sœur aînée ◇ *He's the eldest.* C'est l'aîné.
to **elect** VERB
  élire
election NOUN
  l' **élection** FEM
electric ADJECTIVE
  électrique ◇ *an electric fire* un radiateur électrique ◇ *an electric guitar* une guitare électrique
- **an electric blanket** une couverture chauffante
electrical ADJECTIVE
  électrique
- **an electrical engineer** un ingénieur électricien
electrician NOUN
  l' **électricien** MASC ◇ *He's an electrician.* Il est électricien.
electricity NOUN
  l' **électricité** FEM
electronic ADJECTIVE
  électronique

electronics NOUN
l' **électronique** FEM ◇ *My hobby is electronics.* Ma passion, c'est l'électronique.

elegant ADJECTIVE
élégant

elephant NOUN
l' **éléphant** MASC

eleven NUMBER
onze ◇ *She's 11.* Elle a onze ans.

eleventh ADJECTIVE
onzième ◇ *the 11th floor* le onzième étage ◇ *the 11th of August* le onze août

else ADVERB
d'autre ◇ *somebody else* quelqu'un d'autre ◇ *nobody else* personne d'autre ◇ *nothing else* rien d'autre
- **something else** autre chose
- **anything else** autre chose ◇ *Would you like anything else?* Désirez-vous autre chose?
- **I don't want anything else.** Je ne veux pas rien d'autre.
- **somewhere else** ailleurs
- **anywhere else** autre part

e-mail NOUN
le **courrier électronique**

embankment NOUN
le **talus**

embarrassed ADJECTIVE
gêné ◇ *I was really embarrassed.* J'étais vraiment gêné.

embarrassing ADJECTIVE
gênant ◇ *It was so embarrassing.* C'était tellement gênant.

embassy NOUN
l' **ambassade** FEM ◇ *the British Embassy* l'ambassade de Grande-Bretagne ◇ *the French Embassy* l'ambassade de France

to **embroider** VERB
broder

embroidery NOUN
la **broderie** ◇ *I do embroidery.* Je fais de la broderie.

emergency NOUN
l' **urgence** FEM ◇ *This is an emergency!* C'est une urgence!
- **in an emergency** en cas d'urgence
- **an emergency exit** une sortie de secours
- **an emergency landing** un atterrissage forcé
- **the emergency services** les services d'urgence

to **emigrate** VERB
émigrer

emotion NOUN
l' **émotion** FEM

emotional ADJECTIVE
(*person*)
émotif MASC
émotive FEM

emperor NOUN
l' **empereur** MASC

to **emphasize** VERB
- **to emphasize something** insister sur quelque chose
- **to emphasize that...** souligner que...

empire NOUN
l' **empire** MASC

to **employ** VERB
employer ◇ *The factory employs 600 people.* L'usine emploie six cents personnes.

employee NOUN
l' **employé** MASC
l' **employée** FEM

employer NOUN
l' **employeur** MASC

employment NOUN
l' **emploi** MASC

empty ADJECTIVE
see also empty VERB
vide

to **empty** VERB
see also empty ADJECTIVE
vider
- **to empty something out** vider quelque chose

to **encourage** VERB
encourager
- **to encourage somebody to do something** encourager quelqu'un à faire quelque chose

encouragement NOUN
l' **encouragement** MASC

encyclopedia NOUN
l' **encyclopédie** FEM

end NOUN
see also end VERB
1 la **fin** ◇ *the end of the film* la fin du film ◇ *the end of the holidays* la fin des vacances
- **in the end** en fin de compte ◇ *In the end I decided to stay at home.* En fin de compte j'ai décidé de rester à la maison.
- **It turned out all right in the end.** Ça s'est bien terminé.
2 le **bout** ◇ *at the end of the street* au bout de la rue ◇ *at the other end of the table* à l'autre bout de la table
- **for hours on end** des heures entières

to **end** VERB
see also end NOUN
finir ◇ *What time does the film end?* À quelle heure est-ce que le film finit?
- **to end up doing something** finir par

faire quelque chose ◇ *I ended up
walking home.* J'ai fini par rentrer chez
moi à pied.

ending NOUN
la **fin** ◇ *It was an exciting film,
especially the ending.* C'était un film
passionnant, surtout la fin.

endless ADJECTIVE
interminable ◇ *The journey seemed
endless.* Le voyage a paru
interminable.

enemy NOUN
l' **ennemi** MASC
l' **ennemie** FEM

energetic ADJECTIVE
énergique (*person*)

energy NOUN
l' **énergie** FEM

engaged ADJECTIVE
1 **occupé** (*busy, in use*) ◇ *I phoned, but
it was engaged.* J'ai téléphoné, mais
c'était occupé.
2 **fiancé** (*to be married*) ◇ *She's
engaged to Brian.* Elle est fiancée à
Brian.
- **to get engaged** se fiancer

engagement NOUN
les **fiançailles** FEM PL ◇ *an engagement
ring* une bague de fiançailles

engine NOUN
le **moteur**

engineer NOUN
l' **ingénieur** MASC ◇ *He's an engineer.*
Il est ingénieur.

engineering NOUN
l' **ingénierie** FEM

England NOUN
l' **Angleterre** FEM
- **in England** en Angleterre
- **to England** en Angleterre
- **I'm from England.** Je suis anglais.

English ADJECTIVE
see also English NOUN
anglais ◇ *I'm English.* Je suis anglais.
- **English people** les Anglais

English NOUN
see also English ADJECTIVE
l' **anglais** MASC (*language*) ◇ *Do you
speak English?* Est-ce que vous parlez
anglais?
- **the English** les Anglais

Englishman NOUN
l' **Anglais** MASC

Englishwoman NOUN
l' **Anglaise** FEM

to **enjoy** VERB
aimer ◇ *Did you enjoy the film?* Est-ce
que vous avez aimé le film?
- **to enjoy oneself** s'amuser ◇ *I really
enjoyed myself.* Je me suis vraiment
bien amusé. ◇ *Did you enjoy yourselves
at the party?* Est-ce vous vous êtes bien
amusés à la fête?

enjoyable ADJECTIVE
agréable

enlargement NOUN
l' **agrandissement** MASC (*of photo*)

enormous ADJECTIVE
énorme

enough PRONOUN, ADJECTIVE
assez de ◇ *enough time* assez de
temps ◇ *I didn't have enough money.*
Je n'avais pas assez d'argent. ◇ *Have
you got enough?* Tu en as assez? ◇ *I've
had enough!* J'en ai assez!
- **big enough** suffisamment grand
- **warm enough** suffisamment chaud
- **That's enough.** Ça suffit.

to **enquire** VERB
- **to enquire about something** se
renseigner sur quelque chose ◇ *I am
going to enquire about train times.* Je vais
me renseigner sur les horaires de trains.

to **enter** VERB
entrer
- **to enter a room** entrer dans une pièce
- **to enter a competition** s'inscrire à une
compétition

to **entertain** VERB
recevoir (*guests*)

entertainer NOUN
l' **artiste de variétés** MASC/FEM

entertaining ADJECTIVE
amusant

enthusiasm NOUN
l' **enthousiasme** MASC

enthusiast NOUN
- **a railway enthusiast** un passionné des
trains
- **She's a DIY enthusiast.** C'est une
passionnée de bricolage.

enthusiastic ADJECTIVE
enthousiaste

entire ADJECTIVE
entier MASC
entière FEM
◇ *the entire world* le monde entier

entirely ADVERB
entièrement

entrance NOUN
l' **entrée** FEM
- **an entrance exam** un concours
d'entrée
- **entrance fee** le prix d'entrée

entry NOUN
l' **entrée** FEM
- **"no entry" (1)** (*on door*) "défense
d'entrer"

PTO

- "no entry" (2) (*on road sign*) "sens interdit"
- an entry form une feuille d'inscription

entry phone NOUN
l' **interphone** MASC

envelope NOUN
l' **enveloppe** FEM

envious ADJECTIVE
envieux MASC
envieuse FEM

environment NOUN
l' **environnement** MASC

environmental ADJECTIVE
écologique

environment-friendly ADJECTIVE
écologique

envy NOUN
see also envy VERB
l' **envie** FEM

to **envy** VERB
see also envy NOUN
envier ◇ *I don't envy you!* Je t'envie pas!

epileptic NOUN
l' **épileptique** MASC/FEM

episode NOUN
l' **épisode** MASC (*of TV programme, story*)

equal ADJECTIVE
égal
(**égaux** MASC PL)

equality NOUN
l' **égalité** FEM

to **equalize** VERB
égaliser (*in sport*)

equator NOUN
l' **équateur** MASC

equipment NOUN
l' **équipement** MASC ◇ *fishing equipment* l'équipement de pêche ◇ *skiing equipment* l'équipement de ski

equipped ADJECTIVE
- equipped with équipé de
- to be well equipped être bien équipé

equivalent NOUN
l' **équivalent** MASC
- equivalent to équivalent à

error NOUN
l' **erreur** FEM

escalator NOUN
l' **escalier roulant** MASC

escape NOUN
see also escape VERB
l' **évasion** FEM (*from prison*)

to **escape** VERB
see also escape NOUN
s'échapper ◇ *A lion has escaped.* Un lion s'est échappé.
- to escape from prison s'évader de prison

escort NOUN
l' **escorte** FEM ◇ *a police escort* une escorte de police

Eskimo NOUN
l' **Esquimau** MASC
l' **Esquimaude** FEM
- the Eskimos les Esquimaux

especially ADVERB
surtout ◇ *It's very hot there, especially in the summer.* Il fait très chaud là-bas, surtout en été.

essay NOUN
la **dissertation** ◇ *a history essay* une dissertation histoire

essential ADJECTIVE
essentiel MASC
essentielle FEM
◇ *It's essential to bring warm clothes.* Il est essentiel d'apporter des vêtements chauds.

estate NOUN
la **cité** (*housing estate*) ◇ *I live on an estate.* J'habite dans une cité.

estate agent NOUN
l' **agent immobilier** MASC

estate car NOUN
le **break**

etc ABBREVIATION (= *et cetera*)
etc.

Ethiopia NOUN
l' **Éthiopie** FEM
- in Ethiopia en Éthiopie

ethnic ADJECTIVE
[1] **ethnique** (*racial*) ◇ *an ethnic minority* une minorité ethnique
[2] **folklorique** (*clothes, music*)

EU NOUN (= *European Union*)
l' **Union européenne**

Eurocheque NOUN
l' **eurochèque** MASC

Europe NOUN
l' **Europe** FEM
- in Europe en Europe
- to Europe en Europe

European ADJECTIVE
see also European NOUN
européen MASC
européenne FEM

European NOUN
see also European ADJECTIVE
(*person*)
l' **Européen** MASC
l' **Européenne** FEM

to **evacuate** VERB
évacuer

eve NOUN
- Christmas Eve la veille de Noël
- New Year's Eve la Saint-Sylvestre

even ADVERB

see also **even** ADJECTIVE

même ◇ *I like all animals, even snakes.* J'aime tous les animaux, même les serpents.
- **even if** même si ◇ *I'd never do that, even if you asked me.* Je ne ferais jamais ça, même si tu me le demandais.
- **not even** même pas ◇ *He never stops working, not even at the weekend.* Il n'arrête jamais de travailler, même pas le week-end.
- **even though** bien que

bien que *has to be followed by a verb in the subjunctive.*

◇ *He's never got any money, even though his parents are quite rich.* Il n'a jamais d'argent, bien que ses parents soient assez riches.
- **even more** encore plus ◇ *I liked Boulogne even more than Paris.* J'ai encore plus aimé Boulogne que Paris.

even ADJECTIVE

see also **even** ADVERB

régulier MASC
régulière FEM
◇ *an even layer of snow* une couche régulière de neige
- **an even number** un nombre pair
- **to get even with somebody** prendre sa revanche sur quelqu'un ◇ *He wanted to get even with her.* Il voulait prendre sa revanche sur elle.

evening NOUN

le **soir** ◇ *in the evening* le soir
◇ *yesterday evening* hier soir
◇ *tomorrow evening* demain soir
- **all evening** toute la soirée
- **Good evening!** Bonsoir!

evening class NOUN

le **cours du soir**
(les **cours du soir** PL)

event NOUN

l' **événement** MASC
- **a sporting event** une épreuve sportive

eventful ADJECTIVE

mouvementé

eventually ADVERB

finalement

ever ADVERB
- **Have you ever been to Germany?** Est-ce que tu es déjà allé en Allemagne?
- **Have you ever seen her?** Vous l'avez déjà vue?
- **I haven't seen her.** Je ne l'ai jamais vue.
- **the best I've ever seen** le meilleur que j'aie jamais vu
- **for the first time ever** pour la première

fois
- **ever since** depuis que ◇ *ever since I met him* depuis que je l'ai rencontré
- **ever since then** depuis ce moment-là

every ADJECTIVE

chaque ◇ *every pupil* chaque élève
- **every time** chaque fois ◇ *Every time I see him he's depressed.* Chaque fois que je le vois il est déprimé.
- **every day** tous les jours
- **every week** toutes les semaines
- **every now and then** de temps en temps

everybody PRONOUN

tout le monde ◇ *Everybody had a good time.* Tout le monde s'est bien amusé. ◇ *Everybody makes mistakes.* Tout le monde peut se tromper.

everyone PRONOUN

tout le monde ◇ *Everyone opened their presents.* Tout le monde a ouvert ses cadeaux. ◇ *Everyone should have a hobby.* Tout le monde devrait avoir un passe-temps.

everything PRONOUN

tout ◇ *You've thought of everything!* Tu as pensé à tout!
- **Have you remembered everything?** Est-ce que tu n'as rien oublié?
- **Money isn't everything.** L'argent ne fait pas le bonheur.

everywhere ADVERB

partout ◇ *I looked everywhere, but I couldn't find it.* J'ai regardé partout, mais je n'ai pas pu le trouver. ◇ *There were policemen everywhere.* Il y avait des policiers partout.

evil ADJECTIVE

mauvais

ex- PREFIX

ex- ◇ *his ex-wife* son ex-femme

exact ADJECTIVE

exact

exactly ADVERB

exactement ◇ *exactly the same* exactement le même ◇ *Not exactly.* Pas exactement.
- **It's exactly 10 o'clock.** Il est dix heures précises.

to **exaggerate** VERB

exagérer

exaggeration NOUN

l' **exagération** FEM

exam NOUN

l' **examen** MASC ◇ *a French exam* un examen de français ◇ *the exam results* les résultats des examens MASC

examination NOUN

l' **examen** MASC

to **examine** VERB
examiner ◇ *He examined her passport.* Il a examiné son passeport. ◇ *The doctor examined him.* Le docteur l'a examiné.

examiner NOUN
l' **examinateur** MASC
l' **examinatrice** FEM

example NOUN
l' **exemple** MASC
→ **for example** par exemple

excellent ADJECTIVE
excellent ◇ *Her results were excellent.* Elle a eu d'excellents résultats.
→ **It was excellent fun.** C'était vraiment super.

except PREPOSITION
sauf ◇ *everyone except me* tout le monde sauf moi
→ **except for** sauf
→ **except that** sauf que ◇ *The weather was great, except that it was a bit cold.* Il a fait un temps superbe, sauf qu'il a fait un peu froid.

exception NOUN
l' **exception** FEM
→ **to make an exception** faire une exception

exceptional ADJECTIVE
exceptionnel MASC
exceptionnelle FEM

excess baggage NOUN
l' **excédent de bagages** MASC

to **exchange** VERB
échanger ◇ *I exchanged the book for a video.* J'ai échangé le livre contre une vidéo.

exchange rate NOUN
le **taux de change**

excited ADJECTIVE
excité

exciting ADJECTIVE
passionnant

excuse NOUN
see also **excuse** VERB
l' **excuse** FEM

to **excuse** VERB
see also **excuse** NOUN
→ **Excuse me!** Pardon!

to **execute** VERB
exécuter

execution NOUN
l' **exécution** FEM

executive NOUN
le **cadre** (*in business*) ◇ *He's an executive.* Il est cadre.

exercise NOUN
l' **exercice** MASC
→ **an exercise bike** un vélo d'appartement
→ **an exercise book** un cahier

exhausted ADJECTIVE
épuisé

exhaust fumes PL NOUN
les **gaz d'échappement** MASC PL

exhaust pipe NOUN
le **tuyau d'échappement**

exhibition NOUN
l' **exposition** FEM

ex-husband NOUN
le **ex-mari**

to **exist** VERB
exister

exit NOUN
la **sortie**

exotic ADJECTIVE
exotique

to **expect** VERB
1 **attendre** ◇ *I'm expecting him for dinner.* Je l'attends pour le dîner. ◇ *She's expecting a baby.* Elle attend un bébé.
2 **s'attendre à** ◇ *I didn't expect that from him.* Je ne m'attendais pas à cela de lui.
3 **supposer** ◇ *I expect he'll be late.* Je suppose qu'il sera en retard.
→ **I expect so.** Je suppose.

expedition NOUN
l' **expédition** FEM

to **expel** VERB
→ **to get expelled** (*from school*) se faire renvoyer

expenses PL NOUN
les **frais** MASC PL

expensive ADJECTIVE
cher MASC
chère FEM

experience NOUN
l' **expérience** FEM

experienced ADJECTIVE
expérimenté

experiment NOUN
l' **expérience** FEM

expert NOUN
le **spécialiste**
la **spécialiste**
◇ *He's a computer expert.* C'est un spécialiste en informatique.
→ **He's an expert cook.** Il cuisine très bien.

to **expire** VERB
expirer

to **explain** VERB
expliquer

explanation NOUN
l' **explication** FEM

to **explode** VERB

exploser
to **exploit** VERB
exploiter
exploitation NOUN
l' **exploitation** FEM
to **explore** VERB
explorer (place)
explorer NOUN
l' **explorateur** MASC
l' **exploratrice** FEM
explosion NOUN
l' **explosion** FEM
explosive ADJECTIVE
see also **explosive** NOUN
explosif MASC
explosive FEM
explosive NOUN
see also **explosive** ADJECTIVE
l' **explosif** MASC
to **express** VERB
exprimer
- **to express oneself** s'exprimer ◇ It's
  not easy to express oneself in a foreign
  language. Ce n'est pas facile de
  s'exprimer dans une langue étrangère.
expression NOUN
l' **expression** FEM ◇ It's an English
  expression. C'est une expression
  anglaise.
extension NOUN
[1] l' **annexe** FEM (of building)
[2] le **poste** (telephone)
In France phone numbers are broken into groups
of two digits where possible.
- **Extension 3137, please.** Poste trente et
  un trente-sept, s'il vous plaît.
extent NOUN
- **to some extent** dans une certaine
  mesure
exterior ADJECTIVE
extérieur
extinct ADJECTIVE
- **to become extinct** disparaître
- **to be extinct** avoir disparu ◇ The

species is almost extinct. Cette espèce a
presque disparu.
extinguisher NOUN
l' **extincteur** MASC (fire extinguisher)
extortionate ADJECTIVE
exorbitant
extra ADJECTIVE, ADVERB
supplémentaire ◇ an extra blanket
une couverture supplémentaire
- **to pay extra** payer un supplément
- **Breakfast is extra.** Il y a un
  supplément pour le petit déjeuner.
- **It costs extra.** Il y a un supplément.
extraordinary ADJECTIVE
extraordinaire
extravagant ADJECTIVE
(person)
dépensier MASC
dépensière FEM
extreme ADJECTIVE
extrême
extremely ADVERB
extrêmement
extremist NOUN
l' **extrémiste** MASC/FEM
eye NOUN
l' **œil** MASC
(les **yeux** PL)
◇ I've got green eyes. J'ai les yeux verts.
- **to keep an eye on something** surveiller
  quelque chose
eyebrow NOUN
le **sourcil**
eyelash NOUN
le **cil**
eyelid NOUN
la **paupière**
eyeliner NOUN
l' **eye-liner** MASC
eye shadow NOUN
l' **ombre à paupières** FEM
eyesight NOUN
la **vue**

E

F

fabric NOUN
le **tissu**
fabulous ADJECTIVE
formidable ◇ *The show was fabulous.* Le spectacle était formidable.
face NOUN
see also face VERB
[1] le **visage** (*of person*)
[2] le **cadran** (*of clock*)
[3] la **paroi** (*of cliff*)
- **on the face of it** à première vue
- **in the face of these difficulties** face à ces difficultés
- **face to face** face à face
- **a face cloth** un gant de toilette
to **face** VERB
see also face NOUN
faire face à (*place, problem*)
- **to face up to something** faire face à quelque chose ◇ *You must face up to your responsibilities.* Vous devez faire face à vos responsabilités.
facilities PL NOUN
l' **équipement** MASC SING ◇ *This school has excellent facilities.* Cette école dispose d'un excellent équipement.
- **toilet facilities** les toilettes FEM
- **cooking facilities** la cuisine équipée SING
fact NOUN
le **fait**
- **in fact** en fait
factory NOUN
l' **usine** FEM
to **fade** VERB
[1] **passer** (*colour*) ◇ *The colour has faded in the sun.* La couleur a passé au soleil
- **My jeans have faded.** Mon jean est délavé.
[2] **baisser** ◇ *The light was fading fast.* La lumière baissait rapidement.
[3] **diminuer** ◇ *The noise gradually faded.* Le bruit a diminué peu à peu.
to **fail** VERB
see also fail NOUN
[1] **rater** ◇ *I failed the history exam.* J'ai raté l'examen d'histoire.
[2] **échouer** ◇ *In our class, no one failed.* Dans notre classe, personne n'a échoué.
[3] **lâcher** ◇ *My brakes failed.* Mes freins ont lâché.
- **to fail to do something** ne pas faire quelque chose ◇ *She failed to return her library books.* Elle n'a pas rendu ses

livres à la bibliothèque.
fail NOUN
see also fail VERB
- **without fail** sans faute
failure NOUN
[1] l' **échec** MASC ◇ *feelings of failure* un sentiment d'échec SING
[2] le **raté**
la **ratée**
◇ *He's a failure.* C'est un raté.
[3] la **défaillance** ◇ *a mechanical failure* une défaillance mécanique
faint ADJECTIVE
see also faint VERB
faible ◇ *His voice was very faint.* Sa voix était très faible.
- **to feel faint** se trouver mal
to **faint** VERB
see also faint ADJECTIVE
s'évanouir ◇ *All of a sudden she fainted.* Tout à coup elle s'est évanouie.
fair ADJECTIVE
see also fair NOUN
[1] **juste** ◇ *That's not fair.* Ce n'est pas juste.
[2] (*hair*)
blond ◇ *He's got fair hair.* Il a les cheveux blonds.
[3] (*skin*)
clair ◇ *people with fair skin* les gens qui ont la peau claire
[4] (*weather*)
beau MASC
belle FEM
◇ *The weather was fair.* Il faisait beau.
[5] (*good enough*)
assez bon MASC
assez bonne FEM
◇ *I have a fair chance of winning.* J'ai d'assez bonnes chances de gagner.
[6] (*sizeable*)
considérable ◇ *That's a fair distance.* Ça représente une distance considérable.
fair NOUN
see also fair ADJECTIVE
la **foire** ◇ *They went to the fair.* Ils sont allés à la foire.
- **a trade fair** une foire commerciale
fairly ADVERB
[1] **équitablement** ◇ *The cake was divided fairly.* Le gâteau a été partagé équitablement.
[2] **assez** (*quite*) ◇ *That's fairly good.* C'est assez bien.
fairness NOUN

la **justice**
fairy NOUN
la **fée**
fairy tale NOUN
le **conte de fées**
faith NOUN
[1] la **foi** ◇ *the Catholic faith* la foi
catholique
[2] la **confiance** ◇ *People have lost
faith in the government.* Les gens ont
perdu confiance dans le gouvernement.
faithful ADJECTIVE
fidèle
faithfully ADVERB
▸ **Yours faithfully...** (*in letter*) Veuillez
agréer mes salutations distinguées...
fake NOUN
> *see also* fake ADJECTIVE

le **faux** ◇ *The painting was a fake.* Le
tableau était un faux.
fake ADJECTIVE
> *see also* fake NOUN

faux MASC
fausse FEM
  ◇ *She wore fake fur.* Elle portait une
fausse fourrure.
fall NOUN
> *see also* fall VERB

la **chute** ◇ *a fall of snow* une chute
de neige ◇ *She had a nasty fall.* Elle a
fait une mauvaise chute.
▸ **the Niagara Falls** les chutes du Niagara
to **fall** VERB
> *see also* fall NOUN

[1] **tomber** ◇ *He tripped and fell.* Il a
trébuché et il est tombé.
[2] **baisser** ◇ *Prices are falling.* Les
prix baissent.
▸ **to fall down (1)** (*person*) tomber
  ◇ *She's fallen down.* Elle est tombée.
▸ **to fall down (2)** (*building*) s'écrouler
  ◇ *The house is slowly falling down.* La
maison est en train de s'écrouler.
▸ **to fall for (1)** se laisser prendre à
  ◇ *They fell for it.* Ils s'y sont laissé
prendre.
▸ **to fall for (2)** tomber amoureux de
  ◇ *She's falling for him.* Elle est en
train de tomber amoureuse de lui.
▸ **to fall off** tomber de ◇ *The book fell
off the shelf.* Le livre est tombé de
l'étagère.
▸ **to fall through** tomber à l'eau ◇ *Our
plans have fallen through.* Nos projets
sont tombés à l'eau.
false ADJECTIVE
faux MASC
fausse FEM
▸ **a false alarm** une fausse alerte

▸ **false teeth** les fausses dents
fame NOUN
la **renommée**
familiar ADJECTIVE
familier MASC
familière FEM
  ◇ *a familiar face* un visage familier
▸ **to be familiar with something** bien
connaître quelque chose ◇ *I'm
familiar with his work.* Je connais bien ses
œuvres.
family NOUN
la **famille**
▸ **the Cooke family** la famille Cooke
famine NOUN
la **famine**
famous ADJECTIVE
célèbre
fan NOUN
[1] l' **éventail** MASC (*hand-held*)
[2] le **ventilateur** (*electric*)
[3] le/la **fan** (*of person, band*) ◇ *I'm a fan
of Take That.* Je suis une fan de Take
That.
[4] le/la **supporter** (*of sport*) ◇ *football
fans* les supporters de football
fanatic NOUN
le/la **fanatique**
to **fancy** VERB
▸ **to fancy something** avoir envie de
quelque chose ◇ *I fancy an ice cream.*
J'ai envie d'une glace.
▸ **to fancy doing something** avoir envie
de faire quelque chose
▸ **He fancies her.** Elle lui plaît.
fancy dress NOUN
le **déguisement** ◇ *He was wearing
fancy dress.* Il portait un déguisement.
▸ **a fancy-dress ball** un bal costumé
fantastic ADJECTIVE
fantastique
far ADJECTIVE, ADVERB
loin ◇ *Is it far?* Est-ce que c'est loin?
▸ **far from** loin de ◇ *It's not far from
London.* Ce n'est pas loin de Londres.
  ◇ *It's far from easy.* C'est loin d'être
facile.
▸ **How far is it?** C'est à quelle distance?
▸ **How far is it to Geneva?** Combien y
a-t-il jusqu'à Genève?
▸ **How far have you got?** (*with a task*) Où
en êtes-vous?
▸ **at the far end** à l'autre bout ◇ *at the
far end of the room* à l'autre bout de la
pièce
▸ **far better** beaucoup mieux
▸ **as far as I know** pour autant que je
sache
fare NOUN

⟦1⟧ le **prix du billet** (*on trains, buses*)
⟦2⟧ le **prix de la course** (*in taxi*)
- **half fare** le demi-tarif
- **full fare** le plein tarif
Far East NOUN
l' **Extrême-Orient** MASC
- **in the Far East** en Extrême-Orient
farm NOUN
la **ferme**
farmer NOUN
l' **agriculteur** MASC
l' **agricultrice** FEM
◦ *He's a farmer.* Il est agriculteur.
farmhouse NOUN
la **ferme**
farming NOUN
l' **agriculture** FEM
- **dairy farming** l'industrie laitière
fascinating ADJECTIVE
fascinant
fashion NOUN
la **mode**
- **in fashion** à la mode
fashionable ADJECTIVE
à la mode ◦ *Jane wears very
fashionable clothes.* Jane porte des
vêtements très à la mode. ◦ *a
fashionable restaurant* un restaurant à
la mode
fast ADJECTIVE, ADVERB
⟦1⟧ **vite** ◦ *He can run fast.* Il sait
courir vite.
⟦2⟧ **rapide** ◦ *a fast car* une voiture
rapide
- **That clock's fast.** Cette pendule
avance.
- **He's fast asleep.** Il est profondément
endormi.
fat ADJECTIVE
see also **fat** NOUN
gros MASC
grosse FEM
fat NOUN
see also **fat** ADJECTIVE
⟦1⟧ le **gras** (*on meat, in food*) ◦ *It's very
high in fat.* C'est très gras.
⟦2⟧ la **matière grasse** (*for cooking*)
fatal ADJECTIVE
⟦1⟧ (*causing death*)
mortel MASC
mortelle FEM
◦ *a fatal accident* un accident mortel
⟦2⟧ (*disastrous*)
fatal ◦ *He made a fatal mistake.* Il a
fait une erreur fatale.
father NOUN
le **père** ◦ *my father* mon père
father-in-law NOUN
le **beau-père**

(les **beaux-pères** PL)
fault NOUN
⟦1⟧ la **faute** (*mistake*) ◦ *It's my fault.*
C'est de ma faute.
⟦2⟧ le **défaut** (*defect*) ◦ *There's a fault in
this material.* Ce tissu a un défaut.
- **a mechanical fault** une défaillance
mécanique
faulty ADJECTIVE
défectueux MASC
défectueuse FEM
◦ *This machine is faulty.* Cette machine
est défectueuse.
favour NOUN
le **service**
- **to do somebody a favour** rendre
service à quelqu'un ◦ *Could you do
me a favour?* Tu peux me rendre
service?
- **to be in favour of something** être pour
quelque chose ◦ *I'm in favour of
nuclear disarmament.* Je suis pour le
désarmement nucléaire.
favourite ADJECTIVE
see also **favourite** NOUN
favori MASC
favorite FEM
◦ *Blue's my favourite colour.* Le bleu est
ma couleur favorite.
favourite NOUN
see also **favourite** ADJECTIVE
⟦1⟧ le **favori**
⟦2⟧ la **favorite** ◦ *Liverpool are
favourites to win the Cup.* L'équipe de
Liverpool est favorite pour la coupe.
fear NOUN
see also **fear** VERB
la **peur**
to **fear** VERB
see also **fear** NOUN
craindre ◦ *You have nothing to fear.*
Vous n'avez rien à craindre.
feather NOUN
la **plume**
feature NOUN
la **caractéristique** (*of person, object*)
◦ *an important feature* une
caractéristique essentielle
February NOUN
février MASC
- **in February** en février
fed VERB see **feed**
fed up ADJECTIVE
- **to be fed up with something** en avoir
marre de quelque chose ◦ *I'm fed up
of waiting for him.* J'en ai marre de
l'attendre.
to **feed** VERB
donner à manger à ◦ *Have you fed*

the cat? Est-ce que tu as donné à
manger au chat?
- **He worked hard to feed his family.** Il
travaillait dur pour nourrir sa famille.
to **feel** VERB
  1 **se sentir** ◇ *I don't feel well.* Je ne
  me sens pas bien. ◇ *I feel a bit lonely.*
  Je me sens un peu seul.
  2 **sentir** ◇ *I didn't feel much pain.* Je
  n'ai presque rien senti.
  3 **toucher** ◇ *The doctor felt his
  forehead.* Le docteur lui a touché le
  front.
- **I was feeling hungry.** J'avais faim.
- **I was feeling cold, so I went inside.**
J'avais froid, donc je suis rentré.
- **I feel like...** (*want*) J'ai envie de...
  ◇ *Do you feel like an ice cream?* Tu
  as envie d'une glace?
feeling NOUN
  1 la **sensation** (*physical*) ◇ *a burning
  feeling* une sensation de brûlure
  2 le **sentiment** (*emotional*) ◇ *a feeling
  of satisfaction* un sentiment de
  satisfaction
feet PL NOUN *see* **foot**
fell VERB *see* **fall**
felt VERB *see* **feel**
felt-tip pen NOUN
  le **stylo-feutre**
female ADJECTIVE
  see also female NOUN
  1 **femelle** ◇ *a female animal* un
  animal femelle
  2 **féminin** ◇ *the female sex* le sexe
  féminin
female NOUN
  see also female ADJECTIVE
  la **femelle** (*animal*)
feminine ADJECTIVE
  féminin
feminist NOUN
  le/la **féministe**
fence NOUN
  la **barrière**
fern NOUN
  la **fougère**
ferocious ADJECTIVE
  féroce
ferry NOUN
  le **ferry**
fertile ADJECTIVE
  fertile
fertilizer NOUN
  l' **engrais** MASC
festival NOUN
  le **festival** ◇ *a jazz festival* un festival
  de jazz
to **fetch** VERB

  1 **aller chercher** ◇ *Fetch the bucket.*
  Va chercher le seau.
  2 **se vendre** (*sell for*) ◇ *His painting
  fetched £5000.* Son tableau s'est vendu
  cinq mille livres.
fever NOUN
  la **fièvre** (*temperature*)
few ADJECTIVE, PRONOUN
  peu de (*not many*) ◇ *few books* peu
  de livres
- **a few (1)** quelques ◇ *a few hours*
  quelques heures
- **a few (2)** quelques-uns ◇ *How many
  apples do you want?–A few.* Tu veux
  combien de pommes?–Quelques-unes.
- **quite a few people** pas mal de monde
fewer ADJECTIVE
  moins de ◇ *There are fewer people
  than there were yesterday.* Il y a moins
  de monde qu'hier. ◇ *There are fewer
  pupils in this class.* Il y a moins d'élèves
  dans cette classe.
fiancé NOUN
  le **fiancé** ◇ *He's my fiancé.* C'est mon
  fiancé.
fiancée NOUN
  la **fiancée** ◇ *She's my fiancée.* C'est
  ma fiancée.
fiction NOUN
  les **romans** MASC PL (*novels*)
field NOUN
  1 le **champ** (*in countryside*) ◇ *a field of
  wheat* un champ de blé
  2 le **terrain** (*for sport*) ◇ *a football field*
  un terrain de football
  3 le **domaine** (*subject*) ◇ *He's an
  expert in his field.* C'est un expert dans
  son domaine.
fierce ADJECTIVE
  1 **féroce** ◇ *The dog looked very
  fierce.* Le chien avait l'air très féroce.
  2 **violent** ◇ *The wind was very fierce.*
  Le vent était très violent. ◇ *a fierce
  attack* une attaque violente
fifteen NUMBER
  quinze ◇ *I'm fifteen.* J'ai quinze ans.
fifth ADJECTIVE
  cinquième ◇ *the fifth floor* le
  cinquième étage
- **the fifth of August** le cinq août
fifty NUMBER
  cinquante ◇ *He's fifty.* Il a cinquante
  ans.
fifty-fifty ADJECTIVE, ADVERB
  moitié-moitié ◇ *They split the prize
  money fifty-fifty.* Ils ont partagé l'argent
  du prix moitié-moitié.
- **a fifty-fifty chance** une chance sur
  deux

F

fight NOUN

see also fight VERB

[1] la **bagarre** ◇ *There was a fight in the pub.* Il y a eu une bagarre au pub.

[2] la **lutte** ◇ *the fight against cancer* la lutte contre le cancer

to **fight** VERB

see also fight NOUN

[1] **se battre** ◇ *They were fighting.* Ils se battaient.

[2] **lutter contre** ◇ *The doctors tried to fight the disease.* Les médecins ont essayé de lutter contre la maladie.

◇ *He fought against the urge to smoke.* Il a lutté contre son envie de fumer.

fighting NOUN

les **bagarres** FEM PL ◇ *Fighting broke out outside the pub.* Des bagarres ont éclaté devant le pub.

figure NOUN

[1] le **chiffre** (*number*) ◇ *Can you give me the exact figures?* Pouvez-vous me donner les chiffres exacts?

[2] la **silhouette** (*outline of person*) ◇ *Hélène saw the figure of a man on the bridge.* Hélène a vu la silhouette d'un homme sur le pont.

- **She's got a good figure.** Elle est bien faite.

- **I have to watch my figure.** Je dois faire attention à ma ligne.

[3] le **personnage** (*personality*) ◇ *She's an important political figure.* C'est un personnage politique important.

to **figure out** VERB

[1] **calculer** ◇ *I'll try to figure out how much it'll cost.* Je vais essayer de calculer combien ça va coûter.

[2] **voir** ◇ *I couldn't figure out what it meant.* Je n'arrivais pas à voir ce que ça voulait dire.

[3] **cerner** ◇ *I can't figure him out at all.* Je n'arrive pas du tout à le cerner.

file NOUN

see also file VERB

[1] le **dossier** (*document*) ◇ *Have we got a file on the suspect?* Est-ce que nous avons un dossier sur le suspect?

[2] la **chemise** (*folder*) ◇ *She keeps all her letters in a cardboard file.* Elle garde toutes ses lettres dans une chemise en carton.

[3] le **classeur** (*ring binder*)

[4] le **fichier** (*on computer*)

[5] la **lime** (*for nails, metal*)

to **file** VERB

see also file NOUN

[1] **classer** (*papers*)

[2] **limer** (*nails, metal*) ◇ *to file one's nails* se limer les ongles

to **fill** VERB

remplir ◇ *She filled the glass with water.* Elle a rempli le verre d'eau.

- **to fill in (1)** remplir ◇ *Can you fill this form in please?* Est-ce que vous pouvez remplir ce formulaire s'il vous plaît?

- **to fill in (2)** boucher ◇ *He filled the hole in with soil.* Il a bouché le trou avec de la terre.

- **to fill up** remplir ◇ *He filled the cup up to the brim.* Il a rempli la tasse à ras bords.

- **Fill it up, please.** (*at petrol station*) Le plein, s'il vous plaît.

film NOUN

[1] le **film** (*movie*)

[2] la **pellicule** (*for camera*)

film star NOUN

la **vedette de cinéma** ◇ *He's a film star.* C'est une vedette de cinéma.

filthy ADJECTIVE

dégoûtant

final ADJECTIVE

see also final NOUN

[1] (*last*)

dernier MASC

dernière FEM

◇ *our final farewells* nos derniers adieux

[2] (*definite*)

définitif MASC

définitive FEM

◇ *a final decision* une décision définitive

- **I'm not going and that's final.** Je n'y vais pas, un point c'est tout.

final NOUN

see also final ADJECTIVE

la **finale** ◇ *Boris Becker is in the final.* Boris Becker va disputer la finale.

finally ADVERB

[1] **enfin** (*lastly*) ◇ *Finally, I would like to say...* Enfin, je voudrais dire...

[2] **finalement** (*eventually*) ◇ *They finally decided to leave on Saturday instead of Friday.* Ils ont finalement décidé de partir samedi au lieu de vendredi.

to **find** VERB

[1] **trouver** ◇ *I can't find the exit.* Je ne trouve pas la sortie.

[2] **retrouver** (*something lost*) ◇ *Did you find your pen?* Est-ce que tu as retrouvé ton crayon?

- **to find something out** découvrir quelque chose ◇ *I'm determined to find out the truth.* Je suis décidé à découvrir la vérité.

- **to find out about (1)** (*make enquiries*) se renseigner sur ◇ *Try to find out about the cost of a hotel.* Essaye de te renseigner sur le prix d'un hôtel.
- **to find out about (2)** (*by chance*) apprendre ◇ *I found out about their affair.* J'ai appris leur liaison.

fine ADJECTIVE, ADVERB
see also fine NOUN
[1] **excellent** (*very good*) ◇ *He's a fine musician.* C'est un excellent musicien.
- **to be fine** aller bien ◇ *How are you? –I'm fine.* Comment ça va?–Ça va bien.
- **I feel fine.** Je me sens bien.
- **The weather is fine today.** Il fait beau aujourd'hui.
[2] **fin** (*not coarse*) ◇ *She's got very fine hair.* Elle a les cheveux très fins.

fine NOUN
see also fine ADJECTIVE
[1] l' **amende** FEM ◇ *She got a £50 fine.* Elle a eu une amende de cinquante livres.
[2] la **contravention** (*for traffic offence*) ◇ *I got a fine for driving through a red light.* J'ai eu une contravention pour avoir grillé un feu rouge.

finger NOUN
le **doigt**
- **my little finger** mon petit doigt

fingernail NOUN
l' **ongle** MASC

finish NOUN
see also finish VERB
l' **arrivée** FEM (*of race*) ◇ *We saw the finish of the London Marathon.* Nous avons vu l'arrivée du marathon de Londres.

to finish VERB
see also finish NOUN
[1] **finir** ◇ *I've finished!* J'ai fini!
- **to finish doing something** finir de faire quelque chose
[2] **terminer** ◇ *I've finished the book.* J'ai terminé ce livre. ◇ *The film has finished.* Le film est terminé.

Finland NOUN
la **Finlande**
- **in Finland** en Finlande
- **to Finland** en Finlande

Finn NOUN
le **Finlandais**
la **Finlandaise**

Finnish ADJECTIVE
see also Finnish NOUN
finlandais

Finnish NOUN
see also Finnish ADJECTIVE

le **finnois** (*language*)

fire NOUN
see also fire VERB
[1] le **feu**
(les **feux** PL)
◇ *He made a fire to warm himself up.* Il a fait du feu pour se réchauffer.
- **to be on fire** être en feu
[2] l' **incendie** MASC (*accidental*) ◇ *The house was destroyed by fire.* La maison a été détruite par un incendie.
[3] le **radiateur** (*heater*) ◇ *Turn the fire on.* Allume le radiateur.
- **the fire brigade** les pompiers MASC PL
- **a fire alarm** un avertisseur d'incendie
- **a fire engine** une voiture de pompiers
- **a fire escape** un escalier de secours
- **a fire extinguisher** un extincteur
- **a fire station** une caserne de pompiers

to fire VERB
see also fire NOUN
tirer (*shoot*) ◇ *She fired twice.* Elle a tiré deux fois.
- **to fire at somebody** tirer sur quelqu'un ◇ *The terrorist fired at the crowd.* Le terroriste a tiré sur la foule.
- **to fire a gun** tirer un coup de feu
- **to fire somebody** mettre quelqu'un à la porte ◇ *He was fired from his job.* Il a été mis à la porte.

fireman NOUN
le **pompier** ◇ *He's a fireman.* Il est pompier.

fireplace NOUN
la **cheminée**

fireworks PL NOUN
le **feu d'artifice** SING ◇ *Are you going to see the fireworks?* Est-ce que tu vas voir le feu d'artifice?

firm ADJECTIVE
see also firm NOUN
ferme ◇ *to be firm with somebody* se montrer ferme avec quelqu'un

firm NOUN
see also firm ADJECTIVE
l' **entreprise** FEM ◇ *He works for a large firm in London.* Il travaille pour une grande entreprise à Londres.

first ADJECTIVE, ADVERB
see also first NOUN
[1] **premier** MASC
première FEM
◇ *the first of September* le premier septembre ◇ *the first time* la première fois
- **to come first** (*in exam, race*) arriver premier ◇ *Rachel came first.* Rachel est arrivée première.
[2] **d'abord** ◇ *I want to get a job, but*

first I have to pass my exams. Je veux trouver du travail, mais d'abord je dois réussir à mes examens.
- **first of all** tout d'abord

first NOUN

see also **first** ADJECTIVE

le **premier**
la **première**
◇ *She was the first to arrive.* Elle est arrivée la première.
- **at first** au début

first aid NOUN

les **premiers secours** MASC PL
- **a first aid kit** une trousse de secours

first-class ADJECTIVE

[1] **de première classe** ◇ *She has booked a first-class ticket.* Elle a réservé un billet de première classe.
[2] **excellent** ◇ *a first-class meal* un excellent repas
- **a first-class stamp**

In France there is no first-class or second-class postage. However letters cost more to send than postcards, so you have to remember to say what you are sending when buying stamps.

firstly ADVERB

premièrement ◇ *Firstly, let's see what the book is about.* Premièrement, voyons de quoi parle ce livre.

fish NOUN

see also **fish** VERB

le **poisson** ◇ *I caught three fish.* J'ai pêché trois poissons. ◇ *I don't like fish.* Je n'aime pas le poisson.

to **fish** VERB

see also **fish** NOUN

pêcher
- **to go fishing** aller à la pêche ◇ *We went fishing in the River Dee.* Nous sommes allés à la pêche sur la Dee.

fisherman NOUN

le **pêcheur** ◇ *He's a fisherman.* Il est pêcheur.

fishing NOUN

la **pêche** ◇ *My hobby is fishing.* La pêche est mon passe-temps favori.

fishing boat NOUN

le **bateau de pêche**

fishing rod NOUN

la **canne à pêche**

fishing tackle NOUN

le **matériel de pêche**

fist NOUN

le **poing**

to **fit** VERB

see also **fit** ADJECTIVE, NOUN

[1] **être la bonne taille** (*be the right size*)
◇ *Does it fit?* Est-ce que c'est la bonne taille?

In French you usually specify whether something is too big, small, tight etc.

- **These trousers don't fit me.** (1) (*too big*) Ce pantalon est trop grand pour moi.
- **These trousers don't fit me.** (2) (*too small*) Ce pantalon est trop petit pour moi.

[2] **installer** (*fix up*) ◇ *He fitted an alarm in his car.* Il a installé une alarme dans sa voiture.

[3] **adapter** (*attach*) ◇ *She fitted a plug to the hair dryer.* Elle a adapté une prise au sèche-cheveux.

- **to fit in** (1) (*match up*) correspondre
◇ *That story doesn't fit in with what he told us.* Cette histoire ne correspond pas à ce qu'il nous a dit.
- **to fit in** (2) (*person*) s'adapter ◇ *She fitted in well at her new school.* Elle s'est bien adaptée à sa nouvelle école.

fit ADJECTIVE

see also **fit** VERB, NOUN

en forme (*in condition*) ◇ *He felt relaxed and fit after his holiday.* Il se sentait détendu et en forme après ses vacances.

fit NOUN

see also **fit** ADJECTIVE, VERB

- **to have a fit** (1) (*epileptic*) avoir une crise d'épilepsie
- **to have a fit** (2) (*be angry*) piquer une crise de nerfs ◇ *My Mum will have a fit when she sees the carpet!* Ma mère va piquer une crise de nerfs quand elle va voir la moquette!

fitted carpet NOUN

la **moquette**

fitted kitchen NOUN

la **cuisine aménagée**

fitting room NOUN

la **cabine d'essayage**

five NUMBER

cinq ◇ *He's five.* Il a cinq ans.

to **fix** VERB

[1] **réparer** (*mend*) ◇ *Can you fix my bike?* Est-ce que tu peux réparer mon vélo?

[2] **fixer** (*decide*) ◇ *Let's fix a date for the party.* Fixons une date pour la soirée. ◇ *They fixed a price for the car.* Ils ont fixé un prix pour la voiture.

[3] **préparer** ◇ *Janice fixed some food for us.* Janice nous a préparé à manger.

fixed ADJECTIVE

fixe ◇ *at a fixed time* à une heure fixe ◇ *at a fixed price* à un prix fixe ◇ *a fixed-price menu* un menu à prix fixe

- **My parents have very fixed ideas.** Mes parents ont des idées très arrêtées.

fizzy ADJECTIVE
gazeux MASC
gazeuse FEM
◇ *I don't like fizzy drinks.* Je n'aime pas les boissons gazeuses.

flabby ADJECTIVE
flasque

flag NOUN
le **drapeau**
(les **drapeaux** PL)

flame NOUN
la **flamme**

flamingo NOUN
le **flamant rose**

flan NOUN
1 la **tarte** (*sweet*) ◇ *a raspberry flan* une tarte aux framboises
2 la **quiche** (*savoury*) ◇ *a cheese and onion flan* une quiche au fromage et aux oignons

flannel NOUN
le **gant de toilette** (*for face*)

to **flap** VERB
battre de ◇ *The bird flapped its wings.* L'oiseau battait des ailes.

flash NOUN
see also flash VERB
le **flash**
(les **flashes** PL)
◇ *Has your camera got a flash?* Est-ce que ton appareil photo a un flash?
• **a flash of lightning** un éclair
• **in a flash** en un clin d'œil

to **flash** VERB
see also flash NOUN
1 **clignoter** ◇ *The police car's blue light was flashing.* Le gyrophare de la voiture de police clignotait.
2 **projeter** ◇ *They flashed a torch in his face.* Ils lui ont projeté la lumière d'une torche en plein visage.
• **She flashed her headlights.** Elle a fait un appel de phares.

flat ADJECTIVE
see also flat NOUN
1 **plat** ◇ *a flat roof* un toit plat
◇ *flat shoes* des chaussures plates
2 **crevé** (*tyre*) ◇ *I've got a flat tyre.* J'ai un pneu crevé.

flat NOUN
see also flat ADJECTIVE
l' **appartement** MASC ◇ *She lives in a flat.* Elle habite un appartement.

to **flatter** VERB
flatter

flavour NOUN
1 le **goût** (*taste*) ◇ *This cheese has a very strong flavour.* Ce fromage a un goût très fort.

2 le **parfum** (*variety*) ◇ *Which flavour of ice cream would you like?* Quel parfum de glace est-ce que tu veux?

flavouring NOUN
le **parfum**

flew VERB *see* fly

flexible ADJECTIVE
flexible ◇ *flexible working hours* les horaires flexibles

to **flick** VERB
appuyer sur ◇ *She flicked the switch to turn the light on.* Elle a appuyé sur le bouton pour allumer la lumière.
• **to flick through a book** feuilleter un livre

to **flicker** VERB
trembloter ◇ *The light flickered.* La lumière a trembloté.

flight NOUN
le **vol** ◇ *What time is the flight to Paris?* À quelle heure est le vol pour Paris?
• **a flight of stairs** un escalier

to **fling** VERB
jeter ◇ *He flung the dictionary onto the floor.* Il a jeté le dictionnaire par terre.

to **float** VERB
flotter ◇ *A leaf was floating on the water.* Une feuille flottait sur l'eau.

flock NOUN
• **a flock of sheep** un troupeau de moutons
• **a flock of birds** un vol d'oiseaux

flood NOUN
see also flood VERB
1 l' **inondation** FEM ◇ *The rain has caused many floods.* La pluie a provoqué de nombreuses inondations.
2 le **flot** ◇ *He received a flood of letters.* Il a reçu un flot de lettres.

to **flood** VERB
see also flood NOUN
inonder ◇ *The river has flooded the village.* La rivière a inondé le village.

flooding NOUN
les **inondations** FEM PL

floor NOUN
1 le **sol** ◇ *a tiled floor* un sol carrelé
• **on the floor** par terre
2 l' **étage** MASC (*storey*) ◇ *the first floor* le premier étage
• **the ground floor** le rez-de-chaussée
• **on the third floor** au troisième étage

floppy disk NOUN
la **disquette**

florist NOUN
le/la **fleuriste**

flour NOUN
la **farine**

F

to **flow** VERB
  [1] **couler** (river)
  [2] **s'écouler** (flow out) ○ Water was flowing from the pipe. De l'eau s'écoulait du tuyau.
flower NOUN
  see also flower VERB
  la **fleur**
to **flower** VERB
  see also flower NOUN
  fleurir
flown VERB *see* fly
flu NOUN
  la **grippe** ○ She's got flu. Elle a la grippe.
fluent ADJECTIVE
  ◆ He speaks fluent French. Il parle couramment le français.
flung VERB *see* fling
flush NOUN
  see also flush VERB
  la **chasse d'eau** (of toilet)
to **flush** VERB
  see also flush NOUN
  ◆ to flush the toilet tirer la chasse
flute NOUN
  la **flûte** ○ I play the flute. Je joue de la flûte.
fly NOUN
  see also fly VERB
  la **mouche** (insect)
to **fly** VERB
  see also fly NOUN
  [1] **voler** ○ The plane flies at a speed of 400 km per hour. L'avion vole à quatre cents kilomètres à l'heure.
  [2] **aller en avion** (passenger) ○ He flew from Paris to New York. Il est allé de Paris à New York en avion.
  ◆ to fly away s'envoler ○ The bird flew away. L'oiseau s'est envolé.
foal NOUN
  le **poulain**
focus NOUN
  see also focus VERB
  ◆ to be out of focus être flou ○ The house is out of focus in this photo. La maison est floue sur cette photo.
to **focus** VERB
  see also focus NOUN
  mettre au point ○ Try to focus the binoculars. Essaye de mettre les jumelles au point.
  ◆ to focus on something (1) (with camera, telescope) régler la mise au point sur quelque chose ○ The cameraman focused on the bird. Le caméraman a réglé la mise au point sur l'oiseau.
  ◆ to focus on something (2) (concentrate)

se concentrer sur quelque chose ○ Let's focus on the plot of the play. Concentrons-nous sur l'intrigue de la pièce.
fog NOUN
  le **brouillard**
foggy ADJECTIVE
  ◆ It's foggy. Il y a du brouillard.
  ◆ a foggy day un jour de brouillard
foil NOUN (kitchen foil)
  le **papier d'aluminium** ○ She wrapped the meat in foil. Elle a enveloppé la viande dans du papier d'aluminium.
fold NOUN
  see also fold VERB
  le **pli**
to **fold** VERB
  see also fold NOUN
  plier ○ He folded the newspaper in half. Il a plié le journal en deux.
  ◆ to fold something up plier quelque chose
  ◆ to fold one's arms croiser ses bras ○ She folded her arms. Elle a croisé les bras.
folder NOUN
  [1] la **chemise** ○ She kept all her letters in a folder. Elle gardait toutes ses lettres dans une chemise.
  [2] le **classeur** (ring binder)
folding ADJECTIVE
  ◆ a folding chair une chaise pliante
  ◆ a folding bed un lit pliant
to **follow** VERB
  suivre ○ She followed him. Elle l'a suivi. ○ You go first and I'll follow. Va devant, je te suis.
following ADJECTIVE
  suivant ○ the following day le jour suivant
fond ADJECTIVE
  ◆ to be fond of somebody aimer beaucoup quelqu'un ○ I'm very fond of her. Je l'aime beaucoup.
food NOUN
  la **nourriture**
  ◆ We need to buy some food. Nous devons acheter à manger.
  ◆ cat food la nourriture pour chat
  ◆ dog food la nourriture pour chien
fool NOUN
  l' **idiot** MASC
  l' **idiote** FEM
foot NOUN
  [1] le **pied** (of person) ○ My feet are aching. J'ai mal aux pieds.
  [2] la **patte** (of animal) ○ The dog's foot was injured. Le chien était blessé à la

patte.
- **on foot** à pied
  3 le **pied** (12 inches)
  In France measurements are in metres and centimetres rather than feet and inches. A foot is about 30 centimetres.
- **Dave is 6 foot tall.** Dave mesure un mètre quatre-vingt.
- **That mountain is 5000 feet high.** Cette montagne fait mille six cents mètres de haut.

football NOUN
1 le **football** (game) ◇ *I like playing football.* J'aime jouer au football.
2 le **ballon** (ball) ◇ *Paul threw the football over the fence.* Paul a envoyé le ballon par dessus la clôture.

football player NOUN
le **joueur de football**
la **joueuse de football**
◇ *He's a famous football player.* C'est un joueur de football célèbre.

footpath NOUN
le **sentier** ◇ *Jane followed the footpath through the forest.* Jane a suivi le sentier à travers la forêt.

footprint NOUN
la **trace de pas** ◇ *He saw some footprints in the sand.* Il a vu des traces de pas sur le sable.

footstep NOUN
le **pas** ◇ *I can hear footsteps on the stairs.* J'entends des pas dans l'escalier.

for PREPOSITION
There are several ways of translating **for**. *Scan the examples to find one that is similar to what you want to say.*
1 **pour** ◇ *a present for me* un cadeau pour moi ◇ *the train for London* le train pour Londres ◇ *He works for the government.* Il travaille pour le gouvernement. ◇ *I'll do it for you.* Je vais le faire pour toi. ◇ *Can you do it for tomorrow?* Est-ce que vous pouvez le faire pour demain? ◇ *Are you for or against the idea?* Êtes-vous pour ou contre cette idée? ◇ *Oxford is famous for its university.* Oxford est célèbre pour son université.
When referring to periods of time, use **pendant** *for the future and completed actions in the past, and* **depuis** *(with the French verb in the present tense) for something that started in the past and is still going on.*
2 **pendant** ◇ *He worked in France for two years.* Il a travaillé en France pendant deux ans. ◇ *She will be away for a month.* Elle sera absente pendant un mois. ◇ *There are road works for*

three kilometres. Il y a des travaux pendant trois kilomètres.
3 **depuis** ◇ *He's been learning French for two years.* Il apprend le français depuis deux ans. ◇ *She's been away for a month.* Elle est absente depuis un mois.
When talking about amounts of money, you do not translate **for**.
◇ *I sold it for £5.* Je l'ai vendu cinq livres. ◇ *He paid fifty pence for his ticket.* Il a payé son billet cinquante pence.
- **What's the French for "lion"?** Comment dit-on "lion" en français?
- **It's time for lunch.** C'est l'heure du déjeuner.
- **What for?** Pour quoi faire? ◇ *Give me some money!—What for?* Donne-moi de l'argent!—Pour quoi faire?
- **What's it for?** Ça sert à quoi?
- **for sale** à vendre ◇ *The factory's for sale.* L'usine est en vente.

to **forbid** VERB
défendre
- **to forbid somebody to do something** défendre à quelqu'un de faire quelque chose ◇ *I forbid you to go out tonight!* Je te défends de sortir ce soir.

forbidden ADJECTIVE
défendu ◇ *Smoking is strictly forbidden.* Il est strictement défendu de fumer.

force NOUN
see also **force** VERB
la **force** ◇ *the force of the explosion* la force de l'explosion
- **in force** en vigueur ◇ *No-smoking rules are now in force.* Un règlement qui interdit de fumer est maintenant en vigueur.

to **force** VERB
see also **force** NOUN
forcer ◇ *They forced him to open the safe.* Ils l'ont obligé à ouvrir le coffre-fort.

forecast NOUN
- **the weather forecast** la météo

foreground NOUN
le **premier plan** ◇ *in the foreground* au premier plan

forehead NOUN
le **front**

foreign ADJECTIVE
étranger MASC
étrangère FEM

foreigner NOUN
l' **étranger** MASC
l' **étrangère** FEM

to **foresee** VERB
prévoir ◇ *He had foreseen the problem.* Il avait prévu ce problème.

forest NOUN
la **forêt**

forever ADVERB
[1] **pour toujours** ◇ *He's gone forever.* Il est parti pour toujours.
[2] **toujours** (*always*) ◇ *She's forever complaining.* Elle est toujours en train de se plaindre.

forgave VERB *see* **forgive**

to **forge** VERB
contrefaire ◇ *She tried to forge his signature.* Elle a essayé de contrefaire sa signature.

forged ADJECTIVE
faux MASC
fausse FEM
◇ *forged banknotes* des faux billets

to **forget** VERB
oublier ◇ *I've forgotten his name.* J'ai oublié son nom. ◇ *I'm sorry, I completely forgot!* Je suis désolé, j'ai complètement oublié!

to **forgive** VERB
- **to forgive somebody** pardonner à quelqu'un ◇ *I forgive you.* Je te pardonne.
- **to forgive somebody for doing something** pardonner à quelqu'un d'avoir fait quelque chose ◇ *She forgave him for forgetting her birthday.* Elle lui a pardonné d'avoir oublié son anniversaire.

fork NOUN
[1] la **fourchette** (*for eating*)
[2] la **fourche** (*for gardening*)
[3] la **bifurcation** (*in road*)

form NOUN
[1] le **formulaire** (*paper*) ◇ *to fill in a form* remplir un formulaire
[2] la **forme** (*type*) ◇ *I'm against hunting in any form.* Je suis contre la chasse sous toutes ses formes.
- **in top form** en pleine forme
- **She's in the fourth form.** Elle est en troisième.

formal ADJECTIVE
[1] (*occasion*)
officiel MASC
officielle FEM
◇ *a formal dinner* un dîner officiel
[2] (*person*)
guindé
[3] (*language*)
soutenu ◇ *In English, "residence" is a formal term.* En anglais, "residence" est un terme soutenu.

- **formal clothes** une tenue habillée
- **He's got no formal education.** Il n'a pas fait beaucoup d'études.

former ADJECTIVE
ancien MASC
ancienne FEM
◇ *a former pupil* un ancien élève ◇ *the former Prime Minister* l'ancien Premier ministre

fort NOUN
le **fort**

forth ADVERB
- **to go back and forth** aller et venir
- **and so forth** et ainsi de suite

fortnight NOUN
- **a fortnight** quinze jours ◇ *I'm going on holiday for a fortnight.* Je pars en vacances pendant quinze jours.

fortunate ADJECTIVE
- **to be fortunate** avoir de la chance ◇ *He was extremely fortunate to survive.* Il a eu énormément de chance de survivre.
- **It's fortunate that I remembered the map.** C'est une chance que j'aie pris la carte.

fortunately ADVERB
heureusement ◇ *Fortunately, it didn't rain.* Heureusement, il n'a pas plu.

fortune NOUN
la **fortune** ◇ *Kate earns a fortune!* Kate gagne une fortune!
- **to tell somebody's fortune** dire la bonne aventure à quelqu'un

forty NUMBER
quarante ◇ *He's forty.* Il a quarante ans.

forward ADVERB
see also forward VERB
- **to move forward** avancer

to **forward** VERB
see also forward ADVERB
faire suivre ◇ *He forwarded all Janette's letters.* Il a fait suivre toutes les lettres de Janette.

foster child NOUN
l' **enfant adoptif** MASC
l' **enfant adoptive** FEM

fought VERB *see* **fight**

foul ADJECTIVE
see also foul NOUN
infect ◇ *The weather was foul.* Le temps était infect. ◇ *What a foul smell!* Quelle odeur infecte!

foul NOUN
see also foul ADJECTIVE
la **faute** ◇ *Ferguson committed a foul.* Ferguson a fait une faute.

found VERB *see* **find**

to found VERB
  fonder ◇ *Baden Powell founded the Scout Movement.* Baden Powell a fondé le mouvement scout.
foundations PL NOUN
  les **fondations** FEM PL
fountain NOUN
  la **fontaine**
fountain pen NOUN
  le **stylo à encre**
four NUMBER
  quatre ◇ *She's four.* Elle a quatre ans.
fourteen NUMBER
  quatorze ◇ *I'm fourteen.* J'ai quatorze ans.
fourth ADJECTIVE
  quatrième ◇ *the fourth floor* le quatrième étage
- **the fourth of July** le quatre juillet
fox NOUN
  le **renard**
fragile ADJECTIVE
  fragile
frame NOUN
  le **cadre** (*for picture*)
France NOUN
  la **France**
- **in France** en France
- **to France** en France
- **He's from France.** Il est français.
frantic ADJECTIVE
- **I was going frantic.** J'étais dans tous mes états.
- **to be frantic with worry** être folle d'inquiétude
fraud NOUN
  ⒈ la **fraude** (*crime*) ◇ *He was jailed for fraud.* On l'a mis en prison pour fraude.
  ⒉ l' **imposteur** MASC (*person*) ◇ *He's not a real doctor, he's a fraud.* Ce n'est pas un vrai médecin, c'est un imposteur.
free ADJECTIVE
  see also free VERB
  ⒈ **gratuit** (*free of charge*) ◇ *a free brochure* une brochure gratuite
  ⒉ **libre** (*not busy, not taken*) ◇ *Is this seat free?* Est-ce que cette place est libre? ◇ *Are you free after school?* Tu es libre après l'école?
to free VERB
  see also free ADJECTIVE
  libérer
freedom NOUN
  la **liberté**
to freeze VERB
  ⒈ **geler** ◇ *The water had frozen.*

L'eau avait gelé.
  ⒉ **congeler** (*food*) ◇ *She froze the rest of the raspberries.* Elle a congelé le reste des framboises.
freezer NOUN
  le **congélateur**
freezing ADJECTIVE
- **It's freezing!** Il fait un froid de canard! (*informal*)
- **I'm freezing!** Je suis gelé! (*informal*)
- **3 degrees below freezing** moins trois
freight NOUN
  la **cargaison** (*goods*)
- **a freight train** un train de marchandises
French ADJECTIVE
  see also French NOUN
  français ◇ *He's French.* Il est français. ◇ *She's French.* Elle est française.
French NOUN
  see also French ADJECTIVE
  le **français** (*language*) ◇ *Do you speak French?* Est-ce que tu parles le français?
- **the French** (*people*) les Français
French beans PL NOUN
  les **haricots verts**
French fries PL NOUN
  les **frites** FEM PL
French horn NOUN
  le **cor (d'harmonie)** ◇ *I play the French horn.* Je joue du cor.
French kiss NOUN
  le **baiser profond**
French loaf NOUN
  la **baguette**
Frenchman NOUN
  le **Français**
Frenchwoman NOUN
  la **Française**
frequent ADJECTIVE
  fréquent ◇ *frequent showers* des averses fréquentes
- **There are frequent buses to the town centre.** Il y a beaucoup de bus pour le centre ville.
fresh ADJECTIVE
  frais MASC
  fraîche FEM
- **I need some fresh air.** J'ai besoin de prendre l'air.
to freshen up VERB
  faire un brin de toilette ◇ *I'd like to go and freshen up.* Je voudrais faire un brin de toilette.
to fret VERB
  se tracasser ◇ *Philip was fretting about his exams.* Philip se tracassait au sujet de ses examens.

Friday NOUN
le **vendredi** ◇ *on Friday* vendredi
◇ *on Fridays* le vendredi ◇ *every Friday* tous les vendredis ◇ *last Friday* vendredi dernier ◇ *next Friday* vendredi prochain

fridge NOUN
le **frigo**

fried ADJECTIVE
frit ◇ *fried vegetables* des légumes frits
• **a fried egg** un œuf sur le plat

friend NOUN
l' **ami** MASC
l' **amie** FEM

friendly ADJECTIVE
1 **gentil** MASC
gentille FEM
◇ *She's really friendly.* Elle est vraiment gentille.
2 **accueillant** ◇ *Liverpool is a very friendly city.* Liverpool est une ville très accueillante.

friendship NOUN
l' **amitié** FEM

fright NOUN
la **peur** ◇ *I got a terrible fright!* Ça m'a fait une peur terrible!

to **frighten** VERB
faire peur à ◇ *Horror films frighten him.* Les films d'horreur lui font peur.

frightened ADJECTIVE
• **to be frightened** avoir peur ◇ *I'm frightened!* J'ai peur!
• **to be frightened of something** avoir peur de quelque chose ◇ *Anna's frightened of spiders.* Anna a peur des araignées.

frightening ADJECTIVE
effrayant

fringe NOUN
la **frange** (*of hair*) ◇ *She's got a fringe.* Elle a une frange.

Frisbee ® NOUN
le **Frisbee** ® ◇ *to play Frisbee* jouer au Frisbee

fro ADVERB
• **to go to and fro** aller et venir

frog NOUN
la **grenouille**
• **frogs' legs** les cuisses de grenouille

from PREPOSITION
de ◇ *Where do you come from?* D'où venez-vous? ◇ *I come from Perth.* Je viens de Perth. ◇ *a letter from my sister* une lettre de ma sœur ◇ *The hotel is one kilometre from the beach.* L'hôtel est à un kilomètre de la plage.
• **from...to...** de...à... ◇ *He flew from London to Paris.* Il a pris l'avion de Londres à Paris. ◇ *from 1 o'clock to 2* d'une heure à deux heures ◇ *The price was reduced from £10 to £5.* Ils ont réduit le prix de dix livres à cinq.
• **from...onwards** à partir de... ◇ *We'll be at home from 7 o'clock onwards.* Nous serons chez nous à partir de sept heures.

front NOUN
see also **front** ADJECTIVE
le **devant** ◇ *the front of the house* le devant de la maison
• **in front** devant ◇ *a house with a car in front* une maison avec une voiture devant ◇ *the car in front* la voiture de devant
• **in front of** devant ◇ *in front of the house* devant la maison ◇ *the car in front of us* la voiture devant nous
• **in the front** (*of car*) à l'avant ◇ *I was sitting in the front.* J'étais assis à l'avant.
• **at the front of the train** à l'avant du train

front ADJECTIVE
see also **front** NOUN
1 **de devant** ◇ *the front row* la rangée de devant
2 **avant** ◇ *the front seats of the car* les sièges avant de la voiture
• **the front door** la porte d'entrée

frontier NOUN
la **frontière**

frost NOUN
le **gel**

frosty ADJECTIVE
• **It's frosty today.** Il gèle aujourd'hui.

to **frown** VERB
froncer les sourcils ◇ *He frowned.* Il a froncé les sourcils.

froze VERB see **freeze**
surgelé (*food*)
• **frozen chips** des frites surgelées

frozen ADJECTIVE
see also **freeze**
surgelé (*food*) ◇ *frozen chips* des frites surgelées

fruit NOUN
le **fruit**
• **fruit juice** le jus de fruits
• **a fruit salad** une salade de fruits

fruit machine NOUN
la **machine à sous**

frustrated ADJECTIVE
frustré

to **fry** VERB
faire frire ◇ *Fry the onions for 5 minutes.* Faites frire les oignons pendant cinq minutes.

frying pan NOUN
la **poêle**

fuel NOUN
le **carburant** (for car, aeroplane) ◇ to run out of fuel avoir une panne de carburant

to **fulfil** VERB
réaliser ◇ Robert fulfilled his dream to visit China. Robert a réalisé son rêve de visiter la Chine.

full ADJECTIVE, ADVERB
[1] **plein** ◇ The tank's full. Le réservoir est plein.
[2] **complet** MASC
complète FEM
◇ He asked for full information on the job. Il a demandé des renseignements complets sur le poste.
→ **your full name** vos nom et prénoms ◇ My full name is Ian John Marr. Je m'appelle Ian John Marr.
→ **I'm full.** (after meal) J'ai bien mangé.
→ **at full speed** à toute vitesse ◇ He drove at full speed. Il conduisait à toute vitesse
→ **There was a full moon.** C'était la pleine lune.

full stop NOUN
le **point**

full-time ADJECTIVE, ADVERB
à plein temps ◇ She's got a full-time job. Elle a un travail à plein temps. ◇ She works full-time. Elle travaille à plein temps.

fully ADVERB
complètement ◇ He hasn't fully recovered from his illness. Il n'est pas complètement remis de sa maladie.

fumes PL NOUN
les **fumées** FEM PL ◇ The factory gave out dangerous fumes. L'usine rejetait des fumées dangereuses.
→ **exhaust fumes** les gaz d'échappement

fun ADJECTIVE
see also fun NOUN
marrant ◇ She's a fun person. Elle est marrante.

fun NOUN
see also fun ADJECTIVE
→ **to have fun** s'amuser ◇ We had great fun playing in the snow. Nous nous sommes bien amusés à jouer dans la neige.
→ **for fun** pour rire ◇ He entered the competition just for fun. Il a participé à la compétition juste pour rire.
→ **to make fun of somebody** se moquer de quelqu'un ◇ They made fun of him. Ils se sont moqués de lui.
→ **It's fun!** C'est chouette!

→ **Have fun!** Amuse-toi bien!

funds PL NOUN
les **fonds** MASC ◇ to raise funds collecter des fonds

funeral NOUN
l' **enterrement** MASC

funfair NOUN
la **fête foraine**

funny ADJECTIVE
[1] **drôle** (amusing) ◇ It was really funny. C'était vraiment drôle.
[2] **bizarre** (strange) ◇ There's something funny about him. Il est un peu bizarre.

fur NOUN
[1] la **fourrure** ◇ a fur coat un manteau de fourrure
[2] le **poil** ◇ the dog's fur le poil du chien

furious ADJECTIVE
furieux MASC
furieuse FEM
◇ Dad was furious with me. Papa était furieux contre moi.

furniture NOUN
les **meubles** MASC PL ◇ a piece of furniture un meuble

further ADVERB, ADJECTIVE
plus loin ◇ London is further from Manchester than Leeds is. Londres est plus loin de Manchester que Leeds.
→ **How much further is it?** C'est encore loin?

further education NOUN
l' **enseignement postscolaire** MASC

fuse NOUN
le **fusible** ◇ The fuse has blown. Le fusible a sauté.

fuss NOUN
l' **agitation** FEM ◇ What's all the fuss about? Qu'est-ce que c'est que toute cette agitation?
→ **to make a fuss** faire des histoires ◇ He's always making a fuss about nothing. Il fait toujours des histoires pour rien.

fussy ADJECTIVE
difficile ◇ She is very fussy about her food. Elle est très difficile sur la nourriture.

future NOUN
[1] l' **avenir** MASC ◇ What are your plans for the future? Quels sont vos projets pour l'avenir?
→ **in future** à l'avenir ◇ Be more careful in future. Sois plus prudent à l'avenir.
[2] le **futur** (in grammar) ◇ Put this sentence into the future. Mettez cette phrase au futur.

G

to **gain** VERB
- **to gain weight** prendre du poids
- **to gain speed** prendre de la vitesse

gallery NOUN
le **musée** ◇ *an art gallery* un musée d'art

to **gamble** VERB
jouer ◇ *He gambled £100 at the casino.* Il a joué cent livres au casino.

gambler NOUN
le **joueur**

gambling NOUN
le **jeu** ◇ *He likes gambling.* Il aime le jeu.

game NOUN
1 le **jeu**
(les **jeux** PL)
◇ *The children were playing a game.* Les enfants jouaient à un jeu.
2 le **match** (*sport*) ◇ *a game of football* un match de football
- **a game of cards** une partie de cartes

gang NOUN
la **bande**

gangster NOUN
le **gangster**

gap NOUN
1 le **trou** ◇ *There's a gap in the hedge.* Il y a un trou dans la haie.
2 l' **intervalle** MASC ◇ *a gap of four years* un intervalle de quatre ans

garage NOUN
le **garage**

garden NOUN
le **jardin**

gardener NOUN
le **jardinier** ◇ *He's a gardener.* Il est jardinier.

gardening NOUN
le **jardinage** ◇ *Margaret loves gardening.* Margaret aime le jardinage.

gardens PL NOUN
le **jardin public** SING

garlic NOUN
l' **ail** MASC

garment NOUN
le **vêtement**

gas NOUN
le **gaz**
- **a gas cooker** une cuisinière à gaz
- **a gas cylinder** une bouteille de gaz
- **a gas fire** un radiateur à gaz
- **a gas leak** un fuite de gaz

gate NOUN
1 le **portail** (*of garden*)
2 la **barrière** (*of field*)

3 la **porte** (*at airport*)

gateau NOUN
le **gâteau à la crème**

to **gather** VERB
se rassembler (*assemble*) ◇ *People gathered in front of Buckingham Palace.* Les gens se sont rassemblés devant Buckingham Palace.
- **to gather speed** prendre de la vitesse ◇ *The train gathered speed.* Le train a pris de la vitesse.

gave VERB *see* **give**

gay ADJECTIVE
homosexuel MASC
homosexuelle FEM

to **gaze** VERB
- **to gaze at something** fixer quelque chose du regard ◇ *He gazed at her.* Il l'a fixée du regard.

gear NOUN
1 la **vitesse** (*in car*) ◇ *in first gear* en première vitesse ◇ *to change gear* changer de vitesse
2 le **matériel** ◇ *camping gear* le matériel de camping
- **your sports gear** (*clothes*) tes affaires de sport

gear lever NOUN
le **levier de vitesse**

geese PL NOUN *see* **goose**

gel NOUN
le **gel**
- **hair gel** le gel pour les cheveux

gem NOUN
la **pierre précieuse**

Gemini NOUN
les **Gémeaux** MASC PL ◇ *I'm Gemini.* Je suis Gémeaux.

general NOUN
see also general ADJECTIVE
le **général**
(les **généraux** PL)

general ADJECTIVE
see also general NOUN
général
(**généraux** MASC PL)
- **in general** en général

general election NOUN
les **élections législatives** FEM PL

general knowledge NOUN
les **connaissances générales** FEM PL

generally ADVERB
généralement ◇ *I generally go shopping on Saturday.* Généralement, je fais mes courses le samedi.

generation NOUN

la **génération** ⋄ *the younger generation* la nouvelle génération
generator NOUN
le **générateur**
generous ADJECTIVE
généreux MASC
généreuse FEM
⋄ *That's very generous of you.* C'est très généreux de votre part.
Geneva NOUN
Genève
◆ **in Geneva** à Genève
◆ **to Geneva** à Genève
◆ **Lake Geneva** le lac Léman
genius NOUN
le **génie** ⋄ *She's a genius!* C'est un génie!
gentle ADJECTIVE
doux MASC
douce FEM
gentleman NOUN
le **monsieur**
(les **messieurs** PL)
⋄ *Good morning, gentlemen.* Bonjour messieurs.
gently ADVERB
doucement
gents NOUN
les **toilettes pour hommes** FEM PL
⋄ *Can you tell me where the gents are, please?* Pouvez-vous me dire où sont les toilettes, s'il vous plaît?
◆ **"gents"** (*on sign*) "messieurs"
genuine ADJECTIVE
[1] **véritable** (*real*) ⋄ *These are genuine diamonds.* Ce sont de véritables diamants.
[2] **sincère** (*sincere*) ⋄ *She's a very genuine person.* C'est quelqu'un de très sincère.
geography NOUN
la **géographie**
germ NOUN
le **microbe**
German ADJECTIVE
see also German NOUN
allemand
German NOUN
see also German ADJECTIVE
[1] (*person*)
l' **Allemand** MASC
l' **Allemande** FEM
[2] (*language*)
l' **allemand** ⋄ *Do you speak German?* Parlez-vous allemand?
Germany NOUN
l' **Allemagne** FEM
◆ **in Germany** en Allemagne
◆ **to Germany** en Allemagne

to **get** VERB
> *There are several ways of translating* get. *Scan the examples to find one that is similar to what you want to say.*
[1] **avoir** (*have, receive*) ⋄ *I got lots of presents.* J'ai eu beaucoup de cadeaux. ⋄ *He got first prize.* Il a eu le premier prix. ⋄ *Jackie got good exam results.* Jackie a eu de bons résultats aux examens. ⋄ *How many have you got?* Combien en avez-vous?
[2] **aller chercher** (*fetch*) ⋄ *Quick, get help!* Allez vite chercher de l'aide!
[3] **attraper** (*catch*) ⋄ *They've got the thief.* Ils ont attrapé le voleur.
[4] **prendre** (*train, bus*) ⋄ *I'm getting the bus into town.* Je prends le bus pour aller en ville.
[5] **comprendre** (*understand*) ⋄ *I don't get the joke.* Je ne comprends pas cette blague.
[6] **aller** (*go*) ⋄ *How do you get to the castle?* Comment est-ce qu'on va au château?
[7] **arriver** (*arrive*) ⋄ *He should get here soon.* Il devrait arriver bientôt.
[8] **devenir** (*become*) ⋄ *to get old* devenir vieux
◆ **to get something done** faire faire quelque chose ⋄ *to get one's hair cut* se faire couper les cheveux
◆ **to get something for somebody** trouver quelque chose pour quelqu'un ⋄ *The librarian got the book for me.* Le bibliothécaire m'a trouvé le livre.
◆ **to have got to do something** devoir faire quelque chose ⋄ *I've got to tell him.* Je dois le lui dire.
◆ **to get back (1)** rentrer ⋄ *What time did you get back?* Tu es rentré à quelle heure?
◆ **to get back (2)** récupérer ⋄ *He got his money back.* Il a récupéré son argent.
◆ **to get in** rentrer ⋄ *What time did you get in last night?* Tu es rentré à quelle heure hier soir?
◆ **to get into** monter dans ⋄ *Sharon got into the car.* Sharon est montée dans la voiture.
◆ **to get off** descendre de (*vehicle, bike*) ⋄ *Isobel got off the train.* Isobel est descendue du train.
◆ **to get on (1)** (*vehicle*) monter dans ⋄ *Phyllis got on the bus.* Phyllis est montée dans le bus.
◆ **to get on (2)** (*bike*) enfourcher ⋄ *Carol got on her bike.* Carol a enfourché son vélo.
◆ **to get on with somebody** s'entendre

G

avec quelqu'un ◇ *He doesn't get on with his parents.* Il ne s'entend pas avec ses parents. ◇ *We got on really well.* Nous nous sommes très bien entendus.

+ **to get out** sortir ◇ *Hélène got out of the car.* Hélène est sortie de la voiture. ◇ *Get out!* Sortez!

+ **to get something out** sortir quelque chose ◇ *She got the map out.* Elle a sorti la carte.

+ **to get up** se lever ◇ *What time do you get up?* Tu te lèves à quelle heure?

ghetto blaster NOUN
le **radiocassette portable**

ghost NOUN
le **fantôme**

giant ADJECTIVE
see also giant NOUN
énorme ◇ *They ate a giant meal.* Ils ont mangé un énorme repas.

giant NOUN
see also giant ADJECTIVE
le **géant**
la **géante**

gift NOUN
1 (*present*)
le **cadeau**
(les **cadeaux** PL)
2 (*talent*)
le **don**

+ **to have a gift for something** être doué pour quelque chose ◇ *Dave has a gift for painting.* Dave est doué pour la peinture.

gifted ADJECTIVE
doué ◇ *Janice is a gifted dancer.* Janice est douée pour la danse.

gift shop NOUN
la **boutique de cadeaux**

gigantic ADJECTIVE
gigantesque

gin NOUN
le **gin**

ginger NOUN
see also ginger ADJECTIVE
le **gingembre** ◇ *Add a teaspoon of ginger.* Ajoutez une cuillère à café de gingembre.

ginger ADJECTIVE
see also ginger NOUN
roux MASC
rousse FEM
◇ *Chris has ginger hair.* Chris a les cheveux roux.

giraffe NOUN
la **girafe**

girl NOUN
1 la **fille** ◇ *They've got a girl and two boys.* Ils ont une fille et deux garçons.

2 la **petite fille** (*young*) ◇ *a five-year-old girl* une petite fille de cinq ans
3 la **jeune fille** (*older*) ◇ *a sixteen-year-old girl* une jeune fille de seize ans ◇ *an English girl* une jeune Anglaise

girlfriend NOUN
1 la **copine** (*lover*) ◇ *Damon's girlfriend is called Justine.* La copine de Damon s'appelle Justine.
2 l' **amie** FEM (*friend*) ◇ *She often went out with her girlfriends.* Elle sortait souvent avec ses amies.

to **give** VERB
donner

+ **to give something to somebody** donner quelque chose à quelqu'un ◇ *He gave me £10.* Il m'a donné dix livres.

+ **to give something back to somebody** rendre quelque chose à quelqu'un ◇ *I gave the book back to him.* Je lui ai rendu le livre.

+ **to give something out** distribuer quelque chose ◇ *The teacher gave out the books.* Le professeur a distribué les livres.

+ **to give in** céder ◇ *His Mum gave in and let him go out.* Sa mère a cédé et l'a laissé sortir.

+ **to give up** laisser tomber ◇ *I couldn't do it, so I gave up.* Je n'arrivais pas à le faire, alors j'ai laissé tomber.

+ **to give up doing something** arrêter de faire quelque chose ◇ *He gave up smoking.* Il a arrêté de fumer.

+ **to give oneself up** se rendre ◇ *The thief gave himself up.* Le voleur s'est rendu.

+ **to give way** céder la priorité (*in traffic*)

glad ADJECTIVE
content ◇ *She's glad she's done it.* Elle est contente de l'avoir fait.

to **glance** VERB
see also glance NOUN

+ **to glance at something** jeter un coup d'œil à quelque chose ◇ *Peter glanced at his watch.* Peter a jeté un coup d'œil à sa montre.

glance NOUN
see also glance VERB
le **coup d'œil** ◇ *at first glance* au premier coup d'œil

to **glare** VERB

+ **to glare at somebody** lancer un regard furieux à quelqu'un ◇ *He glared at me.* Il m'a lancé un regard furieux.

glaring ADJECTIVE

- **a glaring mistake** une erreur qui saute aux yeux

glass NOUN

le **verre** ◇ *a glass of milk* un verre de lait

glasses PL NOUN

les **lunettes** FEM ◇ *Jean-Pierre wears glasses.* Jean-Pierre porte des lunettes.

glider NOUN

le **planeur**

gliding NOUN

le **vol à voile** ◇ *My hobby is gliding.* Je fais du vol à voile.

global ADJECTIVE

mondial

(**mondiaux** MASC PL)

- **on a global scale** à l'échelle mondiale

global warming NOUN

le **réchauffement de la planète**

globe NOUN

le **globe**

glove NOUN

le **gant**

glove compartment NOUN

la **boîte à gants**

glue NOUN

la **colle**

go NOUN

see also go VERB

- **to have a go at doing something** essayer de faire quelque chose ◇ *He had a go at making a cake.* Il a essayé de faire un gâteau.
- **Whose go is it?** À qui le tour?

to **go** VERB

see also go NOUN

① **aller** ◇ *I'm going to the cinema tonight.* Je vais au cinéma ce soir.

② **partir** (*leave*) ◇ *Where's Pierre? —He's gone.* Où est Pierre?—Il est parti.

③ **s'en aller** (*go away*) ◇ *I'm going now.* Je m'en vais.

④ **marcher** (*vehicle*) ◇ *My car won't go.* Ma voiture ne marche pas.

- **to go home** rentrer à la maison ◇ *I go home at about 4 o'clock.* Je rentre à la maison vers quatre heures.
- **to go for a walk** aller se promener ◇ *Shall we go for a walk?* Si on allait se promener?
- **How did it go?** Comment est-ce que ça s'est passé?
- **I'm going to do it tomorrow.** Je vais le faire demain.
- **it's going to be difficult.** Ça va être difficile.

to **go after** VERB

suivre ◇ *Quick, go after them!* Vite,

suivez-les!

to **go away** VERB

s'en aller ◇ *Go away!* Allez-vous-en!

to **go back** VERB

> *Use* **rentrer** *only when you are entering a building, usually your home; otherwise use* **retourner**.

① **retourner** ◇ *We went back to the same place.* Nous sommes retournés au même endroit.

② **rentrer** ◇ *Is he still here?—No, he's gone back home.* Est-ce qu'il est encore là?—Non, il est rentré chez lui.

to **go by** VERB

passer ◇ *Two policemen went by.* Deux policiers sont passés.

to **go down** VERB

① **descendre** (*person*) ◇ *to go down the stairs* descendre l'escalier

② **baisser** (*decrease*) ◇ *The price of computers has gone down.* Le prix des ordinateurs a baissé.

③ **se dégonfler** (*deflate*) ◇ *My airbed kept going down.* Mon matelas pneumatique se dégonflait constamment.

- **My brother's gone down with flu.** Mon frère a attrapé la grippe.

to **go for** VERB

attaquer (*attack*) ◇ *Suddenly the dog went for me.* Soudain, le chien m'a attaqué.

- **Go for it!** (*go on!*) Vas-y, fonce!

to **go in** VERB

entrer ◇ *He knocked on the door and went in.* Il a frappé à la porte et il est entré.

to **go off** VERB

① **exploser** (*bomb*) ◇ *The bomb went off.* La bombe a explosé.

② **se déclencher** (*alarm, gun*) ◇ *The fire alarm went off.* L'avertisseur d'incendie s'est déclenché.

③ **sonner** (*alarm clock*) ◇ *My alarm clock goes off at seven every morning.* Mon réveil sonne à sept heures tous les matins.

④ **tourner** (*food*) ◇ *The milk's gone off.* Le lait a tourné.

⑤ **partir** (*go away*) ◇ *He went off in a huff.* Il est parti de mauvaise humeur.

to **go on** VERB

① **se passer** (*happen*) ◇ *What's going on?* Qu'est-ce qui se passe?

② **continuer** (*carry on*) ◇ *The concert went on until 11 o'clock at night.* Le concert a continué jusqu'à onze heures du soir.

- **to go on doing something** continuer à [PTO]

faire quelque chose ◦ *He went on reading.* Il a continué à lire.
- **to go on at somebody** être sur le dos de quelqu'un ◦ *My parents always go on at me.* Mes parents sont toujours sur mon dos.
- **Go on!** Allez! ◦ *Go on, tell me what the problem is!* Allez, dis-moi quel est le problème!

to **go out** VERB
☐ **sortir** *(person)* ◦ *Are you going out tonight?* Tu sors ce soir?
- **to go out with somebody** sortir avec quelqu'un ◦ *Are you going out with him?* Est-ce que tu sors avec lui?
② **s'éteindre** *(light, fire, candle)* ◦ *Suddenly the lights went out.* Soudain, les lumières se sont éteintes.

to **go past** VERB
- **to go past something** passer devant quelque chose ◦ *He went past the shop.* Il est passé devant la boutique.

to **go round** VERB
- **to go round a corner** prendre un tournant
- **to go round to somebody's house** aller chez quelqu'un
- **to go round a museum** visiter un musée
- **to go round the shops** faire les boutiques
- **There's a bug going round.** Il y a un microbe qui circule.

to **go through** VERB
traverser ◦ *We went through Paris to get to Rennes.* Nous avons traversé Paris pour aller à Rennes.

to **go up** VERB
☐ **monter** *(person)* ◦ *to go up the stairs* monter l'escalier
② **augmenter** *(increase)* ◦ *The price has gone up.* Le prix a augmenté.
- **to go up in flames** s'embraser ◦ *The whole factory went up in flames.* L'usine toute entière s'est embrasée.

to **go with** VERB
aller avec ◦ *Does this blouse go with that skirt?* Est-ce que ce chemisier va avec cette jupe?

goal NOUN
le **but** ◦ *to score a goal* marquer un but ◦ *His goal is to become the world champion.* Son but est de devenir champion du monde.

goalkeeper NOUN
le **gardien de but**

goat NOUN
la **chèvre**
- **goat's cheese** le fromage de chèvre

god NOUN
le **dieu**
(les **dieux** PL)
◦ *I believe in God.* Je crois en Dieu.

gold NOUN
l' **or** MASC ◦ *They found some gold.* Ils ont trouvé de l'or. ◦ *a gold necklace* un collier en or

goldfish NOUN
le **poisson rouge** ◦ *I've got five goldfish.* J'ai cinq poissons rouges.

golf NOUN
le **golf** ◦ *My dad plays golf.* Mon père joue au golf.
- **a golf club** un club de golf

golf course NOUN
le **terrain de golf**

gone VERB *see* **go**

good ADJECTIVE
☐ **bon** MASC
bonne FEM
◦ *It's a very good film.* C'est un très bon film. ◦ *Vegetables are good for you.* Les légumes sont bons pour la santé.
- **to be good at something** être bon en quelque chose ◦ *Jane's very good at maths.* Jane est très bonne en maths.
② *(kind)*
gentil MASC
gentille FEM
◦ *They were very good to me.* Ils ont été très gentils avec moi. ◦ *That's very good of you.* C'est très gentil de votre part.
③ *(not naughty)*
sage ◦ *Be good!* Sois sage!
- **for good** pour de bon ◦ *One day he left for good.* Un jour il est parti pour de bon.
- **Good morning!** Bonjour!
- **Good afternoon!** Bonjour!
- **Good evening!** Bonsoir!
- **Good night!** Bonne nuit!
- **It's no good complaining.** Cela ne sert à rien de se plaindre.

goodbye EXCLAMATION
au revoir!

Good Friday NOUN
le **Vendredi saint**

good-looking ADJECTIVE
beau MASC
belle FEM
(**beaux** MASC PL)
◦ *He's very good-looking.* Il est très beau.

goods PL NOUN
les **marchandises** FEM *(in shop)*
- **a goods train** un train de marchandises

goose NOUN
l' **oie** FEM

gorgeous ADJECTIVE
1 **superbe** ◇ *She's gorgeous!* Elle est superbe!
2 **splendide** ◇ *The weather was gorgeous.* Il a fait un temps splendide.

gorilla NOUN
le **gorille**

gossip NOUN
see also gossip VERB
1 les **cancans** MASC PL (*rumours*) ◇ *Tell me the gossip!* Raconte-moi les cancans!
2 la **commère** (*woman*) ◇ *She's such a gossip!* C'est une vraie commère!
3 le **bavard** (*man*) ◇ *What a gossip!* Quel bavard!

to **gossip** VERB
see also gossip NOUN
1 **bavarder** (*chat*) ◇ *They were always gossiping.* Elles étaient tout le temps en train de bavarder.
2 **faire des commérages** (*about somebody*) ◇ *They gossiped about her.* Elles faisaient des commérages à son sujet.

got VERB *see* **get**

government NOUN
le **gouvernement**

to **grab** VERB
saisir

graceful ADJECTIVE
élégant

grade NOUN
la **note** (*at school*) ◇ *He got good grades in his exams.* Il a eu de bonnes notes à ses examens.

gradual ADJECTIVE
progressif MASC
progressive FEM

gradually ADVERB
peu à peu ◇ *We gradually got used to it.* Nous nous y sommes habitués peu à peu.

graduate NOUN
le **diplômé**
la **diplômée**

graffiti PL NOUN
les **graffiti** MASC

grain NOUN
le **grain**

gram NOUN
le **gramme**

grammar NOUN
la **grammaire**

grammar school NOUN
1 le **collège**

2 le **lycée**
In France pupils go to a collège *between the ages of 11 and 15, and then to a* lycée *until the age of 18. French schools are mostly non-selective.*

grammatical ADJECTIVE
grammatical
(**grammaticaux** MASC PL)

gramme NOUN
le **gramme** ◇ *500 grammes of cheese* cinq cents grammes de fromage

grand ADJECTIVE
somptueux MASC
somptueuse FEM
◇ *Samantha lives in a very grand house.* Samantha habite une maison somptueuse.

grandchildren PL NOUN
les **petits-enfants** MASC PL

granddad NOUN
le **papi** ◇ *my granddad* mon papi

granddaughter NOUN
la **petite-fille**

grandfather NOUN
le **grand-père** ◇ *my grandfather* mon grand-père

grandma NOUN
la **mamie** ◇ *my grandma* ma mamie

grandmother NOUN
la **grand-mère** ◇ *my grandmother* ma grand-mère

grandpa NOUN
le **papi** ◇ *my grandpa* mon papi

grandparents PL NOUN
les **grands-parents** MASC PL ◇ *my grandparents* mes grands-parents

grandson NOUN
le **petit-fils**

granny NOUN
la **mamie** ◇ *my granny* ma mamie

grape NOUN
le **raisin**

grapefruit NOUN
le **pamplemousse**

graph NOUN
le **graphique**

to **grasp** VERB
saisir

grass NOUN
l' **herbe** FEM ◇ *The grass is long.* L'herbe est haute.
• **to cut the grass** tondre le gazon

grasshopper NOUN
la **sauterelle**

to **grate** VERB
râper ◇ *to grate some cheese* râper du fromage

grateful ADJECTIVE
reconnaissant

G

grave NOUN
la **tombe**

gravel NOUN
le **gravier**

graveyard NOUN
le **cimetière**

gravy NOUN
la **sauce au jus de viande**

grease NOUN
le **lubrifiant**

greasy ADJECTIVE
gras MASC
grasse FEM
◇ *He has greasy hair.* Il a les cheveux
gras. ◇ *The food was very greasy.* La
nourriture était très grasse.

great ADJECTIVE
1 **génial**
(**géniaux** MASC PL)
◇ *That's great!* C'est génial!
2 **grand** ◇ *a great mansion* un grand
manoir

Great Britain NOUN
la **Grande-Bretagne**
- **in Great Britain** en Grande-Bretagne
- **to Great Britain** en Grande-Bretagne
- **I'm from Great Britain.** Je suis
britannique.

great-grandfather NOUN
l' **arrière-grand-père** MASC

great-grandmother NOUN
l' **arrière-grand-mère** FEM

Greece NOUN
la **Grèce**
- **in Greece** en Grèce
- **to Greece** en Grèce

greedy ADJECTIVE
1 **gourmand** (*for food*) ◇ *I want some
more cake.—Don't be so greedy!* Je veux
encore du gâteau.–Ne sois pas si
gourmand!
2 **avide** (*for money*)

Greek ADJECTIVE
see also Greek NOUN
grec MASC
grecque FEM
◇ *Dionysis is Greek.* Dionysis est grec.
◇ *She's Greek.* Elle est grecque.

Greek NOUN
see also Greek ADJECTIVE
1 (*person*)
le **Grec**
la **Grecque**
2 (*language*)
le **grec**

green ADJECTIVE
see also green NOUN
1 **vert** ◇ *a green car* une voiture
verte ◇ *a green salad* une salade verte

2 **écologiste** (*movement, candidate*)
◇ *the Green Party* le parti écologiste

green NOUN
see also green ADJECTIVE
le **vert** ◇ *a dark green* un vert foncé
- **greens** (*vegetables*) les légumes verts
- **the Greens** (*party*) les Verts MASC

greengrocer's NOUN
le **marchand de fruits et légumes**

greenhouse NOUN
la **serre**
- **the greenhouse effect** l'effet de serre
MASC

Greenland NOUN
le **Groenland**

to **greet** VERB
accueillir ◇ *He greeted me with a kiss.*
Il m'a accueillie en me donnant un
baiser.

greeting NOUN
- **Greetings from Bangor!** Bonjour de
Bangor!

greetings card NOUN
la **carte de vœux**

grew VERB see **grow**

grey ADJECTIVE
gris ◇ *She's got grey hair.* Elle a les
cheveux gris.
- **He's going grey.** Il grisonne.

grey-haired ADJECTIVE
grisonnant

grid NOUN
1 (*in road*)
la **grille**
2 (*of electricity*)
le **réseau**
(les **réseaux** PL)

grief NOUN
le **chagrin**

grill NOUN
see also grill VERB
le **gril** (*of cooker*)
- **a mixed grill** les grillades FEM PL

to **grill** VERB
see also grill NOUN
- **to grill something** faire griller quelque
chose

grim ADJECTIVE
sinistre

to **grin** VERB
see also grin NOUN
sourire ◇ *Dave grinned at me.* Dave
m'a souri.

grin NOUN
see also grin VERB
le **large sourire**

to **grind** VERB
moudre (*coffee, pepper*)

to **grip** VERB

saisir

gripping ADJECTIVE
palpitant (*exciting*)

grit NOUN
le **gravillon**

to **groan** VERB
> see also groan NOUN

gémir ◇ *He groaned with pain.* Il a gémi sous l'effet de la douleur.

groan NOUN
> see also groan VERB

le **gémissement** (*of pain*)

grocer NOUN
l' **épicier** MASC ◇ *He's a grocer.* Il est épicier.

groceries PL NOUN
les **provisions** FEM

grocer's (shop) NOUN
l' **épicerie** FEM

groom NOUN
le **marié** (*bridegroom*) ◇ *the groom and his best man* le marié et son témoin

to **grope** VERB
- **to grope for something** chercher quelque chose à tâtons ◇ *He groped for the light switch.* Il a cherché à tâtons l'interrupteur.

gross ADJECTIVE
dégoûtant (*revolting*) ◇ *It was really gross!* C'était vraiment dégoûtant!

grossly ADVERB
largement ◇ *We're grossly underpaid.* Nous sommes largement sous-payés.

ground NOUN
> see also ground VERB

[1] le **sol** (*earth*) ◇ *The ground's wet.* Le sol est mouillé.
[2] le **terrain** (*for sport*) ◇ *a football ground* un terrain de football
[3] la **raison** (*reason*) ◇ *We've got grounds for complaint.* Nous avons des raisons de nous plaindre.
- **on the ground** par terre ◇ *We sat on the ground.* Nous nous sommes assis par terre.

ground VERB *see* **grind**
> see also ground NOUN

- **ground coffee** le café moulu

group NOUN
le **groupe**

to **grow** VERB
[1] **pousser** (*plant*) ◇ *Grass grows quickly.* L'herbe pousse vite.
[2] **grandir** (*person, animal*) ◇ *Haven't you grown!* Comme tu as grandi!
[3] **augmenter** (*increase*) ◇ *The number of unemployed people has grown.* Le nombre des chômeurs a augmenté.

[4] **faire pousser** (*cultivate*) ◇ *My Dad grows potatoes.* Mon père fait pousser des pommes de terre.
- **to grow a beard** se laisser pousser la barbe
- **to grow up** grandir ◇ *Oh, grow up!* Ne fais pas l'enfant!
- **He's grown out of his jacket.** Sa veste est devenue trop petite pour lui.

to **growl** VERB
grogner

grown VERB *see* **grow**

growth NOUN
la **croissance** ◇ *economic growth* la croissance économique

grub NOUN
la **bouffe** (*informal*)

grudge NOUN
la **rancune**
- **to bear a grudge against somebody** garder rancune à quelqu'un

gruesome ADJECTIVE
horrible

guarantee NOUN
> see also guarantee VERB

la **garantie**
- **a five-year guarantee** une garantie de cinq ans

to **guarantee** VERB
> see also guarantee NOUN

garantir ◇ *I can't guarantee he'll come.* Je ne peux pas garantir qu'il viendra.

to **guard** VERB
> see also guard NOUN

garder ◇ *They guarded the palace.* Ils gardaient le palais.
- **to guard against something** protéger contre quelque chose

guard NOUN
> see also guard VERB

le **chef de train** (*of train*)
- **a security guard** un vigile
- **a guard dog** un chien de garde

to **guess** VERB
> see also guess NOUN

deviner ◇ *Can you guess what it is?* Devine ce que c'est!
- **to guess wrong** se tromper ◇ *Janice guessed wrong.* Janice s'est trompée.

guess NOUN
> see also guess VERB

la **supposition** ◇ *It's just a guess.* C'est une simple supposition.
- **Have a guess!** Devine!

guest NOUN
[1] l' **invité** MASC
l' **invitée** FEM
◇ *We have guests staying with us.* Nous

avons des invités.

[2] (*of hotel*)

le **client**

la **cliente**

guide NOUN

[1] le **guide** (*book, person*) ◇ *We bought a guide to Paris.* Nous avons acheté un guide sur Paris. ◇ *The guide showed us round the castle.* Le guide nous a fait visiter le château.

[2] l' **éclaireuse** FEM (*girl guide*)

• **the Guides** les Éclaireuses

guidebook NOUN

le **guide**

guide dog NOUN

le **chien d'aveugle**

guilty ADJECTIVE

coupable ◇ *to feel guilty* se sentir coupable ◇ *She was found guilty.* Elle a été reconnue coupable.

guinea pig NOUN

le **cobaye**

guitar NOUN

la **guitare** ◇ *I play the guitar.* Je joue de la guitare.

gum NOUN

le **chewing-gum** (*sweet*)

• **gums** (*in mouth*) les gencives FEM

gun NOUN

[1] le **revolver** (*small*)

[2] le **fusil** (*rifle*)

gust NOUN

• **a gust of wind** une rafale de vent

guy NOUN

le **type** ◇ *Who's that guy?* C'est qui ce type? ◇ *He's a nice guy.* C'est un type sympa.

gym NOUN

la **gym** ◇ *I go to the gym every day.* Je vais tous les jours à la gym.

• **gym classes** les cours de gym

gymnast NOUN

le/la **gymnaste** ◇ *She's a gymnast.* Elle est gymnaste.

gymnastics NOUN

la **gymnastique** ◇ *to do gymnastics* faire de la gymnastique

H

habit NOUN
l' **habitude** ◇ *a bad habit* une mauvaise habitude

had VERB *see* **have**

hadn't = had not

hail NOUN
see also hail VERB
la **grêle**

to **hail** VERB
see also hail NOUN
grêler ◇ *It's hailing.* Il grêle.

hair NOUN
1 les **cheveux** MASC PL ◇ *She's got long hair.* Elle a les cheveux longs. ◇ *He's got black hair.* Il a les cheveux noirs. ◇ *He's losing his hair.* Il perd ses cheveux.
- **to brush one's hair** se brosser les cheveux ◇ *I brush my hair every morning.* Je me brosse les cheveux tous les matins.
- **to wash one's hair** se laver les cheveux ◇ *I need to wash my hair.* Il faut que je me lave les cheveux.
- **to have one's hair cut** se faire couper les cheveux ◇ *I've just had my hair cut.* Je viens de me faire couper les cheveux.
- **a hair (1)** (*from head*) un cheveu
- **a hair (2)** (*from body*) un poil
2 le **pelage** (*fur of animal*)

hairbrush NOUN
la **brosse à cheveux**

haircut NOUN
la **coupe**
- **to have a haircut** se faire couper les cheveux ◇ *I've just had a haircut.* Je viens de me faire couper les cheveux.

hairdresser NOUN
le **coiffeur**
la **coiffeuse**
◇ *He's a hairdresser.* Il est coiffeur.

hairdresser's NOUN
le **coiffeur** ◇ *at the hairdresser's* chez le coiffeur

hair dryer NOUN
le **sèche-cheveux**
(les **sèche-cheveux** PL)

hair gel NOUN
le **gel pour les cheveux**

hairgrip NOUN
la **pince à cheveux**

hair spray NOUN
la **laque**

hairstyle NOUN

la **coiffure**

hairy ADJECTIVE
poilu ◇ *He's got hairy legs.* Il a les jambes poilues.

half NOUN
see also half ADJECTIVE
1 la **moitié** ◇ *half of the cake* la moitié du gâteau
2 le **billet demi-tarif** (*ticket*) ◇ *A half to York, please.* Un billet demi-tarif pour York, s'il vous plaît.
- **two and a half** deux et demi
- **half an hour** une demi-heure
- **half past ten** dix heures et demie
- **half a kilo** cinq cents grammes
- **to cut something in half** couper quelque chose en deux

half ADJECTIVE, ADVERB
see also half NOUN
1 **demi** ◇ *a half chicken* un demi-poulet
2 **à moitié** ◇ *He was half asleep.* Il était à moitié endormi.

half-hour NOUN
la **demi-heure**

half-price ADJECTIVE, ADVERB
- **at half-price** à moitié prix

half-time NOUN
la **mi-temps**

halfway ADVERB
1 **à mi-chemin** ◇ *halfway between Oxford and London* à mi-chemin entre Oxford et Londres
2 **à la moitié** ◇ *halfway through the chapter* à la moitié du chapitre

hall NOUN
1 l' **entrée** FEM (*in house*)
2 la **salle** ◇ *the village hall* la salle des fêtes

Hallowe'en NOUN
la **veille de la Toussaint**

hallway NOUN
le **vestibule**

halt NOUN
- **to come to a halt** s'arrêter

ham NOUN
le **jambon**
- **a ham sandwich** un sandwich au jambon

hamburger NOUN
le **hamburger**

hammer NOUN
le **marteau**
(les **marteaux** PL)

hamster NOUN
le **hamster**

hand NOUN

see also hand VERB

1 la **main** (*of person*)

- **to give somebody a hand** donner un coup de main à quelqu'un ◇ *Can you give me a hand?* Tu peux me donner un coup de main?
- **on the one hand..., on the other hand...** d'une part..., d'autre part...

2 l' **aiguille** FEM (*of clock*)

to **hand** VERB

see also hand NOUN

passer ◇ *He handed me the book.* Il m'a passé le livre.

- **to hand something in** rendre quelque chose ◇ *Martin handed his exam paper in.* Martin a rendu sa copie d'examen.
- **to hand something out** distribuer quelque chose ◇ *The teacher handed out the books.* Le professeur a distribué les livres.
- **to hand something over** remettre quelque chose ◇ *She handed the keys over to me.* Elle m'a remis les clés.

handbag NOUN

le **sac à main**

(les **sacs à main** PL)

handbook NOUN

le **manuel**

handcuffs PL NOUN

les **menottes** FEM

handkerchief NOUN

le **mouchoir**

handle NOUN

see also handle VERB

1 la **poignée** (*of door*)

2 l' **anse** FEM (*of cup*)

3 le **manche** (*of knife*)

4 la **queue** (*of saucepan*)

to **handle** VERB

see also handle NOUN

- **He handled it well.** Il s'en est bien tiré.
- **Kath handled the travel arrangements.** Kath s'est occupée de l'organisation du voyage.
- **She's good at handling children.** Elle sait s'y prendre bien avec les enfants.

handlebars PL NOUN

le **guidon** SING

handmade ADJECTIVE

fait à la main

handsome ADJECTIVE

beau MASC

belle FEM

◇ *He's very handsome.* Il est très beau.

handwriting NOUN

l' **écriture** FEM

handy ADJECTIVE

1 **pratique** ◇ *This knife's very handy.* Ce couteau est très pratique.

2 **sous la main** ◇ *Have you got a pen handy?* Est-ce que tu as un stylo sous la main?

to **hang** VERB

1 **accrocher** ◇ *Mike hung the painting on the wall.* Mike a accroché le tableau au mur.

2 **pendre** ◇ *They hanged the criminal.* Ils ont pendu le criminel.

- **to hang around** traîner ◇ *On Saturdays we hang around in the park.* Le samedi nous traînons dans le parc.
- **to hang on** patienter ◇ *Hang on a minute please.* Patientez une minute s'il vous plaît.
- **to hang up (1)** (*clothes*) accrocher ◇ *Hang your jacket up on the hook.* Accrochez votre veste au portemanteau.
- **to hang up (2)** (*phone*) raccrocher ◇ *I tried to phone him but he hung up on me.* J'ai essayé de l'appeler, mais il m'a raccroché au nez.

hang-gliding NOUN

le **deltaplane**

- **to go hang-gliding** faire du deltaplane

hangover NOUN

la **gueule de bois** ◇ *to have a hangover* avoir la gueule de bois

to **happen** VERB

se passer ◇ *What's happened?* Qu'est-ce qui s'est passé?

- **as it happens** justement ◇ *As it happens, I don't want to go.* Justement, je ne veux pas y aller.

happily ADVERB

1 **joyeusement** ◇ *"Don't worry!" he said happily.* "Ne te fais pas de souci!" dit-il joyeusement.

2 **heureusement** (*fortunately*) ◇ *Happily, everything went well.* Heureusement, tout s'est bien passé.

happiness NOUN

le **bonheur**

happy ADJECTIVE

heureux MASC

heureuse FEM

◇ *Janet looks happy.* Janet a l'air heureuse.

- **I'm very happy with your work.** Je suis très satisfait de ton travail.
- **Happy birthday!** Bon anniversaire!

harbour NOUN

le **port**

hard ADJECTIVE, ADVERB

1 **dur** ◇ *This cheese is very hard.* Ce fromage est très dur. ◇ *He's worked very hard.* Il a travaillé très dur.

[2] **difficile** ◇ *This question's too hard for me.* Cette question est trop difficile pour moi.

hard disk NOUN
le **disque dur** (*of computer*)

hardly ADVERB
- **I've hardly got any money.** Je n'ai presque pas d'argent.
- **I hardly know you.** Je te connais à peine.
- **hardly ever** presque jamais

hard up ADJECTIVE
fauché

hare NOUN
le **lièvre**

to **harm** VERB
- **to harm somebody** faire du mal à quelqu'un ◇ *I didn't mean to harm you.* Je ne voulais pas te faire de mal.
- **to harm something** nuire à quelque chose ◇ *Chemicals harm the environment.* Les produits chimiques nuisent à l'environnement.

harmful ADJECTIVE
nuisible ◇ *harmful chemicals* des produits chimiques nuisibles

harmless ADJECTIVE
inoffensif MASC
inoffensive FEM
◇ *Most spiders are harmless.* La plupart des araignées sont inoffensives.

has VERB *see* **have**

hasn't = has not

hat NOUN
le **chapeau**
(les **chapeaux** PL)

to **hate** VERB
détester ◇ *I hate maths.* Je déteste les maths.

hatred NOUN
la **haine**

to **have** VERB
[1] **avoir** ◇ *Have you got a sister?* Tu as une sœur? ◇ *He's got blue eyes.* Il a les yeux bleus. ◇ *I've got a cold.* J'ai un rhume. ◇ *He's done it, hasn't he?* Il l'a fait, non? ◇ *Have you got any money?–No, I haven't!* Est-ce que tu as de l'argent?–Non, je n'en ai pas!
The perfect tense of some verbs is formed with être.
[2] **être** ◇ *They have arrived.* Ils sont arrivés. ◇ *Has he gone?* Est-ce qu'il est parti?
[3] **prendre** ◇ *He had his breakfast.* Il a pris son petit déjeuner. ◇ *to have a shower* prendre une douche
- **to have got to do something** devoir

faire quelque chose ◇ *She's got to do it.* Elle doit le faire.
- **to have a party** faire une fête
- **to have one's hair cut** se faire couper les cheveux

haven't = have not

hay NOUN
le **foin**

hay fever NOUN
le **rhume des foins** ◇ *Do you get hay fever?* Est-ce que vous êtes sujet au rhume des foins?

hazelnut NOUN
la **noisette**

he PRONOUN
il ◇ *He loves dogs.* Il aime les chiens.

head NOUN
see also **head** VERB
[1] (*of person*)
la **tête** ◇ *The wine went to my head.* Le vin m'est monté à la tête.
[2] (*of private or primary school*)
le **directeur**
la **directrice**
[3] (*of state secondary school*)
le **proviseur**
[4] (*leader*)
le **chef** ◇ *a head of state* un chef d'État
- **to have a head for figures** être doué pour les chiffres
- **Heads or tails?–Heads.** Pile ou face? –Face.

to **head** VERB
see also **head** NOUN
- **to head for something** se diriger vers quelque chose ◇ *They headed for the church.* Ils se sont dirigés vers l'église.

headache NOUN
- **I've got a headache.** J'ai mal à la tête.

headlight NOUN
le **phare**

headline NOUN
le **titre**

headmaster NOUN
[1] le **directeur** (*of private or primary school*)
[2] le **proviseur** (*of state secondary school*)

headmistress NOUN
[1] la **directrice** (*of private or primary school*)
[2] le **proviseur** (*of state secondary school*)

headphones PL NOUN
les **écouteurs** MASC

headteacher NOUN
[1] (*of private or primary school*)
le **directeur**
la **directrice**
[2] (*of state secondary school*)
le **proviseur** ◇ *She's a headteacher.* Elle est proviseur.

health NOUN
la **santé**

healthy ADJECTIVE
1 **en bonne santé** (*person*) ◇ *Lesley's a healthy person.* Lesley est en bonne santé.
2 **sain** (*climate, food*) ◇ *a healthy diet* une alimentation saine

heap NOUN
le **tas** ◇ *a rubbish heap* un tas d'ordures

to **hear** VERB
1 **entendre** ◇ *He heard the dog bark.* Il a entendu le chien aboyer. ◇ *She can't hear very well.* Elle entend mal. ◇ *I heard that she was ill.* J'ai entendu dire qu'elle était malade.
• **to hear about something** entendre parler de quelque chose
2 **apprendre** (*news*) ◇ *Did you hear the good news?* Est-ce que tu as appris la bonne nouvelle?
• **to hear from somebody** avoir des nouvelles de quelqu'un ◇ *I haven't heard from him recently.* Je n'ai pas eu de ses nouvelles récemment.

heart NOUN
le **cœur**
• **to learn something by heart** apprendre quelque chose par cœur
• **the ace of hearts** l'as de cœur

heart attack NOUN
la **crise cardiaque**

heartbroken ADJECTIVE
• **to be heartbroken** avoir le cœur brisé

heat NOUN
see also heat VERB
la **chaleur**

to **heat** VERB
see also heat NOUN
faire chauffer ◇ *Heat gently for 5 minutes.* Faire chauffer à feu doux pendant cinq minutes.
• **to heat up (1)** (*cooked food*) faire réchauffer ◇ *He heated the soup up.* Il a fait réchauffer la soupe.
• **to heat up (2)** (*water, oven*) chauffer ◇ *The water is heating up.* L'eau chauffe.

heater NOUN
le **radiateur** ◇ *an electric heater* un radiateur électrique

heating NOUN
le **chauffage**

heaven NOUN
le **paradis**

heavily ADVERB
lourdement ◇ *The car was heavily loaded.* La voiture était lourdement chargée.
• **He drinks heavily.** C'est un gros buveur.

heavy ADJECTIVE
1 **lourd** ◇ *This bag's very heavy.* Ce sac est très lourd.
• **heavy rain** une grosse averse
2 **chargé** (*busy*) ◇ *I've got a very heavy week ahead.* Je vais avoir une semaine très chargée.
• **to be a heavy drinker** être un gros buveur

he'd = he would, he had

hedge NOUN
la **haie**

hedgehog NOUN
le **hérisson**

heel NOUN
le **talon**

height NOUN
1 la **taille** (*of person*)
2 la **hauteur** (*of object*)
3 l' **altitude** FEM (*of mountain*)

heir NOUN
l' **héritier** MASC

heiress NOUN
l' **héritière** FEM

held VERB *see* **hold**

helicopter NOUN
l' **hélicoptère** MASC

hell NOUN
l' **enfer** MASC
• **Hell!** Merde! (*rude*)

he'll = he will, he shall

hello EXCLAMATION
bonjour!

helmet NOUN
le **casque**

to **help** VERB
see also help NOUN
aider ◇ *Can you help me?* Est-ce que vous pouvez m'aider?
• **Help!** Au secours!
• **Help yourself!** Servez-vous!
• **He can't help it.** Il n'y peut rien.

help NOUN
see also help VERB
l' **aide** FEM ◇ *Do you need any help?* Vous avez besoin d'aide?

helpful ADJECTIVE
serviable ◇ *He was very helpful.* Il a été très serviable.

hen NOUN
la **poule**

her ADJECTIVE
see also her PRONOUN
son MASC ◇ *her father* son père
sa FEM ◇ *her mother* sa mère
ses PL ◇ *her parents* ses parents

sa *becomes* **son** *before a vowel sound.*
- **her friend (1)** (*male*) son ami
- **her friend (2)** (*female*) son amie
Do not use **son/sa/ses** *with parts of the body.*
⋄ *She's going to wash her hair.* Elle va se laver les cheveux. ⋄ *She's cleaning her teeth.* Elle se brosse les dents. ⋄ *She's hurt her foot.* Elle s'est fait mal au pied.

her PRONOUN
see also **her** ADJECTIVE
la *becomes* **l'** *before a vowel sound.*
[1] **la** ⋄ *I can see her.* Je la vois.
⋄ *Look at her!* Regarde-la!
l' ⋄ *I saw her.* Je l'ai vue.
Use **lui** *when* her *means* to her.
[2] **lui** ⋄ *I gave her a book.* Je lui ai donné un livre. ⋄ *I told her the truth.* Je lui ai dit la vérité.
Use **elle** *after prepositions.*
[3] **elle** ⋄ *I'm going with her.* Je vais avec elle. ⋄ *He sat next to her.* Il s'est assis à côté d'elle.
elle *is also used in comparisons.*
⋄ *I'm older than her.* Je suis plus âgé qu'elle.

herb NOUN
l' **herbe**

here ADVERB
ici ⋄ *I live here.* J'habite ici.
- **here is...** voici... ⋄ *Here's Helen.* Voici Helen. ⋄ *Here he is!* Le voici!
- **here are...** voici... ⋄ *Here are the books.* Voici les livres.

hero NOUN
le **héros** ⋄ *He's a real hero!* C'est un véritable héros!

heroin NOUN
l' **héroïne** ⋄ *Heroin is a hard drug.* L'héroïne est une drogue dure.
- **a heroin addict** un héroïnomane ⋄ *She's a heroin addict.* C'est une héroïnomane.

heroine NOUN
l' **héroïne** ⋄ *the heroine of the novel* l'héroïne du roman

hers PRONOUN
le sien + MASC NOUN ⋄ *Is this her coat?* *—No, hers is black.* C'est son manteau?—Non, le sien est noir.
la sienne + FEM NOUN ⋄ *Is this her car?* *—No, hers is white.* C'est sa voiture? —Non, la sienne est blanche.
les siens + MASC PL NOUN ⋄ *my parents and hers* mes parents et les siens
les siennes + FEM PL NOUN ⋄ *my reasons and hers* mes raisons et les siennes
- **Is this hers?** C'est à elle? ⋄ *This book is hers.* Ce livre est à elle. ⋄ *Whose is*

this?—It's hers. C'est à qui?–À elle.

herself PRONOUN
[1] **se** ⋄ *She's hurt herself.* Elle s'est blessée.
[2] **elle** (*after preposition*) ⋄ *She talked mainly about herself.* Elle a surtout parlé d'elle.
[3] **elle-même** ⋄ *She did it herself.* Elle l'a fait elle-même.
- **by herself** toute seule ⋄ *She doesn't like travelling by herself.* Elle n'aime pas voyager toute seule.

he's = he is, he has

to **hesitate** VERB
hésiter

heterosexual ADJECTIVE
hétérosexuel MASC
hétérosexuelle FEM

hi EXCLAMATION
salut!

to **hide** VERB
se cacher ⋄ *He hid behind a bush.* Il s'est caché derrière un buisson.
- **to hide something** cacher quelque chose ⋄ *Paula hid the present.* Paula a caché le cadeau.

hide-and-seek NOUN
- **to play hide-and-seek** jouer à cache-cache

hideous ADJECTIVE
hideux MASC
hideuse FEM

hi-fi NOUN
la **chaîne hi-fi**
(les **chaînes hi-fi** PL)

high ADJECTIVE, ADVERB
[1] **haut** ⋄ *It's too high.* C'est trop haut.
- **How high is the wall?** Quelle est la hauteur du mur?
- **The wall's 2 metres high.** Le mur fait deux mètres de haut.
[2] **élevé** ⋄ *a high price* un prix élevé ⋄ *a high temperature* une température élevée
- **at high speed** à grande vitesse
- **It's very high in fat.** C'est très gras.
- **She's got a very high voice.** Elle a la voix très aiguë.
- **to be high** (*on drugs*) être défoncé (*informal*)
- **to get high** se défoncer (*informal*) ⋄ *to get high on crack* se défoncer au crack

high-heeled ADJECTIVE
à hauts talons
- **high-heeled shoes** des chaussures à hauts talons

high jump NOUN
le **saut en hauteur** (*sport*)

highlight NOUN
le **clou** ◇ *the highlight of the evening*
le clou de la soirée

high-rise NOUN
la **tour** ◇ *I live in a high-rise.* J'habite
dans une tour.

high school NOUN
le **lycée**

to **hijack** VERB
détourner

hijacker NOUN
le **pirate de l'air**

hike NOUN
la **randonnée**

hiking NOUN
- **to go hiking** faire une randonnée

hilarious ADJECTIVE
hilarant ◇ *It was hilarious!* C'était
hilarant!

hill NOUN
la **colline** ◇ *She walked up the hill.*
Elle a gravi la colline.

hill-walking NOUN
la **randonnée de basse montagne**
◇ *to go hill-walking* faire de la
randonnée de basse montagne

him PRONOUN
le becomes l' before a vowel sound.
1 **le** ◇ *I can see him.* Je le vois.
◇ *Look at him!* Regarde-le!
l' ◇ *I saw him.* Je l'ai vu.
*Use lui when him means to him, and after
prepositions.*
2 **lui** ◇ *I gave him a book.* Je lui ai
donné un livre. ◇ *I told him the truth.*
Je lui ai dit la vérité. ◇ *I'm going with
him.* Je vais avec lui. ◇ *She sat next to
him.* Elle s'est assise à côté de lui.
lui is also used in comparisons.
◇ *I'm older than him.* Je suis plus âgé
que lui.

himself PRONOUN
1 **se** ◇ *He's hurt himself.* Il s'est
blessé.
2 **lui** ◇ *He talked mainly about
himself.* Il a surtout parlé de lui.
3 **lui-même** ◇ *He did it himself.* Il l'a
fait lui-même.
- **by himself** tout seul ◇ *He was
travelling by himself.* Il voyageait tout
seul.

Hindu ADJECTIVE
hindou ◇ *a Hindu temple* un temple
hindou

hip NOUN
la **hanche**

hippie NOUN
le **hippie**
la **hippie**

hippo NOUN
l' **hippopotame** MASC

to **hire** VERB
see also hire NOUN
1 **louer** ◇ *to hire a car* louer une
voiture
2 **engager** (*person*) ◇ *They hired a
cleaner.* Ils ont engagé une femme de
ménage.

hire NOUN
see also hire VERB
la **location**
- **car hire** location de voitures
- **for hire** à louer

hire car NOUN
la **voiture de location**

his ADJECTIVE
see also his PRONOUN
son MASC ◇ *his father* son père
sa FEM ◇ *his mother* sa mère
ses PL ◇ *his parents* ses parents
sa becomes son before a vowel sound.
- **his friend (1)** (*male*) son ami
- **his friend (2)** (*female*) son amie
*Do not use son/sa/ses with parts of the
body.*
◇ *He's going to wash his hair.* Il va se
laver les cheveux. ◇ *He's cleaning his
teeth.* Il se brosse les dents. ◇ *He's hurt
his foot.* Il s'est fait mal au pied.

his PRONOUN
see also his ADJECTIVE
le sien + MASC NOUN ◇ *Is this his coat?
—No, his is black.* C'est son
manteau?—Non, le sien est noir.
la sienne + FEM NOUN ◇ *Is this his car?
—No, his is white.* C'est sa voiture?
—Non, la sienne est blanche.
les siens + MASC PL NOUN ◇ *my parents
and his* mes parents et les siens
les siennes + FEM PL NOUN ◇ *my reasons
and his* mes raisons et les siennes
- **Is this his?** C'est à lui? ◇ *This book is
his.* Ce livre est à lui. ◇ *Whose is this?
—It's his.* C'est à qui?—À lui.

history NOUN
l' **histoire**

to **hit** VERB
see also hit NOUN
1 **frapper** ◇ *Andrew hit him.* Andrew
l'a frappé.
2 **renverser** ◇ *He was hit by a car.* Il
a été renversé par une voiture.
3 **toucher** ◇ *The arrow hit the target.*
La flèche a touché la cible.
- **to hit it off with somebody** bien
s'entendre avec quelqu'un ◇ *She hit it
off with his parents.* Elle s'est bien
entendue avec ses parents.

hit NOUN

see also hit VERB

[1] le **tube** (song) ◇ Blur's latest hit le dernier tube de Blur

[2] le **succès** (success) ◇ The film was a massive hit. Le film a eu un immense succès.

hitch NOUN

le **contretemps** ◇ There's been a slight hitch. Il y a eu un léger contretemps.

to **hitchhike** VERB

faire de l'auto-stop

hitchhiker NOUN

l' **auto-stoppeur** MASC

l' **auto-stoppeuse** FEM

hitchhiking NOUN

l' **auto-stop** MASC ◇ Hitchhiking can be dangerous. Il peut être dangereux de faire de l'auto-stop.

hit man NOUN

le **tueur à gages**

HIV-negative ADJECTIVE

séronégatif MASC

séronégative FEM

HIV-positive ADJECTIVE

séropositif MASC

séropositive FEM

hobby NOUN

le **passe-temps favori** ◇ What are your hobbies? Quels sont tes passe-temps favoris?

hockey NOUN

le **hockey** ◇ I play hockey. Je joue au hockey.

to **hold** VERB

[1] **tenir** (hold on to) ◇ She held the baby. Elle tenait le bébé.

[2] **contenir** (contain) ◇ This bottle holds one litre. Cette bouteille contient un litre.

- **to hold a meeting** avoir une réunion
- **Hold the line!** (on telephone) Ne quittez pas!
- **Hold it!** (wait) Attends!
- **to get hold of something** (obtain) trouver quelque chose ◇ I couldn't get hold of it. Je n'ai pas réussi à en trouver.

to **hold on** VERB

[1] **tenir bon** (keep hold) ◇ The cliff was slippery but he managed to hold on. La falaise était glissante, mais il est parvenu à tenir bon.

- **to hold on to something** se cramponner à quelque chose ◇ He held on to the chair. Il se cramponnait à la chaise.

[2] **attendre** (wait) ◇ Hold on, I'm coming! Attends, je viens!

- **Hold on!** (on telephone) Ne quittez pas!

to **hold up** VERB

- **to hold up one's hand** lever la main ◇ Pierre held up his hand. Pierre a levé la main.
- **to hold somebody up** (delay) retenir quelqu'un ◇ I was held up at the office. J'ai été retenu au bureau.
- **to hold up a bank** (rob) braquer une banque (informal)

hold-up NOUN

[1] le **hold-up** (at bank)

[2] le **retard** (delay)

[3] le **bouchon** (traffic jam)

hole NOUN

le **trou**

holiday NOUN

[1] les **vacances** FEM PL ◇ Did you have a good holiday? Tu as passé de bonnes vacances? ◇ our holidays in France nos vacances en France

- **on holiday** en vacances ◇ to go on holiday partir en vacances ◇ We are on holiday. Nous sommes en vacances.
- **the school holidays** les vacances scolaires

[2] le **jour férié** (public holiday) ◇ Next Wednesday is a holiday. Mercredi prochain est un jour férié.

[3] le **jour de congé** (day off) ◇ He took a day's holiday. Il a pris un jour de congé.

- **a holiday camp** un camp de vacances

Holland NOUN

la **Hollande**

- **in Holland** en Hollande
- **to Holland** en Hollande

hollow ADJECTIVE

creux MASC

creuse FEM

holy ADJECTIVE

saint

home NOUN

see also home ADVERB

la **maison**

- **at home** à la maison
- **Make yourself at home.** Faites comme chez vous.

home ADVERB

see also home NOUN

à la maison ◇ I'll be home at 5 o'clock. Je serai à la maison à cinq heures.

- **to get home** rentrer ◇ What time did he get home? Il est rentré à quelle heure?

home address NOUN

l' **adresse** FEM ◇ What's your home address? Quelle est votre adresse?

homeland NOUN
la **patrie**
homeless ADJECTIVE
sans abri
- **the homeless** les sans-abri
home match NOUN
le **match à domicile**
homesick ADJECTIVE
- **to be homesick** avoir le mal du pays
homework NOUN
les **devoirs** MASC PL ◇ *Have you done your homework?* Est-ce que tu as fait tes devoirs? ◇ *my geography homework* mes devoirs de géographie
homosexual ADJECTIVE
see also homosexual NOUN
homosexuel MASC
homosexuelle FEM
homosexual NOUN
see also homosexual ADJECTIVE
l' **homosexuel**
honest ADJECTIVE
1 (*trustworthy*)
honnête ◇ *She's a very honest person.* Elle est très honnête.
2 (*sincere*)
franc MASC
franche FEM
◇ *He was very honest with her.* Il a été très franc avec elle.
honestly ADVERB
franchement ◇ *I honestly don't know.* Franchement, je n'en sais rien.
honesty NOUN
l' **honnêteté**
honey NOUN
le **miel**
honeymoon NOUN
la **lune de miel**
honour NOUN
l' **honneur**
hood NOUN
la **capuche** ◇ *a coat with a hood* un manteau à capuche
hook NOUN
le **crochet** ◇ *He hung the painting on the hook.* Il a suspendu le tableau au crochet.
- **to take the phone off the hook** décrocher le téléphone
- **a fish-hook** un hameçon
hooligan NOUN
le **voyou**
hooray EXCLAMATION
hourra!
Hoover ® NOUN
l' **aspirateur** MASC
to **hoover** VERB
passer l'aspirateur ◇ *to hoover the*

lounge passer l'aspirateur dans le salon
to **hope** VERB
see also hope NOUN
espérer ◇ *I hope he comes.* J'espère qu'il va venir. ◇ *I'm hoping for good results.* J'espère avoir de bons résultats.
- **I hope so.** Je l'espère.
- **I hope not.** J'espère que non.
hope NOUN
see also hope VERB
l' **espoir** MASC
- **to give up hope** perdre espoir ◇ *Don't give up hope!* Ne perds pas espoir!
hopeful ADJECTIVE
1 **plein d'espoir** ◇ *I'm hopeful.* Je suis plein d'espoir.
- **He's hopeful of winning.** Il a bon espoir de gagner.
2 (*situation*)
prometteur MASC
prometteuse FEM
◇ *The prospects look hopeful.* Les perspectives semblent prometteuses.
hopefully ADVERB
avec un peu de chance ◇ *Hopefully he'll make it in time.* Avec un peu de chance, il arrivera à temps.
hopeless ADJECTIVE
nul MASC
nulle FEM
◇ *I'm hopeless at maths.* Je suis nul en maths.
horizon NOUN
l' **horizon**
horizontal ADJECTIVE
horizontal
(**horizontaux** MASC PL)
horn NOUN
1 le **klaxon** ◇ *He sounded his horn.* Il a klaxonné.
2 **cor** ◇ *I play the horn.* Je joue du cor.
horoscope NOUN
l' **horoscope**
horrible ADJECTIVE
horrible ◇ *What a horrible dress!* Quelle robe horrible!
horror NOUN
l' **horreur**
horror film NOUN
le **film d'horreur**
horse NOUN
le **cheval**
(les **chevaux** PL)
horse-racing NOUN
les **courses de chevaux** FEM PL
horseshoe NOUN
le **fer à cheval**

hose NOUN
le **tuyau**
(les **tuyaux** PL)
◇ *a garden hose* un tuyau d'arrosage
hosepipe NOUN
le **tuyau d'arrosage**
hospital NOUN
l' **hôpital** MASC
(les **hôpitaux** PL)
◇ *Take me to the hospital!*
Emmenez-moi à l'hôpital! ◇ *in hospital*
à l'hôpital
hospitality NOUN
l' **hospitalité**
hostage NOUN
l' **otage** MASC
+ **to take somebody hostage** prendre
quelqu'un en otage
hostile ADJECTIVE
hostile
hot ADJECTIVE
[1] **chaud** (*warm*) ◇ *a hot bath* un bain
chaud ◇ *a hot country* un pays chaud
*When you are talking about a person being hot,
you use* **avoir chaud.**
◇ *I'm hot.* J'ai chaud. ◇ *I'm too hot.*
J'ai trop chaud.
*When you mean that the weather is hot, you
use* **faire chaud.**
◇ *It's hot.* Il fait chaud. ◇ *It's very hot
today.* Il fait très chaud aujourd'hui.
[2] **épicé** (*spicy*) ◇ *a very hot curry* un
curry très épicé
hot dog NOUN
le **hot-dog**
hotel NOUN
l' **hôtel** ◇ *We stayed in a hotel.* Nous
avons logé à l'hôtel.
hour NOUN
l' **heure** FEM ◇ *She always takes hours
to get ready.* Elle passe toujours des
heures à se préparer.
+ **a quarter of an hour** un quart d'heure
+ **half an hour** une demi-heure
+ **two and a half hours** deux heures et
demie
hourly ADJECTIVE, ADVERB
toutes les heures ◇ *There are hourly
buses.* Il y a des bus toutes les heures.
+ **to be paid hourly** être payé à l'heure
house NOUN
la **maison**
+ **at his house** chez lui
+ **We stayed at their house.** Nous avons
séjourné chez eux.
housewife NOUN
la **femme au foyer** ◇ *She's a
housewife.* Elle est femme au foyer.
housework NOUN

le **ménage**
+ **to do the housework** faire le ménage
hovercraft NOUN
l' **aéroglisseur** MASC
how ADVERB
comment ◇ *How are you?* Comment
allez-vous?
+ **How many?** Combien?
+ **How many...?** Combien de...? ◇ *How
many pupils are there in the class?*
Combien d'élèves y a-t-il dans la classe?
+ **How much?** Combien?
+ **How much...?** Combien de...? ◇ *How
much sugar do you want?* Combien de
sucres voulez-vous?
+ **How old are you?** Quel âge as-tu?
+ **How far is it to Edinburgh?** Combien y
a-t-il de kilomètres d'ici à Édimbourg?
+ **How long have you been here?** Depuis
combien de temps êtes-vous là?
however CONJUNCTION
pourtant ◇ *This, however, isn't true.*
Pourtant, ce n'est pas vrai.
to **howl** VERB
hurler
to **hug** VERB
see also **hug** NOUN
serrer dans ses bras ◇ *He hugged her.*
Il l'a serrée dans ses bras.
hug NOUN
see also **hug** VERB
+ **to give somebody a hug** serrer
quelqu'un dans ses bras ◇ *She gave
them a hug.* Elle les a serrés dans ses
bras.
huge ADJECTIVE
immense
to **hum** VERB
fredonner
human ADJECTIVE
humain ◇ *the human body* le corps
humain
human being NOUN
l' **être humain** MASC
humour NOUN
l' **humour** MASC
+ **to have a sense of humour** avoir le
sens de l'humour
hundred NUMBER
+ **a hundred** cent ◇ *a hundred francs*
cent francs
+ **five hundred** cinq cents
+ **five hundred and one** cinq cent un
+ **hundreds of people** des centaines de
personnes
hung VERB see **hang**
Hungary NOUN
la **Hongrie**
+ **in Hungary** en Hongrie

- to **Hungary** en Hongrie
hunger NOUN
la **faim**
hungry ADJECTIVE
- to be **hungry** avoir faim ◇ *I'm hungry.* J'ai faim.
to **hunt** VERB
1 **chasser** (*animal*) ◇ *People used to hunt wild boar.* On chassait le sanglier autrefois.
- to go **hunting** aller à la chasse
2 **pourchasser** (*criminal*) ◇ *The police are hunting the killer.* La police pourchasse le criminel.
- to **hunt for something** (*search*) chercher quelque chose partout ◇ *I hunted everywhere for that book.* J'ai cherché ce livre partout.
hunting NOUN
la **chasse** ◇ *I'm against hunting.* Je suis contre la chasse.
- **fox-hunting** la chasse au renard
hurricane NOUN
l' **ouragan** MASC
to **hurry** VERB
see also **hurry** NOUN
se **dépêcher** ◇ *Sharon hurried back home.* Sharon s'est dépêchée de rentrer chez elle.
- **Hurry up!** Dépêche-toi!
hurry NOUN
see also **hurry** VERB
- to be in a **hurry** être pressé
- to do something in a **hurry** faire quelque chose en vitesse
- **There's no hurry.** Rien ne presse.

to **hurt** VERB
see also **hurt** ADJECTIVE
- to **hurt somebody (1)** (*physically*) faire mal à quelqu'un ◇ *You're hurting me!* Tu me fais mal!
- to **hurt somebody (2)** (*emotionally*) blesser quelqu'un ◇ *His remarks really hurt me.* Ses remarques m'ont vraiment blessé.
- to **hurt oneself** se faire mal ◇ *I fell over and hurt myself.* Je me suis fait mal en tombant.
- **That hurts.** Ça fait mal. ◇ *It hurts to have a tooth out.* Ça fait mal de se faire arracher une dent.
- **My leg hurts.** J'ai mal à la jambe.
hurt ADJECTIVE
see also **hurt** VERB
blessé ◇ *Is he badly hurt?* Est-ce qu'il est grièvement blessé? ◇ *He was hurt in the leg.* Il a été blessé à la jambe. ◇ *I was hurt by what he said.* J'ai été blessé par ce qu'il a dit.
- **Luckily, nobody got hurt.** Heureusement, il n'y a pas eu de blessés.
husband NOUN
le **mari**
hut NOUN
la **hutte**
hymn NOUN
le **cantique**
hypermarket NOUN
l' **hypermarché**
hyphen NOUN
le **trait d'union**

I

I PRONOUN

1 **je** ◇ *I speak French.* Je parle français.

> je *changes to* j' *before a vowel and most words beginning with "h".*

◇ *I love cats.* J'aime les chats.

2 **moi** ◇ *Ann and I* Ann et moi

ice NOUN

1 la **glace** ◇ *There was ice on the lake.* Il y avait de la glace sur le lac.

2 le **verglas** (on road)

iceberg NOUN

l' **iceberg** MASC

ice cream NOUN

la **glace** ◇ *vanilla ice cream* la glace à la vanille

ice cube NOUN

le **glaçon**

ice hockey NOUN

le **hockey sur glace**

Iceland NOUN

l' **Islande** FEM

- **in Iceland** en Islande
- **to Iceland** en Islande

ice lolly NOUN

la **glace à l'eau**

ice rink NOUN

la **patinoire**

ice-skating NOUN

le **patinage sur glace**

- **to go ice-skating** faire du patin à glace

icing NOUN

la **glaçage** (on cake)

- **icing sugar** le sucre glace

icy ADJECTIVE

glacial

(**glaciaux** MASC PL)

◇ *There was an icy wind.* Il y avait un vent glacial.

- **The roads are icy.** Il y a du verglas sur les routes.

I'd = I had, I would

idea NOUN

l' **idée** FEM ◇ *Good idea!* Bonne idée!

ideal ADJECTIVE

idéal

(**idéaux** MASC PL)

identical ADJECTIVE

identique

identification NOUN

l' **identification** FEM

to **identify** VERB

identifier

identity card NOUN

la **carte d'identité**

idiot NOUN

l' **idiot** MASC

l' **idiote** FEM

idiotic ADJECTIVE

stupide

i.e. ABBREVIATION

c.-à-d. (= c'est-à-dire)

if CONJUNCTION

si ◇ *You can have it if you like.* Tu peux le prendre si tu veux.

> si *changes to* s' *before* il *and* ils.

◇ *Do you know if he's there?* Savez-vous s'il est là?

- **if only** si seulement ◇ *If only I had more money!* Si seulement j'avais plus d'argent!
- **if not** sinon ◇ *Are you coming? If not, I'll go with Mark.* Est-ce que tu viens? Sinon, j'irai avec Mark.

ignorant ADJECTIVE

ignorant

to **ignore** VERB

- **to ignore something** ne tenir aucun compte de quelque chose ◇ *She ignored my advice.* Elle n'a tenu aucun compte de mes conseils.
- **to ignore somebody** ignorer quelqu'un ◇ *She saw me, but she ignored me.* Elle m'a vu, mais elle m'a ignoré.
- **Just ignore him!** Ne fais pas attention à lui!

ill ADJECTIVE

malade (sick)

- **to be taken ill** tomber malade ◇ *She was taken ill while on holiday.* Elle est tombée malade pendant qu'elle était en vacances.

I'll = I will

illegal ADJECTIVE

illégal

(**illégaux** MASC PL)

illegible ADJECTIVE

illisible

illness NOUN

la **maladie**

to **ill-treat** VERB

maltraiter

illusion NOUN

l' **illusion** FEM

illustration NOUN

l' **illustration** FEM

image NOUN

l' **image** FEM ◇ *The company has changed its image.* La société a changé d'image.

imagination NOUN

l' **imagination** FEM

to **imagine** VERB
imaginer ◦ *You can imagine how I felt!* Tu peux imaginer ce que j'ai ressenti! ◦ *Is he angry?–I imagine so.* Est-ce qu'il est en colère?–J'imagine que oui.

to **imitate** VERB
imiter

imitation NOUN
l' **imitation** FEM

immediate ADJECTIVE
immédiat

immediately ADVERB
immédiatement ◦ *I'll do it immediately.* Je vais le faire immédiatement.

immigrant NOUN
l' **immigré** MASC
l' **immigrée** FEM

immigration NOUN
l' **immigration** FEM

immoral ADJECTIVE
immoral
(**immoraux** MASC PL)

impartial ADJECTIVE
impartial
(**impartiaux** MASC PL)

impatience NOUN
l' **impatience** FEM

impatient ADJECTIVE
impatient
- **to get impatient** s'impatienter
  ◦ *People are getting impatient.* Les gens commencent à s'impatienter.

impatiently ADVERB
avec impatience ◦ *We waited impatiently.* Nous avons attendu avec impatience.

impersonal ADJECTIVE
impersonnel MASC
impersonnelle FEM

importance NOUN
l' **importance** FEM

important ADJECTIVE
important

impossible ADJECTIVE
impossible

to **impress** VERB
impressionner ◦ *She's trying to impress you.* Elle essaie de t'impressionner.

impressed ADJECTIVE
impressionné ◦ *I'm very impressed!* Je suis très impressionné!

impression NOUN
l' **impression** FEM ◦ *I was under the impression that...* J'avais l'impression que...

impressive ADJECTIVE

impressionnant

to **improve** VERB
[1] **améliorer** (*make better*) ◦ *They have improved the service.* Ils ont amélioré le service.
[2] **s'améliorer** (*get better*) ◦ *The weather is improving.* Le temps s'améliore. ◦ *My French has improved.* Mon français s'est amélioré.

improvement NOUN
[1] l' **amélioration** FEM (*of condition*) ◦ *It's a great improvement.* C'est une nette amélioration.
[2] le **progrès** (*of learner*) ◦ *There's been an improvement in his French.* Il a fait des progrès en français.

in PREPOSITION, ADVERB

> *There are several ways of translating* in. *Scan the examples to find one that is similar to what you want to say. For other expressions with* in, *see the verbs* go, come, get, give *etc.*

[1] **dans** ◦ *in the house* dans la maison ◦ *in my bag* dans mon sac ◦ *in the sixties* dans les années soixante ◦ *I'll see you in three weeks.* Je te verrai dans trois semaines.
[2] **à** ◦ *in the country* à la campagne ◦ *in school* à l'école ◦ *in hospital* à l'hôpital ◦ *in London* à Londres ◦ *in spring* au printemps ◦ *in the sun* au soleil ◦ *in the shade* à l'ombre ◦ *in a loud voice* à voix haute ◦ *the boy in the blue shirt* le garçon à la chemise bleue ◦ *It was written in pencil.* C'était écrit au crayon.
[3] **en** ◦ *in French* en français ◦ *in summer* en été ◦ *in May* en mai ◦ *in 1996* en dix-neuf cent quatre-vingt seize ◦ *I did it in 3 hours.* Je l'ai fait en trois heures. ◦ *in town* en ville ◦ *in prison* en prison ◦ *in tears* en larmes ◦ *in good condition* en bon état

> *When* in *refers to a country which is feminine, use* en; *when the country is masculine, use* au.

◦ *in France* en France ◦ *in Portugal* au Portugal ◦ *in the United States* aux États-Unis
[4] **de** ◦ *the best pupil in the class* le meilleur élève de la classe ◦ *the best team in the world* la meilleure équipe du monde ◦ *the tallest person in the family* le plus grand de la famille ◦ *at 4 o'clock in the afternoon* à quatre heures de l'après-midi ◦ *at 6 in the morning* à six heures du matin
- **in the afternoon** l'après-midi
- **You look good in that dress.** Tu es jolie avec cette robe.
- **in time** à temps ◦ *We arrived in time*

for dinner. Nous sommes arrivés à temps pour le dîner.
- **in here** ici ⋄ *It's hot in here.* Il fait chaud ici.
- **in the rain** sous la pluie
- **one person in ten** une personne sur dix
- **to be in** (*at home, work*) être là ⋄ *He wasn't in.* Il n'était pas là.
- **to ask somebody in** inviter quelqu'un à entrer

inaccurate ADJECTIVE
inexact

incentive NOUN
- **There is no incentive to work.** Il n'y a rien qui incite à travailler.

inch NOUN
le pouce
In France measurements are in metres and centimetres rather than feet and inches. An inch is about 2.5 centimetres.
- **6 inches** quinze centimètres

incident NOUN
l' incident MASC

inclined ADJECTIVE
- **to be inclined to do something** avoir tendance à faire quelque chose ⋄ *He's inclined to arrive late.* Il a tendance à arriver en retard.

to **include** VERB
comprendre ⋄ *Service is not included.* Le service n'est pas compris.

including PREPOSITION
compris ⋄ *It will be 200 francs, including tax.* Ça coûtera deux cents francs, toutes taxes comprises.

inclusive ADJECTIVE
compris ⋄ *The inclusive price is 200 francs.* Ça coûte deux cents francs tout compris.
- **inclusive of tax** taxes comprises

income NOUN
le revenu

income tax NOUN
l' impôt sur le revenu MASC

incompetent ADJECTIVE
incompétent

incomplete ADJECTIVE
incomplet MASC
incomplète FEM

inconvenience NOUN
- **I don't want to cause any inconvenience.** Je ne veux pas vous déranger.

inconvenient ADJECTIVE
- **That's very inconvenient for me.** Ça ne m'arrange pas du tout.

incorrect ADJECTIVE
incorrect

increase NOUN
see also increase VERB
l' augmentation FEM ⋄ *an increase in road accidents* une augmentation des accidents de la route

to **increase** VERB
see also increase NOUN
augmenter

incredible ADJECTIVE
incroyable

indecisive ADJECTIVE
indécis (*person*)

indeed ADVERB
vraiment ⋄ *It's very hard indeed.* C'est vraiment très difficile.
- **Know what I mean?—Indeed I do.** Tu vois ce que je veux dire?–Oui, tout à fait.
- **Thank you very much indeed!** Merci beaucoup!

independence NOUN
l' indépendance FEM

independent ADJECTIVE
indépendant
- **an independent school** une école privée

index NOUN
l' index MASC (*in book*)

India NOUN
l' Inde FEM
- **in India** en Inde
- **to India** en Inde

Indian ADJECTIVE
see also Indian NOUN
indien MASC
indienne FEM

Indian NOUN
see also Indian ADJECTIVE
(*person*)
l' Indien MASC
l' Indienne FEM
- **an American Indian** un Indien d'Amérique

to **indicate** VERB
indiquer

indigestion NOUN
l' indigestion FEM
- **I've got indigestion.** J'ai une indigestion.

indoor ADJECTIVE
- **an indoor swimming pool** une piscine couverte

indoors ADVERB
à l'intérieur ⋄ *They're indoors.* Ils sont à l'intérieur.
- **to go indoors** rentrer ⋄ *We'd better go indoors.* Nous ferions mieux de rentrer.

industrial ADJECTIVE

industriel MASC

industrielle FEM

industrial estate NOUN

la zone industrielle

industry NOUN

l' industrie FEM ◦ *the tourist industry* l'industrie du tourisme ◦ *the oil industry* l'industrie pétrolière ◦ *I'd like to work in industry.* J'aimerais travailler dans l'industrie.

inefficient ADJECTIVE

inefficace

inevitable ADJECTIVE

inévitable

inexpensive ADJECTIVE

bon marché MASC, FEM, PL ◦ *an inexpensive hotel* un hôtel bon marché ◦ *inexpensive holidays* des vacances bon marché

inexperienced ADJECTIVE

inexpérimenté

infant school NOUN

l' école maternelle FEM

The école maternelle *is a state school for 2-6 year-olds.*

◦ *He's in infant school.* Il est à l'école maternelle.

infection NOUN

l' infection FEM ◦ *a ear infection* une infection de l'oreille

- **a throat infection** une angine

infectious ADJECTIVE

contagieux MASC

contagieuse FEM

◦ *It's not infectious.* Ce n'est pas contagieux.

infinitive NOUN

l' infinitif MASC

infirmary NOUN

l' hôpital MASC

(les hôpitaux PL)

inflatable ADJECTIVE

gonflable (*mattress, dinghy*)

inflation NOUN

l' inflation FEM

influence NOUN

see also influence VERB

l' influence FEM ◦ *He's a bad influence on her.* Il a mauvaise influence sur elle.

to **influence** VERB

see also influence NOUN

influencer

influenza NOUN

la grippe

to **inform** VERB

informer

- **to inform somebody of something** informer quelqu'un de quelque chose

◦ *Nobody informed me of the new plan.* Personne ne m'a informé de ce nouveau projet.

informal ADJECTIVE

1 (*person, party*)

décontracté ◦ *"informal dress"* "tenue décontractée"

2 (*colloquial*)

familier MASC

familière FEM

◦ *informal language* le langage familier

- **an informal visit** une visite non officielle

information NOUN

les renseignements MASC PL

◦ *important information* les renseignements importants

- **a piece of information** un renseignement

- **Could you give me some information about trains to Paris?** Pourriez-vous me renseigner sur les trains pour Paris?

information office NOUN

le bureau des renseignements

infuriating ADJECTIVE

exaspérant

ingredient NOUN

l' ingrédient MASC

inhabitant NOUN

l' habitant MASC

l' habitante FEM

to **inherit** VERB

hériter de ◦ *She inherited her father's house.* Elle a hérité de la maison de son père.

initials PL NOUN

les initiales FEM PL ◦ *Her initials are CDT.* Ses initiales sont CDT.

initiative NOUN

l' initiative FEM

to **inject** VERB

injecter (*drug*)

injection NOUN

la piqûre

to **injure** VERB

blesser

injured ADJECTIVE

blessé

injury NOUN

la blessure

injury time NOUN

les arrêts de jeu MASC PL

injustice NOUN

l' injustice FEM

ink NOUN

l' encre FEM

in-laws PL NOUN

les beaux-parents MASC PL

inn NOUN

l' **auberge** FEM

inner ADJECTIVE
intérieur
- **the inner city** les quartiers déshérités du centre ville

inner tube NOUN
la **chambre à air**

innocent ADJECTIVE
innocent

inquest NOUN
l' **enquête** FEM

inquiries office NOUN
le **bureau des renseignements**

inquisitive ADJECTIVE
curieux MASC
curieuse FEM

insane ADJECTIVE
fou MASC
folle FEM

inscription NOUN
l' **inscription** FEM

insect NOUN
l' **insecte** MASC

insect repellent NOUN
l' **insectifuge** MASC

inside NOUN
see also inside ADVERB
l' **intérieur** MASC

inside ADVERB, PREPOSITION
see also inside NOUN
à l'intérieur ◇ *They're inside.* Ils sont à l'intérieur. ◇ *inside the house* à l'intérieur de la maison
- **to go inside** rentrer
- **Come inside!** Rentrez!

insincere ADJECTIVE
peu sincère

to **insist** VERB
insister ◇ *I didn't want to, but he insisted.* Je ne voulais pas, mais il a insisté.
- **to insist on doing something** insister pour faire quelque chose ◇ *She insisted on paying.* Elle a insisté pour payer.
- **He insisted he was innocent.** Il affirmait qu'il était innocent.

inspector NOUN
l' **inspecteur** MASC (*police*) ◇ *Inspector Jill Brown* l'inspecteur Jill Brown
- **ticket inspector** (*on buses*) le contrôleur

instance NOUN
- **for instance** par exemple

instant ADJECTIVE
immédiat ◇ *It was an instant success.* Ça a été un succès immédiat.
- **instant coffee** le café instantané

instantly ADVERB
tout de suite

instead ADVERB
- **instead of (1)** (*followed by noun*) à la place de ◇ *He went instead of Peter.* Il y est allé à la place de Peter.
- **instead of (2)** (*followed by verb*) au lieu de ◇ *We played tennis instead of going swimming.* Nous avons joué au tennis au lieu d'aller nager.
- **The pool was closed, so we played tennis instead.** La piscine était fermée, alors nous avons joué au tennis.

instinct NOUN
l' **instinct** MASC

institution NOUN
l' **institution** FEM

to **instruct** VERB
- **to instruct somebody to do something** donner l'ordre à quelqu'un de faire quelque chose ◇ *She instructed us to wait outside.* Elle nous a donné l'ordre d'attendre dehors.

instructions PL NOUN
[1] les **instructions** FEM PL ◇ *Follow the instructions carefully.* Suivez soigneusement les instructions.
[2] le **mode d'emploi** SING (*booklet*) ◇ *Where are the instructions?* Où est le mode d'emploi?

instructor NOUN
le **moniteur**
la **monitrice**
◇ *a skiing instructor* un moniteur de ski ◇ *a driving instructor* un moniteur d'auto-école

instrument NOUN
l' **instrument** MASC ◇ *Do you play an instrument?* Est-ce que tu joues d'un instrument?

insufficient ADJECTIVE
insuffisant

insulin NOUN
l' **insuline** FEM

insult NOUN
see also insult VERB
l' **insulte** FEM

to **insult** VERB
see also insult NOUN
insulter

insurance NOUN
l' **assurance** FEM ◇ *his car insurance* son assurance automobile
- **an insurance policy** une police d'assurance

intelligent ADJECTIVE
intelligent

to **intend** VERB
- **to intend to do something** avoir l'intention de faire quelque chose ◇ *I intend to do French at university.* J'ai

l'intention d'étudier le français à l'université.

intense ADJECTIVE
intense

intensive ADJECTIVE
intensif MASC
intensive FEM

intention NOUN
l' intention FEM

intercom NOUN
l' interphone MASC

interest NOUN
see also interest VERB
l' intérêt MASC ◇ to show an interest in something manifester de l'intérêt pour quelque chose
- **What interests do you have?** Quels sont tes centres d'intérêt?
- **My main interest is music.** Ce qui m'intéresse le plus c'est la musique.

to **interest** VERB
see also interest NOUN
intéresser ◇ It doesn't interest me. Ça ne m'intéresse pas.
- **to be interested in something** s'intéresser à quelque chose ◇ I'm not interested in politics. Je ne m'intéresse pas à la politique.

interesting ADJECTIVE
intéressant

interior NOUN
l' intérieur MASC

interior designer NOUN
le/la designer

intermediate ADJECTIVE
(course, level)
moyen MASC
moyenne FEM

internal ADJECTIVE
interne

international ADJECTIVE
international
(internationaux MASC PL)

Internet NOUN
l' Internet MASC ◇ on the Internet sur Internet

to **interpret** VERB
servir d'interprète ◇ Steve couldn't speak French, so his friend interpreted. Comme Steve ne savait pas le français, son ami a servi d'interprète.

interpreter NOUN
l' interprète MASC/FEM

to **interrupt** VERB
interrompre

interruption NOUN
l' interruption FEM

interval NOUN
l' entracte MASC (in play, concert)

interview NOUN
see also interview VERB
[1] l' interview (on TV, radio)
[2] l' entretien MASC (for job)

to **interview** VERB
see also interview NOUN
interviewer (on TV, radio) ◇ I was interviewed on the radio. J'ai été interviewé à la radio.

interviewer NOUN
l' interviewer MASC (on TV, radio)

intimate ADJECTIVE
intime

into PREPOSITION
[1] dans ◇ He got into the car. Il est monté dans la voiture.
[2] en ◇ I'm going into town. Je vais en ville. ◇ Translate it into French. Traduisez ça en français. ◇ Divide into two groups. Répartissez-vous en deux groupes.

to **introduce** VERB
présenter ◇ He introduced me to his parents. Il m'a présenté à ses parents.

introduction NOUN
l' introduction FEM (in book)

intruder NOUN
l' intrus MASC
l' intruse FEM

intuition NOUN
l' intuition FEM

to **invade** VERB
envahir

invalid NOUN
le/la malade

to **invent** VERB
inventer

invention NOUN
l' invention FEM

inventor NOUN
l' inventeur MASC
l' inventrice FEM

investigation NOUN
l' enquête FEM (police)

invigilator NOUN
le surveillant
la surveillante

invisible ADJECTIVE
invisible

invitation NOUN
l' invitation FEM

to **invite** VERB
inviter ◇ He's not invited. Il n'est pas invité.
- **to invite somebody to a party** inviter quelqu'un à une fête

to **involve** VERB
nécessiter ◇ His job involves a lot of travelling. Son travail nécessite de

nombreux déplacements.
- **to be involved in something** (*crime, drugs*) être impliqué dans quelque chose
- **to be involved with somebody** (*in relationship*) avoir une relation avec quelqu'un

IQ NOUN (= *intelligence quotient*)
le **Q.I.** (= *quotient intellectuel*)

Iran NOUN
l' **Iran** MASC
- **in Iran** en Iran

Iraq NOUN
l' **Iraq** MASC
- **in Iraq** en Iraq

Ireland NOUN
l' **Irlande** FEM
- **in Ireland** en Irlande
- **to Ireland** en Irlande
- **I'm from Ireland.** Je suis irlandais.

Irish ADJECTIVE
see also Irish NOUN
irlandais ◇ *Irish music* la musique irlandaise

Irish NOUN
see also Irish ADJECTIVE
l' **irlandais** (*language*)
- **the Irish** (*people*) les Irlandais

Irishman NOUN
l' **Irlandais** MASC

Irishwoman NOUN
l' **Irlandaise** FEM

iron NOUN
see also iron VERB
1 le **fer** (*metal*)
2 le **fer à repasser** (*for clothes*)

iron VERB
see also iron NOUN
repasser

ironic ADJECTIVE
ironique

ironing NOUN
le **repassage** ◇ *to do the ironing* faire le repassage

ironing board NOUN
la **planche à repasser**

ironmonger's (shop) NOUN
la **quincaillerie**

irrelevant ADJECTIVE
hors de propos ◇ *That's irrelevant.* C'est hors de propos.

irresponsible ADJECTIVE (*person*)
irresponsable ◇ *That was irresponsible of him.* C'était irresponsable de sa part.

irritating ADJECTIVE
irritant

is VERB *see* be

Islam NOUN
l' **Islam** MASC

Islamic ADJECTIVE
islamique ◇ *Islamic law* la loi islamique
- **Islamic fundamentalists** les intégristes musulmans

island NOUN
l' **île** FEM

isle NOUN
- **the Isle of Man** l'île de Man
- **the Isle of Wight** l'île de Wight

isolated ADJECTIVE
isolé

Israel NOUN
Israël MASC
- **in Israel** en Israël

Israeli ADJECTIVE
see also Israeli NOUN
israélien MASC
israélienne FEM

Israeli NOUN
see also Israeli ADJECTIVE
l' **Israélien** MASC
l' **Israélienne** FEM

issue NOUN
see also issue VERB
1 la **question** (*matter*) ◇ *a controversial issue* une question controversée
2 le **numéro** (*of magazine*)

to issue VERB
see also issue NOUN
distribuer (*equipment, supplies*)

it PRONOUN
Remember to check if it *stands for a masculine or feminine noun.*
1 **il** ◇ *Where's my book?–It's on the table.* Où est mon livre?–Il est sur la table.
elle ◇ *When does the pool close?–It closes at 8.* La piscine ferme à quelle heure?–Elle ferme à vingt heures.
Use le *or* la *when* it *is the object of the sentence.* le *and* la *change to* l' *before a vowel and most words beginning with "h".*
2 **le** ◇ *There's a croissant left. Do you want it?* Il reste un croissant. Tu le veux?
l' ◇ *It's a good film. Did you see it?* C'est un bon film. L'as-tu vu?
la ◇ *I don't want this apple. Take it.* Je ne veux pas de cette pomme. Prends-la.
l' ◇ *He's got a new car.–Yes, I saw it.* Il a une nouvelle voiture.–Oui, je l'ai vue.
- **It's raining.** Il pleut.
- **It's 6 o'clock.** Il est six heures.
- **It's Friday tomorrow.** Demain c'est vendredi.
- **Who is it?–It's me.** Qui est-ce?–C'est

moi.
- **It's expensive.** C'est cher.

Italian ADJECTIVE

> see also Italian NOUN

  italien MASC
  italienne FEM

Italian NOUN

> see also Italian ADJECTIVE

  1 (*person*)
  l' **Italien** MASC
  l' **Italienne** FEM
  2 (*language*)
  l' **italien** MASC

Italy NOUN

  l' **Italie** FEM
- **in Italy** en Italie
- **to Italy** en Italie

to **itch** VERB

- **It itches.** Ça me démange.
- **My head's itching.** J'ai des
  démangeaisons à la tête.

it'd = it had, it would

item NOUN

  l' **article** MASC (*object*)

itinerary NOUN

  l' **itinéraire** MASC

it'll = it will

its ADJECTIVE

> *Remember to check if its refers to a masculine,
> feminine or plural noun.*

  son MASC ⋄ *What's its name?* Quel
  est son nom?
  sa FEM ⋄ *Every thing in its place.*
  Chaque chose à sa place.
  ses PL ⋄ *The dog is losing its hair.* Le
  chien perd ses poils.

it's = it is, it has

itself PRONOUN

  se

> **se** *changes to* **s'** *before a vowel and most words
> beginning with "h".*

  ⋄ *The heating switches itself off.* Le
  chauffage s'arrête automatiquement.

I've = I have

J

jab NOUN
la **piqûre** (*injection*)

jack NOUN
1 le **cric** (*for car*)
2 le **valet** (*playing card*)

jacket NOUN
la **veste**
- **jacket potatoes** les pommes de terre en robe des champs

jackpot NOUN
le **gros lot**
- **to win the jackpot** gagner le gros lot

jail NOUN
see also jail VERB
la **prison**
- **to go to jail** aller en prison

jail VERB
see also jail NOUN
emprisonner

jam NOUN
la **confiture** ◇ *strawberry jam* la confiture de fraises
- **a traffic jam** un embouteillage

jam jar NOUN
le **pot à confiture**

jammed ADJECTIVE
coincé ◇ *The window's jammed.* La fenêtre est coincée.

jam-packed ADJECTIVE
bondé ◇ *The room was jam-packed.* La salle était bondée.

janitor NOUN
le **concierge** ◇ *He's a janitor.* Il est concierge.

January NOUN
janvier MASC
- **in January** en janvier

Japan NOUN
le **Japon**
- **in Japan** au Japon
- **from Japan** du Japon

Japanese ADJECTIVE
see also Japanese NOUN
japonais

Japanese NOUN
see also Japanese ADJECTIVE
1 (*person*)
le **Japonais**
la **Japonaise**
- **the Japanese** les Japonais
2 (*language*)
le **japonais**

jar NOUN
le **bocal**
(les **bocaux** PL)
◇ *an empty jar* un bocal vide

- **a jar of honey** un pot de miel

jaundice NOUN
la **jaunisse**

javelin NOUN
le **javelot**

jaw NOUN
la **mâchoire**

jazz NOUN
le **jazz**

jealous ADJECTIVE
jaloux MASC
jalouse FEM

jeans PL NOUN
le **jean** SING

Jehovah's Witness NOUN
le **témoin de Jéhovah** ◇ *She's a Jehovah's Witness.* Elle est témoin de Jéhovah.

jelly NOUN
la **gelée**

jellyfish NOUN
la **méduse**

jersey NOUN (*pullover*)
le **pull-over**

Jesus NOUN
Jésus MASC

jet NOUN
le **jet** (*plane*)

jetlag NOUN
- **to be suffering from jetlag** être sous le coup du décalage horaire

jetty NOUN
la **jetée**

Jew NOUN
le **Juif**
la **Juive**

jewel NOUN
le **bijou**
(les **bijoux** PL)

jeweller NOUN
le **bijoutier**
la **bijoutière**
◇ *He's a jeweller.* Il est bijoutier.

jeweller's shop NOUN
la **bijouterie**

jewellery NOUN
les **bijoux** MASC PL

Jewish ADJECTIVE
juif MASC
juive FEM

jigsaw NOUN
le **puzzle**

job NOUN
1 l' **emploi** MASC ◇ *He's lost his job.* Il a perdu son emploi.
- **I've got a Saturday job.** Je travaille le

PTO

samedi.

2 (*chore, task*)

le **travail**

(les **travaux** PL)

◇ *That was a difficult job.* C'était un travail difficile.

job centre NOUN

l' **agence pour l'emploi** FEM

jobless ADJECTIVE

sans emploi

jockey NOUN

le **jockey**

to **jog** VERB

faire du jogging

jogging NOUN

le **jogging**

- **to go jogging** faire du jogging

to **join** VERB

1 **s'inscrire à** (*become member of*) ◇ *I'm going to join the ski club.* Je vais m'inscrire au club de ski.

2 **se joindre à** (*accompany*) ◇ *Do you mind if I join you?* Puis-je me joindre à vous?

joiner NOUN

le **menuisier** ◇ *He's a joiner.* Il est menuisier.

joint NOUN

1 l' **articulation** FEM (*in body*)

2 le **rôti** (*of meat*)

3 le **joint** (*drugs*)

joke NOUN

see also joke VERB

la **plaisanterie**

- **to tell a joke** raconter une plaisanterie

to **joke** VERB

see also joke NOUN

plaisanter ◇ *I'm only joking.* Je plaisante.

jolly ADJECTIVE

jovial

(**joviaux** MASC PL)

Jordan NOUN

la **Jordanie** (*country*)

- **in Jordan** en Jordanie

to **jot down** VERB

noter

jotter NOUN

le **bloc-notes** (*pad*)

journalism NOUN

le **journalisme**

journalist NOUN

le/la **journaliste** ◇ *She's a journalist.* Elle est journaliste.

journey NOUN

1 le **voyage** ◇ *I don't like long journeys.* Je n'aime pas les longs voyages.

- **to go on a journey** faire un voyage

2 le **trajet** (*to school, work*)

- **a bus journey** un trajet en autobus ◇ *The journey to school takes about half an hour.* Il y a une demi-heure de trajet pour aller à l'école.

joy NOUN

la **joie**

joystick NOUN

le **manette de jeu** (*for computer game*)

judge NOUN

see also judge VERB

le **juge** ◇ *She's a judge.* Elle est juge.

to **judge** VERB

see also judge NOUN

juger

judo NOUN

le **judo** ◇ *My hobby is judo.* Je fais du judo.

jug NOUN

le **pot**

juice NOUN

le **jus** ◇ *orange juice* le jus d'orange

July NOUN

juillet MASC

- **in July** en juillet

to **jump** VERB

sauter

- **to jump over something** sauter par-dessus quelque chose

- **to jump out of the window** sauter par la fenêtre

- **to jump off the roof** sauter du toit

jumper NOUN

le **pull-over** (*pullover*)

junction NOUN

le **carrefour** (*of roads*)

June NOUN

juin MASC

- **in June** en juin

jungle NOUN

la **jungle**

junior NOUN

- **the juniors** (*in school*) les élèves des petites classes

junior school NOUN

l' **école primaire** FEM

junk NOUN

le **bric-à-brac** NO PL (*old things*) ◇ *The attic's full of junk.* Le grenier est rempli de bric-à-brac.

- **to eat junk food** manger n'importe comment

- **a junk shop** un magasin de brocante

jury NOUN

le **jury**

just ADVERB

juste ◇ *just after Christmas* juste après Noël ◇ *We had just enough money.* Nous avions juste assez

d'argent. ⋄ *just in time* juste à temps
- **just here** ici
- **I'm rather busy just now.** Je suis assez occupé en ce moment.
- **I did it just now.** Je viens de le faire.
- **He's just arrived.** Il vient d'arriver.
- **I'm just coming!** J'arrive!

- **It's just a suggestion.** Ce n'est qu'une suggestion.

justice NOUN
  la **justice**

to **justify** VERB
  justifier

K

kangaroo NOUN
le **kangourou**

karate NOUN
le **karaté**

keen ADJECTIVE
enthousiaste ◇ *He doesn't seem very keen.* Il n'a pas l'air très enthousiaste.
- **She's a keen student.** C'est une étudiante assidue.
- **to be keen on something** aimer quelque chose ◇ *I'm keen on maths.* J'aime les maths. ◇ *I'm not very keen on maths.* Je n'aime pas trop les maths.
- **to be keen on somebody** (*fancy them*) être très attiré par quelqu'un ◇ *He's keen on her.* Il est très attiré par elle.
- **to be keen on doing something** avoir très envie de faire quelque chose ◇ *I'm not very keen on going.* Je n'ai pas très envie d'y aller.

to **keep** VERB
1 **garder** (*retain*) ◇ *You can keep it.* Tu peux le garder.
2 **rester** (*remain*) ◇ *Keep still!* Reste tranquille!
- **Keep quiet!** Tais-toi!
- **I keep forgetting my keys.** J'oublie tout le temps mes clés.
- **to keep on doing something (1)** (*continue*) continuer à faire quelque chose ◇ *He kept on reading.* Il a continué à lire.
- **to keep on doing something (2)** (*repeatedly*) ne pas arrêter de faire quelque chose ◇ *The car keeps on breaking down.* La voiture n'arrête pas de tomber en panne.
- **"keep out"** "défense d'entrer"

keep-fit NOUN
la **gymnastique d'entretien**
- **I go to keep-fit classes.** Je vais à des cours de gymnastique.

kennel NOUN
la **niche**

kettle NOUN
la **bouilloire**

key NOUN
la **clé**

keyboard NOUN
le **clavier** ◇ *...with Mike Moran on keyboards* ...avec Mike Moran aux claviers

keyring NOUN
le **porte-clés**

kick NOUN
see also **kick** VERB
le **coup de pied**

to **kick** VERB
see also **kick** NOUN
- **to kick somebody** donner un coup de pied à quelqu'un ◇ *He kicked me.* Il m'a donné un coup de pied. ◇ *He kicked the ball hard.* Il a donné un bon coup de pied dans le ballon.
- **to kick off** (*in football*) donner le coup d'envoi

kick-off NOUN
le **coup d'envoi** ◇ *The kick-off is at 10 o'clock.* Le coup d'envoi sera donné à dix heures.

kid NOUN
see also **kid** VERB
le/la **gosse** (*child*)

to **kid** VERB
see also **kid** NOUN
plaisanter ◇ *I'm just kidding.* Je plaisante.

to **kidnap** VERB
kidnapper

kidney NOUN
1 le **rein** (*human*) ◇ *He's got kidney trouble.* Il a des problèmes de reins.
2 le **rognon** (*to eat*) ◇ *I don't like kidneys.* Je n'aime pas les rognons.

to **kill** VERB
tuer ◇ *He was killed in a car accident.* Il a été tué dans un accident de voiture.
- **Luckily, nobody was killed.** Il n'y a heureusement pas eu de victimes.
- **Six people were killed in the accident.** L'accident a fait six morts.
- **to kill oneself** se suicider ◇ *He killed himself.* Il s'est suicidé.

killer NOUN
1 (*murderer*)
le **meurtrier**
la **meurtrière**
◇ *The police are searching for the killer.* La police recherche le meurtrier.
2 (*hit man*)
le **tueur**
la **tueuse**
◇ *a hired killer* un tueur à gages
- **Meningitis can be a killer.** La méningite peut être mortelle.

kilo NOUN
le **kilo** ◇ *10 francs a kilo* dix francs le kilo

kilometre NOUN
le **kilomètre**

kilt NOUN
le **kilt**

kind ADJECTIVE

see also kind NOUN

gentil MASC

gentille FEM

- **to be kind to somebody** être gentil avec quelqu'un
- **Thank you for being so kind.** Merci pour votre gentillesse.

kind NOUN

see also kind ADJECTIVE

la **sorte** ◇ *It's a kind of sausage.* C'est une sorte de saucisse.

kindergarten NOUN

l' **école maternelle** FEM

kindness NOUN

la **gentillesse**

king NOUN

le **roi**

kingdom NOUN

le **royaume**

kiosk NOUN

la **cabine téléphonique** (*phone box*)

kipper NOUN

le **hareng fumé**

kiss NOUN

see also kiss VERB

le **baiser** ◇ *a passionate kiss* un baiser passionné

to **kiss** VERB

see also kiss NOUN

[1] **embrasser** ◇ *He kissed her passionately.* Il l'a embrassée passionnément.

[2] **s'embrasser** ◇ *They kissed.* Ils se sont embrassés.

kit NOUN

[1] les **affaires** FEM PL (*clothes for sport*) ◇ *I've forgotten my gym kit.* J'ai oublié mes affaires de gym.

[2] la **trousse** ◇ *a tool kit* une trousse à outils ◇ *a first aid kit* une trousse de secours ◇ *a puncture repair kit* une trousse de réparations

- **a drum kit** une batterie
- **a sewing kit** un nécessaire à couture

kitchen NOUN

la **cuisine** ◇ *a fitted kitchen* une cuisine aménagée

- **the kitchen units** les éléments de cuisine
- **a kitchen knife** un couteau de cuisine

kite NOUN

le **cerf-volant**

kitten NOUN

le **chaton**

knee NOUN

le **genou**

(les **genoux** PL)

- **He was on his knees.** Il était à genoux.

to **kneel (down)** VERB

s'agenouiller

knew VERB *see* **know**

knickers PL NOUN

la **culotte** SING

- **a pair of knickers** une culotte

knife NOUN

le **couteau**

(les **couteaux** PL)

- **a kitchen knife** un couteau de cuisine
- **a sheath knife** un couteau à gaine
- **a penknife** un canif

to **knit** VERB

tricoter

knitting NOUN

le **tricot** ◇ *I like knitting.* J'aime faire du tricot.

knives PL NOUN *see* **knife**

to **knock** VERB

see also knock NOUN

frapper ◇ *Someone's knocking at the door.* Quelqu'un frappe à la porte.

- **to knock somebody down** renverser quelqu'un ◇ *She was knocked down by a car.* Elle a été renversée par une voiture.
- **to knock somebody out (1)** (*defeat*) éliminer ◇ *They were knocked out early in the tournament.* Ils ont été éliminés au début du tournoi.
- **to knock somebody out (2)** (*stun*) assommer ◇ *They knocked out the watchman.* Ils ont assommé le gardien.

knock NOUN

see also knock VERB

le **coup**

knot NOUN

le **nœud**

- **to tie a knot in something** faire un nœud à quelque chose

to **know** VERB

Use **savoir** *for knowing facts,* **connaître** *for knowing people and places.*

[1] **savoir** ◇ *It's a long way.–Yes, I know.* C'est loin.–Oui, je sais. ◇ *I don't know.* Je ne sais pas. ◇ *I don't know what to do.* Je ne sais pas quoi faire. ◇ *I don't know how to do it.* Je ne sais pas comment faire.

[2] **connaître** ◇ *I know her.* Je la connais. ◇ *I know Paris well.* Je connais bien Paris.

- **I don't know any German.** Je ne parle pas du tout allemand.
- **to know that...** savoir que... ◇ *I know that you like chocolate.* Je sais que tu aimes le chocolat. ◇ *I didn't know that your Dad was a policeman.* Je ne savais pas que ton père était policier.

K

PTO

- **to know about something (1)** (*be aware of*) être au courant de quelque chose ○ *Do you know about the meeting this afternoon?* Tu es au courant de la réunion de cet après-midi?
- **to know about something (2)** (*be knowledgeable about*) s'y connaître en quelque chose ○ *He knows a lot about cars.* Il s'y connaît en voitures. ○ *I don't know much about computers.* Je ne m'y connais pas bien en informatique.
- **to get to know somebody** apprendre à connaître quelqu'un
- **How should I know?** (*I don't know!*) Comment veux-tu que je le sache?
- **You never know!** On ne sait jamais!

know-all NOUN
le/la je-sais-tout ○ *He's such a know-all!* C'est Monsieur je-sais-tout!

know-how NOUN
le savoir-faire

knowledge NOUN
la connaissance

knowledgeable ADJECTIVE
- **to be knowledgeable about something** s'y connaître en quelque chose ○ *She's very knowledgeable about computers.* Elle s'y connaît bien en informatique.

Koran NOUN
le Coran

Korea NOUN
la Corée
- **in Korea** en Corée

kosher ADJECTIVE
kascher MASC, FEM, PL

L

lab NOUN (= *laboratory*)
le **labo**
- a lab technician un laborantin

label NOUN
l' **étiquette** FEM

laboratory NOUN
le **laboratoire**

Labour NOUN
les **travaillistes** MASC PL ◇ *My parents vote Labour.* Mes parents votent pour les travaillistes.
- the Labour Party le parti travailliste

labourer NOUN
le **manœuvre**
- a farm labourer un ouvrier agricole

lace NOUN
1 le **lacet** (*of shoe*)
2 la **dentelle** ◇ *a lace collar* un col en dentelle

lacquer NOUN
la **laque**

lad NOUN
le **gars**

ladder NOUN
l' **échelle** FEM

lady NOUN
la **dame**
- a young lady une jeune fille
- Ladies and gentlemen... Mesdames, Messieurs...
- the ladies' les toilettes pour dames FEM

ladybird NOUN
la **coccinelle**

to **lag behind** VERB
rester en arrière

lager NOUN
la **bière blonde**

laid VERB *see* **lay**

laid-back ADJECTIVE
relaxé

lain VERB *see* **lie**

lake NOUN
le **lac**
- Lake Geneva le lac Léman

lamb NOUN
l' **agneau** MASC
(les **agneaux** PL)
- a lamb chop une côtelette d'agneau

lamp NOUN
la **lampe**

lamppost NOUN
le **réverbère**

land NOUN

see also **land** VERB
la **terre**
- a piece of land un terrain

to **land** VERB
see also **land** NOUN
atterrir (*plane, passenger*)

landing NOUN
1 l' **atterrissage** MASC (*of plane*)
2 le **palier** (*of staircase*)

landlady NOUN
la **propriétaire**

landlord NOUN
le **propriétaire**

landowner NOUN
le **propriétaire terrien**

landscape NOUN
le **paysage**

lane NOUN
1 le **chemin** (*in country*)
2 la **voie** (*on motorway*)

language NOUN
la **langue** ◇ *French isn't a difficult language.* Le français n'est pas une langue difficile.
- to use bad language dire des grossièretés

language laboratory NOUN
le **laboratoire de langues**

lap NOUN
le **tour de piste** (*sport*) ◇ *I ran ten laps.* J'ai fait dix tours de piste en courant.
- on my lap sur mes genoux

laptop NOUN (*computer*)
le **portable**

larder NOUN
le **garde-manger**
(les **garde-manger** PL)

large ADJECTIVE
1 **grand** ◇ *a large house* une grande maison
2 (*person, animal*)
gros MASC
grosse FEM
◇ *a large dog* un gros chien

laser NOUN
le **laser**

lass NOUN
la **jeune fille**

last ADJECTIVE, ADVERB
see also **last** VERB
1 **dernier** MASC
dernière FEM
◇ *last Friday* vendredi dernier ◇ *last week* la semaine dernière ◇ *last summer* l'été dernier
2 **en dernier** ◇ *He arrived last.* Il est ▱

arrivé en dernier.

[3] **pour la dernière fois** ◇ *I've lost my bag. –When did you see it last?* J'ai perdu mon sac. –Quand est-ce que tu l'as vu pour la dernière fois? ◇ *When I last saw him, he was wearing a blue shirt.* La dernière fois que je l'ai vu, il portait une chemise bleue.

- **the last time** la dernière fois ◇ *the last time I saw her* la dernière fois que je l'ai vue ◇ *That's the last time I take your advice!* C'est la dernière fois que je suis tes conseils!
- **last night (1)** (*evening*) hier soir ◇ *I got home at midnight last night.* Je suis rentré à minuit hier soir.
- **last night (2)** (*sleeping hours*) la nuit dernière ◇ *I couldn't sleep last night.* J'ai eu du mal à dormir la nuit dernière.
- **at last** enfin

to **last** VERB

see also **last** ADJECTIVE

durer ◇ *The concert lasts two hours.* Le concert dure deux heures.

late ADJECTIVE, ADVERB

[1] **en retard** ◇ *Hurry up or you'll be late!* Dépêche-toi, sinon tu vas être en retard! ◇ *I'm often late for school.* J'arrive souvent en retard à l'école.

- **to arrive late** arriver en retard ◇ *She arrived late.* Elle est arrivée en retard.

[2] **tard** ◇ *I went to bed late.* Je me suis couché tard.

- **in the late afternoon** en fin d'après-midi
- **in late May** fin mai

lately ADVERB

ces derniers temps ◇ *I haven't seen him lately.* Je ne l'ai pas vu ces derniers temps.

later ADVERB

plus tard ◇ *I'll do it later.* Je ferai ça plus tard.

- **See you later!** A tout à l'heure!

latest ADJECTIVE

dernier MASC

dernière FEM

◇ *their latest album* leur dernier album

- **at the latest** au plus tard ◇ *by 10 o'clock at the latest* à dix heures au plus tard

Latin NOUN

le **latin** ◇ *I do Latin.* Je fais du latin.

Latin America NOUN

l' **Amérique latine** FEM

- **in Latin America** en Amérique latine

Latin American ADJECTIVE

latino-américain

laugh NOUN

see also **laugh** VERB

le **rire**

- **It was a good laugh.** (*it was fun*) On s'est bien amusés.

to **laugh** VERB

see also **laugh** NOUN

rire

- **to laugh at something** se moquer de quelque chose ◇ *They laughed at her.* Ils se sont moqués d'elle.

launderette ® NOUN

la **laverie**

laundry NOUN

le **linge** (*clothes*)

lavatory NOUN

les **toilettes** FEM PL

lavender NOUN

la **lavande**

law NOUN

[1] la **loi** ◇ *The laws are very strict.* Les lois sont très sévères.

- **It's against the law.** C'est illégal.

[2] le **droit** (*subject*) ◇ *My sister's studying law.* Ma sœur fait des études de droit.

lawn NOUN

la **pelouse**

lawnmower NOUN

la **tondeuse à gazon**

lawyer NOUN

l' **avocat** MASC

l' **avocate** FEM

◇ *My mother's a lawyer.* Ma mère est avocate.

to **lay** VERB

lay is also a form of **lie** VERB.

mettre ◇ *She laid the baby in her cot.* Elle a mis le bébé dans son lit.

- **to lay the table** mettre la table
- **to lay something on (1)** (*provide*) organiser quelque chose ◇ *They laid on extra buses.* Ils ont organisé un service de bus supplémentaire.
- **to lay something on (2)** (*prepare*) préparer quelque chose ◇ *They laid on a special meal.* Ils ont préparé un repas soigné.

lay-by NOUN

l' **aire de stationnement** FEM

lazy ADJECTIVE

paresseux MASC

paresseuse FEM

lead NOUN

This word has two pronunciations. Make sure you choose the right translation.

see also **lead** VERB

[1] le **fil** (*cable*)

[2] la **laisse** (*for dog*)

- **to be in the lead** être en tête ◇ *Our*

team is in the lead. Notre équipe est en tête.

[3] le **plomb** *(metal)*

to **lead** VERB

see also lead NOUN

mener ◇ *the street that leads to the station* la rue qui mène à la gare

- **to lead the way** montrer le chemin
- **to lead somebody away** emmener quelqu'un ◇ *The police led the man away.* La police a emmené l'homme.

leaded petrol NOUN

l' **essence au plomb** FEM

leader NOUN

[1] *(of expedition, gang)*

le **chef**

[2] *(of political party)*

le **dirigeant**

la **dirigeante**

lead-free ADJECTIVE

- **lead-free petrol** de l'essence sans plomb

lead singer NOUN

le **chanteur principal**

la **chanteuse principale**

leaf NOUN

la **feuille**

leaflet NOUN

la **brochure**

league NOUN

le **championnat** ◇ *They are at the top of the league.* Ils sont en tête du championnat.

- **the Premier League** la première division

leak NOUN

see also leak VERB

la **fuite** ◇ *a gas leak* une fuite de gaz

to **leak** VERB

see also leak NOUN

fuir *(pipe, water, gas)*

to **lean** VERB

se pencher ◇ *Don't lean over too far.* Ne te penche pas trop. ◇ *She leant out of the window.* Elle s'est penchée par la fenêtre.

- **to lean forward** se pencher en avant
- **to lean on something** s'appuyer contre quelque chose ◇ *He leant on the wall.* Il s'est appuyé contre le mur.
- **to be leaning against something** être appuyé contre quelque chose ◇ *The ladder was leaning against the wall.* L'échelle était appuyée contre le mur.
- **to lean something against a wall** appuyer quelque chose contre un mur ◇ *He leant his bike against the wall.* Il a appuyé son vélo contre le mur.

leap year NOUN

l' **année bissextile** FEM

to **learn** VERB

apprendre ◇ *I'm learning to ski.* J'apprends à skier.

learner NOUN

- **She's a quick learner.** Elle apprend vite.
- **French learners** *(people learning French)* ceux qui apprennent le français

learner driver NOUN

le **conducteur débutant**

la **conductrice débutante**

least ADVERB, ADJECTIVE, PRONOUN

- **the least (1)** *(followed by noun)* le moins de ◇ *It takes the least time.* C'est ce qui prend le moins de temps.
- **the least (2)** *(after a verb)* le moins ◇ *Maths is the subject I like the least.* Les maths sont la matière que j'aime le moins.

When least *is followed by adjective, the translation depends on whether the noun referred to is masculine, feminine or plural.*

- **the least... (1)** le moins... ◇ *the least expensive hotel* l'hôtel le moins cher
- **the least... (2)** la moins... ◇ *the least expensive seat* la place la moins chère
- **the least... (3)** les moins... ◇ *the least expensive hotels* les hôtels les moins chers ◇ *the least expensive seats* les places les moins chères
- **It's the least I can do.** C'est le moins que je puisse faire.
- **at least (1)** au moins ◇ *It'll cost at least £200.* Ça va coûter au moins deux cents livres.
- **at least (2)** du moins ◇ *...but at least nobody was hurt.* ...mais du moins personne n'a été blessé. ◇ *It's totally unfair–at least, that's my opinion.* C'est vraiment injuste–du moins c'est ce que je pense.

leather NOUN

le **cuir** ◇ *a black leather jacket* un blouson en cuir noir

to **leave** VERB

see also leave NOUN

[1] **laisser** *(deliberately)* ◇ *Don't leave your camera in the car.* Ne laisse pas ton appareil-photo dans la voiture.

[2] **oublier** *(by mistake)* ◇ *I've left my book at home.* J'ai oublié mon livre à la maison. ◇ *Make sure you haven't left anything behind.* Vérifiez bien que vous n'avez rien oublié.

[3] **partir** *(go)* ◇ *The bus leaves at 8.* Le car part à huit heures. ◇ *She's just left.* Elle vient de partir.

[4] **quitter** *(go away from)* ◇ *We leave*

London at six o'clock. Nous quittons
Londres à six heures. ◇ *My sister left
home last year.* Ma sœur a quitté la
maison l'an dernier.
- **to leave somebody alone** laisser
quelqu'un tranquille ◇ *Leave me
alone!* Laisse-moi tranquille!

leave NOUN
see also **leave** VERB
1. le **congé** (*from job*)
2. la **permission** (*from army*) ◇ *My
brother is on leave for a week.* Mon frère
est en permission pendant une
semaine.

leaves PL NOUN see **leaf**

Lebanon NOUN
le **Liban**
- **in Lebanon** au Liban

lecture NOUN
see also **lecture** VERB
1. (*public*)
la **conférence**
2. (*at university*)
le **cours magistral**
(les **cours magistraux** PL)

to **lecture** VERB
see also **lecture** NOUN
1. **enseigner** ◇ *She lectures at the
technical college.* Elle enseigne au
collège technique.
2. **faire la morale** ◇ *He's always
lecturing us.* Il n'arrête pas de nous faire
la morale.

lecturer NOUN
le **professeur d'université** ◇ *She's a
lecturer.* Elle est professeur d'université.

led VERB see **lead**

leek NOUN
le **poireau**
(les **poireaux** PL)

left VERB see **leave**

left ADJECTIVE, ADVERB
see also **left** NOUN
1. **gauche** (*not right*) ◇ *my left hand*
ma main gauche ◇ *on the left side of
the road* sur la côté gauche de la route
2. **à gauche** ◇ *Turn left at the traffic
lights.* Tournez à gauche aux prochains
feux.
- **I haven't got any money left.** Il ne me
reste plus d'argent.

left NOUN
see also **left** ADJECTIVE
la **gauche**
- **on the left** à gauche ◇ *Remember to
drive on the left.* N'oubliez pas de
conduire à gauche.

left-hand ADJECTIVE
- **the left-hand side** la gauche ◇ *It's on

the left-hand side.* C'est à gauche.

left-handed ADJECTIVE
gaucher MASC
gauchère FEM

left-luggage office NOUN
la **consigne**

leg NOUN
la **jambe** ◇ *She's broken her leg.* Elle
s'est cassé la jambe.
- **a chicken leg** une cuisse de poulet
- **a leg of lamb** un gigot d'agneau

legal ADJECTIVE
légal
(**légaux** MASC PL)

leggings NOUN
le **caleçon** SING

leisure NOUN
les **loisirs** MASC PL ◇ *What do you do in
your leisure time?* Qu'est-ce que tu fais
pendant tes loisirs?

leisure centre NOUN
le **centre de loisirs**

lemon NOUN
le **citron**

lemonade NOUN
la **limonade**

to **lend** VERB
prêter ◇ *I can lend you some money.*
Je peux te prêter de l'argent.

length NOUN
la **longueur**
- **It's about a metre in length.** Ça fait
environ un mètre de long.

lens NOUN
1. la **lentille** (*contact lens*)
2. le **verre** (*of spectacles*)
3. l' **objectif** MASC (*of camera*)

Lent NOUN
le **Carême**

lent VERB see **lend**

lentil NOUN
la **lentille**

Leo NOUN
le **Lion** ◇ *I'm Leo.* Je suis Lion.

leotard NOUN
le **justaucorps**

lesbian NOUN
la **lesbienne**

less PRONOUN, ADVERB, ADJECTIVE
1. **moins** ◇ *He's less intelligent than
her.* Il est moins intelligent qu'elle.
◇ *A bit less, please.* Un peu moins,
s'il vous plaît.
2. **moins de** ◇ *I've got less time for
hobbies now.* J'ai moins de temps pour
les loisirs maintenant.
- **less than (1)** (*with amounts*) moins de
◇ *It's less than a kilometre from here.*
C'est à moins d'un kilomètre d'ici. ◇ *It

costs less than 100 francs. Ça coûte
moins de cent francs. ◦ less than half
moins de la moitié
- **less than (2)** (in comparisons) moins que
  ◦ He spent less than me. Il a dépensé
  moins que moi. ◦ I've got less than
  you. J'en ai moins que toi. ◦ It cost
  less than we thought. Ça a coûté moins
  cher que nous ne le pensions.

lesson NOUN
  [1] la **leçon** ◦ a French lesson une
  leçon de français ◦ "Lesson Sixteen"
  (in textbook) "Leçon seize"
  [2] le **cours** (class) ◦ The lessons last
  forty minutes each. Chaque cours dure
  quarante minutes.

to **let** VERB
  [1] **laisser** (allow)
- **to let somebody do something** laisser
  quelqu'un faire quelque chose ◦ Let
  me have a look. Laisse-moi voir. ◦ My
  parents won't let me stay out that late.
  Mes parents ne me laissent pas sortir
  aussi tard.
- **to let somebody know** faire savoir à
  quelqu'un ◦ I'll let you know as soon
  as possible. Je vous le ferai savoir dès
  que possible.
- **to let somebody go** lâcher quelqu'un
  ◦ Let me go! Lâche-moi!
- **to let in** laisser entrer ◦ They
  wouldn't let me in because I was under
  18. Ils ne m'ont pas laissé entrer parce
  que j'avais moins de dix-huit ans.

  > To make suggestions using let's, you can ask
  > questions beginning with si on.

  ◦ Let's go to the cinema! Si on allait au
  cinéma?
- **Let's go!** Allons-y!
  [2] **louer** (hire out)
- **"to let"** "à louer"

letter NOUN
  la **lettre**

letterbox NOUN
  la **boîte à lettres**

lettuce NOUN
  la **salade**

leukaemia NOUN
  la **leucémie**

level ADJECTIVE
  > see also level NOUN

  plan ◦ A snooker table must be
  perfectly level. Un billard doit être
  parfaitement plan.

level NOUN
  > see also level ADJECTIVE

  le **niveau**
  (les **niveaux** PL)
  ◦ The level of the river is rising. Le

niveau de la rivière monte.
- **"A" levels** le baccalauréat
  > The French baccalauréat (or bac for short) is
  > taken at the age of 17 or 18. Students have to sit
  > one of a variety of set subject combinations,
  > rather than being able to choose any
  > combination of subjects they want. If you pass
  > you have the right to a place at university.

level crossing NOUN
  le **passage à niveau**

lever NOUN
  le **levier**

liable ADJECTIVE
- **He's liable to lose his temper.** Il se met
  facilement en colère.

liar NOUN
  le **menteur**
  la **menteuse**

liberal ADJECTIVE
  (opinions)
  libéral MASC
  libéraux FEM
- **the Liberal Democrats** le parti
  libéral-démocrate

liberation NOUN
  la **libération**

Libra NOUN
  la **Balance** ◦ I'm Libra. Je suis
  Balance.

librarian NOUN
  le/la **bibliothécaire** ◦ She's a
  librarian. Elle est bibliothécaire.

library NOUN
  la **bibliothèque**

Libya NOUN
  la **Libye**
- **in Libya** en Libye

licence NOUN
  le **permis**
- **a driving licence** un permis de
  conduire

to **lick** VERB
  lécher

lid NOUN
  le **couvercle**

to **lie** VERB
  > see also lie NOUN

  mentir (not tell the truth) ◦ I know
  she's lying. Je sais qu'elle ment.
- **to lie down** s'allonger
- **to be lying down** être allongé
- **He was lying on the sofa.** Il était
  allongé sur le canapé. ◦ When I'm on
  holiday I lie on the beach all day. Quand
  je suis en vacances, je reste allongé sur
  la plage toute la journée.

lie NOUN
  > see also lie VERB

  la **mensonge**

- **to tell a lie** mentir
- **That's a lie!** Ce n'est pas vrai!

lie-in NOUN
- **to have a lie-in** faire la grasse matinée
  ◇ *I have a lie-in on Sundays.* Je fais la grasse matinée le dimanche.

lieutenant NOUN
le **lieutenant**

life NOUN
la **vie**

lifebelt NOUN
la **bouée de sauvetage**

lifeboat NOUN
le **canot de sauvetage**

lifeguard NOUN
le **maître nageur**

life jacket NOUN
le **gilet de sauvetage**

life-saving NOUN
le **sauvetage** ◇ *I've done a course in life-saving.* J'ai pris des cours de sauvetage.

lifestyle NOUN
le **style de vie**

to **lift** VERB
see also **lift** NOUN
soulever ◇ *It's too heavy, I can't lift it.* C'est trop lourd, je ne peux pas le soulever.

lift NOUN
see also **lift** VERB
l' **ascenseur** MASC ◇ *The lift isn't working.* L'ascenseur est en panne.
- **He gave me a lift to the cinema.** Il m'a emmené au cinéma en voiture.
- **Would you like a lift?** Est-ce que je peux vous déposer quelque part?

light ADJECTIVE
see also **light** NOUN, VERB
[1] (*not heavy*)
léger MASC
légère FEM
◇ *a light jacket* une veste légère ◇ *a light meal* un repas léger
[2] (*colour*)
clair ◇ *a light blue sweater* un pull bleu clair

light NOUN
see also **light** ADJECTIVE, VERB
[1] la **lumière** ◇ *to switch on the light* allumer la lumière ◇ *to switch off the light* éteindre la lumière
[2] la **lampe** ◇ *There's a light by my bed.* Il y a une lampe près de mon lit.
- **the traffic lights** les feux MASC
- **Have you got a light?** (*for cigarette*) Avez-vous du feu?

to **light** VERB
see also **light** ADJECTIVE, NOUN

allumer (*candle, cigarette, fire*)

light bulb NOUN
l' **ampoule** FEM

lighter NOUN
le **briquet** (*for cigarettes*)

lighthouse NOUN
le **phare**

lightning NOUN
les **éclairs** MASC PL
- **a flash of lightning** un éclair

to **like** VERB
see also **like** PREPOSITION
[1] **aimer** ◇ *I don't like mustard.* Je n'aime pas la moutarde. ◇ *I like riding.* J'aime monter à cheval.
Note that **aimer** also means to love, so make sure you use **aimer bien** for just liking somebody.
[2] **aimer bien** ◇ *I like Paul, but I don't want to go out with him.* J'aime bien Paul, mais je ne veux pas sortir avec lui.
- **I'd like...** Je voudrais... ◇ *I'd like an orange juice, please.* Je voudrais un jus d'orange, s'il vous plaît. ◇ *Would you like some coffee?* Voulez-vous du café?
- **I'd like to...** J'aimerais... ◇ *I'd like to go to Russia one day.* J'aimerais aller en Russie un jour. ◇ *I'd like to wash my hands.* J'aimerais me laver les mains.
- **Would you like to go for a walk?** Tu veux aller faire une promenade?
- **...if you like** ...si tu veux

like PREPOSITION
see also **like** VERB
comme ◇ *It's fine like that.* C'est bien comme ça. ◇ *Do it like this.* Fais-le comme ça. ◇ *a city like Paris* une ville comme Paris ◇ *It's a bit like salmon.* C'est un peu comme du saumon.
- **What's the weather like?** Quel temps fait-il?
- **to look like somebody** ressembler à quelqu'un ◇ *You look like my brother.* Tu ressembles à mon frère.

likely ADJECTIVE
probable ◇ *That's not very likely.* C'est peu probable.
- **She's likely to come.** Elle viendra probablement.
- **She's not likely to come.** Elle ne viendra probablement pas.

lily of the valley NOUN
le **muguet**

lime NOUN
le **citron vert** (*fruit*)

limit NOUN
la **limite** ◇ *The speed limit is 70 mph.* La vitesse est limitée à cent dix kilomètres à l'heure.

limousine NOUN
la **limousine**

to **limp** VERB
boiter

line NOUN
1 la **ligne** ◇ *a straight line* une ligne droite
2 le **trait** (*to divide, cancel*) ◇ *Draw a line under each answer.* Tirez un trait après chaque réponse.
3 la **voie** (*railway track*)
- **Hold the line, please.** Ne quittez pas.
- **It's a very bad line.** La ligne est très mauvaise.

linen NOUN
le **lin** ◇ *a linen jacket* une veste en lin

liner NOUN
le **paquebot** (*ship*)

linguist NOUN
- **to be a good linguist** être doué pour les langues ◇ *She's a good linguist.* Elle est douée pour les langues.

link NOUN
see also **link** VERB
le **rapport** ◇ *the link between smoking and cancer* le rapport entre le tabagisme et le cancer

to **link** VERB
see also **link** NOUN
relier

lino NOUN
le **linoléum**

lion NOUN
le **lion**

lioness NOUN
la **lionne**

lip NOUN
la **lèvre**

to **lip-read** VERB
lire sur les lèvres

lip salve NOUN
la **pommade pour les lèvres**

lipstick NOUN
le **rouge à lèvres**

liqueur NOUN
la **liqueur**

liquid NOUN
le **liquide**

liquidizer NOUN
le **mixer**

list NOUN
see also **list** VERB
la **liste**

to **list** VERB
see also **list** NOUN
faire une liste de ◇ *List your hobbies!* Fais une liste de tes hobbies!

to **listen** VERB
écouter ◇ *Listen to this!* Écoutez ceci!

◇ *Listen to me!* Écoutez-moi!

listener NOUN
l' **auditeur** MASC
l' **auditrice** FEM

lit VERB *see* **light**

literally ADVERB
vraiment (*completely*) ◇ *It was literally impossible to find a seat.* Il était vraiment impossible de trouver une place.
- **to translate literally** faire une traduction littérale

literature NOUN
la **littérature** ◇ *I'm studying English Literature.* J'étudie la littérature anglaise.

litre NOUN
le **litre**

litter NOUN
les **ordures** FEM PL

litter bin NOUN
la **poubelle**

little ADJECTIVE
petit ◇ *a little girl* une petite fille
- **a little** un peu ◇ *How much would you like?–Just a little.* Combien en voulez-vous?–Juste un peu.
- **very little** très peu ◇ *We've got very little time.* Nous avons très peu de temps.
- **little by little** petit à petit

live ADJECTIVE
see also **live** VERB
1 **vivant** (*animal*)
2 **en direct** (*broadcast*)
- **There's live music on Fridays.** Il y a des musiciens qui jouent le vendredi.

to **live** VERB
see also **live** ADJECTIVE
1 **vivre** ◇ *I live with my grandmother.* Je vis avec ma grand-mère. ◇ *They're not married, they're living together.* Il ne sont pas mariés, ils vivent ensemble.
- **to live on something** vivre de quelque chose ◇ *He lives on benefit.* Il vit de ses indemnités.
2 **habiter** (*reside*) ◇ *Where do you live?* Où est-ce que tu habites? ◇ *I live in Edinburgh.* J'habite à Édimbourg.

liver NOUN
le **foie**

lives PL NOUN
les **vies** FEM

living NOUN
- **to make a living** gagner sa vie
- **What does she do for a living?** Qu'est-ce qu'elle fait dans la vie?

living room NOUN
la **salle de séjour**

lizard NOUN
le **lézard**

load NOUN
see also load VERB
- **loads of** un tas de ◇ *loads of people* un tas de gens ◇ *loads of money* un tas d'argent
- **You're talking a load of rubbish!** Tu ne dis que des bêtises!

to **load** VERB
see also load NOUN
charger ◇ *a trolley loaded with luggage* un chariot chargé de bagages

loaf NOUN
le **pain**
- **a loaf of bread** un pain

loan NOUN
see also loan VERB
le **prêt**

to **loan** VERB
see also loan NOUN
prêter

to **loathe** VERB
détester ◇ *I loathe her.* Je la déteste.

loaves PL NOUN see **loaf**

lobster NOUN
le **homard**

local ADJECTIVE
local
(**locaux** MASC PL)
◇ *the local paper* le journal local
- **a local call** une communication urbaine

loch NOUN
le **loch**

lock NOUN
see also lock VERB
la **serrure** ◇ *The lock is broken.* La serrure est cassée.

to **lock** VERB
see also lock NOUN
fermer à clé ◇ *Make sure you lock your door.* N'oubliez pas de fermer votre porte à clé.

locker NOUN
le **casier**
- **the locker room** le vestiaire
- **the left-luggage lockers** la consigne automatique

locket NOUN
le **médaillon**

lodger NOUN
le/la **locataire**

loft NOUN
le **grenier**

log NOUN
la **bûche** (*of wood*)

logical ADJECTIVE
logique

lollipop NOUN
la **sucette**

lolly NOUN
la **glace à l'eau** (*ice lolly*)

London NOUN
Londres
- **in London** à Londres
- **to London** à Londres
- **I'm from London.** Je suis de Londres.

Londoner NOUN
le **Londonien**
la **Londonienne**

loneliness NOUN
la **solitude**

lonely ADJECTIVE
seul
- **to feel lonely** se sentir seul ◇ *She feels a bit lonely.* Elle se sent un peu seule.

long ADJECTIVE, ADVERB
see also long VERB
long MASC
longue FEM
◇ *She's got long hair.* Elle a les cheveux longs. ◇ *The room is 6 metres long.* La pièce fait six mètres de long.
- **How long?** (*time*) Combien de temps? ◇ *How long did you stay there?* Combien de temps êtes-vous resté là-bas? ◇ *How long have you been here?* Depuis combien de temps êtes-vous ici? ◇ *How long is the flight?* Combien de temps dure le vol?
- **I've been waiting a long time.** J'attends depuis longtemps.
- **It takes a long time.** Ça prend du temps.
- **as long as** si ◇ *I'll come as long as it's not too expensive.* Je viendrai si ce n'est pas trop cher.

to **long** VERB
see also long ADJECTIVE
- **to long to do something** attendre avec impatience de faire quelque chose
- **I'm longing to see my boyfriend again.** J'attends avec impatience de revoir mon copain.

long-distance ADJECTIVE
- **a long-distance call** une communication interurbaine

longer ADVERB
see also long ADJECTIVE
- **They're no longer going out together.** Ils ne sortent plus ensemble.
- **I can't stand it any longer.** Je ne peux plus le supporter.

long jump NOUN
le **saut en longueur**

loo NOUN

les **toilettes** FEM PL ◦ *Where's the loo?* Où sont les toilettes?

look NOUN

see also look VERB

- **to have a look** regarder ◦ *Have a look at this!* Regardez ceci!
- **I don't like the look of it.** Ça ne me dit rien.

to **look** VERB

see also look NOUN

1 **regarder** ◦ *Look!* Regardez!
- **to look at something** regarder quelque chose ◦ *Look at the picture.* Regardez cette image.
  2 **avoir l'air** *(seem)* ◦ *She looks surprised.* Elle a l'air surprise. ◦ *That cake looks nice.* Ce gâteau a l'air bon. ◦ *It looks fine.* Ça a l'air bien.
- **to look like somebody** ressembler à quelqu'un ◦ *He looks like his brother.* Il ressemble à son frère.
- **What does she look like?** Comment est-elle physiquement?
- **Look out!** Attention!
- **to look after** s'occuper de ◦ *I look after my little sister.* Je m'occupe de ma petite sœur.
- **to look for** chercher ◦ *I'm looking for my passport.* Je cherche mon passeport.
- **to look forward to something** attendre quelque chose avec impatience ◦ *I'm looking forward to the holidays.* J'attends les vacances avec impatience.
- **Looking forward to hearing from you...** J'espère avoir bientôt de tes nouvelles...
- **to look round (1)** *(look behind)* se retourner ◦ *I shouted and he looked round.* J'ai crié et il s'est retourné.
- **to look round (2)** *(have a look)* jeter un coup d'œil ◦ *I'm just looking round.* Je jette simplement un coup d'œil.
- **to look round a museum** visiter un musée
- **I like looking round the shops.** J'aime faire les boutiques.
- **to look up** *(word, name)* chercher ◦ *If you don't know a word, look it up in the dictionary.* Si vous ne connaissez pas un mot, cherchez-le dans le dictionnaire.

loose ADJECTIVE

ample *(clothes)*

- **loose change** la petite monnaie

lord NOUN

le **seigneur** *(feudal)*

- **the House of Lords** la Chambre des lords
- **Good Lord!** Mon Dieu!

lorry NOUN

le **camion**

lorry driver NOUN

le **routier** ◦ *He's a lorry driver.* Il est routier.

to **lose** VERB

perdre ◦ *I've lost my purse.* J'ai perdu mon porte-monnaie.

- **to get lost** se perdre ◦ *I was afraid of getting lost.* J'avais peur de me perdre.

loss NOUN

la **perte**

lost VERB *see* lose

lost ADJECTIVE

perdu

lot NOUN

- **a lot** beaucoup
- **a lot of** beaucoup de ◦ *We saw a lot of interesting things.* Nous avons vu beaucoup de choses intéressantes.
- **lots of** un tas de ◦ *She's got lots of money.* Elle a un tas d'argent. ◦ *He's got lots of friends.* Il a un tas d'amis.
- **What did you do at the weekend?–Not a lot.** Qu'as-tu fait ce week-end?–Pas grand-chose.
- **Do you like football?–Not a lot.** Tu aimes le football?–Pas tellement.
- **That's the lot.** C'est tout.

lottery NOUN

la **loterie**

- **to win the lottery** gagner à la loterie

loud ADJECTIVE

fort ◦ *The television is too loud.* La télévision est trop forte.

loudly ADVERB

fort

loudspeaker NOUN

le **haut-parleur**

lounge NOUN

le **salon**

lousy ADJECTIVE

infect ◦ *The food in the canteen is lousy.* La nourriture de la cantine est infecte.

- **I feel lousy.** Je suis mal fichu. *(informal)*

love NOUN

see also love VERB

l' **amour** MASC

- **to be in love** être amoureux ◦ *She's in love with Paul.* Elle est amoureuse de Paul.
- **to make love** faire l'amour
- **Give Delphine my love.** Embrasse Delphine pour moi.
- **Love, Rosemary.** Amitiés, Rosemary.

to **love** VERB

see also love NOUN

1 **aimer** *(be in love with)* ◦ *I love you.* Je t'aime.

L

[2] **aimer beaucoup** (like a lot)
◇ Everybody loves her. Tout le
monde l'aime beaucoup. ◇ I'd love to
come. J'aimerais beaucoup venir.
[3] **adorer** (things) ◇ I love chocolate.
J'adore le chocolat. ◇ I love skiing.
J'adore le ski.

lovely ADJECTIVE
charmant ◇ What a lovely surprise!
Quelle charmante surprise! ◇ She's a
lovely person. Elle est charmante.
◆ **It's a lovely day.** Il fait très beau
aujourd'hui.
◆ **Is your meal OK?–Yes, it's lovely.**
Est-ce que c'est bon?–Oui, c'est
délicieux.
◆ **They've got a lovely house.** Ils ont une
très belle maison.
◆ **Have a lovely time!** Amusez-vous bien!

low ADJECTIVE, ADVERB
(price, level)
bas MASC
basse FEM
◇ That plane is flying very low. Cet avion
vole très bas.
◆ **the low season** la basse saison ◇ in
the low season en basse saison

lower sixth NOUN
la **première** ◇ He's in the lower sixth.
Il est en première.

low-fat ADJECTIVE
allégé ◇ a low-fat yoghurt un yaourt
allégé

loyalty NOUN
la **fidélité**

L-plates PL NOUN
les **plaques de conducteur débutant**
FEM PL

luck NOUN
la **chance** ◇ She hasn't had much luck.
Elle n'a pas eu beaucoup de chance.
◆ **Good luck!** Bonne chance!
◆ **Bad luck!** Pas de chance!

luckily ADVERB
heureusement

lucky ADJECTIVE
◆ **to be lucky (1)** (be fortunate) avoir de la
chance ◇ He's lucky, he's got a job. Il
a de la chance, il a un emploi. ◇ He
wasn't hurt.–That was lucky! Il n'a pas été
blessé.–C'est une chance!
◆ **to be lucky (2)** (bring luck) porter
bonheur ◇ Black cats are lucky in

Britain. Les chats noirs portent bonheur
en Grande-Bretagne.
◆ **a lucky horseshoe** un fer à cheval
porte-bonheur

luggage NOUN
les **bagages** MASC PL

lump NOUN
[1] le **morceau**
(les **morceaux** PL)
◇ a lump of butter un morceau de
beurre
[2] la **bosse** (swelling) ◇ He's got a lump
on his forehead. Il a une bosse sur le
front.

lunatic NOUN
le **fou**
la **folle**
◇ He's an absolute lunatic. Il est
complètement fou.

lunch NOUN
le **déjeuner**
◆ **to have lunch** déjeuner ◇ We have
lunch at 12 30. Nous déjeunons à midi
et demie.

luncheon voucher NOUN
le **ticket-restaurant**

lung NOUN
le **poumon**
◆ **lung cancer** le cancer du poumon

luscious ADJECTIVE
délicieux MASC
délicieuse FEM

lush ADJECTIVE
luxuriant

lust NOUN
le **désir**

Luxembourg NOUN
[1] le **Luxembourg** (country)
◆ **in Luxembourg** au Luxembourg
◆ **to Luxembourg** au Luxembourg
[2] **Luxembourg** (city)
◆ **in Luxembourg** à Luxembourg

luxurious ADJECTIVE
luxueux MASC
luxueuse FEM

luxury NOUN
le **luxe** ◇ It was luxury! C'était un vrai
luxe!
◆ **a luxury hotel** un hôtel de luxe

lying VERB see **lie**

lyrics PL NOUN
les **paroles** FEM PL (of song)

M

mac NOUN
l' **imper** MASC
macaroni NOUN
les **macaronis** MASC PL
machine NOUN
la **machine**
machinery NOUN
les **machines** FEM PL
mackerel NOUN
le **maquereau**
(les **maquereaux** PL)
mad ADJECTIVE
1 (*insane*)
fou MASC
folle FEM
◇ *You're mad!* Tu es fou!
2 (*angry*)
furieux MASC
furieuse FEM
◇ *She'll be mad when she finds out.* Elle
sera furieuse quand elle va s'en
apercevoir.
▪ **to be mad about (1)** (*sport, activity*) être
enragé de ◇ *He's mad about football.*
Il est enragé de foot.
▪ **to be mad about (2)** (*person, animal*)
adorer ◇ *She's mad about horses.*
Elle adore les chevaux.
madam NOUN
madame FEM ◇ *Would you like to
order, Madam?* Désirez-vous
commander, Madame?
made VERB *see* **make**
madly ADVERB
▪ **They're madly in love.** Ils sont
éperdument amoureux.
madman NOUN
le **fou**
magazine NOUN
le **magazine**
maggot NOUN
l' **asticot** MASC
magic ADJECTIVE
see also **magic** NOUN
1 **magique** (*magical*) ◇ *a magic wand*
une baguette magique
2 **super** (*brilliant*)
▪ **It was magic!** C'était super!
magic NOUN
see also **magic** ADJECTIVE
la **magie**
▪ **a magic trick** un tour de magie
▪ **My hobby is magic.** Je fais des tours de
magie.
magician NOUN
le **prestidigitateur** (*conjurer*)

magnificent ADJECTIVE
1 **magnifique** (*beautiful*) ◇ *a
magnificent view* une vue magnifique
2 **superbe** (*outstanding*) ◇ *It was a
magnificent effort.* Ils ont fait un
superbe effort.
maid NOUN
la **domestique** (*servant*)
▪ **an old maid** (*spinster*) une vieille fille
maiden name NOUN
le **nom de jeune fille**
mail NOUN
le **courrier** ◇ *Here's your mail.* Voici
ton courrier.
▪ **e-mail** (*electronic mail*) le courrier
électronique
▪ **by mail** par la poste
main ADJECTIVE
principal
(**principaux** MASC PL)
◇ *the main problem* le principal
problème
mainly ADVERB
principalement
main road NOUN
la **grande route** ◇ *I don't like cycling
on main roads.* Je n'aime pas faire du
vélo sur les grandes routes.
to **maintain** VERB
entretenir (*machine, building*)
maintenance NOUN
l' **entretien** MASC (*of machine, building*)
maize NOUN
le **maïs**
major ADJECTIVE
majeur ◇ *a major problem* un
problème majeur
▪ **in C major** en do majeur
Majorca NOUN
Majorque FEM ◇ *We went to Majorca
in August.* Nous sommes allés à
Majorque en août.
majority NOUN
la **majorité**
make NOUN
see also **make** VERB
la **marque** ◇ *What make is that car?*
De quelle marque est cette voiture?
to **make** VERB
see also **make** NOUN
1 **faire** ◇ *I'm going to make a cake.* Je
vais faire un gâteau. ◇ *He made it
himself.* Il l'a fait lui-même. ◇ *I make
my bed every morning.* Je fais mon lit
tous les matins. ◇ *2 and 2 make 4.*
Deux et deux font quatre.

M

2 **fabriquer** (*manufacture*) ◇ *made in France* fabriqué en France

3 **gagner** (*earn*) ◇ *He makes a lot of money.* Il gagne beaucoup d'argent.

- **to make somebody do something** obliger quelqu'un à faire quelque chose ◇ *My mother makes me do my homework.* Ma mère m'oblige à faire mes devoirs.

- **to make lunch** préparer le repas ◇ *She's making lunch.* Elle prépare le repas.

- **to make a phone call** donner un coup de téléphone ◇ *I'd like to make a phone call.* J'aimerais donner un coup de téléphone.

- **to make fun of somebody** se moquer de quelqu'un ◇ *They made fun of him.* Ils se sont moqués de lui.

- **What time do you make it?** Quelle heure avez-vous?

to **make up** VERB

1 **inventer** (*invent*) ◇ *He made up the whole story.* Il a inventé cette histoire de toutes pièces.

2 **se réconcilier** (*after argument*) ◇ *They had a quarrel, but soon made up.* Ils se sont disputés, mais se sont vite réconciliés.

- **to make oneself up** se maquiller ◇ *She spends hours making herself up.* Elle passe des heures à se maquiller.

make-up NOUN

le **maquillage**

Malaysia NOUN

la **Malaisie**

- **in Malaysia** en Malaisie

male ADJECTIVE

1 **mâle** (*animals, plants*) ◇ *a male kitten* un chaton mâle

2 **masculin** (*person, on official forms*) ◇ *Sex: male.* Sexe : masculin.

- **Most football players are male.** La plupart des joueurs de football sont des hommes.

- **a male chauvinist** un macho

- **a male nurse** un infirmier

Malta NOUN

Malte

- **in Malta** à Malte

- **to Malta** à Malte

mammoth NOUN

see also mammoth ADJECTIVE

le **mammouth**

mammoth ADJECTIVE

see also mammoth NOUN

monstre ◇ *a mammoth task* un travail monstre

man NOUN

l' **homme** MASC ◇ *an old man* un vieil homme

to **manage** VERB

1 **gérer** (*be in charge of*) ◇ *She manages a big store.* Elle dirige un grand magasin. ◇ *He manages our football team.* Il dirige notre équipe de foot.

2 **se débrouiller** (*get by*) ◇ *We haven't got much money, but we manage.* Nous n'avons pas beaucoup d'argent, mais nous nous débrouillons. ◇ *It's okay, I can manage.* Ça va, je me débrouille.

- **Can you manage okay?** Tu y arrives?

- **to manage to do something** réussir à faire quelque chose ◇ *Luckily I managed to pass the exam.* J'ai heureusement réussi à avoir mon examen.

- **I can't manage all that.** (*food*) C'est trop pour moi.

manageable ADJECTIVE

faisable (*task*)

management NOUN

1 la **gestion** (*organization*) ◇ *He's responsible for the management of the company.* Il est responsable de la gestion de la société.

2 la **direction** (*people in charge*) ◇ *"under new management"* "changement de direction"

manager NOUN

1 (*of company*)

le **directeur**

la **directrice**

2 (*of shop, restaurant*)

le **gérant**

la **gérante**

3 (*of team, performer*)

le **manager**

manageress NOUN

la **gérante**

mandarin NOUN

la **mandarine** (*fruit*)

mango NOUN

la **mangue**

mania NOUN

la **manie**

maniac NOUN

le **fou**

la **folle**

◇ *He drives like a maniac.* Il conduit comme un fou.

- **a religious maniac** un fanatique religieux

man-made ADJECTIVE

synthétique (*fibre*)

manner NOUN

la **façon**
- **She behaves in an odd manner.** Elle se comporte de façon étrange.
- **He has a confident manner.** Il a de l'assurance.

manners PL NOUN
les **manières** FEM PL ◇ *good manners* les bonnes manières ◇ *Her manners are appalling.* Elle a de très mauvaises manières.
- **It's bad manners to speak with your mouth full.** Ce n'est pas poli de parler la bouche pleine.

manpower NOUN
la **main-d'œuvre**

mansion NOUN
le **manoir**

mantelpiece NOUN
la **cheminée**

manual NOUN
le **manuel**

to **manufacture** VERB
fabriquer

manufacturer NOUN
le **fabricant**

manure NOUN
le **fumier**

manuscript NOUN
le **manuscrit**

many ADJECTIVE, PRONOUN
beaucoup de ◇ *The film has many special effects.* Le film a beaucoup d'effets spéciaux. ◇ *He hasn't got many friends.* Il n'a pas beaucoup d'amis. ◇ *Were there many people at the concert?* Est-ce qu'il y avait beaucoup de gens au concert?
- **very many** beaucoup de ◇ *I haven't got very many CDs.* Je n'ai pas beaucoup de CD.
- **Not many.** Pas beaucoup.
- **How many?** Combien? ◇ *How many do you want?* Combien en veux-tu?
- **how many...?** combien de...? ◇ *How many francs do you get for £1?* Combien de francs a-t-on pour une livre?
- **too many** trop ◇ *That's too many.* C'est trop.
- **too many...** trop de... ◇ *She makes too many mistakes.* Elle fait trop d'erreurs.
- **so many** autant ◇ *I didn't know there would be so many.* Je ne pensais pas qu'il y en aurait autant.
- **so many...** autant de... ◇ *I've never seen so many policemen.* Je n'ai jamais vu autant de policiers.

map NOUN
[1] la **carte** (*of country, area*)

[2] le **plan** (*of town*)

marathon NOUN
le **marathon** ◇ *the London marathon* le marathon de Londres

marble NOUN
le **marbre** ◇ *a marble statue* une statue en marbre
- **to play marbles** jouer aux billes

March NOUN
mars MASC
- **in March** en mars

march NOUN
see also **march** VERB
la **manifestation** (*demonstration*)

to **march** VERB
see also **march** NOUN
[1] **marcher au pas** (*soldiers*)
[2] **défiler** (*protesters*)

mare NOUN
la **jument**

margarine NOUN
la **margarine**

margin NOUN
la **marge** ◇ *Write notes in the margin.* Écrivez vos notes dans la marge.

marijuana NOUN
la **marijuana**

marital status NOUN
la **situation de famille**

mark NOUN
see also **mark** VERB
[1] la **note** (*in school*) ◇ *I get good marks for French.* J'ai de bonnes notes en français.
[2] la **tache** (*stain*) ◇ *You've got a mark on your skirt.* Tu as une tache sur ta jupe.
[3] le **mark** (*German currency*)

to **mark** VERB
see also **mark** NOUN
corriger ◇ *The teacher hasn't marked my homework yet.* Le professeur n'a pas encore corrigé mon devoir.

market NOUN
le **marché**

marketing NOUN
le **marketing**

marmalade NOUN
la **confiture d'oranges**

maroon ADJECTIVE
bordeaux MASC, FEM, PL (*colour*)

marriage NOUN
le **mariage**

married ADJECTIVE
marié ◇ *They are not married.* Ils ne sont pas mariés. ◇ *They have been married for 15 years.* Ils sont mariés depuis quinze ans. ◇ *a married couple* un couple marié

M

to **marry** VERB

épouser ◇ *He wants to marry her.* Il veut l'épouser.

- **to get married** se marier ◇ *My sister's getting married in June.* Ma sœur se marie en juin.

marvellous ADJECTIVE

1 **excellent** ◇ *She's a marvellous cook.* C'est une excellente cuisinière.

2 **superbe** ◇ *The weather was marvellous.* Il a fait un temps superbe.

marzipan NOUN

la **pâte d'amandes**

mascara NOUN

le **mascara**

masculine ADJECTIVE

masculin

mashed potatoes PL NOUN

la **purée** ◇ *sausages and mashed potatoes* des saucisses avec de la purée

mask NOUN

le **masque**

mass NOUN

1 la **multitude** ◇ *a mass of books and papers* une multitude de livres et de papiers

2 la **messe** (*in church*) ◇ *We go to mass on Sunday.* Nous allons à la messe le dimanche.

- **the mass media** les médias

massage NOUN

le **massage**

massive ADJECTIVE

énorme

to **master** VERB

maîtriser

masterpiece NOUN

le **chef-d'œuvre**
(les **chefs-d'œuvre** PL)

mat NOUN

le **paillasson** (*doormat*)

- **a table mat** un set de table
- **a beach mat** un tapis de plage

match NOUN

see also match VERB

1 l' **allumette** FEM ◇ *a box of matches* une boîte d'allumettes

2 (*sport*)

le **match**
(les **matchs** PL)

◇ *a football match* un match de foot

to **match** VERB

see also match NOUN

être assorti à ◇ *The jacket matches the trousers.* La veste est assortie au pantalon.

- **These colours don't match.** Ces couleurs ne vont pas ensemble.

matching ADJECTIVE

assorti ◇ *My bedroom has matching wallpaper and curtains.* Ma chambre a du papier peint et des rideaux assortis.

mate NOUN

le/la **pote** (*informal*) ◇ *On Friday night I go out with my mates.* Vendredi soir, je sors avec mes potes.

material NOUN

1 le **tissu** (*cloth*)

2 la **documentation** (*information, data*) ◇ *I'm collecting material for my project.* Je rassemble une documentation pour mon dossier.

- **raw materials** les matières premières FEM

mathematics NOUN

les **mathématiques** FEM PL

maths NOUN

les **maths** FEM PL

matron NOUN

l' **infirmière-chef** FEM (*in hospital*)

matter NOUN

see also matter VERB

la **question** ◇ *It's a matter of life and death.* C'est une question de vie ou de mort.

- **What's the matter?** Qu'est-ce qui ne va pas?
- **as a matter of fact** en fait

to **matter** VERB

see also matter NOUN

- **it doesn't matter (1)** (*I don't mind*) ça ne fait rien ◇ *I can't give you the money today.–It doesn't matter.* Je ne peux pas te donner l'argent aujourd'hui.–Ça ne fait rien.
- **it doesn't matter (2)** (*it makes no difference*) ça n'a pas d'importance ◇ *Shall I phone today or tomorrow?–Whenever, it doesn't matter.* Est-ce que j'appelle aujourd'hui ou demain?–Quand tu veux, ça n'a pas d'importance.
- **It matters a lot to me.** C'est très important pour moi.

mattress NOUN

le **matelas**

mature ADJECTIVE

mûr ◇ *She's quite mature for her age.* Elle est très mûre pour son âge.

maximum NOUN

see also maximum ADJECTIVE

le **maximum**

maximum ADJECTIVE

see also maximum NOUN

maximum MASC, FEM, PL ◇ *The maximum speed is one 100 km/h.* La vitesse maximum autorisée est de cent kilomètres à l'heure.

- **the maximum amount** le maximum

May NOUN

mai MASC

- **in May** en mai
- **May Day** le Premier Mai

may VERB

- **He may come.** Il va peut-être venir.
  ◇ *It may rain.* Il va peut-être
  pleuvoir.
- **Are you going to the party?—I don't
  know, I may.** Est-ce que tu vas à la
  soirée?–Je ne sais pas, peut-être.
- **May I smoke?** Est-ce que je peux
  fumer?

maybe ADVERB

peut-être ◇ *maybe not* peut-être pas
◇ *a bit boring, maybe* peut-être un
peu ennuyeux ◇ *Maybe she's at home.*
Elle est peut-être chez elle. ◇ *Maybe
he'll change his mind.* Il va peut-être
changer d'avis.

mayonnaise NOUN

la **mayonnaise**

mayor NOUN

le **maire**

me PRONOUN

me *becomes* m' *before a vowel sound.*

[1] **me** ◇ *Could you lend me your pen?*
Est-ce que tu peux me prêter ton stylo?
m' ◇ *Can you tell me the way to the
station?* Est-ce que vous pouvez
m'indiquer le chemin de la gare?
◇ *Can you help me?* Est-ce que tu
peux m'aider? ◇ *He heard me.* Il m'a
entendu.

moi *is used in exclamations.*

[2] **moi** ◇ *Me too!* Moi aussi!
◇ *Excuse me!* Excusez-moi! ◇ *Look
at me!* Regarde-moi! ◇ *Wait for me!*
Attends-moi! ◇ *Come with me!*
Suivez-moi!

moi *is also used after prepositions and in
comparisons.*

◇ *You're after me.* Tu es après moi.
◇ *Is it for me?* C'est pour moi?
◇ *She's older than me.* Elle est plus
âgée que moi.

meal NOUN

le **repas**

mealtime NOUN

- **at mealtimes** aux heures des repas

to **mean** VERB

see also mean ADJECTIVE *and* means NOUN

vouloir dire ◇ *What does "complet"
mean?* Qu'est-ce que "complet" veut
dire? ◇ *I don't know what it means.* Je
ne sais pas ce que ça veut dire. ◇ *What
do you mean?* Qu'est que vous voulez
dire? ◇ *That's not what I meant.* Ce
n'est pas ce que je voulais dire.

- **Which one do you mean?** Duquel
  veux-tu parler?
- **Do you really mean it?** Tu es sérieux?
- **to mean to do something** avoir
  l'intention de faire quelque chose ◇ *I
  didn't mean to offend you.* Je n'avais pas
  l'intention de vous blesser.

mean ADJECTIVE

see also mean VERB *and* means NOUN

[1] **radin** (*with money*) ◇ *He's too mean
to buy Christmas presents.* Il est trop
radin pour acheter des cadeaux de Noël.
[2] **méchant** (*unkind*) ◇ *You're being
mean to me.* Tu es méchant avec moi.

- **That's a really mean thing to say!** Ce
  n'est vraiment pas gentil de dire ça!

meaning NOUN

le **sens**

means NOUN

see also mean VERB *and* ADJECTIVE

le **moyen** ◇ *He'll do it by any possible
means.* Il le fera par tous les moyens.
◇ *a means of transport* un moyen de
transport

- **by means of** au moyen de ◇ *He got
  in by means of a stolen key.* Il est entré
  au moyen d'une clé volée.
- **by all means** bien sûr ◇ *Can I come?
  –By all means!* Est-ce que je peux
  venir?–Bien sûr!

meant VERB see **mean**

measles NOUN

la **rougeole**

to **measure** VERB

[1] **mesurer** ◇ *I measured the page.*
J'ai mesuré la page.
[2] **faire** ◇ *The room measures 3
metres by 4.* La pièce fait trois mètres
sur quatre.

measurements PL NOUN

[1] les **dimensions** FEM (*of object*)
◇ *What are the measurements of the
room?* Quelles sont les dimensions de
la pièce?
[2] les **mensurations** FEM (*of body*)
◇ *What are your measurements?*
Quelles sont tes mensurations?

- **my waist measurement** mon tour de
  taille
- **What's your neck measurement?** Quel
  est votre tour de cou?

meat NOUN

la **viande** ◇ *I don't eat meat.* Je ne
mange pas de viande.

Mecca NOUN

la **Mecque**

mechanic NOUN

le **mécanicien** ◇ *He's a mechanic.* Il
est mécanicien.

M

mechanical ADJECTIVE
mécanique MASC, FEM

medal NOUN
la **médaille**
- **the gold medal** la médaille d'or

media PL NOUN
les **médias** MASC

medical ADJECTIVE
see also medical NOUN
médical
(**médicaux** MASC PL)
◇ medical treatment les soins médicaux
- **medical insurance** l'assurance maladie
- **to have medical problems** avoir des problèmes de santé
- **She's a medical student.** Elle est étudiante en médecine.

medical NOUN
see also medical ADJECTIVE
- **to have a medical** passer une visite médicale

medicine NOUN
[1] la **médecine** (subject) ◇ I want to study medicine. Je veux faire médecine.
- **alternative medicine** la médecine douce
[2] le **médicament** (medication) ◇ I need some medicine. J'ai besoin d'un médicament.

Mediterranean ADJECTIVE
méditerranéen MASC
méditerranéenne FEM
- **the Mediterranean** la Méditerranée

medium ADJECTIVE
moyen MASC
moyenne FEM
◇ a medium-sized town une ville de taille moyenne ◇ a man of medium height un homme de taille moyenne

medium-sized ADJECTIVE
de taille moyenne ◇ a medium-sized town une ville de taille moyenne

to **meet** VERB
[1] **rencontrer** (by chance) ◇ I met Paul when I was walking the dog. J'ai rencontré Paul alors que je promenais mon chien. ◇ Have you met him before? Est-ce que tu l'as déjà rencontré?
[2] **se rencontrer** ◇ We met by chance in the shopping centre. Nous nous sommes rencontrés par hasard dans le centre commercial.
[3] **retrouver** (by arrangement) ◇ I'm going to meet my friends. Je vais retrouver mes amis.
[4] **se retrouver** ◇ Let's meet in front of the tourist office. Retrouvons-nous devant l'office de tourisme.

- **I like meeting new people.** J'aime faire de nouvelles connaissances.
[5] **aller chercher** (pick up) ◇ I'll meet you at the station. J'irai te chercher à la gare.

meeting NOUN
[1] la **réunion** (for work) ◇ a business meeting une réunion d'affaires
[2] la **rencontre** (socially) ◇ their first meeting leur première rencontre

mega ADJECTIVE
- **He's mega rich.** Il est hyper-riche. (informal)

melody NOUN
la **mélodie**

melon NOUN
le **melon**

to **melt** VERB
fondre ◇ The snow is melting. La neige est en train de fondre.

member NOUN
le **membre**
- **a Member of Parliament** un député

membership card NOUN
la **carte de membre**

memorial NOUN
le **monument** ◇ a war memorial un monument aux morts

to **memorize** VERB
apprendre par cœur

memory NOUN
[1] la **mémoire** ◇ I haven't got a good memory. Je n'ai pas une bonne mémoire.
[2] le **souvenir** (recollection) ◇ to bring back memories rappeler des souvenirs

men PL NOUN see **man**
les **hommes** MASC

to **mend** VERB
réparer

meningitis NOUN
la **méningite**

mental ADJECTIVE
[1] **mental**
(**mentaux** MASC PL)
◇ a mental illness une maladie mentale
[2] (mad)
fou MASC
folle FEM
◇ You're mental! Tu es fou!
- **a mental hospital** un hôpital psychiatrique

to **mention** VERB
mentionner
- **Thank you!—Don't mention it!** Merci!—Il n'y a pas de quoi!

menu NOUN
le **menu** ◇ Could I have the menu please? Est-ce que je pourrais avoir le

menu s'il vous plaît?

merchant NOUN
le **marchand** ◇ *a wine merchant* un marchand de vin

mercy NOUN
la **pitié**

meringue NOUN
la **meringue**

merry ADJECTIVE
- **Merry Christmas!** Joyeux Noël!

merry-go-round NOUN
le **manège**

mess NOUN
le **fouillis** ◇ *My bedroom's usually in a mess.* Il y a généralement du fouillis dans ma chambre.

to **mess about** VERB
- **to mess about with something** (*interfere with*) tripoter quelque chose ◇ *Stop messing about with my computer!* Arrête de tripoter mon ordinateur!
- **Don't mess about with my things!** Ne touche pas à mes affaires!

to **mess up** VERB
- **to mess something up** mettre la pagaille dans quelque chose ◇ *My little brother has messed up my cassettes.* Mon petit frère a mis la pagaille dans mes cassettes.

message NOUN
le **message**

messenger NOUN
le **messager**

messy ADJECTIVE
[1] **salissant** (*dirty*) ◇ *a messy job* un travail salissant
[2] **en désordre** (*untidy*) ◇ *Your desk is really messy.* Ton bureau est vraiment en désordre.
[3] **désordonnée** (*person*) ◇ *She's so messy!* Elle est tellement désordonnée!
- **My writing is terribly messy.** J'ai une écriture de cochon.

met VERB *see* **meet**

metal NOUN
le **métal**
(les **métaux** PL)

meter NOUN
[1] le **compteur** (*for gas, electricity, taxi*)
[2] le **parcmètre** (*parking meter*)

method NOUN
la **méthode**

Methodist NOUN
le/la **méthodiste** ◇ *I'm a Methodist.* Je suis méthodiste.

metre NOUN
le **mètre**

metric ADJECTIVE
métrique

Mexico NOUN
le **Mexique**
- **in Mexico** au Mexique
- **to Mexico** au Mexique

to **miaow** VERB
miauler

mice PL NOUN *see* **mouse**

microchip NOUN
la **puce**

microphone NOUN
le **microphone**

microscope NOUN
le **microscope**

microwave oven NOUN
le **four à micro-ondes**

mid ADJECTIVE
- **in mid May** à la mi-mai

midday NOUN
le **midi**
- **at midday** à midi

middle NOUN
le **milieu** ◇ *in the middle of the road* au milieu de la route ◇ *in the middle of the night* au milieu de la nuit ◇ *the middle seat* la place du milieu

middle-aged ADJECTIVE
d'un certain âge ◇ *a middle-aged man* un homme d'un certain âge
- **to be middle-aged** avoir la cinquantaine
- **She's middle-aged.** Elle a la cinquantaine.

middle-class ADJECTIVE
de la classe moyenne ◇ *a middle-class family* une famille de la classe moyenne

Middle East NOUN
le **Moyen-Orient**
- **in the Middle East** au Moyen-Orient

middle name NOUN
le **deuxième nom**

midge NOUN
le **moucheron**

midnight NOUN
minuit MASC
- **at midnight** à minuit

might VERB
Use **peut-être** to express possibility.
◇ *He might come later.* Il va peut-être venir plus tard. ◇ *We might go to Spain next year.* Nous irons peut-être en Espagne l'an prochain. ◇ *She might not have understood.* Elle n'a peut-être pas compris.

migraine NOUN
la **migraine** ◇ *I've got a migraine.* J'ai la migraine.

mike NOUN
le **micro**

M

mild ADJECTIVE
doux MASC
douce FEM
○ *The winters are quite mild.* Les hivers sont assez doux.

mile NOUN
le **mille**
In France distances are expressed in kilometres. A mile is about 1.6 kilometres.
○ *It's 5 miles from here.* C'est à huit kilomètres d'ici.
- **We walked miles!** Nous avons fait des kilomètres à pied!

military ADJECTIVE
militaire MASC, FEM

milk NOUN
see also milk VERB
le **lait** ○ *tea with milk* du thé au lait

to **milk** VERB
see also milk NOUN
traire

milk chocolate NOUN
le **chocolat au lait**

milkman NOUN
In France milk is not delivered to people's homes.
○ *He's a milkman.* Il livre le lait à domicile.

milk shake NOUN
le **milk-shake**

mill NOUN
le **moulin** *(for grain)*

millimetre NOUN
le **millimètre**

million NOUN
le **million**

millionaire NOUN
le **millionnaire**

to **mimic** VERB
imiter

mince NOUN
la **viande hachée**

to **mind** VERB
see also mind NOUN
1 **garder** ○ *Could you mind the baby this afternoon?* Est-ce que tu pourrais garder le bébé cet après-midi?
2 **surveiller** *(keep an eye on)* ○ *Could you mind my bags for a few minutes?* Est-ce que vous pourriez surveiller mes bagages pendant quelques minutes?
- **Do you mind if I open the window?** Est-ce que je pourrais ouvrir la fenêtre?
- **I don't mind.** Ça ne me dérange pas. ○ *I don't mind the noise.* Le bruit ne me dérange pas.
- **Never mind!** Ça ne fait rien!
- **Mind that bike!** Attention au vélo!
- **Mind the step!** Attention à la marche!

mind NOUN
see also mind VERB
- **to make up one's mind** se décider ○ *I haven't made up my mind yet.* Je ne me suis pas encore décidé.
- **to change one's mind** changer d'avis ○ *He's changed his mind.* Il a changé d'avis.
- **Are you out of your mind?** Tu as perdu la tête?

mine PRONOUN
see also mine NOUN
le mien + MASC NOUN ○ *Is this your coat?–No, mine's black.* C'est ton manteau?–Non, le mien est noir.
la mienne + FEM NOUN ○ *Is this your car?–No, mine's green.* C'est ta voiture? –Non, la mienne est verte.
les miens + MASC PL NOUN ○ *her parents and mine* ses parents et les miens
les miennes + FEM PL NOUN ○ *Your hands are dirty, mine are clean.* Tes mains sont sales, les miennes sont propres.
- **It's mine.** C'est à moi. ○ *This book is mine.* Ce livre est à moi. ○ *Whose is this?–It's mine.* C'est à qui?–À moi.

mine NOUN
see also mine PRONOUN
la **mine** ○ *a coal mine* une mine de charbon ○ *a land mine* une mine terrestre

miner NOUN
le **mineur**

mineral water NOUN
l' **eau minérale** FEM

miniature ADJECTIVE
see also miniature NOUN
miniature ○ *a miniature version* une version miniature

miniature NOUN
see also miniature ADJECTIVE
la **miniature**

minibus NOUN
le **minibus**

minimum NOUN
see also minimum ADJECTIVE
le **minimum**

minimum ADJECTIVE
see also minimum NOUN
minimum MASC, FEM, PL ○ *There's no minimum wage in Britain.* Il n'y a pas de salaire minimum en Grande-Bretagne. ○ *The minimum age for driving is 17.* L'âge minimum pour conduire est dix-sept ans.
- **the minimum amount** le minimum

miniskirt NOUN
la **mini-jupe**

minister NOUN
  [1] le **ministre** (in government)
  [2] le **pasteur** (of church)
minor ADJECTIVE
  mineur ◇ a minor problem un
  problème mineur
- **in D minor** en ré mineur
- **a minor operation** une opération
  bénigne
minority NOUN
  la **minorité**
mint NOUN
  [1] la **menthe** (plant) ◇ mint sauce la
  sauce à la menthe
  [2] le **bonbon à la menthe** (sweet)
minus PREPOSITION
  moins ◇ 16 minus 3 is 13. Seize
  moins trois égale treize. ◇ It's minus
  two degrees outside. Il fait moins deux
  dehors. ◇ I got a B minus. J'ai eu un B
  moins.
minute NOUN
  see also minute ADJECTIVE
  la **minute** ◇ Wait a minute! Attends
  une minute!
minute ADJECTIVE
  see also minute NOUN
  minuscule ◇ Her flat is minute. Son
  appartement est minuscule.
miracle NOUN
  le **miracle**
mirror NOUN
  [1] la **glace** (on wall)
  [2] le **rétroviseur** (in car)
to **misbehave** VERB
  se conduire mal
mischief NOUN
  les **bêtises** FEM PL ◇ My little sister's
  always up to mischief. Ma petite sœur
  fait constamment des bêtises.
mischievous ADJECTIVE
  coquin
miser NOUN
  l' **avare** MASC/FEM
miserable ADJECTIVE
  [1] (person)
  malheureux MASC
  malheureuse FEM
  ◇ You're looking miserable. Tu as l'air
  malheureux.
  [2] (weather)
  épouvantable ◇ The weather was
  miserable. Il faisait un temps
  épouvantable.
- **to feel miserable** ne pas avoir le moral
  ◇ I'm feeling miserable. Je n'ai pas le
  moral.
misfortune NOUN
  le **malheur**

mishap NOUN
  la **mésaventure**
to **misjudge** VERB
  mal juger (person) ◇ I've misjudged
  her. Je l'ai mal jugée.
- **He misjudged the bend.** Il a mal pris le
  virage.
to **mislay** VERB
  égarer ◇ I've mislaid my passport. J'ai
  égaré mon passeport.
misleading ADJECTIVE
  trompeur MASC
  trompeuse FEM
Miss NOUN
  [1] **Mademoiselle**
  (**Mesdemoiselles** PL)
  [2] (in address)
  Mlle
  (**Mlles** PL)
to **miss** VERB
  [1] **rater** ◇ Hurry or you'll miss the bus.
  Dépêche-toi ou tu vas rater le bus.
  ◇ He missed the target. Il a raté la
  cible.
  [2] **manquer** ◇ to miss an opportunity
  manquer une occasion
- **I miss you.** Tu me manques. ◇ I'm
  missing my family. Ma famille me
  manque. ◇ I miss him. Il me manque.
  ◇ I miss them. Ils me manquent.
missing ADJECTIVE
  manquant ◇ the missing part la pièce
  manquante
- **to be missing** avoir disparu ◇ My
  rucksack is missing. Mon sac à dos a
  disparu. ◇ Two members of the group
  are missing. Deux membres du groupe
  ont disparu.
missionary NOUN
  le/la **missionnaire**
mist NOUN
  [1] la **brume** (light)
  [2] le **brouillard** (thick)
mistake NOUN
  see also mistake VERB FEM
  [1] la **faute** (slip) ◇ a spelling mistake
  une faute d'orthographe
- **to make a mistake (1)** (in writing,
  speaking) faire une faute
- **to make a mistake (2)** (get mixed up) se
  tromper ◇ I'm sorry, I made a mistake.
  Je suis désolé, je me suis trompé.
  [2] l' **erreur** FEM (misjudgement) ◇ It was
  a mistake to buy those yellow shoes. J'ai
  fait une erreur en achetant ces
  chaussures jaunes.
- **by mistake** par erreur ◇ I took his
  bag by mistake. J'ai pris son sac par
  erreur.

M

to **mistake** VERB
see also mistake NOUN
- **He mistook me for my sister.** Il m'a prise pour ma sœur.

mistaken ADJECTIVE
- **to be mistaken** se tromper ◇ *If you think I'm going to get up at 6 o'clock, you're mistaken.* Si tu penses que je vais me lever à six heures, tu te trompes.

mistletoe NOUN
le **gui**

mistook VERB *see* **mistake**

mistress NOUN
1 le **professeur** (*teacher*) ◇ *our French mistress* notre professeur de français
2 la **maîtresse** (*lover*) ◇ *He's got a mistress.* Il a une maîtresse.

to **mistrust** VERB
se méfier de

misty ADJECTIVE
brumeux MASC
brumeuse FEM
◇ *a misty morning* un matin brumeux

to **misunderstand** VERB
mal comprendre ◇ *Sorry, I misunderstood you.* Je suis désolé, je t'avais mal compris.

misunderstanding NOUN
le **malentendu**

mix NOUN
see also mix VERB
le **mélange** ◇ *It's a mix of science fiction and comedy.* C'est un mélange de science-fiction et de comédie.
- **a cake mix** une préparation pour gâteau

to **mix** VERB
see also mix NOUN
1 **mélanger** ◇ *Mix the flour with the sugar.* Mélangez la farine au sucre.
2 **combiner** ◇ *He's mixing business with pleasure.* Il combine les affaires et le plaisir.
- **to mix with somebody** (*associate*) fréquenter quelqu'un
- **He doesn't mix much.** Il se tient à l'écart.
- **to mix up** (*people*) confondre ◇ *He always mixes me up with my sister.* Il me confond toujours avec ma sœur.
- **The travel agent mixed up the bookings.** L'agence de voyage s'est embrouillée dans les réservations.
- **I'm getting mixed up.** Je ne m'y retrouve plus.

mixed ADJECTIVE
- **a mixed salad** une salade composée
- **a mixed school** une école mixte
- **a mixed grill** un assortiment de grillades

mixture NOUN
le **mélange** ◇ *a mixture of spices* un mélange d'épices
- **cough mixture** le sirop pour la toux

mix-up NOUN
la **confusion**

to **moan** VERB
râler ◇ *She's always moaning.* Elle est toujours en train de râler.

mobile home NOUN
le **mobile home**

mobile phone NOUN
le **téléphone portatif**

to **mock** VERB
see also mock ADJECTIVE
ridiculiser

mock ADJECTIVE
see also mock VERB
- **a mock exam** un examen blanc

model NOUN
see also model ADJECTIVE
1 le **modèle** (*type*) ◇ *His car is the latest model.* Sa voiture est le tout dernier modèle.
2 la **maquette** (*mock-up*) ◇ *a model of the castle* une maquette du château
3 le **mannequin** (*fashion*) ◇ *She's a famous model.* C'est un mannequin célèbre.

model ADJECTIVE
see also model NOUN
- **a model plane** un modèle réduit d'avion
- **a model railway** un modèle réduit de voie ferrée
- **He's a model pupil.** C'est un élève modèle.

modem NOUN
le **modem**

moderate ADJECTIVE
modéré ◇ *His views are quite moderate.* Ses opinions sont assez modérées.
- **a moderate amount of** un peu de
- **a moderate price** un prix raisonnable

modern ADJECTIVE
moderne

to **modernize** VERB
moderniser

modest ADJECTIVE
modeste

to **modify** VERB
modifier

moisture NOUN
l' **humidité** FEM

moisturizer NOUN
1 la **crème hydratante** (*cream*)
2 le **lait hydratant** (*lotion*)

mole NOUN
  1 la **taupe** (*animal*)
  2 le **grain de beauté** (*on skin*)
moment NOUN
  l' **instant** MASC ⋄ *Could you wait a*
  moment? Pouvez-vous attendre un
  instant? ⋄ *in a moment* dans un
  instant ⋄ *Just a moment!* Un instant!
- **at the moment** en ce moment
- **any moment now** d'un moment à
  l'autre ⋄ *They'll be arriving any*
  moment now. Ils vont arriver d'un
  moment à l'autre.
Monaco NOUN
  Monaco
- **in Monaco** à Monaco
monarch NOUN
  le **monarque**
monarchy NOUN
  la **monarchie**
monastery NOUN
  le **monastère**
Monday NOUN
  le **lundi** ⋄ *on Monday* lundi ⋄ *on*
  Mondays le lundi ⋄ *every Monday*
  tous les lundis ⋄ *last Monday* lundi
  dernier ⋄ *next Monday* lundi prochain
money NOUN
  l' **argent** MASC ⋄ *I need to change*
  some money. J'ai besoin de changer de
  l'argent.
- **to make money** gagner de l'argent
mongrel NOUN
  le **bâtard** ⋄ *My dog's a mongrel.* Mon
  chien est un bâtard.
monitor NOUN
  le **moniteur** (*of computer*)
monk NOUN
  le **moine**
monkey NOUN
  le **singe**
monotonous ADJECTIVE
  monotone
monster NOUN
  le **monstre**
month NOUN
  le **mois** ⋄ *this month* ce mois-ci
  ⋄ *next month* le mois prochain
  ⋄ *last month* le mois dernier
  ⋄ *every month* tous les mois ⋄ *at*
  the end of the month à la fin du mois
monthly ADJECTIVE
  mensuel MASC
  mensuelle FEM
monument NOUN
  le **monument**
mood NOUN
  l' **humeur** FEM
- **to be in a bad mood** être de mauvaise

humeur
- **to be in a good mood** être de bonne
  humeur
moody ADJECTIVE
  1 **lunatique** (*temperamental*)
  2 **maussade** (*in a bad mood*)
moon NOUN
  la **lune** ⋄ *There's a full moon tonight.*
  Il y a pleine lune ce soir.
- **to be over the moon** (*happy*) être aux
  anges
moor NOUN
  | *see also* **moor** VERB |
  la **lande**
to **moor** VERB
  | *see also* **moor** NOUN |
  amarrer (*boat*)
mop NOUN
  le **balai laveur** (*for floor*)
moped NOUN
  le **cyclomoteur**
moral ADJECTIVE
  | *see also* **moral** NOUN |
  moral
  (**moraux** MASC PL)
moral NOUN
  | *see also* **moral** ADJECTIVE |
  la **morale** ⋄ *the moral of the story* la
  morale de l'histoire
- **morals** la moralité
morale NOUN
  le **moral** ⋄ *Their morale is very low.*
  Leur moral est très bas.
more ADJECTIVE, PRONOUN, ADVERB
  When comparing one amount with another, you
  usually use **plus**.
  1 **plus** ⋄ *Beer is more expensive in*
  Britain. La bière est plus chère en
  Grande-Bretagne. ⋄ *Could you speak*
  more slowly? Est-ce que vous pourriez
  parler plus lentement? ⋄ *a bit more* un
  peu plus ⋄ *There isn't any more.* Il n'y
  en a plus.
- **more...than** plus...que ⋄ *He's more*
  intelligent than me. Il est plus
  intelligent que moi. ⋄ *She practises*
  more than I do. Elle s'entraîne plus que
  moi. ⋄ *More girls than boys do French.*
  Il y a plus de filles que de garçons qui
  font du français.
  2 **plus de** (*followed by noun*) ⋄ *There*
  are more girls in the class. Il y a plus de
  filles dans la classe. ⋄ *I get more*
  homework than you do. J'ai plus de
  devoirs que toi. ⋄ *I spent more than*
  500 francs. J'ai dépensé plus de cinq
  cents francs.
  When referring to an additional amount, more
  than there is already, you usually use **encore**.

M

3 **encore** ◇ *Is there any more?* Est-ce qu'il y en a encore? ◇ *Would you like some more?* Vous en voulez encore? ◇ *It'll take a few more days.* Ça prendra encore quelques jours.
4 **encore de** *(followed by noun)*
◇ *Could I have some more chips?* Est-ce que je pourrais avoir encore des frites? ◇ *Do you want some more tea?* Voulez-vous encore du thé?
- **more or less** plus ou moins
- **more than ever** plus que jamais

morning NOUN
le **matin** ◇ *this morning* ce matin ◇ *tomorrow morning* demain matin ◇ *every morning* tous les matins
- **in the morning** le matin ◇ *at 7 o'clock in the morning* à sept heures du matin
- **a morning paper** un journal du matin

Morocco NOUN
le **Maroc**
- **in Morocco** au Maroc

Moscow NOUN
Moscou
- **in Moscow** à Moscou

Moslem NOUN
le **musulman**
la **musulmane**
◇ *He's a Moslem.* Il est musulman.

mosque NOUN
la **mosquée**

mosquito NOUN
le **moustique**
- **a mosquito bite** une piqûre de moustique

most ADVERB, ADJECTIVE, PRONOUN
Use **la plupart de** *when* most (of) *is followed by a plural noun and* **la majeure partie (de)** *when* most (of) *is followed by a singular noun.*
1 **la plupart de** ◇ *most of my friends* la plupart de mes amis ◇ *most people* la plupart des gens ◇ *Most cats are affectionate.* La plupart des chats sont affectueux.
- **most of them** la plupart d'entre eux
- **most of the time** la plupart du temps
2 **la majeure partie de** ◇ *most of the work* la majeure partie du travail ◇ *most of the class* la majeure partie de la classe ◇ *most of the night* la majeure partie de la nuit
- **the most** le plus ◇ *He's the one who talks the most.* C'est lui qui parle le plus.
When most *is followed by adjective, the translation depends on whether the noun referred to is masculine, feminine or plural.*
- **the most... (1)** le plus... ◇ *the most expensive restaurant* le restaurant le

plus cher
- **the most... (2)** la plus... ◇ *the most expensive seat* la place la plus chère
- **the most... (3)** les plus... ◇ *the most expensive restaurants* les restaurants les plus chers ◇ *the most expensive seats* les places les plus chères
- **to make the most of something** profiter au maximum de quelque chose
- **at the most** au maximum ◇ *Two hours at the most.* Deux heures au maximum.

mostly ADVERB
- **The teachers are mostly quite nice.** La plupart des professeurs sont assez gentils.

motel NOUN
le **motel**

mother NOUN
la **mère** ◇ *my mother* ma mère
- **mother tongue** la langue maternelle

mother-in-law NOUN
la **belle-mère**
(les **belles-mères** PL)

Mother's Day NOUN
la **fête des Mères**
Mother's Day is usually on the last Sunday of May in France.

motionless ADJECTIVE
immobile

motivated ADJECTIVE
motivé ◇ *He is highly motivated.* Il est très motivé.

motivation NOUN
la **motivation**

motive NOUN
le **mobile** ◇ *the motive for the killing* le mobile du crime

motor NOUN
le **moteur** ◇ *The boat has a motor.* Le bateau a un moteur.

motorbike NOUN
la **moto**

motorboat NOUN
le **bateau à moteur**

motorcycle NOUN
le **vélomoteur**

motorcyclist NOUN
le **motard**

motorist NOUN
l' **automobiliste** MASC/FEM

motor mechanic NOUN
le **mécanicien garagiste**

motor racing NOUN
la **course automobile**

motorway NOUN
l' **autoroute** FEM ◇ *on the motorway* sur l'autoroute

mouldy ADJECTIVE

moisi

mountain NOUN
la **montagne**
- **a mountain bike** un VTT (= vélo tout-terrain)

mountaineer NOUN
l' **alpiniste** MASC/FEM

mountaineering NOUN
l' **alpinisme** MASC ◇ *I go mountaineering.* Je fais de l'alpinisme.

mountainous ADJECTIVE
montagneux MASC
montagneuse FEM

mouse NOUN
la **souris** *(also for computer)* ◇ *white mice* des souris blanches

mousse NOUN
1 la **mousse** *(food)* ◇ *chocolate mousse* la mousse au chocolat
2 la **mousse coiffante** *(for hair)*

moustache NOUN
la **moustache** ◇ *He's got a moustache.* Il a une moustache.
- **a man with a moustache** un moustachu

mouth NOUN
la **bouche**

mouthful NOUN
la **bouchée**

mouth organ NOUN
l' **harmonica** MASC ◇ *I play the mouth organ.* Je joue de l'harmonica.

move NOUN
see also **move** VERB
1 le **tour** ◇ *It's your move.* C'est ton tour.
2 le **déménagement** ◇ *Our move from Oxford to Luton...* Notre déménagement d'Oxford à Luton...
- **to get a move on** se remuer ◇ *Get a move on!* Remue-toi!

to **move** VERB
see also **move** NOUN
1 **bouger** ◇ *Don't move!* Ne bouge pas! ◇ *Could you move your stuff please?* Est-ce que tu peux bouger tes affaires s'il te plaît?
2 **avancer** ◇ *The car was moving very slowly.* La voiture avançait très lentement.
3 **émouvoir** ◇ *I was very moved by the film.* J'ai été très émue par ce film.
- **to move house** déménager ◇ *We're moving in July.* Nous allons déménager en juillet.
- **to move forward** avancer
- **to move in** emménager ◇ *They're moving in next week.* Ils emménagent la semaine prochaine.

- **to move over** se pousser ◇ *Could you move over a bit?* Est-ce que vous pouvez vous pousser un peu?

movement NOUN
le **mouvement**

movie NOUN
le **film**
- **the movies** le cinéma ◇ *Let's go to the movies!* Si on allait au cinéma?

moving ADJECTIVE
1 **en marche** *(not stationary)* ◇ *a moving bus* un bus en marche
2 **touchant** *(touching)* ◇ *a moving story* une histoire touchante

to **mow** VERB
tondre
- **to mow the lawn** tondre le gazon

mower NOUN
la **tondeuse à gazon**

MP NOUN
le **député** ◇ *She's an MP.* Elle est député.

Mr NOUN
1 **Monsieur** (**Messieurs** PL)
2 *(in address)* **M.** (**MM.** PL)

Mrs NOUN
1 **Madame** (**Mesdames** PL)
2 *(in address)* **Mme** (**Mmes** PL)

Ms NOUN
1 **Madame** (**Mesdames** PL)
2 *(in address)* **Mme** (**Mmes** PL)

There isn't a direct equivalent of Ms *in French. If you are writing to somebody and don't know whether she is married, use* Madame.

much ADJECTIVE, ADVERB, PRONOUN
1 **beaucoup** *(with verb)* ◇ *Do you go out much?* Tu sors beaucoup? ◇ *I don't like sport much.* Je n'aime pas beaucoup le sport. ◇ *I feel much better now.* Je me sens beaucoup mieux maintenant.
2 **beaucoup de** *(followed by noun)* ◇ *I haven't got much money.* Je n'ai pas beaucoup d'argent. ◇ *I don't want much rice.* Je ne veux pas beaucoup de riz.
- **very much (1)** *(with verb)* beaucoup ◇ *I enjoyed the film very much.* J'ai beaucoup apprécié le film. ◇ *Thank you very much.* Merci beaucoup.
- **very much (2)** *(followed by noun)*

M

beaucoup de ◇ *I haven't got very much money.* Je n'ai pas beaucoup d'argent.
- **not much (1)** pas beaucoup ◇ *Have you got a lot of luggage?–No, not much.* As-tu beaucoup de bagages?–Non, pas beaucoup.
- **not much (2)** pas grand-chose ◇ *What's on TV?–Not much.* Qu'est-ce qu'il y a à la télé?–Pas grand-chose. ◇ *What did you think of it?–Not much.* Qu'est-ce que tu en as pensé?–Pas grand-chose.
- **How much?** Combien? ◇ *How much do you want?* Tu en veux combien? ◇ *How much time have you got?* Tu as combien de temps? ◇ *How much is it? (cost)* Combien est-ce que ça coûte?
- **too much** trop ◇ *That's too much!* C'est trop! ◇ *It costs too much.* Ça coûte trop cher. ◇ *They give us too much homework.* Ils nous donnent trop de devoirs.
- **so much** autant ◇ *I didn't think it would cost so much.* Je ne pensais pas que ça coûterait autant. ◇ *I've never seen so much traffic.* Je n'ai jamais vu autant de circulation.

mud NOUN
la **boue**

muddle NOUN
le **désordre** ◇ *The photos are in a muddle.* Les photos sont en désordre.

to **muddle up** VERB
confondre *(people)* ◇ *He muddles me up with my sister.* Il me confond avec ma sœur.
- **to get muddled up** s'embrouiller ◇ *I'm getting muddled up.* Je m'embrouille.

muddy ADJECTIVE
boueux MASC
boueuse FEM

muesli NOUN
le **muesli**

mug NOUN
see also mug VERB
la **grande tasse** ◇ *Do you want a cup or a mug?* Est-ce que vous voulez une tasse normale ou une grande tasse?
- **a beer mug** une chope à bière

to **mug** VERB
see also mug NOUN
agresser ◇ *He was mugged in the city centre.* Il s'est fait agresser au centre ville.

mugger NOUN
l' **agresseur** MASC

mugging NOUN
l' **agression** FEM

muggy ADJECTIVE
lourd ◇ *It's muggy today.* Il fait lourd aujourd'hui.

multiplication NOUN
la **multiplication**

to **multiply** VERB
multiplier ◇ *to multiply 6 by 3* multiplier six par trois

multi-storey car park NOUN
le **parking à plusieurs étages**

mum NOUN
> You use **maman** only when you are talking to your mother or using it as her name; otherwise use **mère**.

1 la **mère** ◇ *my mum* ma mère ◇ *her mum* sa mère
2 la **maman** ◇ *Mum!* Maman! ◇ *I'll ask Mum.* Je vais demander à maman.

mummy NOUN
1 la **maman** *(mum)* ◇ *Mummy says I can go.* Maman dit que je peux y aller.
2 la **momie** *(Egyptian)*

mumps NOUN
les **oreillons** MASC PL

murder NOUN
see also murder VERB
le **meurtre** MASC

to **murder** VERB
see also murder NOUN
assassiner ◇ *He was murdered.* Il a été assassiné.

murderer NOUN
l' **assassin** MASC

muscle NOUN
le **muscle**

muscular ADJECTIVE
musclé

museum NOUN
le **musée**

mushroom NOUN
le **champignon** ◇ *mushroom omelette* l'omelette aux champignons

music NOUN
la **musique**

musical ADJECTIVE
see also musical NOUN
doué pour la musique ◇ *I'm not musical.* Je ne suis pas doué pour la musique.
- **a musical instrument** un instrument de musique

musical NOUN
see also musical ADJECTIVE
la **comédie musicale**

music centre NOUN
la **chaîne stéréo**

musician NOUN
le **musicien**
la **musicienne**

Muslim NOUN
le **musulman**
la **musulmane**
◇ *He's a Muslim.* Il est musulman.

mussel NOUN
la **moule**

must VERB

> *When* must *means that you assume or suppose something, use* **devoir**; *when it means it's necessary to do something, eg* I must buy some presents, *use* **il faut que...**, *which comes from the verb* **falloir** *and is followed by a verb in the subjunctive.*

1 **devoir** *(I suppose)* ◇ *You must be tired.* Tu dois être fatigué. ◇ *They must have plenty of money.* Ils doivent avoir beaucoup d'argent. ◇ *There must be some problem.* Il doit y avoir un problème.

2 **il faut que** ◇ *I must buy some presents.* Il faut que j'achète des cadeaux. ◇ *I really must go now.* Il faut que j'y aille.

• **You mustn't forget to send her a card.** N'oublie surtout pas de lui envoyer une carte.

• **You must come and see us.** *(invitation)* Venez donc nous voir.

mustard NOUN
la **moutarde**

to **mutter** VERB
marmonner

my ADJECTIVE
mon MASC ◇ *my father* mon père
ma FEM ◇ *my aunt* ma tante
mes PL ◇ *my parents* mes parents
ma *becomes* **mon** *before a vowel sound.*

• **my friend (1)** *(male)* mon ami
• **my friend (2)** *(female)* mon amie

> *Do not use* **mon/ma/mes** *with parts of the body.*

◇ *I want to wash my hair.* Je voudrais me laver les cheveux. ◇ *I'm going to clean my teeth.* Je vais me brosser les dents. ◇ *I've hurt my foot.* Je me suis fait mal au pied.

myself PRONOUN
1 **me** ◇ *I've hurt myself.* Je me suis fait mal. ◇ *I really enjoyed myself.* Je me suis vraiment bien amusé.
◇ *...when I look at myself in the mirror.* ...quand je me regarde dans la glace.
2 **moi** ◇ *I don't like talking about myself.* Je n'aime pas parler de moi.
3 **moi-même** ◇ *I made it myself.* Je l'ai fait moi-même.
• **by myself** tout seul ◇ *I don't like travelling by myself.* Je n'aime pas voyager tout seul.

mysterious ADJECTIVE
mystérieux MASC
mystérieuse FEM

mystery NOUN
le **mystère**
• **a murder mystery** *(novel)* un roman policier

myth NOUN
1 le **mythe** *(legend)* ◇ *a Greek myth* un mythe grec
2 l' **idée reçue** FEM *(untrue idea)*
◇ *That's a myth.* C'est une idée reçue.

mythology NOUN
la **mythologie**

M

N

naff ADJECTIVE
   nul MASC
   nulle FEM

to **nag** VERB
   harceler (*scold*) ⋄ *She's always nagging me.* Elle me harcèle constamment.

nail NOUN
   ① l' **ongle** MASC (*on finger, toe*) ⋄ *Don't bite your nails!* Ne te ronge pas les ongles!
   ② le **clou** (*made of metal*)

nailbrush NOUN
   la **brosse à ongles**

nailfile NOUN
   la **lime à ongles**

nail scissors PL NOUN
   les **ciseaux à ongles** MASC

nail varnish NOUN
   le **vernis à ongles**
- **nail varnish remover** le dissolvant

naked ADJECTIVE
   nu

name NOUN
   le **nom**
- **What's your name?** Comment vous appelez-vous?

nanny NOUN
   la **garde d'enfants** ⋄ *She's a nanny.* C'est une garde d'enfants.

nap NOUN
   le **petit somme**
- **to have a nap** faire un petit somme

napkin NOUN
   la **serviette**

nappy NOUN
   la **couche**

narrow ADJECTIVE
   étroit

narrow-minded ADJECTIVE
   borné

nasty ADJECTIVE
   ① **mauvais** (*bad*) ⋄ *a nasty cold* un mauvais rhume ⋄ *a nasty smell* une mauvaise odeur
   ② **méchant** (*unfriendly*) ⋄ *He gave me a nasty look.* Il m'a regardé d'un air méchant.

nation NOUN
   la **nation**

national ADJECTIVE
   national
   (**nationaux** MASC PL)
   ⋄ *He's the national champion.* C'est le champion national.
- **the national elections** les élections législatives

national anthem NOUN
   l' **hymne national**

National Health Service NOUN
   la **Sécurité sociale**
   In France you have to pay for medical treatment when you receive it, and then claim it back from the Sécurité sociale.

nationalism NOUN
   le **nationalisme** ⋄ *Scottish nationalism* le nationalisme écossais

nationalist NOUN
   le/la **nationaliste**

nationality NOUN
   la **nationalité**

national park NOUN
   le **parc national**
   (les **parcs nationaux** PL)

native ADJECTIVE
   natal ⋄ *my native country* mon pays natal
- **native language** la langue maternelle ⋄ *English is not their native language.* L'anglais n'est pas leur langue maternelle.

natural ADJECTIVE
   naturel MASC
   naturelle FEM

naturalist NOUN
   le **naturaliste**

naturally ADVERB
   naturellement ⋄ *Naturally, we were very disappointed.* Nous avons naturellement été très déçus.

nature NOUN
   la **nature**

naughty ADJECTIVE
   vilain ⋄ *Naughty girl!* Vilaine! ⋄ *Don't be naughty!* Ne fais pas le vilain!

navy NOUN
   la **marine** ⋄ *He's in the navy.* Il est dans la marine.

navy-blue ADJECTIVE
   bleu marine MASC, FEM, PL ⋄ *a navy-blue skirt* une jupe bleu marine

Nazi NOUN
   le **Nazi**
   la **Nazie**
   ⋄ *the Nazis* les Nazis

near ADJECTIVE
   see also **near** PREPOSITION
   proche ⋄ *It's fairly near.* C'est assez proche.
- **It's near enough to walk.** On peut facilement y aller à pied.

- **the nearest** le plus proche ◦ *Where's the nearest service station?* Où est la station-service la plus proche? ◦ *The nearest shops were three kilometres away.* Les magasins les plus proches étaient à trois kilomètres.

near PREPOSITION, ADVERB
see also **near** ADJECTIVE
près de ◦ *I live near Liverpool.* J'habite près de Liverpool. ◦ *near my house* près de chez moi
- **near here** près d'ici ◦ *Is there a bank near here?* Est-ce qu'il y a une banque près d'ici?
- **near to** près de ◦ *It's very near to the school.* C'est tout près de l'école.

nearby ADVERB
see also **nearby** ADJECTIVE
à proximité ◦ *There's a supermarket nearby.* Il y a un supermarché à proximité.

nearby ADJECTIVE
see also **nearby** ADVERB
1 **proche** *(close)* ◦ *a nearby garage* un garage proche
2 **voisin** *(neighbouring)* ◦ *We went to the nearby village of Torrance.* Nous sommes allés à Torrance, le village voisin.

nearly ADVERB
presque ◦ *Dinner's nearly ready.* Le dîner est presque prêt. ◦ *I'm nearly 15.* J'ai presque quinze ans.
- **I nearly missed the train.** J'ai failli rater le train.

neat ADJECTIVE
soigné ◦ *She has very neat writing.* Elle a une écriture très soignée.
- **a neat whisky** un whisky sec

neatly ADVERB
soigneusement ◦ *neatly folded* soigneusement plié
- **neatly dressed** impeccable

necessarily ADVERB
- **not necessarily** pas forcément

necessary ADJECTIVE
nécessaire

necessity NOUN
la **chose nécessaire** ◦ *A car is a necessity, not a luxury.* Une voiture est une chose nécessaire et non pas un luxe.

neck NOUN
1 le **cou** *(of body)*
- **a stiff neck** un torticolis
2 l' **encolure** FEM *(of garment)* ◦ *a V-neck sweater* un pull avec une encolure en V

necklace NOUN

le **collier**

to **need** VERB
see also **need** NOUN
avoir besoin de ◦ *I need a bigger size.* J'ai besoin d'une plus grande taille.
- **to need to do something** avoir besoin de faire quelque chose ◦ *I need to change some money.* J'ai besoin de changer de l'argent.

need NOUN
see also **need** VERB
- **There's no need to book.** Il n'est pas nécessaire de réserver.

needle NOUN
l' **aiguille** FEM

needlework NOUN
la **couture** ◦ *We have needlework lessons at school.* Nous avons des cours de couture à l'école.

negative NOUN
see also **negative** ADJECTIVE
le **négatif** *(photo)*

negative ADJECTIVE
see also **negative** NOUN
négatif MASC
négative FEM
◦ *He's got a very negative attitude.* Il a une attitude très négative.

neglected ADJECTIVE
mal tenu *(untidy)* ◦ *The garden is neglected.* Le jardin est mal tenu.

negligee NOUN
le **déshabillé**

neighbour NOUN
le **voisin**
la **voisine**
◦ *the neighbours' garden* le jardin des voisins

neighbourhood NOUN
le **quartier**

neither PRONOUN, CONJUNCTION, ADVERB
aucun des deux
aucune des deux
◦ *Carrots or peas?—Neither, thanks.* Des carottes ou des petits pois?—Aucun des deux merci. ◦ *Neither of them is coming.* Aucun des deux ne vient.
- **neither...nor...** ni...ni... ◦ *Neither Sarah nor Tamsin is coming to the party.* Ni Sarah ni Tamsin ne vient à la soirée.
- **Neither do I.** Moi non plus. ◦ *I don't like him.—Neither do I!* Je ne l'aime pas. —Moi non plus!
- **Neither have I.** Moi non plus. ◦ *I've never been to Spain.—Neither have I.* Je ne suis jamais allé en Espagne.—Moi non plus.

neon NOUN

N

le **néon**
- **a neon light** une lampe au néon

nephew NOUN
le **neveu**
(les **neveux** PL)
◇ *my nephew* mon neveu

nerve NOUN
[1] le **nerf** ◇ *She sometimes gets on my nerves.* Elle me tape quelquefois sur les nerfs.
[2] le **toupet** (*cheek*) ◇ *He's got a nerve!* Il a du toupet!

nerve-racking ADJECTIVE
angoissant

nervous ADJECTIVE
tendu (*tense*) ◇ *I bite my nails when I'm nervous.* Je me ronge les ongles quand je suis tendu.
- **to be nervous about something** appréhender de faire quelque chose ◇ *I'm a bit nervous about flying to Paris by myself.* J'appréhende un peu d'aller toute seule en avion à Paris.

nest NOUN
le **nid**

net NOUN
le **filet** ◇ *a fishing net* un filet de pêche

Netherlands PL NOUN
les **Pays-Bas** MASC
- **in the Netherlands** aux Pays-Bas

network NOUN
le **réseau**
(les **réseaux** PL)

neurotic ADJECTIVE
névrosé

never ADVERB
[1] **jamais** ◇ *Have you ever been to Germany?–No, never.* Est-ce que tu es déjà allé en Allemagne?–Non, jamais. ◇ *When are you going to phone him? –Never!* Quand est-ce que tu vas l'appeler?–Jamais!
Add ne if the sentence contains a verb.
[2] **ne...jamais** ◇ *I never write letters.* Je n'écris jamais. ◇ *I have never been camping.* Je n'ai jamais fait de camping. ◇ *Never leave valuables in your car.* Ne laissez jamais d'objets de valeur dans votre voiture.
- **Never again!** Plus jamais!
- **Never mind.** Ça ne fait rien.

new ADJECTIVE
[1] **nouveau** MASC
nouvelle FEM
(**nouveaux** MASC PL)
◇ *her new boyfriend* son nouveau copain ◇ *I need a new dress.* J'ai besoin d'une nouvelle robe.
[2] (*brand new*)
neuf MASC
neuve FEM
◇ *They've got a new car.* Ils ont une voiture neuve.

newcomer NOUN
le **nouveau venu**
(les **nouveaux venus** MASC PL)
la **nouvelle venue**

news NOUN
[1] les **nouvelles** FEM PL ◇ *good news* de bonnes nouvelles ◇ *I've had some bad news.* J'ai reçu de mauvaises nouvelles. ◇ *It was nice to have your news.* J'ai été content d'avoir de tes nouvelles.
[2] la **nouvelle** (*single piece of news*) ◇ *That's wonderful news!* Quelle bonne nouvelle!
[3] le **journal télévisé** (*on TV*) ◇ *I watch the news every evening.* Je regarde le journal télévisé tous les soirs.
[4] les **informations** FEM PL (*on radio*) ◇ *I listen to the news every morning.* J'écoute les informations tous les matins.

newsagent NOUN
le **marchand de journaux**

newspaper NOUN
le **journal**
(les **journaux** PL)
◇ *I deliver newspapers.* Je distribue des journaux.

newsreader NOUN
le **présentateur**
la **présentatrice**

New Year
le **Nouvel An** ◇ *to celebrate New Year* fêter le Nouvel An
- **Happy New Year!** Bonne Année!
- **New Year's Day** le premier de l'An
- **New Year's Eve** la veille du premier de l'An ◇ *a New Year's Eve party* un réveillon du premier de l'An

New Zealand NOUN
la **Nouvelle-Zélande**
- **in New Zealand** en Nouvelle-Zélande

New Zealander NOUN
le **Néo-Zélandais**
la **Néo-Zélandaise**

next ADJECTIVE, ADVERB, PREPOSITION
[1] **prochain** (*in time*) ◇ *next Saturday* samedi prochain ◇ *next year* l'année prochaine ◇ *next summer* l'été prochain
[2] **suivant** (*in sequence*) ◇ *the next train* le train suivant ◇ *Next please!* Au suivant!
[3] **ensuite** (*afterwards*) ◇ *What shall I*

do next? Qu'est-ce que je fais ensuite?
◇ What happened next? Qu'est-ce
qui s'est passé ensuite?

- **next to** à côté de ◇ next to the bank à
côté de la banque
- **the next day** le lendemain ◇ The
next day we visited Versailles. Le
lendemain nous avons visité Versailles.
- **the next time** la prochaine fois ◇ the
next time you see her la prochaine fois
que tu la verras
- **next door** à côté ◇ They live next
door. Ils habitent à côté. ◇ the people
next door les gens d'à côté
- **the next room** la pièce d'à côté

NHS NOUN
la **Sécurité sociale**
In France you have to pay for medical treatment
when you receive it, and then claim it back from
the Sécurité sociale.

nice ADJECTIVE
1 (kind)
gentil MASC
gentille FEM
◇ Your parents are very nice. Tes
parents sont très gentils. ◇ It was nice
of you to remember my birthday. C'était
gentil de ta part de te souvenir de mon
anniversaire.
- **to be nice to somebody** être gentil
avec quelqu'un
2 (pretty)
joli ◇ That's a nice dress! Qu'est-ce
qu'elle est jolie, cette robe! ◇ Aix is a
nice town. Aix est une jolie ville.
3 (food)
bon MASC
bonne FEM
◇ It's very nice. C'est très bon. ◇ a nice
cup of coffee une bonne tasse de café
- **Have a nice time!** Amuse-toi bien!
- **nice weather** le beau temps
- **It's a nice day.** Il fait beau.

nickname NOUN
le **surnom**

niece NOUN
la **nièce** ◇ my niece ma nièce

Nigeria NOUN
le **Nigéria**
- **in Nigeria** au Nigéria

night NOUN
1 la **nuit** ◇ I want a single room for
two nights. Je veux une chambre à un
lit pour deux nuits.
- **at night** la nuit
- **Goodnight!** Bonne nuit!
- **a night club** une boîte de nuit
2 le **soir** (evening) ◇ last night hier
soir

nightie NOUN
la **chemise de nuit**

nightlife NOUN
- **There's plenty of nightlife.** Il y a plein
de choses à faire le soir.

nightmare NOUN
le **cauchemar** ◇ It was a real
nightmare! Ça a été un vrai cauchemar!
- **to have a nightmare** faire un
cauchemar

nil NOUN
le **zéro** ◇ We won one-nil. Nous avons
gagné un à zéro.

nine NUMBER
neuf MASC
neuve FEM
◇ She's nine. Elle a neuf ans.

nineteen NUMBER
dix-neuf ◇ She's nineteen. Elle a
dix-neuf ans.

ninety NUMBER
quatre-vingt-dix

ninth ADJECTIVE
neuvième ◇ the ninth floor le
neuvième étage
- **the ninth of August** le neuf août

no ADVERB, ADJECTIVE
1 **non** ◇ Are you coming?–No. Est-ce
que vous venez?–Non. ◇ Would you like
some more?–No thank you. Vous en
voulez encore?–Non merci.
2 **pas de** (not any) ◇ There's no hot
water. Il n'y a pas d'eau chaude.
◇ There are no trains on Sundays. Il
n'y a pas de trains le dimanche. ◇ No
problem. Pas de problème.
- **I've got no idea.** Je n'en ai aucune idée.
- **No way!** Pas question!
- **"no smoking"** "défense de fumer"

nobody PRONOUN
1 **personne** ◇ Who's going with you?
–Nobody. Qui t'accompagne?
–Personne.
Add ne *if the sentence contains a verb.*
2 **ne...personne** ◇ There was nobody
in the office. Il n'y avait personne au
bureau.
- **Nobody likes him.** Personne ne l'aime.

noise NOUN
le **bruit** ◇ Please make less noise.
Faites moins de bruit s'il vous plaît.

noisy ADJECTIVE
bruyant

none PRONOUN
1 **aucun** MASC
aucune FEM
◇ How many sisters have you got?–None.
Tu as combien de sœurs?–Aucune.
◇ What sports do you do?–None.

Qu'est-ce que tu fais comme sport?–Je n'en fais aucun.

Add **ne** *if the sentence contains a verb.*

2 **aucun...ne** ◇ *None of my friends wanted to come.* Aucun de mes amis n'a voulu venir.

- **There's none left.** Il n'y en a plus.
- **There are none left.** Il n'y en a plus.

nonsense NOUN

les **bêtises** FEM PL ◇ *She talks a lot of nonsense.* Elle dit beaucoup de bêtises. ◇ *Nonsense!* Ne dis pas de bêtises!

non-smoker NOUN

le **non-fumeur** ◇ *He's a non-smoker.* Il est non-fumeur.

non-smoking ADJECTIVE

non-fumeur ◇ *a non-smoking carriage* une voiture non-fumeurs

non-stop ADJECTIVE, ADVERB

1 **direct** ◇ *a non-stop flight* un vol direct ◇ *We flew non-stop.* Nous avons pris un vol direct.

2 **sans arrêt** ◇ *He talks non-stop.* Il parle sans arrêt.

noodles PL NOUN

les **nouilles** FEM PL

noon NOUN

midi ◇ *at noon* à midi

no one PRONOUN

1 **personne** ◇ *Who's going with you? –No one.* Qui t'accompagne? –Personne.

Add **ne** *if the sentence contains a verb.*

2 **ne...personne** ◇ *There was no one in the office.* Il n'y avait personne au bureau.

- **No one likes him.** Personne ne l'aime.

nor CONJUNCTION

- **neither...nor** ni...ni ◇ *neither the cinema nor the swimming pool* ni le cinéma, ni la piscine
- **Nor do I.** Moi non plus. ◇ *I didn't like the film.–Nor did I.* Je n'ai pas aimé le film.–Moi non plus.
- **Nor have I.** Moi non plus. ◇ *I haven't seen him.–Nor have I.* Je ne l'ai pas vu. –Moi non plus.

normal ADJECTIVE

1 (*usual*)

habituel MASC

habituelle FEM

◇ *at the normal time* à l'heure habituelle

2 (*standard*)

normal

(**normaux** MASC PL)

◇ *a normal car* une voiture normale

normally ADVERB

1 **généralement** (*usually*) ◇ *I normally*

arrive at nine o'clock. J'arrive généralement à neuf heures.

2 **normalement** (*as normal*) ◇ *In spite of the strike, the airports are working normally.* Malgré la grève, les aéroports fonctionnent normalement.

Normandy NOUN

la **Normandie**

- **in Normandy** en Normandie
- **to Normandy** en Normandie

north ADJECTIVE, ADVERB

see also **north** NOUN

1 **nord** MASC, FEM, PL ◇ *the north coast* la côte nord

- **a north wind** un vent du nord

2 **vers le nord** ◇ *We were travelling north.* Nous allions vers le nord.

- **north of** au nord de ◇ *It's north of London.* C'est au nord de Londres.

north NOUN

see also **north** ADJECTIVE

le **nord** ◇ *in the north* dans le nord

North America NOUN

l' **Amérique du Nord** FEM

northeast NOUN

le **nord-est** ◇ *in the northeast* au nord-est

northern ADJECTIVE

- **the northern part of the island** la partie nord de l'île
- **Northern Europe** l'Europe du Nord

Northern Ireland NOUN

l' **Irlande du Nord** FEM

- **in Northern Ireland** en Irlande du Nord
- **to Northern Ireland** en Irlande du Nord
- **I'm from Northern Ireland.** Je viens d'Irlande du Nord.

North Pole NOUN

le **pôle Nord**

North Sea NOUN

la **mer du Nord**

northwest NOUN

le **nord-ouest** ◇ *in the northwest* au nord-ouest

Norway NOUN

la **Norvège**

- **in Norway** en Norvège

Norwegian ADJECTIVE

see also **Norwegian** NOUN

norvégien MASC

norvégienne FEM

Norwegian NOUN

see also **Norwegian** ADJECTIVE

1 (*person*)

le **Norvégien**

la **Norvégienne**

2 (*language*)

le **norvégien**

nose NOUN

le **nez**
(les **nez** PL)
nosebleed NOUN
- **to have a nosebleed** saigner du nez
  ○ *I often get nosebleeds.* Je saigne
  souvent du nez.
nosey ADJECTIVE
- **to be nosey** se mêler de tout ○ *She's
  very nosey.* Elle se mêle de tout.
not ADVERB
  1 pas ○ *Are you coming or not?*
  Est-ce que tu viens ou pas?
- **not really** pas vraiment
- **not at all** pas du tout
- **not yet** pas encore ○ *Have you
  finished?–Not yet.* As-tu fini?–Pas encore.
  Add **ne** *before a verb.*
  2 ne...pas ○ *I'm not sure.* Je ne suis
  pas sûr. ○ *It's not raining.* Il ne pleut
  pas. ○ *You shouldn't do that.* Tu ne
  devrais pas faire ça. ○ *They haven't
  arrived yet.* Ils ne sont pas encore
  arrivés.
  3 non ○ *I hope not.* J'espère que
  non. ○ *Can you lend me £10?–I'm afraid
  not.* Est-ce que tu peux me prêter dix
  livres?–Non, désolé.
note NOUN
  1 la note ○ *to take notes* prendre des
  notes
  2 le mot (*letter*) ○ *I'll write her a note.*
  Je vais lui écrire un mot.
  3 le billet (*banknote*) ○ *a £5 note* un
  billet de cinq livres
to **note down** VERB
  noter
notebook NOUN
  le **carnet**
notepad NOUN
  le **bloc-notes**
notepaper NOUN
  le **papier à lettres**
nothing NOUN
  1 rien ○ *What's wrong?–Nothing.*
  Qu'est-ce qui ne va pas?–Rien.
  ○ *nothing special* rien de particulier
  Add **ne** *if the sentence contains a verb.*
  2 ne...rien ○ *He does nothing.* Il ne
  fait rien. ○ *He ate nothing for breakfast.*
  Il n'a rien mangé au petit-déjeuner.
notice NOUN
  see also notice VERB
  (*sign*)
  le **panneau**
  (les **panneaux** PL)
- **to put up a notice** mettre un panneau
- **a warning notice** un avertissement
- **Don't take any notice of him!** Ne fais
  pas attention à lui!

to **notice** VERB
  see also notice NOUN
  remarquer
notice board NOUN
  le **panneau d'affichage**
  (les **panneaux d'affichage** PL)
nought NOUN
  le **zéro**
noun NOUN
  le **nom**
novel NOUN
  le **roman**
novelist NOUN
  le **romancier**
  la **romancière**
November NOUN
  novembre MASC
- **in November** en novembre
now ADVERB, CONJUNCTION
  maintenant ○ *What are you doing
  now?* Qu'est-ce que tu fais maintenant?
- **just now** en ce moment ○ *I'm rather
  busy just now.* Je suis très occupé en ce
  moment.
- **I did it just now.** Je viens de le faire.
- **He should be there by now.** Il doit être
  arrivé à l'heure qu'il est.
- **It should be ready by now.** Ça devrait
  être déjà prêt.
- **now and then** de temps en temps
nowhere ADVERB
  nulle part ○ *nowhere else* nulle part
  ailleurs
nuclear ADJECTIVE
  nucléaire ○ *nuclear power* l'énergie
  nucléaire ○ *a nuclear power station*
  une centrale nucléaire
nude ADJECTIVE
  see also nude NOUN
  nu
- **to sunbathe nude** faire du bronzage
  intégral
nude NOUN
  see also nude ADJECTIVE
- **in the nude** nu
nudist NOUN
  le/la **nudiste**
nuisance NOUN
- **It's a nuisance.** C'est très embêtant.
- **Sorry to be a nuisance.** Désolé de vous
  déranger.
number NOUN
  1 le nombre (*total amount*) ○ *a large
  number of people* un grand nombre de
  gens
  2 le numéro (*of house, telephone, bank
  account*) ○ *They live at number 5.* Ils
  habitent au numéro cinq. ○ *What's
  your phone number?* Quel est votre

numéro de téléphone? ◇ *You've got the wrong number.* Vous vous êtes trompé de numéro.

3 le **chiffre** (*figure, digit*) ◇ *I can't read the second number.* Je n'arrive pas à lire le deuxième chiffre.

number plate NOUN
la **plaque d'immatriculation**

nun NOUN
la **religieuse** ◇ *She's a nun.* Elle est religieuse.

nurse NOUN
l' **infirmier** MASC
l' **infirmière** FEM
◇ *She's a nurse.* Elle est infirmière.

nursery NOUN
1 la **crèche** (*for children*)
2 la **pépinière** (*for plants*)

nursery school NOUN
l' **école maternelle** FEM
The école maternelle *is a state school for 2-6 year-olds.*

nursery slope NOUN
la **piste pour débutants**

nut NOUN
1 (*peanut*)
la **cacahuète**
2 (*hazelnut*)
la **noisette**
3 (*walnut*)
la **noix**
(les **noix** PL)
4 (*made of metal*)
l' **écrou** MASC

nutmeg NOUN
la **noix de muscade**

nutritious ADJECTIVE
nourrissant

nutter NOUN
- **He's a nutter.** Il est complètement cinglé. (*informal*)

nylon NOUN
le **nylon**

O

oak NOUN
le **chêne** ◇ *an oak table* une table en chêne

oar NOUN
l' **aviron** MASC

oats NOUN
l' **avoine** FEM

obedient ADJECTIVE
obéissant

to **obey** VERB
- **to obey the rules** respecter le règlement

object NOUN
l' **objet** MASC ◇ *a familiar object* un objet familier

objection NOUN
l' **objection** FEM

objective NOUN
l' **objectif** MASC

oblong ADJECTIVE
rectangulaire

oboe NOUN
le **hautbois** ◇ *I play the oboe.* Je joue du hautbois.

obscene ADJECTIVE
obscène

observant ADJECTIVE
observateur MASC
observatrice FEM

to **observe** VERB
observer

obsolete ADJECTIVE
dépassé

obstacle NOUN
l' **obstacle** MASC

obstinate ADJECTIVE
obstiné

to **obstruct** VERB
bloquer ◇ *A lorry was obstructing the traffic.* Un camion bloquait la circulation.

to **obtain** VERB
obtenir

obvious ADJECTIVE
évident

obviously ADVERB
1 **évidemment** (*of course*) ◇ *Do you want to pass the exam?–Obviously!* Tu veux être reçu à l'examen? –Évidemment!
- **Obviously not!** Bien sûr que non!
2 **manifestement** (*visibly*) ◇ *She was obviously exhausted.* Elle était manifestement épuisée.

occasion NOUN
l' **occasion** FEM ◇ *a special occasion* une occasion spéciale
- **on several occasions** à plusieurs reprises

occasionally ADVERB
de temps en temps

occupation NOUN
la **profession**

to **occupy** VERB
occuper ◇ *That seat is occupied.* Cette place est occupée.

to **occur** VERB
avoir lieu (*happen*) ◇ *The accident occurred yesterday.* L'accident a eu lieu hier.
- **It suddenly occurred to me that...** Il m'est soudain venu à l'esprit que...

ocean NOUN
l' **océan** MASC

o'clock ADVERB
- **at four o'clock** à quatre heures
- **It's five o'clock.** Il est cinq heures.

October NOUN
octobre MASC
- **in October** en octobre

octopus NOUN
la **pieuvre**

odd ADJECTIVE
1 **bizarre** ◇ *That's odd!* C'est bizarre!
2 **impair** ◇ *an odd number* un chiffre impair

of PREPOSITION
1 **de** ◇ *some photos of my holiday* des photos de mes vacances ◇ *a boy of ten* un garçon de dix ans

de changes to **d'** *before a vowel and most words beginning with "h".*

d' ◇ *a kilo of oranges* un kilo d'oranges

de + le changes to **du**, *and* **de** + **les** *changes to* **des**.

du ◇ *the end of the film* la fin du film
des ◇ *the end of the holidays* la fin des vacances
2 **en** (*with quantity, amount*) ◇ *He's got four sisters. I've met two of them.* Il a quatre sœurs. J'en ai rencontré deux. ◇ *Can I have half of that?* Je peux en avoir la moitié?
- **three of us** trois d'entre nous
- **a friend of mine** un de mes amis
- **the 14th of September** le quatorze septembre
- **That's very kind of you.** C'est très gentil de votre part.
- **It's made of wood.** C'est en bois.

off ADVERB, PREPOSITION, ADJECTIVE

For other expressions with off, *see the verbs* get, take, turn *etc.*

1 **éteint** (*heater, light, TV*) ◇ *All the lights are off.* Toutes les lumières sont éteintes.

2 **fermé** (*tap, gas*) ◇ *Are you sure the tap is off?* Tu es sûr que le robinet est fermé?

3 **annulé** (*cancelled*) ◇ *The match is off.* Le match est annulé.

- **to be off sick** être malade

- **a day off** un jour de congé ◇ *to take a day off work* prendre un jour de congé

- **She's off school today.** Elle n'est pas à l'école aujourd'hui.

- **I must be off now.** Je dois m'en aller maintenant.

- **I'm off.** Je m'en vais.

offence NOUN

le **délit** (*crime*)

offensive ADJECTIVE

choquant

offer NOUN

see also offer VERB

la **proposition** ◇ *a good offer* une proposition intéressante

- **"on special offer"** "en promotion"

to **offer** VERB

see also offer NOUN

proposer ◇ *He offered to help me.* Il m'a proposé de m'aider. ◇ *I offered to go with them.* Je leur ai proposé de les accompagner.

office NOUN

le **bureau**

(les **bureaux** PL)

◇ *She works in an office.* Elle travaille dans un bureau.

officer NOUN

l' **officier** MASC

official ADJECTIVE

officiel MASC

officielle FEM

off-licence NOUN

le **marchand de vins et spiritueux**

offside ADJECTIVE

hors jeu (*in football*)

often ADVERB

souvent ◇ *It often rains.* Il pleut souvent. ◇ *How often do you go to the gym?* Tu vas souvent à la gym? ◇ *I'd like to go skiing more often.* J'aimerais aller skier plus souvent.

oil NOUN

see also oil VERB

1 l' **huile** MASC (*for lubrication, cooking*)

- **an oil painting** une peinture à l'huile

2 le **pétrole** (*crude oil*) ◇ *North Sea oil*

le pétrole de la mer du Nord

to **oil** VERB

see also oil NOUN

graisser

oil rig NOUN

la **plateforme pétrolière** ◇ *He works on an oil rig.* Il travaille sur une plateforme pétrolière.

oil slick NOUN

la **marée noire**

oil well NOUN

le **puits de pétrole**

(les **puits de pétrole** PL)

ointment NOUN

la **pommade** MASC

okay EXCLAMATION, ADJECTIVE

d'accord (*agreed*) ◇ *Could you call back later?–Okay!* Tu peux rappeler plus tard?–D'accord! ◇ *I'll meet you at six o'clock, okay?* Je te retrouve à six heures, d'accord? ◇ *Is that okay?* C'est d'accord?

- **I'll do it tomorrow, if that's okay with you.** Je le ferai demain, si tu es d'accord.

- **Are you okay?** Ça va?

- **How was your holiday?–It was okay.** C'était comment tes vacances?–Pas mal.

- **What's your teacher like?–He's okay.** Il est comment ton prof?–Il est sympa. (*informal*)

old ADJECTIVE

1 **vieux** MASC

vieille FEM

◇ *an old dog* un vieux chien ◇ *an old house* une vieille maison

vieux *changes to* **vieil** *before a vowel and most words beginning with "h".*

vieil ◇ *an old man* un vieil homme

When talking about people it is more polite to use âgé *instead of* **vieux**.

âgé ◇ *old people* les personnes âgées

2 (*former*)

ancien MASC

ancienne FEM

◇ *my old English teacher* mon ancien professeur d'anglais

- **How old are you?** Quel âge as-tu?

- **He's ten years old.** Il a dix ans.

- **my older brother** mon frère aîné

◇ *my older sister* ma sœur aînée

- **She's two years older than me.** Elle a deux ans de plus que moi.

- **I'm the oldest in the family.** Je suis l'aîné de la famille.

old age pensioner NOUN

le **retraité**

la **retraitée**

◇ *She's an old age pensioner.* Elle est

retraitée.
old-fashioned ADJECTIVE
  1 **démodé** ◇ *She wears old-fashioned clothes.* Elle porte des vêtements démodés.
  2 **vieux jeu** MASC, FEM, PL (*person*) ◇ *My parents are rather old-fashioned.* Mes parents sont plutôt vieux jeu.
olive NOUN
  l' **olive** FEM
olive oil NOUN
  l' **huile d'olive** FEM
Olympic ADJECTIVE
  olympique
◆ **the Olympics** les Jeux olympiques MASC
omelette NOUN
  l' **omelette** FEM
on PREPOSITION, ADVERB
see also **on** ADJECTIVE

There are several ways of translating on. *Scan the examples to find one that is similar to what you want to say. For other expressions with* on, *see the verbs* go, put, turn *etc.*

  1 **sur** ◇ *on the table* sur la table ◇ *on an island* sur une île
  2 **à** ◇ *on the left* à gauche ◇ *on the 2nd floor* au deuxième étage ◇ *I go to school on my bike.* Je vais à l'école à vélo.
◆ **on TV** à la télé ◇ *What's on TV?* Qu'est-ce qu'il y a à la télé?
◆ **on the radio** à la radio ◇ *I heard it on the radio.* Je l'ai entendu à la radio.
◆ **on the bus (1)** (*by bus*) en bus ◇ *I go into town on the bus.* Je vais en ville en bus.
◆ **on the bus (2)** (*inside*) dans le bus ◇ *There were no empty seats on the bus.* Il n'y avait pas de places libres dans le bus.
◆ **on holiday** en vacances ◇ *They're on holiday.* Ils sont en vacances.
◆ **on strike** en grève
With days and dates on *is not translated.*
◇ *on Friday* vendredi ◇ *on Fridays* le vendredi ◇ *on Christmas Day* le jour de Noël ◇ *on June 20th* le vingt juin ◇ *on my birthday* le jour de mon anniversaire
on ADJECTIVE
see also **on** PREPOSITION
  1 **allumé** (*heater, light, TV*) ◇ *I think I left the light on.* Je crois que j'ai laissé la lumière allumée.
  2 **ouvert** (*tap, gas*) ◇ *Leave the tap on.* Laisse le robinet ouvert.
  3 **en marche** (*machine*) ◇ *Is the dishwasher on?* Est-ce que le lave-vaisselle est en marche?

◆ **What's on at the cinema?** Qu'est-ce qui passe au cinéma?
once ADVERB
  une fois ◇ *once a week* une fois par semaine ◇ *once more* encore une fois ◇ *I've been to France once before.* J'ai déjà été une fois en France.
◆ **Once upon a time...** Il était une fois...
◆ **at once** tout de suite
◆ **once in a while** de temps en temps
one NUMBER, PRONOUN
Use un *for masculine nouns and* une *for feminine nouns.*
  1 **un** ◇ *one day* un jour ◇ *Do you need a stamp?–No thanks, I've got one.* Est-ce que tu as besoin d'un timbre? –Non merci, j'en ai un.
  une ◇ *one minute* une minute ◇ *I've got one brother and one sister.* J'ai un frère et une sœur.
  2 **on** (*impersonal*) ◇ *One never knows.* On ne sait jamais.
◆ **this one (1)** celui-ci (*masculine*) ◇ *Which foot is hurting?–This one.* Quel pied te fait mal?–Celui-ci.
◆ **this one (2)** celle-ci (*feminine*) ◇ *Which is the best photo?–This one.* Quelle est la meilleure photo?–Celle-ci.
◆ **that one (1)** celui-là (*masculine*) ◇ *Which bag is yours?–That one.* Lequel est ton sac?–Celui-là.
◆ **that one (2)** celle-là (*feminine*) ◇ *Which seat do you want?–That one.* Quelle place voulez-vous?–Celle-là.
oneself PRONOUN
  1 **se** ◇ *to hurt oneself* se faire mal
  2 **soi-même** ◇ *It's quicker to do it oneself.* C'est plus rapide de le faire soi-même.
one-way ADJECTIVE
◆ **a one-way street** une impasse
onion NOUN
  l' **oignon** MASC ◇ *onion soup* la soupe à l'oignon
only ADVERB, ADJECTIVE, CONJUNCTION
  1 **seul** ◇ *Monday is the only day I'm free.* Le lundi est le seul jour où je suis libre. ◇ *French is the only subject I like.* Le français est la seule matière que j'aime.
  2 **seulement** ◇ *How much was it? –Only 10 francs.* Combien c'était? –Seulement dix francs.
  3 **ne...que** ◇ *We only want to stay for one night.* Nous ne voulons rester qu'une nuit. ◇ *These cassettes are only 30 francs.* Ces cassettes ne coûtent que trente francs.
  4 **mais** ◇ *I'd like the same sweater,*

only in black. Je voudrais le même pull, mais en noir.

- **an only child** un enfant unique

onwards ADVERB

à partir de ◇ *from July onwards* à partir de juillet

open ADJECTIVE

see also **open** VERB

ouvert ◇ *The baker's is open on Sunday morning.* La boulangerie est ouverte le dimanche matin.

- **in the open air** en plein air

to **open** VERB

see also **open** ADJECTIVE

[1] **ouvrir** ◇ *Can I open the window?* Est-ce que je peux ouvrir la fenêtre? ◇ *What time do the shops open?* Les magasins ouvrent à quelle heure?

[2] **s'ouvrir** ◇ *The door opens automatically.* La porte s'ouvre automatiquement. ◇ *The door opened and in came the teacher.* La porte s'est ouverte et le professeur est entré.

opening hours PL NOUN

les **heures d'ouverture** FEM

opera NOUN

l' **opéra** MASC

operation NOUN

l' **opération** FEM ◇ *a major operation* une grave opération

- **to have an operation** se faire opérer ◇ *I have never had an operation.* Je ne me suis jamais fait opérer.

operator NOUN

le/la **standardiste** (*on telephone*)

opinion NOUN

l' **avis** MASC ◇ *in my opinion* à mon avis ◇ *He asked me my opinion.* Il m'a demandé mon avis.

- **What's your opinion?** Qu'est-ce vous en pensez?

opinion poll NOUN

le **sondage**

opponent NOUN

l' **adversaire** MASC/FEM

opportunity NOUN

l' **occasion** FEM

- **to have the opportunity to do something** avoir l'occasion de faire quelque chose ◇ *I've never had the opportunity to go to France.* Je n'ai jamais eu l'occasion d'aller en France.

opposing ADJECTIVE

opposé (*team*)

opposite ADJECTIVE, ADVERB, PREPOSITION

[1] **opposé** ◇ *It's in the opposite direction.* C'est dans la direction opposée.

[2] **en face** ◇ *They live opposite.* Ils habitent en face.

[3] **en face de** ◇ *the girl sitting opposite me* la fille assise en face de moi

- **the opposite sex** l'autre sexe

opposition NOUN

l' **opposition** FEM

optician NOUN

l' **opticien** MASC

l' **opticienne** FEM ◇ *She's an optician.* Elle est opticienne.

optimist NOUN

l' **optimiste** MASC/FEM

optimistic ADJECTIVE

optimiste

option NOUN

[1] le **choix** (*choice*) ◇ *I've got no option.* Je n'ai pas le choix.

[2] la **matière à option** (*optional subject*) ◇ *I'm doing geology as my option.* La géologie est ma matière à option.

optional ADJECTIVE

facultatif MASC

facultative FEM

or CONJUNCTION

[1] **ou** ◇ *Would you like tea or coffee?* Est-ce que tu veux du thé ou du café?

Use **ni...ni** in negative sentences.

◇ *I don't eat meat or fish.* Je ne mange ni viande, ni poisson.

[2] **sinon** (*otherwise*) ◇ *Hurry up or you'll miss the bus.* Dépêche-toi, sinon tu vas rater le bus.

- **Give me the money, or else!** Donne-moi l'argent, sinon tu vas le regretter!

oral ADJECTIVE

see also **oral** NOUN

oral

(**oraux** MASC PL)

- **an oral exam** un oral

oral NOUN

see also **oral** ADJECTIVE

l' **oral** MASC

(les **oraux** PL)

◇ *I've got my French oral soon.* Je vais bientôt passer mon oral de français.

orange NOUN

see also **orange** ADJECTIVE

l' **orange** FEM

- **an orange juice** un jus d'orange

orange ADJECTIVE

see also **orange** NOUN

orange MASC, FEM, PL

orchard NOUN

le **verger**

orchestra NOUN

l' **orchestre** MASC ◇ *I play in the school orchestra.* Je joue dans l'orchestre de l'école.

order NOUN

see also order VERB

[1] l' **ordre** MASC *(sequence)* ◇ *in alphabetical order* dans l'ordre alphabétique

[2] la **commande** *(instruction)* ◇ *The waiter took our order.* Le garçon a pris notre commande.

- **in order to** pour ◇ *He does it in order to earn money.* Il le fait pour gagner de l'argent.

- **"out of order"** "en panne"

to **order** VERB

see also order NOUN

commander ◇ *We ordered steak and chips.* Nous avons commandé un steak frites. ◇ *Are you ready to order?* Vous êtes prêt à commander?

ordinary ADJECTIVE

[1] **ordinaire** ◇ *an ordinary day* une journée ordinaire

[2] **comme les autres** *(people)* ◇ *an ordinary family* une famille comme les autres ◇ *He's just an ordinary guy.* C'est un type comme les autres.

organ NOUN

l' **orgue** MASC *(instrument)* ◇ *I play the organ.* Je joue de l'orgue.

organic ADJECTIVE

biologique *(vegetables, fruit)*

organization NOUN

l' **organisation** FEM

to **organize** VERB

organiser

original ADJECTIVE

original

(**originaux** MASC PL)

◇ *It's a very original idea.* C'est une idée très originale.

- **Our original plan was to go camping.** A l'origine nous avions l'intention de faire du camping.

originally ADVERB

à l'origine

Orkneys PL NOUN

les **Orcades** FEM PL

- **in the Orkneys** dans les Orcades

ornament NOUN

le **bibelot**

orphan NOUN

l' **orphelin** MASC

l' **orpheline** FEM

ostrich NOUN

l' **autruche** FEM

other ADJECTIVE, PRONOUN

autre ◇ *Have you got these jeans in other colours?* Est-ce que vous avez ce jean dans d'autres couleurs? ◇ *on the other side of the street* de l'autre côté de la rue ◇ *the other day* l'autre jour

- **the other one** l'autre ◇ *This one?–No, the other one.* Celui-ci?–Non, l'autre.

- **the others** les autres ◇ *The others are going but I'm not.* Les autres y vont mais pas moi.

otherwise ADVERB, CONJUNCTION

[1] **sinon** *(if not)* ◇ *Note down the number, otherwise you'll forget it.* Note le numéro, sinon tu vas l'oublier. ◇ *Put some sunscreen on, you'll get burned otherwise.* Mets une crème solaire, sinon tu vas attraper des coups de soleil.

[2] **à part ça** *(in other ways)* ◇ *I'm tired, but otherwise I'm fine.* Je suis fatigué, mais à part ça, ça va.

ought VERB

To translate ought to *use the conditional tense of* **devoir**.

◇ *I ought to phone my parents.* Je devrais appeler mes parents. ◇ *You ought not to do that.* Tu ne devrais pas faire ça. ◇ *He ought to win.* Il devrait gagner.

our ADJECTIVE

notre ◇ *Our house is quite big.* Notre maison est plutôt grande.

nos PL ◇ *Our neighbours are very nice.* Nos voisins sont très gentils.

ours PRONOUN

le nôtre + MASC NOUN ◇ *Your garden is very big, ours is much smaller.* Votre jardin est très grand, le nôtre est beaucoup plus petit.

la nôtre + FEM NOUN ◇ *Your school is very different from ours.* Votre école est très différente de la nôtre.

les nôtres + PL NOUN ◇ *Our teachers are strict.–Ours are too.* Nos professeurs sont sévères.–Les nôtres aussi.

- **Is this ours?** C'est à nous? ◇ *This car is ours.* Cette voiture est à nous. ◇ *Whose is this?–It's ours.* C'est à qui?–À nous.

ourselves PRONOUN

[1] **nous** ◇ *We really enjoyed ourselves.* Nous nous sommes vraiment bien amusés.

[2] **nous-mêmes** ◇ *We built our garage ourselves.* Nous avons construit notre garage nous-mêmes.

out ADVERB

There are several ways of translating out. *Scan the examples to find one that is similar to what you want to say. For other expressions with* out, *see the verbs* go, put, turn *etc.*

[1] **dehors** *(outside)* ◇ *It's cold out.* Il fait froid dehors.

② **éteint** (*light, fire*) ◇ *All the lights are out.* Toutes les lumières sont éteintes.
- **She's out.** Elle est sortie.
- **She's out shopping.** Elle est sortie faire des courses.
- **She's out for the afternoon.** Elle ne sera pas là de tout l'après-midi.
- **out there** dehors ◇ *It's cold out there.* Il fait froid dehors.
- **to go out** sortir ◇ *I'm going out tonight.* Je sors ce soir.
- **to go out with somebody** sortir avec quelqu'un ◇ *I've been going out with him for two months.* Je sors avec lui depuis deux mois.
- **out of (1)** dans ◇ *to drink out of a glass* boire dans un verre
- **out of (2)** sur ◇ *in 9 cases out of 10* dans neuf cas sur dix
- **out of (3)** en dehors de ◇ *He lives out of town.* Il habite en dehors de la ville.
- **3 km out of town** à trois kilomètres de la ville
- **out of curiosity** par curiosité
- **out of work** sans emploi
- **That is out of the question.** C'est hors de question.
- **You're out!** (*in game*) Tu es éliminé!
- **"way out"** "sortie"

outdoor ADJECTIVE
en plein air ◇ *an outdoor swimming pool* une piscine en plein air
- **outdoor activities** les activités de plein air

outdoors ADVERB
au grand air

outing NOUN
la **sortie** ◇ *to go on an outing* faire une sortie

outline NOUN
① les **grandes lignes** FEM (*summary*) ◇ *This is an outline of the plan.* Voici les grandes lignes du projet.
② les **contours** MASC PL (*shape*) ◇ *We could see the outline of the mountain in the mist.* Nous distinguions les contours de la montagne dans la brume.

outrageous ADJECTIVE
① (*behaviour*)
scandaleux MASC
scandaleuse FEM
② (*price*)
exorbitant

outset NOUN
le **début** ◇ *at the outset* dès le début

outside NOUN
see also outside ADJECTIVE
l' **extérieur** MASC

outside ADJECTIVE, ADVERB, PREPOSITION

see also outside NOUN
① **extérieur** ◇ *the outside walls* les murs extérieurs
② **dehors** ◇ *It's very cold outside.* Il fait très froid dehors.
③ **en dehors de** ◇ *outside the school* en dehors de l'école ◇ *outside school hours* en dehors des heures de cours

outsize ADJECTIVE
énorme

outskirts PL NOUN
la **banlieue** ◇ *on the outskirts of the town* dans les banlieues de la ville

outstanding ADJECTIVE
remarquable

oval ADJECTIVE
ovale

oven NOUN
le **four**

over PREPOSITION, ADVERB, ADJECTIVE
> When there is movement over something, use **par-dessus**; when something is located above something, use **au-dessus de**.

① **par-dessus** ◇ *The ball went over the wall.* Le ballon est passé par-dessus le mur.
② **au-dessus de** ◇ *There's a mirror over the washbasin.* Il y a une glace au-dessus du lavabo.
③ **plus de** (*more than*) ◇ *It's over twenty kilos.* Ça pèse plus de vingt kilos. ◇ *The temperature was over thirty degrees.* Il faisait une température de plus de trente degrés.
④ **pendant** (*during*) ◇ *over the holidays* pendant les vacances ◇ *over Christmas* pendant les fêtes de Noël
⑤ **terminé** (*finished*) ◇ *I'll be happy when the exams are over.* Je serai content quand les examens seront terminés.
- **over here** ici
- **over there** là-bas
- **all over Scotland** dans toute l'Écosse
- **The baker's is over the road.** La boulangerie est de l'autre côté de la rue.
- **I spilled coffee over my shirt.** J'ai renversé du café sur ma chemise.

overall ADVERB
dans l'ensemble (*generally*) ◇ *My results were quite good overall.* Mes résultats étaient assez bons dans l'ensemble.

overalls PL NOUN
les **bleus de travail** MASC PL

to **overcharge** VERB
- **He overcharged me.** Il m'a fait payer trop cher.
- **They overcharged us for the meal.** Ils

nous ont fait payer de trop pour le repas.

overdone ADJECTIVE
trop cuit (*food*)

overdose NOUN
l' **overdose** FEM (*of drugs*) ◇ *to take an overdose* prendre une overdose

to **overestimate** VERB
surestimer

overhead projector NOUN
le **rétroprojecteur**

to **overlook** VERB
① **donner sur** (*have view of*) ◇ *The hotel overlooked the beach.* L'hôtel donnait sur la plage.
② **négliger** (*forget about*) ◇ *He had overlooked one important problem.* Il avait négligé un problème important.

overseas ADVERB
à l'étranger ◇ *I'd like to work overseas.* J'aimerais travailler à l'étranger.

oversight NOUN
l' **oubli** MASC

to **oversleep** VERB
se réveiller en retard ◇ *I overslept this morning.* Je me suis réveillé en retard ce matin.

to **overtake** VERB
dépasser

overtime NOUN
les **heures supplémentaires** FEM PL
◇ *to work overtime* faire des heures supplémentaires

overweight ADJECTIVE
trop gros MASC
trop grosse FEM

to **owe** VERB
devoir
◆ *to owe somebody something* devoir quelque chose à quelqu'un ◇ *I owe you 50 francs.* Je te dois cinquante francs.

owing to PREPOSITION
en raison de ◇ *owing to bad weather* en raison du mauvais temps

owl NOUN
le **hibou**
(les **hiboux** PL)

to **own** VERB
see also **own** ADJECTIVE
posséder

own ADJECTIVE
see also **own** VERB
propre ◇ *I've got my own bathroom.* J'ai ma propre salle de bain.
◆ *I'd like a room of my own.* J'aimerais avoir une chambre à moi.
◆ *on his own* tout seul ◇ *on her own* toute seule ◇ *on our own* tout seuls

owner NOUN
le/la **propriétaire**

oxygen NOUN
l' **oxygène** MASC

oyster NOUN
l' **huître** FEM

ozone layer NOUN
la **couche d'ozone**

P

PA NOUN
la **secrétaire de direction** (*personal assistant*) ◇ *She's a PA.* Elle est secrétaire de direction.
- **the PA system** (*public address*) les haut-parleurs

pace NOUN
l' **allure** FEM (*speed*) ◇ *He was walking at a brisk pace.* Il marchait à vive allure.

Pacific NOUN
le **Pacifique**

to **pack** VERB
see also pack NOUN
faire ses bagages ◇ *I'll help you pack.* Je vais t'aider à faire tes bagages.
- **I've already packed my case.** J'ai déjà fait ma valise.
- **Pack it in!** (*stop it*) Laisse tomber!

pack NOUN
see also pack VERB
1 le **paquet** (*packet*) ◇ *a pack of cigarettes* un paquet de cigarettes
2 le **pack** (*of yoghurts, cans*) ◇ *a six-pack* un pack de six
- **a pack of cards** un jeu de cartes

package NOUN
le **paquet**
- **a package holiday** un voyage organisé

packed ADJECTIVE
bondé ◇ *The cinema was packed.* Le cinéma était bondé.

packed lunch NOUN
le **repas froid** ◇ *I take a packed lunch to school.* J'apporte un repas froid à l'école.

packet NOUN
le **paquet** ◇ *a packet of cigarettes* un paquet de cigarettes

pad NOUN
le **bloc-notes** (*notepad*)

to **paddle** VERB
see also paddle NOUN
1 **pagayer** (*canoe*)
2 **faire trempette** (*in water*)

paddle NOUN
see also paddle VERB
la **pagaie** (*for canoe*)
- **to go for a paddle** faire trempette

padlock NOUN
le **cadenas**

page NOUN
la **page** (*of book*)

paid VERB *see* pay

paid ADJECTIVE
1 **rémunéré** (*work*)
2 **payé** ◇ *3 weeks' paid holiday* trois semaines de congés payés

pail NOUN
le **seau**
(les **seaux** PL)

pain NOUN
la **douleur** ◇ *A terrible pain.* une douleur insupportable
- **I've got a pain in my stomach.** J'ai mal à l'estomac.
- **to be in pain** souffrir ◇ *She's in a lot of pain.* Elle souffre beaucoup.
- **He's a real pain.** Il est vraiment pénible.

painful ADJECTIVE
douloureux MASC
douloureuse FEM
◇ *to suffer from painful periods* souffrir de règles douloureuses
- **Is it painful?** Ça te fait mal?

painkiller NOUN
l' **analgésique** MASC

paint NOUN
see also paint VERB
la **peinture**

to **paint** VERB
see also paint NOUN
peindre ◇ *to paint something green* peindre quelque chose en vert

paintbrush NOUN
le **pinceau**
(les **pinceaux** PL)

painter NOUN
le **peintre**

painting NOUN
1 la **peinture** ◇ *My hobby is painting.* Je fais de la peinture.
2 (*picture*)
le **tableau**
(les **tableaux** PL)
◇ *a painting by Picasso* un tableau de Picasso

pair NOUN
la **paire** ◇ *a pair of shoes* une paire de chaussures ◇ *a pair of scissors* une paire de ciseaux
- **a pair of trousers** un pantalon
- **a pair of jeans** un jean
- **a pair of pants (1)** (*briefs*) un slip
- **a pair of pants (2)** (*boxer shorts*) un caleçon
- **in pairs** deux par deux ◇ *We work in pairs.* Nous travaillons deux par deux.

Pakistan NOUN
le **Pakistan**
- **in Pakistan** au Pakistan
- **to Pakistan** au Pakistan

- **He's from Pakistan.** Il est pakistanais.

Pakistani NOUN

see also Pakistani ADJECTIVE

le **Pakistanais**

la **Pakistanaise**

Pakistani ADJECTIVE

see also Pakistani NOUN

pakistanais MASC

pakistanaise FEM

pal NOUN

le **copain**

la **copine**

palace NOUN

le **palais**

pale ADJECTIVE

pâle ◇ *a pale blue shirt* une chemise bleu pâle

Palestine NOUN

la **Palestine**

- **in Palestine** en Palestine

Palestinian ADJECTIVE

see also Palestinian NOUN

palestinien MASC

palestinienne FEM

Palestinian NOUN

see also Palestinian ADJECTIVE

le **Palestinien**

la **Palestinienne**

palm NOUN

la **paume** (*of hand*)

- **a palm tree** un palmier

pamphlet NOUN

la **brochure**

pan NOUN

1 la **casserole** (*saucepan*)

2 la **poêle** (*frying pan*)

pancake NOUN

la **crêpe**

panic NOUN

see also panic VERB

la **panique**

to **panic** VERB

see also panic NOUN

s'affoler ◇ *Don't panic!* Pas de panique!

panther NOUN

la **panthère**

panties PL NOUN

le **slip** SING

pantomime NOUN

le **spectacle de Noël pour enfants**

pants PL NOUN

1 le **slip** SING (*briefs*) ◇ *a pair of pants* un slip

2 le **caleçon** SING (*boxer shorts*) ◇ *a pair of pants* un caleçon

paper NOUN

1 le **papier** ◇ *a piece of paper* un morceau de papier ◇ *a paper towel*

une serviette en papier

2 (*newspaper*)

le **journal**

(les **journaux** PL)

◇ *I saw an advert in the paper.* J'ai vu une annonce dans le journal.

- **an exam paper** une épreuve écrite

paperback NOUN

le **livre de poche**

paper clip NOUN

le **trombone**

parachute NOUN

le **parachute**

parade NOUN

le **défilé**

paradise NOUN

le **paradis**

paraffin NOUN

le **pétrole** ◇ *a paraffin lamp* une lampe à pétrole

paragraph NOUN

le **paragraphe**

parallel ADJECTIVE

parallèle

paralysed ADJECTIVE

paralysé

parcel NOUN

le **colis**

pardon NOUN

- **Pardon?** Pardon?

parent NOUN

1 le **père** (*father*)

2 la **mère** (*mother*)

- **my parents** mes parents MASC

Paris NOUN

Paris FEM

- **in Paris** à Paris
- **to Paris** à Paris
- **She's from Paris.** Elle est parisienne.

Parisian ADJECTIVE

see also Parisian NOUN

parisien MASC

parisienne FEM

Parisian NOUN

see also Parisian ADJECTIVE

le **Parisien**

la **Parisienne**

park NOUN

see also park VERB

le **parc**

- **a national park** un parc national
- **a theme park** un parc à thème
- **a car park** un parking

to **park** VERB

see also park NOUN

1 **garer** ◇ *Where can I park my car?* Où est-ce que je peux garer ma voiture?

2 **se garer** ◇ *We couldn't find anywhere to park.* Nous avons eu du

P

mal à nous garer.

parking NOUN
le **stationnement** ◇ *"no parking"* "stationnement interdit"

parking meter NOUN
le **parcmètre**

parking ticket NOUN
le **p.-v.** (*informal*)

parliament NOUN
le **parlement**

parrot NOUN
le **perroquet**

parsley NOUN
le **persil**

part NOUN
[1] la **partie** (*section*) ◇ *The first part of the film was boring.* La première partie du film était ennuyeuse.
[2] la **pièce** (*component*) ◇ *spare parts* les pièces de rechange
[3] le **rôle** (*in play, film*)
- **to take part in something** participer à quelque chose ◇ *A lot of people took part in the demonstration.* Beaucoup de gens ont participé à la manifestation.

particular ADJECTIVE
particulier MASC
particulière FEM
◇ *Are you looking for anything particular?* Est-ce que vous voulez quelque chose de particulier?
- **nothing in particular** rien de particulier

particularly ADVERB
particulièrement

parting NOUN
la **raie** (*in hair*)

partly ADVERB
en partie

partner NOUN
[1] (*in game*)
le/la **partenaire**
[2] (*in business*)
l' **associé** MASC
l' **associée** FEM
[3] (*in dance*)
le **cavalier**
la **cavalière**
[4] (*boyfriend*)
le **compagnon**
la **compagne** (*girlfriend*)

part-time ADJECTIVE, ADVERB
à temps partiel ◇ *a part-time job* un travail à temps partiel ◇ *She works part-time.* Elle travaille à temps partiel.

party NOUN
[1] la **fête** ◇ *a birthday party* une fête d'anniversaire ◇ *a Christmas party* une fête de Noël ◇ *a New Year party* une fête du Nouvel An

[2] la **soirée** (*more formal*) ◇ *I'm going to a party on Saturday.* Je vais à une soirée samedi.
[3] le **parti** (*political*) ◇ *the Conservative Party* le Parti conservateur
[4] le **groupe** (*group*) ◇ *a party of tourists* un groupe de touristes

pass NOUN
see also pass VERB
[1] le **col** (*in mountains*) ◇ *The pass was blocked with snow.* Le col était enneigé.
[2] la **passe** (*in football*)
- **to get a pass** (*in exam*) être reçu ◇ *She got a pass in her piano exam.* Elle a été reçue à son examen de piano. ◇ *I got six passes.* J'ai été reçu dans six matières.
- **a bus pass** une carte de bus

to **pass** VERB
see also pass NOUN
[1] **passer** ◇ *Could you pass me the salt, please?* Est-ce que vous pourriez me passer le sel, s'il vous plaît? ◇ *The time has passed quickly.* Le temps a passé rapidement.
[2] **passer devant** ◇ *I pass his house on my way to school.* Je passe devant chez lui en allant à l'école.
[3] **être reçu** (*exam*) ◇ *Did you pass?* Tu as été reçu?
- **to pass an exam** être reçu à un examen ◇ *I hope I'll pass the exam.* J'espère que je serai reçu à l'examen.

to **pass out** VERB
s'évanouir (*faint*)

passage NOUN
[1] le **passage** (*piece of writing*) ◇ *Read the passage carefully.* Lisez attentivement le passage.
[2] le **couloir** (*corridor*)

passenger NOUN
le **passager**
la **passagère**

passion NOUN
la **passion**

passive ADJECTIVE
passif MASC
passive FEM
- **passive smoking** le tabagisme passif

Passover NOUN
la **Pâque juive** ◇ *at Passover* à la Pâque juive

passport NOUN
le **passeport** ◇ *passport control* le contrôle des passeports

password NOUN
le **mot de passe**

past ADVERB, PREPOSITION
see also past NOUN

après (*beyond*) ◇ *It's on the right, just past the station.* C'est sur la droite, juste après la gare.

- **to go past (1)** passer ◇ *The bus went past without stopping.* Le bus est passé sans s'arrêter.
- **to go past (2)** passer devant ◇ *The bus goes past our house.* Le bus passe devant notre maison.
- **It's half past ten.** Il est dix heures et demie.
- **It's quarter past nine.** Il est neuf heures et quart.
- **It's ten past eight.** Il est huit heures dix.
- **It's past midnight.** Il est minuit passé.

past NOUN

see also past ADVERB

le **passé** ◇ *She lives in the past.* Elle vit dans le passé.
- **in the past** (*previously*) autrefois ◇ *This was common in the past.* C'était courant autrefois.

pasta NOUN

les **pâtes** FFM PL ◇ *Pasta is easy to cook.* Les pâtes sont faciles à préparer.

paste NOUN

la **colle** (*glue*)

pasteurized ADJECTIVE

pasteurisé

pastime NOUN

le **passe-temps**

(les **passe-temps** PL)

◇ *Her favourite pastime is knitting.* Son passe-temps favori est le tricot.

pastry NOUN

la **pâte**
- **pastries** les pâtisseries FEM

patch NOUN

1 la **pièce** ◇ *a patch of material* une pièce

2 la **rustine** (*for flat tyre*)
- **He's got a bald patch.** Il a le crâne dégarni.

patched ADJECTIVE

rapiécé ◇ *a pair of patched jeans* un jean rapiécé

pâté NOUN

le **pâté**

path NOUN

1 le **chemin** (*footpath*)

2 l' **allée** FEM (*in garden, park*)

pathetic ADJECTIVE

lamentable ◇ *Our team was pathetic.* Notre équipe a été lamentable.

patience NOUN

1 la **patience** ◇ *He hasn't got much patience.* Il n'a pas beaucoup de patience.

2 la **réussite** (*card game*) ◇ *to play patience* faire une réussite

patient NOUN

see also patient ADJECTIVE

le **patient**

la **patiente**

patient ADJECTIVE

see also patient NOUN

patient

patio NOUN

le **patio**

patriotic ADJECTIVE

patriote

patrol NOUN

la **patrouille**

patrol car NOUN

la **voiture de police**

pattern NOUN

le **motif** ◇ *a geometric pattern* un motif géométrique
- **a sewing pattern** un patron

pause NOUN

la **pause**

pavement NOUN

le **trottoir**

pavilion NOUN

le **pavillon**

paw NOUN

la **patte**

pay NOUN

see also pay VERB

le **salaire**

to **pay** VERB

see also pay NOUN

1 **payer** ◇ *They pay me more on Sundays.* Je suis payé davantage le dimanche.

2 **régler** ◇ *to pay by cheque* régler par chèque ◇ *to pay by credit card* régler par carte de crédit
- **to pay for something** payer quelque chose ◇ *I paid for my ticket.* J'ai payé mon billet. ◇ *I paid 50 francs for it.* Je l'ai payé cinquante francs.
- **to pay extra for something** payer un supplément pour quelque chose ◇ *You have to pay extra for parking.* Il faut payer un supplément pour le parking.
- **to pay attention** faire attention ◇ *Don't pay any attention to him!* Ne fais pas attention à lui!
- **to pay somebody a visit** rendre visite à quelqu'un ◇ *Paul paid us a visit last night.* Paul nous a rendu visite hier soir.
- **to pay somebody back** rembourser quelqu'un ◇ *I'll pay you back tomorrow.* Je te rembourserai demain.

P

payment NOUN
le **paiement**

payphone NOUN
le **téléphone publique**

PC NOUN (= *personal computer*)
le **PC** ◇ *She typed the report on her PC.* Elle a tapé le rapport sur son PC.

pea NOUN
le **petit pois**

peace NOUN
[1] la **paix** (*after war*)
[2] le **calme** (*quietness*)

peaceful ADJECTIVE
[1] **paisible** (*calm*) ◇ *a peaceful afternoon* un après-midi paisible
[2] **pacifique** (*not violent*) ◇ *a peaceful protest* une manifestation pacifique

peach NOUN
la **pêche**

peacock NOUN
le **paon**

peak NOUN
la **cime** (*of mountain*)
- **the peak rate** le plein tarif ◇ *You pay the peak rate for calls at this time of day.* On paie le plein tarif quand on appelle à cette heure-ci.
- **in peak season** en haute saison

peanut NOUN
la **cacahuète** ◇ *a packet of peanuts* un paquet de cacahuètes

peanut butter NOUN
le **beurre de cacahuètes** ◇ *a peanut-butter sandwich* un sandwich au beurre de cacahuètes

pear NOUN
la **poire**

pearl NOUN
la **perle**

pebble NOUN
le **galet** ◇ *a pebble beach* une plage de galets

peculiar ADJECTIVE
bizarre ◇ *He's a peculiar person.* Il est bizarre. ◇ *It tastes peculiar.* Ça a un goût bizarre.

pedal NOUN
la **pédale**

pedestrian NOUN
le **piéton**

pedestrian crossing NOUN
le **passage pour piétons**

pedestrianized ADJECTIVE
- **a pedestrianized street** une rue piétonne

pedigree ADJECTIVE
de race (*animal*) ◇ *a pedigree dog* un chien de race ◇ *A pedigree labrador.* Un labrador de pure race.

pee NOUN
- **to have a pee** faire pipi

peel NOUN
see also **peel** VERB
l' **écorce** FEM (*of orange*)

to **peel** VERB
see also **peel** NOUN
[1] **éplucher** ◇ *Shall I peel the potatoes?* J'épluche les pommes de terre?
[2] **peler** ◇ *My nose is peeling.* Mon nez pèle.

peg NOUN
[1] (*for coats*)
le **portemanteau**
(les **portemanteaux** PL)
[2] (*clothes peg*)
la **pince à linge**
[3] (*tent peg*)
le **piquet**

Pekinese NOUN
le **pékinois**

pellet NOUN
le **plomb** (*for gun*)

pelvis NOUN
le **bassin**

pen NOUN
le **stylo**

to **penalize** VERB
pénaliser

penalty NOUN
[1] la **peine** (*punishment*)
- **the death penalty** la peine de mort
[2] le **penalty** (*in football*)
[3] la **pénalité** (*in rugby*)
- **a penalty shoot-out** les tirs au but

pence PL NOUN
les **pence** MASC PL

pencil NOUN
le **crayon**
- **in pencil** au crayon

pencil case NOUN
la **trousse**

pencil sharpener NOUN
le **taille-crayon**

pendant NOUN
le **pendentif**

penfriend NOUN
le **correspondant**
la **correspondante**

penguin NOUN
le **pingouin**

penicillin NOUN
la **pénicilline**

penis NOUN
le **pénis**

penknife NOUN
le **canif**

penny NOUN

le **penny**
(les **pence** PL)

pension NOUN
la **retraite**

pensioner NOUN
le **retraité**
la **retraitée**

pentathlon NOUN
le **pentathlon**

people PL NOUN
[1] les **gens** MASC ◇ *The people were nice.* Les gens étaient sympathiques.
◇ *a lot of people* beaucoup de gens
[2] les **personnes** FEM (*individuals*) ◇ *six people* six personnes ◇ *several people* plusieurs personnes
- **How many people are there in your family?** Vous êtes combien dans votre famille?
- **French people** les Français
- **black people** les Noirs
- **People say that...** On dit que...

pepper NOUN
[1] le **poivre** (*spice*) ◇ *Pass the pepper, please.* Passez-moi le poivre, s'il vous plaît.
[2] le **poivron** (*vegetable*) ◇ *a green pepper* un poivron vert

peppermill NOUN
le **moulin à poivre**

peppermint NOUN
la **pastille de menthe** (*sweet*)
- **peppermint chewing gum** le chewing-gum à la menthe

per PREPOSITION
par ◇ *per day* par jour ◇ *per week* par semaine
- **30 miles per hour** trente miles à l'heure

per cent ADVERB
pour cent ◇ *fifty per cent* cinquante pour cent

percolator NOUN
la **cafetière électrique**

percussion NOUN
la **percussion** ◇ *I play percussion.* Je joue des percussions.

perfect ADJECTIVE
parfait ◇ *Chantal speaks perfect English.* Chantal parle un anglais parfait.

perfectly ADVERB
parfaitement

to **perform** VERB
jouer (*act, play*)

performance NOUN
[1] le **spectacle** (*show*) ◇ *The performance lasts two hours.* Le spectacle dure deux heures.

[2] l' **interprétation** FEM (*acting*) ◇ *his performance as Hamlet* son interprétation d'Hamlet
[3] la **performance** (*results*) ◇ *the team's poor performance* la médiocre performance de l'équipe

perfume NOUN
le **parfum**

perhaps ADVERB
peut-être ◇ *a bit boring, perhaps* peut-être un peu ennuyeux ◇ *Perhaps he's ill.* Il est peut-être malade.
- **perhaps not** peut-être pas

period NOUN
[1] la **période** ◇ *for a limited period* pour une période limitée
[2] l' **époque** FEM (*in history*) ◇ *the Victorian period* l'époque victorienne
[3] les **règles** FEM (*menstruation*) ◇ *I'm having my period.* J'ai mes règles.
[4] le **cours** (*lesson time*) ◇ *Each period lasts forty minutes.* Chaque cours dure quarante minutes.

perm NOUN
la **permanente** ◇ *She's got a perm.* Elle a une permanente.
- **to have a perm** se faire faire une permanente

permanent ADJECTIVE
permanent

permission NOUN
la **permission** ◇ *Could I have permission to leave early?* Pourrais-je avoir la permission de partir plus tôt?

permit NOUN
le **permis** ◇ *a fishing permit* un permis de pêche

to **persecute** VERB
persécuter

Persian ADJECTIVE
- **a Persian cat** un chat persan

persistent ADJECTIVE
tenace (*person*)

person NOUN
la **personne** ◇ *She's a very nice person.* C'est une personne très sympathique.
- **in person** en personne

personal ADJECTIVE
personnel MASC
personnelle FEM

personality NOUN
la **personnalité**

personally ADVERB
personnellement ◇ *I don't know him personally.* Je ne le connais pas personnellement. ◇ *Personally I don't agree.* Personnellement, je ne suis pas d'accord.

P

personal stereo NOUN
le **walkman** ®
personnel NOUN
le **personnel**
perspiration NOUN
la **transpiration**
to **persuade** VERB
persuader
- **to persuade somebody to do something** persuader quelqu'un de faire quelque chose ◇ *She persuaded me to go with her.* Elle m'a persuadé de l'accompagner.
pessimist NOUN
le/la **pessimiste** ◇ *I'm a pessimist.* Je suis pessimiste.
pessimistic ADJECTIVE
pessimiste
pest NOUN
le/la **casse-pieds** (*person*) ◇ *He's a real pest!* C'est un vrai casse-pieds!
to **pester** VERB
importuner
pet NOUN
l' **animal familier** MASC ◇ *Have you got a pet?* Est-ce que tu as un animal familier?
- **She's the teacher's pet.** C'est la chouchoute de la maîtresse.
petition NOUN
la **pétition**
petrified ADJECTIVE
pétrifié
petrol NOUN
l' **essence** FEM
- **unleaded petrol** l'essence sans plomb
- **leaded petrol** l'essence au plomb
- **4-star petrol, please.** Du super, s'il vous plaît.
petrol station NOUN
la **station-service**
petrol tank NOUN
le **réservoir d'essence**
phantom NOUN
le **fantôme**
pharmacy NOUN
la **pharmacie**
Pharmacies in France are identified by a special green cross outside the shop.
pheasant NOUN
le **faisan**
philosophy NOUN
la **philosophie**
phobia NOUN
la **phobie**
phone NOUN
see also phone VERB
le **téléphone** ◇ *Where's the phone?* Où est le téléphone? ◇ *Is there a*

phone here? Est-ce qu'il y a un téléphone ici?
- **by phone** par téléphone
- **to be on the phone** être au téléphone ◇ *She's on the phone at the moment.* Elle est au téléphone en ce moment.
- **Can I use the phone, please?** Est-ce que je peux téléphoner, s'il vous plaît?
to **phone** VERB
see also phone NOUN
appeler ◇ *I'll phone the station.* Je vais appeler la gare.
phone bill NOUN
la **facture de téléphone**
phone book NOUN
l' **annuaire** MASC
phone box NOUN
la **cabine téléphonique**
phone call NOUN
l' **appel** MASC ◇ *There's a phone call for you.* Il y a un appel pour vous.
- **to make a phone call** téléphoner ◇ *Can I make a phone call?* Est-ce que peux téléphoner?
phonecard NOUN
la **carte de téléphone**
phone number NOUN
le **numéro de téléphone**
photo NOUN
la **photo**
- **to take a photo** prendre une photo
- **to take a photo of somebody** prendre quelqu'un en photo
photocopier NOUN
la **photocopieuse**
photocopy NOUN
see also photocopy VERB
la **photocopie**
to **photocopy** VERB
see also photocopy NOUN
photocopier
photograph NOUN
see also photograph VERB
la **photo**
- **to take a photograph** prendre une photo
- **to take a photograph of somebody** prendre quelqu'un en photo
to **photograph** VERB
see also photograph NOUN
photographier
photographer NOUN
le/la **photographe** ◇ *She's a photographer.* Elle est photographe.
photography NOUN
la **photo** ◇ *My hobby is photography.* Je fais de la photo.
phrase NOUN
l' **expression** FEM

phrase book NOUN
le **guide de conversation**
physical ADJECTIVE
physique
physicist NOUN
le **physicien**
la **physicienne**
◇ *He's a physicist.* Il est physicien.
physics NOUN
la **physique** ◇ *She teaches physics.*
Elle enseigne la physique.
physiotherapist NOUN
le/la **kinésithérapeute**
physiotherapy NOUN
la **kinésithérapie**
pianist NOUN
le/la **pianiste**
piano NOUN
le **piano** ◇ *I play the piano.* Je joue du
piano. ◇ *I have piano lessons.* Je
prends des leçons de piano.
pick NOUN
see also pick VERB
- **Take your pick!** Faites votre choix!
to **pick** VERB
see also pick NOUN
[1] **choisir** (*choose*) ◇ *I picked the
biggest piece.* J'ai choisi le plus gros
morceau.
[2] **sélectionner** (*for team*) ◇ *I've been
picked for the team.* J'ai été sélectionné
pour faire partie de l'équipe.
[3] **cueillir** (*fruit, flowers*)
- **to pick on somebody** harceler
quelqu'un ◇ *She's always picking on
me.* Elle me harcèle constamment.
- **to pick out** choisir ◇ *I like them all–it's
difficult to pick one out.* Ils me plaisent
tous–c'est difficile d'en choisir un.
- **to pick up (1)** (*collect*) venir chercher
◇ *We'll come to the airport to pick you
up.* Nous irons vous chercher à
l'aéroport.
- **to pick up (2)** (*from floor*) ramasser
◇ *Could you help me pick up the toys?*
Tu peux m'aider à ramasser les jouets?
- **to pick up (3)** (*learn*) apprendre ◇ *I
picked up some Spanish during my
holiday.* J'ai appris quelque mots
d'espagnol pendant mes vacances.
pickpocket NOUN
le **pickpocket**
picnic NOUN
le **pique-nique**
- **to have a picnic** pique-niquer ◇ *We
had a picnic on the beach.* Nous avons
pique-niqué sur la plage.
picture NOUN
[1] l' **illustration** FEM ◇ *Children's*

books have lots of pictures. Il y a
beaucoup d'illustrations dans les livres
pour enfants.
[2] la **photo** ◇ *My picture was in the
paper.* Ma photo était dans le journal.
[3] (*painting*)
le **tableau**
(les **tableaux** PL)
◇ *a famous picture* un tableau célèbre
- **to paint a picture of something**
peindre quelque chose
[4] (*drawing*)
le **dessin**
- **to draw a picture of something**
dessiner quelque chose
- **the pictures** (*cinema*) le cinéma
◇ *Shall we go to the pictures?* On va
au cinéma?
picturesque ADJECTIVE
pittoresque
pie NOUN
la **tourte** ◇ *an apple pie* une tourte
aux pommes
piece NOUN
le **morceau**
(les **morceaux** PL)
◇ *A small piece, please.* Un petit
morceau, s'il vous plaît.
- **a piece of furniture** un meuble
- **a piece of advice** un conseil
pier NOUN
la **jetée**
pierced ADJECTIVE
percé ◇ *I've got pierced ears.* J'ai les
oreilles percées.
pig NOUN
le **cochon**
pigeon NOUN
le **pigeon**
piggy bank NOUN
la **tirelire**
pigtail NOUN
la **natte**
pile NOUN
[1] le **tas** (*untidy heap*)
[2] la **pile** (*tidy stack*)
pill NOUN
la **pilule**
- **to be on the pill** prendre la pilule
pillar NOUN
le **pilier**
pillar box NOUN
la **boîte aux lettres**
pillow NOUN
l' **oreiller** MASC
pilot NOUN
le **pilote** ◇ *He's a pilot.* Il est pilote.
pimple NOUN
le **bouton**

P

pin NOUN
l' **épingle** FEM
- **I've got pins and needles.** J'ai des épingles et des aiguilles.
PIN NOUN (= *personal identification number*)
le **code confidentiel**
pinafore NOUN
le **tablier**
pinball NOUN
le **flipper** ◇ *to play pinball* jouer au flipper
- **a pinball machine** un flipper
to **pinch** VERB
1 **pincer** ◇ *He pinched me!* Il m'a pincé!
2 **piquer** (*informal: steal*) ◇ *Who's pinched my pen?* Qui est-ce qui m'a piqué mon stylo?
pine NOUN
le **pin** ◇ *a pine table* un table en pin
pineapple NOUN
l' **ananas** MASC
pink ADJECTIVE
rose
pint NOUN
la **pinte**
In France measurements are in litres and centilitres. A pint is about 0.6 litres.
- **to have a pint** boire une bière ◇ *He's gone out for a pint.* Il est parti boire une bière.
pipe NOUN
1 la **conduite** (*for water, gas*) ◇ *The pipes froze.* Les conduites d'eau ont gelé.
2 la **pipe** (*for smoking*) ◇ *He smokes a pipe.* Il fume la pipe.
- **the pipes** (*bagpipes*) la cornemuse ◇ *He plays the pipes.* Il joue de la cornemuse.
pirate NOUN
le **pirate**
pirated ADJECTIVE
pirate ◇ *a pirated video* une vidéo pirate
Pisces NOUN
les **Poissons** MASC ◇ *I'm Pisces.* Je suis Poissons.
pissed ADJECTIVE
bourré (*informal*)
pistol NOUN
le **pistolet**
pitch NOUN
see also pitch VERB
le **terrain** ◇ *a football pitch* un terrain de football
to **pitch** VERB
see also pitch NOUN
dresser (*tent*) ◇ *We pitched our tent near the beach.* Nous avons dressé notre tente près de la plage.
pity NOUN
see also pity VERB
la **pitié**
- **What a pity!** Quel dommage!
to **pity** VERB
see also pity NOUN
plaindre
pizza NOUN
la **pizza**
place NOUN
see also place VERB
1 l' **endroit** MASC (*location*) ◇ *It's a quiet place.* C'est un endroit tranquille. ◇ *There are a lot of interesting places to visit.* Il y a beaucoup d'endroits intéressants à visiter.
2 la **place** (*space*) ◇ *a parking place* une place de parking ◇ *a university place* une place à l'université
- **to change places** changer de place ◇ *Tamsin, change places with Delphine!* Tamsin, change de place avec Delphine!
- **to take place** avoir lieu
- **at your place** chez toi ◇ *Shall we meet at your place?* On se retrouve chez toi?
- **to my place** chez moi ◇ *Do you want to come round to my place?* Tu veux venir chez moi?
to **place** VERB
see also place NOUN
1 **poser** ◇ *He placed his hand on hers.* Il a posé la main sur la sienne.
2 **classer** (*in competition, contest*)
plaid ADJECTIVE
écossais ◇ *a plaid shirt* une chemise écossaise
plain NOUN
see also plain ADJECTIVE
la **plaine**
plain ADJECTIVE, ADVERB
see also plain NOUN
1 **uni** (*not patterned*) ◇ *a plain carpet* un tapis uni
2 **simple** (*not fancy*) ◇ *a plain white blouse* un simple chemisier blanc
plain chocolate NOUN
le **chocolat à croquer**
plait NOUN
la **natte** ◇ *She wears her hair in a plait.* Elle a une natte.
plan NOUN
see also plan VERB
1 le **projet** ◇ *What are your plans for the holidays?* Quels sont tes projets pour les vacances? ◇ *to make plans*

faire des projets
- **Everything went according to plan.**
Tout s'est passé comme prévu.
[2] le **plan** (*map*) ◇ *a plan of the campsite* un plan du terrain de camping
- **my essay plan** le plan de mon essai

to **plan** VERB
see also plan NOUN
[1] **préparer** (*make plans for*) ◇ *We're planning a trip to France.* Nous préparons un voyage en France.
[2] **planifier** (*make schedule for*) ◇ *Plan your revision carefully.* Planifiez vos révisions avec soin.
- **to plan to do something** avoir l'intention de faire quelque chose ◇ *I'm planning to get a job in the holidays.* J'ai l'intention de trouver un job pour les vacances.

plane NOUN
l' **avion** MASC ◇ *by plane* en avion

planet NOUN
la **planète**

planning NOUN
la **préparation** ◇ *The trip needs careful planning.* Le voyage nécessite une préparation méticuleuse.
- **family planning** le planning familial

plant NOUN
see also plant VERB
[1] la **plante** ◇ *to water the plants* arroser les plantes
[2] l' **usine** FEM (*factory*)

to **plant** VERB
see also plant NOUN
planter

plaster NOUN
[1] le **pansement adhésif** (*sticking plaster*) ◇ *Have you got a plaster, by any chance?* Vous n'auriez pas un pansement adhésif, par hasard?
[2] le **plâtre** (*for fracture*) ◇ *Her leg's in plaster.* Elle a la jambe dans le plâtre.

plastic NOUN
see also plastic ADJECTIVE
le **plastique** ◇ *It's made of plastic.* C'est en plastique.

plastic ADJECTIVE
see also plastic NOUN
en plastique ◇ *a plastic bag* un sac en plastique ◇ *a plastic mac* un imperméable en plastique

plate NOUN
l' **assiette** FEM (*for food*)

platform NOUN
[1] le **quai** (*at station*) ◇ *on platform 7* sur le quai numéro sept
[2] l' **estrade** FEM (*for performers*)

play NOUN
see also play VERB
la **pièce** ◇ *a play by Shakespeare* une pièce de Shakespeare
- **to put on a play** monter une pièce

to **play** VERB
see also play NOUN
[1] **jouer** ◇ *He's playing with his friends.* Il joue avec ses amis. ◇ *What sort of music do they play?* Quel genre de musique jouent-ils?
[2] **jouer contre** (*against person, team*) ◇ *France will play Scotland next month.* La France jouera contre l'Écosse le mois prochain.
[3] **jouer à** (*sport, game*) ◇ *I play hockey.* Je joue au hockey. ◇ *Can you play pool?* Tu sais jouer au billard américain?
[4] **jouer de** (*instrument*) ◇ *I play the guitar.* Je joue de la guitare.
[5] **écouter** (*record, cassette, music*) ◇ *She's always playing that record.* Elle écoute tout le temps ce disque.

player NOUN
[1] (*of sport*)
le **joueur**
la **joueuse**
◇ *a football player* un joueur de football
[2] (*of instrument*)
le **musicien**
la **musicienne**
- **a piano player** un pianiste
- **a saxophone player** un saxophoniste

playful ADJECTIVE
espiègle

playground NOUN
[1] la **cour de récréation** (*at school*)
[2] l' **aire de jeux** FEM (*in park*)

playgroup NOUN
la **garderie**

playing field NOUN
le **terrain de sport**

playtime NOUN
la **récréation**

playwright NOUN
le **dramaturge**

pleasant ADJECTIVE
agréable

please EXCLAMATION
[1] **s'il vous plaît** (*polite form*) ◇ *Two coffees, please.* Deux cafés, s'il vous plaît.
[2] **s'il te plaît** (*familiar form*) ◇ *Please write back soon.* Réponds vite, s'il te plaît.

pleased ADJECTIVE
content ◇ *My mother's not going to be very pleased.* Ma mère ne va pas être

P

contente du tout. ⋄ *It's beautiful: she'll be pleased with it.* C'est beau: elle va être contente.
- **Pleased to meet you!** Enchanté!

pleasure NOUN
le **plaisir** ⋄ *I read for pleasure.* Je lis pour le plaisir.

plenty NOUN
largement assez ⋄ *I've got plenty.* J'en ai largement assez. ⋄ *That's plenty, thanks.* Ça suffit largement, merci.
- **plenty of (1)** (*a lot*) beaucoup de ⋄ *I've got plenty to do.* J'ai beaucoup de choses à faire.
- **plenty of (2)** (*enough*) largement assez de ⋄ *I've got plenty of money.* J'ai largement assez d'argent. ⋄ *We've got plenty of time.* Nous avons largement le temps.

plot NOUN
see also plot VERB
[1] l' **intrigue** FEM (*of story, play*)
[2] la **conspiration** (*against somebody*) ⋄ *a plot against the president* une conspiration contre le président
[3] le **carré** (*of land*) ⋄ *a vegetable plot* un carré de légumes

to **plot** VERB
see also plot NOUN
comploter ⋄ *They were plotting to kill him.* Ils complotaient de le tuer.

plough NOUN
see also plough VERB
la **charrue**

to **plough** VERB
see also plough NOUN
labourer

plug NOUN
[1] la **prise de courant** (*electrical*) ⋄ *The plug is faulty.* La prise est défectueuse.
[2] le **bouchon** (*for sink*)

to **plug in** VERB
brancher ⋄ *Is it plugged in?* Est-ce que c'est branché?

plum NOUN
la **prune** ⋄ *plum jam* la confiture de prunes

plumber NOUN
le **plombier** ⋄ *He's a plumber.* Il est plombier.

plump ADJECTIVE
dodu

to **plunge** VERB
plonger

plural NOUN
le **pluriel**

plus PREPOSITION, ADJECTIVE
plus ⋄ *4 plus 3 equals 7.* Quatre plus trois égalent sept. ⋄ *three children plus a dog* trois enfants plus un chien
- **I got a B plus.** J'ai eu un Bien.

p.m. ABBREVIATION
- **At 8 p.m.** à huit heures du soir
In France times are often given using the 24-hour clock.
- **At 2 p.m.** à quatorze heures

pneumonia NOUN
la **pneumonie**

poached ADJECTIVE
poché ⋄ *a poached egg* un œuf poché

pocket NOUN
la **poche**
- **pocket money** l'argent de poche MASC ⋄ *£8 a week pocket money* huit livres d'argent de poche par semaine

pocket calculator NOUN
la **calculette**

poem NOUN
le **poème**

poet NOUN
le **poète**

poetry NOUN
la **poésie**

point NOUN
see also point VERB
[1] le **point** (*spot, score*) ⋄ *a point on the horizon* un point à l'horizon ⋄ *They scored 5 points.* Ils ont marqué cinq points.
[2] la **remarque** (*comment*) ⋄ *He made some interesting points.* Il a fait quelque remarques intéressantes.
[3] la **pointe** (*tip*) ⋄ *a pencil with a sharp point* un crayon à la pointe aiguisée
[4] le **moment** (*in time*) ⋄ *At that point, we decided to leave.* À ce moment-là, nous avons décidé de partir.
- **a point of view** un point de vue
- **to get the point** comprendre ⋄ *Sorry, I don't get the point.* Désolé, je ne comprends pas.
- **That's a good point!** C'est vrai!
- **There's no point.** Cela ne sert à rien. ⋄ *There's no point in waiting.* Cela ne sert à rien d'attendre.
- **What's the point?** À quoi bon? ⋄ *What's the point of leaving so early?* À quoi bon partir si tôt?
- **Punctuality isn't my strong point.** La ponctualité n'est pas mon fort.
- **two point five (2.5)** deux virgule cinq (2,5)

to **point** VERB
see also point NOUN
montrer du doigt ⋄ *Don't point!* Ne

montre pas du doigt!
- **to point at somebody** montrer quelqu'un du doigt ◇ *She pointed at Anne.* Elle a montré Anne du doigt.
- **to point a gun at somebody** braquer un revolver sur quelqu'un
- **to point something out (1)** (*show*) montrer quelque chose ◇ *The guide pointed out Notre-Dame to us.* Le guide nous a montré Notre-Dame.
- **to point something out (2)** (*mention*) signaler quelque chose ◇ *I should point out that...* Je dois vous signaler que...

pointless ADJECTIVE
inutile ◇ *It's pointless to argue.* Il est inutile de discuter.

poison NOUN
see also poison VERB
le **poison**

to **poison** VERB
see also poison NOUN
empoisonner

poisonous ADJECTIVE
1 (*snake*)
venimeux MASC
venimeuse FEM
2 (*plant, mushroom*)
vénéneux MASC
vénéneuse FEM
3 (*gas*)
toxique

poker NOUN
le **poker** ◇ *I play poker.* Je joue au poker.

Poland NOUN
la **Pologne**
- **in Poland** en Pologne
- **to Poland** en Pologne

polar bear NOUN
l' **ours blanc** MASC

Pole NOUN
(*Polish person*)
le **Polonais**
la **Polonaise**

pole NOUN
le **poteau**
(les **poteaux** PL)
◇ *a telegraph pole* un poteau télégraphique
- **a tent pole** un montant de tente
- **a ski pole** un bâton de ski
- **the North Pole** le pôle Nord
- **the South Pole** le pôle Sud

pole vault NOUN
le **saut à la perche**

police PL NOUN
la **police** ◇ *We called the police.* Nous avons appelé la police.
- **a police car** une voiture de police

- **a police station** un commissariat de police

policeman NOUN
le **policier** ◇ *He's a policeman.* Il est policier.

policewoman NOUN
la **femme policier** ◇ *She's a policewoman.* Elle est femme policier.

polio NOUN
la **polio**

Polish ADJECTIVE
see also Polish NOUN
polonais

Polish NOUN
see also Polish ADJECTIVE
le **polonais** (*language*)

polish NOUN
see also polish VERB
1 le **cirage** (*for shoes*)
2 la **cire** (*for furniture*)

to **polish** VERB
see also polish NOUN
1 **cirer** (*shoes, furniture*)
2 **faire briller** (*glass*)

polite ADJECTIVE
poli

politely ADVERB
poliment

politeness NOUN
la **politesse**

political ADJECTIVE
politique

politician NOUN
le **politicien**
la **politicienne**

politics PL NOUN
la **politique** SING ◇ *I'm not interested in politics.* La politique ne m'intéresse pas.

pollen NOUN
le **pollen**

to **pollute** VERB
polluer

polluted ADJECTIVE
pollué

pollution NOUN
la **pollution**

polo-necked sweater NOUN
le **pull à col roulé**

polo shirt NOUN
le **polo**

polythene bag NOUN
le **sac en plastique**

pond NOUN
1 l' **étang** MASC (*big*)
2 la **mare** (*smaller*)
3 le **bassin** ◇ *We've got a pond in our garden.* Nous avons un bassin dans notre jardin.

P

pony NOUN
le **poney**
ponytail NOUN
la **queue de cheval** ⋄ *He's got a ponytail.* Il a une queue de cheval.
pony trekking NOUN
◆ **to go pony trekking** faire une randonnée à dos de poney
poodle NOUN
le **caniche**
pool NOUN
[1] la **flaque** (*puddle*)
[2] l' **étang** (*pond*)
[3] la **piscine** (*for swimming*)
[4] le **billard américain** (*game*) ⋄ *Shall we have a game of pool?* Si on jouait au billard américain?
◆ **the pools** (*football*) le loto sportif ⋄ *to do the pools* jouer au loto sportif
poor ADJECTIVE
[1] **pauvre** ⋄ *a poor family* une famille pauvre ⋄ *Poor David, he's very unlucky!* Le pauvre David, il n'a vraiment pas de chance!
◆ **the poor** les pauvres MASC
[2] **médiocre** (*bad*) ⋄ *a poor mark* une note médiocre
poorly ADJECTIVE
souffrant ⋄ *She's poorly.* Elle est souffrante.
pop ADJECTIVE
pop ⋄ *pop music* la musique pop ⋄ *a pop star* un pop star ⋄ *a pop group* un groupe pop ⋄ *a pop song* une chanson pop
popcorn NOUN
le **pop-corn**
pope NOUN
le **pape**
poppy NOUN
le **coquelicot**
popular ADJECTIVE
populaire ⋄ *She's a very popular girl.* C'est une fille très populaire. ⋄ *This is a very popular style.* C'est un style très populaire.
population NOUN
la **population**
porch NOUN
le **porche**
pork NOUN
le **porc** ⋄ *a pork chop* une côtelette de porc ⋄ *I don't eat pork.* Je ne mange pas de porc.
porn NOUN
see also porn ADJECTIVE
le **porno**
porn ADJECTIVE
see also porn NOUN

porno MASC, FEM, PL ⋄ *a porn film* un film porno ⋄ *a porn mag* un magazine porno
pornographic ADJECTIVE
pornographique ⋄ *a pornographic magazine* un magazine pornographique
pornography NOUN
la **pornographie**
porridge NOUN
le **porridge**
port NOUN
[1] le **port** (*harbour*)
[2] le **porto** (*wine*) ⋄ *a glass of port* un verre de porto
porter NOUN
[1] le **portier** (*in hotel*)
[2] le **porteur** (*at station*)
portion NOUN
la **portion** ⋄ *a large portion of chips* une grosse portion de frites
portrait NOUN
le **portrait**
Portugal NOUN
le **Portugal**
◆ **in Portugal** au Portugal
◆ **We went to Portugal.** Nous sommes allés au Portugal.
Portuguese ADJECTIVE
see also Portuguese NOUN
portugais
Portuguese NOUN
see also Portuguese ADJECTIVE
[1] (*person*)
le **Portugais**
la **Portugaise**
[2] (*language*)
le **portugais**
posh ADJECTIVE
chic MASC, FEM, PL ⋄ *a posh hotel* un hôtel chic
position NOUN
la **position** ⋄ *an uncomfortable position* une position inconfortable
positive ADJECTIVE
[1] (*good*)
positif MASC
positive FEM
⋄ *a positive attitude* une attitude positive
[2] (*sure*)
certain ⋄ *I'm positive.* J'en suis certain.
to **possess** VERB
posséder
possession NOUN
◆ **Have you got all your possessions?** Est-ce tu as toutes tes affaires?
possibility NOUN

- **It's a possibility.** C'est possible.
possible ADJECTIVE
  possible ⋄ *as soon as possible*
aussitôt que possible
possibly ADVERB
  peut-être (*perhaps*) ⋄ *Are you coming to the party?–Possibly.* Est-ce que tu viens à la soirée?–Peut-être.
- **...if you possibly can.** ...si cela vous est possible.
- **I can't possibly come.** Je ne peux vraiment pas venir.
post NOUN
  see also post VERB
  1 (*letters*)
  le **courrier** ⋄ *Is there any post for me?* Est-ce qu'il y a du courrier pour moi?
  2 (*pole*)
  le **poteau**
  (les **poteaux** PL)
  ⋄ *The ball hit the post.* Le ballon a heurté le poteau.
to **post** VERB
  see also post NOUN
  poster ⋄ *I've got some cards to post.* J'ai quelques cartes à poster.
postage NOUN
  l' **affranchissement** MASC
postbox NOUN
  la **boîte aux lettres**
postcard NOUN
  la **carte postale**
postcode NOUN
  le **code postal**
poster NOUN
  1 le **poster** ⋄ *I've got posters on my bedrooms walls.* J'ai des posters sur les murs de ma chambre.
  2 l' **affiche** FEM (*advertising*) ⋄ *There are posters all over town.* Il y a des affiches dans toute la ville.
postman NOUN
  le **facteur** ⋄ *He's a postman.* Il est facteur.
postmark NOUN
  le **cachet de la poste**
post office NOUN
  la **poste** ⋄ *Where's the post office, please?* Où est la poste, s'il vous plaît? ⋄ *She works for the post office.* Elle travaille à la poste.
to **postpone** VERB
  remettre à plus tard ⋄ *The match has been postponed.* Le match a été remis à plus tard.
postwoman NOUN
  la **factrice** ⋄ *She's a postwoman.* Elle est factrice.
pot NOUN

  1 le **pot** ⋄ *a pot of jam* un pot de confiture
  2 la **théière** (*teapot*)
  3 la **cafetière** (*coffeepot*)
  4 l' **herbe** FEM (*marijuana*) ⋄ *to smoke pot* fumer de l'herbe
- **the pots and pans** les casseroles
potato NOUN
  la **pomme de terre** ⋄ *potato salad* la salade de pommes de terre
- **mashed potatoes** la purée
- **a baked potato** une pomme de terre en robe des champs
potential NOUN
  see also potential ADJECTIVE
- **He has great potential.** Il a de l'avenir.
potential ADJECTIVE
  see also potential NOUN
  possible ⋄ *a potential problem* un problème possible
pothole NOUN
  le **nid de poule** (*in road*)
pot plant NOUN
  la **plante en pot**
pottery NOUN
  la **poterie**
pound NOUN
  see also pound VERB
  la **livre** (*weight, money*) ⋄ *a pound of carrots* une livre de carottes ⋄ *How many francs do you get for a pound?* Combien de francs a-t-on pour une livre? ⋄ *a pound coin* une pièce d'une livre
to **pound** VERB
  see also pound NOUN
  battre ⋄ *My heart was pounding.* J'avais le cœur qui battait.
to **pour** VERB
  1 **verser** (*liquid*) ⋄ *She poured some water into the pan.* Elle a versé de l'eau dans la casserole.
- **She poured him a drink.** Elle lui a servi à boire.
- **Shall I pour you a cup of tea?** Je vous sers une tasse de thé?
  2 **pleuvoir à verse** (*rain*) ⋄ *It's pouring.* Il pleut à verse.
- **in the pouring rain** sous une pluie torrentielle
poverty NOUN
  la **pauvreté**
powder NOUN
  la **poudre**
power NOUN
  1 le **courant** (*electricity*) ⋄ *The power's off.* Le courant est coupé.
- **a power cut** une coupure de courant
- **a power point** une prise de courant

P

- **a power station** une centrale électrique

  2 l' **énergie** FEM (*energy*) ◇ *nuclear power* l'énergie nucléaire ◇ *solar power* l'énergie solaire

  3 le **pouvoir** (*authority*) ◇ *to be in power* être au pouvoir

powerful ADJECTIVE

puissant

practical ADJECTIVE

pratique ◇ *a practical suggestion* un conseil pratique

- **She's very practical.** Elle a l'esprit pratique.

practically ADVERB

pratiquement ◇ *It's practically impossible.* C'est pratiquement impossible.

practice NOUN

l' **entraînement** MASC (*for sport*) ◇ *football practice* l'entraînement de foot

- **I've got to do my piano practice.** Je dois travailler mon piano.
- **It's normal practice in our school.** C'est ce qui se fait dans notre école.
- **in practice** en pratique
- **a medical practice** un cabinet médical

to **practise** VERB

1 **s'exercer** (*music, hobby*) ◇ *I ought to practise more.* Je devrais m'exercer davantage.

2 **travailler** (*instrument*) ◇ *I practise the flute every evening.* Je travaille ma flûte tous les soirs.

3 **pratiquer** (*language*) ◇ *I practised my French when we were on holiday.* J'ai pratiqué mon français pendant les vacances.

4 **s'entraîner** (*sport*) ◇ *The team practises on Thursdays.* L'équipe s'entraîne le jeudi. ◇ *I don't practise enough.* Je ne m'entraîne pas assez.

practising ADJECTIVE

pratiquant ◇ *She's a practising Catholic.* Elle est catholique pratiquante.

pram NOUN

le **landau**

prawn NOUN

la **crevette**

prawn cocktail NOUN

le **cocktail de crevettes**

to **pray** VERB

prier ◇ *to pray for something* prier pour quelque chose

prayer NOUN

la **prière**

precaution NOUN

la **précaution**

- **to take precautions** prendre ses précautions

preceding ADJECTIVE

précédent

precinct NOUN

- **a shopping precinct** un centre commercial
- **a pedestrian precinct** une zone piétonnière

precious ADJECTIVE

précieux MASC

précieuse FEM

precise ADJECTIVE

précis ◇ *at that precise moment* à cet instant précis

precisely ADVERB

précisément ◇ *Precisely!* Précisément!

- **at 10 a.m. precisely** à dix heures précises

to **predict** VERB

prédire

predictable ADJECTIVE

prévisible

prefect NOUN

French schools do not have prefects. You could explain what a prefect is using the example given.

- **My sister's a prefect.** Ma sœur est en dernière année et est chargée de maintenir la discipline.

to **prefer** VERB

préférer ◇ *Which would you prefer?* Lequel préfères-tu? ◇ *I prefer French to chemistry.* Je préfère le français à la chimie.

preference NOUN

la **préférence**

pregnant ADJECTIVE

enceinte ◇ *She's six months pregnant.* Elle est enceinte de six mois.

prehistoric ADJECTIVE

préhistorique

prejudice NOUN

1 le **préjugé** ◇ *That's just a prejudice.* C'est un préjugé.

2 les **préjugés** MASC PL ◇ *There's a lot of racial prejudice.* Il y a beaucoup de préjugés raciaux.

prejudiced ADJECTIVE

- **to be prejudiced against somebody** avoir des préjugés contre quelqu'un

premature ADJECTIVE

prématuré

- **a premature baby** un prématuré

Premier League NOUN

la **première division** ◇ *in the Premier League* en première division

premises PL NOUN

les **locaux** MASC ⋄ *They're moving to new premises.* Ils vont occuper de nouveaux locaux.

premonition NOUN
  la **prémonition**

preoccupied ADJECTIVE
  préoccupé

prep NOUN
  les **devoirs** MASC PL (*homework*)
  ⋄ *history prep* les devoirs d'histoire

preparation NOUN
  la **préparation**

to **prepare** VERB
  préparer ⋄ *She has to prepare lessons in the evening.* Elle doit préparer ses cours le soir.
  • **to prepare for something** se préparer pour quelque chose ⋄ *We're preparing for our skiing holiday.* Nous nous préparons pour nos vacances à la neige.

prepared ADJECTIVE
  • **to be prepared to do something** être prêt à faire quelque chose ⋄ *I'm prepared to help you.* Je suis prêt à t'aider.

prep school NOUN
  l' **école primaire privée** FEM

Presbyterian NOUN
  see also Presbyterian ADJECTIVE
  le **presbytérien**
  la **presbytérienne**

Presbyterian ADJECTIVE
  see also Presbyterian NOUN
  presbytérien MASC
  presbytérienne FEM

to **prescribe** VERB
  prescrire

prescription NOUN
  l' **ordonnance** FEM ⋄ *You can't get it without a prescription.* On ne peut pas se le procurer sans ordonnance.

presence NOUN
  la **présence**
  • **presence of mind** présence d'esprit

present ADJECTIVE
  see also present NOUN, VERB
  [1] (*in attendance*)
  présent ⋄ *He wasn't present at the meeting.* Il n'était pas présent à la réunion.
  [2] (*current*)
  actuel MASC
  actuelle FEM
  ⋄ *the present situation* la situation actuelle
  • **the present tense** le présent

present NOUN
  see also present ADJECTIVE, VERB

[1] (*gift*)
  le **cadeau**
  (les **cadeaux** PL)
  ⋄ *I'm going to buy presents.* Je vais acheter des cadeaux.
  • **to give somebody a present** offrir un cadeau à quelqu'un
  [2] (*time*)
  le **présent** ⋄ *up to the present* jusqu'à présent
  • **for the present** pour l'instant
  • **at present** en ce moment

to **present** VERB
  see also present ADJECTIVE, NOUN
  • **to present somebody with something** (*prize, medal*) remettre quelque chose à quelqu'un

presenter NOUN
  (*on TV*)
  le **présentateur**
  la **présentatrice**

presently ADVERB
  [1] **bientôt** (*soon*) ⋄ *You'll feel better presently.* Tu vas bientôt te sentir mieux.
  [2] **actuellement** (*at present*) ⋄ *They're presently on tour.* Ils sont actuellement en tournée.

president NOUN
  le **président**
  la **présidente**

press NOUN
  see also press VERB
  la **presse**
  • **a press conference** une conférence de presse

to **press** VERB
  see also press NOUN
  [1] **appuyer** ⋄ *Don't press too hard!* N'appuie pas trop fort!
  [2] **appuyer sur** ⋄ *He pressed the accelerator.* Il a appuyé sur l'accélérateur.

pressed ADJECTIVE
  • **We are pressed for time.** Le temps nous manque.

press-up NOUN
  • **to do press-ups** faire des pompes ⋄ *I do twenty press-ups every morning.* Je fais vingt pompes tous les matins.

pressure NOUN
  see also pressure VERB
  la **pression** ⋄ *He's under a lot of pressure at work.* Il est sous pression au travail.
  • **a pressure group** un groupe de pression

to **pressure** VERB
  see also pressure NOUN

faire pression sur ◇ *My parents are pressuring me.* Mes parents font pression sur moi.

prestige NOUN
le **prestige**

prestigious ADJECTIVE
prestigieux MASC
prestigieuse FEM

presumably ADVERB
vraisemblablement

to **presume** VERB
supposer ◇ *I presume so.* Je suppose que oui.

to **pretend** VERB
- **to pretend to do something** faire semblant de faire quelque chose ◇ *He pretended to be asleep.* Il faisait semblant de dormir.

pretty ADJECTIVE, ADVERB
[1] **joli** ◇ *She's very pretty.* Elle est très jolie.
[2] **plutôt** (*rather*) ◇ *That film was pretty bad.* Ce film était plutôt mauvais.
- **The weather was pretty awful.** Il faisait un temps minable.
- **It's pretty much the same.** C'est pratiquement la même chose.

to **prevent** VERB
empêcher
- **to prevent somebody from doing something** empêcher quelqu'un de faire quelque chose ◇ *They try to prevent us from smoking.* Ils essaient de nous empêcher de fumer.

previous ADJECTIVE
précédent

previously ADVERB
auparavant

prey NOUN
la **proie** ◇ *a bird of prey* un oiseau de proie

price NOUN
le **prix**

price list NOUN
la **liste des prix**

to **prick** VERB
piquer ◇ *I've pricked my finger.* Je me suis piqué le doigt.

pride NOUN
la **fierté**

priest NOUN
le **prêtre** ◇ *He's a priest.* Il est prêtre.

primarily ADVERB
principalement

primary ADJECTIVE
principal
(**principaux** MASC PL)

primary school NOUN
l' **école primaire** FEM ◇ *She's still at*
primary school. Elle est encore à l'école primaire.

prime minister NOUN
le **Premier ministre**

primitive ADJECTIVE
primitif MASC
primitive FEM

prince NOUN
le **prince** ◇ *the Prince of Wales* le prince de Galles

princess NOUN
la **princesse** ◇ *Princess Anne* la princesse Anne

principal ADJECTIVE
see also principal NOUN
principal
(**principaux** MASC PL)

principal NOUN
see also principal ADJECTIVE
le **principal** (*of college*)

principle NOUN
le **principe**
- **on principle** par principe

print NOUN
[1] le **tirage** (*photo*) ◇ *colour prints* des tirages en couleur
[2] les **caractères** MASC (*letters*) ◇ *in small print* en petits caractères
[3] l' **empreinte digitale** FEM (*fingerprint*)
[4] la **gravure** FEM (*picture*) ◇ *a framed print* une gravure encadrée

printer NOUN
l' **imprimante** FEM (*machine*)

print-out NOUN
la **copie papier**

priority NOUN
la **priorité**

prison NOUN
la **prison**
- **in prison** en prison

prisoner NOUN
le **prisonnier**
la **prisonnière**

privacy NOUN
l' **intimité** FEM

private ADJECTIVE
privé ◇ *a private school* une école privée
- **private property** la propriété privée
- **"private"** (*on envelope*) "personnel"
- **a private bathroom** une salle de bain individuelle
- **I have private lessons.** Je prends des cours particuliers.

to **privatize** VERB
privatiser

privilege NOUN
le **privilège**

prize NOUN

le **prix** ◇ *to win a prize* gagner un prix
prize-giving NOUN
la **distribution des prix**
prizewinner NOUN
le **gagnant**
la **gagnante**
pro NOUN
- **the pros and cons** le pour et le contre
  ◇ *We weighed up the pros and cons.*
  Nous avons pesé le pour et le contre.
probability NOUN
la **probabilité**
probable ADJECTIVE
probable
probably ADVERB
probablement ◇ *probably not*
probablement pas
problem NOUN
le **problème** ◇ *No problem!* Pas de
problème!
proceeds PL NOUN
la **recette** SING
process NOUN
le **processus** ◇ *the peace process* le
processus de paix
- **to be in the process of painting the
  kitchen** être en train de faire quelque
  chose ◇ *We're in the process of
  painting the kitchen.* Nous sommes en
  train de peindre la cuisine.
procession NOUN
la **procession** (*religious*)
to **produce** VERB
[1] **produire** (*manufacture*)
[2] **monter** (*play, show*)
producer NOUN
(*of play, show*)
le **metteur en scène**
(les **metteurs en scène** PL)
product NOUN
le **produit**
production NOUN
[1] la **production** ◇ *They're increasing
production of luxury models.* Ils
augmentent la production des modèles
de luxe.
[2] la **représentation** (*play, show*) ◇ *a
production of "Hamlet"* une
représentation de "Hamlet"
profession NOUN
la **profession**
professional NOUN
see also professional ADJECTIVE
le **professionnel**
la **professionnelle**
professional ADJECTIVE
see also professional NOUN
(*player*)
professionnel MASC

professionnelle FEM
◇ *a professional musician* un musicien
professionnel
- **a very professional piece of work** un
  vrai travail de professionnel
professionally ADVERB
- **She sings professionally.** C'est une
  chanteuse professionnelle.
professor NOUN
le **professeur d'université**
- **He's the French professor.** Il est
  titulaire de la chaire de français.
profit NOUN
le **bénéfice**
profitable ADJECTIVE
rentable
program NOUN
see also program VERB
le **programme** ◇ *a computer program*
un programme informatique
to **program** VERB
see also program NOUN
programmer (*computer*)
programme NOUN
[1] l' **émission** FEM (*on TV, radio*)
[2] le **programme** (*of events*)
programmer NOUN
le **programmeur**
la **programmeuse**
◇ *She's a programmer.* Elle est
programmeuse.
programming NOUN
la **programmation**
progress NOUN
le **progrès** ◇ *You're making progress!*
Vous faites des progrès!
to **prohibit** VERB
interdire ◇ *Smoking is prohibited.* Il
est interdit de fumer.
project NOUN
[1] le **projet** (*plan*) ◇ *a development
project* un projet de développement
[2] le **dossier** (*research*) ◇ *I'm doing a
project on education in France.* Je
prépare un dossier sur l'éducation en
France.
projector NOUN
le **projecteur**
promenade NOUN
le **front de mer**
promise NOUN
see also promise VERB
la **promesse** ◇ *He made me a promise.*
Il m'a fait une promesse.
- **That's a promise!** C'est promis!
to **promise** VERB
see also promise NOUN
promettre ◇ *She promised to write.*
Elle a promis d'écrire. ◇ *I'll write, I*

promise! J'écrirai, c'est promis!

promising ADJECTIVE
- **a promising player** un joueur qui a de l'avenir

to **promote** VERB
- **to be promoted** être promu ◇ *She was promoted after six months.* Elle a été promue au bout de six mois.

promotion NOUN
la **promotion**

prompt ADJECTIVE, ADVERB
rapide ◇ *a prompt reply* une réponse rapide
- **at eight o'clock prompt** à huit heures précises

promptly ADVERB
ponctuellement ◇ *We left promptly at seven.* Nous sommes partis ponctuellement à sept heures.

pronoun NOUN
le **pronom**

to **pronounce** VERB
prononcer ◇ *How do you pronounce that word?* Comment est-ce qu'on prononce ce mot?

pronunciation NOUN
la **pronunciation**

proof NOUN
la **preuve**

proper ADJECTIVE
1 **vrai** (*genuine*) ◇ *proper French bread* du vrai pain français ◇ *We didn't have a proper lunch, just sandwiches.* Nous n'avons pas pris de vrai repas, juste des sandwichs.
- **It's difficult to get a proper job.** Il est difficile de trouver un correct travail.
2 **adéquat** ◇ *You have to have the proper equipment.* Il faut avoir l'équipement adéquat. ◇ *We need proper training.* Il nous faut une formation adéquate.
- **If you had come at the proper time...** Si tu étais venu à l'heure dite...

properly ADVERB
1 **comme il faut** (*correctly*) ◇ *You're not doing it properly.* Tu ne t'y prends pas comme il faut.
2 **convenablement** (*appropriately*)
◇ *Dress properly for your interview.* Habille-toi convenablement pour ton entretien.

property NOUN
la **propriété**
- **"private property"** "propriété privée"
- **stolen property** les objets volés

proportional ADJECTIVE
proportionnel MASC
proportionnelle FEM

◇ *proportional representation* la représentation proportionnelle

proposal NOUN
la **proposition** (*suggestion*)

to **propose** VERB
proposer ◇ *I propose a new plan.* Je propose un changement de programme.
- **to propose to do something** avoir l'intention de faire quelque chose
◇ *What do you propose to do?* Qu'est-ce que tu as l'intention de faire?
- **to propose to somebody** (*for marriage*) demander quelqu'un en mariage ◇ *He proposed to her at the restaurant.* Il l'a demandée en mariage au restaurant.

prospect NOUN
la **perspective** ◇ *It'll improve my career prospects.* Ça va améliorer mes perspectives d'avenir.

prospectus NOUN
le **prospectus**

prostitute NOUN
la **prostituée**
- **a male prostitute** un prostitué

to **protect** VERB
protéger

protection NOUN
la **protection**

protein NOUN
la **protéine**

protest NOUN
see also protest VERB
la **protestation** ◇ *He ignored their protests.* Il a ignoré leurs protestations.
- **a protest march** une manifestation

to **protest** VERB
see also protest NOUN
protester

Protestant NOUN
see also Protestant ADJECTIVE
le **protestant**
la **protestante**
◇ *I'm a Protestant.* Je suis protestant.

Protestant ADJECTIVE
see also Protestant NOUN
protestant ◇ *a Protestant church* une église protestante

protester NOUN
le **manifestant**
la **manifestante**

proud ADJECTIVE
fier MASC
fière FEM
◇ *Her parents are proud of her.* Ses parents sont fiers d'elle.

to **prove** VERB
prouver ◇ *The police couldn't prove it.*

La police n'a pas pu le prouver.

proverb NOUN

le **proverbe**

to **provide** VERB

fournir

- **to provide somebody with something**
  fournir quelque chose à quelqu'un
  ◇ *They provided us with maps.* Ils
  nous ont fourni des cartes.

provided CONJUNCTION

à condition que

à condition que *has to be followed by the subjunctive.*

◇ *He'll play in the next match provided he's fit.* Il jouera dans le prochain match, à condition qu'il soit en forme.

provisional ADJECTIVE

provisoire

prowler NOUN

le **rôdeur**

la **rôdeuse**

prune NOUN

le **pruneau**

(les **pruneaux** PL)

pseudonym NOUN

le **pseudonyme**

psychiatrist NOUN

le/la **psychiatre** ◇ *She's a psychiatrist.*
Elle est psychiatre.

psychoanalyst NOUN

le/la **psychanalyste**

psychological ADJECTIVE

psychologique

psychologist NOUN

le/la **psychologue** ◇ *He's a psychologist.* Il est psychologue.

psychology NOUN

la **psychologie**

PTO ABBREVIATION (= please turn over)

T.S.V.P. (= tournez, s'il vous plaît)

pub NOUN

le **pub**

public NOUN

see also public ADJECTIVE

le **public** ◇ *open to the public* ouvert
au public

- **in public** en public

public ADJECTIVE

see also public NOUN

public MASC

publique FEM

- **a public holiday** un jour férié
- **public opinion** l'opinion publique FEM
- **the public address system** les
  haut-parleurs

publicity NOUN

la **publicité**

public school NOUN

l' **école privée** FEM

public transport NOUN

les **transports en commun** MASC PL

to **publish** VERB

publier

publisher NOUN

l' **éditeur** MASC

pudding NOUN

le **dessert** ◇ *What's for pudding?*
Qu'est-ce qu'il y a comme dessert?

- **rice pudding** le riz au lait
- **black pudding** le boudin noir

puddle NOUN

la **flaque**

puff pastry NOUN

la **pâte feuilletée**

to **pull** VERB

tirer ◇ *Pull!* Tirez!

- **He pulled the trigger.** Il a appuyé sur la
  gâchette.
- **to pull a muscle** se froisser un muscle
  ◇ *I pulled a muscle when I was training.*
  Je me suis froissé un muscle à
  l'entraînement.
- **You're pulling my leg!** Tu me fais
  marcher!
- **to pull down** démolir
- **to pull out (1)** arracher *(tooth, weed)*
- **to pull out (2)** déboîter *(car)* ◇ *The
  car pulled out to overtake.* La voiture a
  déboîté pour doubler.
- **to pull out (3)** se retirer *(withdraw)*
  ◇ *She pulled out of the tournament.*
  Elle s'est retirée du tournoi.
- **to pull through** s'en sortir ◇ *They
  think he'll pull through.* Ils pensent qu'il
  va s'en sortir.

pullover NOUN

le **pull-over**

pulse NOUN

le **pouls** ◇ *The nurse felt his pulse.*
L'infirmière a pris son pouls.

pulses PL NOUN

les **légumes secs** MASC

pump NOUN

see also pump VERB

1 la **pompe** ◇ *a bicycle pump* une
pompe à vélo ◇ *a petrol pump* une
pompe à essence

2 la **chaussure de sport** *(shoe)*

to **pump** VERB

see also pump NOUN

pomper

- **to pump up** gonfler *(tyre)*

pumpkin NOUN

le **potiron**

punch NOUN

see also punch VERB

1 le **coup de poing** *(blow)* ◇ *He gave
me a punch.* Il m'a donné un coup de

P

poing.

[2] le **punch** (drink)

to **punch** VERB

see also punch NOUN

[1] **donner un coup de poing à** (hit)
◇ He punched me! Il m'a donné un coup de poing!

[2] **composter** (in ticket machine)
◇ Punch your ticket before you get on the train. Compostez votre billet avant de monter dans le train.

[3] **poinçonner** (by hand) ◇ He forgot to punch my ticket. Il a oublié de poinçonner mon billet.

punch-up NOUN
la **bagarre** (informal)

punctual ADJECTIVE
ponctuel MASC
ponctuelle FEM

punctuation NOUN
la **ponctuation**

puncture NOUN
la **crevaison** ◇ I had to mend a puncture. J'ai dû réparer une crevaison.
• to have a puncture crever ◇ I had a puncture on the motorway. J'ai crevé sur l'autoroute.

to **punish** VERB
punir
• to punish somebody for something punir quelqu'un de quelque chose
• to punish somebody for doing something punir quelqu'un d'avoir fait quelque chose

punishment NOUN
la **punition**

punk NOUN
le/la **punk** (person)
• a punk rock band un groupe de punk rock

pupil NOUN
l' **élève** MASC/FEM

puppet NOUN
la **marionnette**

puppy NOUN
le **chiot**

to **purchase** VERB
acheter

pure ADJECTIVE
pur ◇ pure orange juice du pur jus d'orange ◇ He's doing pure maths. Il fait des maths pures.

purple ADJECTIVE
violet MASC
violette FEM

purpose NOUN
le **but** ◇ What is the purpose of these changes? Quel est le but de ces changements? ◇ his purpose in life

son but dans la vie
• on purpose exprès ◇ He did it on purpose. Il l'a fait exprès.

to **purr** VERB
ronronner

purse NOUN
le **porte-monnaie**
(les **porte-monnaie** PL)

to **pursue** VERB
poursuivre

pursuit NOUN
l' **activité** FEM ◇ outdoor pursuits les activités de plein air

push NOUN
see also push VERB
• to give somebody a push pousser quelqu'un ◇ He gave me a push. Il m'a poussé.

to **push** VERB
see also push NOUN
[1] **pousser** ◇ Don't push! Arrêtez de pousser!
[2] **appuyer sur** (button)
• to push somebody to do something pousser quelqu'un à faire quelque chose ◇ My parents are pushing me to go to university. Mes parents me poussent à entrer à l'université.
• to push drugs revendre de la drogue
• Push off! Dégage!

pushchair NOUN
la **poussette**

pusher NOUN
(of drugs)
le **revendeur**
la **revendeuse**

to **put** VERB
[1] **mettre** (place) ◇ Where shall I put my things? Où est-ce que je peux mettre mes affaires? ◇ She's putting the baby to bed. Elle met le bébé au lit.
[2] **écrire** (write) ◇ Don't forget to put your name on the paper. N'oubliez pas d'écrire votre nom sur la feuille.

to **put away** VERB
ranger ◇ Can you put away the dishes, please? Tu peux ranger la vaisselle, s'il te plaît?

to **put back** VERB
remettre en place (replace) ◇ Put it back when you've finished with it. Remets-le en place une fois que tu auras fini.

to **put down** VERB
[1] **poser** ◇ I'll put these bags down for a minute. Je vais poser ces sacs une minute.
[2] **noter** (in writing) ◇ I've put down a few ideas. J'ai noté quelques idées.

- **to have an animal put down** faire piquer un animal ◇ *We had to have our old dog put down.* Nous avons dû faire piquer notre vieux chien.

to **put off** VERB

1 **éteindre** (*switch off*) ◇ *Shall I put the light off?* Est-ce que j'éteins la lumière?

2 **remettre à plus tard** (*postpone*) ◇ *I keep putting it off.* Je n'arrête pas de remettre ça à plus tard.

3 **déranger** (*distract*) ◇ *Stop putting me off!* Arrête de me déranger!

4 **décourager** (*discourage*) ◇ *He's not easily put off.* Il ne se laisse pas facilement décourager.

to **put on** VERB

1 **mettre** (*clothes, lipstick, record*) ◇ *I'll put my coat on.* Je vais mettre mon manteau.

2 **allumer** (*light, heater, telly*) ◇ *Shall I put the heater on?* J'allume le chauffage?

3 **monter** (*play, show*) ◇ *We're putting on "Bugsy Malone".* Nous sommes en train de monter "Bugsy Malone".

4 **mettre à cuire** ◇ *I'll put the potatoes on.* Je vais mettre les pommes de terre à cuire.

- **to put on weight** grossir ◇ *He's put on a lot of weight.* Il a beaucoup grossi.

to **put out** VERB

éteindre (*light, cigarette, fire*) ◇ *It took them five hours to put out the fire.* Ils ont mis cinq heures à éteindre l'incendie.

to **put through** VERB

passer ◇ *Can you put me through to the manager?* Est-ce que vous pouvez me passer le directeur?

- **I'm putting you through.** Je vous passe la communication.

to **put up** VERB

1 **mettre** (*pin up*) ◇ *The poster's great. I'll put it up on my wall.* Le poster est super. Je vais le mettre au mur.

2 **monter** (*tent*) ◇ *We put up our tent in a field.* Nous avons monté la tente dans un champ.

3 **augmenter** (*price*) ◇ *They've put up the price.* Ils ont augmenté le prix.

4 **héberger** (*accommodate*) ◇ *My friend will put me up for the night.* Mon ami va m'héberger pour la nuit.

- **to put one's hand up** lever la main ◇ *If you have any questions, put up your hand.* Si vous avez une question, levez la main.

- **to put up with something** supporter quelque chose ◇ *I'm not going to put up with it any longer.* Je ne vais pas supporter ça plus longtemps.

puzzle NOUN

le **puzzle** (*jigsaw*)

puzzled ADJECTIVE

perplexe ◇ *You look puzzled!* Tu as l'air perplexe!

puzzling ADJECTIVE

déconcertant

pyjamas PL NOUN

le **pyjama** SING ◇ *my pyjamas* mon pyjama

- **a pair of pyjamas** un pyjama

- **a pyjama top** un haut de pyjama

pyramid NOUN

la **pyramide**

Pyrenees PL NOUN

les **Pyrénées** FEM

- **in the Pyrenees** dans les Pyrénées

- **We went to the Pyrenees.** Nous sommes allés dans les Pyrénées.

P

Q

quaint ADJECTIVE
pittoresque (*house, village*)

qualification NOUN
le **diplôme** ○ *to leave school without any qualifications* quitter l'école sans aucun diplôme
- **vocational qualifications** des qualifications professionnelles

qualified ADJECTIVE
1 **qualifié** (*trained*) ○ *a qualified driving instructor* un moniteur d'auto-école qualifié
2 **diplômé** (*nurse, teacher*) ○ *a qualified nurse* une infirmière diplômée

to **qualify** VERB
1 **obtenir son diplôme** (*for job*) ○ *She qualified as a teacher last year.* Elle a obtenu son diplôme de professeur l'année dernière.
2 **se qualifier** (*in competition*) ○ *Our team didn't qualify.* Notre équipe ne s'est pas qualifiée.

quality NOUN
la **qualité** ○ *a good quality of life* une bonne qualité de vie ○ *good-quality ingredients* des ingrédients de bonne qualité ○ *She's got lots of good qualities.* Elle a beaucoup de qualités.

quantity NOUN
la **quantité**

quarantine NOUN
la **quarantaine** ○ *in quarantine* en quarantaine

quarrel NOUN
see also quarrel VERB
la **dispute**

to **quarrel** VERB
see also quarrel NOUN
se **disputer**

quarry NOUN
la **carrière** (*for stone*)

quarter NOUN
le **quart**
- **three quarters** trois quarts
- **a quarter of an hour** un quart d'heure ○ *three quarters of an hour* trois quarts d'heure
- **a quarter past ten** dix heures et quart
- **a quarter to eleven** onze heures moins le quart

quarter final NOUN
le **quart de finale**

quartet NOUN
le **quatuor** ○ *a string quartet* un quatuor à cordes

quay NOUN
le **quai**

queasy ADJECTIVE
- **to feel queasy** avoir mal au cœur ○ *I'm feeling queasy.* J'ai mal au cœur.

queen NOUN
1 la **reine** ○ *Queen Elizabeth* la reine Élisabeth
2 la **dame** (*playing card*) ○ *the queen of hearts* la dame de cœur
- **the Queen Mother** la reine mère

query NOUN
la **question**

question NOUN
see also question VERB
la **question** ○ *Can I ask a question?* Est-ce que je peux poser une question? ○ *That's a difficult question.* C'est une question difficile.
- **It's out of the question.** C'est hors de question.

to **question** VERB
see also question NOUN
interroger ○ *He was questioned by the police.* Il a été a interrogé par la police.

question mark NOUN
le **point d'interrogation**

questionnaire NOUN
le **questionnaire**

queue NOUN
see also queue VERB
la **queue**

to **queue** VERB
see also queue NOUN
faire la queue
- **to queue for something** faire la queue pour avoir quelque chose ○ *We had to queue for tickets.* Nous avons dû faire la queue pour avoir les billets.

quick ADJECTIVE, ADVERB
rapide ○ *a quick lunch* un déjeuner rapide ○ *It's quicker by train.* C'est plus rapide en train.
- **Be quick!** Dépêche-toi!
- **She's a quick learner.** Elle apprend vite.
- **Quick, phone the police!** Téléphonez vite à la police!

quickly ADVERB
vite ○ *It was all over very quickly.* Ça s'est passé très vite.

quiet ADJECTIVE
1 (*not talkative or noisy*)
silencieux MASC
silencieuse FEM

⋄ *You're very quiet today.* Tu es bien silencieux aujourd'hui. ⋄ *The engine's very quiet.* Le moteur est très silencieux. ② (*peaceful*) **tranquille** ⋄ *a quiet little town* une petite ville tranquille ⋄ *a quiet weekend* un week-end tranquille
- **Be quiet!** Tais-toi!
- **Quiet!** Silence!

quietly ADVERB
① **doucement** (*speak*) ⋄ *"She's dead,"* *he said quietly.* "Elle est morte" dit-il doucement. ② **silencieusement** (*move*) ⋄ *He quietly opened the door.* Il a ouvert la porte sans faire de bruit.

quilt NOUN
la **couette** (*duvet*)

quite ADVERB
① **assez** (*rather*) ⋄ *It's quite warm today.* Il fait assez bon aujourd'hui. ⋄ *I quite liked the film, but...* J'ai trouvé le film assez bon, mais... ② **tout à fait** (*entirely*) ⋄ *I'm not quite sure.* Je n'en suis tout à fait sûr. ⋄ *It's not quite the same.* Ce n'est pas tout à fait la même chose.
- **quite good** pas mal
- **I've been there quite a lot.** J'y suis allé pas mal de fois.
- **quite a lot of money** pas mal d'argent
- **It costs quite a lot to go abroad.** Ça coûte assez cher d'aller à l'étranger.
- **It's quite a long way.** C'est assez loin.
- **It was quite a shock.** Ça a été un sacré choc.
- **There were quite a few people there.** Il y avait pas mal de gens.

quiz NOUN
le **jeu-concours**

quota NOUN
le **quota**

quotation NOUN
la **citation** ⋄ *a quotation from Shakespeare* une citation de Shakespeare

quote NOUN
la **citation** ⋄ *a Shakespeare quote* une citation de Shakespeare
- **quotes** (*quotation marks*) les guillemets MASC ⋄ *in quotes* entre guillemets

Q

R

rabbi NOUN
le **rabbin**

rabbit NOUN
le **lapin**
- **a rabbit hutch** un clapier

rabies NOUN
la **rage**
- **a dog with rabies** un chien enragé

race NOUN

see also race VERB

1 la **course** (*sport*) ⋄ *a cycle race* une course cycliste
2 la **race** (*species*) ⋄ *the human race* la race humaine
- **race relations** les relations interraciales FEM

to **race** VERB

see also race NOUN

1 **courir** ⋄ *We raced to catch the bus.* Nous avons couru pour attraper le bus.
2 **faire la course** (*have a race*)
- **I'll race you!** On fait la course!

racecourse NOUN
le **champ de courses**

racehorse NOUN
le **cheval de course**
(les **chevaux de course** PL)

racer NOUN
le **vélo de course** (*bike*)

racetrack NOUN
la **piste**

racial ADJECTIVE
racial
(**raciaux** MASC PL)
⋄ *racial discrimination* la discrimination raciale

racing car NOUN
la **voiture de course**

racing driver NOUN
le **pilote de course**

racism NOUN
le **racisme**

racist ADJECTIVE

see also racist NOUN

raciste

racist NOUN

see also racist ADJECTIVE

le/la **raciste**

rack NOUN (*for luggage*)
le **porte-bagages**
(les **porte-bagages** PL)

racket NOUN

1 la **raquette** (*for sport*) ⋄ *my tennis racket* ma raquette de tennis
2 le **boucan** (*noise*) ⋄ *They're making a terrible racket.* Ils font un boucan de

tous les diables. (*informal*)

racquet NOUN
la **raquette**

radar NOUN
le **radar**

radiation NOUN
la **radiation**

radiator NOUN
le **radiateur**

radio NOUN
la **radio**
- **on the radio** à la radio
- **a radio station** une station de radio

radioactive ADJECTIVE
radioactif MASC
radioactive FEM

radio cassette NOUN
le **radiocassette**

radio-controlled ADJECTIVE
téléguidé (*model plane, car*)

radish NOUN
le **radis**

RAF NOUN (= *Royal Air Force*)
la **R.A.F.** ⋄ *He's in the RAF.* Il est dans la R.A.F.

raffle NOUN
la **tombola** ⋄ *a raffle ticket* un billet de tombola

raft NOUN
le **radeau**
(les **radeaux** PL)

rag NOUN
le **chiffon** ⋄ *a piece of rag* un chiffon
- **dressed in rags** en haillons

rage NOUN
la **rage** ⋄ *mad with rage* fou de rage
- **to be in a rage** être furieux ⋄ *She was in a rage.* Elle était furieuse.
- **It's all the rage.** Ça fait fureur.

raid NOUN

see also raid VERB

1 (*burglary*)
le **hold-up**
(les **hold-up** PL)
⋄ *There was a bank raid near my house.* Il y a eu un hold-up dans une banque près de chez moi.
2 la **descente** ⋄ *a police raid* une descente de police

to **raid** VERB

see also raid NOUN

faire une descente dans (*police*)
⋄ *The police raided a club in Soho.* La police a fait une descente dans un club de Soho.

rail NOUN

1 la **rampe** (*on stairs*)

2 la **balustrade** (*on bridge, balcony*)
◇ *Don't lean over the rail!* Ne vous penchez pas sur la balustrade!

3 le **rail** (*on railway line*)

- **by rail** en train

railway NOUN
le **chemin de fer** ◇ *the privatization of the railways* la privatisation des chemins de fer

- **a railway line** une ligne de chemin de fer

- **a railway station** une gare

rain NOUN
see also rain VERB
la **pluie** ◇ *in the rain* sous la pluie

to **rain** VERB
see also rain NOUN
pleuvoir ◇ *It rains a lot here.* Il pleut beaucoup par ici.

- **It's raining.** Il pleut.

rainbow NOUN
l' **arc-en-ciel** MASC
(les **arcs-en-ciel** PL)

raincoat NOUN
l' **imperméable** MASC

rainforest NOUN
la **forêt tropicale humide**

rainy ADJECTIVE
pluvieux MASC
pluvieuse FEM

to **raise** NOUN VERB
1 **lever** (*lift*) ◇ *He raised his hand.* Il a levé la main.

2 **améliorer** (*improve*) ◇ *They want to raise standards in schools.* Ils veulent améliorer le niveau dans les écoles.

- **to raise money** collecter des fonds
◇ *The school is raising money for a new gym.* L'école collecte des fonds pour un nouveau gymnase.

raisin NOUN
le **raisin sec**

rake NOUN
le **râteau**
(les **râteaux** PL)

rally NOUN
1 le **rassemblement** (*of people*)

2 le **rallye** (*sport*) ◇ *a rally driver* un pilote de rallye

3 l' **échange** MASC (*in tennis*)

ramble NOUN
la **randonnée** ◇ *to go for a ramble* faire une randonnée

rambler NOUN
le **randonneur**
la **randonneuse**

ramp NOUN
la **rampe d'accès** (*for wheelchairs*)

ran VERB *see* run

ranch NOUN
le **ranch**

random ADJECTIVE

- **a random selection** une sélection effectuée au hasard

- **at random** au hasard ◇ *We picked the number at random.* Nous avons choisi le numéro au hasard.

rang VERB *see* ring

range NOUN
see also range VERB
le **choix** ◇ *There's a wide range of colours.* Il y a un grand choix de coloris.

- **a range of subjects** diverses matières
◇ *We study a range of subjects.* Nous étudions diverses matières.

- **a range of mountains** une chaîne de montagnes

to **range** VERB
see also range NOUN

- **to range from...to** se situer entre...et
◇ *Temperatures in summer range from 20 to 35 degrees.* Les températures estivales se situent entre vingt et trente-cinq degrés.

- **Tickets range from £2 to £20.** Les billets coûtent entre deux et vingt livres.

rank NOUN

- **a taxi rank** une station de taxis

ransom NOUN
la **rançon**

rap NOUN
le **rap** (*music*)

rape NOUN
see also rape VERB
le **viol**

to **rape** VERB
see also rape NOUN
violer

rapids PL NOUN
les **rapides** MASC PL

rapist NOUN
le **violeur**

rare ADJECTIVE
1 **rare** (*unusual*) ◇ *a rare plant* une plante rare

2 **saignant** (*steak*)

rash NOUN
l' **éruption de boutons** FEM ◇ *I've got a rash on my chest.* J'ai une éruption de boutons sur la poitrine.

rasher NOUN
la **tranche** ◇ *an egg and two rashers of bacon* un œuf et deux tranches de bacon

raspberry NOUN

R

la **framboise** ○ *raspberry jam* la confiture de framboises

rat NOUN
le **rat**

rate NOUN
[1] le **tarif** (*price*) ○ *There are reduced rates for students.* Il y a des tarifs réduits pour les étudiants.
[2] le **taux** (*level*) ○ *the divorce rate* le taux de divorce ○ *a high rate of interest* un taux d'intérêt élevé

rather ADVERB
plutôt ○ *I was rather disappointed.* J'étais plutôt déçu. ○ *£20! That's rather a lot!* Vingt livres! C'est plutôt cher!
- **rather a lot of** pas mal de ○ *I've got rather a lot of homework to do.* J'ai pas mal de devoirs à faire.
- **rather than** plutôt que ○ *We decided to camp, rather than stay at a hotel.* Nous avons décidé de camper plutôt que d'aller à l'hôtel.
- **I'd rather...** J'aimerais mieux... ○ *I'd rather stay in tonight.* J'aimerais mieux rester à la maison ce soir. ○ *Would you like a sweet?–I'd rather have an apple.* Tu veux un bonbon?–J'aimerais mieux une pomme.

rattle NOUN
le **hochet** (*for baby*)

rattlesnake NOUN
le **serpent à sonnette**

to **rave** VERB
see also rave NOUN
s'extasier ○ *They raved about the film.* Ils se sont extasiés sur le film.

rave NOUN
see also rave VERB
la **rave** (*party*)
- **rave music** le rave

raven NOUN
le **corbeau**
(les **corbeaux** PL)

ravenous ADJECTIVE
- **to be ravenous** avoir une faim de loup ○ *I'm ravenous!* J'ai une faim de loup!

raving ADJECTIVE
- **raving mad** fou à lier ○ *She's raving mad!* Elle est folle à lier.

raw ADJECTIVE
cru (*food*)
- **raw materials** les matières premières FEM

razor NOUN
le **rasoir** ○ *some disposable razors* des rasoirs jetables
- **a razor blade** une lame de rasoir

RE NOUN

l' **éducation religieuse** FEM

reach NOUN
see also reach VERB
- **out of reach** hors de portée ○ *The light switch was out of reach.* L'interrupteur était hors de portée.
- **within easy reach of** à proximité de ○ *The hotel is within easy reach of the town centre.* L'hôtel se trouve à proximité du centre-ville.

to **reach** VERB
see also reach NOUN
[1] **arriver à** ○ *We reached the hotel at 7 p.m.* Nous sommes arrivés à l'hôtel à sept heures du soir.
- **We hope to reach the final.** Nous espérons aller en finale.
[2] **parvenir à** (*decision*) ○ *Eventually they reached a decision.* Ils sont finalement parvenus à une décision.
- **He reached for his gun.** Il a tendu la main pour prendre son revolver.

to **react** VERB
réagir

reaction NOUN
la **réaction**

reactor NOUN
le **réacteur** ○ *a nuclear reactor* un réacteur nucléaire

to **read** VERB
lire ○ *I don't read much.* Je ne lis pas beaucoup. ○ *Have you read "Animal Farm"?* Est-ce que tu as lu "La ferme des animaux"? ○ *Read the text out loud.* Lis le texte à haute voix.

reader NOUN
(*person*)
le **lecteur**
la **lectrice**

reading NOUN
la **lecture** ○ *Reading is one my hobbies.* La lecture est l'une de mes activités favorites.

ready ADJECTIVE
prêt ○ *She's nearly ready.* Elle est presque prête. ○ *He's always ready to help.* Il est toujours prêt à rendre service.
- **a ready meal** un plat cuisiné
- **to get ready** se préparer ○ *She's getting ready to go out.* Elle est en train de se préparer pour sortir.
- **to get something ready** préparer quelque chose ○ *He's getting the dinner ready.* Il est en train de préparer le dîner.

real ADJECTIVE
[1] **vrai** ○ *He wasn't a real policeman.* Ce n'était pas un vrai policier. ○ *Her*

real name is Cordelia. Son vrai nom est Cordelia.

2 **véritable** ◇ *It's real leather.* C'est du cuir véritable. ◇ *It was a real nightmare.* C'était un véritable cauchemar.

- **in real life** dans la réalité

realistic ADJECTIVE
réaliste

reality NOUN
la **réalité**

to **realize** VERB
- **to realize that...** se rendre compte que... ◇ *We realized that something was wrong.* Nous nous sommes rendu compte que quelque chose n'allait pas.

really ADVERB
vraiment ◇ *She's really nice.* Elle est vraiment sympathique. ◇ *Do you want to go?–Not really.* Tu veux y aller? –Pas vraiment.
- **I'm learning German.–Really?** J'apprends l'allemand.–Ah bon?
- **Do you really think so?** Tu es sûr?

rear ADJECTIVE
see also **rear** NOUN
arrière MASC, FEM, PL ◇ *a rear wheel* une roue arrière

rear NOUN
see also **rear** ADJECTIVE
l' **arrière** MASC ◇ *at the rear of the train* à l'arrière du train

reason NOUN
la **raison** ◇ *There's no reason to think that...* Il n'y a aucune raison de penser que...
- **for security reasons** pour des raisons de sécurité
- **That was the main reason I went.** C'est surtout pour ça que j'y suis allé.

reasonable ADJECTIVE
1 **raisonnable** (*sensible*) ◇ *Be reasonable!* Sois raisonnable!
2 **correct** (*not bad*) ◇ *He wrote a reasonable essay.* Sa dissertation était correcte.

to **reassure** VERB
rassurer

reassuring ADJECTIVE
rassurant

rebellious ADJECTIVE
rebelle

receipt NOUN
le **reçu**

to **receive** VERB
recevoir

receiver NOUN
le **combiné** (*of phone*)
- **to pick up the receiver** décrocher

recent ADJECTIVE
récent

recently ADVERB
ces derniers temps ◇ *I've been doing a lot of training recently.* Je me suis beaucoup entraîné ces derniers temps.

reception NOUN
la **réception** ◇ *Please leave your key at reception.* Merci de laisser votre clé à la réception. ◇ *The reception will be at a big hotel.* La réception aura lieu dans un grand hôtel.

receptionist NOUN
le/la **réceptionniste**

recession NOUN
la **récession**

recipe NOUN
la **recette**

to **reckon** VERB
penser ◇ *What do you reckon?* Qu'est-ce que tu en penses?

reclining ADJECTIVE
- **a reclining seat** un siège inclinable

recognizable ADJECTIVE
reconnaissable

to **recognize** VERB
reconnaître ◇ *You'll recognize me by my red hair.* Vous me reconnaîtrez à mes cheveux roux.

to **recommend** VERB
conseiller ◇ *What do you recommend?* Qu'est-ce que vous me conseillez?

to **reconsider** VERB
reconsidérer

record NOUN
see also **record** VERB
1 le **disque** (*recording*) ◇ *my favourite record* mon disque préféré
2 le **record** (*sport*) ◇ *the world record* le record du monde
- **in record time** en un temps record ◇ *She finished the job in record time.* Elle a terminé le travail en un temps record.
- **a criminal record** un casier judiciaire ◇ *He's got a criminal record.* Il a un casier judiciaire.
- **records** (*of police, hospital*) les archives FEM ◇ *I'll check in the records.* Je vais vérifier dans les archives.
- **There is no record of your booking.** Il n'y a aucune trace de votre réservation.

to **record** VERB
see also **record** NOUN
enregistrer (*on film, tape*) ◇ *They've just recorded their new album.* Ils viennent d'enregistrer leur nouveau disque.

R

recorded delivery NOUN
- **to send something recorded delivery**
envoyer quelque chose en recommandé

recorder NOUN
la **flûte à bec** (*instrument*) ◇ *She plays the recorder.* Elle joue de la flûte à bec.
- **a cassette recorder** un magnétophone à cassettes
- **a video recorder** un magnétoscope

recording NOUN
l' **enregistrement** MASC

record player NOUN
le **tourne-disque**

to **recover** VERB
se remettre ◇ *He's recovering from a knee injury.* Il se remet d'une blessure au genou.

recovery NOUN
le **rétablissement**
- **Best wishes for a speedy recovery!**
Meilleurs vœux de prompt rétablissement!

rectangle NOUN
le **rectangle**

rectangular ADJECTIVE
rectangulaire

to **recycle** VERB
recycler

recycling NOUN
le **recyclage**

red ADJECTIVE
1 **rouge** ◇ *a red rose* une rose rouge
◇ *red meat* la viande rouge
- **a red light** (*traffic light*) un feu rouge
◇ *to go through a red light* brûler un feu rouge
2 (*hair*)
roux MASC
rousse FEM
◇ *Tamsin's got red hair.* Tamsin a les cheveux roux.

Red Cross NOUN
la **Croix-Rouge**

redcurrant NOUN
la **groseille**

to **redecorate** VERB
1 **retapisser** (*with wallpaper*)
2 **refaire les peintures** (*with paint*)

red-haired ADJECTIVE
roux MASC
rousse FEM

red-handed ADJECTIVE
- **to catch somebody red-handed**
prendre quelqu'un la main dans le sac
◇ *He was caught red-handed.* Il a été pris la main dans le sac.

redhead NOUN
le **roux**
la **rousse**

to **redo** VERB
refaire

to **reduce** VERB
réduire ◇ *at a reduced price* à prix réduit
- **"reduce speed now"** "ralentir"

reduction NOUN
la **réduction** ◇ *a 5% reduction* une réduction de cinq pour cent
- **"huge reductions!"** "prix sacrifiés!"

redundancy NOUN
le **licenciement** ◇ *There were fifty redundancies.* Il y a eu cinquante licenciements.
- **his redundancy payment** ses indemnités de licenciement

redundant ADJECTIVE
- **to be made redundant** être licencié
◇ *He was made redundant yesterday.* Il a été licencié hier.

reed NOUN
(*plant*)
le **roseau**
(les **roseaux** PL)

reel NOUN
la **bobine** (*of thread*)

to **refer** VERB
- **to refer to** faire allusion à ◇ *What are you referring to?* À quoi faites-vous allusion?

referee NOUN
l' **arbitre** MASC

reference NOUN
1 l' **allusion** FEM ◇ *He made no reference to the murder.* Il n'a fait aucune allusion au meurtre.
2 les **références** FEM (*for job application*)
◇ *Would you please give me a reference?* Pouvez-vous me fournir des références?
- **a reference book** un ouvrage de référence

to **refill** VERB
remplir à nouveau ◇ *He refilled my glass.* Il a rempli mon verre à nouveau.

refinery NOUN
la **raffinerie**

to **reflect** VERB
refléter (*light, image*)

reflection NOUN
le **reflet** (*in mirror*)

reflex NOUN
le **réflexe**

reflexive ADJECTIVE
réfléchi ◇ *a reflexive verb* un verbe réfléchi

refresher course NOUN
le **cours de recyclage**

refreshing ADJECTIVE

rafraîchissant

refreshments PL NOUN
les **rafraîchissements** MASC PL

refrigerator NOUN
le **réfrigérateur**

to **refuel** VERB
se ravitailler en carburant ◇ *The plane stops in Boston to refuel.* L'avion s'arrête à Boston pour se ravitailler en carburant.

refuge NOUN
le **refuge**

refugee NOUN
le **réfugié**
la **réfugiée**

refund NOUN
see also refund VERB
le **remboursement**

to **refund** VERB
see also refund NOUN
rembourser

refusal NOUN
le **refus**

to **refuse** VERB
see also refuse NOUN
refuser

refuse NOUN
see also refuse VERB
les **ordures** FEM
- **refuse collection** le ramassage des ordures

to **regain** VERB
- **to regain consciousness** reprendre connaissance

regard NOUN
see also regard VERB
- **Give my regards to Alice.** Transmettez mon bon souvenir à Alice.
- **Louis sends his regards.** Vous avez le bonjour de Louis.
- **"with kind regards"** "bien cordialement"

to **regard** VERB
see also regard NOUN
- **to regard something as** considérer quelque chose comme
- **as regards...** concernant...

regarding PREPOSITION
relatif à MASC
relative à FEM
◇ *the laws regarding the export of animals* les lois relatives à l'exportation des animaux
- **Regarding John,...** Quant à John,...

regiment NOUN
le **régiment**

region NOUN
la **région**

regional ADJECTIVE

régional
(**régionaux** PL)

register NOUN
see also register VERB
le **registre d'absences** (*in school*)

to **register** VERB
see also register NOUN
s'inscrire (*at school, college*)

registered ADJECTIVE
- **a registered letter** une lettre recommandée

registration NOUN
1 l' **appel** MASC (*roll call*)
2 le **numéro d'immatriculation** (*of car*)

regret NOUN
see also regret VERB
le **regret**
- **I've got no regrets.** Je ne regrette rien.

to **regret** VERB
see also regret NOUN
regretter ◇ *Give me the money or you'll regret it!* Donne-moi l'argent, sinon tu vas le regretter!
- **to regret doing something** regretter d'avoir fait quelque chose ◇ *I regret saying that.* Je regrette d'avoir dit ça.

regular ADJECTIVE
1 **régulier** MASC
régulière FEM
◇ *at regular intervals* à intervalles réguliers ◇ *a regular verb* un verbe régulier
- **to take regular exercise** faire régulièrement de l'exercice
2 (*average*)
normal
(**normaux** PL)
◇ *a regular portion of fries* une portion de frites normale

regularly ADVERB
régulièrement

regulation NOUN
le **règlement**

rehearsal NOUN
la **répétition**

to **rehearse** VERB
répéter

rein NOUN
la **rêne** ◇ *the reins* les rênes

reindeer NOUN
le **renne**

to **reject** VERB
rejeter (*idea, suggestion*) ◇ *We rejected that idea straight away.* Nous avons immédiatement rejeté cette idée.
- **I applied but they rejected me.** J'ai posé ma candidature mais ils l'ont

R

rejetée.

relapse NOUN

la **rechute** ◇ to have a relapse faire une rechute

related ADJECTIVE

apparenté (people) ◇ We're related. Nous sommes apparentés.

- **The two events were not related.** Il n'y avait aucun rapport entre les deux événements.

relation NOUN

[1] (person)

le **parent**

la **parente**

◇ He's a distant relation. C'est un parent éloigné. ◇ my close relations mes parents proches

Remember that in French, mes parents usually only refers to your mother and father.

- **my relations** ma famille
- **I've got relations in London.** J'ai de la famille à Londres.

[2] (connection)

le **rapport** ◇ It has no relation to reality. Cela n'a aucun rapport avec la réalité.

- **in relation to** par rapport à

relationship NOUN

les **relations** FEM PL ◇ We have a good relationship. Nous avons de bonnes relations.

- **I'm not in a relationship at the moment.** Je ne sors avec personne en ce moment.

relative NOUN

le **parent**

la **parente**

◇ my close relatives mes proches parents

- **all her relatives** toute sa famille

relatively ADVERB

relativement

to **relax** VERB

se détendre ◇ I relax listening to music. Je me détends en écoutant de la musique.

- **Relax! Everything's fine.** Ne t'en fais pas! Tout va bien.

relaxation NOUN

la **détente** ◇ I don't have much time for relaxation. Je n'ai pas beaucoup de moments de détente.

relaxed ADJECTIVE

détendu

relaxing ADJECTIVE

reposant

- **I find cooking relaxing.** Cela me détend de faire la cuisine.

relay NOUN

- **a relay race** une course de relais

to **release** VERB

see also release NOUN

[1] **libérer** (prisoner)

[2] **divulguer** (report, news)

[3] **sortir** (record, video)

release NOUN

see also release VERB

la **libération** (from prison) ◇ the release of Nelson Mandela la libération de Nelson Mandela

- **the band's latest release** le dernier disque du groupe

relegated ADJECTIVE

déclassé (sport)

relevant ADJECTIVE

approprié (documents)

- **That's not relevant.** Ça n'a aucun rapport.
- **to be relevant to something** être en rapport avec quelque chose

◇ Education should be relevant to real life. L'enseignement devrait être en rapport avec la réalité.

reliable ADJECTIVE

fiable ◇ a reliable car une voiture fiable ◇ He's not very reliable. Il n'est pas très fiable.

relief NOUN

le **soulagement** ◇ That's a relief! Quel soulagement!

to **relieve** VERB

soulager ◇ This injection will relieve the pain. Cette piqûre va soulager la douleur.

relieved ADJECTIVE

soulagé ◇ I was relieved to hear... J'ai été soulagé d'apprendre...

religion NOUN

la **religion** ◇ What religion are you? Quelle est votre religion?

religious ADJECTIVE

[1] **religieux** MASC

religieuse FEM

◇ my religious beliefs mes croyances religieuses

[2] **croyant** ◇ I'm not religious. Je ne suis pas croyant.

reluctant ADJECTIVE

- **to be reluctant to do something** être peu disposé à faire quelque chose

◇ They were reluctant to help us. Ils étaient peu disposés à nous aider.

reluctantly ADVERB

à contrecœur ◇ She reluctantly accepted. Elle a accepté à contrecœur.

to **rely on** VERB

compter sur ◇ I'm relying on you. Je compte sur toi.

to **remain** VERB
> **rester**
- **to remain silent** garder le silence

remaining ADJECTIVE
> **le reste de** ◦ *the remaining ingredients* le reste des ingrédients

remains PL NOUN
> les **restes** MASC PL ◦ *the remains of the picnic* les restes du pique-nique
> ◦ *human remains* des restes humains
- **Roman remains** les ruines romaines

remake NOUN
> le **remake** (*of film*)

remark NOUN
> la **remarque**

remarkable ADJECTIVE
> **remarquable**

remarkably ADVERB
> **remarquablement**

to **remarry** VERB
> **se remarier** ◦ *She remarried three years ago.* Elle s'est remariée il y a trois ans.

remedy NOUN
> le **remède** ◦ *a good remedy for a sore throat* un bon remède contre le mal de gorge

to **remember** VERB
> **se souvenir de** ◦ *I can't remember his name.* Je ne me souviens pas de son nom. ◦ *I don't remember.* Je ne m'en souviens pas.
> *In French you often say "don't forget" instead of remember.*
> ◦ *Remember your passport!* N'oublie pas ton passeport! ◦ *Remember to write your name on the form.* N'oubliez pas d'écrire votre nom sur le formulaire.

Remembrance Day NOUN
> le **jour de l'Armistice** MASC ◦ *on Remembrance Day* le jour de l'Armistice

to **remind** VERB
> **rappeler** ◦ *It reminds me of Scotland.* Cela me rappelle l'Écosse. ◦ *I'll remind you tomorrow.* Je te le rappellerai demain. ◦ *Remind me to speak to Daniel.* Rappelle-moi de parler à Daniel.

remorse NOUN
> le **remords** ◦ *He showed no remorse.* Il a manifesté aucun remords.

remote ADJECTIVE
> **isolé** ◦ *a remote village* un village isolé

remote control NOUN
> la **télécommande**

removable ADJECTIVE
> **amovible**

removal NOUN
> le **déménagement** (*from house*)
- **a removal van** un camion de déménagement

to **remove** VERB
> ⓵ **enlever** ◦ *Please remove your bag from my seat.* Est-ce que vous pouvez enlever votre sac de mon siège?
> ⓶ **faire partir** (*stain*) ◦ *Did you remove the stain?* Est-ce que tu as fait partir la tache?

rendezvous NOUN
> le **rendez-vous**
> (les **rendez-vous** PL)

to **renew** VERB
> **renouveler** (*passport, licence*)

renewable ADJECTIVE
> **renouvelable** (*energy, resource*)

to **renovate** VERB
> **rénover** ◦ *The building's been renovated.* Le bâtiment a été rénové.

renowned ADJECTIVE
> **renommé**

rent NOUN
> *see also* rent VERB
> le **loyer**

to **rent** VERB
> *see also* rent NOUN
> **louer** ◦ *We rented a car.* Nous avons loué une voiture.

rental NOUN
> la **location** ◦ *Car rental is included in the price.* Le prix comprends la location d'une voiture.

to **reorganize** VERB
> **réorganiser**

rep NOUN (= *representative*)
> le **représentant**
> la **représentante**

to **repair** VERB
> *see also* repair NOUN
> **réparer**
- **to get something repaired** faire réparer quelque chose ◦ *I got the washing machine repaired.* J'ai fait réparer la machine à laver.

repair NOUN
> *see also* repair VERB
> la **réparation**

to **repay** VERB
> **rembourser** (*money*)

repayment NOUN
> le **remboursement**

to **repeat** VERB
> *see also* repeat NOUN
> **répéter**

repeat NOUN
> *see also* repeat VERB
> la **reprise** ◦ *There are too many repeats on TV.* Il y a trop de reprises à

la télé.

repeatedly ADVERB
  à plusieurs reprises

repellent NOUN
- **insect repellent** l'insectifuge MASC

repetitive ADJECTIVE
  (movement, work)
  répétitif MASC
  répétitive FEM

to **replace** VERB
  remplacer

replay NOUN
  see also replay VERB
- **There will be a replay on Friday.** Le match sera rejoué vendredi.

to **replay** VERB
  see also replay NOUN
  rejouer (match)

replica NOUN
  la **réplique**

reply NOUN
  see also reply VERB
  la **réponse**

to **reply** VERB
  see also reply NOUN
  répondre

report NOUN
  see also report VERB
  [1] le **compte rendu** (of event)
  [2] le **reportage** (news report) ◇ a report in the paper un reportage dans le journal
  [3] le **bulletin scolaire** (at school) ◇ I got a good report this term. J'ai un bon bulletin scolaire ce trimestre.

to **report** VERB
  see also report NOUN
  [1] **signaler** ◇ I reported the theft to the police. J'ai signalé le vol au commissariat.
  [2] **se présenter** ◇ Report to reception when you arrive. Présentez-vous à la réception à votre arrivée.

reporter NOUN
  le **reporter** ◇ I'd like to be a reporter. J'aimerais être reporter.

to **represent** VERB
  représenter

representative ADJECTIVE
  représentatif MASC
  représentative FEM

reproduction NOUN
  la **reproduction**

republic NOUN
  la **république**

repulsive ADJECTIVE
  repoussant

reputation NOUN
  la **réputation**

request NOUN
  see also request VERB
  la **demande**

to **request** VERB
  see also request NOUN
  demander

requirement NOUN
  la **condition requise**
- **What are the requirements for the job?** Quelles sont les conditions requises pour le poste?
- **entry requirements** (for university) les critères d'entrée

to **rescue** VERB
  see also rescue NOUN
  sauver

rescue NOUN
  see also rescue VERB
  [1] le **sauvetage** ◇ a rescue operation une opération de sauvetage
- **a mountain rescue team** une équipe de sauvetage en montagne
  [2] le **secours** ◇ the rescue services les services de secours
- **to come to somebody's rescue** venir au secours de quelqu'un ◇ He came to my rescue. Il est venu à mon secours.

research NOUN
  [1] la **recherche** (experimental) ◇ He's doing research. Il fait de la recherche.
  [2] les **recherches** FEM PL (theoretical) ◇ She's doing some research in the library. Elle fait des recherches à la bibliothèque.

resemblance NOUN
  la **ressemblance**

reservation NOUN
  la **réservation** (booking) ◇ I've got a reservation for two nights. J'ai une réservation pour deux nuits. ◇ I'd like to make a reservation for this evening. J'aimerais faire une réservation pour ce soir.

reserve NOUN
  see also reserve VERB
  [1] (place)
  la **réserve** ◇ a nature reserve une réserve naturelle
  [2] (person)
  le **remplaçant**
  la **remplaçante**
  ◇ I was reserve in the game last Saturday. J'étais remplaçant dans le match de samedi dernier.

to **reserve** VERB
  see also reserve NOUN
  réserver ◇ I'd like to reserve a table for tomorrow evening. J'aimerais réserver une table pour demain soir.

reserved ADJECTIVE

  réservé ◇ *a reserved seat* une place réservée ◇ *He's quite reserved.* Il est assez réservé.

resident NOUN

  le **résident**

  la **résidente**

residential ADJECTIVE

  résidentiel MASC

  résidentielle FEM

  ◇ *a residential area* un quartier résidentiel

to **resign** VERB

  donner sa démission

resistance NOUN

- **He was in the resistance.** Il faisait de la résistance.
- **the French Resistance** la Résistance

to **resit** VERB

  repasser ◇ *I'm resitting the exam in December.* Je vais repasser l'examen en décembre.

resolution NOUN

  la **résolution**

- **Have you made any new year's resolutions?** Tu as pris de bonnes résolutions pour l'année nouvelle?

resort NOUN

  la **station balnéaire** (*at seaside*) ◇ *It's a resort on the Costa del Sol.* C'est une station balnéaire sur la Costa del Sol.

- **a ski resort** une station de ski
- **as a last resort** en dernier recours

resource NOUN

  la **ressource**

respect NOUN

  see also respect VERB

  le **respect**

to **respect** VERB

  see also respect NOUN

  respecter

respectable ADJECTIVE

  [1] **respectable**

  [2] **correct** (*standard, marks*)

respectively ADVERB

  respectivement

responsibility NOUN

  la **responsabilité**

responsible ADJECTIVE

  [1] (*in charge*)

  responsable

- **to be responsible for something** être responsable de quelque chose ◇ *He's responsible for booking the tickets.* Il est responsable de la réservation des billets.
- **It's a responsible job.** C'est un poste à responsabilités.

  [2] (*mature*)

  sérieux MASC

  sérieuse FEM

  ◇ *You should be more responsible.* Tu devrais être un peu plus sérieux.

rest NOUN

  see also rest VERB

  [1] le **repos** (*relaxation*) ◇ *five minutes' rest* cinq minutes de repos

- **to have a rest** se reposer ◇ *We stopped to have a rest.* Nous nous sommes arrêtés pour nous reposer.

  [2] le **reste** (*remainder*) ◇ *I'll do the rest.* Je ferai le reste. ◇ *the rest of the money* le reste de l'argent

- **the rest of them** les autres ◇ *The rest of them went swimming.* Les autres sont allés nager.

to **rest** VERB

  see also rest NOUN

  [1] **se reposer** (*relax*) ◇ *She's resting in her room.* Elle se repose dans sa chambre.

  [2] **ménager** (*not overstrain*) ◇ *He has to rest his knee.* Il doit ménager son genou.

  [3] **appuyer** (*lean*) ◇ *I rested my bike against the window.* J'ai appuyé mon vélo contre la fenêtre.

restaurant NOUN

  le **restaurant** ◇ *We don't often go to restaurants.* Nous n'allons pas souvent au restaurant.

- **a restaurant car** un wagon-restaurant

restful ADJECTIVE

  reposant

restoration NOUN

  la **restauration**

to **restore** VERB

  restaurer (*building, picture*)

to **restrict** VERB

  limiter

result NOUN

  le **résultat** ◇ *my exam results* mes résultats d'examen ◇ *What was the result? One nil.* Quel a été le résultat? –Un à zéro.

to **retire** VERB

  prendre sa retraite ◇ *He retired last year.* Il a pris sa retraite l'an dernier.

retired ADJECTIVE

  retraité ◇ *She's retired.* Elle est retraitée.

- **a retired teacher** un professeur à la retraite

retirement NOUN

  la **retraite**

to **retrace** VERB

- **to retrace one's steps** revenir sur ses pas ◇ *I retraced my steps.* Je suis revenu sur mes pas.

R

return NOUN

> see also return VERB
>
> ☐1 le **retour** ◇ *after our return* à notre retour
- **the return journey** le voyage de retour
- **a return match** un match retour
> ☐2 l' **aller retour** MASC (*ticket*) ◇ *A return to Avignon, please.* Un aller retour pour Avignon, s'il vous plaît.
- **in return** en échange ◇ *...and I help her in return* ...et je l'aide en échange
- **in return for** en échange de
- **Many happy returns!** Bon anniversaire!

to **return** VERB

> see also return NOUN
>
> ☐1 **revenir** (*come back*) ◇ *I've just returned from holiday.* Je viens de revenir de vacances.
- **to return home** rentrer à la maison
> ☐2 **retourner** (*go back*) ◇ *He returned to France the following year.* Il est retourné en France l'année suivante.
> ☐3 **rendre** (*give back*) ◇ *She borrows my things and doesn't return them.* Elle m'emprunte mes affaires et ne me les rend pas.

reunion NOUN
> la **réunion**

to **reuse** VERB
> **réutiliser**

to **reveal** VERB
> **révéler**

revenge NOUN
> la **vengeance** ◇ *in revenge* par vengeance
- **to take revenge** se venger ◇ *They planned to take revenge on him.* Ils voulaient se venger de lui.

to **reverse** VERB

> see also reverse ADJECTIVE
>
> **faire marche arrière** (*car*) ◇ *He reversed without looking.* Il a fait marche arrière sans regarder.
- **to reverse the charges** (*telephone*) appeler en PCV
> *In France, reversing the charges is only possible for international calls.*
> ◇ *I'd like to make a reverse charge call to Britain.* Je voudrais appeler la Grande-Bretagne en PCV.

reverse ADJECTIVE

> see also reverse VERB
>
> **inverse** ◇ *in reverse order* dans l'ordre inverse
- **in reverse gear** en marche arrière

to **revise** VERB
> **réviser** ◇ *I haven't started revising yet.* Je n'ai pas encore commencé à réviser.
- **I've revised my opinion.** J'ai changé d'opinion.

revision NOUN
> les **révisions** FEM PL ◇ *Have you done a lot of revision?* Est-ce que tu as fait beaucoup de révisions?

to **revive** VERB
> **ranimer** ◇ *The nurses tried to revive him.* Les infirmières ont essayé de le ranimer.

revolting ADJECTIVE
> **dégoûtant**

revolution NOUN
> la **révolution**
- **the French Revolution** la Révolution française

revolutionary ADJECTIVE
> **révolutionnaire**

revolver NOUN
> le **revolver**

reward NOUN
> la **récompense**

rewarding ADJECTIVE
> **gratifiant** ◇ *a rewarding job* un travail gratifiant

to **rewind** VERB
> **rembobiner** ◇ *to rewind a cassette* rembobiner une cassette

rheumatism NOUN
> le **rhumatisme**

Rhine NOUN
> le **Rhin**

Rhone NOUN
> le **Rhône**

rhubarb NOUN
> la **rhubarbe** ◇ *a rhubarb tart* une tarte à la rhubarbe

rhythm NOUN
> le **rythme**

rib NOUN
> la **côte**

ribbon NOUN
> le **ruban**

rice NOUN
> le **riz**
- **rice pudding** le riz au lait

rich ADJECTIVE
> **riche**
- **the rich** les riches MASC

to **rid** VERB
- **to get rid of** se débarrasser de ◇ *I want to get rid of some old clothes.* Je veux me débarrasser de vieux vêtements.

ride NOUN

> see also ride VERB
- **to go for a ride (1)** (*on horse*) monter à cheval
- **to go for a ride (2)** (*on bike*) faire un tour en vélo ◇ *We went for a bike ride.*

Nous sommes allés faire un tour en vélo.
- **It's a short bus ride to the town centre.** Ce n'est pas loin du centre-ville en bus.

to **ride** VERB

see also ride NOUN

monter à cheval (on horse) ◇ *I'm learning to ride.* J'apprends à monter à cheval.
- **to ride a bike** faire du vélo ◇ *Can you ride a bike?* Tu sais faire du vélo?

rider NOUN

1 (on horse)
le **cavalier**
la **cavalière**
◇ *She's a good rider.* C'est une bonne cavalière.
2 (on bike)
le/la **cycliste**

ridiculous ADJECTIVE

ridicule ◇ *Don't be ridiculous!* Ne sois pas ridicule!

riding NOUN

l' **équitation** FEM
- **to go riding** faire de l'équitation
- **a riding school** une école d'équitation

rifle NOUN

le **fusil** ◇ *a hunting rifle* un fusil de chasse

rig NOUN
- **an oil rig** une plate-forme pétrolière

right ADJECTIVE, ADVERB

see also right NOUN

There are several ways of translating right. *Scan the examples to find one that is similar to what you want to say.*

1 (factually correct, suitable)
bon MASC
bonne FEM
◇ *the right answer* la bonne réponse ◇ *It isn't the right size.* Ce n'est pas la bonne taille. ◇ *We're on the right train.* Nous sommes dans le bon train.
- **Is this the right road for Arles?** Est-ce que c'est bien la route pour aller à Arles?
2 (correctly)
correctement ◇ *Am I pronouncing it right?* Est-ce que je prononce ça correctement?
- **to be right (1)** (person) avoir raison ◇ *You were right!* Tu avais raison!
- **to be right (2)** (statement, opinion) être vrai ◇ *That's right!* C'est vrai!
3 (accurate)
juste ◇ *Do you have the right time?* Est-ce que vous avez l'heure juste?
4 (morally correct)
bien ◇ *It's not right to behave like that.* Ce n'est pas bien d'agir comme ça.

- **I think you did the right thing.** Je pense que tu as bien fait.
5 (not left)
droit ◇ *my right hand* ma main droite
6 (turn, look)
à droite ◇ *Turn right at the traffic lights.* Tournez à droite aux prochains feux.
- **Right! Let's get started.** Bon! On commence.
- **right away** tout de suite ◇ *I'll do it right away.* Je vais le faire tout de suite.

right NOUN

see also right ADJECTIVE

1 le **droit**
- **You've got no right to do that.** Vous n'avez pas le droit de faire ça.
2 la **droite** (not left)
- **on the right** à droite ◇ *Remember to drive on the right.* N'oubliez pas de conduire à droite.
- **right of way** la priorité ◇ *It was our right of way.* Nous avions la priorité.

right-hand ADJECTIVE
- **the right-hand side** la droite ◇ *It's on the right-hand side.* C'est à droite.

right-handed ADJECTIVE

droitier MASC
droitière FEM

rim NOUN

la **monture** ◇ *glasses with wire rims* des lunettes avec une monture métallique

ring NOUN

see also ring VERB

1 l' **anneau** MASC
(les **anneaux** PL)
◇ *a gold ring* un anneau en or
2 la **bague** (with stones) ◇ *a diamond ring* une bague de diamants
- **a wedding ring** une alliance
3 le **cercle** (circle) ◇ *to stand in a ring* se mettre en cercle
4 le **coup de sonnette** (of bell) ◇ *I was woken by a ring at the door.* J'ai été réveillé par un coup de sonnette.
- **to give somebody a ring** appeler quelqu'un ◇ *I'll give you a ring this evening.* Je t'appellerai ce soir.

to **ring** VERB

see also ring NOUN

1 **téléphoner** ◇ *Your mother rang this morning.* Ta mère a téléphoné ce matin.
- **to ring somebody** appeler quelqu'un ◇ *I'll ring you tomorrow morning.* Je t'appellerai demain matin.
- **to ring somebody up** donner un coup

R

de fil à quelqu'un
2 **sonner** ◇ *The phone's ringing.* Le téléphone sonne.
- **to ring the bell** (*doorbell*) sonner à la porte ◇ *I rang the bell three times.* J'ai sonné trois fois à la porte.
- **to ring back** rappeler ◇ *I'll ring back later.* Je rappellerai plus tard.
ring binder NOUN
le **classeur**
ring road NOUN
1 la **rocade** (*ordinary road*)
2 le **périphérique** (*motorway*)
rink NOUN
1 la **patinoire** (*for ice-skating*)
2 la **piste** (*for roller-skating*)
to **rinse** VERB
rincer
riot NOUN
see also riot VERB
l' **émeute** FEM
to **riot** VERB
see also riot NOUN
faire une émeute
to **rip** VERB
1 **déchirer** ◇ *I've ripped my jeans.* J'ai déchiré mon jean.
2 **se déchirer** ◇ *My skirt's ripped.* Ma jupe s'est déchirée.
ripe ADJECTIVE
mûr
rip-off NOUN
- **It's a rip-off!** C'est de l'arnaque! (*informal*)
rise NOUN
see also rise VERB
1 la **hausse** (*in prices, temperature*) ◇ *a sudden rise in temperature* une hausse subite de température
2 l' **augmentation** FEM (*pay rise*)
to **rise** VERB
see also rise NOUN
1 **augmenter** (*increase*) ◇ *Prices are rising.* Les prix augmentent.
2 **se lever** ◇ *The sun rises early in June.* Le soleil se lève tôt en juin.
riser NOUN
- **to be an early riser** être matinal
risk NOUN
see also risk VERB
le **risque**
- **to take risks** prendre des risques
- **It's at your own risk.** C'est à vos risques et périls.
to **risk** VERB
see also risk NOUN
risquer ◇ *You risk getting a fine.* Vous risquez de recevoir une amende.
- **I wouldn't risk it if I were you.** À votre

place, je ne prendrais pas ce risque.
risky ADJECTIVE
risqué
rival NOUN
see also rival ADJECTIVE
le **rival**
(les **rivaux** PL)
la **rivale**
rival ADJECTIVE
see also rival NOUN
1 **rival** ◇ *a rival gang* une bande rivale
2 **concurrent** ◇ *a rival company* une société concurrente
rivalry NOUN
la **rivalité** (*between towns, schools*)
river NOUN
1 la **rivière** ◇ *The river runs alongside the canal.* La rivière longe le canal.
2 le **fleuve** (*major*) ◇ *the rivers of France* les fleuves de France
- **the river Seine** la Seine
Riviera NOUN
- **the French Riviera** la Côte d'Azur
- **the Italian Riviera** la Riviera italienne
road NOUN
1 la **route** ◇ *There's a lot of traffic on the roads.* Il y a beaucoup de circulation sur les routes.
2 la **rue** (*street*) ◇ *They live across the road.* Ils habitent de l'autre côté de la rue.
road map NOUN
la **carte routière**
road sign NOUN
le **panneau de signalisation**
(les **panneaux de signalisation** PL)
roadworks PL NOUN
les **travaux** MASC PL
roast ADJECTIVE
rôti ◇ *roast chicken* le poulet rôti ◇ *roast potatoes* les pommes de terre rôties
- **roast pork** le rôti de porc
- **roast beef** le rôti de bœuf
to **rob** VERB
- **to rob somebody** voler quelqu'un ◇ *I've been robbed.* On m'a volé.
- **to rob somebody of something** voler quelque chose à quelqu'un ◇ *He was robbed of his wallet.* On lui a volé son portefeuille.
- **to rob a bank** dévaliser une banque
robber NOUN
le **voleur**
- **a bank-robber** un cambrioleur de banques
robbery NOUN

le **vol**
- **a bank robbery** un hold-up
- **armed robbery** le vol à main armée

robot NOUN
le **robot**

rock NOUN
1. la **roche** (*substance*) ◇ *They tunnelled through the rock.* Ils ont creusé un tunnel dans la roche.
2. le **rocher** (*boulder*) ◇ *I sat on a rock.* Je me suis assis sur un rocher.
3. la **pierre** (*stone*) ◇ *The crowd started to throw rocks.* La foule s'est mise à lancer des pierres.
4. le **rock** (*music*) ◇ *a rock concert* un concert de rock ◇ *He's a rock star.* C'est une rock star.
5. le **sucre d'orge** (*sweet*) ◇ *a stick of rock* un bâton de sucre d'orge
- **rock and roll** le rock'n'roll

rockery NOUN
la **rocaille**

rocket NOUN
la **fusée** (*firework, spacecraft*)

rocking chair NOUN
le **rocking-chair**

rocking horse NOUN
le **cheval à bascule**

rod NOUN
la **canne à pêche** (*for fishing*)

rode VERB *see* **ride**

role NOUN
le **rôle**

role play NOUN
le **jeu de rôle**
(les **jeux de rôles** PL)
◇ *to do a role play* faire un jeu de rôle

roll NOUN
see also **roll** VERB
1. le **rouleau**
(les **rouleaux** PL)
◇ *a roll of tape* un rouleau de ruban adhésif ◇ *a toilet roll* un rouleau de papier hygiénique
2. le **petit pain** (*bread*)

to **roll** VERB
see also **roll** NOUN
rouler
- **to roll out the pastry** abaisser la pâte

roll call NOUN
l' **appel** MASC

roller NOUN
le **rouleau**
(les **rouleaux** PL)

rollercoaster NOUN
les **montagnes russes** FEM PL

roller skates PL NOUN
les **patins à roulettes** MASC

roller-skating NOUN

le **patin à roulettes**
- **to go roller-skating** faire du patin à roulettes

rolling pin NOUN
le **rouleau à pâtisserie**

Roman ADJECTIVE, NOUN
romain (*ancient*) ◇ *a Roman villa* une villa romaine ◇ *the Roman empire* l'empire romain
- **the Romans** les Romains

Roman Catholic NOUN
le/la **catholique** ◇ *He's a Roman Catholic.* Il est catholique.

romance NOUN
1. les **romans d'amour** MASC PL (*novels*) ◇ *I read a lot of romance.* Je lis beaucoup de romans d'amour.
2. le **charme** (*glamour*) ◇ *the romance of Paris* le charme de Paris
- **a holiday romance** une idylle de vacances

Romania NOUN
la **Roumanie**
- **in Romania** en Roumanie

Romanian ADJECTIVE
roumain

romantic ADJECTIVE
romantique

roof NOUN
le **toit**

roof rack NOUN
la **galerie**

room NOUN
1. la **pièce** ◇ *the biggest room in the house* la plus grande pièce de la maison
2. la **chambre** (*bedroom*) ◇ *She's in her room.* Elle est dans sa chambre.
- **a single room** une chambre pour une personne
- **a double room** une chambre pour deux personnes
3. la **salle** (*in school*) ◇ *the music room* la salle de musique
4. la **place** (*space*) ◇ *There's no room for that box.* Il n'y a pas de place pour cette boîte.

roommate NOUN
le/la **camarade de chambre**

root NOUN
la **racine**

rope NOUN
la **corde**

rose VERB *see* **rise**

rose NOUN
la **rose** (*flower*)

to **rot** NOUN VERB
pourrir

rotten ADJECTIVE
pourri (*decayed*) ◇ *a rotten apple* une

pomme pourrie
- **rotten weather** un temps pourri
- **That's a rotten thing to do.** Ce n'est vraiment pas gentil.
- **to feel rotten** être mal fichu (*informal*)

rough ADJECTIVE

1 (*surface*)
rêche ◦ *My hands are rough.* J'ai les mains rêches.

2 (*game*)
violent ◦ *Rugby's a rough sport.* Le rugby est un sport violent.

3 (*place*)
difficile ◦ *It's a rough area.* C'est un quartier difficile.

4 (*water*)
houleux MASC
houleuse FEM
◦ *The sea was rough.* La mer était houleuse.

5 **approximatif** MASC
approximative FEM
- **I've got a rough idea.** J'en ai une idée approximative.
- **to feel rough** ne pas être dans son assiette ◦ *I feel rough.* Je ne suis pas dans mon assiette.

roughly ADVERB
à peu près ◦ *It weighs roughly 20 kilos.* Ça pèse à peu près vingt kilos.

round ADJECTIVE, ADVERB, PREPOSITION
see also **round** NOUN

1 **rond** ◦ *a round table* une table ronde

2 **autour de** (*around*) ◦ *We were sitting round the table.* Nous étions assis autour de la table. ◦ *She wore a scarf round her neck.* Elle portait une écharpe autour du cou.

- **It's just round the corner.** (*very near*) C'est tout près.
- **to go round to somebody's house** aller chez quelqu'un ◦ *I went round to my friend's house.* Je suis allé chez mon ami.
- **to have a look round** faire un tour ◦ *We're going to have a look round.* Nous allons faire un tour.
- **to go round a museum** visiter un musée
- **round here** près d'ici ◦ *Is there a chemist's round here?* Est-ce qu'il y a une pharmacie près d'ici?
- **He lives round here.** Il habite dans les parages.
- **all round** partout ◦ *There were vineyards all round.* Il y avait des vignobles partout.
- **all year round** toute l'année

- **round about** (*roughly*) environ ◦ *It costs round about £100.* Cela coûte environ cent livres. ◦ *round about 8 o'clock* à huit heures environ

round NOUN
see also **round** ADJECTIVE

1 la **manche** (*of tournament*)

2 le **round** (*of boxing match*)

- **a round of golf** une partie de golf
- **a round of drinks** une tournée ◦ *He bought a round of drinks.* Il a offert une tournée.

roundabout NOUN

1 le **rond-point** (*at junction*)

2 le **manège** (*at funfair*)

route NOUN

1 l' **itinéraire** MASC ◦ *We're planning our route.* Nous établissons notre itinéraire.

2 le **parcours** (*of bus*)

routine NOUN

- **my daily routine** mes occupations quotidiennes

row NOUN
see also **row** VERB

1 la **rangée** ◦ *a row of houses* une rangée de maisons

2 le **rang** (*of seats*) ◦ *Our seats are in the front row.* Nos places se trouvent au premier rang.

- **five times in a row** cinq fois d'affilée

3 le **vacarme** (*noise*) ◦ *What's that terrible row?* Qu'est-ce que c'est que ce vacarme?

4 la **dispute** (*quarrel*)

- **to have a row** se disputer ◦ *They've had a row.* Ils se sont disputés.

to **row** VERB
see also **row** NOUN

1 **ramer** ◦ *We took turns to row.* Nous avons ramé à tour de rôle.

2 **faire de l'aviron** (*as sport*)

rowing NOUN
l' **aviron** MASC (*sport*) ◦ *My hobby is rowing.* Je fais de l'aviron.

- **a rowing boat** un bateau à rames

royal ADJECTIVE
royal
(**royaux** MASC PL)

- **the royal family** la famille royale

to **rub** VERB

1 **frotter** (*stain*)

2 **se frotter** (*part of body*) ◦ *Don't rub your eyes!* Ne te frotte pas les yeux!

- **to rub something out** effacer quelque chose

rubber NOUN

1 le **caoutchouc** ◦ *rubber soles* des semelles en caoutchouc

2 la **gomme** (*eraser*) ◇ *Can I borrow your rubber?* Je peux emprunter ta gomme?
- **a rubber band** un élastique MASC

rubbish NOUN

see also rubbish ADJECTIVE

1 les **ordures** FEM PL (*refuse*) ◇ *When do they collect the rubbish?* Quand est-ce qu'ils ramassent les ordures?

2 la **camelote** (*junk*) ◇ *They sell a lot of rubbish at the market.* Ils vendent beaucoup de camelote au marché.

3 les **bêtises** FEM PL (*nonsense*) ◇ *Don't talk rubbish!* Ne dis pas de bêtises!
- **That's a load of rubbish!** C'est vraiment n'importe quoi! (*informal*)
- **a rubbish bin** une poubelle
- **a rubbish dump** une décharge

rubbish ADJECTIVE

see also rubbish NOUN

nul MASC

nulle FEM

◇ *This magazine is rubbish!* Ce magazine est nul! ◇ *They're a rubbish team!* Cette équipe est nulle!

rucksack NOUN

le **sac à dos**

rude ADJECTIVE

1 (*impolite*)

impoli ◇ *It's rude to interrupt.* C'est impoli de couper la parole aux gens.

2 (*offensive*)

grossier MASC

grossière FEM

◇ *a rude joke* une plaisanterie grossière ◇ *He was very rude to me.* Il a été très grossier avec moi.
- **a rude word** un gros mot

rug NOUN

1 le **tapis** ◇ *a Persian rug* un tapis persan

2 la **couverture** (*blanket*) ◇ *a tartan rug* une couverture écossaise

rugby NOUN

le **rugby** ◇ *I play rugby.* Je joue au rugby.

ruin NOUN

see also ruin VERB

la **ruine** ◇ *the ruins of the castle* les ruines du château
- **in ruins** en ruine

to **ruin** VERB

see also ruin NOUN

1 **abîmer** ◇ *You'll ruin your shoes.* Tu vas abîmer tes chaussures.

2 **gâcher** ◇ *It ruined our holiday.* Ça a gâché nos vacances.

3 **ruiner** (*financially*)

rule NOUN

1 la **règle** ◇ *the rules of grammar* les règles de grammaire
- **as a rule** en règle générale

2 le **règlement** (*regulation*) ◇ *It's against the rules.* C'est contre le règlement.

ruler NOUN

la **règle** ◇ *Can I borrow your ruler?* Je peux emprunter ta règle?

rum NOUN

le **rhum**

rumour NOUN

la **rumeur** ◇ *It's just a rumour.* Ce n'est qu'une rumeur.

run NOUN

see also run VERB

le **point** (*in cricket*) ◇ *to score a run* marquer un point
- **to go for a run** courir ◇ *I go for a run every morning.* Je cours tous les matins.
- **I did a ten-kilometre run.** J'ai couru dix kilomètres.
- **on the run** en fuite ◇ *The criminals are still on the run.* Les criminels sont toujours en fuite.
- **in the long run** à long terme

to **run** VERB

see also run NOUN

1 **courir** ◇ *I ran five kilometres.* J'ai couru cinq kilomètres.
- **to run a marathon** participer à un marathon

2 **diriger** (*manage*) ◇ *He runs a large company.* Il dirige une grosse société.

3 **organiser** (*organize*) ◇ *They run music courses in the holidays.* Ils organisent des cours de musique pendant les vacances.

4 **couler** (*water*) ◇ *Don't leave the tap running.* Ne laisse pas couler le robinet.
- **to run a bath** faire couler un bain

5 **conduire** (*by car*) ◇ *I can run you to the station.* Je peux te conduire à la gare.
- **to run away** s'enfuir ◇ *They ran away before the police came.* Ils se sont enfuis avant l'arrivée de la police.
- **Time is running out.** Il ne reste plus beaucoup de temps.
- **to run out of something** se trouver à court de quelque chose ◇ *We ran out of money.* Nous nous sommes trouvés à court d'argent.
- **to run somebody over** écraser quelqu'un
- **to get run over** se faire écraser ◇ *Be careful, or you'll get run over!* Fais attention, sinon tu vas te faire écraser!

rung VERB *see* ring

R

runner NOUN
le **coureur**
la **coureuse**

runner beans PL NOUN
les **haricots verts** MASC PL

runner-up NOUN
le **second**
la **seconde**

running NOUN
la **course** ◇ *Running is my favourite sport.* La course est mon sport préféré.

runway NOUN
la **piste**

rural ADJECTIVE
rural
(**ruraux** MASC PL)

rush NOUN
see also rush VERB
la **hâte**
- **In a rush.** à la hâte

to **rush** VERB
see also rush NOUN
1 **se précipiter** (*run*) ◇ *Everyone rushed outside.* Tout le monde s'est précipité dehors.
2 **se dépêcher** (*hurry*) ◇ *There's no need to rush.* Ce n'est pas la peine de se dépêcher.

rush hour NOUN
les **heures de pointe** FEM PL ◇ *in the rush hour* aux l'heures de pointe

rusk NOUN
la **biscotte**

Russia NOUN
la **Russie**
- **in Russia** en Russie
- **to Russia** en Russie

Russian ADJECTIVE
see also Russian NOUN
russe

Russian NOUN
see also Russian ADJECTIVE
1 le/la **Russe** (*person*)
2 le **russe** (*language*)

rust NOUN
la **rouille**

rusty ADJECTIVE
rouillé ◇ *a rusty bike* un vélo rouillé
◇ *My French is very rusty.* Mon français est très rouillé.

ruthless ADJECTIVE
sans pitié

rye NOUN
le **seigle**
- **rye bread** le pain de seigle

S

Sabbath NOUN
- [1] le **dimanche** (*Christian*)
- [2] le **sabbat** (*Jewish*)

sack NOUN
see also sack VERB
le **sac**
- **to get the sack** être mis à la porte

to **sack** VERB
see also sack NOUN
- **to sack somebody** mettre quelqu'un à la porte ⋄ *He was sacked.* On l'a mis à la porte.

sacred ADJECTIVE
sacré

sacrifice NOUN
le **sacrifice**

sad ADJECTIVE
triste

saddle NOUN
la **selle**

saddlebag NOUN
la **sacoche**

sadly ADVERB
- [1] **tristement** ⋄ *"She's gone," he said sadly.* "Elle est partie," a-t-il dit tristement.
- [2] **malheureusement** (*unfortunately*) ⋄ *Sadly, it was too late.* Malheureusement, il était trop tard.

safe NOUN
see also safe ADJECTIVE
le **coffre-fort** ⋄ *She put the money in the safe.* Elle a mis l'argent dans le coffre-fort.

safe ADJECTIVE
see also safe NOUN
- [1] **sans danger** ⋄ *Don't worry, it's perfectly safe.* Ne vous inquiétez pas, c'est absolument sans danger.
- **Is it safe?** Ça n'est pas dangereux?
- [2] **sûr** (*machine, ladder*) ⋄ *This car isn't safe.* Cette voiture n'est pas sûre.
- [3] **hors de danger** (*out of danger*) ⋄ *You're safe now.* Vous êtes hors de danger maintenant.
- **to feel safe** se sentir en sécurité
- **safe sex** le sexe sans risques

safety NOUN
la **sécurité**
- **a safety belt** une ceinture de sécurité
- **a safety pin** une épingle de nourrice

Sagittarius NOUN
le/la **Sagittaire** ⋄ *I'm Sagittarius.* Je suis Sagittaire.

Sahara NOUN
- **the Sahara Desert** le Sahara

said VERB *see* **say**

sail NOUN
see also sail VERB
la **voile**

to **sail** VERB
see also sail NOUN
- [1] **naviguer** (*travel*)
- [2] **prendre la mer** (*set off*) ⋄ *The boat sails at eight o'clock.* Le bateau prend la mer à huit heures.

sailing NOUN
la **voile** ⋄ *His hobby is sailing.* Son passe-temps, c'est la voile.
- **to go sailing** faire de la voile
- **a sailing boat** un voilier
- **a sailing ship** un grand voilier

sailor NOUN
le **marin** ⋄ *He's a sailor.* Il est marin.

saint NOUN
le **saint**
la **sainte**

sake NOUN
- **for the sake of** dans l'intérêt de

salad NOUN
la **salade**
- **salad cream** la mayonnaise
- **salad dressing** la vinaigrette

salami NOUN
le **salami**

salary NOUN
le **salaire**

sale NOUN
les **soldes** MASC PL (*reductions*) ⋄ *There's a sale on at Harrods.* C'est les soldes chez Harrods.
- **on sale** en vente
- **The factory's for sale.** L'usine est en vente.
- **"for sale"** "à vendre"

sales assistant NOUN
le **vendeur**
la **vendeuse**
⋄ *She's a sales assistant.* Elle est vendeuse.

salesman NOUN
- [1] le **représentant** (*sales rep*) ⋄ *He's a salesman.* Il est représentant.
- **a double-glazing salesman** un représentant en doubles vitrages
- [2] le **vendeur** (*sales assistant*)

sales rep NOUN
le **représentant**
la **représentante**

saleswoman NOUN
- [1] la **représentante** (*sales rep*) ⋄ *She's a saleswoman.* Elle est représentante.

S

2 la **vendeuse** (*sales assistant*)

salmon NOUN
le **saumon**

salon NOUN
le **salon** ◇ *a hair salon* un salon de coiffure ◇ *a beauty salon* un salon de beauté

saloon car NOUN
la **berline**

salt NOUN
le **sel**

salty ADJECTIVE
salé

to **salute** VERB
saluer

Salvation Army NOUN
l' **armée du Salut** FEM

same ADJECTIVE
même ◇ *the same model* le même modèle ◇ *at the same time* en même temps
- **They're exactly the same.** Ils sont exactement pareils.
- **It's not the same.** Ça n'est pas pareil.

sand NOUN
le **sable**

sandal NOUN
la **sandale** ◇ *a pair of sandals* une paire de sandales

sand castle NOUN
le **château de sable**
(les **châteaux de sable** PL)

sandwich NOUN
le **sandwich** ◇ *a cheese sandwich* un sandwich au fromage

sandwich course NOUN
le **cours avec stage pratique**

sang VERB *see* **sing**

sanitary towel NOUN
la **serviette hygiénique**

sank VERB *see* **sink**

Santa Claus NOUN
le **père Noël**

sarcastic ADJECTIVE
sarcastique

sat VERB *see* **sit**

satchel NOUN
le **cartable**

satellite NOUN
le **satellite**
- **a satellite dish** une antenne parabolique
- **satellite television** la télévision par satellite

satisfactory ADJECTIVE
satisfaisant

satisfied ADJECTIVE
satisfait

Saturday NOUN

le **samedi** ◇ *on Saturday* samedi ◇ *on Saturdays* le samedi ◇ *every Saturday* tous les samedis ◇ *last Saturday* samedi dernier ◇ *next Saturday* samedi prochain
- **I've got a Saturday job.** Je travaille le samedi.

sauce NOUN
la **sauce**

saucepan NOUN
la **casserole**

saucer NOUN
la **soucoupe**

Saudi Arabia NOUN
l' **Arabie Saoudite** FEM
- **in Saudi Arabia** en Arabie Saoudite

sauna NOUN
le **sauna**

sausage NOUN
1 la **saucisse**
2 le **saucisson** (*salami*)
- **a sausage roll** un friand à la saucisse

to **save** VERB
1 **mettre de côté** (*save up money*) ◇ *I've saved £50 already.* J'ai déjà mis cinquante livres de côté.
2 **économiser** (*spend less*) ◇ *I saved £20 by waiting for the sales.* J'ai économisé vingt livres en attendant les soldes.
- **to save time** gagner du temps ◇ *We took a taxi to save time.* Nous avons pris un taxi pour gagner du temps. ◇ *It saved us time.* Ça nous a fait gagner du temps.
3 **sauver** (*rescue*) ◇ *Luckily, all the passengers were saved.* Heureusement, tous les passagers ont été sauvés.
4 **sauvegarder** (*on computer*) ◇ *I saved the file onto a diskette.* J'ai sauvegardé le fichier sur disquette.
- **to save up** mettre de l'argent de côté ◇ *I'm saving up for a new bike.* Je mets de l'argent à côté pour un nouveau vélo.

savings PL NOUN
les **économies** FEM PL ◇ *She spent all her savings on a computer.* Elle a dépensé toutes ses économies en achetant un ordinateur.

savoury ADJECTIVE
salé ◇ *Is it sweet or savoury?* C'est sucré ou salé?

saw VERB *see* **see**

saw NOUN
la **scie**

sax NOUN
le **saxo** (*informal*) ◇ *I play the sax.* Je joue du saxo.

saxophone NOUN
le **saxophone** ◦ *I play the saxophone.*
Je joue du saxophone.

○ **say** VERB
dire ◦ *What did he say?* Qu'est-ce
qu'il a dit? ◦ *Did you hear what she
said?* Tu as entendu ce qu'elle a dit?
- **Could you say that again?**
Pourriez-vous répéter s'il vous plaît?
- **That goes without saying.** Cela va sans
dire.

saying NOUN
le **dicton** ◦ *It's just a saying.* C'est
juste un dicton.

scale NOUN
[1] l' **échelle** FEM (*of map*) ◦ *a
large-scale map* une carte à grande
échelle
[2] l' **ampleur** FEM (*size, extent*) ◦ *a
disaster on a massive scale* un désastre
d'une ampleur incroyable
[3] la **gamme** (*in music*)

scales PL NOUN
la **balance** SING (*in kitchen, shop*)
- **bathroom scales** le **pèse-personne** SING

scampi PL NOUN
les **scampi** MASC PL

scandal NOUN
[1] le **scandale** (*outrage*) ◦ *It caused a
scandal.* Ça a fait scandale.
[2] les **ragots** MASC PL (*gossip*) ◦ *It's just
scandal.* Ce ne sont que des ragots.

Scandinavia NOUN
la **Scandinavie**
- **in Scandinavia** en Scandinavie

Scandinavian ADJECTIVE
scandinave

scar NOUN
la **cicatrice**

scare NOUN
see also **scare** VERB
la **panique**
- **a bomb scare** une alerte à la bombe

○ **scare** VERB
see also **scare** NOUN
- **to scare somebody** faire peur à
quelqu'un ◦ *He scares me.* Il me fait
peur.

scarecrow NOUN
l' **épouvantail** MASC

scared ADJECTIVE
- **to be scared** avoir peur ◦ *I was
scared stiff.* J'avais terriblement peur.
- **to be scared of** avoir peur de ◦ *Are
you scared of him?* Est-ce que tu as peur
de lui?

scarf NOUN
[1] l' **écharpe** FEM (*long*)
[2] le **foulard** (*square*)

scary ADJECTIVE
effrayant ◦ *It was really scary.*
C'était vraiment effrayant.

scene NOUN
[1] les **lieux** MASC PL (*place*) ◦ *The police
were soon on the scene.* La police est
vite arrivée sur les lieux. ◦ *the scene of
the crime* les lieux du crime
[2] le **spectacle** (*event, sight*) ◦ *It was an
amazing scene.* C'était un spectacle
étonnant.
- **to make a scene** faire une scène

scenery NOUN
le **paysage** (*landscape*)

scent NOUN
le **parfum** (*perfume*)

schedule NOUN
le **programme** ◦ *a busy schedule* un
programme chargé
- **on schedule** comme prévu
- **to be behind schedule** avoir du retard

scheduled flight NOUN
le **vol régulier**

scheme NOUN
[1] le **truc** (*idea*) ◦ *a crazy scheme he
dreamed up* un truc farfelu qu'il a
inventé
[2] le **projet** (*project*) ◦ *a council
road-widening scheme* un projet
municipal d'élargissement des routes

scholarship NOUN
la **bourse**

school NOUN
l' **école** FEM
- **to go to school** aller à l'école

schoolbook NOUN
le **livre scolaire**

schoolboy NOUN
l' **écolier** MASC

schoolchildren NOUN
les **écoliers** MASC PL

schoolgirl NOUN
l' **écolière** FEM

science NOUN
la **science**

science fiction NOUN
la **science-fiction**

scientific ADJECTIVE
scientifique

scientist NOUN
(*doing research*)
le **chercheur**
la **chercheuse**
◦ *She's a scientist.* Elle est chercheuse.
- **He trained as a scientist.** Il a une
formation scientifique.

scissors PL NOUN
les **ciseaux** MASC PL ◦ *a pair of scissors*
une paire de ciseaux

S

to **scoff** VERB
bouffer (*eat*) ◇ *My brother scoffed all the sandwiches.* Mon frère a bouffé tous les sandwichs.

scooter NOUN
1 le **scooter**
2 la **trottinette** (*child's toy*)

score NOUN
see also **score** VERB
le **score** ◇ *The score was three nil.* Le score était trois à zéro.

to **score** VERB
see also **score** NOUN
1 **marquer** (*goal, point*) ◇ *to score a goal* marquer un but
• **to score 6 out of 10** obtenir un score de six sur dix
2 **compter les points** (*keep score*) ◇ *Who's going to score?* Qui va compter les points?

Scorpio NOUN
le **Scorpion** ◇ *I'm Scorpio.* Je suis Scorpion.

Scot NOUN
l' **Écossais** MASC
l' **Écossaise** FEM

Scotland NOUN
l' **Écosse** FEM
• **in Scotland** en Écosse
• **to Scotland** en Écosse
• **I'm from Scotland.** Je suis écossais.

Scots ADJECTIVE
écossais ◇ *a Scots accent* un accent écossais

Scotsman NOUN
l' **Écossais** MASC

Scotswoman NOUN
l' **Écossaise** FEM

Scottish ADJECTIVE
écossais ◇ *a Scottish accent* un accent écossais

scout NOUN
le **scout** ◇ *I'm in the Scouts.* Je suis scout.

scrambled eggs PL NOUN
les **œufs brouillés** MASC PL

scrap NOUN
see also **scrap** VERB
1 le **bout** ◇ *a scrap of paper* un bout de papier
2 la **bagarre** (*fight*)
• **scrap iron** la ferraille

to **scrap** VERB
see also **scrap** NOUN
abandonner (*plan, idea*) ◇ *In the end the plan was scrapped.* Finalement le projet a été abandonné.

scrapbook NOUN
l' **album** MASC

to **scratch** VERB
see also **scratch** NOUN
se gratter ◇ *Stop scratching!* Arrête de te gratter!

scratch NOUN
see also **scratch** VERB
l' **égratignure** FEM (*on skin*)
• **to start from scratch** partir de zéro

scream NOUN
see also **scream** VERB
le **hurlement**

to **scream** VERB
see also **scream** NOUN
hurler

screen NOUN
l' **écran** MASC

screwdriver NOUN
le **tournevis**

to **scribble** VERB
griffonner

to **scrub** VERB
récurer ◇ *to scrub a pan* récurer une casserole

sculpture NOUN
la **sculpture**

sea NOUN
la **mer**

seafood NOUN
les **fruits de mer** MASC PL ◇ *I don't like seafood.* Je n'aime pas les fruits de mer.

seagull NOUN
la **mouette**

seal NOUN
see also **seal** VERB
1 le **phoque** (*animal*)
2 le **cachet** (*on letter*)

to **seal** VERB
see also **seal** NOUN
1 **sceller** (*document*)
2 **coller** (*letter*)

seaman NOUN
le **marin**

to **search** VERB
see also **search** NOUN
fouiller ◇ *They searched the woods for her.* Ils ont fouillé les bois pour la trouver.
• **to search for something** chercher quelque chose ◇ *He searched for gold.* Il cherchait de l'or.

search NOUN
see also **search** VERB
la **fouille**

search party NOUN
l' **expédition de secours** FEM

seashore NOUN
le **bord de la mer** ◇ *on the seashore* au bord de la mer

seasick ADJECTIVE

- **to be seasick** avoir le mal de mer

seaside NOUN

le **bord de la mer** ◇ *at the seaside* au bord de la mer

season NOUN

la **saison** ◇ *What's your favourite season?* Quel est ta saison préférée?

- **out of season** hors saison ◇ *It's cheaper to go there out of season.* C'est moins cher d'y aller hors saison.
- **during the holiday season** en période de vacances
- **a season ticket** une carte d'abonnement

seat NOUN

le **siège**

seat belt NOUN

la **ceinture de sécurité**

sea water NOUN

l' **eau de mer** FEM

seaweed NOUN

les **algues** FEM PL

second ADJECTIVE

see also **second** NOUN

deuxième ◇ *on the second page* à la deuxième page

- **to come second** (*in race*) arriver deuxième
- **to travel second class** voyager en seconde
- **the second of March** le deux mars

second NOUN

see also **second** ADJECTIVE

la **seconde** ◇ *It'll only take a second.* Ça va prendre juste une seconde.

secondary school NOUN

[1] le **collège**

[2] le **lycée**

In France pupils go to a **collège** *between the ages of 11 and 15, and then to a* **lycée** *until the age of 18.*

second-class ADJECTIVE, ADVERB

[1] **de seconde classe** (*ticket, compartment*)

- **to travel second class** voyager en seconde

[2] **à tarif réduit** (*stamp, letter*) ◇ *to send something second-class* envoyer quelque chose à tarif réduit

secondhand ADJECTIVE

d'occasion ◇ *a secondhand car* une voiture d'occasion

secondly ADVERB

deuxièmement

- **firstly...secondly...** d'abord...ensuite... ◇ *Firstly, it's too expensive. Secondly, it wouldn't work anyway.* D'abord, c'est trop cher. Ensuite, ça ne marcherait quand même pas.

secret ADJECTIVE

see also **secret** NOUN

secret MASC

secrète FEM

◇ *a secret mission* une mission secrète

secret NOUN

see also **secret** ADJECTIVE

le **secret** ◇ *It's a secret.* C'est un secret. ◇ *Can you keep a secret?* Tu sais garder un secret?

- **in secret** en secret

secretary NOUN

le/la **secrétaire** ◇ *She's a secretary.* Elle est secrétaire.

secretly ADVERB

secrètement

section NOUN

la **section**

security guard NOUN

le **vigile** ◇ *She's a security guard.* Elle est vigile.

to **see** VERB

voir ◇ *I can't see.* Je n'y vois rien. ◇ *I saw him yesterday.* Je l'ai vu hier. ◇ *Have you seen him?* Est-ce que tu l'as vu?

- **See you!** Salut!
- **See you soon!** À bientôt!
- **to see to something** s'occuper de quelque chose ◇ *The window's stuck again. Can you see to it please?* La fenêtre est encore coincée. Tu peux t'en occuper s'il te plaît?

seed NOUN

la **graine** ◇ *sunflower seeds* des graines de tournesol

to **seem** VERB

avoir l'air ◇ *She seems tired.* Elle a l'air fatiguée. ◇ *The shop seemed to be closed.* Le magasin avait l'air d'être fermé.

- **That seems like a good idea.** Ce n'est pas une mauvaise idée.
- **It seems that...** Il paraît que... ◇ *It seems she's getting married* Il paraît qu'elle va se marier.
- **There seems to be a problem.** Il semble y avoir un problème.

seen VERB *see* **see**

seesaw NOUN

le **tapecul**

see-through ADJECTIVE

transparent

to **select** VERB

sélectionner

selection NOUN

la **sélection**

self-assured ADJECTIVE

sûr de soi ◇ *He's very self-assured.* Il est très sûr de lui.

S

self-catering ADJECTIVE
- a self-catering apartment un appartement de vacances

self-centred ADJECTIVE
égocentrique

self-confidence NOUN
la confiance en soi ◇ He hasn't got much self-confidence. Il n'a pas très confiance en lui.

self-conscious ADJECTIVE
- to be self-conscious (1) (embarrassed) être mal à l'aise ◇ She was really self-conscious at first. Elle était vraiment mal à l'aise au début.
- to be self-conscious (2) (shy) manquer d'assurance ◇ He's always been rather self-conscious. Il a toujours manqué un peu d'assurance.

self-contained ADJECTIVE
- a self-contained flat un appartement indépendant

self-control NOUN
le sang-froid

self-defence NOUN
l' autodéfense FEM ◇ self-defence classes les cours d'autodéfense
- She killed him in self-defence. Elle l'a tué en légitime défense.

self-discipline NOUN
l' autodiscipline

self-employed ADJECTIVE
- to be self-employed travailler à son compte ◇ He's self-employed. Il travaille à son compte.
- the self-employed les travailleurs indépendants

selfish ADJECTIVE
égoïste ◇ Don't be so selfish. Ne sois pas si égoïste.

self-respect NOUN
l' amour-propre MASC

self-service ADJECTIVE
- It's self-service. (café, shop) C'est un self-service.
- a self-service restaurant un restaurant self-service

to **sell** VERB
vendre ◇ He sold it to me. Il me l'a vendu.
- to sell off liquider
- The tickets are all sold out. Il ne reste plus de billets.
- The tickets sold out in three hours. Tous les billets ont été vendus en trois heures.

sell-by date NOUN
la date limite de vente

selling price NOUN
le prix de vente

Sellotape ® NOUN
le scotch ®

semi NOUN
la maison jumelée ◇ We live in a semi. Nous habitons dans une maison jumelée.

semicircle NOUN
le demi-cercle

semicolon NOUN
le point-virgule

semi-detached house NOUN
la maison jumelée ◇ We live in a semi-detached house. Nous habitons dans une maison jumelée.

semi-final NOUN
la demi-finale

semi-skimmed milk NOUN
le lait demi-écrémé

to **send** VERB
envoyer ◇ She sent me a birthday card. Elle m'a envoyé une carte d'anniversaire.
- to send back renvoyer
- to send off (1) (goods, letter) envoyer
- to send off (2) (in sports match) renvoyer du terrain ◇ He was sent off. On l'a renvoyé du terrain.
- to send off for something (1) (free) se faire envoyer quelque chose ◇ I've sent off for a brochure. Je me suis fait envoyer une brochure.
- to send off for something (2) (paid for) commander quelque chose par correspondance ◇ She sent off for a book. Elle a commandé un livre par correspondance.
- to send out envoyer

sender NOUN
l' expéditeur MASC
l' expéditrice FEM

senior ADJECTIVE
haut placé
- senior management les cadres supérieurs
- senior school le lycée
- senior pupils les grandes classes

senior citizen NOUN
la personne du troisième âge (les personnes du troisième âge PL)

sensational ADJECTIVE
sensationnel MASC
sensationnelle FEM

sense NOUN
[1] le bon sens (wisdom) ◇ Use your common sense! Un peu de bon sens, voyons!
- It makes sense. C'est logique.
- It doesn't make sense. Ça n'a pas de sens.

[2] le **sens** (faculty) ◇ the five senses les cinq sens
- **the sense of touch** le toucher
- **the sense of smell** l'odorat MASC
- **the sixth sense** le sixième sens
- **sense of humour** le sens de l'humour
  ◇ He's got no sense of humour. Il n'a aucun sens de l'humour.

senseless ADJECTIVE
insensé

sensible ADJECTIVE
raisonnable ◇ Be sensible! Sois raisonnable!
- **It would be sensible to check first.** Il serait sage de vérifier d'abord.

sensitive ADJECTIVE
sensible ◇ She's very sensitive. Elle est très sensible.

sensuous ADJECTIVE
sensuel MASC
sensuelle FEM

sent VERB see **send**

sentence NOUN
  see also sentence VERB
  [1] la **phrase** ◇ What does this sentence mean? Que veut dire cette phrase?
  [2] la **condamnation** (judgment)
  [3] la **peine** (punishment) ◇ the death sentence la peine de mort
- **He got a life sentence.** Il a été condamné à la réclusion à perpétuité.

to **sentence** VERB
  see also sentence NOUN
- **to sentence somebody to life imprisonment** condamner quelqu'un à la réclusion à perpétuité
- **to sentence somebody to death** condamner quelqu'un à mort

sentimental ADJECTIVE
sentimental
(sentimentaux MASC PL)

separate ADJECTIVE
  see also separate VERB
séparé ◇ I wrote it on a separate sheet. Je l'ai écrit sur une feuille séparée.
- **The children have separate rooms.** Les enfants ont chacun leur chambre.
- **on separate occasions** à différentes reprises

to **separate** VERB
  see also separate ADJECTIVE
  [1] **séparer**
  [2] **se séparer** (married couple)

separately ADVERB
séparément

separation NOUN
la **séparation**

September NOUN

septembre MASC
- **in September** en septembre

sequel NOUN
la **suite** (book, film)

sequence NOUN
  [1] l' **ordre** MASC
- **in sequence** par ordre
- **a sequence of events** une succession d'événements
  [2] la **séquence** (in film)

sergeant NOUN
  [1] le **sergent** (army)
  [2] le **brigadier** (police)

serial NOUN
le **feuilleton**

series NOUN
  [1] la **série** ◇ a TV series une série télévisée
  [2] la **suite** (of numbers)

serious ADJECTIVE
  [1] **sérieux** MASC
sérieuse FEM
  ◇ You look very serious. Tu as l'air sérieux.
- **Are you serious?** Sérieusement?
  [2] **grave** (illness, mistake)

seriously ADVERB
sérieusement ◇ No, but seriously... Non, mais sérieusement...
- **to take somebody seriously** prendre quelqu'un au sérieux
- **seriously injured** gravement blessé
- **Seriously?** Vraiment?

sermon NOUN
le **sermon**

servant NOUN
le/la **domestique**

to **serve** VERB
  see also serve NOUN
  [1] **servir** ◇ Dinner is served. Le dîner est servi. ◇ It's Agassi's turn to serve. C'est à Agassi de servir.
  [2] **purger** (prison sentence)
- **to serve time** être en prison
- **It serves you right.** C'est bien fait pour toi.

serve NOUN
  see also serve VERB
le **service** (tennis)
- **It's your serve.** C'est à toi de servir.

to **service** VERB
  see also service NOUN
réviser (car, washing machine)

service NOUN
  see also service VERB
  [1] le **service** ◇ Service is included. Le service est compris.
  [2] la **révision** (of car)
  [3] l' **office** MASC (church service)

S

- **the Fire Service** les sapeurs-pompiers
- **the armed services** les forces armées

service area NOUN
l' **aire de service** FEM

service charge NOUN
le **service** ◇ *There's no service charge.*
Le service est compris.

serviceman NOUN
le **militaire** ◇ *He's a serviceman.* Il
est militaire.

service station NOUN
la **station-service**
(les **stations-service** PL)

serviette NOUN
la **serviette**

session NOUN
la **séance**

set NOUN
see also **set** VERB
[1] le **jeu**
(les **jeux** PL)
◇ *a set of keys* un jeu de clés ◇ *a
chess set* un jeu d'échecs
- **a train set** un train électrique
[2] le **set** (*in tennis*)

to **set** VERB
see also **set** NOUN
[1] **mettre à sonner** (*alarm clock*) ◇ *I
set the alarm for 7 o'clock.* J'ai mis le
réveil à sept heures.
[2] **établir** (*record*) ◇ *The world record
was set last year.* Le record du monde a
été établi l'année dernière.
[3] **se coucher** (*sun*) ◇ *The sun was
setting.* Le soleil se couchait.
- **The film is set in Morocco.** L'action du
film se déroule au Maroc.
- **to set off** partir ◇ *We set off for
London at 9 o'clock.* Nous sommes
partis pour Londres à neuf heures.
- **to set out** partir ◇ *We set out for
London at 9 o'clock.* Nous sommes
partis pour Londres à neuf heures.
- **to set sail** prendre la mer
- **to set the table** mettre le couvert

settee NOUN
le **canapé**

to **settle** VERB
[1] **résoudre** (*problem*)
[2] **régler** (*argument, account*)
- **to settle down** (*calm down*) se calmer
- **Settle down!** Du calme!
- **to settle in** s'installer
- **to settle on something** opter pour
quelque chose

seven NUMBER
sept ◇ *She's seven.* Elle a sept ans.

seventeen NUMBER
dix-sept ◇ *He's seventeen.* Il a

dix-sept ans.

seventh ADJECTIVE
septième ◇ *the seventh floor* le
septième étage
- **the seventh of August** le sept août

seventy NUMBER
soixante-dix

several ADJECTIVE, PRONOUN
plusieurs ◇ *several schools* plusieurs
écoles
- **several of them** plusieurs ◇ *I've seen
several of them.* J'en ai vu plusieurs.

to **sew** VERB
coudre
- **to sew up** (*tear*) recoudre

sewing NOUN
la **couture** ◇ *I like sewing.* J'aime faire
de la couture.
- **a sewing machine** une machine à
coudre

sewn VERB *see* **sew**

sex NOUN
le **sexe**
- **to have sex with somebody** coucher
avec quelqu'un
- **sex education** l'éducation sexuelle FEM

sexism NOUN
le **sexisme**

sexist ADJECTIVE
sexiste

sexual ADJECTIVE
sexuel MASC
sexuelle FEM
◇ *sexual discrimination* la
discrimination sexuelle ◇ *sexual
harassment* le harcèlement sexuel

sexuality NOUN
la **sexualité**

sexy ADJECTIVE
sexy MASC, FEM, PL

shabby ADJECTIVE
miteux MASC
miteuse FEM

shade NOUN
[1] l' **ombre** FEM
- **in the shade** à l'ombre ◇ *It was 35
degrees in the shade.* Il faisait
trente-cinq à l'ombre.
[2] la **nuance** (*colour*) ◇ *a shade of blue*
une nuance de bleu

shadow NOUN
l' **ombre** FEM

to **shake** VERB
[1] **secouer** ◇ *She shook the rug.* Elle a
secoué le tapis.
[2] **trembler** (*tremble*) ◇ *He was
shaking with cold.* Il tremblait de froid.
- **to shake one's head** (*in refusal*) faire
non de la tête

- **to shake hands with somebody** serrer la main à quelqu'un   ◇ *They shook hands.* Ils se sont serré la main.

shaken ADJECTIVE
secoué   ◇ *I was feeling a bit shaken.* J'étais un peu secoué.

shaky ADJECTIVE
tremblant (*hand, voice*)

shall VERB
- **Shall I shut the window?** Vous voulez que je ferme la fenêtre?
- **Shall we ask him to come with us?** Si on lui demandait de venir avec nous?

shallow ADJECTIVE
peu profond (*water, pool*)

shambles NOUN
la **pagaille**   ◇ *It's a complete shambles.* C'est la pagaille complète.

shame NOUN
la **honte**   ◇ *The shame of it!* Quelle honte!
- **What a shame!** Quel dommage!
- **It's a shame that...** c'est dommage que...

  c'est dommage que *has to be followed by a verb in the subjunctive.*
  ◇ *It's a shame he isn't here.* C'est dommage qu'il ne soit pas ici.

shampoo NOUN
le **shampooing**   ◇ *a bottle of shampoo* une bouteille de shampooing

shandy NOUN
le **panaché**

shan't = shall not

shape NOUN
la **forme**

share NOUN
see also share VERB
l' **action** FEM (*in company*)   ◇ *They've got shares in British Gas.* Ils ont des actions in British Gas.

share VERB
see also share NOUN
partager   ◇ *to share a room with somebody* partager une chambre avec quelqu'un
- **to share out** distribuer   ◇ *They shared the sweets out among the children.* Ils ont distribué les bonbons aux enfants.

shark NOUN
le **requin**

sharp ADJECTIVE
1 **tranchant** (*razor, knife*)
2 **pointu** (*spike, point*)
3 **intelligent** (*clever*)   ◇ *She's very sharp.* Elle est très intelligente.
- **at two o'clock sharp** à deux heures pile

shave VERB

se **raser** (*have a shave*)
- **to shave one's legs** se raser les jambes

shaver NOUN
- **an electric shaver** un rasoir électrique

shaving cream NOUN
la **crème à raser**

shaving foam NOUN
la **mousse à raser**

she PRONOUN
elle   ◇ *She's very nice.* Elle est très gentille.

shed NOUN
la **remise**

she'd = she had, she would

sheep NOUN
le **mouton**

sheepdog NOUN
le **chien de berger**
(les **chiens de berger** PL)

sheer ADJECTIVE
pur   ◇ *It's sheer greed.* C'est de la pure avidité.

sheet NOUN
le **drap** (*on bed*)
- **a sheet of paper** une feuille de papier

shelf NOUN
1 l' **étagère** FEM (*in house*)
2 le **rayon** (*in shop*)

shell NOUN
1 le **coquillage** (*on beach*)
2 la **coquille** (*of egg, nut*)
3 l' **obus** MASC (*explosive*)

she'll = she will

shellfish NOUN
les **fruits de mer** MASC PL

shell suit NOUN
le **survêtement**

shelter NOUN
- **to take shelter** se mettre à l'abri
- **a bus shelter** un arrêt d'autobus

shelves PL NOUN *see* **shelf**

shepherd NOUN
le **berger**

sheriff NOUN
le **shérif**

sherry NOUN
le **xérès**

she's = she is, she has

Shetland Islands NOUN
les **îles Shetland** FEM PL

shield NOUN
le **bouclier**

shift NOUN
see also shift VERB
le **service**   ◇ *His shift starts at 8 o'clock.* Il prend son service à huit heures.
◇ *the night shift* le service de nuit
- **to do shift work** faire les trois-huit

S

to **shift** VERB

> see also shift NOUN
>
> **déplacer** (*move*) ◇ *I couldn't shift the wardrobe on my own.* Je n'ai pas pu déplacer l'armoire tout seul.

- **Shift yourself!** Pousse-toi de là! (*informal*)

shifty ADJECTIVE

> 1 **louche** (*person*) ◇ *He looked shifty.* Il avait l'air louche.
>
> 2 **fuyant** (*eyes*)

shin NOUN

> le **tibia**

to **shine** VERB

> **briller** ◇ *The sun was shining.* Le soleil brillait.

shiny ADJECTIVE

> **brillant**

ship NOUN

> 1 le **bateau**
> (les **bateaux** PL)
>
> 2 le **navire** (*warship*)

shipbuilding NOUN

> la **construction navale**

shipwreck NOUN

> le **naufrage**

shipwrecked ADJECTIVE

- **to be shipwrecked** faire naufrage

shipyard NOUN

> le **chantier naval**

shirt NOUN

> 1 la **chemise** (*man's*)
>
> 2 le **chemisier** (*woman's*)

shit EXCLAMATION

> **Merde!** (*rude*)

to **shiver** VERB

> **frissonner**

shock NOUN

> le **choc**

- **to get a shock (1)** (*surprise*) avoir un choc
- **to get a shock (2)** (*electric*) s'électrocuter
- **an electric shock** une décharge

shocked ADJECTIVE

> **choqué** ◇ *He'll be shocked if you say that.* Tu vas le choquer si tu dis ça.

shocking ADJECTIVE

> **choquant** ◇ *It's shocking!* C'est choquant!

- **a shocking waste** un gaspillage épouvantable

shoe NOUN

> la **chaussure**

shoelace NOUN

> le **lacet**

shoe polish NOUN

> le **cirage**

shoe shop NOUN

> le **magasin de chaussures**

shone VERB *see* **shine**

shook VERB *see* **shake**

to **shoot** VERB

> 1 **abattre** (*kill*) ◇ *He was shot by a sniper.* Il a été abattu par un franc-tireur.
>
> 2 **fusiller** (*execute*) ◇ *He was shot at dawn.* Il a été fusillé à l'aube.
>
> 3 **tirer** (*gun*) ◇ *Don't shoot!* Ne tirez pas!

- **to shoot at somebody** tirer sur quelqu'un
- **He shot himself with a revolver.** (*dead*) Il s'est suicidé d'un coup de revolver.
- **He was shot in the leg.** (*wounded*) Il a reçu une balle dans la jambe.
- **to shoot an arrow** envoyer une flèche

> 4 **tourner** (*film*) ◇ *The film was shot in Prague.* Le film a été tourné à Prague.
>
> 5 **shooter** (*in football*)

shooting NOUN

> 1 les **coups de feu** MASC PL ◇ *They heard shooting.* Ils ont entendu des coups de feu.

- **a shooting** une fusillade

> 2 la **chasse** (*hunting*) ◇ *to go shooting* aller à la chasse

shop NOUN

> le **magasin** ◇ *a sports shop* un magasin de sports

shop assistant NOUN

> le **vendeur**
>
> la **vendeuse**
>
> ◇ *She's a shop assistant.* Elle est vendeuse.

shopkeeper NOUN

> le **commerçant**
>
> la **commerçante**
>
> ◇ *He's a shopkeeper.* Il est commerçant.

shoplifting NOUN

> le **vol à l'étalage**

shopping NOUN

> les **courses** FEM PL (*purchases*) ◇ *Can you get the shopping from the car?* Tu peux aller chercher les courses dans la voiture?

- **I love shopping.** J'adore faire du shopping.
- **to go shopping (1)** (*for food*) faire des courses
- **to go shopping (2)** (*for pleasure*) faire du shopping
- **a shopping bag** un sac à provisions
- **a shopping centre** un centre commercial

shop window NOUN

> la **vitrine**

shore NOUN

le **rivage**
- **on shore** à terre

short ADJECTIVE

[1] **court** ◇ *a short skirt* une jupe courte ◇ *short hair* les cheveux courts
- **too short** trop court ◇ *It was a great holiday, but too short.* C'étaient des vacances super, mais trop courtes.

[2] **petit** (*person, period of time*) ◇ *She's quite short.* Elle est assez petite. ◇ *a short break* une petite pause ◇ *a short walk* une petite promenade
- **to be short of something** être à court de quelque chose ◇ *I'm short of money.* Je suis à court d'argent.
- **at short notice** au dernier moment
- **In short, the answer's no.** Bref, la réponse est non.

shortage NOUN

la **pénurie** ◇ *a water shortage* une pénurie d'eau

short cut NOUN

le **raccourci** ◇ *I took a short cut.* J'ai pris un raccourci.

shorthand NOUN

la **sténo**

shortly ADVERB

bientôt

short notice NOUN
- **at short notice** au dernier moment

shorts PL NOUN

le **short** SING
- **a pair of shorts** un short

short-sighted ADJECTIVE

myope

short story NOUN

la **nouvelle**

shot VERB *see* **shoot**

shot NOUN

[1] (*gunshot*)

le **coup de feu**

(les **coups de feu** PL)

[2] (*photo*)

la **photo** ◇ *a shot of Edinburgh castle* une photo du château d'Édimbourg

[3] (*vaccination*)

le **vaccin**

shotgun NOUN

le **fusil de chasse**

(les **fusils de chasse** PL)

should VERB

> When **should** means "ought to", use **devoir**.

devoir ◇ *You should take more exercise.* Vous devriez faire plus d'exercice. ◇ *He should be there by now.* Il devrait être arrivé maintenant. ◇ *That shouldn't be too hard.* Ça ne devrait pas être trop difficile.
- **should have** avoir dû ◇ *I should*

have told you before. J'aurais dû te le dire avant.

> When **should** means "would", use the conditional tense.

- **I should go if I were you.** Si j'étais vous, j'irais.
- **I should be so lucky!** Ça serait trop beau!

shoulder NOUN

l' **épaule** FEM
- **a shoulder bag** un sac à bandoulière

shouldn't = should not

to **shout** VERB

> *see also* shout NOUN

crier ◇ *Don't shout!* Ne criez pas!
◇ *"Go away!" he shouted.*
"Allez-vous-en!" a-t-il crié.

shout NOUN

> *see also* shout VERB

le **cri**

shovel NOUN

la **pelle**

show NOUN

> *see also* show VERB

[1] le **spectacle** (*performance*)

[2] l' **émission** FEM (*programme*)

[3] le **salon** (*exhibition*)

to **show** VERB

> *see also* show NOUN

[1] **montrer**
- **to show somebody something** montrer quelque chose à quelqu'un ◇ *Have I shown you my new trainers?* Je t'ai montré mes nouvelles baskets?

[2] **faire preuve de** (*prove*) ◇ *She showed great courage.* Elle a fait preuve de beaucoup de courage.
- **It shows.** Ça se voit. ◇ *I've never been riding before.–It shows.* Je n'ai jamais fait de cheval.–Ça se voit.
- **to show off** frimer (*informal*)
- **to show up** (*turn up*) se pointer ◇ *He showed up late as usual.* Il s'est pointé en retard comme d'habitude.

shower NOUN

[1] la **douche**
- **to have a shower** prendre une douche

[2] l' **averse** FEM (*of rain*)

showerproof ADJECTIVE

imperméabilisé

showing NOUN

la **projection** (*of film*)

shown VERB *see* **show**

show-off NOUN

le **frimeur**

la **frimeuse**

shrank VERB *see* **shrink**

to **shriek** VERB

hurler

S

shrimps PL NOUN
les **crevettes** FEM PL

to **shrink** VERB
rétrécir (clothes, fabric)

Shrove Tuesday NOUN
le **mardi gras**

to **shrug** VERB
- **to shrug one's shoulders** hausser les épaules

shrunk VERB see **shrink**

to **shudder** VERB
frissonner

to **shuffle** VERB
- **to shuffle the cards** battre les cartes

to **shut** VERB
fermer ◦ What time do you shut? À quelle heure est-ce que vous fermez? ◦ What time do the shops shut? À quelle heure est-ce que les magasins ferment?
- **to shut down** fermer ◦ The cinema shut down last year. Le cinéma a fermé l'année dernière.
- **to shut up (1)** (close) fermer
- **to shut up (2)** (be quiet) se taire ◦ Shut up! Tais-toi!

shutters NOUN
les **volets** MASC PL

shuttle NOUN
la **navette**

shuttlecock NOUN
le **volant** (badminton)

shy ADJECTIVE
timide

Sicily NOUN
la **Sicile**
- **in Sicily** en Sicile
- **to Sicily** en Sicile

sick ADJECTIVE
[1] **malade** (ill) ◦ He was sick for four days. Il a été malade pendant quatre jours.
[2] **de mauvais goût** (joke, humour) ◦ That's really sick! C'est vraiment de mauvais goût!
- **to be sick** (vomit) vomir ◦ I feel sick. J'ai envie de vomir.
- **to be sick of something** en avoir assez de quelque chose ◦ I'm sick of your jokes. J'en ai assez de tes plaisanteries.

sickening ADJECTIVE
écœurant

sick leave NOUN
le **congé de maladie**

sickness NOUN
la **maladie**

sick note NOUN
[1] le **mot d'absence** (from parents)
[2] le **certificat médical** (from doctor)

sick pay NOUN
l' **indemnité de maladie** FEM

side NOUN
[1] le **côté** (of object, building, car) ◦ He was driving on the wrong side of the road. Il roulait du mauvais côté de la route.
[2] le **bord** (of pool, river, road) ◦ by the side of the lake au bord du lac
[3] le **flanc** (of hill)
[4] l' **équipe** FEM (team)
- **He's on my side. (1)** (on my team) Il est dans mon équipe.
- **He's on my side. (2)** (supporting me) Il est de mon côté.
- **side by side** côte à côte
- **the side entrance** l'entrée latérale
- **to take sides** prendre partie

sideboard NOUN
le **buffet**

side-effect NOUN
l' **effet secondaire** MASC

side street NOUN
la **petite rue transversale**

sideways ADVERB
[1] **de côté** (look, be facing)
[2] **de travers** (move)
- **sideways on** de profil

sieve NOUN
la **passoire**

sigh NOUN
see also **sigh** VERB
le **soupir**

to **sigh** VERB
see also **sigh** NOUN
soupirer

sight NOUN
[1] la **vue** ◦ to have poor sight avoir une mauvaise vue
- **to know somebody by sight** connaître quelqu'un de vue
[2] le **spectacle** ◦ It was an amazing sight. C'était un spectacle étonnant.
- **in sight** visible
- **out of sight** hors de vue
- **the sights** (tourist spots) les attractions touristiques
- **to see the sights of London** visiter Londres

sightseeing NOUN
le **tourisme**
- **to go sightseeing** faire du tourisme

sign NOUN
see also **sign** VERB
[1] (notice)
le **panneau**
(les **panneaux** PL)
◦ There was a big sign saying "private". Il y avait un grand panneau indiquant "privé".

- **a road sign** un panneau
  2 (*gesture, indication*)
  le **signe** ◇ *There's no sign of improvement.* Il n'y a aucun signe d'amélioration.
- **What sign are you?** (*star sign*) Tu es de quel signe?

to **sign** VERB

see also sign NOUN

signer

- **to sign on (1)** (*as unemployed*) s'inscrire au chômage
- **to sign on (2)** (*for course*) s'inscrire

signal NOUN

see also signal VERB

le **signal**
(les **signaux** PL)

to **signal** VERB

see also signal NOUN

- **to signal to somebody** faire un signe à quelqu'un

signalman NOUN

l' **aiguilleur** MASC

signature NOUN

la **signature**

significance NOUN

l' **importance** FEM

significant ADJECTIVE

important

sign language NOUN

le **langage par signes**

signpost NOUN

le **poteau indicateur**

silence NOUN

le **silence**

silent ADJECTIVE

silencieux MASC
silencieuse FEM

silicon chip NOUN

la **puce électronique**

silk NOUN

see also silk ADJECTIVE

la **soie**

silk ADJECTIVE

see also silk NOUN

en soie ◇ *a silk scarf* un foulard en soie

silky ADJECTIVE

soyeux MASC
soyeuse FEM

silly ADJECTIVE

bête

silver NOUN

l' **argent** MASC ◇ *a silver medal* une médaille d'argent

similar ADJECTIVE

semblable

- **similar to** semblable à

simple ADJECTIVE

1 **simple** ◇ *It's very simple.* C'est très simple.
2 (*simple-minded*)
simplet MASC
simplette FEM
◇ *He's a bit simple.* Il est un peu simplet.

simply ADVERB

simplement ◇ *It's simply not possible.* Ça n'est tout simplement pas possible.

simultaneous ADJECTIVE

simultané

sin NOUN

see also sin VERB

le **péché**

to **sin** VERB

see also sin NOUN

pécher

since PREPOSITION, ADVERB, CONJUNCTION

1 **depuis** ◇ *since Christmas* depuis Noël ◇ *since then* depuis ce moment-là ◇ *I haven't seen him since.* Je ne l'ai pas vu depuis.

- **ever since** depuis ce moment-là
  2 **depuis que** ◇ *I haven't seen her since she left.* Je ne l'ai pas vue depuis qu'elle est partie.
  3 **puisque** (*because*) ◇ *Since you're tired, let's stay at home.* Puisque tu es fatigué, restons à la maison.

sincere ADJECTIVE

sincère

sincerely ADVERB

- **Yours sincerely... (1)** (*in business letter*) Veuillez agréer l'expression de mes sentiments les meilleurs...
- **Yours sincerely... (2)** (*in personal letter*) Cordialement...

to **sing** VERB

chanter ◇ *He sang out of tune.* Il chantait faux. ◇ *Have you ever sung this tune before?* Vous avez déjà chanté cet air-là?

singer NOUN

le **chanteur**
la **chanteuse**

singing NOUN

le **chant**

single ADJECTIVE

see also single NOUN

célibataire (*unmarried*)

- **a single room** une chambre pour une personne
- **not a single thing** rien du tout

single NOUN

see also single ADJECTIVE

1 l' **aller simple** MASC (*ticket*) ◇ *A single to Toulouse, please.* Un aller simple pour Toulouse, s'il vous plaît.

2 le **45 tours** (record)
- a CD single un CD single

single parent NOUN
- **She's a single parent.** Elle élève ses enfants toute seule.
- **a single parent family** une famille monoparentale

singles PL NOUN
le **simple** SING (in tennis) ◇ the women's singles le simple dames

singular NOUN
le **singulier** ◇ in the singular au singulier

sinister ADJECTIVE
sinistre

sink NOUN
see also sink VERB
l' **évier** MASC

to **sink** VERB
see also sink NOUN
couler

sir NOUN
monsieur MASC
- **Yes sir.** Oui, Monsieur.

siren NOUN
la **sirène**

sister NOUN
1 la **sœur** ◇ my little sister ma petite sœur
2 l' **infirmière en chef** FEM (nurse)

sister-in-law NOUN
la **belle-sœur**
(les **belles-sœurs** PL)

to **sit** VERB
s'asseoir
- **to sit on something** s'asseoir sur quelque chose ◇ She sat on the chair. Elle s'est assise sur la chaise.
- **to sit down** s'asseoir
- **to be sitting** être assis
- **to sit an exam** passer un examen

sitcom NOUN
la **comédie de situation**
(les **comédies de situation** PL)

site NOUN
1 le **site** ◇ an archaeological site un site archéologique
- **the site of the accident** le lieu de l'accident
2 le **camping** (campsite)
- **a building site** un chantier

sitting room NOUN
le **salon**

situated ADJECTIVE
- **to be situated** être situé ◇ The village is situated on the side of a hill. Le village est situé sur le flanc d'une colline.

situation NOUN
la **situation**

six NUMBER
six ◇ He's six. Il a six ans.

sixteen NUMBER
seize ◇ He's sixteen. Il a seize ans.

sixth ADJECTIVE
sixième ◇ the sixth floor le sixième étage
- **the sixth of August** le six août

sixty NUMBER
soixante

size NOUN
France uses the European system to show clothing and shoe sizes.
1 la **taille** (of object, clothing) ◇ What size do you take? Quelle taille est-ce que vous faites?
- **I'm a size ten.** Je fais du trente-huit.
2 la **pointure** (of shoes)
- **I take size six.** Je fais du trente-neuf.

to **skate** VERB
1 **faire du patin à glace** (ice-skate)
2 **faire du patin à roulettes** (roller-skate)

skateboard NOUN
le **skateboard**

skateboarding NOUN
le **skateboard** ◇ to go skateboarding faire du skateboard

skates NOUN
les **patins** MASC PL

skating NOUN
le **patin à glace** ◇ to go skating faire du patin à glace
- **a skating rink** une patinoire

skeleton NOUN
le **squelette**

sketch NOUN
see also sketch VERB
le **croquis** (drawing)

to **sketch** VERB
see also sketch NOUN
- **to sketch something** faire un croquis de quelque chose

to **ski** VERB
see also ski NOUN
skier ◇ Can you ski? Tu sais skier?

ski NOUN
see also ski VERB
le **ski**
- **ski boots** les chaussures de ski FEM
- **a ski lift** un remonte-pente
- **ski pants** le fuseau SING
- **a ski pole** un bâton de ski
- **a ski slope** une piste de ski
- **a ski suit** une combinaison de ski

to **skid** VERB
déraper

skiing NOUN
le **ski** ◇ to go skiing faire du ski

- **to go on a skiing holiday** aller aux
  sports d'hiver
skilful ADJECTIVE
  adroit
skilled ADJECTIVE
- **a skilled worker** un ouvrier spécialisé
skimmed milk NOUN
  le **lait écrémé**
skimpy ADJECTIVE
  1 **minuscule** (clothes)
  2 **maigre** (meal)
skin NOUN
  la **peau**
  (les **peaux** PL)
- **skin cancer** le cancer de la peau
skinhead NOUN
  le/la **skinhead**
skinny ADJECTIVE
  maigre
skin-tight ADJECTIVE
  collant
skip NOUN
  see also skip VERB
  la **benne** (container)
to **skip** VERB
  see also skip NOUN
  sauter ◇ to skip a meal sauter un
  repas
- **to skip a lesson** sécher un cours
skirt NOUN
  la **jupe**
skittles NOUN
  les **quilles** FEM PL ◇ to play skittles
  jouer aux quilles
to **skive** VERB
  tirer au flanc (be lazy)
- **to skive off** sécher (informal) ◇ to
  skive off school sécher les cours
skull NOUN
  le **crâne**
sky NOUN
  le **ciel**
skyscraper NOUN
  le **gratte-ciel**
  (les **gratte-ciel** PL)
slack ADJECTIVE
  1 **lâche** (rope)
  2 **négligent** (person)
to **slag off** VERB
- **to slag somebody off** dire du mal de
  quelqu'un
to **slam** VERB
  claquer ◇ The door slammed. La
  porte a claqué. ◇ She slammed the
  door. Elle a claqué la porte.
slang NOUN
  l' **argot** MASC
slap NOUN
  see also slap VERB

la **claque**
to **slap** VERB
  see also slap NOUN
- **to slap somebody** donner une claque à
  quelqu'un
slate NOUN
  l' **ardoise** FEM
sledge NOUN
  la **luge**
sledging NOUN
- **to go sledging** faire de la luge
sleep NOUN
  see also sleep VERB
  le **sommeil**
- **I need some sleep.** J'ai besoin de
  dormir.
- **to go to sleep** s'endormir
to **sleep** VERB
  see also sleep NOUN
  dormir ◇ I couldn't sleep last night.
  J'ai mal dormi la nuit dernière.
- **to sleep with somebody** coucher avec
  quelqu'un
- **to sleep together** coucher ensemble
sleeping bag NOUN
  le **sac de couchage**
  (les **sacs de couchage** PL)
sleeping car NOUN
  le **wagon-lit**
  (les **wagons-lits** PL)
sleeping pill NOUN
  le **somnifère**
sleepy ADJECTIVE
- **to feel sleepy** avoir sommeil ◇ I was
  feeling sleepy. J'avais sommeil.
- **a sleepy little village** un petit village
  tranquille
sleet NOUN
  see also sleet VERB
  la **neige fondue**
to **sleet** VERB
  see also sleet NOUN
- **It's sleeting.** Il tombe de la neige
  fondue.
sleeve NOUN
  1 la **manche** ◇ long sleeves les
  manches longues ◇ short sleeves les
  manches courtes
  2 la **pochette** (record sleeve)
sleigh NOUN
  le **traîneau**
  (les **traîneaux** PL)
slept VERB see **sleep**
slice NOUN
  see also slice VERB
  la **tranche**
to **slice** VERB
  see also slice NOUN
  couper en tranches

S

slick NOUN
- **an oil slick** une marée noire

slide NOUN
> see also **slide** VERB
1. le **toboggan** (*in playground*)
2. la **diapositive** (*photo*)
3. la **barrette** (*hair slide*)

to **slide** VERB
> see also **slide** NOUN
glisser

slight ADJECTIVE
léger MASC
légère FEM
- *a slight problem* un léger problème
- *a slight improvement* une légère amélioration

slightly ADVERB
légèrement

slim ADJECTIVE
> see also **slim** VERB
mince

to **slim** VERB
> see also **slim** ADJECTIVE
faire un régime (*be on a diet*) - *I'm slimming.* Je fais un régime.

sling NOUN
l' **écharpe** FEM - *She had her arm in a sling.* Elle avait le bras en écharpe.

slip NOUN
> see also **slip** VERB
1. l' **erreur** FEM (*mistake*)
2. le **jupon** (*underskirt*)
3. la **combinaison** (*full-length underskirt*)
- **a slip of paper** un bout de papier
- **a slip of the tongue** un lapsus

to **slip** VERB
> see also **slip** NOUN
glisser - *He slipped on the ice.* Il a glissé sur le verglas.
- **to slip up** faire une erreur (*make a mistake*)

slipper NOUN
le **chausson**
- **a pair of slippers** des chaussons

slippery ADJECTIVE
glissant

slip-up NOUN
l' **erreur** FEM

slope NOUN
la **pente**

sloppy ADJECTIVE
1. **bâclé** (*work*)
2. **négligé** (*person, appearance*)

slot NOUN
la **fente**

slot machine NOUN
1. la **machine à sous** (*for gambling*)
2. le **distributeur automatique** (*vending machine*)

slow ADJECTIVE, ADVERB
1. **lent** - *He's a bit slow.* Il est un peu lent.
2. **lentement** - *to go slow* (*person, car*) aller lentement - *Drive slower!* Conduisez plus lentement!
- **My watch is slow.** Ma montre retarde.

to **slow down** VERB
ralentir

slowly ADVERB
lentement

slug NOUN
la **limace**

slush NOUN
la **neige fondue**

sly ADJECTIVE
rusé (*person*)
- **a sly smile** un sourire sournois

smack NOUN
> see also **smack** VERB
la **tape**

to **smack** VERB
> see also **smack** NOUN
- **to smack somebody** donner une tape à quelqu'un

small ADJECTIVE
petit
- **small change** la petite monnaie

smart ADJECTIVE
1. **chic** (*elegant*)
2. **intelligent** (*clever*)
- **a smart idea** une idée astucieuse

smash NOUN
> see also **smash** VERB
l' **accident** MASC

to **smash** VERB
> see also **smash** NOUN
1. **casser** (*break*) - *I've smashed my watch.* J'ai cassé ma montre.
2. **se briser** (*get broken*) - *The glass smashed into tiny pieces.* Le verre s'est brisé en mille morceaux.

smashing ADJECTIVE
formidable - *I think he's smashing.* Je le trouve formidable.

smell NOUN
> see also **smell** VERB
l' **odeur** FEM
- **the sense of smell** l'odorat MASC

to **smell** VERB
> see also **smell** NOUN
1. **sentir mauvais** - *That old dog really smells!* Qu'est-ce qu'il sent mauvais, ce vieux chien!
- **to smell of something** sentir quelque chose - *It smells of petrol.* Ça sent l'essence.
2. **sentir** (*detect*) - *I can't smell anything.* Je ne sens rien.

smelly ADJECTIVE
 qui sent mauvais ○ *He's got smelly feet.* Il a les pieds qui sentent mauvais.
smile NOUN
 see also smile VERB
 le sourire
to **smile** VERB
 see also smile NOUN
 sourire
smoke NOUN
 see also smoke VERB
 la fumée
to **smoke** VERB
 see also smoke NOUN
 fumer ○ *I don't smoke.* Je ne fume pas. ○ *He smokes cigars.* Il fume le cigare.
smoker NOUN
 le fumeur
 la fumeuse
smoking NOUN
- **to give up smoking** arrêter de fumer
- **Smoking is bad for you.** Le tabac, est mauvais pour la santé.
- **"no smoking"** "défense de fumer"
smooth ADJECTIVE
 1 (*surface*)
 lisse
 2 (*person*)
 mielleux MASC
 mielleuse FEM
smudge NOUN
 la bavure
smug ADJECTIVE
 suffisant
to **smuggle** VERB
 passer en contrebande
smuggler NOUN
 le contrebandier
 la contrebandière
smuggling NOUN
 la contrebande
smutty ADJECTIVE
 cochon MASC
 cochonne FEM
 ○ *a smutty story* une histoire cochonne
snack NOUN
 l' en-cas MASC
 (les en-cas PL)
- **to have a snack** prendre un en-cas
snack bar NOUN
 le snack-bar
snail NOUN
 l' escargot MASC
snake NOUN
 le serpent
to **snap** VERB
 casser net (*break*) ○ *The branch snapped.* La branche a cassé net.

- **to snap one's fingers** faire claquer ses doigts
snapshot NOUN
 la photo
to **snarl** VERB
 gronder (*animal*)
to **snatch** VERB
- **to snatch something from somebody** arracher quelque chose à quelqu'un ○ *He snatched the keys from my hand.* Il m'a arraché les clés des mains.
- **My bag was snatched.** On m'a arraché mon sac.
to **sneak** VERB
- **to sneak in** entrer furtivement
- **to sneak out** sortir furtivement
- **to sneak up on somebody** s'approcher de quelqu'un sans faire de bruit
to **sneeze** VERB
 éternuer
to **sniff** VERB
 1 renifler ○ *Stop sniffing!* Arrête de renifler!
 2 flairer ○ *The dog sniffed my hand.* Le chien m'a flairé la main.
- **to sniff glue** sniffer de la colle
snob NOUN
 le/la snob
snooker NOUN
 le billard ○ *to play snooker* jouer au billard
snooze NOUN
 le petit somme ○ *to have a snooze* faire un petit somme
to **snore** VERB
 ronfler
snow NOUN
 see also snow VERB
 la neige
to **snow** VERB
 see also snow NOUN
 neiger ○ *It's snowing.* Il neige.
snowball NOUN
 la boule de neige
 (les boules de neige PL)
snowflake NOUN
 le flocon de neige
 (les flocons de neige PL)
snowman NOUN
 le bonhomme de neige
 (les bonshommes de neige PL)
 ○ *to build a snowman* faire un bonhomme de neige
SO CONJUNCTION, ADVERB
 1 alors ○ *The shop was closed, so I went home.* Le magasin était fermé, alors je suis rentré chez moi. ○ *So, have you always lived in London?* Alors, vous avez toujours vécu à Londres?

- **So what?** Et alors?
  ② **donc** (*so that*) ◦ *It rained, so I got wet.* Il pleuvait, donc j'ai été mouillé.
  ③ **tellement** (*very*) ◦ *It was so heavy!* C'était tellement lourd! ◦ *He was talking so fast I couldn't understand.* Il parlait tellement vite que je ne comprenais pas.
- **It's not so heavy!** Ça n'est pas si lourd que ça!
- **How's your father?–Not so good.** Comment va ton père?–Pas très bien.
- **so much** (*a lot*) tellement ◦ *I love you so much.* Je t'aime tellement.
- **so much..., so many...** tellement de... ◦ *I've got so much work.* J'ai tellement de travail. ◦ *I've got so many things to do today.* J'ai tellement de choses à faire aujourd'hui.
  ④ **aussi** (*in comparisons*) ◦ *He's like his sister but not so clever.* Il est comme sa sœur mais pas aussi intelligent.
- **so do I** moi aussi ◦ *I love horses.–So do I.* J'aime les chevaux.–Moi aussi.
- **so have we** nous aussi ◦ *I've been to France twice.–So have we.* Je suis allé en France deux fois.–Nous aussi.
- **I think so.** Je crois.
- **I hope so.** J'espère bien.
- **That's not so.** Ça n'est pas le cas.
- **so far** jusqu'à présent ◦ *It's been easy so far.* Ça a été facile jusqu'à présent.
- **so far so good** jusqu'ici ça va
- **ten or so people** environ dix personnes
- **at five o'clock or so** à environ cinq heures

to **soak** VERB
   tremper
   soaked ADJECTIVE
   trempé ◦ *By the time we got back we were soaked.* Nous sommes rentrés trempés.
   soaking ADJECTIVE
   trempé ◦ *By the time we got back we were soaking.* Nous sommes rentrés trempés.
- **soaking wet** trempé ◦ *Your shoes are soaking wet.* Tes chaussures sont trempées.
   soap NOUN
   le **savon**
   soap opera NOUN
   le **feuilleton à l'eau de rose**
   (les **feuilletons à l'eau de rose** PL)
   soap powder NOUN
   la **lessive**
to **sob** VERB

   sangloter ◦ *She was sobbing.* Elle sanglotait.
sober ADJECTIVE
   sobre
to **sober up** VERB
   dessoûler
soccer NOUN
   le **football** ◦ *to play soccer* jouer au football
- **a soccer player** un joueur de football
social ADJECTIVE
   social
   (**sociaux** MASC PL)
   ◦ *a social class* une classe sociale
- **I have a good social life.** Je vois beaucoup de monde.
socialism NOUN
   le **socialisme**
socialist ADJECTIVE
   see also **socialist** NOUN
   socialiste
socialist NOUN
   see also **socialist** ADJECTIVE
   le/la **socialiste**
social security NOUN
   ① l' **aide sociale** FEM (*money*)
- **to be on social security** recevoir de l'aide sociale
   ② la **sécurité sociale** (*organization*)
social worker NOUN
   ① (*woman*)
   l' **assistante sociale** FEM ◦ *She's a social worker.* Elle est assistante sociale.
   ② (*man*)
   le **travailleur social**
   (les **travailleurs sociaux** PL)
   ◦ *He's a social worker.* Il est travailleur social.
society NOUN
   ① la **société** ◦ *We live in a multi-cultural society.* Nous vivons dans une société multiculturelle.
   ② le **club** ◦ *a drama society* un club de théâtre
sociology NOUN
   la **sociologie**
sock NOUN
   la **chaussette**
socket NOUN
   la **prise de courant**
   (les **prises de courant** PL)
soda NOUN
   le **soda** (*soda water*)
sofa NOUN
   le **canapé**
soft ADJECTIVE
   ① (*fabric, texture*)
   doux MASC
   douce FEM

2 (*pillow, bed*)
mou MASC
molle FEM
* **soft cheeses** les fromages à pâte molle
3 (*hair*)
fin
* **to be soft on somebody** (*be kind to*) être indulgent avec quelqu'un
* **a soft drink** une boisson non alcoolisée
* **soft drugs** les drogues douces FEM
* **a soft option** une solution de facilité
software NOUN
le **logiciel**
soggy ADJECTIVE
1 (*soaked*)
trempé ◇ *a soggy tissue* un mouchoir trempé
2 (*not crisp*)
mou MASC
molle FEM
◇ *soggy chips* des frites molles
soil NOUN
la **terre**
solar power NOUN
l' **énergie solaire** FEM
sold VERB *see* **sell**
soldier NOUN
le **soldat** ◇ *He's a soldier.* Il est soldat.
solicitor NOUN
1 (*for lawsuits*)
l' **avocat** MASC
l' **avocate** FEM
◇ *He's a solicitor.* Il est avocat.
2 (*for wills, property*)
le **notaire** ◇ *She's a solicitor.* Elle est notaire.
solid ADJECTIVE
1 (*not hollow*)
massif MASC
massive FEM
◇ *solid gold* l'or massif
2 **solide** ◇ *a solid wall* un mur solide
* **for three hours solid** pendant trois heures entières
solo NOUN
le **solo** ◇ *a guitar solo* un solo de guitare
solution NOUN
la **solution**
solve VERB
résoudre
some ADJECTIVE, PRONOUN
> When **some** means "*a certain amount of*", use **du**, **de la** or **des** *according to the gender of the* French *noun that follows it.* **du** *and* **de la** *become* **de l'** *when they are followed by a noun starting with a vowel.*
1 **du** ◇ *Would you like some bread?*

Voulez-vous du pain?
de la ◇ *Would you like some beer?* Voulez-vous de la bière?
de l' ◇ *Have you got some mineral water?* Avez-vous de l'eau minérale?
des ◇ *I've got some Blur albums.* J'ai des albums de Blur.
* **Some people say that...** Il y a des gens qui disent que...
* **some day** un de ces jours
* **some day next week** un jour la semaine prochaine
2 **certains** (*some but not all*) ◇ *Are these mushrooms poisonous?–Only some.* Est-ce que ces champignons sont vénéneux?–Certains le sont.
* **some of them** quelques-uns ◇ *I only sold some of them.* J'en ai seulement vendu quelques-uns.
* **I only took some of it.** J'en ai seulement pris un peu.
* **I'm going to buy some stamps. Do you want some too?** Je vais acheter des timbres. Tu en veux aussi?
* **Would you like some coffee?–No thanks, I've got some.** Tu veux du café?–Non merci, j'en ai déjà.
somebody PRONOUN
quelqu'un ◇ *Somebody stole my bag.* Quelqu'un a volé mon sac.
somehow ADVERB
* **I'll do it somehow.** Je trouverai le moyen de le faire.
* **Somehow I don't think he believed me.** Quelque chose me dit qu'il ne m'a pas cru.
someone PRONOUN
quelqu'un ◇ *Somebody stole my bag.* Quelqu'un a volé mon sac.
something PRONOUN
quelque chose ◇ *something special* quelque chose de spécial ◇ *Wear something warm.* Mets quelque chose de chaud. ◇ *That's really something!* C'est vraiment quelque chose! ◇ *It cost £100, or something like that.* Ça a coûté cent livres, ou quelque chose comme ça.
* **His name is Pierre or something.** Il s'appelle Pierre, ou quelque chose comme ça.
sometime ADVERB
un de ces jours ◇ *You must come and see us sometime.* Passez donc nous voir un de ces jours.
* **sometime last month** dans le courant du mois dernier
sometimes ADVERB
quelquefois ◇ *Sometimes I think she*

hates me. Quelquefois j'ai l'impression qu'elle me déteste.

somewhere ADVERB
quelque part ◇ *I left my keys somewhere.* J'ai laissé mes clés quelque part. ◇ *I'd like to go on holiday, somewhere sunny.* J'aimerais aller en vacances, quelque part où il fait du soleil.

son NOUN
le **fils**

song NOUN
la **chanson**

son-in-law NOUN
le **gendre**

soon ADVERB
bientôt ◇ *very soon* très bientôt
- **soon afterwards** peu après
- **as soon as possible** aussi tôt que possible

sooner ADVERB
plus tôt ◇ *Can't you come a bit sooner?* Tu ne peux pas venir un peu plus tôt?
- **sooner or later** tôt ou tard

soppy ADJECTIVE
sentimental
(**sentimentaux** MASC PL)

soprano NOUN (*singer*)
le/la **soprano**

sorcerer NOUN
le **sorcier**

sore ADJECTIVE
see also **sore** NOUN
- **It's sore.** Ça fait mal.
- **That's a sore point.** C'est un point sensible.

sore NOUN
see also **sore** ADJECTIVE
la **plaie**

sorry ADJECTIVE
désolé ◇ *I'm really sorry.* Je suis vraiment désolé. ◇ *I'm sorry, I haven't got any change.* Je suis désolé, je n'ai pas de monnaie. ◇ *I'm sorry I'm late.* Je suis désolé d'être en retard.
- **Sorry!** Pardon!
- **Sorry?** Pardon?
- **I'm sorry about the noise.** Je m'excuse pour le bruit.
- **You'll be sorry!** Tu le regretteras!
- **to feel sorry for somebody** plaindre quelqu'un

sort NOUN
la **sorte** ◇ *What sort of bike have you got?* Quelle sorte de vélo as-tu?

to **sort out** VERB
1 **ranger** (*objects*)
2 **résoudre** (*problems*)

so-so ADVERB
comme ci comme ça ◇ *How are you feeling?–So-so.* Comment est-ce que tu te sens?–Comme ci comme ça.

soul NOUN
1 l' **âme** FEM (*spirit*)
2 la **soul** (*music*)

sound NOUN
see also **sound** VERB, ADJECTIVE
1 le **bruit** (*noise*) ◇ *Don't make a sound!* Pas un bruit! ◇ *the sound of footsteps* des bruits de pas
2 le **son** ◇ *Can I turn the sound down?* Je peux baisser le son?

to **sound** VERB
see also **sound** NOUN, ADJECTIVE
- **That sounds interesting.** Ça a l'air intéressant.
- **It sounds as if she's doing well at school.** Elle a l'air de bien travailler à l'école. ◇ *That sounds like a good idea.* C'est une bonne idée.

sound ADJECTIVE, ADVERB
see also **sound** NOUN, VERB
bon MASC
bonne FEM
 ◇ *That's sound advice.* C'est un bon conseil.
- **sound asleep** profondément endormi

soundtrack NOUN
la **bande sonore**

soup NOUN
la **soupe** ◇ *vegetable soup* la soupe aux légumes

sour ADJECTIVE
aigre

south ADJECTIVE, ADVERB
see also **south** NOUN
1 **sud** MASC, FEM, PL ◇ *the south coast* la côte sud
2 **vers le sud** ◇ *We were travelling south.* Nous allions vers le sud.
- **south of** au sud de ◇ *It's south of London.* C'est au sud de Londres.

south NOUN
see also **south** ADJECTIVE
le **sud** ◇ *in the south* dans le sud
 ◇ *the South of France* le sud de la France

South Africa NOUN
l' **Afrique du Sud** FEM
- **in South Africa** en Afrique du Sud
- **to South Africa** en Afrique du Sud

South America NOUN
l' **Amérique du Sud** FEM
- **in South America** en Amérique du Sud
- **to South America** en Amérique du Sud

southeast NOUN
le **sud-est** ◇ *southeast England* le

sud-est de l'Angleterre

southern ADJECTIVE
- **the southern part of the island** la partie sud de l'île
- **Southern England** le sud de l'Angleterre

South Pole NOUN
le **pôle Sud**

South Wales NOUN
le **sud du Pays de Galles**

southwest NOUN
le **sud-ouest**   ◇ *southwest France* le sud-ouest de la France

souvenir NOUN
le **souvenir**
- **a souvenir shop** une boutique de souvenirs

soya NOUN
le **soja**

soy sauce NOUN
la **sauce de soja**

space NOUN
1 la **place**   ◇ *There isn't enough space.* Il n'y a pas suffisamment de place.
- **a parking space** une place de parking
2 l' **espace** MASC (*universe, gap*)
◇ *Leave a space after your answer.* Laissez un espace après votre réponse.

spacecraft NOUN
l' **engin spatial** MASC

spade NOUN
la **pelle**
- **spades** (*in cards*) le pique SING   ◇ *the ace of spades* l'as de pique

Spain NOUN
l' **Espagne** FEM
- **in Spain** en Espagne
- **to Spain** en Espagne

Spaniard NOUN
l' **Espagnol** MASC
l' **Espagnole** FEM

spaniel NOUN
l' **épagneul** MASC

Spanish ADJECTIVE
see also Spanish NOUN
espagnol   ◇ *She's Spanish.* Elle est espagnole.

Spanish NOUN
see also Spanish ADJECTIVE
l' **espagnol** MASC (*language*)
- **the Spanish** les Espagnols

to **spank** VERB
- **to spank somebody** donner une fessée à quelqu'un

spanner NOUN
la **clé anglaise**

spare ADJECTIVE
see also spare VERB, NOUN
de rechange   ◇ *spare batteries* des piles de rechange

to **spare** VERB
see also spare ADJECTIVE, NOUN
- **Can you spare a moment?** Vous pouvez m'accorder un instant?
- **I can't spare the time.** Je n'ai pas le temps.
- **There's no room to spare.** Il n'y a plus de place.
- **We arrived with time to spare.** Nous sommes arrivés en avance.

spare NOUN
see also spare ADJECTIVE, VERB
- **a spare** un autre   ◇ *I've lost my key. –Have you got a spare?* J'ai perdu ma clé.–Tu en as une autre?
- **a spare part** une pièce de rechange
- **a spare room** une chambre d'amis
- **spare time** le temps libre   ◇ *What do you do in your spare time?* Qu'est-ce que tu fais pendant ton temps libre?
- **spare wheel** une roue de secours

sparkling ADJECTIVE
pétillant (*water*)
- **sparkling wine** le mousseux

sparrow NOUN
le **moineau**
(les **moineaux** PL)

spat VERB *see* spit

to **speak** VERB
parler   ◇ *Do you speak English?* Est-ce que vous parlez anglais?
- **to speak to somebody** parler à quelqu'un   ◇ *Have you spoken to him?* Tu lui as parlé?   ◇ *She spoke to him about it.* Elle lui en a parlé.
- **spoken French** le français parlé

speaker NOUN
1 l' **enceinte** FEM (*loudspeaker*)
2 l' **intervenant** MASC (*in debate*)

special ADJECTIVE
spécial
(**spéciaux** MASC PL)

specialist NOUN
le/la **spécialiste**

speciality NOUN
la **spécialité**

to **specialize** VERB
se spécialiser   ◇ *We specialize in skiing equipment.* Nous nous spécialisons dans les articles de ski.

specially ADVERB
1 **spécialement**   ◇ *It's specially designed for teenagers.* C'est spécialement conçu pour les adolescents.
- **not specially** pas spécialement   ◇ *Do you like opera?–Not specially.* Tu aimes

l'opéra?–Pas spécialement.
[2] **surtout** ⋄ *It can be very cold here,
specially in winter.* Il peut faire très froid
ici, surtout en hiver.
species NOUN
l' **espèce** FEM
specific ADJECTIVE
[1] (*particular*)
particulier MASC
particulière FEM
⋄ *certain specific issues* certains
problèmes particuliers
[2] (*precise*)
précis ⋄ *Could you be more specific?*
Est-ce que vous pourriez être plus
précis?
specifically ADVERB
[1] **spécialement** ⋄ *It's specifically
designed for teenagers.* C'est
spécialement conçu pour les
adolescents.
[2] **particulièrement** ⋄ *in Britain, or
more specifically in England* en
Grande-Bretagne, ou plus
particulièrement en Angleterre
‣ **I specifically said that...** J'ai clairement
dit que...
specs, spectacles PL NOUN
les **lunettes** FEM PL
spectacular ADJECTIVE
spectaculaire
spectator NOUN
le **spectateur**
la **spectatrice**
speech NOUN
le **discours** ⋄ *to make a speech* faire
un discours
speechless ADJECTIVE
muet MASC
muette FEM
⋄ *speechless with admiration* muet
d'admiration
‣ **I was speechless.** Je suis resté sans
voix.
speed NOUN
la **vitesse** ⋄ *a three-speed bike* un
vélo à trois vitesses ⋄ *at top speed* à
toute vitesse
‣ **to speed up** accélérer
speedboat NOUN
la **vedette**
speeding NOUN
l' **excès de vitesse** MASC ⋄ *He was
fined for speeding.* Il a reçu une
contravention pour excès de vitesse.
speed limit NOUN
la **limitation de vitesse**
‣ **to break the speed limit** faire un excès
de vitesse

speedometer NOUN
le **compteur**
to **spell** VERB
see also spell NOUN
[1] **écrire** (*in writing*) ⋄ *How do you
spell that?* Comment est-ce que ça
s'écrit?
[2] **épeler** (*out loud*) ⋄ *Can you spell
that please?* Est-ce que vous pouvez
épeler, s'il vous plaît?
‣ **I can't spell.** Je fais des fautes
d'orthographe.
spell NOUN
see also spell VERB
‣ **to cast a spell on somebody** jeter un
sort à quelqu'un
‣ **to be under somebody's spell** être
sous le charme de quelqu'un
spelling NOUN
l' **orthographe** FEM ⋄ *My spelling is
terrible.* Je fais beaucoup de fautes
d'orthographe.
‣ **a spelling mistake** une faute
d'orthographe
to **spend** VERB
[1] **dépenser** (*money*)
[2] **passer** (*time*) ⋄ *He spent a month in
France.* Il a passé un mois en France.
spice NOUN
l' **épice** FEM
spicy ADJECTIVE
épicé
spider NOUN
l' **araignée** FEM
to **spill** VERB
[1] **renverser** (*tip over*) ⋄ *He spilled his
coffee over his trousers.* Il a renversé
son café sur son pantalon.
[2] **se répandre** (*get spilt*) ⋄ *The soup
spilled all over the table.* La soupe s'est
répandue sur la table.
spinach NOUN
les **épinards** MASC PL
spine NOUN
la **colonne vertébrale**
spinster NOUN
la **célibataire**
spire NOUN
la **flèche**
spirit NOUN
[1] le **courage** (*courage*)
[2] l' **énergie** (*energy*)
spirits PL NOUN
les **alcools forts** MASC PL ⋄ *I don't drink
spirits.* Je ne bois pas d'alcools forts.
‣ **to be in good spirits** être de bonne
humeur
spiritual ADJECTIVE
religieux MASC

religieuse FEM
◇ *the spiritual leader of Tibet* le chef religieux du Tibet

spit NOUN
see also spit VERB
la **salive**

to **spit** VERB
see also spit NOUN
cracher
- **to spit something out** cracher quelque chose

spite NOUN
see also spite VERB
- **in spite of** malgré
- **out of spite** par méchanceté

to **spite** VERB
see also spite NOUN
contrarier ◇ *He just did it to spite me.* Il a fait ça juste pour me contrarier.

spiteful ADJECTIVE
1 (*action*)
méchant
2 (*person*)
rancunier MASC
rancunière FEM

to **splash** VERB
see also splash NOUN
éclabousser ◇ *Careful! Don't splash me!* Attention! Ne m'éclabousse pas!

splash NOUN
see also splash VERB
le **plouf** ◇ *I heard a splash.* J'ai entendu un plouf.
- **a splash of colour** une touche de couleur

splendid ADJECTIVE
splendide

splint NOUN
l' **attelle** FEM

splinter NOUN
l' **écharde** FEM

to **split** VERB
1 **fendre** (*break apart*) ◇ *He split the wood with an axe.* Il a fendu le bois avec une hache.
2 **se fendre** ◇ *The ship hit a rock and split in two.* Le bateau a percuté un rocher et s'est fendu en deux.
3 **partager** (*divide up*) ◇ *They decided to split the profits.* Ils ont décidé de partager les bénéfices.
- **to split up (1)** (*couple*) rompre
- **to split up (2)** (*group*) se disperser

to **spoil** VERB
1 **abîmer** (*object*)
2 **gâcher** (*occasion*)
3 **gâter** (*child*)

spoiled ADJECTIVE
gâté ◇ *a spoiled child* un enfant gâté

spoilsport NOUN
le/la **trouble-fête**

spoke VERB *see* **speak**

spoke NOUN
le **rayon** (*of wheel*)

spoken VERB *see* **speak**

spokesman NOUN
le **porte-parole**
(les **porte-parole** PL)

spokeswoman NOUN
le **porte-parole**
(les **porte-parole** PL)

sponge NOUN
l' **éponge** FEM
- **a sponge bag** une trousse de toilette
- **a sponge cake** un biscuit de Savoie

sponsor NOUN
see also sponsor VERB
le **donateur**
la **donatrice**

to **sponsor** VERB
see also sponsor NOUN
parrainer ◇ *The festival was sponsored by...* Le festival a été parrainé par...

spontaneous ADJECTIVE
spontané

spooky ADJECTIVE
1 **sinistre** (*eerie*)
- **a spooky story** une histoire qui fait froid dans le dos
2 **étrange** (*strange*) ◇ *a spooky coincidence* une étrange coïncidence

spoon NOUN
la **cuiller**
- **a spoonful** une cuillerée

sport NOUN
le **sport** ◇ *What's your favourite sport?* Quel est ton sport préféré?
- **a sports bag** un sac de sport
- **a sports car** une voiture de sport
- **a sports jacket** une veste sport
- **Go on, be a sport!** Allez, sois sympa!

sportsman NOUN
le **sportif**

sportswear NOUN
les **vêtements de sport** MASC PL

sportswoman NOUN
la **sportive**

sporty ADJECTIVE
sportif MASC
sportive FEM
◇ *I'm not very sporty.* Je ne suis pas très sportif.

spot NOUN
see also spot VERB
1 la **tache** (*mark*) ◇ *There's a spot on your shirt.* Il y a une tache sur ta chemise.

S

2 le **pois** (*in pattern*) ⋄ *a red dress with white spots* une robe rouge à pois blancs

3 le **bouton** (*pimple*) ⋄ *He's covered in spots.* Il est couvert de boutons.

4 le **coin** (*place*) ⋄ *It's a lovely spot for a picnic.* C'est un coin agréable pour un pique-nique.

- **on the spot (1)** (*immediately*) sur-le-champ ⋄ *They gave her the job on the spot.* Ils lui ont offert le poste sur-le-champ.

- **on the spot (2)** (*at the same place*) sur place ⋄ *Luckily they were able to mend the car on the spot.* Heureusement ils ont pu réparer la voiture sur place.

to **spot** VERB
> see also spot NOUN

repérer ⋄ *I spotted a mistake.* J'ai repéré une faute.

spotless ADJECTIVE
immaculé

spotty ADJECTIVE
(*pimply*)
boutonneux MASC
boutonneuse FEM

spouse NOUN
l' **époux** MASC
l' **épouse** FEM

to **sprain** VERB
> see also sprain NOUN

- **to sprain one's ankle** se faire une entorse à la cheville

sprain NOUN
> see also sprain VERB

l' **entorse** FEM ⋄ *It's just a sprain.* C'est juste une entorse.

spray NOUN
> see also spray VERB

la **bombe** (*spray can*)

to **spray** VERB
> see also spray NOUN

1 **vaporiser** ⋄ *to spray perfume on one's hand* se vaporiser du parfum sur la main

2 **traiter** (*crops*)

3 **peindre avec une bombe** (*graffiti*) ⋄ *Somebody had sprayed graffiti on the wall.* Quelqu'un avait peint des graffitis avec une bombe sur le mur.

spread NOUN
> see also spread VERB

- **cheese spread** le fromage à tartiner
- **chocolate spread** le chocolat à tartiner

to **spread** VERB
> see also spread NOUN

1 **étaler** ⋄ *to spread butter on a slice of bread* étaler du beurre sur une tranche de pain

2 **se propager** (*disease, news*) ⋄ *The news spread rapidly.* La nouvelle s'est propagée rapidement.

- **to spread out** (*people*) se disperser ⋄ *The soldiers spread out across the field.* Les soldats se sont dispersés dans le champ.

spreadsheet NOUN
le **tableur** (*computer program*)

spring NOUN
1 le **printemps** (*season*)
- **in spring** au printemps
2 le **ressort** (*metal coil*)
3 la **source** (*water hole*)

spring-cleaning NOUN
le **grand nettoyage de printemps**

springtime NOUN
le **printemps**
- **in springtime** au printemps

sprinkler NOUN
l' **arroseur** MASC (*for lawn*)

sprint NOUN
> see also sprint VERB

le **sprint**

to **sprint** VERB
> see also sprint NOUN

courir à toute vitesse ⋄ *She sprinted for the bus.* Elle a couru à toute vitesse pour attraper le bus.

sprinter NOUN
le **sprinteur**
la **sprinteuse**

sprouts PL NOUN
- **Brussels sprouts** les choux de Bruxelles MASC PL

spy NOUN
> see also spy VERB

l' **espion** MASC
l' **espionne** FEM

to **spy** VERB
> see also spy NOUN

- **to spy on somebody** espionner quelqu'un

spying NOUN
l' **espionnage** MASC

to **squabble** VERB
se chamailler ⋄ *Stop squabbling!* Arrêtez de vous chamailler!

square NOUN
> see also square ADJECTIVE

1 le **carré** ⋄ *a square and a triangle* un carré et un triangle

2 la **place** ⋄ *the town square* la place de l'hôtel de ville

square ADJECTIVE
> see also square NOUN

carré ⋄ *two square metres* deux mètres carrés

- **It's 2 metres square.** Ça fait deux

mètres sur deux.

squash NOUN

see also squash VERB

le **squash** (*sport*) ◇ *I play squash.* Je joue au squash.

- **a squash court** un court de squash
- **a squash racket** une raquette de squash
- **orange squash** l' **orangeade** FEM
- **lemon squash** la citronnade

to **squash** VERB

see also squash NOUN

écraser ◇ *You're squashing me.* Tu m'écrases.

to **squeak** VERB

① **pousser un petit cri** (*mouse, child*)
② **grincer** (*creak*)

to **squeeze** VERB

① **presser** (*fruit, toothpaste*)
② **serrer** (*hand, arm*)

- **to squeeze into some tight jeans** rentrer tout juste dans un jean serré

to **squint** VERB

see also squint NOUN

loucher

squint NOUN

see also squint VERB

- **He has a squint.** Il louche.

squirrel NOUN

l' **écureuil** MASC

to **stab** VERB

poignarder

stable NOUN

see also stable ADJECTIVE

l' **écurie** FEM

stable ADJECTIVE

see also stable NOUN

stable ◇ *a stable relationship* une relation stable

stack NOUN

le **pile** ◇ *a stack of books* une pile de livres

stadium NOUN

le **stade**

staff NOUN

① le **personnel** (*in company*)
② les **professeurs** MASC PL (*in school*)

stage NOUN

① la **scène** (*in plays*)
② l' **estrade** FEM (*for speeches, lectures*)

- **at this stage (1)** à ce stade ◇ *at this stage in the negotiations* à ce stade des négociations
- **at this stage (2)** pour l'instant ◇ *At this stage, it's too early to comment.* Pour l'instant, il est trop tôt pour se prononcer.
- **to do something in stages** faire quelque chose étape par étape

to **stagger** VERB

chanceler

stain NOUN

see also stain VERB

la **tache**

to **stain** VERB

see also stain NOUN

tacher

stainless steel NOUN

l' **inox** MASC

stain remover NOUN

le **détachant**

stair NOUN

la **marche** (*step*)

staircase NOUN

l' **escalier** MASC

stairs PL NOUN

l' **escalier** MASC SING

stale ADJECTIVE

rassis (*bread*)

stalemate NOUN

le **pat** (*in chess*)

stall NOUN

le **stand** MASC ◇ *He's got a market stall.* Il a un stand au marché.

- **the stalls** (*in cinema, theatre*) l'orchestre MASC

stammer NOUN

le **bégaiement**

- **He's got a stammer.** Il bégaie.

to **stamp** VERB

see also stamp NOUN

affranchir (*letter*)

- **to stamp one's foot** taper du pied

stamp NOUN

see also stamp VERB

① le **timbre** ◇ *My hobby is stamp collecting.* Je collectionne les timbres.

- **a stamp album** un album de timbres
- **a stamp collection** une collection de timbres

② le **tampon** (*rubber stamp*)

to **stand** VERB

① **être debout** (*be standing*) ◇ *He was standing by the door.* Il était debout à la porte.
② **se lever** (*stand up*)
③ **supporter** (*tolerate, withstand*) ◇ *I can't stand all this noise.* Je ne supporte pas tout ce bruit.

- **to stand for (1)** (*be short for*) être l'abréviation de ◇ *"BT" stands for "British Telecom".* "BT" est l'abréviation de "British Telecom".
- **to stand for (2)** (*tolerate*) supporter ◇ *I won't stand for it!* Je ne supporterai pas ça!
- **to stand in for somebody** remplacer quelqu'un

- **to stand up** (*get up*) se lever

standard ADJECTIVE

  see also standard NOUN

  1 **courant** ◇ *standard French* le français courant

  2 **ordinaire** (*equipment*)

- **the standard procedure** la procédure normale

standard NOUN

  see also standard ADJECTIVE

  le **niveau**

  (les **niveaux** PL)

  ◇ *The standard is very high.* Le niveau est très haut.

- **the standard of living** le niveau de vie
- **She's got high standards.** Elle est très exigeante.

stand-by ticket NOUN

  le **billet stand-by**

standpoint NOUN

  le **point de vue**

stands PL NOUN

  la **tribune** FEM (*at sports ground*)

stank VERB *see* **stink**

staple NOUN

  see also staple VERB

  l' **agrafe** FEM

to **staple** VERB

  see also staple NOUN

  agrafer

stapler NOUN

  l' **agrafeuse** FEM

star NOUN

  see also star VERB

  1 l' **étoile** FEM (*in sky*)

  2 la **vedette** (*celebrity*) ◇ *He's a TV star.* C'est une vedette de la télé.

- **the stars** (*horoscope*) l' horoscope MASC

to **star** VERB

  see also star NOUN

  être la vedette ◇ *to star in a film* être la vedette d'un film

- **The film stars Glenda Jackson.** Le film a pour vedette Glenda Jackson.
- **...starring Johnny Depp** ...avec Johnny Depp

to **stare** VERB

- **to stare at something** fixer quelque chose

stark ADVERB

- **stark naked** complètement nu

start NOUN

  see also start VERB

  1 le **début** ◇ *It's not much, but it's a start.* Ce n'est pas grand chose, mais c'est un début.

- **Shall we make a start on the washing-up?** On commence à faire la vaisselle?

  2 le **départ** (*of race*)

to **start** VERB

  see also start NOUN

  1 **commencer** ◇ *What time does it start?* À quelle heure est-ce que ça commence?

- **to start doing something** commencer à faire quelque chose ◇ *I started learning French three years ago.* J'ai commencé à apprendre le français il y a trois ans.

  2 **créer** (*organization*) ◇ *He wants to start his own business.* Il veut créer sa propre entreprise.

  3 **organiser** (*campaign*) ◇ *She started a campaign against drugs.* Elle a organisé une campagne contre la drogue.

  4 **démarrer** (*car*) ◇ *He couldn't start the car.* Il n'a pas réussi à démarrer la voiture. ◇ *The car wouldn't start.* La voiture ne voulait pas démarrer.

- **to start off** (*leave*) partir ◇ *We started off first thing in the morning.* Nous sommes partis en début de matinée.

starter NOUN

  l' **entrée** FEM (*first course*)

to **starve** VERB

  mourir de faim ◇ *People were literally starving.* Les gens mouraient littéralement de faim.

- **I'm starving!** Je meurs de faim!

state NOUN

  see also state VERB

  l' **état** MASC

- **he was in a real state** il était dans tous ses états
- **the state** (*government*) l'État
- **the States** (*USA*) les États-Unis MASC

to **state** VERB

  see also state NOUN

  1 **déclarer** (*say*) ◇ *He stated his intention to resign.* Il a déclaré son intention de démissionner.

  2 **donner** (*give*) ◇ *Please state your name and address.* Veuillez donner vos nom et adresse.

stately home NOUN

  le **château**

  (les **châteaux** PL)

statement NOUN

  la **déclaration**

station NOUN

  la **gare** (*railway*)

- **the bus station** la gare routière
- **a police station** un poste de police
- **a radio station** une station de radio

stationer's NOUN

  la **papeterie**

statue NOUN
la **statue**

to **stay** VERB
see also stay NOUN
1 **rester** (*remain*) ○ *Stay here!* Reste ici!
+ **to stay in** (*not go out*) rester à la maison
+ **to stay up** rester debout ○ *We stayed up till midnight.* Nous sommes restés debout jusqu'à minuit.
2 **loger** (*spend the night*) ○ *to stay with friends* loger chez des amis ○ *Where are you staying?* Où est-ce que vous logez?
+ **to stay the night** passer la nuit
+ **We stayed in Belgium for a few days.** Nous avons passé quelques jours en Belgique.

stay NOUN
see also stay VERB
le **séjour** ○ *my stay in France* mon séjour en France

steady ADJECTIVE
1 **régulier** MASC
régulière FEM
○ *steady progress* des progrès réguliers
2 **stable** ○ *a steady job* un emploi stable
3 **ferme** (*voice, hand*)
4 **calme** (*person*)
+ **a steady boyfriend** un copain
+ **a steady girlfriend** une copine
+ **Steady on!** Doucement!

steak NOUN (*beef*)
le **steak** ○ *steak and chips* un steak frites

to **steal** VERB
voler

steam NOUN
la **vapeur** ○ *a steam engine* une locomotive à vapeur

steel NOUN
l' **acier** MASC ○ *a steel door* une porte en acier

steep ADJECTIVE
raide (*slope*)

steeple NOUN
le **clocher**

steering wheel NOUN
le **volant**

step NOUN
see also step VERB
1 le **pas** (*pace*) ○ *He took a step forward.* Il a fait un pas en avant.
2 la **marche** (*stair*) ○ *She tripped over the step.* Elle a trébuché sur la marche.

to **step** VERB
see also step NOUN
+ **to step aside** faire un pas de côté

+ **to step back** faire un pas en arrière

stepbrother NOUN
le **demi-frère**

stepdaughter NOUN
la **belle-fille**
(les **belles-filles** PL)

stepfather NOUN
le **beau-père**
(les **beaux-pères** PL)

stepladder NOUN
l' **escabeau** MASC

stepmother NOUN
la **belle-mère**
(les **belles-mères** PL)

stepsister NOUN
la **demi-sœur**

stepson NOUN
le **beau-fils**
(les **beaux-fils** PL)

stereo NOUN
la **chaîne stéréo**
(les **chaînes stéréo** PL)

sterling ADJECTIVE
+ **£5 sterling** cinq livres sterling

stew NOUN
le **ragoût**

steward NOUN
le **steward**

stick NOUN
see also stick VERB
1 le **bâton**
2 la **canne** (*walking stick*)

to **stick** VERB
see also stick NOUN
coller (*with adhesive*) ○ *Stick the stamps on the envelope.* Collez les timbres sur l'enveloppe.
+ **I can't stick it any longer.** Je n'en peux plus.

sticker NOUN
l' **autocollant** MASC

sticky ADJECTIVE
1 **poisseux** MASC
poisseuse FEM
○ *to have sticky hands* avoir les mains poisseuses
2 **adhésif** MASC
adhésive FEM
○ *a sticky label* une étiquette adhésive

stiff ADJECTIVE, ADVERB
rigide (*rigid*)
+ **to have a stiff back** avoir mal au dos
+ **to feel stiff** avoir des courbatures
+ **to be bored stiff** s'ennuyer à mourir
+ **to be frozen stiff** être mort de froid
+ **to be scared stiff** être mort de peur

still ADVERB
see also still ADJECTIVE
1 **encore** ○ *I still haven't finished.* Je

n'ai pas encore fini. ◇ *Are you still in bed?* Tu es encore au lit?
- **better still** encore mieux
  2 **quand même** (*even so*) ◇ *She knows I don't like it, but she still does it.* Elle sait que je n'aime pas ça, mais elle le fait quand même.
  3 **enfin** (*after all*) ◇ *Still, it's the thought that counts.* Enfin, c'est l'intention qui compte.

still ADJECTIVE
see also still ADVERB
- **Keep still!** Ne bouge pas!
- **Sit still!** Reste tranquille!

sting NOUN
see also sting VERB
la **piqûre** ◇ *a bee sting* une piqûre d'abeille

to **sting** VERB
see also sting NOUN
piquer ◇ *I've been stung.* J'ai été piqué.

stingy ADJECTIVE
pingre

to **stink** VERB
see also stink NOUN
puer ◇ *It stinks!* Ça pue!

stink NOUN
see also stink VERB
la **puanteur**

to **stir** VERB
remuer

to **stitch** VERB
see also stitch NOUN
coudre (*cloth*)

stitch NOUN
see also stitch VERB
1 le **point** (*in sewing*)
2 le **point de suture** (*in wound*) ◇ *I had five stitches.* J'ai eu cinq points de suture.

stock NOUN
see also stock VERB
1 la **réserve** (*supply*)
2 le **stock** (*in shop*) ◇ *in stock* en stock
- **out of stock** épuisé
3 le **bouillon** ◇ *chicken stock* du bouillon de volaille

to **stock** VERB
see also stock NOUN
avoir (*have in stock*) ◇ *Do you stock camping stoves?* Vous avez des camping-gaz?
- **to stock up** s'approvisionner ◇ *to stock up with something* s'approvisionner en quelque chose

stock cube NOUN
le **cube de bouillon**

stocking NOUN
le **bas**

stole, stolen VERB *see* **steal**

stomach NOUN
l' **estomac** MASC

stomachache NOUN
- **to have a stomachache** avoir mal au ventre

stone NOUN
1 (*rock*)
la **pierre** ◇ *a stone wall* un mur en pierre
2 (*in fruit*)
le **noyau**
(les **noyaux** PL)
◇ *a peach stone* un noyau de pêche
In France, weight is expressed in kilos. A stone is about 6.3 kg.
- **I weigh eight stone.** Je pèse cinquante kilos.

stood VERB *see* **stand**

stool NOUN
le **tabouret**

to **stop** VERB
see also stop NOUN
1 **arrêter** ◇ *a campaign to stop whaling* une campagne pour arrêter la chasse à la baleine
2 **s'arrêter** ◇ *The bus doesn't stop there.* Le bus ne s'arrête pas là. ◇ *I think the rain's going to stop.* Je pense qu'il va s'arrêter de pleuvoir.
- **to stop doing something** arrêter de faire quelque chose ◇ *to stop smoking* arrêter de fumer
- **to stop somebody doing something** empêcher quelqu'un de faire quelque chose
- **Stop!** Stop!

stop NOUN
see also stop VERB
l' **arrêt** MASC ◇ *a bus stop* un arrêt de bus
- **This is my stop.** Je descends ici.

stopwatch NOUN
le **chronomètre**

store NOUN
see also store VERB
1 le **magasin** (*shop*) ◇ *a furniture store* un magasin de meubles
2 la **réserve** (*stock, storeroom*)

to **store** VERB
see also store NOUN
1 **garder** ◇ *They store potatoes in the cellar.* Ils gardent de pommes de terre dans la cave.
2 **enregistrer** (*information*)

storey NOUN
l' **étage** MASC ◇ *a three-storey building*

un immeuble à trois étages

storm NOUN
1. la **tempête** (gale)
2. l' **orage** MASC (thunderstorm)

stormy ADJECTIVE
orageux MASC
orageuse FEM

story NOUN
l' **histoire** FEM

stove NOUN
1. la **cuisinière** (in kitchen)
2. le **réchaud** (camping stove)

straight ADJECTIVE
1. **droit** ◦ a straight line une ligne droite
2. **raide** ◦ straight hair les cheveux raides
3. **hétéro** (heterosexual)
- **straight away** tout de suite
- **straight on** tout droit

straightforward ADJECTIVE
simple

strain NOUN
see also strain VERB
le **stress**
- **It was a strain.** C'était éprouvant.

to **strain** VERB
see also strain NOUN
se faire mal à ◦ I strained my back. Je me suis fait mal au dos.
- **to strain a muscle** se froisser un muscle

strained ADJECTIVE
froissé (muscle)

stranded ADJECTIVE
- **We were stranded.** Nous étions coincés.

strange ADJECTIVE
bizarre ◦ That's strange! C'est bizarre!

stranger NOUN
l' **inconnu** MASC
l' **inconnue** FEM
◦ Don't talk to strangers. Ne parle pas aux inconnus.
- **I'm a stranger here.** Je ne suis pas d'ici.

to **strangle** VERB
étrangler

strap NOUN
1. la **courroie** (of bag, camera, suitcase)
2. la **bretelle** (of bra, dress)
3. la **lanière** (on shoe)
4. le **bracelet** (of watch)

straw NOUN
la **paille**
- **That's the last straw!** Ça, c'est le comble!

strawberry NOUN
la **fraise** ◦ strawberry jam la confiture

de fraises ◦ a strawberry ice cream une glace à la fraise

stray NOUN
- **a stray cat** un chat perdu

stream NOUN
le **ruisseau**
(les **ruisseaux** PL)

street NOUN
la **rue** ◦ in the street dans la rue

streetlamp NOUN
le **réverbère**

street plan NOUN
le **plan de la ville**

streetwise ADJECTIVE
dégourdi

strength NOUN
la **force**

to **stress** VERB
see also stress NOUN
souligner ◦ I would like to stress that... J'aimerais souligner que...

stress NOUN
see also stress VERB
le **stress**

to **stretch** VERB
1. **s'étirer** (person, animal) ◦ The dog woke up and stretched. Le chien s'est réveillé et s'est étiré.
2. **se détendre** (get bigger) ◦ My sweater stretched when I washed it. Mon pull s'est détendu au lavage.
3. **tendre** (stretch out) ◦ They stretched a rope between two trees. Ils ont tendu une corde entre deux arbres.
- **to stretch out one's arms** tendre les bras

stretcher NOUN
le **brancard**

stretchy NOUN
élastique

strict ADJECTIVE
strict

strike NOUN
see also strike VERB
la **grève**
- **to be on strike** être en grève
- **to go on strike** faire grève

to **strike** VERB
see also strike NOUN
1. **sonner** (clock) ◦ The clock struck three. L'horloge a sonné trois heures.
2. **faire grève** (go on strike)
3. **frapper** (hit)
- **to strike a match** frotter une allumette

striker NOUN
1. le/la **gréviste** (person on strike)
2. le **buteur** (footballer)

striking ADJECTIVE
1. **en grève** (on strike) ◦ striking miners

S

les mineurs en grève

[2] **frappant** (*noticeable*) ⋄ *a striking difference* une différence frappante

string NOUN

[1] la **ficelle** ⋄ *a piece of string* un bout de ficelle

[2] la **corde** (*of violin, guitar*)

to **strip** VERB

see also strip NOUN

se déshabiller (*get undressed*)

strip NOUN

see also strip VERB

la **bande**

➤ **a strip cartoon** une bande dessinée

stripe NOUN

la **rayure**

striped ADJECTIVE

à rayures ⋄ *a striped skirt* une jupe à rayures

stripper NOUN

le **strip-teaseur**

la **strip-teaseuse**

stripy ADJECTIVE

rayé ⋄ *a stripy shirt* une chemise rayée

to **stroke** VERB

see also stroke NOUN

caresser

stroke NOUN

see also stroke VERB

l' **attaque** FEM ⋄ *to have a stroke* avoir une attaque

stroll NOUN

➤ **to go for a stroll** aller faire une petite promenade

strong ADJECTIVE

[1] **fort** ⋄ *She's very strong.* Elle est très forte.

[2] **résistant** (*material*)

strongly ADVERB

fortement ⋄ *We recommend strongly that...* Nous recommandons fortement que...

➤ **He smelt strongly of tobacco.** Il sentait fort le tabac.

➤ **strongly built** solidement bâti

➤ **I don't feel strongly about it.** Ça m'est égal.

to **struggle** VERB

see also struggle NOUN

se débattre (*physically*) ⋄ *He struggled, but he couldn't escape.* Il s'est débattu, mais il n'a pas pu s'échapper.

➤ **to struggle to do something (1)** (*fight*) se battre pour faire quelque chose ⋄ *He struggled to get custody of his daughter.* Il s'est battu pour obtenir la garde de sa fille.

➤ **to struggle to do something (2)** (*have difficulty*) avoir du mal à faire quelque chose

struggle NOUN

see also struggle VERB

la **lutte** (*for independence, equality*)

➤ **It was a struggle.** Ça a été laborieux.

stub NOUN

le **mégot** (*of cigarette*)

stubborn ADJECTIVE

têtu

to **stub out** VERB

écraser (*cigarette*)

stuck VERB *see* **stick**

stuck ADJECTIVE

coincé (*jammed*) ⋄ *It's stuck.* C'est coincé.

➤ **to get stuck** rester coincé ⋄ *We got stuck in a traffic jam.* Nous sommes restés coincés dans un embouteillage.

stuck-up ADJECTIVE

coincé (*informal*)

stud NOUN

[1] la **boucle d'oreille** (*earring*)

[2] le **clou** (*on football boots*)

student NOUN

l' **étudiant** MASC

l' **étudiante** FEM

studio NOUN

le **studio** ⋄ *a TV studio* un studio de télévision

➤ **a studio flat** un studio

to **study** VERB

[1] **faire des études** (*at university*) ⋄ *I plan to study biology.* J'ai l'intention de faire des études de biologie.

[2] **travailler** (*do homework*) ⋄ *I've got to study tonight.* Je dois travailler ce soir.

stuff NOUN

[1] le **truc** (*substance*) ⋄ *I need some stuff for hay fever.* J'ai besoin d'un truc contre le rhume des foins.

[2] les **trucs** MASC PL (*things*) ⋄ *There's some stuff on the table for you.* Il y a des trucs sur la table pour toi.

[3] les **affaires** FEM PL (*possessions*) ⋄ *Have you got all your stuff?* Est-ce que tu as toutes tes affaires?

stuffy ADJECTIVE

mal aéré (*room*)

➤ **It's really stuffy in here.** On étouffe ici.

to **stumble** VERB

trébucher

stung VERB *see* **sting**

stunk VERB *see* **stink**

stunned ADJECTIVE

sidéré (*amazed*) ⋄ *I was stunned.* J'étais sidéré.

stunning ADJECTIVE

superbe

stunt NOUN
  la **cascade** (*in film*)
stuntman NOUN
  le **cascadeur**
stupid ADJECTIVE
  stupide ◇ *a stupid joke* une
  plaisanterie stupide
- **Me, go jogging? Don't be stupid!** Moi,
  faire du footing? Ne dis pas de bêtises!
to **stutter** VERB
  see also stutter NOUN
  bégayer
stutter NOUN
  see also stutter VERB
- **He's got a stutter.** Il bégaie.
style NOUN
  le **style** ◇ *That's not his style.* Ça n'est
  pas son style.
subject NOUN
  [1] le **sujet** ◇ *The subject of my project*
  was the Internet. Le sujet de mon projet
  était l'Internet.
  [2] la **matière** (*at school*) ◇ *What's your*
  favourite subject? Quelle est ta matière
  préférée?
submarine NOUN
  le **sous-marin**
subscription NOUN
  l' **abonnement** MASC (*to paper, magazine*)
- **to take out a subscription to** s'abonner
  à
to **subsidize** VERB
  subventionner
subsidy NOUN
  la **subvention**
substance NOUN
  la **substance**
substitute NOUN
  see also substitute VERB
  (*person*)
  le **remplaçant**
  la **remplaçante**
to **substitute** VERB
  see also substitute NOUN
  substituer ◇ *to substitute A for B*
  substituer A à B
subtitled ADJECTIVE
  sous-titré
subtitles PL NOUN
  les **sous-titres** MASC PL ◇ *a French film*
  with English subtitles un film français
  avec des sous-titres en anglais
subtle ADJECTIVE
  subtil
to **subtract** VERB
  retrancher ◇ *to subtract 3 from 5*
  retrancher trois de cinq
suburb NOUN
  la **banlieue** ◇ *a suburb of Paris* une

banlieue de Paris ◇ *They live in the*
suburbs. Ils habitent en banlieue.
suburban ADJECTIVE
  de banlieue ◇ *a suburban train* un
  train de banlieue
subway NOUN
  le **passage souterrain** (*underpass*)
to **succeed** VERB
  réussir ◇ *to succeed in doing*
  something réussir à faire quelque chose
success NOUN
  le **succès** ◇ *The play was a great*
  success. La pièce a eu beaucoup de
  succès.
successful ADJECTIVE
  réussi ◇ *a successful attempt* une
  tentative réussie
- **to be successful in doing something**
  réussir à faire quelque chose
- **He's a successful businessman.** Ses
  affaires marchent bien.
successfully ADVERB
  avec succès
successive ADJECTIVE
- **on four successive occasions** quatre
  fois de suite
such ADJECTIVE, ADVERB
  si ◇ *such nice people* des gens si
  gentils ◇ *such a long journey* un
  voyage si long
- **such a lot of** tellement de ◇ *such a*
  lot of work tellement de travail
- **such as** (*like*) comme ◇ *hot countries,*
  such as India les pays chauds, comme
  l'Inde
- **not as such** pas exactement ◇ *He's*
  not an expert as such, but... Ce n'est pas
  exactement un expert, mais...
- **There's no such thing.** Ça n'existe pas.
  ◇ *There's no such thing as the yeti.*
  Le yéti n'existe pas.
such-and-such ADJECTIVE
  tel ou tel MASC
  telle ou telle FEM
  ◇ *such-and-such a place* tel ou tel
  endroit
to **suck** VERB
  sucer ◇ *to suck one's thumb* sucer
  son puce
sudden ADJECTIVE
  soudain ◇ *a sudden change* un
  changement soudain
- **all of a sudden** tout à coup
suddenly ADVERB
  [1] **brusquement** (*stop, leave, change*)
  [2] **subitement** (*die*)
  [3] **soudain** (*at beginning of sentence*)
  ◇ *Suddenly, the door opened.*
  Soudain, la porte s'est ouverte.

S

suede NOUN
le **daim** ◇ *a suede jacket* une veste en daim

to **suffer** VERB
souffrir ◇ *She was really suffering.* Elle souffrait beaucoup.
- **to suffer from a disease** avoir une maladie ◇ *I suffer from hay fever.* J'ai le rhume des foins.

to **suffocate** VERB
suffoquer

sugar NOUN
le **sucre** ◇ *Do you take sugar?* Est-ce que vous prenez du sucre?

to **suggest** VERB
suggérer ◇ *I suggested they set off early.* Je leur ai suggéré de partir de bonne heure.

suggestion NOUN
la **suggestion** ◇ *to make a suggestion* faire une suggestion

suicide NOUN
le **suicide**
- **to commit suicide** se suicider

suit NOUN
see also **suit** VERB
1 le **costume** (*man's*)
2 le **tailleur** (*woman's*)

to **suit** VERB
see also **suit** NOUN
1 **convenir à** (*be convenient for*)
◇ *What time would suit you?* Quelle heure vous conviendrait?
- **That suits me fine.** Ça m'arrange.
- **Suit yourself!** Comme tu veux!
2 **aller bien à** (*look good on*) ◇ *That dress really suits you.* Cette robe te va vraiment bien.

suitable ADJECTIVE
1 **convenable** ◇ *a suitable time* une heure convenable
2 **approprié** (*clothes*) ◇ *suitable clothing* des vêtements appropriés

suitcase NOUN
la **valise**

suite NOUN
la **suite** (*of rooms*)
- **a bedroom suite** les meubles de chambre à coucher

to **sulk** VERB
bouder

sulky ADJECTIVE
boudeur MASC
boudeuse FEM

sum NOUN
1 le **calcul** (*calculation*) ◇ *She's good at sums.* Elle est bonne en calcul.
2 la **somme** (*amount*) ◇ *a sum of money* une somme d'argent

to **summarize** VERB
résumer

summary NOUN
le **résumé**

summer NOUN
l' **été** MASC
- **in summer** en été
- **summer clothes** les vêtements d'été
- **the summer holidays** les vacances d'été

summertime NOUN
l' **été** MASC
- **in summertime** en été

summit NOUN
le **sommet**

to **sum up** VERB
résumer

sun NOUN
le **soleil** ◇ *in the sun* au soleil

to **sunbathe** VERB
se bronzer

sunblock NOUN
l' **écran total** MASC

sunburn NOUN
le **coup de soleil**

sunburnt ADJECTIVE
- **I got sunburnt.** J'ai attrapé un coup de soleil.

Sunday NOUN
le **dimanche** ◇ *on Sunday* dimanche ◇ *on Sundays* le dimanche ◇ *every Sunday* tous les dimanches ◇ *last Sunday* dimanche dernier ◇ *next Sunday* dimanche prochain

Sunday school NOUN
le **catéchisme**
le catéchisme, *the French equivalent of* Sunday school, *takes place during the week after school rather than on a Sunday.*
◇ *to go to Sunday school* aller au catéchisme

sunflower NOUN
le **tournesol**

sung VERB *see* **sing**

sunglasses PL NOUN
les **lunettes de soleil** FEM PL

sunk VERB *see* **sink**

sunlight NOUN
le **soleil**

sunny ADJECTIVE
ensoleillé ◇ *a sunny morning* une matinée ensoleillée
- **It's sunny.** Il fait du soleil.
- **a sunny day** une belle journée

sunrise NOUN
le **lever du soleil**

sunroof NOUN
le **toit ouvrant**

sunscreen NOUN
la **crème solaire**

sunset NOUN
le **coucher du soleil**
sunshine NOUN
le **soleil**
sunstroke NOUN
l' **insolation** FEM ◇ *to get sunstroke*
attraper une insolation
suntan NOUN
le **bronzage**
- **suntan lotion** le lait solaire
- **suntan oil** l'huile solaire FEM
super ADJECTIVE
formidable
superb ADJECTIVE
superbe
supermarket NOUN
le **supermarché**
supernatural ADJECTIVE
surnaturel MASC
surnaturelle FEM
superstitious ADJECTIVE
superstitieux MASC
superstitieuse FEM
to **supervise** VERB
surveiller
supervisor NOUN
[1] *(in factory)*
le **surveillant**
la **surveillante**
[2] *(in department store)*
le **chef de rayon**
supper NOUN
le **dîner**
supplement NOUN
le **supplément**
supplies PL NOUN
les **vivres** MASC PL *(food)*
to **supply** VERB
see also supply NOUN
fournir *(provide)*
- **to supply somebody with something**
fournir quelque chose à quelqu'un
◇ *The centre supplied us with all the
equipment.* Le centre nous a fourni tout
l'équipement.
supply NOUN
see also supply VERB
la **provision** ◇ *a supply of paper* une
provision de papier
- **the water supply** *(to town)*
l'approvisionnement en eau MASC
supply teacher NOUN
le **suppléant**
la **suppléante**
to **support** VERB
see also support NOUN
[1] **soutenir** ◇ *My mum has always
supported me.* Ma mère m'a toujours
soutenu.

[2] **être supporter de** ◇ *What team do
you support?* Tu es supporter de quelle
équipe?
[3] **subvenir aux besoins de** *(financially)*
◇ *She had to support five children on
her own.* Elle a dû subvenir toute seule
aux besoins de cinq enfants.
support NOUN
see also support VERB
le **soutien** *(backing)*
supporter NOUN
[1] le **supporter** ◇ *a Liverpool supporter*
un supporter de Liverpool
[2] le **sympathisant**
la **sympathisante**
◇ *a supporter of the Labour Party* un
sympathisant du parti travailliste
to **suppose** VERB
imaginer ◇ *I suppose he's late.*
J'imagine qu'il est en retard.
◇ *Suppose you won the lottery.*
Imaginez que vous gagniez à la loterie.
- **I suppose so.** J'imagine.
- **to be supposed to do something** être
censé faire quelque chose ◇ *You're
supposed to show your passport.* On est
censé montrer son passeport.
supposing CONJUNCTION
si ◇ *Supposing you won the lottery...*
Si tu gagnais à la loterie...
surcharge NOUN
la **surcharge**
sure ADJECTIVE
sûr ◇ *Are you sure?* Tu es sûr?
- **Sure!** Bien sûr!
- **to make sure that...** vérifier que...
◇ *I'm going to make sure the door's
locked.* Je vais vérifier que la porte est
fermée à clé.
surely ADVERB
- **Surely you've been to London?**
J'imagine que tu es allé à Londres, non?
- **The shops are closed on Sundays,
surely?** J'imagine que les magasins
sont fermés le dimanche, non?
surf NOUN
le **ressac**
surface NOUN
la **surface**
surfboard NOUN
la **planche de surf**
(les **planches de surf** PL)
surfing NOUN
le **surf** ◇ *to go surfing* faire du surf
surgeon NOUN
le **chirurgien** ◇ *She's a surgeon.* Elle
est chirurgien.
surgery NOUN
le **cabinet médical** *(doctor's surgery)*

S

- **surgery hours** les heures de consultation FEM

surname NOUN
le **nom de famille** (les **noms de famille** PL)

surprise NOUN
la **surprise**

surprised ADJECTIVE
surpris ◇ *I was surprised to see him.* J'ai été surpris de le voir.

surprising ADJECTIVE
surprenant

to **surrender** VERB
capituler

surrogate mother NOUN
la **mère porteuse**

to **surround** VERB
encercler ◇ *The police surrounded the house.* La police a encerclé la maison. ◇ *You're surrounded!* Vous êtes encerclé!

- **surrounded by** entouré de ◇ *The house is surrounded by trees.* La maison est entourée d'arbres.

survey NOUN
l' **enquête** FEM (*research*)

surveyor NOUN
[1] l' **expert en bâtiment** MASC (*of buildings*)
[2] le/la **géomètre** (*of land*)

survivor NOUN
le **survivant**
la **survivante**
◇ *There were no survivors.* Il n'y a pas eu de survivants.

to **suspect** VERB
see also suspect NOUN
soupçonner

suspect NOUN
see also suspect VERB
le **suspect**
la **suspecte**

to **suspend** VERB
[1] **exclure** (*from school, team*) ◇ *He's been suspended.* Il s'est fait exclure.
[2] **suspendre** (*from job*)

suspense NOUN
[1] l' **attente** FEM (*waiting*) ◇ *The suspense was terrible.* L'attente a été terrible.
[2] le **suspense** (*in story*) ◇ *a film with lots of suspense* un film avec beaucoup de suspense

suspension NOUN
[1] l' **exclusion** FEM (*from school, team*)
[2] la **suspension** (*from job*)

suspicious ADJECTIVE
[1] **méfiant** ◇ *He was suspicious at first.* Il était méfiant au début.

[2] **louche** (*suspicious-looking*) ◇ *a suspicious person* un individu louche

to **swallow** VERB
avaler

swam VERB *see* **swim**

swan NOUN
le **cygne**

to **swap** VERB
échanger ◇ *Do you want to swap?* Tu veux échanger? ◇ *to swap A for B* échanger A contre B

to **swat** VERB
écraser

to **sway** VERB
osciller

to **swear** VERB
jurer (*make an oath, curse*)

swearword NOUN
le **gros mot**

sweat NOUN
see also sweat VERB
la **transpiration**

to **sweat** VERB
see also sweat NOUN
transpirer

sweater NOUN
le **pull**

sweaty ADJECTIVE
[1] **en sueur** (*person, face*) ◇ *I'm all sweaty.* Je suis en sueur.
[2] **moite** (*hands*)

Swede NOUN
(*person*)
le **Suédois**
la **Suédoise**

swede NOUN
le **rutabaga** (*vegetable*)

Sweden NOUN
la **Suède**
- **in Sweden** en Suède
- **to Sweden** en Suède

Swedish ADJECTIVE
see also Swedish NOUN
suédois ◇ *She's Swedish.* Elle est suédoise.

Swedish NOUN
see also Swedish ADJECTIVE
le **suédois** (*language*)

to **sweep** VERB
balayer
- **to sweep the floor** balayer

sweet NOUN
see also sweet ADJECTIVE
[1] le **bonbon** (*candy*) ◇ *a bag of sweets* un paquet de bonbons
[2] le **dessert** (*pudding*) ◇ *What sweet did you have?* Qu'est-ce que vous avez mangé comme dessert?

sweet ADJECTIVE
see also **sweet** NOUN
[1] (not savoury)
sucré
[2] (kind)
gentil MASC
gentille FEM
◇ That was really sweet of you. C'était vraiment gentil de ta part.
[3] (cute)
mignon MASC
mignonne FEM
◇ Isn't she sweet? Comme elle est mignonne!
◆ **sweet and sour pork** le porc à la sauce aigre-douce
sweetcorn NOUN
le **maïs doux**
sweltering ADJECTIVE
◆ **It was sweltering.** Il faisait une chaleur étouffante.
swept VERB see **sweep**
to **swerve** VERB
faire une embardée ◇ He swerved to avoid the cyclist. Il a fait une embardée pour éviter le cycliste.
swim NOUN
see also **swim** VERB
◆ **to go for a swim** aller se baigner
to **swim** VERB
see also **swim** NOUN
nager ◇ Can you swim? Tu sais nager?
◆ **She swam across the river.** Elle a traversé la rivière à la nage.
swimmer NOUN
le **nageur**
la **nageuse**
◇ She's a good swimmer. C'est une bonne nageuse.
swimming NOUN
la **natation** ◇ Do you like swimming? Tu aimes la natation?
◆ **to go swimming** (in a pool) aller à la piscine
◆ **a swimming cap** un bonnet de bain
◆ **a swimming costume** un maillot de bain
◆ **a swimming pool** une piscine
◆ **swimming trunks** le maillot de bain
swimsuit NOUN
le **maillot de bain**
swing NOUN
la **balançoire** (in playground, garden)

Swiss ADJECTIVE
see also **Swiss** NOUN
suisse ◇ Sabine's Swiss. Sabine est suisse.
Swiss NOUN
see also **Swiss** ADJECTIVE
le/la **Suisse** (person)
◆ **the Swiss** les Suisses
switch NOUN
see also **switch** VERB
le **bouton** (for light, radio etc)
to **switch** VERB
see also **switch** NOUN
changer de ◇ We switched partners. Nous avons changé de partenaire.
to **switch off** VERB
[1] **éteindre** (electrical appliance)
[2] **arrêter** (engine, machine)
to **switch on** VERB
[1] **allumer** (electrical appliance)
[2] **mettre en marche** (engine, machine)
Switzerland NOUN
la **Suisse**
◆ **in Switzerland** en Suisse
swollen ADJECTIVE
enflé (arm, leg)
to **swop** VERB
échanger ◇ Do you want to swop? Tu veux échanger? ◇ to swop A for B échanger A contre B
sword NOUN
l' **épée** FEM
swore, sworn VERB see **swear**
swum VERB see **swim**
swung VERB see **swing**
syllabus NOUN
le **programme** ◇ on the syllabus au programme
symbol NOUN
le **symbole**
sympathetic ADJECTIVE
compréhensif MASC
compréhensive FEM
to **sympathize** VERB
◆ **to sympathize with somebody** comprendre quelqu'un
sympathy NOUN
la **compassion**
syringe NOUN
la **seringue**
system NOUN
le **système**

S

T

table NOUN

la **table** ◇ *to lay the table* mettre la table

tablecloth NOUN

la **nappe**

tablespoon NOUN

la **grande cuillère**

- a **tablespoonful of sugar** une cuillerée à soupe de sucre

tablet NOUN

le **comprimé**

table tennis NOUN

le **ping-pong** ◇ *to play table tennis* jouer au ping-pong

tabloid NOUN

le **quotidien populaire**

tackle NOUN

see also tackle VERB

① le **tacle** (*in football*)

② le **plaquage** (*in rugby*)

- **fishing tackle** le matériel de pêche

to **tackle** VERB

see also tackle NOUN

① **tacler** (*in football*)

② **plaquer** (*in rugby*)

- **to tackle a problem** s'attaquer à un problème

tact NOUN

le **tact**

tactful ADJECTIVE

plein de tact

tactics PL NOUN

la **tactique** SING

tactless ADJECTIVE

- **to be tactless** manquer de tact ◇ *a tactless remark* une remarque qui manque de tact

tadpole NOUN

le **têtard**

tag NOUN

l' **étiquette** FEM (*label*)

tail NOUN

la **queue**

- **Heads or tails?** Pile ou face?

tailor NOUN

le **tailleur**

to **take** VERB

① **prendre** ◇ *Are you taking your new camera?* Tu prends ton nouvel appareil photo? ◇ *He took a plate from the cupboard.* Il a pris une assiette dans le placard. ◇ *It takes about an hour.* Ça prend environ une heure.

② **emmener** (*person*) ◇ *He goes to London every week, but he never takes me.* Il va à Londres toutes les semaines,

mais il ne m'emmène jamais.

- **to take something somewhere** emporter quelque chose quelque part ◇ *Do you take your exercise books home?* Vous emportez vos cahiers chez vous? ◇ *Don't take anything valuable with you.* N'emportez pas d'objets de valeur.

- **I'm going to take my coat to the cleaner's.** Je vais donner mon manteau à nettoyer.

③ **demander** (*effort, skill*) ◇ *that takes a lot of courage* cela demande beaucoup de courage

- **It takes a lot of money to do that.** Il faut beaucoup d'argent pour faire ça.

④ **supporter** (*tolerate*) ◇ *He can't take being criticized.* Il ne supporte pas d'être critiqué.

⑤ **passer** (*exam, test*) ◇ *Have you taken your driving test yet?* Est-ce que tu as déjà passé ton permis de conduire?

⑥ **faire** (*subject*) ◇ *I decided to take French instead of German.* J'ai décidé de faire du français au lieu de l'allemand.

to **take after** VERB

ressembler à ◇ *She takes after her mother.* Elle ressemble à sa mère.

to **take apart** VERB

- **to take something apart** démonter quelque chose

to **take away** VERB

① **emporter** (*object*)

② **emmener** (*person*)

- **to take something away** (*confiscate*) confisquer quelque chose

- **hot meals to take away** des plats chauds à emporter

takeaway NOUN

① le **plat à emporter** (*meal*)

② le **restaurant qui vend des plats à emporter** (*shop*) ◇ *a Chinese takeaway* un restaurant chinois qui vend des plats à emporter

to **take back** VERB

rapporter ◇ *I took it back to the shop.* Je l'ai rapporté au magasin.

- **I take it all back!** Je n'ai rien dit!

to **take in** VERB

comprendre (*understand*) ◇ *I didn't really take it in.* Je n'ai pas vraiment compris.

to **take off** VERB

① **décoller** (*plane*) ◇ *The plane took off twenty minutes late.* L'avion a décollé avec vingt minutes de retard.

2 **enlever** (*clothes*) ◇ *Take your coat off.* Enlevez votre manteau.

takeoff NOUN
le **décollage** (*of plane*)

to **take out** VERB
sortir (*from container, pocket*)
- **He took her out to the theatre.** Il l'a emmenée au théâtre.

to **take over** VERB
prendre la relève ◇ *I'll take over now.* Je vais prendre la relève.
- **to take over from somebody** remplacer quelqu'un

talcum powder NOUN
le **talc**

tale NOUN
le **conte** FEM (*story*)

talent NOUN
le **talent** ◇ *She's got lots of talent.* Elle a beaucoup de talent.
- **to have a talent for something** être doué pour quelque chose ◇ *He's got a real talent for languages.* Il est vraiment doué pour les langues.

talented ADJECTIVE
- **She's a talented pianist.** C'est une pianiste de talent.

talk NOUN
see also **talk** VERB
1 l' **exposé** MASC (*speech*) ◇ *She gave a talk on rock climbing.* Elle a fait un exposé sur la varappe.
2 la **conversation** (*conversation*) ◇ *I had a talk with my Mum about it.* J'ai eu une petite conversation avec ma mère à ce sujet.
3 les **racontars** MASC (*gossip*) ◇ *It's just talk.* Ce sont des racontars.

to **talk** VERB
see also **talk** NOUN
parler ◇ *to talk about something* parler de quelque chose
- **to talk something over with somebody** discuter de quelque chose avec quelqu'un

talkative ADJECTIVE
bavard

tall ADJECTIVE
1 **grand** (*person, tree*)
- **to be 2 metres tall** mesurer deux mètres
2 **haut** (*building*)

tampon NOUN
le **tampon**

tan NOUN
le **bronzage** ◇ *She's got an amazing tan.* Elle a un bronzage superbe.

tangerine NOUN
la **mandarine**

tank NOUN
1 le **réservoir** (*for water, petrol*)
2 le **char d'assaut** (*military*)
- **a fish tank** un aquarium

tanker NOUN
1 le **pétrolier** (*ship*)
- **an oil tanker** un pétrolier
2 le **camion-citerne** (*truck*)
- **a petrol tanker** un camion-citerne

tap NOUN
1 le **robinet** (*water tap*)
2 la **petite tape** (*gentle blow*)

tap-dancing NOUN
les **claquettes** FEM PL ◇ *I do tap-dancing.* Je fais des claquettes.

to **tape** VERB
see also **tape** NOUN
enregistrer (*record*) ◇ *Did you tape that film last night?* As-tu enregistré le film hier soir?

tape NOUN
see also **tape** VERB
1 la **cassette** ◇ *a tape of Sinead O'Connor* une cassette de Sinead O'Connor
2 le **scotch** ® (*sticky tape*)

tape deck NOUN
le **magnétophone**

tape measure NOUN
le **mètre à ruban**

tape recorder NOUN
le **magnétophone**

target NOUN
la **cible**

tarmac NOUN
le **macadam** (*on road*)

tart NOUN
la **tarte** ◇ *an apple tart* une tarte aux pommes

tartan ADJECTIVE
écossais ◇ *a tartan scarf* une écharpe écossaise

task NOUN
la **tâche**

taste NOUN
see also **taste** VERB
le **goût** ◇ *It's got a really strange taste.* Ça a un goût vraiment bizarre. ◇ *a joke in bad taste* une plaisanterie de mauvais goût
- **Would you like a taste?** Tu veux goûter?

to **taste** VERB
see also **taste** NOUN
goûter ◇ *Would you like to taste it?* Vous voulez y goûter?
- **to taste of something** avoir un goût de quelque chose ◇ *It tastes of fish.* Ça a un goût de poisson.

T

- **You can taste the garlic in it.** Ça a bien le goût d'ail.

tasteful ADJECTIVE
  de bon goût

tasteless ADJECTIVE
  [1] **fade** (*food*)
  [2] **de mauvais goût** (*in bad taste*) ◇ *a tasteless remark* une remarque de mauvais goût

tasty ADJECTIVE
  savoureux MASC
  savoureuse FEM

tattoo NOUN
  le **tatouage**

taught VERB *see* **teach**

Taurus NOUN
  le **Taureau** ◇ *I'm Taurus.* Je suis Taureau.

tax NOUN
  [1] les **impôts** MASC PL (*on income*)
  [2] la **taxe** (*on goods, alcohol*)

taxi NOUN
  le **taxi**
- **a taxi driver** un chauffeur de taxi

taxi rank NOUN
  la **station de taxis**

TB NOUN
  la **tuberculose**

tea NOUN
  [1] le **thé** ◇ *a cup of tea* une tasse de thé
- **a tea bag** un sachet de thé
  [2] le **dîner** (*evening meal*)
- **We were having tea.** Nous étions en train de dîner.

to **teach** VERB
  [1] **apprendre** ◇ *My sister taught me to swim.* Ma sœur m'a appris à nager. ◇ *That'll teach you!* Ça t'apprendra!
  [2] **enseigner** (*in school*) ◇ *She teaches physics.* Elle enseigne la physique.

teacher NOUN
  [1] (*in secondary school*)
  le **professeur** ◇ *a maths teacher* un professeur de maths ◇ *She's a teacher.* Elle est professeur.
  [2] (*in primary school*)
  l' **instituteur** MASC
  l' **institutrice** FEM
  ◇ *He's a primary school teacher.* Il est instituteur.

teacher's pet NOUN
  le **chouchou**
  la **chouchoute**

tea cloth NOUN
  le **torchon**

team NOUN
  l' **équipe** FEM ◇ *a football team* une équipe de football ◇ *She was in my*

team. Elle était dans mon équipe.

teapot NOUN
  la **théière**

tear NOUN
  see also **tear** VERB
  la **larme** ◇ *She was in tears.* Elle était en larmes.

to **tear** VERB
  see also **tear** NOUN
  [1] **déchirer** ◇ *Be careful or you'll tear the page.* Fais attention, tu vas déchirer la page.
  [2] **se déchirer** ◇ *It won't tear, it's very strong.* Ça ne se déchire pas, c'est très solide.
- **to tear up** déchirer ◇ *He tore up the letter.* Il a déchiré la lettre.

tear gas NOUN
  le **gaz lacrymogène**

to **tease** VERB
  [1] **tourmenter** (*unkindly*) ◇ *Stop teasing that poor animal!* Arrête de tourmenter cette pauvre bête!
  [2] **taquiner** (*jokingly*) ◇ *He's teasing you.* Il te taquine.
- **I was only teasing.** Je plaisantais.

teaspoon NOUN
  la **petite cuillère**
- **a teaspoonful of sugar** une cuillerée à café de sucre

teatime NOUN
  l' **heure du dîner** FEM (*in evening*) ◇ *It was nearly teatime.* C'était presque l'heure du dîner.
- **Teatime!** À table!

tea towel NOUN
  le **torchon**

technical ADJECTIVE
  technique
- **a technical college** un lycée technique

technician NOUN
  [1] le **technicien**
  [2] la **technicienne**

technique NOUN
  la **technique**

techno NOUN
  la **techno** (*music*)

technological ADJECTIVE
  technologique

technology NOUN
  la **technologie**

teddy bear NOUN
  le **nounours**

teenage ADJECTIVE
  [1] **pour les jeunes** ◇ *a teenage magazine* un magazine pour les jeunes
  [2] **adolescent** (*boys, girls*) ◇ *She has two teenage daughters.* Elle a deux filles adolescentes.

teenager NOUN
l' **adolescent** MASC
l' **adolescente** FEM

teens PL NOUN
- **She's in her teens.** C'est une adolescente.

tee-shirt NOUN
le **tee-shirt**

teeth PL NOUN
les **dents**

to **teethe** VERB
faire ses dents

teetotal ADJECTIVE
- **I'm teetotal.** Je ne bois jamais d'alcool.

telecommunications PL NOUN
les **télécommunications** FEM PL

telephone NOUN
le **téléphone** ◇ *on the telephone* au téléphone
- **a telephone box** une cabine téléphonique
- **a telephone call** un coup de téléphone
- **the telephone directory** l'annuaire MASC
- **a telephone number** un numéro de téléphone

telescope NOUN
le **télescope**

television NOUN
la **télévision**
- **on television** à la télévision
- **a television licence** une redevance de télévision
- **a television programme** une émission de télévision

to **tell** VERB
dire
- **to tell somebody something** dire quelque chose à quelqu'un ◇ *Did you tell your mother?* Tu l'as dit à ta mère? ◇ *I told him that I was going on holiday.* Je lui ai dit que je partais en vacances.
- **to tell somebody to do something** dire à quelqu'un de faire quelque chose ◇ *He told me to wait a moment.* Il m'a dit d'attendre un moment.
- **to tell lies** dire des mensonges
- **to tell a story** raconter une histoire
- **I can't tell the difference between them.** Je n'arrive pas à les distinguer.

to **tell off** VERB
gronder

telly NOUN
la **télé** ◇ *to watch telly* regarder la télé
- **on telly** à la télé

temper NOUN
le **caractère** ◇ *He's got a terrible temper.* Il a un sale caractère.
- **to be in a temper** être en colère

- **to lose one's temper** se mettre en colère ◇ *I lost my temper.* Je me suis mis en colère.

temperature NOUN
la **température** (*of oven, water, person*)
- **The temperature was 30 degrees.** Il faisait trente degrés.
- **to have a temperature** avoir de la fièvre

temple NOUN
le **temple**

temporary ADJECTIVE
temporaire

to **tempt** VERB
tenter ◇ *I'm very tempted!* Je suis très tenté!
- **to tempt somebody to do something** persuader quelqu'un de faire quelque chose

temptation NOUN
la **tentation**

tempting ADJECTIVE
tentant

ten NUMBER
dix ◇ *She's ten.* Elle a dix ans.

to **tend** to VERB
- **to tend to do something** avoir tendance à faire quelque chose ◇ *He tends to arrive late.* Il a tendance à arriver en retard.

tennis NOUN
le **tennis** ◇ *Do you play tennis?* Vous jouez au tennis?
- **a tennis ball** une balle de tennis
- **a tennis court** un court de tennis
- **a tennis racket** une raquette de tennis

tennis player NOUN
le **joueur de tennis**
la **joueuse de tennis**
◇ *He's a tennis player.* Il est joueur de tennis.

tenor NOUN
le **ténor**

tenpin bowling NOUN
le **bowling** ◇ *to go tenpin bowling* jouer au bowling

tense ADJECTIVE
see also **tense** NOUN
tendu

tense NOUN
see also **tense** ADJECTIVE
- **the present tense** le présent
- **the future tense** le futur

tension NOUN
la **tension**

tent NOUN
la **tente**
- **a tent peg** un piquet de tente
- **a tent pole** un montant de tente

tenth ADJECTIVE

dixième ◇ *the tenth floor* le dixième étage
- **the tenth of August** le dix août

term NOUN
1. le **trimestre** (*at school*)
2. le **terme** ◇ *a short-term solution* une solution à court terme
- **to come to terms with something** accepter quelque chose

terminal ADJECTIVE
see also terminal NOUN
incurable (*illness, patient*)

terminal NOUN
see also terminal ADJECTIVE
un terminal (*of computer*)
- **an oil terminal** un terminal pétrolier
- **an air terminal** une aérogare

terminally ADVERB
- **to be terminally ill** être condamné

terrace NOUN
1. la **terrasse** (*patio*)
2. la **rangée de maisons** (*row of houses*)
- **the terraces** (*at stadium*) les gradins MASC

terraced ADJECTIVE
- **a terraced house** une maison mitoyenne

terrible ADJECTIVE
épouvantable ◇ *My French is terrible.* Mon français est épouvantable.

terrier NOUN
le **terrier**

terrific ADJECTIVE
super (*wonderful*) ◇ *That's terrific!* C'est super!
- **You look terrific!** Tu es superbe!

terrified ADJECTIVE
terrifié ◇ *I was terrified!* J'étais terrifié!

terrorism NOUN
le **terrorisme**

terrorist NOUN
le/la **terroriste**
- **a terrorist attack** un attentat terroriste

test NOUN
see also test VERB
1. l' **interrogation** FEM (*at school*) ◇ *I've got a test tomorrow.* J'ai une interrogation demain.
2. l' **essai** MASC (*trial, check*) ◇ *nuclear tests* les essais nucléaires
3. l' **analyse** FEM (*medical*) ◇ *a blood test* une analyse de sang ◇ *They're going to do some more tests.* Ils vont faire d'autres analyses.
- **driving test** l'examen du permis de conduire ◇ *He's got his driving test tomorrow.* Il passe son permis de conduire demain.

to **test** VERB
see also test NOUN
1. **essayer** ◇ *to test something out* essayer quelque chose
2. **interroger** (*class*) ◇ *He tested us on the new vocabulary.* Il nous a interrogés sur le nouveau vocabulaire.
- **She was tested for drugs.** On lui a fait subir un contrôle antidopage.

test match NOUN
le **match international**

test tube NOUN
l' **éprouvette** FEM

tetanus NOUN
le **tétanos** ◇ *a tetanus injection* un vaccin contre le tétanos

textbook NOUN
le **manuel** ◇ *a French textbook* un manuel de français

textiles NOUN
les **textiles** MASC PL ◇ *a textiles factory* une usine textile

Thames NOUN
la **Tamise**

than CONJUNCTION
que ◇ *She's taller than me.* Elle est plus grande que moi. ◇ *I've got more books than him.* J'ai plus de livres que lui.
- **more than ten years** plus de dix ans
- **more than once** plus d'une fois

to **thank** VERB
remercier ◇ *Don't forget to write and thank them.* N'oublie pas de leur écrire pour les remercier.
- **thank you** merci
- **thank you very much** merci beaucoup

thanks EXCLAMATION
merci!
- **thanks to** grâce à ◇ *Thanks to him, everything went OK.* Grâce à lui, tout s'est bien passé.

that ADJECTIVE, PRONOUN, CONJUNCTION
Use ce *when* that *is followed by a masculine noun, and* cette *when* that *is followed by a feminine noun.* ce *changes to* cet *before a vowel and before most words beginning with "h".*
1. **ce** ◇ *that book* ce livre
cet ◇ *that man* cet homme
cette ◇ *that woman* cette femme
- **that road** cette route
- **THAT road** cette route-là
- **that one (1)** celui-là (*masculine*) ◇ *This man?–No, that one.* Cet homme-ci? –Non, celui-là.
- **that one (2)** celle-là (*feminine*) ◇ *Do you like this photo?–No, I prefer that one.* Tu aimes cette photo?–Non, je préfère celle-là.

2 ça ◇ *You see that?* Tu vois ça?
- **What's that?** Qu'est-ce que c'est?
- **Who's that?** Qui est-ce?
- **Is that you?** C'est toi?
- **That's...** C'est... ◇ *That's my French teacher.* C'est mon prof de français. ◇ *That's what he said.* C'est ce qu'il a dit.

In relative phrases use **qui** *when* that *refers to the subject of the sentence, and* **que** *when it refers to the object.*

3 qui ◇ *the man that saw us* l'homme qui nous a vus ◇ *the man that spoke to us* l'homme qui nous a parlé ◇ *the dog that bit her* le chien qui l'a mordue

4 que ◇ *the man that we saw* l'homme que nous avons vu ◇ *the man that we spoke to* l'homme à qui nous avons parlé

que *changes to* **qu'** *before a vowel and before most words beginning with "h".*

◇ *the dog that she bought* le chien qu'elle a acheté ◇ *He thought that Henri was ill.* Il pensait qu'Henri était malade. ◇ *I know that she likes chocolate.* Je sais qu'elle aime le chocolat.
- **It was that big.** Il était grand comme ça.
- **It's about that high.** Il est à peu près haut comme ça.
- **It's not that difficult.** Ça n'est pas si difficile que ça.

thatched ADJECTIVE
- **a thatched cottage** une chaumière

the ARTICLE

Use **le** *with a masculine noun, and* **la** *with a feminine noun. Use* **l'** *before a vowel and most words beginning with "h". For plural nouns always use* **les**.

le ◇ *the boy* le garçon
l' ◇ *the man* l'homme MASC ◇ *the orange* l'orange FEM ◇ *the habit* l'habitude FEM
la
◇ *the girl* la fille
les ◇ *the children* les enfants

theatre NOUN
le théâtre

theft NOUN
le vol

their ADJECTIVE
leur
(leurs PL)
◇ *their house* leur maison ◇ *their parents* leurs parents

theirs PRONOUN
le leur + MASC NOUN ◇ *It's not our*

garage, *it's theirs.* Ce n'est pas notre garage, c'est le leur.
la leur + FEM NOUN ◇ *It's not our car, it's theirs.* Ce n'est pas notre voiture, c'est la leur.
les leurs + PL NOUN ◇ *They're not our ideas, they're theirs.* Ce ne sont pas nos idées, ce sont les leurs.
- **Is this theirs?** C'est à eux? ◇ *This car is theirs.* Cette voiture est à eux. ◇ *Whose is this?—It's theirs.* C'est à qui?—À eux.

them PRONOUN
1 les ◇ *I didn't see them.* Je ne les ai pas vus.

Use **leur** *when* them *means* to them.

2 leur ◇ *I gave them some brochures.* Je leur ai donné des brochures. ◇ *I told them the truth.* Je leur ai dit la vérité.

Use **eux** *or* **elles** *after a preposition.*

3 eux MASC ◇ *It's for them.* C'est pour eux.
elles FEM ◇ *Ann and Sophie came—Graham was with them.* Ann et Sophie sont venues—Graham était avec elles.

theme NOUN
le thème

themselves PRONOUN
1 se ◇ *Did they hurt themselves?* Est-ce qu'ils se sont fait mal?
2 eux-mêmes MASC
elles-mêmes FEM
◇ *They did it themselves.* Ils l'ont fait eux-mêmes.

then ADVERB, CONJUNCTION
1 ensuite (*next*) ◇ *I get dressed. Then I have breakfast.* Je m'habille. Ensuite je prends mon petit déjeuner.
2 alors (*in that case*) ◇ *My pen's run out.—Use a pencil then!* Il n'y a plus d'encre dans mon stylo.—Alors utilise un crayon!
3 à l'époque (*at that time*) ◇ *There was no electricity then.* Il n'y avait pas l'électricité à l'époque.
- **now and then** de temps en temps ◇ *Do you play chess?—Now and then.* Vous jouez aux échecs?—De temps en temps.
- **By then it was too late.** Il était déjà trop tard.

therapy NOUN
la thérapie

there ADVERB
1 là ◇ *Put it there, on the table.* Mets-le là, sur la table.
- **over there** là-bas

- **in there** là
- **on there** là
- **up there** là-haut
- **down there** là-bas
- **There he is!** Le voilà!

   2 **y** ○ *He went there on Friday.* Il y est allé vendredi. ○ *Paris? I've never been there.* Paris? Je n'y suis jamais allé.

- **There is...** Il y a... ○ *There's a factory near my house.* Il y a une usine près de chez moi.
- **There are...** Il y a... ○ *There are five people in my family.* Il y a cinq personnes dans ma famille.
- **There has been an accident.** Il y a eu un accident.

therefore ADVERB
  donc

there's = there is, there has

thermometer NOUN
  le **thermomètre**

Thermos ® NOUN
  le **thermos** ®

these ADJECTIVE, PRONOUN
  1 **ces** ○ *these shoes* ces chaussures
- **THESE shoes** ces chaussures-là
  2 **ceux-ci** MASC ○ *I want these!* Je veux ceux-ci!
  celles-ci FEM ○ *I'm looking for some sandals. Can I try these?* Je cherche des sandales. Je peux essayer celles-ci?

they PRONOUN

> *Check if* **they** *stands for a masculine or feminine noun.*

  ils ○ *Are there any tickets left?–No, they're all sold.* Est-ce qu'il reste des billets?–Non, ils sont tous vendus.
  elles ○ *Do you like those shoes?–No, they're horrible.* Tu aimes ces chaussures?–Non, elles sont affreuses.
- **They say that...** On dit que...

they'd = they had, they would
they'll = they will
they're = they are
they've = they have

thick ADJECTIVE
  1 (*not thin*)
  épais MASC
  épaisse FEM
- **The walls are one metre thick.** Les murs font un mètre d'épaisseur.
  2 (*stupid*)
  bête

thief NOUN
  le **voleur**
  la **voleuse**

thigh NOUN
  la **cuisse**

thin ADJECTIVE

  1 **mince** (*person, slice*)
  2 **maigre** (*skinny*)

thing NOUN
  1 la **chose** ○ *beautiful things* de belles choses
  2 le **truc** (*thingy*) ○ *What's that thing called?* Comment s'appelle ce truc?
- **my things** (*belongings*) mes affaires FEM
- **You poor thing!** Mon pauvre!

to **think** VERB
  1 **penser** (*believe*) ○ *I think you're wrong.* Je pense que vous avez tort. ○ *What do you think about the death penalty?* Que pensez-vous de la peine de mort?
  2 **réfléchir** (*spend time thinking*) ○ *Think carefully before you reply.* Réfléchis bien avant de répondre. ○ *What are you thinking about?* À quoi tu penses? ○ *I'll think about it.* Je vais y réfléchir.
  3 **imaginer** (*imagine*) ○ *Think what life would be like without cars.* Imaginez la vie sans voitures.
- **I think so.** Oui, je crois.
- **I don't think so.** Je ne crois pas.
- **I'll think it over.** Je vais y réfléchir.

third ADJECTIVE
> *see also* **third** NOUN

  troisième ○ *the third day* le troisième jour ○ *the third time* la troisième fois ○ *I came third.* Je suis arrivé troisième.
- **the third of March** le trois mars

third NOUN
> *see also* **third** ADJECTIVE

  le **tiers** ○ *a third of the population* un tiers de la population

thirdly ADVERB
  troisièmement

Third World NOUN
  le **tiers monde**

thirst NOUN
  la **soif**

thirsty ADJECTIVE
- **to be thirsty** avoir soif

thirteen NUMBER
  treize ○ *I'm thirteen.* J'ai treize ans.

thirty NUMBER
  trente

this ADJECTIVE, PRONOUN
> *Use* **ce** *when* **this** *is followed by a masculine noun, and* **cette** *when* **this** *is followed by a feminine noun.* **ce** *changes to* **cet** *before a vowel and before most words beginning with "h".*

  1 **ce** ○ *this book* ce livre
  cet ○ *this man* cet homme
  cette ○ *this woman* cette femme
- **this road** cette route

- **THIS road** cette route-là
- **this one (1)** celui-ci (*masculine*) ◇ *Pass me that pen.–This one?* Passe-moi ce stylo.–Celui-ci?
- **this one (2)** celle-ci (*feminine*) ◇ *Of the two photos, I prefer this one.* Des deux photos, c'est celle-là que je préfère.
  2 **ça** ◇ *You see this?* Tu vois ça?
- **What's this?** Qu'est-ce que c'est?
- **This is my mother.** (*introduction*) Je te présente ma mère.
- **This is Gavin speaking.** (*on the phone*) C'est Gavin à l'appareil.

thistle NOUN
le **chardon**

thorough ADJECTIVE
minutieux MASC
minutieuse FEM
◇ *She's very thorough.* Elle est très minutieuse.

thoroughly ADVERB
à fond (*examine*)

those ADJECTIVE, PRONOUN
1 **ces** ◇ *those shoes* ces chaussures
- **THOSE shoes** ces chaussures-là
  2 **ceux-là** MASC ◇ *I want those!* Je veux ceux-là!
  celles-là FEM ◇ *I'm looking for some sandals. Can I try those?* Je cherche des sandales. Je peux essayer celles-là?

though CONJUNCTION, ADVERB
bien que
bien que *has to be followed by a verb in the subjunctive.*
◇ *Though it's raining...* Bien qu'il pleuve...
- **He's a nice person, though he's not very clever.** Il est sympa, mais pas très malin.

thought VERB *see* **think**

thought NOUN
l' **idée** FEM (*idea*) ◇ *I've just had a thought.* Je viens d'avoir une idée.
- **It was a nice thought, thank you.** C'est gentil de ta part, merci.

thoughtful ADJECTIVE
1 (*deep in thought*)
pensif MASC
pensive FEM
◇ *You look thoughtful.* Tu as l'air pensif.
2 (*considerate*)
prévenant ◇ *She's very thoughtful.* Elle est très prévenante.

thoughtless ADJECTIVE
- **He's completely thoughtless.** Il ne pense absolument pas aux autres.

thousand NUMBER
- **a thousand** mille ◇ *a thousand francs* mille francs

- **£2000** deux mille livres
- **thousands of people** des milliers de personnes

thread NOUN
le **fil**

threat NOUN
la **menace**

to **threaten** VERB
menacer ◇ *to threaten to do something* menacer de faire quelque chose

three NUMBER
trois ◇ *She's three.* Elle a trois ans.

three-dimensional ADJECTIVE
à trois dimensions

threw VERB *see* **throw**

thrifty ADJECTIVE
économe

thrill NOUN
l' **émotion** FEM (*excitement*)

thrilled ADJECTIVE
- **I was thrilled.** (*pleased*) J'étais absolument ravi.

thriller NOUN
le **thriller**

thrilling ADJECTIVE
palpitant

throat NOUN
la **gorge** ◇ *to have a sore throat* avoir mal à la gorge

to **throb** VERB
- **a throbbing pain** un élancement
- **My arm's throbbing.** J'ai des élancements dans le bras.

throne NOUN
le **trône**

through PREPOSITION, ADJECTIVE, ADVERB
1 **par** ◇ *through the window* par la fenêtre ◇ *I know her through my sister.* Je la connais par ma sœur. ◇ *to go through Birmingham* passer par Birmingham
- **to go through a tunnel** traverser un tunnel
  2 **à travers** ◇ *through the mist* à travers la brume ◇ *through the crowd* à travers la foule ◇ *The window was dirty and I couldn't see through.* La fenêtre était sale et je n'arrivais pas à voir à travers.
- **a through train** un train direct
- **"no through road"** "impasse"

throughout PREPOSITION
- **throughout Britain** dans toute la Grande-Bretagne
- **throughout the year** pendant toute l'année

to **throw** VERB
lancer ◇ *He threw the ball to me.* Il

m'a lancé le ballon.
- **to throw a party** organiser une soirée
- **That really threw him.** Ça l'a
  décontenancé.
- **to throw away (1)** (*rubbish*) jeter
- **to throw away (2)** (*chance*) perdre
- **to throw out (1)** (*throw away*) jeter
- **to throw out (2)** (*person*) mettre à la
  porte ◇ *I threw him out.* Je l'ai mis à la
  porte.
- **to throw up** vomir

thug NOUN
le **voyou**

thumb NOUN
le **pouce**

to **thump** VERB
- **to thump somebody** donner un coup
  de poing à quelqu'un

thunder NOUN
le **tonnerre**

thunderstorm NOUN
l' **orage** MASC

thundery ADJECTIVE
orageux MASC
orageuse FEM

Thursday NOUN
le **jeudi** ◇ *on Thursday* jeudi ◇ *on*
Thursdays le jeudi ◇ *every Thursday*
tous les jeudis ◇ *last Thursday* jeudi
dernier ◇ *next Thursday* jeudi
prochain

thyme NOUN
le **thym**

tick NOUN
1 la **coche** (*mark*)
2 le **tic-tac** (*of clock*)
- **in a tick** dans une seconde

ticket NOUN
Be careful to choose correctly between **le ticket**
and **le billet.**
1 le **ticket** (*for bus, tube, cinema, museum*)
◇ *an underground ticket* un ticket de
métro
2 le **billet** (*for plane, train, theatre, concert*)
- **a parking ticket** un p.-v.

ticket inspector NOUN
le **contrôleur**
la **contrôleuse**

ticket office NOUN
le **guichet**

to **tickle** VERB
chatouiller

ticklish ADJECTIVE
chatouilleux MASC
chatouilleuse FEM
◇ *Are you ticklish?* Tu es chatouilleux?

to **tick off** VERB
- **to tick something off** cocher quelque
  chose

- **to tick somebody off** enguirlander
  quelqu'un

tide NOUN
la **marée**
- **high tide** la marée haute
- **low tide** la marée basse

tidy ADJECTIVE
see also **tidy** VERB
1 **bien rangé** (*room*) ◇ *Your room's*
very tidy. Ta chambre est bien
rangée.
2 **ordonné** (*person*) ◇ *She's very tidy.*
Elle est très ordonnée.

to **tidy** VERB
see also **tidy** ADJECTIVE
ranger ◇ *Go and tidy your room.* Va
ranger ta chambre.
- **to tidy up** ranger ◇ *Don't forget to tidy*
up afterwards. N'oubliez pas de ranger
après.

tie NOUN
see also **tie** VERB
la **cravate** (*necktie*)
- **It was a tie.** (*in sport*) Ils ont fait match
  nul.

to **tie** VERB
see also **tie** NOUN
1 **nouer** (*ribbon, shoelaces*)
- **to tie a knot in something** faire un
  nœud à quelque chose
2 **faire match nul** (*in sport*) ◇ *They*
tied three all. Ils ont fait match nul,
trois à trois.
- **to tie up (1)** (*parcel*) ficeler
- **to tie up (2)** (*dog, boat*) attacher
- **to tie up (3)** (*prisoner*) ligoter

tiger NOUN
le **tigre**

tight ADJECTIVE
1 **moulant** (*tight-fitting*) ◇ *tight clothes*
les vêtements moulants
2 **juste** (*too tight*) ◇ *This dress is a bit*
tight. Cette robe est un peu juste.

to **tighten** VERB
1 **tendre** (*rope*)
2 **resserrer** (*screw*)

tightly ADVERB
fort (*hold*)

tights PL NOUN
le **collant** SING

tile NOUN
1 (*on roof*)
la **tuile**
2 (*on wall, floor*)
le **carreau**
(les **carreaux** PL)

tiled ADJECTIVE
1 **en tuiles** (*roof*)
2 **carrelé** (*wall, floor, room*)

till NOUN
> *see also* till PREPOSITION

la **caisse**

till PREPOSITION, CONJUNCTION
> *see also* till NOUN

1 **jusqu'à** ◇ *I waited till ten o'clock.*
J'ai attendu jusqu'à dix heures.
- **till now** jusqu'à présent
- **till then** jusque-là

> *Use* **avant** *if the sentence you want to translate contains a negative, such as "not" or "never".*

2 **avant** ◇ *It won't be ready till next week.* Ça ne sera pas prêt avant la semaine prochaine. ◇ *Till last year I'd never been to France.* Avant l'année dernière, je n'étais jamais allé en France.

time NOUN
1 l' **heure** FEM (*on clock*) ◇ *What time is it?* Quelle heure est-il? ◇ *What time do you get up?* À quelle heure tu te lèves? ◇ *It was two o'clock, French time.* Il était deux heures, heure française.
- **on time** à l'heure ◇ *He never arrives on time.* Il n'arrive jamais à l'heure.
2 le **temps** (*amount of time*) ◇ *I'm sorry, I haven't got time.* Je suis désolé, je n'ai pas le temps.
- **from time to time** de temps en temps
- **in time** à temps ◇ *We arrived in time for lunch.* Nous sommes arrivés à temps pour le déjeuner.
- **just in time** juste à temps
- **in no time** en un rien de temps ◇ *It was ready in no time.* Ça a été prêt en un rien de temps.
3 le **moment** (*moment*) ◇ *This isn't a good time to ask him.* Ce n'est pas le bon moment pour lui demander.
- **for the time being** pour le moment
4 la **fois** (*occasion*) ◇ *this time* cette fois-ci ◇ *next time* la prochaine fois ◇ *two at a time* deux à la fois
- **How many times?** Combien de fois?
- **at times** parfois
- **a long time** longtemps ◇ *Have you lived here for a long time?* Vous habitez ici depuis longtemps?
- **in a week's time** dans une semaine ◇ *I'll come back in a month's time.* Je reviendrai dans un mois.
- **Come and see us any time.** Venez nous voir quand vous voulez.
- **to have a good time** bien s'amuser ◇ *Did you have a good time?* Vous vous êtes bien amusés?
- **2 times 2 is 4** deux fois deux égalent quatre

time bomb NOUN
la **bombe à retardement**

time off NOUN
le **temps libre**

timer NOUN
le **minuteur**

time-share NOUN
l' **appartement en multipropriété** MASC

timetable NOUN
1 l' **horaire** MASC (*for train, bus*)
2 l' **emploi du temps** MASC (*at school*)

time zone NOUN
le **fuseau horaire**

tin NOUN
1 la **boîte** ◇ *a tin of soup* une boîte de soupe ◇ *a biscuit tin* une boîte à biscuits
2 la **boîte de conserve** (*empty*) ◇ *The bin was full of tins.* La poubelle était pleine de boîtes de conserve.
3 l' **étain** MASC (*type of metal*)

tinned ADJECTIVE
en boîte (*food*) ◇ *tinned peaches* des pêches en boîte

tin opener NOUN
l' **ouvre-boîte** MASC

tinsel NOUN
les **guirlandes de Noël** FEM PL

tinted ADJECTIVE
teinté (*spectacles, glass*)

tiny ADJECTIVE
minuscule

tip NOUN
> *see also* tip VERB

1 (*money*)
le **pourboire** ◇ *Shall I give him a tip?* Je lui donne un pourboire?
2 (*advice*)
le **tuyau**
(les **tuyaux** PL)
◇ *a useful tip* un bon tuyau (*informal*)
3 (*end*)
le **bout** ◇ *It's on the tip of my tongue.* Je l'ai sur le bout de la langue.
- **a rubbish tip** une décharge
- **This place is a complete tip!** Quel fouillis! (*informal*)

to **tip** VERB
> *see also* tip NOUN

donner un pourboire à ◇ *Don't forget to tip the taxi driver.* N'oubliez pas de donner un pourboire au chauffeur de taxi.

tiptoe NOUN
- **on tiptoe** sur la pointe des pieds

tired ADJECTIVE
fatigué ◇ *I'm tired.* Je suis fatigué.
- **to be tired of something** en avoir assez de quelque chose

tiring ADJECTIVE
fatigant

T

tissue NOUN
le **kleenex** ® ◇ *Have you got a tissue?*
Tu as un kleenex? ®

title NOUN
le **titre**

title role NOUN
le **rôle principal**

to PREPOSITION
à + **le** *changes to* **au.** à + **les** *changes to* **aux.**
☐ **à** ◇ *to go to Paris* aller à Paris ◇ *to go to school* aller à l'école ◇ *a letter to his mother* une lettre à sa mère ◇ *the answer to the question* la réponse à la question
au ◇ *to go to the theatre* aller au théâtre
aux ◇ *We said goodbye to the neighbours.* Nous avons dit au revoir aux voisins.
◆ **ready to go** prêt à partir
◆ **ready to eat** prêt à manger
◆ **It's easy to do.** C'est facile à faire.
◆ **something to drink** quelque chose à boire
◆ **I've got things to do.** J'ai des choses à faire.
◆ **from...to...** de...à... ◇ *from nine o'clock to half past three* de neuf heures à trois heures et demie
☐ **de** ◇ *the train to London* le train de Londres ◇ *the road to Edinburgh* la route d'Édimbourg ◇ *the key to the front door* la clé de la porte d'entrée
◆ **It's difficult to say.** Il est difficile à dire.
◆ **It's easy to criticize.** C'est facile de critiquer.

When referring to someone's house, shop or office, use **chez**.

☐ **chez** ◇ *to go to the doctor's* aller chez le docteur ◇ *to go to the butcher's* aller chez le boucher ◇ *Let's go to Anne's house.* Si on allait chez Anne?

When to *refers to a country which is feminine, use* **en**; *when the country is masculine, use* **au**.

☐ **en** ◇ *to go to France* aller en France
au ◇ *to go to Portugal* aller au Portugal
☐ **jusqu'à** (*up to*) ◇ *to count to ten* compter jusqu'à dix
☐ **pour** (*in order to*) ◇ *I did it to help you.* Je l'ai fait pour vous aider.
◇ *She's too young to go to school.*
Elle est trop jeune pour aller à l'école.

toad NOUN
le **crapaud**

toadstool NOUN
le **champignon vénéneux**

toast NOUN

☐ le **pain grillé** ◇ *a piece of toast* une tranche de pain grillé
☐ le **toast** (*speech*) ◇ *to drink a toast to somebody* porter un toast à quelqu'un

toaster NOUN
le **grille-pain**
(les **grille-pain** PL)

tobacco NOUN
le **tabac**

tobacconist's NOUN
le **bureau de tabac**
(les **bureaux de tabac** PL)

toboggan NOUN
la **luge**

tobogganing NOUN
◆ **to go tobogganing** faire de la luge

today ADVERB
aujourd'hui ◇ *What did you do today?* Qu'est-ce tu as fait aujourd'hui?

toddler NOUN
le **bambin**

toe NOUN
le **doigt de pied**

toffee NOUN
le **caramel**

together ADVERB
☐ **ensemble** ◇ *Are they still together?*
Ils sont toujours ensemble?
☐ **en même temps** (*at the same time*)
◇ *Don't all speak together!* Ne parlez pas tous en même temps!
◆ **together with** (*with person*) avec

toilet NOUN
les **toilettes** FEM PL

toilet paper NOUN
le **papier hygiénique**

toiletries PL NOUN
les **articles de toilette** MASC PL

toilet roll NOUN
le **rouleau de papier hygiénique**
(les **rouleaux de papier hygiénique** PL)

token NOUN
◆ **a gift token** un bon-cadeau

told VERB *see* **tell**

tolerant ADJECTIVE
tolérant

toll NOUN
le **péage** (*on bridge, motorway*)

tomato NOUN
la **tomate** ◇ *tomato soup* la soupe à la tomate

tomboy NOUN
le **garçon manqué** ◇ *She's a real tomboy.* C'est un vrai garçon manqué.

tomorrow ADVERB
demain ◇ *tomorrow morning* demain matin ◇ *tomorrow night* demain soir
◆ **the day after tomorrow** après-demain

ton NOUN

la **tonne** ◇ *That old bike weighs a ton.*
Ce vieux vélo pèse une tonne.
tongue NOUN
la **langue**
- **to say something tongue in cheek** dire
quelque chose en plaisantant
tonic NOUN
le **Schweppes** ® (*tonic water*)
- **a gin and tonic** un gin tonic
tonight ADVERB
1 **ce soir** (*this evening*) ◇ *Are you going
out tonight?* Tu sors ce soir?
2 **cette nuit** (*during the night*) ◇ *I'll
sleep well tonight.* Je dormirai bien cette
nuit.
tonsillitis NOUN
l' **angine** FEM
tonsils PL NOUN
les **amygdales** FEM PL
too ADVERB, ADJECTIVE
1 **aussi** (*as well*) ◇ *My sister came too.*
Ma sœur est venue aussi.
2 **trop** (*excessively*) ◇ *The water's too
hot.* L'eau est trop chaude. ◇ *We
arrived too late.* Nous sommes arrivés
trop tard.
- **too much (1)** (*with noun*) trop de
◇ *too much noise* trop de bruit
- **too much (2)** (*with verb*) trop ◇ *At
Christmas we always eat too much.* À
Noël nous mangeons toujours trop.
- **too much (3)** (*too expensive*) trop cher
◇ *Fifty francs? That's too much.*
Cinquante francs? C'est trop cher.
- **too many** trop de ◇ *too many
hamburgers* trop de hamburgers
- **Too bad!** Tant pis!
took VERB *see* **take**
tool NOUN
l' **outil** MASC
- **a tool box** une boîte à outils
tooth NOUN
la **dent**
toothache NOUN
le **mal de dents** ◇ *to have toothache*
avoir mal aux dents
toothbrush NOUN
la **brosse à dents**
toothpaste NOUN
le **dentifrice**
top NOUN
see also top ADJECTIVE
1 le **haut** (*of page, ladder, garment*) ◇ *at
the top of the page* en haut de la page
- **a bikini top** un haut de bikini
2 le **sommet** (*of mountain*)
3 le **dessus** (*of table*)
- **on top of** (*on*) sur ◇ *on top of the
cupboard* sur le placard

- **There's a surcharge on top of that.** Il a
un supplément en plus.
- **from top to bottom** de fond en comble
◇ *I searched the house from top to
bottom.* J'ai fouillé la maison de fond
en comble.
4 le **couvercle** (*of box, jar*)
5 le **bouchon** (*of bottle*)
top ADJECTIVE
see also top NOUN
grand (*first-class*) ◇ *a top surgeon* un
grand chirurgien
- **a top model** un top model
- **He always gets top marks in French.** Il
a toujours d'excellentes notes en
français.
- **the top floor** le dernier étage ◇ *on
the top floor* au dernier étage
topic NOUN
le **sujet** ◇ *The essay can be on any
topic.* Cette dissertation peut être sur
n'importe quel sujet.
topical ADJECTIVE
d'actualité ◇ *a topical issue* un sujet
d'actualité
topless ADJECTIVE
aux seins nus (*model*)
- **to go topless** enlever le haut
top-secret ADJECTIVE
top secret MASC
top secrète FEM
◇ *top-secret documents* des documents
top secrets
torch NOUN
la **lampe de poche**
tore, torn VERB *see* **tear**
tortoise NOUN
la **tortue**
torture NOUN
see also torture VERB
la **torture** ◇ *It was pure torture.*
C'était une vraie torture.
to **torture** VERB
see also torture NOUN
torturer ◇ *Stop torturing that poor
animal!* Arrête de torturer cette pauvre
bête!
Tory ADJECTIVE
see also Tory NOUN
conservateur MASC
conservatrice FEM
◇ *the Tory government* le
gouvernement conservateur
Tory NOUN
see also Tory ADJECTIVE
le **conservateur**
la **conservatrice**
- **the Tories** les conservateurs
to **toss** VERB

- **to toss pancakes** faire sauter les crêpes
- **Shall we toss for it?** On joue à pile ou face?

total ADJECTIVE

> see also **total** NOUN

total

(**totaux** MASC PL)

- **the total amount** le total

total NOUN

> see also **total** ADJECTIVE

le **total**

(les **totaux** PL)

- **the grand total** le total

totally ADVERB

complètement ◇ He's totally useless. Il est complètement nul.

touch NOUN

> see also **touch** VERB

- **to get in touch with somebody** prendre contact avec quelqu'un
- **to keep in touch with somebody** ne pas perdre contact avec quelqu'un
- **Keep in touch!** Donne-moi de tes nouvelles!
- **to lose touch** se perdre de vue
- **to lose touch with somebody** perdre quelqu'un de vue

to **touch** VERB

> see also **touch** NOUN

toucher ◇ Don't touch that! Ne touche pas à ça!

touchdown NOUN

l' **atterrissage** MASC

touched ADJECTIVE

touché ◇ I was really touched. Ça m'a beaucoup touché.

touching ADJECTIVE

touchant

touchline NOUN

la **ligne de touche**

touchy ADJECTIVE

susceptible ◇ She's a bit touchy. Elle est susceptible.

tough ADJECTIVE

1 **dur** ◇ It was tough, but I managed OK. C'était dur, mais je m'en suis tiré. ◇ It's a tough job. C'est dur.

- **The meat's tough.** La viande est coriace.

2 (strong)

solide ◇ tough leather gloves de solides gants en cuir ◇ She's tough. She can take it. Elle est solide. Elle tiendra le coup.

3 (rough, violent)

dangereux MASC

dangereuse FEM

- **He thinks he's a tough guy.** Il se prend pour un gros dur.

- **Tough luck!** C'est comme ça!

toupee NOUN

le **postiche**

tour NOUN

> see also **tour** VERB

1 la **visite** (of town, museum) ◇ We went on a tour of the city. Nous avons visité la ville.

- **a package tour** un voyage organisé

2 la **tournée** (by singer, group) ◇ on tour en tournée

- **to go on tour** faire une tournée

to **tour** VERB

> see also **tour** NOUN

- **Paul Weller's touring Europe.** (singer, artiste) Paul Weller est en tournée en Europe.

tour guide NOUN

le/la **guide**

tourism NOUN

le **tourisme**

tourist NOUN

le/la **touriste**

- **tourist information office** l'office de tourisme MASC

tournament NOUN

le **tournoi**

towards PREPOSITION

1 **vers** (in the direction of) ◇ He came towards me. Il est venu vers moi.

2 **envers** (of attitude) ◇ my feelings towards him mes sentiments envers lui

towel NOUN

la **serviette**

tower NOUN

la **tour**

- **a tower block** une tour

town NOUN

la **ville** ◇ a town plan un plan de ville

- **the town centre** le centre-ville
- **the town hall** la mairie

toy NOUN

le **jouet** ◇ a toy shop un magasin de jouets

- **a toy car** une petite voiture

trace NOUN

> see also **trace** VERB

la **trace** ◇ There was no trace of the robbers. Il n'y avait pas de trace des voleurs.

to **trace** VERB

> see also **trace** NOUN

décalquer (draw)

tracing paper NOUN

le **papier calque**

track NOUN

1 le **chemin** (dirt road)

2 la **voie ferrée** (railway line)

3 la **piste** (in sport) ◇ two laps of the

track deux tours de piste

[4] la **chanson** (*song*) ⋄ *This is my favourite track.* C'est ma chanson préférée.

[5] les **traces** FEM PL (*trail*) ⋄ *They followed the tracks for miles.* Ils ont suivi les traces pendant des kilomètres.

to **track down** VERB
- **to track somebody down** retrouver quelqu'un ⋄ *The police never tracked down the killer.* La police n'a jamais retrouvé l'assassin.

tracksuit NOUN
le **survêtement**

tractor NOUN
le **tracteur**

trade NOUN
le **métier** (*skill, job*) ⋄ *to learn a trade* apprendre un métier

trade union NOUN
le **syndicat**

trade unionist NOUN
le/la **syndicaliste**

tradition NOUN
la **tradition**

traditional ADJECTIVE
traditionnel MASC
traditionnelle FEM

traffic NOUN
la **circulation** ⋄ *The traffic was terrible.* Il y avait une circulation épouvantable.

traffic jam NOUN
l' **embouteillage** MASC

traffic lights PL NOUN
les **feux** MASC

traffic warden NOUN
le **contractuel**
la **contractuelle**

tragedy NOUN
la **tragédie**

tragic ADJECTIVE
tragique

trailer NOUN
[1] la **remorque** (*vehicle*)
[2] la **bande-annonce** (*film advert*)

train NOUN
see also train VERB
[1] le **train**
[2] la **rame** (*on underground*)

to **train** VERB
see also train NOUN
s'entraîner (*sport*) ⋄ *to train for a race* s'entraîner pour une course
- **to train as a teacher** suivre une formation d'enseignant
- **to train an animal to do something** dresser un animal à faire quelque chose

trained ADJECTIVE

- **She's a trained nurse.** Elle est infirmière diplômée.

trainee NOUN
[1] (*in profession*)
le/la **stagiaire** ⋄ *She's a trainee.* Elle est stagiaire.
[2] (*apprentice*)
l' **apprenti** MASC
l' **apprentie** FEM
⋄ *a trainee plumber* un apprenti plombier

trainer NOUN
[1] (*sports coach*)
l' **entraîneur** MASC
[2] (*of animals*)
le **dompteur**
la **dompteuse**

trainers PL NOUN
les **baskets** FEM PL ⋄ *a pair of trainers* une paire de baskets

training NOUN
[1] la **formation** ⋄ *a training course* un stage de formation
[2] l' **entraînement** MASC (*sport*)

tram NOUN
le **tramway**

tramp NOUN
le **clochard**
la **clocharde**

trampoline NOUN
le **trampoline**

tranquillizer NOUN
le **tranquillisant** ⋄ *She's on tranquillizers.* Elle prend des tranquillisants.

transfer NOUN
la **décalcomanie** (*sticker*)

transfusion NOUN
la **transfusion**

transistor NOUN
le **transistor**

transit lounge NOUN
la **salle de transit**

to **translate** VERB
traduire ⋄ *to translate something into English* traduire quelque chose en anglais

translation NOUN
la **traduction**

translator NOUN
le **traducteur**
la **traductrice**
⋄ *Anita's a translator.* Anita est traductrice.

transparent ADJECTIVE
transparent

transplant NOUN
la **greffe** ⋄ *a heart transplant* une greffe du cœur

transport NOUN

> see also transport VERB

le **transport** ◦ public transport les transports en commun

to **transport** VERB

> see also transport NOUN

transporter

trap NOUN

le **piège**

trashy ADJECTIVE

nul MASC

nulle FEM

◦ a really trashy film un film vraiment nul

traumatic ADJECTIVE

traumatisant ◦ It was a traumatic experience. Ça a été une expérience traumatisante.

travel NOUN

> see also travel VERB

les **voyages** MASC PL

to **travel** VERB

> see also travel NOUN

voyager ◦ I prefer to travel by train. Je préfère voyager en train.

- **I'd like to travel round the world.** J'aimerais faire le tour du monde.
- **We travelled over 800 kilometres.** Nous avons fait plus de huit cents kilomètres.
- **News travels fast!** Les nouvelles circulent vite!

travel agency NOUN

l' **agence de voyages** FEM

travel agent NOUN

- **She's a travel agent.** Elle travaille dans une agence de voyages.

traveller NOUN

1 (on bus, train, plane)

le **voyageur**

la **voyageuse**

2 (gypsy)

le/la **nomade**

traveller's cheque NOUN

le **chèque de voyage**

travelling NOUN

- **I love travelling.** J'adore les voyages.

travel sickness NOUN

le **mal des transports**

tray NOUN

le **plateau**

(les **plateaux** PL)

to **tread** VERB

marcher ◦ to tread on something marcher sur quelque chose

treasure NOUN

le **trésor**

treat NOUN

> see also treat VERB

1 le **petit cadeau** (present)

2 la **gâterie** (food)

- **to give somebody a treat** faire plaisir à quelqu'un

to **treat** VERB

> see also treat NOUN

traiter (well, badly)

- **to treat somebody to something** offrir quelque chose à quelqu'un ◦ He treated us to an ice cream. Il nous a offert une glace.

treatment NOUN

le **traitement**

to **treble** VERB

tripler ◦ The cost of living there has trebled. Le coût de la vie y a triplé.

tree NOUN

l' **arbre** MASC

to **tremble** VERB

trembler

trend NOUN

la **mode** (fashion)

trendy ADJECTIVE

branché

trial NOUN

le **procès** (in court)

triangle NOUN

le **triangle**

tribe NOUN

la **tribu**

trick NOUN

> see also trick VERB

1 le **tour** ◦ to play a trick on somebody jouer un tour à quelqu'un

2 le **truc** FEM (knack) ◦ It's not easy: there's a trick to it. Ce n'est pas facile: il y a un truc.

to **trick** VERB

> see also trick NOUN

- **to trick somebody** rouler quelqu'un

tricky ADJECTIVE

délicat

tricycle NOUN

le **tricycle**

trifle NOUN

le **diplomate** (dessert)

to **trim** VERB

> see also trim NOUN

1 **égaliser** (hair)

2 **tondre** (grass)

trim NOUN

> see also trim VERB

la **coupe d'entretien** (haircut) ◦ to have a trim se faire faire une coupe d'entretien

trip NOUN

> see also trip VERB

le **voyage** ◦ to go on a trip faire un voyage ◦ Have a good trip! Bon

voyage!
- **a day trip** une excursion d'une journée

to **trip** VERB

> see also trip NOUN

trébucher (*stumble*)

triple ADJECTIVE
triple

triplets PL NOUN
les **triplés** MASC PL (*boys*)
(les **triplées** FEM PL) (*girls*)

trivial ADJECTIVE
insignifiant

trolley NOUN
le **chariot**

trombone NOUN
le **trombone** ◇ *I play the trombone.* Je
joue du trombone.

troops PL NOUN
les **troupes** MASC PL ◇ *British troops* les
troupes britanniques

trophy NOUN
le **trophée** ◇ *to win a trophy* gagner
un trophée

tropical ADJECTIVE
tropical ◇ *The weather was tropical.*
Il faisait une chaleur tropicale.

to **trot** VERB
trotter

trouble NOUN
le **problème** ◇ *The trouble is, it's too
expensive.* Le problème, c'est que c'est
trop cher.
- **to be in trouble** avoir des ennuis
- **What's the trouble?** Qu'est-ce qui ne
va pas?
- **stomach trouble** troubles gastriques
- **to take a lot of trouble over something**
se donner beaucoup de mal pour
quelque chose
- **Don't worry, it's no trouble.** Mais non,
ça ne me dérange pas du tout.

troublemaker NOUN
l' **élément perturbateur** MASC

trousers PL NOUN
le **pantalon** SING

trout NOUN
la **truite**

truant NOUN
- **to play truant** faire l'école buissonnière

truck NOUN
le **camion**
- **a truck driver** un camionneur ◇ *He's
a truck driver.* Il est camionneur.

true ADJECTIVE
vrai
- **That's true.** C'est vrai.
- **to come true** se réaliser ◇ *I hope my
dream will come true.* J'espère que mon
rêve se réalisera.

- **true love** le grand amour

trumpet NOUN
la **trompette** ◇ *She plays the trumpet.*
Elle joue de la trompette.

trunk NOUN
1. le **tronc** (*of tree*)
2. la **trompe** (*of elephant*)
3. la **malle** (*luggage*)

trunks PL NOUN
- **swimming trunks** le maillot de bain

trust NOUN

> see also trust VERB

la **confiance** ◇ *to have trust in
somebody* avoir confiance en
quelqu'un

to **trust** VERB

> see also trust NOUN

- **to trust somebody** faire confiance à
quelqu'un ◇ *Don't you trust me?* Tu
ne me fais pas confiance? ◇ *Trust me!*
Fais-moi confiance!

trusting ADJECTIVE
confiant

truth NOUN
la **vérité**

truthful ADJECTIVE
- **She's a very truthful person.** Elle dit
toujours la vérité.

try NOUN

> see also try VERB

l' **essai** MASC ◇ *his third try* son
troisième essai
- **to have a try** essayer
- **It's worth a try.** Ça vaut la peine
d'essayer.
- **to give something a try** essayer
quelque chose

to **try** VERB

> see also try NOUN

1. **essayer** (*attempt*) ◇ *to try to do
something* essayer de faire quelque
chose
- **to try again** refaire un essai
2. **goûter** (*taste*) ◇ *Would you like to try
some?* Voulez-vous goûter?
- **to try on** essayer (*clothes*)
- **to try something out** essayer quelque
chose

T-shirt NOUN
le **tee-shirt**

tube NOUN
le **tube**
- **the Tube** (*underground*) le métro

tuberculosis NOUN
la **tuberculose**

Tuesday NOUN
le **mardi** ◇ *on Tuesday* mardi ◇ *on
Tuesdays* le mardi ◇ *every Tuesday*
tous les mardis ◇ *last Tuesday* mardi

T

dernier ◇ *next Tuesday* mardi prochain
- **Shrove Tuesday, Pancake Tuesday** le mardi gras

tug-of-war NOUN
la **lutte à la corde**

tuition NOUN
les **cours** MASC PL
- **private tuition** les cours particuliers

tulip NOUN
la **tulipe**

tumble dryer NOUN
le **sèche-linge**
(les **sèche-linge** PL)

tummy NOUN
le **ventre**

tuna NOUN
le **thon**

tune NOUN
l' **air** MASC (*melody*)
- **to play in tune** jouer juste
- **to sing out of tune** chanter faux

Tunisia NOUN
la **Tunisie**
- **in Tunisia** en Tunisie

tunnel NOUN
le **tunnel**
- **the Tunnel** (*Chunnel*) le tunnel sous la Manche

Turk NOUN
le **Turc**
la **Turque**

Turkey NOUN
la **Turquie**
- **in Turkey** en Turquie
- **to Turkey** en Turquie

turkey NOUN
1 la **dinde** (*meat*)
2 le **dindon** (*live bird*)

Turkish ADJECTIVE
see also Turkish NOUN
turc MASC
turque FEM

Turkish NOUN
see also Turkish ADJECTIVE
le **turc** (*language*)

turn NOUN
see also turn VERB
1 le **tournant** (*bend in road*)
- **"no left turn"** "défense de tourner à gauche"
2 le **tour** (*go*) ◇ *It's my turn!* C'est mon tour!

to **turn** VERB
see also turn NOUN
1 **tourner** ◇ *Turn right at the lights.* Tournez à droite aux feux.
2 **devenir** (*become*) ◇ *to turn red* devenir rouge

- **to turn into something** se transformer en quelque chose ◇ *The frog turned into a prince.* La grenouille s'est transformée en prince.

to **turn back** VERB
faire demi-tour ◇ *We turned back.* Nous avons fait demi-tour.

to **turn down** VERB
1 **refuser** (*offer*)
2 **baisser** (*radio, TV, heating*) ◇ *Shall I turn the heating down?* Je baisse le chauffage?

to **turn off** VERB
1 **éteindre** (*light, radio*)
2 **fermer** (*tap*)
3 **arrêter** (*engine*)

to **turn on** VERB
1 **allumer** (*light, radio*)
2 **ouvrir** (*tap*)
3 **mettre en marche** (*engine*)

to **turn out** VERB
- **It turned out to be a mistake.** Il s'est avéré que c'était une erreur.
- **It turned out that she was right.** Il s'est avéré qu'elle avait raison.

to **turn round** VERB
1 **faire demi-tour** (*car*)
2 **se retourner** (*person*)

to **turn up** VERB
1 **arriver** (*arrive*)
2 **monter** (*heater*)
- **Could you turn up the radio?** Tu peux monter le son de la radio?

turning NOUN
- **It's the third turning on the left.** C'est la troisième à gauche.
- **We took the wrong turning.** Nous n'avons pas tourné au bon endroit.

turnip NOUN
le **navet**

turquoise ADJECTIVE
turquoise MASC, FEM, PL (*colour*)

turtle NOUN
la **tortue**

tutor NOUN
le **professeur particulier** (*private teacher*)

TV NOUN
la **télé**

tweezers PL NOUN
la **pince à épiler** SING

twelfth ADJECTIVE
douzième ◇ *the twelfth floor* le douzième étage
- **the twelfth of August** le douze août

twelve NUMBER
douze ◇ *She's twelve.* Elle a douze ans.
- **twelve o'clock (1)** (*midday*) midi
- **twelve o'clock (2)** (*midnight*) minuit

twenty NUMBER
  vingt ∘ *He's twenty.* Il a vingt ans.
twice ADVERB
  deux fois
- **twice as much** deux fois plus ∘ *He gets twice as much pocket money as me.* Il a deux fois plus d'argent de poche que moi.
twin NOUN
  le **jumeau** (*boy*)
  la **jumelle** (*girl*)
  (les **jumeaux** PL, les **jumelles** FEM PL)
- **my twin brother** mon frère jumeau
- **her twin sister** sa sœur jumelle
- **identical twins** les vrais jumeaux
- **a twin room** une chambre à deux lits
twinned ADJECTIVE
  jumelé ∘ *Stroud is twinned with Châteaubriant.* Stroud est jumelée avec Châteaubriant.
to **twist** VERB
  ① **tordre** (*bend*)
  ② **déformer** (*distort*) ∘ *You're twisting my words.* Tu déformes ce que j'ai dit.

twit NOUN
  le **crétin**
  la **crétine**
two NUMBER
  deux ∘ *She's two.* Elle a deux ans.
type NOUN
  see also type VERB
  le **type** ∘ *What type of camera have you got?* Quel type d'appareil photo as-tu?
to **type** VERB
  see also type NOUN
  taper à la machine ∘ *Can you type?* Tu sais taper à la machine?
- **to type a letter** taper une lettre
typewriter NOUN
  la **machine à écrire**
typical ADJECTIVE
  typique ∘ *That's just typical!* C'est typique!
tyre NOUN
  le **pneu**
- **the tyre pressure** la pression des pneus

T

U

UFO NOUN

l' **OVNI** MASC (= objet volant non identifié)

ugh EXCLAMATION

pouah!

ugly ADJECTIVE

laid

ulcer NOUN

l' **ulcère** MASC

- **a mouth ulcer** un aphte

Ulster NOUN

l' **Irlande du Nord** FEM

- **in Ulster** en Irlande du Nord

ultimate ADJECTIVE

suprême ◇ *the ultimate challenge* le défi suprême

- **It was the ultimate adventure.** C'était la grande aventure.

ultimately ADVERB

au bout du compte ◇ *Ultimately, it's your decision.* Au bout du compte, c'est votre décision.

umbrella NOUN

1 le **parapluie**
2 le **parasol** (*for sun*)

umpire NOUN

1 l' **arbitre** MASC (*in cricket*)
2 le **juge de chaise** (*in tennis*)

UN NOUN

l' **ONU** FEM (= Organisation des Nations Unies)

unable ADJECTIVE

- **to be unable to do something** ne pas pouvoir faire quelque chose ◇ *I was unable to come.* Je n'ai pas pu venir.

unacceptable ADJECTIVE

inacceptable

unanimous ADJECTIVE

unanime ◇ *a unanimous decision* une décision unanime

unavoidable ADJECTIVE

inévitable

unaware ADJECTIVE

- **to be unaware (1)** (*not know about*) ignorer ◇ *I was unaware of the regulations.* J'ignorais le règlement.
- **to be unaware (2)** (*not notice*) ne pas se rendre compte ◇ *She was unaware that she was being filmed.* Elle ne s'était pas rendu compte qu'on la filmait.

unbearable ADJECTIVE

insupportable

unbeatable ADJECTIVE

imbattable

unbelievable ADJECTIVE

incroyable

unborn ADJECTIVE

- **the unborn child** le fœtus

unbreakable ADJECTIVE

incassable

uncanny ADJECTIVE

étrange ◇ *That's uncanny!* C'est étrange!

- **an uncanny resemblance** une ressemblance troublante

uncertain ADJECTIVE

incertain ◇ *The future is uncertain.* L'avenir est incertain.

- **to be uncertain about something** ne pas être sûr de quelque chose

uncivilized ADJECTIVE

barbare

uncle NOUN

l' **oncle** MASC ◇ *my uncle* mon oncle

uncomfortable ADJECTIVE

pas confortable ◇ *The seats are rather uncomfortable.* Les sièges ne sont pas très confortables.

unconscious ADJECTIVE

sans connaissance

unconventional ADJECTIVE

peu conventionnel MASC

peu conventionnelle FEM

under PREPOSITION

1 **sous** ◇ *The cat's under the table.* Le chat est sous la table. ◇ *The tunnel goes under the Channel.* Le tunnel passe sous la Manche.

- **under there** là-dessous ◇ *What's under there?* Qu'est-ce qu'il y a là-dessous?

2 **moins de** (*less than*) ◇ *under 20 people* moins de vingt personnes ◇ *children under 10* les enfants de moins de dix ans

underage ADJECTIVE

- **He's underage.** Il n'a pas l'âge réglementaire.

undercover ADJECTIVE, ADVERB

secret MASC

secrète FEM

◇ *an undercover agent* un agent secret

- **She was working undercover.** Elle travaillait sous une fausse identité.

to **underestimate** VERB

sous-estimer ◇ *I underestimated her.* Je l'ai sous-estimé.

underground ADJECTIVE, ADVERB

see also **underground** NOUN

1 **souterrain** ◇ *an underground car park* un parking souterrain

2 **sous terre** ◇ *Moles live*

underground. Les taupes vivent sous terre.

underground NOUN
see also underground ADJECTIVE
le **métro** ◦ *Is there an underground in Lille? Est-ce qu'il y a un métro à Lille?*

to **underline** VERB
souligner

underneath PREPOSITION, ADVERB
[1] **sous** ◦ *underneath the carpet* sous la moquette
[2] **dessous** ◦ *I got out of the car and looked underneath.* Je suis descendu de la voiture et j'ai regardé dessous.

underpaid ADJECTIVE
sous-payé ◦ *I'm underpaid.* Je suis sous-payé.

underpants PL NOUN
le **slip** SING

underpass NOUN
[1] le **passage souterrain** (*for people*)
[2] le **passage inférieur** (*for cars*)

to **understand** VERB
comprendre ◦ *Do you understand?* Vous comprenez? ◦ *I don't understand this word.* Je ne comprends pas ce mot. ◦ *Is that understood?* C'est compris?

understanding ADJECTIVE
compréhensif MASC
compréhensive FEM
◦ *She's very understanding.* Elle est très compréhensive.

undertaker NOUN
l' **entrepreneur des pompes funèbres** MASC

underwater ADJECTIVE, ADVERB
sous l'eau ◦ *This sequence was filmed underwater.* Cette séquence a été filmée sous l'eau.
• **an underwater camera** un appareil photographique de plongée
• **underwater photography** la photographie subaquatique

underwear NOUN
les **sous-vêtements** MASC PL

to **undo** VERB
[1] **défaire** (*buttons, knot*)
[2] **déballer** (*parcel*)

to **undress** VERB
se déshabiller (*get undressed*) ◦ *The doctor told me to get undressed.* Le médecin m'a dit de me déshabiller.

uneconomic ADJECTIVE
pas rentable

unemployed ADJECTIVE
au chômage ◦ *He's unemployed.* Il est au chômage. ◦ *He's been unemployed for a year.* Ça fait un an qu'il est au chômage.

• **the unemployed** les chômeurs MASC

unemployment NOUN
le **chômage**

unexpected ADJECTIVE
inattendu ◦ *an unexpected visitor* un visiteur inattendu

unexpectedly ADVERB
à l'improviste ◦ *They arrived unexpectedly.* Ils sont arrivés à l'improviste.

unfair ADJECTIVE
injuste ◦ *It's unfair to girls.* C'est injuste pour les filles.

unfamiliar ADJECTIVE
• **I heard an unfamiliar voice.** J'ai entendu une voix que je ne connaissais pas.

unfashionable ADJECTIVE
démodé

unfit ADJECTIVE ◦ *I'm rather unfit at the moment.* Je ne suis pas en très bonne condition physique en ce moment.

to **unfold** VERB
déplier ◦ *She unfolded the map.* Elle a déplié la carte.

unforgettable ADJECTIVE
inoubliable

unfortunately ADVERB
malheureusement ◦ *Unfortunately, I arrived late.* Malheureusement, je suis arrivé en retard.

unfriendly ADJECTIVE
pas aimable ◦ *The waiters are a bit unfriendly.* Les serveurs ne sont pas très aimables.

ungrateful ADJECTIVE
ingrat

unhappy ADJECTIVE
malheureux MASC
malheureuse FEM
◦ *He was very unhappy as a child.* Il était très malheureux quand il était petit.
• **to look unhappy** avoir l'air triste

unhealthy ADJECTIVE
[1] (*person*)
maladif MASC
maladive FEM
[2] (*place, habit*)
malsain
[3] (*food*)
pas sain

uniform NOUN
l' **uniforme** MASC ◦ *the school uniform* l'uniforme scolaire

uninhabited ADJECTIVE
inhabité

union NOUN
le **syndicat** (*trade union*)

Union Jack NOUN
le **drapeau du Royaume-Uni**
unique ADJECTIVE
unique
unit NOUN
　1 l' **unité** FEM　○ *a unit of measurement*
une unité de mesure
　2 l' **élément** MASC (*piece of furniture*)
○ *a kitchen unit* un élément de
cuisine
United Kingdom NOUN
le **Royaume-Uni**
United Nations NOUN
l' **O.N.U.** FEM (= Organisation des
Nations Unies)
United States NOUN
les **États-Unis** MASC PL
* **in the United States** aux États-Unis
* **to the United States** aux États-Unis
universe NOUN
l' **univers** MASC
university NOUN
l' **université** FEM　○ *She's at university.*
Elle va à l'université. ○ *Do you want to
go to university?* Tu veux aller à
l'université? ○ *Lancaster University*
l'université de Lancaster
unleaded petrol NOUN
l' **essence sans plomb** FEM
unless CONJUNCTION
* **unless he leaves** à moins qu'il ne
parte ○ *I won't come unless you phone
me.* Je ne viendrai pas à moins que tu
ne me téléphones.
unlike PREPOSITION
contrairement à ○ *Unlike him, I really
enjoy flying.* Contrairement à lui,
j'adore prendre l'avion.
unlikely ADJECTIVE
peu probable ○ *It's possible, but
unlikely.* C'est possible, mais peu
probable.
to **unload** VERB
décharger ○ *We unloaded the car.*
Nous avons déchargé la voiture. ○ *The
lorries go there to unload.* Les camions y
vont pour être déchargés.
to **unlock** VERB
ouvrir ○ *He unlocked the door of the
car.* Il a ouvert la portière de la voiture.
unlucky ADJECTIVE
* **to be unlucky (1)** (*number, object*) porter
malheur ○ *They say thirteen is an
unlucky number.* On dit que le nombre
treize porte malheur.
* **to be unlucky (2)** (*person*) ne pas avoir
de chance ○ *Did you win?–No, I was
unlucky.* Vous avez gagné?–Non, je n'ai
pas eu de chance.

unmarried ADJECTIVE
célibataire (*person*) ○ *an unmarried
mother* une mère célibataire
* **an unmarried couple** un couple non
marié
unnatural ADJECTIVE
pas naturel MASC
pas naturelle FEM
unnecessary ADJECTIVE
inutile
unofficial ADJECTIVE
　1 (*meeting, leader*)
non officiel MASC
non officielle FEM
　2 (*strike*)
sauvage
to **unpack** VERB
　1 **défaire** ○ *I unpacked my suitcase.*
J'ai défait ma valise.
　2 **déballer ses affaires** ○ *I went to my
room to unpack.* Je suis allé dans ma
chambre pour déballer mes affaires.
○ *I haven't unpacked my clothes yet.*
Je n'ai pas encore déballé mes affaires.
unpleasant ADJECTIVE
désagréable
to **unplug** VERB
débrancher
unpopular ADJECTIVE
impopulaire
unpredictable ADJECTIVE
imprévisible
unreal ADJECTIVE
incroyable (*incredible*) ○ *It was unreal!*
C'était incroyable!
unrealistic ADJECTIVE
peu réaliste
unreasonable ADJECTIVE
pas raisonnable ○ *Her attitude was
completely unreasonable.* Son attitude
n'était pas du tout raisonnable.
unreliable ADJECTIVE
pas fiable (*car, machine*) ○ *It's a nice
car, but a bit unreliable.* C'est une belle
voiture, mais elle n'est pas très fiable.
* **He's completely unreliable.** On ne
peut pas du tout compter sur lui.
to **unroll** VERB
dérouler
unsatisfactory ADJECTIVE
insatisfaisant
to **unscrew** VERB
dévisser ○ *She unscrewed the top of
the bottle.* Elle a dévissé le bouchon de
la bouteille.
unshaven ADJECTIVE
mal rasé
unskilled worker ADJECTIVE
le **manœuvre**

unstable ADJECTIVE
instable

unsteady ADJECTIVE
mal assuré (walk, voice)
- **He was unsteady on his feet.** Il marchait d'un pas mal assuré.

unsuccessful ADJECTIVE
vain (attempt)
- **to be unsuccessful in doing something** ne pas réussir à faire quelque chose ◇ *an unsuccessful artist* un artiste qui n'a pas réussi

unsuitable ADJECTIVE
inapproprié (clothes, equipment)

untidy ADJECTIVE
1. **en désordre** ◇ *My bedroom's always untidy.* Ma chambre est toujours en désordre.
2. **débraillé** (appearance, person) ◇ *He's always untidy.* Il est toujours débraillé.
3. **désordonné** (in character) ◇ *He's a very untidy person.* Il est très désordonné.

to untie VERB
1. **défaire** (knot, parcel)
2. **détacher** (animal)

until PREPOSITION, CONJUNCTION
1. **jusqu'à** ◇ *I waited until ten o'clock.* J'ai attendu jusqu'à dix heures.
- **until now** jusqu'à présent ◇ *It's never been a problem until now.* Ça n'a jamais été un problème jusqu'à présent.
- **until then** jusque-là ◇ *Until then I'd never been to France.* Jusque-là je n'étais jamais allé en France.

*Use **avant** if the sentence you want to translate contains a negative, such as "not" or "never".*

2. **avant** ◇ *It won't be ready until next week.* Ça ne sera pas prêt avant la semaine prochaine. ◇ *Until last year I'd never been to France.* Avant l'année dernière, je n'étais jamais allé en France.

unusual ADJECTIVE
1. **insolite** ◇ *an unusual shape* une forme insolite
2. **rare** ◇ *It's unusual to get snow at this time of year.* Il est rare qu'il neige à cette époque de l'année.

unwilling ADJECTIVE
- **to be unwilling to do something** ne pas être disposé à faire quelque chose ◇ *He was unwilling to help me.* Il n'était pas disposé à m'aider.

to unwind VERB
se détendre (relax)

unwise ADJECTIVE
imprudent (person) ◇ *That was rather unwise of you.* C'était plutôt imprudent

de votre part.

to unwrap VERB
déballer ◇ *After the meal we unwrapped the presents.* Après le repas nous avons déballé les cadeaux.

up PREPOSITION, ADVERB

For other expressions with up, see the verbs go, come, put, turn etc.

en haut ◇ *up on the hill* en haut de la colline
- **up here** ici
- **up there** là-haut
- **up north** dans le nord
- **to be up** être levé (out of bed) ◇ *We were up at 6.* Nous étions levés à six heures. ◇ *He's not up yet.* Il n'est pas encore levé.
- **What's up?** Qu'est-ce qu'il y a? ◇ *What's up with her?* Qu'est-ce qu'elle a?
- **to get up** (in the morning) se lever ◇ *What time do you get up?* À quelle heure tu te lèves?
- **to go up** monter ◇ *The bus went up the hill.* Le bus a monté la colline.
- **to go up to somebody** s'approcher de quelqu'un ◇ *She came up to me.* Elle s'est approchée de moi.
- **up to** (as far as) jusqu'à ◇ *to count up to fifty* compter jusqu'à cinquante ◇ *up to three hours* jusqu'à trois heures ◇ *up to now* jusqu'à présent
- **It's up to you.** C'est à vous de décider.

upbringing NOUN
l' **éducation** FEM

uphill ADVERB
- **to go uphill** monter

upper sixth NOUN
- **the upper sixth** la terminale ◇ *She's in the upper sixth.* Elle est en terminale.

upright ADJECTIVE
- **to stand upright** se tenir droit

upset NOUN
see also upset ADJECTIVE, VERB
- **a stomach upset** une indigestion

upset ADJECTIVE
see also upset NOUN, VERB
contrarié ◇ *She's still a bit upset.* Elle est encore un peu contrariée.
- **I had an upset stomach.** J'avais l'estomac dérangé.

to upset VERB
see also upset NOUN, ADJECTIVE
- **to upset somebody** contrarier quelqu'un

upside down ADVERB
à l'envers ◇ *That painting is upside down.* Ce tableau est à l'envers.

upstairs ADVERB

U

en haut ○ *Where's your coat?–It's upstairs.* Où est ton manteau?–Il est en haut.
- **to go upstairs** monter

uptight ADJECTIVE
tendu ○ *She's really uptight.* Elle est très tendue.

up-to-date ADJECTIVE
[1] **moderne** (*car, stereo*)
[2] **à jour** (*information*) ○ *an up-to-date timetable* un horaire à jour
- **to bring something up to date** moderniser quelque chose

upwards ADVERB
vers le haut ○ *to look upwards* regarder vers le haut

urgent ADJECTIVE
urgent ○ *Is it urgent?* C'est urgent?

urine NOUN
l' **urine** FEM

US NOUN
les **U.S.A.** MASC PL

us PRONOUN
nous ○ *They helped us.* Ils nous ont aidés. ○ *They gave us a map.* Ils nous ont donné une carte.

USA NOUN
les **U.S.A.** MASC PL

use NOUN
see also **use** VERB
- **It's no use.** Ça ne sert à rien. ○ *It's no use shouting, she's deaf.* Ça ne sert à rien de crier, elle est sourde.
- **It's no use, I can't do it.** Il n'y a rien à faire, je n'y arrive pas.
- **to make use of something** utiliser quelque chose

to **use** VERB
see also **use** NOUN
utiliser ○ *Can we use a dictionary in the exam?* Est-ce qu'on peut utiliser un dictionnaire à l'examen?
- **Can I use your phone?** Je peux téléphoner?

- **to use the toilet** Aller aux W.C.
- **to use up (1)** finir ○ *We've used up all the paint.* Nous avons fini la peinture.
- **to use up (2)** (*money*) dépenser
- **I used to live in London.** J'habitais à Londres autrefois.
- **I used not to like maths, but now...** Avant, je n'aimais pas les maths, mais maintenant...
- **to be used to something** avoir l'habitude de quelque chose ○ *He wasn't used to driving on the right.* Il n'avait pas l'habitude de conduire à droite. ○ *Don't worry, I'm used to it.* Ne t'inquiète pas, j'ai l'habitude.
- **a used car** une voiture d'occasion

useful ADJECTIVE
utile

useless ADJECTIVE
nul MASC
nulle FEM
○ *This map is just useless.* Cette carte est vraiment nulle. ○ *You're useless!* Tu es nul!
- **It's useless!** Ça ne sert à rien!

usual ADJECTIVE
habituel MASC
habituelle FEM
- **as usual** comme d'habitude

usually ADVERB
[1] **en général** (*generally*) ○ *I usually get to school at about half past eight.* En général, j'arrive à l'école vers huit heures et demie.
[2] **d'habitude** (*when making a contrast*) ○ *Usually I don't like wear make-up, but today is a special occasion.* D'habitude je ne me maquille pas, mais aujourd'hui c'est spécial.

utility room NOUN
la **buanderie**

U-turn NOUN
le **demi-tour** ○ *to do a U-turn* faire demi-tour

V

vacancy NOUN
  [1] le **poste vacant** (*job*)
  [2] la **chambre disponible** (*room in hotel*)
  • "no vacancies" (*on sign*) "complet"
vacant ADJECTIVE
  libre
vaccinate VERB
  vacciner
vacuum VERB
  passer l'aspirateur ◇ *to vacuum the*
  hall passer l'aspirateur dans le couloir
vacuum cleaner NOUN
  l' **aspirateur** MASC
vagina NOUN
  le **vagin**
vague ADJECTIVE
  vague
vain ADJECTIVE
  vaniteux MASC
  vaniteuse FEM
  ◇ *He's so vain!* Qu'est-ce qu'il est
  tellement vaniteux!
  • **in vain** en vain
Valentine card NOUN
  la **carte de la Saint-Valentin**
Valentine's Day NOUN
  la **Saint-Valentin**
valid ADJECTIVE
  valable ◇ *This ticket is valid for three*
  months. Ce billet est valable trois mois.
valley NOUN
  la **vallée**
valuable ADJECTIVE
  [1] **de valeur** ◇ *a valuable picture* un
  tableau de valeur
  [2] **précieux** MASC
  précieuse FEM
  ◇ *valuable help* une aide précieuse
valuables PL NOUN
  les **objets de valeur** MASC PL ◇ *Don't*
  take any valuables with you. N'importez
  pas d'objets de valeur.
value NOUN
  la **valeur**
van NOUN
  la **camionnette**
vandal NOUN
  le/la **vandale**
vandalism NOUN
  le **vandalisme**
vandalize VERB
  saccager
vanilla NOUN
  la **vanille**
  • **vanilla ice cream** la glace à la vanille
vanish VERB

disparaître
variable ADJECTIVE
  variable
varied ADJECTIVE
  varié
variety NOUN
  la **variété**
various ADJECTIVE
  plusieurs ◇ *We visited various villages*
  in the area. Nous avons visité plusieurs
  villages de la région.
to **vary** VERB
  varier
vase NOUN
  le **vase**
VAT NOUN (= *value added tax*)
  la **TVA** (= taxe sur la valeur ajoutée)
VCR NOUN (= *video cassette recorder*)
  le **magnétoscope**
VDU NOUN (= *visual display unit*)
  la **console**
veal NOUN
  le **veau**
vegan NOUN
  le **végétalien**
  la **végétalienne**
  ◇ *I'm a vegan.* Je suis végétalien.
vegetable NOUN
  le **légume** ◇ *vegetable soup* la soupe
  aux légumes
vegetarian ADJECTIVE
  see also vegetarian NOUN
  végétarien MASC
  végétarienne FEM
  ◇ *I'm vegetarian.* Je suis végétarien.
  ◇ *vegetarian lasagne* les lasagnes
  végétariennes
vegetarian NOUN
  see also vegetarian ADJECTIVE
  le **végétarien**
  la **végétarienne**
  ◇ *I'm a vegetarian.* Je suis végétarien.
vehicle NOUN
  le **véhicule**
vein NOUN
  la **veine**
velvet NOUN
  le **velours**
vending machine NOUN
  le **distributeur automatique**
Venetian blind NOUN
  le **store vénitien**
verb NOUN
  le **verbe**
verdict NOUN
  le **verdict**

vertical ADJECTIVE
vertical
(**verticaux** MASC PL)

vertigo NOUN
le **vertige** ◇ *I get vertigo.* J'ai le vertige.

very ADVERB
très ◇ *very tall* très grand ◇ *not very interesting* pas très intéressant
◆ **very much** beaucoup

vest NOUN
le **maillot de corps**

vet NOUN
le/la **vétérinaire** ◇ *She's a vet.* Elle est vétérinaire.

via PREPOSITION
en passant par ◇ *We went to Paris via Boulogne.* Nous sommes allés à Paris en passant par Boulogne.

vicar NOUN
le **pasteur** ◇ *He's a vicar.* Il est pasteur.

vice NOUN
l' **étau** (*for holding things*) MASC

vice versa ADVERB
vice versa

vicious ADJECTIVE
1 **brutal**
(**brutaux** MASC PL)
◇ *a vicious attack* une agression brutale
2 **méchant** (*dog, person*)
◆ **a vicious circle** un cercle vicieux

victim NOUN
la **victime** ◇ *He was the victim of a mugging.* Il a été victime d'une agression.

victory NOUN
la **victoire**

to **video** VERB
see also video NOUN
1 **enregistrer** (*from TV*)
2 **filmer** (*with video camera*)

video NOUN
see also video VERB
1 la **vidéo** (*film*) ◇ *to watch a video* regarder une vidéo ◇ *a video of my family on holiday* une vidéo de ma famille en vacances ◇ *It's out on video.* C'est sorti en vidéo.
2 la **cassette vidéo** (*video cassette*) ◇ *She lent me a video.* Elle m'a prêté une cassette vidéo.
3 le **magnétoscope** (*video recorder*) ◇ *Have you got a video?* Tu as un magnétoscope?
◆ **a video camera** une caméra vidéo
◆ **a video cassette** une cassette vidéo
◆ **a video game** un jeu vidéo ◇ *He*

likes playing video games. Il aime les jeux vidéo.
◆ **a video recorder** un magnétoscope
◆ **a video shop** un vidéoclub

Vietnam NOUN
le **Viêt-Nam**
◆ **in Vietnam** au Viêt-Nam

Vietnamese ADJECTIVE
vietnamien MASC
vietnamienne FEM

view NOUN
1 la **vue** ◇ *There's an amazing view.* Il y a une vue extraordinaire.
2 l' **avis** MASC (*opinion*) ◇ *in my view* à mon avis

viewer NOUN
le **téléspectateur**
la **téléspectatrice**

viewpoint NOUN
le **point de vue**

vile ADJECTIVE
dégoûtant (*smell, food*)

villa NOUN
la **villa**

village NOUN
le **village**

villain NOUN
1 le **malfrat** (*criminal*)
2 le **méchant** (*in film*)

vine NOUN
la **vigne**

vinegar NOUN
le **vinaigre**

vineyard NOUN
le **vignoble**

viola NOUN
l' **alto** MASC ◇ *I play the viola.* Je joue de l'alto.

violence NOUN
la **violence**

violent ADJECTIVE
violent

violin NOUN
le **violon** ◇ *I play the violin.* Je joue du violon.

violinist NOUN
le/la **violoniste**

virgin NOUN
la **vierge** ◇ *to be a virgin* être vierge

Virgo NOUN
la **Vierge** ◇ *I'm Virgo.* Je suis Vierge.

virtual reality NOUN
la **réalité virtuelle**

virus NOUN
le **virus**

visa NOUN
le **visa**

visible ADJECTIVE
visible

visit NOUN

see also visit VERB

[1] la **visite** (to museum)

[2] le **séjour** (to country) ◇ Did you enjoy your visit to France? Ton séjour en France s'est bien passé?

• my last visit to my grandmother la dernière fois que je suis allé voir ma grand-mère

to **visit** VERB

see also visit NOUN

[1] **rendre visite à** (person) ◇ to visit somebody rendre visite à quelqu'un

[2] **visiter** (place) ◇ We'd like to visit the castle. Nous voudrions visiter le château.

visitor NOUN

[1] (tourist)

le **visiteur**

la **visiteuse**

[2] (guest)

l' **invité** MASC

l' **invitée** FEM

• to have a visitor avoir de la visite

visual ADJECTIVE

visuel MASC

visuelle FEM

to **visualize** VERB

imaginer

vital ADJECTIVE

vital

(**vitaux** MASC PL)

vitamin NOUN

la **vitamine**

vivid ADJECTIVE

(colour)

vif MASC

vive FEM

• to have a vivid imagination avoir une imagination débordante

vocabulary NOUN

le **vocabulaire**

vocational ADJECTIVE

professionnel MASC

professionnelle FEM

• a vocational course un stage de formation professionnelle

vodka NOUN

la **vodka**

voice NOUN

la **voix**

volcano NOUN

le **volcan**

volleyball NOUN

le **volley-ball** ◇ to play volleyball jouer au volley-ball

volt NOUN

le **volt**

voltage NOUN

le **voltage**

voluntary ADJECTIVE

volontaire (contribution, statement)

• to do voluntary work travailler bénévolement

volunteer NOUN

see also volunteer VERB

le/la **volontaire**

to **volunteer** VERB

see also volunteer NOUN

• to volunteer to do something se proposer pour faire quelque chose

to **vomit** VERB

vomir

to **vote** VERB

voter

voucher NOUN

le **bon** ◇ a gift voucher un bon d'achat

vowel NOUN

la **voyelle**

vulgar ADJECTIVE

vulgaire

V

W

wafer NOUN
la **gaufrette**

wage NOUN
le **salaire** ◇ *He collected his wages.* Il a retiré son salaire.

waist NOUN
la **taille**

waistcoat NOUN
le **gilet**

to **wait** VERB
attendre
- **to wait for something** attendre quelque chose
- **to wait for somebody** attendre quelqu'un ◇ *I'll wait for you.* Je t'attendrai.
- **Wait for me!** Attends-moi!
- **Wait a minute!** Attends!
- **to keep somebody waiting** faire attendre quelqu'un ◇ *They kept us waiting for hours.* Ils nous ont fait attendre pendant des heures.
- **I can't wait for the holidays.** J'ai hâte d'être en vacances.
- **I can't wait to see him again.** J'ai hâte de le revoir.

waiter NOUN
le **serveur**

waiting list NOUN
la **liste d'attente**

waiting room NOUN
la **salle d'attente**

waitress NOUN
la **serveuse**

to **wake up** VERB
se **réveiller** ◇ *I woke up at six o'clock.* Je me suis réveillé à six heures.
- **to wake somebody up** réveiller quelqu'un ◇ *Please would you wake me up at seven o'clock?* Pourriez-vous me réveiller à sept heures?

Wales NOUN
le **pays de Galles**
- **in Wales** au pays de Galles
- **to Wales** au pays de Galles
- **I'm from Wales.** Je suis gallois.
- **the Prince of Wales** le prince de Galles

to **walk** VERB
see also **walk** NOUN
1. **marcher** ◇ *He walks fast.* Il marche vite.
2. **aller à pied** (*go on foot*) ◇ *Are you walking or going by bus?* Tu y vas à pied ou en bus? ◇ *We walked 10 kilometres.* Nous avons fait dix kilomètres à pied.
- **to walk the dog** promener le chien

walk NOUN
see also **walk** VERB
la **promenade** ◇ *to go for a walk* faire une promenade
- **It's 10 minutes' walk from here.** C'est à dix minutes d'ici à pied.

walkie-talkie NOUN
le **talkie-walkie**

walking NOUN
la **randonnée** ◇ *I did some walking in the Alps last summer.* J'ai fait de la randonnée dans les Alpes l'été dernier.

walking stick NOUN
la **canne**

Walkman ® NOUN
le **baladeur**

wall NOUN
le **mur**

wallet NOUN
le **portefeuille**

wallpaper NOUN
le **papier peint**

walnut NOUN
la **noix**
(les **noix** PL)

to **wander** VERB
- **to wander around** flâner ◇ *I just wandered around for a while.* J'ai flâné un peu.

to **want** VERB
vouloir ◇ *Do you want some cake?* Tu veux du gâteau?
- **to want to do something** vouloir faire quelque chose ◇ *I want to go to the cinema.* Je veux aller au cinéma. ◇ *What do you want to do tomorrow?* Qu'est-ce que tu veux faire demain?

war NOUN
la **guerre**

ward NOUN
la **salle** (*room in hospital*)

warden NOUN
(*of youth hostel*)
le **directeur**
la **directrice**

wardrobe NOUN
l' **armoire** FEM (*piece of furniture*)

warehouse NOUN
l' **entrepôt** MASC

warm ADJECTIVE
1. **chaud** ◇ *warm water* l'eau chaude
- **It's warm in here.** Il fait chaud ici.
- **to be warm** (*person*) avoir chaud ◇ *I'm too warm.* J'ai trop chaud.
2. **chaleureux** MASC
chaleureuse FEM

◇ *a warm welcome* un accueil chaleureux
- **to warm up (1)** *(for sport)* s'échauffer
- **to warm up (2)** *(food)* réchauffer ◇ *I'll warm up some lasagne for you.* Je vais te réchauffer des lasagnes.

to warn VERB
prévenir ◇ *Well, I warned you!* Je t'avais prévenu!
- **to warn somebody to do something** conseiller à quelqu'un de faire quelque chose

warning NOUN
l' **avertissement** MASC

Warsaw NOUN
Varsovie

wart NOUN
la **verrue**

was VERB *see* **be**

wash NOUN
see also wash VERB
- **to have a wash** se laver ◇ *I had a wash.* Je me suis lavé.
- **to give something a wash** laver quelque chose ◇ *He gave the car a wash.* Il a lavé la voiture.

to wash VERB
see also wash NOUN
1 **laver** ◇ *to wash something* laver quelque chose
2 **se laver** *(have a wash)* ◇ *Every morning I get up, wash and get dressed.* Tous les matins je me lève, je me lave et je m'habille.
- **to wash one's hands** se laver les mains
- **to wash one's hair** se laver les cheveux
- **to wash up** faire la vaisselle

washbasin NOUN
le **lavabo**

washing NOUN
le **linge** ◇ *dirty washing* du linge sale
- **Have you got any washing?** Tu as du linge à laver?
- **to do the washing** faire la lessive

washing machine NOUN
la **machine à laver**

washing powder NOUN
la **lessive**

washing-up NOUN
- **to do the washing-up** faire la vaisselle

washing-up liquid NOUN
le **produit à vaisselle**

wasn't = was not

wasp NOUN
la **guêpe**

waste NOUN
see also waste VERB
1 le **gaspillage** ◇ *It's such a waste!* C'est vraiment du gaspillage!

- **It's a waste of time.** C'est une perte de temps.
2 les **déchets** MASC *(rubbish)* ◇ *nuclear waste* les déchets nucléaires

to waste VERB
see also waste NOUN
gaspiller ◇ *I don't like wasting money.* Je n'aime pas gaspiller de l'argent.
- **to waste time** perdre du temps ◇ *There's no time to waste.* Il n'y a pas de temps à perdre.

wastepaper basket NOUN
la **corbeille à papier**

watch NOUN
see also watch VERB
la **montre**

to watch VERB
see also watch NOUN
1 **regarder** ◇ *to watch television* regarder la télévision ◇ *Watch me!* Regarde-moi!
2 **surveiller** *(keep a watch on)* ◇ *The police were watching the house.* La police surveillait la maison.
- **to watch out** faire attention
- **Watch out!** Attention!

water NOUN
see also water VERB
l' **eau** FEM

to water VERB
see also water NOUN
arroser ◇ *He was watering his tulips.* Il arrosait ses tulipes.

waterfall NOUN
la **cascade**

watering can NOUN
l' **arrosoir** MASC

watermelon NOUN
la **pastèque**

waterproof ADJECTIVE
imperméable ◇ *Is this jacket waterproof?* Ce blouson est-il imperméable?
- **a waterproof watch** une montre étanche

water-skiing NOUN
le **ski nautique** ◇ *to go water-skiing* faire du ski nautique

wave NOUN
see also wave VERB
1 la **vague** *(in water)*
2 le **signe** *(of hand)* ◇ *We gave him a wave.* Nous lui avons fait signe.

to wave VERB
see also wave NOUN
faire un signe de la main ◇ *to wave at somebody* faire un signe de la main à quelqu'un
- **to wave goodbye** faire au revoir de la

W

[PTO]

main ◇ *I waved her goodbye.* Je lui ai fait au revoir de la main.

wavy ADJECTIVE
ondulé ◇ *wavy hair* les cheveux ondulés

wax NOUN
la **cire**

way NOUN
1 la **façon** (*manner*) ◇ *She looked at me in a strange way.* Elle m'a regardé d'une façon étrange.
- **This book tells you the right way to do it.** Ce livre explique comment il faut faire.
- **You're doing it the wrong way.** Ce n'est pas comme ça qu'il faut faire.
- **in a way...** dans un sens...
- **a way of life** un mode de vie
2 le **chemin** (*route*) ◇ *I don't know the way.* Je ne connais pas le chemin.
- **on the way** en chemin ◇ *We stopped for lunch on the way.* Nous nous sommes arrêtés pour déjeuner en chemin.
- **It's a long way.** C'est loin. ◇ *Paris is a long way from London.* Paris est loin de Londres.
- **Which way is it?** C'est par où?
- **The supermarket is this way.** Le supermarché est par ici.
- **Do you know the way to the hotel?** Est-ce que vous savez comment aller à l'hôtel?
- **He's on his way.** Il arrive.
- **"way in"** "entrée"
- **"way out"** "sortie"
- **by the way...** au fait...

we PRONOUN
nous ◇ *We're staying here for a week.* Nous restons une semaine ici.

weak ADJECTIVE
faible

wealthy ADJECTIVE
riche

weapon NOUN
l' **arme** FEM

to **wear** VERB
porter (*clothes*) ◇ *She was wearing a hat.* Elle portait un chapeau.
- **She was wearing black.** Elle était en noir.

weather NOUN
le **temps** ◇ *What was the weather like?* Quel temps a-t-il fait? ◇ *The weather was lovely.* Il a fait un temps magnifique.

weather forecast NOUN
la **météo**

we'd = we had, we would

wedding NOUN
le **mariage**
- **wedding anniversary** l'anniversaire de mariage MASC
- **wedding dress** la robe de mariée

Wednesday NOUN
le **mercredi** ◇ *on Wednesday* mercredi ◇ *on Wednesdays* le mercredi ◇ *every Wednesday* tous les mercredis ◇ *last Wednesday* mercredi dernier ◇ *next Wednesday* mercredi prochain

weed NOUN
la **mauvaise herbe** ◇ *The garden's full of weeds.* Le jardin est plein de mauvaises herbes.

week NOUN
la **semaine** ◇ *last week* la semaine dernière ◇ *every week* toutes les semaines ◇ *next week* la semaine prochaine ◇ *in a week's time* dans une semaine
- **a week on Friday** vendredi en huit

weekday NOUN
- **on weekdays** en semaine

weekend NOUN
le **week-end** ◇ *at weekends* le week-end ◇ *last weekend* le week-end dernier ◇ *next weekend* le week-end prochain

to **weigh** VERB
peser ◇ *How much do you weigh?* Combien tu pèses? ◇ *First, weigh the flour.* Tout d'abord, pesez la farine.
- **to weigh oneself** se peser

weight NOUN
le **poids**
- **to lose weight** maigrir
- **to put on weight** grossir

weightlifter NOUN
l' **haltérophile** MASC

weightlifting NOUN
l' **haltérophilie** FEM

weird ADJECTIVE
bizarre

welcome NOUN
see also welcome VERB
l' **accueil** MASC ◇ *They gave her a warm welcome.* Ils lui ont fait un accueil chaleureux.
- **Welcome!** Bienvenue! ◇ *Welcome to France!* Bienvenue en France!

to **welcome** VERB
see also welcome NOUN
- **to welcome somebody** accueillir quelqu'un
- **Thank you!—You're welcome!** Merci!—De rien!

well ADJECTIVE, ADVERB
see also well NOUN
  1 **bien** ◇ *You did that really well.* Tu as très bien fait ça.
- **to do well** réussir bien ◇ *She's doing really well at school.* Elle réussit vraiment bien à l'école.
- **to be well** (*in good health*) aller bien ◇ *I'm not very well at the moment.* Je ne vais pas très bien en ce moment.
- **Get well soon!** Remets-toi vite!
- **Well done!** Bravo!
  2 **enfin** ◇ *It's enormous! Well, quite big anyway.* C'est énorme! Enfin, c'est assez grand.
- **as well** aussi ◇ *We worked hard, but we had some fun as well.* Nous avons travaillé dur, mais nous nous sommes bien amusés aussi. ◇ *We went to Chartres as well as Paris.* Nous sommes allés à Paris et à Chartres aussi.

well NOUN
see also well ADJECTIVE
le **puits**
(les **puits** PL)

we'll = we will

well-behaved ADJECTIVE
sage

well-dressed ADJECTIVE
bien habillé

wellingtons PL NOUN
les **bottes en caoutchouc** FEM PL

well-known ADJECTIVE
célèbre ◇ *a well-known film star* une vedette de cinéma célèbre

well-off ADJECTIVE
aisé

Welsh ADJECTIVE
see also Welsh NOUN
gallois ◇ *She's Welsh.* Elle est galloise.
- **Welsh people** les Gallois MASC

Welsh NOUN
see also Welsh ADJECTIVE
le **gallois** (*language*)

Welshman NOUN
le **Gallois**

Welshwoman NOUN
la **Galloise**

went VERB *see* go

were VERB *see* be

we're = we are

weren't = were not

west NOUN
see also west ADJECTIVE
l' **ouest** MASC ◇ *in the west* dans l'ouest

west ADJECTIVE, ADVERB
see also west NOUN
  1 **ouest** MASC, FEM, PL ◇ *the west coast* la côte ouest
- **west of** à l'ouest de ◇ *Stroud is west of Oxford.* Stroud est à l'ouest d'Oxford.
  2 **vers l'ouest** ◇ *We were travelling west.* Nous allions vers l'ouest.
- **the West Country** le sud-ouest de l'Angleterre

western NOUN
see also western ADJECTIVE
le **western** (*film*)

western ADJECTIVE
see also western NOUN
- **the western part of the island** la partie ouest de l'île
- **Western Europe** l'Europe de l'Ouest

West Indian ADJECTIVE
see also West Indian NOUN
antillais ◇ *She's West Indian.* Elle est antillaise.

West Indian NOUN
see also West Indian ADJECTIVE
  1 l' **Antillais** MASC
  2 l' **Antillaise** FEM (*person*)

West Indies PL NOUN
les **Antilles** FEM PL
- **in the West Indies** aux Antilles

wet ADJECTIVE
mouillé ◇ *wet clothes* les vêtements mouillés
- **to get wet** se faire mouiller
- **dripping wet** trempé
- **wet weather** le temps pluvieux
- **It was wet all week.** Il a plu toute la semaine.

wetsuit NOUN
la **combinaison de plongée**
(les **combinaisons de plongée** PL)

we've = we have

whale NOUN
la **baleine**

what ADJECTIVE, PRONOUN
  1 (*which*)
quel MASC
quelle FEM
  ◇ *What subjects are you studying?* Quelles matières est-ce que tu fais?
  ◇ *What colour is it?* C'est de quelle couleur? ◇ *What's the capital of Finland?* Quelle est la capitale de la Finlande? ◇ *What a mess!* Quel fouillis!
  2 **qu'est-ce que** ◇ *What are you doing?* Qu'est-ce que vous faites?
  ◇ *What did you say?* Qu'est-ce que vous avez dit? ◇ *What is it?* Qu'est-ce que c'est? ◇ *What's the matter?* Qu'est-ce qu'il y a?
  3 **qu'est-ce qui** ◇ *What happened?*

Qu'est-ce qui s'est passé? ◇ *What's bothering you?* Qu'est-ce qui te préoccupe?

In relative phrases use **ce qui** *or* **ce que** *depending on whether* what *refers to the subject or the object of the sentence.*

④ *(subject)*
ce qui ◇ *I saw what happened.* J'ai vu ce qui est arrivé. ◇ *I know what's bothering you.* Je sais ce qui te préoccupe.

⑤ *(object)*
ce que ◇ *Tell me what you did.* Dites-moi ce que vous avez fait. ◇ *I heard what he said.* J'ai entendu ce qu'il a dit.

➤ **What?** *(what did you say)* Comment?
➤ **What!** *(shocked)* Quoi!

wheat NOUN
le **blé**

wheel NOUN
la **roue**

➤ **the steering wheel** le volant

wheelchair NOUN
le **fauteuil roulant**

when ADVERB, CONJUNCTION
quand ◇ *When did he go?* Quand est-ce qu'il est parti? ◇ *She was reading when I came in.* Elle lisait quand je suis entré.

where ADVERB, CONJUNCTION
où ◇ *Where's Emma today?* Où est Emma aujourd'hui? ◇ *Where do you live?* Où habites-tu? ◇ *Where are you going?* Où vas-tu? ◇ *a shop where you can buy croissants* un magasin où l'on peut acheter des croissants

whether CONJUNCTION
si ◇ *I don't know whether to go or not.* Je ne sais pas si y aller ou non.

which ADJECTIVE, PRONOUN
① **quel** MASC
quelle FEM
◇ *Which flavour do you want?* Quel parfum est-ce que tu veux?

When asking which one *use* **lequel** *or* **laquelle**, *depending on whether the noun is masculine or feminine.*

➤ **I know his brother.—Which one?** Je connais son frère.–Lequel?
➤ **I know his sister.—Which one?** Je connais sa sœur.–Laquelle?
➤ **Which would you like?** Lequel est-ce que vous voulez?
➤ **Which of these are yours?** Lesquels sont à vous?

In relative phrases use **qui** *or* **que** *depending on whether* which *refers to the subject or the object of the sentence.*

② **qui** *(subject)* ◇ *the CD which is playing now* le CD qui passe maintenant
③ **que** *(object)* ◇ *the CD which I bought today* le CD que j'ai acheté hier

while CONJUNCTION
see also **while** NOUN
① **pendant que** ◇ *You hold the torch while I look inside.* Tiens la lampe électrique pendant que je regarde à l'intérieur.
② **alors que** ◇ *Isobel is very dynamic, while Kay is more laid-back.* Isobel est très dynamique, alors que Kay est plus relax.

while NOUN
see also **while** CONJUNCTION
le **moment** ◇ *after a while* au bout d'un moment

➤ **a while ago** il y a un moment ◇ *He was here a while ago.* Il était là il y a un moment.
➤ **for a while** pendant quelque temps ◇ *I lived in London for a while.* J'ai vécu à Londres pendant quelque temps.
➤ **quite a while** longtemps ◇ *quite a while ago* il y a longtemps ◇ *I haven't seen him for quite a while.* Ça fait longtemps que je ne l'ai pas vu.

whip NOUN
see also **whip** VERB
le **fouet**

to **whip** VERB
see also **whip** NOUN
① **fouetter** *(person, animal)*
② **battre** *(eggs)*

whipped cream NOUN
la **crème fouettée**

whisk NOUN
le **fouet**

whiskers PL NOUN
les **moustaches** FEM PL

whisky NOUN
le **whisky**
(les **whiskies** PL)

to **whisper** VERB
chuchoter

whistle NOUN
see also **whistle** VERB
le **sifflet**

➤ **The referee blew his whistle.** L'arbitre a sifflé.

to **whistle** VERB
see also **whistle** NOUN
siffler

white ADJECTIVE
blanc MASC
blanche FEM
◇ *He's got white hair.* Il a les cheveux

blancs.
- **white wine** le vin blanc
- **white bread** le pain blanc
- **white coffee** le café au lait
- **a white man** un Blanc
- **a white woman** une Blanche
- **white people** les Blancs

Whitsun NOUN

la **Pentecôte**

who PRONOUN

[1] **qui** ◇ *Who said that?* Qui a dit ça? ◇ *Who is Jacques Chirac?* Qui est Jacques Chirac?

In relative phrases use **qui** *or* **que** *depending on whether* who *refers to the subject or the object of the verb.*

[2] **qui** (*subject*) ◇ *the man who saw us* l'homme qui nous a vus ◇ *the man who spoke to us* l'homme qui nous a parlé

[3] **que** (*object*) ◇ *the man who we saw* l'homme que nous avons vu ◇ *the man who she married* l'homme qu'elle a épousé

whole ADJECTIVE

see also whole NOUN

tout ◇ *the whole class* toute la classe ◇ *the whole afternoon* tout l'après-midi

- **a whole box of chocolates** toute une boîte de chocolats
- **the whole world** le monde entier

whole NOUN

see also whole ADJECTIVE

- **The whole of Wales was affected.** Le pays de Galles tout entier a été touché.
- **on the whole** dans l'ensemble

wholemeal ADJECTIVE

complet MASC
complète FEM

- **wholemeal bread** le pain complet

whom PRONOUN

qui ◇ *Whom did you see?* Qui avez-vous vu? ◇ *the man to whom I spoke* l'homme à qui j'ai parlé

whose PRONOUN, ADJECTIVE

[1] **à qui** ◇ *Whose is this?* À qui est-ce? ◇ *I know whose it is.* Je sais à qui c'est. ◇ *Whose book is this?* À qui est ce livre?

[2] **dont** (*after noun*) ◇ *the girl whose picture was in the paper* la jeune fille dont la photo était dans le journal

why ADVERB

pourquoi ◇ *Why did you do that?* Pourquoi avez-vous fait ça? ◇ *That's why he did it.* Voilà pourquoi il a fait ça. ◇ *Tell me why.* Dis-moi pourquoi.

- **I've never been to France.–Why not?**

Je ne suis jamais allé en France. –Pourquoi?

- **All right, why not?** D'accord, pourquoi pas?

wicked ADJECTIVE

[1] (*evil*)
méchant

[2] (*really great*)
génial
(**géniaux** MASC PL)

wicket NOUN

le **guichet** (*stumps*)

wide ADJECTIVE, ADVERB

large ◇ *a wide road* une route large

- **wide open** grand ouvert ◇ *The door was wide open.* La porte était grande ouverte. ◇ *The windows were wide open.* Les fenêtres étaient grandes ouvertes.
- **wide awake** complètement réveillé

widow NOUN

la **veuve** ◇ *She's a widow.* Elle est veuve.

widower NOUN

le **veuf** ◇ *He's a widower.* Il est veuf.

width NOUN

la **largeur**

wife NOUN

la **femme** ◇ *She's his wife.* C'est sa femme.

wig NOUN

la **perruque**

wild ADJECTIVE

[1] (*not tame*)
sauvage ◇ *a wild animal* un animal sauvage

[2] (*crazy*)
fou MASC
folle FEM
◇ *She's a bit wild.* Elle est un peu folle.

wildlife NOUN

la **nature** ◇ *I'm interested in wildlife.* Je m'intéresse à la nature.

will NOUN

see also will VERB

le **testament** ◇ *He left me some money in his will.* Il m'a laissé de l'argent dans son testament.

will VERB

see also will NOUN

- **I'll show you your room.** Je vais te montrer ta chambre.
- **I'll give you a hand.** Je vais t'aider.

Use the French future tense when referring to the more distant future.

- **I will finish it tomorrow.** Je le finirai demain.
- **It won't take long.** Ça ne prendra pas longtemps.

W

- **Will you wash up?–No, I won't.** Est-ce que tu peux faire la vaisselle?–Non.
- **Will you help me?** Est-ce que tu peux m'aider?
- **Will you be quiet!** Voulez-vous bien vous taire!
- **That will be the postman.** Ça doit être le facteur.

willing ADJECTIVE
- **to be willing to do something** être prêt à faire quelque chose

to **win** VERB
> *see also* win NOUN

gagner ◇ *Did you win?* Est-ce que tu as gagné?
- **to win a prize** remporter un prix

win NOUN
> *see also* win VERB

la **victoire**

to **wind** VERB
> *see also* wind NOUN

[1] **enrouler** (*rope, wool, wire*)
[2] **serpenter** (*river, path*) ◇ *The road winds through the valley.* La route serpente à travers la vallée.

wind NOUN
> *see also* wind VERB

le **vent** ◇ *There was a strong wind.* Il y avait beaucoup de vent.
- **a wind instrument** un instrument à vent
- **wind power** l'énergie éolienne FEM

windmill NOUN
le **moulin à vent**
(les **moulins à vent** PL)

window NOUN
[1] (*of building*)
la **fenêtre**
[2] (*in car, train*)
la **vitre**
- **a shop window** une vitrine
[3] (*window pane*)
le **carreau**
(les **carreaux** PL)
◇ *to break a window* casser un carreau
◇ *a broken window* un carreau cassé

windscreen NOUN
le **pare-brise**
(les **pare-brise** PL)

windscreen wiper NOUN
l' **essuie-glace** MASC
(les **essuie-glace** PL)

windy ADJECTIVE
(*place*)
venteux MASC
venteuse FEM
- **It's windy.** Il y a du vent.

wine NOUN
le **vin** ◇ *a bottle of wine* une bouteille de vin ◇ *a glass of wine* un verre de vin
- **white wine** le vin blanc
- **red wine** le vin rouge
- **a wine bar** un bar à vin
- **a wine glass** un verre à vin
- **the wine list** la carte des vins

wing NOUN
l' **aile** FEM

to **wink** VERB
- **to wink at somebody** faire un clin d'œil à quelqu'un ◇ *He winked at me.* Il m'a fait un clin d'œil.

winner NOUN
le **gagnant**
la **gagnante**

winning ADJECTIVE
- **the winning team** l'équipe gagnante
- **the winning goal** le but décisif

winter NOUN
l' **hiver** MASC
- **in winter** en hiver

winter sports PL NOUN
les **sports d'hiver** MASC PL

to **wipe** VERB
essuyer
- **to wipe one's feet** s'essuyer les pieds ◇ *Wipe your feet!* Essuie-toi les pieds!
- **to wipe up** essuyer

wire NOUN
le **fil de fer**

wisdom tooth NOUN
la **dent de sagesse**
(les **dents de sagesse** PL)

wise ADJECTIVE
sage

to **wish** VERB
> *see also* wish NOUN

- **to wish for something** souhaiter quelque chose ◇ *What more could you wish for?* Que pourrais-tu souhaiter de plus?
- **to wish to do something** désirer faire quelque chose ◇ *I wish to make a complaint.* Je désire porter plainte.
- **I wish you were here!** Si seulement tu étais ici!
- **I wish you'd told me!** Si seulement tu m'en avais parlé!

wish NOUN
> *see also* wish VERB

le **vœu**
(les **vœux** PL)
◇ *to make a wish* faire un vœu
- **"best wishes"** (*on greetings card*) "meilleurs vœux"
- **"with best wishes, Kathy"** "bien amicalement, Kathy"

wit NOUN
l' **esprit** MASC (*humour*)

with PREPOSITION
1 **avec** ◇ *Come with me.* Venez avec moi. ◇ *He walks with a stick.* Il marche avec une canne.
- **a woman with blue eyes** une femme aux yeux bleus
2 **chez** (*at the home of*) ◇ *We stayed with friends.* Nous avons logé chez des amis.
3 **de** ◇ *green with envy* vert de jalousie ◇ *to shake with fear* trembler de peur ◇ *Fill the jug with water.* Remplis la carafe d'eau.

within PREPOSITION
- **The shops are within easy reach.** Les magasins sont à proximité.
- **within the week** avant la fin de la semaine

without PREPOSITION
sans ◇ *without a coat* sans manteau ◇ *without speaking* sans parler

witness NOUN
le **témoin** ◇ *There were no witnesses.* Il n'a pas eu de témoins.

witty ADJECTIVE
spirituel MASC
spirituelle FEM

wives PL NOUN *see* **wife**

woke up, woken up VERB *see* **wake up**

wolf NOUN
le **loup**

woman NOUN
la **femme** ◇ *a woman doctor* une femme médecin

won VERB *see* **win**

to **wonder** VERB
se demander ◇ *I wonder why she said that.* Je me demande pourquoi elle a dit ça. ◇ *I wonder what that means.* Je me demande ce que ça veut dire. ◇ *I wonder where Caroline is.* Je me demande où est Caroline.

wonderful ADJECTIVE
formidable

won't = **will not**

wood NOUN
le **bois** (*timber, forest*) ◇ *It's made of wood.* C'est en bois. ◇ *We went for a walk in the wood.* Nous sommes allés nous promener dans le bois.

wooden ADJECTIVE
en bois ◇ *a wooden chair* une chaise en bois

woodwork NOUN
la **menuiserie** ◇ *My hobby is woodwork.* Je fais de la menuiserie.

wool NOUN
la **laine** ◇ *It's made of wool.* C'est en laine.

word NOUN
le **mot** ◇ *a difficult word* un mot difficile
- **What's the word for "shop" in German?** Comment dit-on "magasin" en allemand?
- **in other words** en d'autres termes
- **to have a word with somebody** parler avec quelqu'un
- **the words** (*lyrics*) les paroles ◇ *I really like the words of this song.* J'adore les paroles de cette chanson.

word processing NOUN
le **traitement de texte**

word processor NOUN
la **machine de traitement de texte**

wore VERB *see* **wear**

work NOUN
see also **work** VERB
le **travail**
(les **travaux** PL)
◇ *She's looking for work.* Elle cherche du travail. ◇ *He's at work at the moment.* Il est au travail en ce moment.
- **It's hard work.** C'est dur.
- **to be off work** être en congé
- **He's out of work.** Il est sans emploi.

to **work** VERB
see also **work** NOUN
1 **travailler** (*person*) ◇ *She works in a shop.* Elle travaille dans un magasin. ◇ *to work hard* travailler dur
2 **marcher** (*machine, plan*) ◇ *The heating isn't working.* Le chauffage ne marche pas. ◇ *My plan worked perfectly.* Mon plan a marché impeccablement.
- **to work out (1)** (*exercise*) faire de l'exercice ◇ *I work out twice a week.* Je fais de l'exercice deux fois par semaine.
- **to work out (2)** (*turn out*) marcher ◇ *In the end it worked out really well.* Au bout du compte, ça a très bien marché.
- **to work out (3)** (*figure out*) arriver à comprendre ◇ *I just couldn't work it out.* Je n'arrivais pas du tout à comprendre.
- **It works out at £10 each.** Ça fait dix livres chacun.

worker NOUN
(*in factory*)
l' **ouvrier** MASC
l' **ouvrière** FEM
- **He's a factory worker.** Il est ouvrier.

W

- **She's a good worker.** Elle travaille bien.

work experience NOUN

le **stage** ◇ *I'm going to do work experience in a factory.* Je vais faire un stage dans une usine.

working-class ADJECTIVE

ouvrier MASC

ouvrière FEM

◇ *a working-class family* une famille ouvrière

works NOUN

l' **usine** FEM *(factory)*

worksheet NOUN

la **feuille d'exercices**

workshop NOUN

l' **atelier** MASC ◇ *a drama workshop* un atelier de théâtre

workstation NOUN

le **poste de travail**

(les **postes de travail** PL)

world NOUN

le **monde**

- **He's the world champion.** Il est champion du monde.

worm NOUN

le **ver**

worn VERB *see* **wear**

worn ADJECTIVE

usé ◇ *The carpet is a bit worn.* La moquette est un peu usée.

- **worn out** *(tired)* épuisé

worried ADJECTIVE

inquiet MASC

inquiète FEM

◇ *She's very worried.* Elle est très inquiète.

- **to be worried about something** s'inquiéter pour quelque chose ◇ *I'm worried about the exams.* Je m'inquiète pour les examens.

- **to look worried** avoir l'air inquiet ◇ *She looks a bit worried.* Elle a l'air un peu inquiète.

to **worry** VERB

s'inquiéter

- **Don't worry!** Ne t'inquiète pas!

worse ADJECTIVE, ADVERB

1 **pire** ◇ *It was even worse than that.* C'était encore pire que ça. ◇ *My results were bad, but his were even worse.* Mes notes étaient mauvaises, mais les siennes étaient encore pires.

2 **plus mal** ◇ *I'm feeling worse.* Je me sens plus mal.

to **worship** VERB

vénérer *(God)*

- **He really worships her.** Il est en adoration devant elle.

worst ADJECTIVE

see also **worst** NOUN

- **the worst** le plus mauvais ◇ *the worst student in the class* le plus mauvais élève de la classe ◇ *He got the worst mark in the whole class.* Il a eu la plus mauvaise note de toute la classe.

- **my worst enemy** mon pire ennemi

- **Maths is my worst subject.** Je suis vraiment nul en maths.

worst NOUN

see also **worst** ADJECTIVE

le **pire** ◇ *The worst of it is that...* Le pire c'est que...

- **at worst** au pire

- **if the worst comes to the worst** au pire

worth ADJECTIVE

- **to be worth** valoir ◇ *It's worth a lot of money.* Ça vaut très cher. ◇ *How much is it worth?* Ça vaut combien?

- **It's worth it.** Ça vaut la peine. ◇ *Is it worth it?* Est-ce que ça vaut la peine? ◇ *It's not worth it.* Ça ne vaut pas la peine.

would VERB

- **Would you like a biscuit?** Vous voulez un biscuit?

- **Would you like to go and see a film?** Est-ce que tu veux aller voir un film?

- **Would you close the door please?** Vous pouvez fermer la porte, s'il vous plaît?

- **I'd like...** J'aimerais... ◇ *I'd like to go to America.* J'aimerais aller en Amérique. ◇ *Shall we go and see a film?—Yes, I'd like that.* Si on allait voir un film?—Oui, j'aimerais bien.

- **I said I would do it.** J'ai dit que je le ferais.

- **If you asked him he'd do it.** Si vous lui demandiez, il le ferait.

- **If you had asked him he would have done it.** Si vous le lui aviez demandé, il l'aurait fait.

wouldn't = would not

wound NOUN

see also **wound** VERB

la **blessure**

to **wound** VERB

see also **wound** NOUN

blesser ◇ *He was wounded in the leg.* Il a été blessé à la jambe.

to **wrap** VERB

emballer ◇ *She's wrapping her Christmas presents.* Elle est en train d'emballer ses cadeaux de Noël.

- **Can you wrap it for me please?** *(in shop)* Vous pouvez me faire un papier cadeau, s'il vous plaît?

- **to wrap up** emballer
wrapping paper NOUN
le **papier cadeau**
wreck NOUN
see also **wreck** VERB
[1] le **tas de ferraille** (*vehicle, machine*)
◦ *That car is a wreck!* Cette voiture
est un tas de ferraille!
[2] la **loque** (*person*) ◦ *After the exams I
was a complete wreck.* Après les
examens j'étais une véritable loque.
to **wreck** VERB
see also **wreck** NOUN
[1] **démolir** (*building, vehicle*) ◦ *The
explosion wrecked the whole house.*
L'explosion a démoli toute la maison.
[2] **ruiner** (*plan, holiday*) ◦ *The trip was
wrecked by bad weather.* Le voyage a
été ruiné par le mauvais temps.
wreckage NOUN
[1] les **débris** MASC PL (*of vehicle*)
[2] les **décombres** MASC PL (*of building*)
wrestler NOUN
le **lutteur**
la **lutteuse**
wrestling NOUN
la **lutte**
wrinkled ADJECTIVE
ridé
wrist NOUN
le **poignet**
to **write** VERB
écrire ◦ *to write a letter* écrire une
lettre
- **to write to somebody** écrire à
quelqu'un ◦ *I'm going to write to her in
French.* Je vais lui écrire en français.
- **to write down** noter ◦ *I wrote down
the address.* J'ai noté l'adresse.

- **Can you write it down for me, please?**
Vous pouvez me l'écrire, s'il vous plaît?
writer NOUN
l' **écrivain** MASC ◦ *She's a writer.* Elle
est écrivain.
writing NOUN
l' **écriture** FEM ◦ *I can't read your
writing.* Je n'arrive pas à lire ton
écriture.
- **in writing** par écrit
written VERB *see* **write**
wrong ADJECTIVE, ADVERB
[1] (*incorrect*)
faux MASC
fausse FEM
◦ *The information they gave us was
wrong.* Les renseignements qu'ils nous
ont donnés étaient faux.
- **the wrong answer** la mauvaise réponse
- **You've got the wrong number.** Vous
vous êtes trompé de numéro.
[2] (*morally bad*)
mal ◦ *I think hunting is wrong.* Je
trouve que c'est mal de chasser.
- **to be wrong** (*mistaken*) se tromper
◦ *You're wrong about that.* Tu te
trompes.
- **to do something wrong** se tromper
◦ *You've done it wrong.* Tu t'es
trompé.
- **to go wrong** (*plan*) mal tourner
◦ *The robbery went wrong and they
got caught.* Le cambriolage a mal
tourné et ils ont été pris.
- **What's wrong?** Qu'est-ce qu'il y a?
- **What's wrong with her?** Qu'est-ce
qu'elle a?
wrote VERB *see* **write**

W

X

to X-ray VERB
see also X-ray NOUN
- **to X-ray something** faire une radio de quelque chose ◦ *They X-rayed my arm.* Ils ont fait une radio de mon bras.

X-ray NOUN
see also X-ray VERB
la **radio** ◦ *to have an X-ray* passer une radio

Y

yacht NOUN
1 le **voilier** (*sailing boat*)
2 le **yacht** (*luxury motorboat*)
yard NOUN
la **cour** (*of building*) ◦ *in the yard* dans la cour
to yawn VERB
bâiller
year NOUN
l' **an** MASC ◦ *last year* l'an dernier ◦ *next year* l'an prochain
- **to be 15 years old** avoir quinze ans
- **an eight-year-old child** un enfant de huit ans

In French secondary schools, years are counted from the sixième (*youngest*) *to* première *and* terminale (*oldest*).

◦ *the first year* la sixième ◦ *the second year* la cinquième ◦ *the third year* la quatrième ◦ *the fourth year* la troisième ◦ *the fifth year* la seconde
- **She's in the fifth year.** Elle est en seconde.
- **He's a first-year.** Il est en sixième.

to yell VERB
hurler
yellow ADJECTIVE
jaune
yes ADVERB
1 **oui** ◦ *Do you like it?—Yes.* Tu aimes ça?—Oui.
- **Would you like a cup of tea?—Yes please.** Voulez-vous une tasse de thé? —Je veux bien.

Use si *when answering negative questions.*
2 **si** ◦ *Don't you like it?—Yes!* Tu n'aimes pas ça?—Si! ◦ *You're not Swiss, are you?—Yes I am!* Tu n'es pas suisse, si?—Si!

yesterday ADVERB
hier ◦ *yesterday morning* hier matin ◦ *yesterday afternoon* hier après-midi ◦ *yesterday evening* hier soir ◦ *all day yesterday* toute la journée d'hier
yet ADVERB
encore
- **not yet** pas encore ◦ *It's not finished yet.* Ce n'est pas encore fini.

- **not as yet** pas encore ◦ *There's no news as yet.* Nous n'avons pas encore de nouvelles.
- **Have you finished yet?** Vous avez fini?

yob NOUN
le **loubard**
yoghurt NOUN
le **yaourt**
yolk NOUN
le **jaune d'œuf**
(les **jaunes d'œuf** PL)
you PRONOUN

Only use tu *when speaking to one person, and when the person is your own age. If in doubt use* vous.

1 **vous** (*polite form or plural*) ◦ *Do you like football?* Est-ce que vous aimez le football? ◦ *Can I help you?* Est-ce que je peux vous aider?
2 **tu** (*familiar singular*) ◦ *Do you like football?* Tu aimes le football?

vous *never changes, but* tu *has different forms. When* you *is the object of the sentence use* te *not* tu. te *becomes* t' *before a vowel sound.*

3 **te** ◦ *I know you.* Je te connais. ◦ *I gave it you.* Je te l'ai donné.
t' ◦ *I saw you.* Je t'ai vu. ◦ *I'll help you.* Je vais t'aider.

toi *is used instead of* tu *after a preposition and in comparisons.*

4 **toi** ◦ *It's for you.* C'est pour toi.
◦ *I'll come with you.* Je viens avec toi.
◦ *She's younger than you.* Elle est plus jeune que toi.

young ADJECTIVE
jeune
- **young people** les jeunes
younger ADJECTIVE
plus jeune ◦ *He's younger than me.* Il est plus jeune que moi.
- **my younger brother** mon frère cadet
- **my younger sister** ma sœur cadette
your ADJECTIVE

Only use ton/ta/tes *when speaking to one person, and when the person is your own age. If in doubt use* votre/vos.

1 *(polite form or plural)*
votre ◇ *your house* votre maison
vos PL ◇ *your seats* vos places
2 *(familiar singular)*
ton MASC ◇ *your brother* ton frère
ta FEM ◇ *your sister* ta sœur
tes PL ◇ *your parents* tes parents
ta *becomes* ton *before a vowel sound.*
- **your friend (1)** *(male)* ton ami
- **your friend (2)** *(female)* ton amie
Do not use **votre/vos** *or* **ton/ta/tes** *with parts
of the body.*
  ◇ *Would you like to wash your hands?*
Est-ce que vous voulez vous laver les
mains? ◇ *Do you want to wash your
hair?* Tu veux te laver les cheveux?

yours PRONOUN
Only use **le tien/la tienne/les tiens/les
tiennes** *when talking to one person of your own
age. If in doubt use* **le vôtre/la vôtre/les vôtres.**
The same applies to **à toi** *and* **à vous.**
1 **le vôtre** + MASC NOUN ◇ *I've lost my
pen. Can I use yours?* J'ai perdu mon
stylo. Je peux utiliser le vôtre?
la vôtre + FEM NOUN ◇ *I like that car. Is it
yours?* J'aime cette voiture-là. C'est la
vôtre?
les vôtres + PL NOUN ◇ *my parents and
yours* mes parents et les vôtres
- **Is this yours?** C'est à vous? ◇ *This
book is yours.* Ce livre est à vous.
  ◇ *Whose is this?–It's yours.* C'est à
qui?–À vous.
- **Yours sincerely...** Veuillez agréer
l'expression de mes sentiments les
meilleurs...
2 **le tien** + MASC NOUN ◇ *I've lost my
pen. Can I use yours?* J'ai perdu mon
stylo. Je peux utiliser le tien?
la tienne + FEM NOUN ◇ *I like that car. Is
it yours?* J'aime cette voiture-là. C'est

la tienne?
les tiens + MASC PL NOUN ◇ *my parents
and yours* mes parents et les tiens
les tiennes + FEM PL NOUN ◇ *My hands
are dirty, yours are clean.* Mes mains
sont sales, les tiennes sont propres.
- **Is this yours?** C'est à toi? ◇ *This
book is yours.* Ce livre est à toi.
  ◇ *Whose is this?–It's yours.* C'est à
qui?–À toi.

yourself PRONOUN
Only use **te** *when talking to one person of your own
age; use* **vous** *to everyone else. If in doubt use* **vous.**
1 **vous** *(polite form)* ◇ *Have you hurt
yourself?* Est-ce que vous vous êtes fait
mal? ◇ *Tell me about yourself!*
Parlez-moi de vous!
2 **te** *(familiar form)* ◇ *Have you hurt
yourself?* Est-ce que tu t'es fait mal?
After a preposition, use **toi** *instead of* **te.**
3 **toi** *(familiar form)* ◇ *Tell me about
yourself!* Parle-moi de toi!
4 **toi-même** ◇ *Do it yourself!* Fais-le
toi-même!
5 **vous-même** ◇ *Do it yourself!*
Faites-le vous-même!

yourselves PRONOUN
1 **vous** ◇ *Did you enjoy yourselves?*
Vous vous êtes bien amusés?
2 **vous-mêmes** ◇ *Did you make it
yourselves?* Vous l'avez fait
vous-mêmes?

youth club NOUN
le **centre de jeunes**

youth hostel NOUN
l' **auberge de jeunesse** FEM
(les **auberges de jeunesse** PL)

Yugoslavia NOUN
la **Yougoslavie**
- **in the former Yugoslavia** en
ex-Yougoslavie

Z

zany ADJECTIVE
loufoque
zebra NOUN
le **zèbre**
zebra crossing NOUN
le **passage clouté**
zero NOUN
le **zéro**
Zimbabwe NOUN
le **Zimbabwe**
- **in Zimbabwe** au Zimbabwe
Zimmer frame ® NOUN
le **déambulateur**
zip NOUN

la **fermeture éclair** ®
(les **fermetures éclair** PL)
zit NOUN
le **bouton**
zodiac NOUN
le **zodiaque** ◇ *the signs of the z~*
les signes du zodiaque
zone NOUN
la **zone**
zoo NOUN
le **zoo**
zoom lens NOUN
le **zoom**

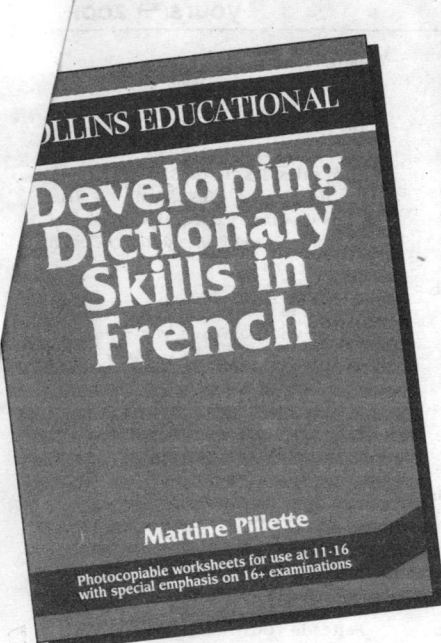

DEVELOPING DICTIONARY SKILLS IN FRENCH

The National Curriculum states that students "should be taught to use dictionaries and reference materials" and students are now entitled to take a dictionary into examinations. Thus, the need for students to use (and not misuse!) a bilingual dictionary has never been more pressing.

This pack of photocopiable masters provides ready-to-use and fun activities to develop dictionary skills. Examples are taken from *Collins Pocket French Dictionary* but the materials can be used alongside any reputable bilingual dictionary.

- The easy way to meet the new NC requirements for dictionary usage
- Crosses age ranges and abilities: KS3 and KS4, less able and more able
- Fully photocopiable
- Ideal for use in the classroom or at home

May 1996   0 00 320194 5   48pp   £25.00

Contents

The activities contained in the pack cover a wide range of topic areas and help students develop a variety of dictionary skills including: learning how a dictionary is organized - finding the appropriate translation - using a dictionary in an exam - when not to use a dictionary.